SCOTT H. BELS[...]R

# CRIMINAL

# *Justice*

## SECOND EDITION

THE TRUE ADMINISTRATION OF JUSTICE IS THE

# Kendall Hunt
publishing company

**Kendall Hunt**
publishing company

www.kendallhunt.com
*Send all inquiries to:*
4050 Westmark Drive
Dubuque, IA 52004-1840

# DEDICATION

I want to first thank my mom and dad for their guidance and wisdom. I would not be the man I am today without them. I want to thank my wife, Amanda. Your love and support gets me through almost anything. I want to thank my two boys, Clayton and Dillon. They both have entered college and are turning out to be fine young men. I cannot be any prouder of them. I also want to thank my teaching assistant, Megan Stidd. Lastly, I want to thank my brother and friend, Ernie Kuehne Jr., who we affectionately call "Big E." You have a kind heart and serve as a motivating force for me to be the best in my career endeavors. I cannot thank you enough.

SB

I want to thank Dr. Belshaw for his wisdom and putting his trust in me with our endeavor. I want to thank my wife, Gayle, for her patience during this process and her love and support.

LD

# BRIEF CONTENTS

# CONTENTS

## SECTION 2: LAW ENFORCEMENT IN THE 21ST CENTURY

# SECTION 3: THE AMERICAN COURT SYSTEM

# SECTION 4: THE CONSEQUENCES OF CRIME: CORRECTIONS

# SECTION 5: SPECIAL TOPICS IN CRIMINAL JUSTICE

# PREFACE

Crime and justice are ever-present and often debated topics in modern society. The public is often attracted to media coverage of celebrities in court and other high-profile cases in the criminal justice system. In the media, cases that involve violence and drug use remain popular—"if it bleeds, it leads." In addition to an apparent interest in sensationalized media, each of us has also developed personal beliefs and ideologies about crime and justice.

Given that the vast majority of the work completed by the criminal justice system is completed without media attention, we must ask whether these sensationalized cases reflect the true criminal justice system. Even more important—do opinions and beliefs created in response to these outliers parallel those developed through careful research? Even when focusing on more mundane crime stories, do the media accurately describe the justice system, crime, and social control? What are the realities of criminal justice, and what are the myths?

In short, how does the criminal justice system really function on an everyday basis, and how do we as citizens interact with the system? *Criminal Justice* aims to answer these questions while providing a clear understanding of many aspects of the U.S. criminal justice system. Readers will develop a thorough knowledge of the elements involved in the criminal justice system, from the start of the process to the end. We also hope readers will begin to understand the complexity of the criminal justice system and the breadth of the challenges faced by justice professionals.

Readers will recognize controversies faced by the criminal justice system. "Real world" examples are offered throughout the text, in each case highlighting difficult choices faced by our society, the justice system, and those attempting to develop a clear and unbiased policy. Ideally, these examples will help readers gain the critical thinking skills needed to reach logical conclusions regarding these controversies.

## Learning about Criminal Justice

How do we learn about criminal justice? From what sources do we get this information? How do we filter the massive amount of information available to us on a given subject—especially one as controversial as criminal justice?

This text has taken a few new directions in regard to these questions. First of all, we acknowledge that much of what we know is socially constructed. We also acknowledge that each of us—whether consciously or unconsciously—tends to place ideological blinders on ourselves as we allow preconceived notions to affect our perceptions.

Criminologists are familiar with Herbert Packer's discussion of "crime control" and "due process." Classroom presentation of Packer's version of these concepts typically involves discussion of the "crime control assembly line" and the "due process obstacle course." While assembly lines have value, efficiency may not be an acceptable goal for the justice system. Similarly, obstacle courses can be a great challenge, but a justice system based on constant indecision is not sustainable.

Again, each of us has developed deeply held views about crime, justice, and the justice system. As a result, each of us occupies a unique point on the crime control/due process continuum. While not perfectly correlated with "liberal" and "conservative," our attitudes toward due process and crime control will impact our interpretation of what we know about the justice system—and what we are willing and able to learn. Some of us are due process people. Others are crime control people. These perspectives cause us to engage our filters, often discounting ideas inconsistent with our beliefs.

Bias reduction is the first step in our efforts to learn about crime and justice. Where do you stand? Like it or not, each of us has a political perspective on the issues raised in this text. Readers should realize they have reached this point through a long process of filtering. We want readers to reflect on what positions they hold and why they hold them. We also encourage readers to adopt alternative points of view and understand criminal justice issues from a variety of perspectives.

## Organization of the Text

The authors of each chapter include a range of perspectives. Some perspectives will be easy to agree with. Readers may be tempted to discount other ideas on purely ideological grounds.

Some perspectives will also be questioned due to the source. While we will not cite Wikipedia, we are not inclined to totally dismiss Internet research, especially when much scholarly research and communication is closed to the general public. In spite of the potential to adopt more open models, most scholarly journals continue to restrict access. As a result, the vast majority of citizens, including our students, use the Internet as their primary research tool.

Professors joke about the student perspective that "if it isn't on Google, it doesn't exist." Since our students will not have lifetime access to the university library, there is some truth to this statement. Rather than discount the obvious value of information available with a web search, we hope we have been selective enough with our resources to help students learn to recognize authoritative information. If readers disagree with facts or positions found here each of us has discovered an opportunity to learn.

Our goal is to provide a balanced, full-scale perspective of the criminal justice system, supplemented by scholarly support from criminal justice experts, researchers, and theorists. The contributing authors of this textbook are criminal justice professors and scholars, each with perspectives developed through years of study and experience. Many of the topics discussed in this book are inherently controversial and political. While the editor and each individual author do not necessarily agree with every sentiment shared in this text, we hope to present and promote a robust, well-rounded discussion.

Above all, we wish to give students the facts they need, the skills to find more, and the ability to critically analyze the bias inherent in policy choices—ideally based on fact, research, reason, and compassion. We hope this text provides a rich and rewarding learning experience for learners and educators.

Most criminal justice students have very little prior knowledge about, or experience with, the criminal justice system. Thus, this textbook is designed to introduce the many facets of the criminal justice system in a logical, readily understandable manner. *Criminal Justice* consists of 14 chapters grouped into five overarching sections. We begin with an overview of the criminal justice system, including a brief examination of theories of crime and social control. We then examine the various players and processes of the system, beginning with police and policing, then moving to the courtroom, then finally the corrections system. Our introduction to criminal justice then moves to special topics in criminal justice, including juvenile justice, victimology, and issues related to terrorism, cybercrime, and a variety of contemporary and future challenges.

## Section 1: Overview of the Criminal Justice System

**Chapter 1, Introduction to Criminal Justice**, helps students become acclimated with the structure, organization, history, and goals of the criminal justice system. This chapter invites students to engage in a scholarly examination of the system and consider how political ideologies play a role in one's perspective. This chapter will compare and contrast criminal justice with other social science disciplines, discuss how the U.S. criminal justice system was created, describe the network of agencies within the system, analyze policy choices and their motivations, and walk through the steps in the criminal justice process.

**Chapter 2, Theories of Crime and Behavior**, reviews the extent to which crime occurs and the theoretical propositions used to explain criminal behavior. This chapter will differentiate between criminal behavior and deviance, report crime trends and statistics in the United States, discuss several methods of acquiring crime data, and review scholarly theories of the causes of crime.

## Section 2: The Policing of Crime

**Chapter 3, Policing in America**, focuses on the role of policing and police systems in the criminal justice system. This chapter provides background information on the history of policing in the United States, including the constant efforts to reform law enforcement and improve police accountability and professionalism. The chapter also identifies local, state, and federal law enforcement agencies and describes the education and training requirements of police and other law enforcement professionals.

**Chapter 4, Policing: Roles, Functions, and Challenges**, describes the experience of contemporary law enforcement officers in the United States. The chapter outlines the many roles, duties, and functions of police officers and police departments, and distinguishes among different styles of policing. This chapter also examines the challenges that police officers face regarding discretion, stress, ethics, and corruption.

## Section 3: The American Court System

**Chapter 5, The Court System in the United States**, explores the American judiciary as a whole, focusing upon the courts themselves at all levels. This chapter discusses the history and background of the courts, including their colonial origins in English common law, and a detailed discussion of the structure of the court system as it exists today. The chapter additionally examines criminal procedure and due process for criminal defendants and gives an overview of the structure and organization of the American courtroom. This chapter describes the various participants in a courtroom and their respective roles, and examines how these roles are interconnected. The chapter also discusses the importance of the jury in criminal trials.

**Chapter 6, Sentencing and Judgment**, examines the overall philosophy and goals of sentencing for criminal offenders and analyzes the range of sentencing options available. The chapter discusses determinate and indeterminate sentencing and "truth in sentencing," and explains the role of presentence investigations.

## Section 4: The Consequences of Crime: Corrections

**Chapter 7, Prisons and Jails**, focuses on the role of corrections in the criminal justice system. This chapter examines the history of corrections, discusses why there is a prohibition on cruel and unusual punishment, determines differences between prisons and jails, examines custody levels, and discusses the issues and controversies of prison privatization.

**Chapter 8, Prison Life**, discusses the concept of correctional facilities as total institutions and the roles and subcultures of both inmates and correctional workers within jails and prisons. This chapter discusses the implications of relying on incarceration, including the economic realities, and reviews various forms of community-based alternatives to incarceration.

**Chapter 9, Special Issues in Corrections**, covers many of the unique challenges regarding the corrections system. This includes a discussion of the range of rehabilitative needs faced by prison inmates and the advantages and challenges of prison rehabilitation programs. This chapter evaluates how well inmates are prepared for their return to society, discusses the factors that influence recidivism rates, and examines if and how the corrections system can address the needs of those released from prison.

## Section 5: Special Topics in Criminal Justice

**Chapter 10, Juvenile Justice**, gives an overview of the juvenile justice system, including the history of juvenile justice in the United States and the differences between the juvenile and adult systems. This chapter outlines the different types of juvenile corrections and explains theories and patterns of both juvenile delinquency and juvenile victimization. The chapter also analyzes debates regarding the treatment and punishment of juvenile offenders.

**Chapter 11, Victimology and Victims' Rights**, explores the study of victimology, including the costs and effects of victimization and how victimization is measured. The chapter also discusses the Victims' Rights Movement and its relation to victimology, and examines the future of victims' rights in terms of legislation and social policy.

**Chapter 12, Domestic and International Terrorism**, discusses the differences between domestic and international terrorism as well as the differences between revolutionary and sub-revolutionary groups. It identifies the differences between the Taliban, ISIS, Al-Qaeda, and Daesh. The chapter also explains the components of state-directed, state-supported, non-state actors and lone terrorists.

**Chapter 13, The Future of Criminal Justice**, focuses on upcoming challenges and considerations that the criminal justice system will face moving forward. Issues discussed include effective and ineffective models of intervention, perceptions of the death penalty in the United States and internationally, trends in drug laws, and the liberty and security implications of technology and social networking. This chapter also explores the growing reliance on global coordination and information sharing between criminal justice entities.

## Special Features

This textbook includes a number of chapter-specific features designed to enhance and extend understanding of the content.

- Each chapter includes one **Career Connections** feature that profiles a specific profession related to the chapter, explaining what the job entails and how it connects to criminal justice. This feature is a valuable resource for students who are planning to pursue a career in criminal justice.
- Each chapter also includes an **Ethics and Professionalism** feature, which highlights a real-life or hypothetical ethical dilemma relevant to the chapter and invites discussion of how to address the dilemma.
- Brief **Critical Thinking** questions are scattered throughout the text and in the end-of-chapter materials. These questions invite students to discuss their thoughts and opinions on relevant criminal justice issues.
- Most chapters include **Exhibits**, which are documents and legislation related to criminal justice topics, such as excerpts from Supreme Court decisions.
- At the end of each chapter is a list of **Media** links, which highlight web sites and other media resources that students are encouraged to explore for further information on the topics discussed in the chapter.
- Both students and instructors have access to **online content** that is integrated chapter by chapter with the text to maximize the principles and enrich student learning. The web access code is included on the inside front cover of the textbook and provides the purchaser of the book the ability to reference all of the online material, including features such as a descriptive **PowerPoint presentation** for each chapter of the book, **flash cards**, and a **test bank**.

## Features of This Text

**Criminal Justice**   presents material in a format that provides a clear understanding of many aspects of the U.S. criminal justice system. Readers will have a thorough knowledge of the elements involved in the criminal justice system, from the start of the process to the end.

**Key Terms list**   directs you to important terminology addressed in the chapter

**Chapter Objectives**   focus on the overall concepts, theories, and skills of the chapter

**Web Icons**   direct you to additional online material relating to text content

**Opening Case Study**   offers a vivid illustration of content that will be discussed throughout the chapter

**Career Connections**   profile a specific profession related to the chapter, offering valuable information for those planning to pursue a career in criminal justice

**Critical Thinking questions**   offer an opportunity to discuss opinions on different criminal justice issues

**Running Glossary**   provides easily accessible definitions to all key terms

**Media links**   offer websites and other resources for exploring further information on the chapter topics

**Endnotes**   comprehensively list all sources and research utilized in each chapter

**Exhibits**   illustrate documents and legislation related to criminal justice topics

**Ethics and Professionalism feature**   showcases an ethical dilemma and invites discussion of it

**Chapter Summary**   succinctly summarizes and reinforces chapter content

# ABOUT THE EDITORS

**Scott H. Belshaw** is currently an Associate Professor of Criminal Justice at the University of North Texas in Denton, Texas. Dr. Belshaw holds a Ph.D. in Juvenile Criminal Justice from Prairie View A&M University. He earned his Bachelor of Science in Social Sciences from the University of Houston-Downtown. He also holds both a Master of Arts in Liberal Arts from Houston Baptist University and a Master of Arts in Criminology from the University of Houston-Clear Lake. Dr. Belshaw's criminal justice experience includes working many years with the Harris County Texas Community Supervision and Corrections Department serving as a probation officer, gang intelligence officer, and court liaison probation officer. Dr. Belshaw has published books on organized crime and constitutional law. He has published numerous research articles in criminal justice journals. Dr. Belshaw is currently serving as the Director of the Cyber Forensics Lab at the University of North Texas.

**Lee DeBoer** holds a Master's Degree in Criminal Justice from University of North Texas-Denton, Texas. He earned his Bachelor of Science degree in criminal justice from Texas A&M University-Texarkana, a member of the Texas A&M University System. He is currently ABD (all but dissertation) and working on his dissertation about the effects of student perceptions on the fear of crime regarding campus safety and carrying concealed handguns on a university campus. He is currently a professor of criminal justice at Collin College in McKinney, Texas. He also serves as an adjunct professor of criminal justice at the University of North Texas in Denton, Texas. He has also served as an adjunct professor in criminal justice at Brown Mackie College in Bedford, Texas. He currently serves on the Para-legal Advisory Board at Collin College and serves on the Interdisciplinary Committee on Race, Poverty and Crime at Collin College. He continues to serves as faculty advisor for the Gamma Alpha Epsilon American Criminal Justice Association student organization at Collin College. He also served as a legal studies instructor for Frisco I.S.D. at their Career and Technical Education Center instructing high school students in criminal justice studies. Prior to entering academia, Lee DeBoer served as a Master Peace Officer for the City of Pittsburg and the City of Farmersville in the State of Texas. During his tenure working in the City of Pittsburg, He worked in criminal investigations, inventory of criminal evidence, and Uniform Crime Report statistics reporting.

## About the Contributing Authors

**Elyshia Aseltine** is an Assistant Professor of Criminal Justice and Criminology at Lycoming College in Williamsport, Pennsylvania. She joined the Lycoming faculty after earning her Ph.D. in sociology at the University of Texas at Austin. Her research focuses on juvenile justice, courts, and policing in the United States and Africa.

**Kathryn A. Branch** is an Assistant Professor in the Department of Criminology and Criminal Justice at the University of Tampa. Dr. Branch's research focuses on gendered forms of violence (i.e., sexual assault and intimate partner violence). Her current research studies the secondary impact of gendered forms of violence on support providers (i.e., friends and professors) and the role of social support in intimate partner violence victimization and perpetration.

**Chris Capsambelis** has over 30 years of experience in the field of law enforcement. He is a former police sergeant with ten years of police experience. He spent another ten years training police officers in both Pennsylvania and Florida. He holds a Master of Arts degree in Criminology and a Doctor of Philosophy degree in Measurement and Evaluation. Currently, he is an Associate Professor of Criminology at the University of Tampa.

**Petter Lovaas** has his B.S. in Information Technology Management from the University of Minnesota, and his M.S. and D.Sc. in Information Assurance and Computer Security from Dakota State University. Dr. Lovaas currently teaches in the Computer and Information Sciences Department at Niagara University as an assistant professor, teaching Computer Forensics and Computer Security courses. Dr. Lovaas also has extensive experience in information security consulting with the banking and financial sector.

**David Olson** is a Professor of Criminal Justice and Criminology at Loyola University Chicago, and previously served as Department Chair and Director of Loyola's interdisciplinary Forensic Science Program. Dr. Olson is also a Special Assistant to the Cook County Sheriff. For nearly 20 years, Dr. Olson worked at the Illinois Criminal Justice Information Authority, where he was the director of Illinois' Statewide Drug and Violent Crime Control Strategy Impact Evaluation Program. Dr. Olson received his B.S. in Criminal Justice from Loyola University Chicago, his M.A. in Criminal Justice from the University of Illinois at Chicago, and his Ph.D. in Political Science/Public Policy Analysis from the University of Illinois at Chicago. In 2011, Dr. Olson was presented with the Hans W. Mattick Award for outstanding accomplishments in the field of criminology and criminal justice research.

**Craig P. Rahanian** assumed the duties of his current position as Superintendent of the American Battle Monuments Commission Brookwood on 12 July 2010. Mr. Rahanian is accredited with the United States Diplomatic Mission London to the United Kingdom. Prior to this assignment Mr. Rahanian was assigned for eleven years to the United States Mission to France at three different posts. He served for six years as the Superintendent of ABMC Somme, France and served as a Deputy Superintendent in Meuse –Argonne and Brittany, France. He was awarded the Department of the Navy Superior Public Service for his work in the Meuse-Argonne and the Department of the Army Commanders award for Civilian Service.

**Mr. Rahanian** was appointed a Career Civilian U.S. Government Supervisory Officer in 2004. He holds a Bachelor of Arts Degree in History and a Graduate Certification in Mediation from the University of Houston. He holds a Diploma from the United States Army Command and General Staff College, and is a graduate of France's Institute of Advanced Studies in National Defence, L'Institut des Hautes Etudes de Défense Nationale. He is currently working on a Masters in Criminal Justice at the University of North Texas.

**Stephen L. Rayle** is an Associate Professor of Criminal Justice at Valencia College in Orlando, Florida. He received his Doctorate in Education at Nova Southeastern University as well as a Master's Degree in Criminal Justice. He has nearly ten years of experience with the Florida Department of Corrections. Dr. Rayle enjoys public service and is currently the Chairman of the Orlando Citizen's Police Review Board.

**Mitch D. Sigal** is a seasoned investigator with over 20 years of Law Enforcement experience at the city, county, and federal levels. His experience includes patrol, narcotics, and money laundering, and he has significant training and experience in Death Investigation and Disaster Management. Mr. Sigal's writing experience includes over five articles on "The Link Between Animal Abuse, Child Abuse, and Domestic Violence," co-authoring a violence prevention manual that has been sold and employed in several states across the United States, and grants for violence prevention programs as well as new technology in the field of forensics.

**Omar Syed** is a Lecturer in the Department of Criminal Justice for Texas State University in San Marcos, Texas. In addition, he is an attorney for the University of Texas System's Office of General Counsel, where he advises the 15 University of Texas System institutions on criminal law, employment law, and tort law matters. Before holding these appointments, Mr. Syed served as an Assistant United States Attorney for the District of Minnesota, where he prosecuted defendants charged with federal narcotics, firearms and white-collar offenses.

**Megan Houck Timmins** is a Senior Law and Policy Analyst at the University of Maryland Center for Health and Homeland Security (CHHS). She graduated from the University of Maryland School of Law and was admitted to the Maryland Bar in 2007. In addition, Megan graduated *magna cum laude* from St. Mary's College of Maryland in 2004, with a B.A. in Economics. Prior to joining CHHS, Megan worked on bankruptcy and white collar crime matters in the private sector and on issues related to higher education institutions with the Maryland Office of the Attorney General. She also studied international and comparative criminal justice in Aberdeen, Scotland.

**Michael Richard Vesely** is a Senior Law and Policy Analyst at the University of Maryland Center for Health and Homeland Security (CHHS). He graduated with honors from the University of Maryland School of Law and was admitted to the Maryland Bar in 2006. At CHHS, Michael has worked as an instructor for the Department of Homeland Security and has worked with federal, state, local, and private sector partners in numerous areas of national security, including counterterrorism. He has also worked for the State Department's Antiterrorism Assistance Program assisting various international allies of the United States to develop and enhance their own domestic security programs.

# SECTION 1
## OVERVIEW OF THE CRIMINAL JUSTICE SYSTEM

**Chapter 1**
Introduction to Criminal Justice

**Chapter 2**
Theories of Crime and Behavior

© corgarashu/Shutterstock.com

# Introduction to Criminal Justice

## KEY TERMS

| | | |
|---|---|---|
| Community corrections | Criminal justice system | Misdemeanor |
| Conflict model | Decriminalize | Net-widening |
| Consensus model | Department of Justice (DOJ) | Norms |
| Courtroom workgroup | Due process model | Plea bargain |
| Crime | Exclusionary rule | Policing |
| Crime control model | Felony | White-collar crime |

# CHAPTER OBJECTIVES

1 Distinguish criminal justice from other social science disciplines.

2 Discuss how the U.S. criminal justice system was created.

3 Understand the justice system as a network of agencies focused on understanding and responding to crime.

4 Analyze a range of policy choices, including the motivations for these choices.

5 Describe the steps involved in the justice process.

## Case Study: O.J. Simpson and Cameron Todd Willingham

Can money buy freedom? Most are familiar with the murder trial of O.J. Simpson, a former professional football player and actor. On June 12, 1994, Nicole Brown Simpson, Simpson's former wife and mother of two of his children, and her friend Ronald Goldman were brutally murdered. O.J. Simpson was charged and pleaded not guilty to both murders. After preliminary hearings regarding admissibility of evidence, the trial began; nearly nine months later, the jury found Simpson not guilty of both murders.

Simpson's sizable team of defense attorneys, referred to as the "Dream Team," included high-profile attorneys and DNA experts. The defense questioned the DNA evidence and further raised doubts about the prosecution's case by insinuating that Detective Mark Fuhrman was a racist who had planted evidence to implicate Simpson in the murders.

Simpson's acquittal shocked the nation and caused many who had watched the televised trial to question the inefficiencies and ineffectiveness of the criminal justice system.

Unlike the high-profile Simpson murder trial, which lasted for months, few are familiar with the case of Texas citizen Cameron Todd Willingham. On December 23, 1991, Willingham's home caught fire and Willingham was able to escape with minor burns. His three young daughters were killed and Willingham was charged in their deaths. Prosecutors sought the death penalty and, eight months after the deaths of his daughters, Willingham was convicted of capital murder and sentenced to death.[1]

At trial an expert witness testified that an accelerant had been used to purposely light the house on fire.[2] Further bolstering the prosecution's case, a jailhouse informant testified that Willingham described squirting lighter fluid around the house and lighting it on fire. Willingham's two attorneys, who were appointed to represent him, failed to find a fire expert to counter the prosecution's claims and only presented one witness, a babysitter who did not believe Willingham could have killed his daughters.[3]

Willingham appealed his conviction. The Court of Criminal Appeals of Texas affirmed the judgment and sentence of the trial court. Federal courts granted a temporary stay, but an appeal to the U.S. Supreme Court was denied. The only remaining option was for the Texas governor to grant him clemency.

Willingham's supporters contacted Dr. Gerald Hurst, a scientist and fire investigator, who reviewed the files and was alarmed at the fire marshal's high rate of arson findings. Hurst dismissed the conclusion that the fire's patterns suggested use of an accelerant.[4] He concluded that faulty wiring or a space heater caused the accidental fire. Despite the new evidence that was provided to the governor that indicated the deaths of Willingham's daughters was accidental, Willingham's request for clemency was denied. He was executed on February 17, 2004.

Afterwards, more questions were raised about his innocence and the media took notice of his case. The *Chicago Tribune* wrote an article in December 2004, and *The New Yorker* wrote one in 2009. In 2006, the Innocence Project submitted the case for review to the Texas Forensic Science Commission.[5] In 2008, the commission agreed to review the case, and a final report was issued on April 15, 2011. The report recognized that the science used to convict Willingham was faulty, but it did not exonerate him. The report proposes changes that need to take place in arson cases.[6] Texas has still not admitted that they executed an innocent man, and in the eyes of the law, Willingham remains guilty of the deaths of his daughters.

The cases of Simpson and Willingham displayed two very different sides of the criminal justice system. While the protracted, high-profile Simpson case received overwhelming media and public attention, the reality of the criminal justice system is that most cases—like Willingham's—are decided in quick fashion in courtrooms across the country every day, often at the expense of the defendant's due process rights. Errors can occur on both sides of the spectrum: guilty people will sometimes go free, while innocent people may be unjustly ruled guilty. The strengths and weaknesses of the criminal justice system will be explored in depth in this chapter and this book as a whole. While the media and common opinion often provide easy answers, you are encouraged to look deeper at crime, justice, and the systems used in a justice system charged with protecting both our liberty and security.

## What Is Criminal Justice?

The **criminal justice system,** which comprises the police, courts, and correctional facilities, is how the government enforces social norms, laws, and justice. Criminal justice is also an academic discipline. It is important to understand and study the criminal justice system, in a reasoned and scientifically accurate manner, because this knowledge helps explain how the police, judicial, and correctional systems interact as a part of the larger justice system. Ideally, this knowledge will then lead to intelligent and effective policy choices.

Criminal justice incorporates the study of other social sciences such as sociology, psychology, political sciences, and law. While interdisciplinary, the study of criminal justice is closely related to, and intertwined with, the study of sociology. *Sociologists* are individuals who study society and apply their findings for the benefit of society. *Criminologists* use sociological skills to study crime and criminals, often with the goal of advancing theoretical knowledge. Criminal justice scholars have similar goals, often focusing on the benefits and consequences of policy choices.

By analyzing what programs have worked and failed, lawmakers can design policies and programs where they are really needed.

*Criminal justice researchers* look at how the decisions of one part of the justice system, widely defined, affect the other parts. These researchers seek to understand how the system adapts to new trends and how the system can handle any problems that arise. Like sociologists and other social scientists, criminal justice researchers pull from many different disciplines to analyze and understand why a problem is occurring. However, while many other disciplines merely look at ideology and the theoretical—trying to postulate how an individual, group, or system would hypothetically react in a given situation based on theory—criminal justice looks at how the system actually is reacting. Criminal justice operates within the confines of the real world based on evidence and statistics. Ideally, the criminal justice system, which includes researchers at many levels, examines what is currently happening and analyzes and responds to these behaviors as necessary.

However, we also know that our justice system, as part of our political system, may not always rely on evidence. It is important to look at actual programs and their success—or lack thereof—to better understand what works and what does not. Theory-based research is just that—theory. By looking at actual numbers, what has been successful, and what has failed, better social policy may evolve. With issues as politicized as crime and justice, policy decisions will ideally be rooted in facts, data, and reasoned analysis. Political debate is an important part of the policy process, which leads criminal justice to maintain a multidisciplinary focus. By studying media, politics, education, medicine, and other social institutions, criminal justice scholars integrate other disciplines' findings into their research, ideally leading to a better understanding of crime and the justice system. Simply put, a greater understanding of the justice system can help make the system more effective. By recognizing the needs and problems faced by victims, lawbreakers, and the accused, lawmakers can design policies, programs, and initiatives to address those problems.

# Two Models of the Criminal Justice System

The Constitution of the United States was designed to protect citizens from the power of the government. However, the processes necessary to ensure these rights may conflict with the goal of removing dangerous people from the general population. As indicated in the Simpson and Willingham cases, the justice system attempts to strike a balance between liberty and security. Laws protect people's freedoms and do not allow infringements without cause. For example, some liberty is lost due to speed limits, but this loss is determined to be an acceptable cost for ensuring security and safety.

Much more freedom or liberty is lost when a person is convicted of a crime. In order for this loss to be considered acceptable, there must be a specific, understandable, and predictable process for determining guilt before an individual's liberty can be taken away by the state. This is the basis for due process protections.

The justice system is also responsible for protecting the freedom and security of a large number of citizens. Due to concerns about time and cost, the system has developed a number of formal and informal processes that are intended to ensure efficient operation. Case backloads, cost, and constitutional guarantees of a speedy trial have each contributed to the development of an efficient system for processing criminal cases. Whether the system has become too efficient is the subject of much debate.

In 1968, Herbert Packer, in his book, *The Limits of the Criminal Sanction,*[7] elucidated the value systems within the **criminal justice system**. The **crime control model** focuses on controlling crime and protecting citizens in the most efficient way possible. Packer wrote, "The value system that underlies the Crime Control Model is based on the proposition that the repression of criminal conduct is by far the most important function to be performed by the criminal process."[8] The **due process model** focuses on fairness, the rights of all Americans, and the process through which criminal guilt is established.

**Criminal justice system**
The police, courts, and correctional departments.

**Crime control model**
A model of the criminal justice system that focuses on controlling crime and protecting the public in the most efficient way.

**Due process model**
A model of the criminal justice system that focuses on protecting the rights of the accused.

Both the Simpson and Willingham cases went through the full "obstacle course" that is the American judicial system, although the Willingham case initially moved through the courts at a rapid pace. The due process obstacle course is the result of the court's efforts to make sure a defendant's rights have not been violated. This model, with an emphasis on rights, contrasts with the crime control "assembly line," which strives for efficiency whenever possible, including plea bargaining and other efforts to move cases quickly—including the potential to minimize evidence that is not consistent with the prosecutor's case.

To declare one of these models superior to the other requires a judgment grounded in ideological difference. Conservative values are reflected in the crime control model, while the due process model reflects values more commonly held by liberals. The last 50 years have marked a shift in dominant values, leading to policy choices consistent with Packer's models.

During the 1960s, the due process model dominated the justice system. This was a relatively liberal period in the United States, and rulings of the Warren Court greatly expanded the rights of those accused of crime. *The Warren Court refers* to the U.S. Supreme Court led by Chief Justice Earl Warren from 1953 to 1969. The Warren Court was a liberal-leaning bench and is most noted for expanding civil rights and civil liberties. The political climate began to shift to more conservative values in the mid-1970s. This ideological shift, which continues to this day, resulted in an environment in which conservatives have been able to create criminal justice policies more consistent with Packer's crime control model.

While a logical argument can be made for the benefits of either model, the reality is that an ideological choice has been made. Politicians, supported by much of the public, have embraced a tough-on-crime attitude that includes longer sentences, reduced protections from biased investigations, and fewer opportunities to question police and court practices. However, both models remain active in today's justice system. The O.J. Simpson case can be seen as an example of using due process protections to the benefit of the accused. This was possible, in part, due to the defendant's wealth, power, and prestige. Simpson had the luxury of being able to force his accusers to navigate the due process obstacle course. The final verdict in Simpson's criminal case was rendered almost 16 months after the murders.

Under the Warren Court, the due process model dominated the criminal justice system.

In contrast, Willingham's death sentence was issued just eight months after the murders. While some may define the lengthy appeal process that followed the conviction as an obstacle course, the obstacles did not prevent the execution of a man who may have been innocent. The Willingham case is an example of a reduced emphasis on due process typical of the majority of criminal justice cases. While high-profile trials such as Simpson's demonstrate the perils of the obstacle course, often leading to criticism, the vast majority of cases are more similar to the Willingham example. In this example, a very efficient process resulted in an execution, in spite of evidence of innocence.

The differences between the Simpson and Willingham cases demonstrate how equally serious cases can be handled differently by the justice system. Not every case is handled the same way, despite what many people believe. The public's understanding of the justice system comes from many sources: these may include reading a textbook as part of a formal learning experience, but they also include the media and informal discussions with those who have not and will not engage in a structured effort to understand the justice system. As a result, media and popular representations of a high-profile defendant's due process rights may obscure the reality that efficient processes, much more like an assembly line, dominate less publicized trials.

This chapter examines the history and goals of the justice system, the importance of engaging in a scholarly examination of this system, and how the system is organized. Students are encouraged to reflect on their political ideology and the ways they have learned about the justice system as they read this text. In addition to providing a framework for debate about how the justice system should be structured, Packer's models allow for reflection on how individuals' political ideologies may lead to discounting information inconsistent with those values. The examination of the justice system begins with Packer's models, as they will provide a framework for thinking about many of the issues to be introduced in this text. Relying on this model, readers are encouraged to examine their own biases in search of a fact-based review of the criminal justice system.

## Crime Control Model

In his examination of the crime control and due process models, Packer offers a clear discussion of the issues raised in the debate about the efficiency of the justice system versus protections for constitutionally guaranteed rights. According to Packer, those who adopt the crime control model argue that punishment and repression of criminal conduct are the most important functions of the justice system. Controlling criminal activity is the most important job of law enforcement, and the system should function quickly and efficiently, much like an assembly line. Proponents of the assembly line model believe that efficiency is key because "the failure of law enforcement to bring criminal conduct under tight control is viewed as leading to the breakdown of public order and thence to the disappearance of an important condition of human freedom."[9]

This model focuses on the efficiency of the criminal justice system to screen suspects, determine guilt, and assign appropriate punishments for those suspects who have been convicted. Efficiency does not require that a suspect be apprehended, tried, and found guilty quickly. Rather, it means that every case should be tried with the proper amount of man-hours devoted to it. The proper amount of man-hours devoted to a case can vary depending upon the severity of the crime, whether it was witnessed or not, and the number of individuals who are involved.

In order for the crime control model to be successful in a country that wants a high conviction rate but does not necessarily want to devote more resources and training to the criminal justice system, suspects must be apprehended and convicted at a high rate. As Packer stated in *The Limits of the Criminal Sanction*, "There must then be a premium on speed and finality."[10]

Proponents of the crime control model believe that the judicial system should move swiftly and efficiently, much like a factory's assembly line.

# Due Process Model

In contrast to the efficiency of an assembly line, due process protections result in an obstacle course. By viewing the criminal justice system as an assembly line, Packer emphasizes that each stage of the criminal justice process is a decision point. Due to the emphasis on efficiency, each decision has the potential to prevent the quick disposal of cases. In contrast, the due process model focuses on protecting the rights of the accused. These rights are protected through constraints on police, courts, and corrections that make it more difficult to prove guilt. In this model, fairness is the primary goal of the justice process. According to Packer, "Each of its successive stages is designed to present formidable impediments to carrying the accused any further along in the process."[11] This process focuses less on crime control and much more on the defendant's rights as they are protected under the Constitution. There are major differences between the two models that can be seen at their earliest stages. Packer wrote, "The Crime Control Perspective, as we have suggested, places heavy reliance on the ability of investigative and prosecutorial officers, acting in an informal setting in which their distinctive skills are given full sway, to elicit and reconstruct a tolerably accurate account of what actually took place in an alleged criminal event. The Due Process Model rejects this premise and substitutes for it a view of informal, non-adjudicative fact-finding that stresses the possibility of error."[12]

The due process model sets out to protect the rights of the accused.

In the due process model, facts are continuously questioned and analyzed, and a case is not considered fully adjudicated until a hearing has been held in the fact-finding context. Proponents of the due process model argue that this is the better model because the goal is to eliminate as many mistakes and wrongful convictions as possible. This is the opposite of the crime control model. The crime control model emphasizes finality, even accepting that a certain number of wrongful convictions will occur when dealing with a large volume of cases. Further differences can be emphasized by the deference that the due process model gives to the letter of the law. The due process model requires that certain standards be met; if they are not, then there are consequences.

The idea that a person is presumed innocent until proven guilty is an essential tenet of the American judicial system and the due process system. The State must prove the defendant is guilty beyond a reasonable doubt. The defendant has no burden in proving his or her case. It is the State's responsibility to convince the judge or jury that the defendant is indeed guilty of the crime of which he or she is accused.

## Crime Control vs. Due Process Model in the Courts

The merits and effectiveness of the crime control model and the due process model are in constant debate. The Supreme Court case of *Whren v. United States*, for example, illustrates these contrasting philosophies. On June 23, 1993, plainclothes officers were patrolling a "high drug area" in Washington, D.C., when they noticed a Pathfinder stopped at a stop sign with two young male African-American occupants. The driver of the car was looking at something in the passenger's hand and remained at the stop sign for over 20 seconds. The car then made a right-hand turn without signaling and sped off. The officers followed and approached the car, identifying themselves as police. An officer noticed that the passenger, Michael Whren, was holding two plastic bags of what appeared to be cocaine.[13] Whren and the driver, James Brown, were arrested and charged with violating various drug laws. The two were eventually convicted of drug-related offenses.

The case was appealed to the Supreme Court. Whren and Brown's defense attorneys argued the legality of the stop and the subsequent seizure of the drugs. The defense argued that the officers had probable cause to believe that traffic laws had been violated but did not have probable cause to search the vehicle for illegal drugs. They believed that the officers used the minor traffic violations as a pretext to search the vehicle and that the officers' behavior deviated from normal police behavior. However, the court declined to overturn the convictions and affirmed the decision of the lower court. In the Supreme Court decision *Whren v. United States*, the court held that "the temporary detention of a motorist upon probable cause to believe that he has violated the traffic laws does not violate the Fourth Amendment's prohibition against unreasonable search and seizures, even if a reasonable officer would not have stopped the motorist absent some additional law enforcement objective."[14]

Proponents of the crime control model would point out that these men were charged and found guilty of drug charges because they had cocaine in plain view. Officers must have probable cause in order to search, but if something is in plain view—as the cocaine was—they may seize it, and that can serve as the probable cause to search the vehicle. The bags could be seized by the police and later could be used by the prosecution. The bags of cocaine would not be subject to the **exclusionary rule**, which states that illegally obtained evidence can be excluded from trial. The crime control model says that the convictions of Whren and Brown were the correct result because they incarcerated drug users and enhanced the security of the public.

**Exclusionary rule** A legal mandate applied when a piece of evidence has been obtained in a manner that violates the rights of the defendant under due process.

Those who identify more strongly with the due process model may claim that this stop was actually an example of profiling. Due process advocates argue that the stop occurred because the police took the defendants' race, vehicle, and location into account. The police did not witness any illegal activity before the stop, which violated the defendants' due process rights. Further, due process advocates argue that the liberty of the public is diminished when police are allowed to initiate an investigation with merely a suspicion that race, location, and vehicle type equate to illegal activity.

The Supreme Court, and the judiciary as a whole, can be a powerful agent of social control and maintaining the public's due process rights. In the near future, as more questions arise regarding the rights of the government to maintain order and an individual's due process rights, the judiciary will play a more prominent role as it sorts through the various legal questions.

## The Public's Perspective

The public's perception of the criminal justice system can be described as cynical at best, especially when they hear statistics that for every 1,000 crimes, only about 20 people are sent to prison.[15] However, over a 30-year period, crime rates decreased from 51.2 incidences of violent crime per 100,000 people in 1994 to the lowest recorded level of 18.6 incidences per 100,000 people in 2015.[16] Statistics on homicide rates show further decline, at 4.8 incidences per 100,000 people in 2010, a low rate not seen since the 1960s.[17]

Despite the decreasing crime rates, the number of adults in the correctional population has continued to increase. In 1970, there were fewer than 200,000 inmates in state and federal prisons. By mid-2003, the number had increased to more than 1.2 million inmates. Additionally, nearly 700,000 inmates were held in local jails.[18]

As the judicial system continues to incarcerate people and limit their liberty, it is important to ask why. To limit someone's *liberty*—or their freedom to make decisions and choices—is not a decision that the judicial system takes lightly. Limiting a person's liberty is done to ensure the security of the public. The public wants to know they will be safe and is often willing to take away an individual's liberty so the collective can feel safer.

The media plays a large role in skewing the public's perception of the criminal justice system by focusing on cases such as that of O.J. Simpson in which offenders escape punishment because of their celebrity status. Constant coverage of crime on television and on the Internet further skews the public's perception of crime. From 1992 to 1996, the number of homicides decreased by 20%, but there was a 721% increase in the major news channels' homicide coverage.[19] Media coverage has the greatest impact on how the public perceives crime. Nearly 76% of citizens form their opinions on crime based on what they see in the media.[20] Because of this, from 1992 to 1993 the public believed that crime was the number one problem facing the nation. Media coverage of "sexy" stories that will grab the public's attention is often not proportionate to reality. For instance, nearly 70% of the news stories

Media coverage of high-profile crimes such as homicide influences the public's perception that crime has increased.

broadcast or published in California discuss violence that involves youth, when in reality, only 14% of violent crime arrests in the state actually involve youths.[21]

Politicians have sensed the public's dissatisfaction with the criminal justice system and often run campaigns on this platform. Politicians argue that they will be tougher on crime than their predecessors and will implement changes to the system that will result in more convictions. Politicians running for re-election will often tout statistics showing that during their terms crime has dropped and the number of convictions has increased.

Fictionalized law shows on television have brought the courtroom into the public's homes week after week and show an incredibly simplified and fast moving judicial system. This unrealistic portrayal of the criminal justice system can affect the public's understanding and opinions of the process and can even affect public policy.

**Critical Thinking**

Would you rather live in a society that risks the chance that guilty people will go free in order to protect innocents, or a society that accepts the reality that they will occasionally punish innocent people in order to be sure no guilty people are allowed to go free?

## History of the Criminal Justice System in America

America's criminal justice system has its roots in the English common law system. This system did not differentiate between misdemeanors, felonies, and common law crimes like today's judicial system does. It recognized when someone committed a crime—or broke a community standard—and punished them accordingly.

In the United States, as the country became unified and governments were put into place, the criminal justice system evolved because laws became codified and penalties were attached. The criminal justice system began to recognize differences in the seriousness of crimes, and classified them as misdemeanors or felonies. Generally, **misdemeanors** were minor criminal offenses that were punished less severely than felonies, usually with a fine or a prison term of less than one year.[22] **Felonies** were more serious crimes, which typically carried prison sentences of longer than one year.[23]

**Misdemeanor** A lesser crime that is punishable by jail time for up to one year and/or a fine.

**Felony** A crime that is punishable by imprisonment in excess of a year or by death.

How, and for what length of time, people should be punished for the crimes they commit has long been debated. In 1764, Italian philosopher Cesare Beccaria wrote *On Crime and Punishments*, a treatise that advocated for publicized laws and consistent punishments for crimes.[24] In 1829, England passed the Metropolitan Police Act and formed the London Metropolitan Police. Fifty years earlier, in 1789, the United States established the U.S.

Marshals Service.[25] The first modern police force in the United States was the Boston police department, established in 1838, and followed shortly thereafter by the New York police department.[26]

The **Department of Justice (DOJ)** was founded in 1870. This department within the executive branch of the federal government is designed to enforce the laws of the United States. Within the DOJ is the Office of the Attorney General, which serves as the legal department for all cases that concern the federal government. The attorney general and the deputy attorney general plan and enact department policies and programs and supervise and direct the department's organizational units.[27] There are numerous other offices within the DOJ that often serve specialized functions including appellate work, national security, etc., and employ units of lawyers with specific specialties depending upon the crime being committed.

In 1931, the National Commission on Law Observance and Enforcement, more commonly known as the Wickersham Commission after its chairman George W. Wickersham, published the *Report on Lawlessness in Law Enforcement*.[28] The report was the first major investigation into police misconduct and alleged that the police were misusing their power and using brutality to force confessions and admissions from suspected criminals. Although police departments disagreed with the report's findings, the Wickersham Commission's findings nevertheless spurred dramatic changes, including the formation of internal affairs commissions to investigate police misconduct and Supreme Court decisions that limited police officers' use of physical force. A thorough summary of the Wickersham Commission's report is given in Chapter 3 of this book.

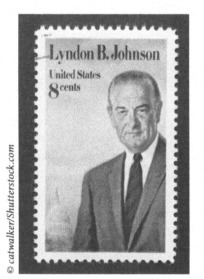

President Johnson's Commission on Law Enforcement and Administration of Justice provided increased assistance to local law enforcement.

President Lyndon B. Johnson, in 1967, appointed the President's Commission on Law Enforcement and Administration of Justice to provide increased federal law enforcement efforts, to provide assistance to local law enforcement efforts, and to provide a comprehensive analysis of crime and its origins in the United States.[29]

In 1968, Congress passed the Safe Streets and Crime Control Act, which established the Law Enforcement Assistance Administration (LEAA).[30] The LEAA, which was abolished in 1982, distributed federal funding for educational programs, research, and local crime initiatives to state and local law enforcement agencies.

The Supreme Court's 1966 ruling in *Miranda v. Arizona* was a hugely important legal decision granting criminal defendants a number of rights upon arrest. Defendants must be informed that they have the right to remain silent; anything they say can and will be used against them in court; they have the right for an attorney to be present before and during questioning; and if they cannot afford an attorney, an attorney will be appointed to them to be present before and during questioning.[31] A waiver of these rights is only valid if the defendant waives them freely, knowingly, and intelligently. Miranda rights are explored further in subsequent chapters of this book.

Another significant decision occurred five years before *Miranda,* in 1961. In *Mapp v. Ohio*, the Supreme Court ruled that a defendant has a right to protection against unreasonable searches and seizures in both federal court and state court.[32] If a government agent (i.e., a police officer or someone working on behalf of the government) obtains evidence in violation of the search and seizure doctrine encased within the Fourth Amendment of the U.S. Constitution, the evidence will not be admissible in a state court.[33]

A defendant's right to an attorney was clarified in the 1963 case *Gideon v. Wainwright*.[34] If the defendant cannot afford an attorney, then the government must appoint one to serve in court on the defendant's behalf. The idea of a public defender's office devoted to providing representation to

## Career Connections: Defense Attorney

Defense attorneys, like prosecutors, must complete law school and pass the bar exam for the specific state in which they practice law. Criminal defense attorneys can enter into private practice, in which clients pay their fees; alternatively, they can become members of the Office of the Public Defender and be paid a salary. Attorneys for the Office of the Public Defender are required to provide their legal services on any case to which they are assigned. In cases in which the office already represents a co-defendant, the case is given to a private attorney, who is paid by the office and may use all resources available to the office.

Frequently, defense attorneys face difficult challenges when working on a case, both inside and outside of the courtroom. They often do not have the resources that are available to the prosecution. They must rely on the prosecution to have turned over all exculpatory evidence or potentially exculpatory evidence, and they must conduct independent investigations with significantly less funds or manpower than those available to the state.

Defense attorneys have an ethical obligation to provide the most effective defense to each client, devoting a significant amount of time and resources to each case. The defense attorney's legal strategy and approach will, by necessity, vary depending on the circumstances of the case. In cases in which the defendant's guilt is very much in doubt, the attorney will argue motions to suppress witness statements and to exclude potentially damaging evidence, while gathering evidence to support the defendant's innocence such as alibi or character witnesses. In cases in which the defendant's innocence will likely be difficult to ascertain in court, the defense attorney may opt to pursue plea negotiations with the prosecution to limit the amount of time the client will have to spend incarcerated.

The defense attorney's job requires him or her to be realistic about every case and to give a thorough and exhaustive effort regardless of the circumstances of the case or client. Being knowledgeable and creative are essential characteristics for any defense attorney. The attorney must be quick-thinking and prepared for a variety of situations that may arise in the courtroom. The attorney must be intimately familiar with court procedures and provide comprehensive, objective counsel to his or her client about the legal proceedings—even if the advice is not necessarily what the client wants to hear.

defendants who cannot afford private counsel is revolutionary and fairly recent. Both the federal and state criminal justice systems employ public defenders whose sole job is to represent defendants. *Gideon v. Wainwright* and the roles of public defenders and defense attorneys are discussed further in Chapter 5.

**Critical Thinking**

Imagine that you are a defense attorney for the Office of the Public Defender and are assigned to defend an accused child molester. What challenges might you face, and how could you overcome them to represent the defendant fairly?

## Scope and Size of Today's Justice System

With the world's population consistently on the rise, it is not surprising that the scope of the criminal justice system has grown steadily larger. In 2012 governments at the federal, state, and local levels in the United States spent an estimated $265 billion on law enforcement, corrections, and court services.[35] As of 2014, there were 6,851,000 people under correctional supervision in the U.S.[36] This number includes adults who were in jail or prison and on probation or parole. Of that number, 516,900 were African-American males who were serving time in state or federal prisons and local jails.[37] Of those men, 241,381 were between the ages of 25 and 29.[38]

A huge workforce is needed in order to supervise these individuals. A 2010 study indicated that between the local, state, and federal systems, the justice system employed over 2.4 million persons with a total payroll of close to 11.7 billion for the month of March 2010 alone. Only 11.6% were federal employees, slightly over a third (36.4%) were state employees, and more than half (57.1) worked at the local level.[39]

But who bears the costs of the criminal justice system? Statistics indicate that 55% of all justice system expenses are funded by local governments, and nearly 28.9% by state governments.[40] Over the years, the amount of money spent per capita has increased. In 1982, the per capita expenditure across federal, state, and local governments was $158. By 2010 this had increased nearly four times to $682. At the same time, judicial and legal services increased from $34 to $139 per U.S. resident, and police protection from $84 to $309.[41] While it may seem that the local government is bearing a disproportionate burden, most of the money that local government spends is for police protection, which is primarily funded by local governments instead of state governments.

© CLICKMANIS/Shutterstock.com

Police departments are primarily funded by local rather than state governments.

The economy, too, can have a significant influence on how programs are structured within the criminal justice system. During times of economic crisis, policy changes are often rampant as lawmakers search for more cost-effective solutions for the criminal justice system. These cheaper alternatives, however, can lead to less effective treatments for offenders. For example, lawmakers may restructure policies cutting down on court-mandated rehab for drug-addicted defendants in favor of the less expensive alternative of housing them in correctional facilities where they receive little help. As a result, these offenders may be more likely, upon release, to recommit an offense.

Several alternative programs and diversionary classes have been made available to offenders in an effort to decrease the number of offenders going through the criminal court system. However, this system has actually had the opposite effect and has resulted in **net-widening**—the number of offenders within the court system has increased, because the criminal justice system has expanded the number of offenders it must supervise.

**Net-widening**
A phenomenon in which the number of offenders within the court system increases as the criminal justice system expands the number of offenders it must supervise.

## What Is Crime?

Crime is considered a social phenomenon that occurs when a person breaks a law or rule of the society in which he or she lives. More specifically, a **crime** is a legally prohibited action that injures the public welfare or morals or the interests of the state. These definitions reflect the idea that a crime is an action that violates the social norm. While the criminal justice system delineates a formalized way of preventing crimes, social **norms** are the informal process of controlling society's behavior. Societal laws and practices have made it difficult for convicted criminals to find employment, vote, be approved for credit, etc. By stigmatizing bad behavior and increasing the difficulty of achieving success in society when one has been convicted of a crime, the criminal justice system aims to deter people from committing crimes.

**Crime** A legally prohibited action that injures the public welfare or morals or the interests of the state.

**Norms** Social expectations for appropriate behavior.

It is important to understand the distinction between crime and deviance. Deviance is an action that violates a social norm but does not necessarily violate an established law. Such behaviors may be frowned upon by society but are not criminal.

The concept that committing a crime is something to be avoided is ingrained in people since early childhood. Parents instill in young children the idea that for every action there is a consequence, either positive or negative. Parents teach this by rewarding good behavior and punishing bad behavior. A child who successfully completes his or her chores may be rewarded with an allowance or another privilege, whereas a child who hits a younger sibling will be punished. From an early age, children learn in a very direct way that there is a code of behavior to which they are expected to conform.

**Consensus model** The idea that when a group comes together to form a society, they will have mutually shared values and norms and will come to a consensus about what is a crime.

The **consensus model** states that members of a society naturally reach a basic agreement regarding shared norms and values.[42] Even a diverse group will have similar norms and values and will endeavor to put into place a structure that emphasizes the norms they value. Laws add structure to a community or group of people, detailing for the society which behaviors are acceptable and expected and which are not.

The consensus model asserts that an action becomes criminal once a society agrees that said behavior is criminal. Durkheim (1893) stated that an act becomes criminal "when it offends strong and defined states of the collective conscience."[43] Stealing a car, for example, is a crime because society has decided that it values an individual's right to his or her property, and that the lawful owner of the property has the right to dictate how and by whom the property is used. When an offender interferes with the owner's rights by taking the property without permission (in this case, stealing a car), society has decided that the act violates a value or norm that it finds to be important. To discourage potential offenders from repeating this action, society deems the action criminal and promises punishment for violators.

The opposing **conflict model** assumes that different segments of society—divided by social class, age, race, income, etc.—have different norms and value systems and perpetually struggle against each other for control of society.[44] This model states that there is no stability in what is "the norm," and that criminal activity is determined by whichever group holds the power at that moment.[45] An example of the conflict model in practice is the debate over abortion. The Supreme Court's decision in *Roe v. Wade* marked a dramatic shift on the subject in the United States by allowing women to have an abortion if they so choose.[46] This norm, however, is certainly not unanimously agreed upon in American society, with different factions of the public holding contrasting opinions on abortion, often segmented by political ideology. In a 2011 poll, 68% of Republicans identified themselves as "pro-life," compared to 32% of Democrats.[47] For many years, Republicans have advocated passing legislation that would prohibit any type of abortion with a few very narrow exceptions, but have not been able to do so because they have never had the overwhelming majority they have needed to change policy. Now that Congress will have a majority of Republicans in 2017, Congress will be able to do so, or at least makes some changes on the issue of abortion.

The conflict model holds that diverse societies cannot always reach a general consensus about what is and what is not criminal. In order for a behavior or action to become criminalized, it must go through a lengthy political process that includes considerable debate between the factions. If one group can obtain a majority, the behavior or action will either remain criminalized or will effectively be **decriminalized**. If neither group can obtain a majority, there is no resolution.

## The Formal Criminal Justice Process

The criminal justice system consists of three major components: law enforcement (or **policing**), the court system, and the correctional system. Each component serves a specific purpose within the criminal justice process, though few cases actually make it through the entire formal process.

The following is a brief overview of the process from start to finish, which will be explored in further detail throughout the book.

The formal criminal justice process begins with *initial contact*, during which law enforcement is first notified that an alleged crime has occurred and is first brought into contact with the potential offender. Initial contact should not be confused with custody or arrest.

Once the police have been notified of an alleged crime, they conduct an *investigation* to assure that the alleged crime did in fact occur, that the offender can be correctly identified, and that there is sufficient evidence to support a conviction in the matter.

An investigation may ultimately lead to an *arrest* or multiple arrests. There must be probable cause to legally arrest the suspect. An arrest can be made in a few instances: if the officer has witnessed a crime, if an officer has probable cause to believe an individual committed a crime based upon the statement of another individual, or when an arrest warrant has been issued.

Upon being arrested, a suspect is in police *custody*. At this stage the police may take a photo (mug shot) of the suspect and gather further personal information about them, including taking their fingerprints. Suspects in police custody may also be obligated to stand in a lineup for witness identification and may be subject to interrogation from officers. A suspect has a right to an attorney while being questioned.

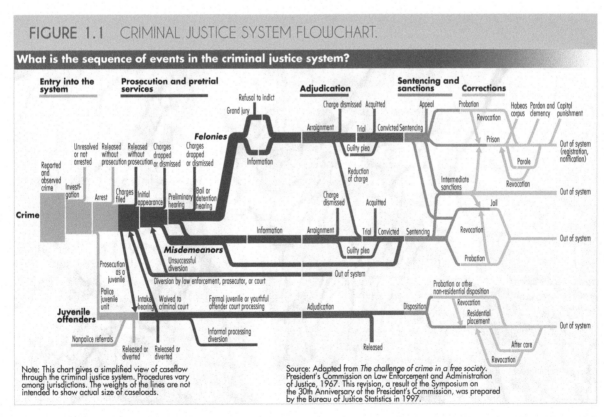

**FIGURE 1.1** CRIMINAL JUSTICE SYSTEM FLOWCHART.

**What is the sequence of events in the criminal justice system?**

Note: This chart gives a simplified view of caseflow through the criminal justice system. Procedures vary among jurisdictions. The weights of the lines are not intended to show actual size of caseloads.

Source: Adapted from *The challenge of crime in a free society*. President's Commission on Law Enforcement and Administration of Justice, 1967. This revision, a result of the Symposium on the 30th Anniversary of the President's Commission, was prepared by the Bureau of Justice Statistics in 1997.

© Prath/Shutterstock.com

Policing, including crime scene investigation, is the first component of the criminal justice process.

A suspect formally becomes a defendant when he or she is *charged* by the state. The state can do this by filing an indictment, which is a formal written statement by the prosecuting attorney charging a person with an offense. Alternatively, in lieu of an indictment, the state can file a statement of probable cause, which is written by a police officer and describes why the defendant is being charged. The type of crime generally dictates how the state will charge the crime. Chapters 3 and 4 provide a thorough description and analysis of the policing and law enforcement process.

Once a suspect is arrested and charged, the suspect and the case then interact with the second component of the justice process: the court system. After being charged, the defendant faces a *preliminary hearing* or *grand jury hearing*. This process varies from state to state, but all are based on a similar foundation. A group of citizens, sitting as the grand jury, must determine that there is appropriate probable cause for a suspect to be charged and for a case to move forward to trial.[48] Some states allow the defendant to be present and to testify; other states allow only the prosecution to argue its case. If the grand jury finds there is enough evidence for the case to proceed, they consequently *indict the defendant.*

*An arraignment* generally marks the defendant's initial appearance in court, as the defendant will appear before the court that will try his or her case. Defendants are informed of the charges against them, including the minimum and maximum punishments and fines they may be facing.[49] Defendants are informed of their constitutional right to have bail set and their constitutional right to a speedy trial. Some courts, though not all, will set a trial date at an arraignment.

A defendant is granted a right to a *bail hearing*, during which the judge can set a monetary bail that will allow for the defendant to be released from jail and to secure his or her presence at all further court dates.[50] Judges are not required to set a monetary bail, and may instead choose to hold the defendant on a no-bail status based upon the severity of the crime. Alternatively, the court can order that a defendant be released on his or her own recognizance or, if a minor, into the custody of a parent or guardian.

Under the Sixth Amendment, the defendant has a right to a trial, but this is not considered an inalienable right. If the defendant or state chooses, he or she can enter into plea negotiations. Between 90% to 95% of all criminal cases end in a **plea bargain**—an agreement on a sentence without a trial verdict.[51] Plea bargains are considered to be contracts between the defendant and the state.[52]

**Plea bargain**
An agreement between the state and defense on a plea and sentence.

Prosecutors may have a variety of motivations for entering into plea negotiations based upon the strength of the case, the severity of the case, and the defendant's background. In some cases, the prosecution may be uncertain whether a trial will result in a conviction; by offering the defendant a deal, the prosecution can guarantee that the defendant receives some manner of punishment. The prosecution may also offer a plea bargain if there are concerns about potential witnesses—for instance, if a witness's credibility with jurors may be troublesome or the witness/victim is a young child whom the prosecution does not want to force to testify in court. Defendants, for their part, will enter into plea negotiations in an effort to protect themselves from harsher punishment.

The ultimate decision rests with the defendant. A defense attorney cannot accept a plea deal without the permission of his or her client. A defendant who has accepted a plea deal may agree to plead to one of the crimes charged and have the rest dismissed, plead guilty to a lesser count, or agree to enter a plea of guilty because he or she wants to limit the amount of time spent in jail. In 2000, guilty pleas accounted for nearly 95% of all felony convictions in state courts.[53]

If the parties do not enter into successful plea negotiations, the next step in the criminal justice process is for the prosecution to bring the defendant to trial. The defendant, and the defendant alone, has the right to choose whether he or she will be tried by a jury or a judge.[54] At trial, the prosecution must prove to a judge or jury that the defendant committed the crime beyond a reasonable doubt.[55] The defendant has the right to confront and cross-examine witnesses and to present witnesses in his or her own defense. The defendant is not required to put on a case. The burden of proof in criminal cases lies with the prosecution, not the defendant, and the trier of fact (the judge or jury) decides whether the state has met its burden.[56]

Some trials may result in a *hung jury*—a jury that is unable to agree on a unanimous decision regarding the guilt or innocence of a defendant. When a hung jury occurs, the prosecution is faced with the choice of whether or not to retry the defendant. If the prosecution chooses to retry the case, the court will set a new trial date. In cases where the defendant has been incarcerated while awaiting trial, the judge may elect to hold a new bail hearing or release the defendant on his or her own recognizance. If the prosecution chooses not to retry the defendant, the prosecution will dismiss the case or place it on the stet docket, and the defendant will be released.

If a defendant is found guilty, the case then progresses to sentencing or *disposition*. In this stage, the defendant is sentenced by the court for the crimes for which he or she was convicted. Disposition can occur immediately after the verdict or can be delayed. A defendant may choose to delay disposition so that a pre-sentence investigation can be done. During the sentencing phase, the defendant can present factors of mitigation, and the victim has the right to give a victim impact statement.

An agent within the correctional system will conduct a *pre-sentence investigation report* to compile background information on the defendant. This exhaustive report examines the defendant's educational background, family background, past medical history, and past criminal history, information that the agent uses to makes recommendations to the sentencing judges. Those recommendations may include whether or not the defendant is likely to offend again and his or her amenability to treatment and rehabilitation.

The judge can take the pre-sentence recommendation report into advisement when determining the defendant's sentence. The judge can also take into account mitigating factors about the defendant's history to structure a sentence that will both protect the public and help rehabilitate the defendant. Many different sentencing options are available to judges, including a fine, probation, incarceration, or some combination of these options. The judge may sentence the defendant to incarceration in prison for a specific duration, after which the defendant is free to reenter society. The judge might instead deliver a sentence that would incarcerate the defendant and then place him or her on probation upon release. The judge can also place the defendant on straight probation with no prison term.

The defendant still has many rights after sentencing, including the right to appeal. On appeal, an appellate court will review the transcript and evidence to confirm that the defendant received a fair trial. The appellate courts will assure there was sufficient evidence to sustain a verdict and will determine whether evidence was properly admitted and if any reversible error occurred. A defendant may only appeal issues that were preserved at trial when an objection was made.

Defendants also are granted post-conviction rights. The defendant may assert in a post-conviction petition that he or she received ineffective assistance of counsel at trial. At a hearing, both the prosecution and the defense have the ability to call witnesses, and the prosecution will call the defendant's trial attorney. By filing a post-conviction claim for ineffective assistance of counsel, the defendant has waived attorney-client privilege and the attorney may testify about any communications between them. Chapters 4 and 5 of this book provide a comprehensive account of the structure, process, and players of the court system.

© OFFSTOCK/Shutterstock.com

A convicted criminal may be placed in jail or prison, sentenced to probation, or a combination of the two.

A defendant who is found guilty and sentenced falls under the jurisdiction of the department of corrections. The correctional system comprises a multitude of facilities and systems, including jail and prison, parole, and probation systems, which will be discussed at great length in Chapters 6, and 7.

Upon the defendant's release from jail or prison, he or she may serve a term of probation. While on probation, the defendant is required to abide by specific rules and conditions, which may include submitting to drug testing and treatment, checking in with probation agents, and avoiding certain locations and people. Defendants, upon their release, may be part of a **community corrections** program and be required to reside at a halfway house. This helps the defendant gradually make the often difficult transition from a secured facility to complete freedom.

**Community corrections**
A halfway house, rehab facility, or home detention that helps an individual move from a correctional facility to complete freedom.

**Critical Thinking**

Ninety percent of all criminal cases end in plea negotiations. Do you consider this justice being served or a shortcut to a conviction?

**Learn More:** Video on "The Plea Bargain" https://www.youtube.com/watch?v=pw6jtwpxlss

## The Informal Criminal Justice System

Many cases are settled in an informal pattern of cooperation between the prosecution, defense, and judge. The informal judicial system relies heavily upon other members of the **courtroom workgroup**, a concept developed by Eisenstein and Jacob (1970)[57] and explored further in Chapter 4 Beyond the judge, the courtroom workgroup consists of the judge's staff—the court clerk, the judge's law clerk, and the court reporter—as well as the prosecution and defense attorneys. The courtroom workgroup collaborates to move cases through the criminal justice system quickly, fairly, and effectively, which in many instances means that a case will not go through the entire extended process of the formal criminal justice system.

**Courtroom workgroup** The judge, courtroom staff, prosecutor, and defense attorney.

The informal justice system relies heavily upon the relationships between the prosecution and defense counsel. The legal community is small, and many of the prosecutors and defense counsel have worked alongside each other for years. Longtime members of the defense bar know when and under what circumstances the prosecution will be willing to engage in plea negotiations. This skill is invaluable to defendants who elect to pursue a plea bargain.

A variety of informal systems and functions exist throughout the criminal justice process. Police discretion is one notable example. *Discretion*, which will be discussed at length in chapter 4 allows a law enforcement officer to use his or her best judgment when deciding how to proceed with a criminal investigation. An officer's discretion may help determine, for example, whether to make a traffic stop, how to interrogate a suspect or person of interest, how to handle an infraction, and so on. While there are certain limits and guidelines regarding police discretion, in general these situations follow an informal process and are not rigidly structured or formally codified.

*Community policing*, too, is part of the informal criminal justice system. Community members may work together with law enforcement to identify and solve local problems, such as setting up a neighborhood watch program to provide extra security for a neighborhood that has suffered a number of burglaries. Community involvement is not a specifically delineated process of the formal criminal justice system, but can nevertheless play an essential role in deterring or responding to crime. Chapters 3 and 4 discuss the structure and implications of community policing.

Victims of crime may go through an informal process of restorative justice (explored in Chapter 6 in which they attempt to recover from their victimization. In many cases, this process does not involve any formal systems such as police, courts, or corrections, but may instead consist of communications between the victim and the offender to repair the social damage caused by a criminal act.

## Continuing Challenges

This chapter began with a discussion of Packer's two models of criminal justice: crime control and due process. These models illustrate the need to balance freedom and security. In essence, the question that the criminal justice system and members of society ask themselves is how much freedom they are willing to sacrifice in the effort to increase safety and security. For example, establishing a national DNA registry could lead to a nearly 100% conviction rate for sexual predators when DNA is present. An individual who was suspected of a crime—and not yet convicted—would be required to give a DNA sample, which would be entered into the national data bank. Law enforcement could use this national DNA database to identify a perpetrator of any crime for which DNA evidence was present. Ideally, the efficient rate of convictions would most likely deter those responsible for sexual assaults. However, because a DNA registry would include information about people's health, including their predisposition to cancer and other diseases, individuals would be compelled to give up many freedoms in order to increase security. Do the benefits of the DNA database outweigh citizens' losses of certain liberties? These are the kinds of controversies that are subject to perpetual debate among policy makers and the public.

New advancements may also allow society to predict future criminality, perhaps leading to efforts to proactively prevent crimes from occurring. While a predictive model may sound appealing, anticipating crime and taking steps to prevent it from occurring could again lead to a deprivation of individuals' rights. In this scenario, the balance of freedom and security has tilted heavily toward security.

One contemporary example of the preference for security is the presence of street gangs. Street gangs have increasingly moved out of the cities and into the suburbs, expanding their drug distribution areas, increasing their revenue, and recruiting new members. Today, there are approximately 1 million gang members and more than 20,000 criminally active gangs throughout the United States.[58] As a response, the public has demanded more security.

Many of those worried by gangs are also calling for tougher gun control. Each year, 30,000 people are killed by gunfire in the United States.[59] Close to 95% of all gang-related homicides are carried out with firearms.[60] States have tried to make stricter laws regarding who is allowed to purchase and own guns. Illinois, Pennsylvania, Hawaii, and Rhode Island have some of the strictest gun laws. Each requires a background check, safety locks, and other safety measures.

The criminal justice system faces challenges from more contemporary criminal acts such as **white-collar crime**—crimes against businesses by people in high-profile positions. White-collar crimes are largely hidden, but American corporations lose about 7% of their annual revenue to fraud, amounting to about $1 trillion of the 2008 gross domestic product.[61]

**White-collar crime** Crimes against businesses by people in high-profile positions.

Modern technologies, too, have transformed the scope of crime. The prevalence of the Internet has allowed for cybercrime to develop. *Cybercrime* involves the targeting of computer systems or networks upon which the public has become increasingly more dependent. These crimes include computer fraud, copyright infringement, distributing illegal sexual material, Internet securities fraud, e-tailing fraud, identity fraud, and cyber vandalism. Cybercrime is uniquely challenging to the criminal justice system because it is difficult to detect through traditional law enforcement channels and is rapidly, continually evolving. Learning to counteract cybercrime demands new technical skills from law enforcement, and new laws and agencies have been created to deal with the constantly changing cyber community. Cybercrime and its effects on the criminal justice system are further explored in Chapter 13 of this book.

The public's demand for safety has especially escalated since the devastating terrorist attacks on the United States on September 11, 2001. The use of terrorism to promote political agendas is a growing concern. Today's terrorists have diverse motivations and sponsors and view their causes as a global war against the values and traditions of their enemies. The criminal justice system, specifically at the federal level, has strongly responded to terrorism. One of the biggest responses since 9/11 has been the development of the Department of Homeland Security, whose purpose is to reduce the country's vulnerability to terrorism, prevent terrorist attacks, and minimize damage and improve recovery if an attack occurs. Chapter 12 provides a comprehensive analysis of the U.S. and international governments' efforts to protect against terrorism.

© Prazis Images/Shutterstock.com

The federal government and the criminal justice system have responded strongly to the threat of terrorism.

As more and more attention is called to these and other contemporary challenges to criminal justice, the public's call for greater safety measures is the rallying point for change. Remember that the ever-present struggle between liberty and security once inspired the country's forefathers to rebel against the British and establish the United States as an independent nation. Today, the government continually attempts to find the right balance between assuring the safety of its citizens and restricting infringements on their civil rights.

As you continue to familiarize yourself with the structure and process of the criminal justice system throughout the book, consider how criminal justice has continued to adapt and evolve based on real-world circumstances. How will the struggle between security and liberty ultimately be resolved? What does the future hold for the criminal justice system and American society as a whole?

## Jodi Arias: A Sensationalized Case

During the summer of 2008, Jodi Arias was accused of murdering her ex-boyfriend Travis Alexander in his apartment. His body was discovered in his Mesa, Arizona home in his shower. Travis was found by friends who were concerned about his whereabouts since they had not heard from him for several days. On June 9, 2008, his friends found his body in the shower. He had been brutally murdered—Travis had been stabbed around 27 times, shot in the head and his throat had been slashed from ear to ear. Investigators later determined that the murder had occurred five days before his body was found, on June 4, 2008. [65.]

Jodi Arias was born in Salinas, California and was age 28 at the time when she made national headlines when the police charged her with murdering Travis, her ex-boyfriend in 2008. Thirty years old, Travis Alexander was a motivational speaker and insurance salesperson who a Mormon and a Riverside, California native. The two met each other at a Las Vegas convention in 2006, while he was a resident in Arizona and Jodi was residing in Palm Desert, California. Shortly after meeting each other, they became boyfriend and girlfriend. However, only after five months of knowing each other, they went their separate ways in late June 2007, but they still maintained a sexual relationship with one another.

Approximately five years later in January 2013, the testimony in Arias's trial began which was aired live to the public and thus became a media sensation.[65] The trial lasted four months with Arias spending 18 days on the witness stand; the jurors reached a unanimous decision in the case on May 8, 2013: Jodi was found guilty of first-degree murder. During the sentencing phase of the trial, the jury became deadlocked over the terms of punishment. A second jury was selected and in March 2015, the second jury was unable to agree on Arias's sentence as well, thus removing the option of the death penalty Judge Sherry Stephens finally determining the extent of a life sentence without the possibility of parole after 25 years in April 2015 for Arias. On April 13, Arias expressed her remorse for her actions in a statement. There was talk of an appeal underway, but in the meantime, Arias will serve time at the Arizona State Prison Complex-Perryville.[65.]

# Chapter Summary

- Criminal justice is the study of the interactions between the police, courts, and correctional facilities. Criminal justice looks at how these interactions shape the criminal justice system and looks to see how these interactions play out in the real world based on evidence and statistics.

- Crime control refers to both the formal and informal ways that society looks to control criminal behavior. Formal controls on criminal behavior include incarceration and probation, while informal controls are done through societal norms. Individuals who are subject to formal crime control are guaranteed certain procedures and rights under due process. Due process protects defendants' constitutional rights to a speedy trial, innocent until proven guilty, the right to an attorney, etc.

- The crime control model argues that punishment and repression of criminal conduct is the most important function of the justice system. Controlling criminal activity is the most important job of law enforcement and the system should function quickly and efficiently—like an assembly line. At each point in the assembly line, there is an opportunity to end the case. The due process model focuses on protecting the rights of the accused. This results in an obstacle course in which each decision has the potential to prevent the quick disposal of cases.

- The criminal justice system in the United States has a long and ever-changing history that has seen each branch of the system become more centralized and unified. In the past, policing systems varied from one locality to another, but now they all use a very similar structure and process. The judicial system has changed as well, as the elements of crimes and the penalties for crimes have been codified in the law and the consequences for breaking the laws have become more consistent. Correctional facilities, too, have undergone extensive changes to become more centralized as prison populations have grown.

- A crime is a wrong against society as proclaimed by law and, if committed under certain circumstances, punishable by society. The consensus model assumes that when a group gathers to form a society, the society will naturally form shared values and norms. The conflict model assumes that within a society there will be different segments, separated by social class, income, age, and race, that will have different values and norms and will engage in a struggle to define what is criminal. The group in power will decide what behavior is criminal.

- There are many different steps in the judicial process—both formal and informal. The formal steps include initial contact, investigation, arrest, custody, charging, preliminary hearing, arraignment, bail/detention, trial, sentencing/disposition, appeal, correctional treatment, release, and post-release. Informal processes are those that deter from the formal process, such as plea bargains, which are agreed upon by the prosecution and defense to move cases quickly and fairly without going through the full formal process.

- The criminal justice system faces continuing challenges in addressing modern, technologically advanced crimes, as well as satiating a public that demands greater security at the expense of civil liberties.

## Critical Thinking?

1. Do you believe that programs designed to give offenders life skills help the recidivism rate? Why or why not?

2. Who or what do you think has the biggest influence on how we as a society view crime? Is it our communities? Television shows? The news?

3. Many states, in an effort to be tougher on crime, have enacted a "three-strikes" rule regarding drugs. On the third conviction, the prosecutor may seek a minimum mandatory sentence that the offender will have to serve. The rule only takes into account how many drug convictions the offender has and not the amount of drugs that the offender had in his or her possession. Do you agree with this policy?

4. What is your opinion of plea bargaining? Is it a necessary evil or does it do a disservice to justice?

5. How do you think the prevalence of technology will continue to change the way that crimes occur and the way we view crimes?

6. Frequently, defendants will ask for a delayed disposition so that a pre-sentencing investigation can be completed. Do you think a judge should take the defendant's background into account when sentencing the defendant for a crime, or should every defendant face the same consequence for the same crime?

7. What are some ways that the United States conducts racial profiling?

8. Compare the cases of Todd Willingham, Troy Davis, and O.J. Simpson. What was the media's role in each case? Does it color your perception of the judicial system?

9. What are the differences between the conflict and consensus models?

10. Do you believe in the crime control model or the due process model? Why? Which model plays a bigger role in our legal system?

# Media

**Department of Justice:** http://www.justice.gov/criminal/
The United States Department of Justice website gives an overview of the federal criminal justice system, its players, and current news.

**National Association of Criminal Defense Attorneys:** http://www.nacdl.org/
The NACDL is the largest association of criminal defense attorneys in the United States. This website gives overviews of recent cases and provides defense attorneys with resources and connections with other defense attorneys in their area.

# Endnotes

[1]   *Willingham v. State*, 897 S.W.2d 351, 354 (1995).

[2]   Ibid.

[3]   Grann, D. (2009, September 7). "Trial by Fire." *The New Yorker*.

[4]   Ibid.

[5]   The Innocence Project. (2011). "Cameron Todd Willingham: Wrongfully Convicted and Executed in Texas." Retrieved from http://www.innocenceproject.org/Content/Cameron_Todd_Willingham_Wrongfully_Convicted_and_Executed_in_Texas.php#summary

[6]   Texas Forensic Science Commission. (2011, April 15). *Report of the Texas Forensic Science Commission: Willingham/Willis Investigation*.

[7]   Packer, H. L. (1968). *The Limits of the Criminal Sanction*. Stanford, CA: Stanford University Press.

[8]   Ibid.

[9]   Ibid.

[10]   Ibid.

[11]   Ibid.

[12]   Ibid.

[13]   *Whren v. United States*, 517 U.S. 806, 808-09 (1996).

[14]   Ibid.

[15]   Department of Justice, Bureau of Justice Statistics. (2003). "Violent Crime Rates Have Declined since 1994, Reaching the Lowest Level Ever Recorded in 2003."

[16]   Ibid.

[17]   Department of Justice, Bureau of Justice Statistics. (2011). "Homicide Trends in the United States, 1980-2008," Retrieved from http://www.bjs.gov/index.cfm?ty=pbdetail&iid=2221

[18]   Department of Justice, Bureau of Justice Statistics. As cited by the Sentencing Project (2004, June 28). Retrieved from http://www.sentencingproject.org/pdfs/1035.pdf

[19]   *Defending Justice: An Activist Resource Kit: Trends in the Criminal Justice System.*

[20]   *The Prison Policy Initiative.* Portland, OR: Bridgetown Printing, 12.

[21]   Defending Justice: *An Activist Resource Kit: Factsheet.*

[22]   Beyer, G. W., & Redden, K. R. (2001). *Modern Dictionary for the Legal Profession* (3rd ed.). Buffalo, NY: W.S. Hein.

[23]   Ibid.

[24]   Beccaria, C. (1764). *On Crime and Punishment.*

[25]   U.S. Marshals Service. (n.d.). *Historical Timeline.* Retrieved from http://www.usmarshals.gov/history/timeline.html

[26]   City of Boston. (2011). *A Brief History of the B.P.D.* Retrieved from http://www.cityofboston.gov/police/about/history.asp

[27]   United States Department of Justice. (n.d.). *Department of Justice Agencies.* Retrieved from http://www.justice.gov/agencies/index-org.html

[28]   United States, Wickersham Commission, Chafee, Z., Polak, W. H., & Stern, C. S. (1931). *Report on Lawlessness in Law Enforcement.* Washington, DC: U.S. Government Printing Office.

[29]   Johnson, L. B. (1965, March 8). "102—Special Message to the Congress on Law Enforcement and the Administration of Justice." *The American Presidency Project.* Retrieved from http://www.presidency.ucsb.edu/ws/index.php?pid=26800#axzz1QsIMq0qt

[30]   The Omnibus Safe Streets and Criminal Control Act of 1968, Pub. L. No. 90-351 (1968).

[31]   *Miranda v. Arizona*, 384 U.S. 436 (1966).

[32]   *Mapp v. Ohio*, 367 U.S. 643 (1961).

[33]   Ibid.

[34]   *Gideon v. Wainwright*, 372 U.S. 335 (1963).

[35]   United States Department of Justice, Bureau of Justice Statistics. (2015). *Employment and Expenditure.* Retrieved from http://www.bjs.gov/index.cfm?ty=dcdetail&iid=286

[36]   Bureau of Justice Statistics, Key Statistics, Total Adult Correctional Population, 1980-2014 on the Internet at www.bjs.gov Retrieved from http://www.bjs.gov/index.cfm?ty=kfdetail&iid=487 .

[37]   United States Department of Justice, Bureau of Justice Statistics. (2014). *Employment and Expenditure.* Retrieved from United States Department of Justice, http://www.bjs.gov/index.cfm?ty=tp&tid=131

[38]   Ibid.

[39]   Bureau of Justice Statistics. (2014) "Justice Expenditure and Employment in the United States-Extracts-Final" (2010), 1–2. Retrieved from http://www.bjs.gov/index.cfm?ty=pbdetail&iid=5049

[40]   Ibid., 1.

41  Ibid., 1–2.

42  Thomas, C. W., Cage, R. J., & Foster, S. C. (1976). "Public Opinion on Criminal Law and Legal Sanctions—An Examination of Two Conceptual Models." *Journal of Criminal Law and Criminology, 67*(1).

43  Durkheim, E. (1893). *The Division of Labor in Society.* New York, NY: The Free Press.

44  Thomas et al., 1976.

45  Ibid.

46  *Roe v. Wade*, 410 U.S. 113 (1973).

47  "Republicans More Unified Than Democrats on Abortion." (2011, June 6). *Gallup Poll.*

48  United States Courts. (n.d.). *Jury Service.* Retrieved from http://www.uscourts.gov/FederalCourts/JuryService.aspx

49  *Black's Law Dictionary.*

50  Ibid.

51  Sandefur, T. (2003, Fall). "In Defense of Plea Bargaining." *Regulation,* 28–31.

52  Ibid., 28.

53  Durose, M. R., & Langan, P. A. (2003). *Felony Sentences in State Courts 2000* (NCJ 198821). Retrieved from http://bjs.ojp.usdoj.gov/index.cfm?ty=pbdetail&iid=913

54  United States Courts. (n.d.). *Criminal Cases.* Retrieved from http://www.uscourts.gov/FederalCourts/Understanding theFederalCourts/HowCourtsWork/CriminalCases.aspx

55  Ibid.

56  Ibid.

57  Eisenstein, J., & Jacob, H. (1970). Felony Justice: *An Organizational Analysis of Criminal Courts.* Boston, MA: Little, Brown.

58  United States Department of Justice. (2009). *2009 National Gang Threat Assessment,* 5.

59  Retrieved from http://webappa.cdc.gov/cgi-bin/broker.exe

60  United States Department of Justice, Bureau of Justice Statistics. (n.d.). *Percent of Homicides Involving Guns by Circumstance, 1976–2005.* Retrieved from http://bjs.ojp.usdoj.gov/content/homicide/d_circumgun.cfm

61  Allen, S. (2011, July 9). "The New ROE: Return on Ethics." *Forbes Magazine.* Retrieved from http://www.forbes.com/2009/07/21/business-culture-corporate-citizenship-leadership-ethics.html

65  Jodi Arias Biography. *Biography.com Editors.* The Biography.com website. A&E Television Networks. Retrieved from http://www.biography.com/people/jodi-arias-21221959

© carl ballou/Shutterstock.com

# Theories of Crime and Behavior

## KEY TERMS

Atavistic man

Biological theories

Chicago School

Classical school

Compurgation

Conflict theory

Crime index

Criminal behavior

Dark figure of crime

Deterrence theory

Developmental pathways

Deviance

Differential association theory

Feminist theories

General deterrence

General strain theory

General theory of crime

Integrated theories

Labeling theory

Left realism

Life course theories

National Incident-Based
 Reporting System
 (NIBRS)

National Crime Victimization
 Survey (NCVS)

Peacemaking criminology

Personality theories

Positivist school

Pre-classical school

Reintegrative shaming

Routine activities theory

Self-report survey

Social control theory

Social disorganization theory

Specific deterrence

Strain theory

Trial by battle

Trial by ordeal

Uniform Crime Reports (UCR)

# CHAPTER OBJECTIVES

1 Differentiate between the concepts of criminal behavior and deviance.

2 Report how much crime there is in the United States and crime trends.

3 Define and discuss the various methods of gathering crime data.

4 Demonstrate an understanding of the causes of crime.

5 Analyze the various theoretical perspectives explaining the causes of crime and their application to behaviors.

# Case Study: Gang Violence

Luis Sanchez was born in Chelsea, Massachusetts, and exposed to the perils and temptations of a gang lifestyle at an early age. His mother had systematically kicked out his older siblings as teenagers, and Sanchez too was nearly legally disowned by his mother, but at age 13 he was considered too young by the court. After being mugged for the first time, Sanchez decided he needed a different means of protection due to his lack of family support. He soon joined a gang and became involved in a variety of criminal activities, including selling illegal drugs such as cocaine and marijuana. Sanchez, fortunately, was able to escape his criminal lifestyle by joining a youth program in Boston in 2004, breaking his gang connections, and becoming a student at Boston College.[1]

Sanchez's case is not at all uncommon: many other young people are in similar situations. Sadly, in many cases, these individuals are unable to escape a life of crime and deviance as Sanchez did. A perennial concern for the criminal justice system in the United States is gang-related crime and violence. Much of the worry consists of trying to determine precisely what events, factors, environment, and inherited traits combine to produce a gang member inclined to commit crime.

Understanding the causes of crime is instrumental in our ability not only to predict future offending, but also to determine the appropriate responses to the crime and the offender. The example of Luis Sanchez illustrates that the causes of crime may be the product of multiple underlying factors (poverty, gang allegiance, drugs, personal quarrels, alcohol). Why do some people in Sanchez's situation join gangs while others do not? This chapter will review the extent to which crime occurs and the various theoretical propositions used to explain the behavior.

## What Is Criminal Behavior?

The concept of crime and its subsequent causes has been debated for centuries. Many theories about the causes and reasons for criminal behavior have been presented. These include the classical perspective, in which offenders are considered to be free will thinkers, and the positivist perspective that looks to the individual or their environment for causes or influences toward crime. Despite these categorical explanations for crime, debate still exists among practitioners, lawmakers, criminologists, and the general public as to what constitutes criminal behavior. More specifically, within this context and framework, one must differentiate between deviance and criminal activity.

The concept of **deviance** is usually defined as behaviors considered outside of or inconsistent with normal behavior for that community or group.[2] Therefore, deviance may differ depending on where you live and the accepted norms, ethics, and morals of the community. Broadly speaking, deviance can be understood from either a positivist or a constructionist point of view. *Positivism* basically asserts that things have distinct, real "essences," and therefore deviant behavior is wrong because it is inconsistent with what is objectively right. In the context of positivist criminology, deviance is thought to be caused by internal and external factors beyond the criminal's control.[3] Related to positivism is *rational choice theory*, which posits that criminals make a cost/benefit analysis to determine whether or not to commit crime.[4] *Constructionist* interpretations of deviance believe that categories of right and wrong, and therefore deviance from them, are social constructs that depend greatly on the perspective of the individual observer.[5] In sociology, deviance refers to actions (or behaviors) that contravene either social norms or written legal codes.

**Criminal behavior**, appropriately, is defined by legislation, statutes, and codes. There are two classifications of these behaviors. The first classification, *mala in se* crimes, covers acts that are deemed illegal because they so violate the norms and moral code of society that they are wrong in and of themselves. Such offenses—murder, for example—are almost universally prohibited. The other classification is behaviors that are deemed illegal not so much due to inherent immorality, but because they are defined as such by those living within that particular society. Essentially, they are crimes because society has enacted laws and statutes that say they are crimes. These are known as *mala prohibitum* crimes. Such crimes are likely to vary from culture to culture (e.g., sex crimes, gambling restrictions, drug and alcohol laws, and so forth).

These two definitions are both incorporated into a legal system based on an understanding of crime that is, to some extent, socially constructed. To be sure, crime can be understood as a codification of deviance: violating social norms, taboos, and laws is often legally criminal. Crime has been succinctly described by Morrison (2006) as "an act or omission that is defined by the

**Deviance** Behaviors considered outside of or inconsistent with normal behavior for a community or group.

**Criminal behavior** Behavior defined by legislation, statutes, and codes.

Mala in se crimes, such as robbery, are almost universally prohibited.

validly passed laws of the nation state in which it occurred so that punishment should follow from the behavior."[6] It is within this framework and context that the criminal justice system operates and functions. Therefore, what constitutes criminal behavior and the appropriate punishments ascribed to those violations of law may change over time.

# Measuring Crime

To understand how much crime there is in the United States, it is important to assess not only the different types of measures that are used but their origins, strengths, and weaknesses. The most frequently used means of data collection are the Uniform Crime Reports (UCR), the National Incident-Based Reporting System (NIBRS), the National Crime Victimization Survey (NCVS), and self-report surveys.

## Uniform Crime Reports (UCR)

Prior to 1930, no centralized program for gathering crime statistics existed. Data that were collected were deemed unreliable because of legislative differences in criminal codes and enforcement practices. Because of the diversity of techniques and procedures, it was nearly impossible to compare crime data in any meaningful way between jurisdictions, let alone states. Law enforcement officers and legislators needed a better way to assemble data to assist with allocation of resources and manpower. This desire to improve data collection efforts was best demonstrated in 1927 by the International Association of Chiefs of Police (IACP). The IACP formed the Committee on Uniform Crime Records to assess the possibility of developing a standardized, centrally located mechanism for gathering crime statistics.[7] Most important was the creation of standardized definitions of crimes. These efforts resulted in the 1929 publication of the first standardized collection of statistics on crimes reported to the police and crimes cleared by arrest.

Beginning in 1930, this tool, known as the **Uniform Crime Reports (UCR)**, was officially implemented on a large-scale basis, with law enforcement agencies volunteering for participation in data collection and reporting to the FBI. The primary purpose of the UCR was to provide uniform definitions for gathering crime data so that results could be compared by month, year, state, and jurisdiction. Since its inception, the UCR has added information on law enforcement officers killed and assaulted on duty as well as hate crime statistics.[8] Today the UCR, which is still a voluntary program, includes approximately 18,000 reporting law enforcement agencies nationally, representing more than 97% of the entire U.S. population.

UCR data are divided into two categories: Part I index offenses and Part II offenses. The Part I **Crime Index** includes a total of eight offenses divided

**Uniform Crime Reports (UCR)** An official data-reporting tool created in 1930 to provide uniform definitions for crime data so that results could be compared by month, year, state, and jurisdiction.

**Crime index** An index reported by the Uniform Crime Reports. Crimes are divided into Part I and Part II index offenses. The Part I index consists of a total of eight offenses divided into the violent crime index and the property crime index. The Part II index comprises a total of 21 categories of less-serious crimes.

into a violent crime index and a property crime index. Part II covers the less serious offenses. (See Figure 2.1 for an overview of the included index offenses.)

In order for an offense to be included in the UCR,[9] it must follow the counting rule, which states that only the most serious offense committed in a single incident is included in the UCR data, although the offender may be charged with more crimes. Additionally, the UCR follows what is known as the hierarchy rule. Offenses are placed in the specific order in which they are supposed to be recorded, beginning with criminal homicide and ranging through runaways in the Part II Offense category. The UCR further distinguishes between time and place. If a criminal event that occurs is a continuation of another event, then the UCR counts those as one single incident. If the criminal events are related but not a single incident, then law enforcement officers must record those as separate incidents.

Data are reported in one of three ways: (1) crimes reported to the police (reported in raw numbers), which includes any offenses that have been reported to the police and have been verified as possible crimes by law enforcement; (2) rates per 100,000 residents, calculated as Total Number of Crimes Reported ÷ Total U.S. Population × 100,000 = Rate per 100,000 Residents; and (3) rate of crime over time or trends. Finally, crimes cleared by arrest are included in the final report. These data include the number of reported offenses where either an arrest was made or at least one person was charged in the incident.[10] Data are further aggregated by community type. These divisions include Standard Statistical Metropolitan Areas (SMSAs); other cities, most of which are not incorporated; and rural counties.[11] Although the data do not allow for individual comparisons by the victim or specific characteristics of crimes, they do allow for comparisons by these types of jurisdictions. Despite every effort to account for all criminal offending, there still exist a number of offenses that go unreported to the police. This category of crime is known as the **dark figure of crime**.

**Dark figure of crime**
Offenses that go unreported to the police.

---

**FIGURE 2.1** UCR OFFENSES

**Part I Offenses**
Part I offense classifications include:

| **Violent Offenses** | **Property Offenses** |
| --- | --- |
| *Murder* | *Burglary* |
| The willful (non-negligent) killing of one human being by another. | The unlawful entry of a structure to commit a felony or theft. |

### Forcible Rape

The carnal knowledge of a female forcibly and against her will. Attempts or assaults to commit rape by force or threat of force are also included; however, statutory rape (without force) and other sex offenses are excluded.

### Robbery

The taking or attempting to take anything of value from the care, custody, or control of a person or persons by force or threat of force or violence and/or by putting the victim in fear.

### Aggravated Assault

Unlawful attack by one person upon another for the purpose of inflicting severe or aggravated bodily injury.

### Larceny-Theft

The unlawful taking, carrying, leading, or riding away of property from the possession or constructive possession of another.

### Motor Vehicle Theft

The theft or attempted theft of a motor vehicle. In the UCR Program, a motor vehicle is a self-propelled vehicle that runs on land surfaces and not on rails.

### Arson

Any willful or malicious burning or attempting to burn, with or without intent to defraud, a dwelling house, public building, motor vehicle or aircraft, personal property of another, etc.

*Information from FBI: http://www2.fbi.gov/ucr/cius2009/index.html*

## Part II Offenses

Part II offenses encompass all other reportable classifications outside those defined as Part I. Law enforcement agencies report to the FBI only arrest data involving the Part II crimes:

1. Other Assaults
2. Forgery and Counterfeiting
3. Fraud
4. Embezzlement
5. Stolen Property: Buying, Receiving, Possessing
6. Vandalism
7. Weapons: Carrying, Possessing, etc.
8. Prostitution and Commercialized Vice
9. Sex Offenses
10. Drug Abuse Violations
11. Gambling
12. Offenses Against the Family and Children
13. Driving Under the Influence
14. Liquor Laws
15. Drunkenness
16. Disorderly Conduct

Although the UCR does provide a mechanism for comparison between jurisdictions and states, there still are some data that are excluded from these efforts. For example, demographic characteristics of the offender are excluded from crimes reported to the police and in most instances with crimes cleared by arrest. The reason for this exclusion is because the witnesses may not be able to accurately account for the offender characteristics or data may not be available in any consistent manner even when crimes are cleared by arrest. Second, law enforcement officers are not required to collect and submit data on crime victims. Third, because data are collected on an aggregate level, individual cases are not followed throughout the system. Therefore, it is impossible to determine whether the offenders were charged in a particular event and/or whether conviction was obtained; UCR data only include whether an arrest has been made or a confirmed suspect has been identified. Finally, the UCR excludes some offense categories, such as the federal offense of kidnapping, that are deemed important. This limits the ability to compare and track data over time.[12]

There are a variety of factors that affect the reporting of crimes from both a law enforcement and an individual perspective. For example, when assessing criminal events, responses to crime by law enforcement are often in reaction to citizen complaints as opposed to the officer witnessing the event themselves. Likewise, many non-serious crimes go unreported. Therefore, inclusion of the most serious criminal offenses makes sense, given the ability to compare across jurisdiction and offense categories. This also includes the difficulty with the type of crime, even if serious. For example, the crime of rape, although serious by nature, often goes unreported because of the sensitive nature of the event, embarrassment, and fear of reprisal.

Because most crime comes to the attention of law enforcement through the efforts of the victims or witnesses, it is important to consider why a victim may not report a criminal event. Research has suggested that many victims report they believe nothing can be done. Lack of faith in the system to either detect or prosecute may preclude many of them from going through the "hassle" of reporting the event. Some victims report they believe their victimization is not important enough to occupy the law enforcement community's time and they do not want to bother the police with such trivial matters. Other victims report that the incident is a personal or private matter that should be handled within the family or between friends, while others fear reprisal. In some cases, the relationship between the victim and offender is such that the victim does not want harm to come to the offender. Crimes that occur between strangers are most likely to be reported. Finally, victims indicate that they report their victimization to others such as family members or social services for assistance with the event.[13]

Law enforcement officials report that there are a variety of factors that affect whether an offense is recorded. Influences such as funding decisions may dictate whether an agency wishes to participate in the UCR at all. Most federal and state funding initiatives require that law enforcement participate in either the UCR or NIBRS (see the next section for a more detailed explanation of NIBRS). While in theory the UCR is a voluntary program, these funding requirements all but force an agency to participate.

Community desires or needs will also influence whether an agency processes a crime officially or unofficially, particularly for less serious offenses. Communities that have seen an increase in certain types of offense categories (e.g., drug usage), may choose to "crack down" on these offenses and formally prosecute violators. Communities may also face political pressures to reduce crime.

Other extralegal factors may play a role, such as the sex, age, and race of the offender and whether the dispatcher names the offense when notifying law enforcement officers.[14]

One of the key benefits of participating in the UCR program is the ability to examine crime trends within a single jurisdiction. These data may be particularly important to a chamber of commerce or tourism bureau that uses the information to market a community.[15] Data may also be used to examine homicide trends across jurisdictions. These trend data can be very beneficial in determining or making staffing decisions or informing legislators to craft new anti-crime policies.[16] Further data may be used to inform the public about crime trends and to encourage appropriate support and response to crime prevention techniques. Finally, researchers use UCR data to test theories and to identify causes of crime.[17]

## National Incident-Based Reporting System (NIBRS)

**National Incident-Based Reporting System (NIBRS)** A national crime data collection program created and implemented during the 1980s in an effort to enhance the methodology for collecting, analyzing, and publishing crime data.

Because of changes in the nature and complexity of crime since the UCR's inception, the law enforcement community during the 1970s began studying the benefits and limitations of the UCR program. The result of this study was the creation of the **National Incident-Based Reporting System (NIBRS)**. The goal of the NIBRS program was to enhance the quantity and quality of the information provided and to enhance the methodology for collecting, analyzing, and publishing crime data.[18] In the most recent *Crime in the United States* report, the FBI stated that for 2012 a total of 6,115 law enforcement agencies reported their UCR crime statistics via NIBRS out of 18,290 total police agencies participating in the UCR program. Although participation is more limited than the UCR reporting program, many state and local agencies are in various stages of transitioning from the UCR to NIBRS. One impediment to this transition is the limited resources available for technology upgrades and training. Data for the NIBRS are not currently reported as separate categories. Instead they are incorporated into the UCR reports and included in the annual *Crime in the United States* publication.

There are a significant number of key differences between the UCR and the NIBRS systems. The NIBRS system includes an expanded offense reporting tool.[19] The program includes a total of 22 offense categories made up of 46 crimes. An additional 11 offenses are included in a group B category (see Figure 2.2 for a list of the offenses in Groups A and B). This expanded list of NIBRS offenses does not follow a hierarchy rule. The NIBRS is an incident-based system.[20] Information is collected on all individual incidents and arrests. Prescribed data allow for the researcher to collect information on each individual offense such as the type, age, sex, race, ethnicity, and residence status of the victim as well as the type of offense and injury sustained. The same type of information is included on the offender, along with the elements of the crime.

The NIBRS uses new and revised definitions from the UCR, such as the definition of rape. The NIBRS also includes new definitions of offense categories that are not represented by the UCR. The NIBRS system provides an opportunity for more specificity in the criminal acts. This includes the ability to compare offenses by individual characteristics as well as business crimes, residency status, weapons used, injuries incurred, etc. The NIBRS system includes a category representing crimes against society, which are *mala prohibitum* categories of crime such as drug offenses, gambling, prostitution, etc. Unlike the UCR, which only records the distinction between attempted and completed crimes in cases of forcible rape and murder, the NIBRS system distinguishes between attempted and completed for each offense category.

In addition, the NIBRS gives the ability to conduct correlations between the offense categories, property, victims, offenders, and arrestees. These linkages are both explicit and implicit. There are implied linkages between the victim and the offender within the offense category and explicit linkages to the crimes committed against the victim. The NIBRS includes the victim-offender relationship. Unlike the UCR, which only records this information for homicides, the NIBRS reporting system records victim-offender relationships for all crimes against persons and robbery.

Another key difference between the two systems is that the NIBRS reports more of the circumstances surrounding the event. In the UCR, information about the circumstances of the event is only included for homicides. NIBRS has expanded this system to include circumstantial information on assaults as well as homicides.

© Peter Schulzek/Shutterstock.com

Both the UCR and NIBRS include circumstantial information on homicides.

The NIBRS incorporates the hotel rule in a different way. For the UCR, the general hotel rule relates to the number of dwellings and how burglaries are reported. If there are a number of burglaries in one complex and they are likely to be reported by the manager, then they are counted as one offense. With the NIBRS, these data are expanded to include rental storage units and to include the number of rooms, units, or storage compartments that were victimized.

Lastly, the NIBRS and UCR report data to the FBI in different ways. For the UCR program, local agencies are permitted to use manual forms to submit data. State agencies must record their data on magnetic tapes. For the NIBRS system, all reporting agencies must record their data on magnetic strips.[21]

## National Crime Victimization Survey (NCVS)

**National Crime Victimization Survey (NCVS)** A survey conducted on households in the United States that includes detailed descriptions of criminal events, including the victim, potential precipitating factors, consequences of the event, and the offender.

Victimization surveys give researchers and policymakers the opportunity to delve further into a criminal incident from the perspective of the victim. Although a variety of different victimization surveys have been developed, the most widely used ongoing effort is known as the **National Crime Victimization Survey (NCVS)**. First administered in 1973 and originally known as the National Crime Survey (NCS), the NCVS is conducted on

---

**FIGURE 2.2** NATIONAL INCIDENT-BASED REPORTING SYSTEM (NIBRS) OFFENSE CATEGORIES

**Group A Offense Categories**

1. Arson
2. Assault Offenses
3. Bribery
4. Burglary/Breaking & Entering
5. Counterfeiting/Forgery
6. Destruction/Damage/Vandalism
7. Drug/Narcotic Offenses
8. Embezzlement
9. Extortion/Blackmail
10. Fraud Offenses
11. Gambling Offenses
12. Homicide Offenses
13. Kidnapping/Abduction
14. Larceny/Theft Offenses
15. Motor Vehicle Theft
16. Pornography/Obscene Material
17. Prostitution Offenses

18. Robbery

19. Sex Offenses, Forcible

20. Sex Offenses, Non Forcible

21. Stolen Property Offenses

22. Weapon Law Violations

## Group B Offense Categories

1. Bad Checks

2. Curfew/Loitering/Vagrancy Violations

3. Disorderly Conduct

4. Driving Under the Influence

5. Drunkenness

6. Family Offenses, Nonviolent

7. Liquor Law Violations

8. Peeping Tom

9. Runaway

10. Trespass of Real Property

11. All Other Offenses

*For more information on NIBRS see National Incident Based Reporting System, Volume 1: Data Collection Guidelines (2000) at http://www.fbi.gov/about-us/cjis/ucr/nibrs/nibrs_dcguide. pdf (p. 11)*

households in the United States by the U.S. Census Bureau on behalf of the Bureau of Justice Statistics. The NCVS may be used to accomplish a variety of different goals from a crime prevention perspective. Most importantly, it is used to tap into the dark figure of crime, enhance the ability to compare victimizations by types of areas and over time, provide uniform definitions of crime, and include detailed descriptions of the criminal event, including the victim, potential precipitating factors, consequences of the event, and offender.[22] Each year, data are obtained from a nationally representative sample of about 90,000 households, comprising nearly 160,000 persons, on the frequency, characteristics, and consequences of criminal victimization in the United States.[23]

The key to the NCVS is that the study population is the household as opposed to the individuals. Should the individuals move, the address/house will remain in the study for a maximum of three years. Each member of the household age 14 and older is interviewed directly and asked to report the frequency and details of individual victimization(s), including characteristics of the victims and crimes both reported and not reported to law enforcement. Children ages 12 and 13, or individuals who are older and physically unable to participate, are interviewed via a proxy. The proxy also reports household victimizations.[24]

© Brian A Jackson/Shutterstock.com

The NCVS records data on property victimizations, such as burglary, as well as personal victimizations.

There are two types of counts that are collected from the NCVS: incidents of crime and victimizations. Incidents of crime correspond with the UCR categories, while victimizations include the number of victimizations the individual experiences[25]; the relationship between the offender and the victim; the month, date, and location; self-protective actions; losses incurred; the consequences of victimization; whether the offense is reported and why or why not; the presence of weapons, drugs, and alcohol; and the demographic information of both the victim and the offender.[26]

The advantages of the NCVS include the ability to record data on the individual level for personal crimes and the household level for household crimes.[27] Because the NCVS data are only recorded for a sample of households, not all victimizations are included in the data set or the data collection instrument. Likewise, not all cities are represented in the sample; therefore, you cannot estimate crime rates for most of the United States, nor can you estimate crimes for most cities.

As with any data collection effort, there are various problems associated with the NCVS. First, one of the most common problems associated with any form of interview data collection effort is the *interviewer effect*. There is always the potential for the interviewee to become bored or resistant to the interview process. There is also a possibility that the interviewer has very little to give the participant in terms of rewards for participating in the study. One of the ways to verify the information provided in the study is to conduct reverse records checks for those offenses that were reported to the police.

A second problem associated with the NCVS is telescoping.[28] *Telescoping* refers to remembering events as occurring more recently (forward telescoping) or further in the past (backward telescoping) than when they actually occurred. Time bounding the survey instruments is one way to minimize this shortcoming of the data collection effort.

Household movement, also known as *mover-stayer*, is a third problem with the NCVS. Because the NCVS tracks household crime, if the residents at the current address move away, the study does not follow them. Instead, the new residents will be included in the study. This is of particular concern for time bounding as well as differences in lifestyle. Time bounding is an issue because the survey is ongoing and the first interview with the new residents will not be time bounded, so telescoping is a real concern. Likewise, lifestyle differences may skew data for increases or decreases in reported victimization. For example, should the original study group be elderly, the research demonstrates that these individuals are among the least likely to be victimized, particularly by personal crimes. Should a young college-age couple with no children move into the residence, because of their lifestyle difference (out later, access to entertainment, etc.), they are more likely to be victimized than the previous residents.

A fourth problem is sampling error. Although the sample includes 90,000 households in the United States, these households may not represent all demographics and regions, such as rural areas. To account for differences, researchers must use very high confidence intervals (meaning the range for margin of error is quite large) to obtain significance.

A final problem arises with the proxy interviews themselves or response bias. For example, if there is only one person over the age of 14 in a household, that person is responsible for reporting all crime committed within the household. If the representative for the household is the perpetrator, such as in domestic offenses, these crimes are not likely to be reported, thus resulting in response bias.

### Career Connections: Survey Researcher

Survey researchers, along with market researchers, are primarily responsible for finding out what people think. In general, they collect statistical data about people and their opinions; as a result, they spend the balance of their time designing and implementing surveys. This requires precision, diligence, and attention to detail, since data analysis is an important part of their job. Additionally, they must be able to work well as part of a research team, and be able to communicate effectively when reporting their findings.[29]

Survey researchers come from diverse backgrounds; there is no specific academic or professional path they must travel. Typically, researchers will have at minimum a bachelor's degree in order to enter the field. Advancement or a more technical position might necessitate a master's degree or doctorate.[30] A background in the social sciences is common, as well as some exposure to business, psychology, marketing, and sociology. Due to the central role of statistical data gathering and analysis in their work, survey researchers must possess a strong background in quantitative analysis. Math and science courses, with sampling theory and survey design as part of the curriculum, will be helpful in acquiring the necessary analytical and mathematical skills, especially in statistics and data analysis.

Survey researchers use questionnaires and surveys to collect information about people, including their beliefs, behaviors, thoughts, and personal data. They should therefore be adept at interacting with people, interviewing, and writing reports to present and summarize their findings.[31] Students interested in careers as survey researchers should investigate the possibility of an internship with a consulting firm, nonprofit organization, or government agency to gain practical experience with conducting surveys and gathering data.

Professional survey researcher.

There are many employment opportunities for survey researchers in both the government and the private sector. Survey researchers can find work as consultants for management, scientific, and technical companies. They work in market research, public opinion polling, and data gathering. Many work in academia, at colleges or universities.[32] Given the pace of globalization and the demographic shift in the U.S. toward a more diverse population, it is vitally important to have accurate information on foreign populations and how they affect the 21st-century economy. According to the Bureau of Labor Statistics, employment in survey (and market) research is likely to grow 28% from 2008 to 2018, making its growth far bigger than most other fields.[33]

## Self-Report Measures

**Self-report survey** A data collection effort asking participants to report the number of criminal offenses or activities they have committed.

Another method of collecting data is the **self-report survey**. There is no one standard method for collecting data using the self-report method. However, this technique was developed and began being used more frequently during the 1950s. Probably the most frequently recognized historical study was conducted by Short and Nye (1957, 1958) and the National Youth Survey. More recently, the Office of Juvenile Justice and Delinquency Prevention (OJJDP) has supported a multi-site, multi-year study to follow youth throughout their childhood and into adulthood in three specific locations: Denver, Colorado; Rochester, New York; and Pittsburgh, Pennsylvania.[34] Another study funded by OJJDP in Maricopa County, Arizona, has explored possible ways to stop youth offending.[35] Results from these recent studies have been used to inform policy and establish best practices in the juvenile justice field.

As stated, there is no one standardized technique for collecting or counting self-report data. Typically, convenience samples are drawn from school-aged populations. These populations are either given a survey instrument or are interviewed to determine the prevalence and incidence of delinquent or criminal offending. *Prevalence* refers to one or more persons reporting the same offense or behavior during the reference period, while *incidence* refers to the reporting of one delinquent or criminal behavior during the reference period.[36] Advantages of using a self-report survey include tapping into the dark figure of crime, collecting more detailed information on the participants/delinquents, and collecting information on the causes or motivations behind the offending.

Although self-report studies provide another tool for tapping into offenses that are not known to the police, there are still a number of weaknesses that must be taken into consideration when using self-report studies or measures. First, because the majority of self-report studies include a convenience sample of school-aged youth, it is possible that these data do not reflect the larger community and cannot be generalized to all youth. Second, there exists the possibility for overreporting or underreporting delinquent or criminal activity. One way to validate the responses is to include a random records check; this technique gives researchers an opportunity to verify the accuracy of results, or at least establish confidence intervals to draw conclusions. Third, many self-report studies have been criticized for low response rates and usability of returned surveys. Fourth, there is some debate about which type of methodology should be used to collect data (e.g., surveys versus interviews). This is most important when you are asking participants to report their delinquent or criminal behaviors. For participants, this may be a concern when they have actually violated the law and fear that researchers will report their behavior. From a research standpoint, an ethical dilemma may arise between protecting the confidentiality of the participants and having an implied and sometimes stated duty to report criminal behavior. One final weakness of self-report studies is that because there is no one single technique, it is nearly impossible to compare results across studies.

# Crime Statistics

Given the various data collection efforts, it is important to understand the various crime trends from both officially reported offense data and victimization data. This section of the chapter reviews the crime data recorded in the Uniform Crime Reports (UCR) and the National Crime Victimization Survey (NCVS).

According to the UCR, in 2015 there were more than 9.1 million Part I index offenses committed. Of those, approximately 87% were property offenses while 13% were violent offenses. Larceny-theft accounted for 71.4% of all property offenses, while aggravated assault accounted for 63.8% of all violent crime.

More than 10.7 million arrests were made in 2015. Drug abuse violations accounted for the largest number of arrests (1,488,707), while larceny-theft (1,160,390) and driving under the influence (1,089,171) followed. The five-year property crime trends (see Figure 2.3) revealed an 13% decrease, while violent offenses (see Figure 2.4) declined 0.7% during that same time period and 16.5% during a 10-year time period. Males accounted for nearly 73.1% of all persons arrested, while "69.7 percent of all persons arrested were white, 26.6 percent were black, and the remaining 3.6 percent were of other races."[38]

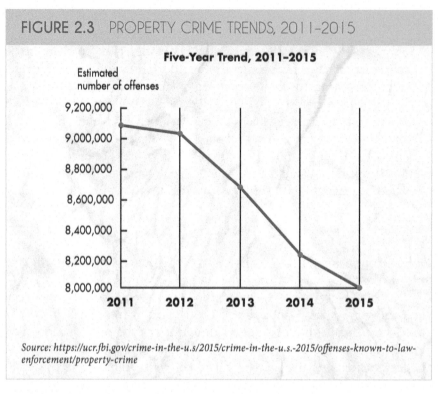

**FIGURE 2.3** PROPERTY CRIME TRENDS, 2011–2015

Source: https://ucr.fbi.gov/crime-in-the-u.s/2015/crime-in-the-u.s.-2015/offenses-known-to-law-enforcement/property-crime

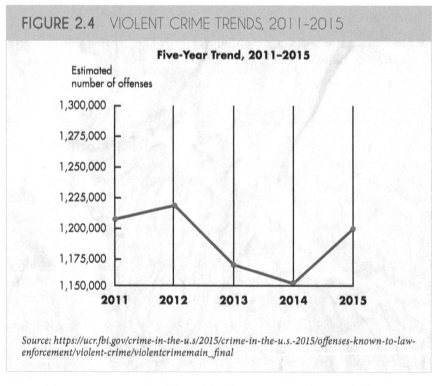

**FIGURE 2.4** VIOLENT CRIME TRENDS, 2011–2015

Source: https://ucr.fbi.gov/crime-in-the-u.s/2015/crime-in-the-u.s.-2015/offenses-known-to-law-enforcement/violent-crime/violentcrimemain_final

According to the NCVS, there were an estimated 14.6 million violent and property victimizations in the United States in 2015.[39] The reported victimizations included an estimated total of 5 million violent victimizations and 14.6 million property crimes. Similar to the UCR data, the NCVS indicated a 6.6% decrease in violent crimes and a 4.4% decrease in property offenses between 2014 and 2015 (see Figure 2.5 for criminal victimization trends).

**Critical Thinking**

How might data collected from the UCR and NCVS shape policy?

## FIGURE 2.5 VIOLENT CRIMINAL VICTIMIZATION

| Type of violent crime | Number | | Rate per 1,000 persons age 12 or older | |
|---|---|---|---|---|
| | 2014* | 2015 | 2014* | 2015 |
| **Violent crime**[3] | 5,359,570 | 5,006,620 | 20.1 | 18.6 |
| Rape/sexual assaultb | 284,350 | 431,840‡ | 1.1 | 1.6‡ |
| Robbery | 664,210 | 578,580 | 2.5 | 2.1 |
| Assault | 4,411,010 | 3,996,200 | 16.5 | 14.8 |
| Aggravated assault | 1,092,090 | 816,760‡ | 4.1 | 3.0‡ |
| Simple assault | 3,318,920 | 3,179,440 | 12.4 | 11.8 |
| Domestic violence[c] | 1,109,880 | 1,094,660 | 4.2 | 4.1 |
| Intimate partner violence[d] | 634,610 | 806,050‡ | 2.4 | 3.0 |
| Stranger violence | 2,166,130 | 1,821,310 | 8.1 | 6.8 |
| Violent crime involving injury | 1,375,950 | 1,303,290 | 5.2 | 4.8 |
| **Serious violent crime**[e] | 2,040,650 | 1,827,170 | 7.7 | 6.8 |
| Serious domestic violence[c] | 400,030 | 460,450 | 1.5 | 1.7 |
| Serious intimate partner violence[d] | 265,890 | 333,210 | 1.0 | 1.2 |
| Serious stranger violence | 930,690 | 690,550‡ | 3.5 | 2.6 |
| Serious violent crime involving weapons | 1,306,900 | 977,840† | 4.9 | 3.6‡ |
| Serious violent crime involving injury | 692,470 | 658,040 | 2.6 | 2.4 |

**Note:** Detail may not sum to total because of rounding. Total population age 12 or older was 252,242,520 in 2008 and 254,105,610 in 2009. Total number of households was 121,141,060 in 2008 and 122,327,660 in 2009.

~Not applicable.

*Difference is significant at the 95%-confidence level. Differences are described as higher, lower, or different in text.

**Difference is significant at the 90%-confidence level. Differences are described as somewhat, slightly, marginally, or some other indication in text.

[a]Victimization rates are per 1,000 persons age 12 or older per 1,000 households.

[b]Percent change calculated based on unrounded estimates.

[c]Excludes murder because the NCVS is based on interviews with victims and therefore cannot measure murder.

[d]Includes rape/sexual assault, robbery, and aggravated assault.

[e]See *Methodology* for discussion on changes in the rate of rape/sexual assault between 2008 and 2009.

[f]Includes pocket picking, completed purse snatching, and attempted purse snatching.

Source: Truman, J. L. & Rand, M. R. (2010). *Criminal victimization, 2009. National Crime Victimization Survey* (NCJ 231327). Washington, DC: U.S. Department of Justice, Bureau of Justice Statistics.

## Drop in Crime Rates

The data cited above demonstrate that there has been a general drop in the overall crime rate in recent years. This is unusual at first glance, as logically a poor economy would seem to correlate with an increase in crime, but the recent statistics are consistent with the overall trend toward a decrease in crime since the 1990s.[40] Explaining this drop in crime rates is a challenge, with no clear consensus as to an explanation. Tufts University sociology professor John Conklin, in his book *Why Crime Rates Fell*, asserts that the drop is due to the fact that more Americans are incarcerated than ever before.[41] For Conklin, the simple drop in the number of criminals on the street means fewer of them are able to commit crime. A more controversial theory, espoused by economist Stephen Levitt, is that the legalization of abortion in the early 1970s was one of the main causative factors in the decrease in crime.[42] In short, he argued that fewer unwanted children in the 1970s and 1980s led to fewer criminals from the 1990s until today.

# Correlates of Crime

Sociologists, and criminologists in particular, are especially interested in the study of the causes and correlates of crime. *Causes* are the factors that directly precipitate criminal offense. *Correlates* are factors that are mutually related, but are not necessarily causal. The important distinction is that correlation does not necessarily imply causation. The most prominent correlates for criminal offending that are of interest to researchers are age, race, socioeconomic status, education, and previous exposure to violence. Each of these correlates/causes has differing levels of empirical support.[43]

## Age

Crime is most common in the second and third decades of the life of the offender.[44] This is a long-accepted tenet of criminology. The aggregate number of arrests in a society may change over a period of time, but the basic breakdown of the relative magnitudes of age groups remains fairly consistent. The 25–29 age group continues to have the highest arrest rate with 1,379,975 arrests in 2015.[45] Moreover, according to Hirschi and Gottfredson, the relationship between age and crime is consistent across both race and sex,[46] which would tend to suggest that it is almost a constant (it does not vary across different categories).

## Race

Race is one of the most studied correlates of crime in the U.S. There are many theories about the relationship between race and crime, most of which are concerned with environmental and social factors. Relatively few researchers advocate for biological reasons to explain race as a cause of crime.[47] The disproportionately large representation of minorities in both arrest and victimization reports is generally accepted,[48] while the root causes of that disparity are hotly debated. Generally speaking, areas that are racially diverse tend to experience higher crime rates.[49] While the majority of arrests are white offenders, African-Americans are represented at a rate two to three times their presence in the general population.[50]

## Socioeconomic/Education Status

Generally speaking, higher socioeconomic status (affluence, education, health, etc.) correlates with lower rates of criminal offense.[51] Criminality correlates highly with unemployment and high frequency of career change. However, it should be borne in mind that so-called "white-collar" crime is a poignant reality, in addition to violent crime and petty theft. The effects of such crime can be equally devastating: doctors cheat on Medicare, lawyers misappropriate funds, business owners run Ponzi schemes, and industrialists dispose of hazardous waste in illegal and unsafe ways.[52] Therefore, explaining criminality solely by reference to the socioeconomic status of the offender is insufficient (although not without merit).

## Previous Exposure to Violence

A final potential correlate for deviance is previous exposure to violence. Children who are exposed to violence at a young age are especially vulnerable to offending as adults.[53] The trauma of witnessing violence at a young age may cause mental stress that leads to delinquency or violent behavior.[54]

# Theories of Crime

Each of us brings to the world our own unique ideological viewpoints, based upon traditions or what we inherently "know" to be true. How do these ideological foundations affect criminological theory? As Lilly, Cullen, and Ball (2007) note, why is it that crime is higher in some communities?[55] Why is it that some people break the law and others do not? Why is it that people, regardless of economic status, commit crimes? From a criminological viewpoint, it is important that we delve into this behavior to capture answers and offer solutions. Criminological theory should guide efforts to react to deviant and/or criminal behavior and prevent it from occurring. Most importantly, theory should inform policy.

Understanding theory is critical in exploring every facet of the criminal justice system, from prevention to crime detection, enforcement, prosecution, sentencing, punishment, incarceration, and re-entry. Theory should help establish the consequences for criminal offending and deviant behavior. Historically, criminological theory can be categorized into three different schools of thought: the pre-classical school, the classical school, and the positivist school.

## Pre-Classical School

Prior to modern-day naturalistic explanations of crime and criminal behavior, crime was understood as a concept of spiritualism and retribution. It was believed that crime was caused by supernatural forces as opposed to natural forces. This was the **pre-classical school** of thought. During the Middle Ages in Europe, the old adage "the devil made me do it" was the guiding philosophy for determining what was considered a crime. Individuals turned to religion and the Bible to determine what constituted violations of law. Crimes that today are not considered illegal—possibly just deviant, or not enforced at all—were worthy of retributive responses, including death or excruciating pain. Likewise, crime and offenses were considered to be private matters, and the responses to these private matters were handled by the individuals and their families.

One response to criminal offenses and punishment was the **trial by battle**. Trials by battle were handled by the victim and the offender. Since it was a private matter, the victim or a chosen member of the victim's family would battle with the offender or a chosen member of the offender's family to determine guilt. The belief was that if offenders were innocent, they would win or not be harmed, therefore proving their innocence.

Another variation of handling the matter privately was the **trial by ordeal**. The trial by ordeal method for proving innocence involved the use of extremely painful or life-threatening methods for punishment. The belief was that if you were innocent, then God would protect you. Examples of punishments included dunking individuals or burying them in heavy stones.

The final example of punishment as a private matter was **compurgation**. In this method of handling offenses, individuals who could find a reputable person in their community to speak on their behalf would be found innocent. This practice led to distinctions by class and in some instances the truly guilty never being held accountable. It should be obvious to a modern observer that the cure did not always logically follow from the cause.

The primary shortcoming of any spiritualistic explanation of crime is that it cannot be scientifically proven. Naturalistic explanations, on the other hand, rely on science to explain the causes of crime. Evidence suggests that as early as 460 B.C., Hippocrates was pointing to the brain as an "independent organ of the mind."[56] Since naturalistic explanations could be used to explain behavior, they could also be used to scientifically study criminal offending. Naturalistic explanations were used to scientifically advance the understanding of behavior during the 16th and 17th centuries in Europe with the development of the classical school of thought.

## Classical School of Thought

The Enlightenment brought an end to the use of brutal and arbitrary punishments. In his 1764 publication, *On Crimes and Punishments,* Cesare Beccaria, known as the father of classical criminology, proposed the removal

---

**Pre-classical school** A school of thought that held that crime was caused by supernatural forces as opposed to natural forces.

**Trial by battle** A mechanism for privately resolving disputes during the pre-classical time period, in which the victim or a chosen member of the victim's family would battle with the offender or a chosen member of the offender's family to determine guilt.

**Trial by ordeal** A method of handling conflict privately during the pre-classical time period, in which proving innocence involved the use of extremely painful or life-threatening methods of punishment.

**Compurgation** A method of handling offenses during the pre-classical time period, in which individuals who could find a reputable person in their community to speak on their behalf would be found innocent.

of harsh punishments and a focus on deterrence principles, in which the offense was punished rather than the offender. The Enlightenment philosophers argued that individuals were free-will thinkers who had the ability to weigh the costs of the punishment with the benefits of the offense. Known also as the *pleasure-pain principle*, this placed the responsibility for behavior on the offender. Further, these philosophers believed that the creation and enforcement of laws should be equal and follow the utilitarian principle of the greatest good for the greatest number. Beccaria and his fellow philosophers further contended that each person in a society agreed implicitly to adhere to the social contract, in which they forfeited certain rights to those in charge in exchange for protection. There was the belief that the government had a right to punish, and that failure to do so was a violation of the social contract.

One of the most important tenets put forth by Beccaria was the idea that punishments should be just, and no greater than the harm caused to society. This tenet called for an end to brutal responses to seemingly minor offenses. More specifically, Beccaria was opposed to the use of the death penalty as a punishment. Instead, he advocated for what we now know as deterrence. **Deterrence theory** is based upon the premise that for any punishment to be effective, it must be swift, severe, and certain. If these three conditions are met, the argument goes, then crime will diminish. There are two forms of deterrence: general and specific. The goal of **general deterrence** is to deter the public from committing future criminal acts by ensuring that punishment is focused on potential criminals as opposed to the individual. The goal of **specific deterrence** is to deter a particular individual from committing future criminal acts by focusing the punishment on that individual.[57]

Jeremy Bentham, in his work, *Introduction to the Principles of Morals and Legislation,* extended the work of Beccaria to include the concept of utility or utilitarianism. "Bentham further specified the idea of utility, or utilitarianism, which emphasizes maximization of pleasure and minimization of pain. This can be viewed on both the individual and aggregate level. On the individual level, this means that an individual will engage (or not engage) in activity that maximizes pleasure and minimizes pain, as perceived by the individual prior to the act. On the aggregate scale utilitarianism argues that the state or government will implement laws that benefit the 'greatest good for the greatest number.'"[58]

Although the **classical school** was an advancement from the spiritualistic view of crime and punishment, it still often resulted in harsh punishments. As scientific exploration and knowledge grew, so too did the pursuit of science to explain criminal behavior. Despite losing favor in recognition of what is now known as the positivist school, the views of the classical school have been revitalized in theories such as routine activities theory.

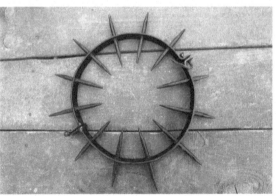

Archaic methods of punishment and deterrence involved extremely painful or life-threatening acts.

**Deterrence theory**
A theory of punishment based upon the premise that in order for any punishment to be effective it must be swift, severe, and certain. There are two forms of deterrence: general and specific.

**General deterrence**
A form of deterrence used to deter the populace from committing future criminal acts by ensuring that the principles of punishment are focused on potential criminals as opposed to the individual.

**Specific deterrence**
A form of deterrence used to deter an individual from committing future criminal acts by focusing the punishment on that individual.

**Classical school**
A philosophy of crime that placed the responsibility for behavior on the offender.

© ID1974/Shutterstock.com

**Routine activities theory** A theory of criminal offending positing that crime is a function of opportunity—the convergence of a motivated offender, a suitable target, and a lack of guardianship.

**Routine activities theory** posits that crime is a function of opportunity. More specifically, as Lawrence Cohen and Marcus Felson (1979) contend, crime occurs when a motivated offender, a suitable target, and a lack of guardianship all converge.[59] Crime as a function of everyday life becomes most prevalent when an individual's routine, either the mundane or the normal, creates a circumstance where these elements converge. Using elements of crime prevention through environmental design allows potential victims to address the issues of routine and mundane behavior.

The *theory of rational choice* contends that traditional theories fail to recognize the merit of choice in criminal acts. Rational choice theorists believe that acts made by offenders are sequenced and purposeful. Under this theory, the criminal act is the result of a rational choice made in the course of a cost/benefit analysis; if the potential gains exceed the punishment, the perpetrator will commit the crime. This perspective advocates for situational crime prevention to reduce opportunities for crime and victimization.[60]

## Positivist School

The classical school, though popular, still came under attack by scientists who argued that not all behavior is reflective of free-will thinking or rational decision-making. Rather, some behavior occurs as a result of factors outside of the control of individuals. This idea led to the formation of the **positivist school** of thought, a philosophy based on biological, psychological, and sociological theories of crime.

**Positivist school** A school of thought on crime arguing that some behavior occurs as a result of factors outside the control of individuals.

**Biological theories** Theoretical propositions that look to the body to identify individuals who are predisposed to criminal offending.

## Biological Theories of Crime

The first **biological theories** of criminal offending were geared toward the elimination of certain groups or classes of individuals. Most notable was the development of *eugenics*, which focused on monitoring and controlling the deviant population through sterilization. Many of the techniques used in such monitoring were essentially pseudoscience, such as craniometry and phrenology.

One example of using biological explanations was the development of craniometry as a field of exploration. Scientists studying craniometry believed they could identify superior versus inferior groups by the size of the skull, and applied this belief to racialized propaganda.[61] The belief was that the skull mirrored the shape of the brain and therefore predicted superiority. Most studies by craniometrists found that white western Europeans were most likely to have the largest skulls and therefore to be superior. This proposition held true until one key researcher, K.F. Gauss, died and an autopsy revealed that his skull and brain were smaller than average. Scientists have subsequently tended to emphasize factors other than the size of the skull or brain, such as the complexity of its development.[62]

Eventually the study of craniometry waned and gave way to phrenology, the study of the bumps on an individual's head. Borrowing from craniometry, phrenologists believed that the skull mirrored the shape of the brain; therefore, skulls that did not conform to the norm were deemed inferior and predictive of criminal offending. Although phrenology as a predictor of criminal offending was not supported by scientific research, more recent studies have revealed a connection between trauma to the left temporal lobe above the ear and violent offending.

Another example of early biological propositions was physiognomy, the study of facial and other features that led to the development of problem behaviors such as criminal offending. The study of facial and body features led to the argument that certain races and ethnicities were superior to others. Such arguments were often made implicitly; for example, James Redfield in *Comparative Physiognomy* (1852) compared the features of different races with different animals, in terms of both appearance and character.[63]

The final proposition that set the framework for the study of biology and crime was the work of Charles Darwin in *The Origin of Species*. In this work, Darwin argued that man evolved from earlier primitive species, and that certain individuals within the species would thrive while others would fail to thrive. This led to the conclusion that there were certain ethnic groups that were essentially throwbacks to an earlier time and therefore inferior. Although Darwin did not specifically study criminality, he did lay the groundwork for the study and application of these principles to understanding the causes of crime.

Cesare Lombroso conducted the first major scientific study of crime, incorporating tenets of all the previously mentioned biological theories. Lombroso first presented his ideas in 1876 and argued that criminal behavior could be differentiated from what one considers to be normal behavior. He contended that individuals who participated in criminal offending were throwbacks from a primitive time, also known as the **atavistic man**. He argued that individuals most likely to be criminals could be identified through recognition of at least five *stigmata* or characteristics, including both physical and extraphysical abnormalities such as "ears of unusual size, sloping foreheads, excessively long arms, receding chins, and twisted noses."[64] He also contended that individuals who displayed tattoos and had a family history of epilepsy and other disorders were more likely to be criminal.[65] Further, Lombroso argued that offenders could be classified into four major categories: "(a) born criminal or people with atavistic characteristics; (b) insane criminals including idiots, imbeciles, and paranoiacs as well as epileptics and alcoholics; (c) occasional criminals or criminaloids, whose crimes are explained primarily by opportunity, although they too have innate traits that predispose them to criminality; and (d) criminals of passion, who commit crimes because of anger, love, or honor and are characterized by being compelled to crime by an 'irresistible force.'"[66, 67]

**Atavistic man**
An identification of individuals participating in criminal activity as throwbacks from a primitive time.

Although Lombroso's theory did not withstand the test of time, his ideas continued to guide researchers. For example, the ideas put forth by Lombroso were further expanded by Raffaele Garofalo. Garofalo shared the belief that certain physical characteristics indicated a criminal nature: for instance,

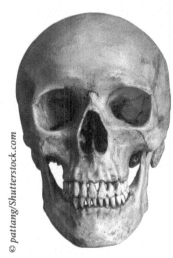

Scientists studying craniometry believed they could identify superior versus inferior groups by the size of the skull.

he thought criminals had less sensitivity to physical pain, demonstrated by the fact that prisoners frequently received tattoos while in prison. Enrico Ferri continued these ideas but included a sociological and psychological component, stating that a combination of many biological, social, and organic factors caused delinquency.[68]

More recent research explored the connection between criminality and inherited traits. One widely cited study was conducted by Richard Dugdale.[69] Dugdale identified a family of individuals, the Jukes (not their real name), who were known to participate in criminal activity. He studied these individuals to determine whether there were specific traits that were inherited by families. He concluded that the poor environment in which the Jukes lived was responsible for their criminality, and that "environment tends to produce habits which may become hereditary."[70]

Another biological explanation for crime was put forth by William Sheldon.[71] Sheldon argued that criminals could be distinguished from the normal population based upon physical characteristics that made them more prone to criminality. He identified three specific body types, known as *somotypes*, that he used to classify the general population. The first body type classification was the *endomorph*: these individuals were characterized as having heavier builds and moving slower. The second type of body classification was the *ectomorph*, tall and slim. The final body type, *mesomorphs*, were best characterized by their overall athletic appearance and build. These individuals were very strong and tended to be aggressive. Sheldon argued that most criminal offenders would be classified as mesomorphs. Further studies and research revealed little or no empirical support for these propositions. Therefore, this theory lost intellectual credibility (though it remains present in ingrained cultural stereotypes).

Researchers have also explored the influence of genetics on criminal offending, questioning whether crime is a function of nature (genetics) or nurture (environment). One way this phenomenon has been studied has been through twin studies. Early studies of twin behavior revealed a significant relationship between identical twins (monozygotic, or MZ) and crime, whereas the relationship between criminal associations and fraternal twins (dizygotic, or DZ) was not significant. A review of relevant studies conducted between 1929 and 1961 found that 60% of MZ twins shared criminal behavior patterns compared to only 30% of DZ twins. Karl Christiansen studied 3,586 male twin pairs and found a 52% concordance for MZ pairs and 22% for DZ twins.[72]

Another way to explore these connections between nature and nurture is through adoption studies. The most frequently cited study on adopted children was conducted by Hutchings and Mednick.[73] They analyzed 1,145 adopted male children born in Copenhagen, Denmark, between 1927 and 1941. They were most interested in looking at the connection between biological or adoptive parents. A total of 143 criminal adoptees (that is, children whose biological fathers had criminal records) were matched with 143 non-criminal adoptees. Results revealed that adopted youth whose biological fathers had criminal records were 24.5% more likely to have a criminal conviction.

## Psychological Theories of Crime

Psychological theories, in general, deal with individual traits that manifest themselves in criminal behavior. For the purposes of this chapter, psychoanalytical and personality theories will be reviewed. More recent expansions of psychological concepts combine these propositions with biological and sociological theories.

**Psychoanalytical** perspectives have their roots in the works of Sigmund Freud. Freud argued that all behavior is motivated by wishes and desires found within our unconscious (or subconscious) minds. It is the interplay between the id, ego, and superego that dictates which unconscious desires will be fulfilled.[74] In Freudian terms, the id includes the unconscious wishes developed in the early stages of life. The superego includes the unconscious wishes developed from watching others around us, such as our parents. The ego serves as the mediator between the id and the superego, translating complex wishes and desires with realistic expectations on a daily basis.[75]

© Lightspring/Shutterstock.com

Sigmund Freud correlated crime to the interplay between the id, ego, and superego.

A frequently cited example of Freud's work in practice is August Aichhorn's 1925 book *Wayward Youth* (translated into English in 1935). Aichhorn described how he utilized Freud's work to resolve chronic delinquent behaviors in youth in both conventional and individual settings. He recognized the interplay between the ego and the superego, arguing that an ill-developed superego led to delinquent activity. For Aichhorn, the key to addressing delinquent activity was moral education. His techniques could be used in a training school setting in small groups. Long-term follow-up studies of youth who worked with Aichhorn revealed changes in behavior after only one session.[76]

Personality theory is another way that psychological perspectives have been used in a criminal justice setting. Unlike psychoanalytical theories that explore the involvement of unconscious wishes and desires, **personality theories** look to explain criminal behavior as expressions of impulsiveness, aggression, or sensation-seeking. A variety of tools have been used in criminal justice settings to identify problems and disorders associated

**Personality theories**
Theories of crime that look to explain criminal behavior as an expression of impulsiveness, aggression, or sensation-seeking.

with personality. These include the Minnesota Multiphasic Personality Inventory (MMPI), the California Psychological Inventory (CPI), and the Hare Psychopathy Checklist (PCL-R).

Another psychological theory is behavioral and/or learning theory using operant conditioning. This therapeutic approach uses reinforcers (both positive and negative) to encourage individuals to perform desired social behaviors.[77]

> **Critical Thinking**
>
> What policy/policies to prevent crime would a psychological theorist most likely support?

## Sociological Theories of Crime

By the early 1900s the city of Chicago, Illinois, had experienced unprecedented growth that ultimately would change the face of the United States. Immigrants from all over the world were flocking to the city in the hope of a better life. This cultural and structural shift prompted faculty members and students from the University of Chicago to explore and study the impact of growth on the city during the 1920s. The result was a specialized body of work in urban sociology that has come to be known as the **Chicago School**,[78] which made use of the city to study "alcoholism, homelessness, suicide, psychoses and poverty." Robert Park, a journalist and sociologist by training, played a significant role in reviewing and covering how the city developed. He focused specifically on the assimilation of immigrants into the general population of the United States, seeing Chicago as a crucible for the process of civilization and a way to view it "under a microscope."[79]

**Chicago School**
A specialized body of work in urban sociology that made use of the city of Chicago to study alcoholism, homelessness, suicide, psychoses, and poverty.

Ernest Burgess, a colleague of Robert Park, sought to graphically depict the outward growth of the city of Chicago. Unlike previous researchers, Burgess contended that there was a distinct pattern to the city's growth.[80] According to Burgess's **concentric zone theory**, the development of the city of Chicago could be divided into five distinct zones or rings. Zone I was the Loop, or the business district. This zone was the heart of the industrial complex. There was a great deal of transportation in and out of the city, including rail and waterways. Zone II, known as the zone in transition, was located just adjacent to the business district. This zone was best defined by deteriorated housing, tenement conditions, continual displacement of residents, and a high rate of turnover by the immigrant population, and was the least desirable place to live in the city.[81] Zone III, working men's homes and multiple-family dwellings, was an area where apartment buildings and modest homes were found. Zone IV, known as the residential zone (single-family homes), consisted of nicer apartments and higher-priced homes. Zone V, known as the commuter zone, was a suburban area.[82]

Park and Burgess's descriptions of the development and growth of Chicago led Clifford Shaw and Henry McKay, sociologists employed by the state of Illinois, to explore the effect of the city's growth patterns on juvenile delinquency. Shaw and McKay[83] proposed that communities with higher rates of social ills—including a breakdown in family composition, dilapidated buildings, unsupervised teenagers, high rates of poverty, high rates of residential mobility, and ethnic heterogeneity—were most likely to experience high rates of crime and delinquency. They postulated that the controls or bonds that would keep youth from committing delinquent acts would be diminished because of these social ills, therefore resulting in increases in delinquent and criminal activity. Communities characterized by intact homes and neighborhoods were known to be more socially organized. Known as **social disorganization theory**, this theory laid the foundation for looking at the causes of crime in the environment, not just at the individual level.

**Social disorganization theory** A theoretical proposition stating that communities with higher rates of social ills, such as breakdown in family composition, dilapidated buildings, unsupervised teenagers, high rates of poverty, high rates of residential mobility, and ethnic heterogeneity, are most likely to experience high rates of crime and delinquency.

To test their theory, Shaw and McKay[84] reviewed juvenile court records, commitments to correctional schools, alleged delinquency handled by police or probation, and juvenile arrests and commitments. Using census data, juvenile court records, and housing and welfare records, they confirmed that crime flourished in zones I and II of Chicago. The highest rates of delinquency were found in communities with the highest rates of social ills that failed to regulate behavior and had the most unsupervised teens. This theoretical premise became the foundation for many advancements in understanding crime and behavior.

In Burgess's concentric zone theory, Chicago's Zone II was characterized by deteriorated and abandoned buildings.

In 1930, Edwin Sutherland joined the faculty of the University of Chicago. Rejecting the individual explanation of crime, Sutherland argued that crime was a product of the social environment in which individuals gained their values from those around them.[85] Sutherland proposed that criminal behavior was learned like all other conventional behavior. In his **differential association theory**, Sutherland identified nine different propositions to explain learning:

**Differential association theory** A sociological theory positing that crime is a product of the social environment whereby values are gained from those around individuals.

1. "Criminal behavior is learned.
2. Criminal behavior is learned in interaction with other persons in a process of communication.
3. The principal part of the learning of criminal behavior occurs within intimate personal groups.
4. When criminal behavior is learned, the learning includes (a) techniques of committing the crime, which sometimes are very complicated, sometimes are very simple; [and] (b) the specific direction of motives, drives, rationalizations, and attitudes.
5. The specific direction of motives and drives is learned from definitions of legal codes as favorable and unfavorable.

6. A person becomes delinquent because of an excess of definitions favorable to violation of law over definitions unfavorable to violation of law. This is the principle of differential association.

7. Differential associations may vary in frequency, duration, priority, and intensity.

8. The process of learning criminal behavior by association with criminal and anti-criminal patterns involves all the mechanisms that are involved in any other learning.

9. While criminal behavior is an expression of general needs and values, it is not explained by those general needs and values since noncriminal behavior is an expression of the same needs and values."[86]

During the 1930s, the Chicago School dominated thought and explanations for crime and criminal behavior. Robert K. Merton, however, rejected these ideas. He was influenced by an understanding of the breakdown of norms and values (normlessness) that was termed "anomie" by Emile Durkheim.[87] Merton expanded upon this, and proposed that when individuals failed to conform to cultural values or achieve financial success, they turned to crime and deviance. In other words, society puts pressure on individuals to live up to certain cultural norms, which can frustrate and put strain on those who are unable to meet those norms. Merton's theory was known as **strain theory**.

Strain theory was further expanded in Lloyd Ohlin's study of delinquent boys. As a student of Merton, he contended that delinquent youth banded together by abandoning middle-class values and creating their own separate sets of values.[88] Richard Cloward (also a student of Merton's) later joined with Ohlin to extend this notion, arguing that the social environment generated pressure for deviance. They argued that the high level of strain experienced by lower-class youth permitted them to adopt illegitimate means for obtaining their goals. In organized slums, younger members of the slums modeled older youth and formed a separate subculture. Similarly, some drug-involved youth further separated themselves as a distinct subculture.[89]

During the 1990s, strain theory was further expanded by Robert Agnew in his **general strain theory**.[90] According to Agnew, Merton did not include all of the strains that existed in an individual's life. Agnew argued that strain could be categorized into three distinct types: 1) "strain as the failure to achieve positively valued goals (traditional strain)"[91]; 2) "strain as the removal of positive stimuli from the individual"; and 3) "strain as the presentation of negative stimuli."[92] The more strain individuals were exposed to, the more likely they were to participate in delinquent or criminal activity.

Control theories seek to add a component of motivation. Like strain theory, social control theory has its roots in the work of Emile Durkheim. Durkheim contended that crime is a normal function of society that serves to unite individuals against a common threat. He further argued that a

**Strain theory** A theoretical proposition contending that crime rates are produced by an individual's inability to conform to cultural values or achieve monetary success through accepted norms.

**General strain theory** An expansion of strain theory stating that the more strain individuals are exposed to, the more likely they are to participate in delinquent or criminal activity. Types of strain include the failure to achieve positive goals, the removal of positive stimuli, and the presentation of negative stimuli.

society without crime is by definition abnormal. Crime and deviance, therefore, serve to establish the moral boundaries for those living within the community.

There are a number of variations of control theories. One of the most significant is Travis Hirschi's **social control theory**. Unlike other theories that sought to explain why individuals committed crimes, Hirschi's theory sought to understand why individuals chose *not* to participate in delinquent or criminal activity. Hirschi characterized the social bond as having four elements. The first, *attachment*, involved identification, emotional bond, concern, and respect for peers or parents, as well as engagement in activities with peers, supervision and intimate communications by parents, attitudes toward school, and concern and sensitivity for the opinions of parents, peers, and teachers. The second element, *involvement*, involved time-consuming activities such as work, sports, recreation, hobbies, and homework, as well as nonactive leisure time, lack of boredom, and time spent interacting with friends. The third element, *commitment*, involved investment in education, career, family, and society, as well as academic and educational competence, aspirations, and expectations, achievement orientation, expected occupation, and importance of reputation. The fourth element, *belief*, involved respect for authorities and law, and the absence of neutralizations. Many have argued that social control theory may be best for explaining less serious forms of delinquency.[93]

**Social control theory**
A theoretical proposition that contends that the more strongly individuals are bonded to their community, the less likely they are to participate in delinquent activity.

Social disorganization theory holds that communities with higher rates of social ills—including high rates of poverty—are most likely to experience high rates of crime and delinquency.

In 1990, Travis Hirschi diverged from his original theory of social control and bonding when he, along with Michael Gottfredson, proposed the **general theory of crime**. Departing from Hirschi's original theoretical premise, they argued that crime was not controlled by bonds to society, but rather by an individual's inability to demonstrate self-control. Crime and other analogous behaviors such as smoking, drinking, driving fast, having multiple sexual partners, etc., provide short-term gratification for those with low self-control. These behaviors begin in early childhood and continue on into later adulthood. Individuals with low self-control are more impulsive, participate in risk-taking behavior, are self-centered, have extreme tempers, and are more physically active.[94] These individuals typically fail at life events that require delayed gratification, such as marriage, education, employment, or other activities that require planning. Crime in general is a not a planned event; rather, offenders act on impulse as a mechanism for gratifying their needs. Gottfredson and Hirschi (1990) contended that there were 10 elements of social control that kept individuals from committing and participating in criminal activity. Those elements of self-control are as follows:[95]

**General theory of crime**
A theoretical proposition that crime is not controlled by bonds to society, but rather by an individual's ability to demonstrate self-control. Under this theory, crime in general is not a planned event; rather, offenders act on impulse as a mechanism for gratifying their needs.

# 10 Elements of Social Control

1. Criminal acts provide immediate gratification of desires.
2. Criminal acts provide easy or simple gratification of desires.
3. Criminal acts are exciting, risky, or thrilling.
4. Crimes provide few or meager long-term benefits.
5. Crimes require little skill or planning.
6. Crimes often result in pain or discomfort for the victim.
7. Crimes require the interaction of an offender with people or their property.
8. The major benefit of many crimes is not pleasure but relief from momentary irritation.
9. Crimes involve the risk of violence and physical injury of pain and suffering on the part of the offender.
10. The risk of criminal penalty for any given criminal act is small but this depends in part on the circumstances of the offense.

Opponents of the general theory of crime have argued that many of the theoretical principles involve circular reasoning. For example, how do we know whether an individual is impulsive or just acting out? This theory further fails to account for personality disorders, racial and gender issues, moral beliefs, and ecological or individual differences. Similarly, this theory purports that behavior does not change over time, and that once an individual demonstrates low self-control, this behavior will continue throughout his or her lifetime. However, other theoretical propositions, such as life course theory, have demonstrated that criminal propensity can change.

Some criminological theories focus on the criminal self as it develops through its relation to others. In 1902, Charles Horton Cooley proposed the idea of the "looking-glass self," which postulated that the self was determined by the perception of others and society's interpersonal interactions.[96] Cooley was a direct influence on George Herbert Mead, a sociologist commonly associated with the Chicago School. Mead saw the self in symbolic terms, specifically as a symbol that can be understood only in its relationship to society as a whole.[97] For Mead, the self is, in some sense, disintegrated by its encounter with society, and then reconstituted as a response to it.[98] Cooley's and Mead's ideas directly influenced labeling theory.

**Labeling theory**
A theoretical tradition in which criminals become set in their roles as criminals as a result of their stigmatized status.

**Labeling theory** was developed by Edwin Lemert. He argued that when an individual is labeled by society as deviant or criminal, the individual is likely to accept the label as true and begin to self-identify as an offender. These individuals are more likely to continue this form of behavior.

Howard Becker further advanced the concept of labeling, arguing that there are four distinct categories of individuals: conformists, pure deviants, falsely accused, and secret deviants.[99] The *conformist* abides by all of the rules and laws of society. The *pure deviant* commits criminal acts and is caught.

The *falsely accused* individual does not commit criminal acts, but instead is falsely accused of crimes, typically as a result of factors such as socioeconomic status, sex, age, race, etc. The *secret deviant* commits acts but is not formally caught and processed; there are a significant number of individuals who fall within this category.[100]

Another variation of labeling theory, known as *radical nonintervention,* was put forth by Edwin Schur, who argued that juveniles who violated delinquency laws should receive no punishment or intervention. Schur contended that any intervention would label an individual as delinquent and would therefore make him or her more likely to commit delinquent behavior—a sort of self-fulfilling prophecy.

Edwin Lemert's labeling theory contends that when an individual is labeled by society as deviant, the individual is likelier to self-identify as an offender.

More recently, the concept of labeling has been extended into John Braithwaite's theory of **reintegrative shaming**. In *Crime, Shame and Reintegration* (1989), Braithwaite contends that punishments designed to stigmatize the offender are counterproductive.[101] Instead of reducing crime, these efforts may in fact further encourage delinquent or criminal offending. Publicly shaming offenders may lead them to be alienated from society and make it difficult, if not impossible, for them to reintegrate. With this in mind, Braithwaite argues that societies should use reintegrative shaming, whereby offenders are punished—therefore repaying their debt to society—and then forgiven for their transgressions and reintegrated back into society. This reintegrative shaming technique has been shown to reduce criminal activity in other countries.[102]

**Reintegrative shaming** A process whereby offenders are punished, therefore repaying their debt to society, and then forgiven for their transgressions and reintegrated back into society.

**Conflict theory** emphasizes how power is used to create conflict in society.[103] This theory builds off the works of Karl Marx and Friedrich Engels, who argued that capitalist societies create power structures that produce struggles for more money and wealth. This power struggle results in conflict and crime.[104] Power is typically associated with wealth and resources; therefore, those with the most wealth in society are more likely to create the laws, maintain control, and have power over the lower classes.[105]

As Reiman and Leighton (2010) contend, the "repressive" nature of law helps maintain the current criminal justice system. In the Marxist tradition, those in power establish a system that fills the needs of the "haves" at the expense of the "have-nots."[106] A variety of different forms of conflict theory exist. More recent versions of conflict theory include peacemaking criminology and left realism.

**Conflict theory** A theory concerned with how power is maintained in a society rather than how individuals function within that continuum. Conflict theory holds that those with the most wealth in society are more likely to create the laws, maintain control, and have power over the lower classes.

> ### Critical Thinking
> What policy/policies to prevent crime would a conflict theorist most likely support?

**Peacemaking criminology** A theory proposing the use of mediation, love, respect, and forgiveness to resolve societal conflicts and reduce recidivism and crime.

**Left realism** A philosophical approach advocating for more minimal responses or sanctions for street-level crimes and less serious offenses, and more stringent responses and social control for white-collar crimes and crimes against society.

**Feminist theories** Theoretical explanations of crime, justice, and the entire criminal justice system from an androgynous perspective.

**Peacemaking criminology** utilizes the concepts of religion, spiritualism, and forgiveness to resolve the conflict that exists within society. Richard Quinney and Harold Pepinsky[107] argued that the keys to reducing recidivism and crime were mediation, love, respect, and forgiveness. They recognized that conflict would continue to exist in any society, but advocated that responses should come from a place of forgiveness.[108]

Another modern-day variation of conflict theory is known as **left realism**. Developed in Britain in the 1980s, left realism branched off from the traditional focus on understanding crime as a class issue and focused on what it deemed the "real aspects of crime."[109] Left realists sought to understand the etiology of everyday crimes that were being committed by the working classes. They advocated for more minimal responses or sanctions for less serious offenses—such as drug use, prostitution, minor property offenses, and victimless crimes—and more stringent responses and social control for white-collar crimes and crimes against society.[110] According to Akers and Sellers (2009), left realism is a philosophical approach that in essence calls for the dismantling of the entire criminal justice system.[111] This approach has been criticized for a variety of reasons. Most notably, the lack of empirical research classifies this approach as philosophical rather than theoretical. Also, this approach calls for punishment responses to offenses rather than rehabilitation or forgiveness, which does not hold to the values of other types of conflict theory.[112]

**Feminist theories** of criminal justice seek to extend the understanding of criminal justice from an androgynous perspective. Many traditional criminological theories fail to take into account that women commit crimes for different reasons than men and they respond to treatment differently as well. No one single feminist perspective exists, but for the purposes of this chapter, a general description of feminist theory will be provided. Feminist theorists argue that the disparities in treatment of men and women in the criminal justice system are as important, if not more important, than the disparities in race and class. Traditional theories of crime have focused on patriarchal explanations.

The *chivalry hypothesis* states that women and girls are treated more leniently in the criminal justice system. This is dismissed by most feminists, though, who instead argue that there is a paternalistic approach in which women are treated on the opposite ends of the continuum—either very leniently or very harshly as a mechanism of control.

Daly and Chesney-Lind (1988)[113] contended that women's roles in society differ fundamentally from those of men, and that these differences in how men and women are viewed in society greatly impact both our understanding of behavior and responses to it.

Another area of feminist literature that has gained recent attention is the *gendering of crime*. This is the exploration of how gender and the roles ascribed to both men and women influence the types of offenses committed.

As Messerschmidt contends, boys and men are raised to be masculine. A sense of being a "man" is defined by "toughness" or assertion. Women, unlike men, take on socially ascribed roles of being the "nurturer" or homemaker. Therefore, if these roles are fulfilled, men should be committing more violent acts as opposed to women, who would be responsible for more property-related offenses.[114]

**Integrated theories** stem from the idea that there are many different theories about crime. Many of these theories fall short because they lack empirical support or because they do not thoroughly explain the causes of crime. One way to address these shortcomings is to combine the most powerful components of each theory into a new theoretical proposition, known as an integrated theory.[115] Theory integration seeks to combine elements of two or more theories into one explanation.

**Integrated theories**
Theories that identify the most powerful elements of other theories and combine two or more of them into one explanation.

Theory integration may combine elements such as control and social learning theories to explain why gangs are formed, or combine strain with social learning theories to explore the impact of the weakening of the social bonds on conventional society.[116]

Wilson and Herrnstein (1985),[117] in their book, *Crime and Human Nature*, proposed an integrated biosocial theory that combined biology with psychology. These authors proposed that biology affects how an individual reacts to their social environment. More specifically, they contended that parents play a crucial role in how children respond to their environment. Individuals seek approval from those closest to them (peers, friends, family) as a mechanism to support acceptable behavior. Wilson and Herrnstein further believed that for punishment to be effective, it must begin with parents and be state-reinforced as a deterrent.

A second variation of integrated theory is the integrated strain-control paradigm developed by Elliott et al. (1985).[118] Elliott and his colleagues proposed that theories of strain, control, and learning could be combined to create a more robust explanation of juvenile offending. For example, they proposed that "(1) strain (in the family and school) weakens (2) social bonds to conventional society, which in turn promotes (3) strong bonds to delinquent peers. It is these strong bonds to delinquent peers, therefore, that are principal factors in (4) the commission of delinquent behavior."[119] They further contended that strong attachments to conventional activities such as school or church reduced the propensity toward crime and delinquency.

Women commit crimes for different reasons than men and respond to treatment differently.

In general, integrated theories have been criticized for a variety of reasons. One of the biggest concerns is that combining two different theories may violate their own assumptions: for instance, control theories seek to explain why individuals do not commit crime, while learning theories seek to explain why they do.[120]

The study of criminal behavior has traditionally focused on the causes of offending among youth or young adults. Theories fail to follow the paths of offending from birth through death. One exception to this rule has arisen in the development of **life course theories**. The life course theorists contend that criminal offending is influenced by two specific patterns of behavior. First, crime is dependent upon the state of the perpetrator: that is, it is malleable based upon previous experiences that influence the individual. Second, crime and behavior are governed by traits that are not changeable, such as impulsivity, age, etc.[121] Individuals establish patterns of behavior in infancy through attachments and reinforcements with parents or caregivers. These attachments or the ability to bond with positive influences continue on into adulthood.

One of the most influential studies of the life course perspective was developed by Robert Sampson and John Laub.[122] They found that criminal or delinquent offending does not occur in a vacuum. Rather, this behavior is influenced by one's environment and structural characteristics such as poverty, residential mobility, family size, and other factors. The family serves as the strongest instrument of control in a child's life through monitoring and attachments. Children reared in unstable homes with few bonds are more likely to grow into adults who have few stable bonds such as employment or marriage. Despite these deficits, research demonstrates that it is not impossible for individuals to overcome these barriers. If individuals are able to establish meaningful bonds in adulthood, these elements may function as "turning points" in their lives to keep them from continuing down a path of crime and delinquency. As noted by Sampson and Laub, it is these informal social controls and bonds that are most important in reducing or preventing crime throughout an individual's lifetime.

> **Critical Thinking**
> What policy/policies to prevent crime would a life course theorist most likely support?

In 1986, the Office of Juvenile Justice and Delinquency Prevention commissioned a study on the causes of delinquency. As part of this study, researchers from the University of Colorado, the University of Pittsburgh, the University of Albany, and the State University of New York interviewed over 4,000 youth at regular intervals, collecting information on their characteristics and behaviors. Information gathered from the study of all-male youth conducted by the team at the University of Pittsburgh helped identify three distinct pathways to crime: the authority conflict pathway, the covert pathway, and the overt pathway.[123] These **developmental pathways** were characterized by differences between these youths and normal offenders.

**Life course theories** The contention that criminal offending is influenced by an individual's previous experiences as well as traits or characteristics that are not changeable, such as impulsivity, age, etc.

**Developmental pathways** A description of the various paths a youth may take into delinquent or criminal offending. These pathways include the authority conflict pathway, the covert pathway, and the overt pathway.

Damaging property is a characteristic of the covert pathway of juvenile crime.

---

**FIGURE 2.6** THREE PATHWAYS TO BOYS' DISRUPTIVE BEHAVIOR AND DELINQUENCY

*Source: Kelley, B. T., Loeber, R., Keenan, K. & DeLamatre, M. (1997). Developmental pathways in boys' disruptive and delinquent behavior (NCJ 165692). Juvenile Justice Bulletin. Washington, DC: Office of Juvenile Justice and Delinquency Prevention, p. 9.*

---

For certain youth, disruptive behavior would manifest itself early in life and continue throughout their lifetime. Research revealed that for stubborn behavior, the median age was nine, with some displaying these characteristics as early as the age of three.

Figure 2.6 illustrates the distinct pathways to crime. The first pathway, the *authority conflict pathway*, begins when a child displays stubborn behavior at an early age. This leads to defiance (such as doing things one's own way and disobedience) and then to an avoidance of authority (such as staying out late or running away). The second pathway, the *covert pathway*, begins with minor dishonest or deceitful behavior (such as lying, shoplifting, or damaging property). This behavior then escalates to more serious crimes, ranging from joyriding, pocket picking, and larceny to using stolen credit cards, breaking and entering, dealing drugs, and stealing cars. The third pathway, the *overt pathway*, includes aggressive acts such as annoying others and bullying, and eventually leads to physical fighting and violent crimes (attacking someone, robbery).[124]

As further noted by the study, of most concern were the issues related to those whose offending persisted over time. Youth who experienced both family dysfunction and neurological problems were most likely to continue down these paths.[125]

## Chapter Summary

- Society differentiates between the concepts of deviance and criminal behavior. Deviance is defined as behaviors considered outside of or inconsistent with normal behavior for a community or group, while criminal behavior is defined by legislation, statutes, and codes. It is important to understand these differences in terms of how society and the criminal justice system respond to illicit activities and behaviors.

- In 1930, the Federal Bureau of Investigation began collecting data on crimes reported to the police and crimes cleared by arrest on a voluntary wide-scale basis. This information is collected in the Uniform Crime Reports (UCR), and divided into Part I and Part II offenses. Part I index offenses are the most serious crimes committed in the United States.

- During the 1980s, the FBI sought to rectify some of the problems encountered with the UCR. The result was the creation of the National Incident-Based Reporting System (NIBRS). There are 13 key differences between the UCR and the NIBRS systems. Unlike the UCR, the NIBRS system includes a total of 22 offense categories made up of 46 crimes. This is an incident-based system that allows for the inclusion of both completed and attempted offenses. Although this is an enhanced version of the UCR, to date it has not been implemented widely. All data collected by the NIBRS system are collapsed into the UCR categories for reporting.

- The National Crime Victimization Survey (NCVS), first administered in 1973 and originally known as the National Crime Survey (NCS), is conducted by the U.S. Census Bureau on behalf of the Bureau of Justice Statistics on households in the United States. The most important functions of NCVS are to tap into the dark figure of crime, enhance the ability to compare victimizations by type of area and over time, provide uniform definitions of crime, and include detailed descriptions of the criminal event, including the victim, potential precipitation, consequences of the event, and the offender.

- Another method for collecting data is the self-report survey. There is no one standard method for collecting data using the self-report method. However, this technique was developed and began being used more frequently during the 1950s. Data from self-report surveys are used to identify the number of crimes not reported to the police.

- Understanding theory is critical for exploring every facet of the criminal justice system, ranging from prevention to crime detection, enforcement, prosecution, sentencing, punishment, incarceration, and re-entry. Theory should establish the context in which consequences are developed for criminal offending and deviant behavior.

- Prior to the modern-day naturalistic explanations of crime and criminal behavior, crime was understood as a concept of spiritualism and retribution. This school of thought is known as the pre-classical school. At that time, it was believed that crime was caused by supernatural forces as opposed to natural forces. Therefore, punishments were considered a private matter and handled as such.

- The Enlightenment brought an end to the use of brutal and arbitrary punishments. Cesare Beccaria set forth a series of propositions advocating the removal of harsh punishments and a focus on deterrence principles whereby the offense was punished versus the offender. The Enlightenment philosophers argued that individuals were free-will thinkers who had the ability to weigh the costs of the punishment with the benefits of the offense. This "pleasure-pain principle" placed the responsibility for behavior on the offender.

- With the development and use of scientific principles, a new realm of theoretical understanding developed known as the positivist school of thought. These theories are best understood in terms of the following categories: biological, psychological, sociological, critical, feminist, peacemaking, and left realist. In all of these explanations, theorists contend that criminal behavior can be explained by forces either inherent within the individual or as a response to societal conditions.

## Critical Thinking?

1. As noted in the beginning of the chapter, distinct differences exist between behaviors that are considered deviant and those considered criminal. Historically, behaviors such as drug use or prostitution were once legal but considered deviant. What factors do you believe should be taken into consideration when deciding whether behavior is illegal? What are some of the unintended/intended consequences of criminalizing behavior?

2. As noted in the statistics presented from both the UCR and the NCVS, crime rates have declined since 2008. What do these statistics reveal to us about crime reduction strategies? How might these data be used on a local and state level to respond to crime?

3. You have just been elected mayor in your community. You ran on a platform of reducing both spending and crime in your community. Given what you know about crime and its causes, how might you accomplish this task?

4. In the case study example provided at the beginning of the chapter, how might biological theory explain the shooting? Create a policy using biological theory that would prevent this crime from occurring in the future.

5. In the case study example provided at the beginning of the chapter, how might psychoanalytical theory explain the shooting? Create a policy using psychoanalytical theory that would prevent this crime from occurring in the future.

6. In the case study example provided at the beginning of the chapter, how might social disorganization theory explain the shooting? Create a policy using social disorganization theory that would prevent this crime from occurring in the future.

7. In the case study example provided at the beginning of the chapter, how might life course theory explain the shooting? Create a policy using life course theory that would prevent this crime from occurring in the future.

8. In the case study example provided at the beginning of the chapter, how might the general theory of crime explain the shooting? Create a policy using the general theory of crime that would prevent this crime from occurring in the future.

9. In the case study example provided at the beginning of the chapter, how might conflict theory explain the shooting? Create a policy using conflict theory that would prevent this crime from occurring in the future.

## Media

**Bureau of Justice Statistics:** http://www.ojp.usdoj.gov/bjs
The Department of Justice website discusses the methodology of crime statistics and provides archived results from the past.

**The National Center for Victims of Crime:** http://www.ncvc.org/ncvc/Main.aspx
The NCVC is a resource and advocacy organization for victims.
This website has useful information for both researchers and victims.

**National Crime Victimization Survey:** http://bjs.ojp.usdoj.gov/index.cfm?ty=dcdetail&iid=245

The NCVS is the crime victims' survey favored by victimologists. It allows researchers to track trends in victimization.

**National Criminal Justice Reference Service:** http://www.ncjrs.gov
The NCJRS is a federally funded, comprehensive website run by the Office of Justice Programs. It contains information relating to the Justice Department for research and public policy.

**National Institute of Justice:** http://www.ojp.usdoj.gov/nij/
The National Institute of Justice is dedicated to using science to help understand and reduce crime.

**Occupational Outlook Handbook, 2010–11 Edition:** http://www.bls.gov/oco/
This government-run site, published by the Bureau of Labor Statistics, details careers and their future outlook.

**U.S. Department of Justice:** http://www.usdoj.gov
The official website of the Department of Justice includes information about the roles of the department and the attorney general.

**Uniform Crime Reports:** http://www.fbi.gov/ucr/ucr.htm
The UCR, published by the FBI, are the most comprehensive statistical reports on reported crime in the United States.

# Endnotes

[1] McCaffrey, F. (2011). "Panel Examines Youth Gang Violence." The Gavel Online. Retrieved from http://bcgavel.com/2011/03/20/gang-violence-examined-presidential-scholars-program-hosts-panel-of-speakers/

[2] Clinard, M. B. (1968). *Sociology of Deviant Behavior* (3rd ed.). New York, NY: Holt, Rinehart, and Winston, 28.

[3] Lombroso, C. (1876). *L'Uomo Delinquente*.

[4] Cornish, D., & Clarke, R. V. (1986). "Introduction." In D. Cornish & R. Clarke (Eds.), *The Reasoning Criminal* (pp. 1–16). New York, NY: Springer-Verlag.

[5] Goode, E. (2001). *Deviant Behavior* (8th ed.). Upper Saddle River, NJ: Prentice Hall.

[6] *Morrison, W. (2006). Criminology, Civilisation and the New World Order. London: Routledge.*

[7] Uniform Crime Reporting Program Staff. (2004). *Uniform Crime Reporting Handbook*. Clarksburg, WV: Federal Bureau of Investigation, 2.

[8] Ibid.

[9] See the Uniform Crime Reporting Handbook at http://www.fbi.gov/about-us/cjis/ucr/additional-ucr- publications/ucr_handbook.pdf for more information on how data are collected and reported to the FBI.

[10] O'Brien, R. M. (1985). *Crime and Victimization Data*. Thousand Oaks, CA: Sage.

[11] Ibid., 22.

[12] Federal Bureau of Investigation (FBI). (2011). *Uniform Crime Reporting Statistics: Their Proper Use*. Retrieved from http://www.fbi.gov/about-us/cjis/ucr/ucr-statistics-their-proper-use

[13] Ibid.

[14] O'Brien, 1985.

[15] FBI, 2011.

[16] Ibid.

[17] Ibid.

[18] FBI. (2000). *National Incident-Based Reporting System, Volume 1: Data Collection Guidelines*. Clarksburg, WV: Federal Bureau of Investigation, 1.

[19] FBI, 2000, 9.

[20] FBI, 2000.

[21] Ibid., 9.

[22] National Archive of Criminal Justice Data (NACJD). (2011). *National Crime Victimization Survey Resource Guide*.

[23] Bureau of Justice Statistics. (2015) Data Collection: *National Crime Victimization Survey (NCVS)* Retrieved from http://www.bjs.gov/index.cfm?ty=dcdetail&iid=245.

[24] NACJD, 2011, 1.

[25] O'Brien, 1985.

[26] NACJD, 2011.

[27] O'Brien, 1985, 47.

[28] NACJD, 2011.

[29] U.S. Department of Labor, Bureau of Labor Statistics. (2009a). "Market and Survey Researchers." *Occupational Outlook Handbook, 2010–11 Edition*. Retrieved from http://www.bls.gov/oco/ocos013.htm#addinfo

[30] Council of American Survey Research Organizations (CASRO). (n.d.). "What Qualifications/Education Do I Need?" *CASRO Careers*. Retrieved from http://www.casro.org/careers/page1.html

[31] U.S. Department of Labor, Bureau of Labor Statistics, 2009a.

[32] CASRO. (n.d.). "Employment Outlook." *CASRO Careers*. http://www.casro.org/careers/page4.html

[33] U.S. Department of Labor, Bureau of Labor Statistics. (2009b). "Occupational Information Included in the Handbook: Job Outlook." *Occupational Outlook Handbook, 2010–11 Edition*. Retrieved from http://www.bls.gov/oco/oco2001.htm#outlook

[34] Thornberry, T. P., Huizinga, D., & Loeber, R. (2004). "The Causes and Correlates Studies: Findings and Policy Implications." *Juvenile Justice Journal, IX(1)*, 3–19.

[35] Mulvey, E. P. (2011). *Highlights from Pathways to Desistance: A Longitudinal Study of Serious Adolescent Offenders* (NCJ 230971). Washington, DC: Office of Juvenile Justice and Delinquency Prevention.

[36] O'Brien, 1985.

37    CNN U.S. (2000, October 5). "Reporting Hate Crimes Presents Dilemma for Many Officials." Retrieved from http://articles.cnn.com/2000-10-05/us/justice.hate.crime_1_crimes-ethnicity-or-national-origin-incidents?_s=PM:US

38    FBI, 2001, 1.

39    Truman, J. L., & Rand, M. R. (2010). *Criminal Victimization*, 2015.October 2016, NCJ 250180. Bureau of Justice Statistics. Retrieved from http://www.bjs.gov/content/pub/pdf/cv15.pdf.

40    FBI. (2006). "Crime in the US, by Volume and Rate per 100,000 Inhabitants, 1986–2005." *Crime in the United States 2005*. Retrieved from http://www2.fbi.gov/ucr/05cius/data/table_01.html

41    Conklin, J. (2003). *Why Crime Rates Fell*. New York, NY: Allyn and Bacon.

42    Levitt, S. D. (2004). "Understanding Why Crime Fell in the 1990s: Four Factors That Explain the Decline and Six That Do Not." *Journal of Economic Perspectives, 18*(1), 163–190.

43    Ellis, L., Beaver, K. M., & Wright, J. (2009). *Handbook of Crime Correlates*. San Diego, CA: Academic Press.

44    Ibid.

45    FBI. (2015) "Arrests by Age" *Crime in the United States 2015*. Retrieved from https://ucr.fbi.gov/crime-in-the-u.s/2015/crime-in-the-u.s.-2015/tables/table-38

46    Gottfredson, M. R., & Hirschi, T. (1990). *A General Theory of Crime*. Stanford, CA: Stanford University Press, 126.

47    For a critical overview of the latter, see Tubman-Carbone, 2009, 50–54.

48    Gabbidon & Greene, 2005a, 31–33; Walsh, 2004, 19–36; Wright, 2009, 143–144.

49    Ellis, Beaver, & Wright, 2009.

50    Gabbidon & Greene, 2005a, 31–33; Walsh, 2004, 22–23, 37–51.

51    Ellis et al., 2009.

52    Gottfredson & Hirschi, 1990, 184.

53    Lauritsen, J. L., Sampson, R. J., & Laub, J. H. (1991). "The Link between Offending and Victimization among Adolescents." *Criminology, 29*, 265–292.

54    Mazerolle, P., Burton, V. S., Cullen, F. T., Evans, T. D., & Payne, G. L. (2000). "Strain, Anger, and Delinquent Adaptations: Specifying General Strain Theory." *Journal of Criminal Justice, 28*(2), 89–102.

55    Lilly, J. R., Cullen, F. T., & Ball, R. A. (2007). *Criminological Theory: Context and Consequences* (4th ed.). Thousand Oaks, CA: Sage.

56    Ibid., 14.

57    Ferris, T. (2005). *Sentencing: Practical Approaches*. Toronto: Lexis-Nexis, 357.

58    Tibbetts, S. G., & Hemmens, C. (2010). *Criminological Theory: A Text/Reader*. Thousand Oaks, CA: Sage, 90.

59    Cohen, L. E., & Felson, M. (1979). "Social Change and Crime Rate Trends: A Routine Activities Approach." *American Sociological Review, 44*, 588–608.

[60] Cornish, D. B., & Clarke, R. V. (Eds.). (1986). *The Reasoning Criminal: Rational Choice Perspectives on Offending.* New York, NY: Springer.

[61] Thomas, D. H. (2001). *Skull Wars: Kennewick Man, Archaeology, and the Battle for Native American Identity.* New York, NY: Basic Books, 38–41.

[62] Cosgrove, K. P., Mazure, C. M., & Staley, J. K. (2007). "Evolving Knowledge of Sex Differences in Brain Structure, Function, and Chemistry." *Biological Psychiatry, 62*(8), 847–855.

[63] Redfield, J. W. "Comparative Physiognomy or Resemblances between Men and Animals: Illustrated."

[64] Lombroso, 1896.

[65] Ibid.

[66] Wolfgang, M. E. (1973). "Cesare Lombroso." In H. Mannheim (Ed.), *Pioneers in Criminology* (2nd ed., pp. 232–291). Montclair, NJ: Patterson Smith.

[67] Lilly et al., 2007, 19.

[68] Ferri, E. (1897/1917). *Criminal Sociology.* Boston, MA: Little, Brown.

[69] Dugdale, R. L. (1910). *The Jukes: A Study in Crime, Pauperism, Disease and Heredity.* New York, NY: G.P. Putnam's Sons.

[70] Ibid., 66.

[71] Sheldon, W. H. (1940). *The Varieties of Human Physique: An Introduction to Constitutional Psychology.* New York, NY: Harper & Brothers.

[72] Moffitt, T. E., Ross, S., & Raine, A. (2011). "Crime and Biology." In J. Q. Wilson & J. Petersilia (Eds.), *Crime and Public Policy* (pp. 53–87). New York, NY: Oxford University Press.

[73] Mednick, S. A., Gabrielli, W. F., & Hutchings, B. (1984). "Genetic Influences in Criminal Convictions: Evidence from an Adoption Cohort." *Science, 224,* 891–894. doi:10.1126/science.6719119

[74] Lester, D., & Van Voorhis, P. (2000). "Psychoanalytic Therapy." In P. Van Voorhis, M. Braswell, & D. Lester (Eds.), *Correctional Counseling & Rehabilitation* (4th ed., pp. 111–128). Cincinnati, OH: Anderson.

[75] Ibid.

[76] Barton-Bellessa, S. M. (2010). "August Aichhorn: Wayward Youth." In F. Cullen & P. Wilcox (Eds.), *Encyclopedia of Criminological Theory.* Thousand Oaks, CA: Sage.

[77] Ibid.

[78] Cavan, R. S. (1983). "The Chicago School of Sociology, 1918–1933." *Urban Life, 11,* 415.

[79] Park, R. E. (1928). "Human Migration and the Marginal Man." *American Journal of Sociology, 33*(6), 890.

[80] McKenzie, R. D., Park, R. E., & Burgess, E. W. (1967). *The City.* Chicago, IL: University of Chicago Press.

[81] Ibid.

[82] Lilly et al., 2007.

[83] Shaw, C. R., & McKay, H. D. (1942). *Juvenile Delinquency in Urban Areas.* Chicago, IL: University of Chicago Press.

84   Ibid.

85   Sutherland, E. (1934). *Principles of Criminology*. Chicago, IL: J.B. Lippincott.

86   Sutherland, E. H., & Cressey, D. R. (1970). *Criminology* (8th ed.). Philadelphia, PA: Lippincott, 75–76.

87   Durkheim, E. (1951). *Suicide: A Study in Sociology*. New York, NY: The Free Press.

88   Ohlin, L. (1956). *Sociology and the Field of Corrections*. New York, NY: Russell Sage Foundation.

89   Cloward, R., & Ohlin, L. (1960). *Delinquency and Opportunity*. New York, NY: The Free Press.

90   Agnew, R. (1992). "Foundation for a General Strain Theory of Crime and Delinquency." *Criminology, 30*(1), 47–87.

91   Ibid., 50.

92   Ibid., 57.

93   Hirschi, T. (1969). *Causes of Delinquency*. Berkeley, CA: University of California Press.

94   Brown, S. E., Esbensen, F., & Geis, G. (2004). *Criminology: Explaining Crime and Its Context* (5th ed.). Cincinnati, OH: Lexis-Nexis.

95   Gottfredson, M. R., & Hirschi, T. (1990). *A General Theory of Crime*. Stanford, CA: Stanford University Press, 89–90.

96   Cooley, C. H. (1902). *Human Nature and the Social Order*. New York, NY: Scribner's.

97   Mead, G. H. (1913). "The Social Self." *Journal of Philosophy, Psychology and Scientific Methods, 10*, 374–380.

98   Ibid., 379.

99   (1963). *Outsiders: Studies in the Sociology of Deviance*. New York, NY: The Free Press.

100  Brown, Esbensen, & Geis, 2004.

101  Braithwaite, J. (1989). *Crime, Shame, and Reintegration*. Melbourne, Australia: Cambridge University Press.

102  Braithwaite, J. (2000). "Shame and Criminal Justice." *Canadian Journal of Criminology, 42*(3), 281–298.

103  Akers, R. L., & Sellers, C. S. (2009). *Criminological Theories: Introduction, Evaluation, and Application* (5th ed.). New York, NY: Oxford University Press.

104  Lilly, J. R., Cullen, F. T., & Ball, R. A. (2011). *Criminological Theory: Context and Consequences* (5th ed.). Thousand Oaks, CA: Sage.

105  Williams, F. P., & McShane, M. D. (2004). *Criminological Theory* (4th ed.) Upper Saddle River, NJ: Prentice Hall.

106  Reiman, J., & Leighton, P. (2010). *The Rich Get Richer and the Poor Get Prison: Ideology, Class, and Criminal Justice* (9th ed.). Boston, MA: Allyn & Bacon.

107  Pepinsky, H., & Quinney, R. (Eds.). (1991). *Criminology as Peacemaking*. Bloomington, IN: Indiana University Press.

[108]    Pepinsky, H. (1999). "Peacemaking Primer." In B. A. Arrigo (Ed.), *Social Justice: Criminal Justice* (pp. 52–70). Belmont, CA: Wadsworth.

[109]    Lilly et al., 2011, 208.

[110]    Ibid.

[111]    Akers & Sellers, 2009.

[112]    Lilly et al., 2011.

[113]    Daly, K., & Chesney-Lind, M. (1988). "Feminism and Criminology." *Justice Quarterly, 5*, 497–538.

[114]    Lilly et al., 2011.

[115]    Barak, G. (1998). *Integrating Criminologies*. Boston, MA: Allyn and Bacon.

[116]    Ibid.

[117]    Wilson, J. Q., & Herrnstein, R. J. (1985). *Crime and Human Nature*. New York, NY: Simon & Schuster.

[118]    Elliot, D. S., Ageton, S. S., & Huizinga, D. (1985). *Explaining Delinquency and Drug Use. Beverly Hills*, CA: Sage.

[119]    Ibid., 94, 146.

[120]    Akers & Sellers, 2009.

[121]    Wright, J. P., Tibbetts, S. G., & Daigle, L. E. (2008). *Criminals in the Making: Criminality across the Life-Course*. Thousand Oaks, CA: Sage, 6.

[122]    Sampson, R. J., & Laub, J. H. (1993). *Crime in the Making: Pathways and Turning Points Through Life*. Cambridge, MA: Harvard University Press.

[123]    Kelley, B. T., Loeber, R., Keenan, K., & DeLamatre, M. (1997). "Developmental Pathways in Boys' Disruptive and Delinquent Behavior" (NCJ 165692). *Juvenile Justice Bulletin*. Washington, DC: Office of Juvenile Justice and Delinquency Prevention, 8–9.

[124]    Ibid.

[125]    Ibid.

# SECTION 2
## LAW ENFORCEMENT IN THE 21ST CENTURY

Chapter 3
Policing in America

Chapter 4
Policing: Roles, Functions, and Challenges

© Yakov Oskanov/Shutterstock.com

# Policing in America

## KEY TERMS

Black codes

Community policing

Constable

Corruption

Early Warning Systems

Extralegal policing

Grass eaters

Law Enforcement Assistance
Administration

*Law Enforcement Bulletin*

Lynch mob

Meat eaters

Miranda rights

Night watches

Pinkertons

Posse

Racial profiling

Sheriff

Slave patrols

SWAT (Special Weapons and
Tactics) team

Texas Rangers

Third degree

Vigilantism

Wickersham Commission
(National Commission
on Law Observance and
Enforcement)

# CHAPTER OBJECTIVES

1 | Describe the history of policing in the United States.

2 | Review significant efforts to reform law enforcement and improve police accountability and professionalism.

3 | Identify the variety of law enforcement agencies located at the local, state, and federal levels.

4 | Describe the education and training requirements of contemporary law enforcement professionals.

## Case Study: Wickersham Commission

Contemporary police are generally held in high regard and perceived as trustworthy and honest by the majority of the American public. This has not always been the case. In fact, the professionalism and public support characteristic of most modern-day policing agencies are the result of many years of reform efforts. Efforts to reform the police have been undertaken by law enforcement agencies and officers themselves, as well as by government officials and concerned community groups.

One of the earliest reports outlining the problems with policing in the United States was the "National Commission on Law Observance and Enforcement," or the Wickersham Commission. The Wickersham Commission was established in May of 1929 by President Hoover. Its purpose was to provide a comprehensive examination of crime and criminal justice in the United States. The commission's membership was bipartisan and included a number of notable legal scholars of the time, such as Roscoe Pound, the dean of Harvard Law School, and Ada Comstock, president of Radcliffe College. The findings of the commission were published in 14 reports[1] and covered a range of topics such as the causes and costs of crime, the enforcement of prohibition laws, and the state of policing and law enforcement. The reports were released to the public in January 1931.

The Wickersham Commission's report was significant because it was the first national publication to highlight a number of shortcomings of American law enforcement agencies in the early 20th century. The report's authors revealed problems with police officer selection and training, effectiveness of police leadership, and law enforcement agencies' success at controlling crime. They also identified three primary concerns with policing that remain today: inappropriate use of force and treatment of suspects, the need for professional and effective police officers, and the necessity of positive community/police relations.

The inappropriate use of force by police officers received significant attention in the commission reports, and the authors describe in detail some of the abusive practices of police officers in the early 1900s, including cases of suspects being savagely beaten or tortured and denied food, drink, or sleep.[2]

While American policing practices and regulations have made significant strides since the days of the Wickersham Commission, the concerns outlined in the report continue to receive the bulk of scholarly attention and are consistently the focus of contemporary police reform initiatives. Though we are moving toward more professional, accountable, and democratic policing in the United States, these issues still exist in modern policing.

# History and Structure of Police Systems

Today, police are generally viewed positively—they are perceived as both honest and effective by the majority of the American public.[3] But the positive light in which contemporary policing is viewed is a relatively recent phenomenon. For much of its history, policing could best be characterized as disorganized, ineffective, and corrupt. Early police officers were poorly paid, ill prepared to address the complexities of crime and disorder, and disrespected by the larger community.[4]

Beginning in the 1900s and continuing today, policing has undergone a series of significant reforms. The objectives of many of these reforms were to transform police officers into unbiased professionals who were capable of upholding the law while enforcing it, and to create well-equipped law enforcement agencies that used their resources effectively to reduce crime. Though there are concerns surrounding American policing that persist today, it has improved significantly since its beginnings.

## History of Policing in the United States

In early American history, the responsibility for policing was left to residents and local and state authorities. Local policing developed in unique ways in different parts of the country. In the Northeast United States, immigrant communities often reproduced the forms of law enforcement most commonly used in Europe. Policing in these areas emphasized the informal enforcement of laws and often relied upon local citizens to act as enforcers.[5] Meanwhile, the practice and legacy of slavery significantly influenced the development of policing in the Southern states. Many of the early policing efforts focused on enforcing slave laws and, after the abolition of slavery, special legal codes designed to regulate the activities of the black population. Policing in the "Wild West" was insufficient, unregulated, and often violent. Due to a lack of formal law enforcement agencies, vigilante groups and private security agencies often performed law enforcement functions on the frontier.

Though historically most policing was locally managed, the federal government did create some law enforcement agencies in early American history.

These agencies tended to focus on offenses such as counterfeiting, interstate or international crimes, and issues related to war, such as spying and draft dodging.

## Policing in the Northeast

Early American colonists typically adopted the English system of shire reeves (now referred to as "sheriffs"), constables, and night watches. These forms of policing emerged in England during the medieval period and remained the most common forms of enforcement well into the mid-1600s. When the first waves of immigrants came to the United States from Europe, they brought these law enforcement practices with them.[6]

**Constable** A local law enforcement officer who was responsible for collecting taxes and enforcing ordinances in the colonial and post-colonial United States, similar to a sheriff; today, constables are typically law enforcement officers in small towns.

**Sheriff** A local law enforcement officer responsible for collecting taxes and enforcing ordinances in the colonial and post-colonial United States, similar to a constable; today, sheriffs serve as law enforcement officers at the county level.

**Night watches** Groups of local, unpaid citizens who would patrol the community at night to deter crime and alert residents of the time, weather, and hazards.

Colonial American **constables** and **sheriffs** were appointed to their positions by the local community. Such positions were not desirable, as they were often unpaid and time-consuming. In order to earn money, constables and sheriffs would take a percentage of the fees collected for serving warrants, making arrests, or collecting fines.[7] In addition, early law enforcement officers were not well respected by the larger community.

Constables were often responsible for forming **night watches** in their colonial towns and cities. They were called night watches because they performed their duties during the night. The first recorded night watch was in Boston in the 1630s, though other Northern cities followed soon after. For much of the colonial period, night watches were sporadically utilized. In fact, Boston was the first city to require a permanent night watch, which it did not do until 1801.[8]

The night watch typically consisted of rotating groups of adult, able-bodied male residents. In addition to watching out for criminal activity, night watches were also required to watch for fires, and to report on the time and on local weather conditions. Night watch duty was not considered a prestigious activity, and men with the political and economic means would often be able to avoid performing this service. This resulted in night watch crews that were either understaffed or staffed by community members of questionable esteem.[9] The system of constables and night watches continued to be the most common form of policing in the Northeastern United States well into the late 1800s.

The primary law enforcement agent in Northeastern cities was the high constable or, in some places, the marshal. It was this person's job to enforce state laws and local ordinances, execute arrest warrants, suppress riots, and maintain general order. These policing executives were often chosen in various ways—some were popularly elected, while others were appointed by the mayor, by members of the local council, or by state governors. These positions were considered undesirable by the general public, and it often proved difficult to find willing and appropriate people to fill them. As in colonial times, constables were not paid, but rather worked on commission. They would earn money by taking a percentage of the revenues they obtained through executing arrest warrants or through the collection of local taxes and fees. Local residents continued to be used to form the ranks of the night watch; however, members of the night watch did not possess police power and were only able to execute an arrest if a crime was committed in their physical presence.

> **Critical Thinking**
> How might working on commission have affected early officers' enforcement of the law?

By the beginning of the 19th century, the United States was experiencing significant social and economic change as a result of the Industrial Revolution. The population was growing dramatically, especially in urban areas, and citizens were experiencing significant economic and political changes. Riots triggered by ethnic tensions and economic insecurity were relatively common in the rapidly growing cities. Local enforcement agents were ill equipped to address mass social unrest, and it was not unusual for the state militia to be called out to restore order to the city.[10]

During the Civil War years (1861 to 1865), urban disruption continued. Perhaps the most memorable of such uprisings was the New York draft riot in 1863. During this protest of President Lincoln's efforts to draft citizens into the Union forces, mobs destroyed property, looted establishments, and killed 1,200 people. The state militia and federal troops were sent to the city to quell the uprising. This is the most violent riot in the United States to date.[11]

By the mid-1800s, local governments began to realize that policing in the form of constables and night watches was inadequate. American cities and towns moved to create their own forms of permanent and professional law enforcement. The British influenced early American efforts to develop a permanent police force. In 1829, British Home Secretary Sir Robert Peel persuaded Parliament to establish a professional police department. As a result of Peel's efforts, 1,000 "bobbies" (the name given to London police officers, in honor of Peel) permanently patrolled the streets of London.

New York City became the first city in the United States to adopt a permanent police force. In 1845, the New York City police force consisted of 800 full-time officers. Other cities followed soon after: Chicago in 1851, Philadelphia and Boston in 1854, and Baltimore in 1857.[12]

**Corruption** within early police forces was rampant.[13] Local government officials had significant control over determining who could be a police officer and over policing activities. Some local officials took advantage of their significant power over law enforcement. Appointments to policing positions were made based on political and ethnic affiliations rather than an individual's skill or commitment to legal principles. Police officers were often uneducated and were rarely screened for suitability

**Corruption** Abuse of police authority for personal gain.

Sir Robert Peel is credited with convincing the British Parliament to institute a permanent police force in London in 1829.

Slave patrols Regulatory groups in the South in the Colonial Era focused on regulating the activities of slaves.

Black codes Laws created after the end of slavery designed to regulate the activities of African-American citizens.

Vigilantism The taking on of law enforcement responsibilities and the dispensing of punishment by private citizens.

Lynch mob A group of individuals seeking to punish someone suspected of having committed a social transgression.

for a law enforcement position. It was not uncommon for individuals with criminal records to become police officers and for police officers to engage in illegal activities.

## Policing in the South

Early policing efforts in the Southern states focused on upholding the slave system and its legal codes.[14] Beginning in the late 1600s, groups of local citizens formed **slave patrols**, whose primary objectives were to track down runaway slaves and return them to servitude, and to stave off potential slave rebellions. Slave patrols were composed of poor, non-slave-owning whites and individuals who were recruited from the state militias. Initially, slave patrols were organized in similar ways to military groups, with an officer who was in charge of a group of men. After the American Revolution, responsibility for the slave patrols shifted to the citizenry, though the patrols never lost their military overtones.

Slave patrols are frequently discussed in slave narratives.[15] These narratives describe the everyday forms of abuse and harassment that slaves would be subjected to by the slave patrols. When traveling off a plantation, for example, slaves were required to carry documentation indicating their owner's approval for their travel. Members of the slave patrol could stop anyone they suspected of being a slave and ask for ownership information and travel authorization. Even when slaves carried the appropriate documentation, they would be subject to verbal and physical abuse by the slave patrol. The slave patrols had tremendous power and could enter any property they desired to without cause or without warrant.

After the Civil War and the formal end of slavery, slave codes aimed at regulating the activities and opportunities of African-Americans were refashioned into "**black codes**." Common laws incorporated into black codes included prohibiting interracial marriages, disallowing African-Americans from testifying against whites in court, and making it illegal for former slaves to own firearms. After the abolition of slavery, those who had served in the slave patrols or in the Confederate Army often assumed posts as police officers.

Regulation of the activities of newly freed slaves was not limited to the formal law enforcement agencies, however, and **vigilantism** was a relatively common practice in the American South after the end of the Civil War.[16] Vigilantism, or the taking on of law enforcement responsibilities and the dispensing of punishment by private citizens, often took the form of a **lynch mob**, a group of individuals seeking to punish someone suspected of having committed a social transgression. Such transgressions could be as minor as an African-American man looking inappropriately at a white woman, and punishments could include hanging, burning at the stake, or shooting.

## Policing in the "Wild West"

For much of the 1800s, the U.S. western frontier was a dangerous and lawless place. Early homesteaders, cattle ranchers, miners, and entrepreneurs who tried to make a living for themselves in the "Wild West" often had to provide for their own protection and enforcement.[17]

In places where there was some law enforcement presence, local law enforcement agents were often as crooked and violent as the individuals they were supposed to control. In fact, it was not uncommon for men who were outlaws themselves to take up the role of local sheriff or marshal, or for men who were once lawmen to return to outlaw activities.

On the frontier, violence by law enforcement was considered a necessity for maintaining social order. Local law enforcement often acted as the investigator, the judge, and, in some cases, the executioner. Punishments were brutal, and law enforcement officers proved their usefulness to the local community through their willingness and ability to dispense these forms of harsh justice.[18] As with police posts in most other parts of the country, law enforcement officers in the West were poorly paid and would often have to find additional means of earning money in order to supplement their meager salaries.

When local sheriffs or marshals were faced with incidents that required additional personnel in order to be effectively addressed, such as tracking a fugitive or quelling large-scale unrest, they would often have to rely on local community members. Local residents were temporarily enlisted by law enforcement agencies to form a posse. Posses allowed under-resourced sheriffs to expand their forces in terms of both bodies and weapons. The challenge for the local officer was to manage the activities of these posses to ensure they acted within the constraints of the law. Often, this was not an easy task.

**Posse** A group of residents temporarily enlisted by law enforcement agencies to assist in law enforcement functions.

Perhaps the most infamous law enforcement agency in the American West is the **Texas Rangers**.[19] The Rangers were first formed by Stephen F. Austin in the 1820s, when Texas was a Mexican territory. Like other law enforcement groups in the West, the Rangers were formed as a self-protection group focused on battling local Native American groups and pursuing cattle thieves and other outlaws. They were similar to a military force in that they had a military organizational structure and they participated in military campaigns (e.g., the Indian Wars and the Mexican Wars). By 1835, there were nearly 200 Rangers performing law enforcement and military functions throughout the region. By 1845, when Texas became the 28th state to join the American Union, the Rangers had become a formalized law enforcement agency.

**Texas Rangers** One of the earliest law enforcement agencies in the American West.

When local law enforcement was available on the frontier, it was often insufficient to meet local needs. **Extralegal policing**—policing that was not regulated or sanctioned by law—was typical in the West. Two types of extralegal

**Extralegal policing** Policing that is not regulated or sanctioned by law.

In addition to law enforcement responsibilities, the Texas Rangers participated in military campaigns.

policing were common: vigilantism and private policing. Citizens would frequently band together to form vigilance committees that served as the mechanism for law enforcement and punishment in remote areas. One of the most notorious vigilante groups was the Regulators of Shelby County, East Texas.[20] This group was initially formed to prevent cattle and horse theft, but began to use its power to harass local residents. In response, members of the community, including several law enforcement officers, formed another group, called the Moderators. The two groups began to wage a war over power and land that ended only after the president of Texas (then a republic independent from Mexico) sent the militia to the area to arrest leaders from both groups and establish peace in the area.

Wealthy groups often responded to the shortage of formal law enforcement officers in the West by hiring their own protective forces. Merchant groups, banks, and mining companies hired private security agencies to protect valuable goods, such as gold and silver, that were being shipped by stagecoach and train across the United States. These goods were especially vulnerable to robbers as they traveled through the sparsely populated or uninhabited places on the frontier.[21]

Though they were not without problems, private protection agencies had several advantages over formal law enforcement. First, they were not limited to a particular area—they were free to pursue suspects across jurisdictions, even across state lines. Second, as for-profit businesses, they had little interest in politics and would complete the jobs for which they were paid. This was not a trivial consideration, as many law enforcement agencies of the time were subject to the whims of political authorities. The downside of private security was that they were not subject to the same forms of legal constraint as formal law enforcement officers. There was little to prevent them from using questionable methods to pursue, apprehend, and even punish suspects.

**Pinkertons** A private investigation and security company formed in the 1880s that assisted in protecting goods, tracking down suspects, and breaking strikes.

Perhaps the most legendary of these private protection agencies was the **Pinkertons**.[22] The Pinkerton National Detective Agency was formed in the mid-1880s by a former presidential security officer, Allan Pinkerton. The motto of the Pinkertons was "The eye that never sleeps." Pinkerton agents were hired by wealthy companies to protect goods, to track down robbers and other criminals, and to break strikes. Though the Pinkerton ranks included skilled detectives, they also included individuals with few reservations about the use of force. For example, when performing a raid in search of the legendary bank robber Jesse James, Pinkerton agents threw a bomb wrapped in fuel-soaked rags into the home where he was believed to be hiding out. James was not in the home at the time, but the bomb ended up killing his younger brother and maiming his mother. This episode serves as a good example of the potential problems associated with using private security as law enforcement.

**Critical Thinking**

Though policing developed differently in the North, South, and West, there are some commonalities. What are the similarities in early American law enforcement approaches in these regions?

## History of Federal Law Enforcement

Most early law enforcement was handled by local or state entities, but there were some federal agencies formed early in American history. Under the first president, George Washington, the U.S. Marshals were created. They were established by the Judiciary Act of 1789, the same act that created the federal court system. One U.S. Marshal was appointed for each of the 13 federal districts. It was the responsibility of each U.S. Marshal to enforce federal laws, to pursue violators of laws enacted by the U.S. Congress or the President, to facilitate federal judicial processing of violators, and to assist in the implementation of punishments meted out by the federal courts within their district. While the number of U.S. Marshals was small, they were granted the authority to deputize others to assist them in the administration of their duties. In addition, U.S. Marshals were given the right to *posse comitatus*, allowing them to summon a posse of men to assist in the pursuit of a fugitive. The activities of U.S. Marshals have varied significantly over time. Prior to the Civil War, U.S. Marshals focused their attention on enforcing the Fugitive Slave Act of 1850. This act required that slaves captured in non-slave states be returned to their owners in slave states. During the Civil War, U.S. Marshals shifted their attention to tracking Confederate spies. Beginning in the 1890s, much of the focus of the U.S. Marshals was on protecting federal judges.[23]

The creation of subsequent federal law enforcement was haphazard, as the U.S. Congress tended to create law enforcement agencies in response to particular crises rather than as part of a strategic plan. The U.S. Secret Service, for example, was created as a part of the Treasury Department in 1865 to deal with growing problems with counterfeit currency and postage stamps. It assumed responsibility for protection of the president after the assassination of President William McKinley at the Pan-American Exposition held in Buffalo, New York, in September 1901.[24]

The Federal Bureau of Investigation (FBI) was created as part of the Department of Justice in 1908 under President Theodore Roosevelt. When the FBI was created, there were a limited number of activities that had been established as federal crimes by the national government. Many of the existing laws focused on issues surrounding banking, immigration, business monopolies, and involuntary servitude. The first substantial federal crime legislation introduced after the formation of the FBI was the Mann Act of 1910, also known as the White Slave Traffic Act. The goal of the Mann Act was to control prostitution and make illegal the transportation of women over state lines for "immoral purposes." Exaggerated concerns about "white slavery" were more likely responses to significant social changes occurring as a result of industrialization, urbanization, and immigration. Women were beginning to move away from their family homes into urban centers where they enjoyed increased autonomy, including sexual autonomy.[25]

© Steve Adamson/Shutterstock.com

It was common for federal law enforcement on the frontier to enlist the help of local citizens to enforce the law.

During World War I, the FBI became responsible for spy operations and foreign intelligence-gathering efforts. A series of new laws were passed that expanded the list of federal crimes that the FBI could investigate. New laws included the 1917 Espionage Act, which prohibited interference with military recruitment, refusal to perform military duty, or disclosure of information related to national defense, and the 1918 Sedition Act, which prohibited public criticism of the American government. After the end of the war, the FBI returned its attention to non-war-related crimes.

In 1924, the Justice Department appointed J. Edgar Hoover as the director of the FBI. Hoover made several changes to FBI personnel processes and to the agency's responsibilities, including requiring all new agents to pass a background screening and physical agility tests, and to have prior training in the law or in accounting. He also established formal training programs for new agents in modern investigative techniques and changed promotion policies so that agents would be promoted based on regular performance evaluations rather than political patronage or seniority.[26]

By 1935, the training programs available to FBI agents were being offered to local and state police forces. Very few local policing agencies offered formal training to their officers at this time. In addition to developing a national training center, the FBI created an Identification Division and Technical Laboratory. The Identification Division became the national collection center for fingerprint cards. Soon, law enforcement agencies from around the country were submitting fingerprint cards to the FBI. The Technical Laboratory was equipped with specialized microscopes as well as extensive data on guns, watermarks, typefaces, and automobile tire designs. These resources were used for forensic analysis in federal investigations and, in some cases, state and local investigations. In the 1930s, the FBI took over responsibility from the International Association of Chiefs of Police for collecting crime statistics from law enforcement agencies across the nation. This program, the Uniform Crime Reports, continues today.[27] Finally, in 1932, the FBI released the first issue of its *Law Enforcement Bulletin*, which included a list of most wanted fugitives and is still published today.

*Law Enforcement Bulletin* A publication of the Federal Bureau of Investigation that includes articles on law enforcement issues as well as information on wanted federal suspects.

The types of law enforcement activities in which the FBI engaged continued to expand throughout the first half of the 20th century as new federal laws were passed that expanded the FBI's jurisdiction. Such laws focused on enforcing the nationwide prohibition of alcoholic beverages, protecting banks from the growing number of robbers, and preventing the transportation of stolen goods and the flight of felons over state borders.

Infamous bank robber John Dillinger evaded the FBI for years.

## Policing from the 20th Century to Today

In the early 1900s, policing agencies across the country suffered from a number of common problems.[28] Police were closely tied to political authorities. Close ties to politicians meant weak boundaries between local politics and policing functions. Policing agencies were often subject to the political whims of local leaders rather than serving the larger needs of their communities. In many places, policing appointments were doled out based on political and ethnic alliances rather than the skill or character of the police officer. When local leadership changed after an election, new leaders would frequently disband the existing police force and replace the officers with individuals from a similar ethnic background or with the same political affiliation.

Local political leadership enjoyed significant power and frequently used this power in inappropriate or illegal ways. Police would assist government officials in rigging elections. They would be used by local politicians to enforce laws against political enemies or be instructed to ignore the criminal activities of political allies. Police officers also engaged in corruption on their own. For example, police officers would solicit payoffs for protecting gambling and prostitution houses. Close ties between police and corrupt political figures and the participation of police in their own illegal endeavors did little to promote trust in, or respect for, police officers.[29]

In addition to corruption, police were often incompetent and ill prepared for the duties of law enforcement.[30] This was due in part to serious problems with the police officer screening and selection processes and, once hired, with their training. Law enforcement agencies and police leadership rarely employed screening processes such as criminal background investigations or physical agility tests to identify strong candidates for police positions. Once hired, officers were given the basic tools for policing, such as a brief handbook and a nightstick, and then sent out into the streets. There was no instruction on criminal law, how to effectively manage physical altercations, or other skills that might be useful for a new officer to possess.

A related problem was that police officers were often responsible for miscellaneous duties that did not fall under the responsibility of other local government groups.[31] In fact, police in the early 1900s were responsible for a broad range of government functions, some of which had little to do with law enforcement, such as cleaning public streets and maintaining street lamps. Some police agencies, such as those in Boston, also had significant social service responsibilities, such as providing food and temporary lodging to homeless people within the city. Early police reformers believed that the primary function of a police officer should be to fight crime and that engagement in tangential or unrelated activities detracted from this function.

One of the most notable early police reformers was August Vollmer.[32] Vollmer began his career in law enforcement in 1905 when he was elected as the town marshal in Berkeley, California. He is best known for advocating the adoption of a "professional" model of policing. A professional police officer, according to Vollmer, was well educated, well trained, and adept at using science and modern technologies to solve crimes and to prevent new ones from occurring. Many of Vollmer's ideas about how the police should function are described in his influential 1936 book, *The Police and Modern Society.*

Vollmer had significant influence over the conclusions drawn about policing in the United States that were included in the **Wickersham Commission**'s reports on law enforcement. Vollmer wrote or directed many of the portions of the reports that focused on policing. The reports highlighted some of the concerns mentioned above, but also included recommendations about improving outdated or ineffective law enforcement technologies, creating a more racially and ethnically diverse police force, and reducing the high levels of abusive policing nationally.[33]

According to the commission's final report, it was a common practice throughout the country for police officers to inflict pain—both physical and mental—on suspects of crime in order to solicit information or confessions. The infliction of pain by police officers in order to solicit evidence about a crime was called the **third degree**. According to the report, the types of physical pain most commonly inflicted by police officers included beating with fists or objects (e.g., rubber hoses, leather straps, and sticks), sleep deprivation, withholding of food, and unsanitary detention facilities. The most common forms of mental suffering inflicted upon suspects by police officers included verbal threats and foul or violent language; illegal detention; preventing contact with family, friends, and legal counsel; and protracted questioning. The typical victim of the third degree was younger than 25, poor, and African-American.[34]

The commission made several recommendations to improve policing, including insulating police agencies from the corrupting influence of politics, improving training and pay of officers, improving policing equipment and recordkeeping, and expanding state-level law enforcement agencies. The Wickersham Commission's reports on policing, however, were overshadowed by the sections of the reports that focused on the enforcement of Prohibition. Prohibition became law in 1919 when the 18th Amendment to the U.S. Constitution banned the sale and manufacture of intoxicating beverages.[35]

Enforcing Prohibition was no easy task.[36] Bootlegging—the illegal manufacture and sale of alcohol—was a lucrative business, and criminal syndicates quickly organized to capitalize on the sale of a commodity that many Americans desired to consume. Federal law enforcement agencies like the Customs Bureau, the U.S. Coast Guard, and the Federal Bureau of Investigation were largely unsuccessful in curbing the smuggling of alcohol (called rum-running) and the growth of illegal bars (called speakeasies) and in keeping up with the creative ways the public came up with to consume alcohol. Enforcement of Prohibition by local police was spotty at best and, in some cases, exacerbated problems of corruption among police officers, as it introduced a new enterprise from which police could take bribes in exchange for protection against enforcement. In addition, the lack of formal regulation over alcohol production often resulted in beverages of low quality or potentially dangerous potency.

The public was becoming increasingly frustrated with criminal justice interventions into their personal lives and with the growth in organized crime that resulted from Prohibition laws. The lack of public support for Prohibition did little to bolster confidence in and public support of law enforcement. In 1933, lawmakers succumbed to public pressure, and Prohibition was repealed by the 21st Amendment.

The Wickersham Commission's reports were the most comprehensive study of the American criminal justice system to date. They were complete with a broad range of recommendations aimed at improving the approach to criminal justice in the U.S., including its methods of policing. Unfortunately, the reports were issued at an inopportune time—the United States had just entered a period of substantial social and economic turmoil, known as the Great Depression. In the midst of a significant national depression, there was little motivation for a sustained focus on the improvement of the criminal justice system. It was not until the 1960s that the criminal justice system again received significant public and political attention.

In the 1960s, the United States was undergoing dramatic social change and experiencing significant episodes of unrest. Both population and crime rates were increasing, as was public fear of crime and disorder.[37] Public fears were exacerbated by a number of assassinations of prominent political figures in the 1960s, including President John F. Kennedy in 1963 and Reverend Martin Luther King, Jr. and New York Senator Robert F. Kennedy in 1968, and by significant media attention to serial killers and mass murderers, including the Boston Strangler, the Zodiac Killer, Charles Manson, and Charles Whitman.

In addition, large-scale urban unrest occurred in a number of cities across the country.[38] According to President Lyndon Johnson's Commission on Law Enforcement and the Administration of Justice, residents in ghetto communities were frustrated by unemployment, discrimination, substandard housing,

*© Underwood Archives/ Contributor/Getty Images*

National Guard troops throw tear gas into the rioters at Kent State protesting the American invasion of Cambodia.

and underfunded schools. These deep-seated frustrations over broader social inequalities were inflamed by poor relationships between the police and members of the community.[39]

Unrest was not restricted to poor, urban areas, however. College and university students across the country participated in sit-ins, protests, and revolutionary acts to express frustrations with discrimination, inequality, and the Vietnam War. One of the most famous episodes of student unrest occurred at Kent State in Ohio on May 4, 1970. During the protest, members of the National Guard fired 61 shots into the crowd, killing four students and wounding nine. The events at Kent State led to protests at more than 700 other colleges across the nation.[40]

As a result of numerous urban riots and incidents like the Kent State shootings, police agencies began to experience significant pressure to change the ways they addressed large-scale protests. Two strategies adopted by policing agencies were improving relationships between the community and the police and adopting crowd control technologies, such as riot gear. These strategies can be seen in contemporary practices such as community policing and SWAT teams.

### Critical Thinking

Military groups such as local militias and the National Guard have been used relatively frequently in American history to deal with large-scale protests. What are the advantages and disadvantages of using the military to quell domestic disturbances?

Wide-scale unrest and increasing crime rates and fear of crime brought renewed attention to policing in the 1960s. One issue that became the focal point of concern for reformers was police/community relations. In "The Challenges of Crime in a Free Society," a report published by a commission organized by President Johnson, the authors recommended improving police/community relations by increasing community participation in police decision-making, creating policing units specifically devoted to community relations, increasing recruitment of officers from diverse backgrounds and from the college-educated, establishing procedures for handling citizen complaints and an internal investigative unit to investigate problematic officers, and establishing policies that limited the use of a firearm to life-or-death situations.[42] Many of these recommendations were reiterated in the 1980s, when policing agencies began to adopt community policing models.

### Exhibit: National Advisory Commission on Civil Disorders 1967 (The Kerner Report)

The Kerner Commission was assembled to determine the causes of the riots that spread across the U.S. in the 1960s. In the following excerpts from the summary of the commission's report, the authors highlight the roles of social inequality and poor police/community relations in creating conditions conducive to rioting:

"We have visited the riot cities; we have heard many witnesses; we have sought the counsel of experts across the country. This is our basic conclusion: Our nation is moving toward two societies, one black, one white—separate and unequal . . . Discrimination and segregation have long permeated much of American life; they now threaten the future of every American . . . Segregation and poverty have created in the racial ghetto a destructive environment totally unknown to most white Americans . . . 'Prior' incidents, which increased tensions and ultimately led to violence, were police actions in almost half the cases; police actions were 'final' incidents before the outbreak of violence in 12 of the 24 surveyed disorders . . . What the rioters appeared to be seeking was fuller participation in the social order and the material benefits enjoyed by the majority of American citizens. Rather than rejecting the American system, they were anxious to obtain a place for themselves in it . . .

Wide-scale unrest, such as the Watts, Los Angeles riot in 1965, brought renewed attention to policing.

The police are not merely a 'spark' factor. To some Negroes police have come to symbolize white power, white racism and white repression. And the fact is that many police do reflect and express these white attitudes. The atmosphere of hostility and cynicism is reinforced by a widespread belief among Negroes in the existence of police brutality and in a 'double standard' of justice and protection—one for Negroes and one for whites."[41]

### Exhibit: Excerpt from "The Challenge of Crime in a Free Society" by the 1967 Commission on Law Enforcement and the Administration of Justice

In the following excerpt, the link between social unrest and poor police/community relations is reiterated:

"Since this is a time of increasing crime, increasing social unrest and increasing public sensitivity to both, it is a time when police work is peculiarly important, complicated, conspicuous, and delicate . . . It is hard to overstate the intimacy of the contact between the police and the community . . . Since police action is so often so personal, it is inevitable that the public is of two minds about the police: Most men both welcome official protection and resent official interference . . . Yet policemen, who as a rule have been well trained to perform . . . have received little guidance from legislatures, city administrations, or their own superiors, in handling these intricate, intimate human situations . . . The peacekeeping and service activities, which consume the majority of police time, receive too little consideration."

"Finally, more than public attitudes toward the police and, by extension, toward the law, are influenced by the way any given policeman performs his duties . . . Most of the recent big-city riots were touched off by commonplace street encounters between policemen and citizens . . . In short, the way any policeman exercises the personal discretion that is an inescapable part of his job can, and occasionally does, have an immediate bearing on the peace and safety of an entire community, or a long-range bearing on the work of all policemen everywhere."[43]

The findings from "The Challenges of Crime" report provided a foundation for the Omnibus Crime Control and Safe Streets Act of 1968. This act was the first comprehensive crime legislation to be introduced by the federal government. It designated federal funds to support local law enforcement agencies to engage in research and evaluation, as well as monies to improve cross-jurisdictional cooperation and support. It also created the **Law Enforcement Assistance Administration (LEAA)** within the Department of Justice as the body responsible for implementing its provisions and for improving policing across the country. The LEAA was abolished in 1982, but while it was in existence it provided millions of dollars in funds and program support to law enforcement agencies across the country.

Concerns over police corruption continued through the 1960s, and several commissions and workgroups conducted investigations of police corruption. The Knapp Commission, which was responsible for investigating corruption within the New York City Police Department, described two types of corrupt police officers: "grass eaters" and "meat eaters."[45] **Grass eaters** were those police officers who engaged in relatively passive forms of inappropriate behavior, such as accepting free goods or services from citizens and local businesses—for example, accepting free coffee from a local diner. **Meat eaters** were characterized as more aggressive in their illegal behavior: for example, a meat eater might solicit money from an offender in exchange for ignoring the individual's criminal activities.

**Law Enforcement Assistance Administration** A body created by the 1968 Omnibus Crime Control and Safe Streets Act to serve as a federal resource for local law enforcement agencies.

**Grass eaters** Those police officers who engage in relatively passive forms of inappropriate behavior by accepting small favors or money for looking the other way when illegal activities are taking place.

**Meat eaters** Police officers who are more aggressive in their illegal behavior and actively search for ways to make money illegally while on duty.

---

**Exhibit: Excerpt from the Omnibus Crime Control and Safe Streets Act of 1968**

This act was designed to improve a number of components of the American criminal justice system. The following excerpt focuses on provisions related to policing:

"Congress finds that the high incidence of crime in the United States threatens the peace, security, and general welfare of the Nation and its citizens. To prevent crime and to insure the greater safety of the people, law enforcement efforts must be better coordinated, intensified, and made more effective at all levels of government.

Congress finds further that crime is essentially a local problem that must be dealt with by State and local governments if it is to be controlled effectively.

It is therefore the declared policy of the Congress to assist State and local governments in strengthening and improving law enforcement at every level by national assistance. It is the purpose of this title to (1) encourage States and units of general local government to prepare and adopt comprehensive plans based upon their evaluation of State and local problems of law enforcement; (2) authorize grants to States and units of local government in order to improve and strengthen law enforcement; and (3) encourage research and development directed toward the improvement of law enforcement and the development of new methods for the prevention and reduction of crime and the detection and apprehension of criminals."[44]

Police themselves were also expressing frustration with their work. Officers in cities around the country participated in strikes and other forms of protest over low wages and poor working conditions. Practices they employed to express their discontent included the "blue flu," where officers would call in sick en masse, and ticket blizzards, where officers would overwhelm government offices and courthouses by writing a large number of non-revenue-generating tickets.

## Critical Thinking

Many states have policies that prohibit crucial personnel, such as police officers and firefighters, from forming unions or participating in strikes. What are the advantages and disadvantages of such policies? Do you agree with the use of these policies? Why or why not?

## Ethics and Professionalism: Early Intervention Systems

Police corruption and abuse of power are serious concerns for many police administrators and local government officials. They can be expensive and result in decreased public confidence in the local police. Often police administrators must develop policies that clearly distinguish between police officer behaviors that are acceptable and those that are not. In addition, they must outline how the department will respond when an officer behaves in an inappropriate or illegal manner.

The newest trend in dealing with problematic officers is the use of **early warning systems (EWS)**. Early warning systems are implemented as a means to identify potentially problematic officers before their behavior becomes very serious. Not all jurisdictions use EWS, and the types of information collected by those agencies that do use EWS vary significantly. Some common types of data monitored by EWS include number and frequency of citizen complaints (including lawsuits), resisting-arrest incidents, use of force incidents, firearm-discharge reports, and pursuits and vehicular accidents. In addition, responses to officers who are identified as problematic by EWS vary—some jurisdictions emphasize punishment, while others emphasize more supportive or corrective types of interventions (e.g., counseling or additional training). Some agencies may utilize both punitive and corrective responses.

**Early Warning Systems**
A means used by police leadership to identify a potentially problematic officer before his or her behavior becomes very serious; sometimes called Early Intervention Systems.

**Critical Thinking**

Imagine that you are the chief of your local police department. What kinds of information do you think should be collected on your department's officers? What responses would you recommend for officers who are identified as potential problems? Would you implement corrective or punitive responses?

## Changes to Policing

A number of court decisions and professional reports in the latter half of the 20th century attempted to change policing in significant ways. For much of the history of policing, the U.S. Supreme Court maintained a hands-off policy, intervening infrequently in issues involving police practices.[46] This changed in the mid-1900s under the tenure of Chief Justice Earl Warren. The Warren Court decisions fundamentally changed policing practices, such as procedures for search and seizure, suspect access to legal counsel, and officers' responsibilities to inform suspects of their rights.

In the case of *Mapp v. Ohio* (1961), the Supreme Court ruled that evidence seized illegally could not be used in a criminal trial. The case began in 1957, when law enforcement officers believed that Cleveland resident Dollree Mapp was hiding a suspect in a bombing incident in her home. When officers first contacted her at her residence, she refused to let them enter without a search warrant. A few hours later, the officers returned, claiming to have obtained a search warrant, and broke down Mapp's door. The officers refused to let Mapp see the document, and at one point she grabbed the sheet from the officer and put it in her dress. The officer wrestled with Mapp to reclaim the piece of paper. During the search of Mapp's home, they uncovered pornographic material. Mapp claimed the materials belonged to a boarder who had since moved. Mapp was charged with possession of obscene material and found guilty at trial. No evidence of a warrant was presented at her trial. The Supreme Court asserted that the pornographic material should have been excluded as evidence, as it was obtained from an illegal search.[47]

In *Escobedo v. Illinois* (1964), the Supreme Court ruled that officers must allow suspects accused of crime the opportunity to consult with an attorney and inform them of their right to remain silent. In this case, 22-year-old Danny Escobedo was questioned regarding his involvement in the fatal shooting of his brother-in-law. Though Escobedo was not formally arrested, he was not allowed to leave police custody. In addition, though he asked repeatedly to speak with his lawyer, officers refused to let Escobedo access counsel. Officers involved in the questioning informed Escobedo that he would be able to leave if he confessed to the murder. Escobedo confessed and was convicted of murder, but the case was later reversed in the Supreme Court. The Supreme Court asserted that, once questioning shifted from being investigatory to accusatory, the suspect had the right to consult with an attorney.[48]

**Miranda rights** The obligation of police officers to inform suspects of their right to remain silent and their right to an attorney.

In 1966, the Supreme Court made its famous ruling on **Miranda rights** in *Miranda v. Arizona*. In this case, Supreme Court justices heard arguments about four cases in which law enforcement officers in California, New York, and Arizona questioned suspects without informing them of their right to counsel. Ernesto Miranda, after whom the famous Supreme Court ruling was named, was a suspect in an Arizona kidnapping and sexual assault. In March 1963, Miranda was arrested by Phoenix police and questioned about the crimes. After a two-hour interrogation, Miranda confessed to the crimes and signed a written confession. The confession included statements from Miranda that he had full knowledge of his legal rights, that he understood that statements he made during the interrogation could be used against him, and that he knowingly waived his rights. Miranda was convicted of kidnapping and rape and sentenced to 20 years in prison. The Supreme Court ruled that the police did not properly inform Miranda of his constitutional rights. As a result of this case, officers are now required to inform suspects of their right to remain silent and that, if they do choose to speak, the information could be used against them. They must also inform them that they have the right to an attorney.[49]

There were two influential advisory boards assembled in the 1970s aimed at reforming policing in the United States. The first, a federal commission

---

FIGURE 3.1 THE USE OF FORCE CONTINUUM USED BY U.S. CUSTOMS AND BORDER PATROL. SIMILAR CONTINUUMS HAVE BEEN ADOPTED BY POLICING AGENCIES NATIONWIDE.

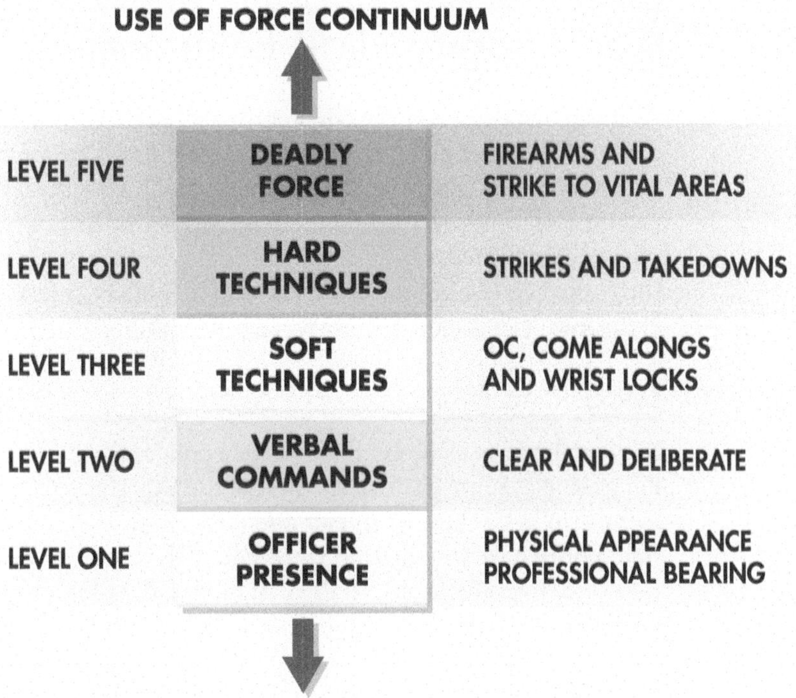

**USE OF FORCE CONTINUUM**

| | | |
|---|---|---|
| LEVEL FIVE | DEADLY FORCE | FIREARMS AND STRIKE TO VITAL AREAS |
| LEVEL FOUR | HARD TECHNIQUES | STRIKES AND TAKEDOWNS |
| LEVEL THREE | SOFT TECHNIQUES | OC, COME ALONGS AND WRIST LOCKS |
| LEVEL TWO | VERBAL COMMANDS | CLEAR AND DELIBERATE |
| LEVEL ONE | OFFICER PRESENCE | PHYSICAL APPEARANCE PROFESSIONAL BEARING |

organized under the newly created LEAA called the National Advisory Commission on Criminal Justice Standards and Goals, made recommendations on a broad array of criminal justice issues, including policing. The second advisory board was assembled by the American Bar Association. Its recommendations focused more narrowly on establishing a set of organizational and behavioral standards for the police. Similar to earlier commissions already discussed, these groups advocated for, among other things, clear policies on the use of force, insulation of police leadership from inappropriate political pressures, a sustained focus on improving police/community relationships, increased training for officers, and increased diversity of police officers. Though these groups' recommendations were not binding, they have influenced police organization and practices. For example, many of the recommendations have been incorporated into the Commission on Accreditation for Law Enforcement's (CALEA) accreditation process.[50] Though accreditation through CALEA is voluntary, nearly every U.S. state has at least two law enforcement agencies that have successfully sought accreditation through CALEA.[51]

---

**Critical Thinking**

Should accreditation by a national body be required of all law enforcement agencies? What are the advantages and disadvantages of requiring accreditation?

---

# Structure and Organization of Contemporary Law Enforcement

As discussed earlier in the chapter, British policing practices had a significant influence on policing in the United States. One important difference between the two countries' approaches to policing is the level of government responsible for its oversight and management. In Britain, policing is largely managed at the federal level by Parliament or other national authorities; in the United States, however, the majority of policing agencies are controlled at the local (e.g., city and county) or state level.

## Local and State-Level Policing

Many states have a combination of state police forces and local police forces. For example, Pennsylvania, the first of the U.S. states to create a state police force, also has a number of city and county law enforcement agencies. The state police have jurisdiction throughout the commonwealth—this means they can investigate criminal activities and enforce traffic laws in any region of the state. Other states, such as California, however, have created state police forces that focus more narrowly on traffic enforcement, leaving criminal investigations to be handled by local and regional law enforcement agencies.[52]

Most of the law enforcement officers in the country work for a local police department. Based on the most recent data from the Bureau of Justice Statistics, as of January 1, 2013, more than 12,000 local police departments in the United States employed an estimated 605,000 persons on a full-time basis. This total included about 477,000 sworn officers (those with general arrest powers) and about 128,000 nonsworn employees. Since 1987, the number of full-time local police employees has increased by about 156,000 (up 35%). The increase includes about 122,000 (up 34%) more local police officers. The New York City Police Department (NYPD) remained the largest local police department in 2013, with 34,454 full-time officers. The NYPD was 1 of 43 local police departments that employed 1,000 or more full-time officers.[53]

The high level of local control in American law enforcement presents both challenges and advantages. Perhaps the most pressing challenges posed by local control are that it makes it difficult to draw conclusions about the state of policing at the state or national level and it limits possibilities for the implementation of needed or desirable systemic changes to policing. Though all law enforcement agencies are accountable to the standards set by the U.S. Constitution, there is significant variance in the policies and practices such agencies choose to adopt. For example, local agencies are free to determine the educational requirements for new recruits, their departmental data collection procedures, their use-of-force policies, etc. These variations may have significant effects on the preparedness of officers, the comprehensiveness (and usefulness) of departmental assessments, and the number and nature of injuries that result from public-police encounters.

The challenges associated with local control may be best illustrated through an example—racial profiling. Racial profiling is a contemporary concern that many states and jurisdictions are attempting to address.[55] Profiling more generally is a relatively common policing strategy. Law enforcement investigators often create "profiles" of individuals who frequently engage in a particular type of criminal activity to aid in their detection. Profiles are developed based on observable characteristics and behaviors. **Racial profiling**, however, entails using race or ethnicity as the primary or only indicator that an individual may be participating in criminal activity. Most of the recent attention to racial profiling has been related to its use in the decision to make a traffic stop.[56]

**Racial profiling** The use of race or ethnicity as the primary or the only indicator that an individual may be participating in criminal activity.

While studying the problem of racial profiling in traffic stops may seem straightforward, there are a number of challenges associated with such studies. One challenge is that procedures for conducting traffic stops may vary from place to place: for example, speeding laws may be consistently enforced in one jurisdiction but under-enforced in another. Another challenge is that agency policies for collecting data about such stops may vary. Some jurisdictions may require officers to collect data on all stops, regardless of outcome, while others agencies may have different policies with regard to the appropriateness of considering the race or ethnicity of a motorist when making traffic stop decisions. Some agencies may have strict policies against the use of race and ethnicity as factors, while others may allow it if other factors are also taken into consideration. These different policies make it difficult to discern broad patterns in racial profiling practices in the United States. They also make it difficult to fashion wide-scale solutions to the problem.

In terms of advantages, local control may allow police departments more flexibility to meet local norms and needs. Local law enforcement agencies are able to determine how to focus their resources based on the needs that are present in their community and to establish forms of policing that work well with the types of populations, issues, and concerns police are most likely to encounter. For example, it may be easier for local law enforcement agencies to determine enforcement priorities based on local concerns and crime patterns, rather than based on goals determined at the state or national level. They also may be able to craft recruitment and promotion policies based on local demographics, applicant pools, and skill sets of their current officers.

**Community policing**
A method of policing that emphasizes community participation in police decision-making and police officer participation in community activities.

The flexibility associated with local control may be beneficial when it comes to implementing **community policing**, a method of policing that has its roots in many of the reform efforts of the 1960s and 70s and that has become increasingly popular since the 1990s.[57] Community policing differs from traditional policing in that it is a proactive, rather than a reactive, approach to law enforcement and problem solving. In a traditional, or reactive, policing model, the police engage with the public in response, or in reaction, to a crime or to a call for assistance. In contrast, community policing requires that police officers be proactive in addressing problems in the community that may lead to crime. Though there is some debate over what exactly constitutes community policing, it is typically described as the engagement of the community in policing efforts as well as the participation of police officers in community affairs. For example, if a particular park is known to be a consistent source of problems in the community, police officers may work with local residents to determine strategies to reduce problems in the area. One solution might be for community members, the police, and the local government to improve lighting and landscaping in the park to make the area more visibly accessible. Police might also work with local community members to establish a citizens' patrol in the area. Members of the citizens' patrols may observe, record, and report suspicious activities to local police for rapid response.

Community policing efforts often include patrols on foot or on bicycles. The belief is that getting officers out of patrol cars and onto the streets will increase officer interaction with community members.

In addition to increased involvement of police with the public, community policing also entails a conception of police officers as problem-solvers rather than as strict enforcers of the law. Though police do deal with violent and serious crimes, more often they are called upon to address minor crimes and interpersonal conflicts.[58] In these cases, the best police response may be something other than issuing a ticket or making an arrest. The problematic individual may be better served by a referral to mental health or drug rehabilitation services or by immediate mediation of the issue.

Community policing has been advanced by its proponents as an effective solution to many of the problems that have plagued policing since its inception. Advocates argue that police involvement in addressing issues of social disorder (rather than a strict focus on crime) will allow the police to better address the underlying causes of crime and, therefore, prevent future crimes from happening. Also, community policing is seen as a means to promote positive public-police relations. If people engage with the police outside of a strict enforcement setting, the community will begin to have more favorable views of police officers.

Despite considerable debate over whether community policing has been effective in reducing crime and fostering positive relationships, it is a popular method of policing. The federal government has devoted significant resources to its implementation in local jurisdictions. In 1994, with the passage of the Violent Crime Control and Law Enforcement Act, $8.8 billion was allotted to hire 100,000 community policing officers throughout the nation.[59] The U.S. Department of Justice continues to fund and sponsor community policing efforts through the Office of Community Oriented Policing Services (COPS).[60] Current data suggest that community policing is unlikely to disappear anytime soon. According to

Military-style police units are becoming increasingly common across the United States.

Bureau of Justice, community policing continued to be an important component of basic law enforcement training in 2013. Nearly all (97%) of academies (which trained 98% of recruits) provided training in this area, up from the 92% observed in 2006. In 2013, recruits were required to complete an average of more than 40 hours of training in community policing. A majority received training on how to identify community problems (77%), the history of community-oriented policing (75%), interacting with youth (62%), using problem-solving models (61%), environmental causes of crime (57%), and prioritizing crime and disorder problems (51%).[61]

In light of the increased focus on community policing, it is surprising that paramilitary or military-style policing is also growing in popularity. In contrast to a community-relations approach, which emphasizes the long-term benefits of positive relationships between the public and law enforcement, military-style police operations emphasize the immediate goal of controlling or suppressing unrest through the use of force. Rather than focusing on increased accountability and engagement with the community, it emphasizes the utilization of sophisticated technologies and strategies similar to those used by the military to root out criminal suspects. The targets of military-style operations are framed as internal security threats or enemy combatants, rather than as problematic or disruptive community members.[62]

The most common manifestation of military-style policing is the special response team, often referred to as **SWAT** (Special Weapons and Tactics Team). The first SWAT team was organized in 1966 by Daryl Gates, who would later become chief of the Los Angeles Police Department. Members of the elite team were selected by Gates and trained in various military tactics by former and current military personnel. In 1969, the newly organized SWAT team engaged in its first substantial conflict with members of the Black Panther Party at their Los Angeles headquarters. Thousands of rounds of ammunition were exchanged in the four-hour conflict, and both sides incurred four wounded each. The incident received substantial news coverage, and led to the creation of similar tactical units across the nation. By 1997, three-fourths of the nation's police departments had military-style units.[63]

Though SWAT teams were initially designed to deal with snipers, hostage situations, or other dangerous confrontations between police and the public, they are now frequently used for more day-to-day policing activities, including drug raids, serving warrants, and patrol.[64] There are a number of criticisms of the increased reliance on paramilitary policing, including the increased potential for injury and loss of life. In addition, the confrontational and aggressive nature of SWAT interactions may be counterproductive to fostering positive police-community relations. Ironically, such an approach to policing may counteract gains being made by community policing efforts.

**Critical Thinking**

Describe how the goals and means of achieving these goals differ between the community policing model and paramilitary policing units.

## Federal Law Enforcement

There are far fewer law enforcement officers employed by the federal government than by local jurisdictions. According to Bureau of Justice Statistics data:

- In September 2008, federal agencies employed approximately 120,000 full-time law enforcement officers who were authorized to make arrests and carry firearms in the United States.

- The four largest agencies, two in the Department of Homeland Security (DHS) and two in the Department of Justice (DOJ), employed 4 in 5 federal officers.

- Women accounted for 15.5% of federal officers with arrest and firearm authority in 2008. This was a slightly lower percentage than in 2004 (16.1%), but higher than in 1996 (14.0%).[65]

Figure 3.2 lists the largest federal law enforcement agencies; border protection and corrections employ the most law enforcement personnel. The list

**FIGURE 3.2** FEDERAL AGENCIES EMPLOYING 250 OR MORE FULL-TIME PERSONNEL WITH ARREST AND FIREARM AUTHORITY, SEPTEMBER 2008

| Agency | Number of full-time officers | Percent change 2004–2008 |
|---|---|---|
| U.S. Customs and Border Protection | 36,863 | 33.1% |
| Federal Bureau of Prisons | 16,835 | 10.7 |
| Federal Bureau of Investigation | 12,760 | 4.2 |
| U.S. Immigration and Customs Enforcement | 12,446 | 19.7 |
| U.S. Secret Service | 5,213 | 9.3 |
| Administrative Office of the U.S. Courts | 4,696 | 13.8 |
| Drug Enforcement Administration | 4,308 | -2.1 |
| U.S. Marshals Service | 3,313 | 2.5 |
| Veterans Health Administration | 3,128 | 29.1 |
| Internal Revenue Service, Criminal Investigation | 2,636 | -5.1 |
| Bureau of Akohol, Tobacco, Firearms and Explosives | 2,541 | 7.1 |
| U.S. Postal Inspection Service | 2,288 | -23.1 |
| U.S. Capitol Police | 1,637 | 6.6 |
| National Park Service – Rangers | 1,404 | -8.6 |
| Bureau of Diplomatic Security | 1,049 | 27.2 |
| Pentagon Force Protection Agency | 725 | 50.4 |
| U.S. Forest Service | 644 | 7.3 |
| U.S. Fish and Wildlife Service | 598 | -15.5 |
| National Park Service – U.S. Park Police | 547 | -10.6 |
| National Nuclear Security Administration | 363 | 24.3 |
| U.S. Mint Police | 316 | -16.0 |
| Amtrak Police | 305 | -3.8 |
| Bureau of India Affairs | 277 | -13.4 |
| Bureau of Land Management | 255 | 2.4 |

Note: Excludes employees based in U.S. territories or foreign countries and offices of inspectors general.
* Limited to federal probation officers employed in federal judicial districts that allow officers to carry firearms.

Source: Bureau of Justice Statistics, Census of Federal Law Enforcement Officers, 2004 and 2008.

also serves as a good illustration of the diversity of law enforcement positions available in the federal government.

Though policing remains a largely local and state responsibility, federal law enforcement agencies are diverse and growing. In addition to the agencies discussed earlier in the chapter (FBI, U.S. Marshals), the federal government oversees a number of other law enforcement agencies, including the

U.S. Bureau of Alcohol, Tobacco, Firearms, and Explosives, the U.S. Drug Enforcement Administration (DEA), and the Department of Homeland Security. These organizations enforce a range of federal laws pertaining to legal and illegal drugs, weapons, and interstate crime.

The Department of Homeland Security is the most recent creation of the national government. On September 11, 2001, four commercial airline jets were hijacked by 19 members of the terrorist group Al-Qaeda. Two of the jets were crashed into the World Trade Center in New York City, and one was crashed into the Pentagon. The final jet was crashed into a field in Shanksville, Pennsylvania, after its crew and passengers diverted the plane from its intended target in Washington, D.C. Three thousand people were killed as a result of the hijackings. Eleven days later, President George W. Bush announced intentions to create an Office of Homeland Security, whose responsibility would be to coordinate anti-terrorism efforts. By November 2002, legislation to establish a permanent Department of Homeland Security was passed.

The creation of the Department of Homeland Security (DHS) was the most massive reorganization of federal agencies since the creation of the U.S. Department of Defense during World War II. The Homeland Security Act of 2002 brought 22 different agencies under the umbrella of the DHS, including, among others, the U.S. Coast Guard, U.S. Secret Service, and

**FIGURE 3.3**   DEPARTMENT OF HOMELAND SECURITY ORGANIZATIONAL CHART

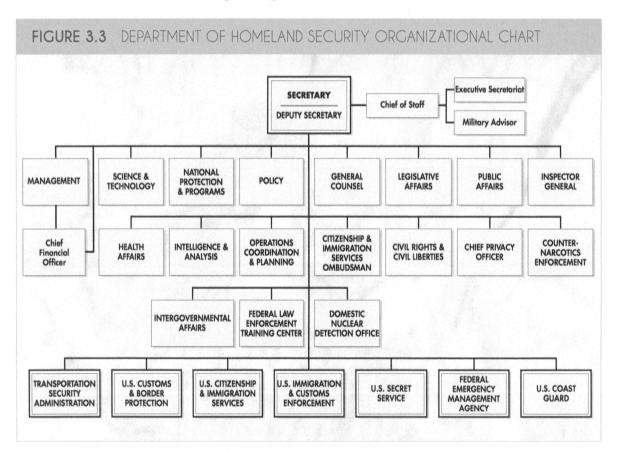

U.S. Immigration and Customs Enforcement (ICE). The ICE is the principal investigative arm of the DHS. Its responsibilities include preventing terrorist attacks, enforcing immigration laws, and securing borders against illegal trade.

After the attacks of 9/11, terrorism became a major focus of federal law enforcement, and significant funding has been directed to terrorism detection and prevention. The federal focus on terrorism prevention and detection has trickled down to local jurisdictions, as evidenced by the increase in the number of terrorism-related trainings offered by local and state training academies. In 2006, 90% of academies provided at least some basic training on issues surrounding terrorism. Examples of training topics include understanding the nature of terrorism, the role of anti-terrorism task forces, and responding to the use of weapons of mass destruction.[66]

---

**Exhibit: Homeland Security Act of 2002**

"The primary mission of the Department is to—

(A) prevent terrorist attacks within the United States;

(B) reduce the vulnerability of the United States to terrorism;

(C) minimize the damage, and assist in the recovery, from terrorist attacks that do occur within the United States;

(D) carry out all functions of entities transferred to the Department, including by acting as a focal point regarding natural and manmade crises and emergency planning;

(E) ensure that the functions of the agencies and subdivisions within the Department that are not related directly to securing the homeland are not diminished or neglected except by a specific explicit Act of Congress;

(F) ensure that the overall economic security of the United States is not diminished by efforts, activities, and programs aimed at securing the homeland; and

(G) monitor connections between illegal drug trafficking and terrorism, coordinate efforts to sever such connections, and otherwise contribute to efforts to interdict illegal drug trafficking."[67]

---

# Becoming a Law Enforcement Officer

The requirements to be a police officer vary from jurisdiction to jurisdiction. Some common requirements of applicants for law enforcement positions include passing written and oral examinations; completion of a minimum level of education; passing background investigations, often including a psychological assessment; and successfully completing physical exams. Some policing agencies also review the credit histories and social networking web pages of applicants. Though the minimum education requirement for most local police departments continues to be a high school diploma, this is changing. Increasingly, police departments are requiring new recruits to have some college credits completed. During 2007, about 30% of local police officers worked for departments where some college education was required.[68]

After passing each of the applicant screening procedures for the appropriate jurisdiction, applicants are typically required to participate in a police training academy. Again, the training requirements for new recruits vary across law enforcement agencies. New recruits may be required to complete trainings in topics such as constitutional or criminal law, self-defense, and diversity/cultural awareness. In 2007, the average local police agency recruit completed 1,370 hours in required training.[70] The number of training hours required for new recruits continues to increase. As mentioned above, the newest addition to mandatory police training programs is terrorism-related trainings. Figure 3.4 describes some of the common types of trainings offered during police academies and the number of hours devoted to the topic.

---

**Exhibit: Requirements for New Recruits in Two Local Police Departments: Reno, Nevada and New York City Police Department[69]**

Reno, Nevada

Based on Nevada Administrative Code Section 289.110.

No person may be appointed to perform the duties of a peace officer unless he/she:

- Has undergone a complete and documented investigation of his/her background which verifies that he/she has good moral character and meets the minimum standards established by the Commission on Peace Officers' Standards and Training (POST);

- Is a citizen of the United States;

- Is at least 21 years of age at the time of his/her appointment;

- Has successfully completed the 12th grade or has been certified by an appropriate authority as having an equivalent education; and

- Has undergone a medical examination performed by a licensed physician who confirms in writing that no physical condition exists that would adversely affect his/her performance of the duties of a peace officer. The employing agency shall inform the examining physician of the specific functions required by the position to be filled.

New York City Police Department

- In order to be considered in the hiring process, candidates must first pass the Police Officer Written Exam

- Have a valid New York driver's license

- Live in one of the city's five boroughs or Nassau, Suffolk, Rockland, Westchester, Putnam, or Orange counties on or before the day of hire.

- Candidates need to pass a drug and alcohol screening, character and background investigation and pay $75 for fingerprinting.

- Candidates must pass all medical, physical, written psychological and oral psychological examinations.

- Candidates can be disqualified if they have been convicted of felony, petit larceny or any offense that shows disrespect for the law or a tendency toward violence. Those who have been dishonorably discharged from the military or terminated from a job for poor behavior or not adjusting to discipline also may be disqualified.

- **Candidate Assessment Division:** Investigators will conduct a background on each candidate to determine the most qualified.

- All qualified candidates will be scheduled at the Candidate Assessment Center located at 235 East 20th Street, New York City, NY to take the following exams to complete the hiring process.

- **Pre-Hire Interview:** This includes a medical exam and an update on the character investigation.

- **Medical Exam:** At this stage, candidates need to document their 60 college credits and a minimum 2.0 GPA, or their two years of military service. The initial character assessment and fingerprinting also take place.

- **Written Psychological Exam:** Candidates must pass this test.

- **Job Standards Test:** Candidates must finish this continuous physical test in 4 minutes and 28 seconds to pass. The "JST" includes sprinting 50 yards and surmounting a barrier; climbing stairs; demonstrating the ability to physically restrain someone; running in pursuit; dragging a 175-pound mannequin 35 feet to simulate a rescue; and pulling the trigger of an unloaded firearm.

- **Oral Psychological Test:** Oral interview.

- **Character Investigation:** Candidates meet with an investigator to go over their application booklet. Supporting documents also may be required at this time.

## Diversity in Law Enforcement

Government commissions, like the Wickersham Commission and President Johnson's 1967 Crime Commission, have often reiterated the need for a police force that reflects the diversity of the community in which it works. Some policing agencies have implemented special programs to recruit candidates from groups that do not typically pursue law enforcement careers, including minorities, women, and homosexuals; however, in many jurisdictions, police officers continue to be predominantly white males.

The first recorded appointment of a female police officer was in 1893 by the Chicago Police Department. Marie Owens was the widow of a male police officer and was appointed to a patrol position upon his death. In 1910, the Los Angeles Police Department appointed its first female police officer, Alice Wells. By 1915, 25 cities had at least one female police officer.[71]

## FIGURE 3.4 MAJOR SUBJECT AREAS INCLUDED IN BASIC TRAINING PROGRAMS IN STATE AND LOCAL LAW ENFORCEMENT TRAINING ACADEMIES, 2013

| Training area | Percent of academies with training | Average number of hours of instruction required per recruit* |
|---|---|---|
| *Operations* | | |
| Report writing | 99% | 25 hrs. |
| Patrol procedures | 98 | 52 |
| Investigations | 98 | 42 |
| Traffic accident investigations | 98 | 23 |
| Emergency vehicle operations | 97 | 38 |
| Basic first aid/CPR | 97 | 24 |
| Computers/information systems | 61 | 9 |
| *Weapons/defensive tactics/use of force* | | |
| Defensive tactics | 99% | 60 hrs. |
| Firearms skills | 98 | 71 |
| Use of force | 98 | 21 |
| Nonlethal weapons | 88 | 16 |
| *Self-improvement* | | |
| Ethics and integrity | 98% | 8 hrs. |
| Health and fitness | 96 | 49 |
| Communications | 91 | 15 |
| Professionalism | 85 | 11 |
| Stress prevention/management | 81 | 6 |
| *Legal education* | | |
| Criminal/constitutional law | 98% | 53 hrs. |
| Traffic law | 97 | 23 |
| juvenile justice law/procedures | 97 | 10 |

*Excludes academies that did not provide this type of instruction.

Source: Bureau of Justice Statistics, Census of Law Enforcement Training Academies, 2013.

Women represented nearly 12% of about 700,000 police officers in the U.S., according to data submitted to the FBI in 2011. That number is up only slightly from 11.2% in 2001.

The FBI's annual report does not track gender breakdowns for police command positions, but the National Association of Women Law Enforcement Executives reported that at last count, there were just 219 women holding chiefs' jobs in the U.S., where there are now more than 14,000 police agencies.

Historically, female police officers' duties differed from those of their male counterparts. Often female police officers were responsible for issues related to children or enforcement of moral norms. For example, female police officers were responsible for runaway children, young girls who were perceived as behaving immorally, and the suppression of negative influences on children (e.g., dancehalls, liquor sales, etc.). In addition to receiving less desirable assignments, female police officers were paid significantly less than male police officers.[72]

Women continue to be underrepresented in law enforcement. However, they are better represented in federal law enforcement than in local law enforcement. As Figure 3.5 indicates, since 2002, women comprise around 15% of all federal law enforcement officers.

As Figure 3.6 demonstrates, women's representation in state and local police departments has shown steady improvement since the 1980s, but their representation in these local departments is lower than their representation in federal law enforcement agencies. In 2007, around 12% of local police officers were women. In the same year, around 6% of state police officers were female. Representation of women in sheriff's departments has been declining since 1997. In 2007, women comprised about 11% of local sheriff forces.

Representation of minorities in federal, state, and local law enforcement varies. As Figures 3.7 and 3.8 reflect, some federal agencies, such as U.S. Customs and Border Protection, have high rates of representation for minority officers. In 2004, U.S. Customs and Border Protection comprised nearly 47% minority officers, the majority of which were Hispanic or Latino. The federal agency with the second highest rate of employment for Hispanic or Latino officers is U.S. Immigration and Customs Enforcement. African-American officers are best represented in the U.S. Capitol Police, Veterans Health Administration, and Federal Bureau of Prisons. Representation of Native American officers typically is less than 1%, with the exception of the National Park Service, in which about 2% of park rangers are Native American. Asians and Pacific Islanders compose between 1% and 5% of most federal law enforcement agencies.

With regard to local police departments, larger departments—departments in areas with populations of 100,000 or more—tend to fare better in terms of employing officers from diverse racial and ethnic backgrounds.

FIGURE 3.5 PERCENTAGE OF WOMEN IN FEDERAL LAW ENFORCEMENT, 1987-2008

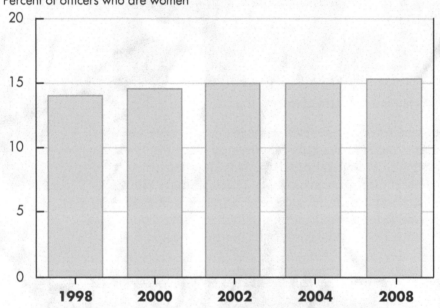

**Percent of federal law enforcement officers who are women, from 1998-2008***

Percent of officers who are women

Note: Data obtained from the BJS Census of Federal Law Enforcement Officers.
*Includes the 53 federal agencies that were consistently organized and consistently reported data on the sex of officers from 1998 to 2008.

**Percent of full-time sworn law enforcement officers who are women among state and local law enforcement agencies, 1987–2007**

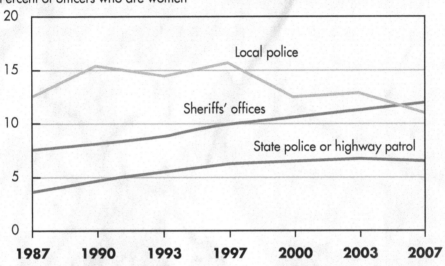

Percent of officers who are women

Note: Data on state police and highway patrol agencies were obtained from the Federal Bureau of Investigation's Uniform Crime Reports. Data on local police departments and sheriffs' offices were obtained from the BJS Law Enforcement Management and Administrative Statistics (LEMAS) series.

**Critical Thinking**

Why do you think women and minorities are less likely to pursue careers in law enforcement? What might be some of the barriers to their participation? Should law enforcement agencies implement programs to increase recruitment for underrepresented populations?

**FIGURE 3.7** FEMALE AND MINORITY FEDERAL OFFICERS IN AGENCIES EMPLOYING 500 OR MORE FULL-TIME OFFICERS, SEPTEMBER 2008

| Agency | Number of officers | Female | Total minority | Percent of full-time federal officers Racial/ethnic minority | | | | |
|---|---|---|---|---|---|---|---|---|
| | | | | American Indian/Alaska Nativesa | Black/African Americana | Asian/Pacific Islandera | Hispanic/Latino origin | Two or more racesa |
| U.S. Customs and Border Protection | 37,482 | 12.1% | 45.3% | 0.4% | 3.5% | 3.3% | 38.0% | -% |
| Federal Bureau of Prisons | 16,993 | 13.6 | 40.0% | 1.4 | 24.1 | 1.6 | 12.9 | 0.0 |
| Federal Bureau of Investigation | 12,925 | 18.8 | 18.1% | 0.4 | 0.4 | 3.9 | 8.1 | 0.2 |
| U.S. Immigration and Customs Enforcement | 12,679 | 15.7 | 37.1% | 0.7 | 8.3 | 3.8 | 24.3 | - |
| U.S. Secret Serviceb | 5,226 | 10.5 | 19.7% | 0.6 | 11.2 | 2.7 | 5.2 | - |
| Administrative Office of the U.S. Courts | 4,767 | 46.2 | 33.8% | 0.6 | 14.3 | 1.8 | 16.5 | 0.7 |
| Drug Enforcement Administration | 4,388 | 9.6 | 19.6% | 0.4 | 7.1 | 2.6 | 9.3 | 0.0 |
| U.S. Marshals Serviceb | 3,359 | 10.2 | 19.4% | 0.7 | 7.4 | 2.2 | 9.6 | 0.1 |
| Veterans Health Administration | 3,175 | 7.8 | 37.2% | 1.7 | 23.5 | 2.6 | 9.4 | 0.0 |
| Internal Revenue Service | 2,655 | 31.5 | 25.5% | 0.1 | 11.0 | 5.7 | 8.5 | 0.2 |

| Agency | | | | | | | | |
|---|---|---|---|---|---|---|---|---|
| Bureau of Alcohol, Tobacco, Firearms and Explosives | 2,562 | 13.0 | 18.9% | 1.1 | 8.5 | 2.1 | 5.8 | 1.6 |
| U.S. Postal Inspection Service | 2,324 | 22.2 | 36.5% | 0.3 | 20.4 | 5.1 | 10.8 | 0.0 |
| U.S. Capitol Police | 1,637 | 18.5 | 37.1% | 0.3 | 29.7 | 2.1 | 4.9 | 0.0 |
| National Park Service-Rangers | 1,416 | 18.6 | 12.7% | 3.0 | 2.1 | 2.2 | 4.8 | 0.6 |
| Bureau of Diplomatic Security | 1,049 | 10.8 | 19.2% | 0.7 | 8.1 | 4.0 | 6.4 | 0.0 |
| Pentagon Force Protection Agency | 725 | 12.4 | 51.2% | 0.8 | 43.0 | 1.5 | 4.3 | 1.5 |
| U.S. Forest Service | 648 | 15.9 | 17.3% | 4.8 | 4.2 | 1.5 | 6.8 | 0.0 |
| U.S. Fish and Wildlife Service | 603 | 8.8 | 15.8% | 3.6 | 1.8 | 2.3 | 7.1 | 0.8 |
| U.S. Park Police | 547 | 13.2 | 21.8% | 0.2 | 11.9 | 3.3 | 5.9 | 0.5 |

Note: Includes personnel with arrest and firearm authority in U.S. territories. Detail may not sum to total due to rounding. See table 5 for sex and race data for personnel in offices of inspectors general.
aExcludes persons of Hispanic/Latino origin.
bPercentages are from 2004 because agency did not provide data for 2008.
-Less than 0.05%

Source: Bureau of Justice Statistics, Census of Federal Law Enforcement Officers, 2008.

## FIGURE 3.8 RACE AND HISPANIC ORIGIN OF FULL-TIME SWORN PERSONNEL IN LOCAL POLICE DEPARTMENTS, BY SIZE OF POPULATION SERVED, 2013

| Population served | Total | White* | Black/ African American* | Hispanic/ Latino | Asian/ Native Hawaiian/ other Pacific Islander*c | American Indian/ Alaska Native* | Two or more races* |
|---|---|---|---|---|---|---|---|
| All sizes | 100% | 72.8% | 12.2% | 11.6% | 2.4% | 0.6% | 0.5% |
| 1,000,000 or more | 100% | 53.4 | 17.0 | 24.7 | 4.4 | 0.2 | 0.3 |
| 500,000-999,999 | 100% | 59.8 | 23.2 | 9.9 | 4.5 | 0.4 | 2.2 |
| 250,000-499,999 | 100% | 67.5 | 18.6 | 11.0 | 2.1 | 0.6 | 0.3 |
| 100,000-249,999 | 100% | 73.9 | 12.3 | 10.7 | 2.5 | 0.3 | 0.3 |
| 50,000-999,999 | 100% | 80.4 | 8.0 | 9.3 | 1.6 | 0.3 | 0.4 |
| 25,000-49,999 | 100% | 86.3 | 5.9 | 5.7 | 0.9 | 0.9 | 0.4 |
| 10,000-24,999 | 100% | 87.8 | 5.1 | 5.7 | 0.7 | 0.4 | 0.3 |
| 2,500-9,999 | 100% | 89.0 | 4.4 | 4.4 | 0.4 | 1.4 | 0.3 |
| 2,499 or fewer | 100% | 84.4 | 6.0 | 5.0 | 0.7 | 3.3 | 0.5 |

Note: Detail may not sum to total because of rounding. See appendix table 19 for standard errors.
‡Excludes persons of Hispanic or Latino origin.

Source: Bureau of Justice Statistics, Law Enforcement Management and Administrative Statistics (LEMAS) Survey, 2013.

## Career Connections: Police Dispatcher

There are a growing number of positions available for civilians in the law enforcement field, including crime analysts, information technology specialists, and researchers, among others. One crucial member of the law enforcement team is the police dispatcher. Dispatchers are often the first responders to citizens in need of police or medical assistance. They serve an essential communication role between the public and the local police. They are responsible for providing support for distressed callers, determining the nature and severity of the problem, and dispatching officers to the scene.

At a minimum, police dispatchers must be able to work well under pressure and possess strong communication and computer skills. Often dispatchers will be required to have some knowledge of first aid in the event that a caller needs immediate medical advice while waiting for emergency personnel. As with many other law enforcement professions, proficiency in more than one language is also desirable. Most dispatchers are required to have a high school education and receive the bulk of their position-specific training on the job.[73] The Bureau of Labor Statistics estimates that emergency call responder positions will increase by 18% by 2018. The mean annual wage for dispatchers is $36,900, and full-time dispatchers are often provided with health and retirement benefits.[74]

# Chapter Summary

- For much of its history, policing could best be characterized as disorganized, ineffective, and corrupt. Early police officers were poorly paid, ill prepared to address the complexities of crime and disorder, and disrespected by the larger community. Early policing efforts often involved local citizens in law enforcement. The United States did not move toward a model of permanent police forces until the mid-1800s.

- Beginning in the 1900s, policing underwent significant reforms. The objectives of many of these reforms were to transform police officers into unbiased professionals who are capable of upholding the law while enforcing it, and to create well equipped law enforcement agencies that used their resources effectively to reduce crime. Police reform efforts reached their peak in the 1960s and 70s.

- Policing is largely a local affair. Local control allows for greater flexibility to meet local needs, but also makes it difficult to implement systemic changes to policing practices and policies.

- Two contradictory trends are occurring in contemporary policing: community policing, which aims at increasing democratic participation in policing processes, and paramilitary policing, which emphasizes aggressive suppression of criminal activity. The effectiveness of these two trends in reducing crime has been heavily debated.

- The process of becoming a police officer varies from jurisdiction to jurisdiction, but often entails passing psychological and physical tests, possessing a clean employment and criminal history, and having a high school diploma or equivalent.

- Women and racial and ethnic minorities are underrepresented in both local and federal law enforcement positions. Women represented nearly 12% of about 700,000 police officers in the U.S., according to data submitted to the FBI in 2011. That number is up only slightly from 11.2% in 2001.

# Critical Thinking?

1. What role have private citizens played in law enforcement historically? What role do they play in the contemporary community policing model?

2. What role has race/ethnicity played in policing throughout its history?

3. Numerous commissions have recommended increasing the diversity of American police personnel. How might increasing the diversity of police forces be beneficial?

4. What are the advantages and disadvantages of local control of policing? Can you think of other issues surrounding local control that were not addressed in the chapter?

5. What role has federal law enforcement played in law enforcement throughout history? Do you think the federal government should play a greater or lesser role in law enforcement in the future? Explain.

6. Policing is a popular topic in contemporary television shows and movies. What kinds of messages about policing are conveyed in modern media about the police? What effect do you think media depictions have on public support or criticism of police?

7. Consider Figure 3.4, which lists the most common topics covered in police academies. Do you think the number of hours devoted to each topic is sufficient? Are there additional topics you think should be offered to new police officers?

8. Imagine this hypothetical situation: Officer Phillips is responsible for patrolling the downtown area of Sunshine City. There are a number of coffee shops on his route, and it is not unusual for Officer Phillips to receive free coffee and pastries from these shops during his shift. Is Officer Phillips's behavior unethical? Explain.

9. Do you think policing agencies should require police officers to have a college education? What are the advantages and disadvantages of such a policy?

10. Though it does not receive much media or scholarly attention, private policing is becoming increasingly popular. Think of your regular routines—how often do you encounter private security or police officers in your normal activities? What do you think are the advantages and disadvantages associated with private policing/security?

## Media

**Bureau of Justice Statistics Law Enforcement Agency Surveys and Data Collections** http://bjs.ojp.usdoj.gov/index.cfm?ty=tp&tid=7#data_collections This website includes results and reports from a number of surveys on law enforcement practices and officer demographics.

**Police Assessment Resource Center** http://www.parc.info/home.chtml PARC is a nonprofit organization that publishes articles related to police oversight and accountability.

**Officer.com** http://www.officer.com This website includes a number of resources related to law enforcement, including job postings, media reports, and listings of upcoming events.

## Endnotes

[1] Wickersham Commission. (1968). *U.S. National Commission on Law Observance and Enforcement*, Montclair, NJ: Patterson Smith.

[2] Chafee, Z., Pollak, W., & Stern, C. (1969). *The Third Degree*. New York: Arno Press & The New York Times, 60–61.

3    Brown, B., & Benedict, W. (2002). "Perceptions of the Police: Past Findings, Methodological Issues, Conceptual Issues and Policy Implications." *Policing, 25,* 543–580.

4    Wadman, R., & Allison, W. (2004). *To Protect and Serve: A History of Police in America.* Upper Saddle River, NJ: Pearson Prentice Hall.

5    Greenberg, M. A. (2005). *Citizens Defending America: From Colonial Times to the Age of Terrorism.* Pittsburgh, PA: University of Pittsburgh Press.

6    Bayley, D. (1998). "The Development of Modern Police." In L. Gaines & G. Cordner (Eds.), *Policing Perspectives: An Anthology* (pp. 59–78). Oxford: Oxford University Press.

7    Stevenson, L. *Policing in America.*

8    Bopp, W., & Schultz, D. (1972). *A Short History of American Law Enforcement.* Springfield, IL: Charles Thomas.

9    Wadman & Allison, 2004.

10   Schneider, J. C. (1980). *Detroit and the Problem of Order, 1830–1880.* Lincoln, NE: University of Nebraska Press.

11   Bernstein, I. (1990). *The New York City Draft Riots of 1863: Their Significance for American Society and Politics in the Age of the Civil War.* Oxford: Oxford University Press.

12   Monkkonen, E. H. (1981). *Police in Urban America.* Cambridge: Cambridge University Press.

13   Walker, S. (1998). *Police in America.* New York, NY: McGraw-Hill.

14   Hadden, S. (2001). *Slave Patrols: Law and Violence in Virginia and the Carolinas.* Cambridge, MA: Harvard University Press.

15   Ibid., 94.

16   Tolnay, S., & Beck, E. M. (1995). *A Festival of Violence: An Analysis of Southern Lynchings, 1882–1930.* Champaign, IL: University of Illinois Press.

17   Prassel, F. (1972). *The Western Peace Officer: A Legacy of Law and Order.* Norman, OK: University of Oklahoma Press.

18   McNab, C. (2009). *Deadly Force: Firearms and American Law Enforcement, From the Wild West to the Streets of Today.* Westminster, MD: Osprey.

19   Prassel, 1972.

20   Utley, R. (2002). *Lone Star Justice: The First Century of the Texas Rangers.* Oxford: Oxford University Press.

21   Cox, M. (2008). *The Texas Rangers.* New York, NY: Forge.

22   O'Neal, B. (2006). *War in East Texas: Regulators vs. Moderators.* Lufkin, TX: Best of East Texas.

23   Mackay, J. (1996). *Allan Pinkerton: The First Private Eye.* New York, NY: John Wiley & Sons.

24   Ibid.

25   Calhoun, F. (1989). *The Lawmen: United States Marshals and their Deputies, 1789–1989.* Washington, DC: Smithsonian Institution Press.

26   Melanson, P., & Stevens, P. (2002). *The Secret Service: The Hidden History of an Enigmatic Agency.* New York, NY: Carroll & Graf.

27    Jeffreys-Jones, R. (2007). *The FBI: A History*. Binghamton, NY: Vail-Ballou Press.

28    Gentry, C. (1991). *J. Edgar Hoover: The Man and the Secrets*. New York, NY: W.W. Norton and Company.

29    Jeffreys-Jones, 2007.

30    Walker, S. (1977). *A Critical History of Police Reform: The Emergence of Professionalism*. Lexington, MA: Lexington Books.

31    Sherman, L. (1974). *Police Corruption: A Sociological Perspective*. New York, NY: Anchor Press.

32    Kappeler, V., Sluder, R., & Alpert, G. (1994). *Forces of Deviance: Understanding the Dark Side of Policing*. Prospect Heights, IL: Waveland Press. Goldstein, H. (1975). *Police Corruption: A Perspective on its Nature and Control*. Washington, DC: Police Foundation.

33    Uchida, C. (1993). "The Development of the American Police: An Historical Overview." In R. Dunham & G. Alpert (Eds.), *Critical Issues in Policing: Contemporary Readings* (2nd ed.). Prospect Heights, IL: Waveland Press.

34    Ibid.

35    Carte, G., & Carte, E. (1975). *Police Reform in the United States: The Era of August Vollmer*. Berkeley, CA: University of California Press.

36    Vollmer, A. (1936). *The Police and Modern Society*. Berkeley, CA: University of California Press.

37    National Commission on Law Observance and Enforcement. (1931a). *Report on Lawlessness in Law Enforcement*. Washington, DC: United States Government Printing Office.

38    National Commission on Law Observance and Enforcement. (1931b). *Report on Police*. Washington, DC: United States Government Printing Office.

39    National Commission on Law Observance and Enforcement. (1931c). *Report on the Enforcement of the Prohibition Laws of the United States*. Washington, DC: United States Government Printing Office.

40    Ibid.

41    Ibid.

42    Beckett, K. (1999). *Making Crime Pay: Law and Order in Contemporary American Politics*. Oxford: Oxford University Press.

43    McPhail, C., Schweingruber, D., & McCarthy, J. (1998). "Policing Protest in the United States: 1960–1995." In D. Della Porta & H. Reiter (Eds.), *Policing Protest: The Control of Mass Demonstrations in Western Democracies*. Minneapolis, MN: University of Minnesota Press.

44    Commission on Law Enforcement and Administration of Justice. (1967). *The Challenge of Crime in a Free Society*. Washington, DC: United States Government Printing Office.

45    Hensley, T. R., & Lewis, J. M. (Eds.). (2003). *Kent State and May 4th: A Social Science Perspective* (3rd ed.). Kent, OH: Kent State University Press.

46    *Report of the National Advisory Commission on Civil Disorders*. New York, NY: Bantam Books, 1–29.

47    Commission on Law Enforcement and Administration of Justice, 1967.

48    Ibid.

49    Federal Communications Commission. (n.d.). Retrieved from http://transition.fcc.gov/Bureaus/OSEC/library/legislative_histories/1615.pdf

50    Chin, G. J. (Ed.). (1997). *New York City Police Corruption Investigation Commissions, 1894–1994*. Buffalo, NY: William S. Hein.

51    Avery, M., Blum, K., & Rudovsky, D. (2010). *Police Misconduct: Law and Litigation* (3rd ed.). Eagan, MN: Westlaw.

52    *Mapp v. Ohio*, 367 U.S. 643 (1961).

53    *Escobedo v. Illinois*, 378 U.S. 478 (1964).

55    Walker, S. (1985). "Setting the Standards: The Efforts and Impact of Blue-Ribbon Commissions on the Police." In W. Geller (Ed.), *Police Leadership in America* (pp. 354–370). Westport, CT: Praeger.

56    Commission on Accreditation for Law Enforcement. (2009). *CALEA 2009 Annual Report*. Retrieved from http://www.calea.org/sites/default/files/2009%20Annual%20Report.pdf

57    *Pennsylvania State Police*. (n.d.). Retrieved from http://www.psp.state.pa.us/portal/server.pt/community/psp/4451

58    Reaves, B. A. (2010). *Local Police Departments, 2007*. Retrieved from http://bjs.ojp.usdoj.gov

59    USACOPS. (n.d.). *California*. Retrieved from http://www.usacops.com/ca/

60    Pampel, F. (2004). *Racial Profiling*. New York, NY: Infobase.

61    Reaves, B. (2016). State and Local Law Enforcement Training Academies, 2013. *Bureau of Justice Statistics*. Retrieved from https://www.bjs.gov/content/pub/pdf/slleta13.pdf.

62    Skogan, W. (Ed.). (2004). *Community Policing: Can It Work?* Belmont, CA: Wadsworth.

63    Moore, M. H., Trojanowicz, R., & Kelling, G. (1988). *Crime and Policing*. Washington, DC: National Institute of Justice. Retrieved from https://www.ncjrs.gov/pdffiles1/nij/111460.pdf

64    Goldstein, H. (1990). *Problem Oriented Policing*. Columbus, OH: McGraw-Hill.

65    Violent Crime Control and Law Enforcement Act, Pub. L. No. 103–322, 108 Stat. 1902 (1994).

66    Oriented Policing Services. (n.d.). *COPS Office: Grants and Resources for Community Policing*. Retrieved from http://www.cops.usdoj.gov/

67    Reaves, B. A. (2009). *State and Local Law Enforcement Training Academies, 2006*. Retrieved from http://bjs.ojp.usdoj.gov

68    Fry, L., & Berkes, L. (1983). "The Paramilitary Police Model: An Organizational Misfit." *Human Organization, 42*, 225–234.

69    Auten, J. H. (1981). "The Paramilitary Model of Police and Police Professionalism." *Police Studies, 4*, 67–78.

70    Kraska, P., & Kappeler, V. (1997). "Militarizing American Police: The Rise and Normalization of Paramilitary Units." *Social Problems, 44*, 1–18.

71    Kraska, P. (Ed.). (2001). *Militarizing the American Criminal Justice System: The Changing Roles of the Armed Forces and the Police*. Boston, MA: Northeastern University Press.

72   Reaves, B. A. (2006). *Federal Law Enforcement Officers, 2004* (NCJ 212750). Retrieved from http://bjs.ojp.usdoj.gov/content/pub/pdf/fleo04.pdf

73   Reaves, 2009.

74   Homeland Security Act of 2002, Pub. L. No. 107-296, 116 Stat. 2135 (2002). Retrieved from http://www.dhs.gov/xlibrary/assets/hr_5005_enr.pdf

75   Reaves, 2010.

76   City of Reno. (n.d.). *Police Recruiting*. Retrieved from http://www.reno.gov/Index.aspx?page=1094 NYPD. (n.d.). *Application Process*. Retrieved from http://www.nyc.gov/html/nypd/html/careers/application_overview.shtml

77   Reaves, 2009.

78   Schulz, D. M. (1995). *From Social Worker to Crimefighter: Women in United States Municipal Policing*. Westport, CT: Praeger.

79   Ibid.

80   U.S. Department of Labor, Bureau of Labor Statistics. (2009). "Police, Fire, and Ambulance Dispatchers." *Occupational Outlook Handbook, 2010–11 Edition*. Retrieved from http://www.bls.gov/oco/ocos343.htm

81   U.S. Department of Labor, Bureau of Labor Statistics. (2011). "Occupational Employment and Wages, May 2010: 43–5031 Police, Fire, and Ambulance Dispatchers." *Occupational Employment Statistics*. Retrieved from http://www.bls.gov/oes/current/oes435031.htm

© GERARD BOTTINO/Shutterstock.com

# Policing: Roles, functions, and challenges

## KEY TERMS

Aggressive patrol

Bias-based profiling

Blue code of silence

Broken windows theory

COMPSTAT

Crime analysis

Crime mapping

Criminal investigation

Deep cover

Directed patrol

Discretion

Excessive force

Field interrogation

Follow-up investigation

Intelligence-led policing

Light cover

Operational styles

Order maintenance

Preliminary investigation

Preventive patrol

Problem-oriented policing

Role

Role conflict

Role expectation

Selective enforcement

Social contract

Symbolic assailant

Thin blue line

# CHAPTER OBJECTIVES

1 Define the various roles and duties that police officers have in enforcing law and maintaining order in society.

2 Distinguish among the different styles of policing used by police officers.

3 Identify the various functions of police departments in America.

4 Explain the components of the police subculture, including issues related to discretion, stress, ethics, and corruption.

## Case Study: Less Lethal or Deadly Force?

Police work can be a dangerous profession, and sometimes the police are required to use physical force to subdue criminals. Historically, the police have carried batons or nightsticks and firearms. In more recent years, new, less lethal technologies have been developed so the police do not have to resort to deadly force. Stun gun technology sends electroshocks into the suspect's body that cause a loss of neuromuscular control and contract the muscles in the body. The most commonly known stun gun used by police departments across the country was developed by TASER International nearly two decades ago. Proponents of the use of the TASER have found it to be a useful tool that has prevented police from having to use deadly force. While these proponents view the use of stun gun technology as preventing deaths of suspects, an alarming number of suspects have died after being "tased." Numerous civil lawsuits have been filed against police departments and stun gun manufacturers, including TASER International, but at present, the courts have ruled against the plaintiffs and found that the deaths were not a direct result of the electroshock weapon.

On September 22, 2005, the Nashville Police Department was called to the Mercy Lounge, a Nashville nightclub, to remove 21-year-old Patrick Lee. When police arrived, Lee was already outside the club and could be observed undressed and rambling incoherently. Earlier in the evening, Lee had reportedly ingested the hallucinogen LSD. In an attempt to control him, police deployed their TASERs and jolted Lee 19 times. Paramedics were called to the scene when Lee was unresponsive, and he died in police custody 39 hours later. When an autopsy was conducted, the medical examiner ruled that Lee's death was caused by a "drug-induced excited delirium." Lee's parents filed a wrongful death lawsuit against the Nashville Police Department, the police officers involved, and TASER International. Eventually, a federal jury cleared all defendants in the lawsuit.

Do you believe the shocking of Patrick Lee 19 times was an excessive use of police force? With the number of deaths that have occurred following the use of electroshock, even though the courts have yet to find its users responsible, should the police still continue to employ this form of less lethal weapon?

## Roles of the Police Officer

Seneviratne (2002) described the role of police officers as being the gate-keepers to the criminal justice system.[1] It is their sworn duty to investigate crimes and arrest the offenders. Their arrests lead offenders through the gates into the criminal justice system. In addition to arresting offenders, police officers have a variety of functions and roles they are expected to perform. Performing these functions and roles does not come without a cost. The nature of police work leads to unique challenges as a result of the powers that police have, the dangers they face, and the temptations all around them. This chapter discusses the roles, functions, and challenges for the police officer in American society.

When citizens think of the police, they most likely envision a uniformed officer who is operating a vehicle marked with emblems and striping and emergency lights mounted on the roof. This description is of the officer who is patrolling a beat and responding to calls for service in the community. Although there are many different law enforcement agencies on the federal, state, and local levels of government, each with its own geographic or criminal responsibility, the patrol officer is the face of law enforcement in America.

The relationship between the public and the government is commonly referred to as the **social contract**. This contract is the agreement into which the public enters with its government allowing it to provide for public safety and security. One form of protection that the public seeks is that of the law enforcement agencies that police America. The police represent a formal state control that is necessary and embodies what Hunter (1985) referred to as public social control.[2] Without the police, the public would be left to its own devices, and crime and victimization would undoubtedly result. The police are said to be a **thin blue line**, named for the color of most police uniforms, between the lawful and the lawless on our streets. Klockars (1985) defined police as "institutions or individuals given the general right to use coercive force by the state within the state's domestic territory."[3]

A **role** is defined as the position one holds within a social structure. The role police officers assume when policing a community can be vague and ambiguous. Take, for example, a community that has an ordinance against doing vehicle repairs on the street. Community residents in an upper-class neighborhood who do not want to see cars sitting on cement blocks and motor oil spills on their streets may call the police department demanding action against a violator. In contrast, residents in a poorer neighborhood may overlook this violation because they know the neighbor doing his own repair work cannot afford to take the car to an automobile repair shop. This example refers to what is termed as **role expectation**. While the residents

**Social contract** An agreement between the public and government in which the public allows the government to provide safety and security.

**Thin blue line** The line between the lawful and the lawless and between social order and chaos on the streets.

**Role** The position one holds within a social structure.

**Role expectation** The behaviors and activities that people expect from a person in a particular role.

of the upper-class neighborhood expect the police to issue a citation for the ordinance violation, the residents in the poorer neighborhood do not. Role expectation is the behavior that is expected of someone in a particular role.

Dunham and Alpert (2010) saw the role of the police officer becoming increasingly more complex and citizens' expectations of the police continually expanding.[4] The expectations of the police officer's role not only reflect the wishes of community residents; the officer must also deal with the expectations of police administrators, political leaders in the community, and sometimes the state legislature. In our example involving vehicle repairs on the street, although residents in the poorer neighborhood do not want violators cited, the police chief may expect officers to cite any violator of the ordinance regardless of where they reside in the community. The mayor of the community may insist that the police department escort funeral processions to the local cemetery as a service to the public, while the officers may not see this role as one that law enforcement should assume. State legislatures have enacted laws restricting police officers' use of discretion when dealing with domestic violence cases: police officers may prefer to mediate a domestic dispute, but they may be required by law to make an arrest in the case.

© Ivan Kokoulin/Shutterstock.com

Role conflict is the conflict between what police officers may prefer to do and what they are expected to do.

**Role conflict** The conflict between what a person may prefer to do and what the person is expected to do.

**Role conflict** can result from the opposing expectations that police officers receive from different sources. Role conflict is the conflict between what police officers may prefer to do and what they are expected to do. While police officers may view themselves as crime fighters, the public may see them as peacekeepers or even "social workers" whose role is to control social problems. They may be expected to serve as social workers and intervene in a domestic dispute, but then have to arrest one of the parties involved because they are legally bound to do so even if they believe arrest may be unwarranted. The police may want to pursue a traffic violator who did not stop after they activated their emergency lights and siren, but not be able to because agency policy prohibits vehicle pursuits of vehicle operators wanted only for a traffic violation. The community and the police department largely base the police officer's role on the social contract that has been agreed upon.

## Controversial Police Roles

The police are expected to ensure that the rights of citizens are not violated and they are afforded their due process. If police engage in unethical or coercive practices, they are only serving to endanger the public and subject citizens to the very risks the police were given power to prevent. Reiman (1985) argued that the police must be accountable to the public they serve for their use of public power.[5]

Police searches, use of force, vehicle pursuits, and citizen encounters can cause controversy among the public if not performed ethically and within the legal boundaries of the law. For example, in the case of *Mapp v. Ohio* (1961), the United States Supreme Court ruled that evidence obtained illegally by the police must be excluded in state prosecutions.[6] Stuntz (1997) found this exclusionary rule, as it is known, to be useful in that it allows the courts to serve as watchdogs for police misconduct regarding the collection of evidence against a suspect. Stuntz called the exclusionary rule the best legal tool available for regulating the police. While critics of the exclusionary rule might focus on a suspect walking out of a court as a result of a legal technicality due to police misconduct, Stuntz stated that the rule is important because the courts see the consequences of the constitutional rules they create for the police.[7]

In contrast, Keenan (1998) noted that another Supreme Court decision of the 1960s involving police searches was widely criticized for being too pro-police.[8] In *Terry v. Ohio* (1968), the court ruled that police have the authority to detain or "stop" a person briefly for questioning and "frisk" the person for weapons if the officer has a reasonable suspicion the person may be armed and dangerous. The court found the "*Terry Rule*" to be necessary for the safety of police officers when dealing with suspicious persons. However, police must have a legitimate reason for conducting a "stop and frisk" so as not to violate an individual's rights against unreasonable search and seizure.[9]

The authority to use force in the line of duty is a second controversial aspect of police work. The videotaped beating of Rodney King in 1991 by several police officers from the Los Angeles Police Department provided the nation with an example of the possible consequences of police use of force. More controversial is the use of deadly force by police. In the landmark *Tennessee v. Garner* (1985) case, the Supreme Court ruled that a police officer may not use deadly force to prevent the escape of a suspect unless probable cause exists that the suspect poses a threat of serious physical injury or death to the officer or other persons present.10 As a result of the *Garner* decision, police departments began to make changes in agency policies regarding the use of deadly force.[11]

Deadly force must be the last resort for the police officer. Unfortunately, police are usually unable to choose the time, place, or circumstances of a potentially deadly encounter. Fyfe (1986) described the split-second syndrome police officers face when they encounter violence, during which time they must diagnose a problem, perform under stress and time constraints, and make an assessment of the justifiability of their actions.[12]

Another controversial role of the police officer involves vehicle pursuits. Alpert (1993) observed that pursuit driving on public streets at excessive speeds is a dangerous police tactic that presents risks to all involved, including the officer, the suspect, and any innocent motorists or pedestrians who may be nearby. Alpert stated that police must balance the need to immediately apprehend a suspect with the likelihood that an accident or injury may occur.[13]

Hicks (2006) warned that police officers are charged with protecting the public, and exposing these members of the public to unnecessary risk is counter to this primary police responsibility. As a result of the danger posed by high-speed police chases, Hicks recommended that police officers be provided with written guidelines regarding the procedures that should be followed when considering the initiation of a vehicle pursuit.[14] The police may argue that policy restrictions imposed on pursuits inhibit their ability to apprehend serious offenders. Many police pursuits initiated for simple traffic violations lead to the apprehension of suspects wanted on felony charges. In a study of police pursuits in the state of Michigan, one-third of pursuits—most of which were initiated for traffic offenses—were found to lead to a felony arrest.[15]

**Bias-based profiling** Selection of individuals based solely on a common trait of a group such as race, ethnicity, gender, sexual orientation, or economic status.

African-Americans are more likely than whites to view police traffic stops as unjustified.

A fourth issue of controversy involves police-citizen encounters and particularly the issue of **bias-based profiling**. Bias-based profiling, previously referred to as racial profiling, is defined as the selection of individuals based solely on a common trait of a group such as race, ethnicity, gender, sexual orientation, or economic status. Race is a significant factor influencing individual attitudes about police, with African-Americans having the most negative attitudes toward police while whites hold the most positive attitudes toward police.[16]

The most common site for a police-citizen encounter is the traffic stop,[17] and the most controversial aspect of those is the phenomenon known as "driving while black."[18] Research has indicated that blacks stopped by the police are more likely than whites to view the stop as unjustified.[19] Brown (2005) wrote that many public surveys have shown that a great number of American citizens believe the police treat African-Americans more harshly than white Americans. In Brown's study of police-suspect encounters in Cincinnati, Ohio, the findings suggest that police base arrest decisions on strict legal criteria when encountering white suspects, but are influenced by demeanor, age, and gender when encountering black suspects.[20]

**Critical Thinking**

Should police officers be permitted to engage in vehicle pursuits for traffic violators who are not suspected of having committed a more serious offense?

## Duties of the Police Officer

In the broadest sense, the role of the police officer is multidimensional. The influence that the community has on the role of police officers requires them to perform a variety of duties. The police are expected to be crime fighters, security guards, peacemakers, lawyers, judges, investigators, social workers, clergymen, psychologists, and medical first responders.

Generally, the role of the police officer falls into four categories of duties:

- Law Enforcement
- Order Maintenance
- Crime Prevention
- Service Provider

These duties that police officers are required to perform are based in large part on the size of the police department and the expectations of the community. Police officers may view themselves as law enforcers, but actually spend most of their time maintaining order in the community. For example, in a large urban police department, the police may deal with a major crime problem that would preclude them from responding to scenes of minor traffic accidents. On the other hand, in a small rural police department, the crime problem may be minimal, so officers are expected to investigate every traffic accident, regardless of how minor it may be. The large urban police department might be exerting most of its efforts maintaining order and enforcing the law, while the smaller rural department is providing services to the community and preventing crime from occurring.

Additionally, the duties police officers perform often overlap. For example, a police officer might be dispatched to the scene of a dispute between two neighbors over the boundary line between their properties. The officer may expect to reach a peaceful resolution to the dispute to maintain order in the neighborhood, but when one neighbor decides to punch the other, the officer may now have to perform a law enforcement duty and arrest the aggressive neighbor. While each category of duties is discussed below, the reality is that the police officer's role includes many overlapping and sometimes conflicting responsibilities.

## Law Enforcement

Enforcing the law is traditionally considered to be the primary responsibility of police officers. Police officers have the power to investigate crimes and arrest offenders. Within these two broad powers are numerous duties, including enforcing traffic laws, interviewing victims of and witnesses to crimes, interrogating persons suspected of committing crimes, collecting physical evidence at crime scenes, conducting undercover and covert operations, and assisting in the prosecution of individuals charged with crimes. When performing these duties, police officers must always be mindful of the legal rights of any accused persons under the United States Constitution to ensure that they have been safeguarded against violations such as unreasonable searches and seizures and notified of their right against self-incrimination and right to counsel.

**Selective enforcement**
The decision made by police as to which laws they wish to enforce and when they choose to enforce them.

Police officers are sworn to uphold and enforce *all* laws, but this can be unrealistic or unwanted. Most police departments practice **selective enforcement** of the law, in which they decide which laws they wish to enforce and when they choose to enforce them. Police departments must allocate manpower and budgetary resources where they can do the most good and deal with the more serious offenses and offenders. Police officer discretion also plays a role in law enforcement. Traffic enforcement efforts usually permit police officers to decide whether to issue a warning or a citation to traffic violators. But at times, the police department may choose to set up a "speed trap" and selectively enforce excessive speed violations, issuing citations to all violators on a particular roadway in the community where they have observed an increase in fatal traffic accidents.

The fact that the public often refers to police officers as "law enforcement officers" suggests that they see this duty as the primary function of the police. In reality, law enforcement takes up a small percentage of time spent by police officers when they are on duty.

## Order Maintenance

The duty of the police officer to act as a peacekeeper and maintain order in the community dates back to the early English watchman with his lantern and baton. Police officers may engage in **order maintenance** more than any other duty that they perform.

**Order maintenance**
A method of policing whereby officers interpret the law and decide on a course of action based on each individual situation when assigning blame and choosing whether or not to arrest.

Order maintenance situations may or may not involve criminal activity. For example, crowd control may be necessary at a public event such as the state fair. In this case, it is unlikely that criminal activity will occur, because these events are typically family-oriented. The police presence is usually meant to ensure that the flow of pedestrian and vehicular traffic remains orderly, though of course unruly persons at the fair would be dealt with and arrested when necessary. In contrast, order maintenance at the site of a political rally involving a hotly debated issue will most likely involve citizens who have a different agenda than those seeking a fun day at the state fair. Arresting drunk or unruly people at the fair is a very different use of state power than arresting protestors engaging in the political process.

Police officers are often dispatched to domestic disputes between individuals such as family members, neighbors, or landlords and tenants. In domestic disputes, police officers intervene and attempt to resolve the situation to the satisfaction of all parties involved. If the problem is unresolved, or one of the parties involved has violated criminal law, then the police may choose to make an arrest. Even loud music complaints or dog barking calls can be resolved by simply issuing warnings to the responsible parties. If the music is turned down and

© 1000 Words/Shutterstock.com

One of the duties of police is maintaining order, such as at a protest, concert, or other gathering.

the dog is kept from barking by its owner, then order is maintained. If not, then it might be necessary for police to make an arrest.

Police officers prefer to deal with order maintenance issues without having to arrest a citizen. Generally, the public favors this approach. But there are times when what began for police as an order maintenance duty becomes a law enforcement duty.

## Crime Prevention

Crime prevention is another duty that the community expects the police to perform. When police officers are on routine patrol in marked patrol vehicles, they are looking for criminal activity that may be in progress. Their mere presence may also deter crime. The public views the high visibility of police as one of the most important ways to prevent crime. It is also common for the police department to increase its visibility in high-crime areas or areas of the community where the public congregates. This is done by use of a variety of patrol techniques. For example, the police may utilize foot patrols and mounted horse patrols on a Saturday night in the nightclub section of the community. These increased patrols can have the effect of inhibiting bar patrons from engaging in criminal activity they may otherwise have attempted if police had not made their presence so evident.

In addition to the use of routine patrols and increased visibility, the police department may engage in activities specifically designed for crime prevention. For example, police units will often conduct speed traps using radar devices to apprehend speeding violators. These traps also serve as a deterrent by discouraging motorists from exceeding the speed limit on roadways known to be locations that police frequently monitor. DUI checkpoints, which are often previously announced in the local newspaper, are meant to prevent vehicle operators from driving while drunk. Even visible foot and vehicle patrols in areas of the community known to be frequented by prostitutes and their potential customers have been useful in dealing with this crime problem.

Finally, many police departments implement organized crime prevention programs. Neighborhood watch programs are designed to encourage neighborhood residents to collaborate with the police department and maintain security in the community. A program for juveniles such as the Police Athletic League (PAL) is another example of crime prevention that targets at-risk youths.

© Maciej Bledowski/
Shutterstock.com

Visher and Weisburd (1998) argued that for decades there was very little positive evidence that police crime prevention strategies worked. These authors reported that in more recent years, there has been reason for optimism, as police departments have begun to focus more on high rate offenders and "hot spots" of crime.[21] Still, even with these newer strategies that target specific offenders and crime areas, the sight of a patrol car passing by a resident's home can provide a sense of security for community residents.

The mere presence of a police car may help prevent crime from occurring in a particular area.

The services provided by the police department typically depend on the size of the department and the amount of time officers can devote to providing service. Kennedy (2002) stated that, as 24/7 agencies, police departments are always available. As such, agencies must prioritize calls and make decisions regarding which calls will be answered and which ones will not. It is expected that the public will seek the assistance of the police when they have been a victim of or witness to a crime, or have been in some other emergency situation. In some communities, it is also expected that the police will perform services for their residents and respond to non-emergency situations. Large police departments may not be able to provide the community with the more personal attention that small departments can.[22] While busier police departments that must respond to numerous emergency calls might offer no assistance to non-emergency callers, a small local police department may respond to both emergency and non-emergency calls.

Police officers act as service providers, performing such tasks as giving directions.

Quite often, the non-emergency service calls to which a police department responds reflect the wishes and expectations of the community. For example, the police department may be expected to assist stranded motorists, provide directions to lost motorists, escort funeral processions, and unlock car doors. A large police department may not have the time to remove cats from trees or provide parenting advice to a distraught parent with a troubled teenager, but the public may expect these types of services from a small-town police department.

# Operational Styles of Policing

**Operational styles** The approaches police officers use to perform their duties.

Several researchers have studied the police officer position in an attempt to determine how officers approach their jobs. These approaches to performing police duties are referred to as **operational styles**. These operational styles can reflect community expectations for police officers, the expectations of police administrators for their departments, and individual police officers' own philosophies on how they should perform their duties. In police departments that do not have a formal agreement on how the community should be policed, individual officers may adopt their own styles.

For example, the community may expect its police officers to adopt a watchman style. This style may be adopted in a very small community where the officers in the police department are familiar with members of the community. The community and the police may agree on informal controls instead of strict enforcement of laws. *Informal social control* refers to a willingness of local residents to actively participate in crime prevention in their neighborhoods.[23] Reisig and Parks (2004) believed the movement toward community policing, which is discussed in further detail later in this chapter, emphasized the positive contribution of police-citizen partnerships that could control crime and build informal social control.[24] Silver and Miller (2004) found that when residents believe police are successful in addressing their crime problems and represent a legitimate institution of public social control, they feel more empowered to partner with police and to engage in their own informal social control.[25] The community and the police department may agree that it is preferable to warn traffic code violators for minor violations instead of issuing citations. The community may prefer that juveniles who are caught in the act of underage drinking should be escorted home to their parents instead of charged with a violation. The community and the police will most likely agree that in serious cases, criminal law must be enforced and offenders charged.

It should be noted that the public's perception of the police department or an individual officer is often determined by the style of policing officers are practicing as a result of the police-citizen contact. The traffic violator who receives a citation may believe that the officer's style is that of an enforcer. This may or may not be valid. Often, the officer is acting in the role of enforcer because strict enforcement of traffic violators at a particular intersection has been ordered due to the high volume of traffic accidents at the location. While an officer would typically practice a watchman style, orders from the police chief have required the use of an enforcer style.

## Wilson's Styles of Policing

Wilson (1968) developed one of the earliest studies of the operational styles of police officers. Wilson found three distinct styles that he termed the watchman style, legalistic style, and service style.

In the *watchman* style, the police officer emphasizes a more informal way of handling disputes within the community. The watchman is most interested in keeping the peace and chooses to arrest only as a last resort to resolve a dispute. This style of policing would be best suited for poorer, economically deprived communities and small towns where informal control is practiced.

Wilson's second style of policing is the *legalistic* style. As the name implies, this style of policing emphasizes strict enforcement of the law and the use of arrests to resolve disputes in the community. Communities with higher crime rates, which are more common within our larger metropolitan areas, would more likely practice the legalistic style of policing, believing that the community will become safer if more offenders are removed from the streets.

The third operational style is Wilson's *service* style. Affluent communities may be more likely to emphasize this style of policing where the police are asked to serve the public's needs. The emphasis of the service style is to assist the community rather than arrest offenders. The use of social service agencies, diversionary programs, and community treatment programs is preferable to the use of the criminal justice system.[26]

## Broderick's Styles of Policing

A second approach to the operational styles of police officers was developed by Broderick (1987). Broderick labeled his officer styles as enforcers, idealists, realists, and optimists.

The *enforcer* has more concern for maintaining the social order and puts little emphasis on the individual rights of citizens or due process. The *idealist* emphasizes social order as well, but unlike the enforcer, places a high value on individual rights and due process. The *realist* places little value on social order or due process and seems to accept society as it is. Finally, the *optimist* values individual rights and due process and is mainly concerned with acting as a public servant, giving a lower value to social control.[27]

## Muir's Styles of Policing

A third classification by Muir (1977) studied the methods by which police officers used their authority on the streets. Muir saw police officers as using *passion*, which was defined as the ability to use force to resolve conflict, or *perspective*, which was described as using force ethically and dealing empathetically with those who are less fortunate. Muir's styles of police officers included the enforcer, reciprocator, avoider, and professional.

The *enforcer* is the police officer who possesses the passion for enforcing laws and has a comfort level with using force to deal with problems. The *reciprocator* lacks any passion for the job, takes little action enforcing law or making arrests, and has a difficult time using force when it is warranted. The *avoider* is the officer who has neither passion nor perspective and takes little action. The *professional* combines the judicious use of passion and the perspective necessary to successfully perform the job.[28]

> **Critical Thinking**
> Among the various styles of policing discussed in the chapter, which type of police officer would you like policing your community?

# Functions of Police

The functions that are carried out by the police are determined based on the size of the police department, the makeup of the community, and the crime problems that the community faces. The following are some of the major functions of a police department.

## Patrol

Patrol is considered to be the backbone of policing. The uniformed police officer in the marked police vehicle patrols the streets of the community and serves as the first responder to calls for service and citizen complaints. In a small police department, it would not be uncommon for all officers, including the police chief, to engage in patrol. In larger police departments that have a variety of specialized functions, patrol officers comprise the largest unit in the department.

The patrol officer is the first police officer dispatched to calls for service. Patrol officers respond to family disputes, neighborhood disputes, traffic accidents, burglar alarms, and any other kind of call that is made to the police department by the residents of the community. In addition to responding to calls for service, the patrol officer is expected to look for criminal activity that might be occurring in the community. The patrol officer's duties can involve investigating crimes such as traffic law violations, driving under the influence, disorderly conduct, domestic violence, burglary, and theft.

### Preventive Patrol

Adams (2006) identified a number of methods that the police employ to patrol the community. The most common method is preventive patrol, which is sometimes referred to as routine or random patrol. **Preventive patrol** involves patrolling the police officer's sector or district in the community on an unpredictable, random basis. The amount of time spent by police officers on preventive patrol is often dependent on the number of calls for service to which they respond. The more time the patrol officer spends answering calls, the less time he or she can spend patrolling the community to prevent crime or look for crimes that may be in progress.[29]

Patrol officers are dispatched to calls for service, including traffic accidents.

**Preventive patrol**
Patrolling the community on an unpredictable and routine or random basis.

Although preventive patrol has been used for centuries, its effectiveness was not studied until 1972 in the well-known Kansas City Preventive Patrol Experiment.[30] This study is still considered to be the most comprehensive look at preventive patrol. The experiment divided the patrol districts in Kansas City, Missouri, into 15 beats, with five beats in each of three different groups. Each of the three groups was similar in demographics and calls for service. The first group of five beats were "proactive beats," in which two to three times the normal level of preventive patrol was conducted. The second group of five beats were "reactive beats," in which no preventive patrol was used, and officers only entered the beats when responding to a call.

Finally, the third group of five beats were the "control beats." Control beats maintained the usual level of preventive patrol that had historically been conducted.

Following the year-long study, the surprising results indicated that neither increasing nor decreasing patrols impacted crime rates in the community. Furthermore, the citizens of Kansas City were unaware that any changes to the way the community was being patrolled had occurred. Citizens' fear of crime, attitudes toward the police, and even their review of police response time to their calls for service remained unchanged. In more recent studies involving police patrol, researchers have found that instead of using a generalized preventive patrol, the focus should be on specific places or "hot spots" where crime is most concentrated.[31,32,33]

The results of the Kansas City Preventive Patrol Experiment caused many police administrators to rethink their positions on the effectiveness of routine patrol. Yet, years after the study, preventive patrol remains the most widely used method for patrolling our communities. As a result of the study, however, alternatives to preventive patrol are being practiced when particular problems in the community warrant their use.

## Directed Patrol

**Directed patrol** Spending an allotted amount of time patrolling a specific area of the community that is considered to be a high-crime area.

A **directed patrol** requires that patrol officers spend an amount of their patrol time in a specified area of the community.[34] These may be known high-crime areas or areas where there has been a noticeable increase in one type of criminal activity. For example, the police department may be aware as a result of crime analysis information that during the three weeks prior to Christmas, the parking lot at the local mall has had an increase in vehicle burglaries and muggings of shoppers. As time permits during the shift, police officers may be ordered to direct frequent patrols through the mall parking lot in order to prevent these crimes from occurring or possibly catch suspects in the act of committing these crimes.

## Foot Patrol

Prior to the use of motorized patrol vehicles, police officers patrolled on foot. Adams (2006) stated that although foot patrol confines police to small areas, it is among the most effective types of patrol.[35] The motorized patrol vehicle has permitted patrol officers to cover more ground and respond more quickly to calls for service. Unfortunately, a negative effect of the use of the patrol vehicle was that police officers began to become more distant and aloof from the community. Foot patrols allow police officers to have more personal contact with the community and move more quietly into areas of the community where the sound of an approaching vehicle may alarm a suspect.

FIGURE 4.1 SCHEMATIC OF 15 BEATS IN KANSAS CITY PATROL EXPERIMENT

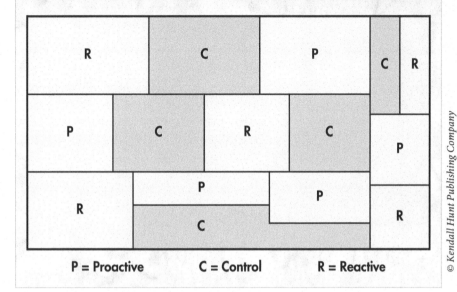

P = Proactive          C = Control          R = Reactive

© Kendall Hunt Publishing Company

Two important studies were conducted in an attempt to determine the possible benefits of the use of foot patrol. The Newark, New Jersey Foot Patrol Experiment found that foot patrols did not affect crime rates, but had a positive impact on citizen satisfaction with foot patrol officers.[36] In a similar study conducted by Trojanowicz (1982) in Flint, Michigan, it was found that citizens also showed an increase in satisfaction with police services and a decrease in fear of crime.[37] Whether or not foot patrol reduces crime is uncertain, but it has led to a more positive relationship between the police and the public.

## Aggressive Patrol

**Aggressive patrol** strategies require patrol officers to maintain a more active or "aggressive" style of policing. Gaines (1996) recommended the use of aggressive patrol because it maximizes police effectiveness in crime reduction.[38] When conducting aggressive patrols, officers are expected to make frequent traffic stops and inquiries of suspicious persons on the streets of the community. The intent of an aggressive patrol is to potentially uncover criminal activity that might otherwise have been missed had officers not stopped the motorist or the pedestrian. For example, stopping a motorist who has not made a complete stop at a stop sign may seem to be an unnecessary and inconvenient action to some residents of the community, but if the stop results in a drunk driving arrest, the residents may feel otherwise. A stop by a patrol officer who conducts a **field interrogation**, which is a temporary detention in order to question

**Aggressive patrol**
Patrolling the community by making frequent and numerous traffic stops and field interrogations of suspicious persons.

**Field interrogation**
A temporary detention of an individual in order to question the individual about a suspicious circumstance.

© Lisa F. Young/Shutterstock.com

Aggressive patrol can lead to arrests of lawbreakers, such as drunk drivers, who otherwise might not have been caught.

a suspicious person, may lead to the arrest of a person who is wanted by the police. Gaines called field interrogation an indispensable part of police efforts to control street crime and disorder.[39]

One concern about the use of aggressive patrols is that police will often stop and question citizens who have not engaged in any criminal activity. These inconvenient stops may anger law-abiding citizens. On the other hand, aggressive patrols that lead to arrests for offenses that might not have been discovered had the police not acted aggressively are often applauded by law-abiding citizens in the community.

## Saturation Patrol

It is sometimes necessary for the police department to increase patrol activity in a particular area of the community. Crime analysis information may indicate an unusual increase in a certain type of crime in that area. It might also be evident that on Friday and Saturday nights, the increased population of patrons in the bar and club areas of the community requires increased police presence. In these instances, the police department may employ saturation patrols, in which they utilize a variety of patrol methods such as routine preventive patrol, directed patrol, and foot patrols to "saturate" the area. Fritsch, Caeti, and Taylor (1999) found that saturation patrols work provided they are directed toward a particular offender, place, victim, or offense. In their study, these researchers found that aggressive curfew and truancy enforcement resulted in significantly reduced gang violence in Dallas, Texas.[40] Saturation patrols can have a crime reduction effect similar to that of aggressive patrols because police visibility may inhibit possible offenders, while the additional police presence may lead to quick apprehension of those persons choosing to commit crime.

### Career Connections: Uniformed Police Officer

Uniformed police officers from municipal, county, or state law enforcement agencies perform a variety of tasks for the community. In general, the duties of a police officer include enforcing the law, assisting the public, investigating crime, and preventing crime. They also maintain order by directing traffic, issuing traffic citations, making arrests, responding to maintenance of public order incidents, and preparing police reports. Each day can be a new challenge and a new adventure. One day, the police officer may conduct traffic stops at a busy intersection, counsel a distressed mother who is dealing with her adolescent son, and conduct an investigation at a residence that has been burglarized. The next day, this same officer may have completely different duties to perform.

In order to become a police officer, a candidate should be a U.S. citizen, be at least 21 years of age, have at least a high school diploma, and be able to pass a criminal history and background check, physical abilities test, and psychological examination. The specific requirements for employment vary from state to state and within each police department. Candidates must also graduate from a state-approved police academy where they are taught the basic requirements for performing the duties of the police officer position.

The ideal police officer candidate should possess strong interpersonal skills, critical thinking and analytical skills, and problem-solving ability. Because police work can be dangerous and very stressful, a successful police officer should also possess excellent physical conditioning and emotional stability. A career as a police officer can be very rewarding. It takes an individual with a strong commitment and a special mix of knowledge, skills, and abilities to choose to become a police officer. The challenges of police work are extraordinary, but the satisfaction that one receives from serving the public can more than compensate.

## Traffic

Vehicular traffic direction is a second function performed by police officers. The police have been given the responsibility for the enforcement of traffic laws, the direction and control of traffic, the investigation of traffic accidents, and the assistance of motorists on the roadways.

Traffic enforcement involves the issuance of citations or warnings for moving and non-moving traffic violations, driver and vehicle licensing violations, and vehicle equipment violations.

The enforcement of traffic laws is usually the responsibility of the patrol officer. When the patrol officer is on routine preventive patrol and not responding to a call for service, observing motorists obeying traffic laws should be of high priority. Many police departments also create organized traffic units with the specific responsibility of traffic law enforcement.

© Paolo Bona/Shutterstock.com

Traffic direction is a function of the patrol officer.

Police officers are responsible for the direction and control of the flow of traffic at busy intersections, at scenes of emergencies such as traffic accidents, or during special community events when an increased number of vehicles can be expected. Parking enforcement is also a responsibility of many police departments that do not have a designated civilian parking enforcement unit.

The responsibility for the investigation of traffic accidents also belongs with the police officer. The police officer's role in accident investigation and reconstruction can affect both criminal and civil liability. A traffic accident may be due to negligence on the part of a motor vehicle operator, which can result in violations of traffic laws or more serious criminal charges such as drunk driving or even vehicular homicide. A police investigation of a traffic accident can also be used by automobile insurance companies to determine the operator who may have been at fault for the accident and affect the civil settlement for any losses as a result of the accident.

Police officers are sometimes called upon to assist motorists when they are on traffic patrol. This assistance may include providing directions to lost motorists, assisting stranded motorists whose vehicles have broken down on the roadway, or changing a flat tire for a motorist.

## Investigations

A third function of the police is to investigate criminal activity. The term *criminal investigation* usually conjures up a vision of a plainclothes detective. In reality, all police officers conduct investigations. Uniformed police officers who are called to domestic disputes investigate to determine if an arrest is warranted. At scenes of traffic accidents, these same officers investigate to determine if any traffic citations should be issued or other more serious charges filed.

### Criminal Investigation

**Criminal investigation** is defined as a lawful investigation to reconstruct the circumstances of an illegal act, determine or apprehend the guilty party, and assist the state's prosecution.

Generally, a criminal investigation process is divided into two separate parts. The **preliminary investigation** consists of evidence-gathering activities that are performed at the scene of a crime immediately after the crime was reported to or discovered by the police. The patrol officer is usually the first responder to a crime scene. This officer is responsible for assessing the situation; determining if a crime has, in fact, been committed; securing the scene; interviewing complainants, witnesses, and victims; making an arrest, if appropriate; arranging for crime scene assistance; and documenting the incident in a report.

If the police department in which the responding officer works does not have a detective unit, the officer will also be responsible for the second part of the criminal investigation. This is referred to as the **follow-up investigation**. The follow-up investigation is the continuation of the preliminary investigation in an attempt to

**Criminal investigation**
A lawful investigation to reconstruct the circumstances of an illegal act, determine or apprehend the guilty party, and assist with the state's prosecution.

**Preliminary investigation**
Evidence-gathering activities performed at the scene of a crime immediately after the crime was reported to or discovered by the police.

**Follow-up investigation**
Continuation of the preliminary investigation in an attempt to reconstruct the circumstances of a crime.

© NEstudio/Shutterstock.com

As part of the criminal investigation process, a police officer may take and analyze fingerprints from suspects.

reconstruct the circumstances of the crime. The results of the preliminary investigation are reviewed; crime scene evidence is analyzed; complainants, witnesses, or victims are re-interviewed; suspects are apprehended; and the prosecutor is assisted with the court case. In a police department that has a detective unit, the follow-up investigation is assigned to one of its detectives.

## Major Case Investigations

### Undercover Investigations

One of the most common forms of criminal investigation conducted by police departments is the undercover or covert investigation. Undercover operations involve the police while a criminal activity is in progress or prior to the crime actually being committed. These operations typically involve crimes such as drug trafficking, gambling, prostitution, and the buying and selling of stolen property.

Police investigators may operate undercover for short periods of time, referred to as **light cover**. A light cover investigation might involve using a male undercover officer to act as a "john" in an attempt to solicit prostitutes in the red light district of the community. In contrast, a **deep cover** operation may involve undercover investigators who infiltrate a criminal organization, gain their confidence, and spend a lengthy period of time gathering intelligence while preparing for major arrests within the organization.

**Light cover** Undercover police operations for a short period of time.

**Deep cover** Undercover police operations for a lengthy period of time.

Undercover operations can be extremely dangerous for police officers. Undercover investigators are often without any communication with fellow police officers, and if their true identity is discovered, it may lead to safety concerns for the officer. Miller (1987) found undercover police work to be extremely emotionally draining for officers and the risks to be greater as the undercover officer penetrates more deeply into an illicit activity. Miller also indicated a concern that undercover officers could be tempted to engage in entrapment, in which an otherwise innocent citizen is coaxed by police to commit a crime they had no intention of committing.[41]

### Terrorism Investigations

Following the September 11, 2001 attacks on the World Trade Center and the Pentagon, the prevention of terrorism has become an important focus of law enforcement in America. The primary responsibility for the war on terrorism has been given to federal law enforcement agencies. The creation of the Department of Homeland Security brought together several federal enforcement agencies to collaborate and share information and intelligence necessary to keep America safe.

The role of most state and local police departments is to assist in this effort by being better trained and equipped to respond to suspicious activity that might uncover a possible terrorist plot. Lyons (2002) wrote that the war on terrorism would place powerful pressure on local police to expand collaborative efforts with state and federal law enforcement agencies. Lyons stated that these efforts require increased information sharing, use of crime analysis, and the development of paramilitary task forces.[42] In addition, community-police partnerships should be encouraged in order to build trust within the community and gain their cooperation. O'Connell (2008) stated that the military and intelligence communities would not be able to succeed in our defense without active cooperation from local police departments that are well informed and well prepared, which requires training and financial support.[43]

## Tools of the Investigator

There have been a number of advances over recent decades that have assisted criminal investigators in bringing criminals to justice. The following are a few of these newer tools of the investigator.

**FIGURE 4.2** ADVANCES IN POLICE TECHNOLOGY IN THE 20TH CENTURY

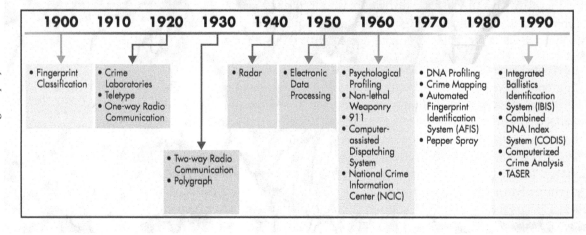

### DNA Profiling

The use of DNA profiling has revolutionized crime fighting and has led to both the conviction and exoneration of criminal defendants. The genetic profile that can be derived from blood, semen, hair, or other bodily substances collected at a crime scene can be matched with DNA samples taken from suspects, giving a high probability of guilt or innocence. DNA profiles can be used at murder scenes where a suspect's blood or tissue may have been left, or at rape scenes where a suspect's semen has been found.

The Combined DNA Index System (CODIS) is a DNA database maintained by the Federal Bureau of Investigation (FBI) that has a collection of samples from biological evidence found at crime scenes and samples from individuals who have been convicted of crimes in states throughout the country. DNA samples have typically been collected from convicted murderers and rapists, but more recently samples have also been taken from convicted burglars. In time, it is believed that DNA samples may be collected from all persons convicted of crimes. Some proponents of the use of the CODIS database would like samples to be taken from all individuals who have been charged with crimes. Just as "mug shots" and fingerprints are taken of arrestees during the booking process, proponents believe that DNA samples should also be collected. Berson (2009) reported that about 20 states and the federal government have already passed legislation requiring DNA collection upon arrest.[44]

---

**Critical Thinking**

Should DNA samples be collected from all arrestees, regardless of the criminal charges, for submission to the CODIS database during the booking process just as fingerprints and photographs are taken today?

---

## Crime Analysis and Mapping

**Crime analysis** involves a systematic collection and analysis of crime data used to support a police department's efforts in crime and disorder reduction and crime prevention. The study of police activities can provide data to analyze current crime trends, patterns, and series.

A related technological advancement to crime analysis is **crime mapping**. Crime mapping involves using geographic information systems to conduct spatial analysis and investigation of crime. Prior to the use of computers, police investigators identified a crime pattern by putting push pins on a map to indicate where crime was occurring. Crime mapping acts as a computerized "push pin" method of tracking crime. Geographic information system (GIS) software tools allow crime analysts to map crime in various ways, such as a simple point map or a three-dimensional visualization.

The more sophisticated computerized crime analysis and mapping systems can identify crime patterns much more rapidly. Many police departments have computerized report writing systems that give the crime analyst instantaneous access to the reports. If a crime pattern is occurring, it becomes apparent much sooner, allowing investigators to compare the evidence that they have gathered in each individual case to look for similarities that may tie the crimes to one offender or group of offenders.

Investigative and patrol units can both benefit from the use of crime analysis and mapping. For example, if it has been determined that a series of convenience store robberies are occurring and it is apparent that they are being committed by the same offender, both units can be positioned at a certain time of day or day of the week as well as a location where the offender is most likely to strike next.

**Crime analysis** A systematic collection and analysis of crime data used to support police efforts in crime and disorder reduction and crime prevention.

**Crime mapping** A process of using geographic information systems to conduct spatial analysis and investigation of crime.

Crime analysis also has other applications. It is being used as a tool to evaluate police department efficiency and effectiveness, crime clearance rates, and tracking of registered sexual offenders.

## Electronic Surveillance

Newer advances in electronic surveillance have greatly enhanced the abilities of police investigators to gather intelligence related to criminal activity. Law enforcement agencies are increasingly using surveillance technologies such as thermal imaging technology, closed circuit television, miniature voice transmitters and video cameras, voice and retinal scanning devices, and more. Still, the wiretap that is used to listen to conversations between persons suspected of crime is the most common electronic surveillance technique for the investigator.

With all of the sophisticated surveillance devices that are available, it is important that procedural safeguards are in place to ensure that citizens' rights against unreasonable searches and seizures are not violated and that a reasonable expectation of privacy is ensured. In *Kyllo v. United States* (2001), the United States Supreme Court addressed the issue of the use of thermal imaging devices by law enforcement. In this case, a federal agent used a thermal imaging device to scan the home of Danny Lee Kyllo, whom they suspected of harvesting marijuana, to determine whether heat emanating from the residence indicated the use of heat intensity lamps. When several relatively high levels of heat were found in areas of the home, agents secured a search warrant and found over 100 marijuana plants. Kyllo was arrested as a result of the use of the thermal imaging device as well as other evidence, and was subsequently convicted. His conviction was appealed based on the evidence gathered by use of the device. The Supreme Court sided with Kyllo, ruling that the warrantless use of thermal imaging technology aimed at a private home to detect the amount of heat within the home constituted an unlawful search and a violation of a citizen's expectation of privacy.[45]

© docent/Shutterstock.com

The use of thermal imaging can help build evidence in a case.

## Psychological Profiling

Psychological profiling has become a tool used by criminal investigators when they suspect that a series of similar crimes are occurring and the pattern seems to indicate the same offender is committing the crimes. Profiling uses major personality and behavioral characteristics of an individual determined by analyzing the series of crimes that have been committed.[46] Psychological profiling is most often used in unsolved cases involving serial murderers or serial rapists, and aids in the investigation by providing investigators with a profile of the characteristics of the probable offender that may be matched to a suspect in the case.

### Automated Fingerprint Identification System

The Automated Fingerprint Identification System (AFIS) is a computerized database system that stores thousands of sets of fingerprints and is used to match and identify latent prints found at crime scenes. This automated system has replaced the older method that required fingerprint examiners to sort through fingerprint cards by hand, which could take several months to review. The FBI has the largest AFIS database, with over 60 million prints on file. Many states have their own AFIS-like systems as well.

### Integrated Ballistics Identification System

The Integrated Ballistics Identification System (IBIS) is a computerized method to digitally compare images of ballistic evidence stored in a large database. When bullets are fired, unique marks can remain on the projectile and on the shell casing. Forensic firearms examiners can then link the projectile and the shell casing with a particular firearm and crime. The IBIS technology allows police investigators to match over 30,000 pieces of firearms evidence currently stored in the database.

## Special Police Functions

All police departments, regardless of size, employ patrol, traffic, and investigations functions. In a small department where it is necessary for all police officers to patrol the community, officers will be required to perform each function.

Other special police functions may include a canine unit, marine unit, aircraft unit, mounted unit, or SWAT team. *Canine units* are used for search and rescue efforts, drug enforcement, and building searches. Police officers may be assigned a canine that is trained to sniff out drugs, follow the trail of a missing or wanted person, or go into buildings or other structures in search of suspects. Marine units are employed by police departments that border lakes, rivers, and other waterways. *Marine unit* officers will enforce vessel safety regulations and investigate cases of drunk operation of vessels. Police departments deploy *aircraft units* for traffic enforcement and searches for missing

Mounted patrol units are often used for crowd control at community events.

and wanted persons. Aircraft units are very expensive to maintain, but can prove invaluable as air support for police officers on the ground. *Mounted units* can be used for crowd control. Mounted patrols are also useful for conducting search and rescue missions in undeveloped areas and natural terrain.

The SWAT team is specially trained to perform in high-risk situations such as barricaded suspect incidents, hostage rescues, and counterterrorism operations. As a result of the Posse Comitatus Act of 1878, the four branches of the military—with the exception of the United States Coast Guard and National Guard units—are not permitted to participate in domestic law enforcement. The military services have served as an auxiliary to law enforcement in drug interdiction and illegal immigration activities and, more recently, to combat domestic terrorism, but the responsibility for dealing with police issues that require a paramilitary presence has been left to SWAT teams.

## Changing Philosophy of Policing

During most of the 20th century, in a period known as the Reform Era, policing in America adopted a professional model that closely resembled the philosophy popular in business and the military. In a historical study of the evolution of policing, Kelling and Moore (1988) viewed it through the framework of a corporate strategy. The authors wrote that the organizational form adopted by police reformers reflected the scientific theory of administration developed by Frederick W. Taylor.[47] This professional model of policing encouraged efficiency, task specialization, chain of command, and written orders and directives. Police officers were expected to respond to calls for service in a timely manner, handle their calls for service as quickly as possible, and return to patrolling the community. Any interaction between the police and the public beyond addressing the reason for the call to police was discouraged because it was assumed that any relationship that might develop could lead to favoritism and corruption.

The turmoil in the 1960s as a result of the Civil Rights Movement and opposition to the Vietnam War led to increased disorder in America. The public viewed nightly news reports depicting the police attempting to quell protests and riots by use of shields and batons. As the crime rate rose steadily over the next two decades, the relationship between the police and the public continued to decline. The public lost trust in the police to solve the crime problem and were angered by what they perceived as an increased use of physical force. Ponsaers (2002) stated the public no longer felt confident that the police could solve their problems. This led many, particularly minority groups, to feel alienated from the police.[48]

Police departments began to implement police-community relations programs in an attempt to heal the strained relationship. Unfortunately, these programs were viewed as little more than "window dressing" and failed to satisfy the community. Kreps and Weller (1973) wrote that the most important factor that led to the expansion of existing community relations programs and the rapid adoption of new programs was the series of urban civil disturbances in the late 1960s. The authors cited a study conducted at Michigan State University in 1967 that found community relations objectives were both ambitious and ambiguous and program goals were too abstract to put into concrete practice. The study also found the public to be suspicious of the conveniently timed adoption of those programs and questioned police motives and sincerity.[49] It began to become apparent that the professional model of policing might have outlived its usefulness. A newer philosophy of policing the community that would foster a partnership between the police and the public was needed to create a safe and secure environment in order to achieve a higher quality of life.[50] The time was right for the implementation of community policing.

## Community Policing

Community policing encourages a partnership between the public and the police for the purpose of working together to identify, prioritize, and solve problems within the community.[51] It is the intent of community policing to deal with the problems of crime and disorder, community decay, and the fear of crime in order to improve the quality of life for community residents.

**Broken windows theory**
A theory involving crime and disorder that states that if a community is allowed to physically deteriorate, an impression will be given that no one cares, causing crime to occur.

The foundation for the implementation of the community policing philosophy was influenced by the **broken windows theory** introduced by James Q. Wilson and George Kelling (1982). Wilson and Kelling argued that when a window is broken in a building and it is not quickly repaired, more windows will likely be broken. The authors theorized that if the community is apathetic toward the destruction occurring within their neighborhoods, they are sending a message to criminals that they can assume control over the neighborhood. In time, as one broken window leads to another, the neighborhood will succumb to physical decay and disorder. Wilson and Kelling believed that police should consider dealing with both minor and major crimes instead of just the more serious crime problems. Concentrated efforts on minor crimes such as vandalism, public drunkenness, and panhandling will help the public begin to feel safer in their neighborhoods. With a reduced fear of crime, citizens begin to develop a feeling of pride and eventually retake ownership of their neighborhoods.[52]

© brackish_nz/Shutterstock.com

The broken windows theory holds that when a community is apathetic toward destruction in their neighborhoods, they are sending a message to criminals that they can assume control over the neighborhood.

Gaines and Kappeler (2009) suggested that one of the two major components of community policing was to develop a relationship with the residents of the community.[53] The police understood that for community policing to truly succeed, cooperation with community residents was imperative. In order to achieve this success, community policing officers were assigned to each neighborhood to forge these partnerships and then work together with residents to address their concerns.

One important result of a partnership between the police and the public is the trust that can develop. The police cannot succeed without the assistance of the public, especially when it comes to solving crime. The public can be the eyes and ears of the police in the community. Police need the public to come forward when they are aware of crimes occurring and who may be committing them. Unfortunately, some community residents pressure other residents not to inform or "snitch" on lawbreakers. This "stop snitching" movement has even found its way into pop culture. Masten (2009) wrote that as a result of a cultural campaign spawned by rap music and clothing, many teens and young adults were refusing to speak to the police even when they had witnessed violent crimes. Masten saw this "stop snitching" phenomenon as part of a deeply rooted distrust toward the police, posing a potential hindrance to America's criminal justice system. The author suggested that police must repair the decades of mistrust built up between the public and the police in order to make the "stop snitching" code less attractive to follow.[54]

The second major component of community policing, as defined by Gaines and Kappeler (2009), is problem solving.[55] Traditionally, when police have responded to calls for service, they have dealt with the incident, but not necessarily with the underlying problem that led to the call. Herman Goldstein (1979) first proposed **problem-oriented policing** to address the concerns of the public. A problem-oriented or problem-solving approach emphasizes identifying a problem, exploring alternatives to deal with the problem, weighing the merits of each alternative, and, finally, implementing the best alternative to solve the problem.[56]

**Problem-oriented policing** An approach to policing in which the underlying causes of crime are identified and addressed.

A problem-solving approach to dealing with community concerns requires both creativity and commitment on the part of the police department. The police and the public must be in agreement regarding the problems in the neighborhood that should be addressed. Cooperation may also be required from other stakeholders in the community, such as business leaders, elected officials, and other public and private agencies that serve the community.

Although some police administrators may claim otherwise, the practice of community policing seems to be waning. Federal funding for community policing efforts, which was once in abundance, has all but dried up. In 2010, the Office of Community Oriented Policing Services (COPS) allocated approximately $600 million to assist law enforcement agencies in their community policing initiatives. That amount of funding is a far cry from the $11 billion that had been allocated at the height of the trend, and thus the decline of the practice may be due more to the funding drying up than to the failure of the philosophy. A study by Zhao, Scheider, and Thurman (2002) found that funding community policing had a positive effect.

The authors examined COPS Office grants awarded between 1994 and 1998 and their effects on crime rates in 6,100 cities in the United States, and their results indicated that funding to medium and large cities had been effective at reducing violent and property crime. Additionally, innovative programs that targeted special crime problems or locations were found to be a most effective contributor to crime reduction.[57]

Still, because federal funding has decreased, many police departments that once displayed an agency-wide commitment to community policing have now resorted to smaller units that operate on an as-needed basis, while some departments have totally abandoned the philosophy, returning to the more traditional incident-based policing.

## Intelligence-Led Policing

The latest movement in policing is the use of crime data analysis to influence decision making. **Intelligence-led policing** uses a business model in which data analysis and criminal intelligence are used to facilitate crime reduction, crime prevention, and enforcement strategies that target the most serious offenders.[58]

**Intelligence-led policing** A business model in which data analysis and criminal intelligence are used to facilitate crime reduction, crime prevention, and enforcement strategies that target the most serious offenders.

The move toward an intelligence-led policing model may be a natural progression in policing from the community policing and problem-oriented models. Both community policing and problem-oriented policing require data collection and crime analysis in order to solve crime problems, although not nearly to the extent that intelligence-led policing utilizes data.

One of the first examples of the use of a data-driven method for determining crime problems took place in the 1990s in New York City.[59] The New York City Police Department became known for the implementation of the COMPSTAT program. **COMPSTAT** is a managerial system that uses criminal intelligence that identifies crime problems and then determines a crime reduction strategy. The system provided timely and accurate intelligence that indicated "hot spots" of crime that police officers were expected to eliminate. Police administrators were then held accountable for the implementation of the reduction strategy and a subsequent reduction in crime. Crime was reduced dramatically in the city, although arguments persist over whether the COMPSTAT program was the primary reason for the reduction. Zimring (2011) credited the COMPSTAT program in New York City with being instrumental in the compilation of data on serious crime that led to police emphasis on "hot spots," drug interdiction, and an aggressive program of street stops and misdemeanor arrests. Zimring also praised the city of New York for choosing not to implement a "broken windows" strategy, which he believed would have concentrated precious resources in marginal neighborhoods rather than neighborhoods with the highest crime rates.[60]

**COMPSTAT** A managerial system that uses criminal intelligence to identify crime problems and determine a crime reduction strategy.

The intelligence-led policing model and its use of crime analysis can provide the foundation for crime prevention and reduction and decisions for directing police resources.

# Challenges for Police Officers

The nature of police work can place great demands on the police officer. Police officers are often called upon to make split-second decisions that sometimes involve use of physical force or even deadly force. The ever present dangers that police officers face can come from many different sources. Every day, police officers risk being killed in the line of duty while serving warrants, conducting traffic stops, responding to domestic violence calls, or interviewing suspicious persons.

Besides the dangers that the job brings, police officers are required to witness the worst that society can offer. The police must investigate the most gruesome suicide or homicide scenes, respond to abuse cases where children may have been physically or sexually assaulted, and reconstruct traffic accidents in which several members of a family may have been killed.

The challenges that police officers face play a part in how they come to view themselves, the public, and their jobs. This can lead to a unique subculture within the police profession, a stress level that is often greater than what is found in other professions, and a temptation toward corruption if they stray from expected ethical and professional boundaries.

## The Police Subculture

Every profession has its own set of values and behavioral patterns that are unique to members of the profession. The police subculture is a product of the responsibilities of the job along with the effects that can result from having carried out these responsibilities. Common attitudes in the police subculture include authoritarianism, cynicism, and solidarity.

### Authoritarianism

Police officers possess a unique power that is not afforded to most professions. The police have the right to arrest individuals, search persons or their belongings, and seize evidence from people. In order to perform these authoritarian duties, police officers are guided by both legal guidelines and their departmental policies. For example, under case law, a police officer who stops a suspicious person may not conduct a warrantless search of the suspect without probable cause to do so.

Additionally, police have the right to use physical force, including deadly force. The police are permitted to utilize physical force when necessary to effect an arrest, although a police officer may be held criminally or civilly liable if the amount of force used is considered to be excessive. Probably the most awesome power that the police officer has is to use deadly force. Of course, this power to use deadly force also comes with responsibility. Deadly force must be the last resort for the police officer.

In the past, police officers only had the baton and the handgun to subdue suspects. In more recent years, new weapons technology has led to the development of nonlethal weapons. Weapons such as rubber bullets and beanbag projectiles have allowed officers to neutralize potentially deadly situations without having to resort to deadly force. The most common type of nonlethal weapon used today by police officers is the Taser technology that sends an incapacitating electric shock to the individual that it strikes.

An important concern regarding police authoritarianism is the abuse of this power. The police must ensure that the rights of citizens are not violated when they engage in arrests, searches, or seizures. They must not use **excessive force**, but only a level of force necessary to effect an arrest or to protect themselves or others from bodily harm. Bohrer and Chaney (2010) wrote that the public's perceptions of police officers involved in shootings are wide and diverse. They point out that while some members of the public believe that if the police shoot someone, the individual probably gave police no choice, many members of the public are quick to assume the police acted inappropriately.[61] Police officers who exceed the authority they have been granted can jeopardize the community's perception of their police department as well as the entire police profession.

**Excessive force**
An amount of physical force beyond that which is necessary to control a suspect.

## Cynicism

Cynicism is a mistrust of human nature and motives. The nature of police work requires that officers view citizens with suspicion. The police interview individuals who will often lie to them. They approach individuals who may be dangerous. Police officers are trained on how to cautiously approach the public on the streets, during traffic stops, or when entering a residence. They are trained to uncover a suspect's lies in order to reach the truth. Through their experience, they can often sense that a suspicious person fits a particular type of individual who may be dangerous. This **symbolic assailant** is an individual whose dress and gestures indicate to the experienced police officer that this person is up to no good.

**Symbolic assailant**
An individual whose dress, behavior, and gestures indicate suspicion and possible danger to a police officer.

Neiderhoffer (1969) conducted a classic study of police cynicism in the New York City Police Department. The study found that cynicism among police officers developed as early as the police academy, when recruits were taught about the ignorance of the public

© somsak suwanput/Shutterstock.com

Police officers may have to use physical force to arrest uncooperative suspects or to protect themselves or others from bodily harm.

and the superiority of the police. Cynicism initially increased sharply and then at a slower rate between years two and six of the police officer's career. After year six, cynicism decreased and leveled off over the remainder of a career.[62]

The unfortunate consequence of police cynicism is that it can cross over into an officer's personal relationships with family and friends. The suspicions that police officers have about people's behaviors and actions may lead them to believe that all people, including those closest to them, should be viewed with suspicion and not be trusted.

## *Solidarity*

The third component of the police subculture is solidarity. Police officers develop a strong connection with other members of the profession. Officers must depend upon their partners for backup and protection. Along with their cynicism and mistrust of the public, this solidarity within the ranks causes an "us versus them" mentality. Police officers close their ranks and insulate themselves from others. Just as cynicism can lead to mistrust of family and friends, police solidarity can lead police officers to become isolated from their relationships outside of the profession.

**Blue code of silence**
The unwritten code of protection among police officers.

One unfortunate result of police solidarity is known as the **blue code of silence**. This is a code of protection among police officers in which they do not report activities of fellow officers that could violate department policy or the law. Police solidarity may be so ingrained within the profession that police officers may be more likely to protect corruption within their ranks—jeopardizing their own careers—than to report corrupt fellow officers.

> **Critical Thinking**
> How can the blue code of silence be eliminated so honest police officers are willing to report dishonest officers?

## Police Discretion

**Discretion** The autonomy a police officer has to choose from a variety of courses of action in various situations.

**Discretion** is defined as a police officer's autonomy to choose from a variety of courses of action in various situations. Alpert, MacDonald, and Dunham (2005) stated that an officer's discretion to choose a course of action such as stopping a citizen usually begins when the officer observes the person appearing suspicious or violating the law.[63] Probably the most common example of the use of police discretion involves traffic stops. Police officers use their discretionary power to determine if a motorist who has been stopped for a traffic violation should be given a warning or issued a citation.

The patrol officer may exercise the greatest discretionary power in the police department. Officers who are on patrol are usually out of the sight of their supervisors. Walker (1993) wrote that most police-citizen encounters occur without outside supervision, which gives the police officer a great deal of discretion.[64] They have the discretion to stop a vehicle operator for a traffic violation in the first place. They have the discretion to stop a suspicious person on the street to conduct a field interrogation. When dispatched to a loud music call, the patrol officer may have the discretion to charge the resident with the appropriate offense or simply order them to turn the music down.

In some instances, police discretion can be controlled and limited. The National Research Council (2003) found that the most important factors associated with police officers' decisions to use their legal authority included the influence of the police organization, legal factors related to the severity of the crime, and the strength of the evidence.[65] The police department may influence the level of discretion that officers have. For example, as discussed earlier in this chapter, the department may have developed a written policy that limits vehicle pursuits. Department-written policies and procedures are often used to control police officers' behavior. At times, special orders may also temporarily limit police discretion. The police chief may have learned that the number of traffic accidents at a particular intersection has increased, and may order all patrol officers to issue citations to any vehicle operator who is observed committing any traffic violation at the intersection, no matter how minor. Even peer pressure among officers within the department may affect police discretion: veteran officers may chastise the newest officer in the department who is giving too many traffic citations to community residents. Alpert, MacDonald, and Dunham (2005) found that officers employed in a police department that emphasized a service approach were less likely to arrest offenders for low-level crimes than officers from a department practicing a legalistic style of policing.[66]

Legislatures can also limit police discretion. State legislatures and local municipalities enact statutes or ordinances. A local community may pass an ordinance that makes it illegal to panhandle on the roadways. The police department may have previously turned a blind eye to the panhandlers, even though they were well aware that many of them were homeless and could be charged with a vagrancy statute violation, but now their discretion will be influenced by this new ordinance.

An example of legislation influencing police discretion occurred as a result of the Minneapolis Domestic Violence Experiment.[67] Historically, the police have used three methods to resolve domestic violence calls: mediate the dispute and leave the partners together, separate the partners by asking one of them to leave the residence for a "cooling off" period, or arrest one of the partners. In the experiment, police were told to either arrest, separate, or mediate incidents on the basis of a random selection. The results of the experiment indicated that those persons who were arrested in the incident were half as likely to reoffend against the victim. These results led many state legislatures across the country to enact mandatory arrest policies for domestic violence perpetrators when an injury to the victim was observed by the police. These new domestic violence laws greatly inhibited police officers' discretion in responding to domestic violence calls. An interesting side note to the results of this landmark experiment was that when similar studies were later conducted, the results did not confirm that arrest was the most effective way to handle domestic violence interventions.

Finally, our courts can also limit police discretion. Decisions made by courts can take away options that police officers may have to deal with criminals on the streets. For example, patrol officers have a limited number of options when they want to conduct warrantless searches of persons, property, and vehicles because the courts have restricted their actions in order to protect the constitutional rights of citizens.

### Additional Factors Affecting Police Discretion

There are a number of factors that can affect a police officer's use of discretion. The seriousness of the crime determines if the police will pursue a case more or less vigorously. Homicide cases are usually investigated with vigor, while a minor neighborhood dispute may not be. The strength of evidence in a case may also affect the extent to which police investigate a crime. Initially, the homicide case will receive strict attention, but once the trail of the killer goes cold, police may have no choice but to move on to other cases.

The nature of the individuals involved in a police encounter may factor into police discretion. The relationship between an offender and the victim may affect the decisions that the police officer makes. For example, in a reported theft case involving two ex-lovers who had lived together, in which the accused was removing some items from the residence that he believed were his property, police officers might choose not to make an arrest. Conversely, a victim who is intent on the offender being arrested may exert influence on police to make the arrest against their better judgment. Police may use the demeanor of an individual as a factor to determine the course of action. A polite and respectful traffic violator may be less likely to receive a citation than an angry and verbally abusive motorist. Sometimes, race, gender, or the income of an individual can play a role in a police officer's decision making. This behavior may be inappropriate, but unfortunately it does sometimes occur. A young male motorist might be more likely to be cited than a young female. An African-American male walking on the streets of a community at 3:00 in the morning may be more likely to be stopped and questioned than a white male, and an affluent resident who complains about juveniles running through his upscale neighborhood may receive more appropriate police action than a long-haired and tattooed trailer park resident making a similar complaint. The National Research Council (2003) found that individual variables such as age, race, social class, or demeanor of a suspect play a minor role in a police officer's decision making.[68] In contrast, Sun and Payne (2004) reported that race is the most important individual factor in police-citizen interactions.[69] Although the research may be mixed, it is important to consider the possible influence of individual variables on the police officer's use of discretion.

# Police Job Stress

Stress can be found to some extent within every vocation and in people's everyday lives. However, Dantzer (1987) stated that law enforcement ranks among the top five most stressful occupations in the world.[70] Police stress is somewhat unique as a result of the nature of the police officer's job. The danger that officers can face, along with the horrors of society that they often witness, can take a great toll on their emotional and physical well-being.

## Sources of Police Stress

For the police officer, there are a number of different sources of stress. One is the physical danger that officers face as an inherent part of the job.[71] It is understandable that one major stressful event can affect a police officer. For example, a use of deadly force situation involving police officers can cause great stress. Shootings in which police officers may see a fellow officer killed or be wounded themselves are very stressful events that can leave lasting emotional scars. When a police officer must use deadly force against a suspect, the officer may find it difficult to deal with afterwards.

However, most police officers will not be involved in events like those just described during their careers. Most stress for the typical officer comes from the continued response to daily calls for service. Responding to calls where they see physical injuries as a result of domestic or child abuse or deadly motor vehicle crashes can leave lasting impressions on a police officer. Even the most routine calls can produce low-grade stressors that, over time, can cause stress for the police officer.

Police stress is sometimes caused by grisly or horrible crime scenes that officers must investigate.

© Prath/Shutterstock.com

The police organization is a second source of stress for police officers. Anderson, Litzenberger, and Plecas (2002) found that within the organizational structure, issues such as lack of group cohesiveness, lack of support from supervisors, and lack of opportunities for promotion make law enforcement an especially stressful job.[72] Police officers usually work in a quasi-military bureaucracy where they have little input into the decision making. They sometimes observe a lack of administrative support and petty department politics. Police officers often view their job as one with inadequate pay and benefits, work schedules that include shift work, weekends, and most holidays, and sometimes periods of monotony and boredom.

A third source of stress for police officers can result from their own personal behaviors. Police officers often develop poor eating habits while on duty as a result of the emergency nature of their job. It can be easy to stop by a fast-food drive-through for a quick lunch between calls for service. Shift work can also affect proper eating habits and lead to fatigue. If the police officer does not eat properly and exercise regularly, poor health can result.

The effects of police stress can be both psychological and physical.[73,74] Stress has been linked to physical disorders such as high blood pressure, ulcers, and heart disease. More common for some police officers is the emotional toll of police stress. The police profession has a high rate of alcoholism, drug abuse, marital problems, and suicide. More police officers commit suicide each year than are killed in the line of duty.

Stress can also affect a police officer's productivity on the job. An officer who has withdrawn from his or her work can become complacent, have lower morale, and feel indifferent toward the job and fellow officers. Post-traumatic stress disorder (PTSD), which is most associated with military personnel, also affects some police officers who have witnessed combat-like situations such as shootings. PTSD can manifest itself in memory loss, loss of concentration, bouts of depression, impulsivity, or anxiety, and can cause recurring nightmares and flashbacks.

## *Management of Police Stress*

Police organizations and each individual police officer within the profession can find ways to manage and reduce stress. Atkinson (2004) stated that stress can be managed by identifying specific strategies in the areas of nutrition, exercise, sleep, and relaxation.[75] Every police officer should be aware of the sources of stress and the effects stress can have. By maintaining a healthy diet and engaging in regular exercise, police officers can do their part to reduce their stress. Family and spiritual support has also been found to be helpful.

Each police department must address police stress by emphasizing stress awareness. Frequent stress reduction training courses should be offered. Support systems such as mental health programs and critical incident stress debriefing teams should also be implemented to assist officers in need of professional assistance.

# Police Ethics

Ethics involves the moral choices that individuals must make regarding good and bad conduct. The social contract that the public has with its government to provide for its safety and security comes with the expectation that those who are asked to provide that protection maintain high standards of ethics, professionalism, and integrity. Generally, the public expects police officers to exhibit even higher standards of behavior than the general population. A lack of ethical behavior on the part of a police officer can lead to corruption. Whenever officers misuse the authority they have been given, they are engaging in some form of corruption.

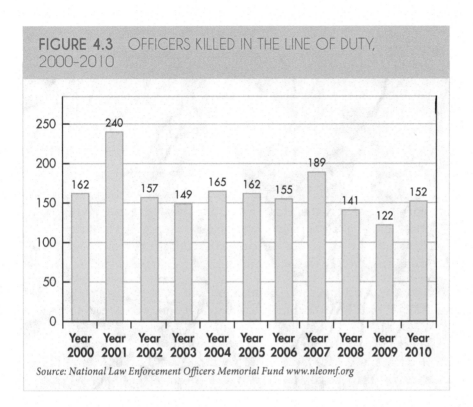

**FIGURE 4.3** OFFICERS KILLED IN THE LINE OF DUTY, 2000–2010

Source: National Law Enforcement Officers Memorial Fund www.nleomf.org

## Forms of Police Corruption

Police corruption may involve unethical acts that violate department policy or illegal acts that violate the law. Corruption within policing may be department-wide, where all members are engaged in corrupt acts or at least aware that they are occurring and turning a blind eye to them. On the other hand, it is more common that individual officers may be engaged in corrupt acts unbeknownst to others in the police department except the corrupt officers' closest confidants. The more common examples of police corruption include the following.

- **Bribery or Extortion**—Accepting offers of cash or gifts from citizens in the form of a bribe for not enforcing laws against them, or demanding remuneration in the form of cash or gifts as a form of extortion for not enforcing the law against citizens.
- **Theft**—Planning burglaries and thefts on or off duty, or taking items of value from scenes of crimes that officers are called to investigate.
- **Alcohol or Drug Abuse**—Consuming alcoholic beverages or taking illegal drugs while on duty or off duty in violation of department policy or the law.
- **Goldbricking**—Avoiding work when on duty by not responding to calls for service, engaging in private business, or sleeping on duty.
- **Gratuities**—Accepting or demanding free or discounted items such as coffee, meals, or entertainment tickets, which may or may not be in return for favorable treatment for the giver at a future time.
- **Sexual Misconduct**—Engaging in sexual acts while on duty, exchanging favors for sex, or sexually harassing coworkers.

There is nothing that shakes the public's confidence in police more than learning that the police have engaged in acts of corruption. Weitzer (2002) found that incidents of police misconduct have a pronounced effect on public opinion, particularly when they involve highly publicized events.[76] Walker (1992) stated that corruption can be controlled with effort from law enforcement, but this requires each police department to take a proactive approach to reducing and controlling it.[77]

Several researchers have suggested ways in which corruption can be controlled.[78,79,80] First, it is important that during the recruitment and selection process, police departments set high standards for police officer candidates and have methods in place to determine the ethical and professional values of the individuals they choose to hire.

Additionally, each police department should have written policies that define what constitutes corrupt acts and a disciplinary apparatus that spells out the actions that will be taken against officers violating established policies. Each police department should require periodic ethics training classes for all officers. A police officers' code of ethics should be prominently placed in the department as a constant reminder to all officers that they have sworn an oath to perform their duties both ethically and professionally.

---

**Exhibit: Law Enforcement Code of Ethics from International Chiefs of Police[81]**

Ethics and Professionalism: Blue Code of Silence

On August 9, 1997, a 30-year-old Haitian immigrant by the name of Abner Louima was arrested by New York City Police Department officers following a disturbance outside a Brooklyn nightclub. While being held at the 70th Precinct stationhouse, Louima was brutalized in the precinct bathroom. He was held down by one officer while the other officer shoved a wooden toilet plunger handle into his rectum and then thrust it into his face. The police officer who assaulted Louima mistakenly believed that he had punched the officer in the head during a street brawl outside the club.

It was reported that several NYPD officers either participated in the assault or witnessed it. After hearing of the incident, then Mayor Rudy Giuliani and Police Commissioner Howard Safir insisted the case would prove that the "blue code of silence" did not exist. The case included allegations of perjury and ultimately resulted in convictions of four police officers—three of which were later overturned on appeal.

Does the "blue code of silence" still exist in policing, all these years after the Louima case? What would cause a police officer to engage in such violent behavior against a suspect? How could other officers look on and allow this to happen without stepping in to stop it? Why would these officers all choose to lie and cover up the incident?

---

Police departments should also have an internal affairs unit that investigates alleged unethical or illegal activities involving police officers. External investigations or reviews by citizen review boards, special investigators or prosecutors, and the courts should be used to ferret out police misconduct when necessary.

Finally, the responsibility for ending police corruption belongs with each individual police officer. One way that can be accomplished is for officers to resist the pressure to adhere to the blue code of silence. Instead, honest police officers should see it as their duty to rid the law enforcement profession of corrupt officers by reporting any unethical or illegal behaviors that they observe.

## Chapter Summary

- The roles police officers assume are based on the issues and problems that are unique to each community. The police officer's role can be vague and ambiguous because the expectations of police administrators, local political leaders, the public, and police officers themselves can conflict. Role conflict results from what police may prefer to do versus what they are expected to do.

- The duties performed by police officers are multidimensional and dependent on community needs. Generally, these duties include law enforcement, order maintenance, crime prevention, and providing service. Enforcing the law is considered to be the primary responsibility of police. Police often act as peacekeepers and maintain order in the community, which may or may not involve dealing with criminal activity. The mere presence of police in the community serves as an important way to prevent crime from occurring in the first place.

- The most common functions performed by police departments include patrol, traffic, and investigations. Routine preventive patrol is the most common form of patrol, but police departments will also use special patrol methods such as directed patrols, foot patrols, aggressive patrols, and saturation patrols. The traffic function includes traffic enforcement, control and direction, accident investigation, and assistance to motorists. Types of police investigations include preliminary investigations, follow-up investigations, and undercover investigations. Advances in technology have provided criminal investigators with a variety of new tools to fight crime. Larger police departments may employ more specialized functions such as canine, marine, aircraft, mounted, and SWAT units.

- The community policing philosophy attempted to encourage a partnership between the public and the police for the purpose of working together to identify, prioritize, and solve community problems. As community policing began to fall out of favor, it was replaced by movement toward an intelligence-led policing philosophy, which emphasizes the use of data analysis and criminal intelligence to facilitate crime reduction, crime prevention, and enforcement strategies that target the most serious offenders.

- The nature of police work puts great demands on the police officer. While every profession has its own set of values and behavioral patterns among its members, the police subculture is quite unique with a composition that includes authoritarianism, cynicism, and solidarity.

- Police officers can suffer from job stress that can come from a variety of sources. Many police officers experience stress resulting from continued responses to daily calls for service. Police stress can also result from the police organization and from an officer's own personal behaviors. Police stress can lead to both psychological and physical problems. Police departments can assist officers in dealing with the problem of stress by offering programs that help to manage stress.

- Police ethics involves the moral choices that police officers make regarding good and bad conduct. Corruption within the police profession occurs when police officers misuse their authority for personal gain. Police corruption can be controlled by use of high selection standards, written policies regarding corruption, internal and external investigation of alleged corruption, ethics training classes, and a code of ethics, as well as dismantling the blue code of silence.

## Critical Thinking?

1. Should electronic devices known as "red light cameras" be used to catch traffic violators running red lights at intersections?

2. Should police officers be permitted to accept gratuities such as a free cup of coffee or a half-price meal when on duty?

3. Among the various methods of patrol, which do you believe works the best to prevent crime and apprehend criminals?

4. What can be done to keep police officers safe on the streets and reduce the number of officers killed in the line of duty?

5. How might police departments eliminate corruption within the ranks of the police?

6. Can you imagine a situation in which it would be acceptable to repeal the Posse Comitatus Act?

7. Explain why you would be in favor of or against giving up some of your individual rights under the Constitution to allow law enforcement to conduct searches and seizures of your personal property without probable cause.

8. Based on the results of the Kansas City Preventive Patrol Experiment, do you believe that police should still conduct routine random patrols throughout the community?

9. Is it a good idea for police officers to be allowed to use discretion in the performance of their duties? Why or why not?

10. When the police conduct an undercover operation in which female police officers are placed in an area known to be frequented by prostitutes and their customers, are they actually encouraging criminal behavior?

## Media

**Law Enforcement News:** www.officer.com
This website provides information on current events in policing and police officer news around the United States.

**Bureau of Justice Statistics:** http://bjs.ojp.usdoj.gov/
The Bureau of Justice Statistics provides comprehensive data on reported criminal activity throughout the country, including frequency of crime and criminal characteristics.

**Franklin Zimring Interview:** http://www.youtube.com/watch?v=EXZgSnKfN5U
In this interview, criminologist Franklin Zimring discusses how New York City dramatically reduced its crime rate.

## (Endnotes)

[1]   Seneviratne, M. (2002). "Ombudsmen and Police Complaints." *The Journal of Social Welfare & Family Law*, 24(2), 195–215.

[2]   Hunter, A. (1985). "Private, Parochial, and Public Social Orders: The Problem of Crime and Incivility in Urban Communities." In G. Suttles & M. Zald (Eds.), *The Challenge of Social Control*. Norwood, NJ: Ablex.

[3]   Klockars, C. B. (1985). *The Idea of Police. Beverly Hills*, CA: Sage.

[4]   Dunham, R. G., & Alpert, G. P. (2010). *Critical Issues in Policing*. Prospect Heights, IL: Waveland Press.

[5]   Reiman, J. (1985). "The Social Contract and the Police Use of Deadly Force." In F. A. Ellison & M. Feldberg (Eds.), *Moral Issues in Police Work*. Savage, MD: Rowman & Littlefield.

[6]   *Mapp v. Ohio*, 367 U.S. 643, 655 (1961).

[7]   Stuntz, W. J. (1997). "The Virtues and Vices of the Exclusionary Rule." *Harvard Journal of Law and Public Policy, 20*(2), 443–455.

[8]   Keenan, J. F. (1998). "The Proper Balance: Exclusion of Evidence or Expulsion of Police Officers." *St. John's Law Review, 72*(3/4), 1376–1384.

[9]   *Terry v. Ohio*, 392 U.S. 1 (1968).

[10]  *Tennessee v. Garner*, 471 U.S. 1 (1985).

[11]  Walker, S., & Fridell, L. (1992). "Forces of Change in Police Policy: The Impact of *Tennessee v. Garner*." *American Journal of Police, 11*(3), 97–112.

[12]  Fyfe, J. J. (1986). "The Split-Second Syndrome and Other Determinants of Police Violence." In A. Campbell & J. Gibbs (Eds.), *Violent Transactions*. New York, NY: Blackwell.

[13]     G. P. (1993). "The Management of Police Pursuit Driving." In W. G. Bailey (Ed.), *The Encyclopedia of Police Science*. New York, NY: Garland.

[14]     Hicks, W. L. (2006). "Police Vehicular Pursuits: A Descriptive Analysis of the State Agencies' Written Policy." *Policing, 29*(1), 106–124.

[15]     Payne, D. M. (1997). "Michigan Emergency Response Study—Phase III. Implications of the Failure to Report Pursuits and Inaccurate Accident Reporting: A Research Note." *Policing, 20*(2), 256–269.

[16]     Weitzer, R., & Tuch, S. A. (2005). "Racially Biased Policing: Determinants of Citizen Perceptions." *Social Forces, 83*(3), 1009–1030.

[17]     Bureau of Justice Statistics. (2001). *Contacts Between Police and the Public: Findings From the 1999 National Survey*. Washington, DC: U.S. Department of Justice.

[18]     Harris, D. (1997). "Driving While Black and Other Traffic Offenses: The Supreme Court and Pretextual Traffic Stops." *Journal of Criminal Law and Criminology, 87*, 544–582.

[19]     Bureau of Justice Statistics, 2001.

[20]     Brown, R. A. (2005). "Black, White and Unequal: Examining Situational Determinants of Arrest Decisions from Police-Suspect Encounters." *Criminal Justice Studies, 18*(1), 151–168.

[21]     Visher, C. A., & Weisburd, D. (1998). "Identifying What Works: Recent Trends in Crime Prevention Strategies." *Crime, Law & Social Change, 28*, 223–242.

[22]     Kennedy, L. W. (2002). "Issues in Managing Citizens' Calls to the Police." *Criminology & Public Policy, 2*(1), 125–128.

[23]     Silver, E. E., & Miller, L. L. (2004). "Sources of Informal Social Control in Chicago Neighborhoods." *Criminology, 42*(3), 551–583.

[24]     Reisig, M. D., & Parks, R. B. (2004). "Can Community Policing Help the Truly Disadvantaged?" *Crime & Delinquency, 50*(2), 139–167.

[25]     Silver & Miller, 2004.

[26]     Wilson, J. (1968). *Varieties of Police Behavior*. Cambridge, MA: Harvard University Press.

[27]     Broderick, J. J. (1987). *Police in a Time of Change*. Prospect Heights, IL: Waveland Press.

[28]     Muir, W. K. (1977). *Police: Street Corner Politicians*. Chicago, IL: University of Chicago Press.

[29]     Adams, T. F. (2006). *Police Field Operations*. Upper Saddle River, NJ: Prentice Hall.

[30]     Kelling, G. L. (1974). *The Kansas City Preventive Patrol Experiment: A Summary Report*. Washington, DC: Police Foundation.

[31]     Weisburd, D., Maher, L., & Sherman, L. (1992). "Contrasting Crime General and Crime Specific Theory: The Case of Hot-Spots of Crime." *Advances in Criminological Theory, 4*, 45–70.

[32]     Sherman, L., & Weisburd, D. (1995). "General Deterrent Effects of Police Patrol in Crime 'Hot-Spots': A Randomized Controlled Trial." *Justice Quarterly, 12*, 626–648.

33   Weisburd, D., & Green, L. (1995). "Policing Drug Hot-Spots: The Jersey City Drug Market Analysis Experiment." *Justice Quarterly, 12*, 711–735.

34   Gaines, L. K. (1996). "Specialized Patrol." In G. W. Cordner, L. K. Gaines, & V. E. Kappeler (Eds.), *Police Operations: Analysis and Evaluation.* Cincinnati, OH: Anderson.

35   Adams, 2006.

36   Pate, A. M., & Skogan, W. G. (1985). *Reducing the Signs of Crime: The Newark Experiment.* Washington, DC: Police Foundation.

37   Trojanowicz, R. (1982). *An Evaluation of the Neighborhood Foot Patrol Study in Flint, Michigan.* East Lansing, MI: Michigan State University.

38   Gaines, 1996.

39   Ibid.

40   Fritsch, E. J., Caeti, T. J., & Taylor, R. W. (1999). "Gang Suppression Through Saturation Patrol, Aggressive Curfew, and Truancy Enforcement: A Quasi-Experimental Test of the Dallas Anti-gang Initiative." *Crime & Delinquency*, 45(1), 122–139.

41   Miller, G. I. (1987). "Observations on Police Undercover Work." *Criminology, 25*(1), 27–46.

42   Lyons, W. "Partnerships, Information and Public Safety: Community Policing in a Time of Terror." *Policing, 25*(3), 530–542.

43   O'Connell, P. E. (2008). "The Chess Master's Game: A Model for Incorporating Local Police Agencies in the Fight Against Global Terrorism." *Policing, 31*(3), 456–465.

44   Berson, S. B. (2009). "Debating DNA Collection." *National Institute of Justice Journal, 264*, 9–13.

45   *Kyllo v. United States*, 533 U.S. 27, 150 L. Ed. 2nd 94, 121 S. Ct. 2038.

46   Douglas, J., Ressler, R. K., Burgess, A. W., & Hartman, C. R. (1986). "Criminal Profiling from Crime Scene Analysis." *Behavioral Sciences and the Law, 4*, 401–421.

47   Kelling, G. L., & Moore, M. H. (1988). "The Evolving Strategy of Policing." *Perspectives on Policing* (NCJ 114213). Washington, DC: National Institute of Justice.

48   Ponsaers, P. (2002). "Reading about 'Community (Oriented) Policing' and Police Models." *Policing, 24*(4), 470–496.

49   Kreps, G. A., & Weller, J. M. (1973). "The Police-Community Relations Movement: Conciliatory Responses to Violence." *The American Behavioral Scientist, 16*(3), 402–412.

50   Ibid.

51   Gaines, L. K., & Kappeler, V. E. (2009). *Community Policing: A Contemporary Perspective.* Cincinnati, OH: Anderson.

52   Wilson, J. Q., & Kelling, G. L. (1982, March). "Broken Windows." *Atlantic Monthly.*

53   Gaines & Kappeler, 2009.

54    Masten, J. (2009). "'Ain't No Snitches Ridin' Wit' Us': How Deception in the Fourth Amendment Triggered the Stop Snitching Movement." *Ohio State Law Journal, 70*(3), 701–753.

55    Ibid.

56    Goldstein, H. (1979). "Improving Policing: A Problem-Oriented Approach." *Crime and Delinquency, 25*, 236–258.

57    Zhao, J., Scheider, M. C., & Thurman, Q. (2002). "Funding Community Policing to Reduce Crime: Have COPS Grants Made a Difference?" *Criminology & Public Policy, 2*(1), 7–32.

58    Ratcliffe, J. H. (2008). *Intelligence-Led Policing.* Cullompton, UK: Willan.

59    Henry, V. E. (2003). *The COMPSTAT Paradigm: Management Accountability in Policing, Business and the Public Sector.* New York, NY: Looseleaf Law Publications.

60    Zimring, F. E. (2011). "How New York Beat Crime." *Scientific American Magazine, 305*(2), 74–75, 79.

61    Bohrer, S., & Chaney, R. (2010). "Police Investigations of the Use of Deadly Force Can Influence Perceptions and Outcomes." *FBI Law Enforcement Bulletin, 79*(1), 1–7.

62    Neiderhoffer, A. (1969). *Behind the Shield.* Garden City, NJ: Doubleday.

63    Alpert, G. P., MacDonald, J. M., & Dunham, R. G. (2005). "Police Suspicion and Discretionary Decision Making During Traffic Stops." *Criminology, 43*(2), 407–434.

64    Walker, S. (1993). Taming the System: *The Control of Discretion in Criminal Justice, 1950–1990.* Oxford: Oxford University Press.

65    National Research Council. (2003). *Fairness and Effectiveness in Policing: The Evidence.* Washington, DC: The National Academies Press.

66    Alpert et al., 2005.

67    Sherman, L. W., & Berk, R. A. (1984). *The Minneapolis Domestic Violence Experiment.* Washington, DC: Police Foundation.

68    National Research Council, 2003.

69    Sun, I., & Payne, B. (2004). "Racial Differences in Resolving Conflicts: A Comparison Between Black and White Police Officers." *Crime & Delinquency, 50*, 516–541.

70    Dantzer, M. L. (1987). "Police-related Stress: A Critique for Future Research." *Journal of Police Criminal Psychology, 3*, 43–48.

71    Anderson, W., Swenson, D., & Clay, D. (1995). *Stress Management for Law Enforcement Officers.* Upper Saddle River, NJ: Prentice Hall.

72    Anderson, G. S., Litzenberger, R., & Plecas, D. (2002). "Physical Evidence of Police Officer Stress." *Policing, 25*(2), 399–420.

73    Rizzolo, D., & Sedrak, M. (2010). "Stress Management: Helping Patients to Find Effective Coping Strategies." *Journal of American Academy of Physician Assistants, 23*(9), 20–24.

74    Atkinson, W. (2004). "Stress: Risk Management's Most Serious Challenge?" *Risk Management,* 51(6), 20–24.

75    Ibid.

[76]  Weitzer, R. (2002). "Incidents of Police Misconduct and Public Opinion." *Journal of Criminal Justice, 30*(5), 397–408.

[77]  Walker, S. (1992). *Police in America*. New York, NY: McGraw-Hill.

[78]  Ivkovic, S. K. (2005). *Fallen Blue Knights: Controlling Police Corruption*. New York, NY: Oxford University Press.

[79]  Arrigo, B. A., & Claussen, N. (2003). "Police Corruption and Psychological Testing: A Strategy for Preemployment Screening." *International Journal of Offender Therapy and Comparative Criminology, 47*(3), 272–290.

[80]  Jones, T. R., Owens, C., & Smith, M. (1995). "Police Ethics Training: A Three-Tiered Approach." *FBI Law Enforcement Bulletin, 64*(6), 22–26.

[81]  http://www.theiacp.org/PoliceServices/ExecutiveServices/Professional Assistance/Ethics/FocusOnEthicsTheLawEnforcementOathofHonor/ tabid/167/Default.aspx

# SECTION 3
## THE AMERICAN COURT SYSTEM

© Billion Photos/Shutterstock.com

# The Court System in the United States

## KEY TERMS

Appellate brief

Bail

Complaint

Court of last resort

Custodial interrogation

Discovery

Due process

*En banc*

Fruit of the poisonous tree

Grand jury

Indictment

Initial appearance

Intermediate appellate court

Judicial review

Jurisdiction

*Nolo contendere*

Plain view

Plea

Probable cause

Reasonable doubt

Recusal

Remand

Speedy Trial Act

Suppression hearing

Trial court

Verdict

Warrant

Writ of certiorari

# Chapter Objectives

1 | Identify the critical steps in the historical development of state and federal court systems in the United States.

2 | Distinguish between the structures of the modern-day state and federal court systems in the United States.

3 | Identify the procedural protections the modern U.S. court system provides to criminal defendants.

4 | Evaluate the adequacy of court procedures provided to criminal defendants.

5 | Examine the importance of juries in the courtroom.

6 | Describe the actual structure of a courtroom.

7 | Identify the various participants (courtroom workgroup) in a courtroom.

8 | Discuss the roles of each of the participants.

9 | Evaluate how each role is connected and vital to the others.

Clarence Gideon's 1961 appeal to the U.S. Supreme Court lead the court to rule persons charged in all state cases must have counsel representation.

# Case Study: Right to Counsel: Gideon v. Wainwright

In 1961, Florida resident Clarence Earl Gideon was accused of breaking and entering into a pool hall with the intention to commit burglary—a combination of offenses that led to felony charges. At his initial court appearance, Gideon requested that the court appoint an attorney to represent him, as he could not afford to hire one. The judge denied the request, saying that the law in Florida at the time provided appointed attorneys only in capital cases. Gideon was forced to represent himself and conduct his own defense. The jury found him guilty, and he was sentenced to five years in prison.

Gideon made effective use of his time in prison. Using the resources available to him in the prison library, he handwrote an appeal to the U.S. Supreme Court and filed a lawsuit against Louie Wainwright, the Secretary of the Florida Department of Corrections. Gideon argued that, as provided by the Sixth Amendment (as applied to the states in the 14th Amendment), the U.S. Supreme Court guaranteed him the right to be represented by counsel, and, therefore, his rights had been violated by the judge's rule to deny him an attorney. Abe Fortas, a well-known attorney from Washington, D.C., was appointed by the U.S. Supreme Court to represent Gideon on the appeal.

The court handed down its unanimous ruling on March 18, 1963: the denial of Gideon's request for appointed counsel did indeed violate his Sixth Amendment right to counsel. The court specified that by requiring Gideon, who was not an attorney, to defend himself, the judicial system had deprived him of his right to due process, as provided for in the Eighth Amendment. Further, the court ruled that the U.S. Constitution does not specify whether a criminal case must be capital or non-capital for the accused to have the right to be represented by counsel; therefore, qualified legal representation must be provided in all cases.[1]

Gideon's appeal was affirmed, and the case was returned to the Florida Supreme Court, who, in turn, returned the case to the trial court. Gideon was retried on the original charges with a court-appointed attorney and found not guilty.

The impact of *Gideon v. Wainwright* was far-reaching. In Florida alone, several thousand inmates who had been convicted in a like manner were set free after the ruling. The decision also led to the creation and continued development of the public defender system in the United States. The ruling ensured that not only must indigent defendants be afforded legal counsel, but those court-appointed attorneys must be effectively trained in defense to provide their clients with as fair a trial as possible. The case also inspired a book, *Gideon's Trumpet*, published in 1965, which detailed Clarence Earl Gideon's fight for fair representation. The Gideon decision was an important ruling that clarified the rights of criminal defendants as outlined in the U.S. Constitution.[2]

To learn more about *Gideon v. Wainwright:* https://www.youtube.com/watch?v=nrcTqx3t8Gg

## Case Study: Presumption of Innocence?

The credibility of North Carolina's criminal justice system was called into question recently by a disturbing revelation. After conducting an audit, the attorney general of the state concluded that the state's Bureau of Investigation had distorted or withheld evidence in the cases of more than 200 potentially innocent men and women.[3] The attorney general's audit uncovered memos indicating that crime lab analysts were trained to help prosecutors; it also indicated that the wrongfully suppressed evidence might have helped absolve certain defendants.[4] Many criminal defendants may have been wrongfully convicted because of the lab's failure to overturn potentially exculpatory evidence.

For a variety of reasons, courts sometimes fail to fulfill one of their primary responsibilities: to safeguard accused individuals from the abuses of overzealous policing and prosecution. Unfortunately, these unprofessional tactics are unlikely to stop unless the courts penalize them—even if it means, in extreme cases, occasionally letting an apparently guilty defendant go free due to these abuses. When courts take these measures, of course, the media and public are unlikely to understand the rationale that can possibly justify them.

Is our court system more error-prone than we can imagine? Perhaps so, and this underscores the continuing need for the procedural and constitutional safeguards that are the hallmark of due process under law. This propensity for error also suggests a much more unsettling problem: that there may be many more innocent people in American prisons than we have long thought. Most people are familiar in some way with the use of DNA evidence to clear persons who were convicted before the technology existed to identify DNA from crime scenes. Several common causes of wrongful conviction include eyewitness misidentification, improper forensics, false or coerced confessions, or informants who provide false testimony.[5]

In the North Carolina cases, the court system failed, for several reasons, to detect professional misconduct by prosecutors and crime labs that led to ill-gotten convictions. Now, the courts will have to fix this, and to revisit many prosecutions that should have concluded long ago. In North Carolina, these errors span many years and include more than 15,000 cases. Why did the court system not detect these problems sooner? At what point does the desire to rapidly convict and punish defendants overwhelm legal safeguards and yield tragic results, falsely incarcerating (or, worse, executing) an innocent person?

## Background History of the U.S. Court System

First and foremost, a court is an official venue for resolving disputes. Every day, courts resolve countless conflicts in criminal and civil matters. Under the principle of government known as *federalism*, created in the United States Constitution, the federal government and individual state governments share power. Similarly, the American judicial system exists in two separate but related systems: state and federal, each with its own courts, structure, and functions.[6]

As we discuss the American court system, we must first understand that there is no single, unified apparatus that controls the judiciary at every level. To many people, this is a surprising fact. In fact, there are more than 15,000 courts in the United States, covering a broad spectrum of functions and geographic jurisdictions. Rather than a uniform system, the American judiciary is better understood as 50 individual state court systems and one separate, national system that is part of the federal government.[7]

There are four principal sources of law in the United States: constitutions, statutes, administrative regulations, and common law, also known as case law.[8] Constitutional law is based on a formally adopted document, or constitution, that defines the broad powers of the government. In the

United States, the supreme law of the land is the U.S. Constitution, which defines the powers held by the federal government, establishes the branches of government, and reserves individual rights to all people who are under the jurisdiction of the United States. Each state also has its own constitution, from which its constitutional law is derived. Statutes are ordinances passed by Congress, state legislatures, and governing bodies at the federal, state, or local level. Administrative regulations, in turn, are rules issued by administrative bodies to exercise and interpret the powers given to them by statutes.[9]

Common law is the oldest source of law in the American legal system. The term *common law* refers to the legal rules formed by the accumulated decisions issued by judges in court cases. The American judicial system traces its roots to its colonial heritage and the legacy of English common law. In England, these decisions were made by judges who traveled across the country and rendered decisions based on rules and social norms common to each area. Common law is unique because it is largely shaped by judges, and not simply by applying statutes passed by a legislature.[10] Colonists carried English common law to the New World and incorporated it into the legal structures of colonial governments.

Significantly, common law also forms precedent, which means it can bind future judges to issue similar rulings in future disputes involving similar facts.[11] This essentially establishes a set of procedures designed to ensure fairness. These procedures are known as *due process*, which essentially means "fair play" in legal contexts.[12] The operating principle of due process is that it is unjust to treat similar facts and actions in a different way on different occasions.[13]

Colonists carried English common law to the New World and incorporated it into the legal structures of colonial governments.

## State Courts

For the most part, colonial courts adhered to the model they inherited from England, though there were some regional differences.[14] Influences such as religion and geography also led to variations in the structure of colonial courts. No attempt was made to unify the colonial courts until after the American Revolution.[15] Most colonies (and, subsequently, the U.S. states they became), of course, were directly influenced by the common law tradition. A notable exception is Louisiana, which today retains an integrated civil law system based on its French and Spanish traditions.[16]

The common law also led to other hallmarks of the American judicial system. In the minds of British subjects, common law came to represent an unassailable natural law that was higher than the laws of men. This view was reinforced by the English Parliament's use of common law to limit the unchecked power of the monarch. Eventually, this use resulted in the passage of significant provisions in English law, including the Bill of Rights, the right of habeas corpus, and the Petition of Right.[17] Each device would find its way into the American judicial system.

The English Bill of Rights in particular would influence American perceptions of justice and democracy. The 1689 Act of Parliament, which established the Bill of Rights in England, contained specific guarantees that later appeared in the U.S. Constitution. The Bill of Rights protected British subjects against excessive bails and fines and cruel and unusual punishment. It also provided jury trials for the accused, and later yielded protections for free speech and parliamentary debate.[18] These protections were incorporated into American state courts, and subsequently into the U.S. Constitution.

### Colonial Judiciary

Before the U.S. Constitution formally established a separation of powers among the three branches of government, judicial power in each colony was vested primarily in the hands of a royal governor. Before the Constitution was ratified, the various state courts existed as colonial judiciaries. By the time of the American Revolution, the colonial judicial system had existed in the same form since the 1720s.[19]

Typically, a justice of the peace, appointed by the royal governor, formed the lowest level of the judiciary. Above him were county courts that adjudicated low-level civil cases and non-capital criminal offenses. The highest-level cases were heard under the jurisdiction of the governor; in some states, the governor appointed a council of judges, while in others, he presided over such a council as a court of appeals.[20] These courts of appeals served as central courts for major offenses, but often traveled only once or twice a year on circuits around the colony.[21] Colonial judiciaries were far more informal than their counterparts in England. Justices of the peace kept few, if any, records. In addition, wealthy members of the community often posted a surety (financial guarantee by one party to assume the debt of another), which would be forfeited if the accused committed another crime.[22]

Colonial courts did not exercise a great deal of power in the colonies. The appeal process from their decisions went to authorities in England, not to the colonial government. Of course, colonial authorities required any laws passed by assemblies or legislatures to accord with English common law. If they did not, they could be overturned by the Privy Council in England, which also could reverse the decisions of colonial judges.[23] Royal governors, the representatives of English control, had the authority to remove judges at their leisure. Additionally, colonial judiciaries were typically less professional and experienced than those in England. Indeed, there were fewer legal experts in the colonies, and judges were often merchants, planters, or wealthy landowners.[24]

Tension began to grow between colonial legislatures and the judicial system controlled by a royal governor—and, by extension, the British Crown. During the colonial period, legislative assemblies in the colonies increasingly asserted themselves as law-making bodies. At the same time, the British government in London began to take a much more active and invasive role in colonial affairs.[25] This was because Britain believed the colonies existed only to provide the home country with resources and wealth, and that the colonists did not enjoy the same rights as British subjects at home.

Royal governors, as proxies of the British crown, performed the functions of the executive, legislative, and judicial branches of government.[26] With every ruling that was handed down by courts, colonists believed the British government was infringing on their rights. Not surprisingly, this untenable arrangement led to the relatively weak functioning of the executive and judicial branches under the first national colonial government. Because the executive and judicial branches were so weak, the legislative branch gained increasing power.

Before and immediately after the American Revolution, legislatures were the strongest branch of American government, dominating both the judicial and executive branches. Legislatures had the power to elect and pay judges, and to overrule their decisions or even impeach them. Legislatures could even amend state constitutions without interference from the courts.[27] Adding to the tension was the fact that legislatures and courts had different economic interests in early America. Members of local legislatures, on one hand, were usually interested in protecting the interests of debtors, especially small farmers. Courts, on the other hand, tended to side with the creditors who filed suit against debtors.[28]

## Formalization of State Court Systems

Conflict existed not only between the legislature and the judiciary, but also between different levels of the court system. As formalized state court systems developed after the American Revolution, a primary source of tension was the division of power between local and national judicial bodies.

Initially, the federal court system was structured to correspond to state lines. This structure was intended to ensure that federal judges would represent the federal court in their home states, with minimal interference from the federal government.[29] This design was a direct response to the inherent distrust of judicial authority that early American leaders retained from their experiences under British rule. They still saw the judiciary as an arbitrary, coercive, powerful system that interfered with their inalienable rights. Federalists created a basic framework for federal courts that would enforce national law.[30]

A second influence on the formalization of the court system was the development of a civil court structure. In the early phases of the American judiciary, the court system was informal enough to allow a great deal of overlap between civil and criminal cases. Justices of the peace met at county courts to hear civil disputes—disputes over contracts, personal injuries, or property—while still holding hearings on petty criminal acts.[31] This overlap of civil and criminal courts continued until the ratification of the U.S. Constitution.

## Federal Courts

Initially, the framers of the U.S. Constitution were ambivalent about the need for federal courts and the amount of power they should grant to the courts. This ambivalence is reflected in Article III of the Constitution, which provides for a single supreme court and gives Congress broad powers to establish lower courts at its discretion.[32] Notably, it provides no further detail on the structure of the courts. However, the experience of the relatively weak judiciary underscored the need for a strong, independent federal judiciary, and the founders became concerned with the rights of individual citizens in relation to the government.

### Articles of Confederation

In the immediate aftermath of the Revolutionary War, the leaders of the new nation were highly suspicious of strong, centralized executive power as a result of their experiences with the British government. In their writings and actions, they demonstrated an obvious preference for legislative power over executive power.[33]

The first federal courts were created, at least in one sense, by the Articles of Confederation, which were adopted in 1778 and ratified in 1781, as the first constitution of the United States of America. The articles did not create a national judiciary. Congress held almost all power, and there was no true executive or judicial branch. Congress did have the authority to create *ad hoc courts that would settle disputes between states, as well as cases involving events on international waters.*[34] However, the seeds of stronger judicial power were present. During the 1780s, state judiciaries were able to declare several state statutes unconstitutional, presaging a later debate over the extent of judicial authority in American government.[35] This debate would reach a climax with the Supreme Court case of *Marbury v. Madison (1803), which established the doctrine of judicial review.*

### U.S. Constitution

For a variety of reasons, the weak and ineffective national government created by the Articles of Confederation lasted only a few years before being replaced. The U.S. Constitution (1787) formally established the federal judiciary as it exists today. Many founders agreed that an independent judiciary was needed to counterbalance potential abuses by the legislative and executive branches. Additionally, they saw a strong judiciary as the most effective way to defend the individual rights guaranteed by the Constitution. The Anti-Federalists (later known as the Jeffersonian-Republicans), who still opposed strong national government, favored a network of self-governing state and local courts instead of a strong, federal "supreme" court that would interpret the Constitution.[36] The Federalists, who advocated strong national government, were successful in arguing that the legislature was the branch most dangerous to the personal freedoms secured by the Constitution. They believed that Congress had been granted a disproportionate amount of power.

The U.S. Constitution instituted the federal judicial system that is in practice today.

The Constitution gave courts the power to prevent the legislature, at both the state and federal levels, from passing bills of attainder (acts of the legislature declaring a person guilty of a crime without a trial) and *ex post facto laws*. In addition, it guaranteed citizens the right to trial by jury, and prohibited the suspension of the right of habeas corpus (the right not to be illegally detained), except in wartime.[37] These basic civil rights and others, collectively known as the "Bill of Rights," compose the first 10 amendments to the Constitution.

The U.S. Constitution also underscored the importance of judicial independence by articulating a clear doctrine of separation of powers. In the English system of government, even today, the legislature retains ultimate authority. American colonists, even before the revolution, began to sharply define the difference between what is considered "legal" and what is considered "constitutional." The British system, by contrast, sees the two concepts as inextricably linked. Americans asserted that the rights and principles outlined by the Constitution take priority over any hasty decisions made by the legislature or the executive.[38]

A crucially important feature of the U.S. Constitution, as compared to the Articles of the Confederation, is the establishment of an independent judiciary. The Constitution is, first and foremost, a "contract" between the people and the government. In the American system, the judiciary is granted the authority and responsibility to guard the freedoms guaranteed by that contract. This authority and responsibility leads directly to the doctrine of judicial review.

The U.S. Constitution authorized two types of federal courts: legislative and constitutional. Legislative courts were established by Congress under

Article I of the Constitution, and serve functions that are both legislative and judicial. They typically have a narrowly defined role and administer a specific statute, such as bankruptcy law. Legislative courts include the Tax Court, the U.S. Court of Appeals for Veterans Claims, the U.S. Court of Appeals for the Armed Forces, and the U.S. Court of Federal Claims. Constitutional courts include the U.S. Supreme Court, circuit courts of appeals, and district courts.

## The Road to Judicial Review

The doctrine of judicial review has become the most powerful tool for the judiciary to take an active role in government. The U.S. Constitution tasked federal courts with upholding and supporting the Constitution.[39] Article III provides that "the judicial power of the United States, shall be vested in one supreme Court, and in such inferior Courts as the Congress may from time to time ordain and establish."[40] The scope of those powers was not clearly or comprehensively described in the Constitution itself, but judicial review has become an established—if somewhat controversial—power of the judiciary.

**Judicial review** The power of the federal judiciary to overturn any legislation or other governmental action ruled inconsistent with the Constitution, Bill of Rights, or federal law.

In the words of David O'Brien, **judicial review** is "the power of the Supreme Court and the federal judiciary to consider and overturn any congressional and state legislation or other official governmental action deemed inconsistent with the Constitution, Bill of Rights, or federal law."[41] This idea was not without controversy. The Jeffersonian-Republicans, the party of Thomas Jefferson, felt the court's power should be limited in regard to the legislature, while the Federalists, the party of John Adams, favored a stronger judiciary.

Since the Constitution did not describe a specific structure for the federal judiciary other than the U.S. Supreme Court, Congress used its authority to establish lower courts by enacting the Judiciary Act of 1789. One clause of that act gave the Supreme Court the power to issue writs of mandamus, which are orders from a higher court compelling a lower court or government officer to perform a specified duty.[42] The act also enabled citizens sued by citizens of another state to transfer the lawsuit to federal circuit court and granted the Supreme Court authority to review the decisions of state courts on appeal.[43]

Nonetheless, there was significant debate about what the U.S. Constitution actually allowed the Supreme Court to do. The Constitution did not explicitly provide the Supreme Court or any of the judiciary the power of judicial review. Article III states that the "judicial Power shall extend to" cases and controversies "arising under this Constitution," implying that the judiciary is empowered to resolve constitutional questions. In addition, Article VI asserts that the Constitution is the "Supreme Law of the Land."[44] But a definitive answer on judicial review would not come until the 1803 U.S. Supreme Court case of *Marbury v. Madison*.

## Marbury v. Madison

The pivotal Supreme Court case that established the doctrine of judicial review is *Marbury v. Madison*.[45] In this case, the Supreme Court first asserted its authority to declare an act of Congress unconstitutional.

## Exhibit: Excerpt from Marbury v. Madison

"It is emphatically the province and duty of the Judicial Department [the judicial branch] to say what the law is. Those who apply the rule to particular cases must, of necessity, expound and interpret that rule. If two laws conflict with each other, the Courts must decide on the operation of each.

"So, if a law [e.g., a statute or treaty] be in opposition to the Constitution, if both the law and the Constitution apply to a particular case, so that the Court must either decide that case conformably to the law, disregarding the Constitution, or conformably to the Constitution, disregarding the law, the Court must determine which of these conflicting rules governs the case. This is of the very essence of judicial duty. If, then, the Courts are to regard the Constitution, and the Constitution is superior to any ordinary act of the Legislature, the Constitution, and not such ordinary act, must govern the case to which they both apply.

"Those, then, who controvert the principle that the Constitution is to be considered in court as a paramount law are reduced to the necessity of maintaining that courts must close their eyes on the Constitution, and see only the law" [e.g., the statute or treaty].

"This doctrine would subvert the very foundation of all written constitutions."[46]

The dispute arose during the transition between the presidency of John Adams and that of Thomas Jefferson. At the close of Adams' presidency, it became clear that Adams' Federalist party was going to lose power. In a political move designed to frustrate the incoming Jefferson administration, Adams spent his last night as president appointing many fellow Federalists—later called "midnight judges"—to judicial positions in and around Washington, D.C. The next day, the Jefferson administration ordered James Madison, the new secretary of state, not to deliver the commissions to the judges, though they had been approved by the Senate. This order prompted one of the newly appointed justices, William Marbury, to file suit for a writ of mandamus in the Supreme Court that would force Madison to deliver the commissions. Marbury based his claim on the Judiciary Act of 1789, which granted the Supreme Court jurisdiction to issue such writs.

The case reached the Supreme Court, and Chief Justice John Marshall determined that it presented three legal issues: did Marbury have a right to the commission, was there a legal remedy, and was a writ of mandamus from the Supreme Court the correct remedy? Marshall answered the first two in the affirmative, but he determined that the third question involved the jurisdiction of the Supreme Court and was, therefore, a constitutional question.[47] Though he agreed that Marbury was entitled to the commission, he ruled that the Judiciary Act of 1789 conflicted with the Constitution, which did not give the Supreme Court original jurisdiction over writs of mandamus. Essentially, Marshall ruled that Congress did not have the authority to add to the original jurisdiction of the Supreme Court.[48]

The result of Marshall's ruling was that a Supreme Court decision partially invalidated an act of Congress by determining that it conflicted with the U.S. Constitution. The ruling strengthened the power of the judiciary by establishing that the legislature could not add to the jurisdiction of the Supreme Court. This precedent also entrenched the checks and balances system in American government.

In the end, as Justice Marshall put it, "it is emphatically the province and the duty of the judicial department to say what the law is."[49] Judicial review, while controversial at first, has in the past two centuries become a fixture of American constitutionalism. The now-accepted doctrine of judicial review allows the judiciary to adjudicate between two contradictory sources of law.[50]

# Court Structure

The American judiciary can best be described as a dual system, including one federal court and 50 state courts. Under this system, federal courts have authority over cases involving an issue of federal law, and state courts have authority over issues of state law.

The separation between the two tiers is not absolute, however. Some cases can be heard in either state or federal court. For example, civil suits in which the parties reside in two different states can be heard in either state or federal court. Narcotics cases and interstate kidnapping charges violate both federal and state statutes. The appeals process can also involve both levels of the judiciary. Those convicted in a state court may appeal to their respective states' appellate courts, to the U.S. Supreme Court, or by petition for a writ of habeas corpus to a federal district court. Detained individuals may petition for a writ of habeas corpus to request their release.

**Jurisdiction** The power of a court to adjudicate a case, issue orders, and render a decision.

To understand the structure of U.S. courts, both state and federal, it is necessary to understand the concept of **jurisdiction**. There are several different kinds of jurisdiction, but—loosely defined—jurisdiction is the power of a court to adjudicate a case, issue orders, and render a decision. The term also refers to the geographic territory over which a court may exercise its power.

**Trial court** A court of original jurisdiction that tries a case and renders a judgment.

Original jurisdiction, as the name implies, is the prerogative of a court—typically, a **trial court**—to be the first to hear a case. Appellate jurisdiction refers to the authority of a higher court to consider an appeal from a decision issued by a trial court. Appellate courts do not hear witness testimony in criminal cases or civil cases. Rather, they consider written and oral appeals about the conduct, procedure, and results of a trial, and then determine if the trial court (or trial court jury) committed errors of fact or law.[51]

Jurisdiction can be further broken down into geographic and subject matter jurisdiction. Subject matter jurisdiction applies in cases where a specific legal issue is in controversy, such as the right of contracts or civil rights. Geographic jurisdiction is the authority of a court to try cases that arise within certain geographical areas, such as a county, city, or state. The state of Maryland, for instance, has no jurisdiction to try a person accused of committing a crime in Pennsylvania.

Geographic jurisdiction can become an issue if a defendant flees a state to avoid prosecution, because the state's prosecutor must request extradition to have the defendant brought to the state in which the crime was committed.[52] In addition, issues of geographic jurisdiction become political when a defendant who commits a capital crime in a state with the death penalty flees to a state that does not impose the death penalty.

## Structure of State Courts

State courts handle the vast majority of cases that occur in the United States. They derive their authority from state constitutions and statutes, which are far more exhaustive than the U.S. Constitution. The 10th Amendment to the Bill of Rights states that the powers not specifically granted to the federal government by the Constitution are reserved to the states or the people.[53] As such, state courts resolve most disputes between private citizens, prosecute most criminal defendants, handle most family disputes, and adjudicate most disputes between citizens and the government.[54]

State court systems, like their federal counterparts, are divided into trial courts and appellate courts. In criminal cases, trial courts arraign defendants, set bail, consider guilty pleas, conduct trials, and impose criminal sentences. In civil cases, trial courts inform plaintiffs and defendants of the complaint filed, perform pretrial procedures, conduct trials, and award damages. To carry out these steps, trial courts often handle factual disputes and hear testimony from witnesses.

Appellate courts correct erroneous decisions of lower courts. Their role is not to determine factual errors or hear witnesses, but rather to determine if the trial court incorrectly interpreted or applied the relevant statute or law. Most rulings of appellate courts become precedent for trial courts. In addition, appellate courts often reassess the application of legal rules, derive new rules for original situations, and interpret ambiguous language in statutes or court opinions.[55]

Appellate courts correct erroneous decisions of lower courts.

In general, the lowest level of a state court system consists of county courts, municipal courts, traffic courts, and magistrates, or judicial officers who perform some administrative tasks of a judge without the same level of authority. These are trial courts of limited jurisdiction. *Limited jurisdiction* refers to the authority of courts over a particular subset of cases.

The next highest level consists of specialized courts that consider juvenile, divorce, family, and housing issues. Superior courts handle serious criminal matters; most trials occur at this level. The highest level is the state supreme court, which has the power to hear appeals from lower courts.

## Municipal Courts, District Courts, and County Courts

Municipal courts, district courts, and county courts are typically trial courts of limited jurisdiction, and often are referred to as *inferior or lower courts. They constitute almost 77% of all courts in the United States.*[56] Courts in this category frequently use abbreviated procedures due to the commonplace nature of the cases they handle. They sometimes exclude attorneys and do not use juries due to the huge volume of civil and criminal matters they arbitrate, many of which are neither complex nor serious (traffic offenses, moving violations, etc.).[57]

Lower courts of this sort nearly always handle misdemeanor crimes, or crimes for which the penalty does not exceed one year of incarceration, and hear civil suits whose amounts do not exceed $15,000. These courts may also handle the preliminary stages of felony cases, which include preliminary hearings, arraignment, bail, and appointment of counsel. As these courts do not handle serious matters, their proceedings are often not officially recorded. Appeals from trial courts of limited jurisdiction usually go to trial courts of general jurisdiction, instead of directly to an appellate court.

The trial court of general jurisdiction for a state is usually called a district or superior court. Most trial courts have unlimited jurisdiction and are therefore the venue for the majority of serious criminal offenses. Still, there is overlap in some states. Usually, courts are divided into judicial districts or circuits, sometimes along political boundaries, such as counties or boroughs. They are much more formal than lower courts, usually featuring a jury trial and attorneys. Major trial courts often have felony jurisdiction, which gives them the power to issue judgments on cases in which preliminary proceedings have occurred in a lower court of limited jurisdiction. These courts also have incidental appellate jurisdiction, so they can hear appeals from lower-level courts and administrative agencies in certain civil or criminal matters.[58]

## The Courtroom Workgroup

Members of the courtroom workgroup collaborate to move cases through the criminal justice system quickly and fairly.

The *courtroom workgroup* plays a hugely important role in criminal justice. This term encompasses the many different players in a courtroom—from the judge to the courtroom staff to the defense and prosecuting attorneys—and the functions of each. The members of the courtroom workgroup perform particular duties to achieve collaborative goals, such as moving cases through the criminal justice system in a timely fashion and ensuring that justice is pursued fairly. Court operation is based not only on the law but also on the judge's decisions as the highest official in the courtroom.[59]

**Defendant** A person charged with a crime.

Workgroups form in all professions, but the courtroom workgroup is unique in that the person at the center—the **defendant**—has very little power. While the system is designed to protect the rights of the accused, the defendant is not involved in most of the proceedings involving the courtroom workgroup. The other participants work together frequently—usually every day—and include the regular courtroom staff, the judge, and any attorneys. These individuals tend to develop a shared set of norms and values from their contact and work. Eisenstein and Jacob (1970) defined the characteristics of the courtroom workgroup as speed, guilt, cohesion, and secrecy.[60] *Speed* indicates the group's desire to dispose of cases quickly rather than administering and dispensing truly fair justice; guilt implies the group's belief that the defendant is indeed guilty, despite the idea from the U.S. Constitution that a defendant is considered innocent until proven guilty. This philosophy is similar to Herbert Packer's Crime Control Model. *Cohesion* is the unity of the individuals as a group, working together toward the common purpose of punishing the defendant; and *secrecy* describes the group's tendency to keep any discussions or negotiations that do not occur in open court private—sometimes even from the defendant. The dynamic of the courtroom workgroup can strongly affect the outcome of a criminal case, sometimes without the defendant knowing what happened.

# The Criminal Trial:

## An Overview

There are two types of criminal trials: a bench trial and a jury trial. A *bench trial* is a trial argued directly in front of a judge without a jury, with the judge making the sole decision as to the defendant's guilt or innocence and possible punishment. A *jury trial* is conducted in front of a jury; the jury listens to all evidence presented and makes the decision as to the guilt or innocence, and later any applicable punishment, of the defendant. The defendant has the right to request either a jury trial or a bench trial, and the choice is generally suggested by the defense attorney as a part of trial strategy.[61] While the U.S. Constitution identifies the right to a jury trial, this was not clarified in all states until the 1968 Supreme Court ruling in *Duncan v. Louisiana. In Duncan*, the defendant was charged with a misdemeanor offense that could have resulted in a maximum sentence of two years' imprisonment and a fine of $300. The trial court rejected the defendant's request for a jury trial based on the Louisiana constitution, which allowed jury trials only in cases that could result in a death sentence or hard labor imprisonment. The Supreme Court ruled in favor of Duncan, saying that his right to a jury trial was guaranteed by the Sixth and 14th Amendments.[62]

When the trial begins, the attorneys for each side make opening statements. The **opening statement** is an opportunity for each attorney to provide the jury with a brief summary of what each side intends to show the jury during the trial. The prosecution, which has the burden of proof—the task of demonstrating the guilt of the defendant—makes the first opening statement. The prosecution endeavors to show the jury that it will **prove beyond a reasonable doubt** that the defendant committed the crime of which he or she is accused.[63] The

**Opening statement** The initial statement of a trial that an attorney makes to the jury, which outlines the argument that will be made during the trial.

**Proof Beyond a Reasonal Doubt** The burden of proof that is put forward by the prosecution used to determine a person's guilt or innocence. The defendant is always presumed to be innocent unless the burden of proof is undeniable. Black's Law Dictionary.

Witnesses help describe the series of events that occurred before, during, and after a crime.

defense attorney, on the other hand, will focus the opening statement on the weaknesses of the state's case, arguing that the defendant's guilt cannot be proved beyond a reasonable doubt. The manner in which the defense attorney makes the opening statement may vary according to trial strategy. Sometimes attorneys may withhold details during opening statements, preferring to allow particular information to be revealed during the course of the trial. Another tactic is to use a very detailed opening statement, which may be delivered forcefully or passionately in an attempt to predispose the jury to accept the defense's argument.[64]

Opening statements are broad, and are not intended—or permitted—to be used as a means for the attorneys to testify or offer evidence. The attorneys from both sides are also bound by "good faith" ethical requirements during opening statements. Each lawyer can mention only the evidence that he or she believes will be presented, and that he or she will be allowed to present during the trial. If either attorney gives the idea that he or she will present evidence that in fact he or she has no intention of presenting, this is not only unprofessional, but has been defined by the U.S. Supreme Court as *professional misconduct*.[65]

**Case-in-chief** The portion of a criminal case presented by the prosecution.

The **case-in-chief** is the argument the state's attorney, who is on the side of the prosecution in criminal proceedings, makes against the defendant. It is the job of the state's attorney to show the jury that the defendant committed, or could have committed, the crime of which he or she has been accused. The case-in-chief is different than the case-as-a-whole, as "the case" includes the entire court case and the arguments for guilt or innocence from both sides, the witnesses, and any experts involved.

## Witness Testimony

**Witness** An individual who gives testimony in court because he or she has information that is pertinent to the case.

**Testimony** The statement of a witness, given under oath, typically in court.

An important part of any criminal trial is the examination of witnesses. This is the primary means by which evidence is introduced in a trial. **Witnesses** have information that helps put together the series of events that occurred before, during, and after the commission of a crime. The **testimony**, or formal statement, from each witness helps paint a picture of what happened, where it happened, how it happened, who caused it to happen, and why it happened. Since the defendant (who may or may not testify), the victim (who may not be able to testify), and the witnesses are the only individuals involved in the trial process who can answer some of these questions definitively, it is important that the judge and jury learn as much information as possible in order to make fair decisions about the defendant's guilt or innocence and any resultant sentence.

Before a witness will be allowed to testify, the attorney questioning the witness must establish that the person is competent to testify. Competency requires that the witness has personal knowledge of the information that he or she will offer and that the witness understands the duty to tell the truth.[66] The trial process relies on the ability of the witness to give accurate and truthful testimony, so it is important to ensure that the witness is capable of telling the truth. This is a practice that developed primarily in the England and Scotland in the 1600s as the adversarial trial process evolved.[67] A **lay witness** is an everyday citizen, who may or may not personally know the defendant or victims involved in the case, who has some personal knowledge about the facts of the case. A spectator at a sporting event who sees an assault occur several seats away would be considered a lay witness if asked to testify in court. It is important to establish that a lay witness is competent and credible to testify because the witness is relaying what occurred that he or she personally witnessed. Incorrect testimony may harm case procedure or the outcome of the case.

Witness competency is also important when an expert witness testifies. An **expert witness** is considered an expert in his or her field of study or work: for example, a physician would be considered an expert in the medical field, while an auto mechanic would be considered an expert in the internal working of automobiles. One accepted legal definition of *expert witnesses is the following: "Persons who through education or experience have developed skill or knowledge in a particular subject so that he or she may form an opinion that will assist the fact finder."*[68] The expert witness must be knowledgeable in his or her field, as the information explained by the expert witness has potential bearing on the guilt or innocence of the defendant. A forensic pathologist who testifies in a murder trial about the manner in which a victim died must be as factual and accurate as possible; the judge or jury needs to understand the facts presented in the case so that a decision of guilt or innocence can be made. Because juries may not be qualified to evaluate the validity of presented scientific evidence, the U.S. Supreme Court ruled in *Daubert v. Merrill Dow Pharmaceuticals (1993) that judges have the duty to perform preliminary evaluations of the scientific basis of any expert testimony prior to allowing the expert to testify in the presence of the jury.*[69]

When a witness is first called to the stand to testify, this is called **direct examination**. If the witness is called to testify by the state's attorney, the witness is referred to as a witness for the prosecution. If the witness is called to the stand and questioned by the defendant's legal counsel, or **defense attorney**, the witness is referred to as a witness for the defense. When the witness is being questioned directly, he or she may be asked questions that may be answered with a simple "yes" or "no," or the witness may be asked "narrative" questions, which allow the witness to tell a version of events in his or her own words. During direct examination, the judge will not allow the attorneys to ask "leading questions," which are questions that suggest the answer within the question. A basic example of such a question would be, "You called the police immediately after hearing the shots, correct?"

**Lay witness** An everyday citizen who has some personal knowledge about the facts of a case.

**Expert witness** A person considered to be an expert in his or her profession or field of study who applies that expertise to the facts or circumstances of a case.

**Direct examination** The act of a witness being first called to the stand to testify.

**Defense attorney** The attorney who represents the defendant in a criminal case.

Any witness who offers testimony in a criminal trial is subject to being cross-examined. **Cross-examination** is the questioning of a witness by someone other than the direct examiner. After a witness for the defense is questioned directly by the defense attorney, the witness is then available to be cross-examined by the **prosecutor**, or the attorney who represents the state and argues the criminal case against the defendant. Cross-examination tests a witness's credibility and memory by challenging facts that have been entered into evidence by the witness's testimony.[70] The cross-examiner may attempt to discredit the witness by questioning the witness's physical or mental status, criminal record, or prior inconsistencies in the witness's statements. Cross-examination may be followed by redirect examination by the state's attorney, which would attempt to clarify anything to which the witness testified under cross-examination. This procedure continues cycling until all of that side's witnesses have been called and all of their evidence presented.[71]

Several Supreme Court rulings have addressed cross-examination of witnesses. In *Ohio v. Roberts* (1980), the court ruled that a statement made by a witness outside of the courtroom could be introduced during trial as long as there were sufficient "indicia of reliability," even if the witness was not available to testify at trial.[72] In the *Roberts* case, the defendant was accused of forging a check and possession of stolen credit cards, both of which belonged to his daughter. While the daughter was subpoenaed five times to testify at trial, she never appeared. The prosecution offered the transcript of the daughter's testimony to the police at trial, and the defendant was convicted, based partly upon the perceived reliability of his daughter's previous statements.[73] In a later ruling, however, the Supreme Court effectively reversed its position in *Roberts* with the 2004 ruling in *Crawford v. Washington*. In *Crawford*, the prosecution introduced during trial a statement previously made to the police by the defendant's wife. The prosecution used the statement of the wife during trial, particularly during closing arguments, and the defendant was convicted. On appeal, the Supreme Court ruled that the defendant's Sixth Amendment right to confront his accuser had been violated because Mrs. Crawford did not actually testify during the trial, preventing the defense attorney from cross-examining her.[74] The *Crawford* decision effectively means that, when a witness is unavailable to testify at trial, previous testimonial statements made by that witness cannot be admitted into evidence unless the defense had the prior opportunity to cross-examine the witness.

© Everett Collection/Shutterstock.com

Rebuttal evidence is introduced during trial to oppose or contradict evidence already submitted by the opposing side.

Another way in which an attorney tests the accuracy of the opposing side's case is during the introduction of rebuttal evidence. *Rebuttal evidence* is evidence that is introduced during trial to oppose or contradict evidence already submitted by the opposing side. Rebuttal evidence is submitted during the side's response to the opposing side's presented case. For example, a witness may testify that he witnessed a robbery at a convenience store on a particular date and time, and then an attorney may introduce into evidence a credit card receipt with the witness's signature proving that he was at another location on the same date and time he claimed to witness the robbery. The receipt would be considered rebuttal evidence.

---

**Critical Thinking**

If a witness can verify testimony given by a previous witness, is it critical that his or her competency to testify can be demonstrated? Why or why not?

---

### Closing Arguments and Jury Instructions

The **closing arguments** of a trial are the final legal arguments presented by the prosecution and the defense before the case is given to the jury for deliberation. The closing argument can be considered a review and summary of what was argued during the case and whether the arguments demonstrate the defendant's guilt or innocence. Because the burden of proof is on the state, meaning that it is up to the state to demonstrate the guilt of the defendant, the prosecutor is allowed to make a reply to the defense's closing argument. The closing argument does not necessarily have a time limit, although one may be imposed by the judge. The attorneys may avoid lengthy closing arguments for fear of confusing the jurors or losing their attention. In bench trials, it is not uncommon for the sides to waive making closing arguments in the presumption that the judge has already arrived at a decision.[75]

**Closing argument** The final legal argument of a case presented separately by the prosecution and the defense before the case is given to the jury for deliberation.

After all the evidence has been presented and closing arguments have ended, the judge gives the charge and instructions to the jury. Typically, the judge and attorneys for both sides will discuss the jury instructions outside the presence of the jury so that changes may be discussed, argued, agreed upon, or ruled upon. While the words may vary between jurisdictions, every judge will remind the jury of the duty to objectively consider only evidence that has been presented during trial when deciding the defendant's guilt or innocence; the importance of impartiality will also be stressed.[76] Most judges will remind the jury that the burden of proof rests on the prosecution and the defense is not obligated to show proof of innocence. The judge will also explain the concept of reasonable doubt by stressing that if jury members are to determine that a defendant is guilty, they must hold no reasonable doubts regarding the person's guilt. Additionally, judges may remind the jury of the legal requirements of the alleged charge: that is, if the defendant is accused of murder, the judge may remind the jury members of what, according to the law, constitutes "murder."

Issues have arisen from time to time concerning whether juries actually understood the instructions given to them by the judge. One study by Wiener, Pritchard, and Weston (1995) demonstrated that juror impartiality can be affected by misunderstanding jury instructions; when jurors were given several versions of instructions in a sample capital case, a strong correlation was found between misunderstanding the jury instructions and the willingness of the jurors to impose the death penalty.[77] It is also typical for jurors to confuse the burden of proof in criminal court—"beyond a reasonable doubt"—with the burden of proof in civil court—"preponderance of the evidence."[78] The American Bar Association has addressed this, stating, "All instructions to the jury should be in plain and understandable language."[79] States are making changes to jury instructions to increase juror understanding of the instructions. States such as Florida and Illinois are now creating standard jury instructions that can be altered according to the specific criteria of each case.[80]

Jury instructions have also been clarified by Supreme Court rulings. In *Pope v. Illinois* (1987), the defendant appealed a guilty verdict based on the assertion that the jury was given erroneous instructions. The defendant, who was a clerk at an adult bookstore, was arrested after selling certain magazines to police. The jury was instructed to determine whether the magazines would be considered obscene by determining how the material would be viewed by ordinary adults in the state of Illinois. The Supreme Court ruled that, although the jury was erroneously instructed to use a particular community standard—the state of Illinois—when considering the social value of the magazines, if no rational juror who had been properly instructed could find social value in the magazines, the guilty conviction should stand.[81]

## The Verdict

When the jury is done deliberating, the foreman will write the verdict on the court's official verdict form. The bailiff will then be notified that a verdict has been reached, and the court will inform all parties to return to the courtroom to hear the verdict. When the parties, audience, and staff return to the courtroom, the jury will be ushered back into the jury box. The foreman hands the jury form to the bailiff, who then gives the form to the judge. The judge makes sure the verdict is properly written and the paperwork is in proper legal order. In some jurisdictions, such as California, the clerk of the court reads the verdict aloud in court. In other jurisdictions, such as North Dakota, the jury foreperson, referred to as the presiding juror, announces the verdict in court.[82] In cases where unanimous verdicts are required of juries, it is easy to know how each juror voted. However, the prosecuting and defense attorneys do have the right to request of the judge that the jury be polled. If this occurs, each juror must announce individually how he or she voted at the conclusion of deliberations.

**Critical Thinking**

What possible issues do you believe could arise from polling a jury after they have found a defendant guilty?

## Intermediate Appellate Courts

All states have at least one appellate court, but some feature more. In states with large caseloads, there are two levels of appellate courts. The highest is a court of last resort, typically a state supreme court. The lower level consists of **intermediate appellate courts**, which alleviate the burden placed on higher courts in the most populous states. These courts relieve the state's highest court (typically a state supreme court) from having to hear every case that generates an appeal.[83] In 1998, 35 states had at least one intermediate court of appeal.[84] These appeals typically are decided by a three-judge panel, although judges occasionally sit **en banc**, a French term that translates to the phrase "on a bench" and implies that all the judges of the court together will decide a case.

The losing side in a criminal or civil case has the right of appeal, and the appeal takes place either in a **court of last resort** or an intermediate appellate court. Intermediate appellate courts generally must hear cases that are appealed to them.

**Intermediate appellate court** The lower level of state appellate courts.

**En banc** A French term indicating that all the judges of an appellate court will together consider an appeal.

**Court of last resort** The highest court of appeal in a state court system: typically, a state supreme court.

## Courts of Last Resort

State supreme courts are the highest level of appellate court and also are referred to as courts of last resort. These courts generally reserve the right to choose which cases they will hear, and they frequently choose cases that carry broad policy and legal implications.[85] Courts of last resort in states without an intermediate level, however, do not get to choose their cases.

All of these courts are composed of five to nine members (most commonly seven) and generally sit *en banc*. Texas and Oklahoma are notable for being the two states to have separate courts of last resort for civil and criminal matters.[86]

State supreme courts are similar to the U.S. Supreme Court in that they interpret state law and have the power to determine whether it violates the state constitution. These courts follow a model similar to the federal model: they require a notice of appeal, require written legal briefs, consider oral arguments by each party's attorneys, and issue a written decision. State supreme courts, like other courts of last resort, do not retry the facts of the case or hear witnesses, but correct errors of law or procedure.[87]

When it is relevant to do so, state supreme courts exercise the authority to interpret the Constitution and, in some instances, federal law. However, if a state court issues an opinion on federal law, its decision is reviewable by the U.S. Supreme Court, whose authority supersedes that of a state court.

The U.S. Supreme Court can review and overrule the state's interpretation of a federal statute or the Constitution.[88]

## Specialized State Courts

© Cheryl Casey/Shutterstock.com

Juvenile courts determine cases involving young offenders, generally those less than 18 years old.

The state court system also includes specialized courts that handle specific types of cases. These courts have limited jurisdiction that covers their specialty, and generally have a single judge hear cases without a jury. Probate courts, for instance, consider the administrative concerns of a deceased person's estate. This usually involves making sure the person's will is executed properly or applying relevant state law if there is no will. Family courts consider divorces, custody disputes, annulments, and alimony. Traffic courts adjudicate speeding tickets and other moving violations.[89]

*Juvenile courts* determine cases involving young offenders, generally those less than 18 years old. Because these offenders are underage, they are not tried in conventional criminal courts. Juvenile courts operate on the premise that sentences should be rehabilitative, rather than punitive, since minors are not as culpable for most criminal acts as an adult would be and can more readily see the error of their ways and remediate their behavior.[90]

## Structure of Federal Courts

In their current form, federal courts have three levels. The lowest level is occupied by federal district courts, which function as trial courts. The middle level includes the U.S. Circuit Courts of Appeals, which consider appeals. The top court is the U.S. Supreme Court, which defines and interprets the U.S. Constitution and statutes passed by the legislative branch.[91]

Federal courts have exclusive jurisdiction over "federal questions." These legal issues arise in suits between citizens of different states, or in suits involving foreign ambassadors or public officials, bankruptcy, patent or trademark law, or crimes specifically punishable by federal statutes. Indeed, any crime mentioned in the Constitution (treason, piracy, counterfeiting) or a federal statute qualifies as a federal question, but most statutory crimes are tried in state courts.[92]

**Career Connections: Federal Judge**

Federal judges sit at the top of the judicial system in the American criminal justice system. They are selected by executive appointment of the president and must be confirmed by at least two-thirds of the U.S. Senate.

This obviously makes the selection process an inherently political one. When a position becomes available, the deputy attorney general of the U.S. Department of Justice conducts a search for qualified lawyers in the state in which the vacancy is located. The initial screening phase involves consulting with local party leaders to ensure that the nominee's political views do not conflict with those of the president.[93]

Federal judges are appointed under Article III of the U.S. Constitution. Judges serve a lifelong term, but can be removed by impeachment. There are no explicit qualifications for a judgeship, but candidates are almost always accomplished attorneys, often working for the government.[94] In addition, it is preferred that judges have a dispassionate demeanor. As arbiters of fairness in the court, judges are expected to be, according to Jackson (1974), "honest, patient, wise, tolerant, compassionate, strong, decisive, articulate, courageous—a list of virtues similar to those in the Boy Scout handbooks."[95]

Some see federal judges as autocratic, but they frequently defer to the advice and opinions of prosecutors and probation officers when it comes to accepting a plea agreement or determining sentencing.[96] In a federal criminal trial, the judge advises the defendant of his or her rights, decides if the defendant should be held in custody until trial, and determines if **probable cause** exists to believe the defendant committed the crime with which he or she is charged. Most defendants (90%) take a plea bargain instead of going to trial, at which point the judge either imposes sentence or waits for a presentence report prepared by a probation officer. If the defendant pleads not guilty, the judge schedules a trial.[97]

**Probable cause**
Reasonable belief that the accused committed the crime with which he or she is charged.

## The Judge and Courtroom Staff

The concept of the courtroom workgroup was introduced earlier in the chapter. Each member of the courtroom workgroup has particular duties in the criminal trial process, all of which combine to dispose of cases as smoothly and efficiently as possible. Following is an overview of the members of the courtroom workgroup.

### The Judge

Many people view the **judge** as the most important person in the courtroom. While there is an expectation of respect that is bestowed on the person holding a judgeship, the judge makes up only one part of the courtroom workgroup.

**Judge** A public officer elected or appointed to administer justice and hear cases in a court of law.

There are different levels of judges: lower court judges, such as justices of the peace; major trial court judges, such as those in district courts; intermediate appellate court judges, who serve in state appellate and superior courts; and

The judge has the responsibility of overseeing fairness in the courtroom.

judges in the courts of last resort, such as the justices in the U.S. Supreme Court. At each level, judges will hear different types of cases. For example, a justice of the peace may preside over charges of traffic violations or school truancy, while the U.S. Supreme Court serves as the final, highest court in the country, hearing appeals that may originate in those local justice of the peace courts. The Supreme Court generally may decide which cases it will review, utilizing the Rule of Four: if four or more justices believe that a case warrants the consideration of the entire court, then the court will review the case.[98]

## Selection of Judges

While most judges obtain their positions by election, federal judges hold their offices for life. Judges are selected in different ways. Federal judges are nominated by the president and then confirmed by the U.S. Senate. This process is outlined in the U.S. Constitution for the Supreme Court justices; the Judiciary Act of 1789 adopted the process for all other federal judicial positions.[99] State, county, and municipal or lower court judges are elected to their positions. This means that candidates must gain the nomination from a political party and then campaign with that party.

President Trump announces Neil Gorsuch as his choice for Supreme Court Justice

## Campaign Financing

Between 1980 and 1986, campaign contributions to candidates in contested appellate court races increased by 250%. During the same period, there was a 450% increase in the number of contributions in excess of $5,000 to candidates in contested appellate court races. The 1988 supreme court elections were the most expensive in Texas history, with twelve candidates for six seats raising $12 million.

Between 1992 and 1997, the seven winning candidates for the Texas Supreme Court raised nearly $9.2 million dollars. Of this $9.2 million, more than 40% was contributed by parties or lawyers with cases before the court or by contributors linked to those parties. The perceived impropriety of judges soliciting and accepting large campaign contributions from attorneys and parties who appear before them has been the subject of numerous newspaper and magazine articles, as well as television broadcasts. In 1987 and again in 1998, 60 Minutes aired segments that examined whether justice was for sale in Texas, and Frontline explored the same question in 1999.

FIGURE 5.1 THE ROAD TO THE SUPREME COURT.

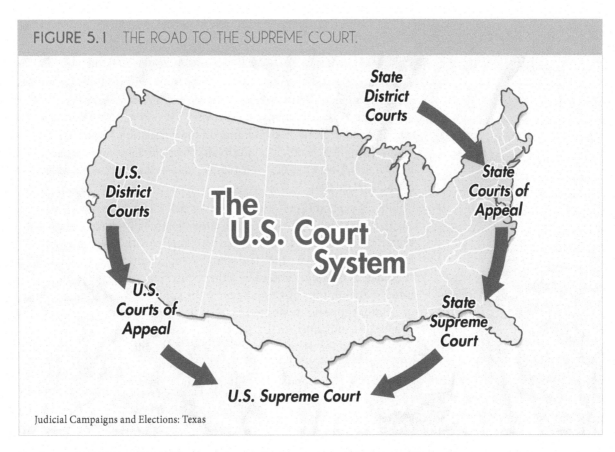

State
District
Courts

U.S.
District
Courts

The
U.S. Court
System

State
Courts of
Appeal

U.S.
Courts of
Appeal

State
Supreme
Court

U.S. Supreme Court

Judicial Campaigns and Elections: Texas

In the early 1980s, plaintiff lawyers were the largest contributors to Texas judicial candidates, but in the late 1980s and 1990s, they were replaced by civil defense attorneys, doctors, insurance companies, and other business interests. In recent years, major contributors to judicial candidates have included the Texas Association of Business and Chambers of Commerce, the Texas Trial Lawyers Association, the Texas Medical Association, Texans for Lawsuit Reform, the insurance industry, energy and natural resources companies, and the Republican and Democratic Parties. Texans for Public Justice, a legal watchdog group founded in 1997, tracks campaign contributions to public officials in Texas, including appellate judges, and has issued a number of reports that examine the relationship between campaign contributions to judges and judicial decisions. Their most recent report, Courtroom Contributions Stain Supreme Court Campaigns, reveals that supreme court candidates receive two thirds of their campaign contributions from lawyers and litigants who appear before them. Other reports include Checks and Imbalances, Payola Justice, and Lowering the Bar.

In 1995, the Judicial Campaign Fairness Act was passed to regulate financing of judicial elections. Under the JCFA:

- Individual contributions to candidates for the supreme court and court of criminal appeals are limited to $5,000. Individual contributions to all other judicial candidates are limited to between $1,000 and $5,000, depending on the population of the judicial district.

- Contributions from law firms and members of law firms are limited to $50 if the aggregate contributions from the firm and its members exceed six times the maximum individual contribution for that judicial office.

- Candidates for the supreme court and court of criminal appeals may accept up to $300,000 in total contributions from PACs. Court of appeals candidates are limited to between $52,500 and $75,000 in total PAC contributions, depending on the population of the judicial district. Total PAC contributions to all other judicial candidates are limited to between $15,000 and $52,500, depending on the population of the judicial district.

- Voluntary expenditure limits are established. Candidates must file a sworn declaration of their intent to either voluntarily comply with or exceed these limits. If a candidate who complies with the expenditure limits is opposed by a candidate who does not comply, the complying candidate is no longer bound by either contribution or expenditure limits. Expenditures by candidates for the supreme court and court of criminal appeals are limited to $2 million. Expenditures by court of appeals candidates are limited to between $350,000 and $500,000, depending on the population of the judicial district. Expenditures by all other judicial candidates are limited to between $100,000 and $350,000, depending on the population of the judicial district.

- Contributions to and expenditures by committees formed to support a judicial candidate, oppose the candidate's opponent, or assist the candidate as an officeholder are considered contributions to and expenditures by the candidate. Contributions to and direct expenditures on behalf of complying candidates from a political party are considered expenditures by the candidate.

- Contribution limits are per candidate, per election. However, the primary election and the general election are considered to be a single election if the candidate is unopposed in the primary *or* if the candidate does not have an opponent on the ballot in the general election. The various contribution limits for that "single election" are increased by 25 percent, but the amount of the increase may only be used for officeholder expenditures. [102]

Due to its political nature, the judge selection process can produce controversy. In Texas, for example, elected judges are allowed to preside over cases in which the involved parties and their lawyers have contributed to the judges' election campaigns. In 2000, a public interest group brought this practice to light, claiming it to be unconstitutional.[100] The trial court ruled against the public interest group, saying that the practice should be solved mutually between the citizens and lawmakers of Texas; the Court of Appeals later affirmed this decision.[101]

**Critical Thinking**

Is it a conflict of interest to permit a judge to preside over a case in which one of the opposing parties is someone who contributed money to the judge's election campaign? Why or why not?

Some state-level judges are appointed by the governor of the state. These positions include the judges for the courts of appeals and sometimes in major district trial courts under certain circumstances. For example, if an elected judge of a district court retires or dies during his or her term, the governor would appoint a replacement. Politics can be involved in this instance as well, as a governor will typically appoint judges who share the same political affiliation.

## Qualifications of Judges

Until the 1960s, many states did not require judges to have education, special training, or other qualifications.[102] This meant that anyone who won an election or was appointed to the position—even someone who did not have a law degree—could become a judge. The New York City Criminal Court Act, implemented in 1962, required judges to reside in the city; to have at least 10 years' experience practicing law in the state of New York; and to pass the state bar exam, although it was possible to do so without obtaining a law degree.[103] Now, almost all states require that a judge in general and appellate court have a juris doctor (or Doctor of Law) degree, be a licensed attorney, and be a member of their state's bar association.

It is important that judges receive ongoing legal training to stay current on changes to laws and the application of the laws. Some entities, such as the Texas Justice Court Training Center at Texas State University, hold state-sponsored training sessions for newly elected judges. This training may address such subjects that are foreign to brand-new judges, such as courtroom and evidentiary procedures, dispute resolution, ethics, and other topics.[104] There are also organizations that provide ongoing training for judges, such as the National Judicial College at the University of Nevada, Reno.[105]

## Duties of Judges

The judge's primary duty is to oversee the standard procedures of the court system to ensure that justice is fairly served. The American Bar Association has laid out a specific description of the duties of the office: "The trial judge has the responsibility for safeguarding both the rights of the accused and the interests of the public in the administration of criminal justice . . . The purpose of a criminal trial is to determine whether the prosecution has established the guilt of the accused as required by law, and the trial judge should not allow the proceedings to be used for any other purpose."[106]

In the courtroom, the judge must make sure that both the prosecution and the defense are given the chance to state their cases, make their arguments, and question the opposing side's witnesses. In each case, the appointed judge decides whether certain pieces of evidence are admissible or inadmissible and gives support for his or her decisions. While the judge has established laws to follow, the judge does have discretion to decide how to apply the laws in his or her courtroom.[107] In this respect, the judge can wield great power over the progression of a criminal case.

During the trial, the judge typically refers to the attorneys of each opposing side as "**counsel**" or "counselor." A counselor is a legal advisor and advocate for one of the sides in a court case. The judge might use this term when addressing the attorneys directly, such as by saying, "Counsel, approach the bench." This is an instruction for each of the attorneys to come to the judge's bench to discuss something with the judge, perhaps out of earshot of the jury and audience. The attorneys may also request to approach the bench by asking the judge for a **sidebar**, which is a discussion held between the judge and the lawyers out of the hearing of the jury.

Deciding whether a piece of evidence is admissible in court depends on several criteria and is one of the more important decisions a trial judge will make. The judge will examine whether the evidence is relevant to the case: that is, whether it is important to the argument being presented by either the prosecution or the defense. The judge also has to consider whether the **probative value** of the evidence outweighs any prejudicial or inflammatory qualities it may have.[108] Evidence has probative value when it is useful and relevant to the case.[109] No matter how useful a piece of evidence may be, it can, however, unfairly sway a jury if it is presented in a way that causes particular anger, sadness, or disgust. For example, a graphic photo of a murder victim's body may be considered inadmissible if it serves no purpose other than to produce an emotional reaction from the jury. Sometimes evidence is admitted in only a limited way. **Limited admissibility** means that the evidence may be used for one specific purpose but cannot be applied in other ways.[110] Continuing the previous example, photos of the murder victim's body may only be admissible if they are shown during the questioning of the medical examiner.

In some state jurisdictions, there is a chief judge who serves as a trial judge and also manages the court system in the local jurisdiction. A chief judge will typically assume the position by tenure or seniority.

While the criminal court judge has the duty to follow and enforce the law in his or her courtroom, how those laws are followed and enforced is partly up to the judge. This is known as *judicial discretion*. A judge may disallow certain testimony in a trial because he or she believes it is not relevant to the case; another judge presiding over the same trial may make a different decision. Judges have the discretion to accept or not accept evidence, pleas, and sentencing agreements made between the prosecution and the defense. This discretion can influence the entire courtroom workgroup. As the prosecutor learns the discretionary tendencies of the judge, the prosecutor learns what preliminary evidence to emphasize during the charging process. As the probation officer learns what types of cases the judge may feel most strongly about, the probation officer may suggest additional or alternative conditions of probation for a particular defendant that may coincide with the judge's beliefs.

**Counsel** A title for an attorney presenting a case in court.

**Sidebar** A discussion conducted during a court hearing between the judge and attorneys outside the hearing of the jury.

**Probative value** Value that is useful in a case.

**Limited admissibility** Evidence that may be used for one specific purpose but cannot be applied in other ways.

## The Court Clerk

The court clerk has many duties that take place both inside and outside the courtroom, performing many different and important jobs. At minimum, the court clerk calls up cases to be heard before the judge and regularly updates the case files for defendants. Before a trial begins, a court clerk may prepare a jury pool for selection and issue jury summonses. During a trial, the clerk will swear in witnesses who are going to testify and can issue subpoenas for witnesses for the defense and the prosecution. The court clerk, or an assistant clerk, also marks exhibits into evidence and maintains proper custody of that evidence while the case is in court. Additionally, the court clerk performs other duties as requested by the judge. In larger jurisdictions, there may be a court clerk in each courtroom, while in smaller jurisdictions, there may be one or two court clerks for the whole courthouse. Some districts have a chief court clerk, often called a court coordinator, who is in charge of making sure the court clerk staff fulfills these duties properly.[111]

Some jurisdictions assign more power to their court clerks, such as the authority to issue warrants for arrest, prepare formal writs and process court-issued documents, and assist with probate matters (i.e., wills and estates). Sometimes young attorneys will serve as court clerks; this level of responsibility can help them gain valuable hands-on experience with various judicial matters. The court clerk can be a powerful position in the courtroom and may sometimes serve as the gateway to discuss case matters with the judge or prosecutor. In addition, a court clerk may have records or know information about a case, or about the judge's tendencies to rule in certain matters, which would be helpful for defense attorneys to know. This, in turn, may affect how the defense attorney formulates the defense.

**Court reporter** A person who uses a shorthand typewriter to record everything that occurs or is said during a court hearing.

**Court record** The official written record of everything that occurs in a court case.

## The Court Reporter

A **court reporter** keeps the official record of everything that happens during a trial. This includes accurately recording everything that is said, whether by the witnesses, the attorneys, or the judge. Some verbal interactions may include objections, instructions the judge gives to the jury, and expert testimony. It is common for a court reporter to read back a portion of the record if instructed by the judge; such instructions may be prompted by a request from the prosecution, the defense, or the jury. The reading of **court records** can help remind courtroom officials of statements made in the courtroom or verify that certain information is included in the official record.

In years past, court reporters were stenographers who used manual shorthand to take detailed notes quickly. Manual shorthand is

The court reporter takes notes of all testimony during trial.

© Lisa F. Young/Shutterstock.com

now largely a thing of the past, and court reporters usually use machine writers to take the transcript of the proceedings. A machine writer looks similar to a small typewriter but has fewer keys, and it is used to type coded letters and combinations of letters rather than entire words and phrases. After the trial has concluded, the court reporter will translate the notes into the official transcript. The notes may be translated visually by the court reporter or scanned by special equipment. In some courts, the court reporter may use computer-aided transcription (CAT) software, which both takes notes and translates those notes into the transcript. Electronic recording equipment, such as audio or video recorders, is used in place of court reporters in some courtrooms, but there are risks to using these machines. Extraneous noises and comments can be recorded and are not easily erased, and the mechanical recorder cannot interrupt proceedings if any testimony is not audible and cannot be recorded properly.

## The Probation Officer

A court probation officer serves as the initial liaison from the local probation department to the defendant who has just been sentenced to probation. Part of a probation officer's duty is to explain the conditions of probation to the defendant for a second time—the judge and defense attorney give the initial explanation—to make sure that the defendant understands. A probation officer will also instruct the defendant on when and where to report for the first probation visit and what to bring to the visit. If there are other procedures, such as reporting for a drug screen or attending a workshop, a probation officer will explain to the defendant how those events will be scheduled as well as handle any associated or monitory paperwork.[112]

Additionally, a probation officer usually serves as an intermediary between the probation department and the judge when dealing with special issues with defendants already on probation. For example, a probation officer from a field office will contact the court probation officer when a probationer tests positive for drugs. The court probation officer will advise the court of the violation and make appropriate recommendations to the field probation officer regarding the handling of the defendant. The court probation officer may also work with the district attorney's office when a defendant returns to court for a probation revocation. A court probation officer is also the court's official custodian of records for the probationer's file while any court hearings are pending. The probation officer becomes familiar with the judge and his or her position on certain types of offenses, as well as the judge's typical rulings on certain criminal matters. In this respect, the probation officer can be a valuable person for a defense attorney to know, especially if the defendant violates probation and must appear before the judge.

## The Bailiff

**Bailiff** A law enforcement officer, such as a sheriff's deputy, assigned to a particular courtroom to assist the judge and courtroom staff in keeping the peace within the courtroom.

A **bailiff** is usually an armed law enforcement officer, typically based in the jurisdiction in which the court is located. For example, a state district court based in a particular county usually has a county sheriff's deputy assigned to that court to serve as the bailiff. A bailiff ensures that order is maintained in the courtroom by instructing spectators and participants to keep discussion at a low volume as well as enforcing any orders or instructions given by the judge.[113] When the judge enters the courtroom, the bailiff announces the judge's arrival as he or she takes the seat at the bench. A bailiff sometimes calls witnesses to testify and may even have to prevent the accused from escaping from custody. A bailiff also controls access to the jury while court is in session and during jury deliberations. When a jury is sequestered, or kept from contact with anyone while a trial is in progress, the bailiff supervises contact between the jury and any non-jury members in an attempt to prevent any outside bias from interfering with the case information given to the jury.

## The Court Process Server

A court process server is responsible for serving subpoenas to witnesses and other persons who are to appear in court. A **subpoena** is a written document that officially notifies someone that he or she must appear in court. A court process server is typically a sheriff's deputy or local law enforcement officer. While a court process server is able to perform law enforcement duties as the court sees necessary, his or her primary function is to serve process.

**Subpoena** A written document that officially notifies someone that he or she must appear in court.

# The Prosecution and Defense

The attorneys for the prosecution and the defense have several things in common. Each attorney will have a certain level of college education, usually having graduated from law school. Attorneys must also comply with the licensing requirements of the state where they want to practice law; this is typically done by taking and passing a bar examination. The bar is the governing body that licenses and regulates attorneys within a particular jurisdiction.

The attorneys for each side play critical roles in the legal process.

## The Prosecution

The prosecution side of judicial proceedings is led by a prosecutor whose primary job is to present a state's case against a defendant. The prosecutor is known by several different names depending on the jurisdiction that he or she represents. The prosecutor may be a district attorney (DA), a county attorney, a state's attorney, or a U.S. attorney. In most states, district attorneys are elected and typically serve four-year terms, although chief federal prosecutors are appointed. In any case, the prosecutor is the lawyer for the government and is the highest law enforcement authority in a particular jurisdiction. When law enforcement officials bring cases to a prosecutor, it is the prosecutor who decides how those cases will be addressed: whether they will be disposed of or dismissed, whether they will be pursued in court, and whether the charges against an accused person may be reduced to a

© Alexander Zavadsky/Shutterstock.com

The state seal is prominently displayed in most state courtrooms.

lesser offense or increased to a more serious charge. In some jurisdictions, prosecutors prepare search and arrest warrants before they are approved and signed by judges.

The role of a prosecutor encompasses many different jobs in one, and each job varies depending on the different stages of the criminal justice process. Prosecutors are involved in various aspects of casework, from investigation, arrest, and trial to sentencing, appeal, and parole, as well as several other additional steps of the judicial process that occur between arrest and trial. Those additional steps may include, but are not limited to, the initial appearance; the preliminary hearing; indictment; arraignment; and pretrial motions. Many prosecutors' offices in the United States have different divisions that handle different types of cases. Each of these divisions may be headed by a chief assistant attorney, who in turn reports to the elected prosecuting attorney. In Franklin County, Ohio, the Criminal Division of the Prosecuting Attorney's Office has 11 different departments, such as the Gang Unit and the Gun Unit, to handle different classifications of criminal offenses.[114]

An initial appearance occurs after a suspect is arrested and becomes a defendant. He or she does not come into contact with a court officer until this appearance. In the initial appearance, the defendant is brought before a magistrate or judge and formally (1) given notice of the charges being brought against him or her, (2) advised of his or her rights, (3) given the opportunity to hire an attorney or request an appointed lawyer, and (4) given the opportunity to request bail. As the agent for the state, a prosecutor is involved in all of these steps, notifying the judge of the charges against the defendant and arguing for a particular bail amount or against bail altogether.

An initial appearance is typically followed by a preliminary hearing, at which the prosecutor for the case must establish probable cause to try the defendant for the crime which he or she is accused of committing. In some instances, a prosecutor will formally notify the court that the case against the defendant will no longer be prosecuted—in other words, charges are dropped. The prosecutor has discretion to decide whether to pursue a case against a defendant. Prosecutorial discretion takes several forms besides the pursuit of charges against a defendant: the prosecutor may offer or accept a plea bargain, may stipulate that the defendant seek counseling or some other treatment before the decision is made to pursue the case, or may dismiss the case entirely.

When judges' discretion, such as on lengths or types of sentences applicable to certain offenses, is limited, discretion often falls by default to the prosecutor. Since the prosecutor is typically voted into office, this can create an ethical conflict. While prosecutors are not supposed to be influenced by political gain or loss that may result from prosecution or non-prosecution of cases, it would be unrealistic to think that this does not occur anywhere in this country. Decisions made by prosecutors are effectively not subject to review by the judicial or administrative processes; this gives prosecutors a great deal of power when deciding whether to proceed with charges against a defendant or in discussion of plea negotiations.[115] Critics argue that the power of the prosecutor's discretion directly contrasts with the ideas of fairness, equity, and accountability upon which the criminal justice system in this country has been based. Still, while plenty of legislation has limited judicial discretion, not much legislation has restrained the discretional power of the American prosecutor.[116]

If a prosecutor decides to proceed with a case, he or she will prepare an information report that demonstrates probable cause to bind over the accused for trial, often called an indictment.[117] In some jurisdictions, such as the state of Texas, the grand jury system is used. In these instances, a prosecutor makes an argument in front of a grand jury to establish probable cause in the hope that the grand jury will return an indictment of the accused. An arraignment may follow.

An *arraignment* has two purposes: to re-inform the defendant of the charges filed against him or her and to give the defendant the chance to enter a plea.[118] According to the Federal Rules of Criminal Procedure, there are three types of pleas allowed: guilty, not guilty, and "no contest," or *nolo contendere.* The phrase *nolo contendere* is Latin and means, "I do not wish to contest." A plea of *nolo contendere* allows for the judge's decision on the defendant's guilt or innocence, while allowing the defendant to refrain from pleading guilty. Defendants in felony charges are arraigned by prosecutors, who bring the accused forward to answer to the indictment or charging instrument. At this stage, a prosecutor may also engage in negotiating a plea with the defendant. This means that the defendant may be allowed to plead guilty to a lesser charge in exchange for a different or reduced sentence.

Before the trial begins, attorneys from both sides may initiate or participate in the arguments of pretrial motions. Pretrial motions may deal with many different issues, such as a request for a trial to be held in a different venue or a motion *in limine*, in which the prosecution seeks to limit the information made available to the defense. A common pretrial motion is a *motion for continuance*, which simply requests that the court postpone the trial to a future date. This motion is generally filed because the requesting side believes there has not been sufficient time to prepare the case for trial.

During a trial, the prosecutor performs his or her primary duty of attempting to prove the defendant's guilt beyond a reasonable doubt. If a defendant is found guilty, sentencing occurs and the prosecutor may recommend a harsher or more lenient sentence, depending on the circumstances of the crime. If a conviction is appealed by the defendant, a prosecutor will typically argue that a conviction was properly obtained and should be upheld. Sometimes, prosecutors may recommend for or against parole for convicted inmates from their jurisdictions when parole reviews arrive. Typically, prosecutors will oppose parole for serious offenders.

## Career Connections: Prosecutor

Working as a prosecutor can be a challenging task. Choosing this field as a career can mean committing to a life of short budgets, large caseloads, and long hours. Prosecutors' salaries may lag well behind those of their peers, and the work can be emotionally taxing. Still, life as a prosecutor can be very fulfilling and rewarding.

Prosecution requires a college degree and three years of law school. Most states require an exam at the conclusion of law school that tests students' overall competency in all of the practice areas they might face. Most prospective prosecutors are required to demonstrate a broad knowledge of legal matters in order to be admitted to the legal bar. They can then be sworn in as lawyers and begin to practice law.

Depending on the size of the jurisdiction, a prosecutor may handle all facets of prosecution or may be able to specialize. Prosecution includes two broad phases: the trial phase and the appellate phase. In large jurisdictions, each phase is handled by separate groups of attorneys working as a team. In smaller jurisdictions, one attorney may handle a particular case throughout both phases. The life cycle of a particular case may vary based on the speed of the jurisdiction and the complexities of the litigation, but the typical life cycle of a case is more than a year.

A prosecutor's job consists of being part social worker, part police officer, and part judge. Prosecutors must be able to handle difficult situations. It is not uncommon for prosecutors to be called out to major crime scenes involving violence and death. Attending autopsies and reviewing crime scene photos may be regular parts of a prosecutor's job. Prosecutors need to have good interpersonal skills, as they deal with law enforcement and victims who may or may not be cooperative. They must be able to make sound decisions quickly. Public speaking is a regular part of the job and a critical skill for effective courtroom litigation.

Prosecution is a career that allows an individual to dramatically impact not only individual lives, but also the community at large. Effectively targeting high-crime areas or violent repeat offenders can make dramatic differences in the day-to-day lives of a prosecutor's constituents. Combining aggressive prosecution techniques with effective public relations campaigns can have a significant deterrent effect within a jurisdiction. Partnering with law enforcement, parent-teacher organizations, and local service organizations can foster educational programs for youth that discourage delinquent behavior that leads to adult criminality.

Students who desire a career in law or prosecution should begin their research and participation in the criminal justice community early. They may seek out internships and service programs with local law enforcement agencies or prosecutor offices. Some police agencies have citizen academies that train local citizens to be ambassadors of law enforcement in the general population and respond to emergencies. Because prosecutorial jobs are becoming harder to acquire, a demonstrated interest in criminal law from an early age can be a tremendous asset when pursuing a prosecutorial job.

Prosecution often leads to other careers. Many prosecutors move on to elected offices such as elected district or county attorneys, judges, legislative positions, or local government officials. Many go on to hold advisory or managerial positions in state and federal government. Many take the extensive trial experience they receive and go on to lucrative private practice careers. Often, prosecutors commit to a lifetime of public service in the prosecutorial field. Prosecutors are in demand in both the private and public sectors.

## The Defense

A defense attorney is a lawyer who represents the accused during the criminal trial process. A defense attorney is typically a trained and educated attorney who may specialize in criminal law. It is the job of the defense to ensure that the rights of the accused are maintained and upheld during the criminal trial process. Prior to trial, a defense attorney will prepare an appropriate and adequate defense to be presented at trial. To prepare for his or her defense, he or she may use the services of outside parties such as experts, witnesses to the crime, character witnesses, and even private investigators.

The Harper Lee novel *To Kill a Mockingbird*, adapted into a movie starring Gregory Peck, featured the classic defense attorney character of Atticus Finch.

Another pretrial job of the defense attorney is negotiating a plea agreement with the state's attorney. A defense attorney will interact frequently, and often intensely, with the defendant before and during trial. These discussions are called privileged communications and are subject to **attorney-client privilege**, meaning that any information shared between a defense attorney and his or her client (the defendant) is kept confidential and does not need to be shared with other members of the court or the public.

During the trial, the defense attorney has the chance to place witnesses on the stand—including the defendant, if that is part of the legal strategy—and ask questions of them. The defense attorney will also have the opportunity to clarify previously testified statements by the state's witnesses by cross-examining them. When an attorney from either side wants to interact directly with a witness, the attorney must ask permission from the judge to **approach the witness**. This allows the attorney to interact more closely with the witness on the stand, including showing evidence to the witness and asking the witness to identify the evidence.

If the accused is found guilty, the defense attorney will argue matters at the sentencing trial and will almost assuredly advise the defendant on any civil issues that may arise as a result of the guilty verdict. A defense attorney may be asked to file an appeal on the conviction, although whether the attorney continues to represent the defendant during the appeal process is typically up to the defendant, in the case of a hired attorney, or the judge, in the case of an appointed attorney or public defender.

There are several types of defense attorneys. A *retained attorney* is one that has been hired to represent a defendant: the defendant, or someone on his or her behalf, will pay money to the attorney in exchange for counsel during the criminal process. Retained attorneys may have a world of resources available to them, including investigators, experts, and support staff, which generally correspond with the defendant's ability to pay for such resources.

Sometimes, a court will appoint a local attorney to represent an indigent defendant during the criminal trial, or appeal, process—a process that was affirmed for all criminal causes following *Gideon v. Wainwright*.

**Attorney-client privilege** The privilege that any information shared between a defense attorney and his or her client is kept confidential and does not need to be shared with other members of the court or the public.

**Approach the witness** An action that occurs when an attorney moves closer to a witness, who is currently on the witness stand, in order to question the witness further or show him or her an exhibit or document. In most jurisdictions, the attorney must request permission from the judge to approach the witness.

## Ethics and Professionalism: Defense Attorneys

As officers of the court, judges and prosecutors are held to ethical standards. Judges must remain impartial and not treat either the defense or the prosecution with hostility, nor must they show favoritism toward either side. Prosecutors must disclose all evidence they will use during trial to the defense, and they are not permitted to allow witnesses or complainants to give false testimony. Judges and prosecutors who do not adhere to the ethical standards imposed upon them by their state bar associations or boards of judicial conduct are subject to sanctions. What, however, about defense attorneys? They are also considered officers of the court, but they are not employed by the government as the judges and prosecutors are. Do defense attorneys have ethical standards that they must follow? Are those ethical standards different than those to which the judges and prosecutors are subjected?

Think about a defense attorney who is representing a man for rape. Not only does the prosecution have enough evidence to show that the defendant committed the rape, but the defendant has also admitted to his attorney that he did commit the rape. How is it ethical for an attorney to defend someone who admittedly committed a terrible crime?

Remember that all persons are afforded certain rights in the U.S. Constitution. Each person is presumed innocent until proven guilty. It is the defense attorney's job to make sure that the defendant receives a fair and impartial trial no matter what the circumstances of the crime may be. The defense attorney will do his or her best to ensure that the prosecution conducts the state's case while following the laws set forth by the state and the federal government. The defense attorney is not present to try to help a guilty criminal go free; the defense attorney helps ensure that the state fulfills its burden of demonstrating the defendant's guilt, as well as ensuring that the defendant's civil rights have not been violated. Think about what would happen if we lived in a country where defendants were not allowed to be represented by counsel and the defendant had the burden to show that he or she did not commit the crime. How would our justice system be different?

---

**Court-appointed attorney** An attorney typically selected from a list of all criminal attorneys in private practice near the jurisdiction who are willing to accept appointed cases.

A **court-appointed attorney** is typically selected from a list of all criminal attorneys in private practice near the jurisdiction who are willing to accept appointed cases. An appointed attorney performs all the services for the defendant that a retained attorney would, but instead of being paid by the defendant or a representative, the appointed attorney is paid by the jurisdiction of the local court. The attorney may submit a voucher detailing his or her work on the case to the local jurisdiction and may be paid by the hour, by the duty performed, or by the court appearance. Fees for appointed attorney work are normally much lower than the fees earned when retained. For example, in Oakland County, Michigan, a court-appointed attorney is paid between $350 and $460 per day for trial appearances.[119] Retained attorneys around the country routinely charge their clients hundreds of dollars per hour for work performed on their cases.

---

**Public defender** An attorney elected in a local jurisdiction to represent indigent defendants in criminal trials.

The ruling in *Gideon v. Wainwright* also helped create the public defender system in the courts, as many defendants cannot afford to hire attorneys to represent them. A **public defender** works much like an appointed attorney, with the exception that a public defender's office is a permanently established office dedicated to represent any indigent defendants in the jurisdiction.

A public defender's office typically employs paralegals, investigators, and other assistants as well as attorneys to conduct the business of defense for the courts. Approximately 64% of counties nationwide now fund public defender programs.[120] Critics of the current public defender system like to demonstrate the inadequate funding the system receives at the state level. The federal public defender system, however, is not experiencing the same problem. The trial defense of Timothy McVeigh, who bombed the Murrah Federal Building in Oklahoma City, cost taxpayers more than $13.8 million. This includes only trial expenses and not appeals.[121]

There are instances in which the court may decide not to appoint an attorney to represent the defendant or refer the case to the local public defender's office. If a defendant claims to be indigent, but is proven to have money or own assets of some amount, such as a car or a home, that can be used to retain an attorney, the judge may deny the request for appointed counsel.

## The Jury

The jury is an important part of the criminal trial process; some may say that, besides the judge, the jury is the most important entity in the court-room. In a jury trial, the jury listens to the evidence presented by both sides and decides whether the defendant is guilty or innocent. In essence, the defendant's life is held in the jury's hands.

Article III of the U.S. Constitution stipulates that "the trial of all crimes . . . shall be by jury." The defendant may choose to waive trial by jury in favor of trial by the judge, as has already been mentioned. In any case where a jury trial is involved, the defendant has been guaranteed by the Supreme Court the right to be judged by a jury of his or her peers.[122]

During the trial, the judge runs the court-room, acting as a judicial umpire and responding to the actions and requests of defense attorneys and prosecutors. Judges have discretion to determine how the law applies to the facts of a specific case. They

© sirtravelalot/Shutterstock.com

A jury is empaneled to hear evidence presented by the prosecution and defense attorneys.

determine which evidence is admissible and which survey questions may be used to select potential jurors, and issue instructions of law to guide the jury in its deliberations.

For many Americans, judges are the most identifiable symbol of justice and fairness in the legal system. As such, judges are invested with a high degree of prestige and respect, as well as a high level of power and responsibility. The Judicial Conference of the United States sets the code of conduct for judges, requiring them to maintain integrity, impartiality, and independence and

**Recusal** The decision by a judge to remove himself or herself from a case if there is a conflict of interest.

to avoid the appearance of impropriety. To meet these standards, judges must **recuse** themselves from cases in which they have a personal interest or connection. Additionally, federal judges must file regular reports of compensation they receive from extrajudicial activities.[123]

## Critical Thinking

Many outcomes in the judicial system (warrants, grand jury indictments, searches, etc.) depend on the definition of probable cause. Is "probable cause" a strong enough basis on which to grant law enforcement and prosecutors such invasive powers? Why or why not?

## U.S. District Courts

U.S. district courts are the federal trial courts. They are courts of limited jurisdiction, as the individual state courts have jurisdiction over the majority of cases. District courts have authority over issues of federal law (a "federal question") and issues between citizens of different states ("diversity jurisdiction"). There are 94 U.S. district courts, with each state having at least one. Districts frequently cover large geographic areas and are subdivided into divisions.

District courts employ anywhere between two and 28 judges per court. The judge determines the issue of law, while the jury (if present) determines issues of fact.[124] In addition, district courts employ magistrates, or federal judges who have the authority to hear lesser charges, conduct trials, accept guilty pleas, and impose sentences. Magistrates are appointed by district judges, but serve a fixed term rather than a lifetime one.[125]

## EXHIBIT: CASE LOAD

During fiscal year 2013, the United States attorneys' offices received 172,024 criminal matters. This represents an increase of 8,193 criminal matters received from law enforcement agencies during the prior year. After review, the offices declined a total of 25,629 criminal matters during the year. The reasons most commonly reported for the declination of these matters included: (1) weak or insufficient evidence, (2) lack of criminal intent, (3) agency request, (4) suspect to be prosecuted by another authority or on other charges, and (4) no federal offense committed.

At the end of fiscal year 2013, a total of 79,735 criminal matters were pending, a decrease of 358 matters when compared to the end of the prior year; of these, 6,790, or nine percent, were matters where the defendant was a fugitive, was in a pre-trial diversion program, was in a mental institution, or was unknown. Of these pending matters, 49,284, or 62 percent, had been pending for 24 months or less, and 58,218, or 73 percent, had been pending for 36 months or less.

During fiscal year 2013, the United States attorneys' offices filed 61,529 criminal cases against 83,825 defendants in United States district courts. This represents a three percent decrease in the number of cases filed and a two percent decrease in the number of defendants filed when compared to the prior year.

The United States Attorneys' offices handled a total of 41,324 criminal matters during fiscal year 2013, in which grand jury proceedings were conducted, representing a two percent decrease when compared to the previous year.

A total of 61,258 cases against 82,092 defendants were also terminated during 2013, representing a six percent decrease in the number of cases terminated and a six percent decrease in the number of defendants terminated, when compared to the prior year. A total of 2,640, or three percent, of the terminated defendants went to trial. This represents a one percent decrease in the number of defendants tried when compared to the prior year. Of the 82,092 defendants terminated during fiscal year 2013, 75,718, or 92 percent, either pled guilty or were found guilty. The rate of conviction remained over 92 percent, as it has since fiscal year 2010.

During fiscal year 2013, a total of 73,397, or 97 percent, of all convicted defendants pled guilty prior to or during trial. This represents the same percentage of convicted defendants who pled guilty when compared to the prior year.

Source: United States Attorneys' Annual Statistical Report (2013). U.S. Department of Justice Executive Office for United States Attorneys. Retrieved from: https://www.justice.gov/sites/default/files/usao/legacy/2014/09/22/13statrpt.pdf

## Circuit Courts of Appeals

The U.S. Circuit Courts of Appeals, created in 1891, are the federal counterparts to the states' intermediate appellate courts; they hear appeals on many cases to ease the burden on the U.S. Supreme Court. The 94 federal districts are subdivided into 12 circuits, with one court of appeals per circuit. Each court hears appeals from district courts and federal administrative agencies. Federal appellate courts also hear appeals involving patent laws, which arise from decisions rendered by the U.S. Court of Federal Claims and the U.S. Court of International Trade.[126]

Federal appellate courts first screen cases to decide whether to dispose of a case or hear it. Cases are heard by panels of three judges, unless the panel is unable to reach a conclusion. In that instance, the court may hear the case *en banc*. After an appellate court decides to hear a case, the attorneys submit written briefs, present their case orally, and answer questions from the judges. The judges then either announce their decision or confer at greater length before rendering a written decision.[127]

Circuit judges are appointed in the same way as district court judges. If a party is dissatisfied with a circuit court of appeals' decision, it may appeal further to the U.S. Supreme Court. However, these requests are rarely granted. Appellate courts also may **remand** cases to a lower court for further proceedings.

**Remand** An appellate court's process of returning a case to a lower court for further proceedings.

## U.S. Supreme Court

The United States Supreme Court is the highest court in the land. It is composed of nine justices who are nominated by the president and confirmed by the U.S. Senate. Like other judges, most U.S. Supreme Court justices are former attorneys (though this is not a prerequisite), and the majority are elevated to the Court from a judgeship in a lower court. The U.S. Supreme Court is a court of discretionary appeal, so it has discretion to decide which cases it will hear. Typically, it selects cases that carry the most profound legal and political ramifications.[128] Also, as an appellate court, it does not hear witness testimony, but instead reviews legal briefs, hears oral arguments by attorneys, and issues written decisions.

**FIGURE 5.3** GEOGRAPHIC BOUNDARIES OF UNITED STATES COURTS OF APPEALS AND UNITED STATES DISTRICT COURTS

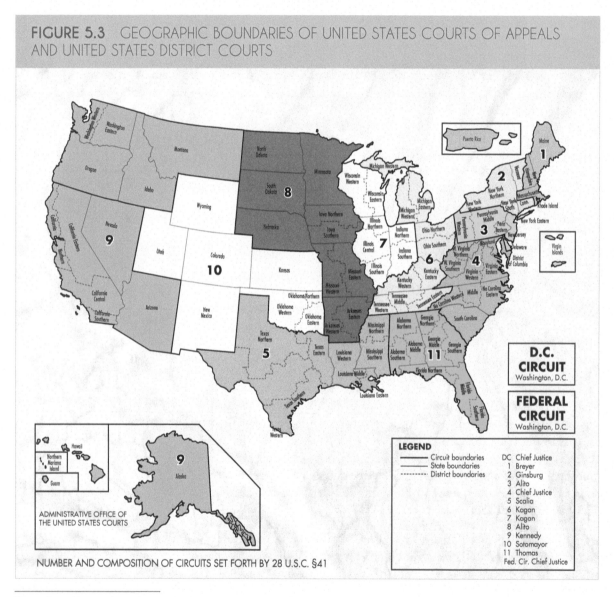

NUMBER AND COMPOSITION OF CIRCUITS SET FORTH BY 28 U.S.C. §41

**Writ of certiorari**

A document issued by the U.S. Supreme Court to confirm that it will review the decision of a federal circuit court of appeals or a state supreme court.

Advancing an appeal to the Supreme Court is not easy; the vast majority of appellants never make it there. The main route to the highest court is through a petition for a **writ of certiorari**, which is a petition filed by a losing party with the Supreme Court, asking it to review the decision of a federal circuit court of appeals or a state supreme court.[129]

The U.S. Supreme Court follows the rule of four: four of the nine justices must vote to hear an appeal, or it will not be heard. Customarily, several criteria must be met in order for an appeal to be heard. First, the plaintiff must have exhausted all other avenues of appeal. Second, the issue must involve a "substantial federal question," as the Supreme Court's jurisdiction is grounded in the U.S. Constitution. Third, the appealed decision must involve an alleged violation of either the Constitution or federal law (the U.S. Code). Finally, the court will not hear cases that ask it to interpret a state's law unless that law violates the U.S.

The U.S. Supreme Court hears between 100 and 200 cases per year.

Constitution. This practice rules out most appeals, as they involve either state criminal statutes or personal civil suits. After applying these criteria and others, the Supreme Court hears oral arguments for 75–80 cases per year, out of 10,000 petitions for writs of certiorari.[130]

*Judicial review,* the power to invalidate acts of Congress, is perhaps the Supreme Court's most significant privilege. It gives the court the authority to interpret authoritatively the supreme law of the land, often to profound social, cultural, and legal effect. The Supreme Court has used this authority about 150 times over acts of Congress, and has invalidated 956 congressional statutes and struck down 1,068 state laws.[131]

## Specialized Federal Courts

The federal court system has fewer specialized courts of limited jurisdiction than do the individual states. Article III courts, such as district and circuit courts of appeals, derive their authority from the U.S. Constitution. These courts include the U.S. Court of Federal Claims, which adjudicates suits against the government, and the U.S. Court of International Trade, which entertains cases involving international trade and tariffs.

A second type of specialized federal court is created by Congress. These include magistrate courts, which handle certain civil and criminal cases at the behest of the parties involved; the U.S. Court of Appeals for the Armed Forces, which handles appeals under the Uniform Code of Military Justice; the U.S. Tax Court; and the U.S. Court of Appeals for Veterans Claims. Additionally, bankruptcy courts have sole jurisdiction over cases that fall under the U.S. Bankruptcy Code.[132]

# Criminal Procedure and Due Process Overview

Criminal procedure and due process are concepts that describe the rights of individuals accused of crimes. **Due process** is a legal doctrine that requires

**Due process** The requirement that an accused person receive notice of the charges made against him or her and the right to respond to those charges before being deprived of life, liberty, or property.

equitable treatment of accused individuals. Its purpose is to prevent uncertainty in the justice system, and to ensure that the process does not conflict with the provisions of the Constitution.[133] The term *criminal procedure* refers to the rules of procedure that the government and courts must follow when enforcing substantive criminal law.

The constitutional basis for criminal procedure and due process is the Bill of Rights in the U.S. Constitution. The amendments that compose the Bill of Rights were designed to alleviate fears that the strong federal government would threaten the freedoms of everyday Americans. There are two different but related types of due process. The first is procedural due process. *Procedural due process* refers to the judicial procedures that prosecutors, police, and the courts must adhere to when charging an individual with a criminal offense.[134]

The Bill of Rights was designed to alleviate fears that the strong federal government would threaten the freedoms of everyday Americans.

The second is substantive due process, a concept more far-reaching than the first. *Substantive due process* entails the right to protection against policies and laws that exceed the government's authority, as it is limited by the Constitution.[135] In the context of criminal procedure, this means rights of due process that are not explicitly listed in the Constitution, but are still fundamental liberties. Congress, therefore, cannot pass statutes that violate those rights.[136] Substantive rights are the affirmative rights of citizens to do or say certain things despite the objections of government. These include, in addition to the rights listed above, freedoms of speech and religion.

Number of Felons Convicted in State Courts. In 2006, nearly one million individuals were convicted of felonies in state courts.

These rights are often not enumerated in the Constitution itself. This makes them basic or, in the words of the Supreme Court itself, "fundamental rights implicit in the concept of ordered liberty."[137] Thus, citizens are protected if the legislature enacts a law that violates substantive due process. For the purposes of criminal procedure, substantive due process requires law enforcement officials to inform defendants, at the time of their arrest, of their right to remain silent and to have an attorney present. This right ensures that defendants do not feel compelled to incriminate themselves.

## Constitutional Guarantees

Other rights embodied in the Bill of Rights are of critical importance. The Fourth Amendment, for example, protects citizens against unreasonable searches and seizures. These protections extend to searches of persons, homes, and documents. According to the common law decisions derived from the Fourth Amendment, a search warrant may be issued by a judge only if the judge decides there is probable cause to do so. Specifically, the judge must believe an individual has committed an offense or possesses evidence of an offense.

## Supreme Court Justification for Jury Trials

The U.S. Constitution guarantees the right to a speedy trial to anyone who is tried in an American courtroom; it is provided in the Sixth Amendment of the Bill of Rights, but it took several rulings from the U.S. Supreme Court to clarify this right. The first ruling to apply the right to speedy trial to the state trial courts was *Klopfer v. North Carolina* in 1967. In this case, the defendant was tried on charges of criminal trespass, but the jury failed to agree on a verdict, resulting in a mistrial. A second trial was supposed to occur, but after one year passed and the second trial did not begin, Klopfer demanded that the trial begin immediately or his case be dismissed. The judge denied Klopfer's request, but granted the state's request to make the case inactive without bringing the defendant to trial, which meant that

The U.S. Supreme Court has clarified the right to a speedy trial in Klopfer v. North Carolina and Barker v. Wingo.

the case could be made active again at any time the state so chose. Klopfer appealed to the North Carolina Supreme Court, which, in turn, ruled that the right to a speedy trial did not mean the state could be forced to prosecute a defendant. Klopfer's case remained inactive, and Klopfer then appealed to the U.S. Supreme Court. The U.S. Supreme Court ruled in Klopfer's favor, simultaneously striking down the North Carolina law that had allowed the indefinite postponement of Klopfer's trial. This judgment extended the speedy trial provision to the states.[138]

The U.S. Supreme Court heard the case of *Barker v. Wingo* in 1972. Prior to this case, courts assumed that a defendant who did not demand a speedy trial was not opposed to waiting. The U.S. Supreme Court held in *Barker* that passively allowing a case to plod slowly through the system does not equate to the defendant's waiver of his or her Sixth Amendment rights. While this ruling did not specify time frames, it did list a number of factors that trial courts need to take into consideration when determining whether the right to a speedy trial has been denied: how long the delay has lasted, why the delay has taken place, the demand of the defendant to have a speedy trial, and any bias against the defendant.[139]

The next year, 1973, yielded the U.S. Supreme Court's ruling in *Strunk v. United States*. This case determined that if a defendant is denied a speedy trial, the appropriate and "only possible remedy" is dismissal of the charges.[140] Several years later, the U.S. Supreme Court clarified in *United States v. Lovasco* that the Sixth Amendment right applies to delays that occur between a defendant's arrest and the trial—not any delays prior to the initial charges and arrest of a defendant.[141]

Another right provided under the Sixth Amendment is the right to a public trial. This right stemmed from the practice of secret trials in Europe, such as the Spanish Inquisition and the Star Chamber in England. In 1948, the U.S. Supreme Court ruled in *In re Oliver* that the failure to allow a defendant a reasonable opportunity to defend himself against a charge of contempt of court violated due process of law. In this case, a man was subpoenaed to testify as a witness to a crime that was being secretly investigated by a one-man grand jury (i.e., a single judge). The judge believed that the man's testimony was false and evasive and promptly charged him with contempt, found him guilty, and sentenced him to 60 days in jail. This process occurred without the witness's knowledge and did not allow him the opportunity to defend himself. The U.S. Supreme Court ruled that the 14th Amendment prevents an accused from being deprived of his or her rights without due process of law; therefore, an accused person cannot be sentenced to prison in secrecy.[142]

## Jury Selection

A defendant has the right to be judged by a jury of his or her peers. The jury must therefore comprise individuals who, in general, reflect the values, rational abilities, and common sense of the average, everyday citizen. A jury of one's peers is supposed to consist of people who are impartial to the case and live in the jurisdiction—typically the county—where the defendant lives. Peer juries are made up of people who represent the community where the alleged crime occurred and where the trial will be held. In 1945, the Supreme Court clarified the meaning of a "jury of one's peers" by stating that while it is unnecessary for each jury to be composed of representatives of every possible economic, racial, religious, gender, and ethnic variable from the community, potential jurors may not be excluded intentionally or systematically due to their social characteristics.[143] The concept of peer juries has origins in the Magna Carta, which guaranteed jury trials for "freemen."[144] This principle was incorporated directly into the U.S. Constitution in Article III, which states: "The trial of all crimes, except in cases of impeachment, shall be by jury."[145] The Sixth Amendment reaffirms Article III by stating, "In all criminal prosecutions, the accused shall enjoy the right to a speedy and public trial by an impartial jury."[146] While federal criminal cases followed suit, some states, such as Louisiana, applied the right to a jury trial selectively. Until 1968, Louisiana granted jury trials only when capital punishment or imprisonment with hard labor were options for sentencing. The Supreme Court ruling in *Duncan v. Louisiana* further applied the jury trial provisions to state-level criminal trials.[147]

Jury members are selected from a master list of all eligible persons in the local jurisdiction of a trial's location. Typically, juries have 12 members, although this is not always the case. State courts are allowed to use as few as six persons in a jury in non-capital cases; federal courts always use 12-member juries. The Supreme Court ruled in *Williams v. Florida* (1970) that states may use juries composed of at least six people in non-capital cases.[39]

There are eligibility requirements for jury service in the United States. In general, jurors must be citizens of the United States and be able to read and write. Jurors must also be older than age 18 and, in most jurisdictions, registered to vote. There are several criteria, which may vary between jurisdictions, that will disqualify someone from being eligible. A serious felony conviction will typically preclude someone from being a juror, for example. Persons such as parents who care for young children during the day, the elderly, or the disabled, who would otherwise be eligible for jury duty, may declare themselves exempt due to physical limitations or personal obligations. This is done on a case-by-case basis and does not permanently exempt the potential juror from service; he or she may be selected again in the future. In the interest of keeping jury panels impartial, as the U.S. Constitution instructs, exemptions are limited at least when preparing the master list.

A *venire*, or *venire facias*, is a writ that summons jurors for service. The potential jurors will report to a designated office or building at a particular date and time. They are interviewed to confirm whether they are eligible and available to serve on a jury. Some are dismissed and sent home, thus fulfilling their jury service. Those who are kept in the jury pool are paid a nominal amount for their service. From the jury pool, several jury panels may be selected and sent to various courtrooms that require juries. A jury panel for a misdemeanor trial will typically be smaller than a jury panel for a felony trial. A felony jury panel could be as many as 36 or more persons. The jury panels are selected at random by the county official, usually a clerk of the court.

A *voir dire* examination is an oath sworn by a potential juror concerning his or her qualifications to serve on a jury. The term *voir dire* means "to speak the truth." During *voir dire*, both the prosecution and the defense will ask potential jurors questions about their personal and professional backgrounds, any prior experience with courts or the legal system, and even personal opinions on current events—which may have relevance for the charge against the defendant. Sometimes the judge will ask jurors questions as well. Any juror who is seen by either side as unacceptable for the jury is typically eliminated by either the challenge for cause or the peremptory challenge. A **challenge for cause** is a specific legal reason to exclude a potential juror. The side that makes the challenge must defend the challenge to the judge, as the challenge typically argues that the juror will be unable to fairly judge the accused for a particular reason. The decision to remove the juror is up to the judge, but there are statutes that specify rules for removing jurors. A **peremptory challenge** is an objection to a potential juror without specifying a reason for the objection. The attorney making the peremptory challenge can make the challenge for any reason, or no reason, and whether a peremptory challenge is made is usually an important part of an attorney's trial strategy. There are limits to the number of jurors who may be eliminated

**Challenge for cause**
A specific legal reason to exclude a potential juror.

**Peremptory challenge**
An attorney's objection to the jury service of a potential juror without a particular argument against the juror.

due to peremptory challenges. New York allows three peremptory challenges, except in particularly serious cases, while Texas allows six.[148]

There are also limitations to peremptory challenges. Using challenges to purposely exclude persons of a particular race, particularly African-Americans, was a common occurrence until the late 20th century, and the Supreme Court upheld the practice in its 1965 ruling, *Swain v. Alabama*.[149] However, in 1986, the Court partially overruled *Swain*, proclaiming in *Batson v. Kentucky* that blacks may not be excluded from juries due to concern that they will decide in favor of a black defendant.[150] The *Batson* ruling was later expanded to include challenges that purposely excluded jurors based on gender; however, the ruling was delivered via a paternity case, *J.E.B. v. Alabama ex rel. T.B.*, not a criminal case.[151] The number of challenges allowed varies from state to state and is controlled by statute.

*Voir dire* continues until the entire jury has been filled, no matter how many challenges occur. Sometimes, alternates are selected. These alternates will sit through the trial with the jury and will take the place of a juror who is forced to leave the trial while it is in progress. Reasons that a juror may leave include illness, family emergency, or disqualification.

**Sequester** To remove the jury, and any alternate jurors, from all possible influences that may affect their abilities to fairly judge the accused.

As soon as the jury is sworn in, the criminal trial officially begins. The judge must decide whether to **sequester** the jury for the duration of the trial. Sequestering a jury theoretically removes the jury, and any alternate jurors, from all possible influences that may affect their abilities to fairly judge the accused. The sequestered jury is housed in a hotel and not allowed visitors. Any magazines or newspapers they read or television shows they watch are censored. Typically, a judge will sequester a jury only in a high-profile case, when inflammatory news stories or tabloid articles may potentially unduly influence the jury. Sequestering a jury puts a strain on the jury members, as they must remain away from their homes, jobs, and families until the trial is over—regardless of whether the trial lasts three days or three months.

With innovations in technology over the last few decades, including the Internet and mobile phones, it has become increasingly difficult to separate the jury from all outside influences that might affect their ultimate decision-making process. Jurors who are sequestered must be monitored more closely now than in years past, due to the wide availability of cell phones and Internet access.

After the state presents its case, the defense may enter a motion for a directed verdict. This motion asserts that the state failed to present a case proving the defendant's guilt beyond a reasonable doubt and asks the judge to acquit the defendant. If the judge approves this motion, he or she typically will direct the jury to acquit the defendant. Even when this motion is not filed by the defense, a trial judge may still order a directed verdict of not guilty. The judge may also order a directed verdict because the prosecutor behaved improperly in some way, or the testimony from the witnesses for the prosecution was not credible.

Once closing arguments have been made, the judge issues orders directly to the jury. These orders include that the jury retire to the jury room; consider the facts, evidence, and testimony presented in court; and decide on a fair verdict. The judge's order will include instructions about the possible verdicts the jury may decide on and the legal definition of reasonable doubt. In some jurisdictions, judges are allowed to review all of the evidence that has been presented to the jury, such as the testimony of each witness. This can be helpful if the trial has been lengthy, but it may inadvertently influence a jury as well if the judge has suggested an opinion about the defendant's innocence or guilt. It can take some time to deliver the instructions to the jury due to the complexities of the laws that must be followed. It is important that judges deliver the jury instructions in a way that all the jurors can understand them and fulfill their duties. Generally, the final instruction given to the jurors is that they may not discuss the facts of the case with anyone other than their fellow jurors during official deliberations.

## Deliberations and Beyond

After the judge's charge has concluded, the jury is removed so that it may begin deliberations. Once the jury retires to the jury room, a foreperson is selected to be the jury's leader. In some courts of law, the first juror selected during *voir dire* is the foreperson. A foreperson typically sits at the head of the table and calls for a vote. Unanimous jury verdicts are required by law in each state except for Oregon and Louisiana. The Oregon Constitution and the Louisiana Codes of Criminal Procedure both allow for non-unanimous jury verdicts in certain non-capital criminal cases. The Supreme Court upheld these state requirements in two 1972 decisions, *Johnson v. Louisiana* and *Apodaca v. Oregon*.[152] There is strength in numbers, however, when it comes to jury deliberation. Twelve unique points of view can expose jury members to different interpretations and opinions about the evidence presented and, thus, discourage them from using only their personal beliefs to select a verdict. Additionally, jurors can work together to refresh improperly or incorrectly recalled memories from the trial.[153]

Jury members are drawn from many different circumstances and situations. They may be schoolteachers, long-haul truck drivers, firefighters, business executives, retired persons, or even students. Because jurors are not always familiar with the legal system, some may not understand legal procedures and complications that arise during the trial process. Even intelligent and well-meaning jurors may not fully understand the judge's charge or some of the jury instructions. Jurors are allowed to ask questions of the court, usually written on paper and delivered to the judge by the bailiff. Communication from the jury is typically read aloud in open court so that it may be entered into the record of the case.

When a jury is unable to generate the required number of votes for a decision, and deliberations have been conducted for some time, the result is a hung jury, which is fairly uncommon. The jury is called into open court and dismissed, and the judge declares a mistrial, allowing the prosecution the choice to drop the case or refile it and attempt to retry the defendant. Juries may be hung due to varying opinions of the significance of a piece of evidence, the meaning of "reasonable doubt," or differing opinions about innocence or guilt.

When a verdict is reached, the jury returns to the courtroom to announce the decision in a formal statement to the court. The jury is then thanked for its service and released by the judge. A prosecutor may request that the court poll the jury members: that is, the judge or bailiff asks each juror whether he or she individually voted for the whole jury's verdict. Polling a jury is typically done to determine whether a juror has been pressured to vote with the remainder of the jurors.

**Jury nullification**
A process that occurs when a jury uses information not provided during a court case to determine the guilt or innocence of a defendant.

One phenomenon in the criminal trial process is **jury nullification**. This occurs when a jury nullifies, or contradicts, the fair and impartial procedure of the trial process in some way. Jury nullification may also occur when a jury does not follow the court's interpretation of the law. A jury may disregard the court's instructions and consider information not presented in court during the trial as evidence in the case. For example, if a defendant claims to have a medical disability that prevented him from being able to commit a murder, and one of the jurors is a medical expert on that disability and subsequently uses personal knowledge to influence the verdict, that is considered jury nullification. A jury may also exercise nullification by refusing to convict the accused because the members believe the penalty is too severe. An example of this would be a case of a young man who shoots his father to prevent the father from committing another incident of spousal abuse on his wife. The jury, feeling that the young man attempted to protect his mother from harm because he knew the beatings would occur again, may find the defendant not guilty.

Judges clearly state in the charge to the jury that jurors are to consider only evidence presented in court, but this does not always occur in a room full of human beings, each with different knowledge and opinions. Attorneys are considered officers of the court with the duty to promote and uphold the law, and many bar associations consider it a breach of ethics for an attorney to make an argument in court that may cause jury nullification. Judges also have the ability to prohibit statements or arguments that request jury nullification. In the *U.S. v. Moylan* (4th Cir. 1969) decision, the right of jury nullification was affirmed, but the Circuit Court also upheld the court's power to disallow statements that informed the jurors of their right of nullification.[154] In a Sixth Circuit Court of Appeals ruling in 1980, the entire panel of judges agreed unanimously that "in criminal cases, a jury is entitled to acquit the defendant because it has no sympathy for the government's position."[155] In contrast, however, the Second Circuit ruled that a juror may be removed, according to Federal Rules of Criminal Procedure 23(b), if there is evidence that he or she intends to nullify the law.[156]

**Bifurcated trial** A criminal trial that has two separate phases: the first phase determines the defendant's guilt or innocence, and the second phase determines the defendant's potential punishment.

Sometimes, the criminal trial is **bifurcated**, or split into two parts. In the first part, the defendant's guilt or innocence is decided; in the second part, the defendant's punishment is argued. Juries do deliberate on a defendant's punishment, and their "verdict" comes in the form of a recommendation to the judge. A jury may sentence a defendant to a particular punishment, only to be overruled by the judge, who sentences the defendant to a different punishment. This does not happen often, however.

## The Accused

While the accused person is at the heart of the criminal trial process, the defendant can be largely unaware of many of the legal aspects of his or her criminal case that occur behind the scenes. There are discussions between the attorneys about evidence that may be presented and witnesses that may be called, as well as negotiations for plea bargains. There may be discussions between the state's attorney, the defense attorney, and the judge about procedural matters that can affect the outcome of the defendant's case but have nothing to do with the offense the accused reportedly committed. The defendant's guilt or innocence lies in the public and private aspects of the trial process and will likely affect the rest of his or her life.

Some defendants are allowed to bond out of jail after arrest. This means that they guarantee, with money, that they will appear at all court hearings during the trial process, including any hearings prior to the beginning of the trial. Defendants may post bond by providing the required amount of cash to the jurisdiction or using the services of a bail bondsman. The defendant will pay a small portion of the bond, usually around 10%, to the bondsman, who will in turn provide proof to the jurisdiction that the defendant has paid bond. The bondsman guarantees the jurisdiction that the defendant will appear for all court hearings. If the defendant fails to appear in court, or "jumps" bond, the bond is revoked by the court, and the bail bondsman is responsible for paying the court the amount of the defendant's bond. If the defendant is subsequently found and brought into custody, he or she will appear in court, and the bondsman will receive a refund of the monies paid to the jurisdiction.

Some defendants are unable to post bond due to financial constraints. Bond amounts can range from $500 for some misdemeanors to $1,000,000 for high-profile cases. Some defendants are not approved for bond by the judge because the judge feels that the defendant will run away or because the judge feels it is safer to society if the defendant remains in jail. Bail is not guaranteed by the U.S. Constitution; however, the Eighth Amendment does state that "excessive bail shall not be required." This means that a judge may not prescribe an outrageous bail amount when compared to the alleged crime. In other words, the Eighth

© Joe Seer/Shutterstock.com

Actress and celebrity defendant Lindsay Lohan faced felony charges for allegedly taking a necklace from a jewelry store.

Amendment prevents judges from assigning a bail amount of $250,000 to a defendant accused of writing a bad check in the amount of $500. Defendants who cannot post bond or do not have an approved bond will remain in jail until trial. **Transport officers** will bring the defendant to court for all court appearances including trial.

A transport officer brings defendants to and from their court appearances.

During a trial, a defendant will sit next to his or her defense attorney at a table near the front of the courtroom. The U.S. Constitution guarantees an accused person the right to confront his or her accuser, meaning a defendant has the right to be present for all witness testimony. During trial, a defendant will frequently confer with the defense attorney to clarify questions or strategy. Whether or not a defendant testifies is also part of the defense's trial strategy. A defendant has the constitutional right to refrain from testifying in court; this is called the right not to incriminate oneself. If a defendant does testify, he or she is subject to the same process of cross-examination by which any other witness must participate.

If a defendant is in custody during the trial process, he or she will return to a supervised room or area when court is not in session. A defendant is allowed to confer with his or her attorney in private but will not have free access to the building. If a defendant needs to use the restroom, for example, someone will accompany him or her to ensure that there is no escape attempt or harm done to anyone—including the harm of a defendant by another party.

After jury deliberations are over and a verdict is delivered in court, a defendant will be released in the case of a not guilty verdict or remanded to the custody of the local jurisdiction in the case of a guilty verdict. Some judges may, depending on circumstances and arguments from the prosecution and defense, release a defendant who has been found guilty for a temporary time so that he or she can manage personal affairs before punishment is assessed. The defendant may be ordered to turn himself or herself in to the authorities on a particular date and time or may be ordered to return to court for sentencing.

A defendant in a criminal trial is arguably in a precarious situation. On the one hand, a defendant is technically innocent until proven guilty. Due to human tendencies and public opinion, a defendant may be perceived as guilty even if the jury returns a verdict of not guilty. Such perception of a defendant can affect the defendant's reputation and everyday activities for the rest of his or her life. The prosecuting attorney has the task of proving the defendant's guilt; often, the prosecutor publicly makes the defendant look like a bad person in addition to showing guilt. This process is sometimes known as a **degradation ceremony**.[157] For example, the prosecutor may take on a very negative attitude when speaking to the jury, using body language such as a curled lip or deep frown to demonstrate his or her distaste for the defendant. Presenting the defendant in the worst light possible is part of the prosecutor's job. The defense attorney will attempt to salvage the defendant's appearance during counterargument.

### Critical Thinking

Do you believe it is fair for a prosecutor to embellish negative statements about the defendant in an attempt to win the sympathy of the jury? Why or why not?

### Exhibit: The Bill of Rights

*Amendment I*

Congress shall make no law respecting an establishment of religion, or prohibiting the free exercise thereof; or abridging the freedom of speech, or of the press; or the right of the people peaceably to assemble, and to petition the Government for a redress of grievances.

*Amendment II*

A well regulated Militia, being necessary to the security of a free State, the right of the people to keep and bear Arms, shall not be infringed.

*Amendment III*

No Soldier shall, in time of peace be quartered in any house, without the consent of the Owner, nor in time of war, but in a manner to be prescribed by law.

*Amendment IV*

The right of the people to be secure in their persons, houses, papers, and effects, against unreasonable searches and seizures, shall not be violated, and no Warrants shall issue, but upon probable cause, supported by Oath or affirmation, and particularly describing the place to be searched, and the persons or things to be seized.

*Amendment V*

No person shall be held to answer for a capital, or otherwise infamous crime, unless on a presentment or indictment of a Grand Jury, except in cases arising in the land or naval forces, or in the Militia, when in actual service in time of War or public danger; nor shall any person be subject for the same offence to be twice put in jeopardy of life or limb; nor shall be compelled in any criminal case to be a witness against himself, nor be deprived of life, liberty, or property, without due process of law; nor shall private property be taken for public use, without just compensation.

*Amendment VI*

In all criminal prosecutions, the accused shall enjoy the right to a speedy and public trial, by an impartial jury of the State and district wherein the crime shall have been committed, which district shall have been previously ascertained by law, and to be informed of the nature and cause of the accusation; to be confronted with the witnesses against him; to have compulsory process for obtaining witnesses in his favor, and to have the Assistance of Counsel for his **defense**.

*(Continued)*

**Exhibit: The Bill of Rights (*Continued*)**

*Amendment VII*

In Suits at common law, where the value in controversy shall exceed twenty dollars, the right of trial by jury shall be preserved, and no fact tried by a jury, shall be otherwise re-examined in any Court of the United States, than according to the rules of the common law.

*Amendment VIII*

Excessive bail shall not be required, nor excessive fines imposed, nor cruel and unusual punishments inflicted.

*Amendment IX*

The enumeration in the Constitution, of certain rights, shall not be construed to deny or disparage others retained by the people.

*Amendment X*

The powers not delegated to the United States by the Constitution, nor prohibited by it to the States, are reserved to the States respectively, or to the people.[158] ]

The Fifth Amendment, in turn, protects citizens from being put on trial twice for the same crime, a practice known as double jeopardy. It also protects individuals against self-incrimination. A defendant who "takes the Fifth" during testimony is using this constitutional right. The Fifth Amendment also guarantees due process. Specifically, the Fifth Amendment requires an individual to be notified of the charges against him or her, and affords him or her the right to answer those charges before being deprived of life, liberty, or property.

The Sixth Amendment guarantees the right to a speedy trial and the right to a trial by jury. Additionally, it allows a defendant to confront his or her accuser in court, to force witnesses to provide testimony, and to be represented by an attorney. The Seventh Amendment provides the right to trial by jury in certain types of civil cases. The Eighth Amendment protects defendants against excessive bail and cruel and unusual punishment.

**Critical Thinking**

Does the Constitution favor the accused at the expense of the victim? If so, what do you think the justifications are for doing so? Explain.

## Constitutional Basis for Due Process

The 14th Amendment guarantees due process to every criminal defendant in the United States. Passed in the aftermath of the Civil War, this amendment initially helped protect the civil rights of African-Americans. It contains a due process clause that prevents states from depriving citizens of life, liberty, and property without the due process of law. This clause is similar to the due process clause found in the Fifth Amendment, but the Fifth Amendment version is understood to apply only to the federal government, while the 14th Amendment version also applies to state and local governments.

The judiciary has repeatedly affirmed that the procedural guarantees in the Bill of Rights—specifically the Fifth, Sixth, and Eighth Amendments—limit what the state can do when it charges and prosecutes an individual. If any of these guarantees or rights are violated or denied, then the individual has been denied due process of law, a violation of his or her constitutional rights. The Supreme Court is the ultimate arbiter of remedies for such violations, as it interprets the Constitution. It ruled in *Chapman v. California* (1967) that "we cannot leave to the States the formulation of . . . remedies designed to protect people from infractions by the States of federally guaranteed rights."[159]

The passage of the 14th Amendment allowed the U.S. Supreme Court to enforce the Bill of Rights against state governments. The 14th Amendment contained what has come to be called the "equal protection clause," which prevents a governmental authority from denying an individual equal protection of the laws, such as laws that guarantee civil rights. It was used to force states to provide the same protection under law to individuals of all races.

## Amount of Due Process

An accused person is afforded rights even beyond those enumerated in the Constitution and state and federal law. For example, the 14th Amendment's due process clause also prohibits practices that fail to meet a standard of fundamental fairness, even if they do not violate a specific provision.[160] Furthermore, the rights of due process, along with the others enumerated in the U.S. Constitution, can never be repealed by the states. Individual states may add additional rights by amending their own constitutions, but they cannot take away or restrict those guaranteed by the Constitution. Additionally, substantive due process significantly strengthens the power

© create jobs 51/Shutterstock.com

Defendants' rights, guaranteed by the U.S. Constitution, are the subject of controversy.

of judicial review. The Supreme Court has retained more extensive discretion in deciding which rights are "substantive" and deserve protection.

## Defendants' Rights

In the American criminal justice system, a defendant is presumed innocent unless and until proven guilty. The burden of proof rests on the prosecution (the state); the prosecution must prove that the defendant is guilty rather than the accused proving they are innocent. In practice, this makes it much more difficult to convict a defendant, as he or she must be proved guilty beyond a **reasonable doubt**. If a judge or jury concludes there is a

**Reasonable doubt** The standard of proof that the state must meet to convict a criminal defendant; if reasonable doubt exists, the defendant must be acquitted.

reasonable doubt the defendant committed the crime, the defendant must be acquitted.

These defendants' rights, and the guarantees enshrined in the U.S. Constitution, were influenced by the fear of tyrannical government. Under the Constitution, everyone is equal in the eyes of the law. The accused must not be painted as the enemy of the state and must be judged by the rule of law (e.g., due process and criminal procedure). The rule of law is crucial because, according to J.H. Skolnick, "its essential element is the reduction of arbitrariness by officials."[161]

Defendants' rights are the subject of controversy. Critics believe that too many guilty people go free because of these rights, while proponents claim that these rights are necessary to spare the innocent from unjust prosecution. Both sides, of course, are correct, as experience has shown that these rights generally protect innocent persons, and on occasion let an apparently guilty person go free. In the words of Judge Henry Friendly, this is not an unjust result, for most Americans "would allow a considerable number of guilty persons to go free than to convict an appreciable number of innocent men."[162]

## Remedies for Violations

While the law provides remedies for violations of judicial procedure or due process, the hope is that these violations never occur. Accordingly, the law provides procedural safeguards to ensure these violations do not occur. For instance, after a suspect is arrested, his or her case must be reviewed by a prosecutor or magistrate. This process ensures that the police follow the rules of due process and have probable cause to believe the arrested person committed the crime with which he or she is being charged.

Another legal tool is the right to petition for a writ of habeas corpus, which allows criminal defendants to compel the government to explain why it has detained them. This writ is a procedural device that protects persons against unjust imprisonment. It does not, however, protect persons against false arrest, so the scope of this power is more limited than commonly imagined.[163]

Another remedy for violations of criminal procedure or due process is the exclusionary rule. This rule holds that evidence is inadmissible in court if it was improperly obtained. The rule rests on the notion that evidence obtained through an unreasonable search and seizure was obtained by violating the civil rights of the suspect. This evidence is called the **fruit of the poisonous tree**, since it is evidence that was tainted from its source.[164]

**Fruit of the poisonous tree** Evidence obtained by law enforcement as a result of an illegal search or seizure.

**Appellate brief** A written memorandum filed by the prosecution or defense attorney to explain why the decision of a lower court was erroneous.

As mentioned in the sections dealing with appellate courts, convicted persons may appeal their convictions to a higher court. All states provide appellate review of some sort, and that right cannot be constrained by the appellant's financial limitations. Accordingly, the state must provide an attorney for the defendant, as well as a trial transcript he or she can use during the appeals process. On appeal, an appellant must demonstrate that the trial court made a legal, not factual, error. His or her arguments also must be presented in an **appellate brief**, which is a written legal argument presented to the panel of judges to persuade them that a legal error was made in the trial court, and the trial court's or trial jury's decision should be reversed.[165]

---

**Ethics and Professionalism: The Disgraced Duke Prosecutor**

Law enforcement officers and prosecuting attorneys are held to a high ethical standard. The 2006 rape allegations filed against the Duke University lacrosse team provide a contemporary example of the dangers wrought by the abuse of prosecutorial power. For his actions during that prosecution, former Durham County, North Carolina District Attorney Mike Nifong was removed from his post and disbarred. As prosecutor, Nifong prosecuted several white Duke lacrosse players who were accused of raping an African-American stripper at an off-campus team party. Although initially praised for his willingness to pursue such a case, Nifong ultimately came under fire for his ethical conduct during the investigation and trial.

Nifong first was criticized for making inflammatory and prejudicial statements, including unfounded accusations about the accused, as well as for omitting exculpatory evidence (evidence tending to exonerate the accused) from the DNA report of the victim's rape. In fact, the full report detected the presence of body fluids from several men who were not charged, and it was later revealed that no DNA evidence implicated the men charged. Nifong claimed this omission was an accident, but his claim was later revealed to be inaccurate, showing his serious breach of the rules of ethics and discovery.

Nifong's misconduct, coupled with the witness's continued changing of her story, ultimately resulted in the charges being dropped.[166] But the damage was done. Nifong was hit with ethics charges by the North Carolina State Bar. He was charged with making prejudicial statements and perpetrating a "systematic abuse of prosecutorial discretion" by withholding the DNA evidence.[167] Nifong was subsequently suspended and disbarred. He was later jailed for one day for contempt of court, and recently filed for bankruptcy after being sued by the accused lacrosse players.

---

## Law Enforcement Investigations

Before setting the machinery of the judicial system in motion, the relevant law enforcement agency (usually local or state police) must conduct its investigation. These investigations, like their later prosecutions, must abide by the rules of due process and criminal procedure.

Criminal procedures vary from state to state, but their grounding principles are found in the U.S. Constitution and Bill of Rights. Although the Constitution regulates searches and seizures, as well as interrogations and the right to counsel, law enforcement agencies may conduct investigations free from the interference of the courts. For example, the Constitution does not require police to articulate a reason for focusing their efforts on a certain suspect before investigating him or her.[168]

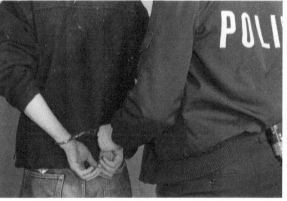

Law enforcement officials must follow specific guidelines when arresting a suspect, including the reading of Miranda rights, to properly protect the suspect's rights.

**Warrant** Legal authorization from a judge to make an arrest, conduct a search, or seize evidence.

Police use two types of **warrants** to investigate and apprehend suspected criminals: an arrest warrant and a search warrant. An arrest warrant is issued by a judge or magistrate and authorizes the arrest of a specific person for a specific crime. The majority of arrests occur "in the field," and these arrests do not require an arrest warrant as long as the officer has probable cause to believe the person being arrested has committed a specific crime for which the arrest is authorized. Common law countries allow police officers to take a person into custody if they believe he or she has committed a felony.

The second type of warrant, a search warrant, authorizes police to search and seize premises for items or information listed specifically in the warrant. With few exceptions, police must have a search warrant before conducting a search and seizure. One exception is that police may search for and seize evidence if the evidence is likely to be destroyed before they can obtain a warrant. They also may search for and seize evidence if a crime is currently being committed, or if the owner of the evidence explicitly consents to the search.[169] Officers can enter only the address listed on the warrant, and search only in the areas and for the items listed.[170]

## Identification

Before entering a residence, police generally are required to announce their entry and intent to search. However, if the police have reason to believe the evidence will be destroyed or they will be injured, they may enter unannounced. If police identify themselves and request the right to search the premises and the suspect or property owner agrees, they generally do not need to obtain a warrant to search the premises.[171]

## Arrest, Search, and Seizure

A person cannot be arrested unless the police have probable cause to believe he or she has committed a crime. Probable cause is determined by the judge who signs the arrest warrant, or by a magistrate after the arrest. In a longer-term investigation in which a grand jury has been convened, the grand jury determines if there is probable cause.[172]

When a police officer makes an arrest and holds the suspect in custody, he or she must read a suspect his or her Miranda rights before asking the suspect any questions relating to the crime. This procedure derives its name from the case of *Miranda v. Arizona* (1966) and safeguards a suspect's rights against self-incrimination under the Fifth Amendment when he or she is subjected to police interrogation.[173] In brief, the Miranda requirements

© sirtravelalot/Shutterstock.com

Officers have the right to stop and question individuals if they see or suspect that a crime or violation has been committed.

are satisfied if officers read suspects a warning, which often is written on a "Miranda card," that they have the right to remain silent, as their words may be used against them, and have the right to an attorney, even if they are unable to afford one.[174]

---

**Exhibit: Miranda Rights**

"In the absence of other effective measures, the following procedures to safeguard the Fifth Amendment privilege must be observed: the person in custody must, prior to interrogation, be clearly informed that he has the right to remain silent, and that anything he says will be used against him in court; he must be clearly informed that he has the right to consult with a lawyer and to have the lawyer with him during interrogation, and that, if he is indigent, a lawyer will be appointed to represent him" (*Miranda v. Arizona*, 1966).

Before questioning a suspect who is in custody, law enforcement officers must issue a Miranda warning (the exact wording of the text varies slightly from state to state, but essentially conforms to the example shown below adapted from the Kansas City Police Department.[175]).

1. You have the right to remain silent.

2. Anything you say can and will be used against you in a court of law.

3. You have the right to talk to a lawyer and have him present with you while you are being questioned.

4. If you cannot afford to hire a lawyer, one will be appointed to represent you before any questioning, if you wish.

5. You can decide at any time to exercise these rights and not answer any questions or make any statements.

The following questions should be asked after the specific warning has been made, and an affirmative reply is returned to each question. This secures a waiver to legally question the suspect, such that their responses will be admissible in court.

1. Do you understand each of these rights I have explained to you?

2. Having these rights in mind, do you wish to talk to us now?

---

## Custodial Interrogations

The Miranda rights of suspects have expanded over time, reflecting a growing concern during the 1960s with **custodial interrogations**, or the questioning of a suspect in custody. Specifically, several of the U.S. Supreme Court's decisions underscore its desire to control custodial interrogations, such as those that occur in a police station, to ensure the police do not harass or intimidate minority defendants and the impoverished, or others who cannot easily pursue traditional avenues of recourse.[176] Miranda rights now apply to people being questioned by the police as part of a criminal investigation, as well as to those arrested. People may waive these rights before speaking to an officer, but all investigations that occur when a person is in custody require the police to notify him or her of the Miranda rights.[177]

**Custodial interrogation** The questioning of a witness by law enforcement while he or she is under arrest.

Similarly, the validity of confessions obtained by law enforcement is interpreted through the lens of the Fifth Amendment to the Constitution, which states that "no person shall be compelled in any criminal case to be a witness against himself."[178] This means that confessions must be voluntary and uncoerced (the suspect must not be under threat of torture, for instance). For the purposes of custodial interrogation, the interrogated person must acknowledge his or her Miranda rights for such a statement to be admissible in court.[179]

## Pretrial Proceedings

Before trial, a defendant appears in the initial, or bail, appearance, as well as in a preliminary hearing.

In a *preliminary hearing* held before a judge, the defense often presents witness testimony to argue there is insufficient evidence to justify the arrest of the accused. Preliminary hearings are used when a grand jury has not returned an indictment, although a grand jury can also be used after a preliminary hearing to approve the prosecutor's case.

The purpose of a grand jury and a preliminary hearing is to ensure there is probable cause to charge a person with a crime.[180] Preliminary hearings are important because they represent the first time someone other than a law enforcement officer or prosecutor has reviewed the case, thus providing a layer of protection against a baseless charge, as well as the unnecessary humiliation of trial. During these hearings, the burden of proof on the prosecution is far less than it is at trial; it merely must prove it has a *prima facie* (at first sight) case, which requires it to show only that there is probable cause to believe a crime was committed by the accused.[181] This standard of proof, probable cause, is the same used by judges to decide whether to issue an arrest or search warrant. Not all states require preliminary hearings, and such hearings are normally reserved for serious felonies.

### The Initial Appearance

**Initial appearance** The court hearing at which a defendant hears the formal charges levied against him or her.

The **initial appearance** in court is the time when a criminal defendant stands in court and hears the formal charges levied against him or her. The defendant enters a plea at this point, most often by declaring himself or herself guilty or not guilty. If the defendant does not yet have an attorney and cannot afford one, the court will appoint one at the public's expense. At this hearing, the official **complaint**, or list of charges brought by the police, is assessed by a magistrate. These first appearances also are known as bail hearings, at which magistrates determine the legality of the arrest and set bail.[182]

**Complaint** A document listing the criminal charges brought against a defendant.

### Grand Jury and Indictment

**Grand jury** A group of 16–23 people that hears evidence and decides if probable cause exists to believe a person has committed a crime.

Grand juries are different from trial juries. **Grand juries** consist of 16–23 people who hear evidence about the crime committed. Usually, a prosecutor presents the evidence to the grand jury in a secret session. The grand jury's task is to determine if probable cause exists to believe that the suspect committed a criminal offense.[183] In felony cases, a grand jury returns a formal charge called an **indictment**, which represents its judgment that there is probable cause to believe the defendant committed a crime.[184]

Grand juries do not, however, decide a defendant's ultimate guilt or innocence; that task is left to the trial judge or trial jury. Additionally, grand jury witnesses are not entitled to have their attorneys present, and the suspect's attorney also has no right to be present, since a grand jury is not a criminal court. Historically, grand juries overwhelmingly return the indictment requested by prosecutors.[185]

## Critical Thinking

Do you think grand juries are necessary in pretrial proceedings, especially if they generally side with prosecutors? Should they be replaced by preliminary hearings? Why or why not?

## Bail

Bail is normally set at the initial appearance or bail hearing stage of the trial. Bail is determined by a judge or magistrate, who considers the seriousness of the crime, the risk the defendant poses to society, and the likelihood that the defendant will flee the court's jurisdiction before trial. If the judge believes the defendant deserves bail, he or she then assigns an amount sufficient to ensure the defendant will appear in court. Bail is usually paid either in cash from the defendant or by bond from a bail bondsman. **Bail** bonds are essentially insurance policies, and the court is the beneficiary if the defendant flees. Excessive bail is prohibited by the Eighth Amendment.

## Discovery

**Discovery** is the court-ordered process by which attorneys learn about their opponents' cases before trial. The discovery process commonly includes depositions (testimony under oath), exchanges of interrogatories (written questions), requests for admissions (requests to admit the truth or falsity of statements), and requests for production of documents.[186]

Discovery is very limited in criminal cases because information procured by the defense conceivably can be used to harass or intimidate prosecution witnesses.[187] Nonetheless, the prosecution is obligated by law to, at a minimum, provide the defense any materials that appear to show the defendant is not guilty. In addition, the prosecution must provide the defense any materials that tend to impeach, or diminish, the credibility of any witnesses who will testify for the prosecution at trial. Police reports, laboratory results, forensic evidence, medical tests, ballistics reports, and witness statements are other categories of information that prosecutors provide to defense attorneys during discovery.

© Andrey_Kuzmin/Shutterstock.com

During discovery, both testimonial evidence, such as an eyewitness account, and physical evidence, such as fingerprints, are presented.

Prosecutors usually are required to disclose more information in discovery than defense attorneys must disclose. Still, prosecutors often seek to limit the materials they disclose, for fear that disclosing certain categories of evidence (such as witness statements) will lead witnesses to be intimidated and deterred from testifying at trial. Broadly speaking, discovery of physical evidence and confessions made by the defendant is considered a right of the defense, but written and recorded witness statements are more problematic.[188]

## Suppression Hearing

**Suppression hearing**
A pretrial hearing where a defendant asks the court to suppress, or disallow, evidence that the police obtained illegally.

A **suppression hearing** is a hearing held if the defense asks the judge to suppress, or disallow, a piece of evidence that it believes the state obtained illegally during the criminal investigation. Usually, motions (requests) to suppress evidence contend that the evidence was obtained only by violating the defendant's Fourth Amendment or Fifth Amendment rights. Defense attorneys may, for example, ask the judge to suppress a confession if the accused was not informed of his or her Miranda rights or was coerced to confess. They also may ask the judge to suppress the evidence gained from a search if the search was conducted without a warrant or otherwise illegally (i.e., fruit of the poisonous tree). If the search was not conducted during an arrest with a warrant or if the evidence was not in **plain view**, then the results of the search may be inadmissible in court.[189]

**Plain view** A method by which police observe physical evidence that is plainly visible to the human eye, without the need for an intrusive search.

Other motions may challenge the accuracy of the indictment, charge the prosecution with entrapment or delay, or contend that the accused already has been acquitted or convicted of the crime charged (double jeopardy). In addition, the defense may lodge motions about the defendant's physical or mental competency to stand trial.[190] A defendant may also claim that his or her right to a speedy trial has been violated, requiring the judge to dismiss the charge.

## Critical Thinking

If evidence obtained through improper procedure turns out to be factually true and is critical to the case, should it be used anyway? Explain.

## Speedy Trials

**Speedy Trial Act** A federal law requiring district courts to ensure that a criminal defendant is brought to trial no later than 100 days after his or her arrest, with some exceptions.

Under the Sixth Amendment, accused individuals have the right to a fair and speedy trial. The goal of this provision is to prevent undue incarceration before trial, reduce anxiety, and ensure that a delay does not hinder the defense. In 1974, Congress passed the **Speedy Trial Act**. With certain exceptions, the act requires district courts to ensure that criminal cases are heard no later than 100 days after the defendant is arrested. Most states have enacted similar statutes, but they have proven difficult to enforce. It is sometimes difficult to prove that a delay is intentional rather than inherent in the system.[191]

Defendants also have the right to a trial by a jury of their peers. The Sixth Amendment enjoins that a speedy trial shall be conducted by an impartial jury in the state where the crime was committed. The phrase "impartial jury" is problematic for due process. Peremptory challenges to a juror's eligibility based on race have been banned,[192] but attorneys still have a great deal of power over who serves on a jury during *voir dire,* when the jury pool is questioned to determine if potential jurors have any specific biases.[193] The jury selection process has been shown by research to be inherently prejudiced against racial minorities, the poor, women, and those of lower educational achievement.[194] This raises a question of fairness in relation to due process: does the makeup of the jury become a right of due process in its own right? Also, whose right is preeminent, that of the victim who has been wronged or the accused on trial?

## Pleas

A **plea** is a defendant's formal, in-court assertion that he or she is guilty or not guilty of the criminal charges.[195] At the arraignment or initial appearance, the accused is advised of his or her rights and invited to enter a plea. Aside from pleading guilty or not guilty, a defendant may plead *nolo contendere*, which means that the defendant does not admit the charges, but will not contest them.[196] A defendant may plead guilty to the charges at any point during the judicial process, as well as negotiate with prosecutors to reach a **plea bargain** agreement, in which the defendant agrees to plead guilty to a lesser charge in exchange for more lenient treatment at the time of sentencing.[197] After a judge accepts a guilty plea, the defendant is sentenced by a judge or jury. Most criminal cases do not result in a finding of guilt or innocence by a judge or jury (**verdict**), but instead are settled by plea bargains.

**Plea** A defendant's in-court statement that he or she is guilty, is not guilty, or will not contest criminal charges.

**Nolo contendere** A plea in which the defendant does not admit the charges, but will not contest them.

**Verdict** Finding of guilt or innocence by a judge or jury.

# Chapter Summary

- The American court system was derived from the common law system inherited from England. From this system, the founding fathers derived their basic understanding of fundamental rights, including habeas corpus, the right to trial by jury, the authority of judicial precedent, and due process. Though there were administrative and procedural differences across the colonies, this common legal heritage was the foundation of the American legal system.

- The U.S. court system consists of two parallel judicial structures: state and federal courts. These structures largely mirror each other; both have lower (trial) courts, which hear evidence, try cases, and reach verdicts, in addition to appeals courts, which review the decisions of lower courts. Federal courts handle "federal questions," which deal with explicitly federal law, and legal issues arising between states.

- The United States Supreme Court is the ultimate legal arbiter in the United States on questions of federal law. It has the prerogative of interpreting the Constitution, the highest law in the land. Legislatures, at any level, are bound to abide by the Constitution. If a law or statute contravenes the Constitution, the Supreme Court may declare it unconstitutional. Cases appealed to the Supreme Court from lower courts may be overturned, thus generating case law that becomes binding precedent for the entire American legal system.

  The criminal trial process is an important function of the criminal justice system. Criminal trials determine the guilt or innocence of an accused person. Criminal trials may be conducted in front of a judge—a "bench trial"—or a jury—a "jury trial." The typical criminal trial consists of opening statements from the defense and prosecution, witness testimony (including direct examination and cross-examination), closing arguments, jury instructions, and the verdict.

- Due process and criminal process provide extensive procedures to safeguard criminal defendants against oppression by the state. The guiding principle is that it is better to let many guilty persons go free than to convict one innocent person. Fundamental, or "natural," rights not explicitly enumerated in the Constitution have been incorporated as substantive due process, largely through the 14th Amendment.

- The Bill of Rights determines the boundaries of "fair play," or due process. The rights enumerated, such as the protections against self-incrimination and unreasonable search and seizure, have been updated to keep pace with the electronic and digital age (e.g., wiretaps).

  *Gideon v. Wainwright* (1963) was an integral Supreme Court decision that not only affirmed that all defendants, even poor ones, are entitled to be represented by counsel, but also spurred the creation of the public defender system.

- The courtroom workgroup includes many important people who are part of the criminal justice process: the judge, the court clerk, the bailiff, the probation officer, the court reporter, and the process server. These individuals ensure that the business of the court runs smoothly.

- The judge, though just one part of the court team, is considered by many the most important person in the courtroom. A judge's primary duty is to oversee the standard procedures of the court system to ensure that justice is fairly served. A judge's responsibilities include making sure that the defense and prosecution both have the opportunity to present their cases, determining the admissibility of evidence, giving instructions to the jury, and using judicial discretion to follow and enforce the law in his or her courtroom.

- The prosecutor is the attorney for the state. The prosecutor makes a criminal case against a defendant and argues that the defendant is guilty of the charges. A prosecutor has many different duties to fulfill in the criminal trial process. Prosecutors are involved in various aspects of casework, from investigation, arrest, and trial to sentencing, appeal, and parole.

- The defense attorney is the attorney who represents the accused. The defense attorney may be hired by the defendant or appointed by a judge. Some counties have a public defender's office. A public defender is an attorney who represents indigent defendants who cannot afford to hire attorneys.

- In a jury trial, the decision of the defendant's guilt or innocence lies in the hands of a jury of the defendant's peers. The jury listens to arguments made during the trial and then deliberates and renders a verdict. Sometimes after a defendant is found guilty, a sentencing trial will be held in front of a jury. The jury will determine the punishment that they recommend to the court for the defendant.

## Critical Thinking?

1. Do the procedural protections afforded to criminal defendants lessen the rights available to other participants in the court system? Explain.

2. Under what circumstances may a law enforcement officer lawfully take the confession of a criminal suspect?

3. Does the requirement of a speedy trial benefit a criminal defendant and the prosecution equally? Discuss.

4. How, if at all, are due process protections affected by the racial, ethnic, and socioeconomic makeup of a trial jury pool?

5. When may a police officer search a person's home without a warrant? Do you think that all searches should require a warrant? Explain.

6. May a person refuse to allow a police officer to enter his or her home if the officer does not have a warrant? Explain.

7. Should victims have a Bill of Rights in the same way that the accused do? Why or why not?

8. Is it fair to allow attorneys to share information during the discovery phase? Explain.

9. Is the right to a speedy trial necessary? Is speed or reaching the truth deliberately more important? Why?

10. Why is the Fifth Amendment important to the accused? How might a person incriminate himself or herself even if he or she did not commit a crime?

11. How do you think trials would be different if our system did not have the presumption of innocence? How might this affect the way trials work?

12. Is it possible for a witness to be competent but not credible? What would be an example of this?

13. Is it important that a judge have experience as an attorney for both the prosecution and the defense? Why or why not?

14. What should be done if a juror lies? What does a "mistrial" really mean for everyone?

15. When might it be in the defendant's best interest to agree, or refuse to agree, to a plea bargain prior to trial? Are the risks in these instances worth it?

16. What is the difference between "not guilty" and "innocent" of a crime? Is there a difference?

17. Do you agree with the concept of limited admissibility of evidence? Why or why not?

18. Legislative efforts to limit judicial discretion shift power from the judge to the prosecutor. How does this affect the intended neutrality of the courtroom process?

19. Is jury nullification an acceptable practice in the criminal trial system? Do you believe it should be allowed? Why or why not?

20. What is the role of the accused in the trial process? Does it matter whether the accused testifies or remains silent?

## Media

**United States Courts http://www.uscourts.gov/Home.aspx**
The website for the federal court system in the United States provides information on federal courts in local areas, as well as educational resources for students and teachers wishing to learn more about the federal judiciary.

**Supreme Court of the United States http://www.supremecourt.gov/**
The website for the U.S. Supreme Court includes resources related to recent decisions, current justices, court history, and the court's docket.

**Rules of Conduct for Lawyers http://www.abanet.org**
The website for the American Bar Association, the regulating body for licensed attorneys in the United States, includes information on the ethical standards to which lawyers must adhere, as well as infractions that could lead to disbarment.

*12 Angry Men* **(1957):** This movie demonstrates the type of interaction and discussion possible during jury deliberation. There is also an example of jury nullification. For a synopsis of the film and detailed descriptions of the different jurors, visit http://www.filmsite.org/twelve.html.

*To Kill a Mockingbird* **(1962):** In this movie, based on the book written by Harper Lee, a defense attorney in the Depression-era American

South defends a black man against undeserved rape charges. While his choice is unpopular with his friends and neighbors, he shows commitment to the integrity of the judicial process and defends his client to the best of his ability. A full description of the story, its characters, and commentary on the racial tensions outlined in the book and movie may be found at http://www.filmsite.org/toki.html.

**Lewis, A. (1966). *Gideon's Trumpet*. New York, NY:** Vintage Books/ Random House This book chronicles the story behind the *Gideon v. Wainwright* (1963) case, which yielded the U.S. Supreme Court's ruling that criminal case defendants have the right to be represented by an attorney, even if they cannot afford to pay. Commentary on the book is available at http://www.nacdl.org/public.nsf/championarticles/A0301p61?OpenDocument.

**Texas Justice Court Training Center:** http://www.tjctc.org/ The official website for the Texas Justice Court Training Center provides legal news and updates for judges, bailiffs, constables, and other courtroom personnel.

**The National Judicial College:** http://www.judges.org/ The agency's official website provides information on continuing education courses, including online offerings, for judges around the country.

## Endnotes

1    *Gideon v. Wainwright*, 372 U.S. 335 (1963).

2    McBride, A. (2006). *Supreme Court History: Expanding Civil Rights; Landmark Cases Gideon v. Wainwright*. Retrieved from http://www.pbs.org/wnet/supremecourt/rights/landmark_gideon.html

3    Locke, M., Neff, J., & Curliss, A. (2010, August 7). *Scathing SBI Audit Says 230 Cases Tainted by Shoddy Investigations*. Retrieved May 13, 2011 from http://www.newsobserver.com/2010/08/19/635632/scathing-sbi-audit-says-230-cases.html

4    Waggoner, M. (2010, September 15). "N.C. Lab Scandal Effects Continue in Court System." *The Herald-Sun*.

5    Innocence Project. (n.d.). *The Causes of Wrongful Conviction*. Retrieved May 15, 2011 from http://www.innocenceproject.org/understand/

6    Mecham, L. R. (2011). *Understanding Federal and State Courts*. Retrieved May 2, 2011 from http://www.uscourts.gov/EducationalResources/Federal-CourtBasics/CourtStructure/UnderstandingFederalAndStateCourts.aspx

7    Neubauer, D. W. (1979). *America's Courts and the Criminal Justice System*. Belmont, CA: Wadsworth, 23.

8    Bergman, P., & Berman-Barrett, S. J. (2008). *Represent Yourself In Court: How to Prepare & Try a Winning Case* (6th ed.). Berkeley: Nolo, 481.

9    Breyer, S., et al. (2001). *Administrative Law & Regulatory Policy* (5th ed.). New York, NY: Aspen.

[10] Garner, B. A. (2001). *A Dictionary of Modern Legal Usage* (revised ed.). New York, NY: Oxford University Press, 177–178.

[11] Arnold-Baker, C. (2008). *The Companion to British History*. London, UK: Loncross Denholm Press, 484.

[12] Orth, J. V. (2002). "Common Law." In K. L. Hall (Ed.), *The Oxford Companion to American Law*. New York, NY: Oxford University Press.

[13] Arnold-Baker, 2008.

[14] Curry, J. A., Riley, R. B., & Battistoni, R. M. (2003). *Constitutional Government: The American Experience* (5th ed.). Dubuque, IA: Kendall Hunt, 35.

[15] Hoffer, P. (2002). "History of American Law: Colonial Period." In K. L. Hall (Ed.), *The Oxford Companion to American Law*. New York, NY: Oxford University Press, 365.

[16] Orth, 2002, 126.

[17] Curry et al., 2003, 31.

[18] Ibid., 36.

[19] Middleton, R. (2002). *Colonial America: A History, 1565–1776* (3rd ed.). Padstow, UK: Blackwell.

[20] Elson, H. W. (1904). *History of the United States of America*. New York, NY: MacMillan, 210–216.

[21] Hoffer, 2002, 366–367.

[22] Ibid., 367.

[23] U.S. Department of Justice (1976). *Two Hundred Years of American Criminal Justice*. Washington, DC: Government Printing Office.

[24] Glick, H., & Vines, K. (1973). *State Court Systems*. Englewood Cliffs, NJ: Prentice-Hall.

[25] Curry et al., 2003.

[26] Glick & Vines, 1973.

[27] Curry et al., 2003, 53.

[28] Neubauer, 1979, 46.

[29] Richardson, R., & Vines, K. (1970). *The Politics of the Federal Courts*. Boston, MA: Little, Brown, 20–21.

[30] Curry et al., 2003, 81.

[31] Hoffer, 2002, 367.

[32] U.S. Constitution, Article III.

[33] Curry et al., 2003, 36.

[34] Ibid., 53.

[35] Graber, M. A. (2002). "Court Systems." In K. L. Hall (Ed.), *The Oxford Companion to American Law*. New York, NY: Oxford University Press, 182–183.

[36] O'Brien, D. M. (2000). *Constitutional Law and Politics: Struggles for Power and Governmental Accountability* (4th ed., vol. 1). New York, NY: W.W. Norton and Company, 46–47.

[37] Curry et al., 2003, 62.

[38] Ibid., 46.

[39] Pittman, R. C. (1953). "Judicial Supremacy in America: Its Colonial and Constitutional History." *Georgia Bar Journal, 16*, 148.

[40] U.S. Constitution, Article III.

[41] O'Brien, 2000, 23.

[42] Garner, B. A. (2004). *Black's Law Dictionary* (8th ed.). St. Paul, MN: Thomson/West, 980.

[43] Adamany, D. (2002). "Judicial Review." In K. L. Hall (Ed.), *The Oxford Companion to American Law.* New York: Oxford University Press, 441.

[44] O'Brien, 2000, 31.

[45] *Marbury v. Madison*, 5 U.S. (1 Cranch) 137 (1803).

[46] 5 U.S. (1 Cranch) at 177–178.

[47] Ritchie, D. A. (2002). "Government, United States." In K. L. Hall (Ed.), *The Oxford Companion to American Law.* New York, NY: Oxford University Press.

[48] O'Brien, 2000.

[49] Adamany, 2002, 441.

[50] Ibid., 444.

[51] Rottman, D. B., Flango, C. R., Cantrell, M. T., & Hansen, R. L. (2000, June). *State Court Organization 1998.* Retrieved May 17, 2011 from http://bjs.ojp. usdoj.gov/content/pub/pdf/sco98.pdf

[52] Black, H. C. (1990). *Black's Law Dictionary* (6th ed.). St. Paul, MN: West, 1557.

[53] U.S. Constitution, Amendment 10.

[54] Hall, M. G. (2002). "Courts, United States: State and Local Courts." In K. L. Hall (Ed.), *The Oxford Companion to American Law.* New York, NY: Oxford University Press, 177.

[55] Wheeler, R., & Whitcomb, H. (1974). "The Literature of Court Administration: A Bibliographical Essay." *Arizona State Law Journal,* 689–722.

[56] *Advanced Report, State Court Caseload Statistics: Annual Report, 1975.* (1978). Williamsburg, VA: National Center for State Courts.

[57] Hall, 2002, 178.

[58] Rottman et al., 2000, 315.

[59] Ulmer, J. (1994). "Trial Judges in a Rural Court Community." *Journal of Contemporary Ethnography, 23,* 79–108.

[60] Eisenstein, J., & Jacob, H. (1970). *Felony Justice: An Organizational Analysis of Criminal Courts.* Boston, MA: Little, Brown.

[61] Stuckey, G. B. (1976). *Procedures in the Criminal Justice System. Columbus, OH: Merrill.*

[62] *Duncan v. Louisiana* 391 U.S. 145 (1968).

[63] *West's Encyclopedia of American Law* (2nd ed.). (2004). Farmington Hills, MI: Gale.

[64] Katz, B. S. (1997). *Justice Overruled: Unmasking the Criminal Justice System.* New York, NY: Warner.

[65] *U.S. v. Dinitz*, 424 U.S. 600, 612 (1976).

66 Federal Rules of Evidence, Rule 601.

67 Schum, D., & Morris, J. (2007, March). "Assessing the Competence and Credibility of Human Sources of Intelligence Evidence: Contributions from Law and Probability." *Law, Probability, & Risk, 6*(1–4), 247–274.

68 Garner, B. (2004). *Black's Law Dictionary* (8th ed.). St. Paul, MN: Thomson West.

69 *Daubert v. Merrill Dow Pharmaceuticals*, 509 U.S. 579 (1993).

70 Jones, D. (1981). *The Law of Criminal Procedure*. Boston, MA: Little, Brown.

71 Jones, 1981.

72 *Ohio v. Roberts*, 488 U.S. 56 (1980).

73 Ibid.

74 *Crawford v. Washington*, 544 U.S. 36 (2004).

75 Jones, 1981.

76 Inciardi, J. (2010). *Criminal Justice* (9th ed.). Boston, MA: McGraw-Hill.

77 Wiener, R., Pritchard, C., & Weston, M. (1995). "Comprehensibility of Approved Jury Instructions in Capital Murder Cases." *Journal of Applied Psychology, 80*(4).

78 Cronan, J. P. (2002). "Is Any of This Making Sense? Reflecting on Guilty Pleas to Aid Criminal Juror Comprehension." *American Criminal Law Review, 39*.

79 American Jury Project. (2005). *Principles for Juries and Jury Trials*. Chicago, IL: American Bar Association.

80 Florida Supreme Court. (n.d.). *Standard Jury Instructions: Criminal Cases*. Retrieved from http://www.floridasupremecourt.org/jury_instructions/index.shtmlIllinois Courts. (2011). *Recent Criminal Jury Instructions*. Retrieved from http://www.state.il.us/court/circuitcourt/CriminalJuryInstructions/default.asp

81 *Pope v. Illinois*, 481 U.S. 497 (1987).

82 North Dakota Supreme Court. (n.d.). *North Dakota Juror's Handbook*. Retrieved from http://www.ndcourts.gov/court/juror.htm

83 Hall, 2002, 178.

84 Rottman et al., 2000, viii.

85 Ibid., 75.

86 Hall, 2002, 178.

87 Mecham, 2011.

88 Carp, R. (2002). Courts, United States: Federal Courts. In K. L. Hall (Ed.), *The Oxford Companion to American Law*. New York: Oxford University Press, 176–177.

89 Ibid.

90 Gluck, Susan Mezey, D. (2002). United States Courts: Juvenile Courts. In K. L. Hall (Ed.), *The Oxford Companion to American Law*. New York: Oxford University Press, 180–182.

91 Carp, 2002, 174.

92 28 U.S.C. § 1331.

93    Grossman, J. (1965). *Lawyers and Judges: The ABA and the Politics of Judicial Selection.* New York, NY: John Wiley.

94    Ibid, 14.

95    Jackson, D. D. (1974). *Judges.* New York, NY: Atheneum, 7.

96    Office of the Federal Defender, Eastern District of California. (n.d.). *Sentencing.* Retrieved from http://www.cae-fpd.org/Client_Sentencing.pdf

97    Mecham, 2011, 19–20.

98    Judiciary Act of 1925, 43 Stat. 936.

99    Richardson, R. J., & Vines, K. N. (1970). *The Politics of Federal Courts.* Boston, MA: Little, Brown.

100    *Public Citizen, Inc., v. Bomer,* 115 F. Supp. 2d 743 (W.D. Tex 2000).

101    Becker, D., & Reddick, M. (2005). *Judicial Selection Reform: Examples from Six States.* Des Moines, IA: American Judicature Society.

102    Inciardi, 2010.

103    New York City Criminal Court Act, Laws of 1962, chap. 697, sec. 22 (1).

104    Texas Justice Court Training Center. (2011). *New Judges Seminar.* Retrieved from http://www.tjctc.org/New-Justices-of-the-Peace/NewJudges.html

105    National Judicial College. (2011). *About the NJC.* Retrieved from http://www.judges.org/about/index.html

106    American Bar Association. (2000). *ABA Standards for Criminal Justice: Special Functions of the Trial Judge* (3rd ed.). Chicago, IL: Author.

107    *Osborn v. Bank* of the United States, 22 U.S. 738 (1824).

108    Friedman, R. (1986). *A Close Look at Probative Value.* 66 B.U.L. Rev. 733.

109    Hill & Hill, 2009.

110    McLaughlin, J. (1989). *Federal Evidence Practice Guide.* Matthew Bender.

111    Holton, N., & Lamar, L. (1991). *The Criminal Courts: Structures, Personnel, and Processes.* New York, NY: McGraw-Hill.

112    Rabe, G., & Champion, D. (2002). *Criminal Courts: Structures, Process, and Issues.* Upper Saddle River, NJ: Prentice Hall.

113    Holton & Lamar, 1991.

114    Franklin County, Ohio. (n.d.) *Franklin County Prosecutor's Office.* Retrieved from http://www.franklincountyohio.gov/Prosecuting_Attorney/

115    Misner, R. L. (1996). "Recasting Prosecutorial Discretion." *The Journal of Law & Criminology, 86*(3).

116    Ma, Y. (2002). "Prosecutorial Discretion and Plea Bargaining in the United States, France, Germany, and Italy: A Comparative Perspective." *International Criminal Justice Review, 12.*

117    LaFave, W. (1965). *Arrest: The Decision to Take a Suspect Into Custody.* Boston, MA: Little, Brown.

118    Inciardi, 2010.

119    Oakland County, Michigan Circuit Court. (2009). *Appointed Attorney Fee Schedule.* Retrieved from http://www.oakgov.com/circuit/assets/docs/division/atty-fee-sched.pdf

120 Smith, S., & DeFrances, C. (1996). *Indigent Defense*. Washington, DC: Bureau of Justice Statistics.

121 "Nationline: McVeigh's Defense Cost Taxpayers $13.8 Million." *USA Today*, July 3, 2001, p. 3A.

122 *Smith v. Texas*, 311 U.S. 128 (1940).

123 Ibid., 13–14.

124 Ibid.

125 28 U.S.C. § 631.

126 Mecham, 2011, 9.

127 Carp, 2002, 117.

128 O'Brien, 2002, 771–776.

129 Ibid., 26.

130 Supreme Court of the United States. (2011). *Frequently Asked Questions*. Retrieved from http://www.supremecourt.gov/faq.aspx#faqgi9

131 O'Brien, 2002, 771.

132 Administrative Office of the U.S. Courts. (2003). *Understanding the Federal Courts*. Retrieved May 8, 2011 from http://www.uscourts.gov/Educational-Resources/FederalCourtBasics/UnderstandingTheFederalCourts.aspx

133 *Murray v. Hoboken Land*, 59 U.S. 272 (1855).

134 Brown, R. L. (2002). "Due Process: Procedural." In K. L. Hall (Ed.), *The Oxford Companion to American Law*. New York, NY: Oxford University Press, 232.

135 Sandefur, T. (2010). *The Right to Earn a Living: Economic Freedom and the Law*. Washington, DC: Cato Institute, 90–100.

136 White, G. E. (2000). *The Constitution and the New Deal*. Cambridge, MA: Harvard University Press, 244–246.

137 *Palko v. Connecticut*, 302 U.S. 319 (1937).

138 *Klopfer v. North Carolina*, 386 U.S. 213 (1967).

139 *Barker v. Wingo*, 406 U.S. 514 (1972).

140 *Strunk v. United States*, 412 U.S. 434 (1973).

141 *United States v. Lovasco*, 421 U.S. 783 (1977).

142 *In re Oliver*, 333 U.S. 257 (1948).

143 *Thiel v. Southern PacificCo.*, 328 U.S. 217 (1946).

144 Magna Carta of 1215.

145 U.S. Constitution, Article III, Sect. 2, Cl. 2.

146 U.S. Constitution, Amendment 14, Sect. 1.

147 *Duncan v. Louisiana*, 391 U.S. 145 (1968).

148 Federal Rules of Criminal Procedure, Rule 24(6).

149 *Swain v. Alabama*, 380 U.S. 202 (1965).

150 *Batson v. Kentucky*, 476 U.S. 79 (1986).

151 *J.E.B. v. Alabama ex rel. T.B.*, 511 U.S. 127 (1994).

152 Glasser, M. (1997). "Letting the Supermajority Rule: Nonunanimous Jury Verdicts in Criminal Trials." *Florida State University Law Review.* Tallahassee, FL: Florida State University Press.

153 Ellsworth, P. (1989). "Are Twelve Heads Better Than One?" *Law and Contemporary Problems, 52,* 205–224.

154 *U.S. v. Moylan,* 417 F2d 1002 (4th Cir. 1969).

155 *U.S. v. Wilson,* 629 F2d 439 (6th Cir. 1980).

156 *U.S. v. Thomas,* 116 F3d 606 (2nd Cir. 1997).

157 Garfinkel, H. (1956). "Conditions of Successful Degradation Ceremonies." *American Journal of Sociology, 61*(5).

158 U.S. Constitution, Amendments 1–10.

159 *Chapman v. California,* 386 U.S. 18, 22 (1967).

160 *In re Winship,* 397 U.S. 358 (1970).

161 Skolnick, J. H. (1966). *Justice Without Trial: Law Enforcement in Democratic Society.* New York, NY: John Wiley, 8.

162 Friendly, H. J. (1968). *The Fifth Amendment Tomorrow: The Case for Constitutional Change.* 37 U. Cin. L. Rev. 671, 694.

163 Krislov, D. R. (2002). "Habeas Corpus." In K. L. Hall (Ed.), *The Oxford Companion to American Law.* New York, NY: Oxford University Press, 349.

164 Dressler, J. (2002). *Understanding Criminal Procedure* (3rd ed.). Newark, NJ: LexisNexis.

165 Mecham, 2011, 26.

166 Washington Post. (2006, December 31). *Prosecutorial Indiscretion.* Retrieved from http://www.washingtonpost.com/wp-dyn/content/article/2006/12/30/AR2006123000886.html?referrer=emailarticle

167 North Carolina State Bar. (2007, June 16). *State Bar Verdict on Nifong.* Retrieved May 19, 2011 from http://www.ncbar.com/Nifong%20Findings.pdf

168 Meyer, L. R. (2002). "Criminal Procedure." In K. L. Hall (Ed.), *The Oxford Companion to American Law.* New York, NY: Oxford University Press, 651–652.

169 *Groh v. Ramirez,* 540 U.S. 551, 564–65 (2004).

170 American Civil Liberties Union. (2010). *Know Your Rights: What to Do If You're Stopped by Police, Immigration Agents or the FBI.* Retrieved from http://www.aclu.org/drug-law-reform-immigrants-rights-racial-justice/know-your-rights-what-do-if-you

171 Ibid.

172 Ibid.

173 *Miranda v. Arizona,* 384 U.S. 436 (1966).

174 Meyer, 2002.

175 Kansas City, MO Police Department. (2006). *Miranda Warning and Miranda Waiver,* pp. 384 U.S. 467–473. Retrieved from http://www.kcpd.org/masterindex/files/PI/PI0605.pdf

176 Meyer, 2002, 652.

177     Curry et al., 2003, ch. X.

178     *Bram v. United States,* 168 U.S. 532, 542 (1897).

179     *Miranda v. Arizona,* 384 U.S. 436 (1966); *California v. Hodari D.,* 499 U.S. 621, 626 (1991).

180     Meyer, 652.

181     *United States v. Sokolow,* 490 U.S. 1 (1989).

182     Meyer, 2002, 652.

183     Mecham, 2011, 39.

184     Ibid, 40.

185     Spain, J. (1961). "The Grand Jury, Past and Present: A Survey." *American Criminal Law Quarterly, 2,* 126–142.

186     Mecham, 2011, 38.

187     Bishop, J. (1978). *Studies in Comparative Civil and Criminal Procedure* (vol. 2). Sydney: Law Reform Commission.

188     Ibid.

189     *Arizona v. Hicks,* 480 U.S. 321 (1987).

190     Meyer, 653.

191     Downs, D. A., & Ruggiero, C. (2002). "Fair Trial, Criminal." In K. L. Hall (Ed.), *The Oxford Companion to American Law.* New York, NY: Oxford University Press, 292.

192     *Batson v. Kentucky,* 476 U.S. 79 (1986).

193     Duhaime, L. (n.d.). "Voir Dire Definition." *Duhaime's Legal Dictionary.* Retrieved from http://www.duhaime.org/LegalDictionary/V/VoirDire.aspx

194     Alker, H. R. Jr., Hosticka, C., & Mitchell, M. (1976). "Jury Selection as a Biased Social Process." *Law & Society Review, 11*(1), 9–41.

195     Mecham, 2011, 43.

196     Bibas, S. (2003, July). "Harmonizing Substantive Criminal Law Values and Criminal Procedure: The Case of Alford and Nolo contendere Pleas." *Cornell Law Review,* 88(6).

197     Ibid.

198     McBride, A. (2006). *Supreme Court History: Expanding Civil Rights; Landmark Cases Gideon v. Wainwright.* Retrieved from http://www.pbs.org/wnet/supremecourt/rights/landmark_gideon.html

198     Ulmer, J. (1994). "Trial Judges in a Rural Court Community." *Journal of Contemporary Ethnography, 23,* 79–108.

199     Eisenstein, J., & Jacob, H. (1970). *Felony Justice: An Organizational Analysis of Criminal Courts.* Boston, MA: Little, Brown.

200     Stuckey, G. B. (1976). *Procedures in the Criminal Justice System.* Columbus, OH: Merrill.

201     *Duncan v. Louisiana* 391 U.S. 145 (1968).

202     *West's Encyclopedia of American Law* (2nd ed.). (2004). Farmington Hills, MI: Gale.

203     Katz, B. S. (1997). *Justice Overruled: Unmasking the Criminal Justice System.* New York, NY: Warner.

204     *U.S. v. Dinitz*, 424 U.S. 600, 612 (1976).

205     Federal Rules of Evidence, Rule 601.

206     Schum, D., & Morris, J. (2007, March). "Assessing the Competence and Credibility of Human Sources of Intelligence Evidence: Contributions from Law and Probability." *Law, Probability, & Risk,* 6(1–4), 247–274.

207     Garner, B. (2004). *Black's Law Dictionary* (8th ed.). St. Paul, MN: Thomson West.

208     *Daubert v. Merrill Dow Pharmaceuticals*, 509 U.S. 579 (1993).

209     Jones, D. (1981). *The Law of Criminal Procedure.* Boston, MA: Little, Brown.

210     Jones, 1981.

211     *Ohio v. Roberts*, 488 U.S. 56 (1980).

212     Ibid.

213     *Crawford v. Washington*, 544 U.S. 36 (2004).

214     Jones, 1981.

215     Inciardi, J. (2010). *Criminal Justice* (9th ed.). Boston, MA: McGraw-Hill.

216     Wiener, R., Pritchard, C., & Weston, M. (1995). "Comprehensibility of Approved Jury Instructions in Capital Murder Cases." *Journal of Applied Psychology, 80*(4).

217     Cronan, J. P. (2002). "Is Any of This Making Sense? Reflecting on Guilty Pleas to Aid Criminal Juror Comprehension." *American Criminal Law Review, 39.*

218     American Jury Project. (2005). *Principles for Juries and Jury Trials.* Chicago, IL: American Bar Association.

219     Florida Supreme Court. (n.d.). *Standard Jury Instructions: Criminal Cases.* Retrieved from http://www.floridasupremecourt.org/jury_instructions/index.shtmlIllinois Courts. (2011). *Recent Criminal Jury Instructions.* Retrieved from http://www.state.il.us/court/circuitcourt/CriminalJuryInstructions/default.asp

220     *Pope v. Illinois*, 481 U.S. 497 (1987).

221     North Dakota Supreme Court. (n.d.). *North Dakota Juror's Handbook.* Retrieved from http://www.ndcourts.gov/court/juror.htm

222     Judiciary Act of 1925, 43 Stat. 936.

223     Richardson, R. J., & Vines, K. N. (1970). *The Politics of Federal Courts.* Boston, MA: Little, Brown.

224     *Public Citizen, Inc., v. Bomer*, 115 F. Supp. 2d 743 (W.D. Tex 2000).

225     Becker, D., & Reddick, M. (2005). *Judicial Selection Reform: Examples from Six States.* Des Moines, IA: American Judicature Society.

226     Tex El. Code Ann. 253.151.

227     Inciardi, 2010.

228     New York City Criminal Court Act, Laws of 1962, chap. 697, sec. 22 (1).

229     Texas Justice Court Training Center. (2011). *New Judges Seminar.* Retrieved from http://www.tjctc.org/New-Justices-of-the-Peace/NewJudges.html

230     National Judicial College. (2011). *About the NJC.* Retrieved from http://www.judges.org/about/index.html

231   American Bar Association. (2000). *ABA Standards for Criminal Justice: Special Functions of the Trial Judge* (3rd ed.). Chicago, IL: Author.

232   *Osborn v. Bank* of the United States, 22 U.S. 738 (1824).

233   Friedman, R. (1986). *A Close Look at Probative Value.* 66 B.U.L. Rev. 733.

234   Hill & Hill, 2009.

235   McLaughlin, J. (1989). *Federal Evidence Practice Guide.* Matthew Bender.

236   Holton, N., & Lamar, L. (1991). *The Criminal Courts: Structures, Personnel, and Processes.* New York, NY: McGraw-Hill.

237   Rabe, G., & Champion, D. (2002). *Criminal Courts: Structures, Process, and Issues.* Upper Saddle River, NJ: Prentice Hall.

238   Holton & Lamar, 1991.

239   Franklin County, Ohio. (n.d.) *Franklin County Prosecutor's Office.* Retrieved from http://www.franklincountyohio.gov/Prosecuting_Attorney/

240   Misner, R. L. (1996). "Recasting Prosecutorial Discretion." *The Journal of Law & Criminology, 86*(3).

241   Ma, Y. (2002). "Prosecutorial Discretion and Plea Bargaining in the United States, France, Germany, and Italy: A Comparative Perspective." *International Criminal Justice Review, 12.*

242   LaFave, W. (1965). *Arrest: The Decision to Take a Suspect Into Custody.* Boston, MA: Little, Brown.

243   Inciardi, 2010.

244   Oakland County, Michigan Circuit Court. (2009). *Appointed Attorney Fee Schedule.* Retrieved from http://www.oakgov.com/circuit/assets/docs/division/atty-fee-sched.pdf

245   Smith, S., & DeFrances, C. (1996). *Indigent Defense.* Washington, DC: Bureau of Justice Statistics.

246   "Nationline: McVeigh's Defense Cost Taxpayers $13.8 Million." *USA Today,* July 3, 2001, p. 3A.

247   *Smith v. Texas,* 311 U.S. 128 (1940).

248   *Klopfer v. North Carolina,* 386 U.S. 213 (1967).

249   *Barker v. Wingo,* 406 U.S. 514 (1972).

250   *Strunk v. United States,* 412 U.S. 434 (1973).

251   *United States v. Lovasco,* 421 U.S. 783 (1977).

252   *In re Oliver,* 333 U.S. 257 (1948).

253   *Thiel v. Southern PacificCo.,* 328 U.S. 217 (1946).

254   Magna Carta of 1215.

255   U.S. Constitution, Article III, Sect. 2, Cl. 2.

256   U.S. Constitution, Amendment 14, Sect. 1.

257   *Duncan v. Louisiana,* 391 U.S. 145 (1968).

258   Federal Rules of Criminal Procedure, Rule 24(6).

259   *Swain v. Alabama,* 380 U.S. 202 (1965).

260   *Batson v. Kentucky,* 476 U.S. 79 (1986).

261     *J.E.B. v. Alabama ex rel. T.B.*, 511 U.S. 127 (1994).

262     Glasser, M. (1997). "Letting the Supermajority Rule: Nonunanimous Jury Verdicts in Criminal Trials." *Florida State University Law Review*. Tallahassee, FL: Florida State University Press.

263     Ellsworth, P. (1989). "Are Twelve Heads Better Than One?" *Law and Contemporary Problems, 52*, 205–224.

264     *U.S. v. Moylan*, 417 F2d 1002 (4th Cir. 1969).

265     *U.S. v. Wilson*, 629 F2d 439 (6th Cir. 1980).

266     *U.S. v. Thomas*, 116 F3d 606 (2nd Cir. 1997).

267     Garfinkel, H. (1956). "Conditions of Successful Degradation Ceremonies." *American Journal of Sociology, 61*(5).

© sakhorn/Shutterstock.com

# Sentencing and Judgment

## KEY TERMS

Aggravating circumstances

Community service

Deferred adjudication

Determinate sentence

Electronic monitoring

Good time credit

House arrest, Incapacitation

Incarceration, Indeterminate
sentence

Intensive supervision probation

Just deserts

Law violation, Mandatory
minimum

Mitigating circumstances

Mitigation specialist

Parole board

Pre-sentence investigation

Pretrial diversion

Rehabilitation, Restitution

Retribution

Sentence

Shock probation

Technical violation

Three-strikes law

Vengeance

# CHAPTER OBJECTIVES

1 Understand the philosophy and goals of criminal sentencing.

2 Describe determinate and indeterminate sentencing.

3 Identify the range of sentencing options.

4 Describe "truth in sentencing" and the motivation for truth-in-sentencing laws.

5 Discuss the role of presentence investigations.

## Case Study: *State of Texas v. Robert Coulson*

On November 13, 1992, the Houston Fire Department discovered five bodies while extinguishing a house fire. The bodies were those of the adoptive parents, two sisters, and brother-in-law (a county sheriff's deputy) of Robert Coulson. Coulson, in an attempt to collect an inheritance from his parents, had subdued each victim with a stun gun, tied their hands and feet, and placed plastic bags over their heads, which caused all the victims to suffocate. Coulson then poured gasoline on the bodies in an attempt to set the house on fire. While the home did catch on fire, the blaze did not entirely engulf the house as planned. It is speculated that while Coulson poured gasoline around the house to destroy evidence, the pilot light from the water heater ignited the gas fumes earlier than Coulson had expected.

An accomplice, Jared Althaus, later confessed to the Harris County District Attorney that he had helped Coulson plan the murders. Althaus described in great detail how he and Coulson left the murder scene and drove to the Althaus family lake house, discarding various pieces of evidence along the way by throwing them out of the car's windows. Coulson maintained that he was at a shopping mall when his family was murdered. Althaus took investigators to the locations along the highway where the tools from the murder scene had been discarded, and each piece of evidence was recovered in the corresponding areas. During the trial, eight witnesses testified against Coulson, who denied their allegations and accused them of lying under oath, but he was subsequently convicted of the murders of his family. At his sentencing, Coulson maintained that he was innocent of the murders. The State argued that Coulson was a manipulative sociopath and only wanted his inheritance. In jail, Coulson reportedly admitted that he did not harbor any resentment toward his family, but felt that the murders were the only way out of his dire financial situation.[1]

Robert Coulson was sentenced to death for the slayings of two of his family members. To avoid a lengthy prison sentence or possibly a sentence of death, Althaus testified against Coulson and received 10 years in prison, a relatively minor sentence considering his alleged involvement with a series of pre-planned murders, in exchange for his cooperation with the district attorney's office. On June 25, 2002, Coulson was executed for the murders of his family members.

Althaus repeatedly denied to investigators that he was inside the Coulson home while the murders were being committed, and said he was sitting in a car outside. Like Coulson, Althaus denied committing the murders. Is it probable, however, that Robert Coulson could have singlehandedly subdued, bound, and killed five adults, one of whom was a trained law enforcement officer?

In this case, two men accused of the same crime received very different sentences. This chapter will explain and discuss sentencing theories and guidelines, disparity in sentencing, plea bargaining, and other issues in sentencing.

# Goals of Sentencing

In the early days of the criminal justice system in the United States, punishments generally followed the philosophy that a person must suffer for committing a crime against society. Historically, the goal of punishing criminals was to cause them to suffer and therefore learn never to commit the offense again. Punishments were generally imposed by taking offenders out of society and placing them in jail cells for the purpose of having them repent to God for their sins. In fact, the word "penitentiary" is based upon this ideal. This is a practice that was introduced to the United States by the Puritans and Quakers, but this philosophy still influences our modern-day criminal justice system. The goals of punishment in the modern criminal justice system in America are to protect society and to rehabilitate the offender. These goals will be covered in detail in the next few pages.

In a criminal proceeding, a defendant who has either pleaded guilty or been found guilty by a judge or jury must have a punishment imposed. These punishments can range from a simple fine to death. For example, in the Robert Coulson case, Coulson was found guilty of murdering his family and sentenced to death, while Coulson's accomplice testified against him and received 10 years in prison. Sentencing is one of the biggest responsibilities of a judge or jury. A **sentence** is a punishment given to an offender by a judge or jury for the crime committed by the offender. Sentencing is the process by which this punishment is determined. All sentences are governed by statutory provisions and vary from state to state and even among local jurisdictions. The states are given the authority to punish criminal defendants; however, the federal government can also punish individuals who are convicted of federal crimes.

**Sentence** A punishment imposed by a judicial body on an offender who has committed a crime.

## Deterrence

Early philosophers such as Cesare Beccaria believed that the only purpose for punishment was the deterrence of crime.[2] Deterrence is a philosophy of punishment that presumes that the punishment inflicted will have the effect of causing criminals to refrain from committing crimes.[3] Deterrence works by influencing the perceptions of potential offenders and, by consequence, their behavior. Punishment can only deter criminals from committing crimes if it is made public. There are two forms of deterrence: general deterrence and special or specific deterrence. *General deterrence* means that by punishing one defendant for a crime, the legal system makes an example of the individual so that other persons will be deterred from committing crimes. Special or *specific deterrence* means that after a defendant is punished for committing a particular crime, that individual will refrain from committing further crimes. Gibbs (1975) further established a difference between absolute and restrictive deterrence. When a person refrains from committing a crime out of fear of being punished for the crime, that individual has been deterred absolutely. When a person limits his or her involvement in committing a crime to reduce the risk of punishment—such as a drug dealer selling smaller amounts of drugs, rather than refraining from the sale of drugs—that person has been deterred restrictively. The individual is still committing the crime, but perhaps on a more limited scale.[4]

Beccaria also asserted that, to be effective, punishment must be swift, certain, and appropriately severe. He believed that punishment for a crime committed must be enacted within a reasonable amount of time after the crime has occurred; if the punishment is delayed for too long, the criminal may not make the connection between the punishment and the crime.[5] For example, if a woman who is arrested on a charge of Driving While Intoxicated (DWI) does not make her first court appearance for six months, will she truly make the connection that her involvement in the justice system is due to her actions? Certainty of punishment means that punishment will be applied, and the potential scope of the punishment is clear to all involved in the process, including the defendant.[6] In the example of the woman arrested for the DWI charge, she should be made to understand the possible range of punishments that she may be subjected to as a result of her crime. Beccaria suggested limitations on the severity of punishments applied: he asserted that the punishment should be proportionate to its corresponding crime, and it should not go beyond the point of severity where it deters others from committing the same crime or prevents the defendant from further harming others.[7] In other words, while the woman charged with DWI did put other individuals at risk by driving drunk, is it appropriate to sentence her, and other persons charged with DWI, to life in prison for the offense?

A complication of general deterrence as a punishment philosophy is that, while it may make sense in theory, its effects cannot be measured by social scientists. This means that whether deterrence works cannot be accurately determined, especially in the cases of people who have been tempted to commit crimes but have refrained from doing so. One cannot easily measure the number of people who have not committed crimes. Only persons who have not been deterred from committing further crimes can be measured, as their repeated crimes are documented by the criminal justice system.[8]

For example, a burglar who commits one burglary and then commits no further crimes was successfully deterred from committing further crimes, while an auto thief who repeatedly commits auto thefts keeps re-entering the criminal justice system.

Specific deterrence, however, does seem to have some impact on the behavior of first-time misdemeanor and white-collar offenders whose arrests and entrances into the criminal justice system cause them embarrassment. The threats of public disgrace and negative effects upon professional and family matters appear to have positive effects on these "small-time" criminals, leading to reductions in further crimes committed by these offenders.[9]

---

### Critical Thinking

Think about Beccaria's points that punishment should be swift, certain, and appropriately severe. What would sentencing be like if only two of those three ideas were applied, such as swift and appropriately severe punishment without certainty? Would criminals know what punishments they faced for their crimes? What if punishment was swift but not certain or appropriately severe? Could that lead, for example, to murderers being executed by police shortly after their arrests?

---

## Retribution

Societies from the ancient Middle East to the American Quakers primarily justified punishment of criminals based on the principle of **retribution**. Some of the oldest examples of retributive punishment are in the Code of Hammurabi, a series of nearly 300 laws and punishments detailed thoroughly under the order of the sixth Babylonian king, Hammurabi, around 1700 B.C. The Code of Hammurabi relies heavily on the concept of "an eye for an eye," as shown by a few examples:

The Code of Hammurabi is one of the oldest known examples of law systems that incorporate retribution.

> If a man puts out the eye of a patrician, his eye shall be put out.
>
> If a man knocks the teeth out of another man, his own teeth will be knocked out.
>
> If a son strikes his father, his hands shall be hewn off.[10]

Retribution suggests that a person who commits a crime should suffer punishment for that crime, and the punishment must be commensurate with the crime. In other words, offenders who commit more heinous crimes receive harsher punishments, while lesser criminals receive more lenient punishments. Someone who commits murder would be put to death under the practice of retribution, and someone who steals money from a store may pay back the money and perhaps any legal costs incurred by the store.

**Retribution** The idea that a criminal should be punished in a manner that is commensurate, or as equal as possible, to the crime committed.

Vengeance is the justification for punishment that draws on the biblical idea of "an eye for an eye." Proponents of vengeance want offenders to pay for what they have done by suffering punishment; a measure of satisfaction is gained from knowing that the criminal has been punished. "**Just deserts**" is a concept that further suggests that the criminal's punishment should be comparable to the crime that was committed. In other words, if a man burns down his neighbor's home, the concept of "just deserts" may force him to lose his home and possessions as well. This justification is based partly on ideas suggested by the German philosopher Immanuel Kant (1724–1804), who stated that offenders should be automatically punished; they have committed crimes, so they "deserve" the punishment.[11] Retribution is the only justification for criminal punishment that focuses on what has happened in the past. All other rationales for punishment hope to influence the future by preventing an offender from committing future crimes.

## Rehabilitation

**Rehabilitation** is a corrections philosophy stating that the offender's behavior and personality can be changed by participation in treatment programs provided by qualified professionals. Offenders are typically put through assessments to determine what issues may be challenging for them, but may also participate in particular types of treatment depending on the nature of the offense and the length of the offender's sentence.[12] Treatment may address more than one issue depending on the offender's identified needs. Examples of rehabilitative treatment may include inpatient substance abuse treatment, participation in 12-step groups, individual psychotherapy, anger management classes, educational or vocational training, and other services.[13] Educational services could include preparation to take a high school equivalency examination, but many prison systems offer inmates the opportunity to complete high school diplomas and even college degrees. Vocational training could include on-the-job training in the prison unit, such as working as a cook in the kitchen or as a mechanic in the garage.

Rehabilitation was the primary rationale for punishing criminals from the 1870s to the 1970s. The goal of rehabilitation was to return offenders to society after **incarceration** as productive, law-abiding citizens. Rehabilitation was de-emphasized in the 1970s in favor of the goals of retribution and incapacitation because the appropriate methods to correct the behavior of offenders are unclear and we do not fully understand what causes crime. This country also experienced a shift away from rehabilitation due to more emphasis on "get tough" policies on crime. While critics suggest that rehabilitation and punishment are not mutually compatible ways to control crime, and that prisons are inappropriate settings to achieve rehabilitation, judges still send offenders to prison for rehabilitation.[14]

## Incapacitation

The removal from society or restriction of the freedom of criminal offenders is called **incapacitation**. In some historical societies, banishment or exile was used to achieve incapacitation. Banishment was utilized in ancient Greece and Rome. When banished, offenders were forced out of a civilized area, leaving them to wander the wilderness, significantly reducing their chances of survival and removing any potential future harm they might cause to their home society. In modern times, foreign nationals may be deported out of the United States if they are convicted of particular crimes. For example, a foreign national who has repeated convictions for drug possession may be deported from the United States to his home country and prevented from returning. The purpose of incapacitation is to make conditions all but impossible for offenders to commit crimes during the period of incapacitation. Prisons are used to incapacitate criminals; incarcerated offenders cannot commit crimes in society outside the prison.

At this time, life imprisonment without parole and execution are the only forms of incapacitation guaranteeing that the offender will no longer commit crimes against the community. The foremost issue concerning incapacitation is that incapacitation by perpetual imprisonment is costly. Additional prisons would need to be built and more employees would need to be hired. Temporary incapacitation—that is, imprisonment until the offender will no longer commit crimes—is unreasonable, as criminality cannot always be predicted. Another issue to consider is the humanity, as well as the practicality, of permanent incapacitation. A criminal permanently ensconced in a prison cell would cause no further harm to society, but permanently imprisoning an offender can be considered cruel and unusual punishment, especially in comparison to the crime. Taking Cesare Beccaria's idea of swift, certain, and appropriately severe punishment into account, is it reasonable to incapacitate all criminals by permanently removing them from society, whether their crimes are small thefts or murders? Permanent incapacitation of offenders also violates their civil rights, which are afforded to all citizens in the U.S. Constitution and its amendments.

## Restorative Justice

Some jurisdictions are making efforts to restore victims of crime as much as possible to their states before the crimes occurred, making them "whole." John Braithwaite, an Australian criminologist, has encouraged the enabling of both the offender and the victim to repair the social damage caused by the crime. This is the concept of restorative justice. Braithwaite stresses that the focus of the mainstream criminal justice system on punishment irreversibly shames the offender and thereby perpetuates criminal association and activity: "When individuals are shamed so remorselessly and unforgivingly that they become outcasts, or even begin to think of themselves as outcasts it becomes more rewarding to associate with others who are perceived in some limited or total way as also at odds with mainstream standards."[15] Sullivan and Tifft (2005) have written that in situations where people have experienced harm, they as victims hope that the one who has caused the harm will accept responsibility for his or her actions, and perhaps offer an apology; acknowledgement of victims' worsened state and subsequent repair of that state—to the extent that it can be repaired—allows the victims to move on.[16] Restorative justice is, essentially, a means for the offender to "make things right" with society by addressing the needs and rights of the victims of the crime.

In the early 1980s, only four states had laws protecting the basic rights of victims in the criminal justice system. Today, every state has some laws protecting victims' rights, thanks largely to the victims' rights movement and increased research in the area. Over 30,000 statutes related to crime victims have been enacted, and federal legislation has been passed to provide basic rights and services to crime victims within the last 25 years.[17]

---

**Critical Thinking**

What are some of the laws in your state to protect victims' rights? Do you believe those laws serve their purpose?

---

**Pre-sentence investigation** A report to the court which outlines the defendant's prior alcohol and drug history, medical history, criminal history, education, and other factors that is given to the judge to assist with determination of sentence. Pre-sentence investigations are generally written by local probation departments.

**Mitigation specialist** A person educated in the social sciences who assists the defendant in obtaining evidence to minimize the impact of punishment. Mitigation specialists are generally social workers or criminologists who compile past history of the defendant's life to assist with the defense.

**Career Connections: Pre-Sentence Investigator**

A pre-sentence investigator compiles a report for the court prior to the sentencing of a defendant. The report, also known as a **pre-sentence investigation**, details the defendant's background and any extenuating circumstances that may have contributed to the criminal behavior, then recommends an appropriate sentence. Some information that may be included in the pre-sentence investigation report includes family history, educational history, economic data, military record, health history, and prior criminal history.

A pre-sentence investigator will interview the defendant, the victim, and any other persons who may contribute relevant information, such as employers, mental health professionals, or even neighbors. Review and compilation of the defendant's records are common to ensure a thorough report. Effective interview skills, critical analysis, and attention to detail are highly desirable qualities for a pre-sentence investigator. A pre-sentence investigator typically has a bachelor's degree in criminal justice or a social or human science, and almost all pre-sentence investigators work for probation departments or the courts. There are, however, persons who conduct pre-sentence investigations for the defense. These individuals are usually known as **mitigation specialists**.

## Types of Sentences

A sentence is the sanction or sanctions imposed upon a convicted criminal by a judicial body such as a jury or a judge. Once the conviction occurs, the court's purpose shifts from impartial case litigation to imposition of sanctions. Different goals of sentencing exist but can intertwine and overlap depending on multiple considerations. The primary goal is to protect the public from the offender; other goals may be to make an example of the offender in an attempt to prevent others from committing the crime, to rehabilitate the offender, or the most obvious and well-known purpose, to punish the offender. In light of the different goals in sentencing, there are also different types of sentences. Some of these sentences may include fines, probation (of which there are different types), and community service, among others.

## Fines

Offenders may be forced to pay fines in place of or in tandem with probation or incarceration. Most traffic offenses and many misdemeanors are traditionally addressed by assessing fines on the offenders. Felony offenders may also be assigned fines, although felony fines are much higher amounts than misdemeanor fines. Sometimes fines are twice the amount of what the offender gained from committing the crime. In New York State, for example, a typical fine imposed for a felony drug conviction is $10,000, even if the offender was in possession of drugs with a street value of far less than $10,000.[18] The imposition of fines has declined somewhat due to two Supreme Court rulings: *Williams v. Illinois* (1970) and *Bearden v. Georgia* (1983). The ruling in *Williams* pronounced that a person cannot be incarcerated longer than the length of the maximum sentence needed to work off a fine the individual was unable to pay. At the time of the ruling, 47 states frequently held defendants beyond the maximum sentence.[19] The *Bearden* decision stated that a sentencing court could not revoke a defendant's probation if a defendant had completed every condition of probation but the payment of fines due to the defendant's inability to pay.[20] This keeps offenders who are on probation from having their probation revoked and going to jail, possibly losing their jobs in the process.

## Probation

Probation, or community supervision, returns an offender to the community under the supervision of an agent of the court or a probation agency. The word "probation" comes from the Latin word *probare*, which means "to test or prove." Probation offers the offender a chance to prove that, if given a second chance, he or she can engage in socially acceptable behavior.

Probationers have been found guilty by the court or have pleaded guilty. The offender who has been placed on probation is not confined in jail or prison and must fulfill conditions of a sentence imposed by the court. When a court sentences a criminal to probation, the judge will set the conditions of probation. The conditions are, in effect, a contract between the court and the probationer. The probation agreement usually comes in the form of general and specific conditions. General conditions are set by law and stipulate the behavior and rules that must be followed by all probationers under the court's jurisdiction. Specific conditions are those additional stipulations that a judge may impose in an effort to customize the probation sentence to fit the individual and crime. General and specific conditions of probation for all states and the federal government may be found online in state and federal government statutes. Probation can include a multitude of conditions, such as community service, participation in therapeutic intervention, and fines.

The concept of probation in the United States was first discussed by John Augustus, a Boston shoemaker, in the early 1840s. The "father of probation" volunteered to pay bail and assume responsibility for certain less serious offenders in exchange for the judge deferring their sentences. Augustus provided the offenders with friendship, support with family and personal issues, and even employment assistance for the period of their release. The offenders later returned to court for sentencing. Augustus would report on their progress toward rehabilitation and request that they be required to pay a fine and court costs rather than being imprisoned. If the judge was satisfied with an offender's performance in the community, the charges were dropped; otherwise, the judge proceeded with the sentence.[21] Augustus worked with the Boston courts for 18 years, never receiving any salary for his efforts. He used his own money and donations from others to support his work.[22] The state of Massachusetts used his basic ideas to pass the country's first official probation law in 1878. Most states allowed probation by 1920, but not until 1957 did all states have probation laws.[23]

Probation is not typically given for dangerous or more serious offenders. In the best situations, probation provides a therapeutic alternative to incarceration, where the offender would be surrounded by more hardcore criminals and hostile situations, making prison a more unlikely place for rehabilitation to take place than the everyday free community. Offenders who are placed on probation and do not successfully complete the court-ordered requirements are violating their probation and are in danger of having their probation revoked. Having probation revoked means the offender typically has to go to jail to complete his or her sentence.

At yearend 2015, an estimated 4,650,900 adults were under community supervision—a decrease of 62,300 offenders from yearend 2014 (Figure 6.1 below). About 1 in 53 adults in the United States was under community supervision at yearend 2015. This population includes adults on probation, parole, or any other post-prison supervision, with probationers accounting for the majority (81%) of adults under community supervision.

There are two general types of probation violations: law and technical. A **law violation** occurs when an offender on probation receives a new criminal charge. For most jurisdictions, the probation officer will be notified when this occurs and will then contact the court to notify the judge of the violation, possibly resulting in the offender being brought in front of the judge to address the violation. A **technical violation** is usually noticed only by the supervising probation officer. Technical violations are less serious than law violations and could include failure to report to the probation officer, failure to make child support payments, or failure to complete other stipulations of probation such as community service hours.[24] The probation

**Law violation** A new criminal charge against an offender on probation.

**Technical violation** A parole violation that is less serious than a law violation and could include failure to report to the probation officer, failure to make child support payments, or failure to complete other stipulations of probation such as community service hours.

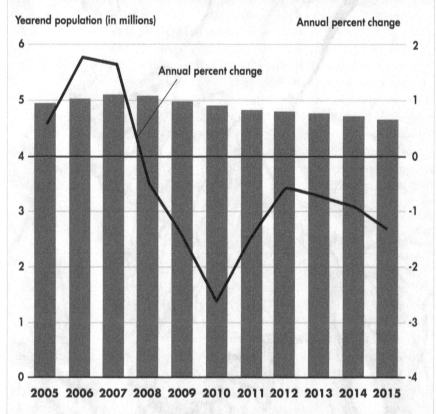

Note: Estimates are based on most recent data and may differ from previously published statistice. See *Methodology*.
Source: Burea of Justic Staistics, Annual Probation Survey and Annual Parole Survey, 2005–2015.
Source: Kaeble, D. & Bonczar, T. (2016). "Probation and Parole in the United States, 2015." Bureau of Justice Statistics. https://www.bjs.gov/content/pub/pdf/ppus15.pdf.

officer typically then has the discretion to cite the probationer for the violation, involve the probationer in more intensive supervision and counseling, or overlook the violation. Technical violation proceedings are started by the supervising officer and typically begin only when the officer has made the decision to approach the court to request that the offender's probation be revoked. Only the court has the final authority to revoke probation, no matter what violations have been committed by the offender.

Probationers are not incarcerated but are also not free citizens. Probationers do not enjoy the full range of

Jail time is one type of sentence a guilty defendant may receive.

protections under the U.S. Constitution that the rest of society enjoys. As part of the probation agreement, probationers agree that the probation officer may enter their homes or places of business unannounced and conduct contraband and weapons searches. They must also submit to drug and alcohol tests. If a probationer is found to be in violation of the probation agreement, he or she may be ordered to jail or prison by the court.

A probationer has not given up all constitutional protections, though. Probationers have a constitutional right to have an attorney represent them during the revocation process.[25] In *Morrissey v. Brewer* (1972) and in *Gagnon v. Scapelli* (1973),[26] the United States Supreme Court recognized limited due process rights of probationers. As part of the rulings, the court established a three-stage procedure that must be followed during revocation proceedings. These stages include a preliminary hearing, the revocation hearing, and sentencing. Often, in lieu of incarceration, the judge will reimpose probation but with stricter terms.

## Deferred Adjudication Probation

**Deferred adjudication**
A type of probation in which the court's decision of the case disposition is delayed while the defendant completes certain requirements of probation.

**Deferred adjudication** is a special type of probation. Adjudication is the court's process of decision making; when something is deferred, it is delayed for a period of time. Deferred adjudication, then, is a type of probation in which the court's decision of the case disposition is delayed while the defendant completes certain requirements of probation. Typically, the defendant pleads "guilty" or "no contest" at the disposition hearing, but no final disposition is recorded with the court until the defendant successfully completes the requirements of probation, or fails to do so and has the probation revoked. If the defendant successfully completes the probation requirements, there may be no formal conviction documented on the defendant's record, as the case is typically dismissed altogether.

**Critical Thinking**

Are there advantages to deferred adjudication probation for the defendant and the prosecution? Are there disadvantages for each? What are they?

## Community Service

**Community service**
Unpaid labor or service to the community as an intermediate sanction ordered by the court.

**Community service** is typically not used as a correctional sentence by itself, but may be a condition of probation for offenders found guilty of lesser offenses, such as shoplifting, first or second drunk driving charges, or minor drug possession. Community service is unpaid work performed for public tax-supported or nonprofit agencies. This form of punishment is consistent with the idea that while each crime has a specific victim, communities as a whole are also victimized by crime. Since crime is an offense against the person as well as the community, service is a good way to offer restitution to the community while reminding the offender of the importance of following rules agreed on by residents of the community. As such, community service is a more restorative process than other forms of punishment. Examples of community service jobs could include picking up trash on state highways, shelving books for the local library, or collecting and organizing canned goods for a food pantry. Community service may be integrated into a probation sentence with the purpose of teaching offenders a specific lesson or exposing them to the possible harm their actions may have caused. For example, a person convicted of cruelty to animals may be sentenced to clean stalls at an animal shelter, or an offender convicted of selling drugs may be ordered to perform community service at a drug abuse treatment program.

Picking up trash in the community is an example of community service.

### Ethics and Professionalism: Innocent of the Crime

As a probation officer for your county, you are ordered by a court to complete a pre-sentence investigative (PSI) report for the court. The defendant pleads guilty to the charge. When you interview the defendant to get his side of the story, he informs you that he is innocent of the charge and he suspects his brother actually committed the crime. The defendant's brother is a parolee who will probably return to prison if he is implicated in another crime. The district attorney's office in your county has enough circumstantial evidence to successfully argue that your defendant committed the crime, and if he is found guilty, there is a good chance that he will go to jail, subsequently losing his job and his home. The defendant has elected to plead guilty to the charge in the hope that he will be placed on probation, allowing him to keep his job and his apartment and potentially preventing his brother from returning to prison.

What do you do? Can the defendant dispute the PSI report while stating he is innocent of the charges? Do you include the defendant's disclosure in your report?

Offenders who have community service as a condition of probation will receive a sentence of a particular amount of hours of community service to complete, such as 50 or 100. The maximum number of community service hours an offender can be ordered to complete varies from state to state; in Texas, for example, an offender can be sentenced to a maximum of 1500 hours of community service for a felony charge.[27] In Illinois, an offender convicted of his first charge of Driving Under the Influence (DUI) without proof of driver's license or insurance is automatically sentenced to 480 hours of community service.[28]

Community service is not currently viewed as an alternative to imprisonment. While community service itself is generally looked upon as positive, the general public does not consider the substitution of a community service sentence for a prison sentence to be punitive enough for most offenders,[29] even though one of the benefits of community service is its value to the public. The state of Georgia reported that in 2007, offenders provided $4.5 million worth of work to the state in the form of community service hours.[30] Another benefit of community service is that it is not costly to implement and monitor. Some proponents, such as Petersilia (2002), argue that community service is beneficial to all parties, as the probation department develops and maintains positive relationships with local agencies by sending them workers, the local agencies benefit from the unpaid work, and the offenders are personally inconvenienced, paying back some of their debts to society.[31]

## Shock Probation

**Shock probation**—technically a misnomer, since probation is designed to be used as an alternative to incarceration—is allowed by some statutes and involves the court sending offenders to prison for a short period of time, usually less than 180 days.[32] This is designed to "shock" offenders by exposing them to the limits of prison life before returning them to the original jurisdiction to be placed on probation. Incarcerating the offenders for a shorter period of time prevents them from absorbing too much of the "hard-core" inmate culture while allowing them to experience the harsh realities of daily prison existence. The first shock probation law in the United States was passed in the state of Ohio in 1965.[33]

There are several pros and cons to shock probation. Offenders who are sentenced to shock probation are made to understand the seriousness of their offenses without being subjected to the effects—as well as the taxpayers' cost—of a lengthy prison sentence. Shock probation also allows offenders who have positive rehabilitation potential to participate in community-based treatment and services, while the court still acknowledges the responsibility for imposing harsher, deterrent sentences in certain circumstances. Economically speaking, the short prison sentences of shock probation are less costly to society than lengthy sentences. On the negative side, shock probation has cost many offenders their jobs and interfered with their family and community support systems. There is also the possibility that even when offenders spend short periods of time in prison, they are exposed to serious offenders and hardened criminals, who generally have deteriorated social skills and hatred of prison life and other prisoners. Offenders may also be stigmatized by being incarcerated, causing confusion of their self-esteem and self-concepts. Whatever the arguments for or against shock probation, as yet, there is no evidence that shock probation reduces recidivism; the research findings on the subject remain inconclusive.

## Intensive Supervision Probation

Some offenders who require additional supervision but may not need outright incarceration may be placed on **intensive supervision probation** (ISP), which includes a higher level of offender supervision, plus a stricter regimen of other services, including such stipulations as treatment programs and community service. Usually the offender is placed on intensive supervision because the probation department has determined that the offender's level of risk and needs require it; however, the court may order the offender directly to an intensive supervision program if the offense warrants, or if the offender was on a less intensive probation regimen but failed to successfully complete its requirements.

Probation officers who supervise intensive offenders typically have much smaller caseloads than other officers, and they may be trained in additional therapeutic interventions. Some of the stricter requirements of ISP may include:

- Multiple office, home, or work visits each week with an officer.
- Mandatory curfews.
- Participation in treatment programs.
- Employment or education requirements.
- Frequent testing for drug and alcohol use.[34]

While intensive supervision probation can help relieve overcrowding in prisons, it is not utilized frequently due to budget constraints and resource limitations. Every additional active intensive supervision officer occupies a spot that could be held by a routine probation officer with a much higher number of clients. Studies of the effectiveness of ISP show mixed results. A study by social scientists Billie Erwin and Lawrence Bennett (1987) examined the intensive supervision probation program in Georgia and found that recidivism rates for probationers on intensive supervision were better than for those on regular probation. The state also saved nearly $7,000 for each defendant assigned to intensive supervision

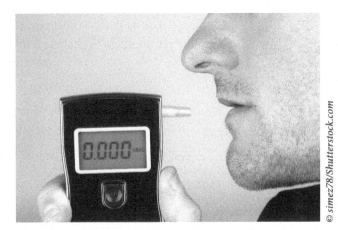

Frequent alcohol and drug testing may be a requirement of intensive supervision probation.

probation rather than prison.[35] Petersilia and Turner (1993) found no clear relationship between more intensive supervision and recidivism. In other words, probationers on intensive supervision were as likely as offenders on regular probation to commit further crimes. Additionally, probationers on ISP had a substantially higher rate of technical violations than those on regular probation. Those offenders in intensive programs, however, came to believe that their chances of getting caught for committing additional crimes while on ISP were high, and they believed that if caught, they would be treated more severely than those on regular probation.[36] Perhaps this secondary effect of ISP led some offenders to refrain from further criminal activity, but this is not known.

## Restitution

**Restitution** is an aspect of probation or punishment that requires the offender to repay the victim, or the victim's family, for the harm that was caused.

**Restitution** Punishment that requires the offender to repay the victim for the harm that was caused, generally through monetary remuneration or community service.

The idea of restitution is to attempt to make the victim or the family of the victim whole again, theoretically restoring things to their original state. Restitution is generally provided by monetary remuneration (paying money to the family) or performing community work service, such as working in nursing homes, alcohol and drug treatment centers, or juvenile counseling or mentoring programs. Restitution not only compensates the crime victims for injuries and other losses, but also forces the offender to take responsibility for the crime committed. Restitution also allows the victim to be included in the process of administering justice.

Critics of restitution programs believe that these programs are punitive rather than rehabilitative because offenders may be subjected to additional sanctions that they cannot fulfill. Some feel that restitution negates any deterrent effects of the offender's sentence because it allows the offender to "pay off" the offense like a traffic ticket or late fee. White-collar criminals are usually sentenced to restitution payments with high dollar amounts to compensate for the large amount of monetary damage their crimes cause victims. The media attention given to white-collar crime also suggests that white-collar restitution amounts compensate for the shorter prison sentences given to these criminals. In other words, the general public seems to feel that white-collar restitution amounts "hit them where it hurts"—in the criminals' wallets.

---

**Critical Thinking**

Do you believe restitution as it is practiced today serves the purpose of making the victim, or the victim's family, whole again? Why or why not?

---

## House Arrest and Electronic Monitoring

**House arrest** A method of punishment in which the defendant is kept under close supervision in his or her own home rather than in prison.

House arrest—also known as home detention, home confinement, and several other names—is a program in which the offender is required to remain in the home except at prearranged and preapproved times, such as to attend work, school, or treatment services. **House arrest** is stricter and seemingly more punitive than ISP, but they may be used in combination. House arrest may also be used as an alternative to pretrial incarceration in jail. While house arrest of some form has probably been implemented by parents since ancient times, it was not used in the United States as an official sanction for criminal activity until the mid-1980s.[37] It became a popular punishment idea due to prison overcrowding. House arrest was not readily considered a reasonable alternative to incarceration because without 24-hour surveillance by law enforcement or court officers, there was no perceived way to ensure that a defendant would comply with the stipulations of home confinement.

**Electronic monitoring** A form of technology used with house arrests to track and limit an offender's movement outside the home with telephone or radio signals.

House arrest became more common with the advent of widely available **electronic monitoring** equipment, which enabled the needed 24-hour surveillance. Electronic monitoring is not a form of detention, but rather a form of technology that tracks and limits an offender's movement outside the home using telephone or radio signals. There are two primary types of electronic monitoring systems used today: continuous monitoring and programmed contact. With the continuous monitoring system, the offender wears a device—typically a type of anklet—programmed to emit continuous signals to a nearby receiver at certain intervals. The receiver communicates with the monitoring agency's computer and cross-checks the offender's location with his or her schedule, which is programmed into the computer, to determine if the offender is in the right place at the required time. With the programmed contact system, the agency's computer makes telephone calls to the offender's approved locations at either random or preprogrammed times, and the offender must respond promptly to those calls to verify his or her location.[38] The type of device utilized governs the offender's response. Some devices require the offender to speak, using voice verification to complete the response. Others require the offender to insert a wrist-worn monitor into a verifier device attached to the telephone. Whatever type of monitoring system is used, each device worn by the offender is usually programmed to detect if it has been tampered with. If an offender tries to remove the device, a signal is sent to the monitoring computer reporting the attempted removal. Offenders who try to remove their monitoring devices may be subjected to more restrictions or incarcerated, as removing the device constitutes failure to comply with the monitoring stipulations.

Supporters state that house arrest and electronic monitoring are more cost-effective than incarceration while allowing the offenders to have more individual supervision than traditional probation. Offenders on electronic monitoring, by not being sent to prison, are spared from the potentially harmful effects of exposure to hardened criminals, some of which were discussed in the section on shock probation. Participants in combined house arrest and electronic monitoring programs are five times more likely to successfully complete their programs and are 50% less likely to abscond from their sentences.[39]

Critics of house arrest and monitoring think that these methods interfere with the offenders' rights to privacy and protection from unreasonable search and seizure as afforded by the U.S. Constitution. This interference, critics say, is also thrust upon those who live in the residence with the offender. Criminologists Rolando del Carmen and Joseph Vaughn (1992) commented, "A review of decided cases in probation and parole indicates that while the use of electronic devices raises constitutional issues, its constitutionality will most likely be upheld by the courts, primarily based on the concept of diminished rights [for offenders]."[40] An offender who is on electronic monitoring experiences a decrease in freedoms, namely the freedom to come and go as one pleases, because he or she is potentially being "watched" at all hours of the day. Other opponents believe that house arrest and electronic monitoring are unfair to economically disadvantaged offenders, who are not as apt to have homes and telephones where the monitoring devices must be installed. Offenders being monitored must also pay costly fees for the monitoring devices and services, which is more difficult for disadvantaged offenders. Another problem with house arrest and electronic monitoring is that while offenders are not allowed to abscond from the program, many still do and may commit more crimes. An examination of Florida's house arrest program revealed that between 1983 and 2008, offenders in the program killed approximately 462 people and committed over 720 sex crimes; approximately 32% of the murderers and 17% of the sex offenders had absconded from their monitoring programs at the time their crimes were committed.[41]

## Pretrial Diversion

Some jurisdictions offer judges the option to sentence offenders to a **pretrial diversion**, which operates much like a probation sentence. The defendant makes at least one court appearance and, depending on the defendant's personal situation and the crime itself, could be recommended by the district attorney to participate in a pretrial diversion. There is no trial and no plea by the defendant. The defendant sees a pretrial officer—who is a probation officer—and performs whatever tasks are assigned by the court. If the offender completes the tasks satisfactorily, the case is typically dismissed without ever going to trial. Pretrial diversions can last for various periods of time depending on judicial preference and local or state laws.

One example of how a pretrial diversion works might be in the instance of an 18-year-old who has been charged with possession of marijuana but has never previously been in trouble. The offender might be sentenced to complete a substance abuse evaluation, urine drug screens, monthly visits with a pretrial officer, and community service hours, all to be done within six months. If the offender completes all of these tasks within the allotted amount of time and does not test positive for substances, the district attorney would then drop the charges.

## Capital Punishment: The Death Penalty

Perhaps the most controversial, hotly debated topic in sentencing for several decades has been capital punishment, also known as the death penalty. A capital crime is a crime that is punishable, according to legislation, by putting the guilty offender to death. Capital crimes, such as the murders committed by Robert Coulson described at the beginning of this chapter, are the most heinous of crimes. Capital punishment is different from any other criminal sanctions not just in its nature but also in its legal process.

### History of Capital Punishment in the United States

When Europeans settled America, they brought the legal systems and processes from their homelands. The English Penal Code was adopted by the British colonies on America's Atlantic coast and included over

50 capital offenses. The adaptation of the rules varied between colonies, so not every colony executed offenders for the same crimes. As an example, the Massachusetts Bay colony observed 12 crimes that were punishable by death. One of these 12 crimes, murder, is still punishable by death in many states today, but several other current-day lesser crimes were capital offenses in colonial days, including witchcraft, rebellion, and sodomy. In the Massachusetts Bay statute, capital punishment was justified for each crime by a supporting quote from the Bible, and the colony later added arson and grand larceny to the approved list of capital offenses. On the less deadly side of the spectrum, the Great Act of 1682 in Pennsylvania listed only treason and murder as crimes punishable by death.[42]

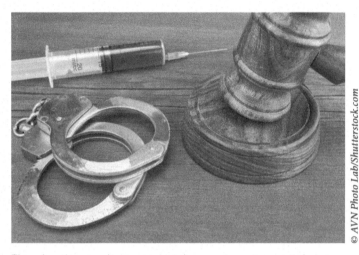

The death penalty is one of the most controversial topics in sentencing.

© AVN Photo Lab/Shutterstock.com

In colonial America, capital punishment was neither rare nor considered cruel and unusual. It was widely accepted as an effective and efficient way to handle criminals; an executed criminal does not live to commit further crimes. The earliest documented lawful execution in the American colonies happened in Virginia in 1608. Captain George Kendall, a prominent citizen in the colony, was found guilty of spying for Spain and executed. Even execution of juveniles was permitted in colonial days.[43]

When the Eighth Amendment of the Constitution was created to ban cruel and unusual punishment, banning the death penalty was apparently not an issue under consideration. The creators of the Constitution were probably thinking of ghastly forms of execution such as boiling in hot oil or impaling with spikes as cruel and unusual.

As time progressed, capital punishment changed. After approximately 1890, the death penalty became an increasingly popular sentence. The 1930s was the peak period for the death penalty: over 1,500 executions occurred in the United States during that decade. After that, use of the death penalty steadily declined, with less than 200 executions carried out in the 1960s.[44] In the southern states, African-Americans were far more likely to be sentenced to death than whites. In mid-1830s Virginia, there were five legislated capital crimes for whites and over 70 for African-Americans. The number of death sentences can be partially explained by the sheer number of states with capital statutes in their penal codes and the offenses listed by state that are punishable by death. In 1961, 48 states had capital offense statutes. Of those [48, 47] considered homicide to be a capital offense; 16 considered rape to be capital; four considered train robbery to be capital; and two considered espionage to be capital.[45]

## The Supreme Court Weighs In

The first argument before the Supreme Court which presented the idea that punishment of offenders could be cruel and unusual was in the case of *O'Neil v. Vermont* (1892). The petitioner faced a sentence of a total of 19,915 days—nearly 55 years—in jail for over 300 separate illegal sales of liquor. The sentence imposed by the court in Vermont was upheld because the Supreme Court found that there was no federal dilemma involved in the case, as the Eighth Amendment did not limit state sentences. Three justices strongly dissented with the opinion, and one, Justice Stephen J. Field, stated that punishment more severe than the crime it was intended to punish was cruel and unusual.[46] The Supreme Court did not hear another cruel and unusual punishment case until 1910, when *Weems v. United States* was decided. The court reversed a sentence imposed upon an offender who made false entries into official government records: 15 years of hard labor, ankle chains, the permanent loss of certain civil rights, and other stipulations. The court determined that the sentence was severely disproportionate to the offense, and *Weems* became the first case in which the court negated a criminal sentence on Eighth Amendment grounds.[47]

Justices of the U.S. Supreme Court have made important case decisions affecting the death penalty.

A barrage of court battles over certain parts of capital punishment, as well as the capital sentence itself, occurred between 1968 and 1972. The initial case decision indicating that the death penalty might be in jeopardy was Witherspoon v. Illinois (1968). In this case, a court in Illinois had allowed a guilty verdict and subsequent death sentence to be handed down by a jury after the state's attorney had methodically excluded all members from the jury pool who were against, or possibly against, capital punishment. The Supreme Court agreed with Witherspoon, ruling that the "death-qualified jury"—meaning that every single jury member was ready, willing, and able to sentence the defendant to die—was not a proper representation of the community as a whole, and therefore violated the Eighth Amendment.[48]

More death penalty challenges made their way to the Supreme Court. States observed an informal moratorium on executions while awaiting the court rulings: in other words, no executions were carried out during this time. The landmark decision finally came on June 29, 1972, when for the first time in history, the Supreme Court set aside death sentences. Three cases, *Furman v. Georgia, Jackson v. Georgia, and Branch v. Texas*, led the court to decide that the capital punishment statutes in those cases were indeed unconstitutional. In those cases, the juries had been given full discretion to decide between imposing the death penalty or a lesser punishment in those capital cases. The majority ruling was five justices to four, and every single justice wrote an opinion—an extremely rare occurrence. The majority justices ruled that those statutes constituted "cruel and unusual punishment" under the Eighth and 14th Amendments because the death penalty was arbitrarily and unfairly imposed against non-whites. This ruling did not declare the death penalty unconstitutional, but rather the methods by which it was administered.[49] The decision in these cases (known collectively as the *Furman* decision) negated the death penalty laws of approximately 35 states, and over 600 inmates had their death sentences set aside and commuted to prison terms. By late 1974, however, 30 states had enacted new death penalty laws that conformed to the *Furman* ruling. Some states mandated capital punishment upon conviction for certain crimes, while others listed specific rules that judges and juries had to follow when deciding whether execution was the appropriate sentence for a specific case.

Another Supreme Court ruling affecting the death penalty was, like the *Furman* decision, a collection of court cases. In *Gregg v. Georgia*, the court addressed the new bifurcated trial structure in the state of Georgia: after defendants were convicted in first-degree murder cases, the punishment was determined in a separate court process. The law at the time in Georgia mandated the judge or jury to take into account any additional **aggravating circumstances** or **mitigating circumstances**, such as a murder occurring while the defendant was attempting to avoid being arrested; a murder of a corrections officer, an on-duty law enforcement officer, or a firefighter; a murder committed in exchange for money; or a murder committed while a rape, armed robbery, burglary, kidnapping, or act of arson occurred. The Supreme Court upheld the Georgia law, saying that because juries had to consider another circumstance in addition to the guilty finding, they were prevented from assessing death sentences with their previous wild abandon. In two companion cases, *Proffitt v. Florida* and *Jurek v. Texas*, the court upheld procedures in those states similar to Georgia's. By handing down these three rulings, the Supreme Court restated that capital punishment laws were indeed constitutional as long as those state laws provided clear and unbiased criteria for judges and juries to follow when determining whether to sentence the guilty party to death.[50]

After the collective *Furman* and *Gregg* decisions, state-sponsored executions resumed. The first state to complete an execution was Utah, on January 17, 1977. Gary Gilmore, convicted of the robbery and murder of a hotel manager, was executed by firing squad. At the time of his sentencing, Utah had two methods of execution—firing squad or hanging—and the judge allowed Gilmore his choice.[51] Since Gilmore's execution, more than half of the executions completed in the United States have occurred in only three states: Texas, Virginia, and Oklahoma.[52]

**Aggravating circumstances**
Circumstances that go above and beyond the basic requirements for a crime to be considered serious; the facts or situations that increase the seriousness of a criminal act.

**Mitigating circumstances**
Circumstances that do not justify a criminal act, but make the crime less reprehensible and may be used to reduce the sentence in a criminal trial.

In 1977, several states legally retired hanging, electrocution, and lethal gas as methods of execution and replaced them with death by lethal injection. Supporters of this method argued that it would be a far more humane mode of execution, as the prisoner would fall asleep, and death would be virtually instantaneous. The American Medical Association argued against lethal injection and issued instructions to its member doctors to refrain from taking part in the act, pointing out that the role of a doctor is to protect and save life, not end it.[53] The first inmate to die in the United States by state-supported lethal injection was Charles Brooks, Jr. He was put to death in Huntsville, Texas, on December 7, 1982, for committing capital murder in 1976.[54]

In 1994, a federal court ruled that execution by lethal gas was in violation of the Eighth Amendment clause on cruel and unusual punishment. The presiding judge cited as evidence doctor reports and eyewitness accounts of many past executions, all of which stated that the dying inmates were still conscious for a minute or more once the gas was administered. Consequently, the inmates could be suffering intense physical pain, including the deprivation of air akin to the experience of being strangled or drowning. This ruling stipulated that all future executions in California would be done by lethal injection.[55] The Supreme Court has declared death by electrocution to be constitutional, but due to the gruesomeness of the act, most states do not allow it. As of November 2016, only Washington and New Hampshire still offer hanging for executions; seven states offer electrocution; five states allow lethal gas; and one allows death by firing squad. Nineteen states and the District of Columbia have no death penalty.[56] However, most states use lethal injection.

Death sentences, executions, and public support for capital punishment all continued historic declines in 2016. American juries imposed the fewest death sentences in the modern era of U.S. capital punishment, since the Supreme Court declared existing death penalty statutes unconstitutional in 1972. The 30 new death sentences imposed in 2016 represent a 39 percent decline from 2015's already 40-year low of 49. The 20 executions in 2016 marked the lowest number in a quarter century, according to a report released by the Death Penalty Information Center (DPIC). National public opinion polls also showed support for capital punishment at a 40-year low. [66]

"America is in the midst of a major climate change concerning capital punishment. While there may be fits and starts and occasional steps backward, the long-term trend remains clear," according to Robert Dunham, DPIC's Executive Director. "Whether it's concerns about innocence, costs, and discrimination, availability of life without parole as a safe alternative, or the questionable way in which states are attempting to carry out executions, the public grows increasingly uncomfortable with the death penalty each year." [66]

For the first time in more than 40 years, no state imposed ten or more death sentences. Only five states imposed more than one death sentence. California imposed the most (9) followed by Ohio (4), Texas (4), Alabama (3), and Florida (2). Death sentences continued to be clustered in *two percent* of counties nationwide, with Los Angeles County imposing four death sentences, the most of any county. But death sentences were down 39 percent, even in those two-percent counties. [66]

The 20 executions conducted in 2016 marked a decline of more than 25 percent since the previous year, when there were 28 executions. Only five states conducted executions in 2016, the fewest number of states to do so since 1983. Two states—Georgia, which had the most executions (9), and Texas, which had the second highest number (7)—accounted for 80 percent of all executions in the U.S. Although Georgia carried out more executions than at any other time since the 1950s, juries in that state have not imposed any new death sentences in the past two years. [66]

## Limits to the Death Penalty

Subsequent Supreme Court rulings have imposed limits on which crimes may appropriately generate death sentences and have further clarified capital punishment as a whole. Figure 6.2 is a list of many of these rulings.

**FIGURE 6.2   SUPREME COURT RULINGS ON THE DEATH PENALTY**

| | |
|---|---|
| *Coker v. Georgia (1977)* | Rape without murder does not warrant a death sentence. [59] |
| *Eberheart v. Georgia (1977)* | Kidnapping when the victim does not die does not warrant a death sentence. [60] |
| *Ford v. Wainwright (1986)* | States are prevented from executing death row inmates who have developed diagnosed mental illnesses while they are on death row. [61] |
| *McCleskey v. Kemp (1987)* | State death penalty laws are constitutional even when research shows that they may have been applied in a racially biased or prejudicial manner. While racial discrimination exists, it must be demonstrated in individual and separate cases. [62] |
| *Thompson v. Oklahoma (1988)* | States may not execute persons who were under the age of 16 when they committed their offenses unless the states in which the offenses occurred had established a clear, set minimum age for the death penalty. [63] |
| *Stanford v. Kentucky (1989)* | It is not a violation of the Eighth Amendment to impose the death penalty upon a defendant who committed his or her crime at the age of 16 or 17 years. [64] |
| *Atkins v. Virginia (2002)* | It is considered cruel and unusual punishment to execute the mentally retarded, since it cannot be determined that they understood their crimes, much less their sentences. [65] |
| *Roper v. Simmons (2005)* | The *Stanford* ruling was overturned. It is now unconstitutional to sentence a juvenile (person under the age of 18 years) to death. [66] |
| *Kennedy v. Louisiana (2008)* | Child rape in which the child victim does not die does not warrant a death sentence. [67] |

Proponents of the death penalty argue that it is, practically speaking, cheaper to execute offenders than to house them in prison for life, which could be many years. Due to state and federal laws, however, all defendants sentenced to death enter a mandatory appeal process, which has several steps and can take quite a few years. There are multiple sets of documents filed in multiple levels of courts, which must be reviewed by judges and attorneys in those courts, and verbal arguments are taken in some of those courts. The appellate courts are usually in wholly different cities or states than the attorneys' offices and the defendant's prison unit. The entire process is costly, from filing court documents, to traveling to and appearing in the courts, to corresponding with the defendant and his or her legal team. Since a judge appoints the defendant's legal team, the costs fall to the taxpayers. The average amount of time a prisoner spends on death row before being executed is long: 10.6 years in Texas (TDCJ) and at least 12 years in Florida (Florida Dept. of Corrections) and Arizona (Arizona Dept. of Corrections).[57] Most quantitative studies of the economic argument for the death penalty have shown that the death penalty exerts a much higher cost to taxpayers than life imprisonment, due to the costs of the appeals process. The state can spend up to $5 million per appeal.[58]

Probably the most hotly argued reason to discontinue the death penalty is the justifiability of punishing someone who has killed by killing that individual. Murder is against the law, yet many opponents of the death penalty consider capital punishment to be state-sanctioned murder. Cesare Beccaria advocated against capital punishment, writing, "The death penalty cannot be useful because of the example of barbarity it gives to men . . . it seems absurd to me that the laws . . . which punish homicide should themselves commit it."[68] Supporters of capital punishment might argue that by killing another individual, the offender has stolen the victim's right to live, and has thereby forfeited his or her own right to live.[69]

There is also the argument that since the death penalty is irreversible, innocent persons may be executed. Research by Radelet and Bedau determined that between 1972 and 1996, 86 death row inmates were released prior to their executions due to doubts about their guilt.[70] These inmates were tried, found guilty, sentenced to death, and later released due to their erroneous convictions. The number of convicted death row inmates receiving exonerations has increased as well, from three per year from 1973 to 1999, to five per year from 2000 through 2007.[71] Opponents of the death penalty argue that one innocent person executed is too many.

Another issue regarding the death penalty is whether it is applied fairly to all races in this country. Since 1976, approximately 35% of executed offenders have been black, despite the black population in the United States being approximately 15% of the total population. Of the current death row offenders in this country, nearly four times as many offenders were convicted in cases involving white victims as were convicted in cases involving non-white victims.[72] Research published in 1989 by Radelet revealed the startling statistic that less than 0.2% of known, sanctioned executions in the United States were of a white individual for committing a crime against a black individual.[73] Updated statistics show that compared to 16 white offenders in the United States who were executed for killing black victims, there have been 253 black offenders executed for killing white victims.[74]

Public support in the U.S. for the death penalty reached its lowest point in 1966, during the height of the Vietnam War and American political activism; the highest was in 1984.[75] Several issues have arisen over time that have led an increasing number of people to question the validity and appropriateness

While a jury may recommend a sentence, the judge may overrule the recommendation and pronounce a different sentence.

of the death penalty. The fact that putting an offender to death is absolutely irreversible raises huge concerns for many death penalty abolitionists. Some offenders who were on death row have been released after new DNA testing technology proved their innocence of the crimes for which they were convicted. One study showed that out of over 4,500 death penalty cases examined, more than two-thirds contained serious legal discrepancies, such as incompetent defense counsel or corrupt prosecution.[76] Many death penalty states now offer sentences of "life without parole" for offenders who are convicted of capital offenses but are not sentenced to death. Life without parole effectively imparts the benefits of the death penalty—deterrence from committing future murders and no re-release into society—without taking the life of the accused.[77] Since 1998, the number of death sentences pronounced per year has dropped by more than half: 294 offenders were sentenced to death in 1998, while 112 were sentenced to death in 2009. [78] In 2016, 30 people were sentenced to death in America, and 20 people were executed. [57]

## Special Issues in Sentencing

The **indeterminate sentence** is the most common type of sentence. It has fixed minimum and maximum terms for imprisonment. The paroling authority determines the amount of time the inmate serves. When a defendant is sentenced to, for example, one to five years' imprisonment or 20 years to life, those are indeterminate sentences.

The indeterminate sentence is based on the idea of teaching offenders to learn to refrain from criminal behavior so they can be returned to society as productive, law-abiding citizens. Theoretically, the indeterminate sentence should meet each defendant's rehabilitative needs. After the inmate is incarcerated, the rehabilitation begins, and the inmate is imprisoned until he or she can demonstrate signs of rehabilitation. The paroling authority, or **parole board**, has the duty to assess the extent to which the offender has

**Indeterminate sentence** A prison sentence that consists of a range of years (such as "five to ten years"). The state parole board holds hearings that determine when, during that range, the convicted person will be eligible for parole.

**Parole board** The governmental board that will determine if an offender receives parole and under what conditions.

been rehabilitated or not rehabilitated and orders the offender's release or return to prison. The readiness of the offender for his or her release theoretically lies with the individual and varies according to the individual's participation in rehabilitation and improvement while incarcerated.[79]

While indeterminate sentencing became popular in the 1950s and 1960s, it lost steam in the 1970s and 1980s. Many offenders who had been deemed to be rehabilitated recidivated, causing politicians and the general public to lose faith in the justice system.[80] Many inmates learned how to "play the game" and behave like they were rehabilitated in order to convince parole officials that they could be released into society. They participated in available treatment programs and learned how to use the appropriate verbiage to obtain their release.[81] As justice system reforms occurred, the decision-making authority regarding the length of an inmate's sentence moved from the parole board and prison staff to the prosecutors and lawmakers when the determinate sentence was introduced.

**Determinate sentence**
A sentence for a specific criminal act that is determined by the state legislature; a sentence that requires a specific amount of time, as ordered by the trial judge, for a person to serve in prison.

Offenders sanctioned with **determinate sentences** have fixed spans of incarceration and know precisely when they will be released, which eliminates the need for parole boards. The federal government and some states have established guidelines for determinate sentencing, while other states have sentencing commissions. The purpose of determinate sentencing is not so much rehabilitation as it is incapacitation: its main purpose is to keep criminals out of society. Stories about lenient judges and liberal parole boards releasing offenders back into society when they were not successfully rehabilitated caused legislators to create sentencing laws that controlled criminal justice professionals' discretion in any particular case. Many of these laws stated that the length of an inmate's sentence would not be determined by any person, such as the judge or the parole board, but by the actual crime committed.[82] In Texas, the parole board is appointed by the governor.

While it appears that determinate sentencing is advantageous because it creates uniformity in sentencing, removing any focus from factors such as race, gender, and social class, unintended consequences have been created. With the removal of discretion and decision-making power from those professionals closely involved with the case, the potential to apply the most appropriate sentence for an offender with extenuating or mitigating circumstances is also removed. This means the welfare of society and the offender's punishment cannot be balanced effectively, as in the case of a young man who kills his father to prevent him from repeatedly beating his wife. Legislators also presumably did not take into account the effect that determinate sentencing would have on correctional resources. Prison overcrowding has grown rampant in this country, with limits to even the number of beds in prisons. While many legislators assume a "get tough on crime" agenda in order to get elected or remain in office, the same legislators are loath to increase resource allocation in order to appropriately address overcrowding in jails and prisons. As a result, the civil and human rights of prisoners are violated.[83]

Another effect of determinate sentencing is that it has caused a power shift from the judge to the prosecutor. With determinate sentencing laws limiting the judge's discretion in sentence imposition, the power of the prosecutor to decide what charges can be filed against the defendant has increased. This has unintentionally caused a ripple effect, as defendants who are unwilling to accept longer determinate sentences for some crimes may be pressured into accepting plea bargains for lesser crimes. This gives the prosecutor a huge amount of leverage in coercing defendants and their attorneys to accept plea bargains, particularly in cases involving sex or drug offenses.[84]

## Mandatory Minimums

The concept of the mandatory minimum sentence came about during the "war on drugs," which took hold particularly during the 1980s. A **mandatory minimum** sentence is governed by the lawmakers in each state and prescribes a set span of imprisonment for drug offenses such as possession or distribution. Other crimes can have punishments dictated by mandatory minimums, such as armed robbery with a gun. All 50 states and the federal government now have at least one mandatory minimum sentencing law. Mandatory minimums do not always work, however, because judges and other officials have the authority to alter those sentences. Mandatory minimum sentencing also does not take into account any special circumstances particular to one crime, forcing defendants who may be small-time or first-time offenders into the hardened culture of prison life with hardcore, repeat offenders.

**Mandatory minimum**
A sentence that is imposed by the state legislature with no discretion given by the trial judge. The defendant is required by law to serve a certain amount of time in the state penitentiary.

**Three-strikes law**
A specific legislative mandate that requires offenders, after their third conviction for any offense, to serve a minimum amount of time in incarceration.

## Three-Strikes Law

In the legal systems of some states, if an offender commits three felonies, he or she earns a sentence of life in prison. These "three-strikes" laws earn their collective name from the game of baseball, in which the at-bat is over if the batter earns three strikes. Washington was the first state to pass a **three-strikes law**, in 1993. Washington's Persistent Offender Accountability Act allows for offenders who have committed three felonies to be sent to prison for life without parole. California followed suit in 1994 with what has been deemed one of the most encompassing three-strikes laws. Under California law, some of the felonies considered "strikes" are sexual abuse of a child, kidnapping, murder, or rape. The first two felonies must be in the serious felony category; any third felony committed dooms the offender to a mandatory

In the legal systems of some states, if an offender commits three felonies, he or she earns a sentence of life in prison.

© Paul Hippauf/Shutterstock.com

life sentence.[85] Over half of the states, as well as the federal government, have three-strikes provisions in their laws. Opponents of three-strikes laws believe they constitute cruel and unusual punishment. One example is the Supreme Court ruling in *Ewing v. California*, in which Gary Ewing's third felony was the theft of three golf clubs. While it was argued that the life sentence was severely disproportionate to the crime, the court upheld the law, and Ewing is currently serving a sentence of 25 years to life.[86]

On November 6, 2012 California voters approved Proposition 36, which substantially amended the law with two primary provisions:

1. The requirements for sentencing a defendant as a third-strike offender were changed by requiring the new felony to be a serious *or violent felony* with two or more prior strikes to qualify for the 25-year-to-life sentence as a third-strike offender; and

2. The addition of a means by which designated defendants *currently serving* a third-strike sentence may petition the court for reduction of their term to a second-strike sentence, if they would have been eligible for second strike sentencing under the new law. * Source: *California's Three Strikes Sentencing Law* (2016). California Courts. The Judicial Branch of California. http://www.courts. ca.gov/20142.htm.

## Truth in Sentencing

Truth-in-sentencing laws mandate that offenders serve a substantial, or even a majority, of their sentences. These laws were enacted because prisoners typically serve less time in prison than their original sentences stipulated due to time off for good behavior or parole. Inmates are also released early due to prison overcrowding, and in some states, inmates who learn a trade or complete school could get time taken off their sentences. The truth-in-sentencing laws restrict **good time credits**, which in turn increases the percentage of a sentence an inmate serves. Most states have adopted truth-in-sentencing laws, and three states require that 100% of a minimum sentence must be served prior to an inmate becoming eligible to be released.[87]

**Good time credit** The amount of time that a state penitentiary gives the offender for maintaining good behavior while incarcerated; time that is taken off the sentence.

## Federal Sentencing Guidelines

Sentencing guidelines may be developed by sentencing commissions made up of criminal justice professionals and private citizens. Sentencing guidelines are a way to restrict judges' discretion. Both state and federal jurisdictions have guidelines in place that serve as general rules on which judges may base sentences. While the guidelines used to be considered mandatory, after the Supreme Court ruling in *United States v. Booker,* the guidelines are considered advisory only.[88] This means that judges may use the sentencing guidelines when determining a defendant's sentence, but this is no longer required.

The United States Congress created the U.S. Sentencing Commission in 1985. This commission creates, maintains, and changes federal sentencing guidelines to prevent sentencing disparities at the federal level. The guidelines are suggestions based on the defendant's conduct during the commission of the offense and the defendant's criminal history. There are 43 offense levels, six criminal history categories based on points, and four sentencing zones: A, B, C, and D. The offense levels rank different types of offenses by severity. Sentencing zones group the lengths of sentences into types and lengths of sentences, from least severe to most severe. Zone A includes sentences ranging from zero to six months; Zone B includes sentences ranging from one to seven months up to six to 12 months, with the possibility of using alternate methods of confinement, split sentences, or incarceration only; Zone C sentences range from eight to 14 months up to 10 to 16 months, with the possibility of a split sentence only if at least one half of the minimum sentence is served while incarcerated; and Zone D includes all sentences ranging from 12 to 18 months up to life in prison, with all time required to be served in prison.[89] New sentencing guidelines implemented resulted in increased similarity of sentences between offenders and sent more federal defendants to prison for shorter periods of time. Figure 6.3 is a table of sentencing guidelines.

**FIGURE 6.3** 2016 FEDERAL SENTENCING GUIDELINES (IN MONTHS OF IMPRISONMENT).[90]

| | Offense Level | Criminal History Category (Criminal History Points) | | | | | |
| | | I (0 or 1) | II (2 or 3) | III (4, 5, 6) | IV (7, 8, 9) | V (10, 11, 12) | VI (13 or more) |
|---|---|---|---|---|---|---|---|
| Zone A | 1 | 0–6 | 0–6 | 0–6 | 0–6 | 0–6 | 0–6 |
| | 2 | 0–6 | 0–6 | 0–6 | 0–6 | 0–6 | 1–7 |
| | 3 | 0–6 | 0–6 | 0–6 | 0–6 | 2–8 | 3–9 |
| | 4 | 0–6 | 0–6 | 0–6 | 2–8 | 4–10 | 6–12 |
| | 5 | 0–6 | 0–6 | 1–7 | 4–10 | 6–12 | 9–15 |
| | 6 | 0–6 | 1–7 | 2–8 | 6–12 | 9–15 | 12–18 |
| | 7 | 0–6 | 2–8 | 4–10 | 8–14 | 12–18 | 15–21 |
| | 8 | 0–6 | 4–10 | 6–12 | 10–16 | 15–21 | 18–24 |
| Zone B | 9 | 4–10 | 6–12 | 8–14 | 12–18 | 18–24 | 21–27 |
| | 10 | 6–12 | 8–14 | 10–16 | 15–21 | 21–27 | 24–30 |
| | 11 | 8–14 | 10–16 | 12–18 | 18–24 | 24–30 | 27–33 |
| Zone C | 12 | 10–16 | 12–18 | 15–21 | 21–27 | 27–33 | 30–37 |
| Zone D | 13 | 12–18 | 15–21 | 18–24 | 24–30 | 30–37 | 33–41 |
| | 14 | 15–21 | 18–24 | 21–27 | 27–33 | 33–41 | 37–46 |
| | 15 | 18–24 | 21–27 | 24–30 | 30–37 | 37–46 | 41–51 |
| | 16 | 21–27 | 24–30 | 27–33 | 33–41 | 41–51 | 46–57 |
| | 17 | 24–30 | 27–33 | 30–37 | 37–46 | 46–57 | 51–63 |

| Offense Level | I | II | III | IV | V | VI |
|---|---|---|---|---|---|---|
| 18 | 27–33 | 30–37 | 33–41 | 41–51 | 51–63 | 57–71 |
| 19 | 30–37 | 33–41 | 37–46 | 46–57 | 57–71 | 63–78 |
| 20 | 33–41 | 37–46 | 41–51 | 51–63 | 63–78 | 70–87 |
| 21 | 37–46 | 41–51 | 46–57 | 57–71 | 70–87 | 77–96 |
| 22 | 41–51 | 46–57 | 51–63 | 63–78 | 77–96 | 84–105 |
| 23 | 46–57 | 51–63 | 57–71 | 70–87 | 84–105 | 92–115 |
| 24 | 51–63 | 57–71 | 63–78 | 77–96 | 92–115 | 100–125 |
| 25 | 57–71 | 63–78 | 70–87 | 84–105 | 100–125 | 110–137 |
| 26 | 63–78 | 70–87 | 78–97 | 92–115 | 110–137 | 120–150 |
| 27 | 70–87 | 78–97 | 87–108 | 100–125 | 120–150 | 130–162 |
| 28 | 78–97 | 87–108 | 97–121 | 110–137 | 130–162 | 140–175 |
| 29 | 87–108 | 97–121 | 108–135 | 121–151 | 140–175 | 151–188 |
| 30 | 97–121 | 108–135 | 121–151 | 135–168 | 151–188 | 168–210 |
| 31 | 108–135 | 121–151 | 135–168 | 151–188 | 168–210 | 188–235 |
| 32 | 121–151 | 135–168 | 151–188 | 168–210 | 188–235 | 210–262 |
| 33 | 135–168 | 151–188 | 168–210 | 188–235 | 210–262 | 235–293 |
| 34 | 151–188 | 168–210 | 188–235 | 210–262 | 235–293 | 262–327 |
| 35 | 168–210 | 188–235 | 210–262 | 235–293 | 262–327 | 292–365 |
| 36 | 188–235 | 210–262 | 235–293 | 262–327 | 292–365 | 324–405 |
| 37 | 210–262 | 235–293 | 262–327 | 292–365 | 324–405 | 360–life |
| 38 | 235–293 | 262–327 | 292–365 | 324–405 | 360–life | 360–life |
| 39 | 262–327 | 292–365 | 324–405 | 360–life | 360–life | 360–life |
| 40 | 292–365 | 324–405 | 360–life | 360–life | 360–life | 360–life |
| 41 | 324–405 | 360–life | 360–life | 360–life | 360–life | 360–life |
| 42 | 360–life | 360–life | 360–life | 360–life | 360–life | 360–life |
| 43 | life | life | life | life | life | life |

Commentary to Sentencing Table

Application Notes:
1.  The Offense Level (1–43) forms the vertical axis of the Sentencing Table. The Criminal History Category (I–VI) forms the horizontal axis of the Table. The intersection of the Offense Level and Criminal History Category displays the Guideline Range in months of imprisonment. "Life" means life imprisonment. For example, the guideline range applicable to a defendant with an Offense Level of 15 and a Criminal History Category of III is 24–30 months of imprisonment.
2.  In rare cases, a total offense level of less than 1 or more than 43 may result from application of the guidelines. A total offense level of less than 1 is to be treated as an offense level of 1. An offense level of more than 43 is to be treated as an offense level of 43.
3.  The Criminal History Category is determined by the total criminal history points from Chapter Four, Part A, except as provided in §§4B1.1 (Career Offender) and 4B1.4 (Armed Career Criminal). The total criminal history points associated with each Criminal History Category are shown under each Criminal History Category in the Sentencing Table.

## Victim Characteristics That Affect Punishment

Some crimes are determined to be more heinous than others depending on the circumstances of the crime or even the characteristics of the victims. For example, the difference between murder and capital murder in some states can be the age or mental capacity of the victim. In Texas, the murder of a peace officer is considered a capital offense, as is a murder committed during the commission of abuse of a minor under the age of 16 years in Wyoming.

## Plea Bargaining

Plea bargaining is a process involving the prosecutor and the accused or the defense counsel. During this process, the parties discuss the stipulations under which the defendant will plead guilty to a charge in exchange for some kind of concession, or trade-off, from the prosecutor or the judge.[91] One or more of several things may happen as the result of plea bargaining. The charges the defendant is facing may be reduced, which leads to a reduction in the defendant's sentence. If the defendant is charged with multiple crimes, the number of crimes may be reduced, also leading by default to a reduction in the defendant's sentence. The prosecutor can choose to recommend that the judge be lenient on the defendant, which could reduce the defendant's sentence from jail or prison time to probation. And finally, in cases involving crimes with negative or inflammatory labels—such as sex crimes—the charge may be reduced to a less incendiary one, thus sparing the defendant from several hardships that may arise due to the label.

Plea bargaining has advantages for both the state and the accused. The financial costs of prosecuting the defendant are reduced. Cases that are taken to plea bargain do not go to trial, which not only saves the government money but also increases the efficiency of the courts.[92] The prosecution is also able to dedicate its time and resources to more involved and serious cases. For the defendant, the possibility of jail time during the pretrial and trial periods is reduced, as are the costs of legal representation. The defendant also increases his or her chances of receiving a reduced sentence.

There are issues with plea bargaining, the foremost being the possibility that an innocent person who faces a harsh sentence if found guilty agrees to plead guilty and accept a lighter punishment rather than risk going to prison or worse. When a defendant accepts a plea bargain, he or she also waives the constitutional rights to trial and appeal. Opponents of plea bargaining argue that by accepting a less severe charge or punishment, the defendant has defeated the system.[93]

The Supreme Court formally upheld the practice of plea bargaining, saying that it served the interests of both the court and the defendant, in *Brady v.*

"Let's take some of the pleading out of your plea bargain."

*United States* in 1970.[94] The Supreme Court has also supported the position of the prosecution in the plea bargaining process with its ruling in *North Carolina v. Alford*. In this ruling, the court announced that a judge can accept a guilty plea from a defendant who declares his or her innocence if the defendant makes the plea both voluntarily and with understanding of the plea, and if there is enough factual evidence to demonstrate that the defendant is guilty.[95]

The only state without plea bargaining is the state of Alaska.

In 1975, Alaska Attorney General Avrum Gross banned plea bargaining in Alaska. The Judicial Council's initial evaluation of the ban found that plea bargaining, both charge and sentence bargaining, was substantially curtailed, and that despite the dire predictions of unmanageable caseloads and backlogged trials, disposition times for criminal cases actually improved. Although few thought that the policy still would be in effect fifteen years later, the Alaska Judicial Council's most recent evaluation of the ban, completed in 1990, shows that the ban continues to affect virtually every important aspect of Alaska's criminal justice system. The ban as it exists today in Alaska differs in several important respects from its original form. The changes in the ban can be linked to two major historical developments. In 1980, a new criminal code and presumptive sentencing went into effect in Alaska, both reflecting societal changes in thinking about crime and punishment. In 1985 and 1986, changes in personnel and declines in state revenues combined to create new opportunities and impetus for charge bargaining. Thus, by 1990, the written guidelines for the policy prohibiting plea bargaining remained unchanged from their 1986 version, but attorneys and judges throughout the state agreed that charge bargaining had become fairly common in most courts.[96]

## Race and Gender

Race and gender are examples of extralegal factors that can affect sentencing. Extralegal factors are aspects concerning the defendant, the victim, or the crime that may not be clearly defined by law and, thus, are not supposed to be taken into consideration when assessing a sentence; however, this is sometimes not the case. Examples of extralegal factors include race, gender, socioeconomic status, and class status. The two perhaps most controversial of these factors, race and gender, will be addressed in this section.

In the United States, there is a disproportionate percentage of non-whites in prison. As of June 30, 2010, the U.S. incarceration rate was 732 per 100,000 residents. But when you break down the statistics, as shown in Figure 6.4, you see that incarceration has a disproportionate share of non-whites and is not an equal opportunity punishment.

**FIGURE 6.4** U.S. INCARCERATION RATES BY RACE AND ETHNICITY, 2010.

United States incarceration rates by race and ethnicity, 2010
(number of people incarcerated per 100,000 people in that group)

Source: Calculated by the Prison Policy Initiative from Bureau of Justice Statistics, Correctional Population in the U.S., 2010 & U.S. Cenus 2010 Summary File 1.

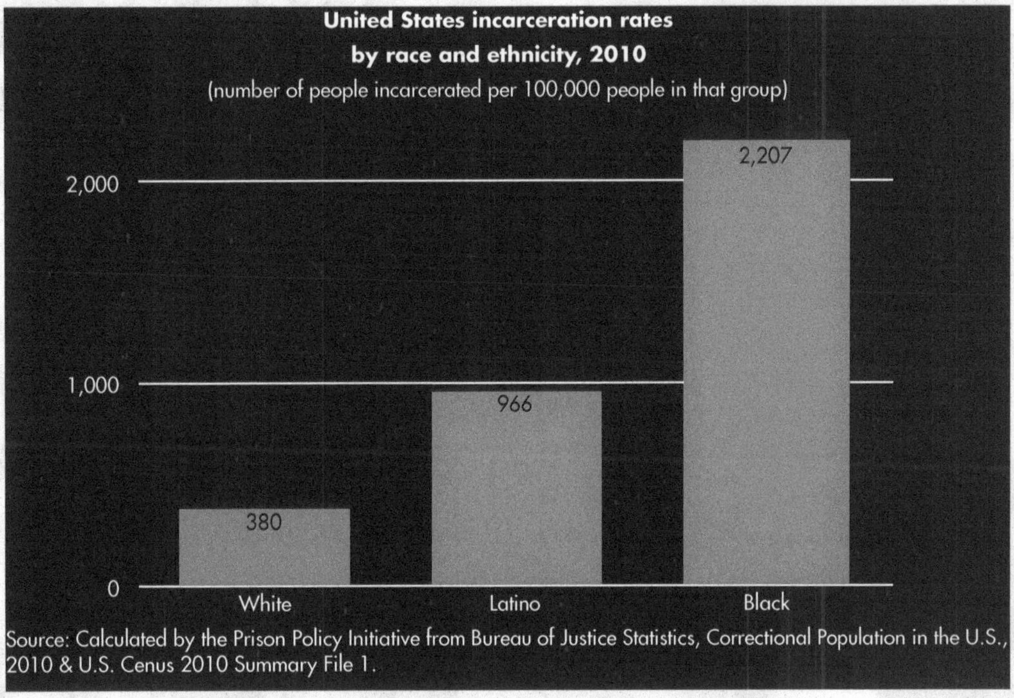

At the end of 2010, there were 2,266,800 people in U.S. prisons and jails. For the second year in a row, the total prison population fell slightly, although some states and the federal system continued to increase the number of people incarcerated. [97]

As of June 30, 2010, the U.S. incarceration rate was 732 per 100,000 residents. But when you break down the statistics you see that incarceration is not an equal opportunity punishment. The graph above illustrates the young Black and Latino male are disproportionately incarcerated. Put those factors together and you have almost 9% of Black men in their late 20s behind bars and almost 4% of Latino men of that age are incarcerated.[97]

Gender is another important consideration in sentencing, especially since the fastest-growing population in prisons is women. There has been a tremendous increase in female prisoners since 1995. Two-thirds of women in prison are non-white, only one-third of women sentenced to prison have graduated from high school or gotten a GED prior to entering prison, and many of them suffer from major depression or other serious psychological disorders. Being sentenced to prison does not seem to act as a deterrent: 65% of women in prison have been found guilty of prior criminal charges. One of the reasons for the increase of women in prisons may be the changes in sentencing laws relating especially to drug offenses. Nearly one-third of female inmates in state prison facilities and over one-half of women sentenced to federal prisons are incarcerated for drug-related and nonviolent crimes.[97] Figures 6.5 and 6.6 show numbers from the Bureau of Justice Statistics demonstrating the overall growth of the female prison population for the years 2006, 2013, and 2014.

**FIGURE 6.5** FEMALE PRISONERS UNDER THE JURISDICTION OF STATE OR FEDERAL CORRECTIONAL AUTHORITIES, BY JURISDICTION, DECEMBER 31, 2006, 2013, AND 2014

| Jurisdiction | | 2006 | 2013 | 2014 | % Change 2006-2014 | % Change 2013-2014 |
|---|---|---|---|---|---|---|
| U.S. Total | | 103,337 | 104,301 | 106,232 | 2.8% | 1.9% |
| Federal/b | | 11,116 | 12,720 | 12,560 | 13.0% | -1.3% |
| State | | 92,221 | 91,581 | 93,672 | 1.6% | 2.3% |
| | Alabama | 1,960 | 2,567 | 2,442 | 24.6% | -4.9% |
| | Alaska/c | 242 | 256 | 263 | 8.7% | 2.7% |
| | Arizona/d | 2,783 | 3,387 | 3,550 | 27.6% | 4.8% |
| | Arkansas | 1,041 | 1,319 | 1,393 | 33.8% | 5.6% |
| | California | 11,581 | 6,297 | 6,382 | -44.9% | 1.3% |
| | Colorado/e | 2,302 | 1,815 | 1,908 | -17.1% | 5.1% |

| | | | | |
|---|---|---|---|---|
| Connecticut/c | 799 | 668 | 637 | -20.3% | -4.6% |
| Delaware/c,d | 229 | 233 | 214 | -6.6% | -8.2% |
| District of Columbia | -- | -- | -- | -- | -- |
| Florida | 6,485 | 7,271 | 7,303 | 12.6% | 0.4% |
| Georgia | 3,557 | 3,525 | 3,475 | -2.3% | -1.4% |
| Hawaii/c,f | 499 | 347 | 309 | -38.1% | -11.0% |
| Idaho | 777 | 1,066 | 1,026 | 32.0% | -3.8% |
| Illinois/g | 2,720 | 2,916 | 2,888 | 6.2% | -1.0% |
| Indiana | 2,161 | 2,835 | 2,875 | 33.0% | 1.4% |
| Iowa | 789 | 703 | 740 | -6.2% | 5.3% |
| Kansas | 638 | 691 | 721 | 13.0% | 4.3% |
| Kentucky | 1,989 | 2,183 | 2,420 | 21.7% | 10.9% |
| Louisiana | 2,377 | 2,228 | 2,075 | -12.7% | -6.9% |
| Maine | 133 | 136 | 142 | 6.8% | 4.4% |
| Maryland | 1,020 | 887 | 890 | -12.7% | 0.3% |
| Massachusetts/h | 422 | 443 | 426 | 0.9% | -3.8% |
| Michigan | 2,170 | 2,059 | 2,123 | -2.2% | 3.1% |
| Minnesota | 562 | 723 | 736 | 31.0% | 1.8% |
| Mississippi | 1,558 | 1,405 | 1,197 | -23.2% | -14.8% |
| Missouri | 2,579 | 2,782 | 3,106 | 20.4% | 11.6% |
| Mantuan | 354 | 412 | 388 | 9.6% | -5.8% |
| Nebraska | 378 | 360 | 428 | 13.2% | 18.9% |
| Nevada | 1,128 | 1,085 | 1,085 | -3.8% | 0.0% |
| New Hampshire | 153 | 212 | 244 | 59.5% | 15.1% |
| New Jersey/g | 1,428 | 1,025 | 1,019 | -28.6% | -0.6% |
| New Mexico | 627 | 640 | 659 | 5.1% | 3.0% |
| New York | 2,810 | 2,337 | 2,308 | -17.9% | -1.2% |
| North Carolina | 1,883 | 2,239 | 2,444 | 29.8% | 9.2% |
| North Dakota | 157 | 149 | 187 | 19.1% | 25.5% |
| Ohio/e | 3,701 | 4,150 | 4,208 | 13.7% | 1.4% |
| Oklahoma | 2,351 | 2,742 | 2,801 | 19.1% | 2.2% |
| Oregon | 1,012 | 1,285 | 1,276 | 26.1% | -0.7% |
| Pennsylvania | 2,200 | 2,655 | 2,693 | 22.4% | 1.4% |
| Rhode Island/c,f | 70 | 79 | 68 | -2.9% | -13.9% |
| South Carolina | 1,480 | 1,296 | 1,285 | -13.2% | -0.8% |
| South Dakota | 348 | 441 | 408 | 17.2% | -7.5% |

| | | | | | |
|---|---|---|---|---|---|
| Tennessee | 1,958 | 2,452 | 2,609 | 33.2% | 6.4% |
| Texas | 11,569 | 12,001 | 12,690 | 9.7% | 5.7% |
| Utah | 602 | 662 | 662 | 10.0% | 0.0% |
| Vermont/c | 105 | 96 | 105 | 0.0% | 9.4% |
| Virginia/g | 2,893 | 2,849 | 3,015 | 4.2% | 5.8% |
| Washington/e | 1,472 | 1,442 | 1,439 | -2.2% | -0.2% |
| West Virginia | 569 | 801 | 828 | 45.5% | 3.4% |
| Wisconsin | 1,357 | 1,169 | 1,305 | -3.8% | 11.6% |
| Wyoming | 243 | 260 | 277 | 14.0% | 6.5% |

Note: Jurisdiction refers to the legal authority of state or federal correctional officials over a prisoner regardless of where the prisoner is held. State methods of enumeration may change over time. Consult the state notes for particular years to ensure parity between years and jurisdictions. As of December 31, 2001, sentenced felons from the District of Columbia are the responsibility of the Federal Bureau of Prisons.
a/Counts based on prisoners with sentences of more than 1 year under the jurisdiction of state or federal correctional officials.
b/Includes inmates held in nonsecure privately operated community corrections facilities and juveniles held in contract facilities.
c/Prisons and jails form one integrated system. Data include total jail and prison populations.
d/Prison jurisdiction population based on custody counts.
e/Includes some prisoners sentenced to 1 year or less.
f/Counts include dual jurisdiction cases where the inmate is currently housed in another jurisdiction's facilities.
g/Includes some prisoners sentence to 1 year.
h/Counts exclude prisoners sentenced to more than 1 year but held in local jails or houses of correction in the Commonwealth of Massachusetts; please see individual years' Prisoners in YYYY for an accounting of these people.

Source: Bureau of Justice Statistic, National Prisoners Statistic Program, 1978-2014.

**FIGURE 6.6**  PRISONERS UNDER THE JURISDICTION OF STATE OR FEDERAL CORRECTIONAL AUTHORITIES, DECEMBER 31, 2003-2013.

| Year | Total | Federal[a] | State | Male | Female |
|---|---|---|---|---|---|
| 2003 | 1,468,601 | 173,059 | 1,295,542 | 1,367,755 | 100,846 |
| 2004 | 1,497,100 | 180,328 | 1,316,772 | 1,392,278 | 104,822 |
| 2005 | 1,525,910 | 187,618 | 1,338,292 | 1,418,392 | 107,518 |
| 2006 | 1,568,674 | 193,046 | 1,375,628 | 1,456,366 | 112,308 |
| 2007 | 1,596,835 | 199,618 | 1,397,217 | 1,482,524 | 114,311 |
| 2008 | 1,608,282 | 201,280 | 1,407,002 | 1,493,670 | 114,612 |
| 2009 | 1,615,487 | 208,118 | 1,407,369 | 1,502,002 | 113,485 |
| 2010 | 1,613,803 | 209,771 | 1,404,032 | 1,500,936 | 112,867 |
| 2011 | 1,598,968 | 216,362 | 1,382,606 | 1,487,561 | 111,407 |
| 2012 | 1,570,397 | 217,815 | 1,352,582 | 1,461,625 | 108,772 |
| 2013[b] | 1,574,741 | 215,866 | 1,358,875 | 1,463,454 | 111,287 |

| Percent change | | | | | |
|---|---|---|---|---|---|
| Average annual, 2003-2012 | 0.7% | 2.2% | 0.5% | 0.7% | 1.0 |
| 2012-2013 | 0.3 | -0.9 | 0.5 | 0.1 | 2.3 |

*Note: Jurisdiction refers to the legal authority of state of federal correctional officials over a prisoner, regardless of where the prisoner is held.*
*a Includes inmates held innsecure privately operated community corrections facilities and juveniles held in contract facilities.*
*b Total and state estimates include imputed counts for Nevada. In addition, Alaska did not submit sex-specific jurisdiction counts to NPS in 2013. See Methodology for Imputation strategy.*

*Source: Bureau of Justice Statistics, National Prisoner Statistics Program, 2003-2013.*

# Chapter Summary

- There is no single primary guiding principle for sentencing, so most practices tend to blend multiple schools of thought. Common theories behind sentencing in the United States are deterrence, incapacitation, rehabilitation, and retribution. Alternatives or partners to sentencing include fines, probation, rehabilitative programs, and community service. Additional options for sentencing, depending on the circumstances of the offense, include imprisonment and the death penalty.

- Deterrence attempts to prevent crime by making examples of offenders in the hope of deterring others from committing crime, or by inflicting punishment on a person with the intent to impart the lesson that crime is not worth committing. Rehabilitation attempts to change the behavior and thinking of offenders by providing them with services that will help change their behavior. Restorative justice seeks to return the crime victims as closely as possible to their original states before the crime was committed. Incapacitation attempts to control crime by removing the offender from the community.

- Retribution refers to the idea that individuals who commit crimes should be punished to a degree commensurate with the seriousness of the crime. Vengeance and "just deserts" fall under retribution: vengeance suggests that satisfaction will be gained simply by punishing the criminal, while "just deserts" intends for the punishment to be comparably equal to the crime.

- The death penalty has been under review for many years to determine whether aspects of it constitute cruel and unusual punishment. The Supreme Court has further clarified stipulations of the death penalty with numerous rulings, but the two most groundbreaking rulings were *Furman v. Georgia* (1972) and *Gregg v. Georgia* (1976). Furman negated the enforcement of state death penalty laws on Eighth Amendment grounds, causing a halt to executions and the commutations of many death sentences to life in prison. *Gregg* upheld the revised laws, which required a multiple-step process in order for judges or juries to assess a death sentence on an inmate.

- Other issues to consider in sentencing are truth in sentencing, mandatory minimum sentences, characteristics of the victim, three-strikes laws, race, and gender. Whether each aspect has measurable effects on sentencing is being studied on a regular basis. Available data is typically a minimum of two to three years old due to reporting and measurement limitations.

## Critical Thinking?

1. Should offense type influence a probation officer's recommendation in the pre-sentence investigation report? Explain why or why not.
2. If deterrence does not work on capital offenders, why do states still utilize the death penalty?
3. How does the law apply rehabilitation and retribution at the same time?
4. Compare and contrast the various sentencing theories. Would the same theory that applies to a large metropolitan city also apply to a rural village in Alaska?
5. What is the purpose of a jury that is death penalty qualified?
6. Who should sentence, the judge or the jury?
7. The concept of jury nullification was introduced in Chapter 5. How might jury nullification affect the sentencing process?
8. In many cases, offenders are offered plea bargains by the prosecuting attorneys. Do you feel that the plea bargain process is fair to all parties involved in the case? The accused? The victim(s)? Why or why not?
9. Do gender and race play a role in sentencing procedures and, if so, how much?
10. Why do you think sentencing disparities still exist?

## Media

**Free Sentencing Guidelines Calculator:** http://www.sentencing.us/ Based on 2010 guidelines, this website allows users to get an idea of the length of a federal prison sentence based on the crime committed and special circumstances that may apply.

**The Death Penalty Information Center:** http://www.deathpenaltyinfo. org/ The Death Penalty Information Center is a nonprofit organization that provides the media and the general public with facts and information relating to capital punishment.

**Texas Department of Criminal Justice:** http://www.tdcj.state.tx.us/ and Florida Department of Corrections: http://www.dc.state.fl.us/ The official websites for some state correctional systems offer a wealth of information, including statistics, about their prison systems.

**Death Penalty Blog:** http://www.deathpenaltyblog.com Written by attorneys from Florida and Texas, the Death Penalty Blog shares news articles about legislation and other current events relating to capital punishment.

The Growth of Incarceration in the U.S. https://www.youtube.com/watch?v=I-kFNDlzL9k. This video illustrates the findings of the NRC report The Growth of Incarceration in the United States: Exploring Causes and Consequences. The nation's reliance on imprisonment has not clearly improved public safety and may have had large unwanted consequences for society. A change in course is needed. The report urges policymakers to reconsider sentencing policies and to seek crime-control strategies that are more effective, with better public safety benefits and fewer unwanted consequences.

## Endnotes

[1]    Riddle, L. (1997). *Ashes to Ashes. New York, NY: Pinnacle Books.*

[2]    Beccaria, C. (1764). *Dei Delitti e delle Pene. (Of Crimes and Punishment)*

[3]    Ibid., 32–24.

[4]    Gibbs, J. (1975). *Crime, Punishment, and Deterrence. New York, NY: Elsevier.*

[5]    Beccaria, 1764.

[6]    Ibid.

[7]    Ibid.

[8]    Zimring, F., & Hawkins, G. (1973). *Deterrence.* Chicago, IL: University of Chicago Press.

[9]    Pontell, H. (1994). *A Capacity to Punish: The Ecology of Crime and Punishment.* Bloomington, IN: Indiana University Press.

[10]   King, L. W. (2005). *The Code of Hammurabi: Translated by L.W. King.* New Haven, CT: Yale University Press.

[11]   Kant, I. (1790). *The Science of Right.*

[12]   Texas Department of Corrections. (2004). *Offender Orientation Handbook.* Mississippi Department of Corrections. *(2009). Inmate Handbook,* State of Washington Department of Corrections. (2008). *Reception, Initial Classification, and Custody Facility Plan.*

[13]   Inciardi, 2010.

[14]   Bohm & Haley, 2010.

[15] Braithwaite, J. (1989). *Crime, Shame, and Reintegration.* New York, NY: Cambridge University Press.

[16] Sullivan, D., & Tifft, L. (2005). *Restorative Justice: Healing the Foundations of Our Everyday Lives* (2nd ed.). Boulder, CO: Lynne Reiner Publishing.

[17] U.S. Department of Justice, Office for Victims of Crime. (2004, December). "New Directions from the Field: Victims' Rights and Services for the 21st Century." *OVC Bulletin.* Washington, D.C.

[18] New York State Unified Court System. (2010). *Statistics.*

[19] *Williams v. Illinois,* 399 U.S. 235 (1970).

[20] *Bearden v. Georgia,* 33 CrL 3103 (1983).

[21] Petersilia, J. (1998). "Probation and Parole." In M. Tonry (Ed.), *The Handbook of Crime and Punishment.* New York, NY: Oxford University Press. New York City Department of Probation. (n.d.). History of Probation. Retrieved from http://www.nyc.gov/html/prob/html/about/history.shtml

[22] Center on Juvenile and Criminal Justice. (n.d.). *The History of the Presentence Report.* Retrieved from http://www.cjcj.org/files/the_history.pdf

[23] National Probation Association. (1939). *John Augustus, First Probation Officer.* New York.

[24] Inciardi, 2010.

[25] *Mempa v. Rhay,* 389 U.S. 128 (1967).

[26] *Morrissey v. Brewer,* 389 U.S. 128 (1972). *Gagnon v. Scarpelli,* 411 U.S. 778 (1973).

[27] *Texas Code of Criminal Procedure,* Art. 42.12.

[28] Illinois General Assembly. (2011). 625 ILCS 5/11–501.

[29] Inciardi, 2010.

[30] Georgia Department of Corrections, Probation Division. *FY 2007 Annual Report.* Atlanta, GA.

[31] Petersilia, J. (2002). *Reforming Probation & Parole in the 21st Century.* Lanham, MD: American Correctional Association.

[32] Waldron, J., & Angelino, H. (1977). "Shock Probation: A Natural Experiment on the Effect of a Short Period of Incarceration." *Prison Journal, 57.*

[33] Ohio Department of Rehabilitation and Correction. (2005). *Ohio Adult Parole Authority: 1965–2005.*

[34] The Judicial Branch of Arizona. (2011). *Intensive Probation Supervision.*

[35] Erwin, B., & Bennett, L. (1987). *New Dimensions in Probation: Georgia's Experience with Intensive Probation Supervision.* National Institute of Justice Research in Brief.

[36] Petersilia, J., & Turner, S. (1993). *Evaluating Intensive Supervision Probation/Parole: Results of a Nationwide Experiment.* National Institute of Justice Research in Brief.

[37] Ball, R., & Lilly, J. (1986). "A Theoretical Examination of Home Incarceration." *Federal Probation, 50,* 17–24.

[38] Gowen, D. (2001). "Remote Location Monitoring—A Supervision Strategy to Enhance Risk Control." *Federal Probation, 65*(2).

39    Florida Department of Corrections. (2007). *Annual Statistics for Fiscal Year 2005–2006.*

40    Del Carmen, R., & Vaughn, J. (1992). "Legal Issues in the Use of Electronic Surveillance in Probation." In T. Ellsworth (Ed.), *Contemporary Community Corrections.* Prospect Heights, IL: Waveland Press.

41    Bureau of Probation & Parole Field Services, Florida Department of Corrections. (2008).

42    Bohm, R. (2007). *Deathquest III: An Introduction to the Theory and Practice of Capital Punishment in the United States* (3rd ed.). Cincinnati, OH: Anderson.

43    The Death Penalty Information Center.

44    Teeters, N., & Zibulka, C. (1974). "Executions Under State Authority: 1864–1967." In W. Bowers (Ed.), *Executions in America. Lexington, MA: Heath.*

45    Bedau, H. (1964). *The Death Penalty in America.* Chicago, IL: Aldine.

46    *O'Neil v. Vermont,* 144 U.S. 323 (1892).

47    *Weems v. United States,* 217 U.S. 349 (1910).

48    *Witherspoon v. Illinois,* 391 U.S. 510 (1960).

49    *Furman v. Georgia, Jackson v. Georgia, Branch v. Texas,* 408 U.S. 238 (1972).

50    *Gregg v. Georgia,* Proffitt v. Florida, Jurek v. Texas, 428 U.S. 153.

51    Katz, L. (1980). *The Justice Imperative.* Cincinnati, OH: Anderson.

52    The Death Penalty Information Center.

53    Ibid.

54    Reinhold, R. (1982, December 7). "Technician Executes Murderer in Texas by Lethal Injection." *The New York Times.*

55    *Fierro v. Gomez,* 56 CrL 1085 (1994)

56    The Death Penalty Information Center.

57    The Death Penalty Information Center.

58    Ibid.

59    *Coker v. Georgia,* 433 U.S. 584 (1977).

60    *Eberheart v. Georgia,* 433 U.S. 917 (1977).

61    *Ford v. Wainwright,* 477 U.S. 399 (1986).

62    *McCleskey v. Kemp,* 481 U.S. 279 (1987).

63    *Thompson v. Oklahoma,* 487 U.S. 815 (1987-1988).

64    *Stanford v. Kentucky,* 492 U.S. 361 (1989).

65    *Atkins v. Virginia,* 536 U.S. 304 (2002).

66    *Roper v. Simmons,* 543 U.S. 551 (2005).

67    *Kennedy v. Louisiana,* 554 U.S. 407 (2008).

68    Beccaria, 1764.

69    Pojman, L., & Reiman, J. (1998). *The Death Penalty: For and Against.* Lanham, MD: Rowman & Littlefield.

70 Radelet, M., Lofquist, W., & Bedau, H. (1996). "Prisoners Released from Death Rows Since 1970 Because of Doubts About Their Guilt." *T.M. Cooley Law Review, 13 (907)*.

71 The Death Penalty Information Center.

72 Stull, B. (2009). *Race and Death Penalty Links Run Deep and Wide*. New York, NY: American Civil Liberties Union.

73 Radelet, M. (1989). "Executions of Whites for Crimes Against Blacks." *Sociological Quarterly, 30, 529–44*.

74 The Death Penalty Information Center.

75 Ibid.

76 Liebmann, J., Fagan, J., & West, V. (n.d.). "A Broken System: Error Rates in Capital Cases, 1973–1995." *The Justice Project*. Retrieved April 12, 2011, from http://www.thejusticeproject.org

77 Bedau, H., Radelet, M., & Putnam, C. (2004). "Convicting the Innocent in Capital Cases: Criteria, Evidence, and Interference." *Drake Law Review, 52*, 587–603.

78 Bureau of Justice Statistics. (2010). *Capital Punishment 2009*. Washington, D.C.

79 Tonry, M. (1999). "Fragmentation of Sentencing and Corrections in the United States." *Research in Brief—Sentencing & Corrections: Issues for the 21st Century*. Washington, D.C.: National Institute of Justice.

80 Lab, S., & Whitehead, J. (1990). "From 'Nothing Works' to 'The Appropriate Works': The Latest Stop in the Search for the Secular Grail." *Criminology, 28, 405–418*.

81 Jacobs, J. (1977). *Statesville: The Penitentiary in Mass Society*. Chicago, IL: University of Chicago Press.

82 Ulner, J. (1997). *Social Worlds of Sentencing: Court Communities Under Sentencing Guidelines*. Albany, NY: State University of New York Press.

83 Austin, J., & Irwin, J. (1997). *It's About Time: America's Imprisonment Binge* (3rd ed.). Belmont, CA: Wadsworth.

84 Harris, J., & Jesilow, P. (2000). "It's Not the Old Ball Game: Three Strikes and the Courtroom Workgroup." *Justice Quarterly, 17*, 185–204.

85 Fischer, C. (2003). "Supreme Court Allows Penalties Under California 3-Strikes Law." *Corrections Journal, 1*(3).

86 *Ewing v. California, 538 U.S. 11 (2003)*.

87 *California's Three Strikes Sentencing Law* (2016). California Courts. The Judicial Branch of California. Retrieved fhttp://www.courts.ca.gov/20142. htm.

87 Durose, M., & Langan, P. (2004). "Felony Sentences in State Courts, 2002." *Bureau of Justice Statistics Bulletin. Washington, D.C.*

88 *United States v. Booker*, 543 U.S. 200 (2005).

89 Kitchens, C. (2010, August). "Federal Sentencing Data and Analysis Issues." *United States Sentencing Commission Research Notes*.

90 United States Sentencing Commission. (2016). *2016 Federal Sentencing Guidelines Manual*.

91     Bibas, S. (2004). "Plea Bargaining Outside the Shadow of Trial." *Harvard Law Review, 117*(8), 2463–2547.

92     Ibid.

93     Nagel, I., & Schulhofer, S. (1992). "A Tale of Three Cities: An Empirical Study of Charging and Bargaining Practices Under the Federal Sentencing Guidelines." *Southern California Law Review, 66,* 501–530.

94     *Brady v. United States,* 397 U.S. 742 (1970).

95     *North Carolina v. Alford,* 40 U.S. 25 (1970).

96     Carns, T. & Kruse, J. (1991). *Alaska's Plea Bargaining Ban: Re-Evaluated.* Retrieved from http://www.ajc.state.ak.us/reports/plea91Exec.pdf.

97     Wagner, P. (2012). *Incarceration is not an equal opportunity punishment.* Prison Policy Initiative. Retrieved from https://www.prisonpolicy.org/articles/notequal.html.

97     Schmalleger & Smykla, 2011.

# SECTION 4
## THE CONSEQUENCES OF CRIME: CORRECTIONS

© Ana Aguirre Perez/Shutterstock.com

# Prisons and Jails

## KEY TERMS

Absconder

Auburn System

Bridewells

Classification officer

Conditional release

Correctional officer

Correctional institution

Deterrence

Disciplinary report

Early release

Escape

Inmate

Institutional capacity

Jail

Juvenile

Offender

Panopticon

Pardon

Pennsylvania System

Prison

Recidivism

Sanctuary

Special Housing Unit (SHU)

Supervised release

Youthful offender

# CHAPTER OBJECTIVES

1 Understand the historical events preceding the modern prison system.

2 Identify the Eighth Amendment and its prohibition on cruel and unusual punishment.

3 Differentiate between prisons and jails.

4 Differentiate between minimum, medium, maximum, and supermax prisons.

5 Discuss the privatization of correctional facilities.

## Case Study: Guantánamo Bay Naval Base

The terrorist attacks of September 11, 2001 and the wars in Afghanistan and Iraq have populated arguably the most notorious prison of modern times. The detention center at Guantánamo Bay Naval Base, presumably outside of U.S. legal jurisdiction, has been accused of violating the human rights of its detainees. This special-purpose prison does not hold criminals. It holds terrorists and others who have waged war against the United States. In 2009, President Barack Obama signed an order to close the Guantánamo Bay detention facility within one year. Eight years later, the facility remains in operation, with 41 prisoners currently being held there.

In a 2002 Department of Defense news briefing, Vice Admiral John Stufflebeem stated in reference to those imprisoned at Guantánamo Bay, "These are the worst of the worst, and if let out on the street, they will go back to the proclivity of trying to kill Americans and others." The detainees were captured fighting for Al-Qaeda or the Taliban, and were not recognized as lawful warriors under international law.[1] By February 10, 2009, 581 tribunals had been held, and it was determined that the 539 current detainees were properly classified as enemy combatants.[2]

Unlike criminals, prisoners of war are not detained as punishment. They are held for security and for strategic and tactical necessity. Though their purposes may be different, the role of detention remains comparable for both criminal prisons and prisoner of war facilities. Most countries recognize that the detention of enemy forces is a legitimate wartime function that serves to prevent detainees from returning to the battlefield.

The Department of Defense is committed to a safe, secure, and humane detention experience for its detainees. Detainees receive three meals per day, comfortable sleeping implements, running water, full uniform and hygiene products, mail privileges, a library, recreation, and religious supplies and opportunity.[3] These amenities are similar to those afforded inmates in U.S. jails and prisons.

The Guantánamo Bay detention center has gained notoriety in part because some Americans and their congressional representatives believe that the detainees are not receiving full constitutional protections.[4] Some have proposed that the detainees be transferred to federal prisons and tried in criminal courts. Here, the detainees would receive the full protection of the U.S. Constitution. These protections are so important to Americans that many feel these rights should be extended even to those considered enemies of the United States. Others, though, do not believe that constitutional protections should apply to these prisoners or other terrorist suspects.

The top-security detention facility at Guantánamo Bay has been compared to America's supermax prisons. Many of the security measures are similar, especially those that subject some inmates to long-term restrictions on social interaction and meaningful activity. Experts studying the supermax and Guantánamo inmates assert that even inmates with no prior mental health issues may become considerably ill from long-term isolation. Comparisons of inmates in isolation with inmates who are allowed regular social interaction demonstrate higher rates of psychiatric and psychological health problems among those in isolation.[5]

Experts note that Guantánamo Bay and the nation's supermax prisons share many of the same practices and procedures, and therefore, cause similar injuries to the inmates' mental health.[6] The wisdom of inflicting psychological trauma on the Guantánamo Bay detainees and in America's supermax prisons is in question, especially since most of those supermax inmates are expected to one day return to open society in America.

The detention center at Guantánamo Bay is introduced here as an extreme example of an American top-security detention facility. While it serves a different purpose than criminal prisons, and its detainees are classified as terrorists and not as prisoners, it demonstrates how difficult and harsh the living conditions may be for extreme and difficult populations.

> Over the eight years of the Obama administration, President Obama attempted to honor his original campaign promise to close Guantánamo Bay down. A total of 779 prisoners have been held by the U.S. military at Guantánamo since the prison opened on January 11, 2002. Of those, 729 have been released or transferred, including one who was transferred to the U.S. to be tried, and nine have died, the most recent being Adnan Latif, in September 2012. As of May 2017, 41 men are still held in the detention center, and five of these men have been recommended for release by high-level governmental review processes. Ten men were released to Oman on January 16, 2017, and four more men were released on Jan. 19, 2017, Obama's last day in office."[7]

# The History of Prisons and Jails

Throughout history, societies have found ways to punish individuals who break laws and commit crimes. Individuals and governments both have employed a variety of methods to prevent and to punish the transgressions of these **offenders**. Within the last few hundred years, detention has been an acceptable method of punishment.

**Offender** One who breaks a rule or commits a crime.

**Prison** A correctional facility that confines those convicted of felonies; may hold both misdemeanants and felons convicted of federal crimes.

**Jail** A correctional facility that holds people accused of or convicted of crimes.

Incarceration is now one of the most widespread criminal punishments throughout the world. Though the details differ widely among countries of the world, most use incarceration for punishment or pretrial detention. As detention methods have advanced, the types of facilities used to detain individuals have evolved as well. The most common of these detention facilities are known as **prisons** and **jails**.

In early American history, jails were used primarily to hold for trial those who could not make bail or those who were unable to pay debts.[7] The living conditions in these primitive houses of detention bred most every form of immorality one can imagine. Men, women, and children of all ages were thrown together in undisciplined and poorly supervised micro-communities where the strong overpowered the weak. There was little medical treatment and most were poorly fed. More often than not, those who did manage to eat did so because family or other benefactors delivered food to the jail. Those lacking outside support often suffered significantly.[8]

© ermess/Shutterstock.com

A pillory device, which secured the head and hands in an uncomfortable position, was used to inflict physical punishment and public humiliation.

At trial, those convicted were regularly sentenced to public humiliation such as the stocks and pillories. Other punishments included whippings, transportation, banishment, branding, amputation, or even death. The offenders would rarely see the jail again after conviction. The jail was used as detention for trial; then the real punishment would be imposed.

**Recidivism** The rate of repeat crime by offenders; the rate of relapse back into criminal activity or behavior.

Eventually, society began to recognize the cruelty they were inflicting on others in the name of justice. The public began to demand punishments that were more sophisticated and more effective in reducing **recidivism**, or repeat crime by offenders. Forcing offenders to repent or to offer penitence eventually became the new method of punishment. Thus, the inspiration for the penitentiary was born.

This fresh and novel plan for a house of penitence spread throughout the early American colonies. The Constitution of Pennsylvania in 1776 decreed that "houses ought to be provided for punishing by hard labour, those who shall be convicted of crimes."[9] The "House of Hard Labour" requirement led to the development of the Walnut Street Jail, which is widely recognized as the first jail or prison where one would be incarcerated as punishment for crimes.

## Early Punishments

History is rife with imaginative techniques to punish criminals. Codified punishment of criminals goes back to ancient Sumerian (1860 B.C.) and Babylonian (1750 B.C.) codes. Both codes contained descriptions of crimes and the punishment meted out to those who committed them. These penalties included whipping, servitude, mutilation, and death.[10]

The Codex Justinianus, or Code of Justinian, in sixth-century Rome was an attempt to codify all possible crimes with an appropriate balance of punishment. The "scales of justice" metaphor is assumed to have developed in this period, as they are depicted in art of the time. The Code of Justinian vanished with the fall of the Roman Empire.

Several decades after the Codex Justinianus, Greece enacted the Code of Draco. This harsh form of criminal law provided the same criminal penalties for citizens and slaves alike. It also allowed any citizen to prosecute an offender. Equal enforcement among citizens was an important advancement in the treatment of criminals. Public interest and public order were now recognized as superior to individual revenge and harm.[11] The Code of Draco has found its way into the modern lexicon through the eponymous term *draconian,* meaning markedly harsh or cruel.

The Inquisition, an invention of the Catholic Church in the Middle Ages, established a tribunal to seek out offenders and heretics and then to determine their innocence or guilt. The Inquisition, which lasted about 500 years, expected those charged to demonstrate their innocence rather than to have guilt proven by evidence at trial. The Inquisition also officially recognized the concept of free will. The concept of free will means that individuals choose their actions and are responsible for them; this concept can be found in our modern system of justice.

At least since the Code of Hammurabi (18th century B.C.) and the Sumerians a thousand years earlier, forms of criminal punishment included death, torture, mutilation, branding, fines, and the loss of property.[12] Ancient Mediterranean societies in the first century B.C. practiced banishment and slavery.[13] These criminal punishments existed in many forms throughout much of human history. In the 17th and 18th centuries in America, creative punishments such as the stocks and pillories were used. Often, the public was invited to watch and even to participate in the punishment of an offender.

The death penalty has long been imposed as a punishment against offenders. Trials, sometimes nothing more than a summary judgment from a group of interested citizens, would merely take offenders straight to their punishment. Punishment of death was accomplished by both crude and sophisticated methods. Impaling, beating, drowning, hanging, crucifixion, and burning at the stake have all been used as methods of execution.[14]

As technology advanced, instruments of death such as the guillotine were invented. Many of these executions were performed in public.

The guillotine is an instrument of capital punishment by beheading. French physician Joseph-Ignace Guillotin proposed the mechanism as a more humane form of capital punishment in 1789. The guillotine was subsequently invented by Antoine Louis in 1792 during the French Revolution.[16]

Often, there would be a festival of sorts with public executions as the main attraction, especially if there were several condemned prisoners. In some cases, the public would be invited to participate in the execution process. Stoning is one of those participatory punishments and is still used in some parts of the world. Though the details may vary among eras and cultures, the condemned would be prepared for stoning by tightly binding their limbs and then burying them halfway or more in the ground. The public would then hurl rocks at the fated individuals until they died.[15]

Lesser punishments also involved the public. In colonial America, the pillory and the stocks were used for minor offenses, and they were often staged as community entertainment. Stocks, which held the offender's wrists and ankles while he or she sat on a stool, and the pillory, which locked around a standing offender's neck and wrists, were forms of public humiliation. After an offender was placed in the device, a flogging was often administered. The public would take part by yelling, spitting, and throwing garbage at the offender. At times, the offender might even have his or her ears nailed to the wooden pillory.[17] Those in the crowd were encouraged to get creative in their efforts at destroying the dignity of the offender. Young boys were especially creative with this form of amusement.

## Critical Thinking

Historical punishments for minor crimes involved state-sponsored humiliation. Though practices such as stocks and pillories are now prohibited, some argue that state-sponsored humiliation remains through online arrest records, prisoners working on roadsides, DUI offenders placing stickers on their cars to alert others, and even some offenders being sentenced to carry placards or post signs in public areas identifying them by their crime. Do you think that these public notices and actions should be allowed? Are these just "modern" forms of the pillory?

Mutilation was another method of criminal punishment. Often, the type of mutilation was determined by the crime. A thief's hand might be cut off; liars or people who talked too much might have their tongues cut out; a rapist might also receive a targeted amputation. Branding, a form of mutilation, would burn a word or a letter onto the offender's body so that she or he could always be recognized. A burglar might have a "B" branded on one hand and possibly another letter on the opposite hand for a subsequent offense. Adulterers, gossips, debtors, and others might all have received similar fates, as creative and even unusual punishments were typical for all levels of crime. Many of these punishments were used in early colonial

America, and some, such as the removal of a thief's hand, are still used in a few parts of the world.

> **Critical Thinking**
> Could mutilation and branding be considered a form of life punishment? In some states, convicted felons often never regain all of their civil rights. Is this a modern form of life punishment even after the sentence has been served?

Such early punishments seem barbaric by today's standards. It is important to note that many of the punishments were not designed to kill, yet nonetheless, they often resulted in death. The ducking stool is a good example of unintended execution. The ducking stool was a contraption whereby the offender, strapped to a seat, would be submerged in a pond or lake. Every so often, a person would be held underwater beyond their capacity to hold their breath and would drown. In some early societies, offenders would even be put to a test of death to prove or disprove guilt. For instance, if someone were deliberately held underwater beyond what was thought survivable and lived, that person would be determined to be innocent.

Not all criminals were mutilated or tortured: some were simply forced to leave their homes. In some ancient societies, when an individual was determined to have committed an egregious offense against the group, the group would force the offender from the tribe. This was a simple yet effective way to keep order within small societies.

Later civilizations, most notably the British Empire, continued this practice and banished criminals in bulk to lands far away. From 1718 to 1775, the British criminal system transported nearly 50,000 convicts to colonial America. With the exception of African slaves, this group of convicted criminals was the largest immigration population to America during the period.[18] The practice was halted when the American colonies asserted their independence from English rule in 1776. However, Captain Cook had discovered the Australian continent in 1770, and it became the new destination for criminal transportation. It is estimated that more than 135,000 people were transported to Australia before this system was abandoned in 1875.[19]

Those early methods were part of the evolution of how criminals are treated in modern society. The U.S. founding fathers who framed the Constitution had a different vision for how people should be treated. They established the Bill of Rights so that those living under the new Constitution would be protected from governmental abuses. One of these rights, a prohibition against cruel and unusual punishment, was formed from the desire to treat convicted criminals humanely and professionalize the criminal justice system. The founding fathers were well aware of the past abuses of offenders, and they therefore sought to prohibit the government from inflicting cruel and unusual treatment on the criminally accused and those convicted of crimes.

© zimmytws/Shutterstock.com

The Eighth Amendment states, "Excessive bail shall not be required, nor excessive fines imposed, nor cruel and unusual punishments inflicted."

In spite of our efforts to treat criminals humanely, we still struggle to define *cruel and unusual*. The death penalty is a good example. Many consider the death penalty to be cruel, and others do not. There is also controversy over the methods used to deliver the death penalty. Some even consider the death penalty to be a practice that should be prohibited.

## Major Figures

The practice of punishing criminals has evolved over the course of human civilization. The evolution of the modern prison and jail system is a result of the collective thoughts and efforts of many, but there have been a few key individuals who have revolutionized or made a lasting impact on the global detainment framework.

### Montesquieu (1689–1755)

Charles-Louis de Secondat, Baron de Montesquieu, or simply Montesquieu, a French nobleman, wrote on the political thought of the day and published it in his work *The Spirit of Laws* in 1748. Montesquieu believed in liberty for every man; however, he also believed in classes and a hierarchy of people, which classified people into three descending categories: monarchy, aristocracy, and commoner. Still, he asserted that no man of any class should be in fear of another.[20]

Montesquieu wrote about the separation of powers in government affairs. His philosophy, taken for granted today, maintained that the legislative, executive, and judicial branches of a government should not unduly be influenced by one another. If any of these were to combine, there could be no liberty.[21]

Much of Montesquieu's writing concerned the structure of governments and the protection of liberty. This was the age of the Enlightenment, which

**Critical Thinking**

The U.S. Constitution's Eighth Amendment prohibits cruel and unusual punishment. This means a punishment must be declared both unusual *and* cruel in order for it to be prohibited. Some states have tightened this requirement in their own constitutions and state that cruel *or* unusual punishment is prohibited. Examine your own state's constitution. Does it prohibit cruel and unusual punishment? If the issue is not addressed, what do you suppose the default prohibition would be?

took place during the 17th and 18th centuries, and man's yearning to be free was a changing force for governments around the world. These philosophies were especially influential on the British colonies as they moved closer and closer to a revolution. James Madison, considered the father of the U.S. Constitution, was heavily influenced by Montesquieu, and much of the Constitution reflects the philosophy of this French nobleman.

## John Howard (1726-1790)

John Howard was an early English prison reformer. Having inherited wealth, Howard traveled throughout Europe. He was captured by French privateers during a voyage to Portugal and was imprisoned. Eventually, he was freed in a prisoner exchange, and it is assumed that this experience was the catalyst for Howard's interest in prison reform.[22]

Appointed as High Sheriff of Bedfordshire, Howard witnessed the appalling conditions of prisons throughout England. He published his findings in his work *The State of Prisons of England and Wales* in 1777, which described, in detail, the conditions he had witnessed. He particularly abhorred the practice of the jailer's fee, which demanded payment for one's detention before release.[23]

Howard proposed many improvements in the prison system. His plans included physical reforms such as improved locations, construction, and furnishings of the prisons. He also insisted on proper diets, fresh water and air, exercise, hygiene, and general health. Moreover, he believed that prison personnel should be of a high quality and prisons should be subjected to independent inspections.[24]

Howard contracted typhus on a prison visit and died in 1790. His legacy remains today in the John Howard Society, a Canadian group that seeks effective solutions to the causes of crime, as well as other groups around the world that invoke his philosophies and remember him as one of the original reformers of modern systems of criminal justice.

## Cesare Beccaria (1738-1794)

Like his contemporaries, Cesare Beccaria was a social reformer who believed in criminal justice transformation. Born to a wealthy family in Milan, Italy, Beccaria anonymously published his work On *Crimes and Punishment* in 1764. Only after this work was widely approved did he claim authorship. Many influential people approved of his treatise: Catherine the Great of Russia, Voltaire, Thomas Jefferson, and Adam Smith all praised his work.

Beccaria believed that a government is right to have laws and punishments so that all obey the social contract, and that those laws should be created by dispassionate, educated, and enlightened males who would create such rational laws to benefit the greatest number in the community. Furthermore, the government has the right and the duty to punish those who violate the law, but punishments should have limits and should fit the degree of the offense. His thoughts on improvements in government, crime, punishment, and human rights influenced methods of punishment and the design of **correctional institutions** around the world.

Beccaria wrote on criminal theory and on how the system should work. He stated that laws should be simply written so that the people and judges do not need to interpret their meaning. He also championed that judges be impartial, suspects be judged by their peers, questions and proceedings at trial be fair, punishment be swift and certain, torture not be used to gain confessions, harsh crimes be punished with longer periods in prison than less harsh crimes, attempting crime be punished, accomplices to crime be punished, and lesser crimes be punished by fines. Moreover, Beccaria was against the death penalty. He asserted that a public murder does nothing to deter a private one.[25]

Much of Beccaria's influence is found in the U.S. Bill of Rights. In the document one will find conventions such as the right to a trial by a jury of one's peers, the right to be informed of accusations, the right to bail, the right to have representation, the right to a speedy trial, the right to confront witnesses, the prohibition on cruel and unusual punishment, and even the right to bear arms, all of which parallel many of Beccaria's reform recommendations. America's forefathers supported the thoughts of the classical criminologists and insisted these principles be codified into the law of the land.

After Beccaria's death, his work lived on and his reputation expanded. He is called the father of classical criminal theory, and many criminologists and other criminal justice experts consider Beccaria's work *On Crimes and Punishment* to be the foundation on which all modern criminology theory is based.[26]

**Correctional institution** A jail or a prison where offenders are confined.

**Panopticon** A circular prison designed with a central observation area so that officers can view all parts of the facility, originally designed by Jeremy Bentham. Variations of this concept are still used in modern correctional facilities so that correctional officers have an unobstructed view of most inmate areas.

**Inmate** An offender or an arrestee in a correctional institution.

## Jeremy Bentham (1748–1832)

Jeremy Bentham is considered one of the first and most significant reformers of criminal punishment and social thought. Schooled as a lawyer, Bentham never practiced law but instead chose to influence social and legal reform. He was a strong supporter of utilitarianism, a form of social thought that—while stated many different ways—essentially means the greatest good for the greatest number.[27] Here, the term *utility* means usefulness or satisfaction.

Bentham also was a reformer in prison design. In order to maximize observation of inmates, he conceived the idea of the **Panopticon**, or all-seeing prison. Designed as a circular building with a watchtower in the middle, the Panopticon afforded the prison guards the ability to see every cell and to observe the **inmates** within. Many contemporary prisons utilize this concept in various forms to maximize the observation of inmates.

© Georgios Kollidas/Shutterstock.com

Modern prisons with a rotunda structure and central guard post are reminiscent of Jeremy Bentham's Panopticon.

Alexis de Tocqueville was a French aristocrat, historian, and philosopher in the early nineteenth century. In 1831, de Tocqueville was granted a commission by King Louis Philippe of France to travel to America and study penitentiaries. The French and other European governments were interested in the new approach in America called rehabilitation, which was the restoration of offenders to a lawful and useful place in society. He traveled with his friend Gustave de Beaumont. Together, they toured the American landscape and wrote about American politics, social systems, and prisons. Though de Beaumont was instrumental in this project and wrote his own books on prison systems, he did not achieve the acclaim of de Tocqueville. The results of their observations were published as *On the Penitentiary System in the United States and its Application in France* and *Democracy in America*. The work *Democracy in America* continues to be printed and is still studied widely, often as assigned reading for those majoring in the political and social sciences, including the study of criminal justice.[28]

Tocqueville and Beaumont focused their work on the Auburn State Prison in New York and the Eastern State Prison in Pennsylvania. In Pennsylvania, inmates were isolated 24 hours a day. The idea was that they would have ample time to read their Bibles and reflect on their lives. At Auburn, the inmates were isolated only at night, and they performed simple labor and ate with other inmates during the day. Though strict silence was enforced at Auburn, there was human contact, unlike at Eastern State. By the middle of the 19th century, the Auburn system was the model for U.S. prisons and the Pennsylvania system became the standard for other countries.[29]

Not content only to observe, de Tocqueville offered his philosophies on most issues. He believed that prisons should rehabilitate and not simply punish. He opposed the death penalty and corporal punishment. He connected poverty with crime, suggesting that those with fewer opportunities would resort to criminal acts. He opposed the constant solitude found at Eastern State and approved of the partial isolation at Auburn. He observed that constant isolation destroyed inmates' spirits and that the interludes of social contact were productive. Additionally, de Tocqueville lamented that though the criminals might be rehabilitated, they would likely return to the conditions that encouraged their criminal activity in the first place.[30]

## Early Forms of Imprisonment

Thanks to advancements in criminal thought, led by de Tocqueville and other reformers, the value of human dignity and life has greatly increased. In most of the industrialized world, prisoners are treated immensely better than in the past. Though prisons are oppressive places and provide for an onerous existence, most countries at least provide prisoners a survivable diet, some medical care, human contact, and some form of classification that separates **juveniles** from adults and men from women.

**Juvenile** A young person, usually a minor.

Incarceration as punishment is a recent development in human history and its treatment of criminals. Early jails were used primarily for the temporary detention of a prisoner before trial. In the early 18th century, England had the gaol (pronounced *jail*, and the source of the modern word *jail*). Upon trial, if an offender were found guilty, he or she would not be returned to the gaol, but instead be subjected to demeaning or abusive forms of punishment as discussed earlier. The concept of "locking up" criminals did not exist until the late 18th century in early America.

Though there may be anecdotal events during which detention was used as a form of punishment, it was most often a byproduct of the intended punishment. In some societies, people of high standing, such as the English nobility, were sentenced to house arrest. In other punishments, detention was only incidental. Consider those sentenced to servitude or to the galleys. These offenders had to be detained somewhere during their sentence or they would simply be able to escape. Some early prison administrators used abandoned mines and quarries to hold inmates, or prisoners.

## The Mamertine Prison

The Mamertine prison, one of the oldest known prisons, was constructed in Rome around 640–618 B.C. Mamertine, also known as the "Prison of Kings," still exists beneath the church of S. Giuseppe dei Falegnami in Rome. It is said to have held St. Peter, who baptized his jailers while imprisoned there.[31]

Mamertine was originally a cistern for water from a nearby spring. Later, it was used for the temporary detention of prisoners of some importance. These higher-level prisoners would eventually be paraded through the streets of Rome and then publicly executed. Others would simply be put to death inside the prison.[32]

## Sanctuaries, Fortresses, Hulks, and Bridewells

**Sanctuary** A sacred place of worship where one can take refuge.

Throughout human history, many other forms of detention have been used. **Sanctuaries** were mentioned in the Old Testament, and this form of safe haven was common through the 12th century. A person accused of a crime could seek sanctuary at a church, and he or she would often be protected from the authorities. Early Christians formalized a policy that if any part of a criminal's body touched the church, then he or she would be given protection from prosecution.[33]

Another historical place of detention and imprisonment is the fortress. Fortresses were simply fortified structures for defense. Though designed to keep enemies out, they were often used to keep criminals in. The criminals would be held until their punishment was decided. Often, they were publicly executed. The Tower of London is an example of a fortress being used as a prison, though that was not its primary purpose.[34]

A *hulk* is a non-functional ship. Ships that were no longer seaworthy were ready-made facilities that were easily used for criminal detention purposes. These opportune facilities have long been used by governments to hold prisoners. As recently as 1997, England used the *Weare*, a decommissioned ship, to relieve prison overcrowding. The ship was never intended to be a permanent facility, and it closed as a prison in 2005.[35]

**Bridewells** were jails in England and Ireland in the 16th century that typically housed petty criminals. The name came from Bridewell Palace, which was originally a home to King Henry VIII; it ultimately became a poorhouse and a correctional facility for prostitutes with the intent of rehabilitation. Soon, *Bridewell* became a common term for any jail or police station in England or Ireland. These poorhouses were at first considered successful, but eventually their conditions and the treatment of prisoners became deplorable. There was no classification of prisoners based on crime, sex, age, or other criteria. Corruption became rampant among staff and inmates alike, and disease and death were common. After public outcry over the conditions, Bridewells were no longer used.

The Tower of London imprisoned infamous historical figures such as William Hastings, Anne Boleyn, and Lady Jane Grey before their ultimate death by beheading.[36]

**Bridewells** Jails and police stations in England and Ireland in the 16th century that typically housed petty criminals.

## The Walnut Street Jail

The Walnut Street Jail was named after the Philadelphia street on which it was located. It was originally constructed in the 18th century to alleviate the overcrowding of another Philadelphia jail, the Old Stone Jail, where men, women, and boys were all housed together. The Walnut Street Jail instituted reforms that are still in use today.

The reforms at the Walnut Street Jail included the classification of inmates according to gender, type of crime, and violent tendencies. It also separated juveniles from adults. In addition, they began attempts at rehabilitation by providing work and trade skills to the inmates. Even with these reforms, the Walnut Street Jail, too, eventually became overcrowded. The Walnut Street Jail continued its service for a number of years as a confinement facility for the more difficult prisoners at the newer Eastern State Prison.

Walnut Street in Philadelphia was home to an overcrowded prison. By 1795, each of the Walnut Street Jail's 18-square-foot cells held 30 to 40 inmates at one time.[38]

The Walnut Street Jail was still being used as a prison during the Constitutional Convention in Philadelphia after the Revolutionary War. Benjamin Franklin, now an old and frail man in poor health, could barely walk, and prisoners from the Walnut Street Jail would carry Franklin on a sedan chair to the convention meetings.[37]

## The Pennsylvania System

The Walnut Street Jail had actually originated before the American Revolution. After the United States gained its independence, this jail on Walnut Street in Philadelphia was expanded to abide by the new Pennsylvania Constitution requiring that "houses ought to be provided for punishing by hard labour."[39] This expansion of the Walnut Street Jail included a cellular construction for housing prisoners, with some cells reserved for the isolation of some of the inmates.

The Philadelphia legislature, having heard the protests of Quakers who rejected the shedding of blood, had created a substitution for corporal punishment. Here, prisoners were classified based on their crimes. Solitary cells were used for those sentenced to absolute isolation by the courts and for those who refused to work. Those inmates in isolation did not perform any labor.

This new method of dealing with criminals was a great leap from past methods used to punish offenders. Offenders who previously would have been sentenced to death were now sentenced to isolation in one of the individual cells at the Walnut Street Jail. Since belligerent inmates and those who refused to work were also forced into isolation, the jail grew quite large by period standards. This became quite expensive.

This system of cellular isolation was soon copied by other states. Maryland, Massachusetts, Maine, New York, New Jersey, and Virginia adopted the Philadelphia form of isolation for certain classes of criminal.[40] These reforms, though well intentioned, did not have the desired results. The prisons found that many of the same individuals kept returning after their release and the expense of housing all of the criminals was "ruinous to the public treasury."[41] It was believed that the solution was simply to add more cells. This, however, involved an even greater expense to the states that chose this method.

Roughly two decades after the advent of the Walnut Street Jail, the Western Penitentiary in Pittsburgh opened. This penitentiary, somewhat modeled after Jeremy Bentham's Panopticon, at first was designed only for the isolation of inmates. Later, inmates were forced to perform some labor within their isolation. Exercise areas were also constructed. Western Penitentiary was considered superior to previous systems, and soon yet another Pennsylvania prison, the Eastern State Penitentiary in Philadelphia, was built not far from the Walnut Street Jail.

The Eastern State Penitentiary was the model for what became known as the **Pennsylvania System**. Here, the Quaker belief that man is inherently

**Pennsylvania System** A penal system advocated by Quakers that used solitary confinement and penitence to reform offenders. Eventually, work such as shoemaking and weaving was allowed to be done in the cells.

good and can be reformed was a foundation for rehabilitation. Proponents of the Pennsylvania System believed that solitary confinement and penitence could reform people into productive and honest citizens.[42]

The Eastern State Penitentiary was constructed similar to Jeremy Bentham's Panopticon, but it was square. Additionally, individual cells had an adjoining outside cell that was used as an exercise yard. This system advocated individual isolation combined with labor. The labor consisted of making crafts in one's cell that were sold to help support the institution. It was assumed that this isolation would prevent corruption through association with other inmates and that prisoners would concentrate more on redemption. Thus, in theory, isolation should require shorter sentences, and it would be less expensive per inmate to run the prison.

## The Auburn System

In 1816, sometime after the Eastern State Penitentiary opened, a new prison was constructed in Auburn, New York. With this new prison came a new prison system. The **Auburn System** was different in many respects from the Pennsylvania System. The cells at Auburn Prison were smaller than those at Eastern State Penitentiary, and they were all enclosed with no individual exercise yard. These cells were for sleeping only, and the inmates worked in a large room with one another. Though silence was strictly enforced, it was thought that the human contact would be good for the inmates and for their rehabilitation.

© Mopic/Shutterstock.com

Both the Pennsylvania and Auburn Systems focused on inmate isolation, a practice that philosophers believed could devastate the human mind.

The discipline at Auburn was harsh by today's standards. Silence was enforced by the whip and with isolation cells. Inmates marched in step when being moved, and they sat facing away from one another during meals. Though this was considered an improvement over Eastern State Penitentiary, the forced silence even when seated next to one another took its toll on the inmates, and by some accounts, on the jailers as well.

**Auburn System** A prison system, also known as the New York System, in which silence is enforced at all times. Inmates work during the day and spend nights in solitary confinement.

These two new prison systems competed somewhat for recognition of superiority.[43] The Pennsylvania System boasted a solitary existence and solitary work, while the Auburn System boasted group work in silence. Nineteenth-century philosophers debated the two systems. Though they disagreed on much, they did agree that isolation without work would devastate the human mind. Total isolation was attempted at various institutions of the time. Inmates often went mad and suicide rates went up. The jailers, it was found, often developed psychological issues as well.[44]

## Notorious Contemporary Prisons

Nothing today can compare with the prisons of the past. The squalid living conditions and the brutality imposed cannot be matched. This does not mean that the modern world is without prisons and jails that have achieved notoriety for their conditions and their contents. Alcatraz Prison, though closed since 1963, is famous for its legendary inmates, and the Maricopa County Jail, still in operation, is known for its tough sheriff, Joe Arpaio.

## Alcatraz

In the early 20th century, the federal prison system included specialized institutions. Some were less restrictive, "easy" prisons that housed the less dangerous inmates, and some were very grim, dungeon-type, supermaximum prisons. These supermaximum prisons held the most notorious and hated criminals of the country. One such prison was built on Alcatraz Island in San Francisco Bay. Alcatraz, also known as "The Rock," was surrounded by swift currents of cold water that, presumably, would kill any prisoner trying to traverse the path to freedom. Thus, the location alone provided its greatest resource; that of being able to contain all of its prisoners and prevent escape.

With one guard to every three prisoners, the inmates at Alcatraz were strictly monitored. At 6:30 A.M., the wake-up call was sounded, and by 7:00 A.M., the prisoners, having dressed, cleaned their cells, and been counted, would march off to the mess hall for the morning meal. Then, it was off to their individual jobs.

The routine at Alcatraz was sternly enforced and rarely varied. The most brutal aspect, at least in Alcatraz's early years, was the forced silence. Many inmates considered this the most unbearable punishment. The silence policy was relaxed in the prison's later years, but it was one of the few rule changes to occur.

Most know Alcatraz Island only for its infamous federal prison. However, Alcatraz was also a civil war fortress, a bird sanctuary, the home of the first lighthouse on the West Coast, and the site of an American Indian occupation in the 1960s.[45] The 1979 movie *Escape from Alcatraz*, which was loosely based on the only known successful escape from the maximum-security prison, further sealed the prison's notoriety. Alcatraz is now a tourist attraction that is visited by hundreds every day.

## Maricopa County's Tent City

Joseph "Joe" Arpaio, the popular yet widely criticized sheriff of Maricopa County, Arizona, has become known as America's toughest sheriff. Sheriff Arpaio runs a jail that has gained notoriety because of his unconventional methods. From forcing inmates to wear pink underwear to housing some of them in tents to endure sweltering heat, the sheriff has earned an extreme reputation among both critics and supporters.

The Maricopa County Jail in Phoenix, Arizona includes a modern, state-of-the-art facility with more than 2,000 beds and seven smaller facilities, including the infamous tent city. According to the Maricopa County Sheriff's Office website, in 1993 Sheriff Arpaio began housing inmates in surplus army tents, due in part to his promises that there would be no **early releases** because of overcrowding.[46] He houses less dangerous inmates in the tents because of the lower level of security. He was able to create this tent city jail with minimal expense. Currently, it can hold up to 2,000 prisoners. Other jail administrators have considered using Arpaio's methods when their own facilities begin to exceed **institutional capacity**, resulting in overcrowding.

The sheriff made a number of other changes to the prison system, such as eliminating coffee to save money, and even bragged that it cost him less per day to feed an inmate than a police dog. He brought back several long-abandoned features from decades past, such as chain gangs and the iconic, stigmatized black-and-white striped jumpsuits. In an attempt to humiliate inmates, Sheriff Arpaio requires them to wear pink underwear and other pink clothing. Additionally, cigarettes, adult magazines, regular television programming, and many other comfort items have been forbidden. The conditions of tent living in the hot and arid Arizona elements can be brutal, and the sheriff considers this a consequence of going to jail. These harsh conditions of detention are expected to have a deterrent effect on offenders. Even though the sheriff has saved the taxpayers much money, critics claim the high legal costs incurred from lawsuits because of his methods negate any savings.[47]

Sheriffs are publicly elected officials, and thus, Sheriff Arpaio must gain support from sufficient numbers of voters to win elections. Arpaio's methods have won him some eager supporters, but also vociferous opponents. Some claim that Arpaio's main objective is publicity. Organizations have developed with the objective of getting rid of Joe Arpaio at the ballot box. These organizations present evidence that the sheriff wastes public funds in his "publicity stunts." They also claim that deputies on county time are assigned as his personal bodyguards, that Arpaio will not debate political opponents, that he is vindictive and abuses his authority, and that he has lied to the public about his biographical information, the costs of lawsuits, and the money he claims to save taxpayers. As evidence, critics tell of Arpaio's claim that an $8.25 million settlement over a dead inmate cost the county nothing because of the jail's liability insurance. What he neglected to say, though, was that the jail had a $1 million deductible.[48]

In 2010, the U.S. Department of Justice sued Arpaio for civil rights violations.[49] There have been other lawsuits as well. The *New York Times* states that according to Maricopa County Risk Management, the sheriff has had over 6,000 claims and lawsuits filed against him since he was first elected, at a cost to taxpayers of over $50 million.[50]

The case study at the beginning of this chapter noted that the detention center at Guantánamo Bay and supermax facilities can be considered extreme

© Chris Curtis/Shutterstock.com

Sheriff Joseph Arpaio brands himself as "America's toughest sheriff."

**Early release** Release from a correctional institution prior to the expiration of an offender's sentence.

**Institutional capacity** The maximum number of inmates an institution can hold.

**Deterrence** The threat of punishment that will result from criminal activity. Deterrence is further categorized into general deterrence, which threatens everyone with criminal sanctions, and specific deterrence, which is a threat to a specific individual who may offend or reoffend.

examples of prisons. The human suffering at these prisons has generated and maintained their notorious reputations. The Maricopa County Jail is similar in that it may be considered an extreme example of an American jail. The jail receives incredible publicity because of the atypical methods used on the inmates and the unreserved behavior of the sheriff.

## Role and Structure of Prisons and Jails

The history of jails and prisons, discussed in the previous section, has brought us to the modern system of corrections. Modern correctional facilities have evolved from past successes and mistakes. Currently, in the United States, there are more than 7 million people incarcerated or under correctional supervision.[51] This is larger than the populations of many states. Since there are so many American citizens incarcerated, the issue of corrections has become a significant issue for all levels of government and the public as well.

Modern correctional facilities exist at the local, state, and federal levels. All have their own missions and roles in criminal justice. Some are old and outdated, and others are modern and very secure. Many have inmate amenities for recreation, education, and training. All have access to medical care. There are also different levels of security, ranging from minimum security to supermaximum prisons. None of the facilities and systems exists without controversy.

Prisoners in America have gained many constitutional rights in the past 50 or so years. Of course, some may argue that these rights were already present, but simply not recognized until the U.S. Supreme Court asserted their existence. Among these rights is access to reasonable medical care. In 1976, the U.S. Supreme Court presented the "deliberate indifference" standard pertaining to correctional facilities and the medical care afforded inmates. The court held that deliberate indifference of correctional staff to an inmate's serious medical illness or injury constitutes cruel and unusual punishment.[52]

In the late 1970s, the American Medical Association addressed this issue by creating a program to assist correctional facilities in establishing proper levels of inmate medical care. This program evolved into what is now known as the National Commission on Correctional Health Care (NCCHC). The not-for-profit NCCHC sets standards and offers education, accreditation, and assistance to correctional facilities. Participation is voluntary, but the program is well established, recognized, and respected; many correctional facilities have adopted the standards of the NCCHC and sought their accreditation.[53]

The U.S. Supreme Court has also ordered that correctional facilities must provide law libraries. An inmate's right to access to a law library and to those skilled in providing legal assistance was established in *Bounds v. Smith*[54]

(1977) and in *Younger v. Gilmore*[55] (1971). The decisions were based on an inmate's widely accepted constitutional right to court access.[56] Subsequent U.S. Supreme Court cases have ruled on this issue even further. *Lewis v. Casey*[57] (1996), for example, may have relaxed some of the privileges gained from the 1971 and 1977 cases. *Lewis* limits access to the types of legal proceedings an inmate may pursue and tightens the rules for an inmate's legal standing in order to file a lawsuit.[58]

---

### Critical Thinking

Correctional administrators tell us that television is a good way for inmates to pass the time and to keep them occupied. Is television for inmates a good idea in prisons and/or jails? What about cable television? Expand some on this concept. What about Internet access, weightlifting, gyms, pool tables, and basketball courts? What about entertainment venues such as comedians and musicians? Are any or all of these a good idea or not? Why?

---

## The Historical Role of Incarceration

Throughout human history, prisoners have been confined for a variety of reasons. Mostly, confinement was used for the temporary detention of individuals until they could be brought to judgment by the governing authority and either released or punished accordingly. If the offender was found guilty, he or she would receive a punishment. As discussed earlier in the chapter, these punishments often included methods that by contemporary standards would be considered cruel and unusual, such as stoning or boiling.

When the American colonies declared themselves independent from English rule, the colonists also insisted that this independence included rules concerning criminal justice. Whereas the British legal system recognized that the monarch was the ultimate source of law, many colonists felt that the ultimate source of law should originate in the people and that leaders should also be bound to laws. British law was, at the time, so merciless that even a petty thief could be put to death. Some higher-class criminals, however, were able to escape justice through a system of patronage. This system allowed offenders to appeal to the crown or others in local authority who would either issue a **pardon**—an exemption from penalty—or otherwise suspend or delay the offender's sentence. The colonists demanded a justice system that treated suspects the same without consideration of their social status.

**Pardon** To forgive, release, or exempt a person from a penalty.

Having won independence in the Revolutionary War, the United States created its own system of laws. Issues of criminal justice are addressed in several sections of the U.S. Constitution. Some of these sections include laws against counterfeiting, treason, and piracy. In addition, there are laws that prohibit federal and state governments from enacting *bills of attainder*, which are edicts that proclaim a person or group guilty without the benefit of a trial, and *ex post facto laws*, which are laws retroactively applied to previous events.

Criminal law was addressed more specifically in the Bill of Rights. The Bill of Rights recognizes the right of people to be free from governmental abuse and codifies this natural human rights acknowledgment into law. Among other things, the Bill of Rights prohibits the government from unreasonably searching or seizing persons or property, from trying someone repeatedly for the same crime, from holding someone "for a capital [death penalty eligible], or otherwise infamous [felony] crime," and from demanding confessions in that a person is not compelled to "be a witness against himself." It also prohibits the government from bringing charges except upon indictment or presentment. Additionally, the Bill of Rights states that an individual has a right to a speedy trial by an impartial jury and punishments deemed cruel and unusual are prohibited.

The provisions in the Bill of Rights were not based on hypothetical situations: they were responses to known abuses from tyrannical governments that the framers of this document intended to prohibit. The text of the Declaration of Independence includes a long list of these "abuses and usurpations." The Bill of Rights was created to protect all citizens from unchecked power and to prevent the government from tyrannical abuses. The Eighth Amendment outlawed cruel and unusual forms of punishment and permitted the modern philosophies of penitence to replace them. Thus, penitentiaries became the new method of punishment.

With the goal of establishing a system based on fair adjudication and punishment, the U.S. founding fathers created the Eighth Amendment to protect the basic human rights of the innocent and the guilty.

At first, the Bill of Rights applied only to federal laws. The states had their own bills of rights, but most were fashioned from those in the U.S. Constitution. It was not until the mid-19th century with the enactment of the 14th Amendment that many of the U.S. Constitutional rights were applied to the states.

## The Role of Incarceration in Contemporary Society

It is a commonly held tenet of criminal justice that people are sent to prison *as* punishment, not *for* punishment. This is a fine distinction, but an important one. In other words, the loss of freedom and many rights is the punishment. Inmates are not to receive punishment in excess of what was ordered by the court.

There have been many correctional ideologies proposed and tried over the centuries. Most of them fall into the categories of punishment, rehabilitation, or prevention. Of course, there is no defined position where one ideology ends before another one begins. They often overlap. For instance, one could easily make a reasonable argument that the goal of both punishment and rehabilitation is prevention.

Punishment of criminals falls into three general categories. The first of these categories is retribution. Retribution has come in many forms through the ages, and is viewed by some as the basest of human qualities. It means getting even, such as in the maxim "an eye for an eye." Banishment, death, and humiliation are all forms of retribution.[59]

The next form of punishment is deterrence. This simple term means a person is deterred from doing wrong because he or she fears the punishment. Deterrence is further broken down into the categories of general and specific deterrence. General deterrence is what all members of society feel that prevents them from doing wrong. This feeling can come from a moral or a religious view, or it can come simply from a fear of being caught. Specific deterrence is a sanction imposed upon a specific person in hopes that the punishment will deter that specific individual from reoffending, or recidivating.[60]

A third reason for punishment is incapacitation. To incapacitate an offender means to remove him or her from the opportunity and availability to commit further criminal acts. This usually means that an offender is locked up, preventing further criminal opportunity and actions.[61]

Rehabilitation, discussed earlier in the chapter, means to restore an offender to a lawful and useful place in society. This, in theory, is accomplished through treatment and education. The treatment model is often referred to as the medical model. In the *medical model*, an offender is viewed as "ill" and in need of treatment. The *educational model* recognizes the offender as disadvantaged and in need of education, training, and discipline. Rehabilitation seems easier in theory than in practice. High rates of recidivism tend to challenge the success of rehabilitation efforts.[62]

The *prevention ideology* is often recognized as something that must begin in early life. Prevention programs attempt to identify early signs of behavior that are statistically tied to criminal behavior. Truancy, dropping out of school, and poor school performance are often viewed as precursors to criminal behavior later in life. Prevention programs attempt to break the path to crime by developing specialized classes, counseling, vocational training, and even alternate schools.[63]

Countless state, federal, appeals, and U.S. Supreme Court cases address issues of prisoner rights. In *Wolff v. McDonnell*, a 1974 case involving prison

## Critical Thinking

Incarcerated individuals lose many of their civil rights, such as the right of liberty, the right to assemble, and in most states, the right to vote. What rights do you believe inmates should be allowed to keep?

inmate rights, Supreme Court Justice Byron White asserted in the majority opinion, "But though [the prisoner's] rights may be diminished by the needs and exigencies of the institutional environment, a prisoner is not wholly stripped of constitutional protections when he is imprisoned for crime. There is no iron curtain drawn between the Constitution and the prisons of this country."[64]

---

**Exhibit:** *Wolff v. McDonnell*

"Petitioners assert that the procedure for disciplining prison inmates for serious misconduct is a matter of policy raising no constitutional issue. If the position implies that prisoners in state institutions are wholly without the protections of the Constitution and the Due Process Clause, it is plainly untenable. Lawful imprisonment necessarily makes unavailable many rights and privileges of the ordinary citizen . . . But though his rights may be diminished by the needs and exigencies of the institutional environment, a prisoner is not wholly stripped of constitutional protections when he is imprisoned for crime. There is no iron curtain drawn between the Constitution and the prisons of this country. Prisoners have been held to enjoy substantial religious freedom under the First and Fourteenth Amendments. They retain right of access to the courts. Prisoners are protected under the Equal Protection Clause of the Fourteenth Amendment from invidious discrimination based on race. Prisoners may also claim the protections of the Due Process Clause. They may not be deprived of life, liberty, or property without due process of law."

---

## A drop in the number of probationers accounted for most of the decrease in the correctional population during 2015.

After a peak in 2007, the U.S. correctional population declined annually through 2015. However, the composition of the population remained stable despite the decreasing size of the population during that time. Between 2007 (58%) and 2015 (56%), probationers accounted for the majority of offenders under correctional supervision (Figure 7.1). Prisoners represented slightly less than a quarter of the U.S. correctional population in 2007 (22%) and 2015 (23%). Parolees (11% in 2007 and 13% in 2015) and jail inmates (11% in both 2007 and 2015) remained the smallest shares of the correctional population during the 8-year period.

### Is It a Prison or a Jail?

In the United States and in many other countries, there are distinct differences between prisons and jails. Jails and prisons are both **correctional institutions**, but have different missions and therefore serve

**FIGURE 7.1** U.S. ADULT CORRECTIONAL POPULATION 2007 AND 2015. THIS FIGURE DEMONSTRATES THAT THE TOTAL NUMBER OF ADULTS UNDER CORRECTIONAL SUPERVISION AS OF 2015 WAS MORE THAN 6.7 MILLION.

| Number of persons supervised by U.S. adult correctional systems, by correctional status, 2007 and 2015 | | | | |
|---|---|---|---|---|
| | 2007 | | 2015 | |
| Correctional populations | Population | Percent of total population | Population | Percent of total population |
| Total[a] | 7,339,600 | 100% | 6,741,400 | 100% |
| Probation[b] | 4,293,000 | 58.5 | 3,789,800 | 56.2 |
| Prison[b] | 1,596,800 | 21.8 | 1,526,800 | 22.6 |
| Parole[b] | 826,100 | 11.3 | 870,500 | 12.9 |
| Local jail[c] | 780,200 | 10.6 | 728,200 | 10.8 |
| Offenders with multiple correctional statuses[d] | 156,400 | : | 174,000 | : |

Note: Counts were rounded to the nearest 100 and include estimates for nonresponding jurisdictions. Detail may not sum to total due to rounding and because offenders with multiple correctional statuses were excluded from the total correctional population.

:Not calculated.

[a]Total was adjusted to exclude offenders with multiple correctional statuses to avoid double counting.

[b]Population as of December 31.

[c]Population as of the last weekday in June.

[d]Some probationers and parolees on December 31 were held in a prison or jail but still remained under the jurisdiction of a probation or parole agency and some parolees were also on probation. In addition, some prisoners were being held in jail. They were excluded from the total correctional population to avoid double counting.

Sources: Bureau of Justice Statistics, Annual Probation Survey, Annual Parole Survey, Annual Survey of Jails, and National Prisoner Statistics Program, 2007 and 2015.

different purposes. *Jails* are usually run by local governments or a county sheriff's office. This is most often determined by the local government or individual state laws. *Prisons* are run by the states and the federal government and are often sprawling complexes with varying degrees of security. Some prisons are run by private organizations, but they are usually under contract with the state. The status of the offender and his or her crime are normally what determines whether the person is in a jail or a prison. In addition, **youthful offenders**—typically offenders under the age of 18—may be tried and sentenced as adults to jail or prison, but most often, juveniles are adjudicated as delinquent and not as criminals. They may then be sent to a juvenile detention facility.

**Youthful offender**
Typically, an offender under 18 years old, though the age requirement can differ among states.

Jails and prisons have evolved significantly over the centuries. In early human history, confinement areas were built from whatever could be used. This often was a natural formation such as a cave. As humankind progressed, cages, special rooms in castles, and even specially built structures would hold prisoners. While some jails today may still be old and poorly built, most jails and prisons are technological wonders with modern security built into the structure. They are designed for maximum observation of inmates by correctional staff. **Escapes** from inside the secure area are very rare. Many of the escapes mentioned in the media are inmates who have simply absconded. **Absconders** are walk-offs from work crews, work release centers, halfway houses, and other inmate areas not inside the main secure facility itself. Typically, the inmates in these other areas are considered less dangerous to society or are nearing the ends of their sentences.[65]

Jails and prisons are now often designed in sections called pods. The goal of the pod system is to maximize observation while sectioning off areas for security reasons. These pods may be used to separate inmates based on gender, classification of their crimes, medical reasons, etc. Additionally, should a disturbance erupt, the officers can secure the area and prevent the spread of violence and therefore maintain control of the facility while addressing the disorder.

## Jails

Jails are multipurpose facilities operated by local governments or sheriffs. Almost all offenders begin their experience with the correctional system in a local jail. Many minor offenders will go no further. For major offenders, jail may be only the first stop in their progression through the correctional system. Most of a jail's population includes those recently arrested, those awaiting trial, and those serving sentences of one year or less. Others found in jail include mentally ill inmates for whom no other facility is available, parolees and probationers awaiting violation hearings, federal prisoners awaiting pickup by marshals, and bail jumpers held overnight by traveling bounty hunters.

Jails are usually the first contact an offender has with the correctional system. When an individual is first arrested, he or she is taken to a jail and is "booked," or has personal information placed in the facility's books. Here, an inmate may be held until trial, known as pretrial detention, or may be given a **conditional release**, which allows the inmate to be released under specific conditions such as an order to enter a treatment program. Others may be released on bail, also known as a bond. Sometimes, charges may be dropped very quickly. Those who are convicted of their offense may be sentenced to jail or prison. Often, sentencing involves probation, which is a form of **supervised release**. Offenders convicted of misdemeanors and sentenced to one year or less of detention usually serve their time in jail. Those convicted of felonies and sentenced to more than one year (at least 366 days) of detention usually go to prison.[66] These situations do have exceptions, as there are few absolutes in criminal justice. Moreover, these procedures are

**Escape** The illegal departure of an offender from legal custody.

**Absconder** One who leaves without authorization. This term is usually used in reference to walk-offs from work crews, work release centers, halfway houses, and other inmate areas not inside the main secure facility.

**Conditional release** The release of a defendant under specific conditions such as an order to enter a treatment program.

**Supervised release** Court-ordered supervision of someone who is awaiting trial or serving probation or parole.

determined by state law, and not all states follow the same practice. For instance, in some states, a misdemeanor sentence can carry a punishment of up to two years of imprisonment, which may be served in a jail. Moreover, some states have indeterminate sentencing laws that mandate a penalty, such as six months to a year or five to 10 years, instead of a determinate amount of time. An inmate may gain an earlier release date based on his or her behavior and efforts to rehabilitate.

Staffing at the jail includes correctional officers, classification officers, medical professionals, and administrative workers. **Correctional officers** are usually academy-trained individuals who meet strict criteria for physical condition, mental condition, and a noncriminal history. **Classification officers** are those who determine the inmate's placement and level of dangerousness. They also calculate sentences as mandated by the courts.

Depending on the size of the jail, there may be a staff of administrative professionals. These individuals perform the back-office functions such as managing funds or ordering supplies. All jails have access to medical care, and jails of significant size often have their own staff for routine medical needs and emergencies. The Eighth Amendment's prohibition on cruel and unusual punishment provides that inmates receive a minimum standard of living, which includes access to medical services.

> **Correctional officer** An officer, also called a prison guard, jail guard, or corrections officer, who oversees and supervises all inmate activity.

> **Classification officer** The officer assigned to determine individual inmate needs and assign them to appropriate custody levels, institutions, and programs.

## Prisons

Prisons are run by the states and the federal government. In some cases, the government oversees a private facility contracted to perform correctional services. Usually, state prisons hold those convicted of felonies who are sentenced to more than one year of imprisonment. States enact their own laws concerning sentencing and correctional facilities, so there is some variation throughout the country. Federal prisons house those convicted of federal crimes, both misdemeanants and felons. Whether the inmate was convicted of a state or a federal crime determines whether he or she goes to a state or a federal prison.

Sometimes, a person is accused of a crime that is prohibited by both state and federal law. Weapons and drug offenses commonly involve both jurisdictions. Since there are state and federal laws against illegal drugs and weapons, offenders may find themselves prosecuted in both state and federal courts. The offender may even be convicted and sentenced in both

**Critical Thinking**
Higher-custody prisons not only keep inmates from escaping, but also prevent inmates from committing crimes while in prison. What kinds of crimes are committed inside of prison? How does prison design help deter or prevent crime from occurring?

jurisdictions. If that occurs, the offender may serve a segmented sentence in both state and federal prison. In practice, however, the jurisdictions often work together to bring a resolution to the case. Sometimes, jurisdictions may defer to the prosecution with the strongest case or the longest sentence. In other cases, one jurisdiction may delay completion of the investigation to see what happens in the other jurisdiction's court before deciding whether to proceed. There may even be a cross-jurisdictional agreement in exchange for a guilty plea.

It is important to note that the Fifth Amendment's prohibition on double jeopardy allows an individual to be convicted in two jurisdictions for the same crime. This is because there are two separate jurisdictions that prohibit the offense. The Fifth Amendment states that no person can be tried twice for "the same offense," but if there are separate offense statutes for a crime on the state and federal levels, then they are not considered the same offense. Thus, an offender may be tried and convicted under both jurisdictions. This is known as the dual sovereignty exception. In *United States v. Lanza,* Chief Justice Howard Taft in delivering the opinion of the court stated, "It follows that an act denounced as a crime by both national and state sovereignties is an offense against the peace and dignity of both, and may be punished by each."[67]

When an inmate is received into most state prison systems, he or she is processed through a classification system. The classification of inmates simply is a means to fit an inmate into a specific category of custody level, medical needs, predisposition to violence or escape, training and educational needs, and other categories as determined by state statute. This classification procedure will determine primarily which security level the inmate requires. Then, after considering the other criteria, the inmate will be assigned to a state prison facility that fits his or her characteristics. The classification procedure usually continues at the receiving facility, and decisions will be made concerning the inmate's abilities, training, counseling, and efforts regarding the inmate's reentry to open society.

Accurate classification of inmates is an admirable goal, and the objectives are achieved to a significant degree. However, institutional needs are the primary forces that determine classification efforts. Often, classification decisions are made based on availability of programs and space at the institution where the inmate's needs would best be served.

## Custody Levels

Inmates are classified to a custody level in jails and in prisons. In jail, the inmate may bond out for pretrial release or may be serving a relatively short sentence of one year or less. In prison, proper classification becomes a continuous process that involves constant reclassification for many inmates based on their behavior and history. These levels of custody usually include minimum, medium, and maximum security. There are others such as community custody, typically for those on parole or probation; death row

**Number of persons supervised by U.S. adult correctional systems, by correctional status, 2000 and 2005-2015**

| Year | Total correctional population[a] | Community supervision | | | | Incarcerated[b] | |
|---|---|---|---|---|---|---|---|
| | | Total[a,c] | Probation | Parole | Total[a] | Local jail | Prison |
| 2000 | 6,467,800 | 4,564,900 | 3,839,400 | 725,500 | 1,945,400 | 621,100 | 1,394,200 |
| 2005 | 7,055,600 | 4,946,600 | 4,162,300 | 784,400 | 2,200,400 | 747,500 | 1,525,900 |
| 2006 | 7,199,600 | 5,035,000 | 4,236,800 | 798,200 | 2,256,600 | 765,800 | 1,568,700 |
| 2007 | 7,339,600 | 5,119,000 | 4,293,000 | 826,100 | 2,296,400 | 780,200 | 1,596,800 |
| 2008 | 7,312,600 | 5,093,400 | 4,271,200 | 826,100 | 2,310,300 | 785,500 | 1,608,300 |
| 2009 | 7,239,100 | 5,019,900 | 4,199,800 | 824,600 | 2,297,700 | 767,400 | 1,615,500 |
| 2010 | 7,089,000 | 4,888,500 | 4,055,900 | 840,800 | 2,279,100 | 748,700 | 1,613,800 |
| 2011 | 6,994,500 | 4,818,300 | 3,973,800 | 855,500 | 2,252,500 | 735,600 | 1,599,000 |
| 2012 | 6,949,800 | 4,790,700 | 3,944,900 | 858,400 | 2,231,300 | 744,500 | 1,570,400 |
| 2013 | 6,899,700 | 4,749,800 | 3,912,000 | 849,500 | 2,222,500 | 731,200 | 1,577,000 |
| 2014 | 6,856,900 | 4,713,200 | 3,868,400 | 857,700 | 2,225,100 | 744,600 | 1,562,300 |
| 2015 | 6,741,400 | 4,650,900 | 3,789,800 | 870,500 | 2,173,800 | 728,200 | 1,526,800 |
| Average annual percent change, 2007-2015 | −1.1% | −1.2% | −1.6% | 0.7% | −0.7% | −0.9% | −0.6% |
| Percent change, 2014-2015 | −1.7% | −1.3% | −2.0% | 1.5% | −2.3% | −2.2% | −2.3% |

Note: Estimates were rounded to the nearest 100 and may not be comparable to previously published BJS reports due to updated information or rounding. Counts include estimates for nonresponding jurisdictions. All probation, parole, and prison counts are not December 31; jail counts are for the last weekday in June. Detail may not sum to total due to rounding and adjustments made to account for offenders with multiple correctional statuses. See Methodology. See the Key Statistics page on the BJS website for correctional population statistics prior to 2000 or other years not included in this table.

[a]Total was adjusted to account for offenders with multiple correctional statuses. See Methodology.

[b]Includes offenders held in local jails or under the jurisdiction of state or federal prisons.

[c]Includes some offenders held in a prison or jail but who remained under the jurisdiction of a probation or parole agency.

Source: Bureau of Justice Statistics, Annual Probation Survey, Annual Parole Survey, Annual Survey of Jails, Census of Jail Inmates, and National Prisoner Statistics Program. 2000 and 2005-2015.

custody; and supermax custody. The various states determine their own categories and criteria for custody levels. For instance, in Florida prisons, most inmates are classified as minimum, medium, or close custody. Maximum custody refers to death row inmates and a few other categories of especially dangerous individuals.

At yearend 2015, an estimated 6,741,400 persons were under the supervision of U.S. adult correctional systems, about 115,600 fewer persons than yearend 2014 (Figure 7.2). This was the first time since 2002 (6,730,900) that the correctional population fell below 6.8 million. The population declined by 1.7% during 2015, which was the largest decline since 2010 (down 2.1%). Additionally, the decrease was a change from a 3-year trend of stable annual rate declines of about 0.6% between 2012 and 2014. About 1 in 37 adults in the United States was under some form of correctional supervision at the end of 2015. This was the lowest rate observed since 1994, when about 1 in 38 adults (1.6 million fewer persons) were under correctional supervision in the nation (not shown).

Minimum and medium custody levels are usually assigned to the least dangerous inmates. Inmates at higher levels may also be reclassified to a lower level if they are nearing the end of their sentence. The theory is that they are less of a trouble and escape risk because they want to complete their time easily and get out. Unfortunately, this theory does not always prove true because many criminals are unable to process this kind of logic. They may be impulsive and unable to understand the consequences of current actions and the result on their future. However, most do finish the end of a sentence quietly. The Bureau of Justice Statistics once estimated that 25% of inmates lost good time credits for good behavior, which means that a full sentence was served without an early release.[68]

Lower-custody institutions are less expensive to operate. Not only is the architecture designed with fewer security barriers, there is usually a lower staff-to-inmate ratio. Since fewer escape attempts and disturbances are expected, fewer security staff are required to supervise the population. When a prison is deemed a close- or maximum-custody institution, there will be more security staff per inmate and the prison design is such that disturbances can be contained in a small area. Escape is nearly impossible. The secure perimeter will often have more than one high fence with razor wire coiled at the bottom and up the side of the fence and topped off as well. The fences are frequently electrified and will contain detection devices to alert control room staff of any movement. In addition, the outside perimeter is patrolled by armed security staff that is in constant contact with the control room, and they will respond to all detected perimeter alerts.

Inmates at most levels of security have jobs that keep them busy on the prison grounds. Most labor in a prison is performed by inmates. Simple jobs such as mowing the grass, picking up trash, cleaning tables at the dining hall, or washing dishes are part of prisoners' daily routines. Skilled inmates may also paint, maintain plumbing and air conditioning, repair structural issues, and maintain prison vehicles. All jobs are supervised by security staff.

## The Supermax

Most prisons have special housing units for disruptive inmates who pose disciplinary problems. Inmates will be placed in one of these units usually after an officer writes a **disciplinary report** describing the offense committed by the inmate. Often, these segregated areas are referred to as the **Special Housing Unit,** or the **SHU,** which is pronounced *shoe*. Inmates needing special housing due to assaultive behavior, escapes, escape attempts, inciting others, gang activity, and other categories of prohibited behavior may be reclassified to a higher custody level. In some states, such inmates will be reclassified to a supermaximum status. This is a management decision in response to an inmate's dangerous and disruptive behavior. The supermax facility may be special housing on the institutional grounds. The supermax that most have heard of is a separate facility designed and staffed exclusively for supermax inmates.

The first supermax prison in this country was Alcatraz. Currently, the only freestanding federal supermax facility is the Administrative Maximum facility in Florence, Colorado, called by some "the Alcatraz of the Rockies." Better known as ADMAX, the prison opened in 1994 and has never incurred a successful escape. Here, the most dangerous and escape-prone long-term inmates live a strict lifestyle that is controlled by officers who operate the prison remotely so that staff/inmate contact is kept to a minimum. As of early 2011, ADMAX houses notorious prisoners such as terrorist Zacarias Moussaoui, Unabomber Theodore Kaczynski, Oklahoma bombing accomplice Terry Nichols, shoe bomber Richard Reid, and FBI agent turned Soviet spy Robert Hanssen.[69]

Many states have supermax facilities constructed on the grounds of existing facilities. There, those deemed the worst of the worst reside. These special housing units are closely monitored and movement is restricted. Inmates in these units are often kept in isolation and are escorted in chains whenever they leave their cells. The supermax inmate is often granted a few hours a week out of the cell for fresh air and exercise in a monitored cage. Even this privilege may be revoked based on the inmate's behavior. Because of the extreme restrictions, the supermax prison is considered by some to be a violation of the Eighth Amendment's prohibition on cruel and unusual punishment. Numerous lawsuits have been filed by inmates and human rights groups. The United Nations has even weighed in on the controversy surrounding supermax prisons, calling for guidelines concerning torture and cruel, inhuman, and degrading treatment and punishment. Specifically, practices such as solitary confinement, excessive use of restraints, and forced psychiatric interventions are viewed as violations by the United Nations.[70]

## Current Notorious Prisons

Many prisons throughout history have achieved notoriety for one reason or another. Some have become famous for alleged human rights violations. The ADMAX prison in Colorado and its extreme conditions is an example of such infamy. Across the nation, other prisons have their own unique characteristics.

**Disciplinary report**
A written report describing the inappropriate behavior or the breaking of institutional rules by an inmate.

**Special Housing Unit (SHU)** Usually an area of confinement within a correctional facility designed to hold the more dangerous or violent inmates, those who are discipline problems, or those who need supervised protection from others.

In California's Marin County, on 275 acres of valuable waterfront property, sits San Quentin Prison. Home to California's only gas chamber and death row, San Quentin is one of the nation's best-known prisons. It was constructed in 1852 by inmate labor, and inmates slept on a ship while the prison was built. With more than 5,000 inmates, San Quentin is one of the largest prisons in the nation. San Quentin's notoriety comes mostly from its legendary depictions in movies and in song. San Quentin has been home to many infamous criminals, such as Richard Ramirez, known as the Night Stalker; Charles Bolles, known as Black Bart; Eldridge Cleaver of the Black Panthers; Charles Manson; and Sirhan Sirhan, who assassinated Robert Kennedy.[71]

Sing Sing Prison in Ossining, New York, is where the phrases "the big house" and "up the river" originated in the American lexicon.[72] Over Sing Sing's nearly two-century existence, it gained notoriety for its historic brutal discipline such as beatings, extended solitary confinement, and withholding of food for even minor violations. Though it is now a fully modern and accredited facility, Sing Sing is legendary in American criminal lore. Famous inmates include Ethel and Julius Rosenberg and bank robber Willie Sutton.

New York is also home to Attica Correctional Facility. Attica gained notoriety in 1971 when a riot erupted in which 29 inmates and 10 correctional officers were killed.[73] By many accounts, among the many grievances that inmates suffered, racial issues seemed to be the touch point that sparked the riots. New York eventually settled with the families of those killed. Nearly $12 million went to the families of the inmates killed, and another $12 million went to the families of those officers who died.[74]

France is home to an especially notorious prison. In 2000, the *New York Times* published an expose about the La Santé prison in Paris. Dr. Veronique Vasseur began working at La Santé in the 1990s and was so shocked by the conditions that she began recording her experiences. Among the atrocities, she found high suicide rates, brutal guards, rapes, bug and rodent infestations, regular beatings, poor medical care, disease, and even the intentional placement of younger inmates in cells knowing they would be raped by men with AIDS.[75] Though conditions may have improved, La Santé can still be found on lists of the most brutal and deadly prisons of the world.

Tibet's Drapchi Prison easily ranks as one of the most notorious prisons on earth. At Drapchi, there are special units for male prisoners, female prisoners, criminals, and political prisoners. The official methods of controlling inmates include torture and other inhumane treatment. Some punishments include standing in the sun for extended periods without moving, running for lengthy times without stopping, and beatings. There are few medical services, especially for the political prisoners. The inmates' diet is poor and barely sustains life, and suicide rates are high. Human rights groups, protest groups, and even international organizations have tried to influence the conditions at Drapchi. However, the Communist regime in China prevents any serious outside investigation or interference. Most information about the prison is gained from former inmates and guards. Conditions are so atrocious that the United Nations Commission on Human Rights has tried, without success, to intervene.[76]

# The Privatization of Prisons

Prisons are very expensive and labor-intensive operations. State governments dedicate tremendous amounts of taxpayer money to correctional systems, both publicly and privately owned. The costs of staffing and running a prison are unlikely to come down anytime soon, if ever. With constant court challenges and demands from the citizenry to improve conditions for prisoners, costs will only increase.[77]

A current movement to reduce costs is to contract out correctional responsibilities to private organizations. Private correctional organizations have contracted with governments at the federal, state, and local levels to assume responsibility for criminal custody and detention functions. There are many successful private correctional organizations operating profitably in the United States. Often, the private facility is paid on a per-inmate basis.

The incentive for governments to turn over correctional functions to private organizations usually involves cost savings for taxpayers. In 2001, the cost for operating state prisons, excluding the cost of the land and the infrastructure, was $100 per U.S. resident.[78] This was up more than 10% from only five years earlier. This trend for increasing expenditures on prisons, operating costs, and inmate expenses will likely continue.

These private companies often promise to deliver reduced costs per inmate and better conditions through cost-efficient construction, cost-efficient operations, and competitive incentives to provide high-quality services while keeping expenses low. This efficiency and competitiveness is expected to leave room for the organization to make a profit. The state governments also expect that the funds paid to the private organizations will be less than the costs of state-run correctional facilities. Some local governments hire private correctional organizations to operate jails as well.[79]

Opponents of privatization point to the many indirect costs for the taxpayer. These costs include contract administration, contract monitoring, and the additional government regulation required. The government also retains legal liability for contractor actions. This alone has the potential for tremendous amounts of taxpayer money to be paid out in legal expenses and for lost or settled lawsuits. Research indicates that these tangential expenses negate any savings expected from the privatization of correctional systems.[80]

On August 18, 2016, Deputy Attorney General Sally Yates, announced that she has instructed the Justice Department to end its use of private prisons. The Justice Department plans to end its use of private prisons after officials concluded the facilities are both less safe and less effective at providing correctional services than those run by the government. Yates stated that prison prisons do not provide the same level of correctional resources, programs, and services. Additionally, they do not save substantially on costs.[81]

While experts said the directive is significant, privately run federal prisons house only a fraction of the overall population of inmates. The vast majority of the incarcerated in America are housed in state prisons rather than federal ones and Yates' memo does not apply to any of those, even the ones that are privately run. Nor does it apply to Immigration and Customs Enforcement and U.S. Marshals Service detainees, who are technically in the federal system but not under the purview of the federal Bureau of Prisons.[81]

In 2013, Yates stated, the prison population began to decline because of efforts to adjust sentencing guidelines, sometimes retroactively, and to change the way low-level drug offenders are charged. She said the drop in federal inmates gave officials the opportunity to reevaluate the use of private prisons.

Yates wrote that private prisons "served an important role during a difficult time period," but they had proven less effective than facilities run by the government The Bureau of Prisons spent $639 million on private prisons in fiscal year 2014, according to the inspectors general's report. [81]

On February 23, 2017, President Donald Trump's administration reinstated the use of private prisons for federal inmates, saying commercial prison operators are needed for the correctional system's "future needs." Trump's new attorney general, Jeff Sessions, officially rescinded the Barack Obama administration's move last August to phase out the management of prisons by private companies, which Obama's justice department had said proved to be inadequate, more dangerous and not cheaper than government-run prisons. Sessions said in an order that the move last year had reversed a longstanding policy at the Federal Bureau of Prisons to have private companies involved, "and impaired the bureau's ability to meet the future needs of the federal correctional system."[82]

The Obama move had only affected a small portion of the US prison system: 13 privately run prisons housing just over 22,000 people, or about 11 percent of the federal prison population. Most are foreign nationals, mainly Mexicans incarcerated for immigration violations. The Trump government has promised a crackdown on crime and illegal immigration, suggesting the prisons bureau could require greater holding capacity in a short time. The 13 prisons are run by three companies: CoreCivic (known until recently as Corrections Corporation of America), GEO Group and Management, and Training Corporation. [82]

The criminal justice system consists of the police, the courts, and corrections. This system is an established government obligation, and some believe that no part of it can be severed from its foundation. Correctional systems traditionally are a government responsibility. The duty of the government to punish lawbreakers is confused when private organizations fulfill the correctional functions. Harvard political scientist John Dilulio is vocal with this view. He says, "It is precisely because corrections involves the deprivation of liberty, precisely because it involves the legally sanctioned exercise of coercion by some citizens over others, that it must remain wholly within public hands."[81]

## A Brief History of Private Correctional Facilities

Modern private prisons appear to have originated from the convergence of two separate events. In the 1970s, the U.S. prison population began to expand somewhat rapidly. A decade later, under the leadership of President Ronald Reagan, the government began to look to the private sector for government solutions. These private-sector solutions were applied to the problem of rising prison populations.

The first known private prison in the United States was San Quentin Prison in California in the 1850s.[82] Even then, the basis for privatization was reduced costs. It was also assumed that there would be less corruption.[83] The first government award for local correctional services occurred in Hamilton County, Tennessee.[84] As of 2009, there were more than 25,000 federal prisoners in private facilities and more than 95,000 in privately operated state facilities.[85]

## Correctional Corporations

Some of the largest private correctional corporations build, manage, and operate prisons with strict government oversight. The CCA claims the title of "America's Leader in Partnership Corrections." The corporation, established in the early 1980s, operates federal, state, and local correctional facilities around the nation. The CCA is a publicly traded corporation that operates about 50% of the private correctional facilities in the nation. This makes CCA the largest private correctional provider, with more than 17,000 employees. The organization also owns and operates TransCor America. TransCor provides inmate transportation services to correctional facilities that need to move inmates from one location to another.[86]

Private prisons have become a very profitable part of the prison-industrial complex. However, saving money for states and the federal government is still in question. A study by Vanderbilt University claims that states can save $13 million to $15 million by contracting out correctional services,[87] while a study by Cornell University demonstrates that the savings are accounting shifts.[88] Many states have taken notice, and those who do not yet use private correctional services are examining the possibility.

Privatization is often criticized because these private organizations may assume custody of healthy populations of inmates and lower-custody inmates. This reduces the costs to the private companies because there are fewer medical expenses and they need less secure facilities and fewer security staff to supervise the inmates. This leaves the more expensive populations, such as the violent, dangerous, elderly, and those with special medical needs, for the government facilities.

Major criticisms of prison privatization often come from criminologists who are convinced that privatization does not result in the promised savings. Comparing the actual costs of private prisons with those of state and federally operated institutions is complex and is often illusory. Cost analysis studies frequently return different results depending on what organization is conducting the study. In addition, the accounting methods and populations can be very different. Since there is no private prison that is exactly like a corresponding government prison, precise cost comparisons are nearly impossible.

To study this issue, in 2007, the National Institute of Justice brought together researchers, private service providers, government prison officials, and proponents and opponents of prison privatization. The study focused on two separate analyses of the same four prisons that produced different results.[89] The privatization study concluded that overhead costs and inmate population sizes were being measured differently between private and government prisons. It found that private prisons were only measuring direct costs—such as staffing, food, medical care, and other services—while government prisons were measuring both direct costs and indirect costs associated with planning, automation, computer services, and budget development. It was assumed that the government would continue to absorb the indirect costs even for those prisons operated by private organizations, thereby eliminating promised savings. The study concluded that, in order to obtain a more accurate measurement of the costs of privatization, these indirect costs should be included in the estimates for private prisons.[90]

## The Hiring and Training of Correctional Officers

Correctional officers provide security and maintain accountability of inmates for detention centers, jails, and prisons. In detention centers, they may be known as detention officers, though *correctional officer* is the generally accepted universal term. The officer must always diligently work to prevent disturbances, assaults, and escapes.

In order to become a correctional officer, one must meet stringent standards. Federal and state requirements mandate that officers have a high school diploma or GED, and some governments require at least a bachelor's degree. Certain states and local governments will also accept military service in lieu of college credit. Others will also accept combinations of college, military, counseling, and supervisory experience.[91]

Recruit officers receive academy training that varies by state. The Federal Bureau of Prisons has its own recruit and training requirements.[92] The American Correctional Association and the American Jail

© Georgios Tsichlis/Shutterstock.com

In 2008, correctional officers and jailors accounted for approximately 454,500 jobs in the United States. Employment in this career is expected to increase 9% by 2018. However, cash-strapped prisons are also using technology to eliminate the staffed towers so prominent at many prisons.

## Career Connections: Correctional Officer

Correctional officers provide security, maintain order, and prevent escapes in detention facilities, jails, and prisons. Employers are state and local governments and private correctional services providers. All officers must be certified by their respective federal and state governments, and recruits must be trained by government-approved training facilities. Most require applicants to have at least a high school diploma, be at least 18 years old and of good character, and have a stable job history. In addition, the correctional officer candidate must not have an extensive or significant criminal history. Some agencies will accept minor violations such as a childhood minor theft incident or misdemeanor drug charges. However, they generally will not tolerate recent charges or allow current officers who commit crimes to remain employed.

The working conditions are sometimes harsh. A correctional officer must be able to perform all job functions in all weather conditions and in sometimes dirty or cramped environments. This occupation can be hazardous and stressful. Correctional officers have one of the highest non-fatal on-the-job occupational injury rates and face the risk of assault daily. Because correctional facilities operate around the clock, officers work at all times, including holidays and weekends. Correctional officers are often required to work overtime. Typically, because of the diverse populations, jails tend to be more dangerous facilities than are prisons. Prisons generally have populations that have been segregated based upon violent tendencies of inmates and have higher staff-to-inmate ratios. Therefore, in general, prisons are safer places to work than are jails.[95]

Association provide accrediting and certification services as well as guidelines for correctional officer training.[93] Officers also receive ongoing education and inservice training provided by their own organizations. Advanced training is also made available to those officers performing specialized functions such as K-9, emergency response teams, special weapons and munitions, and others.

The national occupational outlook for correctional officers is expected to increase by 48,000 between 2008 and 2018.[94] This means that the growth of this field is favorable to those seeking such careers. Mandatory sentencing in many states has increased the correctional inmate populations and, in turn, has increased the need for additional correctional officers. Should the trend for mandatory sentencing reverse, as is being considered in some states for budgetary reasons, the need for correctional officers may decline.

According to the Bureau of Labor Statistics (BLS), the outlook for correctional officers is favorable and is expected to increase by about 9% of current numbers by 2018. This means that an additional 48,000 officers will be needed based on 2008 figures. In 2010, the median salary of correctional officers was $39,040. Supervisors and managers can earn significantly more. The turnover for correctional officers appears to be about average for all occupations.

## FIGURE 7.3 NATIONAL ESTIMATES FOR CORRECTIONAL OFFICERS

**Percentile wage estimates for this occupation: May (2015)**

| Percentile | 10% | 25% | 50% (Median) | 75% | 90% |
|---|---|---|---|---|---|
| Hourly Wage | $13.38 | $15.84 | $19.49 | $26.79 | $35.12 |
| Annual Wage | $27,830 | $32,960 | $40,530 | $55,720 | $73,060 |

*Source: Bureau of Labor Statistics. (2016). Correctional Officers and Jailers. Washington, D.C.: Author.*

All officers in the United States are required to have at least a high school diploma. Some states may require some college or military experience. Local governments may have requirements in addition to what is required for an officer to be certified by the state. Federal prison officers are required to have at least a bachelor's degree or other acceptable work experience in lieu of the degree.

New officers receive academy training in subjects ranging from basic report writing to defensive tactics and weapons training. Federal officers receive training at the Federal Law Enforcement Training Center (FLETC) in Glynco, Georgia. Officers also receive ongoing inservice training and specialized training for those on special teams such as K-9 and emergency response. Both female and male officers receive the same training and must meet the same standards. It has been found that female correctional officers may be especially well suited to defuse potentially violent situations in the early stages.[96]

## FIGURE 7.4 NATIONAL ESTIMATES FOR CORRECTIONAL OFFICERS: AS OF MAY 2015

**States with the highest employment level in this occupation:**

| State | Employment | Employment per thousand jobs | Hourly mean wage | Annual mean wage |
|---|---|---|---|---|
| Texas | 48,280 | 4.17 | $18.37 | $38,210 |
| California | 34,640 | 2.24 | $33.19 | $69,040 |
| New York | 34,140 | 3.80 | $29.41 | $61,160 |
| Florida | 34,470 | 4.35 | $20.83 | $43,330 |
| Georgia | 16,710 | 4.07 | $14.26 | $29,650 |

*Source: Bureau of Labor Statistics. (2016). Correctional Officers and Jailers. Washington, D.C.: Author.*

Most states have public service unions, and correctional officers are often represented by collective bargaining organizations. There are arguments both for and against correctional officer unions. However, unions have a very strong presence, and they negotiate with governments and private correctional organizations for higher wages and increased benefits for members. Contracts also define working conditions and promotional guidelines. In states that do not require union membership as a condition of employment, officers who are not members will still be recipients of most negotiated benefits, just like those officers who are members and who pay union dues.[97]

---

**Career Connections: Correctional Officer**
Should correctional officers be considered professionals or simply skilled workers?

---

**Ethics and Professionalism**
The warden at a major corrections institution has several correctional officer positions he needs to fill. He has more than enough applications because the poor economy has left many people looking for work. As he peruses the applications, he ponders what kind of applicant would best serve the mission of the department.

He has many tools at his disposal, including the usual background checks, psychological exams, and truth detection technologies. However, the warden wants to upgrade the professionalism in his ranks. He contemplates tests such as career aptitude inventories, aggressiveness profiles, and ethical assessments. He also wishes to narrow his selection to those with at least some college experience.

Do you believe that he would get a better-quality officer using these recruitment tools? If the warden uses these new tests, how might the hiring decisions he makes differ from his hiring decisions of the past? Why are ethics important for new officers? Are college-educated officers necessarily better officers?

# Chapter Summary

- Detention has been an acceptable method of punishment for criminal offenders for only a few hundred years. In early American history, jails were used primarily to hold for trial those who could not make bail or those who were unable to pay debts. The living conditions in these early jails were cruel and immoral. Men, women, and children of all ages were thrown together in undisciplined and poorly supervised micro-communities where the strong overpowered the weak. There was little medical treatment and most were poorly fed. Early prisons around the world included the Mamertine Prison as well as fortresses, hulks, workhouses, and Bridewells.

- Early techniques to punish criminals date back to the ancient Sumerians and Babylonians and included whipping, servitude, mutilation, and death. Over the centuries, thanks to reformers such as Montesquieu, John Howard, Cesare Beccaria, Jeremy Bentham, Alexis de Tocqueville, and Gustave de Beaumont, human dignity and life became increasingly valued. In most of the industrialized world, prisoners are treated immensely better than in the past. Though prisons are oppressive places and provide for an onerous existence, most countries at least provide prisoners a survivable diet, some medical care, human contact, and some form of classification that separates juveniles from adults and men from women. The Walnut Street Jail in Philadelphia was one of the first to institute reforms.

- Modern correctional facilities exist at the local, state, and federal levels. Jails are multipurpose facilities operated by local governments or sheriffs and are usually the offender's first contact with the criminal justice system. Prisons are operated by the states and the federal government and usually house offenders who are serving a sentence of more than one year. All correctional facilities have their own missions and roles in criminal justice. Some are old and outdated, and others are modern and very secure. Many have inmate amenities for recreation, education, and training. All have access to medical care. There are also different levels of security, ranging from minimum security to the supermaximum prisons.

- When an inmate is received into most state prison systems, he or she will be processed through a classification system. Classification of inmates simply is a means to fit an inmate into a specific category of custody level, medical needs, predisposition to violence or escape, training and educational needs, and other categories as determined by state statute. This classification procedure will determine primarily which security level the inmate requires. The inmate will be assigned to a state prison facility that fits his or her characteristics.

- Most prisons have special housing units for disruptive inmates who pose disciplinary problems. Inmates needing special housing for assaultive behavior, escapes, escape attempts, inciting others, gang activity, and other categories of prohibited behavior may be reclassified to a higher custody level. In some states, such inmates will be reclassified to a supermaximum status. The supermax facility may be special housing on the institutional grounds or a separate facility for particularly dangerous offenders.

- A current movement to reduce costs is to contract out correctional responsibilities to private organizations. These private companies often promise and may deliver reduced costs per inmate and better conditions through cost-efficient construction, cost-efficient operations, and competitive incentives to provide high-quality services while keeping expenses low. This efficiency and competitiveness is expected to leave room for the organization to make a profit. Privatization is a topic of controversy; while some studies indicate that private prisons save money for states and the federal government, critics believes privatization has not led to the anticipated savings. Studies have noted irregularities in measurements of costs between private prisons and government prisons.

- In order to become a correctional officer, one must meet stringent standards. Federal and state requirements mandate that one have a high school diploma or GED, and some require at least a bachelor's degree. Some state and local governments will also accept military service in lieu of college credit. Others will also accept combinations of college, military, counseling, and supervisory experience.

## Critical Thinking?

1. Why was the Eighth Amendment's prohibition on cruel and unusual punishment incorporated into the Bill of Rights?

2. Is there a difference between the U.S. Constitution's prohibition on cruel and unusual punishment and several state constitutional prohibitions on cruel or unusual punishment?

3. Could supermax prisons be considered cruel and unusual? Could they be considered cruel but not unusual? Or unusual but not cruel?

4. Some people are sent to prison for very long periods, even for life. Do you feel this is a good public expenditure of taxes, or is there a better way to deal with those who violate laws?

5. In 1986, Congress enacted legislation that sentenced offenders differently for possessing different forms of cocaine. Possession of five grams of crack cocaine results in a minimum sentence of five years in federal prison. It takes nearly 100 times that amount in powdered cocaine to receive a comparable sentence. Crack cocaine is found heavily in African-American communities, while powdered cocaine is found primarily in white areas. Is there an issue with disparity in sentencing or is this fair?

6. Civil rights restoration for inmates returning to open society is becoming increasingly popular. What civil rights should be restored and which, if any, should not?

7. With all of the security measures in place, how is it possible that drugs, weapons, and other contraband manage to get into prisons and into prisoners' possession?

8. Since many inmates are able to function well in work release centers and halfway houses, is it a good idea to simply release these inmates to cut down on costs?

9. Do privately owned correctional facilities provide the same services as government-run facilities? Is there any difference as far as criminal justice is concerned?

10. Is the money spent on jails and prisons justified? Is there a better way to punish criminals than by imprisoning them?

## Media

Federal Bureau of Prisons: http://www.bop.gov/ This website contains much information about the correctional system, its history, and references for further reading.

Bureau of Justice Statistics: http://www.bjs.gov/ This government website contains official statistics for all areas of law enforcement.

National Institute of Justice Multimedia: http://www.ojp.usdoj.gov/ nij/journals/media.htm This website contains multimedia from the National Institute of Justice.

Occupational Employment Statistics, Correctional Officer: http://www. bls.gov/oes/current/oes333012.htm. This is the official government website for statistics that may be of interest to those wishing to become correctional officers.

## Endnotes

[1]   JTF-GTMO. (2011). *Overview: Joint Task Force Guantanamo.* Retrieved from http://www.jtfgtmo.southcom.mil/index/Fact%20Sheets/GTMO%20 Overview.pdf

[2]   U.S. Department of Defense (DOD). (2011). *Combatant Status Review Tribunal Summary.* Retrieved from http://www.defense.gov/news/ csrtsummary.pdf

[3]   JTF-GTMO, 2011.

[4]   Congressional Research Service. (2009). *Closing the Guantanamo Detention Center: Legal Issues.* Retrieved from http://www.henrywaxman.house.gov/ UploadedFiles/R40139.pdf

[5]   Human Rights Watch. (2008). *Locked Up Alone: Detention Conditions and Mental Health at Guantanamo.* Retrieved from http://www.defense.gov/ pubs/pdfs/App7.pdf

[6]   Ibid.

[7]   Wilner, T, & Worthington, A. Close Guantanamo. *Prisoners.* Retrieved from http://www.closeguantanamo.org/Prisoners

[7]   Friedman, L. (1993). *Crime and Punishment in American History.* New York, NY: Basic Books.

[8]   Ibid., 50.

9       American Archives. (1776). *Constitution of Pennsylvania*. Retrieved from http://lincoln.lib.niu.edu/cgi-bin/ amarch/getdoc.pl?/var/lib/philologic/databases/amarch/.22309

10      King, L. W. (1997). *Hammurabi's Code*. Retrieved from http://eawc. evansville.edu/index.htm

11      International World History Project. (n.d.). *A History of Ancient Greece: Draco and Solon Laws*. Retrieved from http://history-world.org/draco_and_solon_laws.htm

12      Halsall, P. (1998). "Ancient History Sourcebook: Code of Hammurabi, c. 1780 BCE." *Fordham University*. Retrieved from http://www.fordham. edu/halsall/ancient/hamcode.html

13      Roman Colosseum. (2008). *Roman Punishment*. Retrieved from http:// www.roman-colosseum.info/roman-life/ roman-punishment.htm

14      *Capital Punishment*. (2000). Retrieved from http://autocww.colorado. edu/~toldy2/E64ContentFiles/Law AndCourts/CapitalPunishment.html

15      Alasti, S. (2007). *Comparative Study of Stoning Punishment in the Religions of Islam and Judaism*. Retrieved from http://ggu.academia.edu/SanazAlasti/Papers/195679/Comparative_Study_of_Stoning_Punishments_In_the_Religions_of_Islam_and_Judaism

16      "Guillotine." (2011). *Britannica Online Encyclopedia*. Retrieved from http://www.britannica.com/EBchecked/topic/248765/guillotine

17      Friedman, 1993, 42.

18      Ekirch, R. (1987). *Bound for America: The Transportation of British Convicts to the Colonies*. New York, NY: Oxford University Press.

19      Montgomery, R. (1998). *A History of Correctional Violence*. American Correctional Association.

20      Halsall, P. (1997). "Modern History Sourcebook: Montesquieu: The Spirit of the Laws, 1748." *Fordham University*. Retrieved from http://www.fordham. edu/halsall/mod/montesquieu-spirit.html

21      Ibid.

22      Hay, G. (2011). "Biography of John Howard." *The John Howard Society of Canada*. Retrieved from http://www.johnhoward.ca/about/biography

23      Ibid.

24      Ibid.

25      Beccaria, C. (1764). *Of Crimes and Punishments*. Retrieved from http:// www.constitution.org/cb/crim_pun.htm

26      Ibid.

27      Bentham, J. (1789). "An Introduction to the Principles of Morals and Legislation." *Library of Economics and Liberty*. Retrieved from http://www. econlib.org/library/Bentham/bnthPML1.html#Chapter%20I,%20Of%20the%20 Principle%20of%20Utility

28      De Tocqueville, A. (n.d.). *Democracy in America*. Retrieved from http:// xroads.virginia.edu/~HYPER/DETOC/home.html

29      Ibid.

30      Ibid.

[31]   Hassett, M. (1910). "Mamertine Prison." *The Catholic Encyclopedia*. Retrieved from http://www.newadvent.org/cathen/09579a.htm

[32]   *The Carcer—Mamertine Prison*. (n.d.). Retrieved from http://www.mmdtkw.org/VCarcer.html

[33]   Salvi, S. (2011). *The Original List of Sanctuary Cities, USA*. Retrieved from http://www.ojjpac.org/sanctuary.asp

[34]   Historic Royal Palaces. (2011). *Tower of London*. Retrieved from http://www.hrp.org.uk/TowerOfLondon/stories.aspx

[35]   Morris, S. (2005). "Britain's Only Prison Ship Ends Up on the Beach." *The Guardian*. Retrieved from http://www.guardian.co.uk/uk/2005/aug/12/ukcrime.prisonsandprobation

[36]   Ibid.

[37]   Independence National Historical Park. (2007). *Following in Franklin's Footsteps*. Retrieved from http://www. independenceparkinstitute.com/FranklinDropInPacket6-26-07.pdf

[38]   Johnston, N. (2000). "Prison Reform in Pennsylvania." *The Pennsylvania Prison Society*. Retrieved from http://www.prisonsociety.org/about/history.shtml

[39]   Ibid.

[40]   Stohr, M., Walsh, A., & Hemmens, C. (2009). *Corrections, a Text Reader*. Thousand Oaks, CA: Sage.

[41]   Ibid.

[42]   Northstar Gallery. (n.d.). *Eastern State Penitentiary*. http://northstargallery.com/esp/easternstatehistory01.htm

[43]   Friedman, 1993, 79.

[44]   Ibid., 79–80.

[45]   National Park Service. (2011). "Alcatraz Island: History & Culture." *NPS.gov*. Retrieved from http://www.nps.gov/alca/historyculture/index.htm

[46]   Ibid.

[47]   Overthrow Arpaio. (2009). *Top Ten Reasons to Recall Joe*. Retrieved from http://www.arpaio.com/top-ten/index.php#9 *Maricopa County Sheriff's Office*. (2011). Retrieved from http://www.mcso.org

[48]   *Overthrow Arpaio*. (2009). Retrieved from http://www.arpaio.com

[49]   Lacy, M. (2010, September 2). "Justice Dept. Sues Sheriff Over Bias Investigation." *New York Times*. http://www.nytimes.com/2010/09/03/us/03sheriff.html Wingett, Y., Hensley, J. J., & Kiefer, M. (2010, September 3). "Sheriff Joe Arpaio Sued by Justice Department in Civil-Rights Probe." *AZCentral.com*. Retrieved from http://www.azcentral.com/news/election/azelections/articles/2010/09/02/20100902joe-arpaio-sued-by-justice-department-brk-02-ON.html

[50]   Rangel, C. (2011, May 13). "YOUR Tax Dollars: How Much Does It Cost to Defend the Maricopa County Sheriff's Office?" *ABC15.com*. Retrieved from http://www.abc15.com/dpp/news/local_news/investigations/your-tax-dollars-being-spent-to-fight-sheriff-joe-arpaio%E2%80%99s-lawsuits

[51]   Bureau of Justice Statistics. (2011). *Key Facts at a Glance: Correctional Populations*. Retrieved from http://bjs.ojp.usdoj.gov/content/glance/tables/corr2tab.cfm

52      *Estelle v. Gamble*, 429 U.S. 97 (1976).

53      National Commission on Correctional Health Care. http://www.ncchc.org/index.html

54      *Bounds v. Smith*, 430 U.S. 817 (1977).

55      *Younger v. Gilmore*, 404 U.S. 15 (1971).

56      *Bounds v. Smith*, 1977.

57      *Lewis v. Casey*, 518 U.S. 343 (1996).

58      Ibid.

59      Stanford Encyclopedia of Philosophy. (2008). *Legal Punishment*. Retrieved from http://plato.stanford.edu/entries/legal-punishment/

60      Ibid.

61      Ibid.

62      Ibid.

63      Ibid.

64      *Wolff v. McDonnell*, 418 U.S. 539 (1974).

65      Council of State Governments Justice Center. (2011). *Reentry Policy Council*. Retrieved from http://reentrypolicy.org

66      United States Attorney's Office, District of Minnesota. (2009). *Federal Criminal Prosecution*. Retrieved from http://www.justice.gov/usao/mn/downloads/federal%20criminal%20brochure.2009.final.pdf

67      *U.S. v. Lanza*, 260 U.S. 377 (1922).

68      Tibbs, D. (2006). "Peeking Behind the Iron Curtain: How Law 'Works' Behind Prison Walls." *Southern California Interdisciplinary Law Journal, 16*, 137-182. Retrieved from http://www-bcf.usc.edu/~idjlaw/PDF/16-1/16-1%20Tibbs.pdf
        Bureau of Justice Statistics. (n.d.). *Prison Rule Violators*. Retrieved from http://bjs.ojp.usdoj.gov/index.cfm?ty=gsearch

69      Federal Bureau of Prisons. (2011). *Inmate Locator*. Retrieved from http://www.bop.gov/iloc2/LocateInmate.jsp

70      U.S. Department of Justice, National Institute of Corrections. (1999). *Supermax Prisons: Overview and General Considerations*. Retrieved from http://static.nicic.gov/Library/014937.pdf
        United Nations. (2008). *Torture and other Cruel, Inhuman or Degrading Treatment or Punishment*. Retrieved from http://www.un.org/disabilities/images/A.63.175.doc
        For a cost analysis, see Lawrence, S., & Mears, D. (2004). *Benefit-Cost Analysis of Supermax Prisons*. Retrieved from http://www.hawaii.edu/hivandaids/Benefit-Cost_Analysis_of_Supermax_Prisons.pdf

71      California Department of Corrections and Rehabilitation. (2011). *Adult Facilities Locator: San Quentin State Prison*. Retrieved from http://www.cdcr.ca.gov/Facilities_Locator/SQ-Institution_Stats.html

72      Investigation Discovery. (2011). *Notorious Prisons: Sing Sing Correctional Facility*. Retrieved from http://investigation. discovery.com/investigation/notorious-prisons/sing-sing/sing-sing.html

New York Correction History Society. (n.d.). *Images of America: Sing Sing Prison*. Retrieved from http://www. correctionhistory.org/html/chronicl/state/singsing/cheliindex.html

For further reading and a firsthand account by a Sing Sing correctional officer, see Conover, T. (2000). *Newjack: Guarding Sing Sing*. New York, NY: Random House.

[73]  Jackson, B. (1999). "Attica: An Anniversary of Death." *Artvoice*. Retrieved from http://www.acsu.buffalo.edu/~bjackson/attica.htm

Libcom.org. (2006). *1971: The Attica Prison Uprising*. Retrieved from http://libcom.org/history/1971-the-attica-prison-uprising

National Geographic. (n.d.). *The Final Report: Attica* [Video]. Retrieved from http://channel.nationalgeographic.com/series/final-report/3418/Videos#tab-Videos/05524_00

[74]  Ibid.

[75]  Daley, S. (2000, January 28). "Expose of Brutal Prison Jolts France's Self-Image." *New York Times*. Retrieved from http://www.nytimes.com/2000/01/28/world/expose-of-brutal-prison-jolts-france-s-self-image.html

[76]  Tibetan Center for Human Rights and Democracy. (n.d.). *Drapchi Prison: Tibet's Most Dreaded Prison*. Retrieved from http://www.tchrd.org/publications/topical_reports/drapchi_prison-2001/

News Blaze. (2011, January 5). *Tibetan Political Prisoner Tortured After Speaking To UN*. Retrieved from http:// newsblaze.com/story/20110105080436zzzz.nb/topstory.html

[77]  Bureau of Justice Statistics. (2004). *State Prison Expenditures, 2001* (NCJ 2020949). Retrieved from http://bjs.ojp.usdoj.gov/content/pub/ascii/spe01.txt

[78]  Ibid.

[79]  Austin, J., & Coventry, G. (2001). *Emerging Issues on Privatized Prisons* (NCJ 181249). Retrieved from https://www.ncjrs.gov/pdffiles1/bja/181249.pdf

[80]  Ibid.

[81]  Zapotosky, M. & Harlan, C. (2016). *Justice Department says it will end use of private prisons*. The Washington Post. Retrieved from https://www.washingtonpost.com/news/post-nation/wp/2016/08/18/justice-department-says-it-will-end-use-of-private-prisons/?utm_term=.3f800e3ce23f

[82]  **NDTV.** (2017, February 23). *Donald Trump Reverses Barack Obama Ban On Private Prisons*. Retrieved from http://www.ndtv.com/world-news/donald-trump-reverses-barack-obama-ban-on-private-prisons-1662943.

[81]  Dilulio, J. J. (1986). "Prisons, Profits, and the Public Good: The Privatization of Corrections." *Research Bulletin No. 1*. Huntsville, TX: Sam Houston State University Criminal Justice Center.

[82]  Austin & Coventry, 2001.

[83]  Ibid.

[84]  *Privatization of Prisons*. (2008). Retrieved from http://privatizationofprisons.com

[85]  Bureau of Justice Statistics. (2009). *Correctional Populations in the United States, 2009*. Retrieved from http://bjs.ojp.usdoj.gov/content/pub/pdf/cpus09.pdf

86    Corrections Corporation of America. (2011). *CCA*. Retrieved from http://www.cca.com/

87    Blumstein, J., Cohen, M. A., & Seth, S. (2007). "Do Government Agencies Respond to Market Pressures? Evidence from Private Prisons." *Social Science Research Network*. Retrieved from http://papers.ssrn.com/sol3/papers.cfm?abstract_id=441007

88    McFarland, S., McGowan, C., & O'Toole, T. (2002). *Prisons, Privatization, and Public Values*. Retrieved from http://government.cce.cornell.edu/doc/html/PrisonsPrivatization.htm#_Opponents_of_Privatization:

89    Gaes, G. (2008). "Cost, Performance Studies Look at Prison Privatization." *NJJ Journal, 259*. Retrieved from http://www.nij.gov/journals/259/prison-privatization.htm

90    Ibid.

91    Bureau of Labor Statistics. (2010). *Occupational Outlook Handbook, 2010–2011 Edition: Correctional Officers*. Retrieved from http://www.bls.gov/oco/ocos156.htm

92    Ibid.

93    Ibid.

94    Ibid.

95    Cheeseman, K. A., & Worley, R. (2006). "Women on the Wing: Inmate Perceptions about Female Correctional Officer Job Competency in a Southern Prison System." *Southwest Journal of Criminal Justice, 3*(2), 86–102. Retrieved from http://www.utsa.edu/swjcj/archives/3.2/CheesemanWorley.pdf

96    Ibid.

97    Greenhouse, S. (2011, January 3). "Strained States Turning to Laws to Curb Labor Unions." *New York Times*. Retrieved from http://www.nytimes.com/2011/01/04/business/04labor.html
      *Worthington, A. Close Guantanamo. Retrieved from http://www.closeguantanamo.org/Prisoners

# Prison Life

## KEY TERMS

Day fine

Day reporting center

Deprivation

Doing time

Halfway house

Importation

Indigenous model

Inmate code

Outlaw motorcycle gangs

Pains of imprisonment

Principle of least eligibility

Prison gangs

Prisonization

Street gangs

Total institution

# CHAPTER OBJECTIVES

1 Discuss correctional facilities as total institutions.

2 Understand the roles of both inmate and officer subcultures behind institutional walls.

3. Discuss the implications of relying on incarceration and other corrections-based responses to crime.

4 Discuss the economic realities of incarcerating persons in the United States.

5 Define the various forms of community-based alternatives available.

## Case Study: Richard Speck

On July 13, 1966, the city of Chicago was shaken by the methodical torture, rape, and murder of eight nurses from the South Chicago Community Hospital. One victim survived the attack, and she was later able to provide a detailed description of her assailant. A few days later, 24-year-old Richard Speck saw his likeness and description in a local newspaper. Speck then attempted suicide by slashing his wrists.[1] Apparently, his desire to die was overcome by his will to live, because he called authorities for help.

The police did not realize whom they were assisting as Speck was taken to the hospital. It was not until a doctor noticed the identifying tattoos and compared him to photographs in the newspaper that his identity was known. He was then arrested. Speck was eventually tried and convicted of all eight murders and was sentenced to death.[2] Fortunately for Speck, the United States Supreme Court abolished the death penalty in 1972.[3] His death sentence was subsequently set at consecutive life sentences.

Speck had a lurid history of abuse toward women along with accusations of murder. His abhorrent behavior continued behind the institutional walls at Statesville (Illinois) Correctional Center; his escapades in prison were infamous. While incarcerated, he was included in a study by the Federal Bureau of Investigation Behavioral Science Unit (BSU), which was collecting information to develop a profile of mass murderers.[4]

A homemade video Speck made while in prison that leaked following his death in 1991 from a heart attack showed him having sex with another inmate, waving around $100 bills, and ingesting cocaine. He further bragged about the "good" time he was having while incarcerated. The leaking of this video launched an investigation into the Illinois Department of Corrections.[5] Because the tape had been made years earlier, it was too late to bring any criminal charges; however, the Illinois prison system was prompted to make changes in their operations as a result.

The Richard Speck case is an extraordinary example of life inside prison. Though certainly not a typical representation, it is not particularly shocking to those who have studied and worked in high-security facilities. The appalling aspects of the Speck video are the lack of security and the apparent cooperation of the security staff that allowed the taping session to take place. This experience and countless others worldwide have contributed to the development of modern correctional principles. This chapter examines the prison existence and the way of life for those who reside in prison.

## Prison Culture

Charles Dickens, in *A Walk in a Workhouse*, wrote, "We have come to this absurd, this dangerous, this monstrous pass, that the dishonest felon is, in respect of cleanliness, order, diet, and accommodation, better provided for, and taken care of, than the honest pauper."[6] This is understood to mean that the living conditions of the criminal in the workhouse should be no better than that of the poorest laborer outside of the workhouse.

Early English law attempted to uphold this rule. An early English statute, the Poor Law Amendment Act of 1834 (PLAA)[7], first codified the **principle of least eligibility**. The principle simply means that the conditions provided (in this case, for the poor) by the government should not be better than the existence of the poorest member of society. Only the truly destitute would qualify for aid under the PLAA. This limitation was meant to discourage those who would simply take advantage of the public generosity.

**Principle of least eligibility** The view that those who commit crimes, particularly those in prison, are the least deserving members of society to benefit from government-provided assistance and support, such as education, vocational training, and other forms of support.

The principle of least eligibility has long been society's attitude for those who have been duly incarcerated. Edward Sieh suggests that if imprisonment is to act as a deterrent, then those in the lowest socioeconomic class should lead a better existence than those imprisoned.[8] The attitude that prison should present a harsh existence clashes with many who feel that the imprisoned are treated inhumanely at worst and indifferently at best. Some further believe that the treatment of America's prison and jail populations is unconstitutional.

Indeed, the federal government, along with most state and countless local authorities, has been under court order to improve conditions in prisons and jails.[9] Numerous cases brought before the Supreme Court have challenged the conditions of incarceration, arguing that deprivation of certain liberties constitutes cruel and unusual punishment. One notable case, *Pell v. Procunier* (1974), outlined a benchmark for prisoners' rights, establishing that each inmate "retains those First Amendment rights that are not inconsistent with his status as a prisoner."[10] Two years later, *Estelle v. Gamble* (1976) clarified that prison officials have a responsibility to provide medical care to prisoners because "deliberate indifference" to prisoners' medical needs was a violation of constitutional rights.[11] The concept of "deliberate indifference" has become something of a baseline in determining which prison conditions are deemed unconstitutional and which are legal forms of punishment.

The Supreme Court has ruled on countless issues related to prison policies and prisoners' rights, further delineating which practices are considered acceptable. Some of these rulings have sided with prison policies, such as *Procunier v. Martinez* (1974), which affirmed that prison staff can monitor inmates' mail for security purposes,[12] and *Block v. Rutherford* (1984), which upheld a Los Angeles prison's policy of denying prisoners any outside visitors.[13] Additionally, cases such as *Hudson v. Palmer* (1984) ruled that prisoners do not have a right to privacy and can be subjected to searches.[14] By contrast, other Supreme Court rulings have established prisoners' freedoms, such as *Cruz v. Beto* (1972), which gave inmates the opportunity to pursue their religious faith,[15] and *Wolf v. McDonnell* (1974), which stated that appropriate due process must be followed before sanctions can be levied on a prisoner.[16]

**Critical Thinking**

Should prisoners have a living standard while incarcerated that exceeds that of the poorest in our society? Should they have better medical care? Should they have better recreation? Should they have better food? Stated differently, should the poorest of the honest citizens have better living conditions than convicted felons in prison?

**Exhibit: *Estelle v. Gamble***

"An inmate must rely on prison authorities to treat his medical needs; if the authorities fail to do so, those needs will not be met. In the worst cases, such a failure may actually produce physical 'torture or a lingering death,' ... In less serious cases, denial of medical care may result in pain and suffering which no one suggests would serve any penological purpose. ...

"We therefore conclude that deliberate indifference to serious medical needs of prisoners constitutes the 'unnecessary and wanton infliction of pain,' ... This is true whether the indifference is manifested by prison doctors in their response to the prisoner's needs or by prison guards in intentionally denying or delaying access to medical care or intentionally interfering with the treatment once prescribed."

## Adjusting to Prison Life

When a convicted criminal is first incarcerated, he or she often undergoes a painful adjustment to prison. These experiences were dubbed the "pains of imprisonment" by sociologist Gresham Sykes, who in 1958 published *The Society of Captives*, his study of prison life at the New Jersey State Prison. His work is still considered one of the most important criminological studies conducted, and it laid the foundation for subsequent studies on the effects that prisons have on both inmates and staff.

Sykes explains that the **pains of imprisonment** on a person's personality, though less obvious than physical injuries, are "no less fearful."[17] These pains develop from those deprivations and frustrations that are felt by those who must suffer this threat to self-esteem and personal security. Sykes further notes that this loss of freedom, a scarcity of goods and services, the loss of domestic relationships, and so on, may be acceptable and unavoidable for those imprisoned, but the effects on the inmate must be recognized as serious, just as are physical punishments.[18]

**Pains of imprisonment** Described by Gresham Sykes as the pains that develop from the deprivations and frustrations of those who are incarcerated.

The **deprivation** of liberty, or loss of freedom, is the most obvious of the painful conditions of imprisonment.[19] In a prison, inmates are restricted to their assigned living space, most likely a cell. Sociologist Erving Goffman described prisons as **total institutions**.[20] The prison as a total institution defines the inmate and his or her entire life. Interaction with the world outside of the institution is tightly controlled, and perhaps nonexistent. For the incarcerated, other people have arranged their lives and the inmate must follow the same general routine that the other inmates are required to follow. The inmate's freedom to make choices is limited to what the institution allows.[21] Here, a new cultural and social world develops. Discipline is tightly controlled and rules are abundant. Punishment for infractions is usually swift and more severe than it is for similar violations in open society. Every aspect of the inmate's life is closely monitored, and privacy is minimal. Movement throughout the institution is tightly regulated by a system of permissions, passes, and standardized orderliness. In a total institution, human needs for the entire group are controlled by a bureaucracy.[22]

**Deprivation** Described in Sykes's "pains of imprisonment" as loss of freedom, a scarcity of goods and services, and the loss of domestic relationships for inmates.

**Total institution** An institution that provides everything a person needs for survival, usually at a lower level than what is enjoyed in an open society.

Additionally, the act of imprisonment represents the rejection of the individual from the free society. The inmate (and eventually, the former inmate) has sacrificed his or her status as a trusted member of society. There are certain rights that the inmate will find it difficult or impossible to regain, such as the right to vote, to hold political office, and to obtain certain employment. Sykes suggests that, in order for convicts to endure psychologically, they must find some method of "rejecting [their] rejectors."[23]

© Aerovista Luchtfotografie/
Shutterstock.com

The total institution is a fully self-contained community that provides all required needs and services to its residents.

The deprivation of goods and services, too, is outlined by Sykes as a pain of imprisonment.[24] Attempts to compare the free world with prison are difficult. In prison, the inmate exists in a threadbare environment. Even the floor is usually only bare concrete. The inmate has very few possessions; Bruce Hood, director of the Bristol Cognitive Development

Center in Bristol, England, maintains that prisons remove all belongings deliberately in order to eradicate inmates' sense of self.[25] Goffman describes what happens to an inmate when first introduced to the total institution as a stripping process. This process is one that mortifies, humiliates, degrades, and crushes the self-identity of the new inhabitant. The inmate is stripped of personal physical property that is placed in an area of inaccessible storage. The new inmate will then receive replacement property, such as a prison uniform, that defines his or her new self as an inmate. The effects of this experience are further compounded as the inmate witnesses the mortification process of fellow inmates.[26]

Though basic needs such as food, medical care, and dry living areas are provided, all these resources are strictly supervised and scheduled. An established square footage of living space, defined amounts of calories per day, and scheduled opportunities for exercise and recreation must be considered deprivations from what one is accustomed to in the free world. Though some may claim that the inmate is provided all that is necessary, inmates will define their "material impoverishment" as a painful loss.[27]

Another of Sykes's pains of imprisonment is the deprivation of autonomy. Autonomy, which means one's self-government or self-directing freedom and moral independence,[28] is effectively removed from the inmate through rules and orders that control the inmate's every movement.[29] Every aspect of an inmate's life is regulated. Even the inmate's personal mail may be read by prison staff looking for statements of which the organization does not approve. Moreover, sleeping hours, eating times, and the exact routes taken to different areas of the institution are strictly controlled.

Inmates often express frustration with certain rules, viewing them as nonsensical authoritarian acts on the part of the prison. Inmates may be prohibited from removing anything from the dining hall, even an item such as a packet of sugar that may simply have gone in the trash. Many prisons require that inmates walk down a small painted-off section of the sidewalk while the larger part is reserved for officers and staff. Inmates may also be required to maintain uniform short haircuts and to shave every day. Rules are often enforced without explanation. An inmate may be denied parole one day and told that mail has been delayed another, but rarely given reasons. Moreover, an inmate who demands justification is viewed as a troublemaker and will be treated as such.

This indifference and lack of concern are often institutional policy. The worry is that if prison staff explains the enforcement of the rules to inmates, the inmates may find the explanations unsatisfactory and will begin challenging the situation and arguing with captors. This could then disrupt the power relationship that prison staff must maintain over inmates.[30] This denial of their ability to make choices and the denial of rule and order explanations have profound effects on inmates' psyches. They are rendered helpless, weak, and dependent. The normal self-determining individual has lost his or her autonomy and must somehow develop a method to cope.[31]

Indeed, under Goffman's total institution concept, facilities such as prisons and jails, which protect society from those who are deliberate dangers, present a major division between those who live there and those who work there. This partitioning between staff and inmate is of necessary intent, as they share common sociological worlds with one another. The two sides must spend considerable time together, and each views the other with a great deal of disdain and distrust.[32]

John Irwin, a noted criminologist who himself was incarcerated for an armed robbery in the 1950s, states, "The human density and total lack of privacy expose them to one another in ways that can occur only in total institutions."[33] Everyone witnesses each other's most private activities and habits because the prisoner in a total institution no longer has the privacy once taken for granted.[34]

Irwin notes that the "functionaries" of the criminal justice system, officers and others, contribute to the degradation felt by prisoners because they openly express contempt and hostility toward them.[35] Inmates may view staff as mean and condescending. Staff often views inmates as untrustworthy and secretive. This divide is usually quite wide by design, and even the tones of voice used for communication between the groups are different. Security staff tends to speak to inmates in a firm and commanding tone, while inmates speak to staff in a tone of deference and respect, even if not genuine. Staff members tend to feel superior and inmates, in some ways, feel inferior.[36]

In the total institution, sociological roles are somewhat different from such roles in open society. In an open society, and in the case of the prison staff, people usually work for a particular reward, most often to be paid for their contributions. In a prison, inmates will work not for reward, but from threat of severe punishment if they do not. Another confusion of roles is that of family. The inmate cannot sustain a family existence in the customary sense. Of course, a staff member leaves at the end of a shift and returns to his or her family.[37] This widens the divide even further between the actors in this total institution.

The last of Sykes's pains of imprisonment is the deprivation of security that an inmate must endure. Sykes believes it is strange that society chooses to reduce criminal behavior in offenders by placing them in the company of so many other offenders.[38] Though an individual inmate may not prey on other inmates, it is reasonable for one to believe that others will take advantage of weaker and less resourceful inmates. Therefore, there are those within the criminal population who are considered criminal even to the average inmate. Since the inmate is living with and associating with outlaws of all sorts, it is rational for the inmate to experience, on some level, a lack of personal security.[39]

In prison, the inmate is aware that he or she will likely be faced with another aggressive inmate. The inmate believes that he or she must be prepared to defend person and property. If he or she loses this battle for dominance, the inmate will be considered weak and defenseless. Conversely, should the inmate win this battle, other inmates may seek to gain greater standing by defeating the one who has already earned a reputation for toughness. Since both success and failure in personal battles may bring additional attacks, the inmate never fully gains a sense of security.[40]

Despite these many deprivations, over time, many inmates begin to acclimate themselves to prison life. The term **prisonization** was coined in 1940 by Donald Clemmer, who defined it as "The taking on in greater or lesser degree of the folkways, mores, customs, and general culture of the penitentiary."[41] This refers to the socialization process into the culture and life of a prison inmate. Prisonization also describes those whose prison socialization has become so psychologically ingrained into their personalities that they would have difficulty readjusting to life outside of the prison. Prisonization may be thought of as a subcategory of institutionalization, which describes an excessive dependency on the institution.[42]

Prisonization is a process that does not happen to all incarcerated individuals at the same rate. However, most prisoners do learn a few simple rules, roles, and **inmate codes** very quickly. Inmates learn to behave as good cons **doing time**, meaning they are on their best behavior and are not causing trouble. They learn many informal codes of conduct for being an inmate, such as not getting involved in other inmates' personal affairs, refusing to report another inmate who is breaking rules, never crying or backing down from a fight, never associating with officers, and warning other inmates when an officer is approaching. These informal rules blend into the inmate subculture and allow them to coexist in very cramped and close living arrangements. These learned behaviors aid the progression of the prisonization process.

Prisonization has been identified as one of the variables that frustrate a former inmate's reintegration into open society. Many ex-inmates can never completely regain the social position they held before entering the institution. The stigmatization of being an ex-prisoner creates an individual who is secretive about his or her past and who wishes to conceal particular characteristics of his or her identity.[43] The effects of prisonization often lead inmates to internalize their emotions, which later interferes with their ability to form intimate interpersonal relationships, to find employment, or to gain a sufficient economic level. These frustrations of reintegration have been identified as possible contributing factors in recidivism.[44]

## Inmate Subcultures

The inmate culture and subcultures are defining factors in the prisonization of inmates. There are many subcultures to be found in correctional institutions. These sociological divisions may be positive or negative in nature. It appears that each institution has its own dominant culture and subcultures. The cultures deemed positive are those where inmates offer encouragement and support to other inmates for engaging in programs

---

**Prisonization** The taking on in greater or lesser degree of the customs and general culture of the penitentiary.

**Inmate code** Rules and roles that inmates adopt while incarcerated.

**Doing time** Jargon used by inmates to describe their good behavior.

that reinforce successful reentry and institutional behavior. Other cultures and subcultures are negative and create barriers to successful rehabilitative and reentry efforts. High-security institutions tend to have more negative cultures than do those of lesser security, though this is partly because these high-security institutions tend to have more inmates with strong criminal and anti-authority personalities. The negative cultures create a paradox of sorts. The more difficult the inmates become, the more staff will assert their control. This, in turn, will create a cycle of conflict with little chance of resolution.[45]

The indigenous model evolves from the isolation and loss of freedom an inmate suffers while incarcerated.

According to Kelly Cheeseman of Sam Houston State University, there are two predominant theories regarding inmate subcultures. One is the **importation** model, which simply means that the criminal culture one participates in outside of prison is often how the person will continue to behave inside the prison. Those inmates who were violent on the outside are likely to be violent on the inside. The inmate subcultures are therefore influenced by characteristics and experiences obtained before and outside of prison.[46]

The second of Cheeseman's major subculture theories is the **indigenous model**, also known as the deprivation model.[47] This model holds that those preexisting conditions of deprivation in a prison have a great effect on how the inmate will adjust to prison life. The indigenous model evolves from the isolation, constant monitoring, loss of possessions, and the loss of freedom an inmate experiences.[48] This is consistent with Sykes's pains of imprisonment and the other models discussed in this section. This model refers to the scarcity of all that was known socially and materially to the inmate. The deprivation of human wants and desires and the pains of imprisonment will be the primary factors in the individual's response to incarceration.[49]

According to Dr. Mandeep Dhami, et al., indigenous and importation models both explain how inmates adapt to prison. It has been found that each model may have a greater effect than the other on certain behaviors. Even different characteristics within each model may elicit certain manners of conduct. For instance, when trying to predict which inmates are more likely to violate institutional rules, the importation model—considering age, gender, and marital status—is a better predictor than the indigenous model. However, the importation model characteristics of education, mental illness, and substance abuse are not significant predictors of rule violations. Conversely, some researchers have found that indigenous characteristics, such as security, explain the incidence of violence against staff and other inmates.[50]

**Importation** The tendency for inmates to bring into the prison the criminal culture they participated in outside of prison.

**Indigenous model** A model that refers to the scarcity of all that was previously known socially and materially to the inmate. This model evolves from the isolation, constant monitoring, loss of possessions, and loss of freedom an inmate experiences.

## Gangs

One ever-present subculture in America's jails, prisons, and juvenile facilities, both public and private, is that of gangs. The importation model helps explain this culture. Inmates who belonged to a gang before coming to prison often continue their gang involvement behind bars. In fact, in early 2011, U.S. District Attorney Paul J. Fishman remarked in reference to a gang in New Jersey, "The presence of this gang is unacceptable, whether its leaders are on the streets or behind bars. Prison sentences must mean more than a change of a gang's base of operations."[51] This is a typical challenge that correctional authorities must address when setting gang policy in their institutions.

Inmates typically come from a wide geographic area and they represent all races and socioeconomic groups. Therefore, competing gangs are often imported into prison simply by chance. In addition, it should be noted that not all gangs are first formed on the street. Some gangs originate in prison; they are frequently referred to as "prison gangs." Gangs such as the Black Guerrilla Family and the Aryan Brotherhood are examples of pure prison gangs.[52]

The designation of a gang belongs to the greater category of "Security Threat Group." A *Security Threat Group*, or STG, is defined by the National Gang Crime Research Center as "any group of three or more persons with recurring threatening or disruptive behavior." Some definitions of an STG or a gang require that there be only two participants.[53] On the other hand, federal law defines a gang as numbering at least five participants.[54] However, in the sociological sense, a true social group must have three or more members,[55] so that will be the working definition in this chapter. Regardless of size, the overarching characteristic of an STG is that it poses a threat to the security of the institution.

Defining a gang is even more problematic than agreeing on the minimum number of its members. According to the United States Department of Justice, there is no nationally accepted standard definition of a gang. Therefore, different jurisdictions may have diverse definitions that may even disagree with one another. One measure that is standard in most gang definitions is that the group is involved in ongoing criminal activity.[56]

Gangs comprise all races and ethnicities, and include groups representing immigrants, youths, neighborhoods, motorcycles, drugs, and prisons.[57] Again, the importation theory of prison subcultures explains that many gang members bring their gang activity with them when they are admitted into prison. Therefore, gangs are found at almost all prisons, though statistics show there is more gang activity in state prisons than at their federal counterparts.[58]

### Critical Thinking

How might correctional officers protect weaker inmates? What alternatives for protection exist in a correctional institution?

Gang membership in the U.S. as of September 2008 was estimated at around 1 million. This is an increase of about 20% over 2005. It was estimated that about 90% of those gang members resided in local communities, with the rest being incarcerated in local, state, and federal correctional facilities. The FBI believes that some of the increase in gang membership is attributable to better reporting and identification methods by law enforcement. However, most of the increase is due to gang recruitment efforts and the release of incarcerated gang members. The three basic types of gangs identified by law enforcement are street gangs, prison gangs, and outlaw motorcycle gangs.[59]

## Street Gangs

**Street gangs** are those gangs that originate at the street level. These gangs are a significant security threat group because of the large geographic areas where they proliferate. National and regional-level street gangs have expanded their membership outside the United States to Mexico, Central America, and Canada. Currently, 11 national street gangs have been identified in one or more of these three areas.[60] Street gangs are imported into correctional facilities and are often found in jails and prisons; they will often continue running outside business from inside the prisons.

**Street gangs** Organized criminal networks that originate at the street level.

The Bloods street gang consists of large structured and smaller unstructured gangs that have joined together, forming a single culture. Most Blood members are African-American males, and membership may be as high as 20,000.[61] The Bloods were formed in the 1970s for protection against the Crips.[62]

The Crips street gang is estimated to have up to 35,000 members, mostly African-American males. Their main source of income is drug distribution. Secondary sources come from all manner of felony crime.[63]

Another significant street gang is the Latin Kings, a Chicago-based gang with an estimated membership of 20,000 to 35,000 nationwide. Most of the members are Mexican-American or Puerto Rican males. Again, the gang's main source of income is drug distribution, though the Latin Kings are also known for money laundering activities.[64]

## Prison Gangs

**Prison gangs** are organized criminal networks within the federal and state prison systems. These gangs also operate in communities, where they usually consist of members who belonged to the gang while incarcerated. Prison gangs frequently maintain alliances with other gangs both inside and outside prison, and remain highly influential even while behind bars. When a prison gang member is released from prison, he will often become a representative in his home community and will recruit members to perform criminal activity on behalf of the gang.[65]

**Prison gangs** Organized criminal networks within the federal and state prison systems.

One infamous prison gang, the Aryan Brotherhood, is composed mostly of Caucasian males. It is strongest in the Southwest and Pacific regions of the

United States. The Aryan Brotherhood is extremely violent and is known to commit murder-for-hire. Some of the Aryan Brotherhood membership is aligned with Mexican gangs to smuggle drugs into the Southwest from Mexico.[66]

The Black Guerrilla Family (BGF) prison gang was founded at California's San Quentin State Prison. Its organization is similar to that of a paramilitary organization. It is highly structured with a national charter, code of ethics, and oath of allegiance. The BGF operates mainly in California, Maryland, Missouri, and Georgia. The membership is relatively small, with around 300 members, all African-American males. Their main source of income is drug distribution.[67]

Many gangs use drug distribution and violence as sources of income.

One of the largest and most violent prison gangs is Neta, which began in Puerto Rico and spread to the mainland United States. Neta members in Puerto Rico exist only in prison rather than on the streets. Once a member is released from prison, he is no longer considered a member. Mainland Neta members, however, usually maintain membership after prison release. The main source of income for Neta is drug distribution.[68]

## Outlaw Motorcycle Gangs

**Outlaw motorcycle gangs** Organized criminal networks with a motorcycle lifestyle.

**Outlaw motorcycle gangs** are a serious threat to local public safety because of their extensive criminal activities. They are characteristically quick to use violence. Members engage in drug trafficking, weapons trafficking, and violent crime. They usually have a strong centralized leadership that implements rules, regulates membership, and coordinates criminal activity. It is estimated that there are between 280 and 520 outlaw motorcycle gangs in the United States that have a total membership of around 20,000.

The Hells Angels Motorcycle Club (HAMC) is one of the most well-known of the outlaw motorcycle gangs. This gang comprises about 2,500 members and has chapters in 26 foreign countries. The HAMC indulges in drug distribution, money laundering, extortion, homicide, assault, and motorcycle theft.[69]

Another outlaw motorcycle gang is the Mongols Motorcycle Club (MMC). The MMC is established mostly in the Southwest and Pacific regions. The gang numbers about 300 and consists mostly of Hispanics residing in the Los Angeles area. Many members of the Mongols formerly belonged to street gangs and have a long history of violence. The MMC is allied with several other gangs in opposition to the Hells Angels.[70]

The Outlaws Motorcycle Club consists of more than 1,700 members. Their main source of revenue is drug distribution. They are also involved in such crimes as assault, robbery, kidnapping, money laundering, extortion, fraud, arson, explosives, prostitution, and theft.[71]

## Critical Thinking

Most gangs earn income primarily from the distribution of drugs. The United States expends tremendous resources on the "war on drugs." Do you think that the current methods authorities use in this "war" are effective? How would you do things differently?

## Correctional Officer Subcultures

Within any organization or group of people, cultures and subcultures will ultimately develop. All cultures and subcultures share certain values, beliefs, and norms of behavior, influenced by their leaders, their followers, the national culture, the geographical environment, and the industry.[72] The industry of corrections has developed its own unique culture.

Just as prison inmates have developed their own subcultures, prison staff—particularly correctional officers—have done the same. Correctional officers have an occupation that offers danger every time they go to work. They are surrounded by hostile individuals who have already demonstrated their propensity for breaking laws and not conforming to society's prevailing culture. Officers also face long hours, shift work, and overtime that may or may not be desired.[73] Because prisons and jails never close, this 24-hour industry can make family life challenging. The working schedules are especially challenging for families with young children and even more challenging for single parents.[74]

There are norms of correctional officer behavior that are a part of the officers' code. Correctional officers expect each other to adhere to certain guidelines—some of which are "unwritten" rules. Among these rules: Officers are expected to show positive concern for fellow officers and always come to the aid of another officer in dangerous situations. Officers should always support each other in disputes with inmates and in punishments of inmates, and should never make another officer look bad in front of inmates. Officers are expected to maintain solidarity with each other against outside groups.[75]

## Exhibit: Florida State Correctional Officers' Code of Conduct.

I.  I will never forget that I am a public official sworn to uphold the Constitutions of the United States and the State of Florida.

II. I am a professional committed to the public safety, the support and protection of my fellow officers, and co-workers, and the supervision and care of those in my charge. I am prepared to go in harm's way in fulfillment of these missions.

III.   As a professional, I am skilled in the performance of my duties and governed by a code of ethics that demands integrity in word and deed, fidelity to the lawful orders of those appointed over me, and, above all, allegiance to my oath of office and the laws that govern our nation.

IV.   I will seek neither personal favor nor advantage in the performance of my duties. I will treat all with whom I come in contact with civility and respect. I will lead by example and conduct myself in a disciplined manner at all times.

V.   I am proud to selflessly serve my fellow citizens as a member of the Florida Department of Corrections.

Source: Florida Department of Corrections Website. http://www.dc.state.fl.us/vision.html

Correctional officers are trained to look for and address any signs of trouble.

The officers' code becomes a part of the correctional officers' subculture. This subculture is distinct from the larger culture of the organization that includes civilian staff and the administration. The behaviors of officers are observed and imitated by new recruits, and the culture of the correctional officer passes to newer generations. The new officers develop beliefs and thoughts that are similar to those of officers before them. Sometimes, this can lead to further conflict between officers and inmates. Officers develop a perception that inmates view them as the enemy. Officers typically strongly dislike inmates, and some may look for opportunities to make an inmate's life especially difficult. Moreover, they believe that inmates cannot be trusted.

Still, the subculture also develops positive traits in officers. Officers learn to anticipate trouble at any time. They learn what signs to look for to identify trouble, such as unusual quietness or loudness. An officer who does not develop the proper skills for detecting what is unusual or usual may be excluded from the subculture. Officers will also learn inmate management, though the officer subculture encourages as little interaction with inmates as possible.[76] The correctional officer subculture, like subcultures in other industries, can help the officers handle stress in an occupation that constantly puts them at risk.

There are many studies demonstrating that correctional officers experience higher levels of stress than most other occupations. Often, the correctional officer is required to perform the role of treatment counselor and custody officer at the same time. These seemingly opposite functions can lead to stress and eventually burnout among officers.[77]

Correctional officer role conflict occurs when an officer has conflicting orders. Role conflict also occurs when there is disagreement about how a task should be handled. An additional stressor on correctional officers is role ambiguity, which occurs when an officer does not have enough information about how to perform a particular job function, especially when responsibilities are vague and poorly defined. In some cases, policies are contradictory. These issues seem to afflict correctional officers more than many other occupations and are a significant cause of officer burnout.[78]

### Ethics and Professionalism

Smuggling in prisons is an ongoing concern. Heroin, marijuana, tobacco, other drugs, and weapons can all make their way into prisons throughout the country. Over a five-year stretch, the Bureau of Prisons recorded more than 2,800 positive drug tests for each of those years in federal prisons.[79] The same report recognizes that weapons smuggling is also a serious threat to the security of the institutions. Though there are several mechanisms in place to prevent the entry of contraband into prisons, the found weapons, drugs, and overdoses demonstrate a serious problem.

When officers are caught smuggling drugs, weapons, or other contraband into a jail or a prison, they are usually prosecuted. This general form of deterrence, however, has not stopped the problem. Why would an officer risk his or her occupation, reputation, and personal way of life by trying to introduce contraband into a correctional institution?

Correctional officers face many ethical dilemmas, and they generally receive training on how to handle such situations. The temptation, though, must be too great for some officers to resist.

Consider the following situation. A young officer, already struggling to meet monthly expenses, is soon expecting his first child. Correctional officer pay is not enough to support a growing family and to service the debts already accumulated. A friend of a friend offers him a few thousand dollars a month to take cell phones and drugs to a contact in the prison. Because he knows how the prison security system works, he knows he would likely be able to do so without being caught. It would be easy and profitable. What would you do?

Consider another situation. You are an experienced correctional officer approaching your 20th year. You have known some of your coworkers for most of that time, and many are considered good friends. One day, you see a fellow correctional officer and close friend drop what appears to be a small bag of marijuana while he is adjusting his clothing. What do you do? Do you ignore it? Do you demand to see it? Do you report it? What circumstances would you need to take into account?

## Growth of Corrections

When 2015 ended, the United States held more than 2.1 million people in jails and in prisons throughout the country. In addition, more than 4.6 million were on probation or parole.[80] Both the prison population and the imprisonment rate in the United States are the highest in the world.[81] One will find differences in statistical numbers depending upon the source. The figures above are the official United States government statistics and are more conservative than many others are. Therefore, depending on the source, one may find a much higher prison population and rate of incarceration than what has been quoted here.

In 2000, the United States had 3060 supervised adults per 100,000 in the adult correctional system. In 2015, the number had decreased to 2,710 supervised adults per 100,000 with 1 in 37 adult residents under United States supervision. It may help to think of other countries where, by American standards, people are oppressed and imprisoned without the cherished rights that we enjoy under our laws and customs. Rwanda, Cuba, Russia, and countries known for human rights violations have lower incarceration rates than does the United States.[82] Overall, including probation and parole, one in every 31 adults in this country is under some sort of correctional supervision.[83] Some feel this is a shameful indictment of our system of justice.

The dramatic increase in the prison population has affected the economy. As the rate of incarceration increases, the demand for correctional workers increases as well. Over 470,000 people in the United States were employed in corrections in 2014 according to the Bureau of Labor Statistics. Some rural areas have entire communities with local economies tied to correctional facilities.[84] The U.S. Labor Department projects about a 4% growth for the field of corrections through 2024.[85]

The growth of corrections is tied to several factors. One factor is mandatory sentencing laws, which put criminals behind bars for longer periods than in recent history. Another significant factor is the proliferation of "tough on crime" laws. Current laws that take a hard-line stance on crime have been legislated throughout the country in an effort to reduce crime. Whereas previously an individual might have served a fraction of an imposed sentence, the get-tough laws have created mandatory minimums that are closer to the imposed sentence. Some states now require an inmate to serve at least 85% of a sentence in prison before becoming eligible for probation or parole. Moreover, life sentences, true to their meaning, may mean that the person will never be allowed to go free.[86]

**FIGURE 8.1** COMPARISON OF IMPRISONMENT RATES (SELECTED COUNTRIES).

| Country | Prison Population Rate per/100,000 |
|---|---|
| Seychelles | 799 |
| USA | 666 |
| El Salvador | 574 |
| Cuba | 510 |
| Russian Federation | 436 |

*Source: http://www.prisonstudies.org/highest-to-lowest/prison_population_rate?field_region_taxonomy_tid=All&=Apply*

Some criminologists suggest that the trend to incarcerate more people for longer periods has reached a position where it is no longer effective. One prominent criminologist, James Q. Wilson, states that we have reached a point of diminishing returns on our correctional efforts and investment.[87] Wilson says that judges have always sentenced violent offenders to long sentences, but that we now are "dipping deeper into the bucket of person's eligibility for prison, dredging up offenders with shorter and shorter criminal records."[88] He explains that if we continue to lengthen prison sentences and increase the numbers of people sent to prison, a diminishing marginal return on crime rate reductions will occur. In other words, at some point, imposing longer sentences will have no more effect on the crime rate. Some would argue that this point has already passed.

## Special Populations

All manner of people are represented within the prison population—men, women, the young, the elderly, those with mental illnesses, those with physical illnesses, and those with physical disabilities. Every one of these subsets is represented by all races as well. Many of these special populations are segregated from other populations for security reasons as well as for medical and program functions.

### Female Inmates

Female inmates have special needs that are not typically required by the male population. They require the same generalists and specialists for health needs that any woman outside of prison requires. Moreover, as many as 10% of women are pregnant when they are incarcerated.[89]

The typical female prisoner has been sentenced for a nonviolent crime and is a recidivist, which means she has previously been incarcerated or on probation. Of all female inmates, one-third report that they were under the influence of drugs or alcohol when they were arrested. More than 80% had been drug users at some time in their lives, which is slightly higher than the rate for men, and about 40% had been in drug treatment at some point in their lives. Further, many have a history of sexual abuse.[90]

### Youthful Inmates

While there is a separate system for juvenile justice, some juveniles are tried and convicted in adult courts and sentenced as adults. Many states

© Kasinpoj Wiriyakajorntham/Shutterstock.com

Many facilities have special facilities for youthful offenders to separate them from adult inmates.

have special facilities for youthful offenders. Where this is not practical, the young and weak are typically segregated from the adult population. For example, in Florida, the Youthful Offender Act was passed in 1978. It was designed to improve youth corrections with the goal of successful reentry to open society. Since the act was first passed, it has expanded to provide vocational education and training, counseling, and public service opportunities to young inmates, and requires that the youthful offender attend substance abuse programs.[91]

The Florida Youthful Offender Act applies to those offenders who are under the age of 21 when sentenced. The act also includes those juveniles who have been tried and sentenced as an adult. Moreover, even if a court does not sentence an offender as youthful, the correctional authorities may designate those less than 25 years old as youthful offenders if they are deemed vulnerable in the adult prison population.[92]

### Elderly Inmates

Some researchers, such as Rikard and Rosenberg (2007), estimate that by the year 2020, 21% to 33% of prison residents will be elderly.[93] This increase is partially attributable to medical advances that extend life. However, substance abuse, lack of adequate diet, and poor medical care are found disproportionately in elderly criminals when compared to law-abiding seniors. This lifestyle places elderly offenders' health at about 11.5 years older physically and mentally than their non-incarcerated peers.[94]

An inmate typically is designated elderly at 50 years old. This reflects the physiological age averages discussed in the previous paragraph. Moreover, their elderly status is a reflection of poorer health, including chronic conditions, substance abuse issues, and the fact that they suffer psychological problems more than younger inmates do. An elderly inmate costs roughly three times as much to incarcerate as a younger inmate. They are also more likely to have committed violent acts. Seventy-five percent of elderly inmates are still serving time for their first offense.[95]

### Mentally Ill Inmates

The rate of mental illness among prison inmates is considerable. It is estimated that between 200,000 and 300,000 inmates suffer from mental illnesses, including bipolar disorder, schizophrenia, and major depression.[96] This makes the mentally ill percentage of the prison population two to four times higher than that of the general population.[97]

Mentally ill inmates often find it difficult to comply with the many rules and regulations that control prison populations. Mentally ill inmates tend to break rules at a higher rate than do other inmates. Often, rule breaking is the illness showing itself through aggression and disruptive behavior. These rule violators are regularly punished as discipline problems and without a diagnosis of mental health issues.[98]

Prison authorities have responsibility for the safety and security of staff and inmates. This often does not help the mentally ill inmate who is "acting out" and may be viewed as a discipline problem. Some prison systems have taken measures to diagnose and treat more discipline problems as psychological problems; however, some experts, such as Abramsky and Fellner (2003), maintain that there is an urgent need to reassess the disciplinary procedures as possible mental health issues.[99]

### Chronically Ill Inmates

Another important category of special needs inmates is those with chronic infectious illnesses such as hepatitis B and C, HIV, and AIDS. Much chronic infectious disease is imported into prisons and jails, but other illnesses arise from the sexual activity and drug use that take place in correctional facilities. Therefore, the spread of disease is of significant concern to correctional administrators.[100]

Since many diseases are spread through sexual and drug activity, some researchers have suggested that needle exchanges and condoms should be provided in prisons. Though there are no needle exchange efforts in the United States, some European countries have reported success with these programs. Those countries that have adopted needle exchanges have reported no increase in security issues.[101]

Only a few correctional facilities in the United States provide condoms, but the practice is standard in many other countries, including Canada. There is one such condom distribution program in Washington, D.C. A survey of 100 correctional officers and 300 inmates who participated in the program showed that condom distribution was largely supported and caused no additional security problems. Such prevention measures provide significant protection not only to the inmate population but to the general population as well, because most inmates will return to a life outside of prison.[102]

## Economic Realities

Government at all levels spent about $265 billion on police, courts, and corrections in 2012. Of this, $126 billion went for police protection, $57 billion went for the courts, and $80 billion went for corrections. Breaking it down further reveals that over half of all criminal justice spending came from local governments.[103] These expenses are quite heavy considering

## FIGURE 8.2  CRIMINAL JUSTICE EXPENDITURES BY LEVEL OF GOVERNMENT.

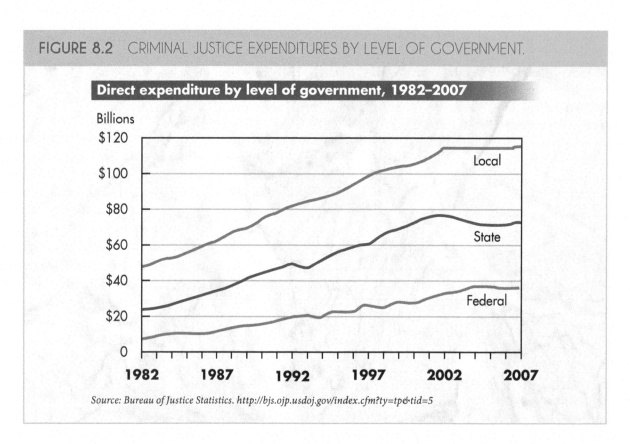

**Direct expenditure by level of government, 1982–2007**

Source: Bureau of Justice Statistics. http://bjs.ojp.usdoj.gov/index.cfm?ty=tp&tid=5

## FIGURE 8.3  EXPENDITURES BY CRIMINAL JUSTICE FUNCTION.

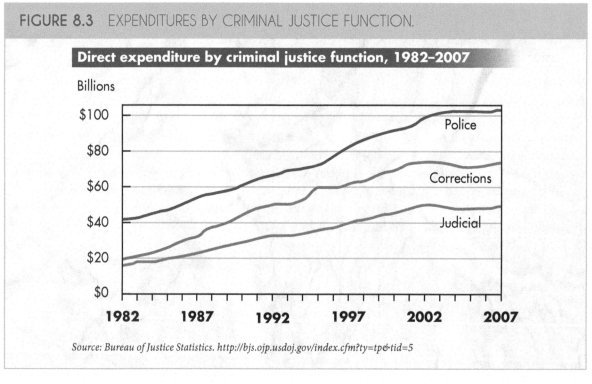

**Direct expenditure by criminal justice function, 1982–2007**

Source: Bureau of Justice Statistics. http://bjs.ojp.usdoj.gov/index.cfm?ty=tp&tid=5

that government budgets at all levels are facing difficult decisions regarding spending and resource allocation in the corrections system.

In 1982, $20 billion was spent on corrections at all levels of government. In 2012, this expense had increased 4 times to $80 billion. The realities of correctional expenses have caused the nation's elected leaders at all levels of government to reconsider how money is spent. Americans want prisons that will hold people accountable for their crimes and keep communities safe. However, citizens also deserve to have their tax money used in appropriate and intelligent ways.

One major reason for the escalating expenditures in corrections is the high rate of recidivism in the United States, which ultimately requires incarcerating the same individuals for multiple stints. A 2009 Pew study demonstrated that more than 40% of inmates will ultimately return to prison for new crimes.[104] For prison systems, reducing these high rates of recidivism is essential in order to help the incarcerated, protect the safety of American communities, and reduce state spending on corrections.

Many prison systems have established programs designed to aid inmates' rehabilitation and produce a positive prison culture that can demonstrably reduce recidivism. These programs include faith-based prisons, GED and college credit opportunities, vocational training, and substance abuse training. These reentry programs implemented at the state and federal levels show great promise for changing offenders' lives.

Many states are already demonstrating success with lowering recidivism through these prison programs. A study for the Florida Department of Corrections found that inmates who complete the programs designed to reduce recidivism are more successful than those who do not. Specifically, the study found that inmates who earned a GED are 8.7% less likely to recidivate, inmates who earn a vocational certificate are 14.6% less likely to recidivate, and inmates who complete substance abuse programs are 6.2% less likely to recidivate.[105]

The federal government, recognizing this pressing need for correctional transformation, has enacted legislation to aid the successful return to society for adults and juveniles leaving prison. In 2008, the Second Chance Act was enacted. The act allows for government agencies and nonprofits to receive grants that will aid in reducing recidivism. Programs such as substance abuse treatment, assistance in finding employment and housing, mentoring, and victim support are made available through these grants.[106] In 2009, $28 million was awarded to grant recipients. The following year saw an even larger allocation of grant money. In October 2010, more than $82 million was awarded to 187 grant recipients to reduce adult and juvenile recidivism, for reentry courts to monitor and provide treatment services, to establish and enhance existing substance abuse treatment programs, to improve education and vocational training at adult and juvenile facilities, to train inmates for technology jobs, and to provide mentors to adult and juvenile offenders.[107]

# Alternatives to Prison

As prison populations continue to expand, governments at all levels look for more ways to control costs. While doing this, they must also attempt to live up to the implied promise of returning repentant former criminals back to the streets as law-abiding citizens. The unfortunate truth, though, evidenced by alarming recidivism rates, is that many former prisoners return to criminal activity.

There are a number of objectives for imprisonment. One is that the convicted criminal is punished through deprivation of liberty. Another is that the criminal is incapacitated from committing further crimes while incarcerated. Presumably, rehabilitation efforts are attempted with the expectation that the individual will leave prison better able to live and work in a law-abiding manner.

Many of those sentenced to jail or prison come from disadvantaged socioeconomic backgrounds. Many are in prison for violent crimes, while others are in prison for nonviolent offenses. Some are incarcerated for traffic offenses or simple possession of illicit substances. Their crimes range from the most horrible imaginable to the relatively mundane and victimless, yet

**FIGURE 8.4** FY2010 SECOND CHANCE ACT GRANT PROGRAM APPLICATION RESULTS

**FY2010 SCA Grant Program Application Results**

| FY10 Grant Program | Total applications received | Total grants awarded | Total amount awarded |
|---|---|---|---|
| Adult Demonstration (101) | 145 | 52 | $27,324,543 |
| Juvenile Demonstration (101) | 39 | 14 | $7,955,996 |
| Reentry Courts (111) | 9 | 9 | $2,651,703 |
| Family-Based Substance Abuse Treatment (113) | 36 | 23 | $6,645,611 |
| Evaluate and Improve Education in Prisons, Jails, and Juvenile Facilities (114) | 12 | 1 | $2,463,635 |
| Technology Career Training Demonstration (115) | 44 | 7 | $4,679,466 |
| Substance Abuse & Criminal Justice Collaboration (201) | 77 | 22 | $11,705,855 |
| Adult Mentoring (211) | 613 | 50 | $13,968,672 |
| Juvenile Mentoring (211) | 214 | 9 | $5,018,909 |
| Total | 1189 | 187 | $82,414,390 |

Source: National Reentry Resource Center.http://www.nationalreentryresourcecenter.org/about/second-chance-act

are still eligible for sentences that may involve incarceration. This can easily compound already difficult issues in many lives. Incarceration interferes with an inmate's employment and family life. It also decreases the inmate's employment prospects after release and limits his or her access to other opportunities, such as an education financed with federal student loans.

Overcrowding of prisons is associated with the spread of infectious diseases such as tuberculosis and HIV. In addition, violence is always a possibility. These fears alone can create health problems associated with stress. Moreover, overcrowding generates the demand for more prison space, meaning more money must again be allocated to build, operate, and maintain these human warehouses.

For these and many other reasons, the criminal justice system utilizes a number of alternatives to prison. The goal of these alternatives, in addition to relieving overcrowding in prisons and giving less severe punishments to offenders who commit less severe crimes, is to move from a punishment model to one of restorative justice and to help reintegrate former criminals back into society.

## Probation and Parole: Effectiveness and Statistics

Probation is the most common form of modern court-imposed punishment. *Probation* is still a sentence, but unlike jail or prison, a sentence of probation is court-ordered supervision that is served while living in the community.[108] Probation may also be a part of a combined sentence in which the community supervision follows incarceration. Probation has three primary goals: rehabilitation, protection of society, and protection of victim rights.[109]

At yearend 2015, an estimated 4,650,900 adults were under community supervision—a decrease of 62,300 offenders from yearend 2014. About 1 in 53 adults in the United States was under community supervision at yearend 2015. This population includes adults on probation, parole, or any other post-prison supervision, with probationers accounting for the majority (81%) of adults under community supervision. The 1.3% decline observed in the adult community corrections population was due to the drop in the probation population. The probation population declined from an estimated 3,868,400 offenders at yearend 2014 to 3,789,800 at yearend 2015. The parole population continued to rise with a 1.5% increase, from 857,700 offenders at yearend 2014 to 870,500 at yearend 2015.[110]

Unlike probation, which is an actual sentence but is served in the community, *parole* is the early supervised release of someone already incarcerated. Often, probationers and parolees are supervised by the same state agencies. Many states and the federal government, however, have abolished parole.[111]

The federal government and many states have shifted away from indeterminate sentences, which establish a range rather than an exact length of a prison term, and now use determinate sentencing, which places mandatory, specifically set sentences on offenders and no longer offers parole. However, some states have defined mandatory sentencing as a percentage of time served. For instance, by statute, some states require that an offender serve at least 85% of a sentence in prison. The other 15% may be served on probation or parole depending on the offender's behavior while in prison. These statutes are known as truth-in-sentencing laws. In 1994, the federal government passed a law that provided funding to states that enacted truth-in-sentencing laws. As of 2008, 35 states qualified to receive the federal funding for truth-in sentencing.[112]

Economically speaking, the probation system is cheaper than incarceration. For example, for the fiscal year of 2012–2013 in the state of Florida, it cost an average of $47.50 per day to house an offender in prison,[113] while monitoring an offender on pretrial release. The cost of supervising a defendant in the community in Broward County is $1.48 per defendant per day, compared to a daily cost of $107.71 for housing a defendant in the Broward County Jail.[114]

**Critical Thinking**

Should states continue to use indeterminate sentencing structures and parole boards to release offenders early? Explain.

## Other Community-Based Alternatives

Community-based alternatives are used effectively for less serious crimes, so-called victimless crimes, and public order crimes. This is also cost-effective in that it does not cost as much to supervise someone in the community as it does to house them in a prison or in a jail. In 2010, at least 26 states have cut the budgets of their corrections departments.[115]

Many of the states that have cut corrections budgets have already increased efficiencies and are now looking to cut costs in other areas.[116] States have reduced inmate healthcare expenses, frozen officer hiring, reduced staff salaries, reduced staff benefits, and eliminated pay increases. Some are considering the consolidation of facilities and forgoing planned expansions.[117]

The largest savings in correctional budgets come from reducing the number of people who come to prison and the length of stay for those who do. Staffing accounts for up to 80% of a prison's budget. In order to reduce staffing, the number of inmates must be reduced. Therefore, states look for ways to close prisons, or at least parts of them, in order to achieve savings. In 2010, states found that they could identify offender populations that could be safely released from prison after serving reduced sentences. Much of these savings can be realized through community-based alternatives to incarceration.[118]

A variety of community-based alternatives are currently in use throughout the United States. House arrest allows an offender to live at his or her residence. The offender is restricted from activity outside the home. Usually, the individual is only allowed to leave for work, school, church, or court-approved activities. The offender is under close scrutiny and there is often electronic monitoring equipment in use to ensure compliance.

Electronic monitoring is often an active system whereby an ankle bracelet transmits a continuous signal to a landline telephone to verify the offender's location. Any deviation or attempts to tamper with the equipment will send a signal to the monitoring station to be reported to the proper authorities.[119] Many agencies are now using more advanced GPS devices, especially for high-risk sex offenders.[120]

© cherezoff/Shutterstock.com

House arrest allows an offender to live at his or her residence, but he or she is restricted from activity outside of the home.

**Halfway houses** are group homes that often house newly released offenders with nowhere else to go. They may not have family, friends, or anyone willing to give them a place to live, at least temporarily. Many halfway houses, however, are specifically for sex offenders; they provide a supervised residence and resources specifically designed for this population.

**Halfway house** A group home often used by newly released offenders who have nowhere else to go. Many halfway houses are specifically designed for sex offenders, providing a supervised residence and resources specifically designed for this population.

**Day reporting centers** are locations for offenders to receive services such as counseling, life skills education, drug abuse treatment, and substance abuse testing. The offender only reports according to a specified schedule and does not live there. These centers also offer access to community services for employment, housing, health services, proper identification, legal support, and wellness.

**Day reporting center** A location for offenders to receive services such as counseling, life skills education, drug abuse treatment, and substance abuse testing. The offender only reports according to a specified schedule and does not live there.

Community service is often an intermediate sanction imposed by a court. Community service is an unpaid service to the community, often at a nonprofit organization that provides a service to society. Sometimes a judge will impose community service that is related to an offender's skill. For instance, a person skilled with animals may work at a pet adoption center or a person with legal skills may work at a community legal aid center.

**Day fines** are popular in some European countries. A day fine is a fine that is based on a person's daily income. The amount of the fine is progressive in relation to the money the offender earns. The more income one has, the higher the fine.

**Day fine** A fine based on a person's daily income; the amount of the fine is progressive in relation to the money the offender earns.

## Critical Thinking

What factors do you think would or should influence a judge's decision to sentence an offender to confinement or to community supervision?

# Career Connections: Correctional Treatment Specialist

The United States Department of Labor publishes statistics and general information for a large number of occupations. Within these pages, the occupation outlook sections offer current and projected future needs. The highest rating outlook for employment in any given occupation is excellent. One of those occupations expected to have excellent growth and opportunity is that of correctional treatment specialist.[121]

Correctional treatment specialists plan educational and occupational programs to improve inmates' likelihood of a successful transition to open society.

Correctional treatment specialists may work from probation offices, jails, or prisons. They evaluate inmate progress, administer psychological tests, and work with probation and parole offices to coordinate inmate releases to community supervision. They also plan educational and occupational programs to improve inmates' likelihood of a successful transition to open society. In addition, they may provide anger management skills, drug and alcohol abuse education, and counseling related to crimes such as sexual offenses.[122]

Daily duties of the correctional treatment specialist may include referring offenders to social services agencies, determining specific needs for rehabilitation, consulting with attorneys and judges, and following up on offender progress. Further, the correctional treatment specialist will confer with the offender's family members to help tend to family business that may impede the inmate's transition or help the offender's family group. The correctional treatment specialist may also be required to testify in court.[123]

The correctional treatment specialist must have specific knowledge and skills. Some of the most important knowledge is that of counseling. The person in this occupation must understand how to use rehabilitative techniques for a population that may not be receptive to treatment and may have other mental ailments. They must also be able to evaluate the effects of treatment. Knowledge of psychology, law, public safety, sociology, computers, and other subjects is considered important.[124]

A bachelor's degree is often a requirement, as is a clean criminal record. Entry into this field may require extensive testing for psychological fitness, physical fitness, and drug use, as well as written exams. One must have good interpersonal skills and good report writing skills. Advancement in this field is often dependent upon experience, performance, and education. A graduate degree may be helpful or required for advancement into the senior ranks.[125]

# Chapter Summary

- Early English law first applied the "principle of least eligibility," meant to discourage anyone from intentionally having themselves completely cared for by the government by making such care no better than the most destitute of society. The principle of least eligibility has long been society's attitude for those who have been duly incarcerated.

- In 1958, sociologist Gresham Sykes presented a study on the effects that prisons have on both inmates and staff. Sykes explains that the pains of imprisonment on a person's personality, though less obvious than are physical injuries, are "no less fearful." Sykes explains that this loss of freedom, a scarcity of goods and services, the loss of domestic relationships, and so on, may be acceptable and unavoidable for those imprisoned, but the effects on the inmate must be recognized as serious, just as are physical punishments.

- Erving Goffman described prisons as total institutions. In the total institution, everything is provided for those who reside there. All aspects of life are conducted within the total institution. Rules are abundant and punishment is swift.

- The term prisonization was first used in 1940 by Donald Clemmer, who defined it as "the taking on in greater or lesser degree of the folkways, mores, customs, and general culture of the penitentiary." This refers to the socialization process into the culture and life of a prison inmate. Prisonization also describes those whose prison socialization has become so psychologically ingrained into their personalities that they would have difficulty readjusting to life outside of the prison.

- There are many subcultures in correctional institutions. The importation model means that the criminal culture one participates in outside of prison is often how the person will continue to behave inside the prison. The indigenous model holds that the preexisting conditions of deprivation in a prison have a great effect on how the inmate adjusts to prison life.

- Gangs present an ongoing problem for correctional facilities. Gangs originate from the street and in prison. The designation of a gang belongs to the greater category of "Security Threat Group," defined by the National Gang Crime Research Center as "any group of three or more persons with recurring threatening or disruptive behavior." The three basic types of gangs identified by law enforcement are street gangs, prison gangs, and outlaw motorcycle gangs.

- The industry of corrections has developed its own unique cultures and subcultures among both inmates and correctional officers. Inmates and officers each adhere to certain unwritten rules to help them adapt to the daily routines of the prison culture.

- When 2015 ended, roughly 2.1 million people were incarcerated in the United States and more than 4.6 million were on probation or parole. Both the prison population and the imprisonment rate in the United States are the highest in the world. Government at all levels spent about $265 billion on police, courts, and corrections in 2012.

- Because of the high cost of incarcerating inmates, states look for alternative methods to punish offenders in order to achieve savings. Such alternatives include probation, parole, and community-based alternatives such as house arrest, halfway houses, day reporting centers, community service, and day fines.

## Critical Thinking?

1. Why is it less expensive to supervise offenders using methods other than incarceration? Should these alternatives be expanded? Why? Is money the only concern?

2. Are those who are incarcerated entitled to free medical care? If so, to what level? Should there be a limit on medical procedures that inmates are allowed to receive?

3. What categories of offender should be subjected to electronic monitoring? What categories of offender should not be candidates for electronic monitoring?

4. How might inmates lessen the pains of imprisonment? How would you attempt to lessen these pains should you be imprisoned?

5. How would you explain the rising prison population?

6. What effects might prison overcrowding have on treatment programs?

7. Do you believe the failure rate of recidivism is too high? What can be done to correct the problem?

8. Gang members in prisons are sometimes separated. What might be an undesirable result of gang member separation?

9. Should a correctional treatment specialist have correctional officer training as well? Should they receive training in defensive tactics?

10. What types of rights should inmates lose? Should there be any loss of rights for those who have completed their sentences? Why or why not?

## Media

**National Institute of Corrections:** http://nicic.gov/
The National Institute of Corrections helps to shape and advance effective correctional practice and public policy.

**American Probation and Parole Association:** http://www.appa-net.org/eweb/

The American Probation and Parole Association is actively involved with probation, parole, and community-based corrections, in both adult and juvenile sectors.

**Bureau of Justice Statistics:** http://www.bjs.gov
This is a premier website for law enforcement and correctional statistics.

# Endnotes

[1]  Secter, B. (1966, July 13). "The Richard Speck Case." *Chicago Tribune.* Retrieved from http://www.chicagotribune.com/news/politics/chi-chicagodays-richardspeck-story,0,4911196.story

[2]  Ibid.

[3]  *Furman v. Georgia,* 408 U.S. 238 (1972). The death penalty was reinstated in *Gregg v. Georgia,* 428 U.S. 153 (1976).

[4]  Olson, J. *Historical Dictionary of the 1960s.*

[5]  Ibid.

[6]  Dickens, C. (1850). *A Walk in a Workhouse.* Retrieved from http://www2.hn.psu.edu/faculty/jmanis/dickens/pieces.pdf

[7]  The Poor Law Amendment Act of 1834." (1834). *The Workhouse.* Retrieved from http://www.workhouses.org.uk/poorlaws/1834act.shtml

[8]  Sieh, E. W. (1989). "Less Eligibility: The Upper Limits of Penal Policy." *Criminal Justice Policy Review, 3*(2), 159–183.

[9]  Rubin, E. L., & Feeley, M. M. (2003, April). "Judicial Policy Making and Litigation against the Government." *University of Pennsylvania Journal of Constitutional Law,* 617.

[10]  *Pell v. Procunier,* 417 U.S. 817, 822 (1974).

[11]  *Estelle v. Gamble,* 429 U.S. 97 (1976).

[12]  *Procunier v. Martinez,* 416 U.S. 396 (1974).

[13]  *Block v. Rutherford,* 486 U.S. 576 (1984).

[14]  *Hudson v. Palmer,* 468 U.S. 517 (1984).

[15]  *Cruz v. Beto,* 405 U.S. 319 (1972).

[16]  *Wolff v. McDonnell,* 94 S.Ct. 2963 (1974).

[17]  Sykes, G. (1958). *The Society of Captives: A Study of a Maximum Security Prison.* Princeton, NJ: Princeton University Press.

[18]  Ibid.

[19]  Ibid.

[20]  Goffman, E. (1961). *Total Institutions.* Retrieved from http://www.markfoster.net/neurelitism/totalinstitutions.pdf

[21]  Ibid.

[22]  Ibid.

[23]  Sykes, 1958.

24    Ibid.

25    "Mine!" *Scientific American Mind, 22*(4), 59.

26    Goffman, 1961.

27    Sykes, 1958.

28    "Autonomy." (2011). *Merriam-Webster Dictionary.* Retrieved from http://www.merriam-webster.com/dictionary/autonomy

29    Sykes, 1958.

30    Ibid.

31    Ibid.

32    Goffman, 1961.

33    Irwin, J. (1992). *The Jail.* Berkeley, CA: University of California Press, 73.

34    Ibid.

35    Ibid., 74.

36    Goffman, 1961.

37    Ibid.

38    Sykes, 1958.

39    Ibid.

40    Ibid.

41    Clemmer, D. (1940). *The Prison Community.* Boston, MA: Christopher Publishing House, 279.

42    O'Toole, M. (Ed.). (2003). "Institutionalization." In *Miller-Keane Encyclopedia and Dictionary of Medicine, Nursing, and Allied Health* (7th ed.). Philadelphia, PA: W.B. Saunders.

43    Goffman, 1961.

44    Harrison, B., & Schehr, R. C. (2004). "Offenders and Post-Release Jobs: Variables Influencing Success and Failure." *Journal of Offender Rehabilitation, 39*(3), 35–68.

45    *Report of the Task Force on Security, Respect.* (2008). Correctional Service Canada.

46    Cheeseman, K. (2003). "Importing Aggression: An Examination and Application of Subculture Theories to Prison Violence." *The Southwest Journal of Criminal Justice, 1*(1), 24–38. Retrieved from http://www.utsa.edu/swjcj/archives/1.1/Cheeseman.pdf

47    Goffman, 1961; Sykes, 1958; Sykes & Messinger, 1960.

48    National Council on Crime and Delinquency. (1994). *Understanding why Inmates are Misclassified.* Retrieved from http://static.nicic.gov/Library/011994.pdf

49    Dhami, M. K., Ayton, P., & Loewenstein, G. (2007). "Adaptation to Imprisonment: Indigenous or Imported?" *Criminal Justice and Behavior.* Retrieved from http://sds.hss.cmu.edu/media/pdfs/loewenstein/AdaptPrisonment-Indigenous.pdf

50    Ibid.

51    United States Attorney District of New Jersey. (2011, January). *Sweeping Racketeering Indictment Charges 15 Members of the Fruit Town and*

*Brick City Brims Bloods Set.* Retrieved from http://www.atf.gov/press/releases/2011/01/012411-new-sweeping-racketeering-indictment-charges-15-members-of-the-fruittown-and-brick-city-brims-bloods-set.pdf

[52] Knox, G. W. (2005). *The Problem of Gangs and Security Threat Groups (STG's) in American Prisons Today: Recent Research Findings from the 2004 Prison Gang Survey.* Retrieved from http://www.ngcrc.com/corr2006.html

[53] Ibid.

[54] 18 U.S.C. § 521.

[55] Knox, 2005.

[56] "Gangs." (2006). *United States Department of Justice Attorney's Bulletin, 54*(3).

[57] Ibid.

[58] Ibid.

[59] FBI National Gang Intelligence Center. (2009). *National Gang Threat Assessment 2009.* Retrieved from http://www.fbi.gov/stats-services/publications/national-gang-threat-assessment-2009-pdf

[60] Ibid.

[61] United States Department of Justice. (2008). *National Drug Intelligence Center, Attorney General's Report to Congress on the Growth of Violent Street Gangs in Suburban Areas.* Retrieved from http://www.justice.gov/ndic/pubs27/27612/appendb.htm

[62] Ibid.

[63] Ibid.

[64] Ibid.

[65] FBI National Gang Intelligence Center, 2009.

[66] Ibid.

[67] United States Department of Justice. (2008). "Appendix B. National-Level Street, Prison, and Outlaw Motorcycle Gang Profiles." *Attorney General's Report to Congress on the Growth of Violent Street Gangs in Suburban Areas.* Retrieved from http://www.justice.gov/ndic/pubs27/27612/appendb.htm

[68] Ibid.

[69] Ibid.

[70] Ibid.

[71] Ibid.

[72] Smircich, L. (1983). "Concepts of Culture and Organizational Analysis." *Administrative Science Quarterly,* 342.

[73] Bureau of Labor Statistics. (2011). "Correctional Officers." *Occupational Outlook Handbook, 2010–11 Edition.* Retrieved from http://www.bls.gov/oco/ocos156.htm

[74] Dial, K. C., & Johnson, W. W. (2008). "Working Within the Walls: The Effect of Care From Coworkers on Correctional Employees." *Professional Issues in Criminal Justice,* 3(2), 17–31. Retrieved from https://kucampus.kaplan.edu/documentstore/docs09/pdf/picj/vol3/issue2/PICJ_Volume3_2_dial.pdf

75    Kauffman, K. (1988). *Prison Officers and Their World.* Cambridge, MA: Harvard University Press, 86.

76    Marquart, J. W., & Crouch, B. M. (1984). "Coopting the Kept: Using Inmates for Social Control in a Southern Prison." *Justice Quarterly, 1,* 491–509.

77    Lambert, E. G., Cluse-Tolar, T., & Hogan, N. L. (2007). "This Job is Killing Me: The Impact of Job Characteristics on Correctional Staff Job Stress." *Applied Psychology in Criminal Justice, 3*(2). Retrieved from http://www.apcj.org/documents/3_2_correctionalstaff.pdf

78    Ibid.

79    Federal Bureau of Prisons. (2003). *The Federal Bureau of Prisons' Drug Interdiction Activities.* Retrieved from http://www.justice.gov/oig/reports/BOP/e0302/final.pdf

80    Bureau of Justice Statistics. (2016). *Correctional Populations in the United States, 2016.* Retrieved from https://www.bjs.gov/content/pub/pdf/cpus15.pdf

81    Walmsley, R. (2008). *World Prison Population List* (8th ed.). Retrieved from http://www.kcl.ac.uk/depsta/law/research/icps/downloads/wppl-8th_41.pdf

82    Ibid.

83    Kirchhoff, S. M. (2010). "Economic Impacts of Prison Growth." *Congressional Research Service.* Retrieved from http://www.fas.org/sgp/crs/misc/R41177.pdf

84    Ibid.

85    Bureau of Labor Statistics, 2011.

86    Ditton, P. M., & Wilson, D. J. (1999). *Truth in Sentencing in State Prisons* (NCJ 170032). Retrieved from http://bjs.ojp.usdoj.gov/content/pub/pdf/tssp.pdf

      Mauer, M., King, R. S., & Young, M. C. (2004). "The Meaning of 'Life': Long Prison Sentences in Context." *The Sentencing Project.* Retrieved from http://www.hawaii.edu/hivandaids/The_Meaning_Life__Long_Prison_Sentences_in_Context.pdf

87    Wilson, J. Q. (1995). "Crime and Public Policy." In J. Q. Wilson & J. Petersilia (Eds.), *Crime* (pp. 489–507). San Francisco, CA: Institute for Contemporary Studies Press.

88    Ibid., 501.

89    Maruschak, L. M. (2011). "Medical Problems of Prisoners." *Bureau of Justice Statistics.* Retrieved from http://www.bjs.gov/content/pub/html/mpp/mpp.cfm

      Law Students for Reproductive Justice. (2008). *Women in Prison.* Retrieved from http://lsrj.org/documents/factsheets/08-09_Women_in_Prison.pdf

90    U. S. Department of Justice. (1999). *Substance Abuse and Treatment, State and Federal Prisoners.*

91    Florida Senate. (2010, October). *Youthful Offender Designation in the Department of Corrections, Interim Report 2011–114.*

92    Ibid.

93    Rikard, R. V., & Rosenberg, E. (2007). "Aging Inmates: A Convergence of Trends in the American Criminal Justice System." *Journal of Correctional Health Care, 13*(3), 150–162.

94    Doughty, P. (1999). *A Concern in Corrections: Special Health Needs.* Oklahoma City, OK: Oklahoma Department of Corrections.

95    Sheppard, R. (2001, April 9). "Growing Old Inside." *Maclean's,* 30–33.

96    Abramsky, S., & Fellner, J. (2003). "Ill Equipped: U.S. Prisons and Offenders with Mental Illness." *Human Rights Watch.* Retrieved from http://www. hrw.org/reports/2003/usa1003/usa1003.pdf

97    Fellner, J. (2006). "A Corrections Quandary: Mental Illness and Prison Rules." *Harvard Civil Rights-Civil Liberties Law Review, 41*(2), 391–412. Retrieved from http://www.law.harvard.edu/students/orgs/crcl/vol41_2/ fellner.pdf

98    Abramsky & Fellner, 2003.

99    Ibid.

100   Hammett, T. M. (2006, June). "HIV/AIDS and Other Infectious Diseases Among Correctional Inmates: Transmission, Burden, and an Appropriate Response." *American Journal of Public Health, 96*(6), 974–978.

101   Ibid.

102   Ibid.

103   Bureau of Justice Statistics. (2015) Justice Expenditure and Employment Extracts, 2012 - Preliminary Justice Expenditure and Employment Extracts, 2012 – Preliminary. Retrieved from https://www.bjs.gov/index. cfm?ty=pbdetail&iid=5239

104   Pew Center on the States. (2010, April). *Prison Count 201.* Washington, D.C.

105   Florida Department of Corrections. (2001). *Analysis of the Impact of Inmate Programsupon Recidivism.*

106   Council of State Governments Justice Center. (n.d.). "Second Chance Act." *National Reentry Resource Center.* Retrieved from http://www. nationalreentryresourcecenter.org/about/second-chance-act

107   Ibid.

108   Glaze, L. E., & Bonczar, T. P. (2010). *Probation and Parole in the United States, 2009* (NCJ 231674). Retrieved from http://bjs.ojp.usdoj.gov/content/ pub/pdf/ppus09.pdf

109   "Probation." (2011). *FindLaw.* Retrieved from http://criminal.findlaw.com/ crimes/criminal_stages/stages-alternative-sentences/probation.html

110   Bureau of Justice Statistics. (2016). *Correctional Populations in the United States, 2015.* Retrieved from https://www.bjs.gov/content/pub/pdf/cpus15.pdf

111   Federal Bureau of Prisons. (2011). *Brief History of the Bureau of Prisons.* Retrieved from http://www.bop.gov/about/history.jsp

112   Ditton & Wilson, 1999.

113   Florida Department of Corrections. (2010). *Annual Statistics for Fiscal Year 2009–2010.*

114   Piquero, A. (2010). *Cost-Benefit Analysis for Jail and Alternatives to Jail.* Florida State University.

115   Scott-Hayward, C. S. (2009). "The Fiscal Crisis in Corrections: Rethinking Policies and Practices." *Center on Sentencing and Corrections.* Retrieved from http://www.pewcenteronthestates.org/uploadedFiles/Vera_state_ budgets.pdf

116    Ibid.

117    Ibid.

118    Ibid.

119    Bottos, S. (2008). "An Overview of Electronic Monitoring in Corrections: The Issues and Implications." *Correctional Service Canada.* Retrieved from http://www.csc-scc.gc.ca/text/rsrch/reports/r182/r182-eng.pdf

120    DeMichele, M., & Payne, B. (2009). "Using Technology to Monitor Offenders: A Community Corrections Perspective." *American Correctional Association.* Retrieved from https://aca.org/fileupload/177/ahaidar/DeMichele_Payne.pdf

121    U.S. Department of Labor. (2011). Retrieved from http://bls.gov

122    Ibid.

123    Occupational Information Network. (n.d.). *Probation and Correctional Treatment Specialists.* Retrieved from http://www.occupationalinfo.org/onet/27305c.html

124    Ibid.

125    Ibid.

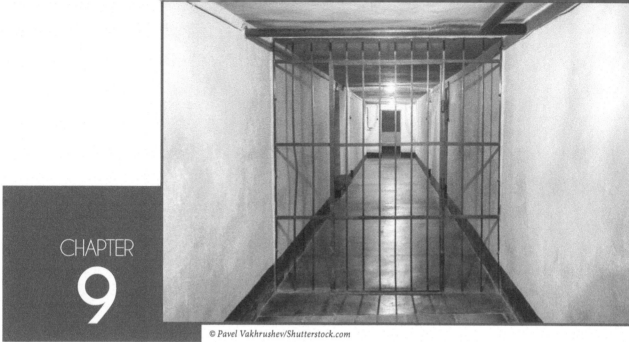

© Pavel Vakhrushev/Shutterstock.com

# Special Issues in Corrections

## KEY TERMS

Aftercare

Barriers to reintegration

Criminogenic needs

Discretionary release

Expungement

Fidelity to program design

Mandatory release

Offender risk

Reentry

Reentry courts

Sanctions

Second Chance Act

Therapeutic Communities (TC)

Victim-offender mediation

Vocational training

Work release centers

# CHAPTER OBJECTIVES

1 Understand why an increased emphasis on rehabilitation is difficult to achieve within prisons.

2 Summarize the range of rehabilitative needs of prison inmates and the degree to which these needs are met in prison.

3 Evaluate the advantages and challenges of the provision of rehabilitative programs within prisons.

4 Evaluate the degree to which inmates are prepared for their return to society.

5 Identify the needs of those released from prison and the means by which these needs can or cannot be met by the justice system.

6 Identify the factors that can influence recidivism rates and prisons' capacity to influence these factors.

7 Critique whether recidivism rates are a good gauge of the effectiveness of prisons.


## Case Study: Return to Society

For the typical person released from prison and attempting to reenter society as a law-abiding citizen, there is a 50-50 chance that they will end up back in prison within a few years.[1] For those who are successful at reentry, there are many factors that support this transition, including a personal commitment to change, participation in rehabilitative programs that are designed based on scientific knowledge about human behavior, and the support of family members and community.

JB, an Illinois inmate in 2010, is one such example. The 35-year-old JB had been on probation numerous times and in and out of jail, and this time he decided he wanted to change. During his processing through the Illinois Department of Corrections, he was asked a series of questions designed to gauge the extent and nature of his substance abuse problem, and his need for treatment. JB had been through this processing system every time he went to prison, and usually only gave the answers he thought the corrections staff wanted to hear. This time, he decided to tell the truth, and described his long-term abuse of alcohol, cocaine, and marijuana. He was determined to be in need of treatment. He met the eligibility criteria to participate in a prison-based drug treatment program, and, fortunately for him, there was a slot open in the program. He was one of the lucky ones—the one out of every five inmates needing treatment who actually receives treatment.[2] During the next 12 months JB participated in daily group treatment led by certified substance abuse counselors, attended **vocational training**, and began to reconnect with his children. Upon release from prison, he was required to attend outpatient treatment multiple times per week, check in with his parole agent, and search for a job so he could support himself. Fortunately, he was placed in a recovery home, a place where he would live in a drug-free environment, during his first four months of the transition back to the free world. After a few months he was able to find a job as a mentor for a youth violence prevention program, moved in with and married a woman he met through a church group he participated in, and was finally able to succeed in the reentry experience at which he had failed so many times before.

LB was a woman sentenced to prison in the same state, around the same time as JB. She too had been through the system multiple times, this time being convicted and sentenced to prison for retail theft. Because of time she spent in jail awaiting her conviction, and good conduct credits, her prison sentence of 18 months would ultimately keep her behind bars for just a few months. During that time, she did not participate in any type of substance abuse treatment program, for two main reasons: she did not disclose her addiction to staff, and her period of incarceration was so short that she would not have moved up the waiting list in time to access treatment while in prison. Upon her release, with little support and no changes in her thinking pattern, she moved in with friends from her past. Within days of her release, she was back to using drugs, with deadly consequences. After just three days of reentry, LB died of a heroin overdose. It is likely that if she had not died, she would have ended up rearrested and back in prison, a fate experienced by so many other people released from prison.

It is important to realize the potential successes of the hundreds of thousands of JBs who leave prison every year, and the extreme tragedy that the LBs and their families experience when rehabilitation and successful reentry are not achieved. For those with a commitment to change, access to effective treatment interventions both while incarcerated and after release, and acceptance and support from family members and society as a whole, successful reentry is possible. Without these positive forces, those reentering society are often destined to continue the cycle of crime and incarceration, with expensive and potentially tragic outcomes for themselves, their families, or their victims.

# Introduction

The media's portrayal of the reentry experiences of those released from prison or jail often focuses on celebrities; the experiences of the typical person trying to reenter society and lead a productive life are usually quite different. In the past two years, prominent NFL football players Michael Vick and Plaxico Burress experienced reentry from prison back to society. Similarly, Lindsay Lohan has been released from jail more than once following sentences for driving under the influence and shoplifting; in 2010, she was released from jail—where she was held in solitary confinement for her own safety—and ordered to enter a drug treatment program. For Vick and Burress, their

**Vocational training** The provision of classes and instruction designed to provide individuals with specific skills for entry into specific labor markets.

reentry included being signed to multimillion-dollar contracts to continue playing football. In Lohan's case, she left jail to enter a private drug treatment program, and after completion, returned to her multimillion-dollar Venice Beach mansion to continue her "reentry" into society.

While these examples of celebrity reentry from incarceration capture the public's attention, they are in reality extremely uncharacteristic of what most people released from prison face. The vast majority of people released from prison in the United States do not have even minimum-wage jobs awaiting them upon release, let alone multimillion-dollar contracts, and often are shunned and ostracized by society, not celebrated and cheered.

The prison population in the United States reflected an average annual change by 1.09% increase from 2000 through 2014, from a total of persons held in custody in state and federal prisons and in local jails. In 2015 the total number of persons in custody was 2,168,400 inmates.[3]

One factor that has maintained these large numbers of adults in prison, and the substantial volume of admissions and exits from prison annually, has been the relatively high rate of recidivism, resulting in what some call the "revolving door" of corrections. About two-thirds (67.8%) of released prisoners were arrested for a new crime within three (3) years, and three-quarters (76.6%) were arrested within five (5) years. ** These high numbers of people returning to communities throughout the United States from prisons, and high rates of recidivism, have led many to call for increased rehabilitative programming in prisons and improved reentry services and support for inmates after their release.[3]

Just as those released from prison face challenges returning to society, prison administrators face challenges as they try to accomplish the multiple goals society has for prisons. There are a few indisputable facts that must be kept in mind when considering **reentry**: 1) most prison inmates have extensive, multiple criminogenic needs when they enter prison, 2) relatively few inmates have these needs met while incarcerated, 3) most people sentenced to prison are eventually released from prison, and 4) the rate at which those released from prison are rearrested and returned to prison suggests that, as a whole, much progress is needed to improve inmate reentry in the United States.

**Reentry** The processes whereby the formerly incarcerated return to society, seeking to establish positive ties to the community and engage in law-abiding behaviors.

For the most part, this chapter focuses on the issues surrounding reentry from state prisons, and not local jails, since most jails serve as pretrial detention facilities and house inmates for relatively shorter periods of incarceration than prisons. However, those released from jail often experience some of the same problems and hurdles associated with reentry as do those coming out of state prisons, with unmet rehabilitative needs, returning to criminogenic environments, and the social stigma of having been incarcerated. Further, in many jurisdictions inmates under the custody of the state prison system serve their sentences in local jails due to crowding in state prisons.

With the increase in the U.S. prison population has come an increase in reentry to society, increased demands on community-based service providers, and increased numbers of individuals under parole supervision.

| Year | Total correctional population[a] | Community supervision | | | Incarcerated[b] | | |
|---|---|---|---|---|---|---|---|
| | | Total[a,c] | Probation | Parole | Total[a] | Local jail | Prison |
| 2000 | 6,467,800 | 4,564,900 | 3,839,400 | 725,500 | 1,945,400 | 621,100 | 1,394,200 |
| 2005 | 7,055,600 | 4,946,600 | 4,162,300 | 784,400 | 2,200,400 | 747,500 | 1,525,900 |
| 2006 | 7,199,600 | 5,035,000 | 4,236,800 | 798,200 | 2,256,600 | 765,800 | 1,568,700 |
| 2007 | 7,339,600 | 5,119,000 | 4,293,000 | 826,100 | 2,296,400 | 780,200 | 1,596,800 |
| 2008 | 7,312,600 | 5,093,400 | 4,271,200 | 826,100 | 2,310,300 | 785,500 | 1,608,300 |
| 2009 | 7,239,100 | 5,019,900 | 4,199,800 | 824,600 | 2,279,700 | 767,400 | 1,615,500 |
| 2010 | 7,089,000 | 4,888,500 | 4,055,900 | 840,800 | 2,279,100 | 748,700 | 1,613,800 |
| 2011 | 6,994,500 | 4,818,300 | 3,973,800 | 855,500 | 2,252,500 | 735,600 | 1,599,000 |
| 2012 | 6,949,800 | 4,790,700 | 3,944,900 | 858,400 | 2,231,300 | 744,500 | 1,570,400 |
| 2013 | 6,899,700 | 4,749,800 | 3,912,900 | 849,500 | 2,222,500 | 731,200 | 1,577,000 |
| 2014 | 6,856,900 | 4,713,200 | 3,868,400 | 857,700 | 2,225,100 | 744,600 | 1,562,300 |
| 2015 | 6,741,400 | 4,650,900 | 3,789,800 | 870,500 | 2,173,800 | 728,200 | 1,526,800 |
| Average annual percent change, 2007–2015 | -1.1% | -1.2% | -1.6% | 0.7% | -0.7% | -0.9% | -0.6% |
| Percent change, 2014–2015 | -1.7% | -1.3% | -2.0% | 1.5% | -2.3% | -2.2% | -2.3% |

Note: Estimates were rounded to the nearest 100 and may not be comparable to previously published BJS reports due to updated information or rounding. Counts include estimates for non responding jurisdictions. All probation, parole, and prison counts are for December 31; jail counts are for the last weekday in June. Detail may not sum to total due to rounding and adjustments made to account for offenders with multiple correctional statuses. See the *Key statistics* page on the BJS website for correctional population statistics prior to 2000 or other years not included in this table.
[a]Total was adjusted to account for offenders with multiple correctional statuses.
[b]Includes offenders held in local jails or under the jurisdiction of state of federal prisons.
[c]Includes some offenders held in a prison or jail but who remained under the jurisdiction of a probation or parole agency.

*Source: Bureau of Justice Statistics, Annual Probation Survey, Annual Parole Survey, Annual Survey of Jails, Census of Jail Inmates, and National Prisoner Statistics Program, 2000 and 2005–2015.*

In fact, in 2009, more than 82,000 state and federal prison inmates—5.1% of the prison population in the United States—were being housed in local jails,[4] despite the fact that jails are primarily designed to provide short-term incarceration for sentenced misdemeanants and pretrial detainees.

**Jail Inmates at Midyear 2014**

### Highlights:

- The number of inmates confined in county and city jails was an estimated 744,600 at midyear 2014, which was significantly lower than the peak of 785,500 inmates at midyear 2008.

- The jail incarceration rate decreased from a peak of 259 per 100,000 in 2007 to 234 per 100,000 at midyear 2014.

- The female inmate population increased 18.1% between midyear 2010 and 2014, while the male population declined 3.2%.

- White inmates accounted for 47% of the total jail population, blacks represented 35%, and Hispanics represented 15%.

- About 4,200 juveniles age 17 or younger were held in local jails at midyear 2014. They accounted for 0.6% of the confined population, down from 1.2% at midyear 2000.[5]

## Rehabilitation and Other Goals of Sentencing

Public policy makers are faced with choices as to how money gets spent.

**Sanctions** Requirements imposed on those convicted of a crime that can range from financial penalties or curfew restrictions to incarceration.

In order to understand the issues and challenges facing those released from prison, it is critical to revisit and emphasize the general goals of sentencing—deterrence, punishment/retribution, incapacitation, and rehabilitation. These multiple goals of sentencing, and prison sentences in particular, create a number of challenges to institutional correctional agencies as they try to meet the expectations of citizens, taxpayers, voters, criminal justice practitioners, and policy makers. Part of what makes this a challenge is the fact that the public has mixed views as to what they expect correctional agencies to focus on, and correctional administrators must also ensure the safety of both staff and inmates.

As described earlier, when convicted offenders are sentenced, imposed **sanctions** may focus on deterrence, retribution, incapacitation, or rehabilitation. In some instances, only one of these goals is sought; in others, judges and prosecutors hope that all of these goals will be achieved simultaneously. Indeed, society as a whole expects multiple goals to be accomplished when someone is sentenced to prison: they want to make sure the person does not escape and therefore cannot commit other crimes while incarcerated (incapacitation), they want the specific person being sentenced to be deterred from future crime as a result of their experience of incarceration (specific deterrence) and for everyone else in society to be deterred as well (general deterrence), they seek punishment that is proportionate to the crime committed (retribution), and they also expect the person to be rehabilitated, through treatment by professionals, while incarcerated.

The public often has varying opinions of what the purpose of prisons should be. In a survey of 1,200 registered voters conducted in 2010 for the Pew Center for the States, 31% of respondents believed the primary purpose of prisons was to protect society (i.e., incapacitation), while 25% felt the primary purpose was rehabilitation, and 20% believed the purpose of prisons was punishment of offenders.[6] However, in a separate survey in 2006 of more than 1,000 adults for the National Council on Crime and Delinquency (NCCD), only 14% thought those coming out of prison were less likely to commit new crimes than before they were incarcerated, more than 50% thought the likelihood of new crimes was the same, and 31% believed those coming out of prison were *more likely* to commit crimes than before they went into prison.[7] These survey results indicate that if the purpose of prisons is to rehabilitate or deter offenders, the American public does not believe this is being accomplished.

### Critical Thinking

What aspect of incarceration do you feel is the most "punitive?" How does access to educational programming, drug treatment, and vocational training relate to punishment?

Thus, depending on the constituency, there are multiple goals correctional administrators and policy makers seek to achieve. Further, the pursuit and accomplishment of these competing goals is often viewed as contradictory and conflicting. For example, empirical evidence indicates that prison-based substance abuse treatment can reduce recidivism,[8] but there is still some political resistance to expanding the provision of treatment, because of either philosophical views (i.e., the notion of state-enforced therapy)[9] or budgetary limitations. Additionally, in some cases, the accomplishment of the rehabilitation goal may impede the accomplishment of the goals of punishment and institutional security. If an inmate is provided with vocational training or educational programming (i.e., rehabilitation), the public may not see this as adequate punishment (i.e., retribution) or may view it as inmates "getting" something law-abiding citizens cannot, or it may pose security concerns related to congregate programs and interpersonal violence between inmates in treatment together.

This conflict was illustrated by the debate over whether prison inmates should have access to college courses, and came to a head with the elimination of Pell grants—federal funding that provided support for college courses—for prison inmates in 1994. Republican Senator Kay Bailey Hutchison of Texas argued against Pell grants, claiming it was unjust for felons to receive support for college courses when up to 100,000 low-income students could not receive similar benefits.[10] This response is illustrative of what has been referred to as the principle of least eligibility, which, as described by Sparks (1996), states that "the level of prison conditions should always compare unfavorably to the material living standards of the laboring poor"[11]—in other words, prison inmates are the least eligible among the American public to receive benefits to which not all law-abiding citizens have access.

This example is also illustrative of how public backlash and political pressure can result in dramatic changes in correctional policy and practice. Before the Pell grant ban was passed, there were 350 college-degree programs for prison inmates, but by 2005, there were only about a dozen college-degree programs in prisons.[12] Further, the timing of this Pell grant ban was part of a widespread public demand to address crime and restrict what many saw as prison inmate privileges. Around the same time as the Pell grant ban for inmates in 1994, Congress also passed the Violent Offender Incarceration/Truth-in-Sentencing (VOI/TIS) Incentive grant program (1994). This program provided states with federal funding if they implemented truth-in-sentencing policies that required those convicted of violent offences sentenced to prison to serve 85% of the court-imposed sentence. Congress also passed the Prison Litigation Reform Act of 1996, which limited the circumstances under which inmates could file petitions in the federal courts.

However, even when correctional administrators and policy makers want to incorporate rehabilitative programming into correctional facilities, doing so can raise concerns regarding staff and inmate safety. From a prison management standpoint, allowing inmates to participate in congregate programs and allowing them movement within a facility are often seen as possible security threats, particularly given the historically limited accuracy of prison classification methods to predict prison violence.[13] In this case, the goal of rehabilitation can be seen as in conflict with the goals of incapacitation and institutional security. The number of empirical studies regarding the relationship between participation in prison-based treatment programs and prison misconduct are small, and have reached different conclusions.[14] Some assessments of the literature have found prison-based treatment programs can reduce prison misconduct,[15] while other assessments have found these have no demonstrable effect—for better or worse—on prison

© Africa Studio/Shutterstock.com

Public policy makers often create new get-tough laws to appease the demands of the public to restrict perceived privileges of prison inmates.

violence or inmate misconduct.[16,17] However, it does not take scholarly research for a prison warden to recognize that leaving inmates in their cells and not allowing them to engage in rehabilitative programs ensures that the goal of incapacitation is accomplished, even at the long-term cost and consequence that once the prisoner is released, he or she will not have received the rehabilitative support needed and will thus be more likely to return to prison.

In addition to the challenges of balancing multiple goals and institutional security and safety, there are other challenges when it comes to the provision of rehabilitative services. One major challenge is the perception by the public and policy makers that rehabilitative services are not effective. These perceptions can be shaped by media coverage, which often include selective observation—finding one person who went through treatment and recidivated and concluding from that observation that treatment does not work. The media and politicians often condemn rehabilitative programs through coverage, or legislative hearings, when someone who completed a prison-based treatment program reoffends, regardless of whether the program is effective as a whole.

Similarly, research on the effectiveness of treatment can also be misused to influence public sentiment away from rehabilitation and toward retribution, deterrence, and incapacitation. One of the most significant examples of this came in the 1970s, when Robert Martinson co-authored the criminological study *Effectiveness of Correctional Treatment: A Survey of Treatment Evaluation Studies* with Lipton and Wolks, in which more than 200 studies on offender rehabilitation were examined and summarized.[18] Martinson also published an article on his own that reached the conclusion that "nothing works."[19] In fact, Jerome Miller, writing in the *Washington Post* in 1989, described this work as "the most politically important criminological study in the past century."[20] Others would later replicate Martinson's research. Gendreau and Ross (1979) used more sophisticated methods of analysis and more examples of programs, and reached different conclusions—treatment did work if it employed specific treatment interventions.[21] However, by then, the momentum to move away from treatment as a correctional goal and toward deterrence, retribution, and incapacitation could not easily be reversed. It would not be until the 1990s that researchers, employing meta-analyses summarizing hundreds and hundreds of evaluations and studies, were able to bring back the notion that treatment programs could be effective if they focused on criminogenic needs, were behavioral in nature and not punishment-oriented, focused on high-risk offenders, were implemented with a high degree of fidelity to the model, included aftercare, and were responsive to the learning styles of the targeted audience.[22]

What also contributed to the influence this research had on public views, and ultimately changes in state sentencing policy and practices, was the timing of the research and larger issues related to crime and crime control occurring in the 1970s. For example, from 1973 to 1979 violent crime reported to the police in the U.S. increased 40%,[23] stoking public concerns about crime and safety. Beginning in the 1970s, there were also increasing concerns that judges and parole boards were either inconsistent or error-prone in sentencing practices or decisions to release offenders. This led many states to adopt sentencing policies that reduced judicial discretion through mandatory prison sentences, and to eliminate parole boards' discretion to release or continue incarcerating inmates through the adoption of determinate sentencing structures.[24] Finally, there was the ongoing concern—continuing today—that prison inmates would feign rehabilitation and "play the game" in order to earn early release. As a result, from the early 1970s, when all states operated under indeterminate sentencing, to 2002, 17 states abandoned indeterminate sentencing structures and discretionary parole,[25] which were based on the belief that rehabilitation was possible if inmates were rewarded with earlier release for their participation. Instead, states shifted toward determinate sentencing, which did not consider or factor in an inmate's efforts at rehabilitation when it came to being released from prison. Under determinate sentencing, prisoners are released once they have served their sentences. The only criteria considered is time served, regardless of whether or not the prisoner has participated in rehabilitative programs and whether or not the prisoner is prepared for reentry into society. Indeed, when the U.S. Supreme Court upheld the federal sentencing guidelines in 1989 in *Mistretta v. United States*,[26] which focused only on the seriousness of the crime and the criminal history of the offender when determining sentence lengths and time to serve, the court had confirmed the "abandonment of rehabilitation in corrections."[27]

The other challenge to rehabilitative programs within prison is that they take time to implement and the results are not seen immediately by the public. This challenge is compounded by what Serin (2005) called prison administrators' "preoccupation with short-term operational goals (i.e., admissions, transfers, accommodation, and the daily routine of the prison) . . . [which] can easily exhaust available fiscal and human resources."[28] It is relatively quick, easy, and highly visible to pass a law that "gets tough on crime." When there is public outrage over a crime, elected officials can draft and pass a new law to increase penalties or make the crime non-probationable, the law is publicly signed, and the public is appeased. Many have pointed to the most recent war on drugs as an example of how elected officials responded to a perceived crime threat with a wide range of both substantive and symbolic legislation, without full consideration of the effectiveness or long-term consequences of these policies.[29] Similar examples of symbolic legislative responses to public crime concerns can be found in sex offender registries.[30] For the most part, sentencing enhancements can be developed, debated, and passed into law during one legislative session. On the other hand, a commitment to the provision of treatment and rehabilitation takes time, a commitment of resources for funding, time for participants to matriculate through, and then years to gauge and show the impact the program has on recidivism. To impatient voters and elected officials, this timeline is not conducive to the politics of crime control. In addition, there is a high likelihood that at least one person who goes through the program will recidivate, or commit a violent crime that may garner public and media attention, and often those individual cases are used to illustrate the ineffectiveness of treatment and justify cuts in treatment budgets in highly political environments.

Staffing patterns of prisons in the United States demonstrate that security, rather than treatment and rehabilitation, is the top priority of correctional facilities. State and federal prisons employed more than 726,268 full time staff in 2012.[31] As would be expected, the majority—66%—of those who work in prisons are correctional officers, and their responsibilities primarily revolve around security, inmate movement within the facility, and ensuring order. Given the 2. 1 million people in prison at yearend 2015 in the United States, it would appear that the ratio of correctional officers to inmates—roughly 1:3—allows for close supervision of inmates by officers. However, the security aspect of prisons operates 24 hours a day, seven days a week, 365 days a year. Since staff do not work 24 hours a day, and get days off, vacations, etc., and not all security staff are in direct contact with inmates (some are in towers, at entrances to the prison, etc.), often a single correctional officer can be responsible for the security and safety of more than 200 inmates at a time. Further, most correctional officers are not trained or qualified to provide inmates with clinical assessment or treatment, educational or vocational training, or counseling services. Those responsibilities fall to doctors, nurses, counselors, chaplains, psychiatrists, psychologists, social workers, classification staff, and teachers, which nationally account for less than 20% of those who work in prisons.[32] For example, there were roughly 12,000 educational staff employed in U.S. prisons in 2005, which translates to a ratio of one educator to 116 inmates nationally.[33] However, with all of these measures of prison staffing, it must be recognized that these ratios of security and treatment staff can vary dramatically from prison to prison. For example, the ratio of education staff to inmates across U.S. prisons in 2005 ranged from 1:20 to 1:1000, and varied by state, prison security classification, and other facility characteristics.[34]

As measured by these staffing patterns, it is clear that the primary emphasis of prisons relates to security and that nationally most inmates have limited access to rehabilitative services provided by educators and counselors. However, it is also clear that these staffing patterns vary dramatically from state to state and from prison to prison. It should also be noted that not included in these figures are rehabilitative staff that may not be employees of the prison, but rather, are contractual service providers or volunteers.

© txking/Shutterstock.com

Correctional officers are trained primarily to provide security, not counseling or rehabilitative programming, and one officer is often responsible for the supervision of more than 50 inmates at a time.

FIGURE 9.2 PRISON STAFFING NUMBERS AND PATTERNS 1984–2005

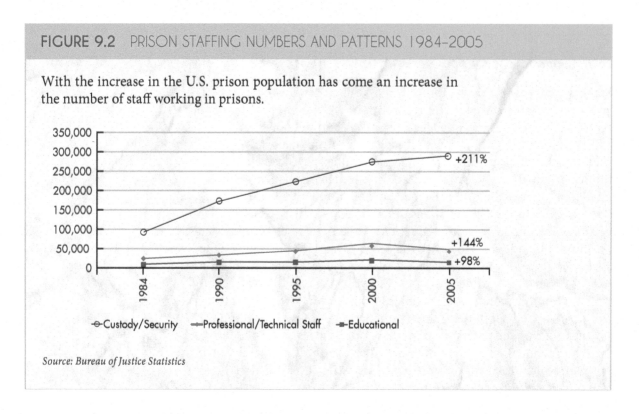

With the increase in the U.S. prison population has come an increase in the number of staff working in prisons.

Source: Bureau of Justice Statistics

This is not to say that prisons operate without any regard for the rehabilitative needs of those admitted to prison. Indeed, most states seek to identify offender needs during the reception and classification process, along with assessments used to make security classification decisions (i.e., **offender risk** for escape and violence toward staff and other inmates). Based on a survey of state correctional systems by the National Institute of Corrections in 2001, almost all states indicated that during the reception and classification process they gauge inmate needs related to medical needs, academic achievement, substance abuse, psychological issues, and other areas that could be the target of rehabilitation programs.[35] Given the focus of prisons on security (i.e., incapacitation and safety), facility placement and classification based on the risks relative to escape and violence within the prison system override most other rehabilitative needs the inmate may have. Additionally, given the crowding in most prison systems, and the fact that the distribution of beds across prisons is for the most part fixed, placement of inmates is often driven more by space availability than treatment needs. While maximum security prisons account for only 20% of all prisons in the United States, they house 36% of all prisoners.[36] On the other hand, minimum security prisons account for more than one-half of all prisons, but house only 21% of all prisoners.[37] These disparities are primarily driven by the fact that the maximum security prisons are extremely large and often hold thousands of inmates, such as Corcoran State Prison in California or Angola State Prison in Louisiana, both of which hold more than 5,000 inmates. In contrast, minimum security facilities usually house fewer than 500 inmates. As a result of these dynamics, inmates classified as medium security risk

**Offender risk** Within the context of prison security, an assessment of the likelihood that an inmate will attempt an escape or assault a staff member or other inmate. Within the context of community-based supervision, an assessment of the likelihood that a former inmate will commit a new crime.

may be housed in maximum security facilities, since this may be where bed space is available, which limits opportunities for access to rehabilitative programming.

---

**Critical Thinking**

If an inmate is considered a high security risk, he or she will likely be housed in a maximum security prison and will not have access to rehabilitative programs due to his or her dangerousness. Discuss the implications of this situation when people are eventually released because they have served their court-imposed sentences, but still remain "dangerous."

---

Thus, from the standpoint of public expectations and prison administrators' immediate need to ensure safety and security, rehabilitative treatment of prisoners may not be an emphasis. Despite this, however, it is clear that those who enter prisons in the United States bring with them a wide array of needs that, if not addressed adequately, will result in a continuation of the cycle of crime and victimization.

Before examining the extent and nature of inmate needs, practitioners and policy makers must recognize that the window to meet these needs is not limited exclusively to the time behind bars. Most of those released from prison will experience a period of supervision in the community upon release. Given this reality, and the complexity and multiplicity of needs for many inmates, there is often more time to address the needs of those reentering society than simply the time they are behind bars. Thus, some of inmates' needs can be addressed during their incarceration, while treatment for some needs can be initiated in prison but would need to be completed or followed up on when the inmate is released. There are also some needs that are beyond the capacity of prisons to address.

Many of the prisons that can hold the largest numbers of inmates were not designed architecturally for the provision of rehabilitative programming.

For example, if an offender is admitted to prison a few credits short of completing high school, or in a position where he or she could be prepared for and pass a GED test, that is a need that could be met while the individual is incarcerated (i.e., completed in nine months) if the resources were available. Similarly, an individual who has a substance abuse disorder or a mental health issue could be provided with treatment while incarcerated (i.e., for 12 months), and in most instances, would need to continue receiving **aftercare**, or continued treatment and recovery support, after release from prison. On the other hand, an individual released from prison may have difficulty in obtaining

**Aftercare** The process of providing continued treatment and recovery support following the conclusion of intensive or residential treatment programming.

employment or being able to find housing because of his or her felony conviction. That is not a need that a prison would be able to easily address, but rather, relates to public policy or society's views of prison releasees. Prison staff, in and of themselves, cannot address or change these realities. Thus, while prisons can have programs to assist inmates in how to conduct job searches, how to be upfront about their criminal background, and how to be effective in job interviews, prison administrators and staff cannot directly change the stigma of being a convicted felon. To accomplish this would require a change in how society views criminality, serving time in prison, or being a convicted felon.

The needs of those in prison in the United States are significant, and many of these relate directly to the likelihood of future recidivism and successful reentry. As seen in Figure 9.3, the majority of those in prison were identified as being substance abusers or drug dependent, having a mental health disorder (often related to their substance abuse), and having prior arrests for violent crimes. In addition, more than one-half were parents of children under the age of 18. Further, a substantial proportion of inmates enter the prison system without a high school diploma or GED, with learning impairments, and with physical health problems. The most frequently cited health problems were arthritis (15% of all inmates), hypertension (14% of all inmates), asthma (9%), heart disease (6%), and hepatitis (5%).[38] In addition, almost 10% of inmates reported previously having tuberculosis.[39] Studies of inmate needs from individual states have highlighted other risks and needs that inmates have. For example, in a study of a drug treatment program in Illinois, Olson and Rozhon (2011) found that 45% of inmates had never held a job longer than two years, despite an average age of 36, and 70% had no valid driver's license or state-issued identification card.[40]

**FIGURE 9.3** 2002-2007 PREVALENCE OF NEEDS AND RISKS AMONG STATE PRISON INMATES IN THE U.S.

|  | **Percent of U.S. State Prisoners** |
| --- | --- |
| 2005 Mental Health Disorder[41] | 56.2% |
| 2005 Psychotic Disorder[42] | 15.3% |
| 2004 Substance Abuse or Dependence[43] | 53.4% |
| 2007 Parent of a Minor Child[44] | 51.9% |
| 2003 No High School Diploma or GED[45] | 39.7% |
| 2007 Learning Impairment[46] | 23.3% |
| 2004 Current Medical Problem[47] | 43.8% |
| 2002 Prior Arrests for Violent Crime[48] | 53.7% |
| 2002 More Than 10 Prior Arrests[49] | 34.2% |

**Critical Thinking**

What criteria would you use to determine which inmates should be given priority access to treatment and rehabilitative programming?

Inmates have extensive needs that must be met in order to improve their chances of successful reentry into society and reduce the cycle of crime and incarceration. Therefore, it is important to consider the degree to which prisons offer rehabilitative programming, and the quality and form of these services. Four key factors play a role in providing prison-based rehabilitative programming: the existence of programming, the capacity of programming, to whom the programming is available, and the quality of programming.

The first factor, the existence of rehabilitative programming, is relatively easy to measure—a program either exists or it does not. In the 2005 census of prisons in the United States, 73% of all prisons had drug or alcohol programs,[50] but the availability of these programs varied considerably from state to state. For example, in five states, 90% or more of the prisons offered some type of drug or alcohol program, whereas in other states fewer than 20% of their prisons had programs.[51] As seen in Figure 9.4, some types of programs appear to be readily available in U.S. prisons, such as high school (secondary education) or GED classes, drug abuse programs, and work programs that provide facility support (i.e., inmate work that supports the operation of the prison, such as laundry, dietary, and maintenance). Other programs are not available in most prisons, such as college classes, parenting classes, or prison industry programs.

A second factor in prison-based rehabilitative programming is the capacity of these programs, which can vary dramatically from prison to prison. For example, there are numerous prisons operating across the country with small individual housing units that provide substance abuse treatment for 50 to 100 inmates. At the other extreme are prisons where all inmates participate in substance abuse treatment, including one of the nation's largest fully dedicated drug treatment prisons, the Sheridan Correctional Center in Illinois, which houses 950 inmates.[52]

A third factor is the quality or integrity of the program. If a program serving 50 inmates is operating as a Therapeutic Community (TC), with highly trained counselors, a rigorous nine-month curriculum, and an aftercare component, research has found that drug use and subsequent criminality will be reduced.[53] **Therapeutic Communities**, as defined by the National Institute on Drug Abuse, are "residential [programs] that use a hierarchical model with treatment strategies that reflect increased levels of personal and social responsibility. Peer influence, mediated through a variety of group processes, is used to help individuals learn and assimilate social norms and develop more effective social skills."[54] Therapeutic Communities are one of the most common drug treatment modalities

**Therapeutic Communities (TC)** Residential programs that help individuals learn social norms and develop more effective social skills.

for prison inmates,[55] and evaluations of specific programs in California,[56] Texas,[57] Delaware,[58] and Illinois[59] have documented that these TCs can substantially reduce post-release recidivism. On the other hand, a correctional boot camp that serves 500 inmates but consists only of an inmate-led self-help group that lasts two weeks would not produce any reductions in recidivism.[60] While the latter program would make it appear that the prison is providing rehabilitation to more inmates, closer inspection might reveal that the intervention is not a substantive attempt at rehabilitation.

---

**FIGURE 9.4** PREVALENCE OF SELECTED PROGRAMS ACROSS STATE AND FEDERAL PRISONS IN THE U.S., 2005

| | Percent of Prisons with Program |
|---|---|
| **Educational Programs** | |
| Secondary Education or GED | 77% |
| Vocational Training | 52% |
| College Classes | 35% |
| **Counseling Programs** | |
| Drug/Alcohol Dependency | 74% |
| Psychological or Psychiatric | 58% |
| Parenting | 48% |
| **Inmate Work Programs** | |
| Facility Support Services | 74% |
| Prison Industries | 31% |

Source: Adapted from Table 6 in Census of State and Federal Correctional Facilities, 2005.

---

**Critical Thinking**

If you were the warden of a prison and had enough money to either provide 25 inmates with intensive, highly effective treatment or provide 200 inmates with less effective programming that occupied them for a few weeks, which would you select and why?

---

Fidelity to program design The degree to which rehabilitative programs are actually delivered in accordance with their pre-operational design.

The current "resurgence" in prison-based treatment has been fueled by a combination of empirical evidence that treatment programs can work if implemented effectively, continued dissatisfaction with the high recidivism rates of those released from prison, and the economic pressures on states to control correctional costs. However, even with "legitimate" programs—those that are provided by trained professionals and last for several weeks—in order for them to work they must be delivered with **fidelity to program design**, or accordance with their pre-operational design, and to the appropriate clients/inmates.

The consensus now is that treatment can reduce recidivism, but not all programs work for all offenders. Further, increased attention and focus on the content and treatment processes has revealed that not all programs operating within prisons have fidelity to the treatment models, and unless programs incorporate specific elements, they will not have the intended effect. For example, in his review of prison-based rehabilitative programs, Genreau (2011) concludes that cognitive-behavioral programs are most reliable in reducing recidivism, whereas programs that are punishment-oriented or focus on building character and self-esteem do not reduce recidivism.[61] Similarly, prison-based substance abuse treatment

Although small group and individual therapy with professional psychologists and counselors can be effective at reducing recidivism, most prisons do not have sufficient resources to provide these types of interventions.

programs need to also include aftercare services for participants following their release in order to sustain and maximize the rehabilitative effects of the programs.[62] Thus, treatment can be effective at rehabilitation, but the public and policy makers should not expect programs to work for everyone. If funding and staffing limitations impede the ability to implement programs with a high degree of fidelity—i.e., if programs are not being delivered as they were designed—they will not have the expected effects on recidivism.

The fourth factor in providing prison-based rehabilitative programs is which inmates have access to them. Given the limited resources and capacity of this treatment, practitioners must make decisions regarding who gets access to which services and who is less of a priority. Generally, correctional treatment programs need to adhere to the principles of risk, need, and responsivity in order to have optimal outcomes.

The *risk* principle is based on the empirical evidence that the largest return on treatment investment comes from targeting the highest-risk offender.[63] By definition, offenders sentenced to prison tend to be higher-risk, at least in the minds of those involved in sentencing decisions, than offenders placed on probation. However, among those in prison, there are varying degrees of risk for subsequent recidivism, and this risk is not necessarily tied to the current conviction offense or the inmate's security classification. Because of this, practitioners need to employ risk assessment instruments when attempting to identify who is at greatest risk of future offending.

The *need* principle is also important to consider when identifying appropriate treatment interventions. Treatment programs must address **criminogenic needs**—those attributes that can be changed and that contribute directly to recidivism, such as education, substance abuse, personality and attitudes, and criminal thinking patterns. To change most of these needs requires considerable time, attention, and trained staff that can develop a strong rapport with the inmate.

**Criminogenic needs** The characteristics of an offender that can be changed through treatment and intervention that are directly related to continued involvement in criminal activity, including drug abuse, interpersonal skills, cognitive functioning, and vocational/employment skills.

The *responsivity* principle relates to the delivery of the intervention and the way it motivates the inmate to change, takes into account the inmate's cognitive abilities and skills, and is sensitive to cultural differences among the participants.[64]

When correctional practitioners make decisions regarding who will participate in treatment programming, they have to consider a number of different dimensions. First is the inmate's security classification. Does the inmate pose a high risk of escape or assault to staff and other inmates? Does allowing the inmate to leave his or her cell to participate in treatment compromise the institutional goals of security? While security classification does not necessarily indicate an inmate's likelihood of recidivating once released from prison, it does indicate the risk of an inmate attempting to escape or harm staff or other inmates.

Another consideration is whether or not the inmate's cognitive ability and mental health would allow him or her to effectively participate in the rehabilitative programming as designed. Very few prison treatment programs are delivered individually to inmates; most use group modalities. Some programs, such as Therapeutic Communities or **victim-offender mediation**, require a certain level of functioning and mental stability that some inmates may not possess.

Program administrators also have to determine if the inmate's participation would be disruptive to the overall group treatment program. One highly disruptive participant can diminish the efficacy of the treatment for the entire group, and therefore prison-based treatment programs are often voluntary to ensure that participants want to be there and will not be disruptive in the hopes of being removed. Because of this, it has been suggested that providers of prison-based treatment modify their programs to address the resistance of non-voluntary participants and their potential for disrupting treatment.[65] In addition, research has also found that in custodial settings, mandated treatments were ineffective at reducing recidivism, while voluntary participation improved outcomes.[66]

Finally, administrators must ensure that inmates are exposed to an appropriate dose of the treatment. *Treatment dosage*—the actual number of hours or treatment sessions—and *treatment duration*—the days from start to finish—are separate concepts, but highly correlated in cognitive-behavioral programs for offenders.[67] Further, the higher the dose of these cognitive-behavioral programs, the lower the subsequent recidivism rates.[68] For some inmates, given the duration and intensity of their substance abuse disorders, treatment lasting nine months may be required in order to have an impact on drug use and criminal behavior. If an inmate will only be in prison for four months, should the inmate be enrolled in a prison-based treatment program when he or she really needs much more therapeutic intervention? This might work effectively if it can be guaranteed the inmate would continue his or her treatment upon release, but often access to treatment post-release cannot be ensured. Indeed, even among prison-based drug treatment programs supported through the federal Residential Substance

Abuse Treatment (RSAT) initiative, which encouraged the programs it funded to include aftercare services,[69] less than one-half of programs placed inmates who received treatment in aftercare upon their release.[70] Another scenario and decision that correctional practitioners and policy makers face is whether those who will never be released or not released from prison for decades should be a treatment priority. While treatment of these individuals may not have an impact on recidivism, it could improve their behavior while incarcerated, thereby increasing staff and other inmate safety and possibly improving the prison atmosphere.

Rehabilitative programs can potentially help reduce correctional costs through two primary mechanisms: shorter lengths of incarceration if participation in and completion of these programs allow for additional sentence reductions or earlier release by parole boards, and a reduction in recidivism and therefore fewer people returning to prison with new sentences. Shorter lengths of stay can be accomplished in states with indeterminate sentencing if inmates' participation in treatment leads to early release, or in determinate sentencing states if inmates receive additional credits toward their sentences for participation in these programs. In 31 states, inmates who participate in rehabilitative programs, such as drug treatment, vocational programming, prison industry, or GED completion, are awarded additional time off their sentences above and beyond traditional day-for-day good conduct credit.[71] In Illinois, an evaluation of the Sheridan Correctional Center's Therapeutic Community found that inmates who participated in the drug treatment program and earned good conduct credits reduced the length of their incarceration by an average of 60 days per inmate. This translates to a cost savings of $2.78 million per year for the program.[72] Additional savings come in the form of lower recidivism (and lower criminal justice processing costs) and lower health care costs; two widely cited studies estimated a savings of $7 for every dollar spent on treatment.[73,74] Therefore, it is evident that in the long run, prison-based rehabilitation can reduce prison populations, crime, and victimization. However, the challenge is that policy makers often do not make decisions based on the long-term view, but rather on the short-term view of fiscal years, or at least the four-year period between election cycles.

Ultimately, the most significant factor that affects offender recidivism and successful reentry is the provision of services and treatment that address the root causes of criminality. These root causes include limited educational achievement and employment/employability, criminal thinking patterns, mental illness, and substance abuse, and are often referred to as criminogenic needs, or risk factors that can be changed through therapeutic intervention.[75] Addressing and reducing these risk factors is ultimately how offenders will reduce their involvement in criminal activity and successfully reintegrate back into society from prison. As with the availability and quality of treatment, the degree to which prisons are able to meet the rehabilitative needs of inmates varies from state to state and prison to prison. However, regardless of the quality and integrity of programming, a significant portion of inmates who have deficiencies do not participate in programming that would improve those areas of risk. For example, in 1997, of those who entered prison without a high school diploma, only 54% participated in any educational programming, and only 32% of all inmates participated in vocational training/programs while incarcerated.[76] Similarly, of those inmates in state prisons in 2004 with mental health problems, only 34% received any treatment.[77]

Substance abuse treatment and aftercare also appear to be lacking for returning inmates. Nationally, in 2004, an estimated 53% of inmates had problems with drug dependence or abuse, but it is projected that only 15% of state prison inmates meeting drug dependence or abuse criteria had participated in substance abuse treatment while in prison.[78] Additionally, despite some increases in funding for prison-based treatment through programs like the federal Residential Substance Abuse Treatment (RSAT) grants, it appears that prison-based substance abuse treatment services decreased in use among prisoners in the 1990s due to the dramatic increases in the number of offenders admitted to prison.[79]

Across the United States, the availability, capacity, and quality of prison-based programming designed to improve inmate reentry and reduce recidivism vary widely, and over time these characteristics of programming have changed. For example, a number of approaches have been used in prisons to address substance abuse treatment needs, including drug education, self-help groups such as Alcoholics Anonymous (AA) or Narcotics Anonymous (NA), group counseling within specific housing units of a prison, and prisons that operate as Therapeutic Communities (TCs). While programming such as drug education and self-help groups are inexpensive and large numbers of inmates can be served through these programs, they lack the components that make up effective interventions. On the other hand, while programs such as prison-based TCs and professional counseling are effective at reducing recidivism, they are extremely expensive and usually only serve a small number of those in need of treatment services. Thus, prison administrators and policy makers are often faced with the choice between providing limited, usually ineffective interventions to large numbers of inmates at a low cost and providing more expensive, effective interventions to a much smaller number of inmates. Often the option of providing "something" to many, even if ineffective, is more symbolic of the effort to improve the reentry process than substantive.

An examination of trends in the proportion of inmates accessing substance abuse treatment programming—distinguishing between drug education versus drug counseling—reveals this shift nationally. In 1991, when there were fewer than 800,000 adults in prison, 36% of those in need of substance abuse treatment received substantive drug

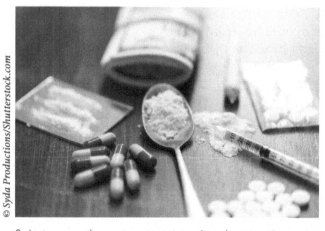

© Syda Productions/Shutterstock.com

Substance abuse treatment is often lacking for inmates returning to society.

treatment (professional counseling or a therapeutic community-type intervention) and about one-quarter (24%) received drug education. Inmates often receive both types of interventions, so there is double counting in the data. However, by 2004, when the prison population in the United States had reached almost 1.5 million, 34% of those in need of drug treatment received drug education, compared to 14% receiving substantive drug treatment. Thus, while a larger proportion of inmates in need are receiving "some" services, most are receiving services that will do little to address their long-term, serious substance abuse problems, which will likely lead to their failing after release from prison and recidivating.

**FIGURE 9.5** PERCENT OF PRISON INMATES IN NEED OF TREATMENT ACCESSING COUNSELING VERSUS SELF-HELP GROUPS, 1991–2004

Over the past 15 years there has been a shift from drug treatment provided by counselors to drug education and self-help groups.

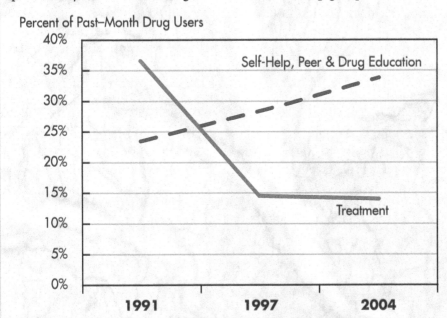

*Treatment defined as "residential" treatment services or professional counseling
Source: Mulola & Karberg (2006): Drug Use and Dependence, State and Federal Prisoners, 2004; Mumola (1999). Substance Abuse and Treatment, State and Federal Prisoners, 1997. U.S. Department of Justice, Bureau of Justice Statistics

In general, most of the research on prison-based TCs and other cognitive-based rehabilitation programs has documented reductions in recidivism, which vary depending on the "dose" of treatment, the characteristics of the prison population served, and the inclusion of other components that address criminogenic needs, such as educational and vocational programming. For example, in one of the most recent reviews of prison-based treatment, it was noted that most TCs examined only served "nonviolent" offenders, and they had better outcomes than those programs that included offenders with violent and nonviolent criminal histories.[80] However, even those programs that included both violent and nonviolent offenders tended to produce lower recidivism rates than when treatment was not provided.[81] Current reviews also concluded that corrections-based TCs that served primarily white and female offenders and that required aftercare experienced better outcomes— lower recidivism rates—than did programs that primarily included minorities and males, and did not require post-release aftercare. Again, though, even these programs had better outcomes than comparison groups with no treatment.[82]

However, despite the empirical evidence that prison-based treatment and aftercare can reduce recidivism rates, there are still a number of barriers that prevent these treatment strategies from being implemented.[83] For example, many programs include restrictions on program eligibility based on the criminal backgrounds of program participants,[84] regardless of treatment need, motivation, or how long ago prohibiting offenses may have been committed. Another challenge has been the ability to attract and retain qualified staff,[85] which can be particularly problematic at prisons located far from metropolitan areas. As described earlier, the conflict within corrections between treatment and punishment also creates tension and challenges between criminal justice personnel (i.e., correctional officers) and treatment personnel (i.e., counselors).[86,87,88] Finally, from a purely financial standpoint, substantive, high-quality prison-based treatment programs, particularly TCs, are expensive to operate in the short run, regardless of the long-term benefits and cost savings.

### Critical Thinking
What is it about the physical design and location of prisons that makes delivering effective correctional programming a challenge?

The capacity of prisons to meet the needs of inmates has been limited, but it is not completely absent. Efforts at rehabilitation exist, but again, in many instances the majority of resources are devoted to security and safety. Indeed, prisons do a very good job at ensuring that the goal of incapacitation is met, and they also are successful at limiting the amount of interpersonal violence between staff and inmates, as well as inmate-on-inmate violence. One indicator of prisons' degree of success at achieving the goal of incapacitation is the extremely small number of inmates that escape from prisons on an annual basis. Although the exact number of escapes from prison throughout the United States has been difficult to determine, given the multiple definitions and reporting processes, in general the rate of escapes is low—less than 0.5 per 100 inmates in 1998—and fell throughout the 1990s.[89] Based on information reported by prisons to the U.S. Department of Justice, in 2005, there were fewer than 100 escapes from prisons that were classified as medium, maximum, or supermax security facilities, which translates to approximately one escape for every 15,000 inmates housed in prisons at those security levels.[90] However, even this low number of escapes makes the prevalence seem higher, since many of these escapes were likely minimum-security inmates who were working in the facility. The majority of "escapes" from prison occur at prisons classified as minimum security, which generally do not have extensive external security perimeters; these escapes are often referred to as "walkaways" or AWOLs (inmates who are on a work-release assignment and do not return by a specified time).

Similarly, prisons' goal of ensuring that staff and inmates are not victimized appears to be met to a relatively high degree. Although there are significant limitations to accurately measuring the extent and nature of prison violence, including inmates not wanting to report victimization due to the inmate code and limited trust of staff, some measures are quite reliable. For example, the number of staff murdered by inmates—one of the most highly reliable measures of prison violence but also the most narrowly defined—totaled fewer than 10 in 2005, which translates to a rate of two murders per 100,000 staff.[91] By comparison, the murder rate in the "free world" of the United States that year was 5.6 per 100,000.[92] Similarly, the inmate-on-inmate murder rate during the period from 2001 to 2004 was four per 100,000 inmates.[93] These low murder rates have not always been the case, however. In the early 1980s, the murder rate in prisons nationally was much higher than in the free world. Through improved methods of inmate classification and an increased focus on staff and inmate safety, the rate of murder in prison has decreased, as shown by Figure 9.6.

When examining the challenges of balancing the rehabilitative needs of inmates, the goals of institutional security and safety, and the larger goal of incapacitation, it is clear that prisons do a very good job at making sure that those sentenced to prison do not escape and that prison staff and inmates are relatively safe from interpersonal violence. The degree to which these goals are accomplished can vary dramatically from prison to prison, but on the whole, the goals of security are accomplished well. On the other hand, the goals of rehabilitation and providing rehabilitative programming to inmates have been less effectively achieved. While many inmates do receive services, the majority of those in need of substance abuse treatment, mental health treatment, and improved educational and vocational skills do not receive these services while incarcerated. As a result, there is very little debate that many individuals released from prison have significant, unmet needs. However, the debate over how to meet these needs, how to balance offender needs with society's demands for safety, who should provide for these needs, and which needs should be addressed first is not settled among policy makers, practitioners, or the public.

FIGURE 9.6 HOMICIDE RATES IN PRISONS FROM 1980–2005

Over the past 30 years, prisons have become safer for both inmates and staff due to improved classification and security processes.

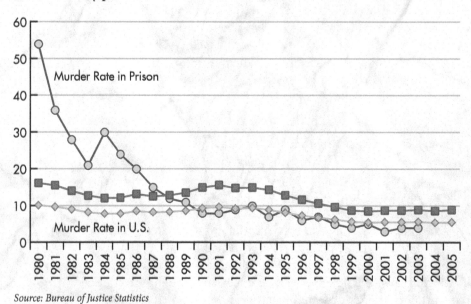

Source: Bureau of Justice Statistics

## EXHIBIT: Mortality in Local Jails and State Prisons, 2000–2012

Bureau of Justice Statistics (BJS) October 2014, NCJ 247448

In 2012, 4,309 inmates died while in the custody of local jails or state prisons—an increase of 2% (67 deaths) from 2011. The number of deaths in local jails increased, from 889 in 2011 to 958 in 2012, which marked the first increase since 2009 (Figure 9.7). The increase in deaths in local jails was primarily due to an increase in illness-related deaths (up 24%). These deaths accounted for 97% of the total increase in deaths in jails and prisons in 2012. The overall mortality rate in local jails increased 4%, from 123 deaths per 100,000 local jail inmates in 2011 to 128 deaths per 100,000 in 2012.

Suicide continued to be the leading cause of death in local jails (40 suicides per 100,000 jail inmates); however, the suicide rate declined 4% in 2012 and has declined 17% since 2000. Heart disease was the leading cause of illness-related deaths in local jails, increasing 14% in 2012.

The rate of AIDS-related deaths in local jails increased from 2 deaths per 100,000 inmates in 2011 to 3 per 100,000 in 2012, the first increase since 2006. Despite the increase in 2012, AIDS-related deaths have decreased 63% in jails since 2000. Most jail jurisdictions (81%) reported no deaths in 2012, which was consistent with previous years. Mortality in jails varied by size of jail population between 2000 and 2012.

The smallest jail jurisdictions had the highest mortality rates, but these jurisdictions averaged less than 1 death annually (Figure 9.8). In 2012, a total of 3,351 deaths (78% of all deaths in correctional facilities) occurred in state prisons, which was nearly equal to the number of deaths in 2011 (3,353). Although the number of deaths in state prisons remained constant, the overall mortality rate in prisons increased 2% in 2012. The increase from 2011 to 2012 was largely due to decrease in the prison population.

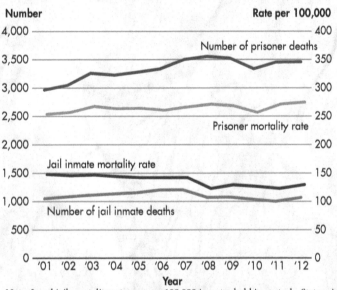

Note: Local jail mortality rates are per 100,000 inmates held in custody. State prison mortality rates are per 100,000 inmates held in custody, including private facilities.

*Sources: Bureau of Justice Statistics, Deaths in Custody Reporting Program, 2001–2012; and National Prisoner Statistics, 2001–2012.*

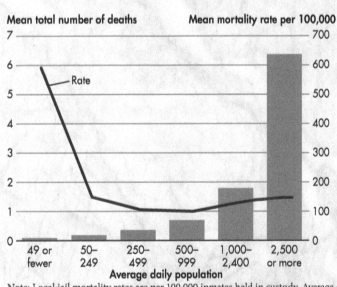

Note: Local jail mortality rates are per 100,000 inmates held in custody. Average daily population is based on average jail inmate population counts from 2000 to 2012.

*Source: Bureau of Justice Statistics, Deaths in Custody Reporting Program, 2000–2012.*

# Return to Society

From 2005 to 2009, more than 700,000 people per year in the United States were released after serving prison sentences and reentered society,[94] more than double the number of people released from prison annually during the 1980s.[95] In recent years, there has been increased emphasis on and interest in improving the reentry process of inmates, primarily driven by concerns over recidivism and increasing correctional budgets. Further, most people returning home from a period of incarceration face considerable **barriers to reintegration** that impede their ability to reestablish citizenship, employment, and housing. As a result, practitioners and policy makers are now seeking ways to improve the transition from prison back to society. Substantial federal funds to assist state and local units of government, as well as nonprofit organizations, have been made available under the federal Second Chance Act to support these efforts.

**Barriers to reintegration** Conditions within the community or society that impede the ability of someone released from prison to reestablish citizenship, employment, and housing.

The U.S. Department of Justice defines *reentry* as "a research-driven process that starts when an offender is initially incarcerated, and ends when the offender has been successfully reintegrated into his or her community as a law-abiding citizen. The reentry process includes the delivery of a variety of program services in both pre- and post-release settings to ensure that the offender safely and successfully transitions from a [correctional facility] to the community."[96] The goal of restoring those in prison to full citizenship and ensuring a smooth transition back to the community has long been a focus of policy makers, but several challenges have arisen. The increased emphasis on punishment, retribution, and incapacitation during the late 1970s through the 1990s is one challenge, but another major issue is the sheer volume of individuals that prisons and agencies serving returning inmates must handle. As a result, the number of people coming out of prison getting services and assistance has grown, but this growth has not kept pace with the number of prison admissions and exits. Thus, the proportion of those receiving rehabilitative services and getting support and assistance in their reentry has decreased.

*The experience of reentry is different for each inmate, and varies based on his or her time in prison, gains made while incarcerated, and family and social support upon release.*

© Skyward Kick Productions/
Shutterstock.com

Increasingly, the process of reentry is not being viewed as something that occurs within the weeks before an inmate is released from prison, but rather, a process of preparing an offender for eventual return to society that often begins with the first contact the justice system has with an offender. Most of those who are ultimately released from prison have spent time on probation, often immediately before their current period of incarceration in prison. For example, more than 375,000 adults on probation in 2009 were negatively discharged from supervision and incarcerated either in jail or prison.[97] In addition, most of those sentenced to prison will have served a fair amount of time in a county jail awaiting trial before the convictions that result in the imposition of a prison sentence: in 2006, the median time between arrest and sentencing for felons in the United States was 265 days, or nearly nine months.[98] Finally, the majority of those released from prison are required to be supervised for a period of time following their release from prison. This perspective is important because many inmates spend relatively little time in prison, but have significant deficits and needs that must be addressed in order to improve their rates of successful reentry and reduce recidivism. Thus, while prisons may have a short period of time to prepare inmates for reentry, the criminal justice system as a whole has a significant amount of time and involvement with these offenders.

The coordination of risk assessment and service delivery would go a long way toward improving the reentry experiences and outcomes of the formerly incarcerated. Any treatment initiated while the offender is on probation or in a county jail awaiting trial should be continued when the offender is incarcerated. Similarly, any information regarding individuals' rehabilitative needs and the progress they may have made while on probation, or in jail or prison, should be shared and communicated to those who work with the individual later in the process. If treatment services are not provided or continued or planned for while an individual is incarcerated, then the prison has not done anything to rehabilitate or initiate the process of rehabilitation.

In order to understand reentry from the inmate's perspective, it is important to recognize that all inmates are unique individuals, with unique circumstances, needs, lengths of time in prison, and environments they will be returning to upon their release from prison. Among inmates released from prison in the U.S. in 2009, the median length of time served overall was 16 months, but for those who served a sentence for a violent crime, the median time served was 29 months.[99] Thus, reentry means something very different for an offender who has served a six-month sentence versus someone who has spent 20 years in prison. Both leave prison having gone through the experience of living within a controlled environment, but for one inmate the world is not much different than when he or she entered prison, whereas for the other, the use of cell phones, the Internet, ATMs, etc., may be completely foreign.

However, for many, their experiences within prison are very similar and have implications for reentry. These individuals are accustomed to living in an environment in which the prison system dictates complete control over when they wake up, when and what they eat, where they sleep, and whom they live with. Relatively little has changed for them in terms of their skills, assets, and thinking patterns. Most inmates who enter prison with a substance abuse problem receive little to no clinical treatment. Although the availability of drugs in prison is much lower than on the streets, this period of sobriety does not change the underlying reasons for the inmates' involvement in crime or use of drugs. Further, this period of sobriety is also not capitalized on through the provision of substantive treatment. Most inmates do not leave prison with markedly higher levels of educational achievement or vocational skills, and most will be going back to the same communities and environments that offered them little opportunity in the first place.

So, while most inmates sentenced to prison will eventually be released, most have not been adequately prepared for their release and reentry into society. The mechanisms of release from prison also have implications for how effectively the reentry process can be managed and facilitated for the formerly incarcerated. Ideally, when people have been deemed dangerous enough to be incarcerated in prison, their incarceration would progress from a highly secure and structured environment to one that provides increased opportunity for rehabilitation, more interaction with society, and increasing levels of personal responsibility for their own care. This would facilitate reentry through progressive stepping down of control and increasing emphasis on independence. From a prison standpoint, this would entail moving from a high-level security status to lower levels of security. Upon release from prison, the former inmates would ideally be provided with a transitional period within a safe, structured environment that would also allow (require) them to seek employment and continue to receive rehabilitative services. These environments are often referred to as halfway houses or work release centers. Although these types of facilities provide inmates with a more gradual transition from the highly regimented, secure setting of prison life to the free world, they also cost more and are less readily available in certain communities than simple release onto parole or post-prison supervision. Another option is for inmates to be released from prison onto electronic monitoring and home confinement. This would then be followed by a period of supervision that would be dictated by the individual risks and needs of the former inmate.

Unfortunately, the experience of most inmates is not close to this ideal. More than a third of inmates incarcerated in the United States are housed in maximum security facilities,[100] which have limited rehabilitative programming, fewer visitation privileges, and other characteristics, such as frequent cell searches, that increase the prisonization of individuals. Relatively few inmates released from prison are transitioned back to the community through **work release centers**, halfway houses, or other monitored residential settings. Instead, prison releasees shift directly from a very highly structured environment in prison where their basic needs are met to "freedom," where suddenly the individual is responsible for meeting his or her own needs. Less than one-quarter (21%) of inmates are housed in minimum security prisons, where access to services and the ability to participate in treatment would be the greatest, and less than 4% are housed in community-based correctional facilities, such as work release centers.[101]

Extensive research has described and gauged the concerns and needs of inmates who are about to be released from prison, as well as the means by

**Work release centers**
Correctional facilities that are designed to provide housing and secure custody of those under the jurisdiction of the prison system, but also allow for inmates to leave during specific periods of time to work or attend vocational or rehabilitative programming in the community.

which these needs are met. The forces that shape the reentry experience of inmates can be grouped into the following categories: the individual-level risks, needs, and attitudes of the formerly incarcerated; the capacity and willingness of friends and family to provide support and assistance to the formerly incarcerated; the capacity and characteristics of the community to which the released inmate is returning; the orientation and resources available to a releasee's parole agent/officer; and finally, the degree to which society as a whole deems the released inmate to be "eligible" for restored citizenship and a second chance.

In most jurisdictions that release inmates to some form of supervision, a risk assessment is performed that often dictates levels of supervision and frequency of contact. Indeed, the assessment of offender risk is a fundamental decision-making process in community corrections.[102] The process and methods used to gauge this risk have evolved considerably over the past 30 to 40 years. Experts have generally identified three "generations" of risk assessment: subjective or clinical judgments by practitioners, actuarial or case classification approaches that employ statistical probabilities of recidivism appropriately matched to supervision levels, and criminogenic/dynamic evaluations.[103] This third approach emphasizes the need to understand offender characteristics that are related to criminal behavior that can be changed through treatment and intervention. These characteristics are dynamic, as opposed to static traits, such as gender and prior criminal behavior.

---

**Ethics & Professionalism**

You are a parole agent supervising a former inmate. The inmate served two years in prison, and had a substance abuse problem before he was incarcerated, but did not access treatment while in prison due to limited availability. The requirement from the parole board is that the inmate be released onto parole, must enroll in a drug treatment program, and must be drug tested randomly while on supervision. You work to identify a program that will enroll the parolee, but he cannot enter the program for another month. You also find out that the parolee tested positive for marijuana after being out of prison for just one week. Legally, you have the ability to use your discretion to return the inmate to prison as a technical violator of parole due to his drug use, or implement graduated sanctions and require the parolee to report more frequently and undergo more frequent drug tests, or do nothing. Which would you do and why? When making this decision, are you concerned more with the costs of continued incarceration, the chances of failure on parole and therefore public safety, the possibility that you will be publicly criticized in the media for making a mistake, or the hope of rehabilitation once treatment is accessed?

Would your decision change if two weeks earlier a colleague had a similar situation, required increased reporting, and the parolee committed an armed robbery that escalated to a murder? Would your decision change if the chances of the above situation occurring are less than 1 in 100? 1 in 1,000? What would be the threshold for you to try to assist the parolee in accessing needed services?

Research shows that information beyond just the formal risk assessment is critical to improving the reentry process. With the renewed interest in and focus on the experiences and needs of those released from prison, a significant amount of research has taken place over the past decade that has been influential in the formation of criminal justice policy and practice.

In their Returning Home study, one of the largest-scale studies of inmate reentry in the United States, the Urban Institute interviewed, surveyed, and tracked thousands of inmates released from prisons across the states of Maryland,[104] Illinois,[105] Ohio,[106] and Texas.[107] The results revealed that not only do inmates leave prison with many of their rehabilitative needs unmet, but they also are forced to rely extensively on family and friends for housing and assistance in seeking employment, and usually return to the same communities they were living in before their incarceration. This is one of the paradoxes of reentry planning and transitioning inmates from prison back to the community—the places that inmates come from often have characteristics that increase the risk of their returning to crime, because they need to protect themselves from violence, need to support themselves, or lack access to mental health or substance abuse treatment. Almost all criminology theories on why offenders commit crime indicate that environmental influences such as social disorganization of neighborhoods, social cohesiveness of communities, and the social disadvantages of neighborhoods affect offenders' decisions to commit another criminal act. In a number of studies examining the characteristics of communities that inmates return to, and how these traits influence recidivism rates, it has been found that returning to a community with concentrated disadvantage increases the odds of recidivism.[108] Even soon-to-be-released inmates recognize that staying away from specific people and places will be critical to their reentry success and staying out of prison in the future.[109] However, given their limited options, most inmates return to the same neighborhoods they came from, and often live with others involved in a pro-criminal lifestyle with antisocial attitudes. Many former inmates feel this is their only option, as most leave prison with nothing more than when they entered, in terms of risks, needs, and deficits.

Another problem that prison releasees face in their communities is that they do not have access to community rehabilitative services. Many of those released from prison are returned to communities where these types of services may be limited or difficult to access, or in more rural communities, may not exist at all because of the small number of people needing such services. In some parts of the United States, those released from prison would need to travel hundreds of miles to access specialized treatment programs or services, even assuming that treatment providers would be willing to enroll/serve someone who may have an extensive history of violence. In more urban areas, programs may be available, but access to these services may be a challenge. Research on prison-based drug treatment has reached a general consensus that post-release aftercare is critical to sustaining the benefits of in-prison treatment,[110] but the access of those released from prison to these services is often limited. The federal Residential Substance Abuse Treatment (RSAT) program encouraged states to ensure that participants in these prison-based treatment programs would receive aftercare,[111] but a number of national evaluations of these programs documented that few jurisdictions were able to provide aftercare for these program participants.[112,113] Indeed, the general conclusion is that most inmates who complete prison-based treatment do not transition back into society with thorough reentry plans or continued services in the community.[114] Some of this difficulty in providing adequate aftercare for inmates stems from the fact that the person released from prison does not always have interest in continuing treatment and often does not have adequate services in his or her community. In some jurisdictions, **reentry courts** have been implemented to ensure that those released from prison with specific requirements are monitored within a judicial setting—a local court—to ensure compliance and to modify conditions as appropriate.

Making aftercare services legally mandatory for released inmates can influence treatment compliance and completion.[115] However, aftercare cannot simply be required: it must also be available and accessible within the communities people are released to, and it requires coordination between correctional facilities, prison-based service providers, and community-based aftercare providers, which does not always happen.[116] Olson and Rozon (2010) found that inmates released back to more rural communities were less likely to access and complete mandatory aftercare following prison-based treatment than those released to more urban areas, other things being equal, and attributed this to lower capacity and availability of services.

Most inmates released from prison return to the same communities where their criminal behavior evolved, with few opportunities, high rates of victimization, and high degrees of social disorganization.

© Fat Jackey/Shutterstock.com

Although the operation of prisons in the United States is primarily the responsibility of state government, the federal government ensures that the constitutional rights of inmates are protected, and supports and conducts research and evaluation to improve the operations of prisons and prison programming. The federal government also provides financial assistance to state governments to develop, implement, and test innovative approaches to improving inmate reentry. The most recent substantive federal act to improve offender reentry was the **Second Chance Act**, which was signed into law on April 9, 2008. Allowed for under this act is the provision of financial support to state, local, and tribal governments, as well as nonprofit groups, to deliver services and programs that improve the reentry of the formerly incarcerated. Congress has appropriated a substantial amount of money to assist state and local criminal justice agencies, service providers, and not-for-profit groups—close to $200 million from 2009 through 2011.[117] But when considering the number of inmates released from prison during that time period—roughly 2 million—much more needs to be done to address the significant needs and barriers inmates face.

**Exhibit: Section III of the Second Chance Act of 2007: Community Safety Through Recidivism Prevention**

The purposes of the Act are—

1. to break the cycle of criminal recidivism, increase public safety, and help States, local units of government, and Indian Tribes, better address the growing population of criminal offenders who return to their communities and commit new crimes;

2. to rebuild ties between offenders and their families, while the offenders are incarcerated and after reentry into the community, to promote stable families and communities;

3. to encourage the development and support of, and to expand the availability of, evidence-based programs that enhance public safety and reduce recidivism, such as substance abuse treatment, alternatives to incarceration, and comprehensive reentry services;

4. to protect the public and promote law-abiding conduct by providing necessary services to offenders, while the offenders are incarcerated and after reentry into the community, in a manner that does not confer luxuries or privileges upon such offenders;

5. to assist offenders reentering the community from incarceration to establish a self-sustaining and law-abiding life by providing sufficient transitional services for as short of a period as practicable, not to exceed one year, unless a longer period is specifically determined to be necessary by a medical or other appropriate treatment professional; and

6. to provide offenders in prisons, jails or juvenile facilities with educational, literacy, vocational, and job placement services to facilitate re-entry into the community.

For many of those released from prison, money is not the only, or most important, force that could improve their outcomes and success. Rather, for many inmates the biggest challenge is overcoming the social and economic stigma of their felony conviction and incarceration. In addition to the significant needs that are unmet by their incarceration—low academic achievement, limited employment history, and substance abuse and mental health disorders—having a felony conviction significantly limits their ability to find employment. Convicted felons are barred from many professions, which vary from state to state, and sometimes from even the most basic of entry-level jobs. For example, in Florida, it was estimated that 40% of public- and private-sector jobs were affected by state-established restrictions on employment of those with criminal records.[118] But even without these prohibitions from employment, many are faced with the challenge of finding employment simply because a felony conviction reported on a job application reduces the chances of being hired. In a study by Pager (2002), it was found that those with a criminal record were one-third to one-half as likely as those without a felony record to be called back for a job interview, and that blacks without a criminal record were less likely to be called back than whites with criminal records.[119] In some states, there have been efforts to address the impact that a felony conviction on a job application can have. Through the so-called "ban the box" initiative, a number of jurisdictions have sought to exclude from job applications the requirement that applicants check a box indicating if they have ever been convicted of a crime/felony. Although legislators and employers remain anxious about the potential liability and risk associated with a person they hire committing a serious crime of violence, no matter how rare the chances of that occurring, some jurisdictions have implemented this policy, at least for public employment. For example, as of early 2011, five states—Hawaii, Massachusetts, Minnesota, New Mexico, and Connecticut—have removed the box asking about felony convictions from state job applications, and at least 20 cities across the country have also implemented this practice on city job applications.[120] Another possible solution to this problem, which has been in place for a long time but is getting renewed interest, is the process of **expungement** of criminal records, in which the official record of an individual's criminal history is prohibited from being disclosed. However, the processes involved in expungement can take considerable time, and for those with multiple convictions, it is not always possible. Despite the increased political attention being paid to the challenges of reentry, political concerns remain about not appearing to be soft on crime.

An even more substantial form of disenfranchisement that those released from prison face is the restriction on voting rights. The degree to which a felony conviction limits someone's right to vote varies from state to state, as does the process to restore this right. For example, in 13 states, upon release from prison, the right of convicted felons to vote is restored provided they register to vote, whereas in 23 other states, a felon can only vote once he or she has completed all aspects of his or her sentence (i.e., completion of parole).[121] In 12 states, the process to regain the right to vote is more complex, including some states where that right can only be reinstated with a pardon from the governor, while others require a certain number of years to elapse since the completion of a prison or probation sentence.[122]

**Expungement** The legal process whereby the official record of an individual's criminal history is prohibited from being disclosed.

---

### Critical Thinking

If you were an employer, what incentives would you need in order to hire someone with a felony conviction?

---

**Discretionary release** The mechanism by which those in prison are released after serving at least a minimum amount of their sentence upon the decision of a parole board.

**Mandatory release** The mechanism by which those in prison must be released after having served their court-imposed sentences, minus any other sentencing credits for which they may be eligible.

Inmates sentenced to prison can be released under three primary methods: parole (**discretionary release**), **mandatory release**, and completion of sentence. As a result of these different release mechanisms, those coming out of prison have varying degrees of what can be required of them by the state. Inmates who have served their full sentences, for the most part, are released without any supervision and few requirements other than those that all law-abiding citizens must live by. They cannot be required to attend drug treatment, participate in educational or vocational programming, or attend anger management classes. On the other hand, inmates released onto parole or some form of supervision following their mandatory or discretionary release are supervised and often have conditions they are expected to abide by, such as treatment programming, urinalysis, and reporting requirements. Because of the concerns that parole boards have regarding releasing inmates before the maximum time has expired, a relatively large portion of inmates released from prison in the United States—25% in 2008—are released from prison "unconditionally," meaning they have no supervision requirements.[123]

A number of states have implemented new programs or policies to try to improve the success of inmates coming out of prison. For example, in Kansas, inmates can work in a government-private partnership program where they earn market-rate pay and are required to save money, pay for a portion of their incarceration, and make restitution.[124] Inmates who participate in this program then have the money they saved available to them when they are released. On average, during 2008 participants in the program earned an average of $13,000 per year, and collectively paid more than $1.6 million in Social Security, federal, and state taxes and more than $2.6 million in "room and board" to the state of Kansas.[125] The fact that participants can save money that they can use upon release gives them some options as to where they will live, with whom they will associate, and the burden, or lack thereof, they place on those with whom they may reside upon release. In comparison, prison releasees who leave prison with the "standard" gate money of $10 to $100, depending on the state, are usually forced to rely on others for all of their needs.

**FIGURE 9.9** PERCENT OF INMATES RELEASED FROM STATE PRISONS IN THE U.S. UNDER MANDATORY PAROLE, DISCRETIONARY PAROLE AND EXPIRATION OF SENTENCE, 1980–2004

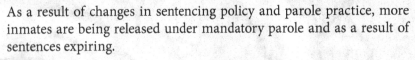

As a result of changes in sentencing policy and parole practice, more inmates are being released under mandatory parole and as a result of sentences expiring.

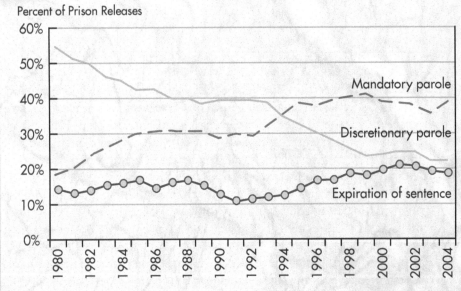

Source: Bureau of Justice Statistics

Still, the prospect of inmates having significant amounts of money saved as a result of their prison labor does not always align with society's expectation that prison be punishment. Illustrative of this is a case in Illinois where an inmate had saved $11,000 over the course of his 25 years of working in a prison industry program, at a rate of about $75 per month. His intention was to provide that money to his daughter, but the state of Illinois moved to seize and use the funds to pay the state back for his incarceration because his account exceeded the threshold of $10,000.[126] Ultimately, the state backed off its effort to seize the funds.

Another factor that affects the reentry experience is the orientation of parole agencies and officers. These agencies may either enforce requirements (i.e., operate as police), refer releasees to needed rehabilitative services and support (i.e., case managers), or work directly with releasees to aid in their rehabilitation and assimilation back into society (i.e., social workers and counselors). These different approaches to the relationship between releasee and parole agent can vary from jurisdiction to jurisdiction, but also from officer to officer. As a result, part of what can influence a prison releasee's success or failure after incarceration is the orientation and emphasis placed on surveillance versus rehabilitation by parole agents.

# Recidivism

In the field of criminal justice, the most frequently used measure to gauge the impact and effectiveness of interventions and rehabilitative programs is the reduction in recidivism, or reduced involvement in criminal behavior, by those who participate in the program. High rates of recidivism have led to calls for increased attention to prison-based programming and enhanced efforts at improving inmate reentry. However, accurately measuring an individual's involvement in crime is very difficult, since many crimes never come to the attention of law enforcement. Thus, for the purposes of criminal justice research, measuring subsequent involvement in crime usually involves analyses of official criminal history information, including rearrests for new crimes, new convictions, or return to prison.

Philosophers ask, "If a tree falls in the forest, but no one is there to hear it, does it make a sound?" Similarly, if someone commits a crime, but is not arrested or returned to prison, can he or she be considered a recidivist?

Some argue that recidivism should be measured by conviction for a crime, because there would have been proof beyond a reasonable doubt that a crime was committed. The limitation with this measure, though, is that when an offender is on active parole, the prosecutor sometimes will not actually file charges or seek a conviction. This can be influenced by both the seriousness of the offense and the response to the new arrest by parole agents and a state's parole board. For example, offenders who are rearrested for drug possession while on parole can have their parole revoked and be returned to prison to serve the remainder of their supervision period. In this case, a prosecutor may not file charges, and therefore not seek a conviction, because the response by the parole agent and parole board achieved the goal of punishment or incarceration. On the other hand, if the crime was more serious, or the prosecutor did not view the parole board's response as sufficient, the prosecutor might choose to file charges and seek a conviction. Thus, some arrests of parolees will result in prosecution being sought, and potentially a conviction being obtained, whereas other cases will not result in additional formal processing through the courts.

Another measure of recidivism is a former inmate's return to prison. This can be influenced by rearrests or other violations of supervision/parole. As described above, inmates rearrested for a new crime while on supervision can be returned to prison because of this new arrest without being convicted, and these are usually considered "technical violations" as opposed to a return to prison for a new crime. Inmates returned to prison for violating the conditions of supervision other than a new arrest can be viewed as "purely" technical violators, and the reasons can include failure to report to their parole agent, not complying with treatment requirements, testing positive for drugs during urinalysis, etc.

Depending on which definition of recidivism is used, combined with practices and policies across the states in what threshold of behavior/violation justifies or requires being returned to prison, recidivism rates can vary dramatically.

However, the public's perception and understanding of recidivism can sometimes be skewed by what they are exposed to in the media. The media often focuses on only the most extreme examples of successes and failures of inmate reentry—those that became very successful following their release from prison or those that experienced horrific outcomes following their release from prison. In reality, most of those released from prison have experiences that fall somewhere in the middle of these two extremes. The reentry experience for most involves some successes and some failures; few experience no hurdles, and few commit horrible crimes of violence and murder. Thus, the reentry experience should be viewed on a scale or continuum, and not as a dichotomy of success or failure. Given the many needs that those coming out of prison often have, successfully addressing one or a few of these needs is often a significant accomplishment in incrementally moving someone from a lifestyle of criminality to the role of law-abiding, income-earning, responsible citizen.

Although somewhat dated, the only nationally representative recidivism rates for individuals released from prison were generated by the U.S. Department of Justice's Bureau of Justice Statistics based on a sample of inmates released from prison in 1994.[127] That study found that 67% of released inmates were rearrested for a new crime within three years and

47% were reconvicted of a new crime. More recent information collected from individual states by the Pew Center for the States found that nationally roughly 43% of inmates released from prison in 2004 were returned to prison within three years, with rates ranging from below 30% in a number of states to more than 50% in others.[128] The authors of the report concluded that comparing recidivism rates from state to state poses a number of challenges, due to differences in parole policies, lengths of supervision, and the nature of parole supervision.

Another problem with comparing rates of recidivism—as measured by official actions within the justice system, such as arrest, conviction, and return to prison—is that these data can be dramatically altered and changed as a result of changes in policies that influence arrests, convictions, and return to prison. For example, if a local police department reduces the number of police officers on patrol due to budgetary cuts or limitations, the number of police available to detect potential illegal behavior by those released from prison decreases. Similarly, if a local police department redeploys more officers to street patrol, or implements a crackdown on street-corner drug sales, the odds of illegal behavior by those released from prison (and everyone else involved in crime) being detected by the police increases. In other words, a decrease in the recidivism rate (as measured by rearrest) could be the result of improved programming and reentry planning by prisons and correctional agencies, or it could be the result of fewer police officers or a change in policing policy, or both. Similarly, if prisons become more effective at assisting inmates as they return to society, but at the same time the police become more sophisticated at detecting illegal behavior or solving crimes, the recidivism rate based on rearrests could remain the same.

Similarly, differences in recidivism rates (as measured by return to prison) vary from state to state, often because of differences in post-prison supervision policies and practices. If one state has no post-prison supervision and another state has extensive supervision, then the latter is likely to have a higher rate of former inmates being returned to prison because technical violations by these individuals can more easily be detected. Even within individual states, these policies and practices can change over time. For example, a state may change its laws related to the duration of post-prison supervision and this may reduce the rate at which former inmates are returned to prison. Although the frequency or prevalence of illegal behavior among former inmates may not change, the capacity of parole agents to detect it and return offenders to prison as technical violators does change.

© IxMaster/Shutterstock.com

Although crimes committed by those released from prison tend to be for nonviolent crimes or drug-law violations, often only the most heinous crimes committed by parolees are covered by the media and shape public perceptions.

An important factor to consider in recidivism is not just how *often* prison releasees reoffend, but *how* they reoffend. While some of the most shocking headlines of the past two decades have involved prison releasees committing horrendous crimes of murder and rape, which then prompted a number of changes to sentencing and prison release policy, the fact remains that these types of violent crimes are rare. Most crimes prison releasees are arrested for are property or drug crimes, indicative of releasees' limited economic opportunity and substance abuse disorders. Among the 1994 releasees the U.S. Department of Justice tracked in their national recidivism study, 33% of the rearrests involved drug-law violations and 34% involved property crimes.[129] Out of all the inmates released in 1994, only 1.4% were rearrested within three years for murder or sexual assault.[130] While these rearrest rates for the most serious forms of violence are relatively low, they still represent significant harm to victims, victims' families, and society as a whole, and often shape the perception of citizens and the electorate as to what types of behaviors those released from prison engage in once free.

Finally, another dimension of recidivism to consider is: who are the offenders, and when do they offend? For the most part, recidivists rearrested for new crimes following their release from prison tend to reoffend relatively soon after release—usually within the first six to 12 months. Nationally, of those rearrested within three years of release, almost one-half of the rearrests occurred within the first six months of release, and two-thirds of those rearrested were rearrested within one year of their release from prison.[131] Again, this is the period when the formerly incarcerated face the most significant changes to their lives—the transition from a highly regimented environment where their basic needs are met by the state to freedom and the expectation that they provide for their own needs. Released inmates who are younger, male, less educated, and have more extensive criminal histories have higher rates of recidivism, regardless of how recidivism is defined.

The degree to which inmates have access to rehabilitative programming is also related to recidivism. Still, rehabilitative programs that seek to improve specific conditions of individuals, such as their education level, substance abuse disorders, interpersonal skills, etc., are not perfect and cannot address larger societal issues and barriers that often challenge the success of those released from prison. Even if offenders' substance abuse problems have been eliminated, they still face significant barriers to employment, as described previously, and the ability to meet their basic needs of food, shelter, and safety.

Research has shown that recidivism rates have been reduced, on average, from 35% to 28% across standardized time periods.[132] These data are promising and encouraging, particularly given all of the other challenges former inmates face when released from prison. However, from a political and public policy standpoint, often these reductions in recidivism are not substantial enough. Often all it takes is for one highly sensationalized case, as rare as it might be, to bring unwarranted criticism to rehabilitative programs, which often results in the programs being eliminated and a "tough" response in terms of criminal justice policy.

**Career Connections: Rehabilitative Professionals**

Employment opportunities working on inmate reentry and rehabilitation include a variety of professions. These range from positions within correctional facilities or prison systems—such as teachers, counselors, psychologists, and parole agents—to positions in social service agencies that work with released inmates in the communities. Those who work in the area of child welfare will often encounter situations where the custodial parent is incarcerated or returning from prison or jail. Similarly, community-based substance abuse treatment and mental health agencies employ counselors and therapists who may work with both prison releasees and those who have not been incarcerated. Increasingly because of the emphasis on reentry, as well as the dedicated funding available through the Second Chance Act, many agencies are creating specialized units to work with those returning from a period of incarceration, including positions within employment agencies, vocational training, and job development.

The credentials needed for positions working within prisons as educators, substance abuse and mental health counselors, psychiatrists, and vocational training professionals vary from state to state as well as position to position. For most of these positions, a bachelor's degree would be the minimum requirement, but some, such as psychiatrists, would require advanced degrees. Others, such as substance abuse counselors, would require certification from state licensing boards that evaluate the credentials of clinical staff. The growing area of employment opportunities providing support for those coming out of prison—community-based treatment providers, job coaches for returning inmates, case managers—are usually within urban areas where many of the inmates are returning after their release, and often do not require college degrees. Indeed, many programs that hire mentors for those coming out of prison seek to hire formerly incarcerated individuals who know the community and can develop rapport with the clients to be served.

# Chapter Summary

- Prisons face the challenge of achieving multiple goals—incapacitation, deterrence, punishment, and rehabilitation—with a diverse population of inmates who have vastly different sentences and conflicting public sentiment regarding what prisons should accomplish. While prisons attempt to balance these multiple goals, they must also seek to ensure that staff and inmates are safe from violence.

- Inmates enter prison with a wide range of needs that, if not addressed, will likely lead to continued involvement in crime. While many prisons have programs to address educational and vocational deficits, substance abuse, and mental health needs of inmates, they are generally small in scale and serve only a fraction of those needing services.

- Inmates released from prison face a variety of challenges as they reenter society, including unmet criminogenic needs, risks associated with the environments they return to, and societal attitudes that make obtaining employment and assimilating back into society a challenge.

- Increased attention to the process of inmate reentry has offered hope that inmates will receive more programming while incarcerated, and assistance and support as they transition from prison life to becoming law-abiding, contributing members of society. Both symbolically and materially, the federal Second Chance Act has changed the tone of the debate regarding inmate reentry in the United States and the need to reduce recidivism.

- Regardless of how it is measured—new arrests, convictions, or return to prison—the recidivism rate of those released from prison is at a level that has resulted in many people questioning the effectiveness of prisons at rehabilitation, although given the multiple goals of prisons, it is clear that rehabilitation has not been the focus of prisons since the 1960s.

## Critical Thinking?

1. Many people point to the high costs of incarceration—roughly $25,000 per year—and the high rate of recidivism—roughly 50% of inmates return to prison within three years of release—and conclude that prisons are not effective. Do you think this is a fair statement?

2. From what you understand about how prisons operate, do you think there are ways to shift the current use of resources away from security staff toward more treatment staff without compromising the security of prisons? Are there opportunities for technology to improve the means by which prison security and/or prisoner rehabilitation is accomplished?

3. What role do you feel society as a whole should play in facilitating inmate reentry and improving the success of those released from prison? To what degree does the stigma of being a convicted felon, or a former inmate, influence successful reentry?

4. To what degree do you feel there is a disconnect between sentencing practices—sentence lengths, time served, determinate versus indeterminate sentencing—and achieving the goals of rehabilitation?

5. Explain why it is important to differentiate between the existence, scale, and quality of prison-based rehabilitative programs. Despite empirical evidence that certain types of programs do not work to reduce recidivism (i.e., drug education programs or self-help groups), why might prisons continue to operate them and offer them to large numbers of inmates?

6. Explain why, despite most prisons having drug abuse programs, most inmates in need of substantive substance abuse treatment do not receive it while incarcerated.

7. When the public considers the effectiveness of prisons, they often point to the recidivism rate and not to other measures of their

effectiveness, such as incapacitation (few escapes) and ensuring safety of staff and inmates (few murders in prison). Why do you think the public fails to consider these dimensions of prison effectiveness?

8. Why do you think that, despite research showing that treatment can reduce recidivism and be cost-effective in the long run, many people still feel treatment does not work?

9. What are the different ways that recidivism has been defined or measured? Which one do you feel is the best measure of whether or not someone released from prison has engaged in illegal activity?

10. If recidivism rates of those released from prison increase (or decrease), explain how that change might have nothing to do with the success or failure of rehabilitative efforts within prisons.

## Media

**The Campbell Collaboration:** https://campbellcollaboration.org/ The Campbell Collaboration's Crime and Justice Reviews website contains objective reviews of the existing research into the effectiveness and efficacy of criminal justice programs and policies.

**The Urban Institute:** http://www.urban.org/projects/reentry-portfolio/index.cfm The Urban Institute's Justice Policy Center website has an extensive collection of national and state-specific reports examining different aspects on inmate reentry, from model programs to original research documenting the experiences of those released from prison.

**The National Reentry Resource Center:** http://www.national reentryresourcecenter.org/ This website contains extensive information on reentry programs and policies across the United States, as well as webinars, announcements of upcoming meetings and training conferences, and links to other sites related to prisoner reentry.

**Bureau of Justice Statistics:** http://bjs.ojp.usdoj.gov/ The U.S. Department of Justice's Bureau of Justice Statistics website allows users to examine recidivism rates of those released from prison based on a nationally representative sample. Users can explore how various demographic, offense, and criminal history characteristics are correlated with different measures of recidivism, such as rearrest, reconviction, and return to prison.

## Endnotes

[1] Pew Center on the States. (2011). *State of Recidivism: The Revolving Door of America's Prisons*. Washington, D.C.: The Pew Charitable Trusts.

[2] Mumola, C. J., & Karberg, J. C. (2006). *Drug Use and Dependence, State and Federal Prisoners, 2004*. Washington, D.C.: U.S. Department of Justice.

3    Bureau of Justice Statistics. (2016) *Correctional Populations in the United States, 2016.* Retrieved from https://www.bjs.gov/content/pub/pdf/cpus15.pdf

3    Travis, J. (2005). *But They All Come Back: Facing the Challenges of Prisoner Reentry.* Washington, D.C.: Urban Institute.

4    West, H. C. (2010). *Prison Inmates at Mid-Year 2009—Statistical Tables.* Washington, D.C.: U.S. Department of Justice.

5    Minton, T. & Zeng, Z. (2015). *Jail Inmates at Midyear 2014.* Bureau of Justice Statistics. NCJ 248629.

6    Pew Center on the States. (2010). *National Research on Public Attitudes Towards Crime and Punishment.* Retrieved from http://www.pewcenteronthestates.org/uploadedFiles/wwwpewcenteronthestatesorg/Initiatives/PSPP/PSPP_National%20Research_web.pdf?n=6608

7    Krisberg, B., & Marchionna, S. (2006). *Attitudes of US Voters toward Prisoner Rehabilitation and Reentry Policies.* National Council on Crime and Delinquency.

8    Mitchell, O., Wilson, D. B., & MacKenzie, D. L. (2006). *The Effectiveness of Incarceration-Based Drug Treatment on Criminal Behavior.* Campbell Collaboration, Criminal Justice Review Group.

9    Cullen, F. T., & Gilbert, K. E. (1982). *Reaffirming Rehabilitation.* Cincinnati, OH: Anderson.

10   Buruma, I. (2005). "Uncaptive Minds." *The New York Times Magazine.*

11   Sparks, R. (1996). "Penal 'Austerity': The Doctrine of Least Eligibility Reborn." In R. Mathews and P. Francis (Eds.), *Prisons 2000* (pp. 74–93). New York, NY: St. Martins.

12   Buruma, 2005.

13   Byrne, J., & Hummer, D. (2007). "In Search of the 'Tossed Salad Man' (and Others Involved in Prison Violence): New Strategies for Predicting and Controlling Prison Violence." *Aggression and Violent Behavior, 12*(5), 531–541.

14   French, S. A., & Gendreau, P. (2006). "Reducing Prison Misconduct: What Works?" *Criminal Justice and Behavior, 33,* 185–218.

15   Ibid.

16   Kinlock, T. W., O'Grady, K. E., & Hanlon, T. E. (2003). "Effects of Drug Treatment on Institutional Behavior." *The Prison Journal, 83*(3), 257–276.

17   Welsh, W. N., McGrain, P., Salamatin, N., & Zajac, G. (2007). "Effects of Prison Drug Treatment on Inmate Misconduct: a Repeated Measures Analysis." *Criminal Justice and Behavior, 34,* 600–615.

18   Lipton, D., Martinson, R., & Wilks, J. (1975). *The Effectiveness of Correctional Treatment.* New York, NY: Praeger.

19   Martinson, R. (1974). "What Works? Questions and Answers about Prison Reform." *The Public Interest, 35,* 22–45.

20   Miller, J. (1989, March). "The Debate on Rehabilitating Criminals: Is It True that Nothing Works?" *Washington Post.*

21   Gendreau, P. & Ross, R.R. (1979). "Effective Correctional Treatment: Bibliotherapy for Cynics." *Crime and Delinquency, 25,* 46–489.

22   Andrews, D. A., & Bonita, J. (2010). *The Psychology of Criminal Conduct* (5th ed.). New Province, NJ: Anderson.

23  Bureau of Justice Statistics. (2011). *Key Facts at a Glance: Four Measures of Serious Violent Crime.* Retrieved from http://bjs.ojp.usdoj.gov/content/glance/tables/4meastab.cfm

24  Stemen, D., Rengifo, A. F., & Wilson, J. A. (2005). *Of Fragmentation and Ferment: the Impact of State Sentencing Policies on Incarceration Rates, 1975–2000.* New York, NY: Vera Institute of Justice.

25  Ibid.

26  *Mistretta v. United States,* 488 U.S. 361 (1989).

27  Miller, 1989.

28  Serin, R. C., & Justice Institute. (2005). *Evidence-Based Practice: Principles for Enhancing Correctional Results in Prisons.* Washington, D.C.: U.S. Department of Justice, National Institute of Corrections, 4.

29  Stolz, B. A. (1992). "Congress and the War on Drugs: An Exercise in Symbolic Politics." *Journal of Crime and Justice, 15*(1), 119–136.

30  Sample, L. L., Evans, M. K., & Anderson, A. L. (2011). "Sex Offender Community Notification Laws: Are Their Effects Symbolic or Instrumental in Nature?" *Criminal Justice Policy Review, 22*(1), 27–49.

30  Bureau of Justice Statistics. (2015). *Census of State and Federal Adult Correctional Facilities, 2015* [Computer file]. ICPSR24642-v2. Ann Arbor, MI: Inter-university Consortium for Political and Social Research.

31  30

32  Sample, L. L., Evans, M. K., & Anderson, A. L. (2011). "Sex Offender Community Notification Laws: Are Their Effects Symbolic or Instrumental in Nature?" *Criminal Justice Policy Review, 22*(1), 27–49.

33  Ibid.

34  Bureau of Justice Statistics. (2005). *Census of State and Federal Adult Correctional Facilities, 2005* [Computer file]. ICPSR24642-v2. Ann Arbor, MI: Inter-university Consortium for Political and Social Research.

35  Hardyman, P. L., Austin, J., & Peyton, J. (2004). *Prisoner Intake Systems: Assessing Needs and Classifying Prisoners.* Washington, D.C.: U.S. Department of Justice, National Institute of Corrections.

36  Stephan, 2008.

37  Ibid.

38  Maruschak, L. M. (2008). *Medical Problems of Prisoners.* Retrieved from http://bjs.ojp.usdoj.gov/index.cfm?ty=pbdetail&iid=1097

39  Ibid.

40  Olson, D., & Rozhon, J. (2011). *A Process and Impact Evaluation of the Southwestern Illinois Correctional Center Therapeutic Community Program During Fiscal Years 2007 through 2010.* Chicago, IL: Illinois Criminal Justice Information Authority.

41  James, D. J., & Glaze, L. E. (2006). *Mental Health Problems of Prison and Jail Inmates.* Washington, D.C.: U.S. Department of Justice.

42  Ibid.

43  Mumola & Karberg, 2006.

44    Glaze, L. E., & Maruschak, L. M. (2008). *Parents in Prison and Their Minor Children*. Washington, D.C.: U.S. Department of Justice.

45    Harlow, C. W. (2003). *Education and Correctional Populations*. Washington, D.C.: U.S. Department of Justice.

46    Maruschak, 2008.

47    Ibid.

48    Langan & Levin, 2002.

49    Ibid.

50    Stephan, 2008.

51    Ibid.

52    Olson & Rozhon, 2011.

53    James & Glaze, 2006.

54    National Institute on Drug Abuse. (2002). *Therapeutic Community— Research Report Series*. Washington, D.C.: Department of Health and Human Services.

55    Lurigio, A. J. (2000). "Drug Treatment Availability and Effectiveness: Studies of the General and Criminal Justice Populations." *Criminal Justice and Behavior, 27*(4), 495–528.

56    Wexler, H, Melnick, G., Lowe, L., & Peters, J. (1999). "Three Year Reincarceration Outcomes for Amity in-Prison Therapeutic Community and Aftercare in California." *The Prison Journal, 79*, 321–336.

57    Knight, K., Simpson, D., Chatham, L., & Camacho, L. (2004). "An Assessment of Prison-Based Treatment: Texas' In-Prison Therapeutic Community Program." *Journal of Offender Rehabilitation, 24*, 75–100.

58    Inciardi, J. A., Martin, S. S., Butzin, C. A., Hooper, R. M., & Harrison, L. D. (1997). "An Effective Model of Prison-Based Treatment for Drug-Involved Offenders." *Journal of Drug Issues, 27*, 261–278.

59    Olson & Rozhon, 2011.

60    Wilson, D. B., MacKenzie, D. L., & Mitchell, F. N. (2005). *Effects of Correctional Boot Camps on Offending*. Campbell Collaboration, Criminal Justice Review Group.

61    Gendreau, P. (2011). "Rehabilitation: What Works to Change Offenders." In F. T. Cullen & C. L. Jonson (Eds.), *Correctional Theory: Context and Consequences*. Los Angeles, CA: Sage.

62    Inciardi, J. A., Martin, S. S., & Butzin, C. A. (2004). "Five Year Outcomes of Therapeutic Community Treatment of Drug Involved Offenders Released from Prison." *Crime and Delinquency, 50*, 88–107.

63    Gendreau, 2011.

64    Andrews & Bonita, 2010.

65    Prendergast, M. L., Farabee, D., Cartier, J., & Henkin, S. (2002). "Involuntary Treatment Within a Prison Setting: Impact on Psychological Change During Treatment." *Criminal Justice and Behavior, 29*(1), 5–26.

66    Parhar, K. K., Wormith, J. S., Derkzen, D. M., & Beauregard, A. M. (200X). "Offender Coercion in Treatment: A Meta-Analysis of Effectiveness." *Criminal Justice and Behavior, 35*(9), 1109–1135.

[67] Langenberger, N. A., & Lipsey, M. W. (2005). "The Positive Effects of Cognitive-Behavioral Programs for Offenders: A Meta-Analysis of Factors Associated with Effective Treatment." *Journal of Experimental Criminology, 1,* 451–476.

[68] Ibid.

[69] Bureau of Justice Assistance. (2007). *Residential Substance Abuse Treatment (RSAT) for State Prisoners Program FY 2008 Formula Grant Announcement.* Washington, D.C.: U.S. Department of Justice.

[70] Lipton, D. S., Pearson, F. S., & Wexler, H. K. (2000). *Final Report: National Evaluation of the Residential Substance Abuse Treatment for State Prisoners Program from Onset to Midpoint.* Washington, D.C.: U.S. Department of Justice, National Institute of Justice.

[71] Lawrence, A. (2009). *Cutting Corrections Costs: Earned Time Policies for State Prisoners.* Denver, CO: National Conference of State Legislatures.

[72] Olson & Rozhon, 2011.

[73] Ettner, S. L., Huang, D., Evans, E., Ash, D. R., Hardy, M., Jourabchi, M., & Hser, Y. (2006). "Benefit-Cost in the California Treatment Outcome Project: Does Substance Abuse Treatment 'Pay for Itself'?" *Health Services Research, 41*(1), 192–213.

[74] Gerstein, D. R., Johnson, R. A., Harwood, H. J., Fountain, D., Suter, N., & Malloy, K. (1994). *Evaluating Recovery Services: The California Drug and Alcohol Treatment Assessment (CALDATA).* Sacramento, CA: California Department of Alcohol and Drug Programs Resource Center.

[75] Gendreau, 2011.

[76] Harlow, 2003.

[77] James & Glaze, 2006.

[78] Mumola & Karberg, 2006.

[79] Mears, D. P., Winterfield, L., Hunsaker, J., Moore, G. E., & White, R. M. (2003). *Drug Treatment in the Criminal Justice System: The Current State of Knowledge.* Washington, D.C.: Urban Institute.

[80] Mitchell et al., 2006.

[81] Ibid.

[82] Ibid.

[83] Mears et al., 2003.

[84] Farabee, D., Prendergast, M., Cartier, J., Wexler, J., Knight, K., & Anglin, M. D. (1999). "Barriers to Implementing Effective Correctional Drug Treatment Programs." *The Prison Journal, 79*(2), 150–162.

[85] Inciardi, J. A., Martin, S. S., Lockwood, D., Hooper, R. H., & Wald, B. A. (1992). "Obstacles to the Implementation and Evaluation of Drug Treatment in Correctional Settings: Reviewing the Delaware KEY Experience." In C. G. Leukenfeld & F. M. Tims (Eds.), *National Institute on Drug Abuse Research Monograph Series #118: Drug Abuse Treatment in Prisons and Jails* (pp. 176–191). Washington, D.C.: U.S. Government Printing Office.

[86] Farabee et al., 1999.

87    Morrissey, J. P., Steadman, H. J., & Kilburn, M. R. (1983). "Organizational Issues in the Delivery of Jail Mental Health Services." *Research in Community and Mental Health, 3,* 291–317.

88    Inciardi et al., 1992.

89    Culp, R. F. (2005). "Frequency and Characteristics of Prison Escapes in the United States: An Analysis of National Data." *The Prison Journal, 85*(3), 270–291.

90    Bureau of Justice Statistics, 2005.

91    Ibid.

92    Bureau of Justice Statistics. (2011). *Homicide Trends in the U.S.* Retrieved from http://www.bjs.gov/content/homicide/overview.cfm#gender

93    Mumola, C. J. (2007). *Medical Causes of Death in State Prisons, 2001–2004.* Washington, D.C.: U.S. Department of Justice.

94    West, H. C., Sabol, W. J., & Greenman, S. J. (2010). *Prisoners in 2009.* Washington, D.C.: U.S. Department of Justice.

95    Mumola, C. J., & Beck, A. J. (1997). *Prisoners in 1996.* Washington, D.C.: U.S. Department of Justice.

96    Bureau of Justice Assistance. (2011). *Second Chance Act Adult Mentoring Grants to Nonprofit Organizations FY 2011 Competitive Grant Announcement.* Washington, D.C.: U.S. Department of Justice.

97    Glaze & Bonzcar, 2010.

98    Rosenmerkel et al., 2010.

99    Bonczar, 2011.

100   Stephan, 2005.

101   Ibid.

102   Holsinger, A. M., Lurigio, A. J., & Latessa, E. J. (2001). "Practitioners' Guide to Understanding the Basis of Assessing Offender Risk." *Federal Probation, 65,* 46–50.

103   Bonta, A. (1996). "Risk-Needs Assessment and Treatment." In A. Harland (Ed.), *Choosing Corrections Options That Work: Defining the Demand and Evaluating the Supply* (pp. 4–54). Thousand Oaks, CA: Sage.

104   LaVigne, N. G., Kachnowski, V., Travis, J., Naser, R., & Visher, C. (2003). *A Portrait of Prisoner Reentry in Maryland.* Washington, D.C.: The Urban Institute.

105   LaVigne, N. G., Mamalian, C. A. Travis, J., Naser, R., & Visher, C. (2003). *A Portrait of Prisoner Reentry in Illinois.* Washington, D.C.: The Urban Institute.

106   LaVigne, N. G., & Thomson, G. L. (2003). *A Portrait of Prisoner Reentry in Ohio.* Washington, D.C.: The Urban Institute.

107   Watson, J., Solomon, A.L., LaVigne, N.G., Travis, J., Funches, M., & Parthasarathy, B. (2004). *A Portrait of Prisoner Reentry in Texas.* Washington, D.C.: The Urban Institute.

108   Hipp, J. R., Petersilia, J., & Turner, S. (2010). "Parolee Recidivism in California: The Effect of Neighborhood Context and Social Service Agency Characteristics." *Criminology, 48*(4), 947–979.

[109] Visher, C., LaVigne, N. G., & Farell, J. (2003). *Illinois Prisoners' Reflections on Returning Home.* Washington, D.C.: The Urban Institute.

[110] Inciardi, Martin, & Butzin, 2004.

[111] Bureau of Justice Assistance, 2007.

[112] Harrison, L. L., & Martin, S. S. (2000). *Residential Substance Abuse Treatment (RSAT) for State Prisoners Formula Grant: Compendium of Program Implementation and Accomplishments.* Newark, DE: Center for Drug and Alcohol Studies.

[113] Lipton et al., 2000.

[114] Mears et al., 2003.

[115] Anglin, M. D., & Hser, Y. I. (1991). "Criminal Justice and the Drug Abusing Offender: Policy Issues of Coerced Treatment." *Behavioral Sciences and the Law, 9*(3), 243–267.

[116] Mears et al., 2003.

[117] Council of State Governments Justice Center. (n.d.). *Second Chance Act.* Retrieved from http://www.reentrypolicy.org/government_affairs/second_chance_act

[118] Mills, L. (2008). *Inventorying and Reforming State-Created Employment Restrictions Based on Criminal Records: A Policy Brief and Guide.* The Annie E. Casey Foundation.

[119] Pager, D. (2002). *The Mark of a Criminal Record.* Dissertation, Department of Sociology, University of Wisconsin, Madison.

[120] Loftus, K. (2011, January 28). "More Public Job Applications Skip the Felony Conviction Box." *Capital News Service of the Michigan State University School of Journalism.*

[121] ProCon.org. (2010). *State Felon Voting Laws.* Retrieved from http://felonvoting.procon.org/view.resource.php?resourceID=286

[122] Ibid.

[123] Sabol, W. J., West, H. C., & Cooper, M. (2010). *Prisoners in 2008.* Washington, D.C.: U.S. Department of Justice.

[124] Kansas Correctional Industries. (n.d.). *Private Prison Industries: Private Companies Employing Kansas Inmates.* Retrieved from http://www.wichitamanufacturers.org/previoustours/EDCF%20Private%20Industry%20Brochure.pdf

[125] Young, M. C. (2011). *Alternative Strategies for Funding Employment-Related Reentry Programs.* Northwestern University Law School.

[126] Sachdev, A. (2011, March 15). "Illinois Seeks to Seize Prisoner's Wages." *Chicago Tribune.*

[127] Langan & Levin, 2002.

[128] Pew Center on the States, 2011.

[129] Langan & Levin, 2002.

[130] Ibid.

[131] Ibid.

[132] Mitchell et al., 2006.

# SECTION 5
## SPECIAL TOPICS IN CRIMINAL JUSTICE

# Juvenile Justice

## KEY TERMS

Adjudication hearing

Age of majority

Amenability hearing

Boot camp

Child Savers movement

Cottage reformatories

Deinstitutionalization

Diminished culpability

Disposition

Drug Abuse Resistance
    Education (D.A.R.E.)

Houses of refuge

Juvenile delinquency

Juvenile waiver hearing

Monitoring the Future

Moral panic

National Youth Survey

*Parens patriae*

Reform schools

Scared-straight programs

Status offenses

# CHAPTER OBJECTIVES

1 Describe the differences between juvenile courts and criminal courts.

2 Discuss the history of the juvenile justice system in the United States.

3 Analyze contemporary debates regarding the treatment and punishment of juvenile offenders.

4 Differentiate between types of juvenile corrections.

5 Explain theories of juvenile delinquency.

6 Examine patterns in juvenile victimization and offending.

## Case Study: Kent v. United States

Prior to the Supreme Court's 1966 ruling in *Kent v. United States*, juveniles had few, if any, rights recognized within the legal system. This changed when the Supreme Court recognized that under the 14th Amendment to the Constitution, a juvenile had due process rights. In *Kent*, the court held that a juvenile has the right to counsel, the right to a hearing, and the right to be informed of what he or she is being charged with.

On September 2, 1961, an intruder entered a woman's apartment in Washington, D.C., stole her wallet, and raped her. Police discovered fingerprints at the scene and matched them to fingerprints taken from Morris A. Kent, a 16-year-old who had been on juvenile probation when he was 14 for house-breaking and an attempted purse-snatching. Kent was taken into custody by police on September 5, 1961. Rather than release Kent to a parent or take him to a juvenile court designee, as required by D.C. law, Kent was taken to police headquarters and interrogated for seven hours. That evening, he was taken to a local children's home, then picked up the next morning for further interrogation by the police. During his interrogations, Kent confessed to the incidents on September 2 and several other offenses. The day after his arrest, Kent's mother retained counsel for her son.

Under the D.C. Juvenile Court Act, Kent was legally a minor and therefore under the jurisdiction of the local juvenile court. The District of Columbia defines a minor as a person under the age of 18. Similar to other jurisdictions, however, Washington, D.C.'s juvenile code allowed for transfer (or waiver) of jurisdiction of a juvenile case to the adult criminal court on a case-by-case basis. To transfer a juvenile, a juvenile court judge was required to conduct a "full investigation" into the child's background and into the circumstances surrounding the offense. The court did not conduct an investigation and neither Kent, Kent's attorney, nor his mother were able to participate in a transfer decision hearing. Further, the court offered no written statement justifying Kent's transfer.

Kent was indicted on eight counts in the District Court and the case went to trial. A jury found Kent guilty on six of the eight counts and he received a total sentence of 30 to 90 years to serve.

After he was found guilty, Kent appealed his conviction and his case was eventually brought before the Supreme Court of the United States. There, the court ruled that the juvenile court's waiver of jurisdiction was procedurally invalid. The court ruled that the juvenile court, by not holding a hearing where Kent, his counsel, and his parents could have participated, violated Kent's fundamental due process rights. This violation made the waiver invalid, and the Supreme Court ordered that the case be remanded back to the juvenile court for a waiver hearing. A waiver can only be valid if the juvenile made it knowingly, intelligently, and voluntarily. The court found that Kent could not have made a knowing, intelligent, and voluntary waiver because he had been denied his due process rights.

*Kent* was one of the first times that the United States Supreme Court stepped in with regards to a juvenile case, and the ruling was significant. The court said that juvenile defendants were afforded rights under the 14th Amendment, including the right to counsel, the right to a hearing, and the right to know what they are being charged with.[1]

## Delinquency

**Delinquency** can refer to many different things. Delinquency can refer to an account that has not been paid or a failure to do something that the law or duty requires. Within the context of this textbook, delinquency will refer to **juvenile delinquency**.

**Juvenile delinquency**
A finding of criminal behavior in the juvenile system.

Juvenile delinquency can include any offense that would be a criminal offense if committed by an adult. Juvenile delinquency also includes status offenses—offenses that are criminal because of the defendant's age. Juvenile courts do not find juvenile defendants guilty or not guilty: instead, they find them either delinquent or not delinquent. In the United States in 2014, just over three out of every 100 youths from ages 10 through 17 were arrested.[2] In 1996, the juvenile arrest rate reached its highest levels in two decades, but by 2014, it had declined 65%.[3]

In order for a juvenile to be found delinquent, the burden of proof is on the state to demonstrate that the juvenile has committed a crime beyond

**Adjudication hearing**
A hearing in which the
juvenile offender is found to
either be delinquent or not
delinquent.

**Status offenses** Offenses
that can only be committed
by a juvenile, not an adult.

a reasonable doubt. This occurs during the **adjudication hearing**, which is the juvenile equivalent to a trial.

A juvenile defendant can be found delinquent by committing either a crime or a status offense. Crimes are illegal acts committed by a person of any age, whereas a **status offense** is an offense that is only illegal or forbidden to a limited number of people—in this case, juveniles. A status offense describes any behavior that is illegal for children yet legal for adults.[4] Examples of status offenses include truancy, consumption of alcohol by a minor, running away from home, incorrigibility, and violating curfew ordinances.[6] In the late 1960s and early 1970s there was a movement, discussed later in this chapter, aimed at removing status offenses from the jurisdiction of the juvenile courts.

Juvenile courts handled 46% of delinquency cases without the filing of a petition, more than half of these non-petitioned cases received some sort of sanction. Juveniles may have agreed to informal probation, restitution, or community service, or the court may have referred them to another agency for services. Although probation staff monitor the juvenile's compliance with the informal agreement, such dispositions generally involve little or no continuing supervision by probation staff.[96]

In 41% of all petitioned delinquency cases, the youth was not adjudicated delinquent. The court dismissed 60% of these cases. The cases dismissed by the court, together with the cases that were dismissed at intake, accounted for 448,200 cases (or 328 of 1,000 cases handled).[96]

In 59% of all petitioned cases, the courts imposed a formal sanction or waived the case to criminal court. Thus, of every 1,000 delinquency cases handled in 2010, 317 resulted in a court-ordered sanction or waiver.[96]

In 2010, 58% (428,200) of the cases that were handled formally (with the filing of a petition) resulted in a delinquency adjudication. In 61% (260,300) of cases adjudicated delinquent in 2010, formal probation was the most severe sanction ordered by the court. In contrast, 26% (112,600) of cases adjudicated delinquent resulted in placement outside the home in a residential facility.[96]

Like crime in general, much of juvenile crime is unreported. In order to better understand how much delinquent or criminal behavior juveniles are engaging in, academics, researchers, and politicians rely upon different methods for gathering information. The most common methods include the use of official records and self-report surveys.

One way that delinquency is measured is with the Uniform Crime Report (UCR). The UCR is an FBI compilation of information from law enforcement agencies from across the country. The UCR relies upon different agencies within each state to submit information about crimes that occur. Additionally, it compiles information from court records and police reports from across the country, and the information is further broken down by state and by major cities within each state.

The most severe sanction ordered in more than 55,000 adjudicated delinquency cases (13%) in 2010 was something other than residential placement or probation, such as restitution or community service

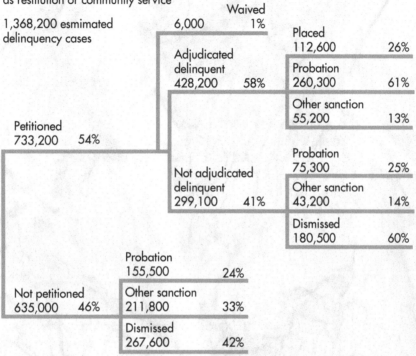

1,368,200 estimated delinquency cases

Waived 6,000 1%

Adjudicated delinquent 428,200 58%

Placed 112,600 26%
Probation 260,300 61%
Other sanction 55,200 13%

Petitioned 733,200 54%

Not adjudicated delinquent 299,100 41%

Probation 75,300 25%
Other sanction 43,200 14%
Dismissed 180,500 60%

Not petitioned 635,000 46%

Probation 155,500 24%
Other sanction 211,800 33%
Dismissed 267,600 42%

Adjudicated cases receiving sanctions other than residential placement or probation accounted for 40 out of 1,000 delinquency cases processed during the year

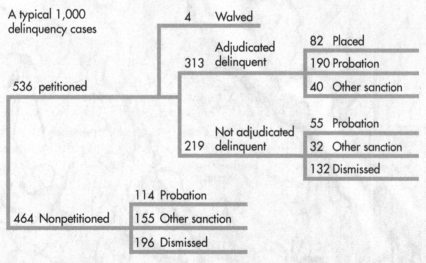

A typical 1,000 delinquency cases

4 Waived

536 petitioned

313 Adjudicated delinquent

82 Placed
190 Probation
40 Other sanction

219 Not adjudicated delinquent

55 Probation
32 Other sanction
132 Dismissed

464 Nonpetitioned

114 Probation
155 Other sanction
196 Dismissed

Notes: Cases are categorized by their most severe or restrictive sanction. Detail may not add to totals because of rounding. Annual case processing flow diagrams for 1985 through 2010 are available online at ojjdp.gov/ojstatbb/court/laqs.asp

*Source: Authors' adaptation of Puzzanchera et al.'s Juvenlo Court Statiscs 2010.*

Delinquency reporting is also done through self-reporting. Self-reporting allows juveniles, and others involved in criminal activity, to report their own criminal activity through anonymous questionnaires. Most commonly, self-reporting questionnaires are handed out at schools and local detention centers. Social scientists then use the answers to track trends. Social scientists like using self-reporting questionnaires because they think that juveniles are less likely to lie about their criminal activity when the answers are anonymous. If juveniles are required to answer out loud and in front of their friends, they may not be as truthful. They could be boasting and exaggerating to impress their friends, or they could be lying to hide their criminal activity. Without peer pressure, their answers are more likely to be truthful.

**Monitoring the Future**
A program that collects data on juveniles and is used by many social scientists.

Another program that collects data on juveniles is **Monitoring the Future**, which annually surveys about 50,000 middle and high school students.[7] Monitoring the Future specifically monitors smoking, drinking, and illegal drug use among students from eighth through 12th grade. The survey asks the same questions each year and looks to see how responses to the questions change over time.

© Sabphoto/Shutterstock.com

Monitoring the Future surveys juveniles regarding smoking, drinking, and illegal drug use.

By following some of the same students year after year and by asking the same questions, Monitoring the Future is able to reflect how behaviors, attitudes, and values change across all age groups, especially as the students leave different environments and transition into new roles. The survey reflects the developmental changes that show up consistently, and shows the inherent differences within class cohorts that remain through all stages of life.

The final way that delinquency is commonly reported is through the **National Youth Survey**. The National Youth Survey is sponsored by the National Institute of Mental Health and contains a multitude of different surveys. Each survey is designed to look at specific issues ranging from gang participation to drug use to families. The questions are designed to find out participants' age, race, languages spoken, extracurricular participation, family income, family background, relationships with parents or guard-

**National Youth Survey**
A compilation of many different surveys measuring gang participation and drug use.

ians, and feelings about drugs, smoking, and alcohol. Researchers look at all of this information and try to understand why some juveniles commit crimes and if there are any factors that would make it more likely for a juvenile to commit a crime.

## The Nature and History of Juvenile Justice

Over the last few decades, the judicial system has dramatically changed the way that it treats children. Historically, in the American legal system children were treated either as property or as adults. The idea that a system should be created to deal with juveniles, and juveniles alone, did not develop until the 20th century.[8] Children under the age of five or six were considered to be the property of their parents: when they were delinquent, they were released to their parents to be dealt with as their parents saw fit. Depending upon the state, as soon as the child turned either five or six, he or she was considered to be an adult in the eyes of the law. It was assumed that a child of that age could form the requisite mens rea, or criminal intent, to be held responsible for their crimes.

Since the 1920s, the Supreme Court has continually recognized the rights of parents and guardians to raise and discipline their children. In 1923, the Supreme Court stated that it was "the natural duty of the parent to give his children education suitable to his station in life."[9] In *Prince v. Common-wealth of Massachusetts*, the Supreme Court reiterated its stance and said, "It is cardinal with us that the custody, care and nurture of the child reside first in the parents, whose primary function and freedom include preparation for obligations the state can neither supply nor hinder. . . . It is in recognition of this that these decisions have respected the private realm of family life which the state cannot enter."[10]

Dating back to the 1500s and 1600s, when children got into trouble that could not simply be disciplined by their parents or families, they could be punished in one of three ways. The first was the apprenticeship system, mostly used for middle- and upper-class children, who would serve as assistants to a skilled craftsman. A second form of punishment, used mainly for poor children, was the binding-out system, in which children could be bound out to any responsible adult for whatever purpose needed. A third form of punishment was church discipline, in which children were flogged, whipped, or branded by church officials. Punishments for children were not significantly different than those for adults.

Early social reformers pushed for changes within the judicial system. Initially, these changes took place outside the confines of the state-run legal system and were funded privately. Social reformers were the champions for change, and in 1825 the first house of refuge was founded. It later was followed by cottage reformatories and reform schools. Houses of refuge were precursors to modern-day juvenile facilities. These houses sought to help juveniles by rehabilitating them, educating them, and teaching them life skills. Cottage reformatories had goals similar to those of the houses of refuge. The main difference between the two was location: a house of refuge was located in the city and a cottage reformatory was located in the country. Juveniles housed in cottage reformatories were taught more agricultural life skills than industrial life skills. Reform schools were juvenile correctional institutes.

In 1899, Cook County in Illinois established the first American juvenile court. In doing so, Illinois was the first state to officially recognize that a child should not be treated the same way as an adult. The early juvenile court was influenced by the British legal doctrine of *parens patriae*.

**Parens patriae**
A legal theory, most often associated with juveniles and the mentally ill, that allows the state to step in and protect those who legally cannot protect themselves. Latin for "the state as a parent."

*Parens patriae*, Latin for "the state as parent," is the idea that the state has a duty to serve as a guardian of juveniles when parents are unable or unwilling to do so.[11] The state assumes the role of the parent and takes responsibility for punishing, guiding, teaching, and educating juveniles. Under the legal doctrine of *parens patriae*, the court is responsible for acting in the best interest of the child. By 1925, juvenile court systems had been established in 48 states.

Prior to 1904, the concept of adolescence had no distinct and formal legal meaning. In 1904, five years after the first juvenile court was established, psychologist Stanley G. Hall published *Adolescence*, an influential book in which he attempted to define adolescence. Hall described adolescence as a "turbulent period of physical, emotional, and sexual development during which youths needed to be shielded from adult duties and expectations."[12] Beginning to understand that juveniles and adults were different led to further development of the juvenile system. Psychology, a growing field at the time, helped bring attention to the differences between children and adults.

In recognizing the inherent differences between adults and children, the juvenile court sought to treat juvenile offenders differently. The juvenile court's mission was fundamentally different from that of the adult criminal court, which was designed to be punitive. Proceedings in adult courts could result in the loss of liberty, or in some cases, life. To ensure that the state does not overstep its authority in causing the loss of liberty or life, defendants within the adult system are protected by due process. In contrast, the juvenile system was designed to rehabilitate. The juvenile court's job was to fashion a **disposition**, or sentence, that would fit that particular juvenile's social and emotional needs.

**Disposition** The sentencing of a defendant.

## The Child Savers Movement

**Child Savers movement**
A movement by a group of reformers in the early 19th century that sought to change the way juveniles were treated by the justice system.

Many of the changes and reforms that came about during the late 19th and early 20th centuries were the result of the **Child Savers movement**. Members of the Child Savers movement were concerned that children were being treated the same as adults. They were outraged that children could receive long prison sentences and be placed in jails with adult criminals, with no distinction between the two. Klein (1998) wrote that the Child Savers movement "believed society's role was not to ascertain whether the child was 'guilty' or 'innocent,' but 'What is he, how has he become what he is, and what had best be done in his interest and in the interest of the state to save him from a downward career.'" In their view, children should not be made to feel that they were under arrest or on trial, but rather that they were the object of the state's care.[13]

Child Savers wanted the state to step in to care for and rehabilitate wayward juveniles. They did not want to see juveniles punished as harshly as their adult counterparts, and believed that intervention and rehabilitation would "save" troubled juveniles. The Child Savers were biased in their efforts, and the majority of their efforts were directed at the poor or children of immigrants. Though middle- and upper-class white children misbehaved, they were shielded from state intervention or control.

Child Savers not only advocated for changes within the legal system, but also developed their own programs to rehabilitate juveniles, to educate them, and to teach them a craft. Many of the programs that were developed by the Child Savers, including orphan trains, houses of refuge, cottage reformatories, and reform schools, will be discussed further in the next section.

---

**Critical Thinking**

At what age should a child be considered criminally responsible?

---

## Orphan Trains

Charles Loring Brace and other New York social reformers founded the Children's Aid Society, one of the major proponents of the orphan trains, in 1853. For the following 75 years, the Children's Aid Society helped to transport over 200,000 abandoned, orphaned, and homeless children from New York City to the Midwest.[14]

Brace's devotion to helping poor children was considered radical at the time. His goal was to transform New York's orphans into productive and contributing members of society by providing them with work opportunities, education, and a welcoming family atmosphere.[15]

Brace wanted to send New York's abandoned, orphaned, and homeless children to live with what he considered moral farm families in the Midwest. This idea was sometimes called "placing out." In placing out, a child was removed from an urban area and placed with a family in the Midwest. Brace believed the best way to help orphans improve their lives was to remove them from the poverty and debauchery of New York City streets.[16] Each orphan, upon being placed on an "orphan train," was given a small suitcase to carry his or her possessions. Often, this was just a change of clothes and nothing else.

The trains, carrying children as young as five and as old as 16, would travel from New York across the country and into Canada and Mexico. Upon arriving in each town, the children would be cleaned up, marched from the train, and taken to the meeting place. The meeting place could be anywhere—from the town square to a barn, a courthouse, or even a church. Usually, the meeting place had a platform where the children all stood. The townspeople were able to examine the children prior to agreeing to adopt them. Some were looking for children to help on the farm and would examine a child's teeth and muscles before selecting them. Still others were looking for young children, some were looking for only girls, and some were looking for boys. Once selected, children went home with their new families. If a child was not selected, he or she re-boarded the train and headed to the next town.

Over 200,000 homeless children were transported from New York City to the Midwest on Orphan Trains.

After settling with their new families, the orphans were encouraged to forget about their old lives in New York. They were asked to forget about their parents, brothers, sisters, grandparents, aunts, uncles, and cousins—most never saw their New York families again.

Orphan Trains were the precursor to state intervention in juveniles' lives and reflective of the middle- and upper-class bias of Child Savers. Poor, urban, and largely immigrant children were taken from big cities and given to farming families. It is questionable whether these children were indeed "homeless" or "abandoned." Brace's beliefs were founded in the idea of *parens patriae*. He and the others in the Children's Aid Society substituted their judgment for the judgment of the parents.

## Houses of Refuge

The New York House of Refuge was the first juvenile reformatory in the country.[17] From the very beginning, the state of New York helped to organize, fund, establish daily procedures, and develop treatment programs. The New York House of Refuge officially opened in 1825 with six boys and three girls, and within a decade it had close to 1,700 inmates.[18] The New York House of Refuge did not close its doors until 1935—110 years after it first began to house inmates.

Within a few years of the New York House of Refuge opening its doors, other houses of refuge opened across the country. All followed similar models and had similar goals. Price (2009) writes: "These houses were created for juveniles who lived in an environment that produced bad habits. These habits were considered a setback for juveniles trying to escape the pressures of committing serious offenses."[19] **Houses of refuge** sought to rehabilitate, educate, and provide vocational training and religion to wayward youth. Children could be committed to the houses for vagrancy or because they had committed petty crimes. They could be committed indefinitely or sentenced for a period of time.

**Houses of refuge** Houses that sought to rehabilitate, educate, and provide vocational training and religion to juvenile offenders and vagrants.

The houses were privately run, but accepted juveniles by court order. The Pennsylvania Supreme Court, in discussing a house of refuge's goal and why a house of refuge was the proper place for wayward youth, stated:

> "The House of Refuge is not a prison, but a school. . . . The object of charity is reformation by training of inmates: by imbuing their minds with principles of morality and religion; by furnishing them with a means to earn a living, and above all, by separating them from the corrupting influences of improper associates. To this end,

may not the natural parents when unequal to the task of education, or unworthy of it, be superseded by the *parens patriae* or common community."[20]

The concept of *parens patriae* has developed into a legal theory, most often associated with juveniles and the mentally ill, that allows the state to step in and protect those who legally cannot protect themselves. Again, the state used this theory to substitute its own decision-making abilities for those of the natural parents.

While houses of refuge fell out of favor almost 110 years after the first one opened, the doctrine of *parens patriae* is still seen today within the modern judicial system in Child In Need of Assistance (CINA) or Child In Need of Supervision cases (CHINS), as well as foster care.

CINA or CHINS cases are generally emergency cases where the state seeks to remove a child or children from the home of their natural parent or guardian. The state seeks to prove that the parent is not the proper person to have custody of the child, and that the child would be safer and better off in the care and custody of the state.

## Cottage Reformatories and Reform Schools

In the mid-to-late 1880s, houses of refuge were facing harsh criticism. Critics focused on the fact that the houses were overcrowded, conditions were harsh, children were abused, and there was little rehabilitation. From these criticisms, the idea for the cottage reformatory was born. The cottage reformatory had many of the same goals as a house of refuge, but operated in a different manner.

**Cottage reformatories**, unlike houses of refuge, were located in rural areas and tried to simulate family. A juvenile sent to a cottage reformatory would find himself or herself in a rural area with approximately 20 to 40 other juveniles. This process of moving a juvenile from the city to the country was commonly referred to as "placing out." The juveniles would then be broken up into smaller groups, and from there, they would go live in "cottages" with cottage parents. Cottage parents were adults that lived in the cottages with a small group of juveniles, helping simulate the family experience for the juveniles. These "parents" would teach them skills—mainly farming and manual labor—and be in charge of educating them. This was different from a house of refuge, which was located in the city and housed hundreds of juveniles in one location.

**Cottage reformatories** Reformatories that taught juveniles farm skills; designed to house 20 to 40 offenders in a cottage with cottage parents.

Following on the heels of the houses of refuge and cottage reformatories, states began to build and fund state-run **reform schools**. In 1847, Massachusetts opened its first reform school. It was followed closely by New York in 1849, and Maine in 1853. Price writes:

**Reform schools** The first state-run schools designed to reform juvenile offenders.

"These schools were founded on strong principles: (1) Young offenders must be segregated from the corrupting influences of adult criminals, (2) Delinquents need to be removed from their environment and imprisoned for their own good and protection; reformatories should be guarded sanctuaries, (3) Delinquents should be assigned to reformatories without trial and with minimal legal requirements . . . (4) Sentences should be indeterminate, so that inmates are encouraged to cooperate in their own reform and recalcitrant delinquents are not allowed to resume their criminal careers, and (5) Reformation should not be confused with sentimentality."[21]

Reform schools remained in effect until the emergence of the modern-day juvenile justice system. Today, reform schools are referred to as juvenile detention centers. Reform schools are different from alternative schools, which will be discussed in more detail later in the chapter.

## Emergence of the Juvenile Courts

In 1899, with the passage of *An Act for the Treatment and Control of Dependent, Neglected, and Delinquent Children*, Cook County, Illinois, established the first juvenile justice system. Within 25 years, 48 states had created a juvenile justice system based on the model started in Cook County.

The newly developed juvenile courts focused less on punishment and more on rehabilitation and socialization. Brink (2004) writes: "Separate juvenile correctional facilities were created that stressed educational and vocational training, sentences were often shorter, courts made greater use of probationary and other diversionary alternatives to incarceration, and the criminal records of juvenile offenders were not made a matter of public record in order to prevent stigmatization that might interfere with successful rehabilitation."[22]

For any criminal acts committed by juveniles, juvenile court holds jurisdiction.[23] In some cases, though, a juvenile court will transfer a juvenile matter to criminal court. A juvenile court may waive jurisdiction over a case, or in some instances, the legislature may mandate juveniles accused of certain crimes to be transferred to criminal court. In some jurisdictions, prosecutors have the power to choose whether to file a case in juvenile or criminal court.[24] These waiver hearings are sometimes called **amenability hearings** because the court must decide whether the juvenile will be amenable to treatment within the juvenile system or needs to be dealt with in the adult system.

**Amenability hearing**
A hearing to determine how well a juvenile offender will respond to treatment within the juvenile system or if the juvenile is better suited to be in the adult system.

**Juvenile waiver hearing**
A hearing held before a judge to determine whether a juvenile will remain in the juvenile system or be transferred to adult criminal court.

Often, the prosecutor and the defense attorney are at odds over which court should have jurisdiction over a case where a juvenile defendant is involved. As discussed earlier, under *Kent v. United States*, a juvenile has the right to a **juvenile waiver hearing.**

Prior to a juvenile waiver hearing, a report is prepared for the judge. The report usually contains information regarding the juvenile defendant's background, including family, education, medical history, and past (if any) criminal record. The report also discusses the age of the defendant at the time the alleged crime occurred, the severity of the crime, and the defendant's amenability to treatment. The judge weighs each factor and decides whether the factor weighs in favor of the prosecution or the defense, or is neutral to both parties. Once the judge has finished weighing each factor, he or she decides whether to retain the case in the adult court or to remand the case back to the juvenile courts.

## Juvenile Court vs. Adult Criminal Court

Most people have some familiarity with the adult criminal court system through firsthand experience or television. They know that a defendant charged with a crime in the adult criminal system has certain trial rights—the right to confront witnesses; the right to a jury or bench trial; the right to remain silent; and the right to counsel. They know that a defendant can be found guilty or not guilty, and that the courtroom is open to the public.

The public's knowledge about the juvenile court system is much more limited. There are significant differences between the two systems. The first difference is the offenders themselves. The

Prior to a juvenile waiver hearing, the judge receives a report containing information about the crime and the juvenile defendant's background.

adult criminal system has exclusive jurisdiction over any defendant who committed a crime while over the age of majority (which varies depending on the state) and concurrent jurisdiction with the juvenile court system with a defendant who committed a crime while under the age of majority. Concurrent jurisdiction occurs when a defendant can be charged in the juvenile system, but, because of age, the severity of the crime, and the offender's prior criminal history, the prosecutor has charged the defendant within the adult criminal system. The defendant can only be tried in the juvenile system or the adult criminal system—not both. In *Breed v. Jones* (1975), the Supreme Court held that once a juvenile had been adjudicated in juvenile court, the juvenile could not be transferred to adult criminal court.[25] This would constitute double jeopardy.

When the adult criminal court and the juvenile court share concurrent jurisdiction over a defendant, a waiver hearing is held. In that hearing, a judge determines whether or not the defendant will be under the jurisdiction of the adult or juvenile system.

If a defendant is to be tried within the adult criminal system, all court proceedings are open to the public and the public has the right to examine the files, unless sealed by court order. If the defendant is placed under the jurisdiction of the juvenile system, the public's right to know is severely limited. Juvenile proceedings can be open or closed to the public, but juvenile records—including information about charges and sentences—are closed.

Accessibility to the public is one of the biggest differences between the juvenile and adult system. The public's accessibility to information regarding proceedings is limited because the goals of the two systems are drastically different. The adult criminal system is looking to punish those who break the law and deter them from doing it again, while the juvenile justice system is looking to rehabilitate. By limiting the public's access to juveniles' records, the juvenile justice system is hoping to allow juveniles to begin their adult lives without any of the baggage or limitations that attach to an adult criminal conviction.

### Critical Thinking

Why do you think that juvenile waiver hearings are so important in the juvenile justice system?

The juvenile justice system offers many offenders access to psychiatric and drug treatment and job training.

Another major difference between the two systems is the programs that are available within the juvenile justice system. The juvenile system has many more programs available to it than the adult system, because the juvenile system is looking to rehabilitate offenders while the adult system is seeking to punish. Within the juvenile system, the offenders have access to psychiatric and drug treatment, job training, and other classes. These programs are designed to give the offenders the best chance of joining society as productive members.

With the emergence of the juvenile courts and the programs associated with them, the hope was that the juvenile system would be able to prevent juvenile offenders from re-offending once they became adults.

### Critical Thinking

Assess the current differences between juvenile and adult courts. Do you believe further changes are needed to juvenile courts? What changes do you think would be appropriate?

# Major U.S. Supreme Court Decisions

*Kent v. United States* was not the only major juvenile justice decision that came from the United States Supreme Court. The 1960s and 1970s saw the Supreme Court issue opinions that directly affected juvenile offenders. During this time, the Supreme Court was especially concerned because it felt that juveniles were receiving the worst of both worlds. In the juvenile system, they were being denied due process rights including the right to counsel, the right to cross-examine and confront witnesses, the right to a hearing, and so forth. *Kent*, and the cases that followed, sought to protect juveniles by guaranteeing them their due process rights.

## In re Gault

In 1967, the United States Supreme Court heard arguments in *In re Gault*.[26] On June 8, 1964, Gerald Francis Gault and his friend Ronald Lewis were taken into custody in Arizona because a complaint had been filed against the two by their neighbor, Mrs. Cook. Mrs. Cook alleged that the boys had telephoned her and made lewd, offensive, and sexually suggestive remarks.[27]

Gerald's parents were at work when he was taken into custody, and they did not learn that he was in custody until his older brother was sent to look for him at the Lewis home. On June 9, a hearing was held in front of a juvenile judge. No record of the hearing was made, and neither of Gerald's parents saw a notice of the hearing. A subsequent hearing was held on June 15, and again no record of the hearing was made.

Mrs. Cook, the complainant against Gerald and Ronald, was not present at the June 9 or the June 15 hearings. At the June 15 hearing, the probation officers filed a "referral report" with the juvenile judge, but the report was not given or disclosed to the Gaults. At the hearing, Gerald was committed as a juvenile delinquent to the State Industrial School until he reached the age of 21. At the time of his commitment, Gerald was 15 years old.

The Gaults appealed the case to the U.S. Supreme Court alleging that Gerald's due process rights were denied. Specifically, they alleged that Gerald, and they, had been denied notice of the charges, their right to counsel, their right to dispute evidence and to cross-examine witnesses, protection against self-incrimination, and a right to a transcript of the proceedings.

The Supreme Court reaffirmed its holding in *Kent v. United States* in *Gault* and addressed each of the Gaults' allegations. First, the court found that the Gaults did not receive adequate notice in the case. "Notice, to comply with due process requirements, must be given sufficiently in advance of scheduled court proceedings so that reasonable opportunity to prepare will be afforded, and it must set for the alleged misconduct with particularity."[28] If the juvenile offender or the offender's parents does not receive notice of a hearing, then the juvenile offender's due process rights have been violated.

Next, the court looked at the Gaults' allegation that they were denied the right to counsel. The court concluded that under the due process clause of the 14th Amendment, "the child and his parents must be notified of the child's right to be represented by counsel retained by them, or if they are unable to afford counsel, that counsel will be appointed to represent the child."[29]

The court then looked to see if Gerald's statements were lawfully obtained. The court found that neither Gerald nor his parents were informed of his right to not make a statement, and they were not informed that Gerald could be committed as a delinquent if he made an incriminating statement. The court found, after a careful examination of the language of the Fifth Amendment and looking at case law from other states, that the "constitutional privilege against self-incrimination is applicable in the case of juveniles as it is with respect to adults."[30] Because it was not made in the presence of counsel or his parents, and he was not made aware of his right to remain silent and to not make incriminating statements, Gerald's confession could not be used against him.

After the court addressed the validity of Gerald's confession, it addressed Gerald's right to confrontation and cross-examination. Mrs. Cook, the complainant, was not present at any of the hearings, and Gerald could not confront her about her complaint or cross-examine her about anything that she said. Both were violations of his due process rights guaranteed under the 14th Amendment.

This case was important to the evolution of juvenile proceedings because the Supreme Court specifically held that juvenile defendants were to be afforded due process rights under the 14th Amendment.

**Exhibit: Excerpt from *In re Gault***

"I think the Constitution requires that he be tried in accordance with the guarantees of all the provisions of the Bill of Rights made applicable to the States by the Fourteenth Amendment. Undoubtedly this would be true of an adult defendant, and it would be a plain denial of equal protection of the laws—an invidious discrimination—to hold that others subject to heavier punishments could because they are children, be denied these same constitutional safeguards. I consequently agree with the Court that the Arizona law as applied here denied to the parents and their son the right of notice, right to counsel, right against self-incrimination, and right to confront the witnesses against young Gault. Appellants are entitled to these rights, not because 'fairness, impartiality and orderliness—in short, the essentials of due process'—require them and not because they are 'the procedural rules which have been fashioned from the generality of due process,' but because they are specifically and unequivocally granted by provisions of the Fifth and Sixth Amendments which the Fourteenth Amendment makes applicable to the States."

### In re Winship

Following *In re Gault*, the Supreme Court's next major decision involving juveniles was decided in 1970, in *In re Winship*.[31] In *Winship*, the court decided the question of "whether proof beyond a reasonable doubt is among the 'essentials of due process and fair treatment' required during the adjudicatory stage when a juvenile is charged with an act which would constitute a crime if committed by an adult."[32] The court decided that under the due process clause, the state was required to prove every element beyond a reasonable doubt in order to find the juvenile delinquent.

Samuel Winship, then 12 years old, was first found delinquent at a 1967 adjudicatory hearing. A judge in New York Family Court found that Winship had stolen $112 from a wallet in a locker. Winship's counsel asserted that the state needed to prove that he was guilty beyond a reasonable doubt, as required in adult criminal court. The judge disagreed and found that he only needed to find Winship delinquent by a preponderance of the evidence as required by New York statutes.

Later, at a disposition hearing, Winship was ordered to be placed in a training school for 18 months, with possible yearly extensions of his commitment until he reached the age of 18—six years later.

The case was appealed to the U.S. Supreme Court, which found that Winship was entitled to be found delinquent by the same standard, beyond a reasonable doubt, as an adult criminal charged with the same offense would.

This case further solidified the juvenile defendant's rights under the 14th Amendment and the due process clause. Most importantly, the decision held that a juvenile defendant could not be found delinquent of a crime unless the state had proved every element of the crime beyond a reasonable doubt. This changed the standard of proof in juvenile proceedings and made a juvenile proceeding more similar to an adult criminal proceeding.

The Supreme Court case of In re Gault held that juveniles were to be afforded due process rights under the 14th Amendment.

## Recent Changes in the Juvenile System

In 1974, Congress brought about changes within the juvenile system by enacting the Juvenile Justice and Delinquency Prevention Act (JJDPA).[33] The original act established the Office of Juvenile Justice and Delinquency Prevention to oversee programs established under the act. It was later updated in 2002. The Act is now expired, but the Coalition for Juvenile Justice Organization is working with Congress to get the Juvenile Justice and Delinquency Prevention Act reauthorized.

This act provided funding for many community-based programs.[34] The JJDPA also set up requirements to assure that status offenders were not housed with delinquents in juvenile correctional facilities. In order for state juvenile justice facilities to receive federal grants, they needed to adhere to the requirements of the JJDPA.[35]

Today, the juvenile justice system does not seek to just rehabilitate and institutionalize. It seeks to rehabilitate through community-based programs to provide juveniles with the skills and tools to operate in the world.

## Deinstitutionalization Movement

**Deinstitutionalization** The process of removing status offenders from the juvenile court system and removing juvenile offenders from adult detention centers.

The **deinstitutionalization** movement developed in the 1970s, seeking to remove many of the nonviolent juvenile offenders and status offenders from being housed in juvenile detention centers, and to remove juvenile offenders from adult detention centers. Proponents of deinstitutionalization were fearful that status offenders and nonviolent offenders would learn violent behaviors while in custody. In 1980, Congress passed legislation prohibiting the United States from detaining juveniles in jails and correctional facilities, and specified that status offenders and nonviolent offenders should be removed from these institutions.[36]

**Exhibit: Excerpt from *In re Winship***

"We turn to the question whether juveniles, like adults, are constitutionally entitled to proof beyond a reasonable doubt when they are charged with violation of a criminal law. The same considerations that demand extreme caution in fact finding to protect the innocent adult apply as well to the innocent child. . . . In sum, the constitutional safeguard of proof beyond a reasonable doubt is as much required during the adjudicatory stage of a delinquency proceeding as are those constitutional safeguards applied in Gault—notice of charges, right to counsel, the rights of confrontation and examination, and the privilege against self-incrimination. We therefore hold, in agreement with Chief Judge Fuld in dissent in the Court of Appeals, 'that, where a 12-year-old child is charged with an act of stealing which renders him liable to confinement for as long as six years, then, as a matter of due process . . . the case against him must be proved beyond a reasonable doubt.'"

**Critical Thinking**

Should juveniles ever be housed in adult prisons? If yes, in what situations?

## Contemporary Juvenile Corrections

The first goal of the juvenile justice system is to rehabilitate. The juvenile justice system hopes that rehabilitation will prevent juvenile offenders from entering the adult criminal justice system. The juvenile justice system has many tools that it employs to first try to rehabilitate and then to punish.

## Juvenile Probation

As with adult offenders, juveniles can be placed on probation. Probation allows the juvenile justice system to keep tabs on offenders while at the same time keeping the offenders out of the more formal institutions like juvenile correction institutes.[37] Probation has ranges of supervision intensity. It can be anywhere from highly intensive to essentially unsupervised.

Probation can follow a period of confinement, but when judges sentence juvenile offenders, they have many options when crafting a sentence. They can give the offender a straight period of confinement; a period of confinement followed by probation; a period of confinement, where either part or all has been suspended, followed by probation; or, finally, a period of straight probation.

While on probation, juvenile offenders are monitored by and have a probation agent who is specifically assigned to their case. While the duties of juvenile probation officers can vary by state or jurisdiction, these responsibilities typically include screening juvenile or family court cases, conducting a pre-sentence investigation of juveniles, and supervising juvenile offenders.[38] An offender who is on an intensive period of supervision may have to contact his or her probation agent a few times per week or every day either by phone or in person. An offender who is under less intensive supervision may only have to see the probation agent once a month.

The juvenile probation agent monitors offenders and makes sure that they are following their probation—if not, the agent will report the violations of probation to the court. Violating probation can lead to serious consequences for juvenile offenders. Periodically, probation agents will send the courts "violation of probation" reports. These reports are designed to keep the courts informed if an offender has violated any of the terms of his or her probation. Upon receiving a violation of probation report, the court will hold an evidentiary hearing in order to decide whether the offender is guilty or not guilty of violating his or her probation.

One of the most common and most serious ways a juvenile offender can violate his or her probation is to be found guilty of another charge. Other ways include not following a certain condition of probation. If the court finds the juvenile offender guilty of violating his or her probation, there are a number of recourses available to the judge. The judge can do one of several things: impose the balance of the offender's suspended sentence if the offender received a split sentence; impose up to the remainder of the suspended sentence if the judge suspended all of the time; continue probation; or terminate probation.

How a judge handles a violation of probation can differ from judge to judge, offender to offender, and case to case. Some judges prefer to continue offenders on probation and give them second chances, especially for minor

## In 2013, 173 Juvenile offenders were in placement for every 100,000 juveniles in the U.S. population

In 2013, the national commitment rate was twice the detention rate, but rates varied by state

| State of offense | Juveniles in placement | Placement rate per 100,000 Total | Detained | Committed | State of offense | Juveniles in placement | Placement rate per 100,000 Total | Detained | Committed |
|---|---|---|---|---|---|---|---|---|---|
| U.S. total | 54,148 | 173 | 57 | 114 | **Upper age 17 (continued)** | | | | |
| **Upper age 17** | | | | | North Dakota | 171 | 253 | 22 | 231 |
| Alabama | 933 | 184 | 72 | 99 | Ohio | 2,283 | 186 | 77 | 109 |
| Alaska | 195 | 241 | 96 | 145 | Oklahoma | 519 | 125 | 57 | 68 |
| Arizona | 882 | 122 | 46 | 73 | Oregon | 1,086 | 281 | 35 | 245 |
| Arkansas | 681 | 215 | 70 | 142 | Pennsylvania | 2,781 | 222 | 35 | 186 |
| California | 8,094 | 197 | 88 | 108 | Rhode Island | 159 | 158 | 27 | 131 |
| Colorado | 1,077 | 197 | 61 | 134 | South Dakota | 333 | 376 | 71 | 302 |
| Connecticut | 279 | 74 | 32 | 41 | Tennessee | 666 | 99 | 33 | 66 |
| Delaware | 159 | 176 | 86 | 90 | Utah | 612 | 160 | 53 | 108 |
| Dist. of Columbia | 228 | 560 | 258 | 302 | Vermont | 27 | 46 | 25 | 20 |
| Florida | 2,802 | 152 | 45 | 106 | Virginia | 1,563 | 188 | 65 | 122 |
| Hawaii | 78 | 60 | 25 | 34 | Washington | 1,014 | 144 | 39 | 105 |
| Idaho | 450 | 236 | 64 | 170 | West Virginia | 510 | 294 | 112 | 178 |
| Indiana | 1,581 | 219 | 89 | 126 | Wyoming | 165 | 279 | 15* | 264 |
| Iowa | 735 | 227 | 53 | 168 | **Upper age 16** | | | | |
| Kansas | 885 | 278 | 89 | 186 | Georgia | 1,557 | 159 | 79 | 79 |
| Kentucky | 774 | 170 | 48 | 120 | Illinois | 1,617 | 134 | 61 | 72 |
| Maine | 162 | 130 | 31 | 99 | Louisiana | 774 | 180 | 51 | 128 |
| Maryland | 771 | 127 | 50 | 78 | Michigan | 1,683 | 183 | 47 | 133 |
| Massachusetts | 393 | 60 | 24 | 36 | Missouri | 1,053 | 191 | 38 | 146 |
| Minnesota | 939 | 165 | 38 | 119 | New Hampshire | 78 | 68 | 13 | 52 |
| Mississippi | 243 | 74 | 30 | 44 | South Carolina | 672 | 159 | 24 | 134 |
| Montana | 150 | 151 | 60 | 84 | Texas | 4,383 | 161 | 65 | 95 |
| Nebraska | 411 | 204 | 67 | 136 | Wisconsin | 816 | 156 | 47 | 107 |
| Nevada | 591 | 201 | 33 | 134 | **Upper age 15** | | | | |
| New Jersey | 888 | 95 | 41 | 54 | New York | 1,650 | 116 | 28 | 87 |
| New Mexico | 402 | 179 | 52 | 127 | North Carolina | 543 | 70 | 19 | 41 |

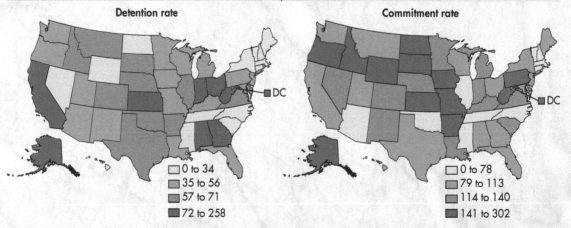

* Rate is based on fewer than 10 juveniles.

**Notes**: Placement rate is the count of juvenile offenders in placement on the census data per 100,000 youth ages 10 throughs the upper age of original juvenile court jurisdiction in each state. U.S. total includes 2,648 youth in private facilities for whom state of offense was not reported and 5 youth who committed their offense in a U.S. territory.

*Data source: Author's analysis of OJJDP's Census of Juveniles inResidential placement for 2013 [machine-readable data files].*

infractions. Still others believe that by placing offenders on probation instead of strictly committing them, they have already given the offenders their second chance, and so if they violate probation, the only way to teach and reform them is to commit them.

In an effort to keep nonviolent juveniles out of juvenile detention centers as part of the deinstitutionalization movement, judges have put juvenile defendants into diversionary programs. The idea of diversionary programs was to divert a portion of the juveniles from the system. As the state created more ways to deal with offenders, it expanded the number of people it supervised, even though these programs were intended to replace or reduce more punitive options. This phenomenon is known as "net-widening," and it is an ongoing issue throughout the criminal justice system, not just the juvenile system.[39]

### Career Connections: Juvenile Probation Officer

A juvenile probation officer supervises juvenile offenders who have been put on probation by a judge in the juvenile court. The juvenile probation officer's responsibilities include supervising juveniles, maintaining communications with judges and law enforcement agencies, and connecting juveniles with needed resources in the community. Juvenile probation officers prepare and maintain case records and various reports, forms, and court documents regarding the juveniles they oversee.

A juvenile probation agent may be required to make inquiries into probationers' problems, antecedents, character, family history, and environment. Further, he or she may make recommendations to the courts through written reports and oral testimony to be used during disposition. Juvenile probation officers also testify at hearings and transport clients between residential and correctional facilities.

A juvenile probation officer must have a bachelor's degree in criminal justice, social work, psychology, or a related field. The median salary for a probation officer in the United States earns approximately $47,149 per year. The most influential factor affecting pay for this group is location, though years of experience and the individual firm have a (lesser) impact as well. Male probation officers are just a bit more common among those who completed the questionnaire than female ones, with male workers composing 52 percent of the field. A large number report receiving medical coverage from their employers and a fair number collect dental insurance. Most probation officers like their work and job satisfaction is high.[40]

## Community-Based Corrections

In the 1980s, the idea of community-based corrections began to take hold. Community-based correctional facilities provide nonviolent offenders with the rehabilitative programs that they need. Funding for community-based corrections was provided by the Juvenile Justice and Delinquency Prevention Act of 1974. The act defined a community-based facility to be a "small, open group home or other suitable place located near the juvenile's home or family and programs of community supervision and service which maintain community and consumer participation in the planning operation, and evaluation of their programs which may include, but are not limited to, medical, educational, vocational, social, and psychological guidance, training, special education, counseling, alcoholism treatment, drug treatment, and other rehabilitative services."[41] Examples of community-based correction centers include residential and group homes.

The goal of the community-based correction facility was to take nonviolent offenders out of the jails and prisons and place them into the community under strict scrutiny. Offenders can enter a community-based correctional program in one of two ways. The first is after they have served all or part of their sentence. Upon release, the offender is released to the custody of the community-based correction program, where that program will monitor the offender and help the offender adjust to life outside of jail or prison walls.

An offender can also enter a community-based correctional program without being incarcerated. The judge, instead of sentencing the offender to jail, can sentence the offender to report directly to the program that has been ordered.

Community-based correctional programs gained popularity for a number of reasons. One of the biggest reasons that judges began sentencing defendants to these programs was because the programs provided for greater supervision than normal probation. Defendants subject to the rules of the community-based programs are usually drug tested, or on house arrest, or living in halfway houses. The programs were designed to help juveniles better adapt to the world that they were going to be released into and to help their families cope with the problems they would soon be facing.

Additionally, community-based correctional programs are much cheaper than housing an inmate in a normal correctional facility. They also help to alleviate overcrowding issues that are prevalent in many of today's correctional facilities.

## Juvenile Detention Centers

Juvenile detention centers (JDCs), sometimes called youth detention centers, house and detain juvenile offenders awaiting their hearing dates and those who have already been adjudicated. Anyone who has committed a crime while under the age of majority can be housed in a juvenile detention center.

**Age of majority** The age at which a person reaches adulthood in the eyes of the law. This age is generally 18, but can vary from state to state.

The **age of majority** is when a person is legally recognized as an adult. This can vary from state to state. For the majority of states, an individual reaches the age of majority at 18, but in other states this age can span from 19 to 21.

Juvenile detention centers were created to separate adult inmates from juvenile offenders. The prevailing thought was that a juvenile offender was not physically or emotionally mature enough to handle the day-to-day trials that being housed in an adult facility would bring. JDCs were originally thought to be safer and easier places for juveniles to be placed.

FIGURE 10.3 AGE OF MAJORITY BY STATE AND UNITED STATES POSSESSION

| State | Age | State | Age |
|-------|-----|-------|-----|
| Alabama | 19 | Nebraska | 19 |
| Alaska | 18 | Nevada | 18 |
| Arizona | 18 | New Hampshire | 18 |
| Arkansas | 18 | New Jersey | 18 |
| California | 18 | New Mexico | 18 |
| Colorado | 18 | New York | 18 |
| Connecticut | 18 | North Carolina | 18 |
| Delaware | 18 | North Dakota | 18 |
| District of Columbia | 18 | Ohio | 18 |
| Florida | 18 | Oklahoma | 18 |
| Georgia | 18 | Oregon | 18 |
| Hawaii | 18 | Pennsylvania | 21 |
| Idaho | 18 | Puerto Rico | 21 |
| Illinois | 18 | Rhode Island | 18 |
| Indiana | 18 | South Carolina | 18 |
| Iowa | 18 | South Dakota | 18 |
| Kansas | 18 | Tennessee | 18 |
| Kentucky | 18 | Texas | 18 |
| Louisiana | 18 | Utah | 18 |
| Maine | 18 | Vermont | 18 |
| Maryland | 18 | Virginia | 18 |
| Massachusetts | 18 | Virgin Islands | 18 |
| Michigan | 18 | Washington | 18 |
| Minnesota | 18 | West Virginia | 18 |
| Mississippi | 21 | Wisconsin | 18 |
| Missouri | 18 | Wyoming | 18 |
| Montana | 18 | | |

Recent studies have shown that JDCs are facing many of the same problems that the adult facilities are facing. Juvenile delinquents are coming in with serious health problems and mental illnesses that the facilities are not capable of handling. Research has found that most juvenile delinquents qualify for at least one diagnosable mental health disorder.[42] High rates of mental health issues have turned the juvenile detention centers from institutions meant to rehabilitate offenders into surrogate mental health facilities.[43] Thus, juvenile detention centers need to develop more programs to help deal with the mental health needs of juveniles.

JDCs are also facing increased scrutiny as they move from being state-run centers to being run by the private sector. In 2009, two judges in Pennsylvania were accused of receiving financial kickbacks from a privately run juvenile detention center for each juvenile that was sent to them. The scheme is alleged to have run from 2004 to 2009, and involved over 5,000 juveniles. The judges are alleged to have made over $2 million in the scheme. In August 2011, one of the judges was sentenced to 28 years in prison for his role. Many of the juveniles who appeared before the judges appeared without counsel, despite the 1976 ruling in *In re Gault* that guaranteed juvenile offenders the right to counsel. Many were first-time offenders, and many had probation agents that recommended they not be sent to detention centers.[44] Despite this, the judges sent the offenders to the privately run facilities.[45] As a result of this scandal, more attention is being paid to who is running JDCs and how many juveniles are being sent to them.

Juvenile detention centers face many of the same problems as adult facilities.

## Trends

Rates of juveniles in residential placement have fallen for more than a decade. In 2013, 173 juveniles per 100,000 population (54,000 total) were in residential placements, compared with 356 per 100,000 in 1997. The rate per 100,000 fell among whites, blacks, and Hispanics about equally (between 50 and 65 percent). (Figure 10.4) In that period, rates of residential placement for Asian youth fell the most (86 percent), while rates for American Indians fell the least (32 percent).97

## FIGURE 10.4

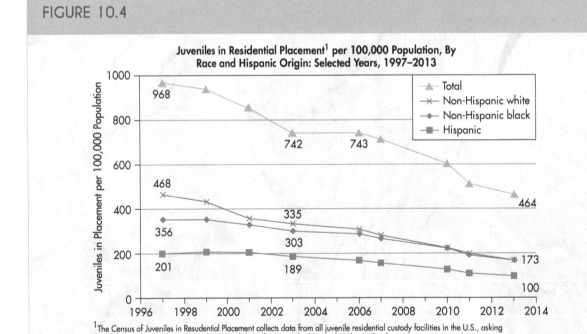

**Juveniles in Residential Placement[1] per 100,000 Population, By Race and Hispanic Origin: Selected Years, 1997–2013**

[1]The Census of Juveniles in Resudential Placement collects data from all juvenile residential custody facilities in the U.S., asking for information on each youth assigned a bed in the facility on the last Wednesday in October.
Rates are calculated per 100,000 juveniles ages 10 through the upper agre of each state's juvenile court jurisdiction.

*Source: National Center for Juvenile Justice (2013). Easy access to the census of juveniles in residential placement 1997–2011, (online tool). Available at: http://www.ojjdp.gov/ojstatbb/ exacjrp/asp/selection.asp*

## Boot Camps and Scared-Straight Programs

During the "get tough" movement, crime deterrent programs such as boot camps and scared-straight programs gained popularity with the public. These programs were designed to "scare" juvenile offenders into behaving correctly.

**Boot camps** are among the most well known of the alternative programs within the juvenile system. These camps follow the model of a military basic-training program and are focused on disciplining juvenile offenders.[46]

Boot camps pride themselves on their military structure. The goal is to "break" troubled juveniles and return them to their parents or guardians as obedient children. While attending boot camps, juvenile offenders are placed within small groups usually composed of other juvenile offenders. One suggested change to the boot camp model is that the boot camp population not be selected by judges, but instead by correctional officials who would select participants based on juveniles who have been sentenced to or already confined in a facility.[47] During his or her time in the program, the juvenile offender focuses on one or two skills instead of a wide range of skills more commonly seen in other programs like community-based programs.[48]

Boot camps do not look to coddle their participants. They believe that participants will benefit from hard work. Boot camps, unlike other programs, do not provide their participants with therapy or other rehabilitative programs.

Some evidence suggests that boot camps may be doing more harm than good. According to a report by the Surgeon General's Office, "Compared to traditional forms of incarceration, boot camps produced no significant effects on recidivism in three out of four evaluations and trends toward increased recidivism in two. The fourth evaluation showed significant harmful effects on youths, with a significant increase in recidivism."[49]

**Scared-straight programs** involve taking juvenile delinquents, or children who may be at risk of becoming delinquent, to adult prison facilities. Scared-straight programs are designed to give participants a firsthand view of prison life and allow them to interact with adult inmates, in the hope that it will deter them from future offending.[50] Scared-straight programs began in the 1970s in New Jersey.[51] The first scared-straight programs featured inmates who were serving life sentences telling juveniles about life in adult prison. The prisoners spared no details, and the juveniles were told stories of rape and murder.[52] These stories aimed to scare juveniles away from a life that would lead them to prison.

Despite reports of early success rates, questions have arisen as to the effectiveness of scared-straight programs. The University of Maryland published an evaluation of over 500 crime prevention programs and found evidence that scared-straight programs were not an effective crime deterrent.[53]

**Boot camp** An alternative to juvenile correctional facilities that follows the model of a military basic-training program and is focused on disciplining juvenile offenders.

**Scared-straight programs** Programs designed to scare juveniles into behaving correctly, including boot camps and juveniles visiting inmates in prisons.

The study showed that juveniles' success in reentering the outside world depends more heavily upon their families, communities, and the labor market. Still, these programs remain in popular use all over the country and the world, in the hope of discouraging juveniles from continuing a downward spiral that will eventually land them in adult jails or prisons.

## Death Penalty for Juveniles

Prior to 2005, seven states—Georgia, Louisiana, Missouri, Oklahoma, South Carolina, Texas, and Virginia—allowed for juveniles to be sentenced to death if they committed their crime prior to the age of majority. Most states did not. In 2005, the Supreme Court case of *Roper v. Simmons*[54] established a clear judgment on this issue.

The defendant, Christopher Simmons, was 17 years and three months old when he planned and committed a murder. On September 8, 1993, Simmons and one other friend entered the home of Mrs. Shirley Crook, bound her in duct tape, and drove her to a state park. Once there, Simmons and his co-defendant threw Mrs. Crook from a bridge and watched her drown.[55]

Simmons, who had begun bragging about the murder, was quickly found and taken into police custody. Upon confessing, Simmons was charged with burglary, kidnapping, stealing, and murder in the first degree. Simmons was charged as an adult, as under Missouri law a juvenile who has turned 17 must be charged as an adult.[56]

At trial, the jury found Simmons guilty of first-degree murder. At the sentencing stage, the state sought to prove three mitigating factors in order to sentence Simmons to death. First, that Simmons committed the murder for the purpose of receiving money. Next, that Simmons committed the murder to avoid or interfere with his lawful arrest. Finally, that the murder was the act of a depraved mind and was outrageously vile, horrible, and inhuman.[57] The jury found that the state had proved its aggravating factors and recommended a sentence of death. Upon their recommendation, the trial judge sentenced Simmons to death.

After his trial concluded and he was sentenced, Simmons appealed to the Missouri Supreme Court and cited the U.S. Supreme Court's decision in *Atkins v. Virginia*,[58] which held that it was a violation of the Eighth Amendment to sentence a mentally retarded person to death.[59] Simmons argued that the reasoning in *Atkins* applied to his case. The Missouri Supreme Court agreed and amended Simmons' sentence to life imprisonment without eligibility for parole, probation, or release unless by an act of the governor.[60]

The modified decision was appealed to the United States Supreme Court, which affirmed the new sentence. It held that no one who committed an offense under the age of 18 shall be put to death for that offense, because it violates the Eighth Amendment that prohibits cruel and unusual punishment.[61] The court focused on three important differences between juveniles and adults. The first was that juveniles tend to lack maturity and do not have a fully developed sense of responsibility, which leads to more poor decisions than in adults. Secondly, juveniles tend to have less control over their environments because they can be easily influenced by peer pressure and other negative influences. Finally, the court recognized that the character of a juvenile is not as well developed as it is in an adult.

The Supreme Court considered all of these factors and concluded that juveniles have **diminished culpability**, or the inability to fully understand the consequences of their actions. The court considered a juvenile's limited culpability to be similar to that of a mentally handicapped defendant. Using the same reasoning as in the *Atkins* decision, the court held that it would violate the cruel and unusual punishment clause to execute a juvenile who was under the age of 18 when the crime was committed.

**Diminished culpability** The inability to fully understand the consequences of an action because of age or cognitive abilities.

This ruling raises new questions for the death-penalty states. If a defendant who is found guilty of committing a murder or any other death-penalty-eligible offense was under the age of 18 at the time of the offense, what is the maximum punishment he or she should be eligible for? Many states have settled on the term of life without the possibility of parole, which means that a defendant will never have the opportunity to be eligible for a parole hearing.[62] A "life without parole" sentence, or LWOP, is different from a sentence of life with the possibility of parole. A "life with" sentence means that a defendant is eligible for parole, after serving a statutory number of years, and may petition the parole board for a parole hearing.

---

**Critical Thinking**

Do you believe that life without possibility of parole is an appropriate sentence for juveniles convicted of violent crimes?

---

**Exhibit:** *Roper v. Simmons*

"Three general differences between juveniles under 18 and adults demonstrate that juvenile offenders cannot with reliability be classified among the worst offenders. First, as any parent knows and as the scientific and sociological studies respondent and his *amici* cite tend to confirm, '[a] lack of maturity and an underdeveloped sense of responsibility are found in youth more often than in adults and are more understandable among the young. These qualities often result in impetuous and ill-considered actions and decisions.' . . .

The second area of difference is that juveniles are more vulnerable or susceptible to negative influences and outside pressures, including peer pressure. . . . This is explained in part by the prevailing circumstance that juveniles have less control, or less experience with control, over their own environment. . . .

The third broad difference is that the character of a juvenile is not as well formed as that of an adult. The personality traits of juveniles are more transitory, less fixed. . . .

These differences render suspect any conclusion that a juvenile falls among the worst offenders. The susceptibility of juveniles to immature and irresponsible behavior means 'their irresponsible conduct is not as morally reprehensible as that of an adult.' Their own vulnerability and comparative lack of control over their immediate surroundings mean juveniles have a greater claim than adults to be forgiven for failing to escape negative influences in their whole environment. The reality that juveniles still struggle to define their identity means it is less supportable to conclude that even a heinous crime committed by a juvenile is evidence of irretrievably depraved character. From a moral standpoint it would be misguided to equate the failings of a minor with those of an adult, for a greater possibility exists that a minor's character deficiencies will be reformed."

## Problematic Issues in Juvenile Justice

In recent years, the public has grown increasingly concerned that the juvenile justice system is not working effectively enough.[63] The media constantly covers violent juvenile crime, and the public is calling for tougher punishment for juvenile offenders. The focus on the rise of gangs and drug and alcohol abuse has contributed to the public's panic, which is sometimes referred to as a **moral panic**.

**Moral panic** A term coined by Stanley Cohen describing the public's irrational fear and concern over a particular issue.

Stanley Cohen, a leading sociologist, coined the phrase "moral panic" in 1972 in his book *Folk Devils and Moral Panics*.[64] He focused on the media's help in causing a moral panic by portraying a group of people—in this instance, juveniles—as a threat to society's values. The media's portrayal of juvenile crime has led the public to believe that troubled youths are the downfall of society. One of the largest contributors to the moral panic is the media's coverage of extreme cases that include children killing children. Although these cases are very rare, the sensationalist way in which the media covers these crimes captures the nation's attention and often leads the public to believe that youth-on-youth violence and murder are more common than they actually are.

But while the public is calling for the juvenile justice system to crack down on violent juvenile offenders, many fail to realize or understand the complexities of the juvenile system. The juvenile system is currently experiencing many of the same problems as adult correctional facilities. Like adult correctional facilities, juvenile correctional facilities are struggling to provide mental health care so desperately needed by inmates. Juvenile correctional facilities have reported high levels of drug abuse. A survey conducted in 2000 found that nearly 56% of boys and 40% of the girls tested positive for drugs at the time of their arrest.[65] Some juvenile offenders are either a member of a gang prior to entering the juvenile system or are a member of a gang by the time they leave.[66]

### Gangs

The Bloods, the Crips, and the Aryan Brotherhood are three of the most well-known gangs, but hundreds of others exist within jails, prisons, juvenile detention centers, and out on the street. An FBI investigation concluded, "Some 20,000 violent street gangs, motorcycle gangs, and prison gangs with nearly one million members are criminally active in the U.S. today. Many are sophisticated and well organized; all use violence to control neighborhoods and boost their illegal money-making activities, which include robbery, drug and gun trafficking, fraud, extortion, and prostitution rings."[67]

Gang members do not just commit violent crimes. Howell (1993) noted that "violent behavior is not the only behavior in which gang members partake. For the most part, gang members 'hang out' and are involved in other normal adolescent social activities, but drinking, drug use, and drug trafficking are also common."[68]

Gang presence, in addition to the streets, jails, prisons, and juvenile detention centers, is also active in schools. According to an August 2010 survey by the National Center on Addiction and Substance Abuse, 45% of high school students say that their school has gangs or students who consider themselves to be part of a gang. For middle school students, this number is 35%.[69]

As the presence of gangs in schools continues to grow, schools must adjust in order to reduce and prevent gang violence within the school. Two different approaches to preventing gangs from having a large presence in schools prevail.

One is the *whole-school approach*. Under the whole-school approach, schools set strict standards of behavior to ensure that gang-related activity is not present in schools. Staff members are trained to identify gang trends and to closely monitor known gang members. Students also must adhere to dress-code policies that forbid gang identifiers or paraphernalia.[70]

Another approach is the *individual gang intervention approach*. The individual gang intervention approach has many of the same aspects of the whole-school approach, but gives extra support to particular students known to be involved in gangs. Under this approach, staff members provide gang-involved students with specific skills and support to help them pull themselves away from gang life.[71]

State legislatures have also passed legislation in hopes of reducing gangs. Many have passed "anti-loitering" laws, which are primarily targeted at juveniles. *Anti-loitering laws* allow for police to break up or arrest groups of people, particularly teenagers, who are hanging out in front of storefronts and on street corners. The fear is that these teenagers are members of gangs and will somehow harm businesses.

© Pressmaster/Shutterstock.com

Gang crime can include robbery and trafficking as well as violent crime.

Anti-loitering laws have come under scrutiny and some, like in Chicago, have been struck down as unconstitutional because they violate citizens' rights to gather on the streets. The right to peaceably assemble is guaranteed by the Constitution under the First Amendment.

Anti-loitering laws are not the only laws that are aimed at juveniles. Both Illinois and New Mexico enacted anti-sagging laws because the public associated low-slung pants with rap music, gangs, and other parts of society it disapproved of.[72] Other states have enacted laws that ban skateboarding because there is a perception that kids on skateboards will destroy property and cause trouble.

Many of these "tough on youth" policies and laws are fueled by moral panics and by the public's perception that certain juveniles are dangerous to society. The public's perception is in some cases shaped by sensationalist media stories on juvenile crime, which do not always provide an accurate portrait of what is actually happening. As a result, many citizens and lawmakers have developed a fear of youth that overestimates the prevalence and frequency of juvenile crime.

## Searches in Schools

The rights of juveniles in schools is an important issue that has been heavily debated in the criminal justice system. What rights does a student have in school that protect him or her against a Fourth Amendment search or seizure? Do schools have to follow the same standards as police when conducting a search? The U.S. Supreme Court has attempted to answer these questions through a series of rulings.

In 1985, in *N.J. v. T.L.O.*, the Supreme Court held that, "under ordinary circumstances, a search of a student by a teacher or other school official will be 'justified at its inception' when there are reasonable grounds for suspecting that the search will turn up evidence that the student has violated or is violating either the law or the rules of the school."[73] This decision affirmed that schools can conduct searches based on reasonable suspicion because of the nature of the location. This is a different standard than the one that police must abide by. Police must have probable cause in order to conduct a search or a seizure.

The Supreme Court further clarified its position on searches within the school in 1995, in *Vernonia School District 47J v. Acton*, a case that dealt with urinalysis of student-athletes.[74] The court determined that conducting urinalysis on student-athletes was reasonable and not an invasion of privacy because student-athletes had been found to be the leaders of drug culture within the schools. The court found that this was reasonable and did not declare these urinalysis tests unconstitutional. However, in 2009, the court did find that a student's rights guaranteed under the Fourth Amendment were violated when she was subjected to a strip search because there was no reasonable suspicion to believe that she was hiding drugs in her underwear.[75]

**Ethics and Professionalism: Searches in Schools**

Consider this scenario. A school principal hears from a student that members of the school's lacrosse team are using drugs. What should the principal do? Does the information from one student qualify as reasonable suspicion sufficient enough to conduct a search of the lacrosse players' bags? Should she gather more information before conducting a search?

Consider a scenario in which the principal decides to search the lacrosse players' bags when they return to the school after playing an away game. As the players exit the team bus, the principal pulls each student aside and asks him to open his bag so that she may search it. After the search is complete, the principal has not found any drugs, but she has discovered that several members of the team are carrying Swiss Army knives. The boys claim that they have the Swiss Army knives because they are tools they use to fix their lacrosse sticks.

Swiss Army knives are classified as weapons under the school's policy, and the policy states that the principal must report all students who have weapons in their possession on school policy. Should the principal report the boys to the police? Should she be legally compelled to do so? What would you do?

## Drugs and Alcohol

Drug use is an ever-present problem in today's society, and juveniles are no exception. Law enforcement agencies have increased their focus on drug crimes, launching undercover investigations to identify drug dealers who sell to minors. Legislatures have passed punitive laws against the use, possession, and sale of illegal drugs.[76]

In the 1970s, President Richard Nixon began America's "War on Drugs." The War on Drugs focuses on reducing the foreign and illegal drug trade with the hope of decreasing the use and production of drugs in America. Forty years after President Nixon began the U.S. government's War on Drugs and 50 years after the United Nations had its first conference on narcotics, the Global Commission on Drug Policy issued a report examining drug policies both nationally and internationally. In the report, the United Nations estimates that consumption of drugs from 1998 to 2008 has steadily increased and that the United States' War on Drugs has had little impact.[77] In 1998, 12.9 million people used opiates; this number grew to 17.35 million people in 2008, an increase of nearly 34.5%.[78] In that same time frame, cocaine use rose 27% and cannabis use rose 8.5%.[79]

Further, the commission compared the Dutch city of Amsterdam, famous for its cannabis cafes, to the U.S. city of San Francisco to see if different regulatory environments affected cannabis use.[80] The commission's report concluded, "Our findings do not support claims that criminalization reduces cannabis use and that decriminalization increases cannabis use . . . With the exception of higher drug use in San Francisco, we found strong similarities across both cities."[81]

Finally, the study concluded that "countries that continue to invest mostly in a law enforcement approach (despite the evidence) should focus their repressive actions on violent organized crime and drug traffickers, in order to reduce the harms associated with the illegal drug market."[82]

**Drug Abuse Resistance Education (D.A.R.E.)**
A program designed to keep kids off drugs by teaching children how to resist peer pressure and avoid drugs and violence.

Los Angeles, California, started the first **Drug Abuse Resistance Education (D.A.R.E.)** program in 1983 to help keep kids off of drugs. The D.A.R.E. program consists of police-officer-led classroom lessons that teach children how to avoid drugs and violence and resist peer pressure. Shortly after the D.A.R.E. program began in 1983, First Lady Nancy Reagan released the "Just Say No" slogan. The slogan was designed to encourage juveniles to just say no to drugs and peer pressure.

Nearly 75% of schools in America have a D.A.R.E. program, but despite its popularity, D.A.R.E. has proven to be counterproductive. Many studies have shown that D.A.R.E. has little lasting impact. Some have even shown higher drug use among suburban youths who had graduated from a D.A.R.E. program. A report by the U.S. Government Accountability Office stated, "In brief, the six long-term evaluations of the D.A.R.E. elementary school curriculum that we reviewed found no significant differences in illicit drug use between students who received D.A.R.E. in the fifth or sixth grade (the intervention group) and students who did not (the control group.)"[83] The report looked at six major evaluations done on the effectiveness of D.A.R.E. Two of the evaluations showed that "D.A.R.E. students showed stronger negative attitudes about illicit drug use and improved peer pressure resistance skills and self-esteem about illicit drug use about 1 year after the intervention. These positive effects diminish over time."[84]

A 2009 National Youth Risk Behavior Survey Overview measured the drug and alcohol use of both male and female juveniles and reported that "72% of students had at least one drink of alcohol on at least 1 day during their life and 41.8% of students had at least one drink of alcohol on at least 1 day during the 30 days before the survey," and "24.2% of students had had five or more drinks of alcohol in a row (i.e., within a couple of hours) on at least 1 day during the 30 days before the survey."[85] Further, it reported that in the 30 days before the survey, 4.5% of students had drunk alcohol on school property.[86]

The same survey, in reporting on drug use, showed that more students used marijuana than any other drug, as "36.8% of students had used marijuana one or more times in their life" and "20.8% of students had used marijuana one or more times during the 30 days before the survey."[87]

Still, despite these somewhat alarming numbers, drug use among juveniles has gone down. In 2009, the national Youth Risk Behavior Survey released a study entitled *Trends in the Prevalence of Marijuana, Cocaine, and Other Illegal Drug Use (1991–2009)*. The survey showed that from 1999–2009, marijuana use among high school students decreased, as did the use of cocaine and other methamphetamines.[88]

## School Violence and Bullying

On April 20, 1999, in Columbine, Colorado, high school students Eric Harris and Dylan Kelbold shot and killed 12 students and one teacher and injured 24 other students before committing suicide at Columbine High School. This incident rocked the nation and made parents across the country question whether schools were really the safest place for children. In 2007, the nation was rocked again when a Virginia Tech student, Seung-Hui Cho, killed 32 people and injured 25 more.

These incidents have led to a greater focus on school violence and school bullying. It is important to note that these extreme examples of school violence are incredibly rare, and that schools in general are safe places for children to be. However, nonviolent examples of bullying can be a problem. Bullying exists at every level of life, from a kid on the playground to a boss in the workplace. One survey showed that approximately 160,000 students leave school early every day because they are afraid of being bullied.[89] Nearly 15% of all students who miss school on any given day do so because they fear being bullied.[90]

With the prominence of Facebook, text messaging, and YouTube, a new form of bullying called "cyberbullying" has emerged. Cyberbullying occurs outside of the classroom and can be done from behind closed doors and not face to face. Cyberbullying occurs when a disparaging remark about someone is spread through electronic means. It can occur through text messages, blogs, personal web pages, emails, cyberstalking, etc.

Regulation and punishment of cyberbullying can be a difficult task. For the most part, cyberbullying takes place outside of the traditional school setting, and it becomes very hard for schools to intervene.[91] Schools that attempt to discipline a student for cyberbullying actions that take place outside of school property and school hours can be sued for exceeding their authority and violating the student's right to free speech.[92] When schools are unable to address the issue, the criminal justice system can step in if the level of harassment rises to a criminal level.

For instance, in September 2010, a Rutgers University freshman, Tyler Clementi, committed suicide after his roommate and his roommate's friend secretly filmed him and a partner having sex and broadcast it on the Internet. The roommate, Dharun Ravi, and friend Molly Wei both faced criminal charges for invasion of privacy for secretly filming Clementi without his or his partner's permission. In May 2011, Wei entered into a plea deal with the prosecution. In exchange for charges against her to be dropped, she had to enter into a pretrial intervention program, perform 300 hours of community service, testify at any proceeding, participate in counseling to deter cyberbullying, and cooperate with authorities.[93] In March 2012, Ravi was tried and convicted for his role. He was sentenced to 30 days in jail, 3 years probation, 300 hours of community service, a $10,000 fine, and counseling on bullying and alternative lifestyles.[94]

Phoebe Prince, an Irish immigrant to the United States, committed suicide in January 2010 after enduring cyberbullying and bullying from classmates. After her death, nine students were charged with a range of felony crimes and have since pleaded to misdemeanors.[95]

## Chapter Summary

- Beginning in 1966 with *Kent v. United States*, and continuing with *Roper v. Simmons*, the United States Supreme Court has issued opinions that change and mold the juvenile system and how juveniles are treated within both the juvenile and adult systems. *Kent*, the first of the decisions, gave juveniles some rights under the due process clause. *In re Gault* and *In re Winship* further solidified juveniles' due process rights, while *Simmons* established that juveniles who committed death-penalty-eligible offenses while under the age of 18 could not be executed for their crimes.

- The concept of what a child is has evolved over time. Children have evolved from being treated as little adults or as the property of their parents to being treated as a distinct class that has its own understandings and limitations. The emergence of adolescence as a distinct time period within a human life helped lead to the formation of the juvenile court system.

- The juvenile court system was first implemented in 1899, in Cook County, Illinois. The juvenile court system first sought to rehabilitate juveniles, but as time went on, the emergence of a "get tough" movement and deinstitutionalization movement moved the juvenile courts away from rehabilitation and into punishment.

- Juvenile courts and adult criminal courts have some similarities and differences. Juvenile courts deal with all juveniles under the state's mandatory age, but these offenders can, after a juvenile waiver hearing, be waived into the adult criminal court. Juvenile courts do not find defendants guilty or not guilty, but rather delinquent or not delinquent. Defendants in adult criminal courts are found guilty or not guilty. In both courts, the state has the burden to prove the defendant's guilt or delinquency beyond a reasonable doubt.

- Probation is a tool used by both juvenile and adult criminal courts as a way to monitor the defendant's behavior. Juvenile defendants can be placed on probation prior to adjudication; after they have gone through the adjudication process and been given a suspended sentence; or after serving part of their sentence.

- The late 19th and early 20th century Child Savers movement can be directly linked to many of the changes that occurred to form a juvenile system. The Child Savers movement was an early form of state intervention and represented an early form of *parens patrie*. Houses of refuge and cottage reformatories were the early versions of juvenile detention facilities.

- Problematic issues still face the juvenile justice system today. The media's focus on crimes committed by juveniles has caused a moral panic in society despite the fact that juveniles commit just a small percentage of all crimes. Providing further issues for the juvenile justice system is the strong presence of gangs within schools and the community.

## Critical Thinking?

1. What differences do you see between a finding of guilt and a finding of delinquency?
2. Should the juvenile court systems rid themselves of status offenses so that they can spend more time focusing on violent offenders?
3. What are some of the major differences between the juvenile courts and the adult criminal courts?
4. Do you think that placing juvenile offenders on probation is a good way to monitor defendants?
5. Do you think that community-based corrections produce results or are a waste?
6. Should there be a minimum age before the court can consider housing a juvenile defendant within an adult correctional facility? Should a juvenile ever be housed in an adult correctional facility?
7. Do you believe boot camps and scared-straight programs are effective? Why or why not?
8. Do you think that the Supreme Court was right, in *Simmons*, when it decided that anyone who committed a death-penalty-eligible offense under the age of 18 could not be subject to the death penalty?
9. What are the major problems you see facing the juvenile justice system today?
10. Should the juvenile justice system focus on rehabilitation or retribution/punishment?

## Media

**Office of Juvenile Justice and Delinquency Prevention:** http://www.ojjdp.gov
The Office of Juvenile Justice and Delinquency Prevention is tasked with trying to improve juvenile justice policies and practices.

**U.S. Department of Education, Office of Safe and Drug-Free Schools:** http://www2.ed.gov/about/offices/list/osdfs/index.html
The Office of Safe and Drug-Free Schools helps to implement programs within the school system that relate to drug and violence prevention and promote the general well-being of students.

Additionally, this organization provides the financial assistance needed for these programs.

**The Coalition for Juvenile Justice:** http://www.juvjustice.org
The Coalition for Juvenile Justice is a group of volunteers devoted to helping juveniles who have been accused within the juvenile justice system. The coalition makes sure that juveniles are treated with care.

**National Council on Crime and Delinquency:** http://www.nccdglobal.org/
By applying research to policy and practice, the National Council on Crime and Delinquency has helped to advise on and design reforms within the juvenile justice system.

**Centers for Disease Control and Prevention's (CDC) Striving to Reduce Youth Violence Everywhere (STRYVE):** http://www.safeyouth.gov/pages/home.aspx
This group takes a public health approach to preventing youth violence.

**Annie E. Casey Foundation:** http://www.aecf.org
This is a private organization founded by Jim Casey, the founder of UPS, to provide grants to organizations that help to meet the needs of vulnerable children and their families.

**National Youth Court Center:** http://www.youthcourt.net
The National Youth Court Center is a central location for information about all youth courts. In youth courts, juveniles who are charged with minor delinquencies and status offenses are sentenced by their peers, who serve as judges, bailiffs, and attorneys.

## Endnotes

1.  *Kent v. United States*, 383 U.S. 541 (1966).

2.  Office of Juvenile Justice and Delinquency Prevention. (2011). "Juvenile Arrest Rate Trends." *Statistical Briefing Book*. Retrieved from http://www.ojjdp.gov/ojstatbb/crime/JAR_Display.asp?ID=qa05200

3.  Ibid.

4.  Steinhart, D. J. (1996). "Status Offenses, The Future of Children." *The Juvenile Court, 6*(3). Retrieved from http://futureofchildren.org/futureofchildren/publications/journals/article/index.xml?journalid=55&articleid=316

6.  Ibid.

7.  *Monitoring the Future*. (2011). Retrieved from http://monitoringthefuture.org/

8.  ABA, Division for Public Education, Part 1: The History of Juvenile Justice.

9.  *Meyers v. State of Nebraska*, 262 U.S. 390 (1923).

10. *Prince v. Commonwealth of Massachusetts*, 321 U.S. 158 (1944).

11. Frontline. (2011). *Child or Adult? A Century Long View*. Retrieved from http://www.pbs.org/wgbh/pages/frontline/shows/juvenile/stats/childadult.html

12. Ehrlich, J. S. (2003). "Shifting Boundaries: Abortion, Criminal Culpability and the Indeterminate Legal Status of Adolescents." *Wisconsin Women's Law Journal*, *18*, 77–116.

13. Klein, E. K. (1998). "Dennis the Menace or Billy the Kid: An Analysis of the Role of Transfer to Criminal Court in Juvenile Justice." *American Criminal Law Review*, *35*, 371–410.

14. *National Orphan Train Complex*. (2011). Retrieved from http://www.orphantraindepot.com

15. The Children's Aid Society. (n.d.). *History*. Retrieved from http://www.childrensaidsociety.org/about/history

16. Ibid.

17. New York State Archives. (n.d.). *New York House of Refuge*. http://www.archives.nysed.gov/a/research/res_topics_ed_reform_history.shtml

18. Ibid.

19. Price, J. R. (2009, Spring). "Birthing Out Delinquents: Alternative Treatment Options for Juvenile Delinquents." *Criminal Law Brief*, 51–57.

20. Ibid.

21. Ibid.

22. Brink, D. O. (2004). "Immaturity, Normative Competence, and Juvenile Transfer: How (Not) to Punish Minors for Major Crimes." *Texas Law Review*, *82*, 1555–1585.

23. Klein, 1998, 373.

24. Ibid., 374.

25. *Breed v. Jones*, 421 U.S. 519 (1975).

26. *In re Gault*, 387 U.S. 1 (1967).

27. Ibid., 4.

28. Ibid., 33.

29. Ibid., 41.

30. Ibid., 55.

31. *In re Winship*, 397 US 358 (1970).

32. Ibid.

33. Juvenile Justice and Delinquency Prevention Act of 1974, Pub. L. No. 93-415.

34. 42 U.S.C. 5601.

35. Weithorn, L. A. (2005, Summer). "Envisioning Second-Order Change in America's Responses to Troubled and Troublesome Youth." *Hofstra Law Review*, *33*, 1305–1506.

36. Holden, G. A., & Kapler, R. A. (1995). "Deinstitutionalizing Status Offenders: A Record of Progress." *Juvenile Justice*, *2*(2), 3–10.

37.  *Black's Law Dictionary* (4th ed.).

38.  Torbet, P. M. (1996). *Juvenile Probation: The Workhorse of the Juvenile Justice System*. Washington, D.C.: U.S. Department of Justice.

39.  *Diversionary Programs: An Overview*. (1999). Retrieved from https://www.ncjrs.gov/html/ojjdp/9909-3/div.html

40.  http://www.bls.gov/oes/current/oes211092.htm#ind  PayScale, Human Capital. Retrieved from http://www.payscale.com/research/US/Job=Probation_Officer_or_Correctional_Treatment_Specialist/Salary

41.  42 U.S.C. 5603 §103(1).

42.  *Prevalence of Mental Health Disorders Among Youth: Youth With Mental Health Disorders: Issues and Emerging Responses*. (2000). Retrieved from https://www.ncjrs.gov/html/ojjdp/jjjnl_2000_4/youth_2.html

43.  Ibid.

44.  Associated Press. (2009). "Pa. Judges Accused of Jailing Kids for Cash." *MSNBC*. Retrieved from http://www.msnbcmsn.com/id/29142654/ns/us_news-crime_and_courts/t/pa-judges-accused-jailing-kids-cash/#.TkiWhr_gVys

45.  Ibid.

46.  Mental Health America. (2011). *Juvenile Boot Camps*. Retrieved from http://www.nmha.org/go/boot-camps

47.  Office of Juvenile Justice and Delinquency Prevention. (1997). *Boot Camps for Juvenile Offenders*, 4.

48.  Ibid., 8.

49.  Surgeon General's Office. (n.d.). "Chapter 5: Ineffective Tertiary Programs and Strategies." *Youth Violence: A Report of the Surgeon General*. Retrieved from http://www.surgeongeneral.gov/library/youthviolence/chapter5/sec6.html

50.  Petrosino, A., Turpin-Petrosino, C., & Buehler, J. (2003, November). "'Scared Straight' and Other Juvenile Awareness Programs for Preventing Juvenile Delinquency." In *The Campbell Collaboration Reviews of Intervention and Policy Evaluations (C2-RIPE)*. Philadelphia, PA: Campbell Collaboration.

51.  Ibid., 4.

52.  Ibid.

53.  Sherman, L. W., Gottfredson, D., MacKenzie, D. L., Eck, J., Reuter, P., & Bushway, S. (1997). *Preventing Crime: What Works, What Doesn't, What's Promising. A Report to the United States Congress*. College Park, MD: University of Maryland.

54.  *Roper v. Simmons*, 543 U.S. 551 (2005).

55.  Ibid.

56.  *Miranda v. Arizona*, 384 U.S. 436 (1966).

57.  *Roper v. Simmons*, 2005.

58.  *Atkins v. Virginia*, 536 U.S. 304 (2002).

59.     *Roper v. Simmons*, 2005.

60.     Ibid.

61.     Ibid.

62.     *Death Penalty Information Center.* (2011). Retrieved from http://www.deathpenaltyinfo.org

63.     McLatchey, S. F. (1999). "Media Access to Juvenile Records: In Search of a Solution." *Georgia State University Law Review, 16*(2), 337–359.

64.     Cohen, S. (2002). *Folk Devils and Moral Panics: The Creation of the Mods and Rockers.* New York, NY: Routledge.

65.     *Principles of Drug Abuse Treatment for Criminal Justice Populations: A Research-Based Guide*, 13.

66.     Howell, J. C. (1998, August). *Youth Gangs: An Overview.* Washington, D.C.: U.S. Department of Justice.

67.     Federal Bureau of Investigation. (2011). *Gangs.* Retrieved from http://www.fbi.gov/about-us/investigate/vc_majorthefts/gangs/gangs

68.     Howell, 1998, 8.

69.     Howell, J. C., & Moore, J. P. (2010). *National Gang Center Bulletin: History of Street Gangs.* 1–25.

70.     Ibid., 4.

71.     Ibid.

72.     Garrison, C. (2011, July 12). "Collinsville Mayor Apologizes for City's New Anti-Sagging Law, Calls It a 'Step Backward.'" *Riverfront Times.* Retrieved from http://blogs.riverfronttimes.com/dailyrft/2011/07/collinsville_sagging_law_mayor_apology.php

73.     *New Jersey v. T.L.O.*, 469 U.S. 325, 341-342 (1985).

74.     *Vernonia School District 47J v. Acton, et ux., etc.*, 515 U.S. 646 (1995).

75.     *Safford Unified School District #1 v. Redding*, 557 U.S. ___ (2009).

76.     Belenko, S. (2000). "The Challenges of Integrating Drug Treatment into the Criminal Justice Process." *Albany Law Review, 3*(3), 833–876.

77.     Global Commission on Drug Policy. (2011). *War on Drugs: Report of the Global Commission on Drug Policy.*

78.     Ibid.

79.     Ibid.

80.     Ibid., 10.

81.     Ibid.

82.     Ibid., 14.

83.     U.S. General Accounting Office. (2003, January 15). *Letter to Senator Richard Durbin.* Retrieved from http://www.gao.gov/new.items/d03172r.pdf

84.     Ibid.

85.     Centers for Disease Control and Prevention. (2011). *YRBSS in Brief.* Retrieved from http://www.cdc.gov/healthyyouth/yrbs/brief.htm

86.     Ibid.

87. Ibid.

88. Centers for Disease Control and Prevention. (2010). "Alcohol & Drug Use." *Healthy Youth!* Retrieved from http://www.cdc.gov/healthyyouth/alcoholdrug/index.htm

89. Bullying Statistics. (n.d.). *Bullying Statistics 2010.* Retrieved from http://www.bullyingstatistics.org/content/bullying-statistics-2010.html

90. Ibid.

91. *Stop Cyberbullying.* (n.d.). Retrieved from http://www.stopcyberbullying.org/prevention/schools_role.html

92. Ibid.

93. Schweber, N. (2011, May 7). "In Fallout of Suicide by Student, a Plea Deal." *The New York Times.* Retrieved from http://www.nytimes.com/2011/05/07/nyregion/in-rutgers-suicide-case-ex-student-gets-plea-deal.html

94. DeMarco, M. and Friedman, A. (2012, May 21). "Dharun Ravi Sentenced to 30 Days in Jail." *The Star-Ledger.* Retrieved from http://www.nj.com/news/index.ssf/2012/05/dharun_ravi_sentenced_for_bias.html

95. Lavoie, D. (2011, April 27). "5 Teens Strike Plea Deal in Phoebe Prince Bullying Case." *The Huffington Post.* Retrieved from http://www.huffingtonpost.com/2011/04/27/phoebe-prince-bullying-case_n_854446.html

96. Sickmund, M. & Puzzanchera, C. (2014). *Juvenile Offenders and Victims:* 2014 National Report. National Center for Juvenile Justice. December 2014.

97. Child Trends, Data Bank. *Juvenile Detention: Indicators on Children and Youth.* December 2015. Retrieved from https://www.childtrends.org/wp-content/uploads/2012/05/88_Juvenile_Detention.pdf.

98. Hockenberry, S. (2016). *Juveniles in Residential Placement, 2013.* Juvenile Justice Statistics. National Report Series Bulletin. Office of Juvenile Justice and Delinquency Prevention.

© Kiev.Victor/Shutterstock.com

# Victimology and Victims' Rights

## KEY TERMS

Civil lawsuit

Compassion fatigue

Compensation

Costs of victimization

Indirect victim

Just world

National Organization for
  Victim Assistance (NOVA)

Repeat victimization

Victimology

Victim advocate

Victim impact statement (VIS)

Victims of Crime Act (VOCA)

Victim precipitation

Victim rights amendment

Victim services

# CHAPTER OBJECTIVES

1 Describe the origins of victimology.

2 Outline the costs of criminal victimization.

3 Describe the ways to remedy the costs.

4 Describe methods used to measure victimization.

5 Discuss the victim's movement and how it increased public interest in crime victims.

# Case Study: Tragedy in Tucson

On January 8, 2011, a gunman opened fire during a town hall meeting held by Democratic Rep. Gabrielle Giffords of Arizona. Rep. Giffords was shot in the head. The gunman shot and killed six people, including a nine-year-old girl and Federal Judge John McCarthy Roll. Thirteen others were wounded. The shooter, 22-year-old Jared Lee Loughner, was subdued by two bystanders at the event. Pima County Sheriff Clarence Dupnik reported that Rep. Giffords was the primary target of the shooting.

The shooting sent ripple effects throughout the community. President Obama told reporters that the events were "a tragedy for Arizona and a tragedy for our entire country. . . . but we don't yet know what provoked this unspeakable act."[1] House Speaker John Boehner, R-OH, said, "I am horrified by the senseless attack on Congresswoman Gabrielle Giffords and members of her staff. An attack on one who serves is an attack on all who serve. Acts and threats of violence against public officials have no place in our society. Our prayers are with Congresswoman Giffords, her staff, all who were injured, and their families. This is a sad day for our country."[2]

The shooting affected the individuals present at the town hall meeting (direct victims), and it also affected family members, friends, community members, concerned citizens, and government officials across the nation (indirect victims). Directly or indirectly, hundreds if not thousands were victims of this heinous crime. Both direct and indirect victims of a crime may experience a wide range of reactions post-victimization, including shock, panic, fear, grief, anger, disbelief, emotional numbness, and feelings of helplessness. These repercussions can extend to vicarious victims, such as friends, family members, and social workers who deal with the aftermath of the crime.

The public is often not aware of services available to victims of crime after a criminal victimization. These services can help victims find counseling, negotiate the criminal justice system, and understand their rights.

## Victimology

Criminology is the study of criminal behavior in both individuals and society. Criminologists attach great importance to the motivations of criminals: who they were, where they came from, how the justice system handled them, and what should become of them.[3] In addition, there is another important element of any crime: the victim. Crime is an offense against an individual victim or victims as well as the state as a whole.

Rooted in criminology, **victimology** is the scientific study of victimization. It is important to note that today victimology is a broad discipline that focuses on several different types of victims, including victims of criminals, oneself, the social environment, technology, and the natural environment. For purposes of this chapter, the discussion will focus on victims of criminals. Victimology does not just focus on the crime itself, but also on addressing the needs and rights of victims once they become a part of the criminal justice system. Victimologists are interested in who is victimized, what the impact of the crime is, the experience of victims in the criminal justice system, and the role a victim may play, if any, in causing the crime. With those factors in mind, consider the case study at the beginning of this chapter. The crime consists of more than just the shooter, the details of the crime (weapon used, location, time of day, etc.), and the shooter's motivations for committing the crime. Investigators of the Representative Giffords shooting, for example, would be interested in why Representative Giffords was targeted, what made her vulnerable, and how best to attend to her needs and rights in the pursuit of justice. Investigators might ask questions about whether or not the offender knew Representative Giffords or any of the other victims, or what about the victims might have provoked a response in the offender. The welfare of the victims after the crime, in particular when they interact with the criminal justice system, would also be of interest to victimologists and other criminologists.

**Victimology** The study of victimization that analyzes the role played by victims in crimes.

Victimologists are also interested in determining the full scope of what constitutes "victimhood." In the opening case study, who are the victims in the Tucson shooting? There are the direct victims who were at the town hall meeting. There are also indirect victims, such as the families of those who were shot, the community, and the state of Arizona (for being deprived of an important public official). In addition, the costs that will result from the crime—financial, emotional, and physical—affect many individuals and groups.[4]

© Piotr Latacha/Shutterstock.com

The current system for handling crime, the criminal justice system, is relatively new.

The understanding of the meaning and purpose of victimology has evolved from an avenue of inquiry within criminology to an independent discipline. Two working definitions of victimology itself could be formulated. The first, which some will argue is outdated, defines victimology as the study of the victim's role in crime events.[5] While this definition may seem overly narrow, criminologists argue that the victim's role stretches from witnessing a crime, or perhaps even causing a crime, through the investigation and trial, and eventually through the parole process and beyond.

A more focused definition of victimology, offered by Andrew Karmen (2004), is "the scientific study of the physical, emotional, and financial harm people suffer because of criminal activities."[6] This includes the crime itself and its results, but may also include victims' experiences at the hands of the criminal justice system. These two definitions encompass the comprehensiveness of the study of victimology.

## The Path from Victim Justice System to Criminal Justice System

The current system for handling crime, the criminal justice system, is relatively new. Early human societies were commonly small, tribal, and organized around a strong family unit, more properly thought of as a "clan," that served as a centering force in human social networks. There was no "state" in the sense of a locus of centralized government that would mete out impartial justice. As Doerner and Lab note, people in early societies tacitly accepted the principle that "victims were expected to fend for themselves."[7] Victims, relying on their families, had a large role in ensuring justice for themselves, as they lived in a world that depended upon personal relationships between individuals and clans. The legal codes that existed provided for either retribution or restitution, and they were enforced due to the fear of feuding and conflict between large families within the community.[8] This "victim justice system" was largely the norm in small societies.

During the Industrial Revolution, which brought rapid urbanization and the rise of the modern city-state, this system began to change. Many citizens, particularly the wealthy, believed they were entitled to restitution paid by offenders to victims.[9] With larger societies and stronger, centralized governmental power, acts of crime were seen as violations against the state instead of an individual victim.[10] State judiciaries levied fines, imposed prison sentences, and determined the outcome of court proceedings. In that way, the "victim justice system" was replaced by the "criminal justice system." The criminal justice system shifted its focus away from victims and toward the offense and the rights of the offender. That said, it must be noted that, today, all states' statutory codes provide extensive basic rights and protections for victims of crime. These statutes have greatly influenced the way victims of crime are treated within the criminal justice system.

---

**Critical Thinking**

How do you feel about the way our system of justice understands crime? Should it be thought of as being against an individual or against society as a whole?

---

## Early Leaders in Victimology

The academic discipline of victimology first emerged during the 1940s as an offshoot of traditional criminology.[11] The focus began to shift to look at the relationship between the victim and offender in the hope of better understanding criminal activity and identifying causes of criminal behavior.

Many individuals laid the groundwork for victimology in the early 20th century. Chief among them were Benjamin Mendelssohn, Hans von Hentig, Marvin Wolfgang, and Menachem Amir. These early pioneers spent much of their careers studying the pathology of offenders, their personal histories and backgrounds, and their relationship with society. Their focus shifted in the 1940s to examining the relationship between victim and offender. These early attempts signaled the beginning of a renewed academic interest in the victim. Much of this early scholarly work focused on creating typologies of victims and assigning various degrees of responsibility to the victim for the criminal act. Some scholars, such as William Ryan (1976), argued that there was a preoccupation with victim blaming during this time period.[12] He asserted that such practices obscured the social inequalities that lay behind crime statistics.[13] The suggestion that victims shared responsibility for or instigated the criminal episode would lead to significant debate within this emerging field. Criticisms from scholars like Ryan were juxtaposed with others who noted that some victims are responsible for their own demise. David Luckenbill (1977), for example, draws upon the work of earlier victimologists and sees homicide as a "situated transaction," in which both the victim and offender play a part. It was already understood that victims sometimes precipitate the violence that kills them, either by throwing the first punch or firing the first shot.[14] Luckenbill, as is typical of many victimologists, was interested in how these roles develop, what patterns of interaction emerge, and what in that transaction eventuates the murder.[15]

The tension between these emphases has informed much of the dialogue in contemporary victimology.

### Benjamin Mendelssohn

Benjamin Mendelssohn was a Romanian lawyer and one of the founders of victimology, beginning in the 1930s. He specialized in penal law, and his initial interest in victims sprang from his need, as a criminal attorney, to demonstrate to the court that the victim had a role in the criminal act.[16] In addition to his contribution of the term *victimology* itself, it was Mendelssohn who first suggested the establishment of an international society dedicated to the field.[17] This eventually was realized with the creation of institutions such as the World Society of Victimology, the American Society of Victimology, and the International Victimology Institute at Tilburg.

Mendelssohn is regarded as the "father" of victimology, not only for contributing the term, but for devising a scale that classified victims based upon what he believed was their level of blame for the crime. Based upon victim questionnaires, Mendelssohn discovered that there was frequently an interpersonal relationship between the victim and the offender.[18] Mendelssohn developed what was, in essence, a continuum of degrees of victim blame. The victim types ranged from "completely innocent victim" to "simulating or imaginary victim." On one end of the spectrum is the completely innocent victim, who in no way provokes or facilitates the offender's attack. At the other end is the imaginary victim, by which Mendelssohn meant a victim who pretended to be victimized.[19]

© Syda Productions/Shutterstock.com

Some would-be criminal offenders instead become victims, such as drug dealers.

People who commit crime are more likely to be victimized than the general population.[20] Mendelssohn, as part of his classification system, also considered situations in which the eventual victim was initially the offender, but lost control of the situation and wound up becoming the victim. Situations in which one drug dealer attacked another, only to lose control of the situation and become injured himself, would fall under this category. This type of victim, one that Mendelssohn called "victim more guilty than offender," would become important to later work done by victimologists such as Amir and Wolfgang.[21]

### Hans von Hentig

Of the early victimologists, Hans von Hentig was among the more influential and controversial. Von Hentig insisted that victims were often involved, even complicit, in putting the criminal act into motion. His theory ran contrary to the prevailing ideology within criminology, which was static and one-dimensional in focusing solely upon the offender.[22] Von Hentig believed that in many cases, "we meet a victim who consents tacitly, co-operates, conspires or provokes. The victim is one of the causative elements."[23] Von Hentig saw a mutual relationship between offender and victim. He grouped his findings into a series of typologies, which are categorized observations put into logical groupings. His typologies described groups of characteristics that explained why some people are more likely to become victims than others. Von Hentig's typologies were similar to Mendelssohn's victim types, but von Hentig was less interested in assigning blame and more interested in asserting that the victim was one of several possible causes of a particular crime, possibly even a precipitating cause, as well as unlocking the relationship between the two.

Indeed, criminals often use victim status or behavior as an attempt to justify their crimes, such as rapists who claim they were perceiving signals from their victims.[24] Of particular interest to victimologists is the presence of drugs and alcohol in sexual assault cases and the role that alcohol played in the perpetrator's understanding of the crime.[25] Some perpetrators try to excuse their actions on the grounds that because the victim was under the influence of alcohol, the offender should be absolved of their crime.[26]

The point of such inquiries is to help understand the genesis of crime, the circumstances surrounding it, and the environmental cues that trigger victimization. Victimology helps researchers understand the role the victim plays in crime. This view of crime resulted in criminological theories like the Routine Activities Theory. Developed by Lawrence Cohen and Marcus Felson (1979), the theory posits that the commission of a crime requires three facilitating factors: a motivated offender, a suitable target, and an absence of capable guardians.[27] These theories enhance the understanding not only of crime, but also of how people can avoid putting themselves in the position to be victimized in the first place.

## Marvin Wolfgang

Marvin Wolfgang is remembered mainly for his contributions to the development of victim precipitation, particularly in what he called the "subculture of violence theory."[28] Wolfgang was one of the first to attempt systematic research to provide empirical support for the assertion that victims contribute to the commission of a crime. As noted earlier, the typologies of Mendelssohn and von Hentig suggested that victims contributed to criminal acts, but neither presented empirical evidence to support his view. Wolfgang studied homicides in Philadelphia for the years 1948–1952. He reported that 26% of the homicides he reviewed resulted from victim precipitation. He defined victim precipitation as "those cases in which the victim was the first to show and use a deadly weapon, to strike a blow."[29]

Wolfgang was specifically interested in violent crime and victimization within Philadelphia's African-American community, as there was a disproportionate level of violence in this community compared to the general population.[30] Wolfgang came to the controversial conclusion that the high rates of homicide among blacks were due to the subculture within the African-American community that emphasized and even valued violence. Wolfgang's studies attempted to analyze the context in which crimes occur, and to illuminate social inequalities that may be the root of the problem. Wolfgang identified several factors typical of what he called victim-precipitated homicides. He found that a great many victims of homicide had a preexisting relationship with their attacker, the homicides were often a product of small disagreements that escalated, and alcohol had often been consumed by the victim. Wolfgang's research suggested that some homicide victims were not completely passive individuals who were preyed upon by aggressive predators.[31]

Wolfgang found that many victims of homicide had a preexisting relationship with their attacker.

### Menachem Amir

Menachem Amir, a student of Marvin Wolfgang, attempted to present an empirical analysis of rape incidents in Philadelphia. He reviewed police reports of rape between 1958 and 1960 and asserted that 19% of all the forcible rapes reported during that time period were victim-precipitated.[32]

Amir's application of the concept of victim precipitation deviated substantially from Wolfgang's initial conception. Wolfgang argued that victim precipitation occurred when a victim first initiated the violence (e.g., the victim was the first to commit or attempt to commit a crime). In contrast, Amir suggested that victim precipitation occurred when factors such as alcohol consumption, flirtatious behavior, revealing clothing, risqué language, being at the wrong place at the wrong time, and personal reputation were present on the part of the victim.[33] Therefore, Amir argued that a woman who drank alcohol or engaged in flirtatious behavior caused her

---

**Critical Thinking**

Do you think that studying the role rape victims play in their own victimization is inherently problematic? Does inquiring about whether or not they "precipitated" the event imply that they are at fault?

own rape. Not surprisingly, Amir's claims were perceived as misogynistic and incendiary. His research was heavily criticized by victim advocates and women's groups as using rape myths to blame victims and giving scientific legitimacy to this practice. Amir's research articulated a view of victim precipitation that remains contentious today.

## Victim Precipitation

Early pioneers in the field of victimology were concerned with the way victims contributed to the criminal act. They suggested that the victim's role could be conscious or unconscious, and could come through carelessness, recklessness, or imprudence.[34] Von Hentig, Mendelssohn, Amir, and others asserted that victims could have a motivational role, which could take the form of attracting, arousing, enticing, inducing, or inciting. They also believed that victims could have a functional role, whether through provoking, precipitating, triggering, facilitating, or actively participating.[35] These varying degrees of victim involvement in the criminal act fall under the heading of victim precipitation.

**Victim precipitation** can be defined as actions on the part of victims that cause, partly or completely, their own victimization.[36] Victim precipitation can be either passive or active. Different victimologists had different interpretations and points of emphasis when discussing victim precipitation. For example, Von Hentig focused more on passive victim precipitation, while Mendelssohn focused on a more active characterization of victim precipitation.

**Victim precipitation**
Actions by the victim, either passive or active, that help to trigger the offense.

The understanding of victim precipitation has evolved over time. Although not emphasized as much as it was in the past, contemporary interpreters still integrate it into their work. For example, David Luckenbill's theory of situated transaction sees crime as a contest of character between victim and offender. Luckenbill accepted that victims could precipitate their own victimization, but felt victimology had not gone far enough in understanding how the relationship developed and the roles played by victims and offenders.[37]

### The Assumptions of Victim Precipitation

As a result of the reactions to Amir's work, victimologists began to challenge the precipitation argument as it had developed to that point. Many suggested that it was important to critically examine the assumptions that provided the foundation for the victim precipitation argument. Franklin and Franklin[38] suggested that there were four main assumptions to consider and critically evaluate. First, victim precipitation assumes that the behavior of the victim can explain the criminal act. Second, victim precipitation assumes that the offender is provoked by signals from the victim. Third, victim precipitation assumes that a victim's behavior is in and of itself enough to instigate a criminal act. Finally, victim precipitation assumes that the victim's intent can be measured by the victimization incident itself, without taking the offender into account.

Critical evaluation of these assumptions reveals several problems. First, certain types of precipitous behavior can occur without leading to any victimization (e.g., dressing provocatively or consuming alcohol to excess does not always lead to rape). Second, offenders often plan their crimes in advance, and are not simply acting in response to stimuli from the victim. Third, offenders may either respond to or ignore the actions of the victim and commit the crime anyway.[39]

Critics argue that studies of victim precipitation only focus on the behavior of the victim, diverting attention away from perpetrators and their responsibility for the crime.[40] Many critics view victim precipitation as

---

**Critical Thinking**

Is the concept of victim precipitation the same as blaming the victim? Is the difference purely semantic? Justify your response with arguments.

---

"victim blaming." For example, Courtney Ahrens (2006) found that rape victims who were perceived as having instigated their own attack were the target of negative reactions from the people who were supposed to help them.[41] Rape victims who disclosed details of their assault often met with suspicion and suggestions that they were at fault.

## The "Just World" Concept and the "Legitimate" Victim

**Just world** A worldview in which everyone gets the consequences they deserve for their actions.

The concept of a "**just world,**" or one in which people get the consequences they deserve for their actions during their lives, also contributes to our understanding of victimhood and deviance. People who adhere to the idea of a just world do not want to believe that innocent people could be victims of random acts of violence and evil. Instead, they believe that the victims must have transgressed or misbehaved in some way to deserve what happened to them. Under this philosophy, the idea that victims are in some way responsible or partially complicit in their own victimizations is reassuring. Because of this, victims are often unfairly stigmatized and are not able to receive the support they need after their victimization. This "just world" belief creates an environment where victims are seen as different from nonvictims and as deficient in some way. The idea of a "culturally legitimate"

---

**Critical Thinking**

What are some examples of culturally legitimate victims? How have these victims been constructed as different and/or deficient from nonvictims?

---

victim[42] is that the victim is in some sense deserving, or "fair game." For example, criminals are often victims of violence themselves,[43] and, as their own involvement in criminal activity makes them less likely to seek help from authorities, they are seen as legitimate targets.[44] This process of creating culturally legitimate victims, though problematic and overly generalized, in some ways makes society believe it is "acceptable" for certain people to be victimized.

## Contemporary Approaches to Victimology

Contemporary victimology tends to approach victimization as largely subjective.[45] This approach emphasizes looking at the specifics of an individual situation, and attending to the perspectives of all involved.[46] For example, the concept of "bystander blaming" has been reintroduced. The "bystander," as Cohen argues, is the third part of a triad of victim, offender, and bystander.[47] In the case of a victim of sexual harassment, the innocent bystander's perspective is considered to give a more complete account of the perspectives and roles in the criminal act.

Another contemporary trend in dealing with victims, as well as criminals, is restorative justice. Restorative justice differs from the traditional model in that it places less emphasis on an adversarial system, such as is found in traditional criminal or civil proceedings. It seeks to repair the damage to all parties involved by facilitating dialogue between victim and offender, and making the offender realize the consequences of his or her actions. The theory acknowledges that three parties are damaged by crime: the victim, the offender, and society. By doing so, it shifts away from the idea of offending as being against the state and toward a notion of

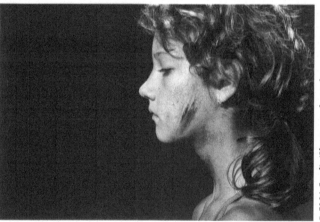

The costs of victimization go beyond just the tangible costs.

offending as being against an individual and the community.[48] Restorative justice also seeks to address the underlying causes that led to the crime in the first place.[49] Restorative justice can be practiced through methods such as victim-offender mediation, family group conferencing, and restorative conferencing, among others. These approaches typically include mediated conferencing between victims, offenders, family members, and friends. They address issues of restitution and consequences.[50]

## Victims' Rights Movement

Victims often feel marginalized and alienated from the criminal justice system. Joanne Wemmers (2008) found that crime victims desire increased recognition and involvement with the criminal justice system.[51] This has led to several initiatives over the past couple of decades that have extended additional rights to crime victims. This victims' rights movement has strived to address the needs of crime victims and help them deal with the trauma of victimization.

## Costs of Victimization

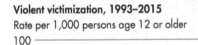

**Costs of victimization** The costs incurred by a victim as a result of victimization. These include financial, emotional, psychological, and social costs.

Victimization imposes tremendous psychological, physical, emotional, and financial costs on the victim, the victim's family, and society as a whole. The **costs of victimization** refer to the costs associated with crime. These costs include not only the direct cost from the criminal event, but the losses that victims and witnesses incur when they enter the criminal justice system. Figure 11.1 breaks down the costs of victimization for the major types of crime into tangible and intangible costs. It should be noted that the costs below reflect only *victim*-related costs; the chart does not address the costs incurred by the criminal justice system.

In 2015, U.S. residents age 12 or older experienced an estimated 5 million violent victimizations, according to the Bureau of Justice Statistics' (BJS) National Crime Victimization Survey (NCVS). There was no statistically

**FIGURE 11.1** TOTAL COST OF VICTIMIZATION: 1993–2015.

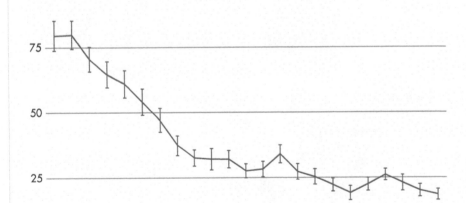

**Violent victimization, 1993–2015**
Rate per 1,000 persons age 12 or older

Note: Estimates include 95% confidence intervals.
*See *Criminal Victimization, 2007* (NCJ 224390, BJS web, December 2008) for information on changes in the 2006 NCVS.

*Source: Bureau of Justice Statistics, National Crime Victimisation Survey (NCVS), 1993–2015.*

significant change in the rate of overall violent crime, defined as rape or sexual assault, robbery, aggravated assault, and simple assault, from 2014 (20.1 victimizations per 1,000 persons age 12 and older) to 2015 (18.6 per 1,000). However, the rate of violent crime in 2015 was lower than in 2013 (23.2 per 1,000). From 1993 to 2015, the rate of violent crime declined from 79.8 to 18.6 victimizations per 1,000 persons age 12 or older. The rates of violent and property crime largely followed similar trends over time. Households in the U.S. experienced an estimated 14.6 million property victimizations in 2015. The overall property crime rate (which includes household burglary, theft, and motor vehicle theft) decreased from 118.1 victimizations per 1,000 households in 2014 to 110.7 victimizations per 1,000 in 2015. A decline in theft accounted for most of the decrease in property crime. [52]

Damaged or lost property at the hands of a criminal offender is part of the first victimization.

### First Victimization

The trauma of the victim at the hands of the offender is often called the "first victimization." At this stage, victims suffer physical injury, property loss, missed time from work, and disruption of their normal lives. Other costs, though more difficult to quantify, include emotional distress and anguish, as well as strained relations with their friends and family due to the trauma of victimization.[52]

### Second Victimization

Entering the criminal justice system can present its own set of challenges to victims. Victims may be subjected to insensitive questioning by detectives and, later, defense attorneys, an unavoidable reality of the criminal justice process. They may discover, after the fact, that their victimizer has been acquitted, with no warning from the state. Similarly, in some cases, victims are not told if the offender makes bail or is paroled after serving only part of the original sentence.[53] While many jurisdictions have attempted to address such problems through policy changes, these issues can sometimes still occur. This leads to what victimologists call the "*second victimization*."[54]

A victim's testimony in a criminal case is often crucial, but as witnesses, victims may endure challenges. When they take the stand, they are frequently cross-examined in an aggressive or hostile manner by defense attorneys. Their personal lives are frequently put on trial and their credibility attacked.[55] Defendants have a constitutional right to confront their accusers, so these situations are often unavoidable and simply part of the process of a robust criminal justice system. Still, these experiences can sometimes cause victims to feel marginalized.

The marginalization of victims was researched by Frank Cannavale in 1976. Cannavale determined that the single greatest impediment to successfully prosecuting a case was that victims were less and less cooperative. They did not want to help the system, as they thought it did not care about their needs.[56] Victims and witnesses often fail to appear in court, despite it being a required civic duty, because they believe it is not worth the high cost and aggravation to do so.

---

**Critical Thinking**

What do you think is the best way to address victims' rights issues? Does providing federal- or state-funded legal support conflict with the rights of the accused? Explain.

---

© Zack Frank/Shutterstock.com

Women's rights leaders fought for changes in the criminal justice system to better respond to victims of rape and sexual assault.

In acknowledging the problem, the justice system has done a great deal to secure cooperation from victims. To prosecute offenders more effectively, the justice system must have witnesses who are willing and happy to help. Witnesses who are confident and informed and benefit from assistance programs are better equipped to deal with the emotionally draining experience of testifying. This leads to lower dismissal rates and higher conviction rates, as well as a restoration of the public's confidence and trust.[57]

## Victims' Rights

Dissatisfaction with the treatment of crime victims by the criminal justice system has been an important force in mobilizing the victims' rights movement. Thirty years ago, victims of crime had few legal rights within the criminal justice system. Over the past several decades, advocates and activists have campaigned for an expansion of victims' rights. Victims often report frustration from participating in the criminal justice system.[58] Early victims' rights advocates equated their struggle with other movements for social justice, including the movements for civil rights, gay rights, women's rights, workers' rights, students' rights, children's rights, patients' rights, and prisoners' rights.[59]

### Special Interest Groups

Numerous special interest groups and advocates for social justice have been linked with the development of victims' rights. The women's rights movement in the 1960s and 1970s fought for changes in a criminal justice system that did not adequately respond to victims of rape and sexual assault. In particular, the criminal justice system did not always attend to the emotional and psychological needs of victims. The women's rights movement helped establish rape crisis centers and domestic violence shelters to better address these needs.[60]

Although possibly the most prominent, women's groups and rape/sexual assault advocates were not the only special interest groups that championed victims' causes. In 1974, Families and Friends of Missing Persons was founded to provide support for the loved ones of missing individuals. Mothers Against Drunk Driving (MADD) followed in 1980, after Candy Lightner's daughter was killed by a drunk driver who was a repeat offender. These organizations usually began as support groups that evolved into a political advocacy role.[61] Many of these organization have been instrumental in shaping federal legislation. See Figure 11.2 for a listing of federal legislation passed.

Several of these groups joined forces to form the **National Organization for Victim Assistance (NOVA)**. Since 1975, NOVA has helped to raise awareness of victims' issues and provided training for those who work with victims.[62] There are many other government and private organizations that exist today to provide assistance and advocacy for victims. For example, the Victim Rights Law Center (VRLC) provides representation for victims of rape and sexual assault, the Identity Theft Resource Center provides information and assistance for victims of identity theft, the National Center on Elder Abuse advocates for the rights of elder Americans, and so forth.

National Organization for Victim Assistance (NOVA) A conglomerate of victims' rights groups that advocate on behalf of victims and victims' issues.

### Career Connections: Guardian ad Litem

A guardian ad litem is, as described by the Children's Guardian Fund, "a volunteer appointed by the court to protect the rights and advocate for the best interests of a child involved in a court proceeding primarily as a result of alleged abuse or neglect."[63] He or she must act as the spokesperson for the child. Such guardians are frequently attorneys, social workers, or simply volunteers. Some states (e.g., Florida) utilize trained volunteers from the community. A guardian ad litem differs from the more commonly known "legal guardian" because they do not control the property of the child and do not furnish the child with a home. Their sole purpose is to act in the best interests of the child.

Such positions are temporary and last only for the duration of the legal proceedings. Guardians come from diverse backgrounds, and the requirements vary by state. Applicants must complete an application, a background check, and an interview, and successfully complete a training course. Guardians spend most of their time (60%) visiting their charges at home or formal meetings.[64] The funding for these programs generally comes from the court's budget.

Guardians are expected to gather information about the conditions and needs of the child. They make recommendations to judges about what they deem to be in the child's best interest in terms of treatment plans and permanent homes in the case of abuse. They also monitor the progress of the child, the case, and the parents (if applicable).

### Federal Initiatives

In 1982, President Reagan established a Presidential Task Force on Victims of Crime. This task force argued for a greater role of crime victims in court and led to the creation of federal legislation establishing a federal Office

© Billion Photos/Shutterstock.com

Advocates have attempted to add a victim rights amendment to the U.S. Constitution.

for Victims of Crime in the U.S. DOJ. In addition, the task force recommended that an amendment to the U.S. Constitution be created giving victims the right to be present and to be heard at all critical stages of judicial proceedings. In 1984, the **Victims of Crime Act (VOCA)** was passed. This allowed the federal government to provide compensation to victims of federal offenses, as well as funds for state governments to use in their own compensation programs. VOCA not only provides funds, but has helped to systematize compensation programs so that there is greater consistency among states.[65]

## Victim Rights Amendment (VRA)

**Victims of Crime Act (VOCA)** An act that allowed federal money to subsidize state compensation programs for victims.

Since the 1982 Presidential Task Force, there have been a number of attempts over the years to incorporate language that would address the rights of victims into the U.S. Constitution. The text of a (recent) version of one **Victim Rights Amendment** is contained below. It was a Proposed Federal VRA for the 108th Congress. The purpose of the amendment was to provide victims with guaranteed rights when they enter the justice system.

**Victim Rights Amendment** A proposed constitutional amendment that would provide victims with guaranteed rights similar to those given to offenders under the Sixth Amendment.

To date, efforts to pass such an amendment have been unsuccessful. Critics have noted that the Seventh Amendment allows victims to sue offenders for restitution, and that this is sufficient.[66] Others felt that the idea was inherently misguided because the purpose of the Bill of Rights is to protect citizens from the government, specifically as it relates to personal freedom and liberty. Victims' issues have nothing to do with freedom, and are therefore outside the scope of the Bill of Rights.[67]

### Federal Constitutional Reform Efforts

There have also been attempts to amend the existing Bill of Rights, specifically the Sixth Amendment, instead of adding an entirely new amendment. Victims' advocates wanted to add the following sentence: "Likewise, the victim, in every criminal prosecution shall have the right to be present and to be heard at all critical stages of judicial proceedings."[71] This, too, met with resistance. Critics argued that the language of the revised amendment did not address property crimes, which was highly problematic because theft is far more prevalent than rape, assault, and murder.[72]

Advocacy groups for victims have had success at the state level. Since 1980, nearly every state has enacted statutes that address basic rights for victims of crime. These typically include the rights to attend court proceedings, to have stolen property returned, to be protected from reprisals by the accused, and to restitution.[73] By the year 2000, 33 states had amended their constitutional charters to address the needs of victims.[74] Advocacy groups hope that these changes to state law will eventually lead to changes to the U.S. Constitution.

---

**Exhibit: Text of the Proposed Amendment (108th Congress)**

The following article is proposed as an amendment to the Constitution of the United States, which shall be valid to all intents and purposes as part of the Constitution when ratified by the legislatures of three-fourths of the several States, and which shall take effect on the 180th day after ratification of this article:

1. Article–SECTION 1. The rights of victims of violent crime, being capable of protection without denying the constitutional rights of those accused of victimizing them, are hereby established and shall not be denied by any State or the United States and may be restricted only as provided in this article.

2. SECTION 2. A victim of violent crime shall have the right to reasonable and timely notice of any public proceeding involving the crime and of any release or escape of the accused; the rights not to be excluded from such public proceeding and reasonably to be heard at public release, plea, sentencing, reprieve, and pardon proceedings; and the right to adjudicative decisions that duly consider the victim's safety, interest in avoiding unreasonable delay, and just and timely claims to restitution from the offender. These rights shall not be restricted except when and to the degree dictated by a substantial interest in public safety or the administration of criminal justice, or by compelling necessity.

3. SECTION 3. Nothing in this article shall be construed to provide grounds for a new trial or to authorize any claim for damages. Only the victim or the victim's lawful representative may assert the rights established by this article, and no person accused of the crime may obtain any form of relief hereunder.

4. SECTION 4. The Congress shall have the power to enforce by appropriate legislation this article. Nothing in this article shall affect the President's authority to grant reprieves or pardons.

5. SECTION 5. This article shall be inoperative unless it shall have been ratified as an amendment to the Constitution by the legislatures of three-fourths of the several States within seven years from the date of its submission to the States by the Congress. This article shall take effect on the 180th day after the date of its ratification.[70]

---

## Federal Victims' Rights Legislation in the U.S.

The federal government has taken an active role in addressing the plight of victims in the United States. Figure 11.2 summarizes key victims' rights legislation passed in the United States since 1974. The biggest piece of federal legislation was the 2004 Crime Victims' Bill of Rights. It incorporates standard rights for victims such as the right to be notified, the right to be included in court proceedings, the right to be heard at plea and parole hearings, the right to confer with the prosecutor from reprisals, and the right to fairness and privacy.

**FIGURE 11.2** KEY FEDERAL VICTIMS' RIGHTS LEGISLATION

**1974** Child Abuse Prevention and Treatment Act

**1980** Parental Kidnapping Prevention Act

**1982** Victim and Witness Protection Act

**1982** Missing Children's Act

**1984** Victims of Crime Act

**1984** Justice Assistance Act

**1984** Missing Children's Assistance Act

**1984** Family Violence Prevention and Services Act

**1985** Children's Justice Act

**1988** Drunk Driving Prevention Act

**1990** Hate Crime Statistics Act

**1990** Victims of Child Abuse Act

**1990** Victims' Rights and Restitution Act

**1990** National Child Search Assistance Act

**1992** Battered Women's Testimony Act

**1993** Child Sexual Abuse Registry Act

**1994** Violent Crime Control and Law Enforcement Act

**1994** Violence Against Women Act

**1996** Community Notification Act ("Megan's Law")

**1996** Antiterrorism and Effective Death Penalty Act

**1996** Mandatory Victims' Restitution Act

**1997** Victims' Rights Clarification Act

**1998** Crime Victims with Disabilities Act

**1998** Identity Theft and Deterrence Act

**2000** Trafficking Victims Protection Act

**2001** Air Transportation Safety and System Stabilization Act (established September 11th Victim Compensation Fund)

**2003** PROTECT Act ("Amber Alert" law)

**2003** Prison Rape Elimination Act

**2003** Fair and Accurate Credit Transactions Act

**2004** Justice for All Act, including Title I The Scott Campbell, Stephanie Roper, Wendy Preston, Louarna Gillis, and Nila Lynn Crime Victims' Rights Act

**2006** Adam Walsh Child Protection and Safety Act

**2010** Tribal Law and Order Act

*Source: https://ovc.ncjrs.gov/ncvrw2015/pdf/Landmarks.pdf*

## Victim Impact Statements (VIS)

One key advancement for victims' rights is the use of victim impact statements. A **victim impact statement (VIS)** allows the victim to actively participate in the sentencing hearing of the offender: it is a statement given at sentencing in which the victim can tell the court exactly how the victimization has affected his or her life. These statements can be delivered in person (known as allocution) or submitted in writing as part of a presentence investigation report (PIR).[75]

**Victim impact statement (VIS)** A statement from the victim to the judge during the sentencing phase of the offender's trial.

Victim impact statements have drawn enough controversy to merit appeals that have gone all the way to the U.S. Supreme Court. In *Booth v. Maryland*, the court reversed a capital sentence because the jury had heard an especially emotional VIS. The impact statement detailed how the slaying of an elderly couple had destroyed the lives of three generations of a family. The court ruled that the use of such a statement was inflammatory and unconstitutional because of its arbitrary nature. The court felt it was wrong to determine the penalty based upon perceptions of a victim's perceived "worth."[76] This ruling was later overturned, however, in *Payne v. Tennessee* in 1991. The case involved the murder of a mother and child; during sentencing the prosecution wanted to enter a VIS detailing the emotional duress of a three-year-old survivor of the attack. The court ruled that a VIS was permissible in a capital case. The grounds for this ruling was that if prosecutors are allowed to present evidence as to the repercussions of the crime on victims, then there is nothing to preclude a jury from hearing it.[77]

© Namning/Shutterstock.com

Victim impact statements allow victims to participate in the trial of the offender.

Balancing the rights of victims with the rights of the accused is not easy. Victim impact statements in particular are controversial. Critics charge that victim impact statements tarnish the objectivity of the judicial process.[78] The emotionally charged testimony of a suffering victim has the potential to be highly prejudicial, especially if their testimony simply talks about what a great person the victim was. Critics assert that judges may be overcome with emotion and accede to pleas from victims who would use a VIS vindictively to exact revenge or unfairly influence sentencing. The claim is not without merit. A particular fear is that the emphasis will shift from offender to victim, leading to unjustly stiff sentences for offenders who commit crimes against especially sympathetic victims.[79]

While victim impact statements remain the subject of controversy, they undeniably give victims a greater voice in the justice system, and the Supreme Court ultimately upheld them. The Supreme Court decided in

*Payne v. Tennessee*[80] that such statements are admissible as testimony during the sentencing phase of the trial. They ruled that such statements were not unconstitutional, and that the punishment should fit the crime.[81] Additionally, advocates for VIS have noted that proper statements help judges and prosecutors to understand in a visceral way the emotional devastation caused by crime, and therefore hand down more appropriate sentences.[82] A study conducted in Australia determined that there was no discernible change in sentencing patterns following the newly implemented use of VIS.[83]

## Remedying the Costs of Crime Victimization

Remedying the costs of victimization can take several forms. The legislative reforms discussed earlier aim to help victims who enter the criminal justice system. However, returning the victim to their pre-victimization state often requires financial restitution. This can take the form of compensation from the state, restitution from the offender, or civil lawsuits. The criminal justice system needs witness testimony to get convictions. A victim may refrain from contact with the criminal justice system because they feel that, financially, they will be better off not participating.[84] Compensation, restitution, and civil lawsuits are all common ways to ease the financial burdens of victims and witnesses.

### Compensation

**Compensation** A financial reward for a wrong incurred at the hands of an offender.

Victim **compensation** involves monetary reimbursement paid by the state to the victim for losses sustained as a result of crime. The primary sources of funds for state compensation are financial assessments imposed on convicted businesses and individuals, bond forfeitures, and fines. Victim compensation is based on the idea that the government has an obligation to care for the safety and well-being of its citizens and to provide a minimum standard of living for citizens. Some advocates and social scientists argue that crime can be attributed to economic and social inequalities such as racism, poverty, and so on. In this way, they argue, the state is in some sense liable for crime.[85] Compensation is one method to recover monetary losses for victims. One of the challenges with compensation is that many states require victims to exhaust all other options (e.g., private insurance) before applying for compensation from the state. As a result, victim compensation is often viewed as a source of last resort.

### Restitution

Restitution, which involves compensation paid to victims by offenders who cause harm through action or negligence, is one of the oldest forms of redress available to victims. The idea is related to the ancient custom of *wergild*, in which compensation was paid to either the victim or the victim's family.[86] The practice also has parallels in the legal codes of Hammurabi and Justinian, as well as Mosaic Law. Restitution is appealing for a number of reasons. It is intuitive: victims should be compensated by their victimizers. Even if the offense is against society, offenders can pay symbolic restitution in the form of money or service to the community. This is important in making the victim(s) whole again.[87]

Restitution has the additional advantage of enticing victims to assist the justice system. If victims and witnesses are reluctant to help the state prosecute offenders because of the financial consequences, then ensuring restitution from offenders may go a long way toward solving the problem. This provides a tangible reward for citizens' cooperation.

There are several drawbacks of offender restitution. Offenders, particularly those who commit theft, frequently do not have enough money to provide immediate restitution, as they are unemployed or incarcerated. In addition, the criminal justice system—in keeping with its idea of crime as committed against the state rather than the victim—is often more concerned with penal fines than compensating victims.[88]

## Civil Suits

A final method of aiding victims, and one provided for by the Bill of Rights, is civil lawsuits. **Civil lawsuits** have the benefit, much like victim impact statements, of empowering victims and letting them participate in the court

**Civil lawsuit** A case in which a plaintiff sues the defendant to recover money damages for negligence or harm.

> **Critical Thinking**
>
> How do you feel about exacting compensation from the state? Is it fair to make taxpayers pay for the actions of offenders?

process, instead of leaving everything to the discretion of a state prosecutor. Victims who seek financial restitution can sue for punitive or compensatory damages. Punitive damages are meant to punish and deter the offender, while compensatory damages are meant to compensate victims for specific costs that they incur.[89]

Civil lawsuits have a number of advantages, aside from empowering the victim. Successful prosecution in a criminal case is difficult. As discussed earlier, the criminal justice system is constitutionally slanted toward the rights of offenders. To get a conviction, the level of proof must be "beyond a reasonable doubt," whereas in civil suits, all that is required is a "preponderance of evidence."[90]

Civil court is not without its problems. Victims are often unaware of this remedy, or have no idea of how to secure an attorney's services. A greater problem is that many victims are unable to afford an attorney, and, therefore, lower-class victims are often unable to pursue civil suits as a method of recourse.[91] Also, many offenders possess few assets, so victims will likely receive very little from the offender even if they win the case.

# Victimization Surveys

The final section of this chapter will focus on the development and use of victimization surveys. As discussed earlier in the chapter, early victimologists recognized that they needed a better way to measure the effects and causes of victimization. As early victimologists suspected, there was a great deal to be learned about criminal acts by collecting data about the victims. Victimization surveys have revealed that crime and victimization both occur in clusters in certain groups and in certain areas.[92] This allows criminologists and victimologists to track trends in crime and victimization, and to assess the risk certain populations have of becoming either victims or victimizers.

## Measuring the Extent of Crime

There are three main sources that victimologists use to statistically assess crime and victimization rates.[93] The first, and oldest, of the major sources of crime data is the Uniform Crime Report. As discussed earlier, the UCR is a collection of official records from police departments, published annually by the FBI, that allows police departments to share information. This allows officials to track the magnitude of crime over time.[94]

The UCR tracks index crimes, which group crimes by the nature of the incident. It also provides geographic data, as it groups offenses by reports that come from the police forces of towns, states, cities, etc.[95] Other tables feature data about the people arrested for these crimes, including sex, age, race, resident status, and past arrest record. This demonstrates that the attention is primarily focused upon the offenders, rather than the victims. Indeed, one shortcoming of the UCR is that it contains limited information about victims. In addition, many crimes go unreported to law enforcement and are not reflected in the UCR. Individuals will not report an act to law enforcement unless they clearly label the act as criminal in their own minds. As a result of these limitations, victimologists look for other sources of data.

Another source is self-report surveys, in which respondents are asked—with the promise of confidentiality—to disclose information about themselves and any crimes they have committed. Even with the inherent risk of exposure, the respondents' replies are eye-opening. It is apparent that much more crime is committed than the official UCR indicates.[96] Self-report surveys also include the demographic and personal information about respondents that the UCR lacks.

Building on this, the next logical step for researchers was to ask people not about offenses they had committed, but about any experiences of victimization in their lives. Victimization surveys went through several iterations before arriving at the National Crime Survey (NCS). The NCS was first administered in 1973 to 100,000 households. Each household was contacted twice a year for three years. The survey was redesigned in 1979, and officially renamed the National Crime Victimization Survey (NCVS) in 1992. Questions were updated for increased accuracy, and to capture as much information as possible about the victim and the circumstances surrounding the criminal event.[97] The survey is more than 20 pages long, and includes questions such as "Have you been robbed in the past six months?" If the response is affirmative, the survey proceeds to ask detailed questions about the experience and the subsequent consequences. Data are categorized into property and personal victimizations. Personal crimes include rape and sexual assault, aggravated and simple assault, robbery, and purse-snatching or pocket-picking. Property crimes include theft, motor vehicle theft, burglary, and vandalism.[98]

## FIGURE 11.3 CRIME IN THE UNITED STATES BY VOLUME AND RATE PER 100,000 INHABITANTS, 1996–2015

| Year | Population[1] | Violent crime[2] | Violent crime rate | Murder and non negligent manslaughter | Murder and nonnegligent manslaughter | Rape (revised definition) | Rape (revised definition) rate[2] | Rape (legacy definition) | Rape (legacy definition) rate[4] | Robbery | Robbery rate | Aggravate assault |
|------|-----------|-----------|------|--------|-----|---------|------|--------|--------|---------|-------|----------|
| 1996 | 265,228,572 | 1,688,540 | 636.6 | 19,645 | 7.4 | | | 96,252 | 36.3 | 535,594 | 201.9 | 1,037,04 |
| 1997 | 267,783,607 | 1,636,096 | 611.0 | 18,208 | 6.8 | | | 96,153 | 35.9 | 498,534 | 186.2 | 1,023,20 |
| 1998 | 270,248,003 | 1,533,887 | 567.6 | 16,974 | 6.3 | | | 93,144 | 34.5 | 447,186 | 165.5 | 976,58 |
| 1999 | 272,690,813 | 1,426,044 | 523.0 | 15,522 | 5.7 | | | 89,411 | 32.8 | 409,371 | 150.1 | 911,74 |
| 2000 | 281,421,906 | 1,425,486 | 508.5 | 15,586 | 5.5 | | | 90,178 | 32.0 | 408,016 | 145.0 | 911,70 |
| 2001[5] | 285,317,559 | 1,439,480 | 504.5 | 16,037 | 5.6 | | | 90,863 | 31.8 | 423,557 | 148.5 | 909,02 |
| 2002 | 287,973,924 | 1,423,677 | 494.4 | 16,229 | 5.6 | | | 33.1 | 420,806 | 146.1 | 891,40 | |
| 2003 | 290,788,976, | 1,383,676 | 475.8 | 16,528 | 5.7 | | | 93,883 | 32.3 | 414,235 | 142.5 | 859,03 |
| 2004 | 293,656,842 | 1,380,088 | 463.2 | 16,148 | 5.5 | | | 95,089 | 32.4 | 401,470 | 136.7 | 847,38 |
| 2005 | 296,507,061 | 1,390,745 | 469.0 | 16,740 | 5.6 | | | 94,347 | 31.8 | 417,438 | 140.8 | 862,22 |
| 2006 | 299,398,484 | 1,435,123 | 479.3 | 17,309 | 5.8 | | | 94,472 | 31.6 | 449,246 | 150.0 | 874,09 |
| 2007 | 301,621,157, | 1,422,970 | 471.8 | 17,128 | 5.7 | | | 92,160 | 30.6 | 447,324 | 148.3 | 866,358 |
| 2008 | 304,059,724 | 1,394,461 | 458.6 | 16,465 | 5.4 | | | 90,750 | 29.8 | 443,563 | 145.9 | 843,683 |
| 2009 | 307,006,550 | 1,325,896 | 431.9 | 15,399 | 5.0 | | | 89,241 | 29.1 | 406,742 | 133.1 | 812,514 |
| 2010 | 309,330,2019 | 1,251,248 | 404.5 | 14,722 | 4.8 | | | 85,593 | 27.7 | 369,069 | 119.3 | 781,844 |
| 2011 | 311,587,816 | 1,206,005 | 387.1 | 14,661 | 4.7 | | | 84,175 | 27.0 | 354,746 | 113.9 | 752,423 |
| 2012 | 313,873,685, | 1,217,07 | 387.8 | 14,856 | 4.7 | | | 85,141 | 27.1 | 355,051 | 113.1 | 762,009 |
| 2013 | 316,497,531 | 1,168,298 | 369.1 | 14,319 | 4.5 | 113,695 | 35.9 | 82,109 | 25.9 | 345,093 | 109.0 | 726,777 |
| 2014[6] | 318,907,401 | 1,153,022 | 361.6 | 14,164 | 4.4 | 118,027 | 37.0 | 84,864 | 26.6 | 322,905 | 101.3 | 731,089 |
| 2015 | 321,418,820 | 1,197,704 | 372.6 | 15,696 | 4.9 | 124,047 | 38.6 | 90,185 | 28.1 | 327,374 | 101.9 | 764,449 |

• 1 Populations are U.S. Census Bureau provisional estimates as of July 1 for each year except 2000 and 2010, which are decennial census counts.
• 2 The violent crime figures include the offenses of murder, rape (legacy definition), robbery, and aggravated assault.
• 3 The figures shown in this column for the offense of rape were estimated using the revised UCR definition of rape.
• 4 The figures shown in this column for the offense of rape were estimated using the legacy UCR definition of rape.
• 5 The murder and nonnegligent homicides that occurred as a result of the events of September 11, 2001, are not included in this table.
• 6 The crime figures have been adjusted.

NOTE: Although arson data are included in the trend and clearance tables, sufficient data are not available to estimate totals for this offense. Therefore, no arson data are published in this table.

Source: https://ucr.fbi.gov/crime-in-the-u.s/2015/crime-in-the-u.s.-2015/tables/table-1

Although the survey focuses on fewer types of crime than the UCR (it does not address kidnapping, extortion, or blackmail, for example), it does provide far more information about the victims and any previous relationship between victims and offenders.[99] The NCVS records information about the number of victimizations, the relationship between the victim and offender (if any), and the losses and consequences incurred by the victimization, among other data.[100]

Of the three major sources of crime data, the NCVS holds the most promise for victimologists.[101] The NCVS is the primary source for the extent and nature of victimization. It provides important details about victims, which may help track patterns in victimizations. The UCR is limited in that it only accounts for crimes that are reported to the police. The NCVS depends upon the victim's perception of events, as opposed to that of a third-party observer. One limitation of the NCVS is that it is a survey, and therefore depends upon honest answers. For that reason there may be underreporting, as people are unlikely to report crimes committed by members of their own family. An additional limitation is that individuals are not asked about crimes that they themselves have committed.[102]

Victimization surveys are the most important tool victimologists have for studying victimization. They provide researchers with the number and types of victims, as well as the biographical information needed to compare trends from one geographical area to another. Additionally, surveys ask questions about feelings and experiences, which help therapists develop treatments to assist in victim recovery programs.[103] Researchers use surveys, in conjunction with the UCR, to try to map trends in crime and victimization. For example, victimologists can compare dates from the UCR and NCVS to determine whether more robberies are leading to homicides. They can determine this by cross-referencing victimization reports of robberies with homicide data from the UCR.[104] The results have concluded that murders during robbery are rare, and usually are not the result of premeditation; the robber's goal is almost always to steal and run.

**Repeat victimization** The recurrence of a crime either in the same place or with the same victim.

Because the NCVS tracks victims over a period of time, it allows researchers to study repeat victimization. Typically, **repeat victimization** is defined as the recurrence of a crime either in the same place or with the same victim. Some crimes are more likely to be repeated than others. For example, women who are victims of intimate partner violence are rarely only victimized by one type of assault and are assaulted repeatedly over time. Analysis also reveals that certain crimes are likely to be repeated within a certain period of time. Fifteen percent of the time, domestic offenders will repeat within 24 hours. The chances increase to 25% over the course of five weeks. Property crime at school is among the most recurring; there is a 70% chance of repeat victimization within one month.[106]

"No change was detected in the rate of serious violent crime from 2014 to 2015. There was no statistically significant change in the rate of serious violent crime, defined as rape or sexual assault, robbery, and aggravated assault, from 2014 (7.7 per 1,000) to 2015 (6.8 per 1,000). . . . The rate of aggravated assault had a decline (90% confidence level), from 4.1 victimizations per

FIGURE 11.4 CRIME VICTIMIZATION

## Violent victimization, by type of violent crime, 2014 and 2015

| Type of violent crime | Number | | Rate per 1,000 persons age 12 or older | |
|---|---|---|---|---|
| | 2014* | 2015 | 2014* | 2015 |
| **Violent crime[a]** | 5,359,570 | 5,006,620 | 20.1 | 18.6 |
| Rape/sexual assault[b] | 284,350 | 431,840‡ | 1.1 | 1.6‡ |
| Robbery | 664,210 | 578,580 | 2.5 | 2.1 |
| Assault | 4,411,010 | 3,996,200 | 16.5 | 14.8 |
| Aggravated assault | 1,092,090 | 816,760‡ | 4.1 | 3.0 |
| Simple assault | 3,318,920 | 3,179,440 | 12.4 | 11.8 |
| Domestic violence[c] | 1,109,880 | 1,094,660 | 4.2 | 4.1 |
| Intimate partner violence[d] | 634,610 | 806,050‡ | 2.4 | 3.0‡ |
| Stranger violence | 2,166,130 | 1,821,310 | 8.1 | 6.8 |
| Violent crime involving injury | 1,375,950 | 1,303,290 | 5.2 | 4.8 |
| **Serious violent crime[e]** | 2,040,650 | 1,827,170 | 7.7 | 6.8 |
| Serious domestic violence[c] | 400,030 | 460,450 | 1.5 | 1.7 |
| Serious intimate partner violence[d] | 265,890 | 333,210 | 1.0 | 1.2 |
| Serious stranger violence | 930,690 | 690,550‡ | 3.5 | 2.6 |
| Serious violent crime involving weapons | 1,306,900 | 977,840† | 4.9 | 3.6‡ |
| Serious violent crime involving injury | 692,470 | 658,040 | 2.6 | 2.4 |

*Note: Detail may not sum to total due to rounding. Total population age 12 or older was 266,665,160 in 2014 and 269,526,470 in 2015.*

*\*Comparison year.*

*†Significant difference from comparison year at 95% confidence level.*

*‡Significant difference from comparison year at 90% confidence level.*

*[a]Excluded homicide because the NCVS is based on interviews with victims and therefore cannot measure murder.*

*[b]BJS has initiated projects examining collection methods for self-report data on rape and sexual assault. See NCVS measurement of rape and sexual assault in Methodology for more information.*

*[c]Includes victimization committed by intimate partners and family members.*

*[d]Includes victimization committed by current or former spouses, boyfriends, or girlfriends.*

*[e]In the NCVS, serious violent crime includes rape or sexual assault, robbery, and aggravated assault.*

*Source: Bureau of Justice Statistics, National Crime Victimization Survey (NCVS), 2014 and 2015.*

1,000 persons in 2014 to 3.0 per 1,000 in 2015. During the same period, the rate of rape or sexual assault increased (90% confidence level), from 1.1 victimizations per 1,000 persons in 2014 to 1.6 per 1,000 in 2015 (see NCVS measurement of rape and sexual assault in Methodology). No measurable change was detected in the rate of simple assault from 2014 (12.4 per 1,000)

| Demographic characteristic of victim | Population | All | Violent victimizations per 1,000 persons age 12 or older | | | | |
| --- | --- | --- | --- | --- | --- | --- | --- |
| | | | Rape/ sexual assault | Robbery | All assault | Aggravated assault | Simple assault |
| **Gender** | | | | | | | |
| Male | 123,071,020 | 21.3 | 0.3† | 2.7 | 18.3 | 3.9 | 14.5 |
| Female | 129,171,510 | 17.3 | 1.3 | 1.7 | 14.3 | 2.8 | 11.5 |
| **Race** | | | | | | | |
| White | 204,683,500 | 18.1 | 0.6 | 1.6 | 15.9 | 3.0 | 12.8 |
| Black | 30,709,860 | 25.9 | 1.9† | 5.5 | 18.5 | 5.2 | 13.3 |
| Other race* | 13,952,240 | 15.2 | 0.9† | 3.0† | 11.3 | 2.8 | 8.5 |
| **Two or more races** | 2,896,930 | 51.6 | 1.9† | 6.8 | 42.9 | 6.8 | 36.1 |
| **Hispanic origin** | | | | | | | |
| Hispanic | 34,506,680 | 16.4 | 0.6† | 3.4 | 12.4 | 3.5 | 8.9 |
| Non-Hispanic | 217,351,750 | 19.7 | 0.8 | 2.0 | 16.9 | 3.3 | 13.6 |
| **Age** | | | | | | | |
| 12–15 | 16,414,550 | 42.2 | 1.6† | 5.5 | 35.2 | 6.1 | 29.0 |
| 16–19 | 17,280,270 | 37.0 | 2.2 | 4.8 | 30.0 | 5.6 | 24.5 |
| 20–24 | 20,547,620 | 37.8 | 2.1 | 5.4 | 30.3 | 8.7 | 21.5 |
| 25–34 | 40,649,500 | 23.4 | 0.7 | 2.3 | 20.5 | 4.0 | 16.5 |
| 35–49 | 65,123,030 | 16.7 | 0.8 | 1.9 | 14.1 | 2.7 | 11.4 |
| 50–64 | 55,116,320 | 10.7 | 0.2† | 0.8 | 9.7 | 2.0 | 7.7 |
| 65 or older | 37,111,240 | 3.1 | 0.2† | 0.2† | 2.7 | 0.4† | 2.3 |

Note: Violent crimes measured by the National Crime Victimization Survey include rape, sexual assault, robbery, and aggravated and simple assault. Because the NCVS interviews persons about their victimizations, murder and manslaughter cannot be included.
†Based upon 10 or fewer sample cases.
*Includes American Indians, Alaska Natives, Native Hawaiians, and other Pacific Islanders.

to 2015 (11.8 per 1,000). No change was detected in the rate of intimate partner violence from 2014 to 2015 The rate of domestic violence, which includes crime committed by intimate partners and family members, was flat from 2014 to 2015. No measurable change was detected from 2014 to 2015 in the rate of intimate partner violence (3.0 per 1,000), which includes victimizations committed by current or former spouses, boyfriends, or girlfriends. However, the number of victimizations committed by an intimate partner increased (90% confidence level) from 2014 to 2015. The rate of serious violent crime involving weapons had a decline (90% confidence level) from 2014 (4.9 per 1,000) to 2015 (3.6 per 1,000). During the same period, the number of serious violent victimizations committed by a stranger decreased (90% confidence level). No statistically significant difference was found in the rate of serious violent crime resulting in physical injury to the victim from 2014 to 2015 (2.4 per 1,000)." , Bureau of Justice Statistics, National Crime Victimization Survey (NCVS), 2014 and 2015.

## Direct and Indirect Victimization

Victimization is not limited merely to those directly victimized. In addition to the particular victim, or victims, of a criminal act, there are secondary victims who are victimized indirectly. **Indirect victims**, or derivative victims, are those affected by traumatic events even though they are not direct victims of crime, as shown in the Gabrielle Giffords case at the beginning of the chapter.[107] These victims include not just friends and family members of direct victims, but all those who are affected by the "ripple effect" of victimization.

### Ripple Effect

Indirect victimization is best illustrated by the "ripple effect." The term, coined by Remer and Ferguson, refers to the effects of victimization, which "spread out like waves from victims to all those with whom they have intimate contact."[108] Furthermore, the trauma felt by victims can negatively affect the social workers and victims' advocates who handle their case. This transference of emotion is called **compassion fatigue** and results in case workers being so emotionally invested in their clients that they are unable to attend to the emotional needs of their own lives.[109] **Victim advocates**, or people trained to help victims handle traumatic events, are particularly susceptible to compassion fatigue. Victim advocates were initially volunteers. As a result of the development of victimology, victim advocacy has become an established profession.[110]

### Underreporting

Underreporting is a problem that affects all three of the main sources of statistics. The UCR overlooks what is termed the "dark figure of crime," which refers to any crime that the police are unaware of.[111] The NCVS is a self-report survey of victimization, and thus relies on the honesty of respondents and does not ask about respondents' criminal behavior. The NCVS also does not interview anyone under the age of 12, and includes no questions about arson or crimes against businesses. If such crimes go unreported, they will not appear in the UCR either, leading to significant underreporting.

### Fear of Crime

Social scientists have long known that fear of crime is a powerful social force in American society. Crime is frequently a centerpiece of political campaigns and evening newscasts,

© SAYAN MOONGKLANG/ Shutterstock.com

Victimization can have a "ripple effect" that spreads to many people.

and ranks highly in polls measuring the importance of certain domestic issues to Americans. This fear has very real consequences. Citizens may feel the need for locks, car alarms, and security systems. Fear of crime has spurred the federal government to spend massive amounts of money on countermeasures. Major public events, such as parades, holidays, and sports games, must have extensive security.

---

**Ethics and Professionalism: Child Services**

You are a case worker with Child Protective Services. One of your clients, Marie, has been successfully working on her case plan for a neglect charge for the past 11 months. Marie has secured employment, gone to treatment, attended all mandatory meetings, attended school, and been to every scheduled visit with her children. On your most recent visit to Marie's home, you saw an empty bottle of alcohol in her garbage can. Alcohol use is in violation of her case plan.

Should you report Marie's violation? Or should you not report her and give her a second chance? If she is found to have violated her case plan, Marie would have to start her case plan from the beginning, resulting in her children remaining out of her custody until she successfully finishes. Her children have been in foster placement for the past 11 months.

---

That fear, though, is misdirected in many cases. People typically imagine a scenario in which a masked hoodlum breaks into their home, bent on inflicting bodily harm upon them. Statistics show, however, that in the case of violent crimes, people are more likely to be victimized by an acquaintance or relative.[112] In 2003, for example, 68% of female victims were victimized by someone who was not a complete stranger. This is particularly true in the case of violent offenses such as rape or assault.[113]

There is something of a paradox among crime victims: Those who are least likely to be victims are the most likely to be afraid. Statistics show that the fear of crime has not diminished over the past 20 years, despite the fact that crime itself has dropped. Over the last two decades, the rate of violent crime in the U.S. has been reduced by half, while property crime has dropped by 60%.[114] Results of a recent Gallup poll suggest that fear of crime is increasing even though crime is decreasing. In 2010, two-thirds of those surveyed said they thought that nationwide crime was on the rise.[115] Ironically, those who self-identified as being the most fearful—women and the elderly—are statistically at a lower risk than the general population.[116]

## The Role of Media

Modern mass media have a profound effect on fear of crime. The media coverage that surrounds the most heinous crimes—which are the most aggressively pursued by journalists—subjects victims to public exposure that can be traumatizing. Female victims in rape cases are particularly vulnerable, as defense attorneys may put their personal lives and past sexual history on trial despite shield laws that should protect this information from being released.

However, the media's influence can be positive as well, particularly when it comes to raising awareness of certain types of victimization. The media's coverage of a high-profile case can help the public become aware of legislation that addresses a particular type of crime or victimization. This can incite the public to clamor for legislative action. For example, the compulsory notification of the community prior to the release of a sex offender, known as "Megan's Law," was the result of the murder of a seven-year-old girl named Megan Kanka. Megan was sexually assaulted and strangled by her neighbor, a two-time convicted sex offender who had recently been released from prison. Nobody in the neighborhood, including Megan's parents, was notified about the background of this man. The media coverage of this case, and the resulting public outcry, led to the creation of Megan's Law.

The media coverage that surrounds the most heinous crimes can subject victims to traumatic public exposure.

It should be acknowledged that the public discourse that surrounds victimization and victims' rights is highly politicized. Politicians are fully aware they will never lose votes by espousing their support for victims. Their support for victims' rights is often calculated to score political points. For example, a bill recently passed in New Mexico to eliminate the death penalty required that savings from not performing executions be transferred to programs for victims.[117] The inclusion of language that supported victims made it politically unpopular to oppose the legislation, and allowed conservative legislators, normally supportive of capital punishment, to back the bill.[118] While this may seem cynical, it is important to remember the politically charged nature of the debate about victimization.

## What Statistics Suggest about Crime

A comprehensive review of statistics from both the UCR and the NCVS reveals some surprising conclusions about crime in the U.S. Firstly, crime is not rising sharply, despite the claims of some politicians. Victimization has actually been declining since 1981, per the NCVS, and violent crime in particular has decreased since 1993.[119] Over the course of the 1990s, the murder rate per 100,000 dropped from 9.8 to 5.6.[120]

Statistics also tell us that offenders and victims often inhabit the same environment, and usually share certain characteristics. Both victims and offenders of crimes that are reported and prosecuted are disproportionately male, young, urban residents, unemployed, unmarried, not in school, and—in the United States—African-American.[121]

### Limitations of the Criminal Justice System

It is, of course, impossible for the criminal justice system to solve all problems related to crime. Many of the causes of crime, both violent crime and property crime, are systemic, due to social inequalities, and cannot be immediately fixed by the actions of the court. Prosecutors and courts are often overworked, and lack the support necessary to effectively attend to every case.

### Attempts to Address the Needs of Victims

The criminal justice system and the government have made progress in their attempts to address the needs of crime victims. States have implemented policies designed to ease the plight of victims during their involvement with the criminal justice system. Some have designed educational programs on sensitive topics such as rape and sexual assault to better equip officials to treat victims properly. Often, states are required to keep the victim informed of the case's progress. Additionally, prosecutors and the police are trained to help victims find the support they need, in the form of rape crisis centers, domestic violence shelters, or victim assistance centers. State compensation programs help victims with medical costs, and judges are encouraged to order offenders to pay restitution to offset the lost value of stolen or destroyed property.[122]

### Future Directions

**Victim services** Programs and support systems for victims of crime.

The past 30 years have shown significant progress in securing rights for crime victims. Today, there are several programs in the United States that offer degrees in victimology and **victim services**. It is important to reiterate that the field of "general victimology" is very broad and focuses on many different types of victims. In this chapter, we have focused on issues and concerns for victims of criminals.

Victimology faces several challenges. First, there is a need to continue dialogue between researchers, legislatures, criminal justice officials, and victims' groups to ensure that the appropriate policies and initiatives are put in place to help crime victims. Second, there is a need for constant monitoring and evaluation of these initiatives to ensure that they are truly effective for victims of crime and to suggest new initiatives that may be needed. For example, mandatory arrest policies for domestic violence swept the nation in the 1990s. In spite of widespread adoption of these policies, research now suggests that these policies may actually cause further harm to victims.[123] Third, there is a need to continue to raise awareness about the challenges that victims of crime face and the role of the criminal justice system in alleviating (or exacerbating) these challenges. This increased awareness can provide a foundation for additional research and the development of programs and policies that address this population's specific needs.

# Chapter Summary

- Victimology is the scientific study of victims and victimization. It grew out of recognition that in order to understand the motivations of criminals, it is necessary to understand the role of the victim in the crime. Understanding the dynamic that exists between offender and victim is key to understanding the genesis of the criminal act.

- Early leaders in victimology included Benjamin Mendelssohn, who classified victims based upon what he believed was their level of blame for the crime; Hans von Hentig, who devised typologies that explained why some people are more likely to become victims than others; and Marvin Wolfgang, whose studies attempted to analyze the context in which crimes occur, and to illuminate social inequalities that may be the root of the problem.

- The costs of victimization are the psychological, physical, emotional, and financial costs to the victim, the victim's family, and society as a whole. This includes the first victimization—the crime at the hands of the offender—and the second victimization, the challenges the victims may face from the criminal justice system.

- The movement to add a Victims' Bill of Rights (VRA) to the U.S. Constitution is ongoing. Laws have been passed in most states to ensure victims have a right to be present at the trial, to be protected from harassment, and to make a statement at sentencing.

- Criminologists and victimologists now study a more statistically comprehensive picture of crime using the UCR, self-report surveys, and victimization surveys. Victimization surveys (such as the National Crime Victimization Survey) help reveal the substantial extent to which crime goes unreported.

- Victimization is not limited merely to those directly victimized. In addition to the direct victims of a criminal act, there are secondary victims who are victimized indirectly. Victimization spreads like a "ripple effect" to all those with whom the direct victims have intimate contact.

# Critical Thinking?

1. How are victims portrayed in the media?
2. Do you think there is ever a situation where it would be appropriate to have crime victims pay for evidence collection? Explain.
3. Compare and contrast the UCR and NCVS. What are the advantages and disadvantages of each?
4. Can both victims' rights and the rights of the accused be fairly protected? Would the Constitution have to be amended in order to do so? Explain your reasoning.

5. Critically evaluate the fairness of civil suits and restitution as recourse methods. Specifically address whether or not the Eighth Amendment protects impoverished victims who may be unable to afford an attorney to pursue a civil suit.

6. Do you think that victim impact statements could be subjective and cause the jury and judge to overlook the objective facts in a case?

7. Explain the difference between restitution and compensation.

8. Should offenders have the right to profit from selling accounts of their crimes to the media? Why or why not?

9. Why do you think certain segments of the population (e.g., the elderly) are highly fearful of victimization when their lifestyle places them at statistically low risk?

10. Explain the effects, both positive and negative, that the media has on public perceptions of crime rates and victims.

## Media

**Office for Victims of Crime:** http://www.ojp.usdoj.gov/ovc
The Department of Justice's page for crime victims provides updates and news on victims' rights as well as contact information for victim support programs.

**National Victim Assistance Academy:** https://www.ovcttac.gov/nvaa/
This website for programs coordinated through the Office of Justice includes resources for training victim advocates and social workers in the United States.

**National Center for Victims of Crime:** http://www.ncvc.org
The NCVC, a research and advocacy group for victims of crime, lobbies for legislation aimed at furthering the cause of victims' rights.

**National Coalition Against Domestic Violence:** http://www.ncadv.org
This organization is dedicated to providing support and raising awareness for victims of domestic violence, especially women and children, and provides support for shelters for battered women.

**Rape Abuse and Incest National Network:** http://www.rainn.org
RAINN, the largest anti-sexual-abuse network in the United States, provides confidential services for victims via rape treatment hotlines and educates the public about sexual assault.

**International Victimology Institute Tilburg:** http://www.victimology.nl
The International Victimology Institute based at Tilburg University in the Netherlands specializes in interdisciplinary research aimed at empowering and supporting victims of crime.

# Endnotes

1   "Remarks by the President on the Shootings in Tucson, Arizona." (2011). *The White House.* Retrieved from http://www.whitehouse.gov/the-press-office/2011/01/08/remarks-president-shootings-tucson-arizona

2   "Boehner Condemns Attack on Congresswoman Gabrielle Giffords." (2011). *Speaker of the House John Boehner.* Retrieved from http://www.speaker.gov/News/DocumentSingle.aspx?DocumentID=219343

3   Karmen, A. (2004). *Crime Victims: An Introduction to Victimology.* Toronto, Canada: Wadsworth.

4   Cole, G., & Smith, C. (2007). *The American System of Criminal Justice.* Belmont, CA: Wadsworth, 38.

5   Siegel, L. J. (2005). *Criminology* (9th ed.). Belmont, CA: Wadsworth, 14.

6   Karmen, 2004, 9.

7   Doerner, W. G., & Lab, S. P. (2008). *Victimology.* Newark, NJ: LexisNexis, 1.

8   Karmen, 2004, 2.

9   Schafer, S. (1968). *The Victim and His Criminal.* New York, NY: Random House.

10   Doerner & Lab, 2008, 2–3.

11   Cole & Smith, 2007, 39.

12   Ryan, W. (1976). *Blaming the Victim.* Vintage.

13   Ibid.

14   Schafer, 1968, 79–83.

15   Luckenbill, D. F. (1977). "Criminal Homicide as a Situated Transaction." *Social Problems, 25*(2), 176–186.

16   Hoffman, H. (1992). "What Did Mendelsohn Really Say?" In S. Ben David & G. F. Kirchhoff (Eds.), *International Faces of Criminology.* Monchengladbach: WSV Publishing.

17   Mendelssohn, B. (1956, July). "The Victimology." *Etudes Internationale de Psycho-sociologie Criminelle.*

18   Ibid., 23–26.

19   Doerner & Lab, 2008, 6–7.

20   Singer, S. (1981). "Homogenous Victim-Offender Populations: A Review and Some Research Implications." *Journal of Criminal Law and Criminology,* 779–788.

21   Doerner & Lab, 2008, 13.

22   Fattah, E. A. (2000). "Victimology: Past, Present and Future." *Criminologie,* 17–46.

23   Hentig, H.V. (1948). *The Criminal and His Victim.* New Haven, CT: Yale University Press, 436.

24   Scully, D., & Marolla, J. (1984). "Convicted Rapists' Vocabulary of Motive: Excuses and Justifications." *Social Problems, 31*(5), 530–544.

25   Groth, N. A. (1979). *Men Who Rape.* New York, NY: Plenum Press.

26    McCaghy, C. (1968). "Drinking and Deviance Disavowal: The Case of Child Molesters." *Social Problems, 16*(1), 43–44.

27    Cohen, L. E., & Felson, M. (1979). "Social Change and Crime Rate Trends: A Routine Activity Approach." *American Sociological Review, 44*(4), 588.

28    Wolfgang, M. E., & Ferracuti, F. (1967). *The Subculture of Violence: Towards an Integrated Theory in Criminology.* London, UK: Tavistock Publications.

29    Ibid.

30    Ibid.

31    Ibid.

32    Amir, M. (1971). *Patterns in Forcible Rape.* Chicago, IL: University of Chicago Press.

33    Doerner & Lab, 2008, 11.

34    Fattah, 2000.

35    Fattah, E. A. (1991). *Understanding Criminal Victimization.* Scarborough: Prentice Hall Canada.

36    Dussich, 120.

37    Luckenbill, 1977.

38    Franklin, C. W., & Franklin, A. P. (1976). "Victimology Revisited: A Critique and Suggestions for Future Direction." *Criminology*, 177–214.

39    Doerner & Lab, 2008, 12.

40    Van Ness, D. W. (1986). *Crime and Its Victims: What We Can Do.* Downers Grove, IL: InterVarsity Press, 29.

41    Ahrens, C. (2006). "Being Silenced: The Impact of Negative Social Reactions on the Disclosure of Rape." *American Journal of Community Psychology, 38*, 263–274.

42    Fattah, 1991.

43    Siegel, 2005.

44    Fattah, 1991.

45    Cole, A. M. (2007). *The Cult of True Victimhood: From the War on Welfare to the War on Terror.* Stanford, CA: Stanford University Press.

46    Ronel, N., Jaishankar, K., & Bensimon, M. (2008). *Trends and Issues in Victimology.* Cambridge, UK: Cambridge Scholars Publishing.

47    Cohen, S. (1993). "Human Rights and Crimes of the State: The Culture of Denial." *Australia and New Zealand Journal of Criminology, 26*, 97–115.

48    Marty Price, J. D. (2001, Fall). "Personalizing Crime." *Dispute Resolution Magazine.*

49    Braithwaite, J. (2002). *Restorative Justice and Responsive Regulation.* New York, NY: Oxford University Press, 249.

50    O'Connell, T., Wachtel, B., & Wachtel, T. (1999). *Conferencing Handbook: The New Real Justice Training Manual.* Pipersville, PA: The Piper's Press.

51    Wemmers, J. (2008). "Victim Participation and Therapeutic Jurisprudence." *Victims and Offenders, 3*(2&3), 165–191.

52    Doerner & Lab, 2008, 58.

53    Cole & Smith, 2007, 48.

54    Campbell, R., & Raja, S. (1999). "Secondary Victimization of Rape Victims: Insights from Mental Health Professionals Who Treat Survivors of Violence." *Violence and Victims, 14*(3), 261–75.

55    Karmen, 2004, 168–169.

56    Cannavale, F. J. (1976). *Witness Cooperation*. Lexington, MA: Institute for Law and Social Research.

57    Rootsaert, D. (1987). *A Prosecutor's Guide to Victim/Witness Assistance*. Alexandria, VA: National District Attorneys Association.

58    President's Task Force on Victims of Crime. (1982). *Final Report*. Washington, D.C.: U.S. Government Printing Office.

59    Viano, E. (1987). "Victim's Rights and the Constitution: Reflections on a Bicentennial." *Crime and Delinquency*, 438–451.

60    Young, M. A. (2009). "History of the Victims Movement in the United States." *International Organization for Victim Assistance*. Retrieved from http://www.iovahelp.org/About/MarleneAYoung/USHistory.pdf

61    Ibid., 72.

62    Doerner & Lab, 2008, 391.

63    Children's Guardian Fund. (n.d.). *Frequently Asked Questions*. Retrieved from http://www.childrensguardianfund.org/faq.html#D

64    Minnesota Judicial Branch, 4th District. (2005). *Guardian Ad Litem Frequently Asked Questions*. Retrieved from http://www.mncourts.gov/Documents/4/Public/Guardian_Ad_Litem/GAL_FAQ.pdf

65    Derene, S. (2005). *Crime Victims Fund Report: Past, Present, and Future*. Washington, D.C.: National Association of VOCA Assistance Administrators.

66    Gahr, E. (1997, March). "Advocates Raise Wide Support for Victims Rights Amendment." *Insight on the News*, 42.

67    Dolliver, J. M. (1987). "Victims' Rights Constitutional Amendment: A Bad Idea Whose Time Should Not Come." *The Wayne Law Review*, 87–93.

71    President's Task Force on Victims of Crime, 1982.

72    Gahr, 1997.

73    Fattah, 2000, 32.

74    Young, 79.

70    Doyle, C. (2004). "Victims' Right Amendment: A Proposal to Amend the United States Constitution in the 108th Congress." *CRS Web*. Retrieved from http://royce.house.gov/UploadedFiles/RL31750.pdf

75    Doerner & Lab, 2008, 408–409.

76    Triebwasser, J. (1987, September 29). "Victims' Non-Impact on Sentence." *Law Enforcement News*, 5.

77    *Payne v. Tennessee*, 501 U.S. 808 (1991).

78    Fattah, 2000, 33.

79    Dugger, A. (1996). "Victim Impact Evidence in Capital Sentencing: A History of Incompatibility." *American Journal of Criminal Law, 23*, 375–404.

80    *Payne v. Tennessee*, 1991.

81    Ibid.

82    Mulholland, C. (1995). "Sentencing Criminals: The Constitutionality of Victim Impact Statements." *Missouri Law Review, 60*, 731–748.

83    Hinton, M. (1995). "Expectations Dashed: Victim Impact Statements and the Common Law Approach to Sentencing in South Australia." *University of Tasmania Law Review*, 81–99.

84    Doerner & Lab, 2008, 83.

85    Childres, R. (1964). "Compensation for Criminally Inflicted Personal Injury." *New York University Law Review*, 455–471.

86    Fattah, 2000, 35.

87    Abel, C., & Marsh, F. (1984). *Punishment and Restitution: A Restitutionary Approach to Crime and the Criminal.* Westport, CT: Greenwood Press.

88    Fattah, 2000, 35.

89    Karmen, 2004, 302–303.

90    *The 1996 Victims' Rights Sourcebook: A Compilation and Comparison of Victims' Rights Laws.* (1996). Retrieved from http://www.ncvc.org/law/sbooks/toc.htm

91    Barbieri, M. (1989). "Civil Suits for Sexual Assault Victims: The Downside." *Journal of Interpersonal Violence, 4*(1), 110–113.

92    Fattah, 2000, 28.

93    O'Brien, R. M. (1985). *Crime and Victimization.* Beverly Hills, CA: Sage.

94    FBI. (1954–2003). *Uniform Crime Report: Crime in the United States (Selected Years 1953–2001).* Washington D.C.: U.S. Government Printing Office.

95    Karmen, 2004, 54.

96    Karmen, 2004, 51.

97    Skogan, W. G. (1990). "The National Crime Survey Redesign." *Public Opinion Quarterly*, 256–272.

98    National Archive of Criminal Justice Data (NACJD). (2011). *National Crime Victimization Survey Resource Guide*, 1.

99    Karmen, 2004, 52.

100   NACJD, 2011.

101   Doerner & Lab, 2008, 27.

102   Cole & Smith, 2007, 29–30.

103   Young, 2009, 120.

104   Cook, P. (1985). "Is Robbery Becoming More Violent? An Analysis of Robbery Murder Trends Since 1968." *Journal of Criminal Law and Criminology*, 480–490.

106   Weisel, D. L. (2005). *Analyzing Repeat Victimization.* Washington, D.C.: Department of Justice, Office of Community Oriented Policing Services.

107   Tomz, J. E., & McGillis, D. (1997). *Serving Crime Victims and Witnesses.* Washington, D.C.: U.S. Department of Justice.

108    Remer, R., & Ferguson, R. (1995). "Becoming a Secondary Survivor of Sexual Abuse." *Journal of Counseling and Development.*

109    Boscarino, J. A., Figley, C. R., & Adams, R. E. (2004). "Evidence of Compassion Fatigue Following the September 11 Terrorist Attacks: A Study of Secondary Trauma among Social Workers in New York." *International Journal of Emergency Mental Health*, 98–108.

110    Weigend, T. (1983). "Problems of Victim/Witness Assistance Programs." *Victimology*, 91–101.

111    Coleman, C., & Moynihan, J. (1996). *Understanding Crime Data: Haunted by the Dark Figure.* Open University Press.

112    Cole & Smith, 2007, 43.

113    Bureau of Justice Statistics. (2003). *Criminal Victimization in the United States—Statistical Tables, 2002.* Retrieved from http://bjs.ojp.usdoj.gov/index.cfm?ty=pbdetail&iid=1154

114    Beam, C. (2011). "Head Case: Crime Rates Have Plummeted over the Last 20 Years. Why Aren't We Less Scared?" *Slate.* Retrieved from http://www.slate.com/id/2284662/

115    Jones, J. M. (2010, November 18). "Americans Still Perceive Crime on the Rise." *Gallup.* Retrieved from http://www.gallup.com/poll/144827/americans-perceive-crime-rise.aspx

116    Cole & Smith, 2007, 46.

117    New Mexico Coalition to Repeal the Death Penalty. (n.d.). *Victims' Families First.* Retrieved from http://www.nmrepeal.org/issues/victims_families_first

118    Death Penalty Focus. (2009). *New Mexico Becomes the 15th State to Eliminate the Death Penalty; Other States Consider Taking Similar Action to Ease Budget Concerns.* Retrieved from http://www.deathpenalty.org/article.php?id=333

119    Cole & Smith, 2007, 30.

120    Karmen, 2004, 44.

121    Gottfredson, M. R. (1984). *Victims of Crime: The Dimensions of Risk.* London, UK: Home Office Research and Planning Unit.

122    Cole & Smith, 2007, 49–50.

123    Iyengar, R. (2006). *Does the Certainty of Arrest Reduce Domestic Violence? Evidence from Mandatory and Recommended Arrest Laws.* Retrieved from http://www.utdt.edu.ar/download.php?fname=_119522597271880400.pdf Iyengar, R. (2007, August 7). "The Protection Battered Spouses Don't Need." *New York Times,* late ed., 19.

© Prazis Images/Shutterstock.com

# Domestic and International Terrorism

Craig P. Rahanian and Scott H. Belshaw, Ph.D.

## KEY TERMS

| | | |
|---|---|---|
| Terrorism | Religious extremism | State-supported |
| International terrorism | Islamic state | Non-State actors |
| Domestic terrorism | Al-Qaeda | Lone wolf terrorists |
| Federal crime of terrorism | Taliban | Crime |
| Terrorists | Daesh | War |
| Revolutionary group | ISIS | Political violence |
| Sub-revolutionary group | Sovereign state | Shaping tool. |
| Establishment | State-directed | |

# CHAPTER OBJECTIVES

1 Define the differences between domestic and international terrorism.

2 Distinguish among the differences between revolutionary and sub-revolutionary groups.

3 Identify the various differences between the Taliban, ISIS, Al-Qaeda, and Daesh.

4 Explain the components of state-directed, state-supported, non-state actors and lone terrorists.

## What is Terrorism?

The answer to the question, "what is terrorism?" is very complex and not straightforward. Where the question is asked and who is referring to "terrorism" help determine how it is defined. The military refers to terrorism as *asymmetrical warfare* or a tactic in unconventional warfare, while the U.S. Department of State defines terrorism as something that is premeditated and violence that is politically motivated. At the same time, the U.S. Department of Justice defines terrorism using more of a crime or law violation language, stating that terrorism is the unlawful use of force against persons or property. The various definitions that are used help define terrorism in the context of how that agency or interest group works to combat terrorism. Even though terrorism is now a U.S. household name after the terrorist acts of 9/11, terrorism has its roots in ancient times. One of the first mentions of asymmetrical warfare that could be defined as terrorism is the splinter Jewish zealot group called the Sicarii. The Sicarii carried out an unconventional warfare-styled campaign to expel the Romans from Judea in around 60 CE. The Sicarii carried sicae, which were small daggers that they concealed in their cloaks. The Sicarii would use their concealed daggers to kill Romans in public places, and then they would just blend into the crowd to escape. Another group that was in operation around 1000 CE was the Hashashin or the Assassins. The Assassins' asymmetrical tactic would be to send a lone assassin into the heart of their enemy to kill or assassinate the leader of the opposition. The lone assassin knew that he or she would be sacrificed during the mission and would not return. Both the Hashashin and the Sicarii are the forerunners of terrorists that we know today. Their history 2000 years earlier is still remembered and studied today. One of the first uses or the word terror was during the French Revolution's Reign of Terror, which ran between 1793 and 1794 CE. During 1793 the French established the Committee of Public Safety, which employed any means to ensure there was no opposition to the revolution. What we are seeing today is not new. These types of tactics have been used for over 2000 years. The principles are the same; only the weapons and the technology have changed.

# Introductory Examples of Terrorism

How does terrorism work? Two examples for consideration: On October 23, 1983 at around 6:22 am, a truck loaded with over 2000 pounds of explosives drove into the U.S. Marine compound in Beirut, Lebanon. The truck exploded, killing 241 U.S military personnel who were part of the 8th Marine Regimental Landing Team. At the same time a suicide bomber in a truck loaded with explosives detonated at the French military barracks, killing 58 French paratroopers. In February 1984, the United States withdrew from Lebanon.

On March 11, 2004 during the morning rush hour in Madrid, Spain, ten bombs were set off by an Al-Qaeda terrorist cell in the Madrid commuter train station, killing 191 and injuring close to 2000 people on their way to work. This attack occurred three day before Spain's general elections. The result of this attack was Spain's presidential incumbent was defeated and Spain pulled its forces out of the Iraq Coalition. These terrorist operations are good examples of how a lone terrorist or a very small terrorist cell can influence governmental decisions, legislation, and a presidential election. Terrorist groups plan their actions to influence a strategic outcome—as happened after these two events.

**FIGURE 12.1** TERRORISM, CRIME, WAR, AND OTHER FORMS OF POLITICAL VIOLENCE

| Primary Independent Variable | Terrorism's Relationship to Variable | Secondary Independent Variables | Types of Activities / Contrast to Terrorism |
|---|---|---|---|
| Crime | Crime is viewed as economically, rather than politically, motivated. | Organized Crime | Terrorizing victims for money or revenge |
| | | Individual Crime | Murder for personal motive |
| War | War is usually perceived as more legitimate and purposeful than terrorism. It is instrumental and not symbolic violence. There are rules and laws of war to be followed by belligerents. Civilians and non-combatants should not be targeted. | Just War | Self defense. Used against tyranny or an aggressor |
| | | Legal War (declared inter state) | Terrorism is not undeclared war |
| | | War Crimes | Terror and illegal acts committed during war by legal combatants |
| | | Civil War | Intra-state between recognized belligerents |
| | | Guerilla War | Guerillas hold territory, fight combatants not civilians, wear uniforms, openly carry weapons |
| | | Insurgency / Low Intensity War | Targets governmental control and power—may illegally target non-combatants |

| Political Violence | Terrorism is form of political violence. It is politically motivated to induce change by producing fear. It is illegal and not recognized as a legitimate form of political violence. | Revolution | Mass overthrow of system |
| | | Riots—Mass Violence | Temporary, spontaneous |
| | | Assassination | Target is single focus / act |
| | | State Repression | Pervasive state terrorism |
| | | Terrorism | Equivalent of war crimes by illegal non-combatants |

(Cunningham, 2003)

# Definitions of Terrorism

## Department of State

**International Terrorism:** Terrorism involving citizens or the territory of more than one country. (As per 22 USCS 2656f. Other definitions in other U.S. laws exist.)

**Terrorism:** Premeditated, politically motivated violence perpetrated against noncombatant targets by subnational groups or clandestine agents. (As per 22 USCS 2656f. Other definitions in other U.S. laws exist.)

## Department of Defense

The unlawful use of violence or threat of violence to instill fear and coerce governments or societies. Terrorism is often motivated by religious, political, or other ideological beliefs and committed in the pursuit of goals that are usually political. (JP 3-07.2)

## U.S. Department of Justice

The FBI defines terrorism as "the unlawful use of force or violence against persons or property to intimidate or coerce a government, the civilian population, or any segment thereof, in furtherance of political or social objectives." (National Institute of Justice)

© Mark Van Scyoc/ Shutterstock.com

The Department of Justice prosecutes terrorism cases.

Title 22 of the U.S. Code, Section 2656f(d) defines terrorism as "premeditated, politically motivated violence perpetrated against noncombatant targets by subnational groups or clandestine agents, usually intended to influence an audience." (National Institute of Justice)

Both of the Justice Department definitions of terrorism share a common theme: the use of force intended to influence or instigate a course of action that furthers a political or social goal. In most cases, National Institute of Justice

(NIJ) researchers adopt the FBI definition, which stresses methods over motivations and is generally accepted by law enforcement communities.

The following laws in the United States Code are used to define and prosecute terrorism by the United States Justice Department.

18 U.S.C. § 2331 defines "international terrorism" and "domestic terrorism" for purposes of Chapter 113B of the U.S. Code, entitled "Terrorism."

**The following are definitions that are quoted directly from the 18 U.S. Code Chapter 113B**

"International terrorism" means activities with the following three characteristics:

- Involve violent acts or acts dangerous to human life that violate federal or state law;
- Appear to be intended (i) to intimidate or coerce a civilian population; (ii) to influence the policy of a government by intimidation or coercion; or (iii) to affect the conduct of a government by mass destruction, assassination, or kidnapping; and
- Occur primarily outside the territorial jurisdiction of the U.S., or transcend national boundaries in terms of the means by which they are accomplished, the persons they appear intended to intimidate or coerce, or the locale in which their perpetrators operate or seek asylum.

"Domestic terrorism" means activities with the following three characteristics:

- Involve acts dangerous to human life that violate federal or state law;
- Appear intended (i) to intimidate or coerce a civilian population; (ii) to influence the policy of a government by intimidation or coercion; or (iii) to affect the conduct of a government by mass destruction, assassination. or kidnapping; and
- Occur primarily within the territorial jurisdiction of the U.S.

**18 U.S.C. § 2332b defines the term "federal crime of terrorism" as an offense that:**

- Is calculated to influence or affect the conduct of government by intimidation or coercion, or to retaliate against government conduct; and
- Is a violation of one of several listed statutes, including § 930(c) (relating to killing or attempted killing during an attack on a federal facility with a dangerous weapon); and § 1114 (relating to killing or attempted killing of officers and employees of the U.S.).
- FISA defines "international terrorism" in a nearly identical way, replacing "primarily" outside the U.S. with "totally" outside the U.S. 50 U.S.C. § 1801(c).

### What U.S. Law Gives the U.S. Government the Jurisdiction to Investigate and Prosecute Terrorism Outside the United States?

In the case of *Filártiga v. Pena-Irala* 630 F.2d 876 (1980), Dr. Joel Filártiga and Dolly Filártiga, Dr. Filartiga's daughter, charged a former Paraguayan official, Americo Peña-Irala, with the wrongful death Joelito Filártiga, Dr. Filártiga's son. The Filártigas and Peña-Irala are both Paraguayans who left Paraguay to live in the United States. This case set the precedent as a landmark case for U.S federal courts to punish non-United States citizens for acts that have been determined as torture committed outside of the United States that are found to be in violation of public international law. This case extends the jurisdictions of United States courts to tortious acts anywhere in the world. This case revisited a long disused law called the Alien Tort Statute (ATS) 1789 under 28 U.S Code 1350 that provides U.S. District courts jurisdiction on any alien for a civil action that violates a treaty of the United States. The circumstance of this case are interesting in that the act of torture and subsequent murder occurred in Paraguay. In March of 1976 in Asunción, Paraguay, Joelito Filáritga, the son of Dr. Joel Filártiga, was kidnaped, tortured, and murdered by Police Inspector Americo Peña-Irala. The Filártiga family filed charges against Peña-Irala in Paraguay. Their case in Paraguay was never heard. Two years later the Filártiga family applied for and received political asylum in the United States, and, at the same time, Dolly Filártiga, the daughter and Joelito's sister, found out that Peña-Irala had been living in the United States unlawfully as an overstay on his tourist visa. Dolly Filártiga reported that Peña-Irala was an over-stay to the Immigration and Naturalization service (INS). The INS promptly acted and commenced deportation procedures for Peña-Irala. While Peña-Irala was being held by the INS pending deportation, the Filártiga family filed a civil case against him claiming that the U.S. Courts had jurisdiction under the Alien Tort Statute of 1789. The Filáritga family won the case against Peña-Irala in the amount of 10 million dollars.

## Who are Terrorists?

The common descriptions used to describe terrorist groups can be broken down by their state affiliation, their identity, their intentions, their ideological beliefs, and their geographic location. The first descriptive nomenclature is: are they affiliated with a country or a state? Their ideological beliefs are analyzed by determining their political and religious beliefs or affiliation. Today the analysis that determines the group's religious affiliation might also determine who is financing them. An example would the group's Muslim sect. The terrorist group known as ISIS, Islamic State, or Daesh is composed of members of the former Ba'ath Party of Iraq. The Ba'ath Party was composed of Sunni Muslims. Areas that are made up of Sunni Muslims like Syria have been supporters of the ISIS movement (Fawaz, 2014). This shows both a state affiliation and a religious affiliation. In the annual U.S. State Department publication of global terrorism called the Country Reports on Terrorism 2015, the State Department lists Iran as one of the state sponsors of terrorism and states that Iran is working closely with Syria to counter the Syrian opposition, and Iran is supporting Shia opposition groups. These relationships are another example of state and religious affiliations.

## Typology of Terrorists

The Defense Security Service Anti-Terrorism Officer course explains that there are three traditional basic categories of terrorist groups: revolutionary, sub-revolutionary, and establishment. Each of the categories of groups is further defined by their objectives.

A *revolutionary group*'s traditional operational objective is to overthrow an existing government. A revolutionary group is composed of political extremists and considers the cause to be of the highest order. Members of this type of group tend to be in their late teens to mid-thirties. They usually claim that they are prepared to die for their cause, but when the group shows failures the members tend to become more concerned with their own survival and escape from being caught by law enforcement. (DSS, ATO II 2013) An example of this was a terrorist group in the United States that was active from the late 1960s until the late 1970s called the Weather Underground. The Weather Underground had the ideology of the destruction of capitalism and United States imperialism, and the establishment of a communist classless society in the United States. This philosophy came out of the Vietnam War era; students at the University of Michigan formed the Weather Underground in opposition to the way the war in Vietnam was being prosecuted, and because they believed that the United States was an imperialist country. By the late 1970s the war in Vietnam was over and the group finally disintegrated and dissolved.

A *sub-revolutionary group* executes operations that are designed to influence an unwilling government into making political, social, and economic changes. (DSS, ATO II) Many of the nationalist groups in the world are sub-revolutionary groups. This typology includes groups like anti-abortion, environmental, and anti-nuclear groups. This type of group's goals are to change a governmental policy or to change what society accepts as a norm.

The third terrorist group typology is called the *establishment,* which is a group that is state-supported whose activities are controlled and condoned by a nation-state. (DSS, ATO II) An example of this would be the Chilean government's use of terrorism to control the population of Chile during and after the military coup in September 1973 in which Salvador Allende was overthrown by Augusto Pinochet. (Church Committee, 1976)

## Religious Extremism and Islamic State

Al-Qaeda, Taliban, Daesh, and Islamic State are common household names today. These groups are commonly referred to as terrorist groups in the west by media and governments. They do not completely fit the common typology of what was known in the past as terrorists because their motivations do not fit into the traditional typology and affiliation. These groups appear to be autonomous from nation state affiliation and support, and could be categorized as non-state actors—with one difference, which is that they are all linked to extreme religious motivations that have as a goal to establish their own state based on their religious belief that God has called them to create an Islamic state that is governed by Allah and sharia law. They leave no room for any other religious belief systems and have assumed the mandate to eradicate all those who do not believe like them. They believe that they have this authority from God which trumps all other forms of authority and gives them the moral authority to take life. (Cunningham, 2003)

The White House in 2015 declared that the Taliban is no longer a terrorist group, instead labeling them as an armed insurgent movement. This re-labeling is a good example of the complexity of the questions of what is and who are terrorists. The implication behind terrorist groups being motivated by the belief that all people who are not of their faith are infidels and targets is profound. This way of thinking even goes as far as to classify those people who do not believe in the same sect of the religion as infidels and legitimate non-believer targets.

Terrorists identify with four different categories of intent on which they act. (DSS, ATO II 2013) They can be grouped by their race or ethnicity, which is defined by an ethnocentric characteristic. They might be grouped by their loyalty to a nation and are motivated by nationalistic beliefs. A group that is revolutionary in nature would be dedicated to the overthrow of a government. A separatist group is motivated by political autonomy. (DSS, ATO II 2013) In what category would you place ISIS/Daesh? Would you categorize Daesh as a separatist group based on religious beliefs'?

### FIGURE 12.2  TERRORISM TYPOLOGY

| State Actors | | | |
|---|---|---|---|
| Action Type | Operational Group | Target Victims | Target Audience |
| Internal Repression | Police, Military, Judicial, Vigilante | Internal individuals and groups considered subversive | Entire or segment of domestic population |
| State-Sponsored | Foreign Affiliate Terrorist Group | Symbolic targets based on shared enemy | Population of shared enemy and allies |
| State Performed | Intelligence Service, Commando Unit | Symbolic targets based on foreign enemy | Population of foreign enemy and allies |

| Non-State Actors | | | |
|---|---|---|---|
| Primary Motivator (Identity) | Orientation | Target Victims | Target Audience |
| Political Ideology | Anarchist | Symbolic targets based on relationship to "system" | Population of System |
| | Marxist | Symbolic targets based on relationship to capitalist-imperialist system | Population of capitalist-imperialist system |
| | Fascist | Symbolic targets based on opposition to fascism (government, middle class, Marxists) | Population of nation-state |
| | Single Issue | Symbolic targets based on issue | Population of issue region (nation-state or region) |
| Ethno-Nationalism | Pro-state | Symbolic targets based on relationship to anti-state revolutionaries | Population of nation-state |
| | Revolutionary | Symbolic targets based on relationship to support of the state | Population of nation-state |
| | Separatist | Symbolic targets based on relationship to state | Population of nation-state |
| | Autonomous | Symbolic targets based on relationship to state | Population of nation-state |
| | Ethnic Vigilante | Symbolic targets based on relationship to ethnic group | Population of issue region (nation-state or region) |
| Religious Extremism | Fundamentalist | Symbolic targets based on relationship to fundamentalist religious worldview | Population of worldview and competing systems (internal cohesion) and those outside worldview (external) |
| | Cults and Sects | Symbolic targets based on relationship to cult or sect | Population of sect region (nation-state or segment) |

(Cunningham, 2003)

# Terrorist Group Affiliation and Relationship

## State Actors

Terrorist groups that have a state affiliation provide an indication of potential targeting and capabilities. There are two sub-groups to state affiliation; they are either state-directed or state-supported. State-supported groups could also have an element of state-directed, depending on their targeting and agenda.

A sovereign state is a nation-state, or what we in America call a country. According to Merriam-Webster dictionary, a state is "a politically organized body of people usually occupying a definite sovereign territory with a political organization that has supreme civil authority and political power that serves as the government with the ability and authority to fully act on behalf of the state."

*State-directed* is a terrorist group that is supported by a country or state. This type of terrorist group's activities are directed by the sponsoring state. The sponsoring state could have members of the sponsoring state's security organization directing its activities, such as targeting, as well as its organizational structure. Examples of state-supported groups are Hezbollah in Lebanon, which has close ties to Iran, and the As-Sa'Iqa group based in Lebanon, which is a military unit of the Palestine Liberation Organization that is supported and manned by elements of the Syrian Army.

State-supported terrorists and terrorist groups receive support from a nation-state. They act on behalf of their supported state in support of that state's agenda. The type of support these groups receive could be a safe haven in the sovereign state, which provides them protection by being inside a sovereign state. They might also receive training facilities, medical support, intelligence, and financial support. An example of this would be the Iranian Revolutionary Guards, which is an arm of the sovereign state of Iran, and is an actual part of the Iranian military. State-supported groups like the Iranian Revolutionary Guards could be employed to provide training to state-directed groups. There are also state-supported groups that are not physically located inside the state that supports them (e.g., Iran's support of terrorist groups in Syria).

## Non-State actors

These are non-state-supported terrorist groups that are not supported by any sovereign state. They have their own agendas, and have their own supply networks. These groups have their own aims and agendas and do not count on any outside support. Since these groups fall outside of the normal channels, they pose the most problematic threat to nation-states. The U.S. government report published in 1988 titled "Terrorist Group Profiles" lists these groups as Maoist ideology or communist in nature, and connected to the countries that they operate in as connected to that country's communist party. Two examples of these types of groups are the "New People's Army" which is the insurgent arm of the Philippine Communist Party, and the Shining Path, which is an insurgent arm to the Peruvian Communist Party. Both groups are similar in that they are proponents of communist ideology and have the goal of overthrowing the current government and establishing a communist regime in their respective countries.

## Lone Terrorists

Lone-wolf or *lone terrorists* are terrorists that act out a terrorist operation by themselves without anyone commanding them. They might have been inspired to perform a terrorist act by an ideology. They might have an association with a domestic terrorist organization that may be engaged in criminal activities. Lone-wolf terrorists, although they may have taken on the beliefs of a domestic terrorist group or may have been inspired by an international group, act alone without direction or guidance from a terrorist group. Domestic terrorist organizations can be white supremacist groups, anarchists, environmental extremists, militia groups, animal rights groups, and extremist religious groups. Lone-wolf terrorists operate in an environment that is extremely difficult for law enforcement to detect, conduct surveillance on, and determine a threat to the public. The common terminology to describe this type of terrorist is that they operate in a way that does not create a very noticeable signature or a small signature that is very difficult for law enforcement to detect. Two examples of lone-wolf terrorists are Anders Breivik in Norway in 2011 and Timothy McVeigh, an American terrorist who is responsible for the Oklahoma City federal building bombing in 1995. Anders Breivik is responsible for a mass shooting and bombing in 2011 in Norway that resulted in the deaths of numerous people. He killed more than eighty youths who were participating in a summer camp that was located on an island called Utoya off the coast of Norway. Breivik published a manifesto titled, "A European Declaration of Independence" where he claimed his reasons for committing these acts was because of the changes in ideology due to political correctness. Breivik goes on the say that "political correctness" is a form of cultural Marxism and Marxism must be eliminated from European society. A more recent example of a lone-wolf terrorist is that of Omar Mateen, a 29-year-old from Florida who claimed allegiance to the Islamic State (ISIS). Mateen in June 2016 killed 49 people in an attack on a gay nightclub in Orlando, Florida. This is an example of the use of the Internet to inspire an individual to committee a lone-wolf terrorist attack. The Mateen attack shows the power of the Internet to communicate an ideology that can radicalize an individual to commit violence, and the difficulty of detection by law enforcement. One question that needs to be clarified is: At what point and by what definition does today's society classify these individuals as lone-world terrorists? Or are they serial killers?

A memorial placed outside the Pulse nightclub after the 2016 shooting.

## Terrorist Operations

Terrorist groups normally are smaller and weaker than the government that they are opposing. While some groups have the funding and training to operate at a more sophisticated level, they still remain weaker than the governments they are in conflict with. This fact means they still have to use asymmetrical tactics and not remain in one place in order to achieve a tactical success. One of the goals of a terrorist group is to achieve some type of publicity. (Taylor and Swanson, 2016) Taylor and Swanson (2016) explain that one of the fastest and cheapest ways to generate publicity is through the Internet. The Internet is a very efficient and effective way of communicating and bringing attention to the group's cause. The group can use the Internet to reach out to current and potential supporters to purchase memorabilia in order generate funds. (Taylor and Swanson, 2016) The Internet can also be used as a *shaping tool*, which is a form of preparation of the battlefield in order to shape public opinion to be favorable to the group's cause, or in the other sense as a way of demoralizing the public with threats of future incidents and operations that will get the news media to stimulate public debate which can be used to weaken the perception that the government can protect its citizens (Taylor and Swanson, 2016) Groups can also take hostages. Hostages can be used as bargaining chips to force the government to negotiate with the group, bringing further publicity to the group and its agenda. (DSS, ATO II, 2013) Today terrorist groups tend to operate in urban environments where they can blend into the community, and have access to communication systems, Internet, money, and transportation. This allows them to go unnoticed, have contacts in a place where they can obtain documentation and have access to public transportation. Terrorist groups use covert organizational structures and communication systems in order to be able to maintain a covert posture for long periods of time, so that their activities are hidden from the public view. These groups develop a strategy that includes the same types of planning cycles that a conventional military unit would employ. The group's operations must follow a plan that includes intermediate and long-term goals to accomplish objectives. A terrorist group's operations must be able to have a series of victories to allow the group to move toward accomplishing their goals. A terrorist group's primary goal is to establish national and international recognition so that they attract financial backers, recruits, and sponsorship. (DSS, ATO II 2013) Terrorists hope to create an atmosphere that is favorable to their cause or just an understanding of their cause when government reacts to terrorist operations by restricting public freedoms and enacting special laws. This overreaction works in their favor.

A military peacekeeping patrol ship safeguards against pirates.

One terrorist tactic that has worked very effectively is the Somali pirates who board large commercial ships demanding ransom and extorting money from the shipping companies. The shipping companies have paid the demands hoping for a nonviolent solution to the problem. The interesting note is that the ships are anchored in the port city of Harardhere, in the Galmudug state of Somalia, while waiting for the insurance companies to pay the ransom. The port is controlled by the al-Shabab terrorists. The Somali pirates have cut al-Shabab into their settlement transactions with the shipping companies' insurers. Aljazeera reported on November 28, 2016 that there was a clash between al-Shabab and Somali pirates over the what is being called the taxation of the Somalis in that area. All commercial ships have insurance policies and are heavily insured. It is the insurance companies that are paying off the Somali pirates' ransom demands. The pirates then pay a cut of taxes to al-Shabab. This process makes the insurance companies terrorist bankroll funders. According to *The Economist* in October 2013, Somali pirates have earned between 339 and 413 million dollars, with the average haul being 2.7 million dollars paid for by insurance policies that commercial shipping companies carry on their operations.

In 1989 the Russians pulled out of Afghanistan. The Afghan Taliban systematically isolated cities and cutoff entire segments of the population from government influence, which made them susceptible to intimidation and Taliban propaganda. This led to the Taliban seizing control in 1996, and maintaining control until the United States' invasion in 2001. Isolating the population creates a chaotic atmosphere and makes it easier for an armed terrorist group to seize control during the chaos. (DSS, ATO II 2013) Isolation, disruption, and chaos discourage foreign investment and assistance. This negatively affects the country's economy, and is a characteristic of Marxist or socialist movements that target western companies and capitalism as the symbols of capitalist imperialism, and provides the reasons behind their actions. This creates a process wherein corporations pull out of the country due to the government being no longer able to protect their business operations, which in turn puts people out of work and then turns the people against the government for not being able to provide them with the security they need to find work and support their families. The population, who are now without employment, have no way to support their families. They become disillusioned and susceptible to being recruited by the terrorist movement. This scenario played out in January 2013 in Amenas, Algeria where Al-Qaeda attacked a natural gas plant and a number of foreign nationals were killed, including three Americans. The plant was a British Petroleum and Norwegian joint venture. The result of this attack and three more years of heightened security and unrest led to the announcement in the *New York Times* in March 2016 that British Petroleum and the Norwegian company of Statoil were pulling all of their employees out of Algeria.

## Chapter Summary

- Terrorism is a very complex and not straightforward. By definition, terrorism has many different definitions depending upon who you ask. It can be caused by religious beliefs or politically motivated. One of the first uses of the word terror was during the French Revolution's Reign of Terror, which ran between 1793 and 1794.
- Crime is viewed as economically, rather than politically motivated. War is usually perceived as more legitimate and purposeful than terrorism. War is instrumental and not symbolic violence. There are rules and laws of war to be followed by belligerents. Civilians

and non-combatants should not be targeted. Terrorism is a form of political violence that is politically motivated to induce some sort of change.

- Both of the Justice Department definitions of terrorism share a common theme: the use of force intended to influence or instigate a course of action that furthers a political or social goal. In most cases, National Institute of Justice (NIJ) researchers adopt the FBI definition, which stresses methods over motivations and is generally accepted by law enforcement communities.

- The common descriptions used to describe terrorist groups can be broken down by their state affiliation, their identity, their intentions, their ideological beliefs, and their geographic location.

- A *revolutionary group*'s traditional operational objective is to overthrow an existing government. A revolutionary group is composed of political extremists and considers the cause to be of the highest order. Members of this type of group tend to be in their late teens to mid-thirties.

- A *sub-revolutionary group* executes operations that are designed to influence an unwilling government into making political, social, and economic changes. Many of the nationalist groups in the world are sub-revolutionary groups. This typology includes groups like anti-abortion, environmental, and anti-nuclear groups.

- Terrorist groups that have a state affiliation provide an indication of potential targeting and capabilities. There are two sub-groups to state affiliation; they are either state-directed or state-supported. State-supported groups could also have an element of state-directed, depending on their targeting and agenda.

- Lone-wolf or *lone terrorists* are terrorists that act out a terrorist operation by themselves without anyone commanding them. They might have been inspired to perform a terrorist act by an ideology. They might have an association with a domestic terrorist organization that may be engaged in criminal activities.

- Terrorist groups normally are smaller and weaker than the government that they are opposing. While some groups have the funding and training to operate at a more sophisticated level, they still remain weaker than the governments they are in conflict with. This fact means they still have to use asymmetrical tactics and not remain in one place in order to achieve a tactical success.

## Critical Thinking?

1. What do terrorists use to increase their attacking power?
2. What terrorist group created the underground video network known as As Sahaab?
3. What are three characteristics found within domestic terrorism?

4. What United States law gives our government the jurisdiction to investigate and prosecute terrorism outside the United States?

5. Why is the French Revolution's Reign of Terror an important event?

6. How does the U.S. Department of Justice define terrorism?

7. Name some terrorist groups that are related to religious affiliations?

8. In 2015 the White House declared what group is no longer considered a terrorist group?

9. What are the two sub-groups called that are related to state affiliations?

10. What are terrorists called that are difficult for law enforcement to detect, conduct surveillance on, and determine to be a threat to the public called?

## Media

**National Counter-Terrorism Center:** https://www.nctc.gov
This website provides information on national counter terrorism. The center leads and integrated the national counterterrorism effort by fusing foreign and domestic counterterrorism information providing terrorism analysis, sharing information with partners across the counterterrorism enterprise, and driving whole-of-government action to secure our national counterterrorism objectives.

**Terrorism:** https://fbi.gov/investigate/terrorism
The National Security Branch leads the FBI's efforts to detect, deter, and disrupt terrorist threats to the United States and its interests. The terrorist threat against the United States remains persistent and acute, and preventing terrorist attacks is the FBI's top priority.

**National Institute of Justice:** https://www.youtube.com/watch?v=IN BHz2Exmsw&list=PLpIlUxHJ-xbrjVvR0keGxr8KMTwk7xFnc
Three internationally-renowned experts from the research and practitioner arenas discuss how community policing can be used to prevent violent extremism and reduce violence within communities.

## Endnotes

Aslan, R. (2013) *Zealot: The Life and Times of Jesus of Nazareth*. New York: Random House.

Aljazeera. (2016, November 28). "Somali Civilians Clash with al-Shabab Over Tax Dispute." Retrieved from http://www.aljazeera.com/news/2016/11/somali-civilians-clash-al-shabab-tax-dispute-161128171031903.html

Breivik, A. B. (2011) "A European Declaration of Independence." Retrieved from https://publicintelligence.net/anders-behring-breviks-complete-manifesto-2083-a-european-declaration-of-independence/

Cunningham, W. G. Jr. (2003). *Terrorism Definitions and Typologies, Terrorism: Concepts, Causes, and Conflict Resolution, Advanced Systems and Concepts Office Defense Threat Reduction Agency and Working Group on War, Violence and Terrorism Institute for Conflict Analysis and Resolution.* (Rev. 1). Fort Belvoir, VA: Defense Threat Reduction Agency.

Defense Security Service. (2013). "Anti-Terrorism Officer II Level Qualification Course Notes GS109.16." Retrieved from http://www.cdse.edu/catalog/elearning/GS109.html

Economist. (2013, October 31). "More Sophisticated Than You Thought." Retrieved from http://www.economist.com/news/middle-east-and-africa/21588942-new-study-reveals-how-somali-piracy-financed-more-sophisticated-you

Gerges, F. A. (2014). "ISIS and the Third Wave of Jihadism, Current History." Retrieved from http://currenthistory.com/Gerges_Current_History.pdf

Forrest, J. J. F., (2015). *The Terrorism Lectures: A Comprehensive Collection for Students of Terrorism, Counterterrorism, and National Security,* 2nd ed. Nortia Press.

Marighella, C. (1969). "Minimanual of the Urban Guerrilla," unpublished original.

Reprint, 1989. Camp Lejeune, NC: II Marine Expeditionary Force G-2.

Molnar, H. (1966). *Human Factors Considerations of Undergrounds in Insurgencies.* Washington, DC: Headquarters, Dept. of the Army.

Molnar, H. (1963). *Undergrounds in Insurgent, Revolutionary, and Resistance Warfare.* Washington, DC: Special Operations Research Office.

Myers, L. W. (1991). *SPYCOMM Covert Communication Techniques of the Underground.* Boulder, CO: Paladin Press.

National Counter-Terrorism Center. "Terrorist Group Profiles." Retrieved from https://www.nctc.gov/site/index.html#

National Institute of Justice. "Terrorism." Retrieved from

https://www.nij.gov/topics/crime/terrorism/Pages/welcome.aspx

http://www.state.gov/j/ct/info/c16718.htm

https://www.fbi.gov/investigate/terrorism

https://www.law.cornell.edu/uscode/text/22/2656f

New York Times. (2016, March 21). "BP and Statoil Pull Employees From Algeria Gas Fields After Attack." Retreived from http://www.nytimes.com/2016/03/22/business/energy-environment/bp-and-statoil-pull-employees-from-algeria-gas-fields-after-attack.html?_r=0

Rogers, R., & Devost, M. G. (2005). *Hacking a Terror Network: The Silent Threat of Covert Channels.* Rockland, MA: Syngress Publishing Inc.

Taylor, R. W., & Swanson, C. R. (2015). *Terrorism, Intelligence and Homeland Security.* Prentice Hall.

US Government Printing Office. (1976). *A Church Committee Report of the Hearings Before Them to Study Governmental Operations with Respect to Intelligence Activities of the United States Senate.* 94 Congress 1 Session Volume 7. Washington, DC: United States Senate..

Chapter 113B United States Code, Terrorism, Retrieved from https://www.law.cornell.edu/uscode/text/18/part-I/chapter-113B

U.S. Department of Defense. (2010, November 24). "Joint Publication 3-07.2: Antiterrorism," Washington, DC: U.S. Department of Defense.

United States Department of State. (2016, June 2). *Country Reports on Terrorism 2015*. Washington, DC: U.S. Bureau of Counterterrorism and Countering Violent Extremism.

CNN. (2016, June 2). "State Department Report Finds Iran is Top State Sponsor of Terror." Retrieved from http://edition.cnn.com/2016/06/02/politics/state-department-report-terrorism/

Sullivan, J. G. (1996). *Embassies Under Siege: Personal Accounts by Diplomats on the Front Line*. Brassey's U.S.

© vchal/Shutterstock.com

# Criminal Justice in a Changing World

## KEY TERMS

Biometrics

Black hat hacker

Business continuity plan

Cybercrime

Cyberterrorism

Department of Homeland Security

Emergency Management Assistance Compact

Extradition

Federal Emergency Management Agency (FEMA)

Government cybercrime

Homeland security

Identity theft

International Court of Justice

INTERPOL

Malware

National Incident Management System (NIMS)

National Response Framework

Patriot Act

Personal cybercrime

Property cybercrime

Stafford Act

Tabletop exercise

Terrorism

Tribunal

United Nations

White hat hacker

# CHAPTER OBJECTIVES

1 Demonstrate the ability to discuss digital evidence and computer forensics.

2 Identify the range of employment possibilities in homeland security, continuity, cybercrime, and information assurance.

3 Identify the primary goals of homeland security initiatives in the United States.

4 Compare and contrast the major types of threats to homeland security the U.S. faces.

5 Analyze international collaboration efforts related to the investigation and prosecution of terrorism.

6 Discuss the International Court of Justice.

## Case Study: The BTK Killer

The serial murderer known as the BTK ("Bind, Torture, Kill") killer first emerged in 1971 when he murdered four members of a Wichita, Kansas family. The BTK killer continued his crimes through the 1980s and '90s. During this time, the killer sent detailed letters to news outlets and law enforcement detailing the murder scenes. He continued this behavior until 1991 when the last known murder was reported. All letters and communication ceased and so did the murders.

In 2004, the BTK killer sent a letter to law enforcement admitting other killings previously not accounted for. From these killings, police were able to retrieve DNA evidence from under the victims' nails and conducted DNA testing on 1,100 men, but had no luck in discovering the BTK killer's identity. From 2004 through 2005, the killer communicated with police and other law enforcement 11 times.

In 2005, the BTK killer sent a floppy disk containing his final letter to a news station, which led to a breakthrough in the case. The disk contained a deleted Microsoft Word document belonging to an author with the first name Dennis. Furthermore, the Word license in question belonged to Christ Lutheran Church in Wichita. During further investigations, investigators discovered the BTK killer was a deacon at the church named Dennis Rader. With the help of Rader's daughter, police ran a DNA test and were able to positively identify Rader as the BTK killer. Without the use of computer forensics tools, Dennis Rader would more than likely never have been convicted.[1]

The investigation of the BTK killer is considered one of the best-known cases utilizing computer forensics investigators. As technology has advanced in the 20th and 21st centuries, the criminal justice system has progressed with it. In 2007, the Department of Homeland Security and Alabama state officials unveiled the National Computer Forensics Institute in Hoover, Alabama. Its purpose is to assist in the computer forensics field analyzing digital evidence.[2]

Advanced technology is just one of the ways in which the U.S. government is striving to protect the homeland from both internal and external threats. Since the beginning of the 21st century, the government has introduced a variety of measures to secure the United States not only from terrorism, but also from cyber warfare and natural disasters. This chapter will explore these 21st century criminal justice issues.

# Homeland Security

**Homeland security** is a widely used term, and one that has garnered increased attention in recent history, particularly following the attacks against the United States on September 11, 2001. Today, the term is used in reference to preparedness, response, and recovery measures taken at national, regional, state, and local levels. Homeland security addresses issues related to terrorism, natural disasters, and anything else that threatens the safety and security of the nation and its people. The growing impact of homeland security in the United States and throughout the world has a far-reaching effect on the criminal justice system, civil liberties, and life safety.

**Homeland security** The preparedness measures taken to protect and ensure the security and safety of the homeland and its citizens.

## History and Goals of Homeland Security in the United States

Broadly speaking, **terrorism** can be defined as the use or threat of violence toward civilians in order to attain political, religious, or ideological goals. However, it is important to note that although this definition is used for our purposes, it is not a universal one. There are many other ways to define the term. For example, the Oxford English Dictionary defines it as "a system of terror" or "a policy intended to strike with terror those against whom it is adopted; the employment of methods of intimidation; the fact of terrorizing or condition of being terrorized."[3] Or, perhaps more helpful in getting to the meaning of the term, the United States Code defines it as "premeditated, politically motivated violence perpetrated against noncombatant targets by subnational groups or clandestine agents."[4]

**Terrorism** The use or threat of violence toward civilians in order to attain political, religious, or ideological goals.

The threat of terrorism has long been a part of history in the United States and around the world. Terrorist incidents have taken place at international venues, U.S. embassies, and on American soil. Perpetrators of these events have been foreign terrorist organizations or individuals and Americans themselves. For example, the first time a U.S. aircraft was hijacked, on May 1, 1961, a Puerto Rican national forced the pilot of a National Airlines flight to land in Cuba, where he was granted asylum.[5] In 1968, the U.S. Ambassador to Guatemala was assassinated by a rebel faction in Guatemala City, and in 1969 the U.S. Ambassador to Brazil was kidnapped by a Marxist revolutionary group.[6] On July 31, 1970, an advisor for the U.S. Agency for International Development was kidnapped in Uruguay; his body was found 10 days later.[7] These unfortunate events are representative of a long series of terrorist incidents, but gave no indication of what was to come later on American soil in Oklahoma City in 1995 and New York City in 2001.

Dylann Roof appears at Centralized Bond Hearing Court on June 19, 2015 in North Charleston, South Carolina.

One of the deadliest terrorist acts committed in the United States was the 1995 Oklahoma City bombing. The bombing, perpetrated by two Americans, targeted a federal building in downtown Oklahoma City, killing 168 people and injuring about 850.[8] However, the deadliest terrorist act committed on American soil took place on September 11, 2001, when attacks on the World Trade Center and the Pentagon killed approximately 3,000 people and gave rise to the most comprehensive reorganization ever taken by the federal government: the establishment of the **Department of Homeland Security (DHS)**.

In June 2015, Dylann Roof attended a Bible study session in a church in Charleston, South Carolina. Did he really come to learn anything sacred or religious or was his attendance a case of cold-blooded murder? After about an hour or so, Dylann drew out his handgun and killed nine group members. What was his rationale? Did he want to start a racial war because he was white and his nine victims were black? In December, a jury convicted him of 33 federal charges for killing nine people as they prayed at the end of a Bible study at the historic Charleston church known as Mother Emanuel.

Most Americans are confused when it comes to domestic terrorism. Would what Dylann did be considered a hate crime or domestic terrorism? More than likely most states would consider this a hate crime because most states do not have statutes on domestic terrorism.

DHS was officially established with the passage of the Homeland Security Act of 2002. The act defines the mission of DHS generally, including protecting the homeland by preventing and reducing the country's vulnerability to terrorist attacks, as well as minimizing damage, assisting in recovery, and acting as the coordinating body for crises and emergency planning at a national level.[9] Because of the wide spectrum of responsibilities housed within DHS, it comprises many federal agencies and offices, such as the Transportation Security Administration (TSA), U.S. Immigration and Customs Enforcement (ICE), U.S. Coast Guard, **Federal Emergency Management Agency (FEMA)**, U.S. Secret Service (USSS), and U.S. Customs and Border Protection (CBP).

**Department of Homeland Security (DHS)** An agency created by the Homeland Security Act of 2002 whose mission is to protect the homeland by preventing and reducing the country's vulnerability to terrorist attacks, as well as minimizing damage, assisting in recovery, and acting as a focal point for crises and emergency planning.

**Federal Emergency Management Agency (FEMA)** An agency within the Department of Homeland Security whose mission is to build, sustain, and strengthen the nation's capability to address all hazards through preparation, response, and recovery measures.

It is important to note that, based on its mission, DHS is not solely focused on terrorism: it is also responsible for coordinating national response to natural disasters and crises. The agency primarily responsible for this function within DHS is **FEMA**. FEMA's mission is to build, sustain, and strengthen the nation's capability to address all hazards through preparation, response, and recovery measures. This mission was put to the test as FEMA took center stage following Hurricane Katrina, which struck the Gulf Coast in August 2005 and was the costliest natural disaster in U.S. history.[10] It killed nearly 2,000 people and displaced hundreds of thousands of families and individuals. FEMA played a major role in coordinating and responding to the disaster, but among its most visible tasks were the deployment of search and rescue teams and providing housing assistance for victims of the storm. Unfortunately, it became apparent that despite its efforts, the agency was suffering from insufficient manpower and lacked a clear understanding of roles and responsibilities in responding to the event. In turn, the government was largely criticized for its delayed and ineffective response.

Hundreds of thousands of families and individuals requested temporary housing from FEMA following the destruction of Hurricane Katrina.

Much like the events of September 11, the devastation of Hurricane Katrina was dramatic and has had a lasting impact on the country. These events exemplify the threats to homeland security faced by the U.S. in the 21st century. Although a manmade event (terrorist attack) is fundamentally different than a natural disaster, both types of threats require preparedness, response, and recovery efforts in order to protect the life and safety of potential victims. These three concepts provide the basis for homeland security and emergency management at all levels of government.

## Preparedness

Federal, state, and local governments place a heavy emphasis on preparedness, and in general, focus on two issues: (1) preparing the government, and its partners, for a coordinated response to a disaster, and (2) encouraging individuals to prepare themselves and their families for a disaster. One of the centerpieces of the federal focus on preparedness is the **National Response Framework (NRF)**, which is a comprehensive national guide for incident management and response to domestic incidents. The NRF takes an all-hazards approach to dealing with incidents: it does not differentiate between a hurricane, a tornado, and a terrorist act, and it accounts for incidents ranging in size from small to catastrophic. Further, the NRF organizes national response by describing the roles of the federal government, states, private sector, and nongovernmental organizations during and after a disaster in an effort to make all response players more prepared in advance of an event.

**National Response Framework (NRF)**
A framework that forms the basis for coordination between all levels of government and the private sector in responding to a disaster. It establishes a comprehensive structure, method, and standard terminology for management of incidents.

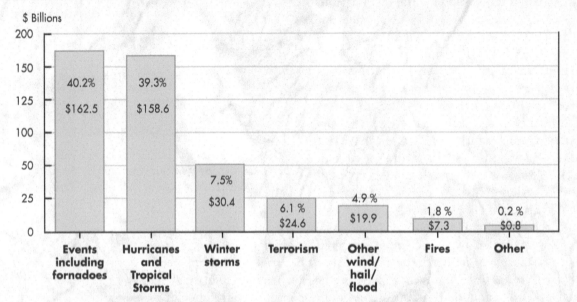

(1) Adjusted for inflation through 2015 by ISO using the GDP implicit price deflator. Excludes catastrophes causing direct losses less than $25 million in 1997 dollars. Excludes flood damage covered by the federally administered National Flood Insurance Program.
(2) Includes other wind, hail, and/or flood losses associated with catastrophes involving tornadoes.
(3) Includes wildland fires.
(4) Includes losses from civil disorders, water damage, utility service disruptions, and any workers compensation catastrophes generating losses in excess of PCS's thershold after adjusting for inflation.

Source: Data from property claim servies (PCS®) a verisk analytics® business

**National Incident Management System (NIMS)** A national system that provides a consistent nationwide approach for government, the private sector, and nongovernmental organizations to work together in preparation, response, and recovery from domestic incidents.

The NRF works hand in hand with the **National Incident Management System (NIMS)**. NIMS provides an overall template for shared management of incidents and can be applied at all levels of government, including state, local, and tribal. A focal point of NIMS is a concept called the *Incident Command System (ICS)*. ICS helps ensure a clear order of command in the management of an incident by assigning planners and responders to defined roles that work with one another and report to a single incident commander. Through the employment of ICS, NIMS streamlines how an incident can and should be managed, and provides a backbone for the specifics of the NRF at a national level. Used in conjunction with one another, NIMS and the NRF aim to integrate emergency management practices at all levels of government into a cohesive national framework.

Although the NRF and NIMS provide a valuable tool for the nation's policy-makers and responders, the government also emphasizes the importance of individuals' participation in preparedness efforts. For example, in 2002, President Bush launched *Citizen Corps*, a program designed to integrate citizens into protecting the nation and supporting first responders in their communities after a disaster.[11] Although the program was launched by the president and FEMA is responsible for its national coordination, it is an excellent example of state and local preparedness efforts as well.

Citizen Corps volunteers work to strengthen community preparedness through state, local, and tribal Citizen Corps Councils.[12] The councils are formed in states and localities throughout the United States and create local strategies to encourage preparedness. They often work directly with state and local emergency management agencies.

Also related to individual preparedness is FEMA's *Ready* program, which highlights preparedness for individuals and their families, businesses, and kids.[13] The program encourages individuals and businesses to have a plan and be informed, because when an incident occurs—whether it is an act of terrorism, an accident, or a natural disaster—it may be several hours, or days, before relief workers can provide assistance. For individuals and families, this means thinking about food, water, first aid, and a plan for staying or evacuating depending on the circumstances. For businesses, this means focusing on continuity, and more specifically, creating a **business continuity plan**.

A business continuity plan helps a business continue its essential functions in order to operate during and after a disaster or other disruptive event. It is largely the same as a *continuity of operations plan*, which is implemented in the public sector. Both of these plans are fundamental to the preparedness of an agency, institution, or business and help the organization streamline its operations so that it can continue to function even with the constraints caused by an event. Most often these constraints relate to the physical structure of an organization—the personnel, equipment, or other tools and materials the organization normally relies on in accomplishing its day-to-day activities. For example, during a snowstorm or following a hurricane, employees may be unable to access the building to report for work. Alternatively, during a pandemic flu it may be unsafe for employees to gather at their normal place of work. Although these events are fundamentally different, they each require plans for allowing business to continue at an alternate location or with alternate staff. A continuity plan allows an organization to prioritize the essentials of its business so that a minimal amount of disruption takes place. Obviously a plan does not prevent disruption from occurring, but it better positions an organization to deal with an event if and when one does occur. And, as with all preparedness initiatives, it is imperative that continuity plans are tested and practiced regularly.

There is a national standard for homeland security exercises called the *Homeland Security Exercise and Evaluation Program (HSEEP)*. According to DHS, HSEEP "provides a standardized methodology and terminology for exercise design, development, conduct, evaluation, and improvement planning."[14] In particular, HSEEP notes seven types of exercises that range in complexity, goals, and outcomes. The least complex, a seminar, simply orients participants to the plan, concept, or idea. The most complex, a full-scale exercise, involves multiple agencies and jurisdictions, and tests many aspects of emergency response and recovery as if an event were actually happening. Though there are several types of exercises that fall somewhere between a seminar and a full-scale exercise, one commonly used option is a **tabletop exercise**. This is a discussion-based exercise related to a

**Business continuity plan**
A plan that helps a business continue its essential functions in order to operate during and after a disaster or other disruptive event.

**Tabletop exercise**
An exercise presenting a hypothetical situation for discussion, used to assess preparedness by allowing participants to discuss how specific plans or policies would be implemented to prevent, respond to, or recover from the scenario.

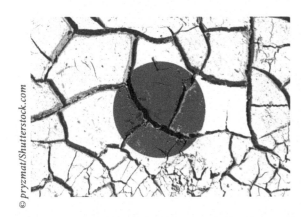

Japan was devastated by a 9.0 earthquake and tsunami on March 11, 2011.

hypothetical situation. It allows participants to talk through a given scenario and discuss how plans or policies would be used to prevent, respond to, or recover from the scenario.

## Response and Recovery

No matter how prepared a nation is, it cannot always prevent a crisis from occurring. Therefore it is equally important for a homeland security program to place emphasis on response and recovery efforts. A real-world example that brings this point to light occurred on March 11, 2011, when one of the most powerful earthquakes in recorded history hit Japan. It was followed by a devastating tsunami. The numbers of dead and missing were estimated to be over 28,000.[15] Prior to the catastrophe, Japan was well prepared in terms of its warning systems, mitigation efforts, and overall individual citizen preparedness to deal with natural disasters, and in particular, earthquakes and tsunamis. However, no amount of preparedness can prevent such a catastrophe, and in the aftermath of the events, the country immediately shifted gears to focus on response and recovery. For Japan, this meant relying on itself and its international partners to respond to the needs of the many survivors, including providing shelter, food, and health services.

In the United States, response and recovery from a disaster almost always begin at a local level, and depending on the severity of the event, can shift to the state and eventually federal levels. As such, all of these players must work together to provide timely and effective responses to an event and continue to play a role in the recovery process. Response and recovery efforts begin nearly immediately during an emergency, and often go hand in hand with a formal disaster or emergency declaration. The federal government has the power to issue a federal disaster declaration, but states have similar, parallel powers. The process of declaring a disaster varies by state, but in general, a governor may declare a state of emergency after consulting with local officials, thus triggering the state's emergency plan. In addition, it is generally true that a state's emergency plan allows for a change in the powers of government to deal most effectively with the emergency at hand. For example, if the disaster includes a threat to public health, many state emergency plans allow the governor, or another appropriate state official, to issue quarantine and isolation orders, which they would not be able to do otherwise.[16]

**Stafford Act**
A congressional act passed in 2009 that provides a method for states to request federal assistance to respond to a disaster. Short for The Robert T. Stafford Disaster Relief and Emergency Assistance Act.

However, if a governor determines that recovery is beyond the state's and localities' capabilities, he or she may request federal assistance under the Robert T. Stafford Disaster Relief and Emergency Assistance Act (**Stafford Act**).[17] In accordance with Stafford Act procedures, the governor must certify that federal assistance is necessary because the magnitude of the disaster exceeds what the state is capable of handling. The governor must also certify that the state executed its emergency plan, and that the state will share costs as needed.[18] In response to this request, FEMA completes a preliminary damage assessment, where personnel from FEMA work with the state's emergency management agency, other county and local officials, and the U.S. Small Business Administration to review damage, costs, and impacts of the disaster in affected areas.[19] Based on this assessment and recommended course of action, the president may issue a formal disaster declaration, thereby bringing the federal government's resources to the aid of the state in need.[20]

## Legal Framework of U.S. Homeland Security and Emergency Management

Ensuring the nation's homeland security requires cooperation from all levels of government, along with nongovernmental organizations, private-sector businesses, and citizens. Because of the complicated nature of providing security and safety to the country, there is an equally comprehensive legal framework that delineates the authorities, powers, and roles of these players.

### Federal Bases of Authority

Arguably the cornerstone of legal authority for modern homeland security in the United States is the Uniting and Strengthening America by Providing Appropriate Tools Required to Intercept and Obstruct Terrorism (USA PATRIOT) Act of 2001. Commonly referred to as the **Patriot Act**, its focus is primarily on providing law enforcement agencies with legal authority to support efforts to fight terrorism. In particular, it addresses law enforcement's authority related to collecting information on and detaining suspected terrorists in an effort to deter terrorists from entering and operating within the U.S.[21] The legislation is quite lengthy, but a few key provisions include:[22]

- Loosening the restrictions between U.S. law enforcement and intelligence officers when sharing information.
- Making it illegal to knowingly harbor terrorists.
- Authorizing "roving wiretaps," allowing law enforcement officials to tap any phone a suspected terrorist might use rather than one specific phone or device.
- Increasing subpoena power for email records of terrorist suspects.
- Greatly expanding the number of border patrol personnel, and other customs and immigration inspectors on U.S. borders.
- Expanding measures against money laundering by requiring identification of certain account holders and additional record keeping and reports for some transactions.
- Eliminating statutes of limitation for prosecuting especially egregious terrorist acts.

**Patriot Act**
A congressional act passed shortly after the September 11, 2001 terrorist attacks in the U.S., focusing primarily on providing law enforcement with legal authority to support efforts to fight terrorism. Short for The Uniting and Strengthening America by Providing Appropriate Tools Required to Intercept and Obstruct Terrorism (USA Patriot) Act.

The Patriot Act sparked controversy because of the content of some of these provisions, but also because of the haste in which it was passed. President Bush announced that he would be seeking passage of the act on September 24, 2001, barely two weeks after the September 11 attacks, and it was signed into law just one month later on October 26, 2001. Many critics of the Patriot Act have questioned the constitutionality of several of its provisions and the methods by which law enforcement agencies would use their new authorities. In particular, critics pointed to the lack of specificity in many of the provisions, which they claimed would allow the government to gather information about and related to citizens not involved in any terrorist activity. For example, the act provides that the FBI can monitor the use of a public computer—at an Internet café or library, for example—if it is being used by a suspected terrorist. Therefore, if an ordinary person used that same computer, the FBI would be permitted to monitor all of that person's Internet usage as part of their investigation and monitoring of the computer.

One of the leading proponents of the Patriot Act, and the U.S. Attorney General at the time, John Ashcroft, argued that these authorities were necessary to fight terrorism effectively. Further, proponents pointed to the fact that the act included several provisions that were to expire on December 31, 2005. However, since that time, Congress and the president have reauthorized the act twice and extended the provisions, thereby continuing to extend the authorities granted to law enforcement agencies.

## Critical Thinking

The Patriot Act sparked much debate in the country regarding the appropriate role of government and limitations, or lack thereof, on its powers. Did Congress act too impulsively in passing this legislation, or was the action appropriate given the mood of the country at the time?

Not long after passing the Patriot Act, Congress passed the Homeland Security Act of 2002, which had sweeping effects on the federal framework relative to homeland security. This legislation officially established the Department of Homeland Security and provided it with a structure and mission. Much like the Patriot Act, this legislation was passed primarily in response to the September 11 attacks and the perceived government inefficiencies that had allowed such an event to occur. Also in response to this perception, and on the heels of the Homeland Security Act of 2002, the White House released Homeland Security Presidential Directive No. 5 (HSPD-5).[23] HSPD-5 tasked DHS with developing a single, comprehensive National Incident Management System, and thus became the underlying authority for the establishment of NIMS and the NRF.[24]

The federal homeland security framework continued to evolve, but did not undergo another major change until Congress passed the Post-Katrina Emergency Management Reform Act of 2006 (Post-Katrina Act).[25] In the aftermath of Hurricane Katrina, many people criticized the government's slow and ineffective response to the disaster. For example, pre-staged resources, such as food and water, were drastically inadequate at shelters, including at the Superdome in Louisiana. These limited resources were quickly depleted, and people with special needs were not adequately addressed, which led to civil unrest in some cases.[26] Critics blamed FEMA's bureaucracy and the fact that many of its preparedness functions had been reassigned to other DHS divisions as part of a department-wide reorganization plan implemented by DHS Secretary Michael Chertoff in 2005. As such, the Post-Katrina Act transferred most of the preparedness functions back to FEMA and elevated the agency's status in the Department by establishing it as a "distinct entity" within DHS.[27] This distinction gave the FEMA administrator direct access to the president and Congress.[28] Specifically, the FEMA administrator is the principal advisor to the president, the secretary of DHS, and the Homeland Security Council on all emergency management matters, and the president is authorized to assign the administrator to serve as a member of the cabinet during disasters.[29]

---

**Exhibit: Patriot Act of 2001**

Title I, Section 102: SENSE OF CONGRESS CONDEMNING DISCRIMINATION AGAINST ARAB AND MUSLIM AMERICANS

(a) FINDINGS.—Congress makes the following findings:

(1) Arab Americans, Muslim Americans, and Americans from South Asia play a vital role in our Nation and are entitled to nothing less than the full rights of every American.

(2) The acts of violence that have been taken against Arab and Muslim Americans since the September 11, 2001, attacks against the United States should be and are condemned by all Americans who value freedom.

(3) The concept of individual responsibility for wrongdoing is sacrosanct in American society, and applies equally to all religious, racial, and ethnic groups.

(4) When American citizens commit acts of violence against those who are, or are perceived to be, of Arab or Muslim descent, they should be punished to the full extent of the law.

(5) Muslim Americans have become so fearful of harassment that many Muslim women are changing the way they dress to avoid becoming targets.

(6) Many Arab Americans and Muslim Americans have acted heroically during the attacks on the United States, including Mohammed Salman Hamdani, a 23-year-old New Yorker of Pakistani descent, who is believed to have gone to the World Trade Center to offer rescue assistance and is now missing.

(b) SENSE OF CONGRESS.—It is the sense of Congress that—

(1) the civil rights and civil liberties of all Americans, including Arab Americans, Muslim Americans, and Americans from South Asia, must be protected, and that every effort must be taken to preserve their safety;

(2) any acts of violence or discrimination against any Americans be condemned; and

(3) the Nation is called upon to recognize the patriotism of fellow citizens from all ethnic, racial, and religious backgrounds.

## USA Freedom Act replaces the USA Patriot Act of 2001

On June 2, 2015, the Uniting and Strengthening America by Fulfilling Rights and Ending Eavesdropping, Dragnet-collection and Online Monitoring Act (or USA Freedom Act) replaced the USA Patriot Act.

The USA Freedom Act renewed many of the Patriot Act's expiring provisions through 2019, albeit with some new limits concerning bulk interception of telecommunication metadata about U.S. citizens.

### What Are Some of the Differences Between the New USA Freedom Act and the USA Patriot Act?

The USA Freedom Act updates and extends several of the expired provisions of the USA Patriot Act. The new Freedom Act includes more limitations due to public outcry of the government intrusion to citizenry privacy rights. Under the old USA Patriot Act, law enforcement agencies could collect many different records from individuals to include phone records, company business records flight manifests, and much more, as so long as government officials believed they were "relevant" to a national security investigation. Under the old Patriot Act the NSA was accused of abusing their power by collecting mega amounts of phone records hoping to find links between suspects they thought to be involved in terrorist activities. NSA argued that this information was necessary as it could lead to the prevention of terrorist acts. However, the government has not been able to provide any examples of where such massive amounts of data surveillance played any key role in stopping a terrorist plot.[99]

As a result, the Freedom Act includes provisions which limit the amount of bulk surveillance of collected information of American citizens. The NSA and other agencies can now only request company records regarding a specific person, account, or device. NSA must show that the entity is associated with a foreign power or terrorist group.[99]

Also, under the USA Freedom Act, intelligence agencies such as the Federal Bureau of Investigation who must be more transparent about the data they are collecting from the public and businesses. Tech companies are no longer subject to gag orders that prevent them from informing customers when their private data is given to the feds.[99]

In addition, the USA Freedom Act allows citizens to lobby the Foreign Intelligence Surveillance Court (FISC), the surveillance-specific court set up under the Foreign Intelligence Surveillance Act of 1978 (FISA). As a result, civil liberties advocates can now force the government to declassify major opinions from the FISC judges.[99]

Even though the USA Freedom Act is an improvement on the USA Patriot Act in terms of individual liberty and privacy, the government can still collect information on a large scale. The lone wolf and roving wiretap provisions remain the same as they were under the Patriot Act.[99] Critics believe that the new USA Freedom Act continues to allow the government to encroach on our privacy rights.

## State and Regional Authorities

State and regional homeland security powers and sources of authority vary across the country, as each state has the power to enact its own laws and regulations. However, it is important to note that in addition to working together with the federal government to respond to a disaster, states often work with one another to respond regionally to a threat or event. The primary vehicle for doing so is the **Emergency Management Assistance Compact (EMAC)**. EMAC is an interstate compact, ratified by Congress, that provides a framework for mutual cooperation.[30] The process of obtaining interstate resources is actually quite simple: once a governor declares a state of emergency, the state may place a request for resources through EMAC, and if assisting states have the resources available, they mobilize and deploy them to the state in need. This mutual cooperation is extremely valuable to states because, while some emergency situations may require additional response and recovery assistance, they may not warrant full federal involvement. At the same time, even for those emergencies that do require federal aid, EMAC can be invoked to supplement federal efforts.

**Emergency Management Assistance Compact (EMAC)** An interstate mutual aid agreement, ratified by Congress, that allows states to assist one another in responding to disasters.

## Impact of Homeland Security Measures in the United States

The increased focus on homeland security in the 21st century has left an indelible mark on the United States. Almost immediately after the September 11 attacks, there was a rise in hate crimes against Muslim-Americans and other targeted groups, as well as a dramatic increase in security measures at airports and other public places. As such, there has been a visible impact on the criminal justice system and the debate regarding civil liberties across the country.

Following the September 11 attacks, there was a rise in hate crimes against Muslims, Sikhs, and people of Arab and South Asian descent. In the first nine weeks after the attacks, more than 700 violent incidents were reported that targeted Arab Americans or those perceived to be Arab Americans, Arabs, and Muslims.[31] In the year following the attacks, from September 11, 2001 to October 11, 2002, there were 80 cases of aircraft passengers being illegally and discriminatorily removed, 800 cases of employment discrimination, and many other instances of discrimination in service and housing, as well as denial of service.[32] In response, the Civil Rights Division of the Department of Justice prioritized the prosecution of perpetrators of these crimes and reached out to the affected communities to educate them about their rights. To date, the Civil Rights Division, the FBI, and the offices of the U.S. Attorneys have investigated more than 800 such incidents and have brought federal charges against 48 defendants, resulting in 44 convictions.[33]

In one 2006 case, a defendant pleaded guilty to threatening the director of the Arab American Institute and other staff members through email and voice mail at their office in Washington, D.C. The defendant received a 12-month prison sentence followed by three years of supervised release. He also received a $10,000 fine and was ordered to complete 100 hours of community service.[34] In another case, four defendants pleaded guilty to plotting to destroy an Islamic education center. The defendants received substantial prison sentences for conspiracy to violate civil rights, firearms violations, attempted destruction of religious property, and conspiracy to detonate explosive devices.[35] In a third case, a defendant pleaded guilty to

Screening of baggage and passengers at airports has dramatically increased since 9/11.

assaulting a Sikh postal carrier with a pellet rifle. The victim suffered a severe neck injury, requiring surgery that caused him to miss work for several months. The defendant was sentenced to a prison term of 70 months and was ordered to pay over $25,000 in restitution.[36] These cases help illustrate the effect that threats to homeland security, and specifically the terrorist events of September 11, have had on the U.S. criminal justice system.

The aftermath of the September 11 attacks also sparked great controversy over civil liberties in the country. As the government increased security measures at airports and surveillance measures in general in an effort to prevent terrorist activities, critics of these measures argued that they had gone too far in curtailing individual rights guaranteed by the U.S. Constitution. Specifically, one issue that has arisen from these concerns is what some perceive to be violations of due process rights. Most often, this issue has come up regarding government scanning and searching procedures at airports. For example, following a passenger's attempt to blow up a plane on Christmas Day in 2010, the United States introduced tougher screening rules for passengers arriving at airports from 14 countries considered high-risk and linked to terrorism. Critics of this policy argued that the screening of individuals based on country of origin was essentially racial profiling and a threat to civil liberties. Similarly, when the government began introducing full-body scanners for all airline passengers, debate arose over not only their effectiveness, but their threat to personal privacy. The United States places a high value on privacy and individual rights, and finding the right balance between keeping the country secure from terrorist threats and respecting those rights has proven to be a complicated task.

**Critical Thinking**

Is a trade-off between civil liberties and security measures necessary to identify and deal with threats to homeland security? Or can threats be dealt with effectively without affecting individual rights?

## International Justice

*International criminal justice* is a movement in the international community to establish appropriate venues, such as criminal courts and tribunals, to respond to violations of international law. Most often, these violations relate to humanitarian law and other gross violations of human rights around the world. Prosecuting such crimes presents a difficult challenge for the international community because each country operates within its own legal structure and bounds. Enforcing international law is an evolving process, and one that requires a unique form of collaboration among many partners.

## The International Court of Justice

Any discussion regarding international justice must include the United Nations and the International Court of Justice. The **United Nations (UN)** is an international organization formed in 1945 by 51 original member states in an effort to promote international peace and security following World War II. It has grown to include 192 member states and is best known for its peacekeeping efforts and humanitarian assistance around the world. The **International Court of Justice (ICJ)**, also established in June 1945 by the charter of the UN, is one of the oldest and most respected institutions in the international community and plays a significant role in enforcing international law.[37] It is the principal judicial organ of the UN and is located at the Peace Palace in The Hague, Netherlands.[38] The ICJ serves two primary roles with respect to international law: settling legal disputes submitted to it by states/countries, and issuing advisory opinions on legal questions referred to it by the UN and other agencies.[39] The court consists of 15 judges, elected to nine-year terms by the United Nations General Assembly and the Security Council.[40] The panel of judges may not include more than one national from the same country at a time, and as a whole it must represent all of the major civilizations and principal legal systems of the world. This makes the ICJ a truly international organization.

The ICJ's impact on the international community is vast. As of March of 2011, 151 cases had been presented to the court since the first case was submitted on May 22, 1947.[41] The first case, *Corfu Channel Case* (*United Kingdom v. Albania*), dealt with a dispute arising from incidents in the Corfu Strait of Albania on October 22, 1946. Two British ships suffered damages and deaths after striking mines in the Albanian waters.[42] The United Kingdom submitted an application to the ICJ to hear the matter,[43] and after the proceedings, in accordance with international law, Albania was ordered to pay compensation to the United Kingdom.[44] The court's decision in that case has been cited numerous times and remains relevant to central questions of international law in the 21st century, such as due diligence, maritime operations, navigation in international waters, and humanitarian concerns. Since its first case, the ICJ has addressed a variety of other matters, including issues such as diplomatic relations, immunities of the state, use of force, and territorial disputes.[45]

© Andrew F. Kazmierski/Shutterstock.com

Countries around the world work together in pursuing international justice.

© Ankor Light/Shutterstock.com

The International Court of Justice acts as a world court on matters of international law.

## International Collaboration: Investigating and Prosecuting Terrorism

Although international justice covers a wide range of topics, one of the primary issues it must address in the 21st century is the investigation and prosecution of terrorism. Sometimes terrorism originates within and affects only one country, but acts of terrorism are increasingly crossing international boundaries. As such, international collaboration to prevent and fight terrorism is of the utmost importance. The following section discusses a variety of tools, including organizations, methods, and venues, that are currently in place to facilitate this collaboration.

### International Policing

**International Criminal Police Organization (INTERPOL)** The world's largest international police organization, which consists of 188 member countries and facilitates cross-border police cooperation.

The **International Criminal Police Organization (INTERPOL)** is charged with facilitating cross-border police cooperation and providing assistance in preventing and combating international crime. INTERPOL, created in 1923, is the world's largest international police organization, composed of 188 member countries.[46] The organization addresses the threat of terrorism by:[47]

1. supporting member countries in combating terrorism, specifically through resources focused on bioterrorism, weapons of mass destruction, firearms and explosives, maritime piracy, and attacks against civil aviation;

2. collecting and exchanging information among member countries about suspected groups and individuals, and coordinating alerts and warnings related to terrorists, criminals, and weapons threats to member countries; and

3. creating the Fusion Task Force. The task force's primary objectives are to "identify active terrorist groups and their members, solicit, collect and share information and intelligence, provide analytical support, and enhance the capacity of member countries to address the threats of terrorism and organized crime."[48]

Similar to INTERPOL, the *European Union Law Enforcement Agency (EUROPOL)* aims to improve cooperation of authorities in member countries to prevent and combat terrorism as well as organized crime and drug trafficking.[49] The agency works closely with non-European Union (EU) partners such as Australia, Canada, the United States, and Norway.[50] Headquartered at The Hague, the organization disseminates information to law enforcement partners who use it to prevent, detect, and investigate suspected terrorists. In particular, EUROPOL produces regular assessments of crime and terrorism in the EU; these Organized Crime Threat Assessments (OCTA) identify and analyze emerging threats. In addition, the agency publishes the EU Terrorism Situation and Trend Report (TE-STAT) annually to provide a detailed account of terrorism in the EU.[51]

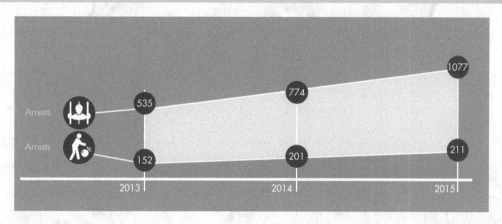

**FIGURE 13.2** NUMBER OF FAILED, FOILED, OR COMPLETED TERRORISM ATTACKS; NUMBER OF ARRESTED SUSPECTS, 2013 TO 2015

Arrests 535    774    1077
Arrests 152    201    211
2013    2014    2015

Source: European Union Terrorism Situation and Trend Report 2016, EUROPOL European Law Enforcement Agency (TE-SAT 2016).

## Extradition Treaties

Extradition treaties can be effective tools to prevent the spread of terrorism because they allow countries to work together to bring criminals to justice despite traditional jurisdictional boundaries. **Extradition** is the formal surrender of a person by one country to another country for the purpose of prosecution or punishment. The United States has over 100 extradition treaties in place with countries around the world.[52] Extradition treaties are bilateral agreements that require one nation to send a person in custody to another country if there is evidence to suggest that the person committed a serious crime that is subject to imprisonment in both countries. However, the content of individual treaties may vary, so it is important that the request for extradition be made in accordance with the applicable terms. For example, treaties provide explicit lists of crimes or offenses for which extradition is appropriate and those for which it may, or even must, be denied.[53] In addition, the terms of most extradition treaties include an exemption for political offenses, thus placing terrorists out of reach for traditional extradition in many cases. The United States has tried to limit this exemption for terrorists by requiring a fugitive to demonstrate that the crime was committed during a violent political disturbance (war, rebellion, etc.) in order to avoid extradition.[54] Other treaties limit the exemption more directly by explicitly excluding terrorist acts from the definition of political crimes. Because of these terms and exemptions, the role of extradition treaties in the context of terrorism is not always clear-cut.

**Extradition** The formal surrender of a person by a country to another country for the purpose of prosecution or punishment.

## United Nations Counter-Terrorism Implementation Task Force (CTITF)

The UN is uniquely positioned to encourage international collaboration because of its international membership. In 2005, the secretary-general of the UN capitalized on this fact and established the Counter-Terrorism Implementation Task Force (CTITF). This task force coordinates counter-terrorism efforts and assists member states in implementing the *UN Global Counter-Terrorism Strategy (Global Strategy)*.[55] Specifically, CTITF works with member states to implement the four pillars of the Global Strategy, which are:[56]

1. "Measures to address conditions conducive to the spread of terrorism;

2. Measures to prevent and combat terrorism;

3. Measures to build states' capacity to prevent and combat terrorism and to strengthen the role of the UN in this regard; and

4. Measures to enact respect for human rights and the rule of law as the fundamental basis of the fight against terrorism."

CTITF operates through working groups devoted to supporting victims of terrorism, responding to terrorist attacks, disrupting terrorists' financing and Internet use, and protecting vulnerable targets and human rights.[57] These working groups assess threats, run exercises, develop partnerships, make recommendations, and bring stakeholders together to fight terrorism more effectively around the world. For example, based on a series of roundtable discussions with banking, intelligence, law enforcement, and criminal justice experts, the Working Group on Tackling the Financing of Terrorism published a report in 2009 covering five specific areas of combating terrorist financing: "(a) the criminalization of terrorist financing; (b) the enhancement of domestic and international cooperation; (c) value transfer systems; (d) non-profit organizations; and (e) the freezing of assets." These recommendations provide best practices for how to effectively reduce terrorists' access to finances in an effort to reduce their ability to commit terrorist acts.[58]

**Tribunal** A specialized venue for enforcing international law. International tribunals can be formed by United Nations charter, Security Council resolution, or international treaty.

## International Courts and Tribunals

International courts and **tribunals** are the primary means for prosecuting terrorism and ensuring the legitimacy of counterterrorism policies and actions.

These special venues may be formed by UN Security Council resolution, UN charter, or international treaty.

The International Court of Justice (ICJ) is a prime example of an international court. As discussed previously in this section, the ICJ is the primary judicial organ of the UN. Formed by UN charter, it deals with all matters related to international law, including protecting human rights.

Another international court is the *International Criminal Court (ICC)*, which was the first permanent, treaty-based criminal court established within the international community. It is governed by the Rome Statute and, like the International Court of Justice, its seat is at The Hague, in the Netherlands.[59] The Rome Statute provides that the ICC "shall have the power to exercise its jurisdiction over persons for the most serious crimes of international concern . . . "[60]

Special courts and tribunals are established to enforce international law.

© heliopix/Shutterstock.com

The International Criminal Tribunal for Rwanda (ICTR) is an example of a tribunal. It was created by UN Security Council Resolution 955 on November 8, 1994.[61] Its purpose was to facilitate national reconciliation and maintain peace in Rwanda in response to genocide and other international law violations that were committed in the country over several months in 1994.[62] Resolutions like this one outline the tribunal's purpose, powers, jurisdiction, structure, composition, and procedural rules. Tribunals like the ICTR are generally established to try crimes related to a specific conflict and committed during a specific time frame.

---

**Exhibit: A Closer Look: The International Criminal Tribunal for Rwanda**

**Formation:** Created by UN Security Council Resolution 955 on November 8, 1994.

**Powers:** ICTR has power to prosecute individuals for violations of international law in Rwanda between January 1 and December 31 of 1994. It also has the power to prosecute citizens of Rwanda who committed such crimes in neighboring countries during the designated timeframe.

**Structure:** There are three trial chambers and one appeals chamber consisting of 16 independent judges, and no two judges may be nationals of the same country. The Office of the Prosecution is in charge of investigation and prosecution for both the trial and appellate level. The Registry administers and manages the Tribunal and provides judicial and legal support for the trial chambers and prosecution. The Tribunal includes a Witness & Victims Support Section, responsible for protecting witness security and ensuring their availability for court procedures. The Tribunal also includes a Defence Counsel & Detention Management Section, which ensures that suspects are provided with competent counsel and that detention of suspects conforms with international standards. Two other sections of the Tribunal include the Court Management Section, which provides support to the three trial chambers and appellate chamber to ensure smooth proceedings, and the

Procurement Section, which procures any goods or services required to support the operations of the ICTR.

**Governing Documents:** The governing documents of the ICTR include the ICTR Statute, annexed to Security Council Resolution 955, other Security Council Resolutions, Bilateral Agreements, and Directives.

**For more information:** Official ICTR Website **http://www.unictr.org/Home/tabid/36/Default.aspx**

Regardless of how an international court or tribunal is formed—whether it is by a UN Security Council resolution, UN charter, or international treaty—it is based on the notion that there is an international presence behind the proceedings. Such entities are excellent examples of international collaboration in the context of investigating and prosecuting terrorism as well as other matters of international law.

## Ethics and Professionalism: Prosecuting International Terrorism

On December 21, 1988, Pan Am Flight 103 exploded over Lockerbie, Scotland. The explosion killed all 243 passengers and 16 crew members as well as 11 Lockerbie residents, resulting in a total of 270 deaths.[63] Following the crash, a massive investigation took place in which the United States and United Kingdom joined forces for three years collecting evidence and interviewing witnesses. The investigation uncovered evidence indicating that explosives were placed in a suitcase originally dispatched from Malta and eventually loaded onto Flight 103 at Heathrow Airport in London. That suitcase contained clothing sold by a shopkeeper in Malta to a man he described as having a Libyan appearance, and whom he later identified as Abdel Baset al-Megrahi, a Libyan intelligence officer and head of security for Libyan Arab Airlines (LAA). The trigger for the explosion was a specific timer of which a substantial quantity had been supplied to Libya.[64]

As a result of this evidence, taken in context with the rest of the case, the court determined that the attacks were perpetrated by Libyan agents. Charges were brought against al-Megrahi and Lamin Khalifah Fhimah, an LAA station manager in Malta. Both al-Megrahi and Fhimah faced a Scottish trial, beginning in May 2000.[65] Fhimah was found not guilty, but Megrahi was convicted of 270 counts of murder and received a life sentence in 2001.[66]

Although Libya's leader, Muammar Gadhafi, claimed no personal involvement in the act, the country admitted responsibility in 2003 and the Gadhafi government agreed to pay the victims' families compensation.[67] Despite his government's admission of responsibility, Gadhafi lobbied for al-Megrahi's release from Scotland. Finally, in 2009 al-Megrahi was released from Scottish prison after he was diagnosed with terminal prostate cancer and given only months to live.[68] He was welcomed as a hero in Libya, where many claimed he was wrongly convicted based on a false identification by the Maltese shopkeeper. Despite his diagnosis, which influenced Scottish officials to grant his release, al-Megrahi survived much longer than the mere months predicted by doctors. In fact, although a London news source reported his death in May 2011, al-Megrahi's lawyer confirmed that he was still alive as of June 2011.

As civil unrest exploded in Libya against the Gadhafi regime in 2011, some former Libyan officials admitted publicly that the Lockerbie bombing was ordered by Gadhafi himself and that he lobbied on behalf of al-Megrahi to cover his own involvement. Some even alleged that al-Megrahi blackmailed Gadhafi into securing his release so that he would not divulge Gadhafi's hand in the event.[69] If the recent allegations concerning Gadhafi's involvement are true, who would prosecute him and in what venue? How should the prior trial and prosecution of al-Megrahi be dealt with? Further, regardless of Gadhafi's alleged involvement, was it appropriate for Scotland to grant al-Megrahi's 2009 release on humanitarian grounds, especially in light of the fact that he was alive years after he was said to have only months to live?

# Computer Crime

With the many technological breakthroughs and advancements over the past few decades, the criminal justice system has taken on an increased focus on cybercrime. **Cybercrime** is a relatively new term used frequently in both the news media and in scholarly articles as these crimes become more prevalent: it refers to crime committed utilizing computers and the Internet. Generally, it involves acquiring a person's or organization's sensitive information. The media has given much attention to issues surrounding cybercrime, particularly cases involving child pornography, unethical hacking, and copyright infringements.[70]

**Cybercrime** Crime committed utilizing a computer and the Internet.

## History of Cybercrime

Cybercrime came into existence even before the establishment of companies such as Microsoft or Apple Computer. In the 1960s and 1970s, a group of students from the Massachusetts Institute of Technology (MIT) created an organization called Tech Model Railroad Club (TMRC) that built sophisticated railroad models. The members of this club created advanced control systems for railroads using computer programming. They were considered the very first **white hat hackers**. Early hackers were considered white hat hackers or ethical hackers because they solved complex computer problems. If either software or hardware were not available, these hackers would develop them and solve the issue at hand. Today we have two types of hackers: white hat hackers and **black hat hackers**. The difference between the two types of hackers is that a white hat hacker values ethical behavior highly and expects this code to be honored by others. A black hat hacker, on the other hand, hacks with malicious intent.[71]

© Eugenio Marongiu/Shutterstock.com

Cybercrime is crime committed utilizing computers and the Internet.

**White hat hacker** An ethical computer hacker who hacks for beneficial reasons, such as solving complex problems.

**Black hat hacker** An unethical computer hacker who hacks with malicious intent to commit a crime.

In 1970, the computer became commercial with the development of the Altair 8800, which is considered the first personal computer (PC). In those days the computer did not come assembled, but rather the user had to build it—and the software—himself or herself. This process allowed early hackers to learn programming.

Hacking became more prevalent with the development of the Internet in the late 1980s. Using Internet access provided by early companies such as AOL, Prodigy, and CompuServe, online criminals and hackers could gain access to other people's personal information.

During the early 1990s, people became increasingly concerned with Internet privacy, or methods of keeping sensitive information safe. Based on these concerns the first encryption software was created, called PGP (Pretty Good Privacy), designed to hide sensitive information for online users. PGP, however, was also utilized by criminals to hide evidence of their crimes.

When the first online bank opened in 1994, the scope of cybercrime shifted and expanded, opening even more doors for cybercriminals. Phishing, cracking of passwords, and stealing people's information have become major threats, not just to the consumer, but to organizations and governments across the world.[72]

## Identity Theft

The *Federal Trade Commission (FTC)* is an independent organization that was created in 1914 to protect consumers. On a daily basis, the FTC polices crimes related to false advertising, credit card fraud, and any matter dealing with consumer protection. In recent years the FTC has also been tasked with investigating crimes relating to identity theft, and has created an entire division dealing only with identity theft.[73] **Identity theft** is the criminal act of stealing someone's identity with malicious intent. These identity thefts most often involve misuse of credit cards.

**Identity theft** The crime of stealing someone's identity and using it for malicious purposes.

Identity theft could be considered the crime of the 21st century because so many Americans are affected by it each year. According to the FTC, 2010 marked the 11th year in a row in which identify theft topped the list of FTC complaints.[74] In 2009, 11.2 million Americans were victims of identity theft, and the cost of these crimes was estimated to be around $54 million. The average cost per record (one person's information) is estimated to be around $200. When an organization is involved in data breaches, the average cost to the organization is $6.6 million. When you consider the fact that thousands of records get stolen at the same time, the amount adds up. For example, in 2008 more than 285 million records were breached, which is more than the combined total from 2001 through 2007. The FTC reported that 83% of these cases could have been avoided through simple and intermediate controls such as software updates, antivirus systems, and compliance with organizational policies and procedures.[75]

There is no "silver bullet" for information protection; there is no single technology or method that can be implemented to make information and assets 100% safe from internal and external threats. However, individuals and organizations can take steps to protect themselves. The National

Security Agency (NSA) has outlined a method for best practices relating to information protection that involves a three-dimensional layered defense approach called Defense-in-Depth (DiD). This method integrates people, process, and technology for better protection for the organization's critical information. One example of a layered defense approach that an organization could use is requiring computer logs (such as log-on times) and auditing those requirements. This process incorporates both technological safeguards (computer logs) and human supervision (auditing) to ensure safety of the organization's information.[76]

## Categories of Computer Crimes

Computer crime can generally be categorized as one of three types: **personal cybercrime**, which includes identity theft and harassment; **property cybercrime**, which includes damage to computer technology caused by malware; and **government cybercrime**, which covers cyberterrorism.[77]

### Personal and Property Cybercrime

Personal cybercrime is probably the category that most people are most familiar with. In addition to identity theft, personal cybercrimes include digital harassment such as *cyberstalking* (using social networking sites, search engines, forums, and discussion boards to pursue a victim), inappropriate email communication, etc.

Property cybercrime is also fairly common. This type of crime involves purposely infecting equipment with some type of malware. **Malware** is short for *malicious software* and is generally designed to disrupt or prevent further use of a system. There are two main groups of malware: viruses and worms, or Trojan horses. Viruses infect executable files on machines; when the executable file is run, the virus spreads to other executable files on the system. Worms are considered a little more complex, as they do not need an executable file to spread. A worm simply attaches to a file such as a Microsoft Word or Excel document, which is why it can spread so quickly when a user is attaching these files to an email. In essence, a worm will scan a computer network for vulnerabilities and will replicate through the vulnerability. Worms need no human interaction to spread and can therefore spread at an incredible speed.

A Trojan horse works a bit differently than a worm or a virus. In general terms, a Trojan horse is attached to a desirable piece of software to "tempt" a user to download and install it using the Internet. Spyware is a common way for a Trojan horse to be distributed. Spyware is self-installing software that gathers information such as Internet searches, shopping preferences, and passwords, and submits this information to a third party for commercial profit.

### Government Cybercrime: Cyberterrorism

**Cyberterrorism** is an unlawful method of attacking and threatening government computer systems and networks, and the information

**Personal cybercrime** Cybercrimes that involve a direct attack on a person, including identity theft and cyber harassment.

**Property cybercrime** Cybercrimes that involve a criminal purposely installing malware on computer equipment.

**Government cybercrime** Cybercrimes that involve attacks on government information systems, including cyberterrorism.

**Malware** Malicious software designed to disrupt or prevent further use of a system.

**Cyberterrorism** An unlawful method of attacking and threatening government computer systems and networks, and the information stored on these systems, to further political or social objectives.

stored on these systems, to further the cyberterrorist's political or social objectives. To fully qualify as cyberterrorism, an incident must result in violence against a person or property. Examples include water contamination, explosions, plane crashes, or other attacks that lead to physical injury, death, or severe economic loss.[78] Cyberspace is constantly under attack, and cyberterrorism is becoming increasingly well known in every country across the world. Counterterrorism organizations in the United States have reported that close to 140 foreign intelligence organizations attempt to hack into official U.S. government agencies on a regular basis.[79]

Cyberterrorism has become more organized, especially by terror organizations such as Hamas, the Islamic Jihad Group, and Al-Qaeda. The terrorist attacks of 9/11 have raised the general public's and government's awareness of the implications of cyberterrorism and terror in general. The U.S. government has created 11 critical infrastructures in an effort to determine where likely terror attacks will occur and how these infrastructures should be protected in the event that cyberterrorism occurs. The 11 infrastructures are electricity distribution, gas production, oil and oil products production, telecommunication, water supply, agriculture, heating, public health, transportation, financial services, and security services.[80] The DHS states that the protection of these critical infrastructures requires cooperation between the public and private sector.

Because people often associate cyberterrorism with terrorist attacks, it is important to discuss whether cyberterrorism is having an impact on the terror rate. Little evidence exists that it is. However, links between the two can be found when discussing money laundering, computer resources, and transit lines. For example, Osama bin Laden, the mastermind behind the 9/11 attacks, was able to use computer resources to communicate through the use of public Internet access.[81]

Cyberterrorism is appealing to terrorist organizations because it can reach a global audience and can potentially make a bigger impact than committing a violent act in a single location.

Obviously, a cyberterrorist's weapon of choice is the computer. The use of the Internet makes it easier for terrorists to meet people with similar thought processes and ideals. Therefore, groups and organizations can actually be entirely created utilizing technology.[82]

Cyberterrorism is appealing to terrorist organizations because it can reach a global audience and can potentially make a bigger impact than committing a violent act in a single location. The Internet is very important both for personal and business use, and it is virtually impossible to close it down completely, so governments must carefully consider how to protect their countries and information from this type of terror.[83] With the use of technology such as honeypots, it is possible for governments and organizations to deter cyberterrorist attacks before they even occur.[84] *Honeypots* are traps that are designed to detect unauthorized access to information systems. Usually a honeypot is designed to look like a system on a network, but is in fact isolated from the rest of the organization's network and is monitored for attacks.[85] Honeypots can prevent unauthorized access of information technology.[86]

## Cybercrime Statistics

The FBI publishes data on cybercrimes in the annual Internet Crime Report, created by the Internet Crime Complaint Center (IC3). In 2015, this report claimed that the FBI receives an average of 24,001 complaints of cybercrime each month. Since its beginnings, the Internet Crime Report has shown a fairly steady increase in annual reports of cybercrimes. In 2000, when IC3 was created, it received almost 17,000 complaints. In 2010 the IC3 had an incident report of 303,000, with an average of 25,000 complaints per month. Figure 13.3 lists the report's findings on the most frequent types of cybercrime.

### FIGURE 13.3  TYPES OF CYBERCRIME

| Type | Percentage |
|------|------------|
| Non-Delivery Payment of Merchandise | 14.4% |
| FBI-Related Scams | 13.2% |
| Identity Theft | 9.8% |
| Computer Crime | 9.1% |
| Miscellaneous Fraud | 8.6% |
| Advance Fee Fraud | 7.6% |
| Spam | 6.9% |
| Auction Fraud | 5.9% |
| Credit Card Fraud | 5.3% |
| Overpayment Fraud | 5.3% |

The IC3 also performs demographic statistics on its reported cases. As of 2015, on top of that list is the state of California, with 14.53% of all cases. Florida with 8.47% and Texas with 7.67% follow. For a detailed report on this data or updated data, refer to the IC3 website.[87] Or go to https://pdf.ic3.gov/2015_IC3Report.pdf.

## Cybercrime Investigations and International Cybercrime

The Internet is considered relatively new, and over the past 25 years this space has changed drastically. Since its creation, the Internet has become affordable and available to nearly everyone. Because of this, several laws and statutes have been created on the state and federal levels that are intended to protect innocent users from crimes committed online.

Enforcing cybercrime laws, however, has proven challenging. There are several reasons for this, the main one being jurisdiction. Because not all state laws are the same, cybercriminals may have to be tried on a federal level instead of at the state level. The area gets even more complex when considering the fact that cybercrime cases often originate outside the United States. Though there are some international regulatory bodies such as the United Nations (UN) and the European Union that set regulatory requirements for their members, other nations have few or no requirements. When crimes originate from a different region or from a less regulated country, it becomes extremely difficult to prosecute a criminal.

Another issue with cybercrimes is anonymity and identity. Before we can even consider jurisdiction, it is necessary to discover where and who the criminal is. Obviously this is a difficult problem with online crimes because there are so many technologies one can use to hide one's identity. There are services that are able to mask an IP address by routing traffic through various servers. This type of technology makes it difficult to track down the criminal.

Finally, the nature of the evidence in cybercrime cases can also make them difficult to investigate and prosecute. The first step in a cybercrime case is to image the evidence (make a duplicate), which is why it is critical to create a hash value before and after the image has been created. A *hash value* is a numerical representation that represents a piece of data. No two hash values are the same; in other words, if someone changes any of the data on the evidence item, such as adding or deleting a file, the hash value will change, and, therefore, will show that the evidence has been tampered with. This is why protecting the evidence and chain of custody become so extremely critical. An investigator can easily contaminate the evidence during the investigation unless precautions are taken.[88]

**Critical Thinking**
The Internet is relatively new and, while there are some regulations and laws regarding this technology, no common laws have been introduced worldwide to make it easier to control and prosecute these types of crimes. How do you suggest the United States should cooperate with most of the world regarding this issue? Is the creation of a worldwide court an option to keep these crimes under control?

## New Technologies in Crime Fighting

Thirty years ago, few people thought that technology and computers would be such a big part of everyday life. Because most people have a computer or at the very least have access to one, by nature, computer crimes have increased. When a cybercrime is committed, it generally involves a computer. This computer and its storage and activities become a place where evidence is stored or recorded. By the early 1990s, computer tools were available to assist in digital investigations; however, these tools were not yet commercially available. As computers continued to evolve, software companies started producing software that was available to individuals and organizations, not just governments. Today there are several computer forensics tools available.

## Computer Forensics Tools

The most common and widely accepted tools on the market today are the Forensics Toolkit (FTK) by AccessData and EnCase by Guidance Software. Both of these software suites are considered premier forensics tools and are acceptable tools for presenting evidence in the court system.

The FTK and EnCase suites include functions and features allowing investigators to acquire and create images. These include registry investigations that contain information regarding browser history, when users log on and off, what devices have been connected to the computer and what documents have been

Computer forensics tools such as FTK and EnCase allow investigators to obtain information on a suspect's browser history, files, and more.

edited or created, as well as password recovery tools. Another critical component in computer forensic investigations is *data carving*, which allows investigators to reconstruct files that are fragmented (deleted or embedded). Data carving can be very time-consuming, but it may be well worth it if the files are critical to the case.

Several cases in the 21st century have been investigated utilizing EnCase and FTK. One of the most famous was the case of the BTK Killer, discussed in the opening case study, where investigators were able to identify Rader based on files recovered from a floppy disk. Another famous case in which computer forensics tools were utilized was the 2005 murder trial of Scott Peterson, who was sentenced to death after being found guilty of murdering his wife and unborn child. During the investigation, investigators utilized the FTK software and GPS data from Peterson's car and cell phone as well as Internet history from his personal and business computers. The data revealed that Peterson had been viewing classified ads for a fishing boat, as well as maps, fishing reports, and charts of currents in the San Francisco Bay area. Peterson also zoomed in on a map close to Brooks Island, near where the remains of his wife and unborn child were later discovered.

The key to an investigation is to collect evidence, and it is important to follow generally acceptable methods when handling evidence. To ensure that the evidence can be accepted by the court system, a forensic investigator must ensure that documentation is kept, and at the very least clearly document where the evidence was stored, who had access to it, and what was done to the evidence during the investigation process. Ensuring proper documentation will ensure that the evidence is not tampered with and is kept in its original state should the case go to court.

The initial step to any investigation is to seize the evidence. Once the evidence is secured, an image of the digital evidence must be created so that the investigator does not work with a live evidence item. Once the image has been created, the investigator can start the digital forensics investigation utilizing FTK or another forensic tool.

As the world moves ahead with new technologies, it is also important that these software suites keep up-to-date to ensure compatibility. FTK has a tool called Mobile Phone Examiner that allows for investigation of cellular devices.

Another upcoming technology that will pose a challenge to computer forensics and businesses as a whole is cloud computing, which is a type of technology that allows for remote storage and other services designed to help an organization. Essentially, it will allow organizations to increase the capacity of their systems quickly with far less resources than acquiring their own technology. Another benefit of cloud computing is savings, as this type of technology does not require additional training, new employees, or acquisition of new software licenses. Cloud computing is designed to extend existing capabilities and is considered a subscription-based service.

Cloud computing is still at an early stage, and research has shown many security threats to this type of service.[89] Most notably, there are so many cloud computing services that it is safe to conclude that not all of them reside in the United States. Hence forensic investigators are likely to face challenges related to control of the evidence, including the collection, preservation, and validation.[90]

© anselmus/Shutterstock.com

With surveillance cameras at malls, airports, subways, and many other public buildings, people are on camera in some form for much of their day.

## Cameras

In the 21st century, criminal justice has changed in more ways than just digital forensics. Today, after 9/11, we live in a world where we are on camera in some form or another for much of our day. Surveillance cameras are located at malls, airports, subways, and many other public buildings.

The Department of Homeland Security has given millions of dollars to states and local law enforcement agencies to purchase high-tech surveillance technologies. In recent years, several cities have received grants and financing from the

DHS. St. Paul, Minnesota received a grant of $1.2 million for the installation of 60 cameras downtown. Pittsburgh, Pennsylvania received a similar grant allowing them to install 83 cameras downtown.[91] Smaller towns have also received funding from the DHS to install surveillance equipment in parks and other public places.

Cameras also have a big impact on police officers and their investigations. For example, car thefts have long been a major problem; in 2006, statistics indicated that a car was stolen in the United States every 26.4 seconds, and only 12.6% of cases were cleared by arrest. New technologies in cameras have allowed police to develop automated license plate recognition systems that can be used by patrol cars or helicopters to track auto thefts. The cameras can scan license plates at a distance and compare them to a database of registered car thefts.[92]

### Should Law Enforcement use Body Cameras?

In June 2015 as a result of recent events between citizens and the police, Congress took symbolic action on police body cameras by supporting and encouraging police agencies to equip their law enforcement officers to wear body cameras while on duty. The resolution was sponsored by Rep. Al Green, D-Texas, in response to the resignation of a Texas police officer accused of police brutality.[100] Due to the recent riots in Ferguson, Missouri and Baltimore, Maryland and other cities, police body cameras have become a popular item of discussion and controversy.

### What are some of the Pros and Cons towards the use of Body Cameras?

### Pros

**Prevent Violence** — A 2013 University of Cambridge study found that when police wear body cameras, both police and respondents are less likely to use violence. The study found a drop in use of force by more than 50 percent. Body cameras could thus make the streets safer for both officers and the general public.[100]

**Accountability** — Officers wearing body cameras would hold police departments accountable for their conduct. Body cameras could reduce the number of cases like Ferguson and Baltimore, where there was no way for the public to know for sure what had happened and having to rely on amateur video to determine the outcomes, when available.[100]

**Human Side of Policing** — Using body cameras continuously could improve the public's view of policing by showing the human side that officers are citizens, too. Police officers could also be more understanding of citizen's complaints and be more sympathetic when dealing with the public.[100]

### Cons

**Privacy** — Some advocates believe that body cameras are an invasion of privacy, as they provide state-owned footage collected by law enforcement officers. When police cameras are running, the cameras capture civilian and police behavior that may not necessarily need to be recorded.

This, most people would agree that this is an invasion of a person's rights. Do you believe that all defendants need to or want their arrests recorded? Do you believe that all bystanders want to be in those videos when shown in court? Isn't this a violation of someone's privacy?[100]

**Limitations** — Shouldn't there be guidelines for police as to when they can turn their cameras on and off?Many current policies encourage the cameras to be turned on only when police are among the public. "The only time people can know that the officers have not been turning on the cameras would be in a scenario where there is a complaint against the officer," Bill Sousa, associate criminology professor at the University of Nevada told the **Huffington Post**. "A technological malfunction or forgetfulness could incriminate officers when misconduct has not occurred."[100] After all, shouldn't citizens be protected from being filmed by the police as long as they have not done anything wrong? However, consider what's in the "best interest of protecting our society", shouldn't this trump our right to privacy?

## Biometrics

**Biometrics** A method of authenticating a person's identity through behavioral or physiological characteristics such as iris scanners and fingerprinting.

Another relatively new technology utilized today for identification is **biometrics**, which is an automated method of recognizing a person based on behavioral or physiological characteristics. Biometric tools can authenticate a person's identity in a variety of ways, such as fingerprints, hand geometry, or handwriting, or by iris, retinal, vein, or voice scanning. Biometrics has become a very popular method of authentication for highly secure areas as identity theft becomes more common and passwords are becoming less secure. Biometrics is used in federal, state, and local governments, as well as in military and commercial applications. Law enforcement and the health care sector have significantly benefited from this technology.[93]

## 3D Imaging Software

© polygraphus/Shutterstock.com

Biometric tools can authenticate a person's identity through fingerprints, hand geometry, and other methods.

Technology is becoming an increasingly larger part of law enforcement as a tool to solve crimes. One of the newer technologies that allows investigators to reconstruct a crime scene is 3D imaging software. This 3D technology is so sophisticated that it is actually possible to recreate a scene where a bullet has been fired and compare that to previous cases involving bullets fired. The Forensic Science Institute in Connecticut, for example, uses the DeltaSphere-3000 3D Scene Digitizer to recreate crime scenes.

3D imaging software can also be used to investigate terrorism. Japan has employed facial-recognition technology to help prevent foreign nationals from committing crimes. Law enforcement organizations in Germany and the United Kingdom are using 3D software to reconstruct three-dimensional images of public places and structures, which assist law enforcement in averting future terrorist attempts.[94]

> **Critical Thinking**
>
> Surveillance is a controversial subject because it breaches the Fourth Amendment to the U.S. Constitution. How would you propose finding a compromise to allow certain forms of surveillance?

## Mobile Devices

With the introduction of a plethora of new mobile devices and operating systems, it is important to consider a few important issues. While these mobile devices (such as the iPad, iPhone, BlackBerry, etc.) have become an integral part of society and how people do business, they do pose a challenge to the computer forensics field as these devices become more complex with features, Internet connectivity, and greater storage capabilities. These devices, similar to PCs, collect information regarding the user and the user's habits such as Internet searches, text messages, and even emails. These may be extremely valuable to investigators, law enforcement, and the court system. Therefore, it is important that investigators strictly adhere to the chain of evidence when performing forensics investigations on mobile devices.[95]

> **Career Connections: Computer Forensics**
>
> Computer forensics is a relatively new field, but the job outlook is very strong. Because of increased usage of digital technology everywhere in our society, and the fact that computer crimes have become a part of everyday life, the need for computer forensics investigators is increasing every year.
>
> Computer forensics experts serve a variety of roles during the criminal investigation. First, these experts uncover and analyze data from digital devices and preserve the data to be used as evidence in court. Uncovering data may entail examining digital evidence on hard drives, storage devices (USB drives, iPods, etc.), cell phones, PDAs, or other electronic devices that may be used in a court setting. Their tasks may include retrieving deleted data in many forms, such as emails, documents, Internet history, and formatted hard disks. During the investigation, a computer forensics expert analyzes and determines the availability and reliability of digital evidence and helps prepare this evidence for trial. A computer forensics expert may work on a variety of cases involving crimes such as hackings, embezzlement, identity theft, and security breaches. The complexity of an investigation can range from a personal computer to an entire network server and its traffic.
>
> An individual who wishes to start in the computer forensics field will need a degree in computer forensics or a related degree such as criminal justice, computer science, information security, or engineering. The individual will likely also need additional computer forensics training. As with any rapidly changing field, it is critical that professionals stay current with training and certifications even after entering the job market.

This type of work requires a person to be very analytical and to have a good foundation in technology, both hardware and operating systems as well as individual software packages such as Microsoft Office. A computer forensics expert is generally tech-savvy and enjoys investigation of digital cases. Computer forensics experts must also be able to communicate effectively, in both non-technical and technical language, and this type of work may require presenting evidence in court to a judge and jury. In addition, computer forensics experts should constantly keep themselves updated on new technological advancements and techniques and current events in the field.[96]

## Freedom vs. Security

With the development of new technologies to combat crime, privacy in society has rapidly decreased. Citizens are constantly the subjects of camera surveillance and other digital monitoring issues that some say interfere with their basic rights, including those granted by the Fourth Amendment.

One study completed by the British government, which has utilized cameras throughout the country, has determined that surveillance has no overall impact on crimes. Studies have also been done in Los Angeles with similar results. However, not all studies agree. Research studies in Chicago, Baltimore, and Washington, D.C. have concluded that in certain areas surveillance has been able to decrease the monthly crime numbers.[97]

Since the events of 9/11, there have been no terrorist attacks on the United States. Many people claim that it is because of the new policies introduced in the months and years following 9/11, including the Patriot Act, discussed earlier in the chapter. While some argue that the Patriot Act is the reason we have not had further attacks, other groups, including the American Civil Liberties Union (ACLU), have taken issue with the Patriot Act. They claim it has taken away some of the privacy rights provided to Americans in the Fourth Amendment.

As the U.S. government continues to establish new policies and utilize new technologies to combat terrorism, cybercrime, and other 21st century criminal justice issues, it is perpetually walking a fine line. Government officials must find the right balance between doing what is necessary to protect the homeland from outside attacks and, at the same time, refraining from infringing on American citizens' rights. This balance of security and freedom remains a controversial issue, and the debate continues to this day.

## Chapter Summary

- The focus on homeland security in the United States has grown since September 11, 2001. It encompasses preparedness, response, and recovery efforts at all levels of government in an effort to protect the safety and security of U.S. citizens. Furthermore, it addresses all threats to the security of the country, including natural disasters such as a hurricane or tornado as well as manmade events such as a terrorist attack.

- The Department of Homeland Security (DHS) was established in 2002 and acts as the coordinating body for response to national incidents. The department is made up of many federal offices and agencies, including the Federal Emergency Management Agency (FEMA). The legal framework, including sources of power and authority, of homeland security in the United States is complex and still evolving. The major pieces of the federal framework are the Patriot Act of 2001 and the Homeland Security Act of 2002. States also have varying sources of authority in this framework, but one unifying document is the Emergency Management Assistance Compact (EMAC), an agreement that allows states to share resources to respond regionally to an event.

- The impact of 21st-century homeland security in the United States may be seen in many facets of society. Following the terrorist attacks on September 11, 2001, there was a rise in hate crimes in the United States against specific groups of people. In response, the government placed a priority on prosecuting perpetrators of these hate crimes. At the same time, in an effort to prevent future terrorist attacks, the government increased surveillance and screening measures at airports. Critics of these measures argue that the government is curtailing civil liberties guaranteed by the U.S. Constitution by threatening privacy rights and due process.

- International criminal justice represents a movement in the international community to enforce international law, including investigating and prosecuting terrorism. Because terrorism is a global threat in the 21st century that crosses international boundaries, it is vital that countries collaborate with one another to identify and deal with terrorists. Special venues such as the International Court of Justice (ICJ), the International Criminal Court (ICC), and specific criminal courts and tribunals exist to enforce violations of international law, including terrorism. These venues are established and run with international support, lending legitimacy to their proceedings. In addition, the international community works together through international policing, extradition treaties, and United Nations efforts to prevent and respond to the threat of terrorism.

- Cybercrime is a new type of crime facing the criminal justice system in the 21st century. Cybercrimes are crimes committed using a computer and Internet resources; they can be classified as personal cybercrime (identity theft, cyberstalking), property cybercrime (malicious software), or government cybercrime (government systems and networks). A common type of cybercrime is identity theft, which is extremely costly and time-consuming for both organizations and victims.

- Cybercrimes can be investigated utilizing computer forensics software. Several types of this software exist in the market today. Both EnCase and the FTK Toolkit are law-enforcement endorsed for investigating cybercrimes.
- Surveillance is increasingly becoming an important issue to the public. Research has shown mixed results as to whether increased surveillance is effective in reducing crimes. Other technologies introduced and designed to deter crimes and which make investigations more accurate and less time-consuming are biometrics and 3D imaging software for reconstruction of crime scenes.

## Critical Thinking?

1. Homeland Security deals with both natural and manmade threats. What are issues common to both and what sets them apart from one another?

2. Is the legal framework that supports current homeland security measures sufficient? Are the roles of federal, state, and local players clearly defined?

3. There has been an increased focus on homeland security in the U.S. since the attacks of September 11, 2001. Is the country better prepared to prevent or respond to such an event today?

4. How can international response to terrorism be improved? Is there sufficient coordination and collaboration to deal with the international threat?

5. The International Court of Justice and the International Criminal Court act as world courts to prosecute violations of international law. With these institutions already in place, is the formation of other specialized international courts and tribunals necessary?

6. What are some of the positives and negatives regarding camera surveillance in today's society?

7. What are some of the challenges a computer forensics investigator faces regarding new technologies?

8. Identify theft is among the most common cybercrimes. What should you do to prevent identity theft, and how can you protect yourself?

9. Why is it important for a computer forensics investigator to be a great communicator? Consider the different venues in which such an investigator may have to communicate.

10. As cybercrime and security breaches become more common, will technology gradually become a less integral part of society? Why or why not?

## Media

**FEMA:** http://www.fema.gov/ FEMA's website offers a wide variety of information regarding the agency's planning, preparedness, response, and recovery efforts, and provides information on what citizens can do to better prepare themselves for an emergency.

**National Response Framework Resource Center:**
https://www.fema.gov/pdf/emergency/nrf/nrf-core.pdf.
The National Response Framework Resource Center provides the most up-to-date information about the federal government's framework for dealing with an emergency on a national level. It acts as a library for documents related to the NRF, including annexes and reference materials.

**The International Criminal Police Organization (INTERPOL):** http://www.interpol.int/ INTERPOL's website has a wealth of information about the organization's structure and initiatives as well as relevant current events. The website is updated frequently with news stories and materials in multiple languages.

**Department of Homeland Security:** https://www.dhs.gov/topic/cybersecurity. This website offers important information regarding homeland protection and cybersecurity.

**Federal Trade Commission:** http://www.ftc.gov/bcp/edu/microsites/idtheft/ The FTC website provides information about identity theft and how to report such crimes.

**Computer Forensics World:** http://www.computerforensicsworld.com/ This website is a great resource for publications, research tools, and other computer forensics questions.

# Endnotes

[1]     Criminal Justice Schools. (2010). *10 Famous Criminal Cases Cracked by Forensics.* Retrieved from http://www.criminaljusticeschools.org/blog/10-famous-cases-cracked-by-forensics

[2]     Department of Homeland Security. (2007). *National Computer Forensic Institute Unveiled.* Retrieved from http://www.dhs.gov/xnews/releases/pr_1173477460607.shtm

[3]     *Oxford English Dictionary.* (n.d.). Retrieved from http://www.oed.com/view/Entry/199608?redirectedFrom=terrorism#eid

[4]     22 U.S.C.§ 2656f(d)

[5]     U.S. Army Timeline of Terrorism.

[6]     Ibid.

[7]     Ibid.

[8]     Oklahoma City National Memorial & Museum. (2011). *A Look at the Numbers.* Retrieved from http://www.oklahomacitynationalmemorial.org/secondary.php?section=5&catid=145

[9]     Homeland Security Act of 2002, 6 U.S.C. §§101-557 (2002).

[10]    Insurance Information Institute. (2011). *Catastrophes: U.S.* Retrieved from http://www.iii.org/facts_statistics/catastrophes-us.html

11   Citizen Corps. (n.d.). *About Citizen Corps.* Retrieved from http://www.citizencorps.gov/about/

12   Ibid.

13   Federal Emergency Management Agency (FEMA). (n.d.). *Ready: Prepare. Plan. Stay Informed.* Retrieved from http://www.ready.gov/

14   Ibid.

15   United Nations Office for the Coordination of Humanitarian Affairs (OCHA). (2011). "Japan Earthquake & Tsunami." *Situation Report No. 16.* Retrieved from http://reliefweb.int/updates?sl=environment-report_listing%252Ctaxonomy_index_tid_content_format-10%252Ctaxonomy_index_tid_source-1503%252Ctaxonomy_index_tid_country-128

16   Catastrophic Health Emergencies Act of Maryland, Md. Health-Gen. Code Ann. § 18-905 (2002).

17   Robert T. Stafford Disaster Relief and Emergency Assistance Act, 42 U.S.C. §§ 5121–5206 (2009).

18   Ibid.

19   Ibid.

20   Ibid.

21   Uniting and Strengthening America by Providing Appropriate Tools Required to Intercept and Obstruct Terrorism Act of 2001 ("Patriot Act"), Pub. L. No. 07–156, 116 Stat. 272 (2001).

22   Bullock, J. A., et al. (2006). *Introduction to Homeland Security.* New York, NY: Elsevier, 41–42.

23   Department of Homeland Security (DHS). (2003, February 28). *Homeland Security Presidential Directive 5: Management of Domestic Incidents.* Retrieved from http://www.dhs.gov/xabout/laws/gc_1214592333605.shtm#1

24   Ibid.

25   Post-Katrina Emergency Management Reform Act of 2006, Pub. L. No. 109–295, 120 Stat. 1355 (2006).

26   Department of Homeland Security Office of Inspector General, Office of Inspections and Special Reviews. (2006, March). *A Performance Review of FEMA's Disaster Management Activities in Response to Hurricane Katrina.* Retrieved from http://www.dhs.gov/xoig/assets/mgmtrpts/OIG_06-32_Mar06.pdf

27   Ibid.

28   Ibid.

29   Ibid.

30   Emergency Management Assistance Compact, Pub. L. No. 104-321, 110 Stat. 3877 (1996).

31   American-Arab Anti-Discrimination Committee. (2003). *Report on Hate Crimes and Discrimination Against Arab Americans: The Post-September 11 Backlash September 11, 2001–October 11, 2002.* Retrieved from http://www.adc.org/PDF/hcr02.pdf

32   Ibid.

33  U.S. Department of Justice. (n.d.). *Initiative to Combat Post-9/11 Discriminatory Backlash*. Retrieved from http://www.justice.gov/crt/legalinfo/discrimupdate.php

34  *United States v. Syring*, 522 F. Supp. 2d 125 (D.D.C. 2007).

35  U.S. Department of Justice, n.d.

36  Ibid.

37  International Court of Justice. (n.d.). *The Court*. Retrieved from http://www.icj-cij.org/court/index.php?p1=1&PHPSESSID=7a3b31f1d2a92d51efc5cb98b1612b96

38  Ibid.

39  Ibid.

40  International Court of Justice (ICJ). (n.d.). *Statute of the International Court of Justice: Chapter 1: Organization of the Court*. Retrieved from http://www.icj-cij.org/documents/index.php?p1=4&p2=2&p3=0#CHAPTER_I

41  International Court of Justice. (2011). *List of Contentious Cases by Date of Introduction*. Retrieved from http://www.icj-cij.org/docket/index.php?p1=3&p2=3

42  Corfu Channel case (*United Kingdom v. Albania*), 1949 I.C.J. Rep. 244. Retrieved from http://www.icj-cij.org/docket/files/1/1663.pdf

43  Corfu Channel case (*United Kingdom v. Albania*), Preliminary Objection, 1948 I.C.J. Rep. 15. Retrieved from http://www.icj-cij.org/docket/files/1/1569.pdf

44  Corfu Channel case (*United Kingdom v. Albania*), 1949 I.C.J. Rep. 244.

45  ICJ, 2011.

46  INTERPOL. (2011a). *About INTERPOL: Overview*. Retrieved from http://www.interpol.int/About-INTERPOL/Overview

47  INTERPOL. (2011b). *Terrorism*. Retrieved from http://www.interpol.int/Crime-areas/Terrorism/Terrorism

48  Ibid.

49  Europol. (2011). *Frequently Asked Questions: What Is Europol's Mission?* Retrieved from https://www.europol.europa.eu/faq

50  Europol. (2010). *Europol Profile*. Retrieved from https://www.europol.europa.eu/sites/default/files/publications/edoc-465620-v1-europol_profile_-_en.pdf

51  Ibid.

52  Garcia, M. J., & Doyle, C. (2010). *Extradition To and From the United States: Overview of the Law and Recent Treaties*. Retrieved from http://www.fas.org/sgp/crs/misc/98-958.pdf

53  Ibid.

54  *Kostotas v. Roche*, 931 F.2d 169, 171 (1st Cir. 1991), citing *Eain v. Wilkes*, 641 F.2d 504, 512 (7th Cir. 1981).

55  United Nations. (2011). *Counter-Terrorism Implementation Task Force*. Retrieved from http://www.un.org/en/terrorism/ctitf/index.shtml

56    Ibid.

57    United Nations. (n.d.). *Working Groups.* Retrieved from http://www.un.org/terrorism/workinggroups.shtml

58    United Nations. (n.d.). *Working Group on Tackling the Financing of Terrorism.* Retrieved from http://www.un.org/terrorism/financing.shtml

59    International Criminal Court. (n.d.). *About the Court.* Retrieved from http://www.icc-cpi.int/Menus/ICC/About+the+Court/

60    International Criminal Court. (2002). *Rome Statute of the International Criminal Court* (I.C.J. Doc. A/CONF.183/9). Retrieved from http://untreaty.un.org/cod/icc/statute/english/rome_statute(e).pdf

61    UN Security Council. (1994). *Resolution 955* (UN Doc. S/RES/955). Retrieved from http://www.unictr.org/Portals/0/English/Legal/Resolutions/English/955e.pdf

62    International Criminal Tribunal for Rwanda. (n.d.). *About ICTR.* Retrieved from http://www.unictr.org/AboutICTR/GeneralInformation/tabid/101/Default.aspx

63    Federal Bureau of Investigation (FBI). (2003). *A Byte Out of History: Solving a Complex Case of International Terrorism.* Retrieved from http://www.fbi.gov/news/stories/2003/december/panam121903

64    BBC News. (2009a). *Megrahi: "A Convenient Scapegoat?"* Retrieved from http://news.bbc.co.uk/2/hi/uk_news/scotland/8211596.stm

65    Scottish Criminal Cases Review Commission. (2007). *News Release: Abdelbaset Ali Mohmed Al Megrahi.* Retrieved from http://www.sccrc.org.uk/ViewFile.aspx?id=293

66    Ibid.

67    FBI, 2003.

68    BBC News. (2009b). *Megrahi: Profile of a Bomber.* Retrieved from http://news.bbc.co.uk/2/hi/uk_news/scotland/7728434.stm

69    Associated Press. (2011). "Report: Gadhafi Ordered Lockerbie Bombing." *MSNBC News.* Retrieved from http://www.msnbc.msn.com/id/41734924/ns/world_news-europe/

70    Babu, M. (2004). "What Is Cybercrime?" *Computer Crime Research Center.* Retrieved from http://www.crime-research.org/analytics/702/

71    Schell, B. H., & Martin, C. (2004). *Cybercrime: A Reference Handbook.* Santa Barbara, CA: ABC-CLIO.

72    Thomas, J. (2006). *Cybercrime: A Revolution in Terrorism and Criminal Behavior Creates Change in the Criminal Justice System.* Retrieved from http://voices.yahoo.com/cybercrime-revolution-terrorism-criminal-53862.html

73    Creditor Web. (2011). *Federal Trade Commission.* Retrieved from http://www.creditorweb.com/definition/federal-trade-commission.html

74    Federal Trade Commission. (2011). *2010 Consumer Complaints.* Retrieved from http://www.ftc.gov/opa/2011/03/topcomplaints.shtm

75   Godwin, G. (2010). "2010 FTC Identity Theft Statistics." *Examiner.com*. Retrieved from http://www.examiner.com/pop-culture-in-detroit/2010-ftc-identity-theft-statistics

76   Lovaas, P. (2010). *A Holistic IT Audit Program*.

77   Babu, 2004.

78   Denning, D. (2000). *Cyberterrorism*. Retrieved from http://www.cs.georgetown.edu/~denning/infosec/cyberterror.html

79   Stanton, T. H. (2008). *Defending Cyberspace*. Retrieved from http://advanced.jhu.edu/bin/g/z/Defending_Cyberspace.pdf

80   DHS. (2003). *Homeland Security Presidential Directive 7: Critical Infrastructure Identification, Prioritization and Protection*. Retrieved from http://www.dhs.gov/xabout/laws/gc_1214597989952.shtm

81   Nagre, D., & Warade, P. (2008a). *Cyber Terrorism*. Retrieved from www.contrib.andrew.cmu.edu/~dnagre/Final_Report_dnagre_pwarade.pdf

82   Gordon, S. (2010). *Cyberterrorism*. Retrieved from www.symantec.com/avcenter/reference/cyberterrorism.pdf

83   Tucher, D. (2000). *The Future of Armed Resistance: Cyberterror? Mass Destruction*. Retrieved from http://www.nps.edu/Academics/Centers/CTIW/files/substate_conflict_dynamics.pdf

84   Science Daily. (2011). *How Do We Fight the War Against Cyber Terrorism?* Retrieved from http://www.sciencedaily.com/releases/2011/04/110411103717.htm

85   Honeynet Project. (2005). *Know Your Enemy: GenII Honeynets*. Retrieved from http://old.honeynet.org/papers/gen2/

86   Science Daily, 2011.

87   FBI. (2010). *2010 IC3 Annual Report*. Retrieved from http://www.ic3.gov/media/annualreports.aspx

88   Nagre, D., & Warade, P. (2008b). *Cyberterrorism: Vulnerabilities and Policy Issues*. Retrieved from http://www.andrew.cmu.edu/user/dnagre/

89   Lawton, G. (2011). "Cloud Computing Poses New Forensic Challenges." *SearchCloudComputing*. Retrieved from http://searchcloudcomputing.techtarget.com/feature/Cloud-computing-crime-poses-unique-forensics-challenges

90   Ibid.

91   Head, T. (n.d.). "Big Brother Is Watching: A History of Government Surveillance Programs." *About.com Civil Liberties*. Retrieved from http://civilliberty.about.com/od/waronterror/tp/Surveillance-History.htm

92   Ibid.

93   Biometric Consortium. (2011). *An Introduction to Biometrics*. Retrieved from http://www.biometrics.org/html/introduction.html

94   Family Home Security. (2011). *The Latest in Crime Fighting Technologies*. Retrieved from http://www.familyhomesecurity.com/the-latest-in-crime-fighting-technology/

95    NIST. (2009). *Mobile Forensics and Security*. Retrieved from http://csrc.nist. gov/groups/SNS/mobile_security/index.html

96    Criminal Justice Careers & Education. (2011). *Computer Forensics Job Description*. Retrieved from http://www.criminaljusticeschoolinfo.com/ computer-forensics-job-description.html

97    Homeland Security News Wire. (2011). *Do Security Cameras Deter Crime?* Retrieved from http://www.homelandsecuritynewswire.com/ do-security-cameras-deter-crime

98    Bischoff, P. (2016). A breakdown of the Patriot Act, Freedom Act, and FISA. Retrieved from https://www.comparitech.com/blog/ vpn-privacy/a-breakdown-of-the-patriot-act-freedom-act-and-fisa/

99    Baum, E. NEWSMAX (2015). 5 Pros and Cons of Police Wearing Body Cameras. Retrieved from http://www.newsmax.com/FastFeatures/ police-body-cameras-pros-and-cons/2015/06/30/id/652871/.

# GLOSSARY

**Absconder**   One who leaves without authorization. This term is usually used in reference to walk-offs from work crews, work release centers, halfway houses, and other inmate areas not inside the main secure facility.

**Actus reus**   The act that is committed in a crime.

**Adjudication hearing**   A hearing in which the juvenile offender is found to either be delinquent or not delinquent.

**Administrative law**   The area of law that controls, creates, and/or governs the administrative and regulatory agencies of the government.

**Aftercare**   The process of providing continued treatment and recovery support following the conclusion of intensive or residential treatment programming.

**Age of criminal responsibility**   The general age at which a juvenile can be found criminally responsible; varies from state to state.

**Age of majority**   The age at which a person reaches adulthood in the eyes of the law. This age is generally 18, but can vary from state to state.

**Aggravating circumstances**   Circumstances that go above and beyond the basic requirements for a crime to be considered serious; the facts or situations that increase the seriousness of a criminal act.

**Aggressive patrol**   Patrolling the community by making frequent and numerous traffic stops and field interrogations of suspicious persons.

**Alibi**   A defense to a criminal charge stating that the accused was somewhere other than at the scene of the alleged crime.

**Alter ego rule**   A criminal defense where one person defends another person who cannot defend themselves.

**Amenability hearing**   A hearing to determine how well a juvenile offender will respond to treatment within the juvenile system or if the juvenile is better suited to be in the adult system.

**Anti-Terrorism Assistance Program (ATAP)**   A State Department program that offers myriad training programs to combat terrorism in at-risk countries.

**Appellate brief**   A written memorandum filed by the prosecution or defense attorney to explain why the decision of a lower court was erroneous.

**Approach the witness**    An action that occurs when an attorney moves closer to a witness, who is currently on the witness stand, in order to question the witness further or show him or her an exhibit or document. In most jurisdictions, the attorney must request permission from the judge to approach the witness.

**Atavistic man**    An identification of individuals participating in criminal activity as throwbacks from a primitive time.

**Attorney-client privilege**    The privilege that any information shared between a defense attorney and his or her client is kept confidential and does not need to be shared with other members of the court or the public.

**Auburn System**    A prison system, also known as the New York System, in which silence is enforced at all times. Inmates work during the day and spend nights in solitary confinement.

**Bail**    A sum of money that the court receives if a defendant flees from court proceedings.

**Bailiff**    A law enforcement officer, such as a sheriff's deputy, assigned to a particular courtroom to assist the judge and courtroom staff and keep the peace.

**Barriers to reintegration**    Conditions within the community or society that impede the ability of someone released from prison to reestablish citizenship, employment, and housing.

**Bias-based profiling**    Selection of individuals based solely on a common trait of a group such as race, ethnicity, gender, sexual orientation, or economic status.

**Bifurcated trial**    A criminal trial that has two separate phases: the first phase determines the defendant's guilt or innocence, and the second phase determines the defendant's potential punishment.

**Biological theories**    Theoretical propositions that look to the body to identify individuals who are predisposed to criminal offending.

**Biometrics**    A method of authenticating a person's identity through behavioral or physiological characteristics such as iris scanners and fingerprinting.

**Black codes**    Laws created after the end of slavery designed to regulate the activities of African American citizens.

**Black hat hacker**    An unethical computer hacker who hacks with malicious intent to commit a crime.

**Blue code of silence**    The unwritten code of protection among police officers.

**Boot camp**    An alternative to juvenile correctional facilities that follows the model of a military basic-training program and is focused on disciplining juvenile offenders.

**Bridewells**    Jails and police stations in England and Ireland in the 16th century that typically housed petty criminals.

**Broken windows theory**    A theory involving crime and disorder that states that if a community is allowed to physically deteriorate, an impression will be given that no one cares, causing crime to occur.

**Business continuity plan**    A plan that helps a business continue its essential functions in order to operate during and after a disaster or other disruptive event.

**Case law**   The entire collection of published legal documents and decisions of the courts; comprises a large portion of the legal rules that apply to modern society.

**Case-in-chief**   The portion of a criminal case presented by the prosecution.

**Causation**   A definitive link between the offender's criminal act and the victim's suffering.

**Challenge for cause**   A specific legal reason to exclude a potential juror.

**Chicago School**   A specialized body of work in urban sociology that made use of the city of Chicago to study alcoholism, homelessness, suicide, psychoses, and poverty.

**Child Savers movement**   A movement by a group of reformers in the early 19th century that sought to change the way juveniles were treated by the justice system.

**Civil law**   A body of laws that regulate non-criminal disputes, derived from Roman law. In civil law, laws are written and codified.

**Civil lawsuit**   A case in which a plaintiff sues the defendant to recover money damages for negligence or harm.

**Classical school**   A philosophy of crime that placed the responsibility for behavior on the offender.

**Classification officer**   The officer assigned to determine individual inmate needs and assign them to appropriate custody levels, institutions, and programs.

**Closing argument**   The final legal argument of a case presented separately by the prosecution and the defense before the case is given to the jury for deliberation.

**Common law**   Law that is based on customs and legal precedents developed in Britain over hundreds of years.

**Community corrections**   A halfway house, rehab facility, or home detention that helps an individual move from a correctional facility to complete freedom.

**Community policing**   A method of policing that emphasizes community participation in police decision-making and police officer participation in community activities.

**Community service**   Unpaid labor or service to the community as an intermediate sanction ordered by the court.

**Compassion fatigue**   Emotional exhaustion as a result of treating traumatized victims.

**Compensation**   A financial reward for a wrong incurred at the hands of an offender.

**Complaint**   A document listing the criminal charges brought against a defendant.

**COMPSTAT**   A managerial system that uses criminal intelligence to identify crime problems and determine a crime reduction strategy.

**Compurgation**   A method of handling offenses during the pre-classical time period, in which individuals who could find a reputable person in their community to speak on their behalf would be found innocent.

**Concurrence**   The combination of actus reus (the commission of the crime) and mens rea (the intent to commit the crime).

**Conditional release**   The release of a defendant under specific conditions such as an order to enter a treatment program.

**Conflict model**   The idea that when a group comes together to form a society there will be differences within the group—i.e., age, race, and socioeconomic differences—that will make it difficult to come to an agreement about what is criminal. The group in power will set the standards.

**Conflict theory**   A theory concerned with how power is maintained in a society rather than how individuals function within that continuum. Conflict theory holds that those with the most wealth in society are more likely to create the laws, maintain control, and have power over the lower classes.

**Consensus model**   The idea that when a group comes together to form a society, they will have mutually shared values and norms and will come to a consensus about what is a crime.

**Constable**   A local law enforcement officer who was responsible for collecting taxes and enforcing ordinances in the colonial and post-colonial United States, similar to a sheriff; today, constables are typically law enforcement officers in small towns.

**Constitutional law**   A judicial interpretation of the U.S. Constitution for court cases.

**Corpus delicti**   The body of evidence; proof that a crime has been committed.

**Correctional institution**   A jail or a prison where offenders are confined.

**Correctional officer**   An officer, also called a prison guard, jail guard, or corrections officer, who oversees and supervises all inmate activity.

**Corruption**   Abuse of police authority for personal gain.

**Costs of victimization**   The costs incurred by a victim as a result of victimization. These include financial, emotional, psychological, and social costs.

**Cottage reformatories**   Reformatories that taught juveniles farm skills; designed to house 20 to 40 offenders in a cottage with cottage parents.

**Counsel**   A title for an attorney presenting a case in court.

**Court of last resort**   The highest court of appeal in a state court system: typically, a state supreme court.

**Court record**   The official written record of everything that occurs in a court case.

**Court reporter**   A person who uses a shorthand typewriter to record everything that occurs or is said during a court hearing.

**Court-appointed attorney**   An attorney typically selected from a list of all criminal attorneys in private practice near the jurisdiction who are willing to accept appointed cases.

**Courtroom workgroup**   The judge, courtroom staff, prosecutor, and defense attorney.

**Crime**   A legally prohibited action that injures the public welfare or morals or the interests of the state.

**Crime analysis**   A systematic collection and analysis of crime data used to support police efforts in crime and disorder reduction and crime prevention.

**Crime control model**   A model of the criminal justice system that focuses on controlling crime and protecting the public in the most efficient way.

**Crime index**   An index reported by the Uniform Crime Reports. Crimes are divided into Part I and Part II index offenses. The Part I index includes a total of eight offenses divided by violent crime index and the property crime index. The Part II index includes a total of 21 categories of crimes.

**Crime mapping**   A process of using geographic information systems to conduct spatial analysis and investigation of crime.

**Criminal behavior**   Behavior defined by legislation, statutes, and codes.

**Criminal investigation**   A lawful investigation to reconstruct the circumstances of an illegal act, determine or apprehend the guilty party, and assist with the state's prosecution.

**Criminal justice system**   The police, courts, and correctional departments.

**Criminal law**   A set of rules and statutes that defines conduct prohibited by the government and establishes punishment for committing prohibited acts.

**Criminogenic needs**   The characteristics of an offender that can be changed through treatment and intervention that are directly related to continued involvement in criminal activity, including drug abuse, interpersonal skills, cognitive functioning, and vocational/employment skills.

**Cross-examination**   The act of challenging a witness's testimony by asking more questions. Cross-examination is conducted by the other side of the case; the prosecution will cross-examine a defense witness, and the defense will cross-examine a witness for the state.

**Custodial interrogation**   The questioning of a witness by law enforcement while he or she is under arrest.

**Customs and Border Protection (CBP)**   The largest law enforcement agency within the U.S. Department of Homeland Security. Its primary mission is to detect, prevent, and apprehend terrorists and terrorist weapons from entering the country through land borders or ports of entry.

**Cybercrime**   Crime committed utilizing a computer and the Internet.

**Cyberterrorism**   An unlawful method of attacking and threatening government computer systems and networks, and the information stored on these systems, to further political or social objectives.

**Damages**   Monetary compensation awarded by the court when someone has wronged another person or their property.

**Dark figure of crime**   Offenses that go unreported to the police.

**Day fine**   A fine based on a person's daily income; the amount of the fine is progressive in relation to the money the offender earns.

**Day reporting center**   A location for offenders to receive services such as counseling, life skills education, drug abuse treatment, and substance abuse testing. The offender only reports according to a specified schedule and does not live there.

**Decriminalize** To legalize something that used to be a crime.

**Deep cover** Undercover police operations for a lengthy period of time.

**Defendant** A person charged with a crime.

**Defense attorney** The attorney who represents the defendant in a criminal case.

**Deferred adjudication** A type of probation in which the court's decision of the case disposition is delayed while the defendant completes certain requirements of probation.

**Degradation ceremony** The tactic of presenting someone in a negative light so that others may look unfavorably upon that individual. A prosecutor may do this to a defendant, or a defense attorney may do this to a witness for the prosecution.

**Deinstitutionalization** The process of removing status offenders from the juvenile court system and removing juvenile offenders from adult detention centers.

**Department of Homeland Security (DHS)** An agency created by the Homeland Security Act of 2002 whose mission is to protect the homeland by preventing and reducing the country's vulnerability to terrorist attacks, as well as minimizing damage, assisting in recovery, and acting as a focal point for crises and emergency planning.

**Department of Justice (DOJ)** A department within the executive branch of the federal government designed to enforce the laws of the United States.

**Deprivation** Described in Sykes's "pains of imprisonment" as loss of freedom, a scarcity of goods and services, and the loss of domestic relationships for inmates.

**Determinate sentence** A sentence for a specific criminal act that is determined by the state legislature; a sentence that requires a specific amount of time, as ordered by the trial judge, for a person to serve in prison.

**Deterrence** The threat of punishment that will result from criminal activity. Deterrence is further categorized into general deterrence, which threatens everyone with criminal sanctions, and specific deterrence, which is a threat to a specific individual who may offend or reoffend.

**Deterrence theory** A theory of punishment based upon the premise that in order for any punishment to be effective it must be swift, severe, and certain. There are two forms of deterrence: general and specific.

**Developmental pathways** A description of the various paths a youth may take into delinquent or criminal offending. These pathways include the authority conflict pathway, covert pathway, and overt pathway.

**Deviance** Behaviors considered outside of or inconsistent with normal behavior for a community or group.

**Differential association theory** A sociological theory positing that crime is a product of the social environment whereby values are gained from those around individuals.

**Diminished culpability** The inability to fully understand the consequences of an action because of age or cognitive abilities.

**Direct examination**   The act of a witness being first called to the stand to testify.

**Directed patrol**   Spending an allotted amount of time patrolling a specific area of the community that is considered to be a high-crime area.

**Disciplinary report**   A written report describing the inappropriate behavior or the breaking of institutional rules by an inmate.

**Discovery**   The court-ordered process by which attorneys learn about their opponents' cases to prepare for trial.

**Discretion**   The autonomy a police officer has to choose from a variety of courses of action in various situations.

**Discretionary release**   The mechanism by which those in prison are released after serving at least a minimum amount of their sentence upon the decision of a parole board.

**Disposition**   The sentencing of a defendant.

**Doing time**   Jargon used by inmates to describe their good behavior.

**Double jeopardy**   A provision of the U.S. Constitution that prohibits state and federal governments from prosecuting individuals for the same crime more than once, or imposing multiple punishments for a single offense.

**Drug Abuse Resistance Education (D.A.R.E.)**   A program designed to keep kids off drugs by teaching children how to resist peer pressure and avoid drugs and violence.

**Due process**   The requirement that an accused person receive notice of the charges made against him or her and the right to respond to those charges before being deprived of life, liberty, or property.

**Due process model**   A model of the criminal justice system that focuses on protecting the rights of the accused.

**Early release**   Release from a correctional institution prior to the expiration of an offender's sentence.

**Early Warning Systems**   A means used by police leadership to identify a potentially problematic officer before his or her behavior becomes very serious; sometimes called Early Intervention Systems.

**Electronic monitoring**   A form of technology used with house arrests to track and limit an offender's movement outside the home with telephone or radio signals.

**Emergency Management Assistance Compact (EMAC)**   An interstate mutual aid agreement, ratified by Congress, that allows states to assist one another in responding to disasters.

**En banc**   A French term indicating that all the judges of an appellate court will together consider an appeal.

**Escape**   The illegal departure of an offender from legal custody.

**Evidence-based models**   Models of intervention proven effective through social scientific research and study.

**Ex post facto**   A law dictating that a person cannot be charged or punished for a crime that occurred before the rule, law, or procedure was created.

**Excessive force**   An amount of physical force beyond that which is necessary to control a suspect.

**Exclusionary rule**   A legal mandate applied when a piece of evidence has been obtained in a manner that violates the rights of the defendant under due process.

**Expert witness**   A person considered to be an expert in his or her profession or field of study who applies that expertise to the facts or circumstances of a case.

**Expungement**   The legal process whereby the official record of an individual's criminal history is prohibited from being disclosed.

**Extradition**   The formal surrender of a person by a country to another country for the purpose of prosecution or punishment.

**Extralegal policing**   Policing that is not regulated or sanctioned by law.

**Federal Emergency Management Agency (FEMA)**   An agency within the Department of Homeland Security whose mission is to build, sustain, and strengthen the nation's capability to address all hazards through preparation, response, and recovery measures.

**Federal Wiretap Act**   An act, also called the Electronic Communications Privacy Act of 1986, that forbids acquiring the contents of electronic communications without users' consent and includes provisions for prohibited activities, government access, and consequences of a violation.

**Felony**   A crime that is punishable by imprisonment in excess of a year or by death.

**Feminist theories**   Theoretical explanations of crime, justice, and the entire criminal justice system from an androgynous perspective.

**Fidelity to program design**   The degree to which rehabilitative programs are actually delivered in accordance with their pre-operational design.

**Field interrogation**   A temporary detention of an individual in order to question the individual about a suspicious circumstance.

**Follow-up investigation**   Continuation of the preliminary investigation in an attempt to reconstruct the circumstances of a crime.

**Forensic science**   The application of physical and social sciences to legal and criminal issues.

**Fruit of the poisonous tree**   Evidence obtained by law enforcement as a result of an illegal search or seizure.

**Fusion center**   An information sharing center that allows a state to assess threats and implement corrective action, while at the same time increasing state and local law enforcement agencies' awareness of terrorist-related activity within their borders.

**General deterrence**   A form of deterrence used to deter the populace from committing future criminal acts by ensuring that the principles of punishment are focused on potential criminals as opposed to the individual.

**General strain theory**    An expansion of strain theory stating that the more strain individuals are exposed to, the more likely they are to participate in delinquent or criminal activity. Types of strain include the failure to achieve positive goals, the removal of positive stimuli, and the presentation of negative stimuli.

**General theory of crime**    A theoretical proposition that crime is not controlled by bonds to society, but rather by an individual's ability to demonstrate self-control. Under this theory, crime in general is not a planned event; rather, offenders act on impulse as a mechanism for gratifying their needs.

**Global Positioning System (GPS)**    A system of satellites that orbit the earth and transmit signals to allow receivers to display accurate location, speed, and time information.

**Good time credit**    The amount of time that a state penitentiary gives the offender for maintaining good behavior while incarcerated; time that is taken off the sentence.

**Government cybercrime**    Cybercrimes that involve attacks on government information systems, including cyberterrorism.

**Grand jury**    A group of 16–23 people that hears evidence and decides if probable cause exists to believe a person has committed a crime.

**Grass eaters**    Those police officers who engage in relatively passive forms of inappropriate behavior by accepting small favors or money for looking the other way when illegal activities are taking place.

**Gross negligence**    Lack of care or obvious disregard for another that results in damage or injury to another.

**Halfway house**    A group home often used by newly released offenders who have nowhere else to go. Many halfway houses are specifically designed for sex offenders, providing a supervised residence and resources specifically designed for this population.

**Homeland security**    The preparedness measures taken to protect and ensure the security and safety of the homeland and its citizens.

**House arrest**    A method of punishment in which the defendant is kept under close supervision in his or her own home rather than in prison.

**Houses of refuge**    Houses that sought to rehabilitate, educate, and provide vocational training and religion to juvenile offenders and vagrants.

**I-24/7**    An information sharing network designed to enable law enforcement officers in every member country to share sensitive police data.

**I-Link**    An operating system that has the ability to identify common aspects of ongoing investigations that are seemingly unrelated.

**Identity theft**    The crime of stealing someone's identity and using it for malicious purposes.

**Importation**    The tendency for inmates to bring into the prison the criminal

**Incapacitation**    A theory of punishment that imprisons offenders to prevent them from committing other crimes while incarcerated.

**Incarceration**    The act of confining a person in a jail or prison facility.

**Indeterminate sentence** A sentence of incarceration without a specific term or ending date. Parole boards or other professionals generally determine when the offender will be released.

**Indictment** A written document issued by a grand jury to indicate that there is probable cause to believe a person has committed a crime.

**Indigenous model** A model that refers to the scarcity of all that was previously known socially and materially to the inmate. This model evolves from the isolation, constant monitoring, loss of possessions, and loss of freedom an inmate will experience.

**Indirect victim** A person who suffers vicarious trauma as a result of crime even though he or she is not a direct victim.

**Infraction** A lesser crime that is usually punishable by a fine.

**Initial appearance** The court hearing at which a defendant hears the formal charges levied against him or her.

**Inmate** An offender or an arrestee in a correctional institution.

**Inmate code** Rules and roles that inmates adopt while incarcerated.

**Institutional capacity** The maximum number of inmates an institution can hold.

**Integrated theories** Theories that identify the most powerful elements of other theories and combine two or more of them into one explanation.

**Intelligence-led policing** A business model in which data analysis and criminal intelligence are used to facilitate crime reduction, crime prevention, and enforcement strategies that target the most serious offenders.

**Intensive supervision probation** A type of probation with a higher level of offender supervision, plus a stricter regimen of other services, including such stipulations as treatment programs and community service.

**Intermediate appellate court** The lower level of state appellate courts.

**International Court of Justice (ICJ)** The primary judicial organ of the UN, established in June 1945.

**International Criminal Police Organization (INTERPOL)** The world's largest international police organization, which consists of 188 member countries and facilitates cross-border police cooperation.

**Israeli Model** A method of interrogation in which the interrogator looks intently into the face of the subject and asks a series of probing personal questions.

**Jail** A correctional facility that holds people accused of or convicted of crimes.

**Joint Terrorism Task Forces** Entities that serve as a clearinghouse of terrorism-related information for a specified region. Task forces are comprised of federal, state, and local law enforcement representatives.

**Judge** A public officer elected or appointed to administer justice and hear cases in a court of law.

**Judicial review** The power of the federal judiciary to overturn any legislation or other governmental action ruled inconsistent with the Constitution, Bill of Rights, or federal law.

**Jurisdiction**    The power of a court to adjudicate a case, issue orders, and render a decision.

**Jurisprudence**    The philosophy of law.

**Jury nullification**    A process that occurs when a jury uses information not provided during a court case to determine the guilt or innocence of a defendant.

**Just deserts**    A philosophy of punishment that states that a person who commits a crime should suffer for that crime; the amount of time or type of punishment for a particular offender is generally proportionate to the type of offense that was committed.

**Just world**    A worldview in which everyone gets the consequences they deserve for their actions.

**Juvenile**    A young person, usually a minor.

**Juvenile delinquency**    A finding of criminal behavior in the juvenile system.

**Juvenile waiver hearing**    A hearing held before a judge to determine whether a juvenile will remain in the juvenile system or be transferred to adult criminal court.

**Labeling theory**    A theoretical tradition in which criminals become set in their roles as criminals as a result of their stigmatized status.

**Law Enforcement Assistance Administration**    A body created by the 1968 Omnibus Crime Control and Safe Streets Act to serve as a federal resource for local law enforcement agencies.

**Law Enforcement Bulletin**    A publication of the Federal Bureau of Investigation that includes articles on law enforcement issues as well as information on wanted federal suspects.

**Law violation**    A new criminal charge against an offender on probation.

**Lay witness**    An everyday citizen who has some personal knowledge about the facts of a case.

**Left realism**    A philosophical approach advocating for more minimal responses or sanctions for street-level crimes and less serious offenses, and more stringent responses and social control for white-collar crimes and crimes against society.

**Legal cause**    In tort law, the behavior or action that causes harm or proximate cause.

**Legalization**    Removing legal barriers to drug possession and use in an effort to make it a regulated and taxable portion of the economy.

**Life course theories**    The contention that criminal offending is influenced by an individual's previous experiences as well as traits or characteristics that are not changeable, such as impulsivity, age, etc.

**Light cover**    Undercover police operations for a short period of time.

**Limited admissibility**    Evidence that may be used for one specific purpose but cannot be applied in other ways.

**Lynch mob**    A group of individuals seeking to punish someone suspected of having committed a social transgression.

**Malware**    Malicious software designed to disrupt or prevent further use of a system.

**Mandatory minimum**    A sentence that is imposed by the state legislature with no discretion given by the trial judge. The defendant is required by law to serve a certain amount of time in the state penitentiary.

**Mandatory release**    The mechanism by which those in prison must be released after having served their court-imposed sentences, minus any other sentencing credits for which they may be eligible.

**Meat eaters**    Police officers who are more aggressive in their illegal behavior and actively search for ways to make money illegally while on duty.

**Mens rea**    The intent to commit a criminal act.

**Michigan Prisoner Reentry Initiative (MPRI)**    A state imitative implemented in 2003 with a mission of equipping released offenders with the tools they need to succeed in the community.

**Miranda rights**    The obligation of police officers to inform suspects of their right to remain silent and their right to an attorney.

**Misdemeanor**    A lesser crime that is punishable by jail time for up to one year and/or a fine.

**Mitigating circumstances**    Circumstances that do not justify a criminal act, but make the crime less reprehensible and may be used to reduce the sentence in a criminal trial.

**Mitigation specialist**    A person educated in the social sciences who assists the defendant in obtaining evidence to minimize the impact of punishment. Mitigation specialists are generally social workers or criminologists who compile past history of the defendant's life to assist with the defense.

**Monitoring the Future**    A program that collects data on juveniles and is used by many social scientists.

**Moral panic**    A term coined by Stanley Cohen describing the public's irrational fear and concern over a particular issue.

**Motive**    In a criminal investigation, a probable reason that a person committed a crime.

**National Crime Victimization Survey (NCVS)**    A survey conducted on households in the United States that includes detailed descriptions of criminal events, including the victim, potential precipitation, consequences of the event, and the offender.

**National Incident Management System (NIMS)**    A national system that provides a consistent nationwide approach for government, the private sector, and nongovernmental organizations to work together in preparation, response, and recovery from domestic incidents.

**National Incident-Based Reporting System (NIBRS)**    A national crime data collection program created and implemented during the 1980s in an effort to enhance the methodology for collecting, analyzing, and publishing crime data.

**National Organization for Victim Assistance (NOVA)**    A conglomerate of victims' rights groups that advocate on behalf of victims and victims' issues.

**National Response Framework (NRF)**    A framework that forms the basis for coordination between all levels of government and the private sector in responding to a disaster. It establishes a comprehensive structure, method, and standard terminology for management of incidents.

**National Youth Survey** A compilation of many different surveys measuring gang participation and drug use.

**Net-widening** A phenomenon in which the number of offenders within the court system increases as the criminal justice system expands the number of offenders it must supervise.

**Night watches** Groups of local, unpaid citizens who would patrol the community at night to deter crime and alert residents of the time, weather, and hazards.

**Nolo contendere** A plea in which the defendant does not admit the charges, but will not contest them.

**Norms** Social expectations for appropriate behavior.

**Offender** One who breaks a rule or commits a crime.

**Offender risk** Within the context of prison security, an assessment of the likelihood that an inmate will attempt an escape or assault a staff member or other inmate. Within the context of community-based supervision, an assessment of the likelihood that a former inmate will commit a new crime.

**Opening statement** The initial statement of a trial that an attorney makes to the jury, which outlines the argument that will be made during the trial.

**Operational styles** The approaches police officers use to perform their duties.

**Order maintenance** A method of policing whereby officers interpret the law and decide a course of action based on each individual situation when assigning blame and choosing whether or not to arrest.

**Outlaw motorcycle gangs** Organized criminal networks with a motorcycle lifestyle.

**Pains of imprisonment** Described by Gresham Sykes as the pains that develop from the deprivations and frustrations of those who are incarcerated.

**Panopticon** A circular prison designed with a central observation area so that officers can view all parts of the facility, originally designed by Jeremy Bentham. Variations of this concept are still used in modern correctional facilities so that correctional officers have an unobstructed view of most inmate areas.

**Pardon** To forgive, release, or exempt a person from a penalty.

**Parens patriae** A legal theory, most often associated with juveniles and the mentally ill, that allows the state to step in and protect those who legally cannot protect themselves. Latin for "the state as a parent."

**Parole** A supervised release from incarceration in lieu of serving a full sentence.

**Parole board** The governmental board that will determine if an offender receives parole and under what conditions.

**Patriot Act** A congressional act passed shortly after the September 11, 2001 terrorist attacks in the U.S., focusing primarily on providing law enforcement with legal authority to support efforts to fight terrorism. Short for The Uniting and Strengthening America by Providing Appropriate Tools Required to Intercept and Obstruct Terrorism (USA Patriot) Act.

**Peacemaking criminology** A theory proposing the use of mediation, love, respect, and forgiveness to resolve societal conflicts and reduce recidivism and crime.

**Penal code**   A set of codified laws in a legal system that describe a crime and its punishment at the state level.

**Pennsylvania System**   A penal system advocated by Quakers that used solitary confinement and penitence to reform offenders. Eventually, work such as shoemaking and weaving was allowed to be done in the cells.

**Peremptory challenge**   An attorney's objection to the jury service of a potential juror without a particular argument against the juror.

**Personal cybercrime**   Cybercrimes that involve a direct attack on a person, including identity theft and cyber harassment.

**Personality theories**   Theories of crime that look to explain criminal behavior as an expression of impulsiveness, aggression, or sensation-seeking.

**Pinkertons**   A private investigation and security company formed in the 1880s that assisted in protecting goods, tracking down suspects, and breaking strikes.

**Plain view**   A method by which police observe physical evidence that is plainly visible to the human eye, without the need for an intrusive search.

**Plea**   A defendant's in-court statement that he or she is guilty, is not guilty, or will not contest criminal charges.

**Plea bargain**   An agreement between the state and defense on a plea and sentence.

**Policing**   Enforcing the law by monitoring suspected criminal activity and apprehending violators of law.

**Positivist school**   A school of thought on crime arguing that some behavior occurs as a result of factors outside the control of individuals.

**Posse**   A group of residents temporarily enlisted by law enforcement agencies to assist in law enforcement functions.

**Pre-classical school**   A school of thought that held that crime was caused by supernatural forces as opposed to natural forces.

**Pre-sentence investigation**   A report to the court which outlines the defendant's prior alcohol and drug history, medical history, criminal history, education, and other factors that is given to the judge to assist with determination of sentence. Pre-sentence investigations are generally written by local probation departments.

**Precedent**   A prior opinion from a court of appeals establishing the legal rule or authority for future questions on the same legal matter.

**Preliminary investigation**   Evidence-gathering activities performed at the scene of a crime immediately after the crime was reported to or discovered by the police.

**Pretrial diversion**   An informal arrangement that involves referring the defendant to rehabilitative programs prior to arraignment in an attempt to address the offense reasonably while offering the defendant the opportunity to keep the offense off his or her criminal record.

**Preventive patrol**    Patrolling the community on an unpredictable and routine or random basis.

**Principle of least eligibility**    The view that those who commit crimes, particularly those in prison, are the least deserving members of society to benefit from government-provided assistance and support, such as education, vocational training, and other forms of support.

**Prison**    A correctional facility that confines those convicted of felonies; may hold both misdemeanants and felons convicted of federal crimes.

**Prison gangs**    Organized criminal networks within the federal and state prison systems.

**Prisonization**    The taking on in greater or lesser degree of the customs and general culture of the penitentiary.

**Probable cause**    Reasonable belief that the accused committed the crime with which he or she is charged.

**Probation**    A supervised release from incarceration in lieu of serving any time or a full term in jail.

**Probative value**    Value that is useful in a case.

**Problem-oriented policing**    An approach to policing in which the underlying causes of crime are identified and addressed.

**Procedural law**    A set of laws that describe the formal steps to be taken in the legal process to protect the rights of all parties.

**Property cybercrime**    Cybercrimes that involve a criminal purposely installing malware on computer equipment.

**Prosecutor**    The attorney, representing the state, who argues the criminal case against the defendant.

**Public defender**    An attorney elected in a local jurisdiction to represent indigent defendants in criminal trials.

**Racial profiling**    The use of race or ethnicity as the primary or the only indicator that an individual may be participating in criminal activity.

**Reasonable doubt**    The standard of guilt that the state must meet to convict a criminal defendant; if reasonable doubt exists, the defendant must be acquitted.

**Recidivism**    The rate of repeat crime by offenders; the rate of relapse back into criminal activity or behavior.

**Recusal**    The decision by a judge to remove himself or herself from a case if there is a conflict of interest.

**Reentry**    The processes whereby the formerly incarcerated return to society, seeking to establish positive ties to the community and engage in law-abiding behaviors.

**Reentry courts**    Courtroom working groups, including judges, prosecutors, defense attorneys, and parole agents, that monitor those released from prison to ensure compliance with conditions of release and respond to violations of these conditions through graduated sanctions and rehabilitative services.

**Reform schools**    The first state-run schools designed to reform juvenile offenders.

**Rehabilitation**   A philosophy of punishment that is based on the idea that the offender's behavior can and will change through treatment programs by professionals. Rehabilitation can involve treating offenders for drug and alcohol issues, anger problems, mental health counseling, and other services.

**Reintegrative shaming**   A process whereby offenders are punished, therefore repaying their debt to society, and then forgiven for their transgressions and reintegrated back into society.

**Remand**   An appellate court's process of returning a case to a lower court for further proceedings.

**Repeat victimization**   The recurrence of a crime either in the same place or with the same victim.

**Restitution**   Punishment that requires the offender to repay the victim for the harm that was caused, generally through monetary remuneration or community service.

**Retribution**   The idea that a criminal should be punished in a manner that is commensurate, or as equal as possible, to the crime committed.

**Role**   The position one holds within a social structure.

**Role conflict**   The conflict between what a person may prefer to do and what the person is expected to do.

**Role expectation**   The behaviors and activities that people expect from a person in a particular role.

**Routine activities theory**   A theory of criminal offending positing that crime is a function of opportunity—the convergence of a motivated offender, a suitable target, and a lack of guardianship.

**Rule of law**   A doctrine that no branch of government or public official may act arbitrarily outside the law. The rule of law dictates that any law enforced by the government must be fair, moral, and just.

**Sanctions**   Requirements imposed on those convicted of a crime that can range from financial penalties or curfew restrictions to incarceration.

**Sanctuary**   A sacred place of worship where one can take refuge.

**Scared-straight programs**   Programs designed to scare juveniles into behaving correctly, including boot camps and juveniles visiting inmates in prisons.

**Second Chance Act**   Federal legislation that authorizes Congress to appropriate funds that support reentry programs across the country, conduct research to evaluate reentry initiatives, and develop model programs and policies to improve the reentry process.

**Selective enforcement**   The decision made by police as to which laws they wish to enforce and when they choose to enforce them.

**Self-defense**   The use of force to protect oneself or one's family from bodily harm from an attacker.

**Self-report survey**   A data collection effort asking participants to report the number of criminal offenses or activities they have committed.

**Sentence**   A punishment imposed by a judicial body on an offender who has committed a crime.

**Sequester**   To remove the jury, and any alternate jurors, from all possible influences that may affect their abilities to fairly judge the accused.

**Sheriff**   A local law enforcement officer responsible for collecting taxes and enforcing ordinances in the colonial and post-colonial United States, similar to a constable; today, sheriffs serves as law enforcement officers at the county level.

**Shock probation**   A type of probation in which the court sends offenders to prison for a short period of time to "shock" them by exposing them to the limits of prison life, then returns them to the original jurisdiction to be placed on probation.

**Sidebar**   A discussion conducted during a court hearing between the judge and attorneys outside the hearing of the jury.

**Slave patrols**   Regulatory groups in the South in the colonial era focused on regulating the activities of slaves.

**Social contract**   An agreement between the public and government in which the public allows the government to provide safety and security.

**Social control theory**   A theoretical proposition that contends that the more strongly individuals are bonded to their community, the less likely they are to participate in delinquent activity.

**Social disorganization theory**   A theoretical proposition stating that communities with higher rates of social ills, such as breakdown in family composition, dilapidated buildings, unsupervised teenagers, high rates of poverty, high rates of residential mobility, and ethnic heterogeneity, are most likely to experience high rates of crime and delinquency.

**Social networking**   A web-based service that allows users to construct personal profiles and connect and communicate with other users.

**Special Housing Unit (SHU)**   Usually an area of confinement within a correctional facility designed to hold the more dangerous or violent inmates, those who are discipline problems, or those who need supervised protection from others.

**Specific deterrence**   A form of deterrence used to deter an individual from committing future criminal acts by focusing the punishment on that individual.

**Speedy Trial Act**   A federal law requiring district courts to ensure that a criminal defendant is brought to trial no later than 100 days after his or her arrest, with some exceptions.

**Stafford Act**   A congressional act passed in 2009 that provides a method for states to request federal assistance to respond to a disaster. Short for The Robert T. Stafford Disaster Relief and Emergency Assistance Act.

**Stare decisis**   The doctrine that a trial court must adhere to appellate decisions or precedents raised in a lower court.

**Status offenses**   Offenses that can only be committed by a juvenile, not an adult.

**Statutory law**   A written law explicitly describing actions that are prohibited.

**Strain theory**   A theoretical proposition contending that crime rates are produced by an individual's inability to conform to cultural values or achieve monetary success through accepted norms.

**Street gangs**   Organized criminal networks that originate at the street level.

**Subpoena** A written document that officially notifies someone that he or she must appear in court.

**Supervised release** Court-ordered supervision of someone who is awaiting trial or serving probation or parole.

**Suppression hearing** A pretrial hearing where a defendant asks the court to suppress, or disallow, evidence that the police obtained illegally.

**SWAT (Special Weapons and Tactics) team** A paramilitary policing unit originally formed to deal with dangerous confrontations, but increasingly being used in everyday policing.

**Symbolic assailant** An individual whose dress, behavior, and gestures indicate suspicion and possible danger to a police officer.

**Tabletop exercise** An exercise presenting a hypothetical situation for discussion, used to assess preparedness by allowing participants to discuss how specific plans or policies would be implemented to prevent, respond to, or recover from the scenario.

**Technical violation** A parole violation that is less serious than a law violation and could include failure to report to the probation officer, failure to make child support payments, or failure to complete other stipulations of probation such as community service hours.

**Terrorism** The use or threat of violence toward civilians in order to attain political, religious, or ideological goals.

**Testimony** The statement of a witness, given under oath, typically in court.

**Texas Rangers** One of the earliest law enforcement agencies in the American West.

**Therapeutic Communities (TC)** Residential programs that help individuals learn social norms and develop more effective social skills.

**Thin blue line** The line between the lawful and the lawless and between social order and chaos on the streets.

**Third degree** The infliction of pain by police officers in order to solicit evidence about a crime.

**Three-strikes law** A specific legislative mandate that requires offenders, after their third conviction for any offense, to serve a minimum amount of time in incarceration.

**Tort** A breach of a civil duty or wrongful act that results in an injury to another or damage to their property.

**Total institution** An institution that provides everything a person needs for survival, usually at a lower level than what is enjoyed in an open society.

**Transport officer** A law enforcement officer who transports inmates to and from court and jail.

**Trial by battle** A mechanism for privately resolving disputes during the pre-classical time period, in which the victim or a chosen member of the victim's family would battle with the offender or a chosen member of the offender's family to determine guilt.

**Trial by ordeal** A method of handling conflict privately during the pre-classical time period, in which proving innocence involved the use of extremely painful or life-threatening methods of punishment.

**Trial court**   A court of original jurisdiction that tries a case and renders a judgment.

**Tribunal**   A specialized venue for enforcing international law. International tribunals can be formed by United Nations charter, Security Council resolution, or international treaty.

**Uniform Crime Reports (UCR)**   An official data-reporting tool created in 1930 to provide uniform definitions for crime data so that results could be compared by month, year, state, and jurisdiction.

**United Nations (UN)**   An international organization formed by 51 member states in 1945 in an effort to promote international peace and security following World War II. The organization has grown to include 192 member states and is best known for its peacekeeping efforts and humanitarian assistance around the world.

**Vengeance**   The idea, based on the biblical philosophy of "an eye for an eye," of seeing that a criminal is punished, and that some satisfaction is taken from the fact that the criminal is punished.

**Verdict**   Finding of guilt or innocence by a judge or jury.

**Victim advocate**   A person who works in victim services to attend to the needs and rights of victims.

**Victim impact statement (VIS)**   A statement from the victim to the judge during the sentencing phase of the offender's trial.

**Victim precipitation**   Actions by the victim, either passive or active, that help to trigger the offense.

**Victim rights amendment**   A proposed constitutional amendment that would provide victims with guaranteed rights similar to those given to offenders under the Sixth Amendment.

**Victim services**   Programs and support systems for victims of crime.

**Victim-offender mediation**   A process facilitated by clinicians or trained personnel whereby crime victims are able to express to the perpetrators how the crime has impacted their lives, and the perpetrators can apologize and explain themselves to the victims.

**Victimology**   The study of victimization that analyzes the role played by victims in crimes.

**Victims of Crime Act (VOCA)**   An act that allowed federal money to subsidize state compensation programs for victims.

**Vigilantism**   The taking on of law enforcement responsibilities and the dispensing of punishment by private citizens.

**Visa**   An official authorization permitting a foreign citizen entry into the United States for either a temporary stay or permanent residence.

**Vocational training**   The provision of classes and instruction design to provide individuals with specific skills for entry into specific labor markets.

**Warrant**   Legal authorization from a judge to make an arrest, conduct a search or seize evidence.

**Wedding cake model of justice**   A four-layer model in which the top layer is celebrated trials, the second layer is major felonies, the third layer is less major felonies, and the fourth layer is misdemeanors.

**White hat hacker**   An ethical computer hacker who hacks for beneficial reasons, such as solving complex problems.

**White-collar crime** Crimes against businesses by people in high-profile positions.

**Wickersham Commission (National Commission on Law Observance and Enforcement)** A commission that published a comprehensive report on the state of the American criminal justice system the 1930s.

**Witness** An individual who gives testimony in court because he or she has information that is pertinent to the case.

**Work release centers** Correctional facilities that are designed to provide housing and secure custody of those under the jurisdiction of the prison system, but also allow for inmates to leave during specific periods of time to work or attend vocational or rehabilitative programming in the community.

**Writ of certiorari** A document issued by the U.S. Supreme Court to confirm that it will review the decision of a federal circuit court of appeals or a state supreme court.

**Youthful offender** Typically, an offender under 18 years old, though the age requirements may be different among the several states.

# INDEX

# THE HISTORY OF ISLINGTON

One thousand copies of this edition have been printed,
of which this is number  *985*

# John Nelson

# The History
## of
# ISLINGTON

*A Facsimile of the First Edition (1811)*
*together with 79 Additional Illustrations*
*and an Introduction by Julia Melvin*

Philip Wilson Publishers

Summerfield Press

© 1980 Philip Wilson Publishers Ltd & Summerfield Press Ltd

First published 1811

This revised edition published 1980 jointly by
Philip Wilson Publishers Ltd & Summerfield Press Ltd
Russell Chambers,
Covent Garden,
London WC2E 8AA

ISBN 0 85667 104 5

Printed and bound by The Scolar Press, Ilkley, West Yorkshire

# CONTENTS

## ACKNOWLEDGEMENTS

The editor, and the publishers, wish to express their gratitude to the Libraries Department of the London Borough of Islington, and most particularly to Mr. E. A. Willats, the Reference Librarian, and to Mr. Arthur Brooks, his deputy, who have supported this republication of Nelson's *History* with enthusiasm and the most generous assistance of their own personal knowledge of the borough's history.

The editor also wishes to thank Mr. John Huddy, of the Map Department of the British Library, and the staff of the Royal Commission on Historical Manuscripts.

VII

# LIST OF ILLUSTRATIONS

The latter two plates are of the old Queen's Head, which until its demolition in 1830,
was one of the finest examples of Elizabethan building within the environs of London

# INTRODUCTION

John Nelson's *History, Topography and Antiquities of the Parish of St Mary Islington* was first published in 1811; it ran into three editions, but has been out of print since 1829.

Very little is known about Nelson, apart from what can be deduced from his *History of Islington*. Unlike his distinguished contemporary, neighbour and friend, John Nichols, FSA, he was not a writer or publisher by profession; but a businessman. He was a resident of Islington, and claims modestly that his prime motive in writing his history was the information and amusement of his neighbours and friends. He was infected with an enthusiasm and love for Islington which is felt by many of those who have rediscovered Islington in the post-Second World War years. He lived, at one time, in rooms in Camden Passage, and T. H. Shepherd painted two watercolours of the exterior and interior of this lodging-house. At the date of the second edition, 1821, he was living in Hornsey Row, now Tyndale Place. He would appear to have devoted his maturity to collecting and studying all the known printed and manuscript sources for an antiquarian study of Islington, and his work carries an authority of scholarship which no subsequent history of Islington approaches. Although he acknowledges his debt to and his great admiration for John Nichols, historian of Leicestershire, editor of the *Gentleman's Magazine* and immensely prolific printer and author, Nelson was innovative: he was the first to approach the problem of writing topographical history with a perambulatory structure, and all the subsequent 19th-century accounts of Islington are heavily derivative of his. Thomas Cromwell's *Walks Through Islington* was the next to appear in 1835, and although by 1843 when Samuel Lewis's *History and Topography of the Parish of St Mary Islington* was first published, Islington had changed into a metropolitan suburb and bore the marks of its quadrupled population, Lewis even quotes word for word from Nelson, and similarly in his later (1854) publication: *Islington as it was and as it is*. Tomkins'

*Perambulation of Islington* (1858) and Thomas Coull's *History and Traditions of Islington* are slim, jejune volumes which plagiarise unashamedly.

John Nelson knew Islington as a village, and describes in clear, even prose the rural environs of the north-east of London at a date immediately preceding the dense development of the 19th century. In the first decade of the 19th century, the ribbon suburban building of Cubitt's Barnsbury, of the Milner-Gibson and Cloudesley Estates and the subsequent march of brick terraces was yet to come. While Nelson's volume duly examines the known evidence for Islington as a pre-Roman settlement, and meticulously analyses it in terms of its manorial divisions, it is by no means dry. He is at his best, perhaps, in recounting its contemporary character as a place of retreat, whether for purposes of entertainment in the spas and pleasure gardens of the 18th and 19th centuries, or for writers, scholars, dissenting clergy and those seeking a *villeggiatura* hard by the gates of London. His annecdotal footnotes and biographical sketches are lively and opinioned: in these is to be found Nelson's own portrait. In a period of successive Tory Governments, and then the long peace of Lord Liverpool's now admired Tory rule, he was a considered radical, and yet also a moderate man, even a recluse. He would appear to have been a member of the Established Church and yet, although a castigator of the activities of non-conformist religious cranks, he greatly sympathised with the band of dissenting clergy that settled round Newington Green in the late 17th century and writes with admiration of the several other Calvinist congregations that were established in Islington in the 18th century. He was strongly prejudiced against the practice of Roman Catholicism.

His taste as a topographical historian was perhaps unfashionable. He decried the current practice of masking 17th-century mouldings and carvings with white paint, and he writes with particular feeling about several fine Elizabethan houses, none of which survived his time.

Nelson's extended descriptions of Mr. Laycock's and Mr. Rhodes' enormous dairy farms have a poignancy for us today which Nelson must have foreseen. Even long after Nelson's death, Islington continued to maintain her position as the dairy of London. However, almost incongruously the brick-fields, smart new terraces and increased land-values have here and there entered Nelson's world of Welsh milk-maids and Holloway cheese-cakes.

Curiously enough Nelson's *History* has a deep relevance for those who know Islington today. The classical squares and crescents, even the close inner-London housing estates are contained within ancient roads, and determined by features belonging to rural Islington: the lie of the land, the reminders of the past in street names and a domestic scale all contribute to Islington's survival as a village.

This edition is extra-illustrated. Seventeen plates were specially commissioned for the first edition, and these are all included with the exception of Hawkesworth's rather uninspired engraving of Dowbiggin's church: for this Rich's prettier re-working (2nd edn., 1821) of the subject has been substituted. Notably, all but two—which were considered inappropriate—of Augustus Pugin's *Views in Islington and Pentonville*, published by Ackermann in 1819, have been added. This is, of course, Augustus Pugin the elder, father of the architect of the Palace of Westminster. Many of those who originally purchased the second edition of Nelson had the Pugins bound in, but this was not invariably so.

The remaining illustrations have been added in order to provide a fine gloss on the text. This republication has been printed as a facsimile from a grangerised copy of the first edition in the private collection of Mr. Philip Wilson. From the manuscript markings in the margins of this copy, it would appear that a mid-19th-century owner was contemplating an extra-illustrated edition very similar to that which is being published now. He too would have included the six illustrations of the New River Head by Wenceslaus Hollar. Nelson's footnote references to rare and striking prints of Canonbury House would have been followed up: in this edition they also add to our knowledge of the appearance of 18th-century Islington. One further comment on the copy from which this edition is printed is perhaps worth making. The Licrece collection in the Islington Central Library includes a richly grangerised copy of Nelson, which contains archival items from the offices and family of John Nichols, FSA. Manuscript markings in both grangerised copies are almost certainly in the same hand, and it is worthy of surmise that it was the publishing house of Nichols that was interested in this venture a hundred and forty years ago.

The coat of arms which was first devised for the original title-page and now also appears as a decorative gilt stamp on the binding, is entirely spurious. It was invented, if we are to believe the story recounted on pp. 35–37, as part of an elaborate entertainment given for Elizabeth I by the Earl of Leicester at Kenilworth in 1575, and may be taken as a paradigm for Islington.

THE

# History, Topography, and Antiquities

OF THE PARISH OF

# St. MARY ISLINGTON,

## IN THE COUNTY OF MIDDLESEX.

INCLUDING

BIOGRAPHICAL SKETCHES OF THE MOST EMINENT AND REMARKABLE PERSONS
WHO HAVE BEEN BORN, OR HAVE RESIDED THERE.

ILLUSTRATED BY SEVENTEEN ENGRAVINGS.

## BY JOHN NELSON.

Old ISELDON, tho' scarce in modern song
Nam'd but in scorn, may boast of honour'd days ;
For many a darling child of Science there
Hath trimm'd his lamp, and wove his laurel crown.
  And ISELDON, as ancient records tell,
In distant time as now, had much to boast
Of other praise, in Nature's bounty rich.
For thither, then, from London's hectic town
Her fam'd chalybeates oft allur'd the sick ;
Her fresh lactarian draughts the babe sustain'd.          Fox.

LAC    CASEUS    INFANS

## LONDON:

PRINTED FOR THE AUTHOR BY JOHN NICHOLS AND SON, RED LION PASSAGE, FLEET STREET ;
AND SOLD BY C. RUSSELL, AT THE CIRCULATING LIBRARY, UPPER STREET, ISLINGTON ;
MESSRS. BLACK, PARRY, AND KINGSBURY, LEADENHALL STREET ; VERNOR, HOOD, AND
SHARPE, POULTRY ; GREENLAND, FINSBURY PLACE ; AND SETCHEL AND SON, KING STREET,
COVENT GARDEN.

1811.

# PREFACE.

THE Author of the following sheets is fully aware of his own inability to add much to the stock of the experienced Antiquary and Topographer,—his chief motive was the information and amusement of his neighbours and friends; his end will therefore be sufficiently answered, if in what he has done he should meet with their kind approbation and support. In justice to himself it must however be observed, that the materials for the present work were for the most part collected and prepared for the press during his hours of relaxation from mercantile pursuits.

In the progress of the volume it has been the Writer's aim to collect all the original information which such time and opportunity afforded; and in this he might probably have been more successful, had his enquiries always met with that attention which he flattered himself the subject deserved; but which opinion he was too often unable to impress upon the minds of those who had it in their power to render him material assistance.

It must however be confessed, that he has availed himself of every printed authority which fell in his way, a circumstance not to be omitted without considerable detriment in a work of this nature; and he hopes that those gentlemen to whose labours he may be indebted will pardon him for that liberty, as he believes he has generally acknowledged his obligation at the bottom of the page.

With respect to the Engravings that accompany the work, they are, with the exception of the eleventh plate, executed by Mr. J. Hawksworth and his sister, both young artists of considerable promise; and the Author feels pleasure in expressing an opinion that they are superior in execution to the plates accompanying the generality of works on Parochial History and Antiquities.

To those persons who have furnished him with information, and favoured his enquiries, he returns his best thanks; particularly to Mrs. Hunt of Canonbury, John Nichols, Esq. (the warm friend and promoter of Antiquarian research;) Jonathan Eade, Esq. John Bentley, Esq. John Scriven, Esq. Mr. Haslam, Messrs. Dowling, Palmer, and Powell, to each of whom he is under particular obligations.

*Islington, May* 1, 1811.

# SUBSCRIBERS

ABBOT, Robert, Esq. Upper-street, Islington.
Arch, John and Arthur, Booksellers, Cornhill.
Ashby, Robert, Esq. Highbury-terrace.
Asperne, Mr. James, Bookseller, 32, Cornhill.
Astbury, William, Esq. Portugal-street, Lincoln's-inn-fields.
Aubert, Anthony, Esq. Woodford, Essex.

Banner, T. P. Esq. Broadstairs, Kent.
Barr, Mr. Balls Pond.
Bedwell, Bernard, Esq. Canonbury.
Bentley, John, Esq. Highbury House.
Bishop, Nathaniel, Esq. Gloucester-place, New-road, Mary-le-bone.
Bowles, Henry-Carington, Esq. Bull's Cross, Enfield.
Britton, John, Esq. F. S. A. Tavistock-place.
Browne, W.-R.-H. Esq. Canonbury-square.
Browne, Mr. John, Pleasant-row, Islington.
Browne, Mr. William, Stanton's wharf, Southwark.
Byng, George, Esq. M. P. Wrotham Park, Middlesex.

Caley, John, Esq. F. S. A. Spa fields.
Canonbury Book Society.
Clark, Mr. Thomas, Crown-street, Finsbury.
Clayton, Rev. John, Highbury-place.
Clingand, Mr. Thomas, Stanton's wharf, Southwark.
Cordell, Mr. 4, Terrace, Upper-street, Islington.
Cowie, Robert, Esq. Highbury-place.
Cowie, John, Esq. Newington-green.
Coxhead, Mr. Bookseller, Holywell-street, Strand.
Cross, Mr. James, Upper-street, Islington.

Davidson, Thomas, Esq. Upper-street, Islington.
Dawson, William, Esq. Oddys-row, Upper-street, Islington.
Derrick, Charles, Esq. Tyndale-place, Islington.
Dowling, Mr. John, Astey's-row, Islington.
Drew, Mr. Hedge-row, Islington.

Eade, Jonathan, Esq. Stoke Newington.
Evans, Rev. John, M. A. Pullin's-row, Islington.

Faulkner, Mr. T. Bookseller, Chelsea.
Flower, Mr. Upper-street, Islington, two copies.
Floyer, Mr. R. Bookseller, 428, Strand.
Foster, J. Esq. Tyndale-place, Islington.

Garton, Mr. Colebrooke-row, Islington.
Gaskin, Rev. George, D. D. Rector of Stoke Newington and St. Bennet
        Gracechurch, and Lecturer of Islington.
Godfrey, Mr. H. Colebrooke-row.
Godwin, Captain, Cross-street, Islington.
Gray, Mr. Robert, Terrace, Upper-street, Islington.
Greenland, Mr. Bookseller, Finsbury-place.

Hall, Mr. David, Lower-street, Islington.
Hawksworth, Mr. Chapel-street, Pentonville.
Hedges, Mr. Henry, Upper-street, Islington.
Hope, John-Thomas, Esq. 37, Upper Seymour-street.
Hopkinson, Benjamin, Esq. Upper Grove, Highbury.
Hood, Mr. Lower-street, Islington.
Horton, William, Esq. Highbury.
Huckin, Mr. John, Upper-street, Islington.
Huddart, Joseph, Esq. F. R. S. Highbury-terrace.
Humphreys, Mr. Thomas, Park-place, Islington.

Jackson, John, Esq. Paradise-row, Islington.
Jennings, Rev. Nathaniel, Upper-street, Islington.

Knight, George, Esq. River-terrace, Islington.
Knight, John, Esq. Upper-street, Islington.

Laycock, Mr. Richard, Sebbon's-buildings, Islington.
Lewis, Rev. Thomas, Wells's-row, Islington.
Lucas, Mr. William, Stapleton-hall, Stroud-green.
Lysons, Rev. Daniel, M. A. F. R. S. F. S. A. and L. S. Rector of Rodmar-
    ton, Gloucestershire.

Mellish, William, Esq. M. P. Bush-hill, Enfield.
Meyers, Mr. J. City-road.
Milner, Mrs. Cross-street, Islington.

Northampton, the Earl of, Castle Ashby, Northamptonshire.
Nares, Rev. Archdeacon, Prebendary of Islington.
Neale, Henry-St.-John, Esq. Frith-street, Soho.
Nichols, John,Esq. F. S. A. Lond. Edinb. & Perth, Canonbury-lane.

Oates, Rev. William, Bray's-place, Islington.
Oldershaw, Mr. Vestry Clerk, Lower-street, Islington.

Palmer, William, Esq. Rufford's-buildings, Upper street, Islington.
Parker, Rev. William, Rector of St. Ethelburga, Bishopsgate, Astey's-row,
    Islington.
Parry Roger, Esq. Colebrooke-row.
Percival, Richard, Esq. Highbury-place.
Percival, Richard, jun. Esq. Highbury-place.
Playfair, Mr. George, Hanover-street, Hanover-square.
Pocock, Mr. John, Whitefryars.
Powell, Mr. Hornsey-row, Islington.
Powell, M. Cross-street, Islington.
Pownall, John, Esq. River-terrace.
Pyman, S. W. Esq. Colebrooke-row.

Randall, Mr. Birchin-lane.
Rhodes, Samuel, Esq. Islington.
Ricardo, Abraham, Esq. Canonbury-lane.

Richardson, Mr. J. M. Bookseller, 23, Cornhill.
Rose, Samuel, Esq. Edinburgh.
Rowe, Mr. 9, Dalby-terrace.
Russell, Mr. Bookseller, 122, Upper-street, Islington.

Sanders, Mr. Thomas, Upper-street, Islington.
Score, Mr. William, Bank of England.
Setchel, Mr. Bookseller, King-street, Covent-garden.
Stevenson, Mr. James, Islington-green.
Stockdale, Mr. F. W. L. East India House.
Strahan, Rev. George, D. D. Vicar of Islington, Rector of Cranham,
    Essex, and Prebendary of Rochester.
Sutherland, Alexander, M. D. Physician to St. Luke's Hospital.
Swaine, Thomas, Esq. Canonbury.
Symonds, Mr. H.-D. Astey's-row.

Taylor, William, Esq. 25, Laurence Pountney-lane.
Taylor, Mr. James, York-place, City-road.
Tibbatts, John, Esq. Tyndale-place.

Walker, Mr. J.-G. Conway-street, Fitzroy-square.
Watson, Mr. Thomas, Bridle-lane, Islington.
Wheble, Mr. John, Warwick-square.
White, William, Esq. Highbury-place.
Whittomore, Mr. Thomas, Upper-street, Islington.
Wickings, William, Esq. Barnesbury-place.
Widt, Mr. G.-W. Lower-street, Islington.
Wilkinson, Charles, Esq. Highbury-place.
Willoughby, Mr. Highbury tavern.
Wilson, Joseph, Esq. Highbury.
Wilson, John, Esq. Upper-street, Islington.
Wilson, Thomas, Esq. Oddys-row, Islington.
Wilson, William, Esq. Nether Worton, Oxon.
Wilson, Mr. Robert, East India Dock House.
Winkles, Mr. Terrace, Lower-street, Islington.
Wood, Matthew, Esq. Alderman of London, Highbury-place.
Wormald, John, Esq. 13, Highbury-place.

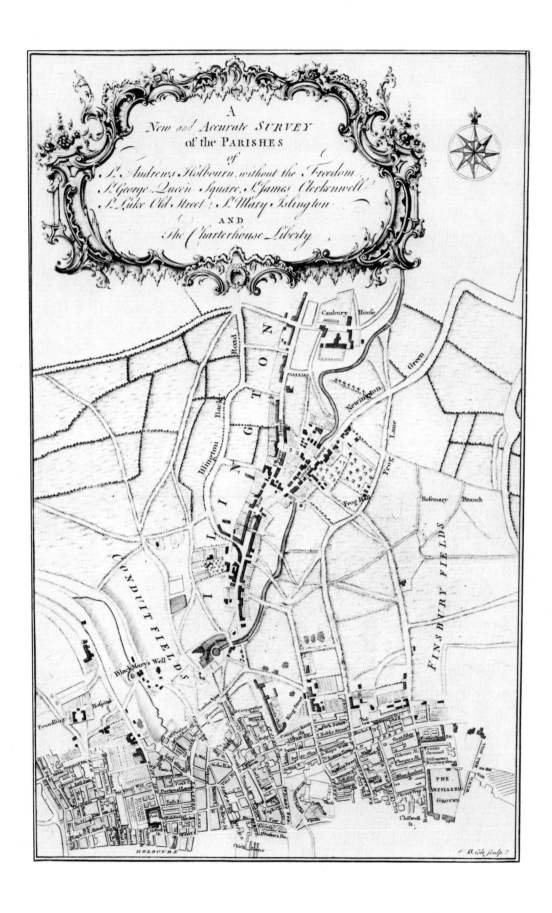

A
*New and Accurate* SURVEY
of the PARISHES
of
*St. Andrews Holbourn, without the Freedom*
*St. George Queen Square, St. James Clerkenwell*
*St. Luke Old Street & St. Mary Islington*
AND
*The Charterhouse Liberty*

Canbury House

ISLINGTON

Road

Back

Islington

Newington Green

Frog Lane

Frog Hall

Rosemary Branch

CONDUIT FIELDS

FINSBURY FIELDS

Black Mary's Well

Hospital

Foundling

King Street

Jack Street
Noble Street

Great Alley

Foster Ground

Dissenters Burying Ground

Blue Anchor

THE ARTILLERY GROUND

WIND MILL HILL

Chiswell St.

HOLBOURN

B. Cole sculp.

Nelson's room in Camden Passage.
Watercolour by T. H. Shepherd, circa 1835.

# HISTORY,

## TOPOGRAPHY, AND ANTIQUITIES

### OF

# ISLINGTON.

---

## INTRODUCTION.

ANTIQUARIAN research, at all times interesting, is found more particularly engaging, when some object with which we are nearly connected, affords the subject of inquiry. The study of our National Antiquities has called forth the talents of the most eminent scholars; and it is generally admitted, that writings on this subject, combining Historical remark with Topographical illustration, are calculated to convey a knowledge of our domestic concerns, in a way the most entertaining and instructive.

To trace the origin and history of a number of those respectable villages that lie scattered throughout the vicinity of London, and which form such delightful appendages to that antient and august city, it is necessary to refer to a very remote period of our metropolitan annals.

In contemplating the establishment of a great city, it will always appear, that within a short space of time the surrounding country begins to experience its effects; for, as the radiance of the sun diffuses vigour and animation wherever his beams extend, so, like that great luminary, a populous and flourishing capital is certain, by its fostering influence, to create a spirit of activity and industry in every surrounding object. The cultivation of the ground, promoted and improved with the rearing of cattle for domestic use, is the first necessary result of that influence, whilst the industrious peasant finds encouragement to his increasing efforts in the metropolitan mart, which is always open to receive the fruits of his toil : hence he derives ample remuneration, in an increase of the comforts and conveniences of life; and the well-peopled city, and the rising village, are soon brought to feel their dependance upon each other.

When London, at a very remote æra, began to increase in extent and population, and to assume a degree of consequence as the mart of trade, and a place of resort for merchants, the quantity of provisions, &c. necessary for its sustenance (though infinitely small in comparison with the luxury of modern times) could not have been produced within its own limits, but must have been necessarily derived from the country adjacent. That these wants were abundantly supplied is evident, since we are informed by Tacitus, in his account of the revolt of the Britons under Boadicea (which happened in the reign of Nero, and about the year 61), that London, though not distinguished by the name of a Roman colony, was a place " famous for concourse of merchants and *provisions*[1]."

In further traces of its history it will be found that in the time of the Emperor Severus (who reigned from 193 to 211), London was

[1] Camden's Britannia, folio, 1695, p. liii. Maitland's London, p. 16. The size and importance of London at the commencement of the Christian æra, may be easily inferred from the circumstance of Suetonius Paulinus marching with so much intrepidity by a dangerous route, and through the heart of an enemy's country, to defend that post against Boadicea, which he found untenable, with an army of 10,000 Romans, well armed and disciplined. See Tacit. Ann. lib. xiv.

distinguished as " a great and wealthy city;" and at the former
period, it is described by the Roman Historian, as " illustrious for
the vast number of merchants who resorted to it, for its widely extended commerce, and for the abundance of every species of commodity which it could supply [1]."

When it is considered that the place which forms the subject of
the following sheets, is scarcely two miles from the centre of the original London; that it is situate upon the *Ermin-street* of the Romans
(one of their principal roads leading from the metropolis), and the
spot where they had a military post; also, that it has, from the earliest period of our history, been celebrated for the richness of its
pastures, and the excellent produce of its dairies, there can remain
little doubt that these circumstances must have rendered it of considerable importance to the Londoners, as well as the garrison there,
who, upon these grounds we may reasonably conjecture, derived a
large proportion of their needful supplies from the luxuriant herbage
of Islington [2].

The farm-houses and buildings (if such they may be called) in
that barbarous age, could have been nothing more than a few hovels
of the most rude and inconvenient form, the peasantry being far
from numerous, and their flocks but thinly scattered : yet there is every
reason to believe, as it respects agriculture and rural economy, that
long before Islington received either a name or a parochial distinc-

---

[1] Tacit. Ann. lib. xiv. c. 33.

[2] Fitzstephen, who died in 1191, in his " Descriptio nobilissimæ Civitatis Lon-
doniæ," notes the following circumstances, which doubtless had existed for centuries before his time, viz. " On the North are fields for pasture and open meadows,
very pleasant, into which the river waters do flow, and mills are turned about with
a delightful noise. The arable lands are no hungry pieces of gravel ground, but
like the rich fields of Asia, which bring plentiful corn, and fill the barns of the
owners with a dainty crop of the fruits of Ceres." Stow's Survey, folio, 1633,
p. 704. By an inquisition taken of the manor of Bernersbury about 1295 (see the
account of that manor), it appears that the estate chiefly consisted of corn land,
with a very small proportion of meadow.

tion, it was a place of some note, and, in a commercial point of view, intimately connected with the city of London.

As the metropolis continued to flourish and increase (which it did to an eminent degree under the Saxon government[1]), while Commerce, smiling on the industrious inhabitants, poured the horn of Plenty into their laps, it may be readily supposed that the manners of the citizen soon became formed, and that, even at this early period, those distinguishing habits and customs which have for centuries marked the civic character, began to prevail: the sedentary or active pursuits of the day called for the recreation or retirement of the evening; and for this purpose, that spot most contiguous to the seat of trade, and possessing peculiar beauty of situation and salubrity of air, was the most likely to attract his attention[2].

That the place we are now contemplating, must in this respect, have excited the early notice of the citizen, there can be little doubt, even were it unknown in the more remote ages; and it may be fairly presumed, that Islington, newly distinguished as a parish, and bearing a name, was a spot often resorted to, either for solace or amusement, by the inhabitants of London.

## ETYMOLOGY, &c.

Few places have experienced more orthographical changes than this village. It has in different antient records been written, Isendune, Isendon, Iseldon, Isleton, Yseldon, and Eyseldon. Some, assigning it a British origin, have derived the name from *Ishel*,

---

[1] Venerable Bede, who flourished about the year 700, observes, that " London was a mart town of great traffic and commerce both by sea and land." Camden's Britannia, p. 314. See also, " An Account of the Trade of the Anglo-Saxons," European Magazine, vol. LIV. p. 13.

[2] William of Malmsbury, who lived in the reign of Stephen, calls London " a city, noble, wealthy, adorned in every part by the riches of the citizens, and frequented by merchants from all parts of the world." Cam. Brit. p. 316.

implying in that language *Lower*, and *don*, from *twyn*, a *forti-fied inclosure;* whence *Ishel don*, the *Lower fortification*[1]. It has been also fancifully derived from the Saxon ʒiʃel, a *hostage*, and ʧun, a *village* or *town*[2]. Others, referring to its cognomen *Isendone*, in the Domesday Survey, which is a Saxon and British compound, signifying *the hill of iron*, derive its etymology from the circumstance of springs of water impregnated with that mineral rising in the vicinity[3]. The present name, Islington, appears to have been generally adopted towards the close of the sixteenth century[4].

The village of Islington is finely situated upon a rising but undulated surface, of rich gravelly and loamy soil, in some parts mixed with clay and sand; and is distant from London, on the Northern side, about one mile on the road to Barnet. The air is remarkably salubrious; and the place is on that account much resorted to by valetudinarians from the metropolis. The parish lies within the Finsbury division of Ossulston hundred, in the county of Middlesex, and is bounded

[1] Hughson's London, vol. VI. p. 373.

[2] See Skynner's Etym. Ling. Angl. and Bailey's Dictionary.

[3] In digging a well for the use of the new houses lately erected on the glebe in the Back Road, large masses of *sulphuret of iron* were found, imbedded in a hard stratum of potter's clay, containing a small portion of *magnesia*, also considerable quantities of a decayed vegetable substance like peat, which on ignition emitted a strong sulphureous smell. The former was also found on sinking a well near the end of Park-street.

[4] In an antient ballad, called, " The Tyrnament of Totenhame, or the wooeing, winning, and wedding of Tibbe the Reve's Daughter there," some of the characters are described as belonging to " *Hisselton.*"

> " Thither came all the men of that countray,
>     Of *Hisselton*, of Higate, and of Hakenay," &c.

A parish within a few miles of Lynn, in the county of Norfolk, has been called *Islington* from a very early period of our history. In Domesday it occurs *Islingetuna;* and in the Ecclesiastical Taxation of Pope Nicholas (A. D. 1290), and all subsequent records, it bears the former name. This name has of late years been also given to a place in the neighbourhood of Birmingham.

by those of Clerkenwell, St. Pancras, Hornsey, Stoke Newington, Hackney, St. Leonard Shoreditch, and St. Luke Old-street. It is three miles two furlongs in length from North-west to South-east; two miles one furlong in breadth from East to West, and 10 miles two furlongs 11 poles in circumference. It contains an area of 3032 acres three roods, of which 2699 acres and 37 perches are almost entirely meadow and pasture, and 333 acres two roods and three perches are occupied by houses, yards, gardens, and wastes. The whole of the arable land throughout the parish, which is included in the above, does not exceed 30 acres, and there are about as many acres of nursery grounds.

Exclusive of the village from which it is named, the parish contains the hamlets of Holloway, Ball's Pond, Battle Bridge, the City Gardens, Kingsland Green, and the greater part of Newington Green [1].

[1] The following is the boundary line observed in the perambulation (which is generally made once in three years); viz. Commence at the stone, South end of the Back road; continue from thence North up the middle of the said road, along the South side of Sermon-lane to the stone at the back gate of White Conduit House (opposite the Spanish Patriots); enter the gate, and continue in a direct line to a stone in the South wall at the front of the house; proceed West along the South bank and wall of White Conduit field (the sewer running by this wall towards Battle Bridge being in Islington parish, and the boundary line thereof); continue along the same to a stone in Smith's (late Gray's) brick field; then turn South along a watercourse to another stone standing upon the same; proceed East of the tile kiln to a stone standing on the foot path at Battle Bridge; cross the road, and proceed in the nearest direction by the West end of a house in the occupation of —— Bourlet, picture-frame maker (which house is numbered 17, and

has on the front $\overset{S}{\underset{1791.}{P\ P}}$ (the mark of St. Pancras parish *) to a stone in the cellar of

a house numbered 26, fronting Gray's-inn-lane road, in the occupation of Elizabeth Reynolds, turner; thence cross the said road to a stone facing the South end of Maiden-lane, and which is placed on the South bank of the old river Fleet

* All the houses from the above mark, forming the angle opposite Maiden-lane between Battle Bridge and Gray's-inn-lane road, though within the parish of Islington, have been time out of mind assessed, and have paid the rates to the parish of St. Pancras. When, or from what cause, this originated, cannot now be ascertained.

The principal Northern road, which is here called the Upper Street, runs through the whole length of the village, and passes on to Highgate through Holloway: from this there is one branching off at the Green, nearly in the centre of the town, which takes the name of the Lower Street, and leads to Stoke Newington and

within the fence where is now a dust hill belonging to John Smith; proceed up the West bank of Maiden-lane by the old hedge-rows to the stone at the entrance of the lane leading to Kentish Town; continue along the West bank to a stone at the top of the lane; then cross the turnpike road at Highgate-hill, and proceed East along the South side of Hornsey-lane to the stone at the North end of Du Val's lane; proceed along the opposite fields, following the hedge-row (which divides this parish from Hornsey), taking in the two wooden dwelling-houses West of Mount Pleasant, to the stone at the West side of the road leading from Crouch-end; then cross the said road, and continue East along the North bank at Mount Pleasant to a stone in the corner of the field; then turn South along the West bank of the fields towards Stroud Green, and West along the old hedge-row, across an inclosure of Mr. Blackall's, to the Hornsey mark on the cart-house at Japan-house (Mr. Blackall's *), and then South to the stone at the North-east corner of Stroud Green †; proceed South along the East bank of Stroud Green to the stone opposite Heame-lane, and thence down the middle of Boarded-river-lane to the bridge where was formerly the Boarded-river; then turn East along the middle of the said lane to a stone at Willan's farm; thence proceed South along the old West bank of the Green-lanes (now a turnpike road) to a stone in the corner of a field; and from thence East to the house of John Freeman, Esq. Newington Green, where the boundary is marked by a flat stone in the yard ‡; cross from thence to the stone at the rails which separate the North side of the Green from the road; then proceed East and South-east along the South-west bank of the Coach and Horses-lane to a stone at the corner of a green lane, and continue South along the East side of the said lane to a stone on the waste; then along the water-course to a stone on Kingsland Green §; proceed along the East side of the

* John Blackall, Esq. pays 1l. to the churchwardens on the day of perambulation, as an acknowledgment, for the privilege of a wall standing on (the waste) parish ground.

† On the day of perambulation the churchwardens provide rolls, cheese, and ale, at this place, for the refreshment of the inhabitants and the charity children forming the procession, which is obligingly distributed at the house of John Blackall, Esq. whose premises on this occasion exhibit a scene of unusual festivity.

‡ Mr. Freeman pays 5s. *per annum* on the perambulation day, for the privilege of his wall standing on parish land.

§ Mr. Elderton, at Kingsland Green, pays 10s. *per annum* for a similar privilege.

Kingsland, also the Green Lanes leading to Enfield; another, called the Back Road, which runs behind the whole extent of the houses on the Western side of the Upper Street, commences at the turnpike near the entrance of the village, and falls into the main road near the toll gate at Ring Cross [1].

said green to Kingsland chapel *, enter the door on the North side, and pass through the same by a door opposite, keeping on the West side of the old Lock Hospital to a stone at the opposite bank; then turn West along the said bank at the back of the houses and premises on the South side of the Ball's Pond road to a stone at the corner of the lane leading to Islington common, and turning South along the East bank of the said lane to the stone at the corner of the common; then turn East to the stone by the water-course, and again South with the bank of the water-course of the common (late a brick field) to the sunk stone at the Rose-mary-branch; turn West to the stone nearly opposite the Rosemary-branch public house, and then, in an oblique line from that stone, to the boundary stone of St. Leonard Shoreditch at the corner of Mr. Rhodes's field; then South-west along the bank to the stone near the porter's resting-block in the Prebend-field; conti-nue South-west along the bank towards the City Gardens; then turn South to the stone near the corner of Fuller's garden, and again to the stone on the West side of the ditch at the City Gardens, following the ditch to another stone close to the arch over the same, and further West to the stone near the new houses (late Keith's garden ground); turn South, pursuing the water-course, and cross the City road to an iron plate having the parish mark at the gate of house No. 5, the East end of St. Vincent's-row; continue in a line to the stone in Neal's cow-house, between the City road and the Goswell-street road, and from thence to a stone in a wall behind the new buildings in Sidney-place; proceed from hence in a line through the house No. 2 in Sidney-street to a stone near the South-west corner of that street in the Goswell-street road, then turn North-west along the North bank of the said road, crossing the New River close by the tool-house to a stone at the point between the City and Goswell-street roads; from thence con-tinue along the middle of the road to the High-street, and thence North to the South end of the Back road, where the perambulation begins.

[1] Edward and Benjamin Baker, two ingenious artists residing at Islington, en-graved and published in 1793 a very neat plan of the village, size 12 inches by 10, containing also a statistical account of the parish, its population, &c.

* On the perambulation day, prayers are read in this chapel by the clergyman attending the procession.

The parish is divided into six liberties or districts, named from the manors in which they are situate; viz.

St. John of Jerusalem;

Upper Barnesbury;

Lower Barnesbury;

Canonbury;

The Prebend; and

Highbury, or Newington Barrow.

The affairs of the parish are governed by a general vestry, composed of not less than thirteen housekeepers, assembled in the vestry-room, after due notice given in the church. There are usually two held in the year, unless particular business renders it necessary for others to be called. The first is on Easter Tuesday, for the purpose of choosing parish officers for the year ensuing; and the other is in the month after Easter, to make and sign the poor's rate[1].

The officers appointed by the vestry, and in whom the management of the parish concerns is vested, are three churchwardens, two overseers of the poor, and an assistant overseer, who is also beadle. Each of the churchwardens has the assistance of a sidesman. There are also a surveyor of highways and foot-paths, and two supervisors of the watch, exclusive of the constables and headboroughs, of whom one constable and one headborough is appointed over each of the several districts before named, except that of St. John of Jerusalem, the officers of which, a constable and two headboroughs, are nominated by the lord of that manor. The general business of the parish, calling the vestries, &c. is conducted by the vestry-clerk.

The quota paid towards the land tax is £.2001. 0s. 10d. the amount redeemed being £.606. 5s. 6d. and the assessed taxes for the year

---

[1] The poor of this parish are supported by virtue of an Act, 17 Geo. III. cap. 5, intituled, " An Act for the better Relief and Employment of the Poor of the Parish " of St. Mary Islington, in the County of Middlesex, and for building a Workhouse " for the said Parish." This act was amended by another passed in April 1802.

ending April 1810, produced about £.19,300. The poor's rates for the last three years have averaged about 2s. 5d. in the pound. An adequate sum is collected for watching and lighting the village and its vicinity [1]; and a fund is also raised annually by composition (in lieu of statute duty), for repairing the parish roads and foot-paths [2]: the rate for this purpose from Lady-day 1808 to Lady-day 1809 produced £.1,840. 8s. 4d. By virtue of the Act of 46 Geo. III. the dust is annually disposed of to the highest bidder: the first year (1806) it produced £.850. 10s.; the next year £.498. 15s.; in 1808 it produced £.450.; in 1809 £.651.; and is at present contracted for at £.840. This money is applied towards the purposes of the Act last mentioned.

The number of inhabitants in this parish, according to the return made to government under the Act passed in the year 1800, (40 Geo. III.) for ascertaining the population of the whole kingdom, amounted to 10,212, being 4,189 males, and 6,023 females. Of the total of these 115 were stated to be employed in agriculture; 892 chiefly in trade, manufactures, or handicraft; and 9,205 not included in either of these classes. The number of houses, according to this return, was 1,665, occupied by 2,228 families, and 80 were uninhabited; making a total of 1745.

[1] By stat. 12 Geo. III. cap. 17, intituled, " An Act for lighting such Part of " the Town of Islington as lies in the Parish of St. Mary Islington, in the County of " Middlesex; and for establishing a regular nightly Watch therein." This was al- " tered and amended by an Act of 46 Geo. III. which also provides " for the re- " moving and preventing nuisances and annoyances within the said town and parish."

[2] By stat. 35 Geo. III. intituled, " An Act for amending, improving, and keep- " ing in repair, the Road leading from the Hamlet of *Highgate*, in the County of " Middlesex, through a certain Lane called *Maiden-lane*, in the Parish of St. Mary " Islington, to a certain Place called *Battle Bridge*, in the same County, and the " several other Highways and Foot-paths in the said Parish of St. Mary Islington " (which are not included in any Turnpike Acts); and to enable the Inhabitants of " the said Parish to raise Money for that and other the Purposes therein men- " tioned."

It is not generally considered that the returns, made under the Population Act were very correct; nor was great accuracy, from the nature of the enquiry, to be expected. With regard to some of the above particulars, the statement is without doubt erroneous. The excess in the number of families in proportion to the houses inhabited, may however be accounted for, by many persons having apartments here, especially during the summer months. On examination into the present state of the parish, as to these particulars, it appears that the number of houses is about 2,200, and the population may be estimated at 14,000 [1].

The following will exhibit a comparative statement of the number of houses and inhabitants that have been estimated to be in Islington parish, at different periods, during the last century; viz.

|  | Houses. | Inhabitants. |
|---|---|---|
| In 1708 [2]. | 325 | |
| 1754 [3]. | 937 | |
| 1788 [4]. | 1,060 | |
| 1793 [5]. | 1,200 | 6,600 |
| 1800 [6]. | 1,745 | 10,212 |
| 1810. | 2,200 | 14,000. |

[1] The parish at this time contains 55 licensed public-houses, 17 bakers' shops, and there are about 40 inhabitants who keep four-wheeled carriages.

[2] New View of London.

[3] Seymour's Survey of London.

[4] MS. of Mr. Biggerstaff, vestry-clerk.

[5] Ibid. and Baker's Plan.

[6] Population Act.

ROADS AND WAYS.

It has been generally supposed, that the Roman military way, called the Ermin, or *Herman-street*[1], led from Cripplegate Northward through Islington, and, as some have thought, nearly in the line of the present high road.  It appears more probable that its route was along the antient bridle-way, leading from Brick-lane, and crossing the City road, whence proceeding by the Eastern side of the village, it passed by Highbury and Hornsey Wood, and continued by way of the Green Lanes towards Enfield.

As it was the custom of that people to make their roads in a line as direct as possible, unless when some local impediment intervened, it is probable that the present road has, in either case, some deviation from the course of their military way.  Mr. Maitland is of opinion[2], that the route of the Herman-street lay over *Stroud Green*, and mentions the appearance of the ground there, as indicative of such a circumstance ; but as in that case it would either have to surmount the acclivity of Highbury, or form an unnecessary curve, this is perhaps not altogether correct.  There is however sufficient reason to believe that it passed near to this village; and it is highly probable that the summer camp belonging to the garrison in London (which is supposed to have been upon the hill at Highbury) was situate not far distant from their military way.

An old road is mentioned by Stow[3], who informs us, that before the erection of Bishopsgate, travellers refusing to take their journey Eastward out at Aldgate, " must then take their way by the North " out at Aldersgate, through Aldersgate-streete and Goswell-streete

[1] Ermin, quod þeneman, signifies *a soldier*, and reþet, Saxon, a *road* or *way*, equivalent to the Latin *via militaris*.

[2] History and Survey of London, p. 16.

[3] Survey of London, p. 33.

" towards *Iseldon*, and by a crosse of stone on their right hand, set
" up for a marke, by the North end of *Golding-lane*, to turne Eastward
" through a long streete, unto this day called *Alde-streete*, to another
" crosse then there standing, where now a smith's forge is placed, by
" *Sewers-ditch* church, and then to turne again North towards To-
" tenham, Enfield, Waltham, Ware, &c."

Mr. Ellis, who quotes the above passage in his History of Shoreditch (p. 103), considers it to have given rise to an opinion, that the
*Herman-street* went in the same direction : but the road described by
Stow was comparatively modern ; and after leaving Aldersgate, passed
from Goswell-street to Shoreditch church, upon the line of the *Via
Iceniana*, which led from Staines, in this county, to Colchester, in
Essex [1]. This was a different road from the *Herman-street*, the route
of which lay Northward, and probably intersected the above about
the spot where afterwards stood the " crosse of stone," mentioned in
the preceding extract.

After quitting the Surrey side of the Thames (which, as Mr. Ellis
conjectures, was most probably by way of Stoney-street, in the parish of St. Mary Overy's), the most likely place for its continuation
on the City side, was the antient *Trajectus*, or water gate of *Dour-
gate* (or Dowgate), where it would embrace the Watling-street.
From this place Cripplegate lay in a Northern direction, the proper
course of the *Herman-street* ; it must therefore, in proceeding from
that gate, have necessarily been continued along the Eastern side of
Islington [2].

---

[1] Stukeley's Itin. Curiosum.

[2] After all that can be said, as to the course of the Roman military ways in this
country, since the lapse of so many centuries, a great deal must necessarily be left in
doubt, or founded on conjecture. The author, in the present instance, cheerfully
adopts the sentiment of the learned author of " Britannia Romana ;" who, after enu-
merating the various speculations of Antiquaries as to the route of the *Herman-
street*, very properly concludes, " I shall leave every man to his own opinion."

The highways and roads connected with this village, were, till of late years, very badly kept, and extremely incommodious. Formerly the avenues leading to Islington from the metropolis (exclusive of the foot paths over the fields) were confined to the road passing from Smithfield through St. John's-street, the Goswell-street road leading from Aldersgate, and the antient bridle-way[1] before mentioned; and these were frequently in the winter time rendered almost impassable.

The former of these seems to have been a road of some consequence at a very early period, owing perhaps in a great measure to its affording the communication between the two priories of St. John of Jerusalem, and St. Bartholomew in Smithfield, with their possessions in this parish. Among the records in the Tower is a patent for " *Pavage* for the highway from Smithfield Bars to Gore's place, *Iseldon*," about the year 1380[2]; and certain customs were granted in the preceding reign for repairing the highway between *Highgate* and Smithfield[3]. Such, however, was the state of the highways in this district, not more than 40 years back, that travellers were frequently obliged in their journeys to and from the metropolis, in the winter season, to remain all night at the inns in the village, as the roads were absolutely dangerous after the close of day. The Red Lion, the Angel, and the Pied Bull, were at that time houses of great resort for persons journeying the Northern road[4].

---

[1] This bridle-way used formerly to be much frequented by travellers, pack horses, &c. Some years ago a toll was collected upon it for the Highgate and Hampstead trust; but persons now pass that way on horseback toll-free to the City. The right of way by this road, over the West end of the *Prebend-field* to Frog-lane, was, some few years since, a matter of contest betweeu the occupier of the field, and Mr. Aubert, of Highbury. The latter gentleman, on this occasion, caused a gate to be cut down, which had been put up by the former to prevent horses passing over. The way has since continued open, and the right undisputed.

[2] First part Pat. 4 Richard II. No. 19.

[3] Second part Pat. 37 Edward III. No. 25.

[4] Ogleby's " Itinerarium Angliæ" (anno 1674) describes the road from London to Holyhead as coming from Cheapside, " through Blowbladder-street, Newgate-

Stow informs us, that Sir Thomas Falconer, Lord Mayor of London in the year 1415, " caused the wall of the City to bee broken " towards the Moore field, and builded the postern called Moore Gate, " for ease of the citizens to walke that way upon *causies* towards Isel- " don and Hoxton [1]." This appears to be the origin of the old highway leading from Moorgate to the Dog-house bar[2]. He also remarks, that in his time, " many faire houses were builded by the highway leading from the priory of St. John's towards Iseldon;" and that persons used to come that way to Clerkenwell church from Highgate, Moswell, &c.

Thomas Sutton, Esq. founder of the Charter-house, gave 40 marks to the mending of the highways between Islington and Newington[3].

street, by Pye-corner, Smithfield, St. John's-street, and, crossing the New River, enter Islington, *full of inns and other public houses*, whence $3\frac{1}{2}$ pass by *Ring-cross* to Lower and Upper Holloway, &c."

Less than half a century ago, it was not uncommon for robberies to be committed, even in the heart of the village : both carriages and foot passengers were frequently stopt in the most daring manner ; and it was usual for persons walking from the City in the evening to wait at the end of St. John's-street, till a sufficient party was collected, who were then escorted to Islington by an armed patrole appointed for that purpose. The annals of the Old Bailey abound with instances of delinquents who have been apprehended for robberies and murders committed in this neighbourhood, till of late years that the police has been kept on a more respectable footing. A quarto sheet, published in 1674, bears the following title: " Four great and hor- " rible murders, or *Bloody News from Islington*; being a full and true relation how a " woman's brains were knocked out with her own patten, robbed, and her throat cut, " on Tuesday the 5th of February instant ; a man beaten to death, the 8th of the " same month ; and a woman drowned herself in a pond at Islington, &c." British Topography.

[1] Survey of London, p. 475.

[2] A toll-gate so called, from being contiguous to the house where the City hounds were kept, near the end of Old-street. The City huntsman had also a dwelling in the fields hard by, about the spot where the Angel public house, in the City road, now stands.

[3] Stow's Survey, p. 480.

The following curious anecdote is related by Strype [1]; viz. " Beyond
" Aldersgate Bars, leaving the Charter-house on the left hand
" stretches up toward ISELDON, commonly called *Islington,* a country
" town hard by, which in the former age was esteemed to be so plea-
" santly seated, that in 1581, Queen Elizabeth (in one of the 12 days)
" on an evening rode that way to take the air, where near the town
" she was environed with a number of begging rogues (as beggars
" usually haunt such places) which gave the Queen much disturbance.
" Whereupon Mr. Stone, one of her footmen, came in all haste to the
" Lord Mayor, and to Fleetwood, the Recorder, and told them the
" same.  The same night did the Recorder send out warrants into the
" same quarters, and into Westminster, and the Dutchy; and in the
" morning he went out himself, and took that day seventy-four rogues,
" whereof some were blind, and yet great usurers, and very rich.  Upon
" Twelfth-day, the Recorder met the Governor of Bridewell; and
" they examined, together, all the abovesaid seventy-four rogues,
" and gave them *substantial payment,* and the strongest they bestowed
" in the milne and the lighters; the rest were dismissed, with a pro-
" mise of double payment if they were met with again."

For several centuries previous to the reign of Charles I., many of
the Nobility, as well as the more opulent Citizens, seem to have had
houses at Islington, and a few other villages North of London, of
which many instances might be adduced, (for the air of the Court
and the West end of the Town was not then found so inviting as at
the present day).  Their dwellings were usually not far distant from
town, which was probably owing to the badness of the roads: it indeed seems clear that they were only passable occasionally.  This state
of the highways (which were equally bad all round the metropolis),
together with their circuitous route, and general inconvenience, rendered it in these times a common thing for great personages travelling
with their equipage, &c. to turn out of the highway, and make the

---

[1] Survey of London, v. II. p. 59.

nearest cut across the fields, to their point of destination. The grounds in this neighbourhood, from their being almost in common, and uninclosed, were particularly convenient in this respect.

In July 1561, Queen Elizabeth went from the Tower, through Houndsditch, to the Spittle, and down Hog-lane " *over the fields*" to the Charter house. From thence in a few days she took her way *over the fields* unto the Savoy; and shortly after she came from Enfield to St. James's: from Islington thither " the hedges and ditches were " cut down to make the *next way* for her[1]."

King James I. on his first coming to London, after the death of Elizabeth, was met at Stamford Hill, by the Lord Mayor and Aldermen, in scarlet gowns and chains of gold, and the principal City Officers, besides " 500 grave citizens," all mounted on horseback, in velvet coats and chains of gold, together with the officers of state, with numerous other attendants, from whence they proceeded *over the fields* to the Charter house. Charles I. on his return from Scotland, in 1641, came by a similar route, across the fields from Newington, by Sir George Whitmore's, at Hoxton, and entered the City by Moorgate, accompanied by his Queen, the Prince of Wales, the Duke of York, and a splendid cavalcade.

In the month of October 1642, the Committee of the Militia of London gave orders, that trenches and ramparts should be made near all the highways leading to the City; as at Islington, in the fields near Pancras church, Mile-end, &c. This work was carried on for several months[2]. In May and June 1643, it was prosecuted with uncommon zeal, as appears by the following extracts from the public papers:

" May 8. The work in the fields to trench the City goes on amain. " Many thousands of men, women, and servants, go out daily

---

[1] Collection of Queen Elizabeth's Progresses, published by Nichols.
[2] England's Memorable Occurrences, Oct. 24—31, 1642.

" to work; and this day there went out a great company of the
" Common Council, and divers other chief men of the City, with
" the greatest part of the trained bands, with spades, shovels, pick-
" axes, &c." [1]

" May 9. This day many thousands of citizens, their wives, and
" families, went out to dig, and all the porters in and about the City,
" to the number of 2,000. — May 23. Five thousand felt-makers
" and cappers went to work at the trenches, near 3,000 porters, with
" a great company of men, women, and children. — May 24. Four
" or five thousand shoe-makers. — June 5. Six thousand taylors [2]."
" — It was wonderful to see how the women and children, and vast
" numbers of people, would come and work about digging and car-
" rying of earth, to make their new fortifications [3]."

On this occasion, a battery and breast-work at Mount Mill, in
the Goswell-street road; another at the end of St. John's street; a
large fort, with four half bulwarks at the New River Upper Pond;
and a small redoubt near Islington Pound; were erected for the protection of the Metropolis on the Northern side [4].

Of the origin of the road over Highgate Hill, we are thus informed
by Norden [5]; viz. " The old and auncient highwaie to *High Bernet*
" from *Port Poole,* now *Gray's Inn,* as also from Clerkenwell,
" was through a lane on the East of *Pancras Church,* called *Long-*
" *wich Lane;* from thence, leaving *Highgate* on the *West,* it
" passed through *Tallingdone-lane,* and so to *Crouch-ende;* and

---

[1] This gave rise to the satirical song, " Roundheaded Cuckolds, come dig,"
which was made by the Cavaliers, in the Civil wars, upon the opposite party, whom
they styled the Roundheads.

[2] Perfect Diurnal, quoted by Lysons.

[3] Whitelocke's Memorials, p. 60.

[4] These fortifications consisted of a strong earthen rampart, flanked with bas-
tions, redoubts, &c. surrounding the whole City and its liberties, including
Southwark.

[5] Speculum Britanniæ.

" thence, through a parke, called *Harnsey Great Parke*, to *Mus-*
" *well-hill*, to *Coanie Hatch, Fryarne Barnet*, and so to *Whet-*
" *stone*. This auncient highway was refused of wayfaring men and
" carriers, by reason of the deepness and dirtie passage in the win-
" ter season. In regarde whereof, it was agreed, betweene the
" Bishop of London and the Countrie, that a newe waie shoulde
" be laide forth through the said Bishop's parke, beginning at
" *Highgate hill*, to leade (as now is accustomed) directly to Whet-
" stone: for which newe waie all cartes, carriers, packmen, and such
" like travellers, yeelde a certain Tole unto the Bishop of London,
" which is now fermed at *£*.40. *per annum;* and for that pur-
" pose was the gate erected on the hill, that through the same all
" travellers shoulde passe, and be the more aptlie staide for the
" same tole [1]."

So lately as the year 1714, when the Act of Parliament passed for
erecting turnpikes on the roads about Islington, Highgate, &c. the
preamble stated them to be " very ruinous, and almost impassable for
" the space of five months in the year." The road from Paddington
to Islington was made by virtue of an Act of Parliament, 29
Geo. II. (1756), after a violent contest between the Duke of Bedford, who opposed it, thinking it would approach too near to
Bedford-house, and the Duke of Grafton, who supported it with all
his power [2].

About the year 1756, a scheme was projected by Charles Dingley,
Esq. [3] for making a new road from the South end of Islington, over

---

[1] According to Camden's account, this road must have been opened upwards of
500 years (Brit. p. 309). The Bishop of London continues to receive the profits
of the tolls paid at the gate, which are now farmed at a much larger sum. The
old gate was taken down, and the road opened, at the joint expence of the Islington and Whetstone trust, in 1769.

[2] Ellis's Campagna of London, p. 102.

[3] A gentleman well known for his unsuccesful attempt to establish in this country
that useful piece of mechanism, the saw-mill.

the fields to the *Dog-house Bar* before mentioned, and thereby to open
a communication between the City and the Western parts of the
Metropolis, by the above mentioned road leading to Paddington.
It being considered that this would greatly facilitate the intercourse
between the City of London, and the Northern and Western
roads; and prove a most valuable accommodation to the inhabitants of
Islington and the adjacent villages; it was speedily carried into effect,
under and by virtue of an Act of Parliament of 1 Geo. III. intituled,
" An Act for making, widening, and repairing, a Road from the
" North-east Side of the Goswell-street Road next Islington, in the
" County of Middlesex, and near to the Road called the *New Road,*
" over the Fields and Grounds to Old-street Road, opposite to *the*
" *Dog-house Bar,* and at and from the *Dog-house Bar* to the End
" of Chiswell-street by the Artillery-ground."

This road being completed, under and by virtue of the above-
mentioned act, was opened on the 29th of June, 1761 [1], by the name
of the City-road; and it continues at this day one of the finest highways leading from the Metropolis [2]. The turnpike at the entrance of
the village was first erected after the making of this road, and it then
stood near the end of White Lion-street, but was removed, about 20
years ago, close to the entrance of the Back Road. This situation
having been found very dangerous to carriages in turning, and the
occasion of many accidents, by reason of the sharpness of the angle,
the gate was again removed, in 1808, to the spot it now occupies,
near midway between its two former positions. The two toll-houses,
and the weighing engine, were completed, by contract, for the
sum of £.700, or thereabouts, paid by the trustees of the high-

---

[1] Entick's History and Survey of London, vol. III. p. 185.

[2] By the Act passed in 1766, for the better paving, lighting, and cleansing the
City of London, &c. tolls are directed to be taken at the gates of the City Road,
Ball's Pond, Islington, Holloway, &c. towards the purposes of that Act. Ibid.
p. 285.

Drawn by Schnebbelie, & Engraved by Hay.

For R. Hughsons Description of London.

*Entrance to* LONDON *from Islington.*

Published by J. Stratford, 112, Holborn Hill, Feb.16.1810.

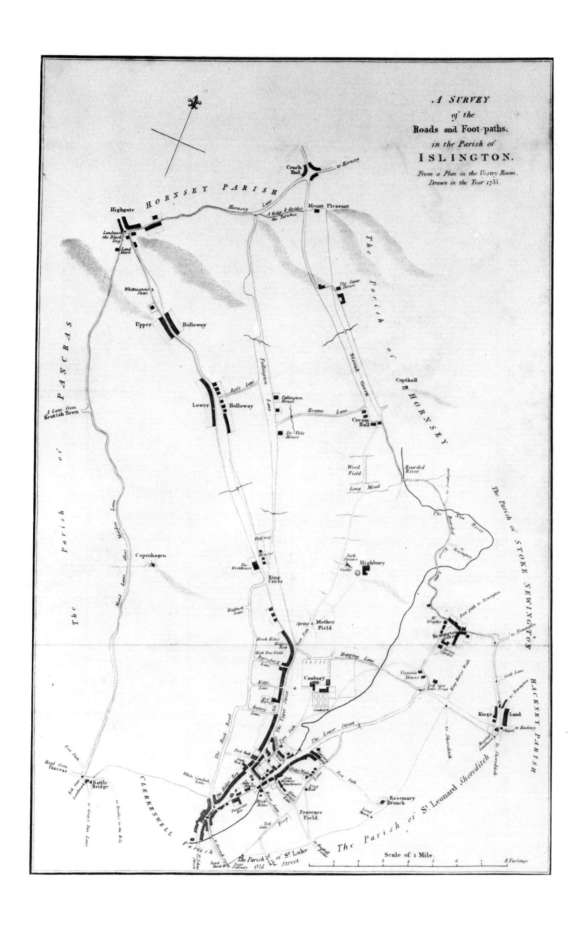

ways, and forms a very handsome entrance into the village from London.

On digging for the foundation of the toll-houses, the ballast and other materials appeared to have been laid upon the road to the depth of six feet. Its thickness in the Lower-street is about five feet, and it averages the same depth in several parts of the Upper-street. The parish of Islington contains six miles four furlongs and seven poles of turnpike roads, seven miles three furlongs and sixteen poles bye roads, and nine miles one furlong and thirty-six poles of foot-paths and church-ways[1]. The former are under the direction of the Hampstead and Highgate trust, and the two latter are maintained at the expence of the parish. The annexed plan of the roads and ways copied from the original in the vestry-room, taken in the year 1735, will give a general idea of the state of the parish, with respect to the number of buildings it contained at that period.

[1] Biggerstaff's MS.

PASTIMES OF THE CITIZENS, &C.

Islington, as it has been before observed, appears to have been for many centuries a place resorted to by the citizens of London. Fitz-stephen, who flourished in the reign of Henry the Second, speaks as to circumstances in its immediate neighbourhood in connexion with the City, and which must have existed (perhaps for many ages) before he wrote his book. " There are," says he, " on the North " part of London, principal fountains of water, sweet, wholesome, " and clear, streaming forth among the glistering pebble stones : in " this number, Holy-well, Clerkenwell, and St. Clement's well, " are of most note, and frequented above the rest, when scholars, " and the youth of the City, take the air abroad in the summer " evenings [1]."

The amusements of the citizens, as described by this antient writer, were confined to the Northern vicinity of the capital; but it appears, that at this period it was not unusual for wrestling matches, shooting, casting the stone, and other pastimes between the citizens and the villagers, to be held at places farther distant from the City than either of the situations above mentioned [2].

Fitzstephen informs us, that in the afternoon the youth of the City were accustomed to go out *into the fields*, with their teachers, to play at ball; the scholars of every school having their particular balls; while " the antient and wealthy citizens came on horseback " to see these youngsters contending at their sport :" that exercises on horseback, to qualify them for military pursuits, were used every

[1] Stow's Survey of London, p. 710.

[2] In the year 1222, 6 Henry III. " on St. James's day, the citizens of London " kept games of defence and wrestling, near to the Hospital of Matilda, at St. Giles's " in the Fields, where they got the mastery of the men of the suburbs." Ibid. p. 77.

*Friday* [1] afternoon in Lent; and that on these occasions the sons of the citizens came out of the City in great numbers. He likewise adds, that the citizens took delight in birds, such as *sparrow-hawks*, *goss-hawks*, &c. and in dogs, for following the sports of the field.

Stow, speaking of the fields in the Northern environs of London, describes them as " commodious for the citizens therein to walke, " shoote, and otherwise to recreate and refresh their dulled spirits, in " the sweet and wholesome ayre." He also mentions, that it was " customary of old time" for the officers of the City, " namely, the " sheriffs, the porters of the King's beame or weigh-house, and other " of the Citie," to be challengers of all men in the suburbs, to wrestle, shoot the standard, broad arrow, and flight, for games, at Clerkenwell, and in Finsbury fields [2].

But among the variety of pastimes used by the citizens in antient times, none seems to have been more attended to than the practice of shooting with the long bow; and the fields extending from the City wall to the vicinity of ISLINGTON, HOXTON, and SHOREDITCH, and known by the name of *Finsbury fields*, were kept in common for that purpose: a right which appears to have been from time immemorial enjoyed by the Londoners in the exercise of their several amusements.

The encouragement of this pastime was a measure of the first political importance, and of which most of our Kings subsequent to the Norman Conquest seemed fully aware, as is evident, from the statutes that were repeatedly enacted for the regulation of the exercise.

In 1365, Edward the Third commanded the Sheriffs of London to make proclamation, that " every one of the said City, strong in " body, at leisure times, on holydays, should use in their recreations " bows and arrows, or pellets, or bolts, and learn and exercise the art.

[1] Some copies of Fitzstephen's tract read *Sunday*.
[2] Stow's Survey of London, p. 85.

" of shooting, forbidding all and singular in our behalf, that they do
" not after any manner apply themselves to the throwing of stones,
" hand-ball, foot-ball, bandy-ball, lambuck, or cock fighting, nor
" such other like vain plays which have no profit in them [1]."

In 1392, an Act passed to oblige servants to shoot with bows and
arrows on holydays and Sundays; and of such consequence was excellence in this art esteemed, that Sir John Fortescue, an eminent
lawyer in the reign of Henry VI. again and again declares, " that
" the mighte of the realme of Englande standyth upon archers [2]."

During the reign of Henry VIII. (who had from early life practiced the manly and athletic exercises, particularly that of the bow)
several statutes were made for the promotion of archery. He
granted, in the 29th year of his reign, a patent to Sir Christopher
Morris, Master of the Ordnance, and others, that they should be
overseers of the science of artillery, " to wit, long bowes, cross
" bowes, and hand gonnes;" with liberty for them and their fraternity
to exercise shooting at all manner of marks and butts, and at the
game of the popinjay, and other games, as at fowl and fowls, as
well in the City and suburbs, and in all other places. In this patent
there was one remarkable passage, viz. that in case any person was
shot or slain in these sports by an arrow shot by any of these
archers, he was not to be sued nor molested, if he had, immediately
before he shot, used the word FAST [3].

Arthur, the elder brother of Henry, was particularly fond of this
exercise; insomuch, that an expert bowman was styled *Prince
Arthur* [4]. In the third year of this reign, every father was directed
to provide a bow and two arrows for his son when he should be seven

[1] Rot. Claus. 39 Edw. III.

[2] Anecdotes of Archery, by E. Hargrove, York, 1792, 12mo, p. 35.

[3] See a copy of this patent in Highmore's History of the Artillery Company,
p. 40.

[4] Barrington's " Observations on the Practice of Archery in England." Archæologia, vol. VII. p. 66.

years old; also, in the sixth year of the same reign, all persons, except the Clergy and Judges, were obliged to shoot at butts [1].

In a splendid shooting match at Windsor, before the King, when the exercise was nearly over, his Majesty, observing one of his guard, named *Barlo*, preparing to shoot, said to him, " Beat them " all, and thou shalt be Duke of Archers." Barlo drew his bow, executed the King's command, and received the promised reward, being created *Duke of Shoreditch*, that being the place of his residence [2]. Several others of the most expert marksmen were in like manner honoured with titles, as *Marquis of Islington*, the *Earl of Pancridge*, &c. taken from those villages where they resided. The title of Duke of Shoreditch descended for several generations with the Captainship of the London Archers.

It is noted by Hall, in his Chronicle, about 6 Henry VIII. that " before this time the inhabitants of the towns about London, as " ISELDON, HOXTON, SHORESDITCH, and others, had so inclosed the " common fields with hedges and ditches, that neither the young men " of the City might shoote, nor the antient persons walke for their " pleasures in those fields, but that either their bowes and arrowes " were taken away or broken, or the honest persons arrested or in- " dighted, saying, that no Londoner ought to go out of the City but " in the highwayes.

" This saying so grieved the Londoners, that suddainly this yeere " a great number of the City assembled themselves in a morning; and " a *turner, in a foole's coate,* came crying thorow the City, *shovels* " *and spades, shovels and spades.* So many of the people followed, " that it was wonder to behold; and within a short space all the

[1] Anecdotes of Archery, p. 45. In an old ballad, written in praise of the Princess Elizabeth, wife of Henry VII. his Majesty is described as employed in a princely amusement.

" See where he *shooteth* at the *buttes,* and with him Lordes three."

Harl. MSS. 367.

[2] Strype's Stow, vol. I. p. 302.

E

" hedges about the City were cast down, and the ditches filled up, and
" every thing made plaine, such was the diligence of these workemen."
The rioters having thus effected their purpose, returned quietly to
their respective homes; " after which," says Hall, " those fields
" were never hedged [1]."

In 1583, there was a splendid shooting match in Smithfield, un-
der the direction of the *Duke of Shoreditch*, Captain of the London
Archers, with his several officers, the Marquisses of Clerkenwell,
Islington, Hoxton, and Shacklewell, the Earl of Pancras, &c.

In the " Remembrance of the worthy Show and Shooting, by the
" Duke of Shoreditch and his Associates, upon Tuesday the 17th of
" September, 1583, by W. M." (London, 12mo, 1682), we are
told, that " the train passed to Shoreditch church, and then turned
" down into *Hogsden fields*, into a faire large green pasture ground
" of goodly compass, where a tent was set up for the Duke and the
" chief citizens [2]." This exercise lasted two days. There were
assembled archers to the amount of 3,000, each having a sash, a long
bow, and four arrows. On the evening of the second day, the vic-
tors were led off the field, mounted on horses, and attended by
200 persons, each bearing a lighted torch in his hand [3].

Paul Hentzner, in his Journey to England, in the reign of Elizabeth, observes, " the English make great use of bows and arrows
" to this day in their exercises." It appears, however, that the
practice was at this period on the decline; for, about the year 1570,
the Bowyers, Fletchers, Stringers, and Arrow-head-makers, peti-

---

[1] Stow's Survey, p. 476. — In 1544, Roger Ascham wrote an excellent treatise,
intituled, " Toxophilus, the Schole or Partitions of Shooting; contayned in Two
" Bookes; pleasaunt for all Gentlemen and Yeomen of Englande for theyr Pas-
" tyme to reade, and profitable for theyr Use to folowe, both in Warre and Peace."
In this work the great excellence of archery above other sports, and its utility in
a political point of view, are ably discussed, while many of the fashionable amusements of the day are justly condemned.

[2] Ellis's History of Shoreditch, p. 171.

[3] Anecdotes of Archery, p. 59.

tioned the Lord Treasurer, as they had the Queen before that time, concerning their *decayed condition*, by reason of the discontinuance of the use of archery, and toleration of unlawful games [1].

In the reign of James I. archery seems to have fallen much into disuse. Stow laments, that it had become " almost cleane left off " and forsaken; for," says he, " by the means of closing in of com- " mon grounds, our archers, for want of roome to shoote abroade, " creepe into bowling alleys, and ordinarie dicing houses, neerer " home, where they have roome enough to hazzard their money at " unlawful games [2]."

To remedy these inconveniences, and give encouragement to this exercise, James, in 1605, directed his letters patent to the Lord Mayor, the Lord Chancellor, and several other eminent persons (in-cluding Sir Thomas Fowler, of Islington), alledging that divers per-sons about the City, possessing lands, &c. had taken away from the archers the exercise of shooting in such fields and closes, as, time out of mind, had been allowed to be shot in, by making banks, hedges, and plucking up the old marks, and making ditches so broad, without bridges, &c.; and directing these commissioners to survey the grounds *within two miles compass* of the City and suburbs as used to have marks, and be used for shooting, and to reduce the same to proper order and condition, as in Henry the Eighth's time [3].

Charles the First appears, from the dedication of a treatise, inti-tuled, " The Bowman's Glory [4]," to have been himself an archer; and, in the eighth year of his reign, he issued a commission, similar to the above, directed to the same persons, and empowering them to prevent the fields near London from being so inclosed as to " inter-

[1] Seymour's Survey of London, vol. II. p. 383.
[2] Survey of London, p. 85.
[3] Highmore's History of the Artillery Company.
[4] " The Bowman's Glory, or Archery revived; giving an Account of the many " signal Favours vouchsafed to Archers and Archery, by King Henry the Eighth,

" rupt the necessary and profitable exercise of shooting," and also
to lower the mounds, where they hindered the view from one mark
to another [1].


" James, and Charles the First, &c. by *William Wood*, 1682," 12mo. This Wood
lies buried in the church-yard of St. James Clerkenwell. His epitaph begins,

> " *Sir* William Wood lies very near this stone,
> In 's day of Archery excell'd by none," &c.

Maitland tells us (History of London, p. 1364), that " the title of *Sir* was only
" a compliment of his brethren archers, by way of pre-eminence for his dexterity
" in shooting." History of Shoreditch, p. 171.

[1] It appears, from the above mentioned warrants from the Crown, that the Artillery Company of London (which seems to have had its origin in the before named
patent of Henry VIII.) has for many centuries possessed a right of assembling
and exercising in these fields. Moreover, they have several times of late years
asserted this right, by removing obstructions, reinstating their marks, &c. as appear by the Company's records, from which the following extracts are made :

" On the Company's march to Baumes on the Accession-day in 1782, they
" found the gate of a large field, in which stood one of their stone marks, near
" *Ball's Pond*, both locked and chained, and four men placed to prevent their
" entrance. The adjutant ordered it to be forced; after which they marched across,
" and opened another gate." History of the Artillery Company, p. 366.

" In 1784, a committee was appointed to ascertain the situation of the butts,
" &c. that the right might not be lost, and report thereon." Ibid. p. 385.

In October the same year, " the Company marched to Finsbury fields to view
" their several stone marks, beginning at *Prebend Mead*, where the *Castle* stone
" stood, and thence extending to *Baumes Fields* and *Islington Common*." They
removed several obstructions, &c. Ibid. p. 393.

In 1786, " considerable encroachments having been made upon the antient
" marks belonging to the Company, the Court (July 30) ordered notice to be given
" to all the occupiers of lands in Baumes and Finsbury fields, between *Peerless*
" *Pool* South, *Baumes Pond* North, *Hoxton* East, and *Islington* West, wherein any
" of their marks were placed, to remove any obstruction to the Company's
" rights." Ibid. p. 396.

Aug. 12, 1786, " the Company, on its march over Baumes and Finsbury fields,
" having pulled down by the pioneers several parts of the fence of a piece of
" ground inclosed about two years since, by Mr. Samuel Pitt, for gardens and

S. Harding delin                                    I Clamp Sculp

To his Grace the Duke of                          Leeds President, & the
*TOXOPHILITE* Society of London,            This Portrait of SIR WILL.ᵐ WOOD,
a Celebrated Archer of the last                Century, from an Original Picture
in the Possession of that Society,             is Respectfully Inscribed by
his Grace's, & their Obed.ᵗ Hum.ᵗᵉ             Servants. S & E Harding.

CENTRUM PETE

London. Pub.ᵈ by E & S. Harding. Pall Mall 21 May 1793.

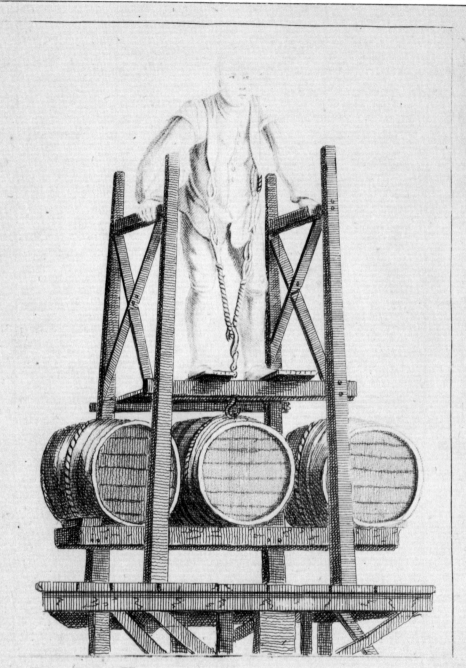

THOMAS TOPHAM, THE STRONG MAN.
*Performing one of his astonishing feats of Strength in Spa-fields 28th of May 1741.*

In 1628, was published, a small volume, intituled, " *Ayme* for
" Finsburie Archers ; or, an Alphabetical Table of the Names of
" every Marke within the same Fields, with their true Distances, ac-
" cording to the Dimensuration of the Line, newly gathered and
" amended, by James Partridge [1]." This book is dedicated, " to all
" that affect the famous exercise of Archerie frequenting Finsburie
" Fields ;" and in the Preface are given " rules touching the use of
" the treatise," with general directions to archers in the pursuit of
that exercise [2].

" summer houses, through which breaches the Company marched from the marks of
" *Guardstone* to *Arnold*, and from *Arnold* to *Absoly* ; and having come to a piece
" of ground lately inclosed with a brick wall, by Messrs. Walker, Ward, and Co.
" (proprietors of the white-lead mill), between the marks of *Bob Peak* and the
" *Levant*, the Company were induced to desist from pulling down, or making a
" breach in the wall, in order to march through, on account of Mr. Maltby (one
" of the partners in the white-lead works) having assured the commanding officer
" of the battalion, that he and his partners, at the time of making the said inclo-
" sure, were ignorant of the Company's right in those fields, but were willing to
" enter into any reasonable terms of accommodation with the Company for what
" they had done.— One of the archers' division was then ordered to shoot an arrow
" over the said inclosure, as an assertion of the Company's right ; which, having
" done, the battalion proceeded on its march to several of the other marks," &c.
Ibid. p. 399.

Again, in 1791, when the long butts on Islington Common were destroyed by
digging gravel, " A detachment marched to the spot (Aug. 12), pursuant to a pre-
" vious notice to the occupiers and commissioners of the roads to remove every
" obstruction, and to replace the marks. These objects were obtained." Ibid.
p. 410.

[1] The first edition of this book was published in 1594, by " I. I. and E. B." and
were sold at the sign of the Swan, in Grub-street. This street was inhabited, in
old times, by the fletchers, bowyers, bowstring-makers, and manufacturers of
every thing relating to archery. It was the last in this part of the town about the
time of Aggas's map of London. Pennant's London.

[2] The marks or butts enumerated in this treatise amount to upwards of 160.
They were chiefly made by posts of wood fixed in the ground, having tops of different forms, and unequal in height. They were scattered over the fields, extending from the City Northward to *Islington Common*, beyond the Rosemary-branch,

In the use of the bow, great dexterity, as well as strength, seems to have been requisite. The English archers made use of a very long bow; and, by stat. 33 Hen. VIII. persons of the age of 24 years were prohibited from shooting at any mark that was not distant 220 yards. The longest distance between the marks in these fields appears to have been 19 score, or 380 yards, and the shortest from mark to mark 9 score, or 180 yards.

An anecdote is related of TOPHAM, *the strong man of Islington,* who, happening to be at a public house to which the Finsbury archers resorted after their exercise [1], considered the long bow as a play-thing

and close to the back of the village on the Eastern side. They are delineated in an engraved plan of Finsbury fields, copied in Malcolm's Londinium Redivivum; vol. IV. p. 26. The following, as a specimen of their names, with the distances in scores and yards, is extracted from the " Ayme for Finsburie Archers," p. 92.

|  | Score. | Yards. |
|---|---|---|
| " Partridge his pillar to Dickman | 14 | 18 |
| Sir Rowland | 10 | 14 |
| Marsh | 9 | — |
| Lurching | 15 | 4 |
| Nelson | 12 | 10 |
| Martin's Mayflower | 14 | 16 |
| Dunstan's Darling | 11 | 17 |
| Beswick's Stake | 11 | 13 |
| Lambert's Goodwill | 12 | 6 |
| Lee's Leopard | 13 | 5 |
| Gosson | 14 | 16 |
| Theefe in the Hedge | 13 | 4 |
| Mildmay's Rose | 9 | 15 |
| Silkeworme | 11 | 2 |
| Lee's Lion | 11 | 7 |
| Gilbert's Goodwill | 10 | 10." |

[1] An old house yet remains fronting the fields at Hoxton, which was formerly much resorted to by the Finsbury archers. It bears for its sign the *Robin Hood,* which has, to the present day, written underneath, the following inscription;

" Ye archers bold, and yeomen good,
" Stop, and drink with Robin Hood;
" If Robin Hood is not at home,
" Stop, and drink with Little John."

fit only for a child; upon which, one of the archers laid him a bowl of punch that he could not draw the arrow two thirds of its length. Topham accepted the bet with the greatest confidence of winning; but, drawing the arrow towards his breast instead of his ear, he was greatly mortified in being obliged to pay the wager, after many fruitless efforts [1].

Partridge, the author of the treatise just mentioned, seems to have been an eminent archer, and to have shewn no small degree of zeal for the exercise. His name is attached to two of the marks mentioned in his book (for they generally bore the name of the person erecting them); and he laments the decay of the art in most places save the City of London, where, as it would seem, archery was yet a familiar exercise, " as appeareth by the daily concourse of citizens, to their " great commendations, in divers companies, in the convenient fields " about the City [2]."

During the grand rebellion, the practice of archery seems to have received no encouragement, but rather to have fallen into disrepute. Sir William D'Avenant, in a mock poem, intituled, " The long Va- " cation in London," describes the shooting matches made between the attornies and proctors, who,

" Each with solemn oath agree,
" To meet in Fields of Finsburie;
" With loynes in canvas bow-case tyde,
" Where arrowes stick with mickle pride;
" With hats pin'd up, and bow in hand,
" All day most fiercely there they stand,
" Like ghosts of ADAM BELL [3], and *Clymme*,
" Sol sets for fear they 'll shoot at him [4]."

[1] Anecdotes of Archery, p. 65.          [2] Ayme for Finsburie Archers.

[3] " *Adam Bell* was the name of a mark in these fields (see Ayme for Finsburie " Archers). *Adam Bell, Clym of the Clough,* and *William of Cloudesley,* were three " noted outlaws, whose skill in archery rendered them as famous in the North of " England, as Robin Hood and his contemporaries were in the midland counties." Bishop Percy's Reliques of English Poetry, 1765, p. 129.

[4] Sir William D'Avenant's Works, folio, 1673, p. 291.

In 1682, there was a most magnificent cavalcade, succeeded by an entertainment given by the Finsbury archers, when the titles of *Duke of Shoreditch, Marquis of Islington, &c.* were bestowed upon the most deserving. Charles the Second was present upon this occasion; but the day being rainy, he was obliged soon to leave the field [1].

By a plan of the fields, representing the state in which they were in the year 1737, it appears that only twenty-four of these antient shooting marks were then standing; for, as archery fell into disuse, they became gradually obliterated and removed. However, so lately as the year 1746, a cow-keeper, named *Pitfield*, was obliged to renew one of them, by virtue of the last mentioned letter of King Charles I. on which the Artillery Company caused this inscription to be cut: " *Pitfield's repentance.*" And since that time, a brick-maker was compelled to make a similar submission [2].

Archery had now degenerated, from being the glory of British warriors, into a mere manly recreation. Finsbury fields were unfrequented by the votaries of this noble art; and the very name of archer seemed forgotten, till, in 1753, targets were erected during the Easter and Whitsun holydays, when the best shooter was styled Captain for the ensuing year; and the second, Lieutenant [3]. Of the original members of this society there were only two living in 1783, viz. Mr. Benjamin Poole, and Mr. Philip Constable; both of whom had frequently obtained these titles. The Society of Archers has been long since incorporated with the Honourable Artillery Company, who, till within these few years, had a company called the *Archers division* attached to their corps.

The two old shooting butts, mentioned in p. 29, which remained till within the last thirty years on the common, near the Rosemary-branch, in this parish, were at that time occasionally used by Toxophilites from the Metropolis. These have given place to a solitary

---

[1] Barrington's Observations, Archæologia, vol. VII.
[2] Ibid.                        [3] Ibid.

target butt, defended with iron plates, for the exercise of ball firing, in an adjoining inclosure : but several vestiges of the old marks may yet be traced in the fields adjacent[1].

In addition to what has been mentioned upon the subject of archery, and in order to trace the connexion between the City of London and the village of Islington, in regard to the pastimes and amusements of the citizens; a few other particulars may not be improperly introduced in this place, and which will serve to shew that the predilection of the *Cockneys* for the cheerful walks and salubrious atmosphere of this place, was as strong three centuries ago as at the present time.

After the demolition of the hedges and ditches about ISELDON, HOXTON, &c. in the sixth year of Henry VIII. as described by Edward Hall (see p. 25), Stow remarks, " But afterward wee saw " the thing in worse case than ever, by means of inclosure for gar- " dens, wherein are builded many faire summer-houses; and, as in " other places of the suburbes, some of them like Midsummer pa- " geants, with towers, turrets, and chimney tops, not so much for " use or profit as for shew and pleasure, and bewraying the vanitie

---

[1] About 20 years since, the practice of archery met with a considerable revival, and was pursued by many of our nobility and gentry as an amusement. A grand annual meeting of the following societies of archers took place on Blackheath in May 1791, viz. the Honourable Artillery Company, in two divisions; the Surrey Bowmen, two divisions; Hainault Foresters; Toxophilites, two divisions; Northumberland Archers; Sherwood Foresters; Kentish Rangers; Kentish Bowmen; Loyal Archers; Woodmen of Arden; Robin Hood Society; Yorkshire Archers; and Woodmen of Hornsey. They were all dressed in green, with half boots. Numbers of ladies were likewise dressed in the uniform of the societies. Some of these were accustomed at this time to frequent a field adjoining Canonbury-house, for the purpose of shooting at a target; and such was the rage for archery, that " The Bowman's Glory" was sold at the price of one guinea and a half: but it has again fallen into disuse, and will not, it is probable, meet again with a similar renovation.

F

" of men's mindes, much unlike to the disposition of the ancient
" citizens, who delighted in the building of hospitals and almes-
" houses for the poore, and therein both employed their wit, and spent
" their wealth, in preferment of the common commoditie of this our
" citie [1]."

The erections above described, and which began to be extended to
most of the villages round the Metropolis, seem to have been something like the *villas* and *country boxes* of our modern citizens [2], and,
as in the present day, to have been called by names, fancifully bestowed on them by their respective builders or proprietors. It also
appears, that, like them, they afforded a subject for the exercise of
the satirical wit of the times. Stow gives the following distich, made
in ridicule of the names of some of them in his time; viz.

> " *Kirbie's Castle,* and *Fisher's Folly,*
> *Spinila's Pleasure,* and *Megses Glory.*"

Concerning which, " and other like buildings about the Citie by
" citizens," he observes, " men have not letted to speake their plea-
" sure [3]."

The proclamation of Queen Elizabeth, in 1580, to prevent the
erection of new buildings within three miles of the City gates, does

---

[1] Survey of London, p. 476.

[2] Norden, in his Speculum Britanniæ, containing a description of the county
of Middlesex, published in 1593, observes, " This shire is plentifullie stored;
" and, as it seemeth, beautified with manie faire and comely buildinges, *especially*
" *of the Merchants of London,* who have planted their houses of recreation not in
" the meanest places; which also they have cunningly contrived, curiously beau-
" tified with divers devices, neatly decked with rare invencions, invironed with
" orchards of sundrie delicate fruites, gardens with delectable walks, arbers,
" allees, and great varietie of pleasing dainties."

[3] Survey of London, p. 175.

not seem to have been much attended to; for several of the old houses in Islington had their origin soon after the time it was issued[1]. The Queen, as it appears from the passage before quoted from Strype, and other circumstances, was very partial to the place, and was, in her little excursions, in the habit of calling upon her wealthy subjects, several of whom, as it will be found, erected houses here, during her reign, for their places of residence or occasional retirement.

Of the fame of this village Elizabeth had heard, in an entertainment given to her Majesty by her favourite Robert Dudley Earl of Leicester at Kenilworth Castle, in the year 1575. The following extract from a speech made by a person who, on this occasion, represented a *Squier Minstrel of Middlesex*, will go in confirmation of what has been before stated as to the supplies afforded many centuries ago to the citizens of London, of an article in those days of no small importance; and which has, from the earliest period, been considered as the staple commodity of this place. This minstrel declared, " How the worshipful village of *Islington*, in *Middlesex*, " well knooen to bee one of the most auncient and best toounz in " Englande, next to London, at thiz day, for the feythful freendship " of long time sheawed, as well at *Cookez feast* in *Aldersgate-*

---

[1] The increase of buildings was again noticed in the Parliament, anno 1656; and an Act was then made, for preventing the multiplying of houses, &c. in and about the suburbs, and within ten miles thereof. The preamble sets forth, how these new buildings, outhouses, and cottages, were found to be mischievous and inconvenient, and a great annoyance and nuisance to the commonwealth. By this Act, for every dwelling-house, outhouse, or other building, erected within ten miles of the City walls, after March 25, 1620, and not having four acres of land occupied therewith, one year's rack rent was enacted to be paid by the occupier, for the use of the commonwealth; and for any new building erected after this Act, the builder was to be fined £.100; and if the same was upheld and continued, the further sum of £.20 every month that the same should be so upheld, for the use of the poor! Seymour's London, vol. II. p. 695. What would our ancestors (who were thus apprehensive of the evils arising from an overgrown capital) say, could they behold the gigantic and still extending Metropolis of the present day?

" *streete* [1], yeerely, upon *Holly-rood* day, az allso at all solemn
" bridealez in the Citie of London all the yeer after, in well serving
" them of furmenty for porage, not oversod till it bee too weak; of
" mylke for theyr flawnez, not yet pild nor chalked; of creame for
" theyr custardes, not frothed nor thykened with floour [2]; and of
" butter for theyr pastiez and pye paste, not made of well curds, nor
" gathered of whey in soomer, nor mingled in winter with salt but-
" ter watered or washt; did obteyn long agoo thez woorshipful armez
" in cooler and foorm az ye see. On a field Argent, as the field and
" groound indeed whearin the milk wivez of this worthy tooun, and
" every man els in hys faculty, doth trade for hys living; on a fess
" tenny three platez, between three mylk tankerds proper; the three
" mylk tankerds as the proper vessel whearin the substauns and
" matter of theyr trade is too and fro transported; the fess tenny,
" which is a cooler betokening dout and suspition, so az suspition
" and good heed taking (as well to theyr markets and servants as to

[1] The *cooks*, or *pastelars*, were incorporated by charter from King Edward IV.
about 1480; and their hall was situate opposite Little Britain, in Aldersgate-street.

[2] These dishes, which may appear somewhat *outré* to those voluptuaries of the
present age, the amateurs of *callipash* and *callipee*, were by no means uncommon at
the tables of the great in the less *refined* periods of our history. Indeed, the
various preparations of milk formed at all times an essential part of the feast.
At a great entertainment given in honour of the nuptials of Henry IV. in the
year 1403, was a dish of " venyson with fermente," also " crustade Lambarde" (a
dish composed of cream, eggs, &c.), and " creme of almaundes;" and at the feast
on the coronation of Catherine, Queen of Henry VI. we find " frumente,"
" whyte potage," " creme motle," and " custard royal." — In a MS account of
preparations for the funeral of Sir John Rudstone, Lord Mayor of London, who
died in 1531 (temp. Hen. VIII.), the following items occur, and which will serve
to shew the price of the articles at that period; viz.

" To the mylke wyffe.          *s.   d.*
" Item, 2 gallones, and 6 dysshes of butter........4   2
" 8 gallons of creme...................................4   0
" 12 gallons of curdde.............................1   6."

Strutt's Manners and Customs of the People of England,
vol. II. p. 101, &c. vol. III. p. 114.

" theyr customerez, that they trust not too farre), may bring them unto
" platez that iz coynnd silver; three, that iz sufficient, and plentie,
" for so that number in armory may well signifie.   For creast, upon
' a wad of ote strawe for a wreath, a boll of firmenty, and in the
" midst of it sticking a doozen of hoorn spoonz in a bunch (as the
" instrument meetest to eat furmenty porage withal), that with a
" little licking wool alweiz bee kept as clen as a dy.   This skoochion
" with beastz very aptly agreeing both to the armz and to the trade
" of the bearers, gloriously supported between a gray mare (a beest
" meetest for carrying of mylk tankerds), hir panell on hir bak, az
" alwais reddy for servis at every feast and brydale at need, her tayl
" splayd at most eaz, and her silly fole, fallow and flaxen mane, after
" the syre.   In the skro undergraven iz thear a proper word, well
" squaring with all the rest. taken out of *Salern's* chapter of things
" that moost noorish a man's body, ' LAC CASEUS INFANS;' that iz,
" goode milke and yoong cheez.   'And thus mooch, gentlemen, and
" pleas you (quoth he), for the armz of our worshipful tooun;' and
" therewithall made a manerly leg, and so held his peas; whereupon
" another good fello of the company sais, 'I am sorry to see how mooch
" the poor Minstrel mistakez the matter; for, indeed, the armez are
" thus: three milk tankerds proper, on a field of clouted creame;
" three green cheeses upon a shelfe of cake bread, the fermenty bool,
" and horn spoonz, becauz their profit comes all by horned beastz,
" supported by a mare with a galled back, and therefore still covered
" with a pannel, fisking with her taile for fleyz, and her sely fole ney-
" ing after the dam for suk.   This word, *lac caseus infans*, that iz,
" ' fresh cheez and creame,' and the common cry that theaz milk wives
" make in London streets, yearly; betwixt Easter and Whitsuntide.
" And this is the very matter; I know it well enough[1].' "

In the succeeding reigns of James and Charles, Islington, in the
summer season, appears to have been a very favourite spot with the

---

[1] Laneham's account of Queen Elizabeth's entertainment at Killingworth (Kenilworth) Castle, anno 1575, printed in Nichols's Queen Elizabeth's Progresses.

Londoners in their pleasures and recreations; and it was the more frequented by reason of the many houses of entertainment open for their
reception [1].   Another inducement arose from the delicious repast, with
which they could so conveniently regale themselves at the neighbouring dairies.   Nor did these pursuits, as it may be supposed, pass
unnoticed by the comic writers of the age.

" The Walks of Islington and Hogsdon, with the Humours of
" Wood-street Compter, a comedy, by Thomas Jordan, Gent." (li-
cenced 1641 [2]), is a low dramatic piece; the principal characters of
which are composed of wild gallants, who make assignations with
city wives; and the humour of the plot lies in the " hair's breadth
" 'scapes" they experience in eluding the vigilance of the " old jealous
" citizen."   The scene is laid at the " *Saracen's Head in Islington*,"
where the parties call for wine; and in the Prologue, we are informed
of the usual cheer belonging to the place in the following lines:

> " Though the scene be Islington we swear,
> " We will not blow ye up with *bottle-beer*;
> " Cram ye with *cream*, and *fools* [3], which sweetly please
> " Ladies of fortune, and young 'prentices,
> " Who (when the supervisors come to find 'um)
> " Quake like the *custard* which they leave behind 'um."

---

[1] In that part of the manor of Highbury at the lower end of Islington were the
following public houses and inns in 1611; viz. the *Rose and Crown, Saracen's Head,
George, Swan, Red Bull, Blue Boar, Prince's Arms,* and the *Cockatrice.*   The following, which do not exist at the present time, were houses of resort within the
memory of some of the oldest inhabitants; viz. the *Angler,* in Angler's Gardens,
*Frog Hall,* in Frog-lane, the *Crown,* Lower-street, *Three Tuns,* Rosoman's-row,
*Colebrooke House, Spotted Dog,* near the turnpike, the *Castle* tea gardens, Colebrooke-row, *Unicorn,* Hedge-row, *Duke's Head,* corner of Cadd's-row, *Hole-in-
the-Wall,* Cross-street, *Castle,* Hornsey-row, and the *Red Cow,* near Sebbon's-
buildings.

[2] Quarto, 1657.

[3] Gooseberry fools

The famous " Drunken Barnaby," in his " Four Journeys to the " North of England," published about the middle of the seventeenth century, has in the following lines noticed some of the houses at Islington.

Barnaby's Latin Itinerary being greatly superior to his English version, the passage is given in the original:

" Veni HOLLOWAY, Pileum Rubrum,
" In cohortem muliebrem ;
" Me Adonidem vocant omnes,
" Meretrices Babylonis ;
" Tangunt, tingunt, molliunt, mulcent,
" At egentem fores pulsant.
  " Veni ISLINGTON ad Leonem,
" Ubi spectans histrionem,
" Sociatam cum choraulis,
" Dolis immiscentem sales,
" Cytharæ repsi in vaginam,
" Quod præstigis dedit finem."

In the Poem before quoted from the Works of Sir William D'Avenant, descriptive of the amusements of the citizens during the long vacation in London, the following lines occur :

" Now damsel young, that dwells in Cheap,
" For very joy, begins to leap ;
" Her elbow small she oft doth rub,
" Tickled with hope of syllabub,
" For mother (who does gold maintaine
" On thumb, and keys in silver chaine),
" In snow white clout wrapt nook of pye,
" Fat capon's wing, and rabbet's thigh ;
" And said to hackney coachman, go,
" Take shillings six — say, I or no ;

" Whither ? (says he) — quoth she, thy teame

" Shall drive to place where groweth CREAME.

" But husband gray, now comes to stall,

" For 'prentice notch'd he strait doth call,

" Where 's dame ? (quoth he) — quoth son of shop,

" She 's gone her cake in milke to sop,

" Ho ! ho ! — to ISLINGTON — enough —

" Fetch Job my son, and our dog *Ruffe ;*

" For there, in pond, through mire and muck,

" We 'll cry, hay, duck — there *Ruffe* — hay, duck," &c. [1]

" The Merry Milkmaid of Islington, or the rambling Gallants de-
" feated," acted at Newmarket [2], is another dramatic piece, of a cast
similar to that of the one before noticed. The scene is also laid
among the fields, and in the public houses at Islington. Amongst
the characters are, a *half-witted knight*, two *town gallants*, a *lost
gentlewoman*, a *tapster*, and a *milkmaid*, the heroine of the piece.
The following extract may not be unamusing :

[1] It was common for the citizens in former times to bring their dogs to the ponds
in this neighbourhood to exercise the sport of *duck hunting.* Master Stephen (in
Ben Jonson's Comedy of Every Man in his Humour) says, " Because I dwell at
" *Hogsden* I shall keep company with none but the archers of Finsbury ! or the
" citizens that come *a-ducking* to Islington ponds !" &c. There is a piece of
ground in the Back road lately built on, which was called the *Ducking Pond field ;*
and the reservoir at the New River Head (as we are informed by Howes, in his
Chronicle) was " in former times an open idell pool, commonly called *The Ducking*
" *Pond.*" Goldsmith, in his Citizen of the World, No. 122, mentions a pond in
the midst of the town, probably alluding to one on the Green, or another formerly
at the front of *Pullin's-row.* The *Wheel Pond*, by White Conduit house, was
till lately famous for this sport. A duck hunt, which was advertized to take place
here last summer, was prevented by the interference of the magistrates.

[2] Quarto, 1681.

*New Tunbridge Wells near Islington.*

Anker Smith sc.

GEORGE COLMAN ESQ.

" SCENE.

" *Lovechange, Sir Jeffery Jolt, Artezhim (the Lady Jolt), and*
*Tapster.*

" *Love.*   What is the reckoning ?

" *Tap.*   Nine and eleven pence.

" *Jeff.*   How 's that ?   Let 's have the particulars.   Mr. Love-
" change shall know how he parts with his money.

" *Tap.*   Why, Sir, cakes two shillings, ale as much, a quart of
" mortified claret eighteen pence, stewed prunes a shilling.

" *Art.*   That 's too dear.

" *Tap.*   Truly, they cost a penny a pound, of the one-handed
" costermonger, out of his wife's fish-basket.—A quart of cream half
" a crown.

" *Art.*   That 's excessive.

" *Tap.*   Not if you consider how many carriers' eggs miscarried
" in the making of it, and the charge of isinglass, and other ingre-
" dients, to make cream of the sour milk.

" *Art.*   All this does not amount to what you demand.

" *Tap.*   I can make more.   Two three-penny papers of sugar a
" shilling ; then you had bread, Sir —

" *Jeff.*   Yes, and drink too, Sir, — my head takes notice of that.

" *Tap.*   'Tis granted, Sir—A pound of sausages, and forty other
" things, make it right, — our bar never errs [1]."

In later times, this village has been equally celebrated for pursuits
of a similar kind.   The Works of Ned Ward, 8vo, 1706, contains
" *A walk to Islington*, with a Description of *New Tunbridge Wells*,
" and *Sadler's Music House*."   And in " The Spleen, or Islington

---

[1] It seems pretty clear, from the speech of *the Squier Minstrel* (see p. 35),
and which is confirmed by the above extract, that, centuries ago, the dealers in

" Spa," a comic piece, by George Colman, acted at Drury-lane Theatre in 1756, are some satirical remarks upon the country-house of a citizen at Islington, and the bustle occasioned by packing up the neats' tongues and cold chicken, preparatory to his wife's journey thither, by the *coach and three*[1], from the end of Cheapside. The feast of " Hot rolls and butter," and the tea-drinking parties at White Conduit House, have been noticed by Goldsmith, in his Essays[2]; and the facetious Bonnel Thornton, in several papers of the *Connoisseur*, has described the Sunday excursions of the citizens to this village, to drink ale, and smoke their pipes, &c.

Notwithstanding the revolutions and changes produced by time in all mundane affairs, Islington, to the present day, maintains its full

---

milk were not unacquainted with the art of adulterating their commodity. It would also appear that the innkeepers of antient times were as great adepts at making out a bill as any *honest* Boniface of the present day.

[1] The stage coaches to Islington 50 years ago were drawn by three horses, on account of the badness of the roads. The inside fare was at that time six pence each person.

[2] Goldsmith is remarkable for the frequent mention made of Islington in his writings. It appears indeed he was very partial to this village, where he spent much of his time, and where at one period he occupied apartments. It was occasionally his custom to enjoy what he called a *shoemaker's holiday*, which was a day of great festivity with the Bard, and was spent in the following innocent manner :

Three or four of his intimate friends rendezvoused at his chambers to breakfast about 10 o'clock in the morning ; at 11 they proceeded by the City road, and through the fields to Highbury barn to dinner ; about six o'clock in the evening they adjourned to White Conduit house to drink tea ; and concluded the evening by supping at the Grecian or Temple Exchange coffee-houses, or at the Globe in Fleet-street. There was a very good ordinary, of two dishes and pastry, kept at Highbury barn at this time (about 40 years ago) at 10*d. per* head, including a penny to the waiter ; and the company generally consisted of literary characters, a few Templars, and some citizens who had left off trade. The whole expences of this day's *fête* never exceeded a crown, and oftener from 3*s.* 6*d.* to 4*s.* for which the party obtained good air and exercise, good living, the example of simple manners, and good conversation. European Magazine, vol. XXIV. p. 172.

share of attractions; nor are its various charms found less inviting to the modern than to the antient citizen. These, at the present time, form a principal part of its inhabitants; and, to the great influx of persons connected with London, may be attributed the number of handsome houses that have been from time to time erected, and which renders it one of the most opulent and respectable villages round the Metropolis. The number of deaths and interments that take place here, has, however, been remarked by some as rather extraordinary, considering the general character of the place for healthfulness and salubrity of air. But this fact may be easily accounted for, when it is considered that the bracing air of Islington is often had recourse to, by persons in the last stages of disease, and frequently when all the power of medicine has been of no effect; thus, there can be little wonder that its piercing keenness, contrasted with the closeness of the City from which they have been removed, may have a contrary effect to the one desired, that of hastening, rather than protracting an event which mankind in general are so anxious to avoid [1].

[1] The great disproportion that appears in the Parish Register between the burials and baptisms, has, without doubt, arisen chiefly from the decease of persons taking place under the circumstances above mentioned. Islington, from the great number of valetudinarians resorting to it, has for many years obtained the name of the *London Hospital*, in like manner as one of our senators lately distinguished the parks, and other open places in the environs of the Metropolis, as " the lungs of " the City."—The late ingenious Dr. Hunter used to relate a story of a lady, who, in an advanced age, and declining state of health, went, by the advice of her physician, to take lodgings in Islington : she agreed for a suite of rooms; and, coming down stairs, observed, that the banisters were much out of repair : "these," she said, "must be mended before she could think of coming to live there." " Madam," replied the landlady, " that will answer no purpose, as the undertakers' " men, in bringing down the coffins, are continually breaking the banisters." — The old lady was so shocked at this funereal intelligence, that she immediately declined all thoughts of occupying the apartments. Monthly Mirror, vol. I. p. 156.

RECORDS, HISTORICAL NOTICES, &c.

In the Domesday Survey, the landed property at Islington is thus described (A. D. 1087): " The Canons of St. Paul's hold two hides " in ISENDONE; the land is one carucate and a half, on which there " is only one plough, but another might be kept half employed. " There are three villans who hold a virgate of land; and there is " pasture for the cattle of the town.  This estate, the present and " former value of which is 40s. has been, time out of mind, parcel of " the demesnes of the Church.  The said Canons hold two other " hides in ISENDONE.  This land furnishes employment for two " ploughs and a half, and is all in culture.  There are four villans, " who hold this land under the Canons, four bordars and thirteen " cottars."  This estate, which was parcel also of the demesnes of the Church, had been valued in King Edward's time at 40s.; but when the Survey was taken at 30s. only.  " GILBERT holds half a " hide of GEOFFREY DE MANDEVILLE.  This land is half a carucate, " and is cultivated to its full extent.  There is one villan and one bor- " dar.  It was valued in King Edward's time at 20s. now at 12s.  It " was formerly the property of GRIM, a servant of King Edward, " who could alien it at pleasure.  DERMAN holds half a hide of the " King.  On this land, which is half a carucate, is one villan.  This " estate is valued at 10s. and was formerly the property of ALGAR, " a servant of King Edward, who had power either to sell or to " devise it.

" RANULF, brother of ILGER, holds TOLENTONE of the King, for " two hides.  The land is two carucates.  One hide is in demesne, " on which is one plough.  The villans have two ploughs.  There " are five villans who hold half a virgate each; two bordars who hold

" nine acres ; one cottar and one slave ; pasture for the cattle of the
" town ; pannage for 60 hogs ; and 5*s.* rents. This manor was valued
" in King Edward's time at 40*s.* when it was granted to Ranulf at
" 60*s.* but is worth now only 40*s.* It was the property of Edwin, a
" servant of King Edward, who had the power of aliening it at
" pleasure."

Lysons's Environs.

" Placita inter Martinum de ISELDON et Priorem Sanctæ Trinitat'
" London', pro 1 messuag' et 24 acr' terr' in *Kenteston.*"

Esch. 10 Ed. I. No. 43.

" RIC'US DE HEDERESTE, pro Abb'e de Valle Regali Westmonas-
" ter', 17 acr' terr' et VI*s.* VIII*d.* redd', ISELDON & Beata Maria at
" Strond."

Ibid. No. 99.

Anno 1341. (14th Edward III.) The Parliament having granted
to the King a subsidy of the ninth and fifteenth of their grain, wool,
and lambs, the following was the Survey or Taxation of the parish of
Islington, made by Commissioners appointed by the Crown, upon
the oaths of the inhabitants. The Record informs us of the number
of landholders in the parish, with the value of a considerable portion
of their possessions at the above period.

## " ISELDON.

" The same (*i. e.* the venditors and assessors) render accompt of
" £10. 13*s.* 4*d.* received of Richard Crollyng, Stephen Lambert,
" William Pursel, Maurice Compayn, Stephen Pursel, and Simon le
" Mareschal, for the ninth of the sheaves, fleeces, and lambs, of the
" parish of ISELDON (the Church whereof is not taxed), to them
" committed, according to the true value of the same, together with
" the ninth of the Prior of the Hospital of the Blessed Mary without
" Bishopsgate, which was worth the same year 6*s.* 8*d.* and with the

" ninth of the Prior of St. Bartholomew in Smithfield in the same,
" which was worth 40s. 10d. of which they have a writ of *Superse-*
" *deas* altogether. — Of the fifteenth nothing for the cause abovesaid.
  " In the ninth of the religious 46s. 8d.
  " Value of the ninth £.10 13s. 4d."

Inquisitiones Nonarum in Cur. Scaccarii, temp. Edw. III.

2 Hen. IV. A. D. 1410.   Anne, wife of James de Northampton,
had dower assigned her out of divers lands at Shoreditch, Hackney,
ISELDON, Newton, and Totenham, &c.

Claus. 4 Hen. IV. m. 17.

A. D. 1463.   Richard Rich, Citizen and Mercer of London, be-
queathed to his son Thomas Rich, all his lands and tenements in
ISELDEN (Islington), and Ratcliff, in Middlesex.   From this Richard
Rich, descended Richard Lord Rich, of Lee, in Essex, sometime
Lord Chancellor, *temp.* Edward VI. the raiser of the noble family of
the Earls of Warwick.

Seymour's Survey of London, vol. I. p. 548.

In the year 1465, the unfortunate King Henry VI. having wandered more than a year after the battle of Hexham, and secreted himself in caves and desert places, " was taken in Cletherwood, beside
" Bungerley, Hippinstons, in Lancashire, by Thomas Talbot, sonne
" and heyre to Sir Edward Talbot, of Bashall, and John Talbot his
" cousin, of Colebry, which deceived him, being at his dinner at
" Waddington Hall, and brought him towards London, with his
" legges bound to the stirrops, where he was met by the Earle of
" Warwicke, and arrested at EYSELDON, and forthwith his gilt spurs
" were taken from his feete.   Doctor Manning, Deane of Windsore,
" Doctor Bedle, and young Ellerton, being in his company, with
" theire feete bound under the horse bellies, were brought tho-
" row the Citty to the Tower of London, where the King was kept
" long time."

Stow's Chronicles.

Edward IV. his fortunate competitor, was shortly afterwards met " betwixt ISELDON and SORESDITCH" by the Lord Mayor and Aldermen of London, who offered congratulations, and received the honour of Knighthood.

In 1487, Henry VII. on his return to London after the defeat of Lambert Simnel and his adherents, " was met in *Harnesey Parke* " by the Maior, Aldermen, Sheriffes, and principal commoners of " the City of London, all on horsebacke, and in one livery, to attend " upon him, when he dubbed Sir William Horne, Maior of London, " Knight; and betwixt ISELDON and London he dubbed Sir Jo. " Percivall, Alderman, Knight."

Stow's Annals.

On the third Sunday in Advent, A. D. 1557, " John Rough[1], " with Cuthbert, Symson, and others, through the craftie and tray- " terous suggestion of a false hypocrite and dissembling brother called " Roger Sergeant, a taylor, were apprehended by the Vice Cham- " layne of the Queene's House at the *Saracen's Head* in ISLINGTON, " where the congregation had then purposed to assemble themselves, " to their godly and accustomable exercises of prayer, and hearing " the Word of God : which pretence, for the safeguard of all the rest, " they get at their examinations, covered and excused by hearing of " a play that was then appointed to be at that place." One of the charges brought against Rough by the infamous Bishop Bonner was, that he had assembled at the house above mentioned, with " one " Cuthbert, a taylor, Hugh, a hosier, and divers others, under the " colour of hearing a play, to have read the Communion Book, and

---

[1] John Rough had been some years a preacher among the fraternity of Black Friars at Stirling, and afterwards Chaplain to the Earl of Arran. He was the means of persuading the celebrated John Knox, the Scotch Reformer, to take to the Ministry. After having experienced many vicissitudes in different countries, he became preacher to a private congregation at Islington, in the last year of Queen Mary's reign, where he was apprehended, and burnt in the manner above stated. See Life of John Knox, by J. Lettice, B. D.

" to have used the accustomed fashion as was in the later days of
" King Edward VI." He was soon after burnt at the stake in
Smithfield.

Richard Roth, Ralph Allerton, James Austoo, and Margery
Austoo, were all burnt in one fire at *Islington* the 15th of September
in the same year.

Fox's Acts and Monuments.

June 27th, 1558. " Secretly, in a back close in the field by the
" town of ISLINGTON, were collected and assembled together a certain
" company of godly and innocent persons, to the number of forty,
" men and women, who there, sitting together at prayer, and vertu-
" ously occupied in the meditation of God's Holy Word: first,
" cometh a certain man to them unknown, who, looking over unto
" them, so stayed and saluted them, saying, that they looked like
" men that meant no hurt. Then one of the said company asked the
" man if he could tell whose close that was, and whether they might
" be so bold there to sit; ' yea,' said he, ' for that ye seem unto me
" such persons as intend no harme,' and so departed. Within a quar-
" ter of an hour after cometh the Constable of ISLINGTON, named
" *King*, warded with six or seven others, accompanying him on the
" same business; one with a bow, another with a bill, and other with
" their weapons likewise. The which six or seven persons the said
" Constable left a little behind him, in a close place, there to be ready
" if need should be, while he, with one with him, should go view
" them before; who, so doing, came through them, looking and
" viewing what they were doing, and what bookes they had; and so
" going a little forward, and returning back againe, bade them deliver
" their bookes. They understanding that he was Constable, refused
" not so to do; with that cometh forth the residue of his fellows above
" touched, who bade them stand, and not depart. They answered
" againe, they would be obedient, and ready to go whithersoever they
" would have them; and so were they first carried to a *brewhouse* but

The Martyrdom of Ralph Allerton James Austoo
Margery Austoo & Richard Roth at Islington

COLONEL JOHN OKEY,
*From a rare Print.*

" a little way off, while that some of the said souldiers ran to the Jus-
" tice next at hand, but the Justice was not at home; whereupon
" they were had to *Sir Roger Cholmley.*   In the mean time, some of
" the women, being of the same number of the aforesaid 40 persons,
" escaped away from them, some in the close, some before they came
" to the brewhouse; for so they were carried, ten with one man,
" eight with another, and with some more, with some less, in such
" sort as it was not hard for them to escape that would.   In fine, they
" that were carried to Sir Roger Cholmley were 27; which Sir Roger
" Cholmley and the Recorder, taking their names in a bill, and calling
" them one by one, so many as answered to their names he sent to
" Newgate.   In the which number of them that answered, and that
" were sent to Newgate, were twenty and two.

" These two and twenty were in the said prison of Newgate seven
" weekes before they were examined, to whom word was sent by
" Alexander the keeper, that if they would hear a mass they should
" all be delivered.   Of these foresaid two and twenty, were burned
" thirteen: in *Smithfield* seven; at *Brainford* six."

Fox's Acts and Monuments.

Certain lands, late parcel of the possessions of Adam Winthorpe,
Esq. valued at £.11. 10s. *per annum*, were sold by the Crown in
Queen Mary's reign (A. D. 1558), to " William Ormested, one of
" the Masters of the Chancery, for 20 yeares purchase, *and not*
" *above*, in consideration that he promyseth to give the land to the
" churche."

Harl. MSS. No. 608.

In a " Taxation of the Lands and Fees in the Countie of Middle-
" sex" *(inter ann.* 1581 and 1594), the following is the return from
the parish of *Islington:*

£.   s.   d.

" William Perriam, Justice of the Common Pleas,
" in lands - - - - - - - - - - - - - - - - - - - - - - - - - - - - - - 30   0   0

|  | £. | s. | d. |
|---|---|---|---|
| " Thomas Stanley, Esq. in lands - - - - - - - - - - - - - | 40 | 0 | 0 |
| " Robert Brokesby, Esq. in lands - - - - - - - - - - - - | 40 | 0 | 0 |
| " Humfrie Smith, Esq. in lands - - - - - - - - - - - - - | 24 | 0 | 0 |
| " Robert Cristifer, Gent. in lands - - - - - - - - - - - - | 20 | 0 | 0 |
| " John Wyldegoose, Gent. in lands - - - - - - - - - - - | 25 | 0 | 0 |
| " Robert Boyse, Gent. in lands - - - - - - - - - - - - - | 20 | 0 | 0 |
| " John Iremonger, Gent. in lands - - - - - - - - - - - - | 10 | 0 | 0 |
| " Arthur Atie, Esq. in goodes - - - - - - - - - - - - - - | 40 | 0 | 0 |
| " Tho. Bodily, Gent. in goodes - - - - - - - - - - - - - | 40 | 0 | 0 |
| " William Meredewe, Gent. in goodes - - - - - - - - - | 20 | 0 | 0" |

Harl. MSS. No. 366.

" In Golding-lane, *Richard Gallard,* of ISLINGTON, Esq. Citizen
" and Painter-stainer of London, founded 13 almeshouses, for so
" many poor people placed in them, rent free. He gave to the poor
" of the same almeshouses 2*d.* the piece weekly, and a load of char-
" coales among them yeerly for ever. He left faire lands about
" ISLINGTON to maintaine his foundation."

Stow's Survey of London, p. 318.

The date of this foundation does not appear. From the smallness
of the allowance, it however must have been of considerable antiquity.

" The Earle of Essex rode from his house in *Seding-lane* (March
" 27th) towards ISELDUNE, Highgate, and to St. Alban's, that
" night," accompanied by a great train of noblemen and gentlemen
on horsebacke, &c. on his journey to Ireland, in the year 1599.

Stow's Chronicle.

" A D. 1653. A plot was started in February, and a great many
" committed to the Tower; among which were Mr. Vowell, a school-
" master at *Islington.* The plot was said to be to assassinate Oliver's
" person. Several were tried before the High Court of Justice; it
" availed them not to deny this charge. Vowell was sentenced to

" be hanged at Charing-cross, and was there executed, July 10;
" when, with a Roman spirit, tempered with Christian patience, he
" suffered his martyrdom, off from a stool fetched from the guard,
" the adjacent neighbours refusing to lend any thing to his death,
" the executioner not having his ladder in readiness."

Heath's Chronicle, folio, 1676.

" Peter Vowell was a Bedfordshire man. At his death he warned
" the soldiery of the dangerous principles they went on in; professed
" openly his adherence to the King (Charles II. in his exile), and
" the Church; commended his soul to God's mercy, and his nume-
" rous family to God's providence, saying, he was sure the King
" should be restored, &c."

Magna Britannia, 4to, 1724, vol. III. p. 43.

" Colonel Okey, a famous commander in Cromwell's army, was
" first a *drayman*, and then a *stoaker*, in the brewhouse in this
" town (ISLINGTON). He was a person of more bulk than brains,
" and more strength than wit. Being entered into the Parliament
" army, he passed through the several military degrees till he became
" a colonel of dragoons, and much in Cromwell's favour, who, un-
" knowing to him, inserted his name amongst the King's Judges,
" in which he was forced to act, for fear of displeasing Cromwell,
" whom yet he left, when he saw him aiming at the government
" alone. At length, upon a foresight of the return of King Charles
" the Second, he fled into Holland, and, with *Miles Corbet* and *John*
" *Banksteap*, settled at Delft, where they were all three seized by
" Sir George Downing, his Majesty's resident at the Hague; and
" being sent to London were sentenced to death, and hanged, drawn,
" and quartered, April 19, 1662, yet his quarters were interred by
" his relations, and not hanged on several gates as the other men's
" were, because in his last speech he had spoken dutifully of his
" Majesty."

Magna Britannia, 4to, 1724, vol. III. p. 43.

In 1662, John Brown devised to the Governors of Christ's, Bridewell, and St. Thomas's Hospitals, all his messuages and lands, with the appurtenances, in *Islington*, known by the sign of the *Nag's Head*, then at the yearly rent of £.60, to the said Governors, and their successors for ever, towards the maintenance of six scholars at Cambridge University taken from Christ's Hospital.

Seymour's Survey of London, vol. I. p. 788.

John Bagford, the Antiquary, and great collector of old English books, prints, &c. died at Islington, May 15, 1716, aged 65. His typographical collections are now deposited in the British Museum [1].

Addison appears to have visited this place for his health. One of his papers in the Spectator (No. 393) was dated from Islington [2].

Daniel Defoe, the well-known author of Robinson Crusoe, and many other works, received his education at Newington Green [3].

Mrs. Mary Drought, of Islington, in 1740, gave £.20, towards erecting a marble font, and purchasing the new branches and chains, in Shoreditch church; also to poor housekeepers, by her will, £.10. [4]

Collins the Poet, while labouring under mental infirmity, was visited at Islington by Dr. Samuel Johnson [5].

Mrs. Foster, grand-daughter of Milton, the immortal author of Paradise Lost, kept *a chandler's shop!* at Lower Holloway, some years, and died at *Islington*, May 9, 1754, in the 66th year of her age; and by her death all Milton's family became extinct. She had

[1] Nichols's Anecdotes of Bowyer, 4to, p. 505.

[2] See " La Bagatella, or Delineations of Home Scenery, by William Fox, jun." demy 8vo, 1801, p. 29. This is a very pleasing poem, by a gentleman who was an inhabitant of Islington. It describes some of the neighbouring scenery in language highly poetical, and contains may sensible remarks, together with some well selected notes, critical and historical.

[3] Dr. Rees's Cyclopædia.

[4] Ellis's History of Shoreditch, p. 279.

[5] Johnson's Life of Collins.

lived many years in a low way, and was at last depressed with poverty and the infirmities of old age. It does not appear that any of her grandfather's admirers took any notice of her till 1750, when, on the 5th April that year, *Comus* was represented at Drury-lane theatre, with a new prologue, written by Johnson, and spoken by Garrick, for her benefit, which produced her about £.130. [1]

JAMES BURGH, an esteemed moral and political writer, kept an academy at Newington Green for 19 years, where he died in 1775. Of many excellent works that he left behind him, " Political Dis-" quisitions," 3 vols. and " Youth's Friendly Monitor," are the best known, and most esteemed [2].

Dr. NICHOLAS ROBINSON, a celebrated physician, and author of several medical works, died at Islington in 1775 [3].

JOSEPH COLLYER, who translated the Messiah, and Noah, from the German, and published some historical and geographical works, died here in 1776. Mrs. COLLYER, who translated the " Death of " Abel," also resided at Islington [4].

ISAAC RITSON, a native of Cumberland, who published a translation of Homer's Hymn to Venus, wrote the preface to Clarke's History of the Lakes, and promised considerable eminence as a literary character, died here in 1789, at the age of 29 [5].

The Rev. GEORGE MARRIOTT, author of various Poems and Sermons, died at Islington in 1793; and the Rev. Mr. VILLETTE (near 30 years ordinary of Newgate) in 1799 [6].

Sir BROOK BOOTHBY, the translator of Sappho, and author of several poetical pieces, also resided here [7].

[1] Newton's Life of Milton.
[2] Dr. Rees's Cyclopædia.
[3] Lysons's Environs.
[4] Ibid.
[5] Lysons's Environs.
[6] Obituary in the European Magazine.
[7] La Bagatella, p. 32.

Mr. JOSEPH WHITE, eminent for his knowledge of Coins, as well as of Natural History, died at his house, adjoining the Old Queen's Head, June 1, 1810.  He possessed a fine series of *Saxon* coins, which he disposed of some time previous to his death [1].

The following corporate and other public bodies possess the under-mentioned lands in this parish, as appears by the terrier; viz.

|  |  | A. | R. | P. |
|---|---|---|---|---|
| The Sons of the Clergy - - - - - Land at Holloway - - - - | | 49 | 2 | 19 |
| Mercers Company - - - - - - - Ditto - - - - - - - - - - - - | | 6 | 2 | 39 |
| Governors of St. Bartholomew's Hospital - - - - - - - - - - - - }Baker's field, Holloway | | 6 | 0 | 0 |
| Drapers Company - - - - - - - A field adjoining the workhouse - - - - - - - | | 6 | 0 | 0 |
| Dean and Chapter of St. Paul's - Broom field, otherwise Even grove - - - - - - - | | 6 | 0 | 31 |
| Brewers Company - - - - - - - - London fields, Du Val's lane | | 21 | 3 | 36 |
| Governors of Christ's Hospital - Skinner's place, and field near Ring Cross - - - - | | 6 | 2 | 25 |
| Ditto - - - - - - - - - - - - - - - - Behind the Nag's Head - | | 3 | 2 | 22 |
| Clothworkers Company - - - - - The Prebend field, in Queen's Head lane, the Lower-street, &c. - - - | | 60 | 0 | 31 |

[1] Obituary in the Gentleman's Magazine.

## MANOR OF ST. JOHN OF JERUSALEM.

It will not be a matter of surprize, that in the days of ignorance and Monkish superstition, (when Priestcraft had attained a
complete ascendency over the minds of the people of this realm, in
regard to their spiritual concerns,) a large proportion of the worldly
possessions of individuals should, in process of time, become transferred to the Church. Acts of this kind were by the religious of
the different orders always impressed upon the minds of their deluded
followers, as the most certain way of insuring a state of happiness in
a future world. To this influence may be attributed the great number of religious foundations with which this country at one time
abounded; it may, in like manner, serve to account for the fact, that
at the Dissolution of the Monasteries, &c. (temp. Henry VIII.) at
least four fifths of the parish of ISLINGTON was in the possession of
the clergy.

The tract of land comprized in this manor was the most considerable of these estates. The name is derived from its having
formed part of the possessions of THE KNIGHTS HOSPITALLERS OF
ST. JOHN OF JERUSALEM, a religious order instituted about the beginning of the twelfth century [1]. The grand house belonging to this
order stood on the site of St. John's square, by Clerkenwell, and of

---

[1] " This order was instituted shortly after Geoffrey of Bouillon had recovered
" Jerusalem. The brethren wore a white cross upon their upper black garment,
" and by solemn profession were bound to serve pilgrims and poor people, in the
" Hospital of St. John of Jerusalem, and to secure the passages thither. They
" charitably buried the dead; they were continual in prayer; mortified themselves
" by watchings and fastings; they were courteous and kind to the poor, whom they
" called their masters, and fed with white bread, while themselves lived with brown,
" and carried themselves with great austerity, whereby they purchased to themselves
" the love and liking of all sorts." Camden's Britannia, p. 322.

which the antient gateway there forms at this time the most striking remains. Such was the real or pretended humility of these Knights, that they at first styled themselves, *Servants to the poor servants of the Hospital at Jerusalem;* and, to express their poverty, took for their seal the representation of two men riding upon one horse; but by the munificence of some of our Kings and Nobility, together with the accession of lands and possessions which they received on the suppression of the Knights Templars (temp. Edward II.), the order was found at the dissolution of religious houses, to be endowed with lands to the yearly value of £.2,385. 12s. 8d. [1]; and about the year 1240 they are said to have possessed 19,000 lordships or manors in different parts of Christendom [2].

In a record of the numerous possessions of this order, about the year 1373, the following occurs:
" Prior Sancti Joh'is Jer'l'm in Angliâ :
  " West Smethefeld;
  " Finchesley;
  " Iseldon;
  " Kentisheton;
  " Canonsburie Maner'; Midd'x [3]."

The Lord Prior had precedence of all the Lay Barons in Parliament, and chief power over all the preceptories and lesser houses of the order throughout England [4]. The patron of this order was St. John the Baptist, from whom they took their denomination.

It does not appear at what time, or in what manner, the Knights obtained this manor. It is, however, probable, that it originated in certain lands annexed to their house by *Jordan Briset* its founder,

---

[1] Dugdale's Monasticon.
[2] Camden's Britannia.
[3] Esch. 47 Edw. III. No. 80, 2d number.
[4] Tanner's Notitia Monasticon.

about the year 1100 ; and that in succeeding times, by the donations
of various benefactors, it arrived at its subsequent great extent.
From the situation of the manor of Bernersbury (which is partly encompassed by that of St. John of Jerusalem), and other circumstances, it seems probable that some of the family of *Berners* made
considerable additions to the possessions of the Knights Hospitallers
in this parish, and which became incorporated with this their capital
manor.

The Prior of St. John of Jerusalem held in the reign of Henry VI.
half a knight's fee in Islington, which had formerly belonged to
William de Vere [1]. These, perhaps, are the lands which constitute
that part of the manor lying between Tallington-lane and the Western extremity of the parish [2].

The adjoining manor of Highbury, which formed a part of their
estates in Islington, became vested in the Priory about the end of the
thirteenth century, which, being added to this manor, gives a tract
of land contiguous to their house, upwards of 12 miles in circumference, and of which they remained possessed till the time of the
Dissolution.

The boundary line of this manor (which extends from Smithfield to
the beginning of Hornsey parish, and includes the whole of the parish
of St. John, and part of that of St. James Clerkenwell) enters Islington at the South-west extremity at Battle Bridge ; and proceeding
through Maiden-lane in the line of the parish boundary, it crosses
Highgate-hill, and continues along Hornsey-lane in the same line to
the top of Du Val's lane ; and from thence down the middle of Du
Val's lane to Ring Cross. The line continues from this place, along
the middle of the Back road, to a certain point in the said road, behind
the Star and Garter, where it branches off Eastward, includes that
house, and then proceeds along the highway of the Upper-street, to
the commencement of the parish boundary [3].

[1] Records in the Exchequer, Book No. 28, Knight's fees.
[2] Lysons's Environs.
[3] As the above Itinerary includes a part of the manor of Bernersbury, which is

I

A List of the Priors of St. John of Jerusalem in England[1].

1. Garnarius, or Garnerius, of Naples, was the first Prior, at the time of the foundation of the Sister house of Buckland, co. Somerset (temp. Hen. II.); the Prioress of which house retained her situation 60 years.   He was Prior of the Hospital in the time of Richard de Balneis, Bishop of London (who died 1162), and also when Richard Fitz-Neal held the same see (*i. e.* between the years 1189 and 1198).   He died the last day of August.

2. Richard de Turk was Prior in the time of the said Prioress; and in his time Walter, the son of Robert, gave the advowson of *Wodeham Walter*, co. Essex, to the Brothers of the Hospital of St. John of Jerusalem in England.   He died 12 August.

interwoven with that of St. John of Jerusalem, it may not be improper to state in this place, that Bernersbury manor, according to a survey lately taken, contains as under:

A. R. P.
121 2 28  Copyholds.
121 0 19  Demesnes situate near the three mile stone at Holloway.

Total 242 3 7

As the situation of this manor, from its irregular distribution, can only be understood by consulting the plan, suffice it to say, that the following are the principal buildings erected upon it: viz. that part of Hedge-row North of the Star and Garter, Upper-street; the houses from the Pied Bull to Mr. Blount's, opposite the church (both inclusive); the houses from the one next beyond Mr. Flower's school to opposite the South end of Hornsey-row; the houses between Park-street and Sebbon's-buildings, together with several pieces of land between the Upper street and the Back road; sundry houses and land opposite the two mile stone on the road to Holloway; Northampton-row, near Ring Cross; house and land adjoining the three mile stone; house and land on Highgate-hill; North-east corner of Maiden-lane; together with a number of fields and parcels of ground between the high road and Maiden-lane.

[1] See Newcourt's Repertorium, vol. I. p. 668.

3. RODOLPHUS DE DYNA was Prior in the time of the said Prioress. He died 13 May.

4. ALANUS, Prior, was raised to the Bishoprick of *Bangor* 16 April, 1195; and died 19 March the following year.

5. GILBERT DE VERE was Prior in the time of the said Prioress, A. D. 1195. He gave to the Sisters of the House of Buckland 100s. *per annum*, out of the manor of *Reynham;* which gift was confirmed by the said Bishop of Bangor. This villa, with its appurtenances, Gilbert gave to the Brothers of this Hospital, to whom he bequeathed his body. He died 13 August.

6. HUGH DE ALNETO was Prior in the time of the said Prioress. He died 23 November.

7. ROBERT THEASARIUS was Prior in the time of the said Prioress. He died 26 October.

8. TERRICUS DE NUSSA, otherwise MUSSA, was Prior in the years 1237 and 1238. He gave to the Sisters of Buckland, and their successors, xxxviii marks and xiis. viii*d.* to be paid at two different periods of the year, on condition that Prayers should be offered up for the repose of the said Terricus and his successors. He died 21 December.

9. ROBERT DE MANNEBY, Prior in 1251 and 1262. He died 14 October.

10. ROGER DE VERE, Prior, gave to the church of Clerkenwell one of the six pots used when Jesus turned water into wine, 1269, and died 15 February, 1270.

11. JOSEPH DE CHAUNCY was Prior in 1274 and 1280, in which last year he gave to the Vicar of *Standon* lands in the same parish. He died 11 March.

12. WILLIAM DE HENLEY was made Prior 10 Feb. 9 Edward I. (1280). He caused the cloister of Clerkenwell to be built 1284; departed beyond sea in 1287; was Prior in 1288; and died 4 February.

13. PETER DE HAKHAM, otherwise HAGHAM, was Prior 20 Edw. I. 1291 and 1293, and died 11 January.

14. WILLIAM DE TOTHALL was Prior in 1297, and died 12 October, 1318.

15. RICHARD DE PAVELEY was Prior in 1318 and 1321 (temp. Edw. I.) and died 3 August.

16. ROBERT DE DYNA, Prior, died 24 November.

17. THOMAS L'ARCHER was Prior in 1323. He died 28 August, 1329.

18. LEONARD DE TYBERTIS succeeded L'ARCHER in 1329. In his time the Hospital received many good gifts. He died the last day of January.

19. PHILIP DE THAME was Prior in 1335 and 1353.

20. JOHN PAVELEY was Prior in 1355 and 1371.

21. ROBERT HALES was Prior in 1372. In 1380 he was appointed Treasurer of the Exchequer by King Richard II. 1 February. (Pat. 4 Richard II. part II.); and was beheaded on Tower-hill, by the Insurgents under Wat Tyler, A. D. 1381.

22. JOHN DE RADINGTON was Prior in 1382 and 1406.

23. WALTER GRENDON was Prior of this Hospital in 1408, 1409, and 1416.

24. WILLIAM HULLES occurs Prior in 1407, 1427, 1429, and 1431.

25. ROBERT MALLORE, Prior in 1432 and 1437.

26. ROBERT BOTYL, Prior in 1439. He vacated the Priorship 16 January 1469.

27. JOHN LANGSTROTHER, Prior, 9 March, 1469.

28. WILLIAM TOURNAY, Prior, 1471 and 1474.

29. ROBERT MOLTON occurs Prior in 1474, 1475, and 1476.

30. JOHN WESTON occurs Prior in 1477, 1478, 1479, 1483, and 1485.

31. JOHN KENDAL occurs Prior in 1491, 1495, and 1500. He vacated the Priorship 18 November, 1501.

32. THOMAS DOCWRA occurs Prior 1 May, 1502, 1517, and 1519.

33. WILLIAM WESTON, last Prior of this Hospital, died the 7th of May : in the same year the Priory was dissolved, viz. 1540. (32 Henry VIII).

The following were also Priors of St. John of Jerusalem, but the dates of their Priorship does not appear, though Newcourt supposes them to have held that office in the reign of Edward I.

Simon Botard, died 3 May.

Elias Smetheton, 27 April.

Stephen Fulborn, 1 January.

Walter, died 27 August.

Sir William Weston, who was Prior when the institution was dissolved, had a pension assigned him of £.1,000. a year, but died the day on which he surrendered this manor, with their other possessions, to the crown. The knights also had pensions granted to them. The site of the Priory was granted 38 Henry VIII. to John Lord Viscount Lisle[1].

This manor continued in the Crown after the Dissolution of Monasteries till the year 1625, when it was granted to Robert Dixon and William Walley, and their heirs, at the yearly rent of £.17. 18s. 10d.[2] It seems to have been immediately conveyed to Justinian Povey, Esq.

---

[1] The Priory church and house at Clerkenwell (the former of which is described as having " a great bell tower, a most curious piece of workmanship, graven, gilt, " and inameled, to the great beautifying of the City") were preserved during the reign of Henry VIII. and employed as a storehouse for the King's " toyles and " tents for hunting, and for the wars, &c." but in the 3d of Edward VI. the chief part of the church, together with the great tower, was " undermined and blowne " up with gunpowder, and the stone thereof imployed in building of the Lord " Protector's house at the Strand." Stow's Survey, p. 483. It is recorded, that Henry bestowed upon the challengers in " a great triumph of justing," held before him and his Queen at Westminster, on May-day, and the four following, A. D. 1546, " a hundred markes, and a house to dwell in, of yeerely revenues out of " the lands of the said Hospital, in reward for their valientness." Stow's Annals.

Philip and Mary re-established a Lord Prior (Sir Thomas Tresham) and some brethren of the order here in 1557, repaired the house, and restored many of the old estates in divers counties to the same, who were again suppressed in the first year of Queen Elizabeth. Tanner's Notitia Monastica.

[2] Fee-farm Rolls, Augmentation Office.

who held it several years. In 1643, Christopher Wase, Esq. of Upper Holloway, died seised of this manor, leaving issue two daughters, Hester, married to Sir William Mainwaring, and afterwards to Sir Henry Blount; and Judith, the wife of George Master, Esq. of Lincoln's-inn. From this period, the manor has been divided into moieties, one of which came into the family of Short[1], and was afterwards devised to Colonel Henry Hasard, who took the name of Short, pursuant to the will of John Short, Esq. His brother, John Garbrand Hasard, afterwards possessed it; and it is now the property of their younger brother Richard Samuel Hasard, who has also taken the name of Short. The other moiety continued in the Master family till the year 1741 or 1742, when it was sold by Thomas Master, Esq. to William Snell, Esq. whose widow is the present possessor.

A house, called the Shipcote, and lands in Islington, then on lease to Henry Ledisman at the annual rent of £.51. 1s. 8d. formerly parcel of the possessions of the Priory of St. John of Jerusalem, were granted by Queen Elizabeth, in 1582, to Robert Earl of Leicester[2].

Lands in this manor descend according to the custom of Borough English, whereby the youngest son of a copyholder inherits, or in default of issue, the younger brother[3]. The fines are arbitrary, and at the will of the lord, whose custom is to take two years improved rent on a descent, and one year and a half on alienation. No heriots are taken. Widows are entitled to dower of the copyhold. The Lord holds a Court Leet and Court Baron on Holy Thursday, and

[1] See Monumental Inscriptions to these families in the old church.

[2] Pat. 24 Eliz. part III. Aug. 9.

[3] It has been observed, that the origin of this custom proceeded from the Lords of certain lands having the privilege to lie with their tenants' wives the first night after marriage; wherefore, in time the tenants obtained this custom, on purpose that their eldest sons (who might be the Lord's bastards) should be incapable to inherit their estates. But Littleton says, the reason of the custom is because the youngest is presumed in law to be least able to provide for himself. Jacob's Law Dictionary.

retains, from antient custom, the privilege of appointing two parish
officers, viz. a constable and headborough, who are placed over that
district of the parish where the manor is situate. The courts were
formerly held at the Angel, facing the City-road, but have been lately
removed to the Lord Vernon's Arms at Pentonville [1].

[1] In the 38th volume of the Gentleman's Magazine is the following copy of a
curious law instrument, about the date of 1615, said to have been found in the
town-chest of Bradfield in Yorkshire, and to relate to a dispute between the
parishioners of Islington and one William Dickinson, bailiff to the then Earl of
Shrewsbury, Gilbert Talbot:

> " At the Court Leet holden before the Fidlers of Islington, upon the feast
> " of Jervas Somersall, Gent. in the chamber of Armes and Scutcheons,
> " couched under the signe of the Angel, there it was enacted as follow-
> " eth, celebrated with dancing:

" That William Dickinson, in consideration of 4d. paid to him by William Re-
" vell, and of respitting his examination in the Chancerie this Trinitie tearme, did
" assume and promisse, in case all matters in question betwixt him and the pa-
" rishioners of Bradfield, were not ended or accorded in the interim, that he would
" appear in Chancery next Michaelmasse tearme, within eight days of All Saints,
" and there heare the judgment of the Doctors of the Court, and be examined
" accordingly, or in default thereof would forfeit to the said William Revell, for
" the use of the said parishioners, £.xxx."

" THOMAS HANSON.
" JERVAS HANSON."

It seems very probable, that this instrument was intended as an undertaking
given in regard to a recovery suffered in the manor of St. John of Jerusalem at
the above period. The circumstance of the Court Leet being mentioned, and the
sign of the *Angel*, the house where the Courts have (till lately) been held for many
years, are alone sufficient to warrant this opinion. — When it is considered that
the *suffering* a recovery (as the word implies) is a feigned law proceeding between parties in perfect amity, and the hilarity and good humour usually prevailing in these Manerial Courts being taken into the account, the drollery introduced into the above may in some degree be accounted for. Further, it may
have arisen from the circumstance of the instrument having been drawn up at the
*feast* usually given on court days in the court-room, and which might at that time
have been hung round with the arms and military equipments of some of the antient

## BATTLE BRIDGE

Is supposed to have been so called from its contiguity to the spot where the celebrated battle was fought between the Roman General Suetonius Paulinus, and Boadicea Queen of the Iceni, A. D. 61; and there are circumstances that seem to make in favour of this opinion[1].

Here was formerly a small bridge over the river *Fleete*, but the highway is now carried over an arch of considerable length, which secludes the stream except in one part near the turnpike, where it is left open as a watering place.

The operations of the Roman General in his arduous contest with that injured and unfortunate Princess, were, it is most probable, confined to the North, or North-western vicinity of London.   Tacitus (who had the most authentic information as to the affairs of Britain) informs us, that after Suetonius had abandoned London as untenable by the small army under his command, he was determined on hazard-

Knights Hospitallers; and on this occasion, it must be allowed, it was not at all unlikely that a party of Fiddlers should assist at the entertainment. — *A propos!* — The Fidlers of Islington appear to have formed a *band* of some *note* about this period; for, in the first scene of " The Walks of Islington and Hogsdon" before quoted, on a question of some moment being put to the drawer at the Saracen's Head by one of the guests, he replies, " I cannot tell, Sir — I'll ask the FIDLERS." — And, in " The Merry Milkmaid of Islington," one of the characters observes, " If I for- " bear my breakfast but two minutes longer, my guts will shrink to *minikins*, which " I'll bequeath to the poor FIDLERS at Islington, for a May-day legacy."

[1] A place on the river Derwent, in the East Riding of Yorkshire, is called by this name, from its having been the scene of a *battle* between Harald Haardred the Norwegian and Harold King of England, just before the arrival of William the Conqueror.   The town of *Battle* in Sussex also derived its name from the *battle* fought there between the two Princes last named, and which terminated the Saxon dynasty in this country.   Camd. Brit.   Etym. Ling. Angl.

View looking towards Pancras from Pentonville.

Published Dec 1793 by J.S. Storer, 2 A Farnham Buildings Upper Town

THE REED MOAT FIELD
ISLINGTON.

Malcolm del et f.

ing a battle, and for that purpose waited the approach of the enemy. It will be readily admitted, that no situation in the neighbourhood of the Capital could afford a more advantageous position, than the high ground in the vicinity of Islington; both in regard to security, and as a post of observation for an army apprehensive of immediate attack, from an immense superiority of force.

The opinion that the scene of this dreadful conflict was not far distant from this spot, is further strengthened, by some considerable remains of an encampment, which may yet be seen in the neighbourhood, and which exhibits sufficient evidence that the situation was an important military post, upon some occasion in the early part of our history. In a field called the *Reed Moat Field*, a little to the Northwest of the workhouse, are the remains of a camp, evidently Roman, and which is generally supposed to have been the position occupied by Paulinus previous to his engagement with the Britons. These remains consist of a Prætorium, &c. (see Plate II. Fig. 2), which in situation, form and size, exactly corresponds with the description of the General's tent, as given by Polybius (book VI.), in his account of the Roman method of castrametation. The site of the Prætorium is an exact square of about 200 feet; the area within the intrenchment being a quadrangle of about 45 yards. The surrounding *fosse* varies in breadth from 20 to 30 feet, which irregularity has been occasioned by encroachments upon the embankment. The *fosse*, which is about 10 or 12 feet deep, is, for the most part, filled with water, and overgrown with sedge.

In the encampment of a Roman army, the General's tent always occupied the most convenient place for prospect and command; so this Prætorium is seated on an elevated spot, embracing an extensive view over the adjacent country on all sides. To make it more convenient in this respect, that side from whence the view was least commanding has been raised by art, and presents a bolder embankment; and there is a visible ridge across the middle of the area where this elevated part

K

begins.    Here is also a raised breast-work or rampart extending for a considerable length on the Western side of the Prætorium, and another on the South.  The position occupied by this camp (supposing it to have been that of Paulinus) will be found strikingly advantageous, when it is considered, that the enemy was expected to make the attack from that side next to the Metropolis [1].

It is probable, that this was the first place of security to which Paulinus retired to unite his scattered forces, and upon which occasion this camp was formed, for it was customary with the Romans to entrench themselves, though they remained but a single night in a place.   The description Tacitus gives of the scene of his operations is very narrow and confined, " *Deligitque locum arctis faucibus & à* " *tergo silvâ clausum; satis cognito, nihil hostium, nisi in fronte et* " *apertam planitiem esse, sine metu insidiarum.*" But the great scene of carnage appears to have been between a couple of eminences, "*Angustias loci pro munimento*[2]."

It is not unlikely that the Roman General abandoned the above encampment, on finding the disparity of his force compared with that of the Britons, with which he had to contend, and fixed upon the narrow spot of ground as best calculated for his little army to act with advantage.   The situation of the valley that lies between the acclivity of Pentonville and the high ground about Gray's-Inn-lane, and where the river Fleete has its course (though now for the most part obscured by buildings), will not, on inspection, be found any thing at va-

---

[1] Since writing the above description, the ground about this spot, including part of the *prætorium,* has been broken up to a considerable depth, to procure clay and sand for brick-making, the latter of which has been found in great abundance.  It is the intention of persons who have taken the ground, to erect a considerable number of houses here ; and notice has been given of an intended application to Parliament for an Act to form a new public road, to lead from the Back road in the direction of the above, and to communicate with other roads which are also projected to be made in the parish of St. Pancras, &c.

[2] Tacit. Ann. lib. XIV. c. 34.

riance with the above description of Tacitus; and an opinion may be fairly hazarded, that the scene of action was confined to this place, in the immediate vicinity of Battle Bridge [1].

As this battle forms a very prominent feature in the early Annals of our Country, and appears so connected with this spot, a brief relation of the circumstances attending it, may not be improper to insert in this place. When London was occupied by a Roman garrison about the period last mentioned, Suetonius Paulinus, proprætor in Britain, was personally employed in an invasion of the Isle of MONA (Anglesey), the principal remaining seat of Druidical superstition. Boadicea Queen of the ICENI, taking advantage of his absence in this expedition, to revenge the injuries received by herself and her daughters in the abuse of their persons, and the grievous oppressions suffered by the whole people under the Roman yoke, became the principal mover of a revolt against that government, which was attended with the most serious consequences to the whole nation.

While Suetonius was engaged in the reduction of Mona, news was brought to him of the revolt of the province, headed by that warlike Princess: meanwhile, the Trinobantes, and other neighbouring powers, being induced to join her standard, an army of 120,000 Islanders was rapidly formed. Their united efforts were soon bent upon the destruction of Camalodunum (Colchester), the nearest Roman colony; which, being unprovided for any sudden attack, and Suetonius yet afar off, was immediately stormed, and reduced to ashes, all within it being previously massacred. The ninth legion, which had ventured to take the field against the insurgents, was next attacked, and defeated. The infantry were almost totally destroyed. The Commander, Petilius Cerealis, at the head of his cavalry, with difficulty regained his camp, where he carefully en-

---

[1] The skeleton of an elephant was discovered on digging in a field at this place by Mr. John Coniers, " a great searcher after Antiquities." Seymour's Survey of London, vol. II. p. 869.

trenched himself, while Cato Decianus, the Procurator, terrified at
the consequences of his infamous conduct towards the Britons in his
administration of affairs during the absence of the Propraetor, made
his escape into Gaul, covered with universal odium.

Suetonius, however, with great firmness and resolution, marched
with all speed, by a dangerous route, and through the midst of the
enemy's country, towards London. As he judged this post to be
untenable, he retired, to unite his scattered forces, accompanied
by such of the inhabitants as chose to follow his fortunes. The
City, being now abandoned to Boadicea, was sacked and burnt, and
those that remained behind, without regard to age or sex, were
indiscriminately sacrificed to the fury of the Britons. Verulamium
(St. Alban's), another colony, shared the same fate; all foreigners
were every where put to the sword; and the cruelties said by Dion
to have been exercised upon some of the sufferers are shocking beyond description.

The rebellion had now attained its utmost height: three Roman
stations laid in ashes, and the blood profusely poured of 70,000 of
her persecutors, had amply revenged the wrongs of Boadicea; the
whole Eastern part of the island was in possession of her partizans,
and her forces in arms had increased to the amazing number of
230,000, when Suetonius, having taken every measure prudence
could suggest in his circumstances, prepared to check this torrent in
its course. After every effort had been tried by the Roman General
to increase the number of his troops, and put them in the best posture of defence, he found his situation still extremely critical; his
entire forces, including auxiliaries, amounting to no more than
10,000 men.

With this army, small as it was, he determined on hazarding a
battle, and therefore waited the approach of the Britons, on " a
" spot of ground, narrow at the entrance, and sheltered in the
" rear by a thick forest. In that situation he had no fear of an
" ambuscade. The enemy, he knew, had no approach but in front;

" an open plain lay before him." According to the usual disposition observed by the Roman armies, the legionaries were stationed in the centre, flanked by the light armed and auxiliary cohorts; the wings being composed of cavalry. Suetonius did not tarry long in expectation of the enemy; the Britons soon appeared, covering the plain in immense numbers. Their wives and children, who had accompanied them to become spectators of a victory already considered as certain, were mounted in heaps on waggons encircling the field in their rear, like an amphitheatre. Boadicea, with her daughters, drove in her chariot along the ranks, renewing the detail of Roman injustice, and encouraging her troops in the most animating language: she besought vengeance for the wrongs sustained by herself and her family, and finished her address by exhorting them to conquer or die, which, she added, was her own resolution. Suetonius, on his side, did not neglect to animate his men by a suitable oration, and the acclamation and cheerful countenance with which it was received, convinced him that he had every thing to hope from the bravery and discipline of his soldiers.

The Britons came on, uttering loud shouts, menaces, and songs of victory; while the Romans, closely drawn up, awaited the onset in perfect silence. Preserving the advantage of the ground, they received the attack of the natives with great firmness; and having expended all their javelins, with dreadful carnage of the enemy, they rushed forward from all parts at once, observing the form of a wedge, the more easily to penetrate such an immense multitude. This charge was seconded by the allies with equal ardour; the first ranks of their opponents were instantly borne down, and hewn in pieces; but the rest crowding to surround the Romans, a bloody contest commenced. The British war-chariots, wherever they succeeded in breaking in among their enemies, occasioned terrible annoyance, till Suetonius, ordering his men to direct their blows at the naked bodies of the drivers, by degrees disembarrassed himself of these troublesome invaders. The action was long maintained with fury on both sides; the Britons, though destitute of order or discipline, fighting with great obstinacy and desperation; but, finally, the superior skill, coolness, and bravery of the Romans, bore down every opposition. Prodigious numbers perished beneath the swords of the legions, or by the charges of the cavalry, who trampled all before them, while the crowds that endeavoured to save themselves by flight, met with an insurmountable impediment in their own waggons, which inclosed them in form of a semicircle. Here the slaughter was terrible; for mercy, in the circumstances of Suetonius, would have been in the highest degree imprudent. The Romans, in the heat of their fury, spared neither age nor sex. Even the beasts of burden, struck through with darts, increased the horrors of the scene, and the heaps of dead, which covered the plain, the fields, and the surrounding forests. Upwards of 80,000 Britons are computed to have perished on this occasion; while of the Romans about 400 were killed, and scarcely so many wounded.

Few victories, even in the most flourishing ages of the Roman republic, deserved to be compared with this of Suetonius; never had any been more decisive. The remaining Britons, terrified at the dreadful chastisement they had received, departed into their respective districts; and Boadicea herself perished soon after the battle, either through chagrin, or, as is the prevailing opinion, she put an end to her life by poison [1].

The stream of water called the river *Fleete*, or Fleet ditch, which passes under the road at Battle Bridge, was more antiently denominated *The River of Wells*, and *Turnmill Brook*. Passing by the end of Islington parish, it proceeds onward to Bagnigge Wells, by the house of correction, and through Clerkenwell, between Turnmill-street and Saffron-hill, under Holborn Bridge and Fleet Market, emptying itself into the Thames at Blackfriars Bridge. In its course

[1] Tacit. Ann. lib. XIV. c. 31. 37; and Dion Cassius, Hist. Rom. lib. LXII. c. 1. 12.

from St. Pancras to London it is mostly arched over or hidden by buildings, and now scarcely any otherwise used than as a common sewer. It has its source from several springs on the South side of the hill between Hampstead and Highgate, by Ken wood, where it forms several large ponds, and from whence the greater part of its water is now carried off by pipes, for the supply of St. Pancras, Kentish Town, and Tottenham Court Road.

Before its waters were thus diverted, it was a very considerable stream, and is supposed to have been once navigable even beyond this place : an anchor is traditionally said to have been found in it, as high up as the site of the Elephant and Castle at Pancras-wash, where the road branches off to Kentish Town [1]. It formerly turned a number of mills in its course, whence it was called Turnmill-brook ; and till within these few years gave motion to the flour and flatting mills, at the back of Field-lane, near Holborn.

Such is the increase of the water in the channel of *Fleete*, after long continued rains or a sudden thaw, when there is much snow on the ground, by reason of the great influx from the adjacent hills, that sometimes at this place it overflows its bounds, breaks up the arches, and inundates the surrounding neighbourhood for a considerable extent. Some years ago an inundation of this kind took place, when several drowned cattle, with butts of beer, and other heavy articles, were carried down the stream, from premises on its banks, into which the flood had entered, and made considerable devastation. But the most considerable overflow that has happened here, within memory, was in the month of January 1809. At this period, when the snow was lying very deep, a rapid thaw came on, and the arches not affording a sufficient passage for the increased body of water, the whole space between Pancras, Somers Town, and the bottom of the hill at Pentonville, was in a short time entirely covered with water. The flood rose to the height of three feet in the middle of the highway,

[1] Beauties of England and Wales, vol. X. p. 70.

the lower rooms of all the houses within that space were completely inundated, and the inhabitants sustained considerable damage in their goods and furniture, which many of them had not time to remove. Two cart-horses were drowned; and for several days, persons were obliged to be conveyed to and from their houses, and receive their provisions, &c. in at the windows, by means of carts.

Battle Bridge consists of a number of small houses, chiefly inhabited by shop-keepers and working people. From its low situation it is in general very miry, and is rendered the more unpleasant by reason of the many noisome trades that are carried on in the neighbourhood, At the back of the houses on the North side of the road is a pottery, for the making of garden and chimney pots, sugar bakers moulds, &c. and a manufactory of a paint or colour called "*Patent Yellow*," carried on by a German, named *Scheldt*. Here is also a receptacle for bones, which are brought here by the itinerant collectors of the metropolis, and sold at 1*s.* 6*d. per* bushel. The oleaginous quality being extracted by boiling, they are afterwards sold to manufacturers of knife-handles, button-moulds, &c. and to farmers for manuring the land.

It is recorded by Stow, that in the reign of Edward the Sixth, " A Miller of Battaile Bridge was set on the pillory in Cheape, and " had both his eares cut off for seditious wordes by him spoken against " the Duke of Somerset[1];" and one " Cliffe, an honest cobler dwelling " at *Battel Bridge*," was supposed to have been the author of " The " Coblers book," which denies the Church of England to be a true Church, and charges her with maintaining idolatry under the name of decency, in the habits, fonts, baptism by women, gang days, saints days, bishoping of children, organs, wafer cakes, &c. printed in 1589[2].

[1] Stow's Chronicles.
[2] Ames's Typographical Antiquities, by Herbert, p. 1687.

## MAIDEN-LANE

Is an antient way leading from Battle Bridge to Highgate-hill; it was formerly the principal road for travellers, being the same called by Norden *Longwich Lane*, (see p. 18). The road he describes as leading to Tallingdon-lane, " leaving Highgate on the " West," appears to have branched off E. and N. E. by way of *Blindlane*, which has all the appearance of an antient road; by this route the above-mentioned acclivity must have been altogether avoided. Maiden-lane is one of the roads kept in repair by the parish of Islington, though formerly half the expence was sustained by the parish of St. Pancras [1].

Near the South end of Maiden-lane is a small meeting-house, belonging to a congregation of Particular Baptists: it is inscribed in front " *Battle Bridge Meeting* [2]," and has been built 30 or 40 years. The present minister is Mr. Sowerby, who resides in Bartholomew Close, London. In this lane are several extensive manufactories, belonging, for the most part, to persons in the Metropolis: they are chiefly of that description which falls under the denomination of nuisances, and have been brought hither by reason of the conve-

---

[1] In 1778 a dispute arose between the two parishes respecting the repair of this road, and which gave rise to legal proceedings, wherein a very considerable sum of money was expended. It appeared that a boundary stone, belonging to Islington, had been incautiously removed from the South side of the lane to the West, thereby including the whole of the road within that parish, after which the people of St. Pancras refused to bear any part of the repairs, which was, by the result of these proceedings, thrown entirely upon the parish of Islington, together with an enormous bill for law expenses, &c.

[2] In Baker's Plan, and the Schedule to the Highway Act, it is called " Trinity " Chapel."

niency of the situation and its proximity to the capital. Here is a manufactory belonging to Messrs. Rood, Heal, and Co. feather dressers, &c. of Compton-street, Soho; a stone blue and mustard manufactory, belonging to Messrs. R. P. Smith, Vaux, and Bell; Warner's coach and cart grease manufactory (part of which has been recently burnt down;) Margett's chemical laboratory; a large manufactory of varnish, carried on by Wallis and Sons, of Long Acre; a soap boiling house, now unoccupied; and a pottery for garden and chimney pots, &c. all of which are on the East side of the lane, and in this parish. Here is also an ale and table-beer brewery, and one or two houses for slaughtering horses.

About midway up this lane, in the fields on the right hand, stands a public house, known for many years by the name of *Copenhagen House*, and traditionally said to have been so called from the circumstance of a Danish Prince or Ambassador having resided here during the great plague. It is a house of considerable resort in the summer time, especially during the hay harvest, when the walks over the fields about it are particularly agreeable. The situation affords a very fine prospect over the Western parts of the Metropolis. Adjoining the house is a small garden, furnished with seats and tables for the accommodation of company, and a fives ground [1].

At the top of this lane is Highgate-hill, whereon stand many large and commodious houses, in a very salubrious air, and enjoying the most delightful prospects. The beauty and healthfulness of this place has for centuries been the theme of eulogium of our poetical and other writers. Norden says, " Upon this hill is most pleasant dwel- " ling, yet not so pleasant as healthful, for the expert inhabitants

---

[1] About fifteen years ago this place was noted for the meetings held in the fields by the *London Corresponding Society.* On the 15th Oct. 1795, a numerous assembly was collected, and three rostra were set up for the elevation of the Speakers. An Address to the Nation, a Remonstrance to the King on the neglect of their former Address, and some resolutions on the state of affairs, were voted by acclamation, after which the meeting dispersed. History of Artillery Company, p. 446.

View *of* HIGHGATE, *in* Middlesex, *taken from Upper* Holloway.

Merigot del.                                                    C. J. Will.....

COPENHAGEN HOUSE.

COPENHAGEN HOUSE, ISLINGTON.

Laycock's Dairy.
Watercolour by C. H. Matthews, circa 1840.

" there report, that divers that have been long visited with sicknes,
" not cureable by physicke, have in short time repayred their health
" in that sweete salutarie aire [1]." One or two houses on the East
side of Hornsey-lane, from their antient appearance, were, it is probable, among the first buildings erected on this spot.

In antient times upon the top of this hill was an hermitage, one of
the hermits whereof caused the causeway to be made between Highgate and Islington [2], taking the gravel from the top of the hill where
is now the pond, " a two handed charity," says Dr. Fuller, "providing
" water on the hill, where it was wanting; and cleanness in the
" valley, which before, especially in winter, was passed with great
" difficulty." This hermitage was in the disposal of the Bishop of
London, for it appears William Lichfield, a poor old hermit, was
presented to it by Robert de Braybrooke, Bishop of London, Feb.
20, 1386 *(in meritum animæ suæ)*; and

William Forte, by Bishop Stokesley, April 20, 1531, in consideration of his services in praying for his soul and the souls of his predecessors and successors, and all the faithful deceased. This man was
the last hermit of Highgate [3].

William Poole, Yeoman of the Crown, in the reign of Edward IV.
founded an hospital for lepers on the lower part of the hill, being
himself stricken with the same distemper [4]. This foundation remained till the time of Henry VIII. as appears by the will of Richard
Cloudesley, noticed in the ensuing pages, wherein he bequeaths 6s. 8d.
" to the poor lazars of *Hyegate* to pray for him by name in their
" bede role."

Our illustrious countryman, the great Lord Bacon, Baron of Veru-
lam and Viscount St. Alban's, whose moral and philosophical works
will transmit his name to the latest posterity with honour, is said to

[1] Speculum Britan.
[2] Tanner's Notitia Monastica.
[3] Newcourt's Repertorium.
[4] Pat. 17 Edw. IV. p. Oct. 26.

have met with his death from the following circumstance near this spot, as it is related by Aubrey in his MSS. now preserved in the Ashmolean Museum at Oxford. Aubrey himself professes to have received his information from Thomas Hobbes of Malmsbury, who was in habits of intimacy with his lordship, and frequently visited him. " The cause of his lordship's death was trying an experiment " as he was takeing the aire in the coach with Dr. Witherborne, a " Scotch man, Phisitian to the King. Towards *High Gate* snow lay " on the ground; and it came into my lord's thoughts why flesh " might not be preserved in snow, as in salt. They were resolved " they would try the experiment presently: they alighted out of the " coach, and went into a poore woman's house at the bottome of " *High-Gate Hill*, and bought a hen and made the woman exente- " rate it, and then stuffed the bodie with snow; and my lord did help " to doe it himself. The snow so chilled him, that he immediately " fell so ill, that he could not return to his lodgings (I suppose then " at Gray's-inn), but went to the Earle of Arundel's house at *High-* " *Gate,* where they put him into a good bed, warmed with a panne; " but it was a dampe bed, that had not been layn in for about a yeare " before, which gave him such a colde, that in two or three dayes, " as I remember he (Hobbes) told me he died of suffocation."

The road over Highgate-hill was formerly very hazardous, and many accidents were occasioned by its steepness and irregular construction. This inconvenience has of late years been somewhat remedied, by raising the road in some parts, and lowering it in others, whereby the surface is now rendered more equal. A number of schemes have at different times been projected for improving this road, or forming a new one, in order to avoid the hill altogether; for this purpose an Act has lately been passed by the Legislature (50 Geo. III.), intituled, " An Act for making and maintaining a " Road, partly by an Archway through the East Side of *Highgate* " *Hill,* communicating with the present Turnpike Road from *London* " to *Barnet,* at *Upper Holloway,* in the Parish of *St. Mary Isling-*

ALTI MELLIORA
MO RA
MEDIO FIRMA CRIA

Hon.ᵐᵒ Franciscᵒ Baconᵒ Baro de Veru: lam. Vice-Comes Sᶜᵗⁱ Albani. Mortuus 9 Aprilis, Anno Dñi. 1626. Annoᵍᵉ Aetat 66.

Engraved by Thomas Dixon from a Drawing by J.P. Neale.    for the Beauties of England & Wales.

HIGHGATE ARCHWAY,
Middlesex.

London, Published by Vernor Hood & Sharpe, Poultry, March 1st 1804.

" *ton*, and near the Brook below the fifth Mile-stone in the Parish of " Hornsey, in the County of Middlesex."

By this Act the proprietors therein named are constituted a body politic and corporate, by the name and style of " *The Highgate* " *Archway Company*," with power to purchase lands, &c. and to raise £.40,000, for making and maintaining the said road and archway, by transferable shares of £.50 each. Should this fund prove insufficient, they are further empowered to raise an additional sum of £.20,000. A proper number of lamps are to be fixed for lighting the archway, and a toll-house and turnpike erected at each end, where the following tolls are to be received; viz.

For every horse, or other beast, drawing a coach, chariot, *d.* landau, &c. - - - - - - - - - - - - - - - - - - - - - - - - - - - - - - - - 6

Every horse, mare, or gelding, not drawing a carriage - - - - 3

Every ass - - - - - - - - - - - - - - - - - - - - - - - - - - - - - - - - - 2

Every foot passenger - - - - - - - - - - - - - - - - - - - - - - - - - 1

The passengers are to be exempt from payment a second time in the same day on producing a proper ticket. A clause in the Act provides, that, if the lessors and lessees of the toll on *Highgate-hill* be damnified or injured in the amount of tolls receivable by such lessee, the amount of such damage shall be ascertained and settled by the Directors of the Company and the parties interested, or by a jury to be summoned by the sheriff.

### UPPER HOLLOWAY

appears to have been the residence of the family of Blount during a considerable part of the sixteenth century. Sir HENRY BLOUNT married the widow of Sir William Mainwaring, who was one of the daughters and coheiresses of Christopher Ware, Esq. lord of this manor as before mentioned, by which means he became possessed of the mansion house, and a moiety of the manerial estate. This gen-

tleman left England in the year 1634, and visited the Turkish domi-
nions in Europe, and also several parts of Egypt.   After some stay at
Grand Cairo, he returned home in 1636, and published an account of
his travels, under the title of " A Voyage into the Levant, &c."
London, 1636, 4to.—Charles I. appointed him one of the band of
pensioners; and in the Civil War he joined the King's party, and
fought on the Royal side at the battle of Edge Hill.   He afterwards
abandoned the King's cause, and engaged in that of the Commonwealth, rendering himself very useful to his country.   In 1651, he
became one of the committee for reforming the practice of the law,
and was very zealous against tythes, and for the reduction of the stipends of all parish ministers to an equal and moderate provision.   His
general knowledge recommended him to the office of one of the Commissioners for advancing the Trade and Navigation of the Commonwealth.   At the Restoration he was favourably received by the King;
and, in 1661, he served the office of High Sheriff for the county of
Hertford (where the family possessed considerable property).   From
this time till his death, in 1682, he lived as a retired English gentleman; but he seems to have acquired from his travels an inclination to
freedom of opinion, and to have adopted several singular and paradox-
ical notions.   Six Comedies, intituled, " Court Comedies," and published under the name of John Lilly, have been ascribed to him.   He
also wrote a Satire, called, " The Exchange Walk," and an Epistle in
praise of Coffee and Tobacco [1].

SIR THOMAS POPE BLOUNT[2], eldest son of the preceding, was
born here Sept. 12, 1649, and educated under the immediate inspection of his father.   Having established an early reputation for learning and worth, he was created a Baronet by Charles II. in 1679.   He
represented the borough of St. Alban, and afterwards the county, in
Parliament; and was always esteemed as a friend of liberty, and a

[1]  Biographia Britannica, &c.
[2]  The grandfather of the above was the first that bore this name, being related to
Sir Thomas Pope, founder of Trinity College, Oxford.

true patron of literature.  Of his erudition he gave evidence in his learned work, intituled, " Censura Celebriorum Authorum," printed at London, in 1690, folio, and reprinted at Geneva, in 1694 and 1710, quarto.  This work is an accurate and useful compilation, containing an account of the characters and writings of both antient and modern poets.  His work, " De Re Poetica," published in 1694, quarto, is a similar compilation, comprehending an account of antient and modern poets.  His Natural History, printed in 1693, 12mo, is a kind of common place book, containing observations, many of which are uncommon, selected from the best modern writers.  Of his talents as an original writer we have a specimen in his " Essays " on various Subjects," 8vo, in which he discusses many curious points, such as the influence of the priesthood; the regard due to the antients; the variety of opinions; the uncertainty of human knowledge; the effects of custom and education, &c.  He died at the family seat at Tittenhanger, in Herts, in 1697, and left a numerous family[1].

CHARLES BLOUNT, brother of the preceding, who was born at Upper Holloway in 1654, also possessed distinguished talents.  As he was the favourite of his father, he encouraged his marrying, and settling in an independent estate at the early age of 18 years.  With the exception of a little treatise, published without his name, and intituled, " Mr. Dryden vindicated, &c." his literary career commenced in 1678 or 1679, with the publication of his " Anima Mundi, or an " Historical Narration of the Opinions of the Antients concerning " Man's Soul after this life, according to unenlightened Nature," in the composition of which, he is said to have been assisted by his father.  This work contained free opinions, which gave great offence; and, though it had been previously licensed, was suppressed by order of Compton, Bishop of London, and during his absence burned by some officious zealot.  Several answers to it were written; and it was

[1] Biographia Britannica.

particularly animadverted upon in the second volume of Nichols's Conference with a Theist. In the same year Mr. Blount published some extracts from Hobbes's Leviathan, in a single sheet, intituled, " Mr. Hobbes's last Words and dying Legacy," and intended to expose, probably, the political principles of this writer. To these his ardent zeal for liberty rendered him peculiarly adverse, and his zealous attachment to this cause was soon after manifested, in a pamphlet under the signature of " Junius Brutus," designed to alarm the nation, with regard to a Popish plot, and the prospect of a Popish successor to the Crown. In 1680, he published his translation of " The two " first Books of Philastratus, concerning the Life of Apollonius Ty- " anæus, with philological Notes on each Chapter," folio, which being considered as a dangerous attempt to reproach and injure the Christian Religion, was immediately suppressed, so that few copies of it could be obtained. This was followed in the same year by a work, intituled, " Great is Diana of the Ephesians, or the Original " of Idolatry, together with the political Institutions of the Gentiles' " Sacrifices ;" which, though professedly written against the impositions of the Heathen Priests, was thought to be aimed at the Christian priesthood, and indirectly against all revelation. The author was now considered as the head of the Deistical sect, and he is charged with having taken great pains, by conversation and correspondence, to propagate and defend his opinions. In a letter to Dr. Sydenham, however, he acknowledged, that, in point of practice, Deism was less satisfactory than the Christian scheme. The clamour occasioned by his former publications made him somewhat more cautious and reserved; and accordingly he studied to conceal his being the author of a treatise, intituled, " Religio Laici," published in 1683, and said by Dr. Leland, in his Deistical writers, v. I. p. 37, to be little more than a translation of Lord Herbert's work under the same title ; and he also abandoned the design which he had formed of writing a Life of Mahomet. From this time he seems to have changed the objects of his study, for in 1684 he published " Janua Scientiarum, or

" an Introduction to Geography, Chronology, Government, History,
" Philosophy, and all genteel sorts of Learning," 8vo, which was
intended to assist young persons, at an early age, in the acquisition
of principles of philosophy and science, without pursuing the tedious
course that had been usually prescribed to them in schools.

Mr. Blount was one of those who cordially concurred in the Revolution; and, in a letter addressed to William Leveson Gower, concerning Corporations, and inserted in the " Oracles of Reason," he
expresses his wish, that those counsellors of the late King who had
injured the independence of Parliament, might be punished, justly
considering the purity of representation as the essence of a free constitution. About this time he wrote his treatise, intituled " A just
" Vindication of Learning, and of the Liberty of the Press;" which
is esteemed one of his best performances, and a summary of all the
principal arguments that can be urged upon this topic. In his zeal
for the cause of King William, he wrote a pamphlet, in 1693, intended to prove the right of William and Mary to the Crown, on the
ground of Conquest; and, in explanation of this design, so dissonant,
one would imagine, with his principles, and no less obnoxious than
ill founded, he declares, that he wrote " with an especial regard to
" such as have hitherto refused the oath, and yet allow of the title of
" Conquest, when consequent to a just war." By this performance
he gave such offence, that on a complaint being brought before the
House of Commons against this pamphlet, intituled, " William and
" Queen Mary Conquerors," it was ordered to be burnt by the hands
of the common hangman; and in the same censure was involved a
Pastoral Letter of Bishop Burnet, in which the same notion was advanced, probably with the same views.

Mr. Blount having lost his wife, became ardently enamoured of
her sister, a lady of great beauty and merit, who seemed disposed to
return his affection; but, as the ecclesiastical laws opposed their union,
he drew up a case, strongly argued, and referred it to certain divines,
who of course gave their opinions against his wishes. As the lady

M

refused to comply after such a determination, Mr. Blount sunk into despair; and at length shot himself through the head. After this act of phrenzy, he languished for some days, receiving no nourishment but from the hands of the object of his affection, till at last death released him, August 1693 [1].

Many of his private letters, and some small tracts, were published together, with a Preface by Gildon, in 1693, before the author's death, in a work intituled, " The Oracles of Reason," which was afterwards reprinted, with some additional pieces, after his decease, in 1695, in a collection of " The Miscellaneous Works of Charles Blount, Esq." by the same Mr. Gildon, who prefixed to it an account of the life and death of the author. The learning of Mr. Blount is unquestionable, and he seems to have possessed a strong and ardent mind; but his early dislike of superstition precipitated him into some very considerable errors, and inclined him to believe all revealed religion to be priestcraft, because he perceived that some priests had converted religion to their own secular advantage. His sentiments on the subject of religion were divulged in his writings without disguise, and sufficiently warrant our referring him to the class of Deists; but the charge of Atheism alledged against him by some foreign divines is certainly unfounded. See an account of Mr. Blount's writings, by Dr. Leland, in the fourth letter of his View of the Deistical writers, vol. I. By this writer we are informed, that Mr. Gildon, who published the " Oracles of Reason," and communicated them to the world, was afterwards, upon mature consideration, convinced of his error, and, in 1705, published his retraction, in a book intituled, " The Deists' "Manual." The greatest part of this book is intended to vindicate the doctrines of the existence and attributes of God, his providence,

---

[1] In the Cæsar MSS. the cause of his death is thus related :

" Aug. 31, 1693. Mr. Charles Blount, of Tittenhanger, in Hartfordshire, died " in London, *felo de se*, five weeks after he had shot himself into the belly with a " pistoll; for the love of Mrs. Hobby (his wive's sister), who was a rich widow." Beauties of England and Wales, vol. VII. p. 282.

and government of the world, the immortality of the soul, and a future state : and his avowed reason was, because many of the Deists, with whom he was well acquainted, did really deny those great principles, which lie at the foundation of all religion, or at least represent them as doubtful and uncertain. And their not admitting natural religion in its just extent formed some of their principal prejudices against the Christian revelation[1].

On the North side of the road at Upper Holloway, are a few antient houses, which it is probable were formerly inhabited by persons of eminence; but nothing now remains to point out who have been their original proprietors or inhabitants. Tradition reports, that Oliver Cromwell resided in one of them (now the Crown public house), which has a modern brick front, but from the internal appearance, must have been built about the beginning of the seventeenth century. It does not appear that the Protector ever had a house in this parish, though he in all probability visited the place; for his contemporary and associate Sir Arthur Hesilrige had, beyond all doubt, a dwelling in Islington, as appears by the following extract from the Journals of the House of Commons:

May 21, 1664-5. " Sir Arthur Hesilrigge, by command of the " House, related the circumstance of an assault made on him by the " Earl of Stamford, and Henry Polton, and Matthew Patsall, his " servants, in the highway leading from *Perpoole-lane* to Clerken- " well, as he was peaceably riding from the House of Commons to " his house in ISLINGTON, by striking him with a drawn sword, and " other offensive instruments, and was enjoined to keep the peace, " and not to send or receive any challenge[2]."

[1] Biographia Britannica.

[2] Sir Arthur was the son of Sir Thomas Hesilrige, of Noseley, in Leicester-shire, who was created a Baronet by James I. in 1622. He was elected Member for the county of Leicester in the Parliament which met Nov. 4, 1640; and soon

Between the Crown and Ring Cross are a number of small houses, built in the cottage style, and which are mostly occupied by citizens as retiring villas. At the end of Du Val's lane is a large manufactory, where cloths and other articles are rendered *water-proof*. A patent was first granted for this invention, in the year 1801, to Messrs. Ackermann, Suardy, and Co. of the Strand, who having soon after disposed of their interest therein to a person at Leeds, the above manufactory was established here by other parties, under the firm of Elizabeth Duke and Co. by whom the business is still carried on. The articles that are here made water-proof, consist for the most part of great coats and cloaks for the army, for which the proprietors have considerable contracts with government. The wide part of the highway where the Back road terminates, near Holloway turnpike, has been, time out of mind, called *Ring Cross*, probably from a cross standing here antecedent to the Reformation.

The parish workhouse stands at a little distance from the Back road, nearly opposite Barnesbury-street. It is a commodious building of brick, and was erected in the year 1777, at the expence of £.3,000, upon a piece of ground given to the parish by Mrs. Amey Hill. It has a spacious garden attached, from which a considerable portion of the vegetables used in the house are supplied. The building at first consisted of a centre and two wings; but, an enlargement being found necessary, the centre was made to project in

became one of the most active leaders of the Republican party, particularly distinguishing himself in the various contests between the King and the Parliament. The Protector and Sir Arthur were upon the most familiar terms; and it appears, that, upon one occasion, Oliver was entertained by the Baronet with great magnificence at Newcastle, when prayers were offered up for the success of the army in Scotland. A letter to Sir Arthur, dated Sept. 3, 1650, written by the Protector, wherein he addresses him, " Deere Sir," is printed in Mr. Nichols's History of Leicestershire, vol. II. part II. p. 744, which work contains an interesting narrative of the share he had in the various proceedings of the Parliament during that important period of our history.

front by an addition made thereto in the year 1802. Before the erection of this house, the poor were maintained in a part of *The Old Soap House* in the Lower-street, and previously in a workhouse on the South side of the road at Holloway, upon the site of North-ampton-place, which also contained the poor belonging to the parish of Hornsey. The number of poor in the workhouse generally averages about 200 [1]; and they are carefully provided with every thing necessary for the comfort and convenience of persons in their situation.

[1] In April 1810, there were 240 persons in the workhouse; of which number 60 individuals were of the age of 70 years, and upwards. In the list of paupers, is an unfortunate female, known by the name of *Jemima Williams*, who was brought hither from a dunghill, where she lay apparently expiring, in the autumn of 1802. She had, for more than twenty years, wandered about the village in a state of mental weakness bordering on insanity, subsisting intirely upon the charity of the inhabitants and such passengers as were moved to pity, by her forlorn and wretched appearance. She was generally known to the inhabitants by the name of *Mad Eleanor*, and the *Queen of Hornsey*. The officers of the parish have never been able to obtain any account of her relatives, or early connexions; it has, however, been asserted, and is the prevailing opinion, that she came of a good family, and possessed considerable fortune, but was shamefully deluded and robbed of all her property by a villain in her younger days. This is said to have been the occasion of that derangement of mind, which led her to the wandering mode of life she afterwards adopted. She would constantly range about the village, to Highbury, Canonbury, &c. having her cheek distended with tobacco, and covered with rags, which were hung in bundles about various parts of her body. She subsisted in the manner before mentioned, always sleeping in the fields, an outhouse, or some doorway, wherever night happened to overtake her.

The following correct description of this unfortunate woman is given by a lady who had daily opportunities of seeing her for the last two years of her miserable wandering : " She appeared to be about 60 years of age, was fed and clothed by " charity. She walked in all weathers from morning till night, and seemed insensi- " ble of the worst. She spoke not unless spoken to; she then answered in a mild " and civil manner. When she was tired she rested her back against a wall, or sat " on steps; she always accepted what was given her with silent civility; but if asked

The following rules and orders, for the better regulation of the workhouse, were agreed upon at a meeting of the trustees of the poor, on the 25th of January, 1798:

1. That the master and mistress do constantly exercise a benevolent tenderness towards all persons in general, but especially the sick and infirm, and the children that shall be committed to their care.

2. That in their respective departments, they do uniformly exert a prudent care, management, and distribution of furniture, utensils, linen, coals, candles, soap, provision, clothing and stores of all sorts, with which they shall be entrusted; and that the master do make a proper entry thereof.

3. That by their own good example, and the authority vested in them from the trustees, they be careful to promote cleanliness, industry, frugality, sobriety, peace and piety in the said house, and to prevent and discourage the contrary vices of sloth, idleness, wastefulness, intemperance, discord and irreligion among the persons over whom they are placed.

4. That they do not admit any person into any other place than one of the rooms in the yard, set apart from the house for the reception of those who shall not appear to be clean or free from infection, till they be first examined by the apothecary, who attends the poor, and properly cleansed and cloathed.

---

" what had reduced her to the necessity of begging, she would refuse the money
" then offered her, and walk away. She seemed always contented, and sometimes
" cheerful. It is supposed, that her name is *Stuart.* I once asked her her name;
" she replied, 'I am called hereabouts Jemima Williams.' — In her we behold a
" striking instance of his providence whose mercy is over all his works; for she cer-
" tainly subsisted very many years without a roof to shelter her from inclement
" skies, or a change of apparel." See a volume of Poems, intituled, " Friendly
" Visits from the Muse, or the Consolations of Solitude," 8vo, 1810, which contains
some verses written upon the above female, under the title of " *Elenora the insane*
" *Fugitive of* ISLINGTON."

5. That the bell be rung, and that they see all the family, except the sick and infirm, be up, dressed, washed and combed by 6 o'clock in the summer mornings, and seven in the winter; and that prayers be read by the master, or such other person as may be appointed by the trustees, morning and evening.

6. That after prayers are read in the morning, the master or mistress do set all to work (who are not reported by the apothecary to be incapable), beginning at seven o'clock from Lady-day to Michaelmas, and from Michaelmas to Lady-day at eight o'clock, and to continue till six o'clock from Lady-day to Michaelmas, and till four o'clock from Michaelmas to Lady-day (meal-times excepted, that is to say, breakfast at nine precisely, and dinner at one, in the common eating-room); and that the said several poor persons be allowed half an hour at breakfast, and one hour at dinner: the master and mistress to attend the whole time of such meals, and to the distribution of the provisions ordered at the said meals, and take care there be no waste.

7. That a portion of the time between breakfast and dinner be set apart for instructing the children in reading, and learning their prayers and catechism.

8. That the several poor persons do go to supper, after their work, in the common eating-room; and after supper to evening prayer; and be all in bed, except the nurses, by nine in the summer, and eight in the winter.

9. That the several meals for the family, be directed by the trustees at their general meetings or committees; that the cloth be laid at every dinner; grace said before and after meat by one of the children; and that the graces and prayers to be used, be severally approved of by the vicar of the parish.

10. That no candles be used in the evenings of the months of May, June, July, and August, except by the master and mistress, or in the infirmaries; and that the master and mistress, in their

proper departments, do see that the candles be put out each night, at a proper hour, in the other months; and that no person be suffered to smoke or read in bed.

11. That no person be admitted to see any poor in the house without leave of the master; and that the master do not permit any person who now is, or at a future time may be, maintained in the workhouse, to go out of the same without an order (in writing) from a churchwarden or overseer of the poor.

12. That no person do presume to beg, within or out of the house, on pain of incurring such punishment, as the trustees shall think proper to inflict on him or her so offending.

13. That all those who are well and able (except such as of necessity must be at home) go in a decent order to the parish church, every Sunday morning and evening, accompanied by the master or mistress, and return in the same manner, *except such as have been otherwise educated, who are to repair to their respective places of worship, under the direction of a proper person appointed by the master;* and those persons who go to church, and do not return home within one quarter of an hour after the master or mistress, be not admitted without the knowledge of the master; and that such of the poor persons who may offend in the above, be mulcted of their allowance of meat, either on that or the next meat day: that the master, every Sunday evening, do read prayers and a sermon to the poor persons in the house, in the eating-room, at six o'clock from Michaelmas to Lady-day, and seven o'clock from Lady-day to Michaelmas.

14. That all poor persons in the house, do quietly bear the just reproofs of the master and mistress, and diligently and willingly perform the work or service they shall from time to time be required to do. That they do not swear, curse, quarrel, give rude language, or be guilty of any indecent behaviour whatever. And if they shall find themselves ill used by the master or mistress, they are at full liberty to complain to the committee of trustees, who will see them redressed.

15. That on the admission of every adult person, the master do

read over to him, or her, all such of the aforegoing rules and orders, as relate to the behaviour of the poor, during their continuance in this house.

16. That in the placing persons into their several wards, as well as in other respects, some distinction be made between such poor who have been creditable housekeepers, and reduced by misfortunes, and the other poor, who become so by vice or idleness.

17. That the master do enter in a book, to be kept for that purpose, the names and ages of all persons now in the house, or that shall from time to time be taken into the house, when they are admitted, when they die, or are discharged.

18. That the key of the outer door of the lodge, be delivered to the master or mistress at nine o'clock in the evening from Lady-day to Michaelmas, and from Michaelmas to Lady-day at eight o'clock.

19. That the master keep an account, in proper books, of the quantity and quality of the materials, which, from time to time, shall be brought in to be manufactured, and from whom; that he shall, upon all proper occasions, settle the accounts for such works with the several employers, and receive from them the amount thereof; he shall duly pay the usual emoluments to the poor employed in such works for their encouragement, and pay the surplus into the hands of such person as the trustees may direct.

20. That the master or mistress do not at any time absent themselves from the workhouse for one whole day without the consent of one of the churchwardens or overseers of the poor; and in such case, that they return on or before nine o'clock in the evening of such day (except on any particular occasion): and further, without such consent of a churchwarden or overseer of the poor, they do not, at any time, absent themselves from the same, after the said hour of nine in the evening.

21. That the master or mistress take care that all the beds, rooms, wards, and other parts of the house be kept clean and decent, and that the same be inspected every morning.

N

22. That the mistress deliver out the soap, and see all the linen of the house brought into the wash-house, washed, got up, and properly mended; that every poor person have a shirt or a shift once in every week; that the beds be clean sheeted once a month; and that no linen be washed or hung up to dry in any of the bed-rooms; that she distribute milk and such other necessaries to the sick as the apothecary shall think proper.

Provisions for the several days, as follow; viz.

| | Breakfast. | Dinner. | Supper. |
|---|---|---|---|
| Sunday | Bread and butter | Boiled beef | Bread & cheese. |
| Monday | Milk porridge | Peas soup | Ditto. |
| Tuesday | Milk porridge | Mutton, legs & should. | Ditto. |
| Wednesday | Broth | Bread and cheese | Ditto. |
| Thursday | Bread and butter | Boiled beef | Ditto. |
| Friday | Milk porridge | Ox heads stewed | Ditto. |
| Saturday | Bread and butter | Bread and cheese | Ditto. |

Allowance as under to each person:

Bread, 14 ounces for the day.

Meat, eight ounces *per* meal.

Butter, two ounces *per* meal.

Cheese, two ounces *per* meal.

On Christmas-day and New-year's-day, roast beef and plumb pudding; and one pint of ale for grown persons, and half a pint for children.

Easter-day, legs of pork and peas puddings, with the same allowance of porter.

Whit Sunday, shoulders of veal, with porter as above.

In the several seasons, peas and bacon, and beans and bacon, with the like allowance of porter [1].

---

[1] Much praise is due to the gentlemen concerned in the management of the poor of this parish, for their promptitude at all times, to add to the comforts of those

Islington Workhouse.

Pub. May 1.1819. for the Proprietor by R. Ackermann. 101. Strand.

View of Islington from the Back Road (Liverpool Road).

The Back road, which formerly passed in a direct line from the South to the front of the workhouse, and thence turned off East to

persons whom necessity compels to solicit their relief; nor can the benevolent spirit of the inhabitants at large be too much commended for the liberality shewn by them on every occasion, when called upon to contribute to the happiness of the indigent. One instance of their bounty is worthy of being recorded; namely, the contribution raised throughout the parish to enable the poorer inhabitants to join in the festivities of the day of Jubilee, when our beloved Monarch entered the 50th year of his reign. Nor does it redound less to their honour, that on this occasion the same philanthropic spirit was found to prevail throughout the whole kingdom. The subscription collected amongst the inhabitants of Islington for this purpose, and for the relief of such persons imprisoned for debt as might be parishioners, amounted to £.746. 10s. which was applied in the following manner, under the direction of a committee appointed for that purpose; viz.

In 1209 families, comprizing 4,200 persons, each adult received on the day of Jubilee, one quartern loaf, one pound of beef, and one shilling and six pence in money; those having children received an additional pound of beef, twenty pounds of potatoes, and three pence in money, for every child. The total expence of the provisions, &c. was as under:

|  | £. | s. | d. |
|---|---|---|---|
| 1979 loaves | 133 | 19 | 9¾ |
| 537 stone of meat | 129 | 19 | 1 |
| 20 tons of potatoes, at 90s. per ton | 90 | 0 | 0 |
| Money distributed | 170 | 16 | 0 |
| Dinner for children in the charity schools | 9 | 11 | 1¼ |
| Dinner for children in Union Chapel school | 5 | 5 | 0 |
| Beer to men delivering potatoes | 0 | 15 | 10 |
| The keeper of Fleet Prison, visiting a prisoner | 0 | 7 | 0 |
| Printing the resolutions of meeting in the vestry | 13 | 9 | 6 |
| Men to deliver them | 4 | 4 | 0 |
| Advertizing them in the newspapers | 2 | 15 | 6 |
| Ringers, for their dinner | 5 | 0 | 0 |
| To poor prisoners in the City gaols | 20 | 0 | 0 |
|  | 586 | 2 | 10 |

The balance was afterwards expended in provisions and coals for the poor, and the relief of sundry individuals belonging to the parish, at the discretion of the committee.

the top of Barnesbury-street [1], was changed into its present course in August 1796, by which alteration two very dangerous angles, which had been the occasion of frequent accidents, were removed.

In the fields Westward of the workhouse, on the evening of Sunday May 7, 1797, between eight and nine o'clock, a barbarous murder was committed on the body of Mr. Fryer, an attorney, of Southampton-buildings, Holborn, who, walking here with a young lady to whom he was soon to have been married, was attacked by three footpads, and shot through the head; after which they robbed him of his watch and money. A reward of £.50 was offered in the London Gazette for the apprehending the murderer; and on the 5th of June following, Clinch and Mackly, two notorious offenders, were executed at Newgate for the crime, but which they persevered in denying to the last. Another malefactor, who was hung some time afterwards, confessed having been the perpetrator of this horrid deed.

### WHITE CONDUIT HOUSE

has been for many years celebrated as a tea-house, and for its beautiful prospect over the fields towards Hampstead, Highgate, &c. It derived its name from an old stone conduit yet remaining here (see Plate II. fig. 1.), and which from the date in front appears to have been erected in the year 1641. It was built over a head of water that supplied the Charter-house, by means of a leaden pipe, which after the erection of Sadler's Wells passed through the basement story of that building. The carved stone in front which bears the above date, exhibits also the initials of Thomas Sutton, founder of the Charter-house, with his arms [2], and other initials, probably those of persons connected with the Hospital. The letters " S. H."

[1] See Baker's Plan.
[2] Or, on a chevron between three annulets as many crescents of the field.

PLATE II.

1362

J. Hawksworth sculp.

White Conduit House, Pentonville.

Pub. May 1 1819. for the Proprietor by R. Ackermann 101 Strand.

WHITE CONDUIT HOUSE. *near* Islington.

Pentonville Chapel.

Collier Street, Pentonville.

Pub. May 1.1819. for the Proprietor by R. Ackermann, 101, Strand.

(Sutton's Hospital) are also to be seen on several stones in the adjoining fields to the North, which point out the direction of the watercourse leading to the conduit. For some years past, the house and premises of the late **Dr. De Valangin** at Pentonville has been supplied with water from this conduit, the Charter-house having discontinued to use it.

The gardens belonging to White Conduit House are laid out in a neat manner, having in the middle a circular bason of water, with boxes around it, decorated with paintings, &c. in which the company sit and take their refreshments. Here are also a bowling-green, Dutch-pin grounds, &c. and a neighbouring field was about twenty years back used as a cricket ground by a society of noblemen and gentlemen, who formed a club here for the exercise of that game. A view of the ground, with the members playing, is contained in Carington Bowles's set of prints of " Manly Recreations," published in the year 1788. The house is spacious, and consists of several handsome and convenient rooms, the principal of which contains a very fine toned organ. The premises are at present occupied by **Mrs. Sharpe** and **Mr. Warren**, who have also an ale and table beer brewery attached to the premises.

This house and gardens were celebrated half a century ago as a place of great resort, not only for the lower orders of the community, but for decent tradesmen and their families, on a Sunday afternoon, to drink tea, &c. The following poem, published in the Gentleman's Magazine, for May 1760, contains a lively, if not altogether a correct picture of the place in its happiest time [1].

[1] Upon the site of Dobney's-place, at the back of Penton-street, formerly stood an old house, called *D'Aubigny's, Dawbeney's,* or *Dobney's,* having a bowling-green and tea-gardens, with ponds, &c. similar to those at White Conduit House, and which were fresh planned and laid out by a person named Johnson, who took the premises in the year 1767. At this place about forty years ago one *Price,* an equestrian performer, did feats of horsemanship, whilst an opponent named *Sampson* exhibited similar performances in a field behind the *Old Hats.* The exhibition

" WHITE CONDUIT HOUSE.

" And to White Conduit House
" We will go, will go, will go.
                                    " Grub-street Register.

" Wish'd Sunday 's come-—mirth brightens every face,
" And paints the rose upon the house-maid's cheek,

of these two heroes, so near to one spot, caused no small degree of jealousy between them, and gave rise to a piece of generalship, that may not be considered
unworthy the notice of our more illustrious politicians.  One of the equestrians procured a female of dashing appearance, and some personal attractions, who, under his
instructions, went as a spectator to witness the performances of his rival : she admired his abilities, as he did her charms, and an intimate connexion was soon
formed between them ; the result of which was, that the unfortunate equestrian
soon finding himself unable to perform feats of horsemanship, was under the necessity of leaving the field to his crafty competitor.  These two persons are the first
performers of equestrian feats that we read of in this country, being antecedent
to the exhibitions of the celebrated Astley.

In the High-street at the entrance of *Islington*, but in Clerkenwell parish, some
old houses yet remain.  The *Angel inn*, facing the City-road, exhibits the appearance of some antiquity in the staircases and galleries which surround the yard.
In this part of the village there were formerly several capital houses of this description : one at the North-east corner of White Lion-street (said to have been a tavern,
and which with the adjoining house appears to have been originally one building)
has lofty stuccoed cielings, similar to others in Islington of the time of Elizabeth
and James the First ; it also contains a stone chimney-piece representing the story
of Orpheus charming the brutes, in relievo.  The house at the opposite corner
bears in front the figure of a lion rampant gardant in bold relief, with the date
1714, when it was built for an inn, bearing that sign ; used principally by drovers
of cattle ; and so continued to be used till part of the house was pulled down, and an
opening made through it into the adjoining street, which bears that name.  The car-
riage-way to the inn yard (which was also the public and principal road to the dwelling-house of Daubeneys bowling-green) was through a part of the present shop,
immediately under the Lion ; and so continued, till the trade of the inn declining,
the building was converted into private dwellings.  These houses are now both occupied by grocers.  The *Peacock*, near the same spot, is at this time a house of
great trade, and where most of the stage coaches that travel this road stop to take
up passengers and parcels.

_Representation of the Noble_ GAME of CRICKET, _as played in the celebrated Cricket Field near White Conduit House_

Published by Alexr Hogg, No 16 Paternoster Row, Aug 1st 1787.

Angel-Inn. Islington.

Angel Inn Yard. Islington.

Pub.ᵈ May 1.1819 for the Proprietor by R. Ackermann. 101. Strand.

" Harriott, or Moll more ruddy. — Now the heart
" Of 'Prentice, resident in ample street,
" Or alley, kennel-wash'd; Cheapside, Cornhill,
" Or Cranbourne, thee for calcuments renown'd,
" With joy distends — his meal meridian o'er,
" With switch in hand, he to the *White Conduit House*
" Hies merry-hearted. — Human beings here,
" In couples multitudinous, assemble,
" Forming the drollest groupe that ever trod
" Fair *Islingtonian* plains. — Male after male,
" Dog after dog succeeding—husbands, wives,
" Fathers, and mothers, brothers, sisters, friends,
" And pretty little boys and girls — around,
" Across the garden's shrubby maze
" They walk, they sit, they stand. -— What crowds press on
" Eager to mount the stairs, eager to catch
" First vacant bench, or chair, in long room plac'd !
" Here prig with prig holds conference polite,
" And indiscriminate the gaudy beau
" And sloven mix. — Here, he who all the week
" Took bearded mortals by the nose, or sat
" Weaving dead hairs, and whistling wretched strain,
" And eke the sturdy youth, whose trade it is
" Stout oxen to contund, with gold-bound hat
" And silken stocking strut. — The red armed belle
" Here shews her tasty gown, proud to be thought
" The butterfly of fashion : and, forsooth,
" Her haughty mistress deigns for once to tread
" The same unhallow'd floor. — 'Tis hurry all,
" And rattling cups and saucers. — Waiter here,
" And waiter there, and waiter here and there
" At once is call'd, Joe, Joe, Joe, Joe, Joe.
" Joe on the right, and Joe upon the left,
" For every vocal pipe re-echoes Joe !

" Alas ! poor Joe ! like Francis in the play,
" He stands confounded, anxious how to please
" The many-headed throng.   But should I paint
" The language, humours, customs of the place,
" Together with all curtseys, lowly bows,
" And compliments extern, 'twould swell my page
" Beyond its limits due. — Suffice it then
" For my prophetic Muse to sing, ' So long
" As Fashion rides upon the wing of Time,
" While tea and cream, and butter'd rolls, can please,
" While rival beaux and jealous belles exist,
" So long, *White Conduit House* shall be thy fame.' "

Some years ago, this house and premises were kept by Mr. Christopher Bartholomew, a person who inherited a good fortune from his parents, and who brought much trade to the place by the taste he displayed in laying out the gardens and walks, and the excellent manner in which he conducted the business of the house.

This person, with every prospect of success and eminence in life, fell a victim to an unconquerable itch for gambling in the lottery. At one time the tea-gardens and premises, as also the Angel Inn mentioned in the preceding note, were his freeholds; he rented land to the amount of £.2000 a year in the neighbourhood of Islington and Holloway; and was remarkable for having the greatest quantity of haystacks of any grower in the neighbourhood of London.  At that time he is believed to have been worth £.50,000, kept his carriage and servants in livery; and, upon one occasion, having been unusually successful at insuring in the lottery, gave a public breakfast at his tea-gardens, " *to commemorate the smiles of Fortune,*" as it was expressed upon the tickets of admission to this *Fête Champetré.*

He at times had some very fortunate hits in the lottery, and which, perhaps, tended to increase the mania which hurried him to his ruin. He has been known to spend upwards of 2000 guineas in a day for insurance, to raise which, stack after stack of his immense crops of hay have been cut down and hurried to market, as the readiest way to obtain the supplies necessary for these extraordinary outgoings. Having at last been obliged to part with his house from accumulated difficulties and embarrassments, he passed the last thirteen years of his life in great poverty, subsisting by the charity of those who knew his better days, and the emolument he received as a Juryman of the Sheriff's Court for the County.

Still his propensity to be engaged in this ruinous pursuit never forsook him: and meeting one day, in the year 1807, with an old acquaintance, he related to him a strong presentiment he entertained, that if he could purchase a particular number in the ensuing lottery (which he was not then in a situation to accomplish) it would prove successful. His friend, after remonstrating with him on the impropriety of persevering in a practice that had been already attended with such evil consequences, was at last persuaded to go halves with him in a sixteenth part of the favourite number, which, being procured, was most fortunately drawn a prize of £.20,000. With the money arising from this extraordinary turn of fortune, he was prevailed upon by his friends to purchase an annuity of £.60 *per annum ;* yet, fatally addicted to the pernicious habit of insurance, he disposed of it, and lost it all. He has been known frequently to apply to those persons who had been served by him in his prosperity, for an old coat, or some other article of cast apparel; and not many days before he died, he solicited a few shillings to buy him necessaries.

A gentleman in his manners, with a mind rather superior to the generality of men, he at one time possessed the esteem of all who knew him; but was reduced from a state of affluence and respectability to wretchedness and want, by following that baneful practice, which, in spite of all laws made to the contrary, will ever exist whilst the government continues to resort to the unwise expedient of inducing the individual to pay £.20 for the liberty of gambling for £.10. Let his fate be a warning to all ranks, particularly to those engaged in trade, not to engage in a pursuit which will ultimately be their ruin; and, when tempted to insure, let them remember the fate of BARTHOLOMEW. He died in a two pair of stairs room, in Angel-court, Windmill-street, Haymarket, in March 1809, aged 68.

The ground adjoining to White Conduit House for a considerable extent is appropriated to the laying of cattle on their way to Smithfield Market. The removal of that market to some spot in this neighbourhood has been a matter of late much agitated in the Court of Common Council, and two Bills have been brought into Parliament for that purpose, but which were both lost by very small majorities in the House of Commons. A field belonging to the New River Company, adjoining to Sadler's Wells, containing about 14 acres, was offered to the City for the Market, at the sum of £.25,000, as was also the Stone-field, belonging to this parish, at £.22,800. These are both eligible spots; and when the abominable nuisance of the market in its present confined situation in the heart of the City is considered, together with the continual damage and expence sustained by the owners of cattle in consequence, it is almost a matter of astonishment that such a measure should meet with the slightest opposition.

## MANOR OF ISELDON BERNERS, OR BERNERSBURY, COMMONLY CALLED BARNESBURY [1].

MR. Lysons thinks it probable that the greater part of the estates at Islington, said in the Domesday Survey to belong to the Church of St. Paul's, came into the Berners family. It is certain that as well as this Manor (which bears the name of the family) they possessed that of Canonbury, and it seems not unlikely that at some former period they also held a part of the manor of St. John of Jerusalem. Ralph de Berners, who died in 1297, was seised of the manor of YSELDON, held under the Bishop of London, as of his castle of Stortford, by a certain quit-rent, and the service of warding the castle [2]. This manor, called in later records Berners, or Bernersbury, in Iseldon, continued in the same family for several generations.

It appears, however, that Humphrey de Bohun, Earl of Hereford, had some interest in this estate about the middle of the fourteenth century [3]. The Berners family, in the reign of Henry VI. held some lands in Islington (being half a knight's fee under the Bo-

[1] For the situation of this Manor, see p. 58.

[2] Esch. 25 Edward I. No. 39. Edward de Berners held the same possessions by military service, vide second and last patent 14 Richard II. In the former record the value and extent of this manor is thus estimated. A capital messuage, with the garden, &c. valued at 18s. 180 acres of arable land, valued at 2d. an acre, five of meadow at 1s. 6d. Rents of assize 26s. 3d. A pair of gilt spurs payable by Thomas Meuse of East Smithfield 6d. Customary rents 71s. 48 hens 4s. 144 days work due from 48 customary tenants 18s. being 1½d. each day's work; the reaping of 48 acres of corn 12s. The carrying of hay 2s. Weeding corn 2s. Profits of Court 6s. 8d. Edmund de Berners, 26 years of age, abroad in Gascony, was son and heir of Ralph.

[3] Esch. 46 Edw. III. No. 10.

huns [1];) being, no doubt, the same estate which is mentioned in the Domesday Survey as held by Gilbert under Geoffrey de Mandeville, whose heirs the Bohuns were [2].

Sir John de Berners died anno 1396, seised of the manor of Berners in Iseldon, valued at *£.24 per annum ;* James, his son and heir, being then 14 years of age [3]. Richard Lord Berners died anno 1412, seised of this manor; a third part of which was held in dower, anno 1417, by Philippa his widow, then married to Thomas Lewkner; the two other parts were in the occupation of the Bishop of London (Kemp.) Margaret, daughter of Lord Berners, seven years of age in 1417, was his heir [4]. Philippa Lady Berners died in 1421. It appears by the inquisition taken after her death [5], that her daughter Margery, then 12 years of age, was married to John Ferriby. Her second husband was Sir John Bourchier, into which family it passed on their intermarriage.

Sir John Bourchier, Lord Berners in right of his wife, died in 1475, and Margaret Lady Berners in 1476, when this manor was inherited by their grandson John, the last Lord Berners, then eight years of age [6], who became Chancellor of the Exchequer, Deputy General of the Town of Calais, &c. He is recorded among the noble authors, having published a translation of Froissart's Chronicle [7].

---

[1] Exchequer Records, Lib. No. 8. knights fees.

[2] Lysons's Environs.

[3] Esch. 50 Edw. III. No. 10.

[4] Esch. 5 Edw. V. No. 8.

[5] Esch. 9 Hen. V. No. 24. Among the profits of the manor enumerated in this record are certain rents called Lord's Silver, amounting to 4s. 5½d. The demesne lands held by Lady Berners in dower are nearly of the same extent as the whole manerial estate described in the inquisition taken after Ralph de Berners' death.

                              Lysons's Environs, London, vol. III. p. 129.

[6] See Esch. 15 Edw. IV. No. 35. The manor was then valued at 20l. *per annum.*

[7] The following is the title of this book, " Here begynnith the firste Volum of " Syr John Froysshart, of the Cronycles of Englande, Fraunce, Spayne, Portyn- " gale, Scotlande, Bretaine, Flaunders, and other places adjoynynge. Translated

"The Golden Boke of Marcus Aurelius." "The Hystory of the "Moost Noble and Valyant Knyght, Arthur, of Lytel Brytayne, &c." Lord Berners died in 1532, leaving issue one daughter, married to Edmund Knyvett, Esq. who had livery of his lands. In 1548 this manor was the property of Thomas Fowler, Gent. [1] in whose family it continued till 1656, when it passed to Sir Thomas Fisher, who married Sarah, the daughter and heir of Sir Thomas Fowler, Bart. and in 1671 it descended to his son Sir Richard Fisher, Bart. [2] Ursula, daughter and eventually heir of Sir Thomas Fisher, by marriage with Sir William Halton, Bart. [3], brought this manor into that family, in which it continued till 1754, when it was devised by Sir William Halton, their grandson, to William Tuffnell Jolliffe, Esq. [4] with whom it continued till his death in 1797, when it became the property (under the intail of Sir William Halton's will) of George Forster Tufnell, Esq. who died in 1798. From him it descended to his son William Tufnell, Esq. who died in 1809, and it is now vested in Trustees for the use of his widow, till his infant son, William Tufnell, shall attain the age of 25 years.

"out of Frenche into our maternall Englysshe tonge, by Johan Bourchier, Knyghte, "Lorde Berners, at the comaundement of oure mooste highe redouted Soveraygne "Lorde Kynge Henry the VIII. Kynge of Englande and of Fraunce, and high de- "fendour of the Christen Faythe, &c. Imprinted at London, in Flete-strete, by "Richard Pynson, Printer to the Kynges Noble Grace, MDXXIII." Among the Cotton MSS. (Vespasian, C. I.) are several Letters written from Spain, by Lord Berners to Cardinal Wolsey.

[1] Chantry Roll for Middlesex in the Augmentation Office, dated that year, in which mention is made of lands held under Thomas Fowler. See also "Clameum "Thomæ Fowler, militis & baronetti, tangens manerium de Barnesbury in com. "Middlesex." Hilarii Rec. A. D. 1650. rot. 13. among the Exchequer Records.

[2] See Kimber's Baronetage, vol. I. p. 487.

[3] Ursula Fisher was second wife of Sir William Halton; his first lady was Mary, daughter of Sir Edward Altham, of Marks Hall, Essex, by whom he had Sir William, his successor. Ibid.

[4] This gentleman obtained an Act of Parliament (8 Geo. III. cap. 3.) to enable him to grant building leases of the demesne lands, &c.

The fines in this manor are arbitrary and at the will of the Lord, whose custom is to take two years improved rent on a descent, and one year and a half on alienation. No heriots are paid, nor are widows intitled to dower. The Court Baron is held at the King's Head, in the Upper-street.

Towards the bottom of Highgate-hill, on the South side of the road, stands an upright stone, inscribed " Whittington Stone," and which marks the situation of another stone that formerly stood here, traditionally said to have been that on which the celebrated Richard Whittington sat down to ruminate on his hard fortune, after having been induced to run away from his master's house and go back to the country, on account of the ill usage which he experienced from the cook maid. The tradition relates, that whilst sitting pensive on this stone, his ears were on a sudden assailed by a peal from Bow bells, which seemed to urge him to return back, in the following distich :

> " Turn again Whittington,
> " Thrice Lord Mayor of London."

Whatever may have been the early history of this celebrated hero, certain it is, from our civic annals, that he served the office of Mayor three times, viz. in the years 1398, 1406, and 1419. He also founded several public edifices and charitable institutions, and was esteemed the richest and most munificent subject in the whole kingdom [1]. The original stone that occupied the above situation lay flat

[1] Some idea of the wealth of this citizen and the little value he set on money, may be had from the following circumstance, which is related by our civic historians. At an entertainment given to Henry V. at Guildhall, after his conquest of France, the King was much pleased with a fire which Sir Richard had caused to be made of choice woods, mixed with cinnamon, cloves, and other spices, and aromatics. The Knight said he would endeavour to make it still more agreeable to his Majesty, and immediately tore and burnt in that fire, the King's bond of 10,000 marks due to the Company of Mercers, another of 1,500 marks due to the Chamber of London, another of 2,000 marks due to the Grocers, another of 3,000 marks due to several other Companies, and divers others, in all to the amount of

**SIR RICHARD WHITTINGTON,**
*Thrice Lord Mayor of London:*
*of famous Memory.*

Chapel of Ease Islington.

Islington Turn-Pike.

Pub. May 1 1819. for the Proprietor by R. Ackermann. 101. Strand.

on the ground, and was broke into two pieces; these were removed
some years since by the Surveyor of the Roads, and placed as curb
stones against the posts at the corner of Queen's Head-lane, in the
Lower-street. Another tradition affirms the stone to have been placed
on the above spot, by the desire of Whittington after he had risen to
wealth and eminence in the City, for the convenience of mounting or
dismounting his horse at the foot of the hill, in the rides which he
was accustomed to take in this neighbourhood, and whence his name
became attached to it.

## HOLLOWAY

appears to have been so called from its situation in the *hollow*, or valley
at the foot of Highgate-hill[1]. At Upper Holloway between the three
and four mile stones, is an old publick house, the "*Mother Red
" Cap*," celebrated by Drunken Barnaby, in the extract before given
from his Itinerary; also "The Half Moon," no less famous a century
ago for excellent cheesecakes. This circumstance, with others relating to Islington, is noticed in a Poem entitled, "A Journey to

£.60,000 sterling (an immense sum in those days), borrowed by the King to pay his
army in France; and then told his Majesty, that he had taken in and discharged all
those debts, and made his Majesty a present of the whole. Entick's London, vol. I.
p. 344.

[1] In an old Comedy, called, "Jacke Drum's Entertainment," 4to. 1601. On the
introduction of a Whitsun Morrice-dance, the following song is given:

" Skip it and trip it nimbly, nimbly,
" Tickle it, tickle it lustily,
" Strike up the taber for the wenches favour,
" Tickle it, tickle it, lustily.
" Let us be seene on *Hygate Greene*
" To dance for the honour of *Holloway*.
" Since we are come hither, let's spare for no leather,
" To dance for the honour of HOLLOWAY."

" Nottingham," in the Gentleman's Magazine for Sept. 1743, of which the following is an extract :

" Slow we set out, for sages have decreed,
" That fair and gently brings the greatest speed;
" Now straggling ISLINGTON behind we leave,
" Where piety laments her learned CAVE [1];
" Now CANBURY's numerous turrets rise to view
" No costly structure if the tale be true *.
" Here Humphreys breath'd his last, the Muses friend,
" Here Chambers found his mighty labours end,
" Here City Doctors bid the sick repair,
" Only, too oft, to die in better air.
    " Through HOLLOWAY *fam'd for cakes* [2], we onward tend.
" While much St. Michael's hermit we commend,
" Whose care a double charity bestow'd,
" Supplying water, as he rais'd the road.
" To HIGHGATE hence, the long ascent we gain,
" Whose various prospects will reward our pain, &c."

* " Reported to have been built for a penny a day."

A little distance from the road side, at Lower Holloway, is a small chapel belonging to a congregation of Independants. It was first built in the year 1804, and was destroyed by fire, Oct. 3, 1807, which was supposed to have been communicated to it by some wicked incendiary, for the apprehending of whom £.100 reward was offered in addition to £.100 by government, but without effect. It was re-built in 1808, and the interior fitted up with the pews, wainscotting, &c., from the chapel in Highbury Grove, and opened a second time, Sept. 27, in that year, when two sermons were preached on the

[1] See List of Vicars.
[2] One of the London cries, within the memory of persons now living, was " *Hol-loway* Cheesecakes," by a man on horseback.

occasion by the Rev. Mr. (now Dr.) Collyer, of Peckham, and the Rev. George Clayton, son of the Rev. John Clayton, of Highbury place. The chapel has no regular minister, but is supplied by students from the Hoxton and other Dissenting academies.

In consequence of the great increase of buildings at Holloway, and the want of water; in 1809 the New River Company not having at that time thought proper to serve the inhabitants, Mr. George Pocock, who had built several houses there, expended near £.2,000 in digging a well (172 feet deep by 5 feet in diameter) in a field at the bottom of *Cornwall-place,* over which he erected a steam engine, and furnished the same with the necessary machinery, &c. for supplying the whole neighbourhood with that useful element.

The well was found to produce water of an excellent quality [1]; and the proprietor, in order to remunerate himself for the great expence which he had already sustained, and was yet likely to sustain before the work could be carried into effect, divided the undertaking into 200 shares of £.50 each, reserving to himself 60 shares for his own benefit. A Company being thus formed, it was incorporated by Act of Parliament 50 Geo. III. intituled, " An Act for supplying with " Water, Upper and Lower Holloway, Highbury, Canonbury, Up- " per Islington, and their respective vicinities, all in the parish of St. " Mary Islington, in the County of Middlesex, and for other purposes " relating thereto." By this Act the Company are empowered to raise £.10,000 for completing the works, and a further sum of £.10,000, should the first not be found sufficient.

As soon as the New River Company found the above Act was likely to pass the Legislature, they went to work, and carried their pipes through Islington, with great expedition, for the purpose of supplying Holloway with water, which was hitherto withheld, notwithstanding the many applications that had for years been made to them, and

[1] The water has been analyzed by two professional gentlemen, who have pronounced it to be of the finest quality, extremely soft, and consequently fit for washing, and every culinary purpose.

P

which the inhabitants were now about to obtain, through the exertions of an individual: they moreover pulled up the pump (mentioned
in the following note) from which the people of Holloway had before procured water, in order to oblige them, if possible, to have the
Company's pipes laid into their premises; but the housekeepers of the
neighbourhood have very properly refused to receive water from the
New River, and are now for the most part supplied from the well of
Mr. Pocock [1].

About the beginning of the last century two malefactors were hung
in chains in this neighbourhood; viz. William Johnson (in 1712), for
shooting the turnkey of Newgate in the open court at the Old Bailey,
while the Judge was sitting; and John Price, otherwise Jack Ketch,
(who had been the public executioner), for murdering Elizabeth
White, a poor woman, who sold gingerbread in Moorfields, in March
1718 [2].

Between the Upper-street and the Back road, facing Union Chapel,
is a very considerable dairy or grass farm, belonging to Mr. Richard
Laycock, who occupies upwards of 500 acres of land in Islington
and its neighbourhood, besides a considerable quantity at Enfield, and
who, from the extent and diversity of his agricultural and other concerns, is, without doubt, the most eminent farmer in the environs of
the Metropolis [3].

---

[1] Half a century back, the whole of Islington, beyond the White Lion, was
without a supply of water from the New River, otherwise than by purchasing it at a
halfpenny *per* pail, of persons who procured it from the stream. The inhabitants
of Holloway, till lately, obtained a precarious supply from a person keeping a cart
for the purpose, and who obtained the water from the River by means of a pump at
the bottom of Hopping-lane, for which privilege a consideration was paid to the
Company, of 20s. *per annum.*

[2] Newgate Calendar.

[3] Some 40 or 50 years ago, there were a number of small grass farms in Islington,
on which the stocks varied from 20 to 100 cows: one of these was on the site of *Elliot's-place* in the Lower-street, another where *Bray's-buildings* now stands, and

The land occupied by the cow-keeper is necessarily meadow and pasture, and which in this parish is found peculiarly excellent, for such whose business it is to supply the dealers of the Metropolis with milk. The great quantity of manure derived from the cow-yard, enables the farmer to give his meadow land frequent dressings; it is therefore always kept in a highly productive state, and is generally mown at least twice in a summer. It is, moreover, his study to procure hay of a soft grassy quality, not letting it stand till the seedling stems rise, but mowing it three or four weeks sooner than it would be advisable to do for the support of horses[1].

Mr. Middleton observes, " In the art of haymaking the Middlesex " farmers are superior to those of any other part of the island, and " may be said indeed to have reduced it to a regular system; even in " the most unfavourable weather the method pursued by them is bet- " ter than any other practised under similar circumstances[2]." The quantity of hay carried from the field in a summer by Mr. Laycock and Mr. Rhodes amounts in a favourable season to several thousand loads[3]: a stack of hay made by Mr. Laycock at his premises in Du Val's-lane, in the summer of 1808 measured 144 feet in length, and contained upwards of 300 loads, and many stacks containing from 100 to 200 loads are for the greatest part of the year to be seen standing upon his farm.

The village and its vicinity in an evening during the haymaking season displays a scene of unusual bustle, occasioned by the number of persons (men and women, who have been through the day em-

others in the Upper-street, at Holloway, &c. These have long since given place to the more extensive concerns of Mr. Rhodes, and Mr. Laycock; who at this time are the only two persons that hold any considerable quantity of land and farming stock in this parish.

[1] See " Middleton's View of the Agriculture of Middlesex."

[2] Ibid.

[3] Hay has been sold within this month (Jan. 1811) in the London markets at the enormous price of ten guineas *per* load, and which might have been bought of as good a quality, during the American war, at less than 40s.

ployed as haymakers in the fields adjacent) returning home from their labour, while the delightful fragrance arising from the numerous loaded waggons and carts on their way to the rick-yard, is equally agreeable to the inhabitants and to the passing stranger. Several hundreds of persons are employed by the two farmers above named, in the haymaking season, for the purpose of mowing and carrying their crops.

The cows kept for the purpose of the dairy, are chiefly of a large size, with short horns, and are distinguished by the name of *Holdernesse* cattle, from a district so called in the East Riding of Yorkshire, but to which the breed has long ceased to be confined.

Mr. Foot, in his Agricultural Report on this County, describes pretty accurately the practice of the Islington farmer, in regard to the management of his stock. " The cows," he observes, " are during the " night confined in stalls : about 3 o'clock in the morning each has a " half bushel basket of grains. From 4 o'clock to half past 6 they " are milked by the retail dealers. When the milking is finished, a " bushel basket of turnips is given to each cow, and very soon after- " wards they have an allotment in the proportion of one truss to ten " cows of the most grassy and soft meadow hay, which has been the " most early mown and cured of the greenest colour. These several " feedings are generally made before 8 o'clock in the morning, at " which time the cows are turned into the cow-yard. About 12 " o'clock they are again confined to their stalls, and served with the " same quantity of grains as they had in the morning. About half " past 1 o'clock in the afternoon the milking recommences, and con- " tinues till near three, when the cows are again served with the same " quantity of turnips ; and about an hour afterwards with the same " distribution of hay as before described. This mode of feeding ge- " nerally continues during the turnip season, which is from the month " of September, till the month of May. During the other months " in the year, they are fed with grains, cabbages, tares, and the " foregoing proportion of rouen or second-cut meadow hay, and are

" continued to be fed and milked with the same regularity as before
" described, until they are turned out to grass, when they continue in
" the field all night; and even, during this season, they are fed with
" grains, which are kept sweet and eatable for a considerable length
" of time, by being buried in pits made for that purpose[1]." There
are about ten bulls to a stock of 200 cows. The calves are generally
sent to Smithfield market at one, two, or three days old, where they
fetch from 25s. to 35s. each. Those cows that give the most milk are
not found in general sufficiently productive to be kept longer than
three or four years, after which time, being rendered unfit for the purposes of the dairy, they are fattened, and sold to the butchers.

The quantity of milk yielded by each cow has been averaged
at nine quarts *per* day. The retail dealer agrees with the cow-
keeper for the produce of a certain number of cows, and takes the
labour of milking them upon himself: for this purpose certain persons are employed in the cow-house, called *milkers*, who are
paid by the retailer. The milk is sold by the cow-keepers of Islington to the retail dealers at about 2s. 6d. for eight quarts (which is
called a *barn* gallon); but, in delivering it to the consumer, a vast
increase takes place, not only in the price, but also in the *quantity*,
which is greatly adulterated with water; and, as there is reason to

---

[1] Mr. Laycock has had at one time on his farm upwards of 10,000 quarters of
grains, preserved in the manner above described; and the cows being accustomed
to this food throughout the year, are found to be partial to it, even when approaching to a state of acidity. Among other articles of food introduced of late years
into the cow-farm, may be reckoned that of *distiller's wash*, which has been given
to the cows in certain proportions, mixed with their dry provender.—Large quantities of *potatoes* are also now consumed; which, as also turnips, are sometimes procured from places many miles distant: indeed, when we consider the vast demand
for every article of provisions for cattle of this description in the environs of
the Metropolis (the number of cows alone being estimated at between 8 and
9,000), it will be a matter of some surprize, to think whence these supplies can be
derived.

suspect, sometimes impregnated with still worse ingredients, to hide the cheat [1].

The milk is conveyed from the cow-house in tin pails, which are principally carried by strong, robust Welch girls; but a considerable number of Irish women are also employed for this purpose. These are the same that retail the milk about the streets of the Metropolis; and it is amazing to witness the labour and fatigue these females will undergo, and the hilarity and cheerfulness that prevails amongst them, and which tends, in a surprizing manner, to lighten their laborious employment. Even in the most inclement weather, and in the depth of winter, they arrive here in parties from different parts of the Metropolis, by three and four o'clock in the morning, laughing and singing to the music of their empty pails: with these they return loaded to town; and the weight they are thus accustomed to carry on their yokes, for a distance of two or three miles, is sometimes from 100 to 130 pounds.

The stock of cows on Mr. Laycock's farm amounts to between 5 and 600, but the number is subject to considerable variation at different times in the year. From the great labour connected with the business of a farm of this description, in the frequent, long, and heavy draught attending the fetching of turnips, potatoes, grains, &c. from places at considerable distance, a large stock of heavy carriages and horses is found absolutely necessary. Upwards of 50 carts and waggons are kept for these and other purposes by Mr. Laycock, and between 70 and 80 horses. The cost of these [2], together

---

[1] " The milk-room is mostly furnished with a *pump*, to which the retail dealers " apply in rotation, not secretly, but openly, and pump water into the milk ves- " sels, at their discretion; the pump being placed there expressly for that purpose, " and but seldom used for any other. A considerable cow-keeper in Surrey has a " pump of this kind, which goes by the name of the *Black Cow*, from its being " painted of that colour; and it is said to yield more than all the rest put together." Middleton's View, p. 423. See also the report of a trial *Brown versus Smidtz* at the Court of Requests, in the Morning Chronicle, January 30, 1811.

[2] Mr. Laycock has, not long since, given 210 *guineas* for the purchase of three

with the numerous other farming requisites, crops of hay, &c., being added to the value of the stock before mentioned, will give some idea of the magnitude and importance of the cow-keeping business, and the scale upon which it is now carried on in this parish.

Several acres of ground contiguous to the farm, have, within these few years, been dug up by Mr. Laycock, for the purpose of brick-making. The quantity of bricks that have been made at Islington, and its neighbourhood, within the last 20 years, is incalculable; and it would appear that the manufacture has been of considerable standing in the place. In a report made to the Lord Treasurer, by Fleetwood, the Recorder of London, about the year 1580, concerning the police of the Metropolis, it was stated, that " the chief allurers" of the rogues and vagabonds of those times were, " the Savoy, and the " *Brick-kilns* near ISLINGTON[1]." Messrs. Scott and Co. have for some years past been considerable manufacturers of bricks, in the fields on the East side of the Lower road leading to Ball's Pond.

In many instances, rows of houses and streets have arisen on the very spot where the chief material for building them has been previously excavated and burnt. The brick earth averages, in general, from four to five feet in depth; and every acre is calculated to produce a million of bricks. A great number of working people, men, women, and children, are engaged in the laborious employment of the brick field, in moulding, turning, stacking, &c. An experienced moulder will make upwards of 10,000 bricks in a day, and it is astonishing to view the dexterity with which the various other parts of the manufacture are conducted. The present price of bricks, exclusive of the charge for carriage, is, for Grey-stocks 40s. *per*

cart-horses; and £.75. is about the present average price of as many prime milch cows.—Most of the carts, waggons, &c. used in the above concern, are made and repaired on the premises, by workmen constantly retained, and who have proper workshops, forges, &c. fitted up for that purpose.

[1] Seymour's Survey of London, vol. II. p. 326.

1000, Place bricks 34s. Second Marl-stock 65s. and best Washed Marl-stocks about 120s.

Between Park-street and Barnesbury street (formerly Kettle-lane and Batty's-lane) is a nursery-ground, containing about five acres, in the occupation of Mr. Townsend[1]. It was first converted to this use in 1806, having previously been the field wherein the Islington Volunteer Cavalry and Infantry performed their exercises. Between this ground and the Upper-street is an old house occupied for many years by the elder Dr. Monro, the celebrated Physician to Bedlam Hospital, and now by Dr. Sequeira; also a spacious dwelling, sometimes called *Harvey's*, from having been long the residence of Jacob Harvey, Esq. a Justice of the Peace, and a most respectable and benevolent man, who died about the year 1770. It was afterwards inhabited by Roger Altham, Esq. a very eminent proctor, and a branch of the Altham family, of Mark's Hall, Essex, and is now

---

[1] The number of acres cultivated as nursery grounds in this parish, has of late been considerably diminished. Two acres, rented by Mr. Townsend, adjoining to *Frog-lane*, as also 10 acres, part of the ground occupied by Mr. Bassington, at *Kingsland*, have been recently cleared for the purpose of building. The number of the Connoisseur, for March 4, 1756, advertizes a fine Auricula, raised by Mr. William Redmond, at ISLINGTON, named the Triumph, at half a guinea each plant. Mr. Barr, of Ball's Pond, exhibited a beautiful *American Aloe* in full blossom, a few summers ago; and " a fine bed of Tulips," belonging to Mr. Gabell, of the City-gardens, has been lately advertized for inspection, at 6d. each person. The following is the whole of the nursery grounds at this time in Islington parish.

|  | A. | R. |
|---|---|---|
| Mr. Bassington, at Kingsland........................................... | 8 | 0 |
| Mr. Barr, Ball's Pond....................................................... | 12 | 0 |
| Mr. Barrow (late Parker's), Holloway................................. | 2 | 1 |
| Mr. Townsend, Barnesbury-street.................................... | 5 | 0 |
| Mr. Watson, Bridle-lane ................................................. | 6 | 0 |
| Sundries, about ............................................................. | 0 | 3 |

Total 34 0

the residence of Mr. Sabine. It bears in front the date 1719, and at the East end 1716, with the initials, E. C. The garden-ground belonging to this house, before Barnesbury-place was erected thereon, extended South to Barnesbury-street. The street last named was only a narrow passage, leading to the workhouse, and vulgarly called *Cut-throat-lane*, till the houses were built on the North side, when it was widened to its present extent.

Somewhat more than 30 years ago, the late Dr. William Pitcairn began a botanical garden contiguous to the house in which he resided (now Mr. Wilson's), opposite Cross-street, and which he cultivated till his decease : this continues to be one of the finest gardens in Islington, and is upwards of four acres in extent. Dr. Pitcairn was born at Dysart, in Scotland, in the year 1711. He graduated at Leyden; and on the 13th of April, 1749, had the degree of Doctor in Physick conferred on him, together with Drs. Conyers and Kennedy, by the University of Oxford, as a mark of gratitude to the founder of the Radcliffe Library, which was then opened. He was the same year admitted a candidate of the Royal College of Physicians in London; was elected a Fellow in the succeeding year; and President in 1775, which he resigned in 1785. He died at Islington, Nov. 25, 1791, at the age of 80 years.

The ground whereon the house occupied by Dr. Strahan, the present vicar, stands, was (previous to the building of that house) the yard, skittle grounds, &c. belonging to the *Old Parr's Head* public house, which was the small edifice adjoining on the North. The old house occupied by Mr. Flower, nearly opposite Rufford's-buildings, appears to have been built in the reign of Elizabeth or James the First. It is chiefly composed of wood and plaster, the cielings are of stucco, in crocket work, with medallions, &c. similar to those in the mansions of Sir Thomas Fowler, in Cross-street, and Alderman Halliday, at Newington-green. In one of the rooms is a chimney-piece, representing the Garden of Eden, with the Tree of Knowledge, and the figures of Adam and Eve. This house has been for many years, a

Q

seminary for the education of youth[1].  About 60 years ago it was kept as a boarding-school for young ladies by Mrs. Science, the wife of an ingenious watch-maker of that name : Mr. John Shield[2], who, after the death of Mrs. S. married her daughter, afterwards opened it as a boys' school, which he conducted for many years with great reputation.  Among his pupils were those two eminent natives[3] of this village, the late William Hawes, M. D. founder of the Humane Society, and John Nichols, Esq. F. S. A. Lond. Edinb. & Perth, who is at this time a parishioner[4].

[1] Islington has been for several ages, a chosen spot for academies for youth of both sexes.  Samuel Clarke, a learned Orientalist, and one of the editors of the Polyglot Bible, was a schoolmaster here about the year 1650 (Athen. Oxon vol. II.), and several of the ejected ministers, men eminent for their piety and learning, appear to have kept schools here during the 17th century; some of them, it is probable, in the house above described.  Among these the *Rev. Thomas Doolittle*, M. A. of Pembroke-hall, Cambridge, rector of St. Alphage, London-wall, kept an academy here about the year 1672, "and fitted several young men for the ministry," (among whom was the eminently pious Matthew Henry).  He died May 24, 1707, aged 77, and was buried at Bunhill-fields.  He was the last of the ejected ministers in London.  Among his works are, " A Treatise of the Lord's " Supper ;" " Young Man's Instructor, and Old Man's Remembrancer ;" " Earth- " quakes explained, and improved ;" " Compleat Body of Divinity," &c.—The Rev. Robert Ferguson, vicar of Godmersham, Kent, some time after his eject-ment, taught University learning at *Islington.*—The Rev. Ralph Button, M. A. Fellow of Merton College, Oxon. and Professor of Geometry in Gresham College, &c. also kept an academy here, where Sir Joseph Jekyll was one of his pupils.  He died in October, 1680, and was buried in the church.—James Burgess, M. A. rec-tor of Ashprington, Devon, kept a boarding-house at Islington, for the sons of citizens who went to a flourishing school kept by Mr. Singleton, and died here about 1663.—George Fowler, M. A. minister of Bridewell, " a man much esteemed and loved in the City," died at his house at Islington.—And Mr. Bruce, an ejected minister, from Marbury, in Cheshire, frequently preached here. *Nonconformist's Mem.*

[2] Mr. Shield died in March 1786.  See an account of him and his family con-nections, in the Gentleman's Magazine for that year, p. 269.

[3] Contemporary with these, at the school of Mr. Shield, though not a native of Islington, was the Rev. William Tooke, F. R. S. the learned and excellent Historian of the Empress Catharine, and of the Russian Empire.

[4] This gentleman, who has attained to considerable eminence in the literary

PLATE III.

The Crown Lower Street.

North View of the Pied Bull.

F.W.L. Stockdale delt.                    Frances Hawksworth sculpt.

To John Bentley Esqr. of Highbury House.

This Plate is Respectfully inscribed by his obliged & obedient Servant  J. Nelson.

Published May 1 1811 by Rodwell Upper Street Islington

Pied Bull Inn Interior, Islington.

Mr. Flower, the present proprietor, has erected a handsome and spacious school-room detached from the old building, and established the reputation of the academy, which may be ranked among the most respectable in the environs of the metropolis. On the South side of the school-room is an old building called the Bath House, from being erected over a cold bath, which is supplied by a spring: this is now used as an appendage to the school.

The Old Pied Bull inn, near the Green, appears from its architecture (see Plate III.)[1] to have been built in the reign of Queen Elizabeth. The parlour, on the right hand of the entrance from the street, seems to have been a principal room, and is ornamented accordingly, in the prevailing taste of that age. A window of this room, looking into the garden, contains the arms of sir John Miller, Knight, of Islington and Devon[2]; impaling those of Grigg, of Suffolk[3]. In the kitchen are the remains of the same arms, with the date of 1624, and another coat[4] (Plate II. fig. 10); also several fragments of heraldry,

world, was born in the year 1745, at the house opposite the church, now occupied by Mr. Blount. In 1763, he published, " ISLINGTON, a Poem," in 4to, a familiar epistle to a schoolfellow, written soon after their separation, with some other poetical essays. Besides the "Bibliotheca Topographica Britannica" (a number of which contains " The History and Antiquities of Canonbury," written by Mr. Nichols, 1788), he has been the editor and publisher of many works of sterling excellence. The Gentleman's Magazine has been conducted and printed by him for more than thirty years, with increasing reputation: he has devoted several of the last years to the writing and publishing an elaborate History of the County of Leicester; and is revising for the press a new edition of the Anecdotes of his friend and partner Mr. William Bowyer, one of the most learned Printers of this or any other Country.

[1] The North side of the building, represented in the annexed engraving, seems to have been originally the front, and which, together with the garden ground adjoining, and the present front, were inclosed by an old wall, within the memory of persons yet living, at which time there was no footpath on that side of the way.

[2] Azure, an inescutcheon between four mascles in saltire Or.

[3] Argent, three lions passant in pale Azure, within a border of the second. Sir John Miller married the daughter of Michael Grigg, of London, and was living at Islington in 1634. Camp. London.

Sable, three bells Argent, for *Porter* (the coat of Sir William Porter, temp.

which have been misplaced at different times in repairing the windows. The first mentioned arms in the parlour window are inclosed within an ornamental border, consisting of two mermaids, each crested with a globe, as many sea-horses supporting a bunch of green leaves over the shield, and the lower part contains a green and a grey parrot, the former eating fruit (Plate II. fig. 9). Adjoining to this is another compartment in the window, representing a green parrot perched on a wreath, under a pediment, within a border of figures and flowers, but which does not seem to have been intended for any armorial ensign.

The chimney-piece of this room contains the figures of Faith, Hope, and Charity, with their usual insignia, in niches, surrounded by a border of cherubim, fruit, and foliage (Plate II. fig. 12). The centre figure, Charity, is surmounted by two Cupids supporting a crown, and beneath is a lion and unicorn couchant. This conceit was probably designed by the artist, in compliment to the reigning Princess Queen Elizabeth. The cieling displays a personification of the five Senses in stucco, with Latin mottoes underneath, as follows: an oval in the centre contains a female figure holding a serpent, which is twining round her right arm, and biting the hand, her left hand holds a stick, the point of which rests on the back of a toad at her feet. The motto to this is TACTVS. Around the above, in smaller ovals, are, a female bearing fruit under her left arm, of which she is eating, as is also an ape seated at her feet, with the word, GVSTVS. Another figure, holding a vizard; at its feet a cat and a hawk, with the motto, VISVS. A figure playing on the lute, with a stag listening; and the motto, AVDITVS. The last figure is standing in a garden, and holding a bouquet of flowers. At her feet is a dog; and the motto, OLFACTVS.

Henry V.), impaling, Sable, on a fess Or, between three owls of the second, as many crosses botonny of the field for *Pennythorne*. The author of the " New View of " London" says, the above arms were emblazoned quarterly on a tomb in the old church, impaled with Ermine, on a canton a mullet, but without any inscription.

It is the general tradition that this house was the residence of the brave, but unfortunate, Sir Walter Raleigh, who was beheaded in the reign of James the First, and whose history is so well known, that it needs no repetition in this place. From the strength and antiquity of this tradition, which may be traced more than a century back, together with the circumstance of this village being frequented by his Royal mistress, and inhabited by several worthies of the time of Elizabeth, there is great reason to believe that the report is not altogether void of foundation. It is true that the arms of Sir Walter have never been found on the premises, while those of Sir John Miller (who, it is certain, resided here in the reign of James) are yet to be seen; these arms, however, bear date eight years after Sir Walter was beheaded, which was most likely the time when Sir John Miller came to reside here. If these premises were ever inhabited by our gallant countryman, it must necessarily have been previous to his commitment to the Tower in 1603, and therefore, it may be presumed, 23 years before the occupation of the premises by Sir John Miller.

It is, indeed, not improbable, that the arms of Sir Walter[1] may have occupied the same border that now contains the arms of the other knight, as such a change could have been easily effected at any time in a leaden casement window. This conjecture is somewhat strengthened by this very border; inasmuch as it is composed of sea-horses, mermaids, parrots, &c. which certainly bear a most appropriate allusion to the character of Sir Walter, as a great navigator and discoverer of unknown countries. The bunch of green leaves before mentioned, has been generally asserted to represent the tobacco plant, of which he is said to have been the first importer into this country[2].

[1] Argent, a bend lozengy Sable.

[2] Camden, in his Annals of the Reign of Elizabeth, says, that, to the best of his knowledge, the first tobacco seen in England was brought from Virginia, by Sir Walter Raleigh, in 1583; and he observes, that, in a few years after, *Tobacco-taverns*, or smoking-houses, were as common in London, as beer-houses, or wine-taverns. Such was the rage for this entertaining exotic on its first introduction,

The time of Sir Walter Raleigh's residence in this house (if such a
conclusion may be drawn from the circumstances here stated) must
have been when he was in high favour with his sovereign Queen Elizabeth; and, perhaps, when his various avocations allowed him but
little opportunity to be the permanent inhabitant of any place: or,
otherwise, he might have built the house at this period for his future
retirement; and this alone was sufficient for tradition to connect his
name with the premises, although they might never have been inha-

that it was even smoked in the theatres, and other public places of amusement,
both by men and women (vide *Malone's History of the English Stage, Hentzner's
Journey to England, &c.*). On the other hand, it was so disgusting to some, that
one Peter Campbell, in his will (Oct. 20, 1616), desired, that his son should be
disinherited of the property bequeathed him thereby, if at any time he should be
found "*taking of Tobacco.*" (Gent. Mag. vol. XXXIX. p. 181.)

The following pleasant story is related of Sir Walter, who, as the writer infers,
by the caution he took in smoking tobacco, did not intend that the practice should
be copied: " Sitting, one day, in a deep meditation, with a pipe in his mouth,
" he inadvertently called to his man, to bring him a tankard of small ale; the
" fellow, coming into the room, threw all the liquor in his master's face, and
" running down stairs, bawled out, *Fire! help! — Sir Walter has studied till his
" head is on fire, and the smoke bursts out of his mouth and nose.* — It is added,
" after this affair Sir Walter made it no secret; and took two pipes just before he
" went to be beheaded." (Gent. Mag. Sept. 1731). The author of the Life of
Sir Walter Raleigh (hereafter mentioned) says, " Being at Leeds, in Yorkshire,
" soon after Mr. *Ralph Thoresby* the Antiquary died, anno 1725, I saw his museum,
" and in it, among his other rarities, what himself has publickly called (in the
" catalogue thereof annexed to his Antiquities of that town) Sir Walter Raleigh's
" *tobacco-box.* From the best of my memory, I can resemble its outward appear-
" ance to nothing more nearly than one of our modern muff-cases; about the same
" height and width, covered with red leather, and opened at top (but with a hinge
" I think), like one of those. In the inside there was a cavity for a receiver of
" glass or metal, which might hold half a pound, or a pound of tobacco, and
" from the edge of the receiver at top, to the edge of the box, a circular stay or
" collar, with holes in it, to plant the tobacco about, with six or eight pipes to
" smoke it in." Mr. Boughey, a tobacconist (who lies buried in Islington church-
yard), kept for many years in his window in Bishopsgate-street, the painted sign of
" Sir Walter Raleigh and his man," taken from the story before mentioned.

bited by him. His taste in architecture and gardening are sufficiently attested by an author, who was witness to the improvements he made upon the *Sherborne* estate granted to him by her Majesty, and which, under his direction, is said to have been rendered, for beauty and magnificence, unparalleled by any in those parts. The author of Sir Walter's life, published 70 years ago, who mentions the above, relates the following circumstances, which may be considered as corroborative of what has been before inferred as to the probability of his having been an inhabitant of this house.

" There is," says he, " no farther from London than *Islington*, " about a bow's shot on this side the church, which though, I think, " it has no such evidences remaining upon its walls, cielings, or " windows, that will prove him to have been its owner, the arms " that are seen there, above a hundred years old, being of a succeed- " ing inhabitant; is yet popularly reported to have been a *villa* of " his. For the present tenant affirms, his landlord was possessed of " some old account books, by which it appears beyond all doubt, this " house and 14 acres of land, now let at about £.70 *per annum*, did " belong to Sir Walter Raleigh, and that the oldest man in the parish " would often declare his father had told him, Sir Walter purposed to " wall in that ground, with intention to keep some of his horses " therein; further, that some husbandmen, ploughing up the same " a few years since, found several pieces of Queen Elizabeth's mo- " ney, whereof they brought (whatever they might reserve to them- " selves) about four-score shillings to their master, the said tenant, in " whose hands I have seen of the said coin. As for the house, it " is, and has been, for many years an inn; so that what it was, is not " clearly to be judged from its present outward appearance, it being " much impaired, or very coarsely repaired, and diminished, perhaps, " from what it might be when persons of distinction lived in " it. However, there are within side some spacious rooms. The " parlour was painted round the uppermost part of the wainscoat, in " about a dozen pannels, with Scripture histories, but now so old " and decayed as to be scarcely distinguishable. There is also a noble

" dining-room, the cieling whereof is all over wrought in *plastick*,
" or fret-work, with representations of the *five Senses;* and the
" chimney-piece with the three principal Christian virtues.   But the
" arms in the window, as well as in that of the hall, are, by the
" present inhabitants, erroneously called Sir Walter Raleigh's, there
" being a date under one of the coats which shews it was *anealed* six
" years after his death; so that we are not sure the decorations afore-
" said were done by his direction, or *that others more rich and*
" *elegant were not in their stead before them*[1]."

Upon the whole, it would appear from these several circumstances
(and nothing having ever been produced to invalidate the opinion),
that this House was originally either the property or residence of that
illustrious character, who has, with great propriety, been called the
*English Xenophon*, whose life was an honour, whose death a disgrace
to his Country; who by his writings contributed materially to the improvement of our language, and which for their intrinsic excellence
continue to be most deservedly the theme of universal panegyric.

> Raleigh, the scourge of Spain, whose breast with all
> The Sage, the Patriot, and the Hero burn'd;
> Nor shrunk his vigour, when a coward reign
> The Warrior fetter'd, and at last resign'd,
> To glut the vengeance of a vanquish'd foe.
>     Then active still, and unrestrained, his mind
> Explor'd the vast extent of ages past,
> And, with his prison hours, enrich'd the world,
> Yet found no times, in all the long research,
> So glorious, or so base, as those he prov'd,
> In which he conquer'd, and in which he bled.
>
> THOMSON.

[1] Life of Sir Walter Raleigh, 8vo, 1740, p. 152.

At what time this house was converted into an inn does not appear. The sign of the Pied Bull, worked in relief on the front towards the South end, bears the date 1730; and which was probably the time when this additional part was made to the building, for here it is not so antient, nor of such an elevation as the other part of the structure. A considerable quantity of land behind the house is divided into sheep-pens and layers for cattle on their way to Smithfield market, for which purposes the situation is very convenient, having an entrance from each of the roads[1]. A Society is held at the Pied Bull, called the TRUE BRITONS, composed of a number of respectable inhabitants of the parish, who meet here three times a week, in the evening, for convivial purposes, and who, imitating the example of their illustrious prototype, —

> Here, through the well-glaz'd tube, from business freed,
> Draw the rich spirit of the Indian weed,
> By turns relieving with the circling draught,
> Each pause of chat, and interval of thought.

The society, which consists of about 40 members, who are admitted by ballot, dine together once a quarter, the dinner being provided by three members, who thus take it in their turns to cater for the occasion. It was first formed at the Half Moon, in the Lower-street, in

[1] The value of land about this spot, and indeed of both land and houses throughout the village, has greatly increased within these few years; in many instances, the sums which have been given are immense. About a year ago 3 acres, 39 poles of ground on this spot, were let for the purpose of cattle-pens, on a seven years lease, at the rent of 100 guineas *per annum!!* And in March 1808, several old houses opposite the Church, in a very dilapidated state, were let by auction on leases of 21 years, at double their former rent; the Lessees being bound to put them in thorough repair. At the same time a close of land of about three acres, behind these houses, rented by Mr. Flower, as a play-ground for his school boys, at £.36, was advanced to the extraordinary sum of £.92 *per annum*, on a new lease, granted to him for the same term.

R

April 1796, was afterwards held for several years at the *Fox*, from whence it was removed to this house, February 14, 1810.

On the South side of the entrance to the inn-yard, stands the Vicarage-house, a square brick and plaster building, now rented of the vicar by Mr. Thompson, who holds the cattle-pens behind the Pied Bull, and who lately kept that house. It is supposed to have been built by Dr. William Cave, who held the living from 1662 to 1691. His initials were found on the front of the building some years since, when the premises were undergoing some repairs. It appears that an old house adjoining, (for many years past in the occupation of Mr. Burton, bricklayer,) was the original house appertaining to the living, before the present one was built, as in the deeds and writings relating thereto, it is called the *Parsonage house*. The other house appears to have been raised upon the garden ground attached to the old premises.

Between Oddys-row and the Back Road is a manufactory of pasteboard, belonging to Mr. Creswick, in which, from 15 to 20 persons are generally employed.

At the South-east corner of Cadd's-row, near the green, was formerly a public house known by the sign of the *Duke's Head*, which towards the middle of the last century was kept by Thomas Topham, better known as " *The Strong Man*," and of whose herculean feats a number of wonderful tales are related. The following account of this extraordinary man, for the most part attested and recorded by two respectable writers, may be considered as having some claim to authenticity.

The father of Topham, who was a carpenter, brought him up to the same trade, but it appears that he quitted it soon after his apprenticeship. When he had attained his full growth, his stature was about five feet ten inches; and he soon began to feel indications of superior strength and muscular power. About the age of 24 he became the host of the Red Lion, near the old Hospital of St. Luke, in which house he failed, probably owing to his inattention to business, and the company with which he became connected from the situation of his dwelling ; for at that time (as Mr. Pennant observes) " Moorfields was the *Gymnasium* of our capital ;" and the famous ring, over which OLD VINEGAR presided, was the great resort of cudgellers, wrestlers, back-sword players, and boxers from all parts of the Metropolis. It also appears, that Topham was unfortunate in his matrimonial connection; and that the inconstancy of his wife was a continual drawback upon his domestic happiness.

The first public exhibition of his extraordinary strength was that of pulling against a horse, lying on his back, and placing his feet against the dwarf wall that divided Upper from Lower Moorfields. He afterwards pulled against two horses ; but his legs being placed horizontally, instead of rising parallel to the traces of the horses, he was jerked from his position, and had one of his knees much bruised and hurt ; whereas, it was the opinion of Dr. Desaguliers, a great mechanic and experimental philosopher, that, had he been in a proper position, he might have kept his situation against the pulling of four horses without the least inconvenience.

The following are among th e feats which Dr. Desaguliers says, he himself saw him perform :—By the strength of his fingers he rolled up a very strong and large pewter dish. He broke seven or eight pieces of a tobacco-pipe, by the force of his middle finger, having laid them on his first and third finger. Having thrust the bowl of a strong tobacco-pipe under his garter, his legs being bent, he broke it to pieces by the tendons of his hams, without altering the bending of his legs. Another bowl of this kind he broke between his first and second finger, by pressing them together sideways. He took an iron kitchen poker, about a yard long and three inches round, and struck upon his bare left arm, between the elbow and the wrist, till he bent the poker nearly to a right angle. With such another poker, holding the ends of it in his hands, and the middle of it against the back of his neck, he brought both ends of it together before him ; and what was yet more difficult, he pulled it almost straight again. He broke a rope of two inches circumference, though, in consequence of his awkward manner, he was obliged to exert four times more strength than was necessary. He lifted a rolling-stone of 800 pounds weight with his hands only; standing in a frame above it, and taking hold of a chain that was fastened thereto[1].

It is probable he kept the Duke's Head in Islington at the time he exhibited the exploit of lifting three hogsheads of water, weighing 1,831 pounds, in Cold Bath Fields, on the 28th of May, 1741, in commemoration of the taking of Porto Bello, by Admiral Vernon, and which he performed in the presence of the Admiral and thousands of spectators[2]. A number of curious and whimsical pranks are related of him, some of which are said to have occurred during the time he kept the Duke's Head.

On his way home one night, finding a watchman fast asleep in his box, he took both on his shoulders, and carrying the load with the greatest ease, at length carefully dropped the guardian of the night and his wooden tenement over the wall of Bunhill Fields Burying-ground, where the poor fellow between sleeping and waking, and doubtful whether he was in the land of the living, in recovering from his fright, seemed to be only waiting for the opening of the graves around him. Another time, sitting at the window of a low public-house, while a butcher from a slaughter-house was passing by with nearly half an ox on his back, Topham relieved him of it with so much ease and dexterity, that the fellow, almost petrified with astonishment, swore, that nothing but the devil could have flown away with his load. Upon another occasion, thinking to enjoy a little sport

---

[1] See A Course of Experimental Philosophy, by J. T. Desaguliers, LL. D. F. R. S. 4to, 1763, vol. l. p. 289.

[2] A print in Kirby's " Wonderful Museum," 8vo, 1803, represents Topham performing this extraordinary feat, which was effected by means of a wooden stage, whereon he stood over the three hogsheads, which he raised several inches by means of a strong rope and tackle passing over his shoulders. The sign at a public-house in East Smithfield, called " *The Strong Man*," exhibits him performing the above feat, also with his feet fixed against a post, in the act of pulling against a dray-horse.

with some bricklayers, by removing part of a scaffold, just before they intended to strike it from a small building, his grasp was so rude, that a part of the front wall following the timber, the fellows conceived it had been the effects of an earthquake, and immediately ran, without looking behind them, into an adjoining field. Here, however, Topham was near paying dearly for his prank: for one of the poles struck him a severe blow on the side, and gave him considerable pain.

Being one time persuaded by an acquaintance to accompany him on board a vessel in the river from the West Indies, and being, when on board, presented with a cocoa nut, he threw one of the sailors into the utmost astonishment, by cracking it close to his ear, with the same facility as one would crack an eggshell. Another time, a race being to be run on the Hackney road, a fellow, with a horse and cart, would persevere in keeping close to the contending parties, much to the displeasure of the spectators in general. Topham, who was one of them, stepping into the road, seized the tail of the cart, and, in spite of all the fellow's exertions in whipping his horse to get forward, he drew them both backwards with the greatest ease; and while the pleasure of the beholders was at the highest point of gratification, the surprize and rage of the driver seemed to be beyond all expression, nothing preventing him from exercising his whip upon the immediate cause of his chagrin, but the fear of being probably pulled or crushed to pieces. Having one day in his tap-room two guests extremely quarrelsome, he bore with their noise and insolence with much patience for a length of time; but they at length proceeded so far, that nothing would satisfy them but fighting the landlord. As they could be appeased no other way, Topham, at length seizing them both by the nape of the neck, with the same facility as if they had been children, he knocked both their heads together, till, perfectly sensible of their error, they became as abject in asking pardon, as they had before been insolent in giving offence.

The following particulars respecting this wonderful man are related by Mr. Hutton, in his " History of Derby:" " We learn, from " private accounts well attested, that Thomas Topham, a man who

" kept a public house at *Islington*, performed surprizing feats of
" strength, as breaking a broomstick of the first magnitude, by
" striking it against his bare arm ; lifting two hogsheads of water ;
" heaving his horse over the turnpike gate ; carrying the beam of a
" house as a soldier his firelock, &c.  But, however Belief might
" stagger, she soon recovered herself, when this second Sampson
" appeared at Derby as a performer in public, at a shilling each per-
" son.  Upon application to Alderman Cooper for leave to exhibit,
" the magistrate was surprized at the feats he proposed ; and as his
" appearance was like that of other men, he requested him to strip,
" that he might examine whether he was made like them ; but he
" was found to be extremely muscular.  What were hollows under
" the arms and hams of others, were filled up with ligaments in
" him.

" He appeared near five feet ten, turned of thirty, well made,
" but nothing singular : he walked with a small limp.  He had for-
" merly laid a wager, the usual decider of disputes, that three horses
" could not draw him from a post which he should clasp with his
" feet ; but the driver giving them a sudden lash, turned them aside,
" and the unexpected jerk had broke his thigh.

" The performances of this wonderful man, in whom were united
" the strength of twelve, were, rolling up a pewter dish, of seven
" pounds weight, as a man rolls up a sheet of paper ; holding a
" pewter quart, at arms length, and squeezing the sides together
" like an egg-shell ; lifting two hundred weight with his little
" finger, and moving it gently over his head.  The bodies he touched
" seemed to have lost their powers of gravitation.  He also broke a
" rope fastened to the floor that would sustain 20 hundred weight ;
" lifted an oak table six feet long with his teeth, though half a hun-
" dred weight was hung to the extremity ; a piece of leather was fixed
" to one end for his teeth to hold, two of the feet stood upon his
" knees, and he raised the end with the weight, higher than that in
" his mouth.  He took Mr. Chambers, Vicar of All Saints, who

" weighed 27 stone, and raised him with one hand; his head being
" laid on one chair, and his feet on another, four people (14 stone
" each) sat upon his body, which he heaved at pleasure.   He struck
" a round bar of iron, one inch diameter, against his naked arm, and
" at one stroke bent it like a bow.   Weakness and feeling seemed
" fled together.

  " Being a master of musick, he entertained the company with *Mad*
" *Tom.*   I heard him sing a solo to the organ in St. Warburgh's
" church, then the only one in Derby; but, though he might per-
" form with judgment, yet the voice, more terrible than sweet,
" scarcely seemed human.   Though of a pacific temper, and the ap-
" pearance of a gentleman, yet he was liable to the insults of the
" rude.   The ostler at the Virgin's Inn, where he resided, having
" given him disgust, he took one of the kitchen spits from the man-
" tel-piece, and bent it round his neck, like a handkerchief; but as
" he did not chuse to tuck the ends in the ostler's bosom, the cum-
" brous ornament excited the laugh of the company, till he conde-
" scended to untie his iron cravat.   Had he not abounded with good
" nature, the men might have been in fear for the safety of their per-
" sons, and the women for that of their pewter shelves; as he could
" roll up both.   One blow with his fist would for ever have silenced
" those heroes of the Bear-garden, Johnson and Mendoza."

This second Sampson, as is before hinted, was not without his
Dalilah; for, after he had left ISLINGTON, and taken another public
house, in Hog-lane, Shoreditch, the infidelity of his wife had such
an effect upon Topham, that, unable to bear the reflections it excited
in his mind, in a fit of phrenzy, after beating her most unmercifully,
and stabbing her in the breast, he inflicted several wounds upon
himself with the same weapon; and, after lingering several days,
died, in the flower of his age, on the 10th of August, 1749.   His
wife afterwards recovered.

MANOR OF HIGHBURY, OR NEWINGTON BARROW.

The manor of Highbury, otherwise Newington Barrow, is divided into two distinct parts; one at the North, and the other at the Southern extremity of the parish, being intersected by the manors of Canonbury and the Prebend. The boundary line of the upper part is as follows: Commence at the parish stone the corner of Hornsey and Du Val's lanes, and continue along the parish boundary by Stroud Green, Newington, and Kingsland Greens, and the Ball's Pond road (by Islington Common), to the Rosemary-branch; proceed from hence along the bank of the field between the Clothworker's almshouses in *Frog-lane*, and the carriage road leading to the Rosemary-branch; cross the lane, and continue, by the South end of the *Barley-mow* public house, through *Paradise-place*; proceed North up the Lower road to *Ball's Pond* turnpike, and West up *Hopping-lane*, by the end of *Highbury-place*, through the turnpike at *Holloway*, and up Du Val's lane to the parish stone first above mentioned. The other part of the manor contains so much of the lower or South end of the parish as is cut off by the watercourse which runs from the Upper-street, and passing the South end of the house No. 1, in *Pullin's-row*, continues through Mr. Rhodes's cow-yard, under the New River, and along the fields, till its junction with the parish boundary at the City-gardens.

This manor appears to be the same with that called by the name of TOLENTONE in the Domesday Survey, at which time it was held of the King by one *Ranulf*, and the manerial rights were valued at

40s. *per annum* [1]. TOLENTONE or Tallington-lane, now called Devil's, or Duval's-lane, divides this manor from that of St. John of Jerusalem, to the Knights of which Order both of these estates subsequently belonged. On the East side of this lane still remains a moated site, where formerly stood TOLENTONE HOUSE, the dwelling appertaining to the Lords of this manor, and which is called in old records, "The Lower Place." It seems probable, that this house having fallen to decay, the mansion was afterwards built on the high ground to the Eastward, and from that circumstance called HIGHBURY, to distinguish it from the old site; which name became afterwards attached to the whole manor.

The spot chosen for this purpose, it is most probable, was the same that had been formerly occupied by the Roman camp, in the vicinity of the Herman-street, as before mentioned. The addition "Newington "Barrow," may serve to confirm this opinion; the latter word being derived from the low Latin *Burgus*, which signifies a fortified place or defence, unless it arose from Alice de Barowe, who was in possession of this manor about the middle of the thirteenth century; though her name might, with the same probability, have originated from the possession of this land, as was frequently the case, both before and after the Norman Conquest.

This Lady Alicia, or Alice de Barowe, gave the entire Lordship of Highbury and Newton to the Priory of St. John of Jerusalem in England [2]. Previously to this grant, in 1271, being then seised of the Manor of Newton, she gave to the Nuns of Saint Mary, Clerkenwell, an annual rent of seven marks, charged upon a house which was held of her by the Prior of St. John of Jerusalem. For this benefaction it was covenanted that Alice de Barowe and her heirs should be for ever remembered in the masses of the Convent [3]. The Prior of St. John

[1] See the preceding extracts from Domesday Book.
[2] Dugdale's Monasticon, vol. II. p. 543.
[3] Cotton MSS. Nero, E. vi. f. 62.

S

of Jerusalem had a charter of free warren in Neweton, dated 1286[1].

The Manor-house of Highbury seems to have been at this time the *refuge,* or country lodging, of the Lord Prior, and so continued until its destruction by the rebels in the reign of Richard the Second. The haughtiness and ambition of the Knights Hospitallers, and the excessive riches they had accumulated, gave such offence to the common people at this period, that, in the insurrection under Wat Tyler, in the year 1381, after totally consuming with fire their magnificent Priory in St. John-street, near Smithfield, " causing it to burne " by the space of seven days together, not suffering any to quench " it[2];" a detachment of the insurgents proceeded with the same intention to the Prior's Country-house at Highbury: *Jack Straw,* one of the leaders in this rebellion, appears to have headed the lawless mob engaged in this outrage, the number of which, as we are informed by Holinshed, was estimated at 20,000, who " tooke in hand " to ruinate that house:" from which circumstance, and having perhaps made the spot a temporary station for himself and his followers, the place was afterwards called *Jack Straw's Castle,* by which name it continues to be generally known to the present day[3].

The Prior's house at Highbury, was, without doubt, a building of considerable beauty, and appears to have been built with stone, and other durable materials; wherefore the banditti found no small difficulty in its demolition, and were obliged to pull down by main force the firmer parts of the house, which the fire could not consume[4]. Sir

---

[1] Cart. 14 Edw. I. No. 8.

[2] Stow's Survey, p. 483.

[3] In Bishop Gibson's edition of Camden's Britannia, folio, 1695, p. 337, a number of plants are described as growing about *Jack Straw's Castle,* near ISLINGTON; and in Ogilby's *Itinerarium Angliæ,* 1698, it is called by that name: a small building is also delineated on the map, which appears to have been the old *Highbury Barn.*

[4] See Thomas of Walsingham; also Cleveland's *Rustic Rampant* (1687).

Robert Hales, the Lord Prior, who had fled to the Tower for safety, was at last, on the taking of that fortress, brought out and beheaded on Tower-hill, together with Simon Sudbury, Archbishop of Canterbury, John Legg, one of the King's Serjeants at Arms, and a Franciscan friar named William Appledore, who was the King's Confessor. After the death of Wat Tyler, and the dispersion of the mob, the King knighted William Walworth (who slew the chief rebel); also three other citizens for his sake; and " upon the sand-hill towards " ISELDONNE were created the Earles Marshall and Pembroke; and " shortly after Nicholas Twiford and Adam Francis, Aldermen, were " also made Knights [1]."

The Manor of Highbury, with their other possessions in this neighbourhood, remained vested in the Knights of St. John, till the dissolution of religious houses under Henry VIII. when all the lands belonging to the Priory being seized by the King, this manor was granted to Thomas Lord Cromwell, together with that of Canonbury in this parish; and upon his attainder, in 1540, they both reverted to the Crown [2]. King Henry VIII. in the 33d year of his reign, granted a lease to Sir Henry Knevet, Knight, of lands at Highbury, at the yearly rent of £51. 4s. The annual value of the whole manor was £69. 11s. [3]

The Manor of Highbury had been settled on the Lady Mary (afterwards Queen) before the death of Edward VI.; and from the time of her accession continued vested in the Crown till the reign of James the First, who, about the time he created his eldest son Henry Prince of Wales, bestowed this manor on him. A Survey of it was made by his Royal Highness's command in the year 1611.

The site of the manor, and certain demesne lands, consisting of about 300 acres, had been leased by Queen Elizabeth, anno 1562, for 21 years, to Sir Thomas Wroth; and the lease was renewed to

[1] Howe's Chronicle.
[2] Record in the Augmentation Office.
[3] Camp. Lond. p. 87.

Richard Wroth, for the same term, in 1584. The same premises were granted, in 1594, for 60 years, in reversion to Sir John Fortescue, one of the Queen's Privy Council, at the annual rent of £51. 6s. 8d. Sir John Spencer afterwards possessed them, and William Lord Compton, who married his daughter (see the account of Canonbury), held, at the time of this Survey, the remainder of Sir John Fortescue's lease [1].

Queen Elizabeth had also granted a lease, in the 5th year of her reign, of the profits of the manerial courts, which amounted to 40s. *per annum*, to Nicholas Chewne, and afterwards to Thomas Owen [2].

The survey and plan of this manor before mentioned, with the report of the Surveyors, &c. is now in the possession of Jonathan Eade, Esq. the present Lord. It is inscribed, " *The Plot of the Mannor* " *of Newington Barrowe, parcel of the possessions of the High and* " *Mighty Prince Henry, Prince of Wales, Duke of Cornewall, and* " *Earle of Chester, &c. taken in July* 1611, *by Rocke Churche* [3]."

The premises are described in this survey as consisting of one yard or close, where antiently was a castle or mansion house, called Highbury Castle, together with two woods, called Highbury Wood and Little St. John's Wood, and other parcels of land adjoining. The estate had increased to more than six times its value in the reign of Henry the Eighth, being at that time estimated at £.453. 19s. 8d. *per annum*. The surveyors stated, " that there had been a capital " mansion, as they had heard, standing within a moat yet remaining, " but that the house was decaied beyond the memory of man."

In the plan attached to this survey, Highbury Barn is delineated as a high building within the Castle yard; Highbury Wood is contigu-

---

[1] Survey of the Manor, A. D. 1611.

[2] Probably the Judge of the Common Pleas Court, and husband of Alice Owen, founder of the Almshouses at the lower end of Islington.

[3] This plan does not contain the detached part of the manor at the South end of the parish, although it is described in the Survey. It was probably drawn upon a separate piece of vellum, and has, in consequence, been lost.

ous on the North, and is parted from St. John's Wood, which is still further Northward, by a strip of land extending from Stroud-bridge almost to Tollington-lane.

A few acres of ground at the corner of Ball's Pond (now Barr's Nursery) were then called " *The Hoppinge*," from which, no doubt, the adjoining lane derived its name [1].

The surveyors likewise stated, that the house then called " *The* " *Devil's House*," in " *Devil's-lane*," was in antient writings known by the name of " *The Lower-place*," being an old house, inclosed with a " mote, and a little orchard within."

At the time of the survey there were eight freeholders in the manor, holding together 113 acres 3 roods, one of whom was Sir James Pemberton, Knight, Lord Mayor of London that year [2]; and the Brewers' Company held two fields containing 18 acres, called the *London-fields*, on the East side of Tollington-lane. The copyholds amounted to 414 acres 3 roods 14 perches; and among the tenants were Sir Henry Slingsby, Knight, Sir James Pemberton, Knight, Sir William Ayliff, Knight, &c. The leaseholders were, Lord Compton, who held the demesne, 426 acres 38 perches, and Sir Nicholas Coote, who held two meadows containing 32 acres 3 roods 6 perches, by letters patent, dated 17 October, 30th of Elizabeth, at 6s. 8d. [3]

It further appears by a Survey in the Augmentation-office, taken by Commissioners during the Commonwealth, anno 1650, that in the parish of Islington there were then existing two woods, one called *Little St. John's Wood*, which consisted of 35 acres, and the other called *Hibery Wood*, of 43 acres 2 roods 16 perches; and the commis-

[1] See Account of Canonbury Manor.

[2] On Lord Mayor's day, 1611, Sir James Pemberton, goldsmith, made a splendid display, which was celebrated in a pamphlet, called " *Chryso Thryambos, The* " *Triumphs of Gold;* being a Description of the Shows at his Inauguration, at the " Charge of the Goldsmiths. Written by Anthony Munday, Citizen and Draper. " Imprinted by William Jaggard, Printer to the City."

[3] Survey, A. D. 1611.

sioners certified, that 371 trees were at that time growing in these woods, the value whereof they estimated to be £148. 8s.

These woods were sold by the Parliament, in 1651, to Henry Mildmay, of Wansted, co. Essex, Esq. second son of Sir Henry Mildmay; and Richard Clutterbuck, of London, Merchant, for £.327. 6s. 4d.[1] They appear to have been soon after extirpated by the purchasers, for from that time no traces of them are to be found; and in the map of the County, *temp. Car. II.* scarcely any trees are marked upon the spot. The opinion that this manor and that of TOLENTONE, described in Domesday, are the same, is considerably strengthened by the circumstance of these woods having existed at Highbury, for no wood is mentioned in that Survey as belonging to any of the Islington estates, except Tolentone; and pannage[2] for the number of hogs there stated, could only have been derived from plantations of wood similar to those growing on this manor. In the time of King Henry the Eighth, Christopher Newton was keeper of these woods, and had a fee of 20s. yearly.

At the death of Henry Prince of Wales, which happened Nov. 6, 1612, this manor came again to the Crown, in which it remained till 14 James I. when the King granted it, in trust, for the use of his surviving son Charles Prince of Wales, who, after he came to the Crown, bestowed it, anno 1629, on Sir Allen Apsley, who sold it the next year to Thomas Austen, Esq. ancestor of Sir John Austen, Bart. who in the year 1723, alienated it to James Colebrooke, Esq. from whom it descended to Sir George Colebrooke, Bart. Banker in London. This gentleman's life interest in this manor was, Feb. 16, 1791, put up to sale, and purchased by Jonathan Eade, Esq. of Stoke Newington, who is now in possession of the reversion, Sir George having died in the month of August 1809[3].

[1] Deed of Sale, in the Augmentation Office, dated Dec. 3, 1651.

[2] *Pannage* is the food that swine feed upon in the woods, as beech mast, acorns, &c.; also the money taken for the food of hogs in the King's forests.

[3] Sir George Colebrooke, Bart. was born at the family seat at Chilham, in the County of Kent, June 14, 1729. At the age of twenty-six he married Mary, only daughter and heiress of Patrick Gaynor, Esq. of the Island of Antigua, with whom

Little St. John's and Highbury wood, which were parcel of the possessions of the Priory of St. John of Jerusalem, and were included

he had a large fortune, and who brought him four sons and three daughters, whereof two daughters and two sons are living. He pursued his studies for some time at the University of Leyden, was chosen Fellow of the Society of Antiquaries, and published a few Literary pieces. He was elected to serve in three successive Parliaments for the borough of Arundel, from 1754 to 1774, and attained to considerable eminence as a merchant and banker in the City of London. The banking concern, of which he was the head, was for several years carried on in Threadneedle-street, at the house now occupied by Prescott and Co. under the firm of " Sir George Cole- " brooke, Lessingham, and Binns." He was appointed Deputy Chairman of the East India Company in 1768; was chosen Chairman in 1769; and was re-elected to that situation in 1771 and 1772. During the time he presided, he was highly instrumental in preventing the newly-acquired territories in the East Indies from being annexed to the Crown, and exerted himself greatly to preserve the independence of the Company, and to secure it from that interference and controul which has been since established.

Having been unsuccessful in a number of mercantile and other speculations, particularly in the articles of salt-petre, alum, and betel-nut, the trading concerns in which he was engaged became greatly embarrassed and involved in debt, and which ultimately led to a stoppage of payment at the banking-house, in the month of March 1773. He, however, managed to get pretty well through his difficulties; and lived during the latter years of his life in ease and independence on his estate at Chilham. He also was enabled, from his East India connexion, to procure for his sons that patronage which has been the means of elevating them to the highest official situations in the Company's service. His son James-Edward (born July 7, 1761, and who inherits the title of Baronet) was some time Judge of Appeals at Moorshedabad, and now holds a high and lucrative post in the civil department in the province of Bengal. A Letter, written by the celebrated Warren Hastings, dated Feb. 8, 1786, speaks of his abilities in the following highly commendatory terms: " I know few young men in the service (and the service may " boast of many who are an honour to it) who possess superior talents, or more cul- " tivated understandings, and few equal to him in the knowledge of the *Persian* " language. I respect his personal character so much, that I feel a regret, almost " approaching to self reproach, in the reflection that, after so many years of official " labour bestowed, where I may be supposed to have had it in my power to recom- " pense, the only return I can now make to him is a mere acknowledgment of his " merits."

in the lease to Sir John Fortescue, were *not* granted with the manor to Sir Allen Apsley in 1629, but still continue in the Crown.

Sir George's youngest son, Henry-Thomas (born June 15, 1765) is now Chief Judge of the Supreme Court of Judicature at Calcutta. Having made himself master of the Sanscrit language, he undertook, on the death of Sir William Jones, to translate a digest of the Hindoo law, for the use of the Courts of Justice. Besides this, he has published a much esteemed work on the Husbandry and internal Commerce of Bengal, and has been since employed in making a Grammar of the Sanscrit. The two former works are recommended by Captain Williamson, in his "*East India Vade-Mecum*," to all persons who may be induced to visit our territories in Hindostan. The office of Chirographer of the Court of Common Pleas was, by Letters Patent, dated March 18, 6 George III. vested in the two sons of Sir George above mentioned, and their elder brother George, who was born Aug. 9, 1759. He was Lieutenant-Colonel of the Somerset Militia; hereditary Keeper of the Castle of Crawford; and afterwards a Major in the Army. He died in the summer of 1809, and was buried at Chilham.

Mary, the eldest daughter of Sir George (born Oct. 26, 1757) married the Chevalier Charles Adrian de Peyron, in the service of Gustavus, King of Sweden; and by him had one son, Charles-Adolphus-Mary. The Chevalier was killed in a duel, in 1784, by the Count de la Marck; upon which melancholy occasion, the King, being at Paris, sent for the mother and child, and not only promised to confer upon the boy, then only three years of age, the office in his household which the father held, but graciously offered to take him into his family, and educate him with his son, the Prince Royal. His Swedish Majesty, on his return to Stockholm, ordered a grant of the office of Gentleman of his Bedchamber to be transmitted, together with a certificate of the boy's parentage and birth, and of its registration in the list of the nobility, by which he, on attaining the proper age, would have a right to a seat in the Diet of Sweden. In 1789, the mother took for her second husband, William Traill, Esq. by whom she has had a son, George-William, born Oct. 2, 1792, and a daughter, Harriet, who is dead.

The Baronet's second daughter, Louisa (born Jan. 1764) married Andrew Sutherland, Esq. Captain in his Majesty's Navy. He died at Gibraltar, in 1795, Commissioner of that Port, leaving issue a daughter, Louisa, and a son, James-Charles-Colebrooke Sutherland, born Nov. 6, 1792, and who is now in the East India Company's service.

Sir George, the venerable head of so promising a progeny, died at Bath Easton, in the County of Somerset, the 5th of August 1809, at the advanced age of 80

The manor of Highbury according to the Survey before mentioned, contains 987 acres 2 roods 18 poles, of which 459 acres and 4 poles were then in demesne, including the two meadows held by Sir Nicholas Coote. Lands in this manor descend according to the custom of *Gavelkind*, being equally divided between male heirs in the same degree of consanguinity : and in default of male heirs, among females in like manner. The copyholders pay a fine *uncertain*, it being arbitrary, and at the will of the lord. The rule observed is to take on descent, a year and a half improved rent on houses, and two years improved rent on land ; and on alienation, one year on houses, and a year and a half on land. No heriots are now demanded, nor has there been for many ages, but 6*s*. 8*d*. appears to have been once paid on that account in the reign of Henry the Seventh. Widows are not entitled to dower of the copyhold. The Court Baron for the manor is held at the *Blue Coat Boy*, in the lower part of Islington, which house is kept by the bailiff.

## HIGHBURY HOUSE.

It is the opinion of Antiquaries, that the Roman garrison of London had a summer camp on the hill at Highbury. From the commanding situation of the place, and other circumstances, this seems highly probable ; nor is it at all unlikely that the moated site of the Prior's house and the present mansion was that of the *prætorium* of such an encampment. There is no historical record relative to this point, nor does it appear that any coins of that people have ever been discovered here; nevertheless, there is every reason to attach credit to the opinion.

years, and was buried in the family mausoleum at Chilham, built by Sir Robert Taylor, the architect, in the year 1755, at the expence of £.2,000 and upwards. This silent depository contains the remains of several deceased branches of the Colebrooke family.

T

Whilst Sir George Colebrooke was in possession of the fee simple of the manor of Highbury, he sold the site of the old mansion within the moat, called " Jack Straw's Castle," and a considerable quantity of land adjoining, to John Dawes, Esq. an eminent stock-broker, who erected, in the year 1781, at the expence of near £10,000. an elegant and commodious house, with suitable offices, on the spot where the Prior's house formerly stood. In digging for the foundation of this building, a number of antient tiles were discovered by the workmen; but whether of Roman manufacture, or Norman (as conjectured by Mr. Ellis[1]) cannot now be ascertained. Mr. Dawes laid out the grounds in a handsome manner, with shrubberies, paddocks, hothouses, green-house, &c. and continued to reside here till his death, January 31, 1788[2], when the house and premises were sold by auction, May 8th following, to William Devaynes, Esq. M. P. and a Director of the East India Company, for £.5,400. The premises were afterwards purchased of that gentleman by Alexander Aubert, Esq. F. R. S. for 6,000 guineas, who, next coming to reside here, made considerable alterations and improvements on the estate.

Among other things, he erected, near to the House, a lofty and spacious observatory, which he furnished with a very complete collection of astronomical instruments, disposed with great judgment, particularly a very fine reflecting telescope by Short, being the largest ever made by that artist, and which was purchased out of the late Topham Beauclerk's collection. The largest and most important instruments, in order to prevent the effect of motion, were insulated from the floors, being placed upon a pier of solid stone carried up from the earth, and rising through the centre of the building. This fabrick was erected to answer completely all the purposes of astronomy, after a plan of his own, and under his own direction, with the

[1] Campag. Lond. p. 89.

[2] He was taken with a fit in the Stock Exchange, and died there. Obituary in European Magazine.

Miss Henrietta Davies delin.

Rawle Sculp

View of HIGHBURY HOUSE the Seat of ALEX.ᴿ AUBERT ESQ.ᴿ

Painted by Drummond

Engraved by Chapman

*Alexr. Aubert, Esqr. F.R.S.*

assistance of his intimate friend John Smeaton, Esq. F. R. S. and Civil Engineer. Here he deposited a select library of choice and valuable books. In a handsome turret erected for the purpose, near the observatory, he also placed a clock of excellent workmanship, which had belonged to the old church of St. Peter le Poor in Broadstreet.

The improvements made on the estate by this gentleman were of the first magnitude; gardens, lawns, shrubberies, and plantations, of every description, were soon brought to environ the dwelling-house; and the old moat, which had, in the gloomy ages of superstition, been only passable by means of a drawbridge, was partially filled up to form a carriage way to the house; it now assumes the appearance of a canal in front of the mansion, over which the weeping willow "bends to the stream," and gives the landscape a very pleasing and picturesque appearance.

After the death of Mr. Aubert (19 Oct. 1805) the house and premises being put up to sale by auction in July 1806[1], were purchased

---

[1] The following descriptive account of this beautiful domain, by no means overcharged, is extracted from the printed particulars delivered at the time of sale; viz. a freehold villa, called HIGHBURY HOUSE, not more than three miles from the metropolis, an observatory with various apartments three stories high, entrance lodge, lawn, paddocks, walks, shrubberies, plantations, pleasure grounds, canal, range of hot houses 70 feet in length, planted with choice vines, peach and nectarine trees, fruiting house, forcing house, green house, kitchen garden, farm yard, and pasture land, coach-house, stable, cow-house, brew-house, &c. &c. the whole inclosed within a ring-fence, and containing in the whole 74 acres, tithe free, of which

| A. | R. | P. | |
|----|----|----|---|
| 28 | 1 | 14 | are freehold. |
| 45 | 2 | 26 | crown land *. |
| 74 | 0 | 0 | |

* Mr. Bentley is a Lessee of the Crown for these 45 acres two roods 26 perches, being a part of the woodlands before described.

by John Bentley, Esq. who now resides upon the estate. This gentleman retains all the large fixed astronomical instruments placed in the observatory by Mr. Aubert, and it may be truly said, that this building, with its apparatus, is the most complete erection of the kind in the whole kingdom belonging to a private individual [1].

Mr. Bentley has also made many improvements on the premises, and has lately inclosed a considerable part of the grounds by a substantial brick wall. The domestic offices are replete with every thing for use and convenience, and the grounds are abundantly stored with choice vegetables of every kind: the pinery and grapery are in the finest order, and extremely productive; there is also a small orangery, and a plantation of tobacco, which, in October 1809, was standing seven feet high: this has, in one season, produced a hogshead of that entertaining exotic, of a very good quality; but the mode of curing and drying the leaves not being sufficiently understood in this country, much of its virtue is on that account lost.

This place is greatly favoured by Nature in the beauty of its situation, which commands delightful prospects of the surrounding country for a considerable extent, including Stamford Hill and Epping Forest, Hornsey Wood, Muswell Hill, Crouch End, Highgate, Ken Wood, Hampstead, and Primrose Hill: from the top of the observatory the view is still more beautiful and extensive. The following extract from a poem, addressed to its late worthy inhabitant, by a lady, contains some brief allusions to the various charms of " Highbury's " transcendant ground."

> Where Nature's hand, redundant but refin'd,
> A second Eden for AUBERT design'd.
> There the pure stream, refreshing as it glides,
> The flowery bosom of the mead divides;

---

[1] A person in the employ of government comes regularly to Highbury at stated times to take astronomical observations, &c.

While through the windows in the crystal wave
We see the watry children, lightly lave.

But see yon lovely haunt, yet more retir'd,
The HERMITAGE, where genius is inspir'd;
Thither retire, and 'neath its moss-grown cell
Bid for a while the giddy world farewell;
Else on the lawn, beside the nodding grove
Where violets and honeysuckles rove,
There let me view the villages around;
Or from the telescope, survey the ground
Where MANSFIELD's Earl repos'd his dying sigh,
And wing'd a better angel to the sky.

HAMPSTEAD and HIGHGATE both, AUBERT, are thine,
Or to thy pow'r they willingly incline, &c. [1]

### ALEXANDER AUBERT, ESQ.

This gentleman, so highly esteemed by all who had the honour of
his acquaintance, was particularly endeared to the inhabitants of
Islington, for his good humour, hospitality, affability, and politeness
upon every occasion. He was a native of the City of London, being

---

[1] Europ. Mag. vol. xxiv. p. 139. See also a view of *Highbury House*, vol. xxxvi.
p. 79. Mr. Ellis justly observes, " that the Manor of Highbury affords a remarkable
" instance of the advantages derived by the nation from the distribution of church
" lands. At the distance of little more than two centuries, a gloomy castle sur-
" rounded by a moat, with a humbler dwelling at a small distance from the former,
" and guarded in the same jealous manner, were all the habitations that Highbury
" could boast : these were the residences of a few imperious men, who revelled in
" the spoil which they procured by credulity, and maintained by oppression. The
" land is now the property of various individuals, who have erected commodious
" houses in different parts of it, and who improve their own happiness, and that
" of others, by a cheerful and social intercourse." *Campagna of London*, p. 89.

born in Austin-friars, May 11, 1730, and received the first rudiments
of his education, at the Cheam Academy, in Surrey, kept by Mr.
Sanxay.  After some time he was removed to a public school at
Geneva, where he remained six or seven years, during which period
he acquired the French and Italian languages to great perfection.
While he was at this seminary, the comet, in the year 1744, made
its appearance; and it was that which first directed his attention to
the study of astronomy, of which he afterwards became a complete
master.

Being destined to a mercantile life, he was first placed in the count-
ing-house of an eminent merchant in the above city, where, after
continuing a short time, he was sent to Leghorn, and remained some
time in the service of a merchant there.  He then removed to Genoa;
after which he made the tour of Italy; and was at Rome at the cele-
bration of the jubilee in 1750.  He resided three years in Italy, and
returned to England, through Switzerland and France, in which
countries he made some stay, both in the provinces and in the capital.
In 1752, he was taken into partnership in the house of his father in
London.

In 1753, he was elected a Director of the London Assurance Company, and some years afterwards was appointed Governor of that
Corporation.

In 1772, he was elected a Fellow of the Royal Society; and in
1784, a Fellow of the Society of Antiquaries.  In 1793, he received
a diploma, creating him a Member of the Imperial Academy of Sciences at Petersburg.

His favourite study being that of astronomy, he spared no expence
nor exertion in its pursuit.  In 1771, he built an observatory at
Loampit-hill, near Deptford, and furnished it with the best instruments of Short, Bird, Dolland, Ramsden, and the most eminent
makers of the time.

Mr. Aubert's knowledge in mechanics was also very considerable.
He was appointed one of the trustees for the completion of Ramsgate

Harbour; and afterwards, in 1787, on the death of Mr. Barker, he was unanimously requested to take the chair: " which being done," says Mr. Smeaton, " the gentlemen (trustees) observed, that, from " the situation of Ramsgate Harbour, and the very great use it has " already been to shipping, there was no doubt that it might be made " of the utmost utility to commercial navigation; but that, as yet, " there remained a great deal to be done, and many works to be car- " ried forward, to bring it to that state of usefulness and perfection " that it is capable of; and that, consequently, it being an affair of " great magnitude and importance to the publick, it required the con- " stant care and attention of a gentleman of abilities and respectabi- " lity; therefore the Board, in the same unanimous and earnest man- " ner, requested Mr. Aubert to take the lead in the management and " direction of the business, and affairs relative thereto, to which re- " quest Mr. Aubert politely assented; at the same time requesting " the gentlemen to assist and support him in every measure tending " to the benefit and public utility of the harbour [1]."

From this time the works at Ramsgate were carried on with un-abated diligence, and Mr. Aubert, with Mr. Smeaton (whom he had prevailed upon to accept the situation of Engineer to this important undertaking), on one occasion descended in a diving-bell to the bot-tom of the sea, where they remained three quarters of an hour, exa-mining the foundation of the pier, &c.[2] By their joint efforts the har-bour soon arrived to a state of perfection, and has been the means of saving many lives, and much property, which would otherwise have been inevitably lost.

Mr. Smeaton was under many obligations to Mr. Aubert, for the friendly assistance rendered him on various occasions. He revised and corrected for publication the account of the building the Edystone Light-house, by that great mechanical genius; and in other respects contributed to his advancement in his profession.

[1] Smeaton's " Historical Report on Ramsgate Harbour," 8vo, 1791, p. 65.

[2] Ibid. p. 77

In 1792, a period when every thing was to be apprehended from the revolutionary spirit that then prevailed, Mr. Aubert was chairman of a society, the object of which was to suppress sedition; and afterwards, at his recommendation, and under his auspices, the inhabitants of Islington formed themselves into a military association towards the defence of the Country against her enemies, foreign and domestic. On the execution of this plan he was elected the chief officer, and was afterwards appointed by his Majesty's commission, Lieutenant-colonel Commandant of the " *Loyal Islington Volunteers.*"

Mr. Aubert had the honour to be acquainted with many of the most illustrious men of the day; and his character and abilities were duly esteemed by his Sovereign: the late able statesman, Mr. Pitt, Mr. Secretary Dundas (now Lord Melville), the Right Honourable George Rose, and many other persons of the highest eminence, have visited his observatory and house at Highbury.

The friend and promoter of science, he fell a victim to that ardent pursuit of knowledge by which he was always actuated. Being on a visit to his friend John Lloyd, Esq. of Wygfair, near St. Asaph, in Wales, he went to examine the nature of the manufacture at a glass house in that neighbourhood, where becoming overheated by too long a stay in the place, a sudden chill seized him on leaving it, the forerunner of a disorder which put a period to his life, the 19th of October, 1805, in the 76th year of his age. His remains, being brought to Islington, were interred in the vault underneath the church[1].

The corps of " LOYAL ISLINGTON VOLUNTEERS" having first originated from the patriotic spirit and example of the gentleman just

[1] Mr. Aubert died a bachelor. In the parlour on the first floor of the Angel and Crown at Islington is a whole length portrait of him, dismounted, and holding his charger, as Commanding Officer of the *Loyal Islington Volunteers*, which corps is represented in the back ground, drawn up in military array. It was painted by Mather Brown, Esq. There is also a good likeness of him in the European Magazine for November 1798, from a painting by Drummond.

spoken of, it may not be improper to take some notice of it in this place. After its formation as before mentioned, which was in the year 1797, the corps continued to increase in numbers and respectability, and was joined by many gentlemen from the City and the adjacent parishes. It consisted of a regiment of infantry, and one of cavalry, the latter being commanded by Captain Anderdon; and the number, within a few months after it was embodied, amounted to upwards of 300 effective members. The uniform consisted of a blue jacket with white facings, scarlet cuffs, collar, and epaulets, and trimmed with silver lace; white kersymere pantaloons, and short gaiters, helmets, and cross belts. Their arms and accoutrements were provided by Government; the expences of the establishment being defrayed by a fund raised amongst themselves for that purpose.

In consequence of an unfortunate dispute having arisen between some of the officers and their Lieutenant-colonel, when the corps had been established nearly four years, the members began to resign; their exercises were discontinued, and the establishment was totally broken up about the beginning of 1801.

The members upon this occasion, to testify the high sense they entertained of the loyalty, ability, and spirited conduct of their commandant, presented him with a superb silver vase, which, for beauty of workmanship, and elegance of design, may be reckoned among the first productions of the arts in this country[1].

---

[1] The cover of this magnificent vessel contains a grand display of military insignia, among which are introduced the particular accoutrements of the corps, the standard of the cavalry, &c. In the centre of these is a figure of *Fame* seated on a mortar, in the act of sounding a trumpet, and supporting the colours of the *Loyal Islington Volunteers*, on the staff of which is the British Cap of Liberty. Vine leaves, grapes, roses, &c. arranged in festoons of singular richness, and beautifully diversified, nearly surround the upper part of the body of the vase, and are collected together in a knot on the principal front by a Bacchanalian head, from which is suspended a shield, with this inscription:

U

At the same time the gentlemen of the Corps presented the Colonel with a copy of the following address, richly emblazoned on vellum,

" This Cup

" was presented by the late Corps of

" Loyal Islington Volunteers

" to Alexander Aubert,  Esq.

" their Lieut.-Col. Commandant,

" in testimony of their respect and esteem

" for him,  in approbation of his firm and

" spirited behaviour in support of the

" honour and independance

" of the corps,  previcus to its general

" resignation,

" and in grateful acknowledgement

" of his judicious and liberal conduct

" upon all occasions

" as their Commander.

―――

" Embodied the 4th of March,  1797 ;

" Unanimously resigned 20th of January,  1801,

" at that period consisting of 314 members,

" Cavalry and Infantry."

On the opposite front is suspended a shield bearing the Colonel's arms *, supported by a band of laurel, over which is placed a head in the Egyptian costume, with a star on the forehead, alluding to his favourite pursuit, the study of astronomy. The body of the vase is gilt, and partly enveloped in a lion's skin, exhibiting the strength and unity of the corps.  This and all the ornaments are richly chased in silver matt.

The handles are each formed of two serpents ; the tails proceed from the upper part in front, and, following the course of the festoons a little way, emerge from them, and proceed in a bold and ample curve towards each other.  The continuation of this curve brings each head to the lowest part of the opposite side, where it is received in a hollow, formed by acanthus leaves, and composing the base of the vase.  The effect of the whole is much heightened by festoons of double chains hanging loose from the body, which pass through the mouths of the serpents,  and

---

* Vide Additions to Edmondson's Heraldry, vol. II.

which was unanimously agreed to by the Corps on the day of their resignation :

" *To* ALEXANDER AUBERT, *Esq. Lieutenant-Colonel-Commandant*
        " *of the Loyal Islington Volunteers.*

 " SIR,
   " WE beg leave to address you, for the last time we shall
" have it in our power as a Volunteer Corps.  We should not depart
" hence with satisfaction to ourselves, were we to neglect this oppor-
" tunity of expressing to you our sentiments.  The very great acti-
" vity you have taken in forming so respectable a corps—the genero-
" sity and unbounded liberality you have always shewn in supporting
" it,—and the very marked ability with which you have commanded
" it, merit our warmest approbation, and our most sincere thanks.
 " In taking our leave of you as our Commander, permit us to assure
" you, Sir, we shall ever entertain a lively remembrance of that po-
" lite attention to us, for which you have been so eminently distin-
" guished; and that you may enjoy long life and happiness, is the
" hearty wish of every LOYAL ISLINGTON VOLUNTEER.

       " JOHN BIGGERSTAFF, Jun',
        " *Secretary to the Corps.*"

After the short interval of peace in 1803, the old threat of invasion being repeated, a meeting of the inhabitants of Islington was
held at Canonbury-tavern, in the month of July that year, " to con-
" sider of the propriety of forming a military association for the
" defence of the country, &c."  A subscription being entered into

are disposed with great taste and judgment.  The pedestal was copied from the
celebrated Bacchanalian Vase in the Villa Borghese at Rome, and on its plinth are
grouped astronomical instruments.  The whole was executed, with great care and
precision, by Mr. Preedy, from the chaste and elegant designs of Mr. Thurston,
and modelled in the purest style of the antique by Mr. Edmund Coffin.  The vase
is now in the possession of Mr. Aubert's family, and is valued at 300 guineas.

by the inhabitants for that purpose, a Volunteer Corps of Infantry was speedily established, which soon arrived to great perfection, in order and discipline, under the instruction of Mr. Dickson, who had formerly served in the army, and was now appointed Adjutant. The following lines are part of some verses addressed to him on the presentation of a sword in December 1804; they were written by a Member of the corps.

> Honour, that guides our Patriot band,
> Presents with an impartial hand,
> A Sword of Merit, where 'tis due,
> To Zeal and Science, found in you.
>     The day is yet but scarcely past,
> Rude was our corps, and form'd in haste;
> Till, model'd by your just design,
> They march, they wheel, and form the line.
> Expert in onset, fierce to close,
> Or pour a volley on their foes;
> Or frequent by manœuvres skill'd,
> Seem bold for conquest in the field, &c.[1]"

This corps was commanded by Mr. Wheelwright, of Highbury, and consisted of about 300 members. The uniform was different to that of the original corps, being a scarlet jacket turned up with black, light blue or grey pantaloons, short gaiters, and beaver caps. The arms and accoutrements were provided by Government. The " *Loyal Islington Volunteers*" continued their exercises till October 1806, when, in consequence of their fund being found insufficient to answer the expences of the establishment, the same was dissolved. A vote of thanks was given to their Commandant; and the Adjutant Dickson, having procured an Ensign's commission in the 82d regi-

---

[1] Monthly Mirror, vol. xix. p. 56.

ment of foot, proceeded with the British army, under Lord Cathcart, to the attack upon Copenhagen, and was killed by a shot from a cannon, near Roeskilde, in the island of Zealand, in the month of August 1807.

## CONDUITS.

Before the establishment of the Water-works at London bridge in 1582, and the subsequent bringing of the New River from Hertford-shire for supplying the City with water, the principal source from which the inhabitants derived that useful element, was the springs rising on the high grounds, on the North and Western sides of the Capital, from which it was conveyed, by pipes, to conduits erected in different parts of the town for its reception. From these the supply was at best but scanty, and the means of obtaining it attended with much inconvenience; being either by fetching it from the conduits, or paying men who made it their business to bring it from thence[1].

[1] One of these persons is characterized by the name of *Cob*, a *water-bearer*, in Ben Jonson's Comedy of *Every Man in his Humour*. The vessels they carried the water in, were called tankards, and held about three gallons; they were hooped round like a pail, and in figure were a frustrum of a cone: they had a small iron handle at the upper end, like that of an ale-house point, and being fitted with a cork, bung, or stopple, were easily portable on the shoulders of a man. One of these vessels is still used in the representation of the above Comedy. The last instance that is recorded of their actual use, was by a servant of James Colebrooke, Esq. (Lord of the manor of Highbury), whose business in town was carried on at a house nearly adjoining the Antwerp-tavern, behind the Royal Exchange. This man, who was his porter, employed to water and sweep the shop, &c. used every morning at 8 o'clock to fetch water from a neighbouring pump in such a tankard as above described. These vessels are frequently mentioned by Stow, and other old writers; and it appears, that vehicles of a similar form, and bearing the same name, were also used for the transporting of milk on horses, and which continue to be used by some milk dealers, for the purpose of conveying it in carts, to the present day. There were also women, whose employment it was to carry water from the con-

These conduits, and the springs from which they derived their supply, were objects of great attention with the Corporation of the City; and some of its members bestowed considerable sums in establishing and keeping them in proper condition.  It was customary, in former times, for the Citizens occasionally to visit the conduit heads, when they had an allowance out of the City Purse for a dinner [1].  It is noted by Strype, that on the 18th September, 1562, " The Lord Mayor, Aldermen, and many worshipful persons, rode " to the conduit-heads to see them, *according to the old custom:* " then they went and hunted a hare before dinner, and killed her; " and thence went to dinner at the head of the conduit, where a great " number were handsomely entertained by the Chamberlain.  After " dinner, they went to hunt the fox.  There was a great cry for a " mile, and at length the hounds killed him at the end of *St. Giles's,* " with great hollowing and blowing of horns at his death; and " thence the Lord Mayor, with all his company, rode through " London, to his place in Lombard-street."

At Highbury, and in its immediate vicinity, there appears to have been some of these conduit-heads belonging to the City.  Sir William Eastfield, Lord Mayor in 1438, " a great benefactor to the water " conduits," caused water to be conveyed from HIGHBERY, in pipes of lead, to the parish of St. Giles without Cripplegate, " where the " inhabitants of those parts incastellated the same in sufficient cis-

---

duits in pails, a more convenient vessel for a woman's use than a tankard.  This may be inferred from Lamb's * gift " to poore women, such as were willing to take " paines," of " 120 pailes therewith to carry and serve water."  See Gent. Mag. for 1783, p. 136; Stow's Survey, p. 93; and Beauties of England and Wales, vol. X. p. 75.

[1] See index to Records of London, date August 1590 and 1591.  Harl. MSS. No. 6597.

* William Lamb, citizen and clothworker, who formed the conduit where Lamb's Conduit-street now stands, and where the spring yet remains.  Part of the water he conveyed from thence through leaden pipes, for the space of 2,000 yards, to another conduit on Snow-hill.

" ternes [1];" and in 1546, water was conveyed " *in great abundance* " from divers springs lying betwixt Hoxton and Iseldon," to a conduit at the West end of the Parish Church of St. Margaret Lothbury [2].

In the antient Survey of this Manor before cited, a piece of ground in the lower part is mentioned under the name of " the Conduit- " field;" and in Camden's Britannia, 1695, " an old stone conduit" is described as situate " between Islington and Jack Straw's Castle," which is also delineated in Ogilby's Book of Roads, 1698. This conduit, which appears to have been the one formed by Sir William Eastfield, yet remains in the field opposite to No. 14, Highbury-place. The conduit-house being removed, it is now arched over with brick, and its situation marked by an upright stone, which also points out the direction of the springs on the higher gronnd from which it receives its supply. From this antient conduit, which remained open as a watering-place for cattle before the building of Highbury-place, many of the houses there are now served with water, a proper communication having been made on building them for that purpose. By these means it flows into wells or reservoirs behind the houses, which also communicate with each other, the lower well receiving the surplus water, when the upper one is filled. The pump at the West end of Hopping-lane is also supplied from the same source.

The Prior's house, and the conduit-heads at Canonbury, appear also to have derived a part of their water from the springs of Highbury, as mentioned in the account of the former place. At the time of digging for the foundation of Highbury-house, in the year 1781, a great collection of pipes, made of red earth baked, resembling those used for the conveyance of water about the time of Queen Elizabeth, were dug up [3], and similar discoveries of leaden pipes have

---

[1] Stow's Survey, p. 302, &c.      [2] Ibid.

[3] Some of these were sold by Leigh and Sotheby in July 1810, amongst the curiosities of the late eminent Antiquary Richard Gough, Esq.

been made at different times in the fields between **Canonbury** and **Highbury**.

The antient method of supplying the City with water by means of the conduits will be better understood from the following

REPORT, made upon a view of *Dalston* and *Islington* Waters :

" To the Honourable the Committee appointed by the Right Honour-
    " able the Lord Mayor, Aldermen, and Commoners, in Common
    " Council assembled.

    " In pursuance of an order of this Committee, dated the thirteenth
" day of this instant *December*, wee have, with the assistance of
" *William Cooper*, one of the Citty labourers, viewed the springs
" and waters at *Dalston* ; and find the same to be reduced to two se-
" verall heads, walled and inclosed, situate in two fields near *Dal-
" ston*, and from thence conveyed, in two pipes of lead, through
" sundry fields, crossing the footway from *Shoreditch* to *Hackney*,
" something Eastward of a tenement there called the *Virginia-
" house* ; and from thence, crossing *Swann-field*, on the West of
" *Brick-lane*, under a tenement now in the occupation of one *Wil-
" liams*, a bricklayer, in *King-street* ; and from thence, crossing the
" same street, under certaine tenements near the *Golden Heart*, into
" *Phœnix-street* ; and from thence, crossing the said street, under a
" tenement at the upper end of *Gray Eagle-street*, in the occupation
" of one *Castle*, and so down the middle of the said street to the
" almshouses at the corner of *Corbutt's-court* ; and from thence, up
" the said court, to the upper end of *Browne's-lane*, eight foot deep,
" where the said two pipes are united into one, which conveys the
" water from thence down a street on the East side of *Spittle-fields*,
" about nine foot deep, and under some tenements at the South-west
" corner of the said street ; and so, cross *White Rowe-street*, and
" under a tenement on the South side the said street, into and cross a
" centre field to the South-west corner thereof, where a stone is
" erected ; and from thence, under a tenement in the occupation of

" one *Gantam*, a wyer-drawer, into *Bell-lane;* and from thence,
" down the middle of the said lane, through *Mountague-street* and
" *Wenford-street*, into *Pettycoat-lane*, and so along the middle of
" the said lane, fifteen foot deep, into *Whitechappel-street;* and
" from thence, up the West side of the said street, (from fourteen to
" eighteen foot deep) to the conduit at *Algate*.

" And we cannot be informed that the said pipes, or any other
" from the said springs, are employed to any other use than the ser-
" vice of the said Conduit, except a quill laid into a tenement in the
" said *Bell-lane*, belonging to one *Sheppard*, to whom (as wee are
" informed by the said *Cooper*) the same was granted by the Citty
" about five years since, in consideration of laying their conduit pipe
" through and under the said tenement, now in the occupation of
" *Gantam*, which then belonged to the said *Sheppard*. And we find
" the said conduit very plentifully supplied with water.

" And we have also, in further pursuance of the said order, viewed
" the springs and water belonging to the Citty neare *Islington;* and
" find the same in two heads, one covered over with stone, in a field
" neare *Jack Straw's Castle*, which is fed by sundry springs in an ad-
" jacent field, and is usually called *The White Conduit*, the water
" whereof is conveyed from thence, in a pipe of lead, through *Cham-
" bery park*, to the other conduit in *Chambery-field;* and from
" thence the water of both the said heads so united is conveyed, in a
" pipe of lead, cross *The New River*, in a cant, into *The Green
" Man fields*, and entering from thence a garden, heretofore be-
" longing to one *Porter*, vintner, at about forty foot distance from
" *Frogg-lane*, into a field on the East side thereof; and from thence,
" cross the North-east corner of a garden at the hither end of *Frogg-
" lane*, into a field belonging to the Company of Clothworkers; and
" from thence, through the field next to, and West of the footway
" from *Islington*, unto the stile by the *Pest-house*, where it crosseth
" the said way, and so along the East side thereof, cross the road at
" *Old-street*, and under the bridge there, into *Bunnhill-fields;* and

x

" from thence, on the West side of the said field, by *The Artillery*
" *garden*, crossing *Chiswell-street*, into and down the middle of
" *Grubb-street*, into *Fore-street*, and so on the South side thereof to
" the conduit at *Cripplegate :* and we cannot find that the said wa-
" ters are employed to any other use than to the service of the said
" conduit.

" Also we humbly certify, that both the said conduit-heads of
" *Dalston* are out of repair ; the first wanting two pillars for the win-
" dow, and a copeing stone ; and the furthest wants one side of a
" stone door case, and a new door, the old being broken by some
" persons that have broke up the inside pavement, and the curb
" stones round the cistern of lead, and taken away about three yards
" of wast pype, and two leaden bosses out of the said cistern theire,
" and the hinges and hooks of the door ; and we find one of the jambs
" of the window is also broke, and the roofe wants repaire in cieling.

" And we conceive that the pipe from the furthest conduit-head to
" that in *Chambery-field* beyond *Islington* is stopped ; for that the
" cistern in the first is full of water, and the water joining to the latter
" is not above a quarter pipe, whereas it hath used to come full pipe ;
" also, that the planks of one of the draines feeding the said furthest
" head is broke about six foot square, and two stones wanting in the
" covering ; and also, the like quantity of plank is broke over the
" cess-poole at the head in *Chambery-field*.   All which we humbly
" certify, this twentieth day of *December*,  Anno Domini 1692.

" Thomas Glentworth.
" James Nalton.
" Ro. Tarlton [1]."

The farm house called *Cream-hall*, standing upon the Crown land,
and which has been known by this name time out of mind, is included in Mr. Bentley's lease from the Crown.   Another house adjoining to Highbury tavern, was also a farm of some consequence,
called Highbury-farm, and was usually considered as the manor-

[1] Appendix to Ellis's History of Shoreditch.

house, till the present mansion was erected upon the antient site by Mr. Dawes. Some of the buildings attached to this farm have been converted into a dwelling-house, now in the occupation of Mr. Horton. Whilst this manor was in the possession of Sir George Colebrooke, Mr. John Wallbank was a considerable farmer at Highbury; and afterwards, both the farms last mentioned were rented by Mr. Thomas Porter, together with several hundred acres of land adjoining, at not more than 37s. *per* acre. He was succeeded by a Norfolk farmer, named Barwell; but the lands and premises which were held by these persons are now distributed among a number of tenants. Mr. Willoughby holds the old Highbury farm-house, and Cream-hall is also rented by him of Mr. Bentley. These farms, or more properly dairies, were almost entirely devoted to the supply of the London milk dealers, which appears to have been the chief business of the farmers in this parish, from time immemorial; and the name of *Cream-hall,* there is no doubt, originated from this circumstance.

The Highbury tavern and tea-gardens, commonly called *Highbury Barn,* arose from what was originally an ale and cake house, upon a very limited scale, and which had been in possession of the family of Mr. Willoughby, who keeps the present tavern, for a number of years. The Court Baron for the Manor used to be held here; and in process of time, the house, from its pleasant situation, being much resorted to by persons from London, and the trade thereby increased beyond the accommodation the place afforded, an extensive barn, belonging to the adjoining farm, was added to the premises, which, fitted up with a handsome interior, forms at the present time the principal room of the tavern [1].

---

[1] Previous to this circumstance the place was called *Highbury Barn,* from being the situation originally occupied by the *barn* belonging to the Manor-house. This term, amongst milk dealers, &c. is synonymous with farm or dairy, whence the term *barn measure,* as applied to milk, in contradistinction to that by which it is retailed to the public.

The bowling-green, trap-ball grounds, and gardens, were laid out by Mr. Willoughby, by whose persevering industry, and the excellent accommodations of the place, the concern has within these few years increased in trade to an extent almost unparalleled [1]. From the grounds the prospect is extensive and beautiful; at one end is a

[1] The business done at this house in the summer months is equal to, if not beyond, that of any similar concern in the metropolis or its environs : a great number of corporate bodies, public charities, clubs, and other societies are accustomed to have their annual and other dinners at this place, where from 1500 to 2000 people can upon occasion be accommodated. A dinner has been dressed here for a company of 800 persons, who all sat down to hot dishes, on which occasion upwards of *seventy* geese were to be seen roasting at one fire. In June 1808 the Society of Ancient Free Masons, having been in procession to Islington Church in their masonic dresses, to the number of 12 or 1400, attended with several bands of musick, &c. about 500 of them dined at Highbury tavern : the Lodge of Jews were entertained at the Pied Bull after their own manner, and the remainder were distributed among the other public houses in the village. A similar procession and feasting were repeated here on the 25th June 1810.

A society that deserves particular remark, has for many years been held at this place. It is a friendly association of Protestant Dissenters, formed about a century ago, and who first combined together at a time when the privileges of that body were imminently endangered by the passing of an act called the *Schism* Bill, which was directly levelled against all those not in conformity with the Established Church; subjecting them to various disabilities, and rendering them liable to severe fines, and even imprisonment. The day on which this iniquitous Act was to have received the royal sanction, Queen Anne died; in consequence of which important event " *The Highbury Society*" (as it is now called) was established; but their meetings were originally held at *Copenhagen-house.* It appears, however, that so far back as the year 1740, *Highbury* was the place where this society held their meetings; concerning which the following particulars, extracted from the printed report of its rise and progress, will not be uninteresting. About the period last mentioned, " The party who walked together from London had a ren-
" dezvous in Moorfields at one o'clock, and at *Dettingen Bridge* (where the house
" known by the name of the Shepherd and Shepherdess now stands) they chalked
" the initials of their names on a post, for the information of such as might fol-
" low. They then proceeded to *Highbury;* and, to beguile the way, it was their
" custom, in turn, to bowl a ball of ivory at objects in their path. This ball has

*Highbury Assembly House, near Islington, kept by Mr. Willoughby.*

Published 12th Sepr 1791 by Robt Sayer & Co. Fleet Street London.

Highbury Barn, Islington.

John Street, Pentonville.

Pub. May 1.1819. for the Proprietor by R. Ackermann, 101. Strand

small plantation of hops, which has been for these few years past cultivated by Mr. Willoughby, who has lately erected a very convenient ale and table-beer brewery on the premises. An assembly is likewise established here, which is supported by the subscriptions of the neighbouring inhabitants, who meet together in the great room once a month during the seasons of winter and spring. In a field adjoining the gardens, is a butt for the exercise of ball firing, similar to one at Canonbury [1].

" lately been presented to the society by Mr. William Field. After a slight re-
" freshment, they repaired to the field for exercise; but in those days of greater
" economy and simplicity, neither wine, punch, nor tea, were introduced, and
" eight pence was generally the whole individual expence incurred.

" A particular game, denominated *Hop Ball*, has from time immemorial formed
" the recreation of the members of this society at their meetings. On a board,
" which is dated 1734, which they use for the purpose of marking the game, the
" following motto is engraven: *Play justly, play moderately, play chearfully; so*
" *shall ye play to a rational purpose.* It is a game not in use elsewhere in the
" neighbourhood of London; but one somewhat resembling it is practised in the
" West of England. The ball used in this game, consisting of a ball of worsted
" stitched over with silk or packthread, has from time immemorial been gra-
" tuitously furnished by one or another of the members of the society.

" The following toast is always given at their annual dinner in August; viz.
" *The glorious first of August, with the immortal memory of King William and his*
" *good Queen Mary, not forgetting Corporal John; and a fig for the Bishop of Cork,*
" *that bottle-stopper.* How this toast first originated has not been ascertained, but
" it seems strongly tinctured with the spirit of the times in which it is supposed
" to have been first adopted. John Duke of Marlborough, the great friend of
" the Protestant and Whig interest, was in all probability the person designated
" by Corporal John." The society dine together weekly, on Saturday, in the winter time, from November to March; and it consists at this time of between 40 and 50 members. *Report of the Committee on the Rise and Progress of the Highbury Society, printed* 1808.

[1] These butts are formed of a huge bank of earth, strengthened with turf and faggot wood, and have been raised in several places contiguous to the metropolis, as at Chalk farm, Montpelier gardens, &c. for the use of the Volunteer Corps.

A way continues from Highbury to a public house called *The Eel Pie House,* on the West bank of the New River, and to *Hornsey Wood House,* places both much frequented in the summer time[1]; and to which the walk from Highbury is remarkably pleasant, being agreeably undulated over hill and vale[2], and carried for some length along the margin of the river. This road, which is in the immediate vicinity of the Herman-street, appears to be an antient public way, the right to which was opposed by James Colebrooke, Esq. when in possession of this manor, he having erected gates for the purpose of stopping the passage; this circumstance gave rise to a law suit, upon the issue of which, the privilege of the public to this road as a thoroughfare was lost[3].

[1] Such is the resort of the lower order of people from the metropolis to *The Eel Pie House* on Palm Sunday, in their way to Hornsey wood, to procure palm, that the host and servants are obliged to be upon the alert at two o'clock in the morning, in order to receive their numerous guests; who, even at this early hour, begin to call for refreshment; generally on that day, more than an extra butt of beer is drawn at the house, with gin and other liquors in proportion.

[2] On the hill near *Cream Hall* is a remarkably distinct echo.

[3] The following are the circumstances which gave rise to this action. There was one Jennings, a quaker, who was originally by profession an ass driver, afterwards became proprietor of some asses in *fee simple,* then a farmer at Crouch-end, and at length lessee of the Manor of Brown's Wood. This man became acquainted with Richard Holland, a leatherseller in Newgate-street, London, who had a *villa* at Hornsey, and was at great pains to obtain the suppression of some tolls demanded in Smithfield market (see Noorthouck's History of London). These two persons determined to oblige Mr. Colebrooke to open the road. Accordingly, one day they sent several teams down the road. When they came to the *Boarded-river,* not finding any body to open the gate, they, without further ceremony, cut it down, drove across the field to the next gate, and did the same there; thence, passing by *Cream-hall,* they came to *Highbury-barn,* where they found a third gate; whereupon they dispatched a messenger to Mr. Wallbank (before mentioned), requesting him to open the same; which he refusing to do, they pulled it up with their horses, and drove it in triumph down the road to Hopping-lane, and thence to *Islington,* where they proclaimed aloud, " that they had come along

Mr. Hopkinson, of Holborn, who holds a considerable estate at Highbury, is making great improvements on the East side of this road, beyond Mr. Willoughby's, where he is erecting some very handsome houses (eight in number), detached from each other, and intersected with ornamental plantations, shrubberies, &c. One of these, intended for his own residence, stands on the brow of the hill, facing *Cream-hall*, and commands the most extensive and delightful prospects. When these buildings are completed, the place is to be called " *Highbury Upper Grove.*"

## NEW RIVER.

About the place where the New River enters this parish, it was formerly conducted over the valley by means of an enormous wooden trough, 462 feet in length and 17 feet high; lined with lead, and supported by strong timbers standing on piers of brick [1], and which went by the name of *The Boarded River*. This mode of conveying the water having been found a very great expence to the Company, from the trough being continually out of repair, and the loss of water sustained in consequence, occasioned them to determine upon its removal, and which was begun upon about Midsummer 1776.

" this old road, which was a thoroughfare, &c." Upon this Wallbank commenced a suit; and, in order effectually to stop the passage, by Mr. Colebrooke's desire, took off the crown of the arch at the *Boarded-river*, and laid it open, raiiing the opening to prevent mischief. At length the suit was brought to an issue; and the plaintiff examined one Richard Glasscock, who had long dwelt at the *Boarded-river house* as a servant to the Company, and swore that there had always been a bar there. The defendant did not appear, and the cause was determined in the plaintiff's favour; in consequence of which this has ever since continued a *via clausa*. Mr. Colebrooke died before the trial came on. See *Gent. Mag. for Nov.* 1784.

[1] See engraved views of a similar aqueduct of the New River at Bush-hill, near Enfield, in the Gentleman's Magazine for September and October 1784.

To effect this, and form a more durable and convenient channel for the stream, the earth underneath and along the sides of the trough was raised by the addition of a great bed of clay, till it arrived at a proper height and level, in which a passage was made for the river, nearly along the old track, and by these means the wooden trough was entirely superseded. Great pains were taken to strengthen the bank, and make it water-tight, as far as possible, by sowing grass down its sides, &c.; and at the top, on the Western side, a strong bed of gravel was laid, which forms a very pleasant terrace along the brink of the river. Underneath this trough, an antient bridle way, falling into the *Herman-street*, had its course; this was not stopped up, but continued by means of a bridge over the stream. Nearly underneath this bridge, and below the bed of the river, is a sub-aquæous arch or culvert, about six feet wide, formed to convey away the land waters, which formerly passed under the *Boarded-river:* these, descending from Highgate and the neighbouring hills, and passing along this valley, proceed through Stoke Newington, crossing the great road, and thence to Hackney, where, having acquired the name of Hackney Brook, it continues onward, and at length falls into the river Lea.

The New River, which has been noticed by topographers at almost every village that it visits in its meandering course, is certainly entitled to some description in a place to which it is so great an ornament, and from whence it is diffused by innumerable subterraneous channels to almost every part of the great Metropolis.

During the reigns of Elizabeth and James, a number of schemes were projected for supplying the Capital with water, the conduits resorted to for that purpose being now found insufficient to answer the increasing demands of an extending Metropolis. Elizabeth granted an Act, which gave the citizens liberty to cut and convey a river from any part of Middlesex or Hertfordshire to the city of London, within the limited time of ten years, but which was never acted upon.

In the early part of James's reign, the citizens procured "An Act "for the bringing in a fresh stream of running water to the North "part of the City of London" (3 Jac. cap. 18), which was followed by another, to explain the said Statute (4 Jac. cap. 12); but the difficulties of the undertaking appeared so great, that they declined to embark any farther in it.

Mr. Hugh Middleton, or Myddelton, a native of Denbigh, and citizen and goldsmith of London (who had considerably enriched himself by a copper, or, according to others, a silver mine, in Cardiganshire), at whose instigation it would seem the City had applied for the Acts last mentioned, made an offer to the Court of Common Council, March 28, 1609, that he would begin this work within two months, they transferring to him the power vested in them by the said two Acts; whereupon the Court accepted his offer, and ordered that a letter of attorney should be made out from the Mayor and Common Council (which was done the 1st of April following), and that indentures should be made and passed between them and him, which was also done the 21st of the same month [1].

Being vested with ample powers from the City, this gentleman, with a spirit equal to the importance of the undertaking, at his own risk and charge began the work; but had not proceeded far, when innumerable and unforeseen difficulties presented themselves. The art of civil engineering was then little understood in this country; and he experienced many obstructions from the occupiers and proprietors of the lands through which he was under the necessity of conducting his stream.

The distance of the springs of Chadwell and Amwell is 20 miles from London; but it was found necessary, in order to avoid the eminences and valleys in the way, to make it run a course of more than 38 miles. "The depth of the trench in some places de- "scended full 30 feet, if not more, whereas in other places it

[1] Lysons's Environs.

Y

" required as sprightfull arte againe to mount it over a valley in a
" trough betweene a couple of hils, and the trough all the while
" borne up by woodden arches, some of them fixed in the ground
" very deepe, and rising in heighth above 23 foot[1]."

The progress of the work, indeed, appears to have been attended
with difficulties almost insurmountable, for the industrious projector
soon found himself so harrassed and impeded by sundry interested
persons in Middlesex and Herts, that he was obliged to petition the
City for a prolongation of the time to accomplish his undertaking.
The Corporation now granted him a term of five, in addition to a
former term of four years; but his difficulties did not terminate here;
for, after having adjusted all his controversies with the landholders in
an amicable manner, and brought the water into the neighbourhood
of Enfield, he was so impoverished by the expence of the undertaking, that he was once more obliged to apply to the City to interest themselves in this great and useful work; and, upon their refusal to embark in so chargeable and hazardous an enterprize, he
applied with more success to the King himself, who, upon a moiety
of the concern being made over to him, agreed to pay half the expence of the work past and to come. It now went on without inter-
ruption, and was finished according to Mr. Middleton's original agreement with the City, when, on the 29th of September, 1613, the
water was let into the bason, now called *The New River Head*, in
the parish of Clerkenwell, which had been prepared for its reception.

" Being brought to the intended cisterne, but not (as yet) the
" water admitted entrance thereinto, on Michaelmasse day, in anno
" 1613, being the day when Sir Thomas Middleton, brother to the
" said Sir Hugh Middleton[2], was elected Lord Maior of London
" for the yeere ensuing, in the afternoone of the same daye *Sir John*
" *Swinerton, Knt.* and Lord Maior of London, accompanied with
" the said *Sir Thomas, Sir Henry Montague, Knt.* Recorder of

[1] Stow's Survey, p. 13.

[2] Sir Hugh Middleton was not created a Baronet till October 1622.

" London, and many of the worthy Aldermen, rode to see the cis-
" terne, and first issuing of the water thereinto, which was performed
" in this manner :

" A troope of labourers, to the number of 60 or more, well appa-
" relled, and wearing green *Monmouth caps*, all alike, carryed
" spades, shovels, pickaxes, and such like instruments of laborious
" imployment, marching after drummes, twice or thrice about the
" cisterne, presented themselves before the mount, where the Lord
" Maior, Aldermen, and a worthy company beside, stood to behold
" them : and one man (in behalf of all the rest) delivered this
" speech :

" Long have we labour'd, long desir'd, and pray'd
" For this great work's perfection; and by th' aid
" Of Heav'n, and good men's wishes, 'tis at length
" Happily conquer'd, by cost, art, and strength.
" And after five yeeres deare expence, in dayes,
" Travaile, and paines, beside the infinite wayes
" Of Malice, Envy, false suggestions,
" Able to daunt the spirits of mighty ones
" In wealth and courage.   This, a worke so rare,
" Onely by one man's industry, cost, and care,
" Is brought to blest effect; so much withstood,
" His onely ayme, the Citie's generall good.
" And where (before) many unjust complaints,
" Enviously seated, caused oft restraints,
" Stops, and great crosses, to our master's charge,
" And the work's hindrance : Favour, now at large,
" Spreads herself open to him, and commends,
" To admiration, both his paines and ends
" (The King's most gracious love).   Perfection draws
" Favour from Princes, and (from all) applause.
" Then, worthy Magistrates, to whose content
" (Next to the State) all this great care was bent;

" And for the publike good (which grace requires),

" Your loves and furtherance chiefly he desires,

" To cherish these proceedings, which may give

" Courage to some that may hereafter live,

" To practise deedes of goodness, and of fame,

" And gladly light their actions by his name.

" — *Clarke* of the worke, reach me the booke, to show,

" How many arts from such a labour flow.

" First, here's the *Overseer*, that tride man,

" An ancient souldier, and an artizan;

" The *Clarke*, next him mathematician,

" The master of the timber worke takes place;

" Next after these, the *Measurer*, in like case

" *Bricklayer* and *Engineer*; and after those,

" The *Borer* and the *Pavier*.   Then it showes

" The *Labourers* next; keeper of *Amwell head*,

" The *Walkers* last : so all their names are read.

" Yet these, but parcels of six hundred more

" That (at one time) have been imployed before;

" Yet these in sight, and all the rest will say,

" That all the weeke they had their royall pay.

" Now for the fruits then : Flow forth precious spring

" So long and dearely sought for, and now bring

" Comfort to all that love thee : loudly sing,

" And with thy chrystal murmurs strook together,

" Bid all thy true *wel wishers* welcome hither.

" At which words the flood gates flew open, the streame ranne gal-
" lantly into the cisterne, drummes and trumpets sounding in tri-
" umphall manner, and a brave peale of chambers gave full issue to
" the intended entertainment [1]."

---

[1] Stow's Survey, p. 13.   A print of letting the water into the basin was published, and a poem, called " THE NEW RIVER," 8vo, *sans date*, was written by

$O$ne of the most difficult parts of the work now remained to be accomplished, which was to convey the water to the various parts of the metropolis. The expence attending this was very great, and it was a considerable time before the water came into general use; but this being effected, it has been of unspeakable benefit to the City and its immediate neighbourhood, since, by the water supplied from this river, a speedy stop has been put to a great number of alarming fires, and the health of the metropolis has been remarkably preserved, by the cleanliness it has introduced, not only in the streets, but into the

William Garbot; *Brit. Topog.* vol. I. p. 428. The bringing this river to London is said to have cost £.500,000; *Entick's London*, vol. II. p. 112. In Goldsmiths' hall there is an original portrait of Sir Hugh Middleton, to which Company he belonged, and to which he bequeathed a share in the New River towards the relief of its poor members.

On a small isle formed by the stream that supplies the river at *Amwell*, a tribute of respectful homage has been paid by Robert Mylne, Esq. to the genius and patriotism of Sir Hugh Middleton. It consists of a votive urn, erected on a monumental pedestal of Portland stone, which is surrounded by a close thicket of mournful trees and evergreens. An inscription is engraven on each side of the pedestal; that on the South is as follows:

" Sacred to the memory of
" Sir Hugh Mydelton, Baronet,
" whose successful care,
" assisted by the patronage of his King,
" conveyed this stream to LONDON;
" an immortal work.
" Since man cannot more nearly
" imitate the Deity,
" than in bestowing health."

The inscription on the North side is a Latin translation of the above: that on the West records the distance of *Chadwell*, the other source of the New River, at two miles, and the meanders of the river from Amwell to London at 40 more: the East side records the dedication of this "humble tribute to the genius, talents, and ele-" vation of mind, which conceived and executed this important aqueduct, by " Robert Mylne, architect, engineer, &c." in the year MDCCC.

dwellings.　Yet so little were the great advantages that are now derived from this river, at that time, understood, that the shares continued to be of very small value, and for the first 19 years after the finishing of the work the annual profit upon each scarcely amounted to 12 *shillings!*

When the New River was first brought to London, it was not foreseen that a deficiency of water might at some future time, especially in the summer months, be attended with great inconvenience.　When this was learnt from experience, the Company borrowed from the overplus of the mill stream of the River Lea; which, after a practice of some years, became a subject of litigation, finally determined by an Act of Parliament about the year 1738.　It was then agreed that the New River Company, on condition of their paying a sum of money towards improving the navigation of the River Lea, and continuing to pay an annuity for the same purpose, should have a certain quantity of water [1] from the mill stream, to be measured by a balance engine and guage, then constructed near *Hertford*, and rebuilt by Mr. Mylne about the year 1770.　The Company have since bought the mill, with the unrestricted use of the water.

By an exact mensuration of the course of the New River, taken by Henry Mill, Engineer and Surveyor to the Company in 1723, it appeared to be 38 miles three quarters and 16 poles in length [2] : it has between 2 and 300 bridges over it, and upwards of 40 sluices in its course, and in divers parts, both over and under the same, considerable currents of land waters, as well as a great number of brooks and

---

[1] An anecdote is recorded of the good bargain made upon this occasion by the engineer of the New River Company, who, after having agreed with the proprietors of the lands in the River Lea, for a cut of two feet of water from that river, at a certain rate, persuaded them to take double the price for a four foot cut, to which the other party assented, not considering, that by such an agreement, the Company, instead of *double*, would receive at least a *quadruple* supply. *London and Environs*, vol. V. p. 40.

[2] Maitland's London.

rivulets, have their passage. From the place where it first enters this parish, beyond Highbury, it pursues a winding course into the parish of Stoke Newington; from thence, crossing the green lanes, it continues to intersect the grounds at some distance from the back of Highbury Grove [1], and through Canonbury fields, to the *Thatched House,* in the Lower-street, whence it proceeds, by a subterraneous passage of about 200 yards in length under the highway, to Cole-brooke-row. At this place it emerges, and passing in front of the houses, continues through the lower part of this manor, and across the City-road, to the reservoir by Sadler's Wells. On approaching the reservoir, there are several small houses erected at a considerable distance from each other on its banks, having cisterns underneath, into which the water runs, and is conveyed by pipes to the adjacent houses, and the more easterly parts of the Metropolis.

The reservoir called *The New River Head* is a circular bason, now thrice its original size, inclosed with a brick wall, whence the water is conveyed by sluices into various large cisterns of brick-work, from which it passes in a subdivided state by means of large wooden pipes, of six or seven inches bore (called mains and riders, and distinguished by names appropriated to their several districts), to all parts of the Metropolis. The distribution of the water from these pipes to the numerous houses which are supplied by it, exhibits a very wonderful system of hydraulics [2].

---

[1] This part of the river is much resorted to in the summer season by persons from London, and others, for the purpose of bathing, a practice which the New River Company and the Magistrates, at the instigation of the neighbouring inhabitants, have endeavoured to put a stop to, but without effect.

[2] In Hughson's History of London, vol. VI. p. 358, is a copy of a lease for 21 years granted in 1616, by *Hugh Myddelton,* to a Citizen and his wife, of a pipe or quill of half an inch bore, for the service of their " *yarde and kitchnie,*" by means of " *tooe* of the smallest swan necked cockes," in consideration of 26s. 8d. and the like sum to be paid yearly.

At the River head are two steam-engines, and a water wheel (the latter turned by the waste water flowing downward to a pond in the Spa-fields), for the purpose of raising the water to a reservoir upon higher ground at Pentonville, called *The Upper Pond*, and which was formerly effected by a windmill, long since removed[1]. From this pond, another of considerable magnitude, near the end of Tottenham-court-road is also supplied, and from which water is conveyed to many parts of the West end of the town, even to Mary-le-bone, &c.—In a field, to the West of the River head, is an iron pipe, 12 feet in height (including a wooden tub placed on its top), and four feet eight inches in circumference, erected on a great main of pipes of the same dimensions. It acts in the double capacity of an air and a waste water pipe, and is very useful in preventing accidents to the pipes, occasioned by the force of water, or compressed air, which before this preventive was very frequent. In the same field is another reservoir, supplied by one main from the New River Head, and which serves the pipes in Pentonville, and its vicinity.

By means of the steam-engine the water has also been lately conveyed over the higher parts of Islington, through a series of main pipes to *Holloway*, for the purpose of supplying that neighbourhood. An auxiliary bason has been lately formed near the River head, abutting on the St. John-street-road, and the Company has been at very great expence in substituting, in many places, main pipes of cast iron of 19 inches in diameter, for the wooden ones before used: a long chain of these has lately been laid down the City-road, from which other pipes branch off in several directions.

At the River head is a house belonging to the Company, origi-

---

[1] The lower part of this windmill is represented in one of a set of prints, published in 1731, called " Divers Views of Noted Places near London," and which is mentioned by Mr. Gough as very rare to be met with. The said book contains eight views at Islington. Vide *British Topography*.

Sir Hugh Myddelton.

*W. Hollar delin: et sculp: 1665.*  By Iflington.

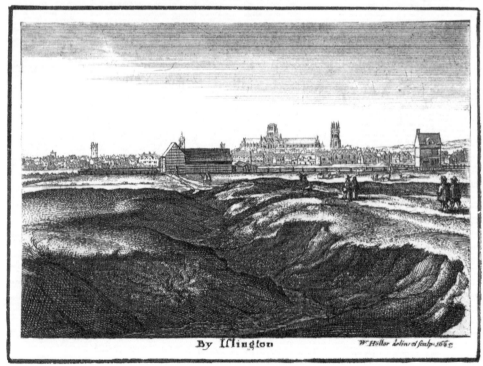

By Iflington  *W Hollar delin et sculp: 1665.*

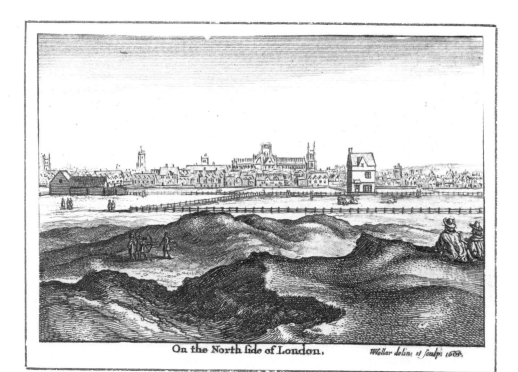

On the North fide of London.  Wßollar delin: et ßculpß 1665.

Waterhoufe by Iflington.  Wß Hollar delin: et ßculpß 1665.

Sould 🙵 by Iohn Ouerton     yͤ Waterhouſe,     Wͦ Hollar fecit 1665.

by the Waterhouſe     Wͦ Hollar delin: et ſculpt: 1665.

nally built in 1613 [1], and repaired and new fronted in 1782, under the direction of Robert Mylne [2], Esq. surveyor and engineer to the Company, who resides here. A large room in this house, with wainscot pannels, was fitted up for the meetings of the Company before the beginning of the last century. On the cieling is a portrait of King William, and the arms of Middleton [3] and Green. Under this room is one of the cisterns before mentioned.

The property of the New River is divided into 72 shares, which division took place soon after the commencement of the undertaking : 36 of these were originally vested in Sir Hugh Middleton, the first projector, who having impoverished himself and his family [4] by a concern which has proved so beneficial to the public as to render his name ever honoured and respected, was obliged to part with his property in the undertaking, which was divided among various persons.

[1] Hollar engraved, in 1665, a set of prints (about five inches by three), consisting of six views at *Islington*, two of " *The Water House*," and four in its vicinity. Three of these contain a distant prospect of the City, taken from this spot, including the cathedral church of St. Paul, &c.

[2] The architect who furnished the design, and superintended the building of Blackfriars bridge, in the year 1760.

[3] Or, on a pile Vert three wolves heads of the field.

[4] Lady Middleton, the mother of the last Sir Hugh Middleton, actually received a pension of £.20 *per annum* from the Goldsmiths' Company, which after her death was, at the solicitation of Mr. Harvey, of Chigwell, in Essex, continued to her son Sir Hugh, but who was in possession of other property. He afforded a melancholy proof of a fact, the truth of which we have too frequent evidence of, namely, that a man may convey his blood, but not his brains, to his posterity. All his employment, and all his amusement, consisted in drinking ale in any company he could pick up. Mr. Harvey took care of him, and put him to board in the house of a sober farmer at or near Chigwell, on whom he could depend; and there he lived, and died, a striking and unhappy contrast to his great ancestor. He was the last heir male of this branch of the family, and with him the title expired. (Gent. Mag. vol. LIV. p. 805.) Some of the family have since been brought to solicit relief from the New River Company, which property owed its existence to the public spirit, and persevering industry of their great progenitor; and a female descendant within these few years obtained an annuity of twenty pounds from the Corporation of London.

These shares are called the Adventurers' shares. The moiety of the undertaking which was vested in the Crown, was by King Charles the First, on account of the then unpromising aspect of the Company's affairs, re-granted to Sir Hugh Middleton, Bart. his heirs and assigns, on condition that they should for ever pay to the King's Receiver General, or into the receipt of the Exchequer, for his Majesty's use, the yearly rent of £.500, which is still paid, and almost entirely out of the King's shares; but the Crown never having had any hand in the management of the concern, the holders of these shares are still excluded from the direction [1].

This great undertaking, which is generally believed to have cost the original proprietors *half a million* sterling, an immense sum in those times, and which was, without doubt, the ruin of its first projector, has risen, by degrees, to be a most valuable and beneficial concern. The Company's charter is dated June 21, 1619 [2]; but no dividend appears to have been made till the year 1633, when the proportionate sum before mentioned, making, together with the dividend for that year, £.15. 3s. 3d. was paid upon each share. At

---

[1] Though King James became a proprietor of one half of the concern, Middleton, to prevent the direction of its affairs from falling into the hands of courtiers, precluded him from having any share in the management, and only allowed him a person to be present at the several meetings, to prevent any injustice to his royal principal. By this preclusion of the holders of the King's shares from the government of the Company, exclusive of their being encumbered with the aforesaid annuity, they are of course not quite so valuable as those of the adventurers. Many of the adventurers' shares being by alienation divided into fractional parts, the Lord Chancellor Cowper, in 1711, decreed, that the possessors of two or more fractional parts of a share may jointly depute a person to represent them in the government of the Company; whereupon every person so deputed becomes capable of being elected one of the 29 representatives of the whole, who are entrusted with the direction of the Company's affairs.

[2] By this charter, Sir Hugh Middleton was appointed the first Governor; Robert Bateman, of London, skinner, Deputy Governor; Rowland Backhouse, of London, mercer, Treasurer; to continue in the said offices till Tuesday next after the feast of All Saints, in 1620: William Lewin was appointed Clerk for life.

this time, however, a call upon the proprietors was expected. The following statement of the dividends that have been since paid at different intervals, will give an idea of the progressive improvement of the concern, and the consequent increase in the value of its shares :

|  | £. | s. | d. |
|---|---|---|---|
| Dividend for the year 1633 | 3 | 4 | 2 |
| 1640 | 33 | 2 | 8 |
| 1680 | 145 | 1 | 8 |
| 1700 | 201 | 16 | 6 |
| 1720 | 214 | 15 | 7 |
| 1794 | 431 | 5 | 8 |

An adventurer's share in the *New River Company* has been sold by public auction for upwards of £.14,000: this, however, was upon occasion of a contest between two parties, each striving to outbid the other. The shares are now considered worth about £.11,500, and the dividends have increased somewhat beyond the sum last above mentioned; but it is probable they have now reached their climax, for the various new Companies of this kind in the environs of the Metropolis, as, the East London, the West Middlesex, and the Holloway Water-works, must inevitably prevent any great extension of the former concern, if not operate much to its disadvantage, in depriving the Company of a considerable portion of the trade they already possess.

The direction is vested in 29 holders of adventurers' shares, who form a board; when a vacancy happens in this number, the remaining 28 elect. The chief officers belonging to the Corporation are, a Governor, Deputy Governor, Treasurer, and Clerk. The present Governor is John Walker, Esq.; the Deputy Governor, Richard Benyon, Esq. M. P.; the Treasurer, Samuel Garnault, Esq.; and the Clerk, John Rowe, Esq.

The business of the Company is transacted at a commodious house, near the river Thames, at the bottom of Dorset-street, Salisbury-square, where the clerk resides. Here is also a spacious wharf for landing timber, and workshops for boring the pipes, &c.

STROUD GREEN,

which lies to the North-west of the situation formerly occupied by *the Boarded River,* is a long piece of common land belonging to the copyholders of Highbury Manor : here stands an old farm house (in Hornsey parish) called *Stapleton Hall,* and which was formerly the property and residence of Sir Thomas Stapleton, of Grey's Court, in the county of Oxon, Bart. an antient family, remarkable for the number of eminent men it has produced. In the building are his initials, with those of his wife, and the date 1609. It was afterwards converted into a publick house, and within memory had in front the following inscription :

" Ye are welcome all
" To Stapleton Hall."

Mr. William Lucas is the present occupier of the house, together with a farm of more than 80 acres of land contiguous thereto.

About 40 years ago there was a Society held at the Queen's Arms Tavern, in Newgate-street, the members of which were accustomed to meet annually at this place in the summer time, to regale themselves on the grass with cakes, ale, &c. They styled themselves " the " Lord Mayor, Aldermen, and Corporation of *Stroud Green;*" and the number of persons that were drawn to the spot on these occasions, produced a scene, similar to that of a country wake or fair; but the practice has been for many years discontinued.

At the top of Duval's-lane is a beautiful eminence, called Mount Pleasant, where stands a boarding school and two gentlemen's houses, enjoying the most delightful and uninterrupted views of the adjacent country, and over the metropolis. In contemplating the beauty of this scene, one cannot help calling to mind that fine exclamation of the Poet, which is not less appropriate to this spot than to many others with which our Island so plentifully abounds.

" Heav'ns ! what a goodly prospect spreads around
" Of hills, and dales, and woods, and lawns, and spires,
" And glittering tow'rs, and gilded streams, 'till all
" The stretching landscape into smoke decays !
" Happy Britannia ! where the Queen of Arts
" Inspiring vigour, Liberty, abroad
" Walks unconfin'd, e'en to thy farthest cots,
" And scatters plenty with unsparing hand."    THOMSON.

In Devil's or *Du Val's* (formerly Tollington) lane, near the end of Heame-lane, is the old moated site before noticed, whereon stands the building which appears, for some centuries, to have obtained the name of *The Devil's House*. In later times, a tradition has prevailed that this was the retreat of the famous *Du Val*, the highwayman, who was executed in the reign of Charles the Second, and that the roads and bye lanes in this neighbourhood, were the frequent scenes of his predatory exploits.

As it is evident from the Survey of 1611 that the house was then called " The Devil's House in Devil's-lane," it is most probable that the name of *Du Val*, by which the place has been for many years more generally called, was afterwards adopted in amendment of the more antient and uncouth term, without any reference to his having resided here, which does not appear from any thing that is left on record, respecting that highly accomplished depredator [1].

[1] The following lines are extracted from " *A Pindaric Ode to the happy Memory* " *of the most renowned Du Val*," written by the ingenious author of Hudibras; and from the nature of the exploits described therein, it would seem not improbable

Between 30 and 40 years ago, the surrounding moat, which was of considerable width, and filled with water, was passed by means of a long wooden bridge. At that time a man named *Fawcett* kept the premises as a public house, and who used to relate the preceding story respecting the etymology of the place. The house, which is chiefly composed of wood, appears from the old chimneys, &c. to be the same that was standing on the spot at the time of the Survey before

that this neighbourhood was laid under contribution by that hero of the road, since it must have afforded as great scope for the exercise of his abilities, as any other round the Metropolis:

> " He, like a lord o' the manor, seiz'd upon
> " Whatever happen'd in his way,
> " As lawful weft and stray,
> " And after, by the custom, kept it as his own.
> " He would have starv'd the mighty town,
> " And brought its haughty spirit down;
> " Have cut it off from all relief;
> " And, like a wise and valiant chief,
> " Made many a fierce assault
> " Upon all ammunition carts,
> " And those that bring up cheese or malt,
> " Or bacon, from remoter parts.
> " No convoy e'er so strong, with food,
> " Durst venture on the desp'rate road;
> " He made th' undaunted waggoner obey,
> " And the fierce higler contribution pay;
> " The savage butcher, and stout drover,
> " Durst not to him their feeble troops discover;
> " And if he had but kept the field,
> " In time had made the City yield.
> " For great towns, like to crocodiles, are found,
> " I' the belly aptest to receive a mortal wound."

" Du Val was executed at Tyburn, Jan. 21, 1669, in his 27th year. —After *lying* " *in state* at the Tangier tavern, in St. Giles's, he was buried in the middle aile of " Covent Garden church: and his funeral was attended with many flambeaux, " and a numerous train of mourners, whereof most were of the beautiful sex."

*Memoirs of Monsieur Du Val,* 4to, 1670.

mentioned; it has lately been fitted up in the modern taste, and the moat nearly filled with earth, and added to the garden which surrounds the dwelling.

The old road through this lane, by way of *Crouch End,* to Whetstone, which in Camden (1695) is mentioned as " *a sloughy lane,*" and which it continued to be till within these few years, has, from a road almost impassable in winter, been converted into a very good public highway at the expence of the parish, and is still receiving further improvements.

## HIGHBURY-PLACE

is one of the finest rows of houses in the environs of the Metropolis : it is inhabited by eminent merchants, and other persons of opulence and respectability. The prospect on both sides is very fine, and the situation remarkably healthy[1]. It consists of 39 houses, built on a large scale, but varying in size; they have all good gardens behind, and allotments of meadow ground in front : to some of the houses there are coach-houses, in a line with the front of the dwellings, others have the same convenience, with stabling, &c. at the back of the premises, to which there is a convenient carriage way extending behind the whole of the houses. The road in front is private, being frequented only by the carriages passing to and from the several dwellings, between the village and Highbury-house.

The ground whereon Highbury-place stands, was the freehold estate of the late John Dawes, Esq. who, from the year 1774 to 1779, granted the same at different times upon building leases, of about 60 years, to Mr. John Spiller, by whom the present houses were all erected. Spiller died at the end house, No. 39, which he had fitted

---

[1] A pair of aquatinta views of Highbury and Canonbury, by F. Jukes, were published about the year 1787.

up for his own residence. The several houses and premises in this place were at first let at very low rents, and it was a considerable time before many of them were occupied; the first tenants of Nos. 2 to 8 inclusive, had leases granted them at from £.34 to £.36 *per annum;* but such is the increased value of the property, that many of the houses here, will now let at thrice the rent paid by the original inhabitants.

The house No. 38 in Highbury-place, was for several years the residence of that old and faithful servant of the publick, ABRAHAM NEWLAND, Esq. Chief Cashier of the Bank of England.

A few of the most prominent traits in the character of this gentleman, whose rise and progress in life, and final settlement in ease and affluence, by his own unremitting industry and unimpeached integrity, may serve as an useful lesson to those who look forward to similar advantages, which they may hope to attain by the like honourable means.

He was the son of William Newland, a baker, of Castle-street, in the parish of St. Mary Overy's, Southwark, where he was born the 23d April, 1730. His education was calculated for the Counting house; and it is related, that at an early age he wrote a fair and legible hand, and shewed great expertness in the application of the rules of arithmetic. He remained with his father till the age of eighteen, when he was appointed a Clerk in the Bank of England, an establishment which afterwards became greatly indebted to his ability and honest integrity, and which the liberality of the persons from time to time concerned in the direction, were not behind hand to appreciate in a proper manner.

It has been said, that, during his early occupations at the Bank, he united, with the profits of his situation, a stipend he derived as organist to one of the churches in the neighbourhood of Southwark; certain it is, he had a great fondness for music, which was his favourite juvenile amusement, but he pursued it merely as an amateur, and towards the latter part of his life he abandoned it altogether.

Pub.d by Ridley from an orig.l Painting by Drummond taken in the 73 Year of his Age

*Abraham Newland, Esq.*

*Chief Cashier,*

OF THE BANK OF ENGLAND.

BANK OF ENGLAND,

Taken by Permission from a Drawing in Possession of J. Soane, Esq.r

NEW THREE PER CENT OFFICE, BANK OF ENGLAND.

At this early period Mr. Newland seems to have been addicted to those gay and irregular pursuits which young men, after the business of the morning is over, being unrestrained by domestic society, and left to their own disposal for the remainder of the day, are too frequently led into.   The play-houses, the opera, concerts, and other fashionable amusements, were now his predominant delight : however, it does not seem that his business was ever neglected, and he appears to have risen by regular gradation in the establishment till January, 1782, when he was appointed Chief Cashier, with a liberal salary annexed to the situation.

In this respectable office he continued, fulfilling the highest duties of the institution, both receiving and inspiring general confidence, until the day of his resignation.   When he was nominated Chief Cashier, the accommodations in the Bank being enlarged, a suite of rooms was devoted to the reception of this principal servant of the establishment ; and so much attached was he to his employment, and so punctually did he acquit himself in relation to it, that for twenty-five years, during which he was engaged, he never slept a single night out of the building.

His mind seemed totally absorbed in the duties of his office, and he appeared only to exist for the service of the Bank ; nay, he has been known to declare that he derived more happiness from a single hour's attendance on the duties of his office, than from a whole day spent in the most convivial and entertaining company.   Indeed, the services he rendered to the concern were of the most important and essential nature; for as the Company of Directors, however great their wisdom and experience, could only be considered as a fluctuating body, and the benefit arising from their deliberations necessarily limited, and requiring a proper agent to put them into execution ; Mr. Newland (whose long and laborious life was devoted to the interests of this great national establishment) was the man always looked up to : in every matter of importance he was consulted as the senior of the

A A

institution, and his opinion in some doubtful questions has been decisive.

Upon the Directors of the Bank ceasing to pay the amount of their notes in specie, by virtue of an Order of the Privy Council in February 1797, Mr. Newland rendered great service to the publick and to government, in the information he afforded as to the circumstances which led to that measure, and the multifarious concerns of the Bank, its money transactions with the Government, &c. For this purpose he underwent an examination before a Committee of the House of Lords in the month of March; when by his replies, wherein he stated himself to be " Chief Cashier and Superintendant of many other departments" in the Bank of England a most distinct and comprehensive view was given of the concerns of the Company, at that critical period. By means of the examinations that were made on this occasion the affairs of the Bank were fully disclosed, and the information was principally derived from. Mr. Newland, and the departments under his immediate controul and superintendance.

A circumstance occurred in the year 1803, which tended much to embitter the declining years of Mr. Newland's life. A person of the name of Aslett, a Clerk in the Bank, had, by his assiduity and attention to business for a series of years, so recommended himself to the notice and patronage of the Chief Cashier, that by his means he had attained to one of the highest situations in the establishment, and would ultimately have succeeded him in that office : it was indeed reported, though probably without any foundation, that this person was the natural son of Mr. Newland, and the patronage afforded him was ascribed to this near and tender relation. For this man Mr. Newland had contracted a particular friendship and regard, and would, in all probability, (if he had not been prevented by his subsequent misconduct,) have continued his patron through life, and left him the bulk of his fortune at his decease ; but such is too often the blindness of mankind to their own best interests, that this person was led to the commission of a crime, which, though it was not followed by an ignominious death, has consigned the remainder of his life to indelible infamy and disgrace.

On the 8th of July in this year the said Robert Aslett was indicted for feloniously secreting and embezzling Exchequer Bills to the amount of several thousand pounds, belonging to the Governor and Company of the Bank. Upon this trial he was acquitted on a point of law, by reason of an informality upon the face of the bills so embezzled: however, in the September Sessions following, being charged upon another indictment, the Jury found the prisoner guilty of the fact, and the point of law as to the validity of the bills stolen was reserved for the opinion of the Judges [1]. Aslett yet remains a prisoner in Newgate; and the shock given to his patron by a developement of this base transaction was felt by him to the last hour of his life, and, as it is generally believed, tended to accelerate his end.

Long before this period Mr. Newland had acquired an ample fortune. His wealth was to be attributed both to the rigid economy of his habits, and to some successful speculations; but, although he was saving, he possessed none of the qualities of the miser; yet, as is too frequently the case with our wealthy citizens and others, his liberality was confined to his own house; and there are few instances to be recorded of his public bounty or munificence.

It has been observed, that at a certain period of life men both acquire and retain singular habits, either of regularity or dissipation. At 15 minutes past nine o'clock in the morning, Mr. Newland was seen constantly at his desk, and was never absent from his duty until three in the afternoon. Though he possessed a handsome house, in a fine situation, and the surrounding neighbourhood most pleasant and inviting, he never enjoyed the pleasures it afforded for many

---

[1] At the following half yearly meeting of the proprietors of Bank Stock, the Chairman stated the loss of the Company, by the depredations of Aslett, to amount to £.320,000.

hours at a time; for, while he retained his situation in the Bank, he constantly slept at his apartments in that building. His usual practice was to repair to Highbury, in his carriage, after dinner; drink tea with his housekeeper; and afterwards perambulate the path along the front of the houses, or take a walk on the gravel way leading to Highbury-barn; returning, invariably, to London in the evening to sleep.

Notwithstanding Mr. Newland's habitual parsimony and retired habits, it is said, that, some time previous to his death, he projected a plan by which he would have abandoned both the one and the other: his domestic establishment was to be raised to £.4,000 a year, and £.2,000 a year he intended to devote to the purposes of extraordinary gratification, of which the exercise of his bounty would have formed no inconsiderable portion. This plan was never adopted; the infirmities of age were hastening fast upon him, and he felt himself ill qualified, under their pressure, to change the direction of his habits.

Had he adopted this plan of life somewhat earlier, it would have been consistent with true wisdom, directed to the important consideration of the means of his own happiness; adopting the resolution at the time he did, brings to mind the story of *Mercator*, in the 102d Number of The Adventurer: " I was envied; but how little can " one man judge of the condition of another! The time was now " coming, in which affluence and splendour could no longer make me " pleased with myself; I had built till the imagination of the architect " was exhausted; I had added one convenience to another, till I " knew not what more to wish or to design; I had laid out my gar- " dens, planted my park, and completed my waterworks; and what " now remained to be done? What, but to look up to turrets, of " which, when they were once raised, I had no further use; to range " over apartments, where time was tarnishing the furniture; to stand " by the cascade, of which I scarcely now perceived the sound; and " to watch the growth of woods, that must give their shade to a " distant generation.

" In this gloomy inactivity is every day begun and ended: the hap-
" piness that I had been so long procuring is now at an end, because
" it has been procured; I wander from room to room till I am weary
" of myself; I ride out to a neighbouring hill in the centre of my
" estate, from whence all my lands lie in prospect round me; I see
" nothing that I have not seen before, and return home disappointed,
" though I knew that I had nothing to expect."

Mr. Newland did not adventure so much in the Stocks as was generally supposed, nor was it by these means that the principal part of
his property was obtained; it was by participating in shares of loans
to the Government, that was the principal source of his wealth, and
which, from the nature of his situation, he could speculate in upon
pretty safe grounds. He was remarkably correct in the expenditure
of his family, and his example in this respect is worthy of being followed. Before the close of every day, the books of account of his
domestic transactions were entered; and the receipts and expences of
each day were regularly and methodically assigned to their proper
places.

After a constant and faithful discharge of his official duties at
the Bank for nearly sixty years, Mr. N. was induced to resign his
situation there, on the 17th of September, 1807, by reason of the infirmities of age; upon this occasion he declined taking an annuity which
was offered him by the Governor and Company, but agreed to accept of
a service of plate, value 1000 guineas. This was a tribute of respect
and acknowledgment for his long and faithful services, and a similar
motive induced them some years before, to have his portrait painted,
which is hung up in one of their principal rooms.

Scarcely had Mr. Newland quitted the situation which he had held
with so much advantage to his fortune, and satisfaction to the public,
for so long a series of years, and before he was put in possession of
the valuable present that was to bear testimony to his deserving conduct; when his mortal career was arrested by the hand of death. He
declined gradually in health from the time of his leaving the Bank,

and departed this life, at Highbury, on the 21st of November, 1807. On the 28th his remains, inclosed in a coffin covered with black velvet, were removed to the parish church of St. Saviour, Southwark, where they were interred, in the Bishop's vault, by the side of his father and sister [1].

Mr. Newland was never married; but had, several years previous to his death, received into his family a lady of the name of Cornthwaite, whose kindness and assiduity relieved him from every domestic trouble, and with whom a near friendship was cemented, which conduced greatly to the comfort and enjoyment of his declining years. His gratitude for her kindness he expressed in his will, by leaving to her (in addition to a handsome legacy) his carriage, furniture, and establishment, and an income from £.60,000 in the stocks, to support her in a respectable independence. His property at the time of his decease amounted to upwards of £.130,000, which he chiefly bequeathed among his relatives, who were, for the most part, in necessitous circumstances.

He was of the middle stature, somewhat athletic in form, of pleasing features and a cheerful aspect; he was sincere in his friendships, and a game at cards and free unreserved communication with a few intimates were among the principal pleasures of his simple life; he possessed naturally high spirits, and was a lively and entertaining companion. His judgment in affairs of business was accurate, his apprehension quick, and his memory remarkably tenacious. In cursory conversation he had an unusual steadiness of attention, and was fond of disputation, even perhaps to a fault. In his politics he was what is familiarly called *a King's Man;* adhering to the Court party invariably, under every change of administration, rather from attachment to the reigning Prince than

[1] The funeral was conducted by Mr. Powell, an eminent undertaker, and many years parish-clerk of Islington. He was the inventor of the original design for a state car, for the funeral of the late Admiral Lord Nelson, and of which he published an engraving.

from any uniform approbation of the measures of the servants of the Crown. It is much to be lamented, that the religious opinions of Mr. Newland were, with too much reason, suspected to be of a very dangerous and Antichristian tendency. Such is, unhappily, too often the case with those, who, like him, are so much absorbed in the affairs of the world, and so intent on its pursuits, that their more serious concerns are excluded from that attention and reflection which they so pre-eminently demand, and which would infallibly lead to a proper estimation of the character of the Deity, and the important duties of our holy religion.

A very excellent likeness of Mr. Newland at the latter part of his life is contained in the European Magazine for January 1803; and a mezzotinto engraving, by Grozer, from his picture in the Bank, exhibits his resemblance at an earlier period [1].

[1] The celebrity which the subject of the above biographical sketch obtained, from his name forming a most prominent feature in the paper currency of the day, gave rise to the following humorous and satirical song from the pen of the ingenious Mr. C. Dibdin, jun. Manager of the Sadler's Wells Theatre:

" There ne'er was a name so bandied by fame,
   " Thro' air, thro' ocean, and thro' land,
" As one that is wrote upon every bank note,
   " You all must know *Abraham Newland.*
      " Oh! Abraham Newland,
      " Notified Abraham Newland!
" I 've heard people say, ' sham Abraham' you may,
" But you musn't sham *Abraham Newland.*

" For Fashion or Arts should you seek foreign parts,
   " It matters not wherever you land,
" Jew, Christian, or Greek, the same language they speak,
   " That's the language of *Abraham Newland.*
      " Oh! Abraham Newland,
      " Wonderful Abraham Newland!
" Tho' with compliments cramm'd,
" You may die and be d—n'd,
" If you hav'n't an *Abraham Newland.*

### HIGHBURY-TERRACE

is situate upon an elevated spot to the North-west of Highbury-place, and consists of 22 houses of different sizes, which were built by several individuals about the year 1789. It is chiefly inhabited by merchants, and persons connected with the City. From hence in a clear day is a very commanding view to the Eastward, embracing Limehouse Church, Greenwich Hospital and Park, and the vessels

" The world is inclin'd to think Justice is blind,
    " But Lawyers know well she can view land ;
" But, Lord, what of that—she 'll blink like a bat,
    " At the sight of an *Abraham Newland !*
        " Oh! Abraham Newland,
        " Magical Abraham Newland !
" Tho' Justice, 'tis known, can see through a mill stone,
" She can't see through *Abraham Newland.*

" You Patriots who bawl, for the good of us all,
    " Kind souls! here like mushrooms they strew land,
" Tho' loud as they drum, each proves Orator Mum,
    " If attack'd by stout *Abraham Newland.*
        " Oh! Abraham Newland,
        " Invincible Abraham Newland!
" No argument's found, in the world half so sound,
" As the logic of *Abraham Newland.*

" If a maid of three score, or a dozen years more,
    " For a husband should chance to sigh thro' land,
" I 'm vastly afraid, she would not die a maid,
    " If acquainted with *Abraham Newland.*
        " Oh! Abraham Newland,
        " Deluding Abraham Newland !
" Tho' crooked and cross, she 'd not be at a loss,
" Thro' the friendship of Abraham Newland.

navigating the river Thames [1].    Between the Terrace and Highbury House are two detached dwellings, finely situated in the midst of spacious gardens, shrubberies, &c.    On digging a well in the ground attached to one of these houses some years since, at the depth of more than 100 feet, a large *stratum* of marine shells was discovered, which on being cut through, in order to procure water, was found to be of great thickness, and many cart loads were excavated and carried from the place.

In the Grove, which runs between the back of Highbury Place and the New River, and is the public coach road to the tavern and the new buildings in the Upper Grove, there stood a Chapel, in which service was performed for some years, but which was superseded on the building Union Chapel on Compton Terrace.    It has lately been converted into a dwelling house.

> " The French say, they 're coming, O sure they 're a humming,
>    " We know what they want if they do land,
> " But we 'll make their ears ring, in defence of our king,
>    " Our country and *Abraham Newland.*
>        " Oh! Abraham Newland!
>        " Useful Abraham Newland!" &c.

[1] This place is the residence of Joseph Huddart, Esq. F. R. S. an elder brother of the Honourable Corporation of the Trinity house, and a gentleman of very considerable mechanical and nautical abilities.    He was formerly a Captain in the East India Company's service, and is the inventor of an improved method of making cables and ropes for shipping, for which purpose he has an extensive manufactory at Limehouse.    A very fine portrait of Captain Huddart, engraved by Stow, from a painting of Hoppner, is prefixed to a quarto volume intituled " *The Oriental Navigator,*" published by Laurie and Whittle, in which work he rendered great assistance to the publishers, as also in a Survey of St. George's Channel, and several other valuable publications on navigation and seamanship.

## NEWINGTON GREEN.

Newington Green forms a square of respectable houses, chiefly inhabited by Gentlemen and Merchants: three sides of the square,
with the inclosed ground in the centre, are in this parish, the North
side being in that of Stoke Newington[1].    On the South side of
the Green are the remains of an old house, now converted into two,
one of which is called "*Mildmay House Boarding School*," and is
kept by Mrs. Moate.    In the Survey A. D. 1611, William Halliday,
Alderman and Mercer of London, held these premises, with orchard,
&c. and a piece of pasture ground behind, called "*The Park*," en-

[1] On this side of the Green is a meeting-house of Protestant Dissenters of the
Presbyterian denomination, built in the year 1708.  Among the ministers of this
place have been several very eminent for their learning and abilities, as Hugh
Worthington, M. A. Dr. Amory, Dr. Price, Dr. Towers, &c.  Mr. Barbauld, husband of the celebrated literary Lady of that name, was late minister there, and
is succeeded by the Rev. Mr. Rees.  Several of the ejected and silenced ministers
were inhabitants of Newington Green towards the close of the seventeenth century.
Among these were the Rev. Luke Milbourn, M. A. whose wife kept a school, by which
she supported herself and her husband, he not being suffered to teach.  Charles
Morton, M. A. ejected from his Rectory of Blisland, Cornwall, kept an academy
here, "where some scores of young ministers were educated by him, as well as
"many other good scholars."  Among his Works are, "*The Gaming Humour con-
"sidered and improved.*"  "*Of Common Place or Memorial Books.*"  "*A Discourse
"on improving the County of Cornwall.*"  "*Considerations on the New River,*" and
several other Treatises, all compendious, he being an enemy to large volumes, and
often saying, "*A great book is a great evil.*"  Mr. Jonathan Grew, of Pembroke
Hall, Cambridge, was engaged for some time in a school here; and the Rev. Mr.
Starkey, of St. John's College, in the same University, spent the latter part of
his life here, where he lived beloved, and died lamented. (Nonconformists' Memorial.)  Anthony Wood in his Athenæ Oxonienses is extremely illiberal and unjust
in his remarks on the characters of most of these eminently pious and worthy men.

NEWINGTON GREEN MEETING HOUSE.
Built 1708.

F.W.L. Stockdale del.                                              Frances Hawksworth sculp.

Old House at Newington Green.

To Jonathan Eade Esq.º of Stoke Newington.
This Engraving is Respectfully inscribed by his much obliged & Obedient Servant   J. Nelson
Published May 1. 1811 by Russell Upper Street Islington.

vironed with pale and quickset, containing 44 acres, and which extended South almost as far as Ball's Pond.

Sir Henry Mildmay (to whom the Parliament granted the woods at Highbury as before mentioned) and who was one of the Judges on the trial of King Charles [1], afterwards became possessed of this estate by marrying the daughter and heir of Alderman Halliday. His estates were forfeited at the Restoration; but this at Newington Green having been settled on his wife, as being her own inheritance, it continued in the family, and is now the property of Sir Henry St. John Mildmay, Bart.

The first floor of this house, in that part which forms the boarding-school, is handsomely wainscotted, with oak : in the school-room is a carved chimney piece of the same wood, having in the centre a shield bearing three esquires' helmets, the arms of Halliday. The cieling, which is wrought in stucco, contains the arms of England, with I. R. the initials of King James, and medallions of Hector, Alexander, &c. The other part of the building, comprising the adjoining house, is similarly ornamented with pannelled wainscot, and has a chimney piece with carved figures, and other decorations, the whole of which in both houses are covered with white paint.

Another large old house was till within these few years standing at the North-west corner of the Green (see Plate IV.), the site of which is now covered by two handsome modern dwellings. It was a quadrangular building, composed chiefly of wood and plaster, having a square court in the centre, and communication to the various apartments all round, by means of small doors opening from one room to another. The premises had been for many years divided into a number of small tenements occupied by poor people, and was called *Bishop's-*

[1] It is a singular circumstance that Sir Henry Mildmay sat in judgment on the King, whilst his brother Anthony was so devoted to that unfortunate and misguided monarch, that he attended his execution as a confidential servant, and was one of those who superintended the interment of his remains at Windsor. *Kimber's Baronetage*, vol. III. p. 215.

*place.*  On its being pulled down, some parts of the old oak wainscoat were found to be richly gilt, and adorned with paintings, but they were almost entirely obliterated from the effects of time.

Tradition throughout the neighbourhood strongly affirms both these houses to have been in the occupation of our capricious monarch, Henry the Eighth, and that this building, wherein he is said to have kept a number of concubines as in a seraglio, was the scene of his illicit amours, whilst the other was appropriated to his occasional residence.  The appearance of the house last described when standing, was certainly indicative of great antiquity, being literally falling to the ground from the gradual operations of time; but as the other, from what remains of it, appears to have been erected by Alderman Halliday, it is probable the tradition refers to a more antient house standing upon the same site; the building represented in the plate may, however, with greater probability be imagined to have been the occasional resort or temporary residence of the King.

There is further reason to believe that this tradition is not wholly void of foundation, inasmuch as this neighbourhood seems to have been a favourite spot with some of the Nobility about that period.  A branch of the family of Dudley, Earl of Warwick, possessed the neighbouring Manor of Stoke Newington; and the following letter of Henry Algernon Percy, Earl of Northumberland *(temp. Henry VIII.)* dated " at Newington Greene," it is very probable was indited at the antient house last described.  This letter was written to the Lord Cromwell, Secretary of State, to exculpate the writer from the pretended suspicions of Henry in regard to a matrimonial contract supposed to have been made between the Earl and Ann Boyleyn, previous to her marriage with the King.

" MASTER SECRETARY,

" This shall be to signify unto you, that I perceive, by " Sir Raynold Carnaby, that there is supposed a pre-contract to bee " betweene the Queene and me.  Whereupon I was not only hereto-

" fore examined, upon mine oath, before the Archbishops of Canter-
" bury and Yorke, but allso received the Blessed Sacrament upon the
" same, before the Duke of Norfolk and other the King's Highness
" Council, learned in the Spiritual Law; assuring you, Mr. Secre-
" tary, by the said oath and blessed body, which afore I received, and
" hereafter intend to receive, that the same may be my *damnation* if
" ever there were any contract or promisse of marriage between her
" and me. At Newington Greene, the 13th day of May, in the 28th
" year of the reign of our Sovereign Lorde King Henry VIIIth.

" Your assured,

" H. Northumberland [1]."

This Earl of Northumberland, who died the following year at
Hackney [2], (whither it is probable he removed from Newington
Green,) is said to have " prodigally given away a great part of his
lands and inheritance *to the King and others* [3]," which, indeed, is
evident from letters of his own writing, still extant; it is therefore
not unlikely that in this manner one or both of these houses might
come into His Majesty's possession.

A very old inhabitant of the Green recollects, that more than half
a century ago, when some of the present houses were erected, several
vestiges of other antient dwellings of considerable magnitude were removed; and the tradition of Henry's resorting to this place is further
supported by the circumstance of a very pleasant path, which winds
from the South-east corner of the Green to the turnpike road by Ball's
Pond, having been called, time immemorial, by the name of " *King*
" *Harrys' Walk* [4]."

---

[1] Collins's Peerage, vol. II. p. 393.

[2] His epitaph in Hackney Church, where he was buried, may be seen in *Weever's
Funeral Monuments*.

[3] Nichols's History of Canonbury, p. 9.

[4] Vide Old Plan of Islington, plate I.

Mr. Samuel Wright, an inhabitant of Newington Green, who died towards the middle of the last century, and who held considerable estates in Leicestershire, and other counties, is entitled to some notice in this place, on account of the charitable distribution made by him of his great wealth at the time of his decease. He gave by his will[1] upwards of £.13,000, besides landed property, to his several relations and friends, and the following sums to charitable uses ; viz.

£.

Item. To six Nonconformist Ministers, of good life and conversation, and not worth £.200 each in the world, each £.100 - - - - - - - - - - - - - - - - - - - - - - - - - - - - 600

Item. To six honest sober Clergymen, of temper and moderate charitable principles to their dissenting brethren, and not worth £.200 a year each, or provided with a living of upwards of £.40 a year, each £.100 - - - - - - - - - - - - - 600

Item. To 40 poor decayed families that have come to poverty purely by losses and misfortunes unavoidable, each £.100 - - - - - - - - - - - - - - - - - - - - - - - - - - - - 4,000

Item. To 40 poor widows, of upwards of 50 years, and not worth £.50 any one of them, each £.50 - - - - - - - - - 2,000

Item. To 40 poor maidens, whose parents formerly lived well, and now come to decay, and have not £.100 each to their portion, each £.100 - - - - - - - - - - - - - - - - - 4,000

Item. To clothe, and put out apprentice 20 poor boys, £.50 each- - - - - - - - - - - - - - - - - - - - - - - - - - 1,000

Item. To the Society for the Reformation of Manners - - - 500

Item. To the Society for propagating the Gospel in Foreign Parts - - - - - - - - - - - - - - - - - - - - - - - - - - 500

Item. To Christ Church Hospital- - - - - - - - - - - - 1,000

Item. To St. Thomas's Hospital - - - - - - - - - - - - 1,000

[1] Printed in Mr. Nichols's History of Leicestershire, vol. II. part II. p. 706.

|  | £. |
|---|---|
| Item. To Bethlehem Hospital- - - - - - - - - - - - - - | 1,000 |
| Item. To the London Workhouse - - - - - - - - - - - - | 1,000 |
| Item. To the prisoners in Ludgate prison - - - - - - - - | 500 |
| Item. To the prisoners in the Fleet prison - - - - - - - - | 400 |
| Item. To the prisoners in the Marshalsea - - - - - - - - | 300 |
| Item. To the prisoners in Whitechapel prison - - - - - - | 300 |
| Item. To the poor at Great Paxton, Lubbenham (co. Leicester), Islington, and Bow (Middlesex), and St. Alphege London, each parish £.50 - - - - - - - - - - - - - - - - | 250 |
|  | Total - - - - 18,950 |

The residue of his personal estate he bequeathed to the widows and orphans of Nonconformist Ministers.

## BALL'S POND

was formerly a spot famous for the exercise of bull-baiting, and other brutal sports ; and therefore much resorted to by the lower order of people from all parts of the Metropolis.  It appears to have derived its name from JOHN BALL, who kept a house of entertainment here about the middle of the seventeenth century, having for its sign *The Salutation*, as displayed on the token issued by him (see Plate V. fig. 3.)[1], with the following inscription : " *John Ball, at the Boarded* " *House neere Newington Green.*"   A large pond, which remained here till within these few years, was, perhaps, at that time frequented

[1] Two other tokens issued by trades-people in this parish are given in the same Plate (fig. 7 and 8), viz. Joane Kettle, at the sign of the three globes in Islington, 1667 ; and Robert Pe . . . . . . . in Islington, confectioner, 1667.   Another token of ——— Fosbrook, Holloway, having on the reverse a man with a coursing-pole, followed by two greyhounds (probably representing the *Green Man)*, was found by the sexton some years since in the new burying-ground.

by *duck-hunters*, &c. and by them coupled with the name of their host.   At this place is a nursery-ground, containing about 12 acres, in the occupation of Mr. Barr.   In the Survey of 1611 this piece of land is called " *The Hopping*," and was at that time the freehold of Lord Compton.

The road leading from the Lower-street, Islington, to Ball's Pond, which before went in a curved line by the bank on the East side, as it appears in Baker's plan, was, in May 1800, thrown into its present course by order of the Highgate and Hampstead trust.

### KINGSLAND HOSPITAL AND CHAPEL.

The foundation of a house for persons afflicted with the leprosy[1] at Kingsland appears to be of considerable antiquity.   So early as the year 1437, John Pope, citizen and barber, by his will gave to " the " Master and Governors of the House of Lepers, called *Le Lokes*[2],

[1] This disorder has been properly termed the *lack-linen disease*, as it certainly was engendered by the want of that most clean and necessary article of apparel, and the consequent wearing of woollen; to which must be added the want of attention to what in the East is made an article of religion, namely ablution, both personal and domestic.   Lazar-houses, or hospitals for lepers, were in antient times established in every suburb of the Metropolis, at Whitehall, Kingsland, London-wall, Clerkenwell, on the sites of Dufour's-place and St. James's palace, in Tothil-fields, Lambeth Marsh, Bermondsey, &c.; and perhaps, from the circumstances already mentioned, no establishments were more necessary.   *Moser's Vestiges, Europ. Mag.* vol. LI. p. 331.

[2] Some have derived this term from *loques*, an obsolete French word, signifying *rags*; but more probably it comes from the Saxon word *Loc* or *Loke*, which implies shut close, or confined, perhaps alluding to the restraint under which the patients were kept in these houses, and which, from the nature of their disease, was, without doubt, absolutely necessary.   Stow calls a similar house (the chapel appertaining to which is yet remaining at the end of Kent-street) the *Loke*, from whence we have the modern term *Lock*, as applied to hospitals of a particular class, by which name the hospital at Kingsland was afterwards called, and which is synonymous with a *spittle*, or *lazar-house*.

" at Kingeslond without London, an annual rent of 6s. 8d. issuing
" out of certain shops situate in Shirborne-lane, toward the sustenta-
" tion of the said house at Kingeslond, for ever [1]."

It appears from the records of St. Bartholomew's Hospital in
London, that soon after the foundation and endowment of that charity in the reign of Henry VIII. certain lock or lazar hospitals were
opened for the reception of persons afflicted with the venereal disease
at a distance from the City, to which places they were sent by the
governors, and thus kept apart from the other patients, the disorder
being in those times considered as contagious, wherefore they were
removed entirely from the capital. Each of these houses was under
the care of a surgeon, a chaplain, and a sister, a nurse, and helper,
and each contained about 20 beds [2].

The Lock Hospital [3] at Kingsland was one of these receptacles,
and appears to have superseded the old " House of Lepers" before mentioned. The Governors of St. Bartholomew's afterwards
erected a more commodious edifice of brick on the old site, which
is now in the occupation of ——— *Boustred*, a corn-dealer: it
has over the door the arms of the Hospital [4]; and there was formerly
at the end a sun-dial, having the following suitable motto: " *Post*
" *voluptatem misericordia.*"

The chapel connected with this house, which stands near the turnpike, at the South-east corner of the road leading to Ball's Pond,
appears from its architecture to have been erected before the Reformation, being, without doubt, the same that was attached to the original lazar-house, with which it had a communication, whereby the
patients entered to attend divine service; and it is said to have been

[1] Strype's Survey of London.

[2] Records of St. Bartholomew's Hospital.

[3] In the Survey of this manor, 1611, it is called " *Kingsland Spittle.*" Another
house of this kind, appertaining to St. Bartholomew's Hospital, was " *The Loke,* in
" Southwark," mentioned in the preceding page.

[4] Party per pale, Argent and Sable, a chevron counterchanged.

C C

so contrived, that when in the chapel they could neither see nor be seen by the rest of the audience [1].

This Hospital continued to be used as an appendage to St. Bartholomew's until the committee recommended (January 27, 1757) " convenience in the new wing for the foul patients, and afterwards " no more to be received in the *out* houses [2]." It appears that the building was now let to some other use; but a petition was presented (February 17, 1761) by Mr. Cookson, Chaplain to the Lock, from the inhabitants at Kingsland, praying, " he might continue the duty " for their accommodation as thentofore." The Committee afterwards ordered " that Mr. Cookson should have the use of the chapel " as desired, on paying a yearly acknowledgement of 6d. into the " poor's box, with leave to take down the patients' pew in the gallery, " and raise the seats at his expence, under the direction of the Hos- " pital Surveyor [3]."

From this time the office of chaplain was discontinued, and Mr. Cookson being no longer upon the establishment, was, by way of recompence, permitted to have free use of the chapel (keeping the same in repair), and to receive what stipend he could collect from the neighbouring inhabitants who attended public worship in the place. In this manner the chapel has been kept open to the present time, the Governors of St. Bartholomew's Hospital continuing to nominate a preacher upon a vacancy.

The chapel is a small stone building, of old English architecture, (see Plate IV.), in extent about 27 feet from East to West by 18 feet from North to South, and not more than 20 feet in height on the outside to the top of the roof; the road about it having been raised so much, that the bottom of the pulpit is upon a level with the highway, and the floor of the area about three feet below it. The roof, which is overgrown with moss and weeds, supports a small turret, with a

[1] London and Environs, vol. III. p. 283.
[2] Records of St. Bartholomew's Hospital.
[3] Ibid.

bell, which is rung by means of string passing through a hole, into the gallery. The pulpit stands in the North-east corner of the build-ing, and the Decalogue, &c. is painted on a large board, in gilt letters, on a black ground, surmounted with gilt cherubim. In the area, are seven double pews and two single ones, and five single pews comprise the whole of the gallery. The communion-table is formed of a plain deal falling slab; and in the chapel is an old pewter salver, on which the arms of St. Bartholomew's Hospital are engraved. The whole of the building is in a very dilapidated state; and the interior, which, from its smallness, is very incommodious, presents a mean and neglected appearance[1]. A closet in the chapel contains an old folio Bible, strongly secured with brass, having Psalms at the end set to music, in the antient square character, and not divided into bars; this has, to all appearance, remained in the place from the days of Henry VIII. or Elizabeth.

From Islington Common is an antient foot-path to London, which leads by the side of an extensive white-lead manufactory, in the posses-sion of Samuel Walker and Co. very considerable iron-masters, at Masborough, near Rotherham, in Yorkshire, and connected with the firm of Walkers, Maltby, and Co. at the Steel-yard in Upper Thames-street. These gentlemen erected here, in the year 1786, a curious windmill for the purpose of grinding lead, differing in two remarkable particulars from common windmills; viz. *first*, that the brick tower of it is crowned with a great wooden cap, to which is affixed, on one side, the flyers; and, on the opposite side, a projecting gallery, ter-minated by a very small machine of four flyers, by means of which the whole top is turned round at pleasure, so as to bring the sails into that direction which is most convenient with respect to the wind; and *secondly*, that instead of four, the usual number of flyers, this was

---

[1] Since writing the above account, the chapel has been new roofed, the interior painted, and otherwise materially repaired, at the expence of the Governors of St. Bartholomew's Hospital.

furnished with five. Another mill, similar to the above, was added about the year 1792, but the flyers of both are now reduced to four, which are so constructed as either to unfurl or take in the sails, by the means above mentioned, as the wind increases or diminishes, and that without having any effect upon their motion while the alteration is taking place.

Between 40 and 50 persons, chiefly women, are employed here in the manufacture of ceruse or white-lead for the use of potters, painters, &c. This article, which forms a considerable branch of trade, is prepared from the blue sheet-lead, with the aid of vinegar, or some strong acid; the vapour of which, by a curious process operating upon the metal, corrodes and reduces it into a white calx, which is afterwards ground in these mills to a proper consistence for use [1].

Part of this manufactory was formerly a public-house, well known as *The Rosemary Branch;* and in 1783, a new " Rosemary Branch" was erected just beyond it, at the meeting of the parishes of Shoreditch and Islington [2]. This is a house principally of summer resort;

---

[1] For an account of this process, see art. CERUSE, in Rees's Cyclopædia, new edition.

[2] Not far from this spot, in Shoreditch parish, is an old square house, having two stories in the roof, antiently called *Bames, Baumes,* or *Balmes,*

" ——————————— the once fam'd abode,
" Of plump Lord Mayor, and oft prais'd Civic cheer,
" The seat of loyal Whitmore * — good old man,
" Who, for his duty to his King, preferr'd
" To pass in prison house his lonesome hours.
  " Far other uses now the mansion claim;
" And where the music and the banquet cheer'd,
" Now mopes the maniac wretch the live-long day,
" And clanks his chains, and weeps, and laughs aloud."

FOX.

---

\* Sir George Whitmore, Lord Mayor of London in 1631, who suffered much for his loyalty in the reign of Charles the First. For a particular account of this house and its inhabitants, see *Ellis's History of Shoreditch*, and *Moser's Vestiges, Europ. Mag.* vol. XLV. p. 90.

but it is also frequented in the winter time by persons for the purpose of skaiting, there being a pond of above an acre, in the ground attached to the premises, and which is chiefly supplied by the waste water of the New River, escaping from a number of main pipes which pass this way, for the serving of Hoxton, Shoreditch, &c. On this piece of water several boats are kept for the amusement of persons frequenting the house, which are let by the proprietor at 6*d. per* head *per* hour.

On the West side of Frog-lane is The Barley-mow public-house, perhaps deserving of notice from having been at one time the temporary residence of that dissipated character, but great natural genius, the celebrated George Morland. This eccentric Being, having called at the house casually about 12 years since, remained in it for several months. During this time, which was for the most part devoted to the bottle and the company of his low-lived associates, he painted a few of his best pictures, some of which came into the possession of his attorney, to whom he was continually indebted for extricating him from the difficulties daily arising from his manifold indiscretions; others fell into the hands of mercenary individuals, who were constantly calling upon and teazing him for some specimen of his art, and which he would often transfer to those who would join with him in his irregular pursuits, for a very trifling consideration.

Whilst at the Barley Mow he frequently applied to the farm-yard opposite, for portions of old cart harness, as saddles, collars, hames, &c. which were regularly copied into his sketch book, and he would send after any rustic-looking character that he chanced to see passing the house, in order to obtain a sitting, and for which the party was generally remunerated with a piece of money, and something to drink. The landlord (Tate), who was himself an artist in the former part of his life, can bear testimony to the masterly manner in which he sketched some of his subjects, and the facility of execution with which he finished others : his pallet knife, his knuckles, and his finger ends, were not unfrequently made subservient to his great skill in producing the most happy effects, and with a dispatch almost incredible.

He would sometimes, in a sober and serious mood, determine to begin and finish a picture in his best style, one that when done should procure him several hundred guineas; for this purpose (according to the nature of the subject fixed upon) he would send to Billinsgate for fine and handsome fish to copy into his work, or explore the ad-joining farm-yard, for animals and objects suited to his purpose; but the same fatality which attended him through life, seldom permitted him to accomplish any work of this kind which he happened to take in hand. The fish would remain in his apartment, till it was equally unfit for the picture and the table; and figures which had per-haps been introduced as prominent objects in the composition, and designed to receive the finest touches of his pencil, were either rubbed out altogether, or, by some happy combination of art, thrown into shadow, or rendered subordinate to the general effect produced in the whole work. By these means the labour was abridged, the picture went sooner to market, and the supply of cash which it produced, though comparatively small, was sufficient to answer the exigencies of the moment, and that was all which gave any concern to this extraordi-nary compound of genius and prodigality.

One anecdote of Morland during his stay here is perhaps not un-worthy of notice. Observing a portrait of Tate, the landlord, hang-ing up in one of the rooms, painted at a time when he wore his own hair, powdered and tied in a *queue*, but which he had been sub-sequently induced to exchange for a peruke, having more the semblance of nature ; Morland remarked that the picture was not like the original by reason of this difference in the head dress, and volun-teered his services to supply his host's counterpart with a handsome brown wig, such as then adorned his head, adding, that if he did not like it when done, he would replace his old head of hair: this alteration

*George Morland, the celebrated Painter.*

Plate IX

*Lower Street Chapel.*

Plate X

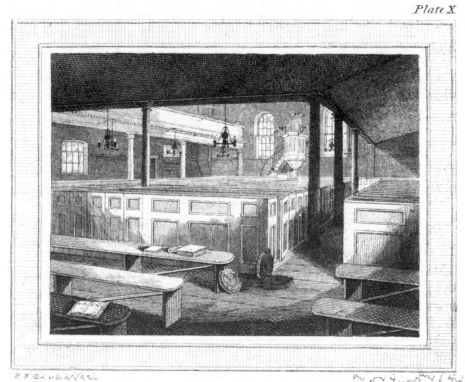

*Interior of the Chapel, Lower Street.*

was agreed to, and the picture now remains in the house, a perfect resemblance of the landlord, and a proof of the skill and versatility of talent of the inimitable but indiscreet artist.

At the lower end of *Green Man's-lane* is an extensive Fur Manufactory, belonging to Thomas Wontner and Sons, hatters, of the Minories, London, where about 60 persons, of which two thirds are women, are employed in separating and sorting the hair of beaver, seal, and other skins, for the making of hats, and a variety of other purposes, to which it is afterwards applied. A kind of cloth of a very fine and soft texture has been lately made from the fine down of the seal, a specimen of which was to be seen on the premises, in a waistcoat worn by one of the persons employed in the business. In the house attached to this manufactory, Dr. Mayersbach, the celebrated water-doctor, at one time resided, and practised as a physician.

Near this spot, at the lower end of Norfolk-street, is another manufactory, where several persons are engaged in the making of *Havannah segars!* from the tobacco-leaf. Between Frog-lane and the Lower-street, are a number of small houses and gardens, forming the Elder-walk, Angler's gardens, Paradise-place, &c.: these are principally inhabited by mechanics in the different branches of the watch-making business, who are employed chiefly by the manufacturers of Clerkenwell. Near the top of Norfolk-street, in the Lower-street, stood an old building, some years ago, occupied by two Dutchmen, as a rectifying-house, for converting English distilled spirit into a compound resembling in flavour the real Hollands geneva; but the undertaking not meeting with success, they soon quitted the premises.

At the corner of Green Man's-lane, in the Lower-street, is a Meeting house, belonging to a congregation of Dissenters of the Independant denomination, which was erected in the year 1744. The building was first promoted by a legacy of £.100. bequeathed by Mr. Pike; and the sum of £.95. was afterwards given by Mr. William Pearcy.

The latter gentleman's donation and death is recorded in the following inscription on a stone fixed in the North wall of the meeting
house:

" In a vault near this place
" lyes interr'd the body of Mr. William Pearcy,
" late of this parish,
" whose love for publick worship induced him
" to give ninety-five pounds towards the
" building of this place, and appointed
" the following lines to be inscribed on
" his stone:
" *This is a faithful saying and worthy of*
" *all acceptation, that Jesus Christ came into*
" *the world to save Sinners, of whom I am chief.*
" He died Sept. 5th, 1746,
" aged 68."

No regular minister was appointed till the year 1761; when the
Reverend John Gawsell was nominated pastor: till this time the congregation had been supplied by the occasional preaching of various
gentlemen in the Independant connection.

In the year 1768, Mr. Gawsell resigned his charge, and retired to
Bury St. Edmunds, where he soon after died of the small pox [1].   The

---

[1] A remarkable example of the futility of human endeavours to avoid the all-wise
dispensations of Providence, is exhibited in the case of this gentleman.   Never
having had the small pox, he was particularly careful to shun every hazard of receiving the contagion.   With this view he left Islington, to retire into the country,
where he hoped to be more secure from danger; but the very means used upon this
occasion communicated the disease, which terminated his life; and which he
had so anxiously endeavoured to escape.   A man employed to pack up his books
and papers for removal, had recently had the disorder in his family, and there
was no doubt that, through his agency, it was conveyed to the minister, who had
scarcely taken possession of his new habitation, when his mortal career was arrested
by the hand of Death.

same year the Reverend Nathaniel Jennings was appointed to the pastoral office; and shortly after, the congregation having much increased, the galleries were erected. Previously to the death of Mr. Gawsell, a part of the congregation had separated, and attended the ministry of the Reverend James Blenchall, D. D. from Dundee, at the old building, about to be described, near the same spot, which was fitted up for the purpose[1]; but an union afterwards took place when the Doctor went to Holland, and afterwards returned to his native place, where he died. Mr. Jennings is at this time minister of the congregation.

## WARD'S PLACE.

Between the meeting-house last mentioned, and Paradise-place, there stood a building of considerable antiquity (see Plate VI.); and which was pulled down, about the year 1800. It was a large irregular fabric, composed of brick, wood, plaister, &c. and appeared from its size, and its internal decorations, which consisted of a variety of ornaments beautifully executed in stucco, carved work, and stained glass, to have been the residence of persons of considerable distinction. On the front, which abutted on the Lower-street, was a board inscribed " *King John's-place;*" and it was the vulgar tradition of the neighbourhood, that it had originally been a palace of that monarch[2]. For

[1] It is perhaps from this circumstance that (in *London and Environs*, vol. III. p. 226) Islington is said to have two Independent Meeting Houses in the Lower-street.

[2] It is curious to hear the number of stories that are related in almost every part of the kingdom, of houses, castles, &c. in the respective neighbourhoods, *said to have been* the habitations of King John, Queen Elizabeth, &c. If we may believe tradition, the former has occupied almost half the antient buildings in the vicinity of London; whilst the name of Elizabeth is as commonly attached to every old house of which the uninformed neighbours cannot tell the origin. Thus we have in Islington, " *King John's Palace,*" " *Queen Elizabeth's Lodge,*" her *Hunting Box*, &c.

some time previous to its demolition it had obtained the name of *Ward's Place* (being divided into several dwellings) and which was afterwards given to the buildings occupying part of the site whereon the old mansion stood.

A number of conjectures have arisen respecting the origin and history of this house [1]; but the most probable appears to be, that it was built by Sir Thomas Lovell, Knight, a person of considerable note in the reigns of Henry VII. and VIII. and who, there is reason to believe, was an inhabitant of Islington [2].    From the armorial bearings of

[1] Vide Gentleman's Magazine for 1791, several numbers.

[2] In 1485, when an Esquire only, he was made Chancellor of the Exchequer for life; and the same year had an annuity of 40 marks, as an Esquire to the King's Body.   In 1473, Henry Heydon, Esq. granted him an annuity of 20s. out of his manor of *Snoryng Parva*, called *Dorkettys*, for his good counsel that he had already and should thereafter give him.   He was first made Banneret in 1487; was knighted at the battle of Stoke; and afterwards installed Knight of the Garter.   In 1502, he was Treasurer of the Household, and President of the Council.   He was one of the executors of Henry the Seventh's will, Constable of the Tower, Surveyor of the Court of Wards, Steward and Marshal of the House to King Henry the Eighth. He built the gate-house at Lincoln's-inn, 1518, and placed on it the King's arms, the Earl of Lincoln's, and his own; where they remain to the present day.   He built *East Herling Hall* in Norfolk; and, in 1508, upon the death of Edmund Lord Roos of Hamlake, without issue, the manor of Worcesters, in the parish of Enfield, came to Sir Thomas Lovel, who had married Isabel, his sister and heir; where, in 1516, he was honoured with a visit by Margaret, Queen Dowager of Scotland, sister to Henry the Eighth, on Ascension-day; and there he died, May 25, 1524; and was buried in a chapel which himself had founded within the Priory of Holywell.

To this priory, which was situate in the parish of Shoreditch, Sir Thomas Lovel appears to have been a great benefactor, as is indicated by the following lines, which, according to Weever, were painted on almost every window of that house.

" Al ye nunnes in Holywel
" Pray for the soul of Sir Thomas Lovel."

But Mr. Blomefield, in the History of Norfolk, gives them differently, and says they

Dudley, (Plate VII. fig. 4.) it seems pretty clear that the house was in the occupation of some branch of that family. These arms, which were executed in stained glass in one of the windows, are *only* applicable to three persons, viz. John Earl of Warwick (mentioned in the account of Canonbury), Ambrose, his son, who also had that earldom, and the celebrated Robert Dudley, Earl of Leicester, the favourite of Queen Elizabeth. The latter Nobleman, it is most likely, was the person who resided here; where, it is probable, he was visited by his royal mistress, and this may, in some degree, elucidate the circumstance of her name being so uniformly connected with the old houses about this spot. It may also serve to account for the introduction of " *the Squier Minstrel*," from " the woorshipful tooun of Islington," in the Earl's entertainment given to the Queen at Kenilworth (see p. 35). [1]

were inscribed on a wall of the priory house.

> All ye nunns of Halliwell,
> Pray ye both day and night
> For the soul of Sir Thomas Lovel,
> Whom Harry the Seventh made knight.

Vide *Ellis's " History and Antiquities of Shoreditch*," which contains a pedigree of the family of Lovell.

[1] This Nobleman, who was one of the most favoured courtiers in the reign of Elizabeth, was restored in blood, and created Earl of Leicester, &c. by her Majesty, in consideration of the sufferings of his family in her father's and sister's reigns. Other circumstances, however, might have contributed to his exaltation. He is described by Naunton as " a very godly person, singular well featured, high foreheaded, and " of a sweet aspect." Speaking of his Letters and Writings he says, " I never yet " saw a style or phrase more seeming religious and fuller of the streams of devo- " tion." The Earl has, however, been charged with practices not altogether becoming the character he professed, for he was suspected of having been the cause of his Lady's death, in 1560, from an ambition of being thought the suitor of the Queen. Other crimes of a very black nature have also been laid to his charge; and Naunton mentions it, as an opinion, that he met his death "by that poison which " he had prepared for others."

Leicester

It appears from the writings relating to this house, and the records of the manor, that the premises were the property of Sir Robert Ducy, Baronet, who was Lord Mayor in 1630. The letters H D, which were cut in very large characters in relief, within the pediment of a principal door, (Plate V. fig. 4.) were perhaps the initials of Sir Hugh Ducy, Knight of the Bath, who married into the neighbouring family of *Fisher* [1], and who it is probable made some alterations in this part of the building.

From the period last mentioned, no particulars of any interest can be traced respecting the premises, till about the year 1740, when Dr.

Leicester seems to have been held in much esteem by his Sovereign; of which he failed not to take due advantage, in endeavouring to carry matters with a very high hand at Court. The following story related by the above author may serve in proof of this, while it affords an excellent trait in the character of Elizabeth, in her regal capacity. " Bowyer, a gentleman of the Black Rod, being " charged by her expresse command to look precisely to all admissions into the " Privy Chamber, one day stayed a very gay Captain and a follower of my Lord of " *Leicester's* from entrance, for that he was neither well known nor a sworn servant " to the Queen. At which repulse, the gentleman, bearing high on my Lord's " favour, told him, he might perchance procure him a discharge. *Leicester* coming " in to the contestation said publikely (which was none of his wont) that he was a " knave, and should not continue long in his office; and so turning about to go into " the Queen, *Bowyer*, (who was a bold gentleman and wel beloved) stept before " him, and fell at her Majesties feet, related the story, and humbly craves her " Grace's pleasure; and whether my Lord of *Leicester* was King, or her Majesty " Queen; whereunto she replyed with her wonted oath (God's death) 'my Lord, I " have wisht you well; but my favour is not so lockt up for you, that others shall " not partake thereof, for I have many servants unto whom I have and will, at my " pleasure, bequeath my favour, and likewise resume the same, and if you think " to rule here, I will take a course to see you forthcoming. I will have here but " one mistris and no master; and look that no ill happen to him, least it be severely " required at your hands;' which so quelled my Lord of *Leicester* that his fained " humility was long after one of his best vertues." *Naunton's Fragmenta Regalia*, 4to, 1642.

[1] See Monumental Inscriptions in the old Church.

PLATE VI.

*Church Spire in Wicker Case.*

*Sir Thomas Fowlers Lodge.*

*Ancient Building formerly in the Lower Street.*

F.W.L. Stockdale del.

Frances Hawksworth sculp.

*To William White Esq.r of Highbury Place.*

*This Plate is Respectfully inscribed by his obliged & most obedient Servant  J. Nelson.*

Published May 1 1811 by Russell Upper Street Islington.

*New River Head*

*Queen Elizabeths Gate at Islington*

*Drawn & Engrav'd by B. Green.*

Poole rented the house for the purpose of inoculation; and it afterwards became an appendage to the Small-pox Hospital in Cold-bath Fields, first instituted by the exertions of that gentleman in the year 1746 [1]. Some time after this, a part of it was used by a congregation of Dissenters, as before mentioned; it was afterwards converted into a soap manufactory, and then, occupied for a time as the parish workhouse. Before the building was pulled down, it had been let out to a number of working people, who occupied the different apartments, at weekly rents.

The variety of interesting specimens of the arts in this country at the beginning of the 16th century, which this house afforded, are deserving of some notice. A chimney piece, about five feet in height represented in Plate V. contained the arms of the City of London, with those of Lovel, quartering Muswel or Mosel [2]; the arms of

---

[1] See Inscription to his memory in the Church-yard; also *London and its Environs,* vol. VI. p. 23.

[2] These arms are described as above by Mr. Ellis (Camp. Lond. p. 96.) who appears to have inspected them in the building. The drawing, however, from which the plate was engraved, does not exactly correspond with the coat of *Lovel;* but the difference between roses and annulets, squirrels and lions rampant, though most important in Heraldry, may not be at all times easily distinguishable in an old and decayed piece of carved work: they are therefore given as they came to the hands of the author, who had not an opportunity of viewing the original. It may be observed here, that the armorial bearings of the above Knight are to be found variously represented. On the Gate-house at Lincoln's Inn the chevron in the first coat is charged with a *rose,* and the chevronels in that of *Muswell* bear each three *cinquefoils.* In some places *five* cinquefoils only are assigned to this coat, while in others six *roses* are given with an *annulet* for difference (vide *Edmondson's Heraldry, Lysons's Environs,* &c.) The first coat in the above shield is similar to that of Sir John Halys, of Essex; but the other quartering not being to be found at the Heralds' Office, as represented in the plate, is somewhat corroborative of its being the arms of *Mosell* or *Muswell,* and consequently that the coat was intended for that of Sir Thomas Lovel.

the priory of St John of Jerusalem; the coat of Gardners, of London, grocer; and the arms of the company of Merchant Adventurers. The coat of Gardners was also finely delineated in stained glass, and otherwise, in various parts of the building. The same is exhibited in Plate VII. fig. 3. as copied from one of the windows, where it was emblazoned within a border of foliage of the most lively colours.

But the most beautiful specimens were exhibited in a variety of scriptural and historical subjects, pourtrayed on the glass windows of an upper room in the house. Of these (Plate VII. fig. 1.) is the device of a person writing at a table and taking an account of the money lying before him, one piece of which he holds in his left hand. The apparatus of his employment, as pen-knife, ink-horn, &c. appear on the table before him, with a speculum, books, &c. Under the table are two recesses, one of which has a bunch of keys appendant to the lock; the furniture and utensils, &c. in the room were pourtrayed with the greatest exactness. The subject represented in this picture is probably intended for that of the *faithful steward*.

The device of a rose tied to a wing (Plate VII. fig. 5.) has the appearance of a rebus, or something emblematical. In connection with fig. 6, it may be understood as bearing allusion to the transient nature of beauty and the certainty of death; as *beauty flies*, *death seizes*, or some such matter. The abbreviated Latin words (fig. 7.) may be Englished, " *All things from above.*" It may be observed that the rose and wing also occurs over the arches of the nave of Enfield Church, in which parish Sir Thomas Lovel resided, likewise upon the tower of the Church at Hadley[1]. It appears very probable that this device belonged to the Company of Merchant Adventurers, whose arms were upon the chimney piece before described, or was adopted by Sir Thomas, or some person or persons belonging to that body. The crest of the Company was a Pegasus, bearing on either *wing* two

[1] Lysons's Environs.

*roses* proper ; and on referring to the arms of the old trading Companies of the City, it will be found, that *wings* (most appropriate emblems of Trade and Commerce) often formed a part of their bearings. Thus, in all probability, the said device may have been placed by such persons in the situations above mentioned, by reason of their having been either inhabitants of the houses, or benefactors to the Churches, where it is found.

The painting (Plate VII. fig. 2.) was also finely executed in stained glass in the window of a room on the ground floor, and is the first of a set taken from the parable of the Prodigal Son, which it is probable adorned a number of the windows, but at the time the above was copied (1789) only the above and two others of the series remained. One of these was a fragment representing the Prodigal Son in excess, (Plate V. fig. 2.) and the other his feeding of swine, each of which were delineated in very lively colours, and encircled with Latin mottos in an antient character.

In the first picture, the prodigal son appears as suppliant, and requesting of his father the portion of goods belonging to him. The elder son also appears represented by the figure in the back ground ; who is putting his part of the divided substance into a casket: behind him stands a domestic, or friend, who, by his hands being familiarly laid on his arm and shoulder, seems to be congratulating him on such acquisition of wealth. The father, a venerable old man, is seated in a sumptuous manner, affectionately grasping one hand of his son, and with the other seems ready to deliver a bag of money to him. At the right he is seen mounted on horseback, and riding from his father's house. The Latin inscription round the picture intimates the prodigal son asking from his father his portion, receives it, and departs happy in his lot.

Here were also many figures of Saints in an upper room, some of them half a yard long, several of which were much mutilated, and others entirely obscured, the windows having been covered with lath and plaister, to decrease the number of lights.

One of these figures (Plate V. fig. 1.) was about nine inches in length, and by the nimbus round his head, and lion at his feet, was probably intended for St. Mark. He bears in his left hand something like the foundation stone of a pillar, which, with the sword, lion, and his armour, seems to bear allusion to the strength, durability and defence of the Gospel[1].

It is somewhat remarkable, that notwithstanding the variety of ornaments and works of art, with which this building in every part abounded, not a single date was to be found. The arms taken for those of Holywell priory, said to have been in one of the windows, (Camp. Lond. p. 96.) were perhaps those of the Priory of St. John of Jerusalem, in whose manor the house was situate. Part of an old wall yet remains at the back of Mr. Jennings's meeting-house, which probably enclosed the garden attached to these premises.

In the lower part of Highbury Manor[2], near Pullen's-row, is an extensive dairy or grass farm, for supplying the London milk dealers,

[1] The author is indebted to the family of the late Matthew Skinner, of Islington, a gentleman of much antiquarian knowledge and research, for the loan of a book of drawings of the different objects in this house, and which were copied by him previous to the demolition of the premises. A quantity of the stained glass that adorned this building, afterwards came into the possession of the late Samuel Ireland, Esq. of Norfolk-street, Strand.

[2] In that part of ISLINGTON which is situate in the parish of Clerkenwell, are the following objects worthy of remark. On the East side of the *St. John's Street Road* is a low range of building, comprising the free school and almshouses, founded and endowed by *Dame Alice Owen*, three years before her death (A. D. 1613) and to which the inscription on her monument in the old Church referred. This foundation is said to have had its origin from a very remarkable circumstance, of which the following traditionary account is extracted from a record belonging to the Brewers' Company.

" Alice Owen was born at Islington in the reign of Queen Mary ; her first hus-
" band was Henry Robinson, Citizen and Brewer of London ; her second husband
" was William Elkin, of London, Alderman ; her third and last husband was Sir
" Thomas Owen, one of her Majesty Queen Elizabeth's Justices of the Court of

Alms Houses. Islington.

Published May.1.1819. for the Proprietor by R. Ackermann.101.Strand.

PLATE V.

1

2

3

AT·THE·BOARDED·
IOHN
BALL

NEWINGTON·GREEN·
HOVSE·NEERE
HIS
PENNY

4

ᕼD

5

6

KETTLE
IOANE

7

ISLINGTON
HER·IN
HIS
HALFE
PENNY
T·K
·1667·

IN·1667
ROBERT·PE
R·M
P

8

CONFECTIONER·ISLINGTON
HIS
HALFE
PENNY
IANE

PLATE VII.

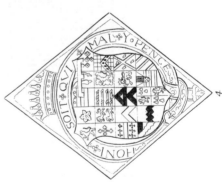

J.Harwickworth, sculp.

Published May 2.1812 by Baldwd, Upper Street Islington.

Colebrooke Row, Islington.

Pub.d May 1, 1819, for the Proprietor by R. Ackermann, 101, Strand.

belonging to Mr. Samuel Rhodes. This farm has been for many years a

"	Common Pleas; lived and died in Bassishaw, made her will the 10th of June
"	1613; died the 26th of November, in the reign of King James I. was buried
"	1613, in the East corner of St. Mary Islington Church, where there is a curious
"	monument erected to her memory.

"	In the reign of Queen Mary it was an exercise for archers to shoot with their
"	bows and arrows at butts; this part of Islington at that time being all open fields
"	and pasture land; and on the same spot of ground where the school now stands,
"	was a woman milking a cow. The Lady Owen, then a maiden gentlewoman,
"	walking by with her maid servant, observed the woman a milking, and had a
"	mind to try the cows paps, whether she could milk, which she did, and at her
"	withdrawing from the cow, an arrow was shot through the crown of her hat (at
"	which time high-crowned hats were in fashion) which so startled her that she then
"	declared, that if she lived to be a Lady she would erect something on that very
"	spot of ground, in commemoration of the great mercy shewn by the Almighty in
"	that astonishing deliverance. This passed on till she became a widow lady; her
"	servant at the time this accident happened, being still living with her Lady, re-
"	minded her Lady of her former words; her answer was, she remembered the af-
"	fair, and would fulfil her promise; upon which she purchased the land from the
"	*Welch Harp* to the *Turk's Head* Islington road, and built thereon, as appears with
"	the arrows fixed on the top."

The school is for the education of 30 boys of the parishes of Islington and
Clerkenwell. The ten almshouses which join the school are for so many widows
of the same parishes, who receive each a yearly allowance with a chaldron and a
half of coals *. The boys are instructed in reading, writing, and arithmetic,
and have books, &c. found them. The plot of ground, a part of which is occupied by the school and almshouses, together with a farm at Orset in Essex, now
let at a very low rent, forms the endowment of these charities. The property is
however likely to be much improved, as the lease of the farm is nearly expired,
and the ground contiguous to the school has been lately let on a building lease.
According to Stow's Survey, p. 111, the expence of purchasing the land, and
building the school, almshouses, &c. amounted to £.1776. The story of the arrow
is there related with some variation from the above, and from the annexed list of
Mrs. Owen's benefactions it also appears that she gave " to Christ's Hospital in Lon-

* The widows, by Mrs. Owen's Statutes, were to receive 16s. 8d. per quarter each, a gown once in two years, and to have 6l. *per annum* allowed between them for fuel; they were to be above 50 years of age, and to have been inhabitants of *Islington* for seven years before their election.

E E

concern of considerable magnitude, and is at this time one of the

" don three score pounds, to the end that twelve pence a-piece weekly might
" be given to certain poor people of ISLINGTON."

This Lady, by her will, left rules for the ordering and government of her school
and almshouses; and gave the entire management thereof, with a discretionary power
of altering the Statutes, to the Brewers Company, the Master and Wardens of which
she enjoined once a year to visit the charity and her tomb in the Church, allowing
them 30 shillings for a dinner.   The arrows mentioned in the preceding account, as
being on the top of the building, were remaining within memory, which circumstance serves to corroborate the story.   Over the outer gate of the building is a
stone with the following inscription :

" These Ten Alms Houses with the Free Grammar School
" adjoining were built and endowed in the year 1613,
" by Lady Alice Owen, and by her will left to the government of the
" Worshipful Company of Brewers of the City of London ;
" In commemoration of which this stone is placed in the year 1788.

" EDWARD BOND, Esq. Master.

" Mr. BENJAMIN SMITH,　⎫
　　　　　　　　　　　　　　⎬ Wardens.
" Mr. SAMUEL WATLINGTON,　⎭

Among the Exchequer Records the following occur, viz.

" Aliciæ Owen Licentia concessa ædificandi Hospitalem in com. Middlesex."   10
Pars Orig. anno 6 Rot° 57 Jac. I.

" Aliciæ Owen viduæ, Licentia concessa fundandi Hospitalem in *Islington*."
4 Pars Orig. anno 8 Rot° 2 Jac. I.

### NEW TUNBRIDGE WELLS, or ISLINGTON SPA.

Near the New River Head is a spring of chalybeate water, in a very pleasant and
retired garden, containing some large and handsome trees.   This spring was, a century ago, much resorted to by our Nobility and Gentry for its medicinal virtues, and
it obtained the above name from its similarity to the waters of Tunbridge Wells in
Kent.   The spring was discovered by Sadler, a Surveyor of the Highways in 1683,
in the garden belonging to a house which he had then just opened for the publick
reception as a musick house.   In the following year a pamphlet was published, intituled, " A true and exact Account of Sadler's Wells, or the new Mineral Water
" lately found out at *Islington*, treating of its Nature and Virtues, together with
" an Enumeration of the chiefest Diseases which it is good for, and against
" which it may be used, and the Manner and Order of taking it.   Published

largest establishments of the kind, in the vicinity of the Metropolis.

" for publick Good, by T. G. Doctor in Physick." London, 1684, 4to, one sheet. This pamphlet gives an account of the discovery, with the virtues of the water, which is there said to be of a ferruginous nature, and much resembling in quality and effects the water of *Tunbridge Wells*; this is confirmed by Dr. Russell, in his Account of Mineral Springs; and Munro calls it a light chalybeate, and one of the best in the neighbourhood of London. The author of the pamphlet says, that the well at *Islington* was famed before the Reformation for its extraordinary cures, and called the *Holy Well*: that the priests of the Priory of Clerkenwell using to attend there, made due advantage of the spring, attributing its virtues to the efficacy of their prayers; and adds, that these superstitions were the occasion of its being arched over and concealed at the time of the Reformation. In this state (he observes) " it " grew out of remembrance" until discovered again by Sadler as above mentioned. In the summer of 1700 the place was in high favour with the publick, at which time dancers were admitted during the whole of the day on Mondays and Thursdays, " provided they did not appear in masks." *Malcolm's Manners and Customs.*

In 1733, their Royal Highnesses the Princesses Amelia and Caroline, frequented these gardens daily in the summer time, for the purpose of drinking the waters, when such was the concourse of Nobility and others, that the proprietor took above £.30, in a morning. On the birth-day of the Princesses, as they passed through the *Spa field* (which was generally filled with carriages), they were saluted with a discharge of 21 guns, a compliment which was always paid them on their arrival; and in the evening there was a great bonfire, and the guns were again discharged several times. On ceasing to visit the gardens, the Princess Amelia presented the Master with 25 guineas, each of the water-servers with three guineas, and one guinea to each of the other attendants. *Gent. Mag.*

These wells have furnished a subject for a number of pamphlets, poems, &c. Among these are, " Islington Wells; or the Three-penny Academy, a Poem," London, 1694, a low Burlesque, most probably by Ned Ward. — " The Humours of " New Tunbridge Wells at *Islington*, a Lyric Poem," 1734, 8vo. — "Experimental " Observations on the Water of the Mineral Spring near *Islington*, commonly " called New Tunbridge Wells," London, 1751. — " The Spleen, or Islington " Spa," a comic piece, of two acts, by George Colman, 8vo, 1776. — And " A " Treatise on the Mineral Spring at the New Tunbridge Wells, near Islington, " with Rules for drinking the Waters, and a Plan of Diet for Invalids labouring " under Chronic Complaints. By the late Hugh Smith, M. D." Printed for J. Howard, at Islington Spa.

## It was for many years carried on by the family of PULLIN, who

The following are some of the chief diseases for which the waters of this place are recommended; viz. nervous, hypochondriac, and hysteric affections; asthmatic complaints; indigestion; female obstructions; chlorosis; swellings; eruptions; &c.

The gardens are still frequented by persons for the benefit of the waters. The subscription is one guinea for the season, or six pence *per* glass, with capillaire. The spring is inclosed by an artificial grotto, composed of flints and shells, which is entered by a rustic gate. Here is also a lodging-house, where invalids may be accommodated with bed and board; and in the gardens is a breakfast-room, about 40 feet long, having at the end a small orchestra. In this room is a printed comparative statement (dated May 1, 1727,) of the specific gravity of the most celebrated mineral waters, from the experiments of Mr. Boyle, in which that of this spring is said to be 3 oz. 4 dr. 36 gr. or seven grains lighter than common water. Here are also some testimonials of the virtues of the spring, said to have been written by persons who experienced its salutary effects. Of these the following may serve as a specimen:

" The two following lines were curiously cut in the bark of one of the trees in " the walks, but now defaced:

> " Obstructum recreat; durum terit; humidum siccat;
> " Debile fortificat, — si tamen arte bibas.

" Which were thus paraphrased by a gentleman who was restored to health by " this water, after an extreme ill state of constitution for more than 30 years, and " drinking almost all the other mineral waters in the kingdom without effect:

> " This water drank with careful art, is found
> " To raise the weak, to make the leprous sound;
> " It gives relief in each obstructive case;
> " Corroding gravel, by its force will pass;
> " Inveterate coughs, tough phlegms it will dispel,
> " And numbers save whose bodies dropsies swell.

" And the same gentleman left the following lines in his apartment here, when " he left it after his cure:

> " For three times ten years I travell'd the globe,
> " Consulted whole tribes of the physical robe;
> " Drank the waters of Tunbridge, Bath, Harrowgate, Dulwich,
> " Spa, Epsom (and all by advice of the College);

View from Pullins Row Islington.

Sadlers Wells.

Pub. May 1, 1819, for the Proprietor, by R. Ackermann, 101 Strand.

Drawn and Engrav'd by J.Greig after a Sketch by S.Prout.

*Sadler's Wells.*

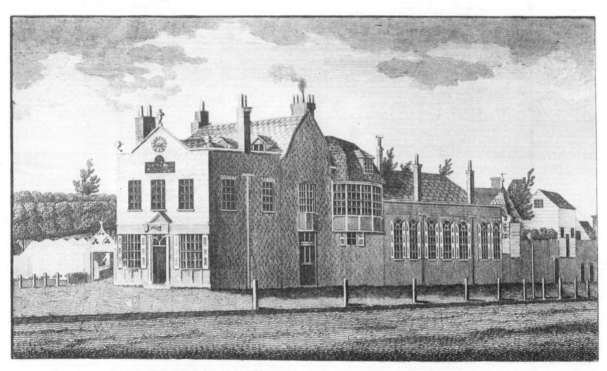

BAGNIGGE WELLS, *near* Battle Bridge, Islington.

EVENING.

Published by John Major 50 Fleet Street, March 31, 1831.

usually kept between 3 and 400 cows, for the service of the

> " But in vain —'till to ISLINGTON waters I came,
> " To try if my cure would add to their fame;
> " In less than six weeks they produc'd a belief,
> " This would be the place of my long-sought relief;
> " Before six weeks more had finish'd their course,
> " Full of spirits and strength I mounted my horse;
> " Gave praise to my God, and rode cheerfully home,
> " Overjoy'd with the thoughts of sweet hours to come.
> " May thou, great Jehovah! give equal success,
> " To all who resort to this place for redress!"

The gardens were opened during the last two summers, on certain evenings, with amusements similar to those of Vauxhall, consisting of music, fire-works, &c. but without much success.

## SADLER'S WELLS.

After the death of Sadler, his music-house and premises came to Francis Forcer, a musician, and vocal performer, whose son was the first who exhibited there the diversions of rope-dancing and tumbling, which he continued till the year 1730, when he died, at an advanced age. The concern was afterwards taken by Mr. Rosoman, an eminent builder, and the house of entertainment, which was at first a wooden erection on the present site (as it is represented in an engraved view, under the name of Sadler's Wells, with the date 1733), was by him, about the year 1765, formed into a more substantial building of brick, as it now appears *. A painting, representing a convivial society, of persons at that time interested in and frequenting the theatre, including portraits of Rosoman the proprietor, and some of the performers, still remains in the bar of the Sir Hugh Middleton's Head. This society, which was called *The Sadler's Wells Club*, contributed much to bring the place into reputation; and having been licensed, in 1753, it assumed the rank of a regular theatre. The amusements of this place were originally exhibited in the open air; and the spectators paid for a ticket on admission, which entitled them to its value in liquor or refreshments. A paper of The Connoisseur, for July 1756, notices the surprizing feats of activity exhibited here; these, with a variety of tricks and other performances, are also described in chap-

---

* The inimitable Hogarth has made choice of this spot for the exercise of his satirical talent at depiction, in his print of " *Bvening*" published in 1738, which contains a back-ground view of Sadler's Wells, and the Sir Hugh Middleton's Head.

dairy [1]. The stock of the present proprietor consists of about 500 cows,

ters V. and VI. of Strutt's Sports and Pastimes. Sadler's Wells has been since famous for the exhibition of burlettas, musical interludes, and pantomimes; and the performances of the celebrated *Richer* on the tight rope. The old custom of supplying the spectators with refreshments was revived a few years back, in the sale of English and foreign wines in the theatre, which were furnished by the managers at a moderate rate. A novel and interesting exhibition, of the *naumachie* kind, has been lately introduced here, the representation of dramatic spectacles on water : for this purpose, the element is introduced from the New River into an immense trough, occupying the whole space of the stage. The besieging of fortifications by sea, naval engagements, &c. are by these means, with the aid of appropriate scenery, exhibited with unusual effect. Since the time of Rosoman, the concern has been in the hands of different persons, particularly Mr. Thomas King the celebrated comedian, and Mr. Wroughton, both of Drury-lane theatre. It is now the joint property of several gentlemen, who each take a part in furnishing the amusements of the place. Of these, the stage pieces and songs are written by Mr. Charles Dibdin, jun. who is stage manager, the scenery is painted by Mr. Andrews, and the music is composed by Reeve. The house opens on Easter Monday, and continues during the summer season. A most fatal and distressing scene took place here on the evening of the 15th of October, 1807. The word *a fight!* vociferated by some persons in the house, was construed by a part of the audience into *a fire!* and, wonderful as it may appear, though neither light nor smoke were seen, nor was it scarcely possible a fire could happen in this theatre, such were the precautions used by the managers, yet a phrenzy took place in the gallery, altogether unaccountable. The entreaties and despairing cries of the managers, with speaking trumpets, that there was no fire, availed nothing; persons regardless of their lives threw themselves over into the pit, and eighteen died from pressure and suffocation on the gallery stairs. Numbers besides, experienced severe bruises and injuries, from the extraordinary pressure of the audience endeavouring to leave the house. Every possible recompense was made to the surviving friends of the unfortunate sufferers by the Proprietors, who entered a prosecution against the persons by whose exclamation the terror had been excited, and divided the produce of two free benefits amongst those deprived of support by the unexpected death of their fathers and husbands.

[1] A vulgar tradition prevails, that the late Mr. Pullin constantly kept near 1000 cows, which number he was desirous to attain, but could never accomplish by reason of one of his stock dying immediately on his attempting to exceed 999. This is

among which are to be seen the most perfect specimens of large and handsome cattle in the environs of the Metropolis, or, perhaps, in the whole kingdom. About 400 acres of land are rented by Mr. Rhodes in this parish, from which immense quantities of hay are procured, as the numerous large stacks of that commodity, which are annually deposited on his premises, near the South end of Colebrooke-terrace, abundantly testify.

On the waste ground in front of this farm, is a pound for strayed cattle, belonging to the lord of the manor; and the *Blue Coat Boy* at the corner of the City-road, where the manerial courts are held, is one of the receiving-houses appointed by the Royal Humane Society.

The City-gardens, near the City-road, contain a number of small houses and cottages, with pieces of ground attached. It is probable, the name was derived from the circumstance of the gardens in this place being rented by the citizens, for their occasional recreation or retirement; as by such they are for the most part occupied at the present day.

At the South-east extremity of the parish, in the highway leading to Aldersgate, somewhat more than two centuries ago, there stood a cross, probably of wood, called *Lambert's Cross*[1]. Erections of this kind were very common in such situations in the times antecedent to the Reformation.

Within these few years, several handsome rows of houses have been built on the sides of the City-road; among these are Nelson-terrace, Duncan-terrace, and St. Vincent's-row, so called in honour of our naval heroes bearing those names. Dalby-terrace has been lately built by a person of that name, who realized considerable property by the manufacture of beer-machines, for the use of public houses, and who for some time resided in the end house abutting on the New River,

totally erroneous, as it does not appear that at any time a greater number have belonged to any one person in Islington than the quantity usually kept by Mr. Rhodes or by Mr. Laycock.

[1] Survey of Highbury Manor, 1611.

and inclosed the piece of ground forming the angle between the two roads. Near this spot a hackney coach stand was first stationed in the year 1808. The piece of ground now occupied by Dalby-terrace, before the houses were built, was a hollow space between the two roads, which are in this place raised considerably above the natural level. This spot, from its convenient situation, was frequently the scene of pugilistic contests between heroes of the fist resorting hither from the Metropolis.

On the 28th of July 1762, one Plackett, a notorious robber, was executed here for robbing and ill treating Mr. Fayne, a Norway merchant, whom he had decoyed towards this place for the perpetration of his design. On this occasion a number of persons were much hurt by the breaking down of the fence, the crowd of people standing on the foot path being by this accident precipitated into the bottom. The place was afterwards for a length of time called *Jack Plackett's Common.*

### MANOR OF CANONBURY.

The Manor of CANONBURY, sometimes corruptly written *Canbury* and *Cambray*, occupies the area contained within the following line, viz. From the watchhouse at the South end of Islington-green, proceed North along the Upper-street, to the entrance of Highbury-place, turn down Hopping-lane to Ball's pond, and continue from thence up the Lower-road to the watchhouse aforesaid [1].

[1] The Survey of this Manor made for the Earl of Northampton in 1806 includes the nursery ground adjoining to Ball's pond, containing 11 acres and 37 perches, occupied by Mr. Barr; but this land is properly within the boundary line of Highbury Manor, and can be considered only as a freehold appendage to his Lordship's estate at Canonbury; the proper extent of which is formed entirely by the publick highway in manner above stated. This plot of ground, which in the Survey of Highbury Manor, A. D. 1611, is described as Lord Compton's Freehold, under the name of "*The Hoppinge*," was probably enfranchised by his Lordship, and added to the Canonbury estate at the time he held the Highbury demesnes, as mentioned in the account of that Manor.

CANONBURY MANOR, according to the Survey of 1806, contains as follows:

|  | A. | R. | P. |
|---|---|---|---|
| Demesnes held by the Earl of Northampton (including the ground at Ball's Pond) | 153 | 2 | 30 |
| Copyhold | 26 | 1 | 1 |
| Sundry Freeholds | 3 | 2 | 26 |
| Waste at Islington Green | 1 | 0 | 6 |
|  | 184 | 2 | 23 |
| Deduct Land at Ball's Pond | 11 | 0 | 37 |
| Total | 173 | 1 | 26 |

F F

There is reason to believe that the Manor of Canonbury formed one of the lay possessions before described from Domesday Book, at the time of the Norman Conquest. It came afterwards into the family of Berners (see p. 99); and making part of their fee, was, as such, included in the grant made to the Priory of *St. Bartholomew* in West Smithfield, by Ralph de Berners, of lands and rents with their appurtenances in ISELDONE held of the said fee[1], and enumerated among several other possessions of that monastery in a confirmation grant of King Henry III. by Letters Patent, bearing date at Winchester June 15th 1253, in the 37th year of his reign[2]. From the record before quoted (p. 56) it would seem that the Prior of St. John of Jerusalem had some interest in this Manor in the reign of Edward III.; this was probably a copyhold possession, for it does not appear that the estate was ever in the hands of that order.

It is most probable that this site being pitched on for a mansion for the Prior of the Canons of St. Bartholomew, it received the name of *Canonbury*, q. d. Canons House, as Canons in Little Stanemore, once the magnificent seat of the Duke of Chandos, had its name from belonging to the Canons of Bentley adjoining, which was a foundation previous to St. Bartholomew's. *Bury* is synonymous with *Bower* or *Burgh*, and signifies generally, a mansion or dwelling place[3]. For this purpose, as Mr. Malcolm observes, " Canonbury was certainly " most convenient and pleasant : we can easily imagine the beautiful " view they must have had from thence, even to the gates of the

---

[1] In a record dated 1373, it is said that Ralph de Berners formerly gave Canonesbury, in *Iseldon*, and a messuage called Cotelers, to the Prior and Convent of St. Bartholomew. Esch. 47 Edw. III. No. 80. 2d numb. *Lysons's Environs.*

[2] Dugd. Monast. vol. II. p. 386.

[3] Nichols's " History and Antiquities of Canonbury, 1788," 4to. The termination BURY is affixed to seats in Hertfordshire and other places : thus, Cashio-BURY means the chief DETACHED SEAT in Cashio hundred ; and Gorham-BURY, the seat of Robert de Gorham, Abbot of St. Alban's. Vide *History of St. Edmund's Bury, &c.*

" Priory, for the smoke of London was not then so dense as it is at
" present, and but very few buildings intervened[1]."

In the Ecclesiastical taxation of Pope Nicholas the Fourth, A. D.
1290, temp. Edward I. " lands and meadows rented of the Prior of St.
" Bartholomew at *Iseldon*" are assessed at £.1. 15s.

Henry le Hayward and Roger de Creton gave (anno 1334) 106
acres of arable land and four of meadow in Iseldon and Kentyshton,
valued at 21s. 6d. *per annum*, to the hospital of St. Bartholomew in
Smithfield, to pray for the soul of John de Kentyshton. A considerable part of this land was held under the Prior and Convent of St.
Bartholomew[2].

A stone yet remains in the wall of that part of the old mansion occupied by Mr. Field, with the date 1362[3] (see Plate II. fig. 4) just
10 years after the Priory of Saint Bartholomew had been exempted by
King Edward the Third from the payment of tenths, fifteenths, and
every other subsidy, on account of the disproportion of their income
to their great expenditure in works of charity[4].

The following is a List of all the Priors of St. Bartholomew, from
the MS Collections of Bishop Kennett, in a copy of Dugdale's Monasticon belonging to the late Mr. Gough[5], and printed in Mr.
Nichols's History of Canonbury.

1. G. Canon of Osney, made Prior of St. Bartholomew, London,
   1213, and a few days after became Monk at Abingdon[6].
2. Licence to elect a Prior 1256, on the cession of Peter, 40 Henry

[1] Londinium Redivivum, vol. I. p. 284.

[2] Esch. 8 Edw. III. No. 19. 2d numb. *Lysons's Environs.*

[3] This is probably the date of the erection of the Prior's first house at Canonbury,
and has been suffered to remain in the building through its various alterations, &c.
to the present time.

[4] Dugd. Monast. vol. II. p. 387.

[5] See the Vetusta Monumenta of the Society of Antiquaries, vol. II. plates xxxvi.
xxxvii.

[6] Chron. Dunstaple, p. 69.

III.  ROBERT, the Sub-prior, was elected, and the King consented Nov. 23d, that year.

3. 1262. GILBERT DE WELEDON was elected 46 Hen. III. and the King gave his consent, and restored the temporalities Nov. 24 [1].

4. 48 Henry III. the King consented to the election of JOHN BACUN Jan 11, 1264 [2].

5. 33 Edward I. Licence to elect a Prior, March 11, 1295, on the death of brother Hugh [3].

6. 10 Edward II. The King was advised of the death of the Prior of St. Bartholomew, and granted licence to elect, Nov. 4, 1317 [4].

7. 24 Edward III. Licence to elect a Prior on the death of John de Pekenden, May 25, 1351.  The King consented to the election of EDMUND DE BRAUGHYNG June 3, and restored the temporalities June 23.

8. 29 Edward III. The Convent besought the King's leave to elect a Prior, on the cession of Edmund de Braughyng, April 18, 1356. The King consented to the election of JOHN DE CARLETON, and restored the temporalities April 22.

9. THOMAS DE WATFORD died June 4, 1381.
   WILLIAM GEDNEY was elected June 10.
   Here were at that time twenty-one monks [5].

10. William Gedney resigned 1390 ; and
    JOHN REPYNGDON, alias EYTON, was elected March 3 [6].

11. Brother JOHN, Prior of St. Bartholomew's, Smithfield, 1407, cited to convocation in St. Frideswide's Church, Oxford, Nov. 23 [7].

---

[1] Pat. 46 Hen. III.

[2] Pat. 48 Hen. III. m. 18.

[3] Pat. 33 Edw. I.

[4] Pat. 10 Edw. II.

[5] Reg. Lond.

[6] Pat. 10 Edw. II.

[7] Reg. Lond. Morant, Essex, vol. II. p. 614, refers to a rental of this house, made when John de Kensington was Prior.

Brother REGINALD, Prior of St. Bartholomew, cited to convocation May 1, 1437 [1].

13. JOHN, Prior of St. Bartholomew, cited to convocation 1439 [2]; so was

14. WILLIAM BOLTON, cited to convocation 1509, 1529 [3]; he died April 15, 1532 [4].

15. ROBERT FULLER, Abbot of Waltham Holy Cross 1532, was elected and held this Priory with his Abbacy as Prior Commendatory. He surrendered this house to the King Oct. 25, 1540, 31 Henry VIII. [5]; and his Abbey of Waltham March 23 the same year.

Both Stow and Weever mistake in calling Bolton the *last* Prior of St. Bartholomew's; for it appears that he had a successor, Robert Fuller, Abbot of Waltham Holy Cross, who was elected in 1532, and held the priory with his abbacy in manner above mentioned.

At the general dissolution of abbeys and religious houses under Henry VIII. the priory of St. Bartholomew, with the manor of Canonbury, among its other appurtenances, was surrendered by Fuller to the King on the 25th October, 1539. A copy of the instrument by which this was effected, with the seal of the priory, is given in Mr. Nichols's interesting work before referred to.

The following is a list of all the Monks who had pensions allowed them on the dissolution, as appears by a large folio volume of pensions given to Monks, remaining in the Augmentation Office.

---

[1] Reg. Lond.        [2] Ibid.

[3] Reg. Fitz James.

[4] He died at his parsonage at Harrow, and was there interred. *Weever's Funeral Monuments*, p. 434.

[5] Willis's Mitred Abbeys, vol. II. p. 125.

|  |  | £. | s. | d. |
|---|---|---|---|---|
| Robert Glasier - - - - Sub-Prior - - - | 15 | 0 | 0 | *per annum.* |
| William Barlowe - - Canon - - - - - | 6 | 13 | 4 | |
| John Smyth - - - - - Canon - - - - - | 6 | 13 | 4 | |
| Henry George - - - - Canon - - - - - | 6 | 13 | 4 | |
| John Smyth, Junior - Canon - - - - - | 6 | 13 | 4 | |
| Christopher Reynolde Canon - - - - - | 6 | 13 | 4 | |
| Peter Wade - - - - - Canon - - - - - | 6 | 13 | 4 | |
| Robert Stokys - - - - Canon - - - - - | 6 | 13 | 4 | |
| Robert Kenham - - - Canon - - - - - | 6 | 13 | 4 | |
| Richard Duffe - - - - Canon - - - - - | 6 | 13 | 4 | |
| John Sutton - - - - - Canon - - - - - | 6 | 13 | 4 | |
| George Chapman - - Canon - - - - - | 5 | 0 | 0 | |
| Matthew Dyll - - - - Canon - - - - - | 5 | 0 | 0 | |

The abbey of Waltham being in like manner surrendered March 23, 1539-40, Fuller retired to London, where he died in a few months [1].

The manor of Canonbury was in 1539, bestowed on Thomas Lord Cromwell, Lord Privy Seal, Vicar General, Lord Great Chamberlain of England, &c. &c. the chief instrument in dissolving the Monasteries, and depressing the Clergy: the adjoining manor of Highbury being also at this time granted to him.

On the 6th of January, 1539-40, the King married the Lady

---

[1] As appears by his will, dated Aug. 14, and proved Nov. 5, 1540, wherein he styles himself "late Abbot of Waltham, and Prior of St. Bartholomew, Smithfield," out of the revenues of which last house, as being most largely endowed, Mr. Willis supposes his pension was paid if he had any allowed him, but his name is not in the list. He bequeathed his body to be buried in Corpus Christi Chapel, in St. Sepulchre's Church without Newgate, and gave some small legacies to Waltham Church, to the Churchwardens of which, Dr. Fuller tells us, his executor paid £.10. by his appointment 1554. *Nichols's History of Canonbury*, p. 7.

Anne of Cleves; an union concerted by Cromwell, who was created Earl of Essex, April 17, 1540, but soon fell from the height of his ambition, and with him the Princess he recommended to the throne, who was divorced July the 6th. The Earl of Essex was committed to the Tower, July the 9th; attainted of high treason and heresy the 19th; and beheaded the 28th, when Canonbury reverted to the Crown. The Queen fortunately escaped with life; obtained letters patent of naturalization, January 9, 1540-41; and a few days after, a handsome jointure, formed principally from the wreck of Cromwell's fortunes. Among other articles, she had an annuity of £.20 from this manor; which, it is presumed, she enjoyed till her death, July 15, 1557. The grant dated January 20, 1540-41, 31 Henry VIII. after reciting various lands, tenements, messuages, &c. &c. adds:

" Et ulterius, de ampliori gratiâ n'râ, damus et concedimus præ-
" fatæ d'næ Annæ de Cleve, unam annuitatem sive annualem reddi-
" tum viginti librarum sterlingarum, exeuntem de manerio n'ro de
" Canberye, in com' n'ro Middlesexiæ, parcellam nuper possessio-
" num dicti Thomæ Cromwell, nuper comitis Essexiæ, solvendum
" annuatim ad festum S'c'i Michaelis Archangeli[1]."

In the Minister's or Bailiff's Accompts 36 Henry VIII. 1545, of the possessions of Thomas Cromwell, Earl of Essex, in the Augmentation Office, under the title "Annuitas," this possession is thus described:

" Et in quadam annuitate per dominum regem concessâ dominæ
" Annæ de Cleve, filiæ Johannis nuper ducis de Cleve, Guligh,
" Gelder & Barry, pro termino vitæ ejusdem dominæ Annæ, si tam-
" diu infra hoc regnum Angliæ habitaverit & moram fecerit, exeunte
" de manerio ibidem per annum, prout in literis ejusdem domini
" regis patentibus eidem dominæ Annæ inde confectis, datis apud
" Westmonasterium 20 die Januarii, anno regni regis Henrici Octavi
" prædicti 31°, plenius apparet, &c. £.20.

[1] Rymer, Fœd. xiv. 713.

The accounts already referred to, under the title of " *Canbury*, com. " Middlesex," do not return any particular sum for the site of the Manor or capital mansion there, " eo quod reservatur ad usum Do- " mini regis per Franciscum Bryan militem, custodum ejusdem, ut di- " citur."   Whence it should seem that it was intended for the residence of the King.   It was granted however by Edward VI. in 1547, the first year of his reign, in exchange for the site of the Priory of Tinmouth, &c. [1]   And in consideration of the sum of £.1252. 6s. 3d. to John Dudley, Earl of Warwick, to whom it was the more desirable, as a branch of the family of Dudley had a lease from the Prebendary of the neighbouring manor of Stoke Newington.

This nobleman mortgaged the Manor of Canonbury in 1549 to John Yorke, Esq. Citizen and Merchant Tailor of London, for the sum of £.1660; but redeemed it in a very short time: for the Earl, by deed of exchange, dated the 18th July, 4 Edward VI. conveyed the same back again to the King [2]; who, after keeping it two years, restored it by a fresh grant to the said John Dudley, then Duke of Northumberland [3]; who, in a few months, was also attainted, and on August 22, 1553, beheaded under Queen Mary.

This last named possessor was the eldest son of Edmund Dudley, Esq. Speaker of the House of Commons in the reign of Henry VII. who, with Sir Richard Empson, was executed in the beginning of the following reign, to appease the popular clamour excited by their extortions.   He was educated in the Court, under the protection of the King, as some compensation for the severity exercised toward his father; and was appointed to the offices of Master of the Armoury in the Tower, and Master of the Horse to Queen Anne of Cleves; created Viscount Lisle, and made Lord Admiral of England in 1542, in which office he gained great reputation at the siege of Boulogne.   Early in

[1] Harl. MSS. Brit. Mus. No. 7389. 1 Edw. VI.
[2] Record in the Augmentation Office.
[3] Ibid.

the reign of Edward VI. he was deprived of the post of Admiral, but was created Earl of Warwick, appointed Great Chamberlain, and raised to the rank of Duke of Northumberland. He prevailed on Edward to entail the succession to the Crown on the Lady Jane Gray (to whom his son Lord Guildford Dudley was married), and was ruined in the attempt to establish that lady on the throne. He is spoken of by some historians as the most powerful subject England ever possessed, but fraudulent, unjust, and of insatiable ambition. He appears to have been as abject in adversity as he was haughty in prosperity, and whilst under sentence of death in the Tower begged for life in the most unbecoming terms. In a letter to the Earl of Arundel, a copy of which is preserved in the Harleian MSS. he exclaims, " Alas, my good Lord, is my crime so heinous that no " redemption but my bloude can washe awaye the spottes thereof? " An old proverb there is, and that most true, that a livinge dogge " is better than a dead lyon. Oh! that it would please her good " grace to give me life, yea, the life of a dogge, that I might live " and kiss her feet [1]."

After the death of the Duke of Northumberland, Queen Mary granted the Manor of Canonbury, anno 1557, to Thomas Lord Wentworth[2]; who, in 1570, alienated it to John, afterwards Sir John Spencer, Knt. and Baronet (son to Richard Spencer of Waldingfield in Suffolk), from his great wealth usually called " *Rich Spen-* " *cer*," of whom a few anecdotes, it is presumed, will not be unacceptable.

Sir John was a Citizen and Clothworker of London, an Alderman of the same City, Sheriff in 1583-4, and elected Lord Mayor at Michaelmas 1594.

He appears to have possessed much public spirit, loyalty,

[1] Campagna of London, p. 90, 91.
[2] Pat. 3 and 4 Philip and Mary, part 9. June 10.

and patriotism, and though connected with many of the leading characters of the Court in that day, was extremely tenacious of the rights and privileges of the City. In 1594, the year of his Mayoralty, a time of great scarcity, in order to provide against a dearth in the City, the Companies were, by the Lord Mayor's means, to buy each of them a certain quantity of corn brought from foreign parts, and to lay it up in their garnet (or granary) in the Bridge-house. Before this object could be effected, an obstacle presented itself, which went nigh to frustrate the provident intentions of the Mayor; for Sir John Hawkins, to whom the care of the Queen's fleet belonged, required at this time the Bridge-house himself, for the bringing in, and laying up there his provisions for the use of the navy, and the ovens likewise there for baking their ship bread. In this strait Sir John sent an earnest message to the Lord Treasurer Burleigh, the great patron of the City, telling him (after a statement of the case) that " they could with no convenience spare the same." And having further pointed out the great necessity the Citizens had at this time for their granaries and ovens, observes, " that he was informed her " Majesty had garnets about Tower-hill, and Whitehall, and West- " minster; and also, that if they would not serve, her Majesty had in " her hands Winchester house, wherein great quantities might be " laid." " But upon this stout answer of the Mayor they told him, " that he should hear more to his further dislike, and he bade them, " that if they did procure any letters for the same, he doubted not " but to answer them to their Lordships (of the Privy Counsels) good " acceptance. And that now having received letters for the same " from some of the Counsel, he humbly prayed the Lord Treasurer's " good favour, that the same garnets being the City's might be em- " ployed for the use of the same, that there might be no want nor " outcry of the poor for bread, or else, that if there fell out a greater " want and dearth of grain than yet there was, and that the City was " unprovided, his Lordship would be pleased to hold him excused,

" and so most humbly submitted himself to his honour's good
" pleasure [1]."

In the following year, for the purpose of ensuring the better safety
of the City, and having met with some opposition from persons interested, he applied by letter to the Privy Council, referring to their
consideration the propriety of stopping up " some five or six small
" postern doors made through the City walls for the ease of some te-
" nements," which he was desirous of removing, as " things dan-
" gerous," and wished " that some letters were directed from their
" Lordships to the parties concerned for reformation in that behalf [2]."

Within the same year, we also find Sir John very active in the suppression of several tumultuous meetings of apprentices and others in
the City, many of whom he committed to the Compter, promising, in
a letter to the Lord Keeper, to proceed against them with all severity.
Five of these " unruly youths" were afterwards executed on Tower-
hill, the scene of their riotous proceedings [3].

One more example of his firmness shall be given. It being reported that the Queen intended to take Sir John Crooke, Recorder
of London, into her service, and promote him, and the Lord Keeper
(Sir John Pickering) having informed one of the Aldermen thereof,
and having likewise told him that the Queen desired the Lord Mayor
to return to her the names of the persons intended to be put in nomination for that office, the Citizens, alarmed at so extraordinary a
proceeding, and fearing it might affect their privileges, nominated
only one person; and the reason for it was thus given, July 23,
1595, to the Lord Treasurer, by Sir John Spencer :

" Right Honourable, and my very good Lord; albeit I presume,
" &c. I have thought good also to let your Lordship know, that
" upon Saturday morning last I was informed by Sir John Harte,
" that he understood from the Right Honourable the Lord Keeper,

[1] Nichols's History of Canonbury.

[2] Ibid.                          [3] Stow's Chronicles.

" that her most excellent Majesty had taken our Recorder from us
" into her Highness's service ; and that her Majesty's pleasure was
" that we should deliver to my Lord Keeper the names of such as
" we would put, in election anew, to the end that her Majesty might
" please to consider of their aptness for the place ; but, notwith-
" standing that, her Highness would please to leave to our own free
" election therein : howbeit, I have spared hitherto to make any pro-
" ceeding accordingly, partly in respect that I understand not by the
" Recorder himself of his remove ; and chiefly, for that the last term
" there was the like rumour, and yet sodenly it died again ; in which
" respect I thought it discretion to have some sufficient warrant or
" note, eyther from my Lord Keeper himself, or some other of your
" Honours, or from the Recorder, before I proceed to any new elec-
" tion ; lest otherwise I should do the gentleman wrong who holdeth
" the place, and seem myself more hasty than there may be cause.

" But, my good Lord, while I have pause herein until I had
" more certain advertisement, the grave Commoners of the City of
" London, hearing a common bruit that a new Recorder was speed-
" ily to be chosen at a Common Council held at Guildhall on Tues-
" day last for other causes, one of them in the behalf made very
" earnest suite, because in all our councils and consultations (which
" are almost daily for one cause or other), the Recorder hath of aun-
" cient tyme bene present as a principal man, both for advice in law,
" and other direction, and now of late those which we have had
" have been for the most part absent ; that therefore myself and the
" Aldermen would take care that we choose no sergeant nor other
" stranger, but only some one that is resident and dwelling among
" us, and acquainted with our customes, and to make choice of our-
" selves as we have bene wont, without sending any names as hath
" bene mentioned.   And thereof very urgent suite was made in Com-
" mon Council on the behalf of the Commoners, whereof I thought
" it my duty to advertize your Lordship, most humbly desiring you
" to be a means that we may herein have our own free election, ac-

" cording to our auncient custome; for that albeit we have lately had
" most worthy men, yet we have found their long and much absence
" a great maihem unto us.

" And for mine own opinion, my good Lord, as also of many others,
" we have one born and dwelling among us whom we have great ex-
" perience of, and think very able to do us service in this behalf:
" his name is Mr. James Altham [1], son of Mr. Altham, late of Es-
" sex, Esq. He is a bencher of Grai's-inn, and one of our ordinary
" sworn councillors of the City, well acquainted with our customes, and
" very well thought of for his honestie and skill in law, both
" throughout the whole City and elsewhere, and being in election
" last time did very narrowly miss it; in which respects, and for the
" good hope we have of him, myself and many others do onely for
" the good of the City earnestly wish him the place, if her Majesty
" shall please to remove the other, nothing doubting but that her
" most excellent Majesty, and your good Lordship, and my other
" Lords, will take a very good liking of him; and therefore, as a
" well-willer to the City, and one that desireth that the continual
" business thereof may be attended as it ought, I am, as far as I
" may, a most earnest and humble petitioner to your good Lordship
" to farther us and him therein by your honourable letters, or such
" other means as to your Honour shall seem good.

" I am also to advertise your Lordship, that having appointed to
" hold a quarter sessions in the borough of Southwark, according to
" the charter of London, this present day, it so happened, by reason
" of Mr. Recorder's absence, and other letts, which the rest of the
" Knights of the City which should associate me, had, as themselves
" say; that there was not one justice to attend that service but my-
" self, albeit there was eight days warning given, with their own

---

[1] Afterwards Sir James Altham, and an eminent lawyer in his time. He was third
son of James Altham, of Mark's-hall, in Essex, Esq. by his first wife, sister and
heir of Sir Thomas Blanke, Knt. and younger brother of Edward Altham, ancestor
of the Althams of Marks-hall.

" consents, and that they were often put in mind of it; whereupon,
" finding that neither by charter nor otherwise I might hold the
" sessions alone, I was inforced to forbear, and to put the same off
" to some other tyme, even when I was ready to go; whereof I
" thought good to let your Lordship understand, both to the end
" your Honour may perceive how necessary our Recorder's daily pre-
" sence is, as also lest your Honour and others might conceive any
" negligence in me from attending the service which appertaineth to
" my place, whereof I would be sorry to omit the least part."

There was, however, no new election; for Sir John Crooke continued in office till 1603, when he was succeeded by Sir Henry Montague, afterwards Earl of Manchester.

In a curious pamphlet, intituled, " *The Vanity of the Lives and*
" *Passions of Men, by D. Papillon, Gent.* 1651," 8vo, occurs the
following remarkable passage : " In Queen Elizabeth's days, a pirate
" of Dunkerk laid a plot, with twelve of his mates, to carry away
" Sir John Spencer; which if he had done, fifty thousand pounds had
" not redeemed him. He came over the seas in a shallop, with
" twelve musketiers, and in the night came into Barking-creek, and
" left the shallop in the custody of six of his men, and with the
" other six came as far as *Islington*, and there hid themselves in
" ditches, near the path in which Sir John came always to his house;
" but, by the providence of God, Sir John, upon some extraordinary
" occasion, was forced to stay in London that night, otherwise they
" had taken him away; and they, fearing they should be discovered,
" in the night-time came to their shallop, and so came safe to Dun-
" kerk again [1]."

The town residence of Sir John Spencer was in Crosby-place, a
large and sumptuous house within the parish of St. Helen, on the
East side of Bishopsgate-street, which had been built by Sir John
Crosby, and was some time the residence of the Duke of Gloucester,

[1] " I have this," says Papillon, " out of a private record."

afterwards King Richard the Third. "This house [1]," says Stow, " Sir John Spencer lately purchased, made great reparations, kept " his mayoralty there, and since builded a most large warehouse near " thereunto;" and here, in 1603, he lodged, and splendidly entertained the French Ambassador the Marquis de Rosny, Great Treasurer of France, and all his retinue. This nobleman, afterwards prime minister, and better known as the Duke of Sully, arrived in England, with a superb train, soon after the accession of King James the First.

Sir John Spencer died at an advanced age, March 30, 1609, and was buried in the church of St. Helen's in Bishopsgate-street. His monument, having the effigies of himself and his lady in recumbent postures, as large as life, with their daughter kneeling at their feet, is situate in the South aile, " as in a chapel by itself," and bears the following inscription :

" Hic situs est Johannes Spencer, Eques auratus,
Civis & Senator Londinensis, ejusdem Civitatis Prætor, an. D'ni MDXCIIII.
Qui ex *Alicia Bromefeldia* uxore, unicam reliquit filiam *Elizabeth*,
*Gulielmo* Baroni *Compton* enuptam.
Obiit 30 die Martii, anno salutis MDCIX.
Socero bene merito *Gulielmus* Baro *Compton* gener posuit."

The church of St. Helen's having lately undergone a thorough repair, this monument appears to have received rather unhandsome treatment; while several others in the church have been restored to

---

[1] On the site of this house, Crosby-square was built in 1678. A part of the edifice yet remains ; consisting of a spacious hall, of elegant architecture, in the pointed style. It is now divided into two stories by a strong floor in the centre, and has been many years in the occupation of Messrs. Holmes, Hall, and Co. packers; and encumbered with their ponderous machines, and merchandize of various descriptions, affords a striking contrast to the elegant appearance it must have had in former times. Engravings of the interior and exterior of this building, both in its antient and present state, may be found among the " Select Views in London " and its Environs," and in Malcolm's " Londinium Redivivum."

their original and proper state, the "faire goodly tombe" of Sir John Spencer, whatever may have been its former beauties, is now entirely obscured by a coat of *white paint.*

The following particulars are part of a letter from Mr. John Beaulieu, a gentleman of fine parts and good judgment, to Mr. Trumbull, resident at Brussels, copied from *Winwood's State Papers,* vol. III. p. 136.   The letter is dated March 22-April 2, 1609-10.

"Upon Tuesday the funerals of Sir John Spencer were made, "where some thousand men did assist, in mourning cloakes or gowns, "amongst which there were 320 poor men, who had every one of them "a basket given them, stored with the particular provisions set down "in this note inclosed[1].   But to expound to you the mysticall mean- "ing of such an anticke furniture, I am not so skilful an Œdipus, "except it doth design the horn of abundance, which my Lord Comp- "ton hath found in that succession.   But that poor Lord is not like "(if God do not help him) to carry it away for nothing, or to grow "very rich thereby, being in great danger to loosé his witts for the "same; whereof being at the very first newes, either through the ve- "hement apprehension of joy for such a plentiful succession[2], or of "carefulness how to take it up and dispose it, somewhat distracted, "and afterwards reasonably well restored[3], he is now of late fallen

[1] The inclosed note is as follows : "A blacke gowne, four pounds of beef, two "loaves of bread, a little bottle of wine, a candlestick, a pound of candles, two "saucers, two spoons, a black pudding, a pair of gloves, a dozen of points *, two "red herrings, four white herrings, six sprats, and two eggs."

[2] Mr. Beaulieu, in a preceding letter to Mr. Trumbull (which is only quoted by Winwood) relates, that "Sir John Spencer died worth at least £.300,000. some say £.500,000. others £.800,000."

[3] Sir Thomas Edmondes, in a letter to Sir Ralph Winwood, March 17, 1609, ex- presses himself to the same effect.   "The Lord Compton hath been so transported

* Pieces of string about eight inches in length, tagged at both ends with bits of tin plate, formerly used to fasten the garments worn on different parts of the body.

" again (but more deeply) into the same frenzy, so that there seemeth
" to be little hope of his recovery. And what shall these thousands
" and millions avail him if he come to lose, if not his soul, at least
" his witts and reason? It is a faire and ample subject *for a divine to*
" *course riches*, and a notable example to the world not to wooe or
" trust so much in them."

In a subsequent letter, dated March the 29th, Mr. Beaulieu gives
the following account:

" Here is dead within these two days, the old Lady Spencer, fol-
" lowing the heels of her husband, who gave away amongst her
" kindred £.13,000 of the £.15,000 which she was to have of my
" Lord Compton; who is now altogether distracted, and so franticke,
" as that he is forced to be kept bound. The administration of his goods
" and lands is committed to the Lords Chamberlaine, Privy Seal, and
" Worcester; who, coming the last week into the City, took an in-
" ventory (in the presence of the Sheriffs) of the goods, amongst
" which (it is said) there were bonds found for 133,000 pounds."

Sir John Spencer had by his Lady Alice Bromfield, one sole
daughter and heiress, Elizabeth, of whom Mr. Nichols mentions a
*tradition*, that she was carried off from Canonbury-house in a baker's
basket, by the contrivance of the before-named William, the second
Lord Compton, Lord President of Wales, to whom, in the year
1594, she was married; and thus the Canonbury estate was carried
into his family [1].

" with joy for the great fortune befallen him by the death of Sir John Spencer, his
" father in law, as the over working of the same in his mind did hinder him from
" taking any rest, whereby he was grown half distracted, but now he is reasonably
" well recovered again."

[1] Mr. Biggerstaff, sen. an old inhabitant, and many years vestry-clerk of Islington parish, used to relate a pleasant anecdote respecting this match, from which it
would appear, that the Knight was so much incensed at the elopement of his
daughter, that he totally discarded her, until a reconciliation took place by the kind

The following letter from her to her Lord, *sans* date, but probably written in or about the year 1617, states her wealth to have been much beyond what in these times we can readily have any conception of [1]:

"MY SWEET LIFE,

"Now I have declared to you my mind for the settling of "your state, I suppose that it were best for me to bethink or consider "with myself what allowance were meetest for me. For, considering "what care I have had of your estate, and how respectfully I dealt "with those, which, both by the laws of God, of nature, and of civil "polity, wit, religion, government, and honesty, you my dear are "bound to, I pray and beseech you to grant me £.1600 *per annum* "quarterly to be paid.

interposition of Queen Elizabeth: to effect which, the following stratagem is said to have been resorted to. When the matrimonial fruit was ripe, the Queen requested that Sir John would, with her, stand sponsor to the first offspring of a young couple, happy in their love, but discarded by their father: the Knight readily complied, and her Majesty dictated his own surname for the Christian name of the child. The ceremony being performed, Sir John assured the Queen, that having discarded his own daughter, he should adopt this boy as his son. The parents of the child being now introduced, the Knight, to his great surprize, discovered that he had adopted his own grandson; who ultimately succeeded his father in his honours, and his grandfather in his wealth.

This nobleman (Spencer) the second Earl, particularly distinguished himself in the perilous reign of Charles I. Having relinquished a life of ease, in an advanced age, he raised a regiment of foot and a troop of horse at his own expence, and fighting in the cause of royalty, was slain at the battle at Hopton Heath, March 19, 1642. At Castle Ashby, the seat of the Earl of Northampton, is a fine portrait of him in armour.

The foregoing story is rational, and not improbable; it is however given merely as a matter of tradition.

[1] Nichols's History of Canonbury. This letter was first printed in the Europ. Mag. for June 1782.

" Also I would (besides that allowance for my apparel) have
" £.600. added yearly (quarterly to be paid) for the performance of
" charitable works; and those things I would not, neither will be
" accountable for.

" Also, I will have three horses for my own saddle, that none shall
" dare to lend or borrow; none lend but I, none borrow but you.

" Also, I would have two gentlewomen, lest one should be sick or
" have some other lett; also, believe that it is an undecent thing for
" a gentlewoman to stand mumping alone, when God hath blessed
" their Lord and Lady with a good estate.

" Also, when I ride a hunting or hawking, or travel from one
" house to another, I will have them attending; so, for either of
" those said women, I must and will have for either of them a horse.

" Also, I will have six or eight gentlemen; and I will have my
" two coaches, one lined with velvet to myself, with four very fair
" horses; and a coach for my women, lined with sweet cloth, one
" laced with gold, the other with scarlet, and laced with watched
" lace and silver, with four good horses.

" Also, I will have two coachmen, one for my own coach, the
" other for my women.

" Also, at any time when I travel, I will be allowed not only car-
" roches and spare horses for me and my women, but I will have such
" carriages, as shall be fitting for all, orderly, not pestering my
" things with my women's, nor their's with chambermaids', nor
" their's with wash-maids'.

" Also, for laundresses, when I travel, I will have them sent away
" before with the carriages, to see all safe; and the chambermaids
" I will have go before with the greens [1], that the chambers may be
" ready, sweet and clean.

---

[1] It was the custom in former times to strew the floors with *green* rushes. See
Blount's Tenures (art. Aylesbury.) Strutt's Manners and Customs, vol. III. p. 72.
Douce's Illustrations of Shakspeare, 8vo, 1807, vol. I. p. 477. Paul Hentzner's Tra-
vels in England, &c.

" Also, for that it is indecent to crowd up myself, with my gentle-
" man-usher in my coach, I will have him to have a convenient horse,
" to attend me either in city or in country; and I must have two foot-
" men; and my desire is, that you defray all the charges for me.

" And for myself, besides my yearly allowance, I would have
" twenty gowns of apparel, six of them excellent good ones, eight of
" them for the country, and six other of them very excellent good ones.

" Also, I would have, to put in my purse, £.2,000, and £.200;
" and so for you to pay my debts.

" Also, I would have £.6,000 to buy me jewels, and £.4,000 to
" buy me a pearl chain.

" Now, seeing I am so *reasonable* unto you, I pray you to find my
" children apparel, and their schooling; and also my servants (men
" and women) their wages.

" Also, I will have my houses furnished, and all my lodging cham-
" bers to be suited with all such furniture as is fit; as beds, stools,
" chairs, suitable cushions, carpets, silver warming-pans, cupboards
" of plate, fair hangings, and such like; so, for my drawing-cham-
" bers in all houses, I will have them delicately furnished, both with
" hangings, couch, canopy, glass, carpet, chair-cushions, and all
" things thereunto belonging.

" Also, my desire is, that you would pay all my debts, build
" Ashby-house, and purchase lands; and lend no money (as you love
" God) to the Lord Chamberlain [1]; who would have all, perhaps
" your life from you. Remember his son, my Lord Walden [2]; what
" entertainment he gave me when you were at Tilt-yard. If you
" were dead, he said he would be a husband, a father, a brother;
" and he said, he would marry me. I protest, I grieve to see the

[1] Thomas Earl of Suffolk, (one of the Committees of Lord Compton's effects;)
see p. 233. He was appointed Lord Treasurer July 10, 1613.

[2] Theophilus Lord Howard of Walden succeeded his father as Earl of Suffolk,
May 28, 1626. *Nichols's History of Canonbury.*

" poor man have so little wit and honesty, to use his friend so vilely.
" Also, he fed me with untruths concerning the Charter-house; but
" that is the least; he wished me much harm.   You know him; God
" keep you and me from such as he is!

" So now that I have declared to you what I would have, and what
" that is that I would not have; I pray, that when you be an Earl, to
" allow me £.1000. more than I now desire, and *double attendance.*

" Your loving wife,

" ELIZA COMPTON."

On August 2, 1618, this noble Lord was created Earl of Northampton [1]; and had issue two daughters, and a son, Spencer, who
succeeded him in titles and estates, and married Mary, daughter to Sir
Francis Beaumont, knt. by whom he had issue six sons and two
daughters.   James, his eldest son succeeded; he was twice married,
but left no issue by the first lady; by the second lady, who was Mary,
daughter of Baptist Viscount Campden, he had three sons and two
daughters.   George, his eldest son and successor, married Jane,
daughter of Sir Stephen Fox, knight, by whom he had six daughters
and four sons; viz. James, fifth Earl, who left no male issue; George,
sixth Earl, who had no issue; Stephen, who died young, and Charles,

---

[1] Hence it appears that the " distraction" mentioned in p. 232 was only temporary.   His death however happened on a sudden, of which S. Meddus, in a letter
dated July 2, 1630, preserved in Peck's Desiderata Curiosa, vol. II. p. 39, has
given the following account: " Yesterday sev'nnight, the Earl of Northampton,
" Lord President of Wales (after he had waited on the King at supper, and had
" also supped), went in a boat with others to wash himself in the Thames, and so
" soon as his legs were in the water but to the knees, he had the colic, and cried
" out, " *Have me into the boat again, or I am a dead man!*" and died a few hours
" after, at his lodgings in the Savoy, within the suburbs of London, on June 24,
" 1630 (6 Car. I.), and was buried at Compton, with his ancestors." *Nichols's
History of Canonbury.*

who married Mary, only daughter of Sir Berkeley Lucy, Bart. by whom he had issue four daughters and two sons. Charles succeeded his uncle, as seventh Earl, but having no male issue, was succeeded by his brother Spencer, the eighth Earl, who married Jane, daughter of Henry Lawton, of Northampton, Esq. by whom he had issue a son and daughter. Charles, the present and ninth Earl, married August 18, 1787, to the eldest daughter of Joshua Smith, of Earl Stoke Park, Wilts, Esq. by whom he has issue now living, a son, Spencer Joshua Alwyne, Lord Compton, born January 1790, and a daughter, Lady Frances-Elizabeth Compton.

The paternal coat of Compton is, Sable, a lion passant gardant Or, between three esquires helmets Argent.

The copyholders in this Manor pay a small fine certain, on death or alienation, with a trifling quit-rent; and the estates descend according to the strict custom of *Gavelkind.* The annual court-baron is held, on the Saturday before Michaelmas, at Canonbury-tavern.

PLATE VIII.

F.W.L. Stockdale del.ᵗ

J. Hawksworth sculp.ᵗ

To John Nichols Esq.ʳ F.S.A. Lond. Edinb. & Perth.

This Engraving of the ANCIENT TOWER at CANONBURY,

Is Respectfully inscribed by his greatly obliged & obedient Servant  J. Nelson

Published May 1.1811 by Russell, Upper Street Islington

PLATE IX

Drawn & Engraved by J. Hawksworth.

To Mrs Hunt, of Canonbury Boarding School.

This Engraving of an *ANCIENT CHIMNEY PIECE* in her House.

Is most Respectfully inscribed by her greatly obliged & obedient humble Servant J. Nelson.

Published May 1. 1811 by Russell, Upper Street, Islington.

### CANONBURY-HOUSE.

" See on the distant slope, majestic shews,

" Old Canonbury's tow'r, an antient pile,

" To various fates assign'd; and where, by turns,

" Meanness and grandeur have alternate reign'd.

" Thither, in later days, hath *genius* fled

" From yonder City, to respire, and die.

" There the sweet Bard of Auburn sat, and tun'd

" The plaintive moanings of his village dirge.

" There learned Chambers treasur'd lore for *men,*

" And Newbery there his A B C's for *babes.*"

Fox.

Canonbury-house, the manerial residence, was originally built for a mansion-house for the Priors of St. Bartholomew, as before mentioned. This edifice was of considerable extent, covering nearly the whole site of ground now called Canonbury-place, and having a park, with spacious garden grounds, and domestic offices.

One large old house, having a tower of brick, about 17 feet square, and 60 feet high, which, both externally and within doors, retains much of its primitive appearance (see Plate VIII.)[1], together with a considerable part of the wall that encompassed the park and garden ground, form at this time the most striking remains of this once noble dwelling.

Stow says, William Bolton (who was Prior of St. Bartholomew from 1509 till his death, April 15, 1532), " builded of new the ma-

---

[1] There is a very picturesque and good engraving of this building in the " Select " Views in London and its Environs."

" nor of Canonbury at Islington, which belonged to the Canons of " that house." It is, however, probable, that he only reinstated the decayed parts of the original mansion, at the same time making considerable improvements on the old foundation, and that the Prior's *new* building was confined to the premises with the brick tower just mentioned. This being complete in itself, and quite detached from the old house, was perhaps built by the Prior, for the advantage of the delightful prospect afforded from its greater height.

Mr. Lysons thinks it probable, that this part of the premises was built by some of the owners of Canonbury since the Reformation; but from Bolton's rebus (a bolt in a tun) appearing in so many parts of the wall[1] connected with the tower, and which is evidently of the same materials and workmanship, there can be no doubt of its having been erected by him. Part of this wall still incloses the ground attached to the Canonbury tavern on the East, dividing it from the open fields, and on the North by the side of *Hopping-lane.* The Western wall branched off from the above somewhat behind the site of Compton-terrace, towards Canonbury-lane. For the erection of the original mansion-house, we may, without doubt, refer to the date (1362) inscribed on the building as before mentioned.

Bolton is represented as a great builder. The Priory of St. Bartholomew, and the Parish Church adjoining, with the lodgings belonging to the Priory, were all either rebuilt or completely repaired by him.

Camden, in his " Remaines," remarks, " It may seeme doubtfull " whether Bolton, Prior of St. Bartholomew, in Smithfield, was " wiser when he invented for his name a bird-bolt through a tunne, " or when he built him an house upon Harrow-hill, for feare of " an inundation after a great conjunction of planets in the watery " triplicate [2].

[1] " On the outside of that wall which faces Wells's-row the bolt in tun is cut " in stone in two places. The tun lies in fess, and the bolt runs through it." *Nichols's History of Canonbury.*—This part of the wall has been long pulled down.

[2] Hall, in his Chronicle, following common tradition, relates that Bolton, fore-

Some interesting parts of the old mansion at Canonbury are yet remaining a little eastward of the tower building, comprising three dwelling-houses, which have been formed out of the antient edifice, with modern fronts, &c. These are the Canonbury boarding-school, kept by Mrs. Hunt, and the houses on each side, occupied by Messrs. Field and Swaine.

From the appearance of these habitations, it is evident that the interior of the mansion-house before re-instated by Prior Bolton was materially altered, and the whole edifice again thoroughly restored by Sir John Spencer, on his coming to reside here about the year 1599. Previously to this time, it appears to have been rented of him by particular individuals.

In the passage of Mr. Field's house, over a door, is the arch represented in Plate II. fig. 6. having a blank escutcheon, and one charged with the rebus of Prior Bolton. There are also over another doorway the armorial bearings of Sir Walter Dennys [1], who was knighted 5 Henry VII. on Prince Arthur's being created Prince of Wales. These are cut in a stone about a yard square, (see Plate II. fig. 2.) and were formerly fixed over a chimney in that part of the old house,

seeing, by astrological prognostications, eclipses in watery signs, and particular conjunctions of the planets, that there would be great floods, built himself on high ground a house at Harrow, and stored it with provisions for two months. But Stow, properly enough, accounts for this fable: that Bolton, being rector of Harrow (as it appears from the archiepiscopal register he was nine or ten years, from Sept. 23, 1522, to his death in 1532), among other improvements at his parsonage-house, built a *dove-house* " to serve him when he had foregone his priory." See *Stow's Survey of London.*

[1] Quarterly, viz. 1st, Azure, three leopards faces vorant fleurs de lis Or, over all a bend of the 2d, for *Dennys.* Second, Or, on a chief Sable, three torteaux, for *Russell.* Third, Argent, a raven proper, within a border Sable bezanté, for *Corbet.* Fourth, Quarterly, 1 and 4, Argent, on a bend Gules, three martlets Or, for *Davers;* 2 and 3, Gules, two bars and a chief Or, the latter charged with two bucks' heads cabossed, for *Popham.* In centre a crescent Or, upon a torteaux, which seems intended for a distinction of brotherhood.

which was adorned with a turret. The stone was taken away some years ago, by Mr. Duval, the mason employed in some alterations of the premises; but has been since restored, and placed in its present situation, with the following inscription underneath :

" These were the arms of Sir Walter Dennys, of Gloucestershire,
" who was made a Knight by bathing at the creation of Arthur,
" Prince of Wales, in November, 1489, and died September 1,
" 21 Henry VII. 1505; and was buried in the church at Olvis-
" ton, in Gloucestershire. He married Margaret, daughter of Sir
" Richard Weston, Knight : to which family Canonbury-house
" formerly belonged. The carving is therefore above 280 years old."

The latter part of this inscription is erroneous, as neither the family of *Dennys*, nor that of *Weston* could have any interest in these premises at the above period, it being antecedent to the dissolution of religious houses, and consequently before the estate came into lay hands. These arms were, in all probability, first placed here by some descendant, of one of these families, who might afterwards have resided at Canonbury; perhaps, one of the *Comptons : Joan*, a daughter of Sir Walter, having married into that family, and Mary, his descendant, was married to a *Fisher*, in the reign of Queen Elizabeth. The Comptons had no interest here till 1610, a century after the death of Sir Walter Dennys.

The circumstance of these arms being improperly marshalled, as noted by Mr. Nichols, (the arms of *Corbet*, the first heiress, married to one of the *Dennys* family, being improperly borne after those of *Russel*) will make somewhat to prove that this carving was executed at a later period than that mentioned in the inscription. Such an error would hardly have escaped the nice observation, as to matters of *etiquette*, in the chivalrous age of Henry the Seventh.

In the house of Mr. Field, is also a very handsome chimney-piece of carved oak, now coated with white paint; and the adjoining boarding-school contains a number of specimens of the taste for stucco work, and ornamental carving, that prevailed about the time of Queen Elizabeth. The cielings of a very fine set of rooms on the first floor are elaborately embellished with a variety of ornaments in stucco, consisting of ships, flowers, foliage, &c. with medallions of Alexander the Great, Julius Cæsar, Titus Vespasian, &c. The arms of Queen Elizabeth are also represented in several places, one of which bears the initials E. R. and the date 1599.

The chimney-pieces in this house are particularly beautiful, and in their original state must have had an extremely rich and grand appearance; but they have all unfortunately been covered with white paint; though, in other respects, they have hitherto escaped meeting with any considerable injury. One of them (Plate IX.) exhibits a very elaborate piece of workmanship in carved oak, containing figures of the Christian and Cardinal Virtues, with other devices; also, the arms of the City of London, with those of Sir John Spencer [1], and the Clothworkers Company, of which he was a member. His name also was probably intended by the monogram or device in the same compartment with the date 1601.

In another room, the chimney-piece is divided into three compartments, containing a male and female figure in long robes, with the arms of Sir John Spencer in the centre, surrounded by tritons, griffins, serpents, fruit, and other ornaments, finely carved, and intersected by beautiful columns, with Corinthian capitals. The whole is supported by two figures, bearing on their heads, baskets of fruit. The arms of Sir John are also carved in several other parts of the chimney-piece, which also bears his crest (an eagle volant) immediately over the fire-place.

These rooms still remain handsomely wainscoated with oak, in square and lozenge pannels, but entirely painted over with white. An old oak staircase is yet standing in this house, which seems to have been erected by Sir John Spencer, at the time of his fitting up

[1] Argent, two bars gemelles, between three eagles displayed proper.

the rooms; also several ponderous oak doors, with massive hinges, bolts, and other fastenings of iron.

The *tout ensemble* of these premises, exhibits a striking contrast of the domestic architecture, and interior decoration of antient and modern times. The lofty and elegant folding sash window, opening to the lawn and shrubbery from a parlour tastefully ornamented with the fashionable furniture of the present day, is here opposed to the substantial oak wainscoat, the heavy stuccoed cieling, and the ponderous chimney ornaments of the 16th century.

Here is also a range of tiled building of some length, which seems to have been the stabling attached to the mansion-house; it has an old oak folding gate, apparently of the time of Sir John Spencer. This is now an appendage to the Canonbury-tavern adjoining; at one end is a bakehouse, where the pastry and rolls are prepared for the use of the house and tea garden; in the centre some stalls for horses yet remain, and the other extremity is chiefly used as a depository for coals, fire-wood and lumber.

The old mansion-house, when in its perfect state, was adorned with a turret, &c. as represented in the annexed engraving[1]; the whole line of the building on the Southern side, is there exhibited as it appeared before the alterations took place. The site of the house will be immediately known by marking the situation of the two octagonal summer houses, which terminate the garden wall in the engraving, as these are yet to be seen in the ground attached to the house of Mr. De Paiva, which slopes down to the river side, from Canonbury-place. On one of them is Prior Bolton's rebus, before mentioned, cut in a stone about 15 inches square, as also in three distant

---

[1] See also a small print of the house, dated 1731, from the book of views mentioned in page 168, and two other views by Chatelain, published in 1750. Likewise an engraving of the same, in a landscape nine inches by sixteen, published by Boydell about ten years after. In the Pepysian Library is an etching of the East view of *Canonbury House.*

Canonbury Tower.

S. View of Canbury House.

## 36

Chatelain delin

J.Roberts sculp.

## The North View of Islington.

Publish'd according to Act of Parliament

Chatelain delin

J. Roberts Sculp.

## The South East View of Cambray House

Publish'd according to Act of Parliament

parts of the old wall connected with them. (See Plate II. figs. 5, 7, 8[1].)

In the garden-ground attached to the house of Mrs. Ancrum, is a cold bath, supplied by one of the antient springs in the neighbourhood. This was a luxury, without doubt, enjoyed many centuries ago, by the holy fathers resident at Canonbury; for it would appear from the numerous heads of excellent water about this spot, that they were abundantly supplied with that element for every purpose to which it could be applied, either of luxury or use.

The few particulars here described are now the only remains of this once magnificent dwelling; the site being for the most part occupied by handsome modern houses, inhabited chiefly by merchants and persons retired from trade. The first step towards its present state was the granting of a lease, in 1770, for the term of 61 years, at a moderate ground-rent, to the late John Dawes, Esq. mentioned in page 138, who built a villa, and three other good dwelling-houses[2], delightfully situated near the New River, on that side of the antient house looking towards the road leading from the Lower-street to Ball's Pond. On other parts of the old site this number has been since increased; and there are at present fourteen houses, with gardens, &c. (exclusive of the tavern); also the old building, with the brick tower, which is occupied by —— Simes, bailiff of the Manor to Lord Northampton.

The lower part of the building last mentioned, which is seven stories in height to the top of the tower, comprizes a large hall, with kitchen and other offices, having two entrances from the North and

[1] See several prints of bird-bolts, and remarks on them, in Douce's Illustrations of Shakspeare, vol. I. p. 164.

[2] The first five new houses built at Canonbury, at the time of their sale, in May 1788, produced a nett annual income of £.200 above the ground-rent; Mr. Dawes resided in one of them, the house now occupied by Mrs. Ancrum, till he purchased the adjoining estate at Highbury, as mentioned in the account of that place. He also added the projecting windows at the West end of the old tower building.

Western sides. On the South it was formerly connected with the mansion by an arched gateway, which formed an entrance to the Court-yard. Behind is a neat garden, containing several fruit-trees, and some excellent vines. The staircase is of oak, of considerable width; it ascends through the tower to the several apartments, of which there are 23 in the building, with convenient closets on the landing-places attached to them. The two principal rooms, which are in the first and second stories of the plaster part of the building, facing Canonbury-lane, form each a square of about 20 feet, and in height 12 feet; they are very handsome in regard to internal decoration, having each a wainscot of oak from the floor to the cieling, in complete preservation, and *as yet* uncovered with paint. These apartments appear also to have been fitted up by Sir John Spencer during the time of his residence at Canonbury. The wainscot of the lower room is divided into small pannels, with fluted pilasters, and an ornamented cornice. Over the fire-place are two compartments of finely carved oak, embellished with lions' heads, escallop shells, and other figures; also a small carved pair of bellows, which, being surrounded by objects more prominent, are only observed upon close inspection. The other room, which is over this, is yet more handsomely ornamented with carved wainscot in the Grecian taste, consisting of pannels intersected with beautifully wrought pilasters. A handsome cornice runs round the top, composed of wreathed foliage and escallop shells. Over the chimney are two female figures carved in oak, representing *Faith* and *Hope*, with the mottos, " FIDES . VIA " DEVS . MEA ;" and " SPES . CERTA . SVPRA." — These are surmounted by a handsome cornice, of pomegranates, with other fruit and foliage, having in the centre the arms of Sir John Spencer. The floors of both rooms are of fir-boards, of very large dimensions; in some parts repaired with oak. The cielings are of plain plaster, and the windows are modern glazed sashes, looking down Canonbury-lane.

The other apartments are smaller in size, and contain nothing particularly worthy of remark. On the white wall of the staircase, near the top of the tower, the following Latin hexameter verses comprizing the abbreviated names of the Kings of England, from William the Conqueror to Charles the First, are painted in Roman characters, an inch in length :

" Will . Con . Will . Rufus . Hen . Stephanus . Henq' . secundus .
" Ri . John . Hen . tert' . Ed . terni . Ricq' . secundus .
" Hen . tres . Ed . bini . Ri . ternus . Septimus . Henry .
" Octavus . post . hunc . Edw . sext . Regina . Maria .
" Elizabetha . soror . succedit . Fr— . Jacobus .
" Subsequitur Charolus ; qui longo tempore vivat !
   " Mors tua, Mors Christi, Fraus Mundi, Gloria Cœli,
   " Et dolor Inferni, sint meditanda tibi."

These lines were, in all probability, the effusion of some poetical inhabitant of an upper apartment in the building, during the time of the monarch last named; such, it would appear, having been no uncommon residents in the place : they are somewhat obliterated from damp at one end, but yet sufficiently legible to be transcribed, with the help of a lighted candle.

From the flat leads on the top of the tower, is one of the most delightful panoramic views to be found near the Metropolis. It embraces an uninterrupted view on all sides, over the adjoining villages, the City of London, and the hills of Hampstead and Highgate, with the surrounding counties for several miles. In a clear day, the meanderings of the Thames may be perceived, with that fine building Greenwich Hospital, and the vessels sailing on the river as far as Gravesend. There is a fish-pond 1 rood 30 poles in extent, on the North part of the building, of considerable depth, encompassed by an old wall, coëval with the house, which, notwithstanding continual depredation, still contains some very good carp and tench.

An absurd tradition prevails in the neighbourhood, that the monks of St. Bartholomew had a subterraneous communication from Canonbury, to the Priory in Smithfield. This story, arising, no doubt, from the vulgar prejudices entertained against the Romish clergy at the time of the Reformation, has gained strength from the discovery, at various times, of brick archways under ground (sufficiently large to admit of a person standing upright) in digging foundations, &c. near the old premises. An excavation of this kind, partly choked up with earth, was, not long since, explored by Mr. Leroux, and found to extend under Canonbury-lane, from the Park, in a Southern direction. It has an open square entrance in the centre, within a few yards of the road side, and becomes gradually contracted towards each extremity, where it ends in a point. From the fine sediment found at the bottom, which has evidently been deposited by water, and from other circumstances, there is no doubt, that this is the remains of one of the old conduit-heads which were formed to receive that element from the springs situate in higher ground, and whence it was conveyed by pipes to the wells and reservoirs belonging to the Prior's house, &c.

One of these conduit-heads yet remains in the field adjoining Canonbury-lane, near that part of the New River, called the Horse-shoe, within a few yards of the bridge; which, after having laid open for many years, has been lately covered by an arch of brick-work, at the expence of Mr. Miller, a respectable surgeon, of Islington; and water, which is much esteemed for its clearness and purity, is still procured from the place by many of the neighbouring inhabitants. Another of these conduit-heads stood formerly not far from the

---

[1] The pipes used for the conveyance of water in those times were in many instances not imbedded in the earth, as is the present custom, but inclosed within a capacious arch of brick-work, into which the workmen could, upon occasion, descend to repair any decay or accident which might happen to them. In a report on the Dog House Conduit (History of Shoreditch, p. 366), Three several springs of water are said to be " conveyed *in draines of brick* to a conduit-house," &c.

above, to the Eastward, which in the old engravings of Canonbury House is represented as a small building similar to that which now covers the head of water at White Conduit House [1].

The Priory in Smithfield was certainly supplied with water from Canonbury; for in 1433 the Master and Brethren of the Hospital gave an annuity of 6s. 8d. to the Prior and Convent of St. Bartholomew, on condition that they should have free use of an aqueduct, the head of which was within the precincts of Canonbury. And a grant of Henry VIII. in 1544 of certain possessions belonging to that house, includes " also the water from the Conduit head of St. Bartholomew, " within the Manor of *Canbury*, co. Midd'x, as enjoyed by Prior " Bolton and his predecessors [2]."

In digging for gravel, &c. in that part of the park lately in the possession of Mr. Leroux, leaden pipes of a large size, connected with these springs, or those of Highbury, have recently been discovered branching in various directions. The old key of the park gate is still in the possession of Mr. Simes, the bailiff, having appended to it an inscription, requesting ladies to take off their pattens; and in the garden ground behind Mr. Field's house, several copper coins have been dug up, but which, having been either lost or intermixed with others, cannot now be described.

The old tower building being quite detached from the neighbouring houses, encompassed with pleasant fields and gardens, and in a most salubrious air, considering its proximity to London, is in the summer time chiefly occupied by persons whose affairs do not permit them to be farther from town, and who come hither for retirement or for health. To such it is now let out in apartments by the present tenant, who by these means, and other domestic accommodations, realizes a handsome annual income.

[1] Balme's House at Hoxton, better known as Sir George Whitmore's, was, time out of mind, till within these few years, supplied with water from a spring in Canonbury-field. *Ellis's History of Shoreditch*, p. 125.

[2] Malcolm's Londinium Redivivum, vol. I. p. 286.

K K

Since the Reformation many illustrious persons have resided at Canonbury. It was rented of Sir John Spencer by William Ricthorne, Esq. who died here in 1582 ; and was afterwards, for a few years, in the possession of Sir Arthur Atye, Public Orator of the University of Oxford, who married his widow[1]. The Charter of incorporation granted to the Butchers Company in 1605 is signed by Thomas Egerton, Baron of Ellesmere, then Lord Chancellor, and dated at Canonbury, where this worthy Peer was then on a visit to Sir John Spencer. The Compton family appears to have resided here after the marriage of the second Lord with the heiress of Sir John Spencer as before mentioned. A daughter of Lord Compton was born here in 1605 [2].

From 1627 to 1635, Canonbury House was rented by the Lord Keeper Coventry[3]. In the Strafford papers is a letter from the Earl of Derby, dated Jan. 29, 1635, from *Canbury Park*, where he was staid from St. James's by the greatest snow he ever saw in England. William Fielding, Earl of Denbigh, died at Canonbury House in 1685 [4].

Several literary characters also appear to have had lodgings in the yet remaining part of this fabrick, since it has been appropriated to that use. Samuel Humphreys died at Canonbury on the 11th of January 1737, aged about 40. " He was," says the Daily Post, " a " gentleman well skilled in the learned languages, and the polite " among the modern. Though he was very conversant in and fond " of history, and every part of the *Belles Lettres*, yet his genius led " him chiefly to poetry, in which (had fortune been as indulgent to " him as nature) he would have left such compositions as must have " delighted late posterity. The admired Mr. Handel had a due es-

[1] Some of his children were baptized at Islington in 1590, 1591, and 1592.

[2] Parish Register.

[3] A son of Sir Thomas Coventry was baptized in 1627. He dates from *Canbury* in 1634. Strafford's Letters, vol. I. p. 447 ; and Harl. MSS. Brit. Mus. No. 7001. *Lysons's Environs.*

[4] Collins's Peerage, edition 1756, vol. II. p. 254.

" teem for the harmony of his numbers ; and the great Mæcenas, the
" Duke of Chandos, shewed the regard he had for his Muse by so ge-
" nerously rewarding him for celebrating his Grace's seat at Canons.
" Some disappointments Mr. Humphreys met with forced him to ap-
" pear as a translator, on which occasion the graceful ease and other
" beauties of his versions gained him no little applause ; but his too
" intense application (for he sometimes wrote the whole night), and
" his never taking any exercise, greatly impaired his health ; and at
" last brought him into a consumption which proved fatal to him.
" His corpse was buried in a private, but decent manner, in Islington
" Church-yard [1]." He wrote Ulysses, an Opera [2], translated Spectacle
de la Nature ; wrote " Canons, a poem," and several other pieces.

Ephraim Chambers, the well-known author of the Cyclopædia,
died here whilst engaged in a continuation of that elaborate work, in
the year 1740.

Dr. Oliver Goldsmith had apartments for some time in the old turret building, where he is supposed to have written some of his works.

The late John Newbery, Esquire, author of several useful books
for children, also resided here, and had under his protection the Poet,
Christopher Smart.

Among the inhabitants of Canonbury may also be reckoned Mr.
Deputy Harrison, many years printer of the London Gazette; Mr.
Robert Horsfield, successor to Messrs. Knaptons, Pope's book-
sellers, and afterwards Treasurer of the Stationers Company ; also
——— Palmer, Esq. a Justice of the Peace, and Train-bearer to Arthur
Onslow, Esq. Speaker of the House of Commons. Dr. John Hill
died at Canonbury in Feb. 1789 [3]. And the Rev. John Williams, LL. D.
40 years a Dissenting Minister at Sydenham, and author of " An En-
" quiry into the Authenticity of the First and Second Chapters of St.
" Matthew's Gospel;" " Thoughts on Subscription to the XXXIX

[1] " Samuel Humphreys, a stranger," was buried at Islington Jan. 15, 1737. *Parish Register.*
[2] See Biographia Dramatica. [3] Obituary, European Magazine.

" Articles ;" " A Concordance to the Greek Testament ;" and " An
" Enquiry and Observations respecting the Discovery of America [1]."

The Canonbury tavern, which stands near the old mansion house,
within the park wall, was, about half a century ago, an inconsiderable ale-house, scarcely more than one fourth of its present size, and
was then kept by Mr. Benjamin Collins, who was Churchwarden
when the new Church was opened in 1754. It afterwards came into
the possession of Mr. James Lane [2], who had been a common soldier,
and who made considerable additions and improvements to the premises. During his time it became a house of some trade during
the pleasant part of the year, and continued increasing in business and
respectability till his death in 1783. It was kept for a short time after
by —— Hemingway; and about the year 1785 was taken by Mr. Sutton, who dying soon after, his widow continued to carry on the business, and make further improvements on the premises, by building
additional rooms, &c. as the trade was found to increase. The bowling green and tea gardens were also laid out by Mrs. Sutton, and
during the time of her keeping the house it entertained more corporate and parochial bodies, clubs, and other dinner parties, than almost
any other tavern in the vicinity of the Metropolis. It still continues
to be a place of great resort for parties of the above description and
others, particularly during the summer season.

The gardens are very pleasant, and are kept in excellent order. They
consist of a shrubbery and bowling green, with Dutch-pin and trap-
ball grounds, and a butt for the exercise of ball-firing, which has of
late been much resorted to by Volunteers and others from the Metropolis. The house was taken by the present occupier Mr. Baxter at
L. D. 1808, upon Mrs. Sutton's retiring from business. The premises are partly enclosed by the old park-wall and the fish-pond be-

[1] Obituary, Gent. Mag.
[2] See Inscriptions in the Church-yard.

Pl. XVIII.

View of Canonbury in its Ancient State.

Published by J. & J. Rundell about the Year 1760

*Drawn & Engraved by S.Rawle.*

## CANNONBURY HOUSE, ISLINGTON.

Canonbury Tavern.

before mentioned. On the former the Eastern side of the house stands erected, and has from thence a beautiful prospect over the fields towards Hackney, Limehouse, &c. The whole of the premises occupies an area of about four acres.

The two houses fronting the fields at the East end of Canonbury-lane, near the old tower, have a handsome appearance, and are very pleasantly situated. The white house has recently been furnished with an attic story, and fitted up throughout in the most elegant style for the residence of —— De Paiva, Esq. The gardens and pleasure grounds are tastefully laid out, and being terminated by the brink of the New River, its serpentine course at this place forms a most agreeable and beautiful boundary. The walks about the fields in this neighbourhood are very pleasant, the ground being for the most part uninclosed and intersected by foot paths, which are found very accommodating to persons passing from different parts of the village to Kingsland, Hackney, Newington-green, &c. [1]

The plot of ground, containing two acres and 20 perches, whereon stand the seven houses and gardens on the South side of Canonbury-lane, with the ten houses and gardens forming Hornsey-row, is a copyhold estate belonging to the parish of Hornsey. A house at the South end of Hornsey-row was formerly a public house, called *The Castle*, the landlord of which sold a mineral water, procured from a spring in his garden.

The new buildings between Canonbury-park and the Upper-street, comprizing Union Chapel and the adjoining houses on Compton-terrace, together with the dwelling-houses forming part of Canonbury-square, within the Park, were erected about five years ago by Mr. H. Leroux, who had obtained a lease from the Lord of the Manor of 19 acres 1 rood and 31 perches of land, extending between Canonbury and Hopping lanes, for the purpose of building.

[1] "The Old Wife and Young Husband," a novel, by Mrs. Meeke, (vol. II. p. 63.) contains some descriptive particulars of the walks in this neighbourhood.

Union Chapel [1], which stands in the centre of the Terrace bearing the family name of the Earl of Northampton, was erected at the period last mentioned, by some gentlemen, forming part of a congregational society of opulent and respectable individuals in this pa-

[1] For the following particulars respecting Union Chapel the author is indebted to a gentleman of the congregation assembling there :

The increasing population of Islington induced some of the inhabitants to devise a plan of general accommodation in a place of Divine Worship.

The necessity of a new Chapel had indeed been long felt and acknowledged throughout the parish ; for while Religion and Morality are essential to the well-being of Society, it is proper that all ranks of people should be furnished with means of religious instruction.

About twelve years ago a number of gentlemen, both of the Established Church, and of various Dissenting communities, laying aside their little unimportant distinctions, united, to forward this laudable object, and open a place of worship to supply the defect they lamented.

They repaired an unfinished Chapel, for a temporary accommodation in High-bury-grove ; but, though this was a considerable convenience to families residing in and near Highbury, it did not answer the purpose generally to the inhabitants of the village.

To erect a capacious and convenient Chapel in a central spot, in which Christians of all denominations might assemble, and to adopt a mode combining every interest, and embracing the most extensive usefulness, was the grand point in view, and on this plan *Union Chapel* was built.

They considered, that amidst the diversity of religious opinion among their countrymen, it was a pleasing fact, that in all the fundamental principles of the Christian Faith, Protestants are generally agreed. That the national Churches of England and Scotland, and the different bodies of Dissenters from each, with the numerous religious Societies termed Methodists, maintain and inculcate the same doctrines.

They deemed it a laudable exercise of prudence and benevolence, to fix upon some rational means of drawing Christians into nearer communion with each other : and, by adopting outward forms of worship with regard to the feelings of their brethren, to promote a spirit of amity and concord amongst all Christian worshippers.

For this end the excellent Liturgy of our Church of England, and the usage of extempore prayer as in the Church of Scotland, and among Dissenters, were adopted alternately, the former on the Sunday mornings, and the latter in the evenings.

rish, in lieu of a place of worship belonging to them situated in High-bury-grove. The concern is divided into proprietors' shares of £.100 each, with pews attached, and which are transferable by sale or otherwise. The Chapel, which is a very neat and commodious brick edifice, with a frontispiece of Portland stone, and crowned with a turret, is capable of conveniently seating 1000 persons: it was first opened for divine service in August 1806, on which occasion two Sermons were preached by the Rev. Mr. Gauntlet, M. A. a Clergyman of the Established Church at Reading, and the Rev. David Bogue, M. A. a Dissenting Minister of Gosport. The galleries are pannelled with fine mahogany, inscribed in gilt letters with passages selected from the Bible, and supported by Tuscan pillars; the roof is sustained by columns of the Composite order, which, with the pews, &c. are painted of a dead white, the walls being coloured with a light blue or grey. The pulpit and reading-desk are of a very handsome form, and composed of fine mahogany and satin wood, as are the whole of the reading slabs in the pews. The altar is formed by pillars and their entablature of the Ionic order, the intercolumns containing the decalogue, &c. in gilt letters, on a black ground.

Service is performed in the Chapel on Sundays in the morning and evening; there is also an evening lecture on Thursdays. The Rev. Thomas Lewis is minister. A school for the clothing and educating

---

The Chapel (as the name imports) belongs *exclusively* to no party; it is open to the Evangelical Ministers of the Church of England and of Scotland, and to all Dissenting communions holding the same doctrines as the National Establishments.

To unite Christians of all denominations, to afford instruction to those who, from the great population of the parish, could not find accommodation for public worship, UNION CHAPEL was erected, on the best model that could be devised; and it has hitherto answered all the purposes intended, more completely than by any more public and expensive scheme, such as a *Parochial Chapel;* which, while it would have created a burdensome charge on the parish, and probably alienated a part of the incumbent's living, would not at the same time have answered the intended purpose, of conciliating, uniting, and accommodating *all* the different classes of Christian Society.

of 50 girls has also been established; likewise, a Sunday school for boys; a society for supplying poor married women with child-bed linen and other necessaries; and another for visiting and relieving the sick poor: these are all supported chiefly by the congregation.

Tyndale-place was built about the year 1792, and received its name from Colonel Tyndale, of a family in the West of England; who, at that time, possessed the copyhold. The adjoining livery-stables, belonging to Mr. John Ions, were burnt down in the summer of 1796, through the carelessness of a boy, by which accident several horses were also burnt. They were afterwards rebuilt, and the riding-house became the head quarters of the Islington Volunteer Cavalry and Infantry, during the existence of that corps, and was appropriated to their drills and exercises in wet weather. The riding-house continues to be an equestrian school, for instructing novices in the art of horsemanship, though occasionally, it has been used for other purposes. Some of the society of Friends, called *Quakers*, have at times assembled here, and invited the inhabitants of the village to attend their religious admonitions.

In a large room on the first floor at the *Old Parr's Head* (which then included the adjoining house) on the Terrace, Upper-street, Henderson, the celebrated player, was in the habit of giving recitations, previously to any theatrical engagement; and it was on an exhibition of his great talents before David Garrick, John Ireland, Esq. and other competent judges, at this house, that he was first induced to adopt the stage as a profession.

Rufford's-buildings is dated in front 1688; and from the accompanying initials $_{NE}^{R}$ seems to have been built by Captain Nicholas Rufford, a gentleman of some eminence in the parish at that period[1].

[1] There is a Rufford's-buildings in the lower part of the village, near the turnpike, bearing the following inscription: " RVFFORDS BVLDINIS," with the above initials, and the date 1685. Nicholas Rufford was churchwarden in 1690. See inscriptions to him and several of his family in the Church-yard.

On this spot, before the present row of houses was built, there is said to have stood an old mansion, which Mr. Ellis conjectures to have been the residence of the *Fowler* family, before they inhabited the house in Cross-street [1].

The parochial Charity School at the corner of Cross-street was en-larged and rebuilt in the year 1788, on the site it has occupied since the pulling down the old Church, to which the school-room was formerly attached. This charity was instituted in the year 1710, for the education and clothing of 30 boys and 20 girls. These schools are supported by annual subscriptions, donations, and collections in the Church, in addition to a stock of £.2000 in the three per cent. an-nuities. They now contain 46 boys and 34 girls, who are supplied with every thing necessary for their education, and brought up in the prin-ciples of the Established Church. The former are taught reading, writing, and arithmetic; the latter, reading, writing, knitting, and plain work. The children are annually clothed, and when of a proper age put out apprentices, or to service in reputable families; with the boys a premium of £.5 is given, and the girls have two pounds allowed for necessaries. On leaving the school both boys and girls are presented with a Bible and Prayer-book.

The affairs of the Charity are managed by a Committee of Trustees, who are annual subscribers of one guinea or upwards; and any person contributing at one time ten guineas or more, is considered a Trustee for life. A set of excellent regulations are drawn up for the govern-ment of the Schools, which are delivered to the children or their pa-rents on their admission to the Charity. There are two collections made at the Church in the year [2], and the present number of annual subscribers is about 170, the whole being (with one or two excep-tions) inhabitants of the parish.

[1] Campagna of London, p. 95.

[2] The largest collection ever made in the Church, was on Sunday May 20, 1810, when £.73 were collected, after two Sermons preached for the benefit of the Cha-rity Schools.

The following is a List of Benefactions to these Schools from the Tables at the West entrance of the Church:

| | | £. | s. | d. |
|---|---|---|---|---|
| 1710 | By an unknown hand.....5 | 0 | 0 | |
| 1712 | Mrs. Lloyd, her legacy..5 | 0 | 0 | |
| 1713 | Mr. Chew's legacy.......10 | 0 | 0 | |
| 1715 | Mr. Hitchcock's legacy..1 | 0 | 0 | |
| 1717 | Dr. Tilly's gift................3 | 0 | 0 | |
| 1718 | Mrs. Anne How, her legacy ..........................5 | 5 | 0 | |
| 1719 | Mrs. Danvers, her legacy 2 | 0 | 0 | |
| | Mrs. Anne West, her legacy ..........................40 | 0 | 0 | |
| | Mrs. Snape, her legacy.3 | 0 | 0 | |
| 1720 | Mrs. Yeats, her gift........5 | 0 | 0 | |
| | By an unknown hand.....4 | 4 | 0 | |
| | Mrs. Beck, her gift......10 | 0 | 0 | |
| | Mrs. Winifred Taylor, her gift....................40 | 0 | 0 | |
| 1721 | Mr. Oswald Hoskins, from a person unknown..50 | 0 | 0 | |
| | Mr. Joseph Calcot, from a person unknown....5 | 5 | 0 | |
| | Mrs. Bridget Cave, her legacy.......................50 | 0 | 0 | |
| | Mr. Richard Stretch's legacy...........................50 | 0 | 0 | |
| 1722 | Mrs. Atkins, her legacy 20 | 0 | 0 | |
| 1724 | Mr. John Best, from a person unknown.......3 | 0 | 0 | |
| | Mrs. Margaret Clarke, her gift....................10 | 0 | 0 | |
| | Mrs. Susanna Galway, her legacy.................5 | 0 | 0 | |
| | Mr. Robert Southam's legacy.......................50 | 0 | 0 | |
| 1725 | Mr. James Ballard, his legacy ..................100 | 0 | 0 | |

| | | £. | s. | d. |
|---|---|---|---|---|
| 1726 | The Rev. Mr. Mills, his gift.......................5 | 0 | 0 | |
| 1728 | In part of Mr. George Liquorish's legacy of £.100 received.......50 | 0 | 0 | |
| 1729 | Mr. Thomas Purley, his legacy ....................20 | 0 | 0 | |
| | Mrs. Anne White, her legacy .......................50 | 0 | 0 | |
| | Mr. William Whitfield's legacy.....................10 | 0 | 0 | |
| | By Mr. James Ballard's bequest of the residue, &c..................31 | 2 | 7½ | |
| 1730 | By a further part of Mr. Liquorish's legacy..12 | 10 | 0 | |
| | Mrs. Bodily....... ............20 | 0 | 0 | |
| | Mr. Fellows...................20 | 0 | 0 | |
| | Philip Oddy, Esq. .....126 | 0 | 0 | |
| | Mr. Emerson..................5 | 5 | 0 | |
| 1745 | Mrs. Muglestone..........30 | 0 | 0 | |
| | Everard Sayer, Esq.....40 | 0 | 0 | |
| 1746 | Mr. Thomas Evans.......20 | 0 | 0 | |
| 1747 | Mrs. Elizabeth Fowler....5 | 0 | 0 | |
| 1748 | Thomas Bridges, Esq..20 | 0 | 0 | |
| 1749 | Mr. William Allam.......16 | 4 | 2 | |
| 1750 | Mr. John Brown............30 | 0 | 0 | |
| | Mr. Bartholomew Pidgeon ..........................10 | 0 | 0 | |
| 1751 | Mr. Altham's gift...........7 | 4 | 2 | |
| | Mr. Stegues..................10 | 0 | 0 | |
| 1752 | Mr. John Litten.............5 | 0 | 0 | |
| | Mr. Burton. ..................3 | 0 | 0 | |
| 1753 | Mr. Thomas Stonestreet, his aunt's executor......5 | 5 | 0 | |

|  | £. | s. | d. |
|---|---|---|---|
| 1754 Mr. Geo. Liquorish, the remaining part £100, 25 | | 0 | 0 |
| 1756 Mrs. Litten................5 | | 0 | 0 |
| 1758 Mr. Bowles................50 | | 0 | 0 |
| 1762 Mrs. Lucy Yeates.........20 | | 0 | 0 |
| Mrs. Lilburne.............10 | | 0 | 0 |
| 1763 Mr. Charles Biddle ......20 | | 0 | 0 |
| Mrs. Thomas.............30 | | 0 | 0 |
| Mr. Cox...................20 | | 0 | 0 |
| Mr. Pamplyn.................5 | | 0 | 0 |
| 1769 Mrs. Berriman.............10 | | 0 | 0 |
| 1774 Mrs. Eliz. Gramer.....100 | | 0 | 0 |
| 1775 Mrs. Henrietta Cooke..10 | | 0 | 0 |
| Mr. John Piggott........100 | | 0 | 0 |
| Mr. Thos. Stonestreet..20 | | 0 | 0 |
| 1777 Mr. Wm. Stonehouse....20 | | 0 | 0 |
| Mr. Richard Lock.........20 | | 0 | 0 |
| 1778 Mr. Christian.............10 | 10 | 0 |
| 1779 Mr. John Locke...........20 | | 0 | 0 |
| 1780 Mrs. Aubeck, 3 per cent. Annuities...............20 | | 0 | 0 |
| 1783 Mr. William Exell, 3 per Cent. Consolidated Bank Annuities.........50 | | 0 | 0 |
| 1784 Mrs. Mary Franklin......30 | | 0 | 0 |
| 1786 Mr. James Crane, *per annum* for ever............5 | | 0 | 0 |
| Mrs. Rosa[d] Marshall, 3 per Cent. Consolidated Bank Annuities......100 | | 0 | 0 |

|  | £. | s. | d. |
|---|---|---|---|
| 1787 Mr. Frederick Hawes, 3 per Cents............100 | | 0 | 0 |
| 1790 Stafford Briscoe, Esq.100 | | 0 | 0 |
| John Lloyd, Esq.........21 | | 0 | 0 |
| 1792 Mr. Wm. Davis...........10 | | 0 | 0 |
| Mrs. Ann Swinscoe.......10 | | 0 | 0 |
| Thos. Cogan, Esq........20 | | 0 | 0 |
| 1793 Mr. William Bennett....50 | | 0 | 0 |
| 1794 Mrs. Rebecca Stonestreet.....................50 | | 0 | 0 |
| 1795 Mrs. Ann Locke...........20 | | 0 | 0 |
| 1797 Everard Heylyn, senior, Esq.............................31 | 10 | 0 |
| 1798 Mrs. Mary Hollis............5 | | 0 | 0 |
| 1801 Mrs. Ann May [1]..........100 | | 0 | 0 |
| 1802 Richard Singleton, Esq.10 | | 0 | 0 |
| 1804 Mr. John Hayes..........100 | | 0 | 0 |
| 1806 An Old Inhabitant[2], whose father was educated in the school.................10 | | 0 | 0 |
| Robert Careless, Esq.100 | | 0 | 0 |
| Mrs. Jane Gibbs............50 | | 0 | 0 |
| 1807 The late Corps of Islington Volunteers.25 | | 0 | 0 |
| John Bentley, Esq.........10 | | 0 | 0 |
| Mrs. Pickford.................50 | | 0 | 0 |
| To which her son added 10 | | 0 | 0 |

In addition to the above, a legacy of £.20. has been lately left to the schools by Daniel Sebbon, Esq.

[1] Ann May was educated in the school, and left a moiety of her savings during a life of servitude, to be divided between this charity and the poor of the parish.

[2] This Old Inhabitant, it since appears, was the Printer of this Volume.

A house near to the Charity School, then in the occupation of Justice Hyde, was partly demolished by the rioters in 1780, and his goods burnt in the street; this outrage was occasioned by his having given offence to the populace by some proceedings in his magisterial capacity.

The boarding school near the bottom of Cross-street, kept by Mrs. Clarke, was formerly one of the most respectable edifices in the village; it was the mansion house belonging to the family of the Fowlers, Lords of the Manor of Barnesbury, and who possessed the copyhold estate on this spot, which has since become vested in the Tufnell family together with that Manor. The above estate contains 10 acres and 24 perches in this Manor, and comprizes the ground whereon the following buildings have been erected; viz. Tufnell-place, Astey's-row, Pleasant-row, the North side of Cross-street, seventeen houses on the South side of Cross-street, including the passage behind, also Little Cross-street, Thatched House-row, and the whole of the terrace in the Lower-street.

The family of Fowler appears to have been one of the most considerable in this parish during the reigns of Elizabeth and James the First, and antecedent to that time the name frequently occurs in records connected with the place. Sir Thomas Fowler, Knt. was one of His Majesties Deputy Lieutenants for the County of Middlesex, a High Commissioner for the Verge, and Justice of the quorum. He married Jane, daughter of Gregory Charlet, Citizen and Tallow Chandler of London, and died Jan. 14, 1624. He appears to have been one of the Jurors upon the trial of the ill-fated Sir Walter Raleigh at Winchester, in Nov. 1603. His son Sir Thomas was created a Baronet May 21, 1628, but the title became extinct at the death of Sir Edmund Fowler, brother to the gentleman last mentioned.

The house is an irregular building, composed chiefly of wood and plaster, with a modern brick front, and has been much altered internally from its original state, but the back front towards the garden yet retains something of its antient character. It appears to have been built in the reign of Queen Elizabeth. The cieling of a back room on the first floor is decorated with the arms of England in the reign of that Princess, with her initials, and the date 1595 in stucco. Also $_{T\ I}^{\ F}$ the initials of Thomas and Jane Fowler with fleur de lis, medallions, &c. in the same style as the cielings at Canonbury House. The rooms are wainscotted with oak in pannels, and till the year 1788 the windows contained some arms, &c. in stained glass, among which were those of Fowler, with the date 1588, but which were taken away about that time, and substituted by plain glass. In pulling down some old houses for a new street intended to be made at the East end of this house, some remains of the antient stabling and offices were lately removed. In these stables a fire broke out on the 17th February 1655 [1], but which does not appear to have done any injury to the dwelling house.

At the extremity of the garden which belonged to this mansion is a small brick building about 15 feet square, absurdly called Queen Elizabeth's lodge (see Plate VI.) This appears to have afforded access to the house through the grounds, and was probably built for a summer house or a porter's lodge at the entrance of the garden, about the time the mansion-house was erected. The arms of Fowler bearing an esquire's helmet, are cut in stone on the West side of the building, near the top, and which proves the time of its erection to have been before the honour of knighthood was conferred upon its owner. On the front next Canonbury fields, are also the arms of Sir Thomas Fowler the younger [2] cut in stone, within a handsome frame of brick work, with his initials, and the date 1655. From the date, it appears that these arms were placed in the building by a subsequent possessor, it being after the death of Sir Thomas Fowler, and when the title had become extinct; perhaps, by his grandson Sir Richard Fisher, Bart. who resided here at the period last mentioned.

[1] Perfect Proceedings, February 22, 1655.

[2] Azure, on a chevron Argent, between three herons Or, as many crosses pattée Gules; in chief, an escutcheon, charged with a sinister hand couped at the wrist, the arms of Ulster, and ensign of Baronetcy.

The building is three stories in height, having a room and closet on each floor, and windows looking into the garden; on which side it has been ornamented with small escutcheons, &c. which are now broken off. The staircase turns spirally round a fir pole, about 24 feet in length, in the small hexagonal part attached to the square building, which pole, standing in the centre, receives the small end of each step, whilst the other end is fixed in the wall. The stairs are of oak; as also the doors, which are strongly rivetted and fastened with iron. On the roof there is a small platform of lead, which gives a pleasing panoramic view of the village, and adjoining fields, with the New River, &c. The lodge, together with part of the garden, is now separated from the dwelling-house, and let to other tenants. The old wall which divides the gardens from the fields at the back of Cross-street, in a line with the lodge, appears to have formerly inclosed the ground attached to the mansion-house. This situation must have afforded a most pleasant and agreeable retreat; enjoying a prospect of the noble mansion and park of Canonbury, with the woods of Highbury on the one side; and the village church, with here and there an intervening house, and an open view over the fields towards the Metropolis, on the other.

The name vulgarly attached to the lodge, arose in all probability from the circumstance of Queen Elizabeth having passed through the same to the dwelling house, when upon a visit to Sir Thomas Fowler, or Sir John Spencer, at Canonbury; or, perhaps, curiosity might have induced her to take a more than ordinary survey of the interior of this little edifice; a thing not unusual with that princess, and this might occasion the inhabitants of the house, or the neighbours, to attach her name to the building, which it continues to bear to the present day. Persons who were thus honoured with the visits of her Majesty, appear to have taken pleasure in coupling her name with particular rooms in their houses; and such was the veneration in which she was held by her subjects, that the arms, initials, &c. of their sovereign, frequently formed a very prominent feature in the decorations of their apartments: instances of this may yet be seen in several of the old houses in this parish.

Near the end of Thatched House-row stands the public house bearing that name, from its being covered with *thatch*. This is a house appointed by the Royal Humane Society for the reception of persons apparently drowned: from its contiguity to the New River, it has been selected for that purpose, and the necessary apparatus for restoring suspended animation is kept ready for use by a medical gentleman living near the spot. Contemplating this subject, it is rather a curious coincidence, that the worthy and philanthropic individual, to whom the country is indebted for the formation of that most useful and laudable institution, drew his first breath within a very few yards of this house.

WILLIAM HAWES, M. D. who first projected, and was, from its establishment to the termination of his life, the chief supporter of the Royal Humane Society, was born near this spot, November 17, 1736. His father for many years kept the house, formerly called *Job's House*, but better known as *The Old Thatched House Tavern;* during which time the premises were burnt by an accidental fire, and rebuilt on the same site, about midway between the present Thatched House and Sir Thomas Fowler's, in Cross-street. This building has lately been pulled down. He received the early part of his education in his native village, at the seminary of honest John Shield, and completed it in St. Paul's school. He was afterwards placed with Mr. Carsan, an ingenious medical practitioner, near Vauxhall; and, at the expiration of his apprenticeship, was, for a short time, an assistant to Mr. Dicks, in the Strand, whom he succeeded in business; and, by his application and unwearied attention to his patients, acquired a considerable degree of reputation and affectionate esteem. In May 1759, he married an amiable woman, who survives to lament his loss, and by whom he had a numerous family.

In 1773, he became deservedly popular, from his incessant zeal in calling the attention of the public to the resuscitation of persons apparently dead, principally by drowning; a subject that had been for 30 preceding years particularly recommended and encouraged by the Editors of that valuable monthly publication the Gentleman's Magazine.

In this he encountered much opposition, and some ridicule. The practicability of *resuscitation* was denied. This he however ascertained, by advertising rewards to persons, who, between Westminster and London bridges, should, within a certain time after the accident, rescue *drowned persons* from the water, and bring them ashore to places appointed for their reception; where means might be used for their recovery, and give immediate notice to him. The public mind being thus awakened to the subject, greater exertions were made by individuals than had ever before been known, and many lives were saved by himself and other medical men; Mr. Hawes, at his own expence, paying the rewards in these cases for 12 months, which amounted to a considerable sum. His excellent friend Dr. Cogan (then somewhat known to the public, and since much better, by some most valuable publications), who had long turned his thoughts to this subject, remonstrated with him on the injury which his private fortune would sustain from a perseverance in these expences; and he at last consented to share them with the publick. Dr. Cogan and he agreed to join their strength; and each of them bringing forward fifteen friends to a meeting at the Chapter Coffee-house, in 1774, the *Humane Society* was instantly formed. In the following year, an admirable sermon was preached in recommendation of it by the Rev. R. Harrison, at St. Bride's church. From this period, the weight and organization of the infant Institution devolved in a great measure on Mr. Hawes, whose undeviating labours, it is hoped, established it for ever; and without which, there would probably not have been at this time, a similar establish-

Eng.ᵈ by Ridley from a miniature in the possession of Dʳ Lettsom

WILLIAM HAWES M.D.

Union Chapel Islington.

Thatched House. Islington.

Humane Societies have now multiplied with every great stream that fructifies the soil of these different regions.

In 1774, he published, " An Account of Dr. Goldsmith's last Illness," whose death he ascribed to the improper administration of a popular medicine; and from this unfortunate event he deduced many useful cautions respecting the exhibition of powerful remedies.

In 1777, appeared his " Address on Premature Death, and Pre-" mature Interment," which he liberally distributed, in order to awaken attention in the public mind against the too early interment of persons supposed to be dead, before it was clearly ascertained that life was totally extinct. This performance had been suggested to his mind even prior to the establishment of the great object of resuscitation, which he afterwards so successfully pursued; and which, in effect, the following declaration confirms :

" At a General Court of the Directors of the Humane Society in " 1776, Dr. Towers sat as Chairman, and after congratulating the " Society on a variety of successful cases of astonishing recoveries, he " thus proceeded :

" To the well-known humanity of his (Mr. Hawes's) disposition, " and to that activity of benevolence for which he was so remarkable, " this society in a great degree owed its origin. The reasonableness " and utility of an institution of this kind had been very early seen by " Mr. Hawes; and therefore he had laboured to promote it with a " diligence and an ardour that would ever do him honour. Indeed, " before the establishment of this Society, he had publicly advertized " rewards for notice to be brought him of any persons in such situa-" tions (within a reasonable distance from his own habitation) as those " who are now the objects of this Institution; which was the strongest " demonstration of his solicitude to promote so benevolent a design ; " and that afterwards, by joining with his worthy colleague Dr. Co-" gan, in adopting the necessary measures for establishing the present " Institution, he had performed a real service to his Country."

In 1780 was published his third edition of an " Examination of the Rev. John Wesley's Primitive Physick;" in which the absurdities and dangerous remedies recommended by that venerable and (on many other accounts) respectable writer, were acutely exposed by a combination of irony and serious argument.

In 1780 or 1781 he removed to Palsgrave-place, and commenced practice as a physician; the degree of Doctor of Medicine having been some time before conferred upon him.

In 1781 Dr. Hawes published " An Address to the Legislature on " the importance of the Humane Society;" and by his steady perseverance and personal endeavours he lived to see most of his objects realized, as conducive to the restoration of suspended animation.

About the same period appeared his " Address to the King and " Parliament of Great Britain, with Observations on the General " Bills of Mortality." These useful and interesting publications gradually raised the reputation of the author, to the notice of the learned as well as benevolent characters.

In the same year he was elected Physician to the Surrey Dispensary; and about the same time commenced his Medical Lectures on suspended animation, and was the first, and perhaps the only person that ever introduced the subject as a part of medical education; which he elucidated under the following heads :

1. To instruct the younger part of the Faculty how to preserve human life in every critical circumstance wherein the vital powers are liable to be suspended; and to urge the importance of the inquiry on every principle of Christianity, national policy, and humanity.

II. To consider the sundry derangements which suspend the action of the principal vital organs, the brain, the heart, or the lungs; together with the various means for restoring their respective functions.

III. An inquiry (so far as relates to the present subject) into the effects of the animal, vegetable, and mineral poisons; their deleterious power in suddenly destroying the vital functions; and the most approved methods of preventing or correcting their baneful effects when received into the human body.

IV. The modes of recovering persons from syncopæ, inebriation, trance, drowning, suffocation by the cord or noxious vapours, intense cold or lightning.

V. Important reflections on still-born children, and the most efficacious modes of restoring vital action.

VI. The various symptoms of apparent death, which sometimes supervene in acute diseases, but which might frequently be surmounted by suitable measures speedily adopted and vigorously pursued; and *lastly* the usual signs of death considered, and those which are *certain*, distinguished from those which are more equivocal, &c.

These lectures were closed by a proposal of bestowing prize medals, suggested by the ardour of his mind, and founded by his munificence; and in October 1782 the gold medal was awarded by four respectable Physicians to Dr. Richard Pearson of Birmingham, and the silver medal to a writer whose paper was signed *Humanitas*. Since that period similar prize medals, bestowed by the Medical Society, have given rise to the invaluable works of Pearson, Goodwin, Coleman, Kite, and Fothergill.

In 1782, Dr. Hawes removed to Eastcheap; and (having been elected Physician to the London Dispensary in 1785) to Bury-street in 1786, and to Spital-square in 1791.

In 1793 when the manufactories of cottons had so far superseded those of silks as to occasion temporary want, and even beggary, among the artizans in Spital-fields, Dr. Hawes singly stood forward; and principally by his activity 1200 families were snatched from ruin. His Address on that occasion, in a Letter to a popular Clergyman, was afterwards made public, to the great benefit of the industrious sufferers whose distress he so feelingly commiserates: as it serves to display the unbounded philanthropy of his heart, it is worthy of being preserved.

REVEREND SIR,

"PERMIT me to address you on the present occasion, and
"to return you my most sincere thanks for your voluntary exertions
"in behalf of the distressed Weavers.

"Believe, Sir, it is not in the power of language to describe their
"long and continued miseries; miseries not brought on by idleness,
"intemperance, or a dissolute course of life, but human wretchedness
"absolutely produced by the want of employment.

"My profession obliges me daily to be an eye-witness of the severe
"distresses, trials, and afflictions of these much-to-be-pitied of our
"fellow creatures. Whole families *without fire, without raiment,*
"and *without food ;* and, to add to the catalogue of human woes,
"three, four, and five, in many families, languishing on the bed of
"sickness.

"I am sure, Sir, you will believe me, when I declare that such
"scenes of complicated woe are too affecting to dwell upon : and
"therefore shall conclude with my most earnest wishes, that, by your
"pleading in their behalf, other Divines may be animated to the same
"pious undertaking, as I am certain that public benevolence will
"prevent the *premature death* of many, will restore health to num-
"bers, and afford the staff of life to thousands.

"I am, Reverend Sir,

"Yours, &c.

"WILLIAM HAWES, Physician
*Spital-square, Nov.* 16, 1793.         "to the London Dispensary."

In 1796, Dr. Hawes favoured the publick with his great work, intituled, "Transactions of the Royal Humane Society from 1774 to
"1784," which was dedicated to the King by Royal permission.

The following character of this amiable and benevolent Physician
emanated warm from the heart of one who tenderly esteemed him, and

who thus feelingly anticipated the chasm occasioned by his passage to the grave. " The writer of these lines hardly dares to indulge a hope " that upon some contemporary who may survive him, the spirit that " actuated the archetype may descend. At this time [1802] he is about " 65 years of age; possessing his usual flow of spirits among his " friends and society in general; but, with all his usual cheerfulness, " if a subject be casually started in his company that excites pity and " demands succour, he is instantly metamorphosed into another being " — his eyes sparkle — his whole body appears in motion — he rises " from his chair — runs up to the individual who represented the case " of human woe — draws him to the corner of the room — and in- " stantly opens his purse, with a request to convey his mite to the ob- " ject of distress; or take his address for future investigation and sub- " sequent aid. In the street, the writer who directs the pen of anec- " dote over these pages hath often seen him hasten up to a poor object, " press something into the cold hand of misery, and as hastily pass " out of sight, like a shadow, to prevent his being known by the re- " ceiver, or thanked by his gratitude: it has however been occasionally " noticed, and been found to constitute an amplitude of succour that must " have surprized as well as gratified the supplicant—surprize height- " ened by ignorance of the donor, and gratitude augmented by the " degree of unexpected liberality. Surprize and gratitude must be " still more elevated were it known that this benefactor is the father " and grandfather of a large progeny; in the circle of which, however, " he is happy in their affection, and, like an antient patriarch, can " rejoice in their esteem.

" I am not aiming at regular biography but cursory characteristic " anecdote; which I mention and claim as an apology for introducing " age before infancy. In youth, liberality is predominant if not pro- " verbial, but it is avarice that most generally accompanies old age; " and happy, and indeed great must be that mind that can triumph " over this worst imbecility of advancing years, and, like Dr. Hawes, " open the heart whenever want appeals to its tender auricles, which

" in him have a portal, through which the warm blood of humane
" affections is preserved in a constant pulsation, and a warm stream
" of beneficent action.

" Absorbed as he has been in promoting and extending. Humane
" Societies over the whole globe, the avenues of his active benefi-
" cence are not dried up, or contracted by them; for his hand is in
" his purse whenever the appeals of misery touch his heart, or the
" importance and wants of philanthropic institutions are presented :
" his time is no less in unison with his activity of mind in devoting
" both to private committees and public meetings, in the promotion
" of private and public charities, and other useful institutions.

" The numerous instances of his promoting the public good, natu-
" rally raised the reputation of so distinguished and beneficent a
" character, both at home and abroad, and occasioned his name to
" be enrolled as an Associate and Honorary Member in several Lite-
" rary Societies ; a NAME that will be enrolled among the great cha-
" racters who have been the benefactors of mankind, and the mind
" that has influenced that *name* will ascend to be enrolled among
" congenial spirits, bearing this passport engraven on the wings that
" enable it to mount upwards : ' *The sick and the prisoner he vi-*
" *sited ; the poor he fed ; widows and the fatherless he consoled and*
" *comforted ; and the apparently dead he raised to life.*'   But that
" the period of departure from works here to reward hereafter may
" long be protracted, is the wish of all those who have experienced
" the undeviating friendship, the cheerful society, and the rational
" conviviality, of the living HAWES."

Such was, in 1802, the lively and the faithful portraiture of a
good and worthy man, who, on the 5th of December, 1808, having
just entered on the 73d year of his age, completed a well-spent life.

There was a simplicity in his manners, the result of an innocent
and unsuspecting mind ; his heart overflowed with the milk of human kindness, and self never entered into his contemplation.   Without possessing, or affecting to possess, any very superior literary

talents, he contrived to furnish to the publick an acceptable work in his "Annual Reports."

His practice had been considerable, and his medical knowledge was respectable. In the resuscitative art he was eminently skilled.

He was an Honorary Member of the Massachusetts Humane Society, and of many others at Edinburgh, Manchester, Bath, &c. &c.; and a Vice President of the London Electrical Dispensary.

The Royal Humane Society is a shining and an eminent proof of his philanthropy; an institution which has been found highly useful, and to establish which, he employed many years of his life.

The moment in which one of the regular Anniversaries of the Society was at an end, he began to meditate plans for the success of the ensuing year. The nomination of succeeding stewards; the augmentation of the list of regular subscribers; and the obtaining of churches and preachers for the benefit of his favourite institution, were never out of his sight; and it is believed that the not being able to obtain for that purpose the grant of the churches of two or three opulent parishes, which he had long been anxiously soliciting (particularly that of *Islington*[1], where a very large proportion of the Society's rewards is unavoidably applied) was a circumstance that gave him more uneasiness, and preyed more upon his mind, than can easily be imagined. So much indeed did the Humane Society engross his attention, that his own immediate interests appeared to him to be subordinate considerations. He was always ready to afford both his pecuniary and his professional assistance to distress: and his name ought to be recorded among those who have added to the character of

---

[1] It is certainly a matter to be regretted, that, under any circumstances, such an accommodation should have been withheld from a Society having so laudable an end in view. It may be proper, however, to remark in this place, that on Dec. 11, 1800, a concert was given for its benefit in the school-room belonging to Mr. Flower in the Upper-street, who conducted the business in a manner that did great credit to his well-known philanthropy and public spirit. The Humane Society on this occasion received a clear benefit of £.63. 5s.

the Nation, by the establishment of an institution founded on the most benevolent principles; and which has been a source of renewed happiness to many who might otherwise have sunk into wretchedness, arising from the untimely loss of their nearest relatives.

His remains were deposited the 13th December in the new cemetery attached to the church-yard at Islington, being attended in three mourning coaches by his three sons, his grandson, his son in law, Mr. Gurney; two other relations, Mr. Bennett and Mr. Townsend; and five of his oldest friends; viz. Dr. Lettsom, Mr. Nichols, Mr. Beaumont, Mr. Milward, and Mr. Jennings. The mournful train was augmented by a handsome testimony of regard and respect from twenty-nine other friends, Managers and Directors of the Royal Humane Society, who volunteered their attendance, and joined the procession at their own expence.

A handsome marble tablet to his memory has since been placed in the Church by the Humane Society, with an inscription bearing testimony to the virtues and usefulness of this amiable and exalted character [1].

The prospect down the Lower-street, looking Northward from the end of Church-street, is in the summer time very pleasing; the irregular disposition of the houses, intersected and enlivened by the variegated foliage of the different sorts of trees that stand before the buildings on each side of the road, gives the scene a very agreeable and picturesque appearance.

[1] For this biographical sketch the present work is indebted to the accounts published in the European and Gentleman's Magazines, drawn up by two of the Doctor's old friends, who attended him to the grave. The former publication (for June 1802) contains his portrait, and a poetical tribute to his memory. A good likeness of Dr. Hawes is also introduced in the picture engraved by Pollard of " *a youth restored* " *from drowning;*" likewise in that painted by Mr. S. Medley, for the London Medical Society.

By virtue of the statute 46 Geo. III. before mentioned, the high-way between the sign of the Carved Lion and the opposite side, which from its narrowness had been the occasion of many accidents, was, in the year 1806, widened to the extent of ten feet and upwards, the ground for that purpose being taken from the garden belonging to the end house of Old Paradise-row by the Green.

In Church-street, is a Chapel belonging to the Calvinistic Methodists, built in the year 1788, on part of a nursery ground formerly in the occupation of Mr. W. Watson. It is a plain brick building, having a small burying ground attached, and was first begun by an individual named Ives, a blacksmith of this parish[1]; some of the materials for its foundation were brought from the ruins of the old Church at Clerkenwell. This person not being able to proceed with the building for want of pecuniary assistance, it was for some time left in an unfinished state, during which time, for the accommodation of several persons desirous of hearing a Minister in the place, the Rev. Mr. Clayton, Mr. Crole of Founders-hall, and some other gentlemen, preached in the Chapel occasionally; and this continued to be the case until the building was finished, and a regular minister appointed. The premises afterwards became the property of Mr. Welch, banker, in Cornhill, who, about the year 1793, granted a lease

---

[1] See inscriptions in the church-yard. Before this time, a character of some notoriety, one Jeremiah Garrett, an itinerant, had been in the habit of *holding forth* at the Old *Rectifying* House, in the Lower-street. His eloquent powers were afterwards displayed in frequent lectures given at the *Old Soap House*, near the same spot; and he occasionally harangued the multitude on the Green from a moveable rostrum, which was carried about from place to place upon the shoulders of the above mentioned Ives. On these occasions Ives acted as clerk, until the preacher's oratory was put an end to by the interference of Justice Cogan, a magistrate residing in the parish. This Garrett has since professed the Antinomian doctrine, and lately had a chapel in *Lant-street*, Southwark. In the title-page to one of his publications he styles himself " *The Weather-beaten Watchman of the Lant-street Mountain !*"

N N

for life to the Rev. Thomas Wills [1], A. B. who resided in Church-row, when that gentleman entered upon the pastoral office, and continued to be minister of the congregation assembling here for several years.

[1] This gentleman was born at Truro in Cornwall, and at an early age was sent to Truro school, where he made the usual proficiency in classical knowledge which boys designed for the University are expected to attain. He was sent at the usual time to Oxford, and entered a Commoner at Magdalen-hall, where he soon cultivated an intimate acquaintance with Dr. Haweis, the present rector of Aldwinkle in Northamptonshire, and author of several valuable works: they followed their studies together, and soon became remarked for their close application to the duties of religion, and their assiduity in acquiring a knowledge of the learned languages. Here he took the degree of A. B. and afterwards became curate to Mr. Walker, at St. Agnes, one of the most populous parishes in Cornwall, and at this place his usefulness amongst that un-enlightened class of people, the tin-miners, became eminently conspicuous, in the reformation produced in their manners when he had been only a short time amongst them.

Being visited in this dreary spot by the indefatigable Countess of Huntingdon, in her peregrinations, an intimate acquaintance took place between them, which led to a matrimonial alliance between the Minister and her Ladyship's niece, Miss Wheeler. He was now induced to give up his cure, and to join in the more extended sphere of her ladyship's numerous Chapels. In these he preached during several journies through various parts of the kingdom, under the patronage and protection of the Countess, who on these occasions defrayed his necessary travelling expenses. Some misunderstanding afterwards happening between Mr. Wills and his patroness, he engaged upon his own account the Chapel in Silver-street, also one in Grub-street, and afterwards the Chapel at Islington. In each of these he performed the clerical office with much ability and usefulness, making occasional tours into the country in various directions. In these employments the latter years of his life were usefully spent, till his bodily health began to suffer; insomuch that he was obliged to sit while preaching, being unable to bear the fatigue of an erect posture. A paralytic affection now attacked him, his eyes began to fail, and imbecility of mind and weakness of body compelled him to quit his pastoral charge, and seek relief from his native air. With this view he retired into Cornwall to the house of an old friend at *Boskenna*, where he lingered for a considerable time, incapable of ministerial labour, and died the 12th of May 1802, in the 63d year of his age. There is a good head of Mr. Wills extant, engraved by Holloway, from a picture by Lawrence; also several others of a smaller size.

HOPE    FAITH

Rev.ᵈ THOˢ WILLS, A.B.
*Chaplain to the Countess of Huntingdon, &*
*Minister at Northampton or Spa Fields Chapel.*

*Accurately Drawn & Engraved (with the permission of Mr. Wills)*
*from the Life — by Mr. Goldar*

Published by Alexr. Hogg Nᵒ 16, Paternoster Row. ___

Islington Chapel.

About the beginning of the year 1800, in consequence of bodily infirmity, and being at that time also Minister of the Chapel in Silver-street, London, Mr. Wills disposed of his interest in the premises to the Rev. Evan-John Jones, who has since been pastor over the congregation assembling here, and also that in Silver-street.  The expences of the Chapel, &c. are defrayed by quarterly collections and monies received from persons occupying seats, which in the preferable part of the building are let at one guinea *per annum*.  With respect to the doctrine preached in this place, it may be stated in the words of the Minister, extracted from a printed address respecting the Charity Schools connected with the Chapel ; viz. " The doctrinal articles of " the Church of England are our basis, not indeed because they are " the Articles of the Established Church, but for a much better reason, " namely, because they are Bible truths, and we love the Church on " that account, retaining for the same reason her service in our " Chapels."

The interior of the Chapel has within these few years been rendered more commodious, and a large room for a " School of Industry" has been added to the building, where 30 girls are clothed, educated, and taught needle-work and knitting, and have each a Bible, with a Prayer and Hymn Book presented to them on leaving the school. This charity is supported by voluntary subscriptions, donations, and collections in the Chapel.  There is likewise a Sunday-school attached to the place, which sometimes consists of 300 children, and a Society for visiting and relieving sick persons and poor women in their lying-in, &c. [1]

[1] The many charitable objects embraced by congregations similar to the above, are sufficiently indicative of their Christian philanthropy, and zeal for the cause of true religion.  Were the ministers of the Established Church more generally endued with a similar spirit, and equally zealous in the cause they take in hand, they would not have occasion so often to deplore the erection of Chapels and Conventicles, and their flocks running after Methodist and Itinerant preachers, to the frequent desertion of their own parish Churches.

In the burial-ground adjoining the Chapel are the following Monumental Inscriptions :

" Thomas Clark, of Throgmorton-street, died 10 July, 1808, aged 49 ; and three children."

"Emmanuel Vaughan, died 4 Sept. 1801, aged 59. Mary his wife, 12 Oct. 1807, aged 68."

" Rev. Joseph Phillips [1], died Aug. 30, 1808, aged 71.
I know in whom I have believed."

"John Cape, died July 16, 1796, aged 46."

" Thomas Mennells, of this parish, citizen of London, died 4 Aug. 1791, in his 62d year."

" Sarah Knight, died Dec. 23, 1809, aged 37."

"Mary Jones, died Nov. 8, 1798, aged 66.
A sinner sav'd by Grace alone,
She pleads no merit of her own;
But, through the Spirit's quick'ning pow'r,
She triumph'd in her dying hour.

And now she 's gone to sing above,
The wonders of redeeming love.

Mary Jones, died 31 Jan. 1808, aged 41;
Jane Jones, died 8 June, 1808, aged 38; daughters of the above.

Earthly cavern, to thy keeping,
We commit our sister's dust ;
Keep it safely, softly sleeping,
Till our Lord demand thy trust.
Sweetly sleep, dear Saints, in Jesus,
Ye with us shall wake from death,
Hold he cannot, though he seize us ;
We his pow'r defy by Faith."

" Mary Pellatt, spinster, of this parish, died 28 Jan. 1791, aged 53.

Father, I give my spirit up,
And trust it in thy hand ;
My dying flesh shall rest in hope,
And rise at thy command."

" Rev. John Marrant [2], died April 15, 1791, aged 35."

[1] Mr. Phillips was an occasional preacher in the Chapel for some years, and assistant or curate to Mr. Wills.

[2] This minister was a converted negro, who preached in the neighbourhood of Whitechapel, and occasionally at this place.

Drawn by Schnebbelie & Engraved by Sparrow.

For D.r Hughson's Description of London

## ISLINGTON.

Published by J. Stratford, at Holborn Hill, July 30th 1808.

Watch House, Islington.

Pub. May 1. 1819 for the Proprietor by R. Ackermann, 101. Strand.

### ISLINGTON-GREEN

was formerly a piece of waste ground uninclosed, and the common depository, or lay-stall, for a great part of the dirt and filth of the town. The watch-house, together with a cage, engine-house, and a pair of stocks, stood about the middle of the green, until the former was erected in its present situation. The ground was taken up for the parish, of the lord of the manor, by trustees appointed for that purpose in the year 1777; when, the nuisances being removed, it was inclosed with posts and rails. The watch-house at the corner was built in 1797, and the engine-house behind, enlarged and rebuilt in 1808; at which time the trees were planted around them.

The Fox public-house, at the North-west corner of the Green, is a very old building, composed chiefly of wood, with gable roof, and pannelled wainscoats of oak. Several years ago, a large tree, surrounded by benches, stood in front of the house, at which time it was kept by a person named George Prince, a man who had received a classical education, and was famous for his home-brewed ale, and for *capping Latin verses.* Near to the Fox is a small ale and table-beer brewery belonging to Mr. Fishwick.

### CHURCH LIVING, &c.

The church living of this parish was appropriated to the nuns of St. Leonard, at Bromley, in this county, to whom it probably was given by William, Bishop of London, their founder, about the time of William the Conqueror. Of the patronage of the church at Islington

" there was of old," says Newcourt[1], " a controversy before Gilbert,
" Bishop of London, between the dean and chapter of St. Paul's on
" the one part, and the nuns of Stratford Bow on the other; which,
" by the authority and assent of the said Bishop, was at last quietly
" determined after this manner, viz. that the said nuns should hold
" this church of *Iseldon*, of the Canons of St. Paul's; and should
" therefore yearly pay to the said Canons one mark; half on the next
" day after the feast of St. Leonard, and half in the Octaves of Pente-
" cost; and that thereupon the said nuns should freely present to this
" church. Which church, it seems, was afterwards appropriated to
" those nuns; and a vicarage here ordained and endowed, of which
" they continued patrons till their suppression, but afterwards it came
" into the hands of private patrons."

At the dissolution of their convent, the rectory and advowson were
granted to Sir Ralph Sadler[2], who alienated them anno 1548, to John
Perse[3]. In 1565, they were conveyed by Thomas Perse to Roger
Martyn[4], and in 1582 by Humphrey Martin to John Cheke[5]. It is
probable that they came into the Stonehouse family before the Civil
War, and were seized among other estates of Sir George Stonehouse,
who suffered considerable losses for his loyalty. In 1646, Sir Walter
Smyth, being then in possession of the rectory of Islington[6], (to the
exclusion, it is presumed, of the legal owner) conveyed it by an in-
denture of that date to Sir Arthur Hesilrige, Sir Thomas Fowler,
Sir Thomas Fisher, and other inhabitants of the place, as feoffees in

---

[1] Repertorium, vol. I. p. 676.

[2] Pat. 32 Hen. VIII. pt. 22. April 21.

[3] Pat. 2 Edw. VI. pt. 1. March 6.

[4] Pat. 7 Eliz. pt. 8. Aug. 17.

[5] Pat. 24 Eliz. pt. 2. Jan. 2.

[6] " 29 Oct. 1646, Walter Smith, of Great Bedwin, co. Wilts, agreed to settle
" £.100. a year on the Church of Islington, for which he was allowed £.400. and
" his fine of £.1085. reduced to £.685." *Impropriations purchased by the Committee
sitting at Goldsmith's-hall for compositions with delinquents.* Sept. 22, 1648.

trust for the vicar and his successors, on whom he settled the great tithes [1]. In 1657, it was ordered by the Committees, that Leonard Cooke, who had been presented to the vicarage in the December preceding [2], should receive the profits of the rectory pursuant to this grant. In the year 1662 the rectory and advowson were certainly vested in the Stonehouse family [3], in which they continued till about the middle of the last century; the late vicar was presented by Richard Holden, esq. in 1768; the present vicar by Richard Smith, esq. The rectory and advowson are now vested in the devisees in trust under Mr. Smith's will [4].

The present incumbent is the Rev. George Strahan, D. D. Rector of Cranham, Essex, and Prebendary of Rochester. The lecturer is the Rev. George Gaskin, D. D. Rector of Stoke Newington, and the united parishes of St. Bennet Gracechurch and St. Leonard Eastcheap; also Secretary to the Society for promoting Christian Knowledge among the Poor. The parish is in ecclesiastical matters subject to the Archdeacon of London. The vicar receives a modus of 4d. *per* acre for land, 2d. *per* cow, and 2d. *per* calf, but no tithes whatever are paid to any other person. The vicarage is rated in the King's Books at £.30. The glebe attached to the living contains 9 acres 2 roods 21 perches; part of which, containing 4 acres 13 perches, situate on the North side of Sermon-lane, in the Back road, has been lately let by Dr. Strahan on building leases of 99 years, by virtue of an Act of Parliament obtained for that purpose; the remainder, containing 5 acres 2 roods and 8 perches, is situate near Ball's Pond. The parsonage house has been already noticed in p. 122.

[1] Parliamentary Surveys, Lamb. MSS. Lib. and Proceedings of the Committees, vol. xxix. pp. 58, 59.

[2] Ibid. vol. III. p. 63.

[3] Newcourt's Repertorium, vol. I.

[4] Lysons's Environs.

The following is a catalogue of the Vicars of Islington parish, from the list published by Mr. Nichols in his History of Canonbury.

1. WALTER GERKIN, the earliest vicar whose name is preserved, died in 1327.

2. EGIDIAC DE FELSTED, 3 non. Oct. 1327.

3. WILLIAM DE SOUTHWERK, Aug. 6, 1332.

4. JOHN SEMAN, (vicar of Fering, Essex), 10 kal. Nov. 1336.

5. THOMAS GUNGE, prid. non. Feb. 1336.

6. HENRY LE CLERKE, 10 kal. Nov. 1337.

7. LAURENCE SPROT, chaplain, April 29, 1384.

8. JOHN COOKE, Feb. 27, 1393, on Sprot's death.

9. WILLIAM HARDY, Sept. 21, 1395; resigned in 1397, on being presented to the rectory of Mesdon, Herts, which rectory he also resigned in 1398.

10. JOHN DAMES, June 8, 1397, (vicar of Ealing.)

11. WILLIAM CHAPELL, (rector of South Hanningfield, Essex;) resigned.

12. WILLIAM CANON, rector of Netteswell, Essex, Aug. 4, 1425; resigned.

13. RICHARD DALLY, Dec. 18, 1427; resigned.

14. JOHN CROXBY, Sept. 27, 1434. He resigned in 1438, and was afterwards vicar of South Mims, Middlesex, 1456; and of East Ham, Essex, 1462.

15. WILLIAM LECHE, Feb. 27, 1438; resigned.

16. JOHN FARLEY, Aug. 14, 1443; resigned.

17. ROBERT SMITH, Nov. 23, 1444; resigned for the rectory of St. Vedast, London, 1448.

18. JOHN FAYLEY, 1448; resigned.

19. JOHN WARDALL, April 16, 1454. He had afterwards the Prebend of Twyford, in the Church of St. Paul, and was admitted rector of Wybourn Magna, Essex, Sept. 17, 1466, all which he held till his death in 1472.

20. THOMAS GOORE, May 5, 1472.

21. EDWARD VAUGHAN, LL. D. of the University of Cambridge, was admitted rector of St. Matthew, Friday-street, London, Jan. 21, 1487, being then Doctor of Laws; but the time of his voiding it appears not. He was collated to the prebend of Re-culverland April 15, 1493, which he resigned in 1499, and had the prebend of Harleston conferred on him Nov. 16 that year, which he resigned in 1503, on succeeding to the treasurership of St. Paul's. He was also prebendary of Broomesbury, but the time of his admission appears not. All which last preferments became void in 1509, by his being promoted to the Bishoprick of St. David's, to which he was consecrated July 22 that year, in which Cathedral Church he built the Chapel of the Holy Trinity a little before his death, at his own charge, and dying in Nov. 1522, was buried in the same.

22. THOMAS WARREN, B. D. Sept. 27, 1509. He died in 1521.

23. JOHN COCKS, or COCKYS, LL. D. March 3, 1521. He was of All Souls College, Oxon; principal of St. George's Hall in St. Mary's parish there, and in 1509 warden or rector of the Church of Elmley, in Kent, rector of St. Mary le Bow, London, in 1522, and Official of the Arches in 1543. He was also princi-pal of Henxey Hall in St. Aldate's parish, Oxon (a place for Ci-vilians); Principal or Chief Moderator or Professor of the Civil Law School in the parish of St. Edward; and died in 1545.

24. JAMES ROBINSON, LL. B. Feb. 26, 1545. According to New-court he had been vicar of North Weld Bassett 1519; of Tot-ham Magna 1527; and rector of Barnston Terling 1543, all in the County of Essex; and attained the rectory of Little Badow, in that County in 1578. But it is not likely that these should all have been the same James Robinson. The vicar of Isling-ton resigned in 1550.

25. WILLIAM JENNINS, April 30, 1550. He had been rector of

Allhallows, Lombard-street, London, 1538; and attained the rectory of St. Pancras Soper-lane in 1570.

26. ANTHONY SYLLIARD, M. A. March 18, 1565.

27. MEREDITH HANMER, son of Thomas Hanmer, of Porkington, in Shropshire, descended from the Hanmers in Flintshire, was born in that County 1544, became chaplain of Corpus Christi College, Oxford, in April 1567; took the degrees in Arts, and after some time spent in that house was at length made vicar of St. Leonard, Shoreditch, Middlesex (Dec. 8, 1581,) where, according to the relation of the inhabitants (as Weever tells us, p. 437), he converted the brass of several antient monuments into coin for his own use. In 1581 and 1582 he took the degrees in Divinity, and in 1583 was admitted vicar of this Church, which he resigned in 1590, and that of Shoreditch before June 22, 1592. He went into Ireland, and at length became Treasurer of the Church of the Holy Trinity (now called Christ Church) in Dublin, which he kept to his dying day, which happened in the year 1604 of the plague. Weever asserts, that he ended his days in Ireland ignominiously, meaning perhaps as a judgment for the sacrilege he committed while vicar of Shoreditch [1]. He was es-

---

[1] In Strype's Annals, vol. III. pp. 216, 217, under the occurrences of the year 1584 is related the scandalization of the Earl of Shrewsbury, that he had got a child by the Queen; and among the witnesses examined before the jury, writes Recorder Fleetwood, in his Diary, " was one Meredith Hanmer, a Doctor of " Divinity, and vicar of *Islyngton*, who dealt as leudly towards my Lord in " speeches, as did the other Walmesley. This Doctor regardeth not an oath; " surely he is a very bad man."

In the Consistorial Acts of the Diocese of Rochester, A. D. 1588—1590, fol. 40. b. is this entry of a charge against Hanmer:

" Dr. Hanmer, vicar of Shoreditch, married Richard Turke, of Dartforde, and " Gertrude, the wife of John Wynd, without banns or license."

It is traditionally preseved by some of the inhabitants of Shoreditch that the Doctor committed suicide, by the halter. *Ellis's History of Shoreditch*, p. 24.

teemed an exact disputant, a good preacher and Grecian, and excellent for Ecclesiastical and Civil Histories. His publications are, 1. " Confutation and Answer of the great Bragge and " Challenge of Mr. Campian, the Jesuit, containing nine articles " by him directed to the Lords of the Privy Council 1581," 8vo. 2. "The Jesuits Banner, displaying their Original and Success, their " Vow, and other their Hypocrisy and Superstition, their Doctrine " and Positions, 1581," 4to. 3. " A Confutation of a brief Cen- " sure upon Two Books, written in answer to Mr. Campian's offer " of Disputation," printed with the Jesuits Banner, &c. 4. " The " Chronicle of Ireland," in two parts, the second of which was printed at Dublin, in 1633, folio. 5. " Sermon at the Bap- " tizing of a Turk, on Matt. v. 15. 1586," 8vo. 6. " An " Ephemeris of the Saints of Ireland." 7. " A Chronography, " with a Supputation of the Years from the Beginning of the " World unto the Birth of Christ, and continued from the Birth " of Christ (where Eusebius chiefly, Socrates, Evagrius, and " Dorotheus, after him do write) unto the twelfth year of the " reign of Mauritius the Emperor, being the full time of 600 " years wanting five after Christ; all chiefly collected out of " Eusebius, Socrates, and Evagrius, 1585," &c. folio. Be- sides these, he hath translated from Greek into English; 1. " The Antient Ecclesiastical Histories of the first 600 years " after Christ, written in the Greek Tongue, by three learned " Historiographers, Eusebius, Socrates, and Evagrius, 1577," 1585, 1619, folio. The dedication, to the Earl of Leicester, which was prefixed to the second edition, is dated from Shore- ditch, the 15th December, 1584. 2. " The Lives, Ends, and " Martyrdoms of the Prophets, Apostles, and Seventy Dis- " ciples of Christ, originally written by Dorotheus, Bishop " of Tyrus;" printed with the former translation. Dr. Han- mer, it appears, had translated all the Church Historians, except Eusebius's four books, concerning the Life of the Emperor Constantine, and the two Orations subjoined thereunto, which were afterwards done by Wye Saltonstal, and printed in a fifth edition of Hanmer's translation, 1650, folio.

28. SAMUEL PROCTOR, B. D. September 5, 1590, rector of Shepperton, 1592.

29. WILLIAM HUNT, M. A. May 10, 1639.

30. LEONARD COOKE.

31. WILLIAM CAVE, August 7, 1662. This learned divine was born in 1637; and educated in St. John's College at Cambridge; M. A. 1660; D. D. 1672. He was successively minister of Haseley in Oxfordshire, Allhallows the Great in London, and Islington. He became chaplain to Charles II. [1]; and in 1684, was installed Canon of Windsor. He was the author of some large and learned works relating to ecclesiastical antiquity; and composed a very useful work, intituled, " Antiquitates Aposto- " lici : or, The History of the Lives, Acts, Deaths, and Martyr- " doms of those who were contemporary with the Apostles, and " of the principal Fathers, within the three first Centuries of " the Church, 1677, London;" folio, which went in a short time through three or four editions. Here the English reader had an opportunity of acquainting himself with some of the principal and most important circumstances which attended the Christian religion, while it was making its way to an establishment under Constantine the Great. In 1689, he published a work of a more extensive nature: " Scriptorum Ecclesiasticorum " Historia Literaria, à Christo Nato usque ad Sæculum XIV. " facili Methodo digesta, Lond." folio. In this work he gives an exact account of all who had written upon Christianity, either for or against it, from Christ to the fourteenth century; mentions the times they lived in, the books they wrote, and the

---

[1] Two sermons of Dr. Cave are in print, preached before the King, 1676, 1684, and one before the Lord Mayor, 1680.

doctrines they maintained; and also enumerates the Councils that were called in every age of the Church. This and the former work gave occasion to a controversy which ensued, and was very warmly agitated between Cave and Le Clerc, who was then writing his " Bibliotheque Universelle," in Holland. Le Clerc charged Dr. Cave with two unfair proceedings : 1. That, instead of writing the Lives of the Fathers, he had written their pane- gyrics. 2. That he had forcibly drawn Eusebius, who was, as he imagined, plainly enough an Arian, over to the side of the orthodox, and made a Trinitarian of him. These were the points debated, and a great deal of good learning, as well as good sense relating to ecclesiastical antiquity, and the authority of the Fathers, was produced on both sides : but which of the two had the better in the dispute, is not a point to be determined here; unless we may just be permitted to say, but without any intention to diminish the value of Dr. Cave's work, that he did not entirely clear himself of the charge. Dr. Cave died in 1713, and was buried at Islington [1].

32. ROBERT GERY, M. A. May 4, 1691. He was rector of All- hallows the Great, London, 1689, and installed a Prebendary of Lincoln Dec. 15, 1701. He published a single Sermon, 1706, 4to.; died Oct. 1, 1707; and was buried at Islington [1].

33. CORNELIUS YEATE, M. A. Archdeacon of Wilts; died April 12, 1720; and was buried at Islington [1]. " He was a gentle- " man of great probity and learning, and generally esteemed for " his exemplary life, which he spent chiefly in inculcating and " practising all Christian virtues." (*Daily Post, April* 14, 1720.)

34. GEORGE CAREY [2], 1720, died at Bath, May 13th, 1733. It is recorded of this gentleman, that on a wet hay-making time, in the year 1725, he went through the parish from house to house,

---

[1] See inscriptions in the church.
[2] His only son was drowned in the New River Aug. 7, 1731.

collecting for the poor haymakers a handsome sum, which he afterwards distributed at the Church [1].

35. RICHARD STREAT, M. A, July 1733; resigned in 1738.

36. GEORGE STONEHOUSE [2], M. A. 1738; married June 1, 1739, Miss Crisp, daughter of Sir John Crisp, Bart.; published a single sermon, 1739, 12mo; and resigned the vicarage in 1740. He died at Bristol in 1793.

37. Sir GILBERT WILLIAMS [3], of Guernevet, Brecon, Bart. and M. A. 1740; vicar also of Sarrat, Herts; died in 1767.

38. RICHARD SMITH, M. A. 1768; died Feb. 16, 1772; and was buried in Islington Church [4].

39. GEORGE STRAHAN, M. A. 1772 (now D. D. and the present vicar;) rector of Thurrock Parva in Essex, by dispensation, 1783 (since resigned); and of Cranham in the same county, by dispensation, 1786; Prebendary of Rochester 1808. This gentleman was honoured with the acquaintance and friendship of the great Dr. Samuel Johnson, who frequently visited him at Islington, and was at his house for a few days during his last illness. He bequeathed Dr. Strahan a part of his library, and left in his hands for publication some posthumous writings, which were afterwards printed under the title of " Prayers and Medi-" tations, composed by Samuel Johnson, LL. D. and published " from his Manuscripts, by George Strahan, M. A." &c. 8vo.

---

[1] Malcolm's Customs and Manners of London.

[2] Mr. Stonehouse, as it appears by the Journals of Whitefield and Wesley, was a favourer of the original Methodists; to whom he used to lend his church; a circumstance which so extremely affected Mr. Scott the then lecturer, that it was supposed to hasten his death, which happened July 18, 1740. Whitefield, however, on one occasion being refused the church, mounted a tomb-stone in the church-yard, and preached a sermon to a very numerous congregation. *Life of Whitefield.*

[3] Sir Gilbert Williams preached one of the sermons before the Sons of the Clergy.

[4] See inscriptions in the church.

Robert Brown, founder of the sect denominated *Brownists*, appears to be the most remarkable among the lecturers of this parish. He was born at Northampton towards the middle of the 16th century; studied divinity at Cambridge; and afterwards became a schoolmaster in Southwark. About the year 1580, he began to inveigh with intemperance, vehemence, and ardour, against the discipline and ceremonies of the Church of England, representing her government as Anti-Christian, her Sacraments as superstitious, her Liturgy as a mixture of Popery and Paganism, and the mission of her Clergy as no better than that of Baal's Priests in the Old Testament. He afterwards preached to a Dutch congregation at Norwich, and gaining many proselytes, partly Dutch and partly English, to his doctrine, his followers formed themselves into a separate Society from the Church, under the denomination of BROWNISTS. He afterwards fled from the persecutions he experienced in this kingdom, and settled at Middleburgh, where he and his followers obtained leave of the States to worship God in their own way.

Having returned to England, he continued to disseminate his opinions with great freedom and zeal, till, being excommunicated for contempt of a summons to appear before the Bishop of Peterborough, he was induced to renounce his principles of separation, returned to the communion of the establishment, and obtained preferment in the Church. His sect, however, long survived his revolt, and many of his opinions were afterwards received and inculcated with more moderation by the *Independants,* which sect appears to have originated in the *Brownists* about the beginning of the 17th century.

Brown is represented as a man of good parts, and some learning; and though of an imperious and ungovernable temper, appears to have been treated with too much severity. He died in Northampton gaol, in 1630, aged above 80 years; after boasting of his persecutions, and that he had been committed to thirty-two prisons, in some of which he could not see his hand at noon-day [1].

[1] Biog. Brit. Neale's History of the Puritans, &c.

## THE OLD CHURCH.

OF the first foundation of a Church at Islington nothing at this period can be ascertained. The old edifice, which was dedicated to the Virgin Mary [1], and stood exactly on the site of the present Church, was a spacious but low built structure, in the old English style of architecture, composed of a rough kind of masonry called Boulder, or an intermixture of flints, pebbles, and chalk, strongly cemented together. The roof was covered with tiles. Its dimensions were as follows:

Length - - - - - - - - - - - 92 feet.
Breadth - - - - - - - - - - - 54 feet.
Height - - - - - - - - - - - 28 feet.
Altitude of the tower and turret 74 feet.

In the tower there were six bells, and a clock on the West front, also a sun dial on the South side, near to the top, bearing the date 1708, and the motto, "*Dum spectas, fugit Hora.*" The West end of the Church was almost obscured by the old school-house, which stood close against the front of the building, under which was the porch, and an adjoining room used for lumber, &c. (see Plate XI.)

Hatton, an eminent surveyor, who wrote the "*New View of London,*" about a century ago, on actual survey of the building remarks, that, as near as could be guessed, from order, materials, and other circumstances, it appeared at that time to have been erected about 200 years. Of the interior of the building he observes, "As to ornament it cannot be expected any considerable should be in so old and

[1] A superstitious image of the Virgin Mary, called *Our Lady of Islington*, appears to have been kept in the Church, and held in high veneration, but which was burnt at the Reformation.

## 37

A View of St Mary's Church Iflington

ISLINGTON CHURCH.

Taken down in 1751

PLATE XI.

*N.W. View of the old Church of S.t Mary, Islington, 1750.*

*N.E. View of the old Church of S.t Mary, Islington, 1750.*

Published May 1.1811 by Russell Upper Street Islington.

" decaying a structure, but what is there to be found is agreeable
" enough [1].

The Church contained three ailes, and was paved throughout with brick and stones intermixed : the floor, to which there was a descent of several steps from the entrance, was raised two steps higher at the altar than in the other parts. The roof was divided into pannels, and immediately over the chancel was painted with clouds, &c. in fresco. The pews were of oak, and the walls wainscotted, in most parts seven feet high, but higher round the communion table, and painted of an olive colour, enriched with gilt mouldings. The East end was adorned with a cornice of carved oak, having a glory in the centre ; and between the two tables of the decalogue, which were painted in black letters on the white wall, there was a spacious window containing some remnants of fine stained glass. The gallery was built in 1663, and the altar-piece in 1671.

On pulling down this structure in 1751, the earliest date that occurred was 1483, which was discovered at the South-east corner of the steeple, but was not visible till the West gallery had been removed. This, it is most probable, was the period of its erection ; and, while it confirms the opinion of Hatton, shews the time of its standing to have been 268 years.

In this year (1751), the building being examined by three surveyors appointed for that purpose, they were of opinion that it was so much dilapidated and gone to decay as to endanger the lives of the inhabitants assembling therein ; that it could not be substantially repaired, but at a very great expence ; and that, even then, it would be found insufficient to accommodate the parishioners. Whereupon an application was made to Parliament by the Vestry for an Act to enable them to pull down and rebuild the structure.

An Act was accordingly passed, which empowered the several trustees therein named to borrow a sufficient sum of money for that purpose, by way of annuities on lives. These annuities were paid by

---

[1] New View of London, 8vo, 1708.

a rate or assessment on the landlords and householders of the parish; the landlord paying two thirds and the tenant the remainder.

In the month of July, a contract was entered into with Mr. G. Steemson for taking down the church, he agreeing to allow £.110 for the old materials, and to clear them away within one month from that time, which was executed accordingly. The tower was found so strongly cemented together, that it set the efforts of the workmen employed in its demolition at defiance. Gunpowder was used in order to dislodge the firmer parts; but being used sparingly, for fear of accident, it had not the desired effect; whereupon the surveyor had recourse to undermining the foundation, first shoaring up the superstructure with strong timbers; these being consumed by a large fire kindled for the purpose, the tower fell to the ground with a tremendous crash. From the great strength and solidity of this part of the fabric, it was considered that it might have stood, perhaps, some centuries longer; but the inhabitants persisted in having it removed, to give place to the new building [1].

Upon the old church [2] being shut up previous to its removal, divine service was regularly performed in a large building near the Fox

[1] Notice was given in the public papers, that any person or family having tombstones or monuments in the church might have them to preserve upon application. The trustees for the new building were mentioned with honour in the public prints, " for the care they took of the monuments and reliques of the dead, to the shame " of some precedents on the like occasion, where the disregard or ill usage of the " dust and bones of their fellow Christians appeared in a scandalous manner." *Gent. Mag.* vol. XXI. p. 378. 426.

[2] From a letter of Vertue the engraver to Dr. Ducarel (Nov. 16th 1750) in the possession of Mr. Nichols, it appears that he had been to Islington in search of Antiquities, and wishes the Doctor to appoint a day to accompany him thither. He remarks that he knew of no print of the Church then extant, but considered that the building might probably contain something worthy of preservation.— A view of the antient Font is given in Plate VII.—A beautiful view of the old Church, drawn by *Pillament*, was sold by auction at Langford's some years ago. *British Topography*, p. 544. Another view of it, including the old School, was engraved

public-house, rented of Henry Harpur, esq. for that purpose, and which had been previously fitted up as a tabernacle, at the expence of £.100, till the new church should be completed. The mode of raising a fund to re-build the church by way of annuities turned out very easy and beneficial to the parish, several of the annuitants having died after receiving a year's interest only. The surviving one died in 1785 [1].

### MONUMENTAL INSCRIPTIONS IN THE OLD CHURCH.

ON the wall, near to the end of the South aile, was a very spacious and costly monument of white and veined marble, adorned with two columns and their entablature of the Corinthian order, also pyramidical figures; and those of the lady, lying on her left side, under an arch, as reading, and of eleven children and grandchildren in a kneeling posture; in the front of the tomb were also enrichments of cherubim, fruit, and leaves, partly gilt, and the whole inclosed by iron railing, with this inscription:

" Under the hope of the resurrection,

Here lyeth the bodie of *Alice Owen,* widowe, the daughter of Thomas Wilkes. She was first married to Henry Robinson, by whom she had sixe sonnes, John, William, Henry, John, Tho-

in 1738, as a ticket for the churchwardens' feast *(Ibid.)*; and a neat view of the West part may be found among the engravings from the works of Chatelain. In the vestry of the present church are two drawings, North-west and South-east views of the old fabric, from which the annexed engraving is taken: they were given to the vestry by Hammond Crosse, esq. in the year 1769. Several views of it were also taken about the year 1734, by Bernard Lens, drawing-master to the Duke of Cumberland, and subsequently by Benjamin Green, an artist of some ability, who resided at Islington, and was drawing-master to Christ's Hospital. In Ellis's Campagna of London, is an aquatinta engraving of the West front.

[1] MS. of the late Mr. Biggerstaff, jun. vestry-clerk, obligingly communicated by Mr. Palmer.

mas, and Henry; which said Henry the younger was married unto Mary, the daughter of Sir William Glover, Knt. Alderman of London; and five daughters, Margaret, married to Sir John Bret, of Edmunton, in the County of Middlesex, Knight; Susan; Ann; and Ann the younger, married to Robert Rich, of Horndon on the Hill, in the County of Essex, Esq. and Alice, married to John Washborne, of Wichinforde, in the County of Worcester, Esq.

The second husband was William Elkin, Esq. Alderman of the City of London, by whom she had issue only Ursula Elkin, married to Sir Roger Owen, of Condover, in the County of Salopp, Knt.

The third husband was Thomas Owen, one of the Judges of the Court of Common Pleas to Queen Elizabeth [1].

This matron, having advaunced and enriched all her children, kept greate hospitalitie: shee also in her lifetime so furthered the publique weale of this state, as her charitable deedes to the Cittie of London, both Universities, Oxford and Cambridge, especialie this towne of Islington, can testifie; a monument of her pietie to future ages beinge extant in the South end of this towne, more worthie and largelie expressing her pietie than these gowlden letters, as much as deedes are above wordes. She having lived religiouslie to God, sufficientlie *for nature, but not for her children and friends*, her just soulle is in the hands of the Almightie, when her bodie departed on the 26th day of November, anno d'ni 1613."

Arms: 1. *Argent, on a mount in base proper, a fig-tree Vert, fruited Or;* Wilkes. 2. *Azure, three roebucks trippant Or, three lozenges Gules on a chevronel Or;* Kemp *impaled with* Wilkes. 3. *Gules, a bar on a fess Argent, between two tigers*

---

[1] A handsome monument to the memory of this lady's third husband, Judge Owen, is erected in the South aile of Westminster-abbey.

*courant Or, three mullets pierced Sable ;* Elkin *impaled with* Wilkes. 4. *Gules, a chevron between three lions rampant Or ;* Owen *impaled with* Wilkes.

Upon a brass plate :

" Here lyeth Thomas Walker, citizen and grocer of London, and Cicele his wife. Thomas deceased the 25th day of the month of July, the year of our Lord God a thousand CCCCLXXXXVI. On whos sowlys J'hu have mercy. Amen."

Upon a plated stone[1] :

" 𝔍 p'ye the Chrysten man that ꝑast yee to see this
to p'ye for the soulls of them that here buryed is |
And remember that in Cryst we be bretherne
the wich hath comaunded ev'y man to p'ye for other ; |
this sayth Robert Midleton ad Johan hys wyf
Here wrappid in claye. Abiding the mercy |
of Almighty God till domesdaye.
W'ch was su'tyme s'unt to S' George Hastyng[2], knight, |
Erle of Huntingdount passid this t'nscitory lyf
in the yere of our Lord God MCCCC . . . . . |
And the . . . day of the moneth of . . . . . .
On whose soull Almighty God have m'cy. Amen."

On a monument on the North side of the chancel :
" *Vivit post funera Virtus.*

" Here lyeth the body of William Richorne, late of Canonbury, Esq. ; which William married with Anne, the daughter of John Quarles, of London, merchant, and dyed without issue the 18th day of November, in the yeere of our Lord God 1582, and in the 54th yeare of his age."

[1] This appeared to have been laid down in the life-time of Robert Middleton, neither the year, month, nor day being set down, but spaces left for that purpose ; the whole was divided into six lines, each ending where the mark | is placed.

[2] Sir George Hastings was created Earl of Huntingdon Dec. 8, 1529.

On a brass plate :

" Here lyeth the body of Gregory Charlet, citizen and tallow-
chandler, of London, who had one only daughter named Jane,
married to Thomas Fowler, of Islington, Esq. which said Gregory was buried the 6th of June 1593, whose soule resteth with
the Lord, ætat. sue 67—."

" Here lyeth the body of Jane Fowler, daughter to Gregory Charlet,
citizen and tallow-chandler, &c. She had issue by the said
Thomas Fowler, two sons, Thomas and Edmund : She was
buried the 14th of October, 1601, whose soul resteth in the
Lord.

Sir Thomas Fowler, Knt. who took to wife Jane Charlet, by whom
he had issue Sir Thomas and Sir Edmund Fowler ; after the
death of Jane, he took to wife Mary, the widow of Sir John
Spencer, of Althrop, in the county of Northampton, Knt.
and mother to the Lord Spencer that now is, by whom he had
no issue. The said Mary departed this life the 5th of January,
1620. He afterwards married Dorothie, the daughter of Sir
Walter Coape, of Kensington, in the county of Middlesex,
Knt. and had by her no issue. The said Sir Thomas departed
this life the 14th of January, 1624. He was one of his Majesty's Deputy Lieutenants of this county of Middlesex ; as also
a high commissioner for the verge, and likewise in the commission of the peace and quorum for this county.

Elizabeth Lady Fowler, late wife of Sir Thomas Fowler the younger,
Knt. the daughter and heir of William Person, of the Inner
Temple, Esq. the 19th September 1628. She had issue by the
same Sir Thomas, four sons and seven daughters.

John Fowler, sole son and heir of Sir Thomas Fowler, of this parish, Knt. and Bart. who married Elizabeth, the daughter and
heir of Aunseline Fowler, of the County of Gloucester, esq.
died without issue the 1st Sept. 1638.

Jane, the daughter of Sir Thomas Fowler, of this parish, Knt. and Bart. and wife of Mr. Richard Corbet, of          , in the County of Lincoln, the 20th day of November 1633, and had issue by the said Corbet two sons, viz. Thomas and Rowland.

Martha, the daughter of Sir Thomas Fowler, Knt. and Bart. the 11th of June, 1634.

Dedicated by Richard Fisher, Bart. to the honoured memory of his grandfather Sir Thomas Fowler, late of this place, Knt. and Bart. and of his Lady Elizabeth, daughter of William Person, Esq. by whom he had one son and four daughters; viz. John, who married Sarah, daughter to John Fowler, of Staffordshire, Esq. who dyed childless; Sarah, married to Sir Thomas Fisher, Knt. and Bart.; Jane, married to Richard Corbet, Esq.; Elizabeth, married to Gerard Gore, Esq.; and Martha, died a virgin. These all sleep in hope of a blessed resurrection, 1678."

" Erected by Sir Richard Fisher, Bart. to the dear remembrance of his father Sir Thomas Fisher, Knt. and Bart. and his beloved Lady Sarah, eldest daughter of Sir Thomas Fowler, Knt. and Bart. by whom he had three sons and three daughters, viz. Thomas, who married Jane, the daughter of Sir John Prescot, Knt.; he had only one son Thomas, who died at the age of 18 years; John dyed young; Sarah, married Sir Hugh Ducie, Knight of the Bath, both deceased; Richard, Susan, and Ursula, are now living, March the 30th 1678."

## Upon a brass plate:

" Mr. William Langham, late one of the prebends of Litchfield, parson of Thurnbie, and Doctor of Physic, who deceased the 16th day of Sept. 1603."

## On a plated grave-stone in the South aile:

" Here lyeth the body of John Markham, esq. one of the Serjeants at Arms to our most gracious Sovereign Lord King James, &c. who dyed the 26th of August, 1610.

He was both gentilke born,  and gentilke bred,
And ere he dyed was well marryed
Unto a vertuous and a loving wife,
Who,  losing him,  loathed her own life;
Whose love hath built this for eternity,
That he may still be had in memory."

### Another plated stone was thus inscribed :

" Thomas Draper,  de Stroud Green,  dum vixit Civis Londineus'.   Postquam omnia Societatis suæ munia obiisset, et in Communi Civitatis Concilio diu  sedis-
set,  placidè decessit in  Domino.   Vir probus, prudens, et pius, &c.   Ob. 23
Octobr. anno Dom. 1611.
        By his wife Sarah he left three  sons and one daughter."
Arms : *Four bendlets Or, on a field parted per fess Argent and Ermine, charged in chief*
*with three fleur de lis Sable.*

On the North side of the chancel was a very spacious marble monument, adorned with four black  columns and entablature ; also the
effigies of  Sir Nicholas Kempe  between those of  his two wives,  in a
kneeling  posture,  and  enrichments of  cherubim,  gilding,  &c. and
this inscription :

" Here lyeth buried the body of Sir Nicholas Kempe, Knt. one of his Majesty's
Justices of the Peace,  and an honourable member of the  High Commission
Court, &c. who  had  to his first wife Cecilia, with  whom  he  lived in blessed
amity near forty years together ; with Sarah  his  second wife six years ; and
having past, with much prosperity, love,  and credit, the reverend years of 72,
he changed this terrestrial  condition for that everlasting state of blessedness,
the third of September, 1624.
        Wise,  loving,  liberal,  religious,  just;
        Those graces fill'd the soul of him whose dust
        Lies here intomb'd : all that praise can bring  forth,
        There are not words enough t'express his worth
        For his good works.   This stone cannot comprise
        Half the particulars of his pieties ;
        What goodness ever was,  is, and to come,
        In mortal man,  that makes up his just sum."
Arms ;  *Gules,  three garbes within a bordure engrailed Or.*

'' Here lieth Dame Sarah Kempe, who was first married to Thomas Draper, Esq˙ after to Sir Nicholas Kempe, Kt. and died the 25 of Julie, 1650, in the 77 year of her age ¹.''

## On a fair stone in the Chancel :

" Hinc
Sperat Resurrectionem
(Filius HARBOTELLI GRIMESTON,
Militis & Baronetti,
Natu tertius),
HENRICUS GRIMESTON.

Anagramma :
*En ! Christi regno sum.*
Qui moritur, vivit Christo : huic mors semita, ductor
Angelus, ad vitam janua Christus erit.
Hac iter ad superos, calcans vestigia lethi,
Intrabam Christi Regia, Templa Dei,
12° die mensis Julii, An. Dom. 1627.''

## On a monument in the South aile :

" To the sacred memory of Anne, late wife of Henry Chitton, Esq. Chester Herald at Arms, eldest daughter of William Bennett, gentleman, by Joice, widow of Richard Joselin, of Newhall Joselins, in Essex, Esq. and daughter of Robert Atkinson, of Stowell, in the County of Gloucester, Esquire. She had four children, whereof three are living; Thomas, Joyce, and Henry; of which last she died in childbed the 8th of May, 1632, in the 27th year of her age, and 4th year of her marriage.

*Mors mihi vita.*
Life is Death's road, and Death Heav'n's gate must be,
Heav'n is Christ's throne, and Christ is life to me ;
The angels of the Lord protect
All those that are his own elect.
*Vivit post funera virtus.*''

---

¹ This stone is now in the pavement close to the wall of the Church at the West front. The inscription, though still legible, is generally printed incorrectly, as it may be seen in the *Monumenta Anglicana*, &c. Le Neve has also given the epitaphs of Edmund Pott and Sir Thomas Fowler with some variations.

**Q Q**

## On the South wall of the Chancel, a black and white marble monument, adorned with the effigies of Hugh Dashfield and a festoon :

" Memoriæ Sacr.  Hic componitur Hugo Dashfield, Wigorniensis, vir pietate in
    Deum,  liberalitate in egenos,  comitate erga omnes insignis.   Cujus industria,
    prudentia, & spectata fides honoratissimo Thomæ Domino Coventriæ (cui tan-
    dem à Carolo rege concredita est Magni Sigilli Custodia) ita placuerunt, ut
    tanto hero, publicisque muniis inserviens, apud ipsum duodecim penè triteri-
    das vixerit, quam hinc excederet, quod quidem naturæ debitum magno cum
    bonorum desiderio (quibus semper prodesse studuit & beneficia præstare liben-
    tius quam polliceri) fidei plenus & spei, cursum persolvit Septembris 17 Ann.
    Dom. 1638, ætat. 59."

## At the East end of the North aile :

" Hic sepelitur Margaretta Savil,  nuper uxor Henrici  Savil,  armigeri,  filia Thomæ
    Fowler,  in hac parochia item armigeri, &c. 15° die post partum editum in ipso
    juventutis flore ex hac vita concessit, anno ætatis suæ 19, 27 mensis Augusti,
    Ann. Dom. MDCXLVI."

" Edmund Pott, of Pott, in the County of Chester, Gent. first married to Sarah,
    daughter  of  Anthony Thompson, of  Cambridge,  Gent. and had issue by her
    two sons and one daughter.   She deceased 1640.   His second wife was Jane,
    the daughter of Joseph Lane, of London, Gent. who had issue by her two sons.
    He deceased March the 28th,  1650."

## On a grave-stone:

" Christopher Wase, of Upper Holloway, Esq. and Judith Master, one  of the
    daughters and coheirs of the said Christopher Wase.  She died the 4th of
    November, 1669, and George Master, son of the abovenamed Judith Master,
    the 6th of June, 1666."

## On a white marble monument on the South side of the chancel :

" Near this place lyeth the body of Judith Master, one of the daughters and coheirs
    of Christopher Wase, of Upper Holloway, Esq. and wife to George Master, of
    Lincoln's-inn, third son of Sir William Master, of Ciceter, in the county of
    Gloucester, Knt.   She was a woman of exemplary virtue : towards God truly
    pious, towards man exactly just.   To her husband, during their ten years
    intermarriage, she was ever a most affectionate and observant wife, a real and

judicious friend, by whom she had many children; but left him only one son. She died the 4th of November, 1669."

Arms of Master: *Gules, a lion rampant gardant Or, impaled with those of* Wase, *barry of six, Argent and Gules.*

" Sarah Fowke, wife of Thomas Fowke, of London, merchant, March 10, 1663. By her he had issue five sons and six daughters."

## In the chancel:

" John Short, citizen and merchant taylor of London, born at Doncaster, in York-shire, who departed this life at Canbury-house, in this parish, the 26th of March, 1689, in the 66th year of his age.

John Short, citizen and draper of London, began this life in Kent, departed this life in the same place as above, in October 1666, aged near 60 years.

*Omnium vereatur urna.*"

## On a pillar on the North side of the church, a black and white marble monument, with this inscription in gold letters:

" Juxta hunc locum humatum jacet corpus Hugonis Ratclyffe, ex hac parochia, armigeri, civis et galeropolæ Londinensis; quondam pileonis Sacræ Majestati Caroli I<sup>mi</sup> beatæ memoriæ, totique familiæ Regali; qui Novembris vicesimo 8° fato functus vitæ æternæ per Christum partæ hæreditatem (ut piè speremus) adiit 1678.

This man had two wives, viz. Margaret, daughter of Gervase Handel, of Wil-ford, in Nottinghamshire, gent.; and Elizabeth, coheir of Thomas Chewning, citizen and skinner, of London. This monument was erected by Chewning Ratcliff, his heir, 1681."

Arms: *Argent, a chevron engrailed Sable between six ogresses, with a crescent on a mullet for difference. On an inescutcheon of pretence, Vert, an eagle displayed Argent.*

## On a flat stone within the rails of the communion-table:

" Here lies Ann Woolnough, daughter of Henry Woolnough, clerk, deceased the 11th of June, 1679, aged 14 years."

## On a grave-stone:

" James Ward, son of Lieutenant James Ward, Esq. and of Frances his wife, 30th April 1686."

### On another:

" Susanna, the wife of John Marsh, of Wilsden, in the County of Middlesex, yeoman, and daughter of Robert Merry, yeoman, the 4th of Sept. 1687."

Under the Communion-table, a marble grave-stone, with this inscription :

" Here lyes the body of Elizabeth Spooner, the wife of Abraham Spooner, citizen
and vintner of London, who was married 20 years to her husband, and lived an
affectionate and faithful wife to him, a diligent and tender mother in the instruction of her children, a kind and careful mistress of her servants, upright and
circumspect in all her conversation, bearing always a conscience void of offence
towards God and Man.

She departed this life, in the full assurance of a better, the 1st of March, 1699,
in the 42d year of her age [1]."

### In the middle aile :

" In a vault near this stone lyeth the body of Richard Cooke, of London, merchant,
who departed this life the 21st of January, 1715, aged 62 years.

.....................................

........ ............................. [covered by a pew]

......................... aged 42 years.

Here also lyeth the body of John Cooke, Esq. eldest son of Richard and Ann
Cooke, who departed this life the 5th of February 1750, aged 53 years."

### On the South side of the chancel :

" Near this place lyes the body of Mrs. Elizabeth Barber, late wife of Robert Barber, of Ashcomb, in the County of Wilts, Esq. who dyed March the 7th, 1724,
aged 59 ; and also her daughter Mary, who dyed December the 3d, 1696, aged
12 weeks."

" Here.........John Fowler............1538.   On whose soule............

Here lyeth Alis Fowler, the wyff of Robert Fowler, Esquire, who dyed 1540[2].

Behold and se, thus as I am so sal ye bee

When ye be dead, and layd in grave,

As ye have done so sal ye have."

---

[1] This stone is now laid down in the Church-yard.

[2] " Divers of this family lie here interred, the ancestors of Sir Thomas Fowler,
" Knt. and Bart. now living, 1630."   *Weever's Funeral Monuments*, p. 538.

" Orate pro Wilielmo Mistelbroke, auditore, qui in servitio regis itinerans, Deo dis-
ponente, apud Denby in MarchiaWalliæ,An. Dom. MCCCCLXXXXII. corpus suum
sacre sepulture reddidit; et pro Catherina uxore sua, cujus corpus sub isto marmore tumulatum fuit; quorum anime in pace Jesu Christi requiescant. Amen."

The Brotherhood of Jesus appears to have been a monkish establishment connected with the Church of Islington, previously to the
Reformation. To this fraternity Richard Cloudesley, a parishioner,
left by will, bearing date 13th Jan. 9 Hen. VIII. certain stipends
charged on lands and premises in this parish, to keep an obit and sing
masses for his soul, &c. which, with other provisions of a superstitious
nature, will be seen more fully from the following extracts from his
will and codicil in the London Registry. This document, while it
serves to illustrate the manners of the times, will also exhibit the arch
priestcraft and blind superstition by which our ancestors were guided
and imposed upon in the times antecedent to the Reformation.

" In the name of God, Amen. In the name of the Holy Trinity,
" Father and Son and Holy Ghost, Amen, the 13th day of the month
" of January the year of our Lord 1517, and the 9th year of the
" reign of King Henry the VIIIth. I Richard, you otherwise called
" Richard Cloudysley, clere of mind and in my good memory being,
" loved be Almighty God, make and ordain my testament or my last
" will in this manner and form as followeth. First, I bequeath and
" recommend my soul unto Almighty God, my Creator and Saviour,
" and his most blessed moder Saint Mary the Virgin, and to all the
" Holy Company of Heaven. My body, after I am past this present
" and transitory life, to be buried within the Church-yard of the pa-
" rish Church of Islington, near unto the grave of my father and
" moder, on whose souls Jesu have mercy. Also I bequeath to the
" high altar of the same Church, for tythes and oblations peradven-
" ture by me forgotten or withholden, in discharging of my conscience,
" 20s. Also I bequeath to the said Church of Islington eight torches,
" price the piece six shillings, four of them after my months mind is
" holden and kept to remain to the brotherhood of Jesu within the

" said Church, and the other four torches to burn at the sacryng of
" the high mass within the said Church as long as they will last.

" Item, I give and bequeath to the common box of the said parish
" 20s.   Item, I give and bequeath to two poor men of the parish of
" Islington, two gowns with the name of *Jesu* upon them, every
" gown price 6s. 8d.   Item, I give and bequeath to two poor men of
" the said parish of Islington two gowns, and the same gowns to have
" *Maria* upon them, in the honour of our blessed Lady, every gown
" price 6s. 8d.   Item, I will that the said gowns be given to such
" honest poor persons as shall honestly wear them while they last,
" and not to sell them or put them to pledge.

" Item, I give and bequeath to the High Altar of the Church of
" St. James, Clerkenwell, 3s. 4d.   Item, I give and bequeath to the
" ladies of the same place 20s. to do for me *placebo & dirige*, with
" a mass of requiem.   Item, to the Church of St. James afore-
" said, the Churches of St. Pancras, Hornsey, Finchley, and Hamp-
" stead, each two torches, price 14s. and to two poor men of the same
" parishes two gowns, price the piece 6s. 8d.   Item, I give and be-
" queath to every parish priest of the Churches aforesaid 20 pence a
" piece, to the intent that they shall pray for me by name openly in
" their Churches every Sunday, and to pray their parishioners to pray
" for me and to forgive me, as I forgive them and all the world.

" Item, I give and bequeath to the prisoners of Newgate in money
" 3s. 4d.   Item, a load of straw price 4s.   Item, to the prisoners
" of the King's Bench 3s. 4d.   Item, a load of straw.   Item, to the
" prisoners of the Marshalsea 3s. 4d. and a load of straw.   Item,
" to the poor men or prisoners of Bedlam 3s. 4d. and a load of straw.
" Item, I will that there be a load of straw laid on me in my grave,
" the price five marks.

" Item, I give and bequeath to the repayring and amending of the
" cawseway between my house that I now dwell in and Islington
" Church 40s.   Item, I will that there be incontinently after my de-
" cease, as hastily as may be, a thousand masses sayd for my soul,

" and that every priest have for his labour 4*d*. Item, I will that there
" be dole for my soul the day of my burying, to poor people 5 marks
" in pence. Item, I will that there be bestowed upon the amending
" the highway between Hyegate-hill and the stony bounds beyond
" Ring Crosse £.20.; and if the said £.20. will not make it sufficient,
" I will there be bestowed thereon other £.20.

" Item, I bequeath to the Poor Lazars of Hyegate, to pray for
" me by name in their bede-role, 6*s*. 8*d*. Also, I bequeath the
" Fryers of Greenwich, to sing a solemn dirge and mass, by note,
" for me, 40*s*. Also, I will a priest to sing for me at Scala Celi at
" the Savoy, by the space of one year after my decease, and he to
" have for his salary £6. 16*s*. 8*d*. Also, I will that, every month
" after my decease, there be an obit kept for me in Islington church,
" and each priest and clerk have for their paines to be taken, as they
" used to have afore this time. And I will there be distributed at
" every obit, to poor people, to pray for my soul, 6*s*. 8*d*.

" I will, that all that now be seised to my use, and to the per-
" formance of my will, or hereafter shall be seised to the same, of
" and in a parcel of ground called the *Stony-field*, otherwise called
" the Fourteen Acres, shall suffer the rent and profits of the same
" from henceforth to be counted to this use ensuing; that is to say, I
" will that, yearly after my decease, the parishioners of the parish of
" Islington, or the more part of them, once in the year, at the pa-
" rish church aforesaid, shall elect and choose six honest and discreet
" men of the said parish, such as they think most meet to have the
" order and distribution of the rent and profit aforesaid, which rent I
" will shall by the said six persons be bestowed in manner and form
" following; that is to say, I will, that there be yearly, for ever, a
" solemn obit to be kept for me within the said church of Islington,
" and that there be spent at the obit 20*s*. And also, that there be
" dealt to poor people of the said parish at every obit, to pray for my
" soul, my wife's soul, and all Christen souls, 6*s*. 8*d*. And further,
" I will that the said six persons shall yeerely pay, or do to be paid,

" to the wardens of the brotherhood of Jesu £.1. 6s. 8d. towards
" maintaining of the masse of Jesu within the said churche; upon
" this condition, that the said wardens shall yeerely, for ever, cause
" a *trental*[1] of masses to be said for my soul in the said churche; and
" further, I will that the aforesaid six persons shall have among them
" for their labour, to see the true performance of the same, yearly,
" at every obite 10s.

   " Also, whereas I have made a surrender into the hands of the Lord
" of St. John's Jerusalem in England, of certain lands and tenements;
" that is to say, of a house and nine acres of land, late Barrell's, and
" a close called Sibley's Field, to the intent that the said Lord shall
" grant again the said lands and tenements to *Robert Fowller*, gent.
" *John Burton, Robert Middleton, Richard Baylley, John Smith,*
" *Denis Ashpoll,* and *John Nutt,* to the performance of this my last
" will : and to the intent I would be prayed for perpetually : I will,
" that the said Robert and others above named shall, within a month
" after my decease, name and appoint an honeste sadde preste, to syng
" for my soule, my father and moders soules, and all Christen soules,
" in the new Chapel called *The Hermitage*, at Islington town's end[2].
" And that the said preste shall say three times in a week *placebo &*
" *dyryge* for my sowle and all Christen sowles; and that, every masse
" he sayeth, he shall say *de profundis* for my sowle and all Christen
" sowles, and pray openly and specially for me by name.   And I will,
" that as long as the said preste is of a good and sadde dispositon, and
" keep his service truly, that the said Robert and others above named
" shall suffer the said preste to have the hole rent of the said lands
" and tenements, bearing the charge to the Lord, and keeping the re-
" parations.

   [1] Thirty masses said for a person deceased, according to the Institution of St.
Gregory.
   [2] This was probably on the site of Mrs. Owen's school and alms-houses, which
piece of ground is described in the writings of the Brewers' Company under the
name of " *The Hermitage Field.*"

" Item, I make and ordain executioners of this my present testa-
" ment and last will, *Thomas Dowrey*[1], Lord of St. John Jerusalem
" in England, *Sir Thomas Lovell, John Fyneux, Knt. Bartholomew*
" *Westby, John More, Richard Hawkes.* And if there shall hap-
" pen any sums of money to remain in the said Lord's hands, Sir
" Thomas Lovell, John More, Bartholomew Westby, or any of them,
" I will that such sums of money shall be bestowed in such good
" deeds of charity as by them shall be advised, for the wealth of my
" soul. Also, I will that my feoffees that now be, or hereafter shall
" be, in the said 14 acres, otherwise called *Stoney's Crofts*, shall
" suffer Robert Middleton, that now is tenant, to have the occupation
" thereof, as he will occupy it, paying yeerely £.4, at two times, in
" the year, to those I have assigned it, and to keep the reparations[2]."

[1] Thomas Docwry, or Docwra, the last Prior but one of the above house. See
p. 60.

[2] After all the provisions made by Cloudesley for the pardon of his sins, and the
repose of his soul, it would seem (at least if we may give credit to the testimony of
an antient writer) that his spirit was not to be lulled to sleep by the Monkish strains so
carefully appointed by him for that purpose. The author alluded to, after speaking of
earthquakes and other similar phenomena of nature, proceeds, "And as to the same
" heavings or tremblements *de terre*, it is sayde, y^t in a certaine fielde neare unto y^e
" parish Church of Islingtoun, in like manner, did take place a wondrous commo-
" tion in uarious partes, y^e earthe swellinge, and turninge uppe euery side towards y^e
" midst of y^e sayde fielde, and, by tradycion of this, it is obserued, y^t one Richard
" De Clouesley lay buryed in or neare y^t place, and y^t his bodie being restles, on
" y^e score of some sinne by him peraduenture committed, did shewe or seeme to
" signifye y^t religious obseruance should there take place, to quiet his departed
" spirit; whereupon certaine exorcisers, if wee may so term y^m, did at dede of
" night, nothing lothe, using divers diuine exercises at torche light, set at rest
" y^e unrulie spirit of y^e sayde Clouesley, and y^e earthe did returne aneare to its
"pristine shape, neuermore commotion procedeing therefrom to this day, and this
" I know of a verie certaintie." *Purlet de Mir. Nat.* X. c. 4.

The following particulars are extracted from the Certificate of the Commissioners for Dissolving Colleges and Chantries, in the Augmentation-office :

" Primo die Januarii, anno primo regni regis Edwardi Sexti 1548.

" The P'oche of ISELDON ; scil't,

" Richard Clowdesley willed and gave unto the said churcheon e closse ther, conteyning XII acres, now in the tenure of Walter Coyny, to th' entente to kepe an obite, and for the mayntenance of a masse, which closse arrentithe yerely £.VII ; whereof,

" At th' obite wᵗ VIS. VIIId. to the pore XXs.

" And to the brotherhedd of Jesus within⎫
" the seid churche, founded at will for ⎬XXVIS. VIIId. ⎫XLVIS. VIIId.
" singing of masses for the seid Clowdesley⎭           ⎭

" And then remayneth clere - - - - - - - - - ¹CXIIIS. IIIId."

" John Englande willed and gave unto the seid churche, for the " keeping of an obite and the meyntenance of an honest priest, one " closse of copyholde land in the seid parishe, in the tenure of Robert " Walker at will, by yeare £.IIII. VIS. VIIId.  In quit-rent to Tho- " mas Fowler, gent. IIs. IXd. ob. q.  And then remaynethe clere " £.IIII. vs. xd. d. q.²

" Memorandum, ther is of Howselyng³ people within the seid pa-

¹ It should be xciijs. ivd.

² Probably iijs. the sum should be £.iv. iijs. xid.

³ *Housel.*  The Holy Eucharist.  JOHNSON.  This means persons supposed to be qualified to receive the Communion.

> But for as moche as man and wife
> Should shew the parish priest ther life ;
> Onis a yere as saith the boke,
> Er any wight his *Housil* toke.  *Chaucer, Rom. Rose.*
>
> I wol forthe, and to him ygone,
> And he shal *Housil* me anone.     *Ibid.*

See also " A Boke of *Howselyng*," or a Worke of Preparation, or of Ordinaunce

" rische the number of CCCCXL. Sir Jamys Robynson[4] is vicar ther,
" and his vicarage is worthe by yere £.xxx."

The Fourteen Acres, or *Stone-field*, bequeathed to the church by Cloudesley, is situate on the West side of the Back-road, and contains, according to a survey hanging in the vestry-room, 16 acres 2 roods 17 perches. These premises, though appropriated by the testator to superstitious uses, escaped being seized by the crown at the dissolution of chauntries, 1 Edward VI. probably by reason that part of the produce was directed to be given to " poor people," or perhaps from motives of respect to the feoffees or the executors of the testator, who were persons of great respectability, and connected with the parish, particularly Sir Thomas Lovel, who, in the preceding reign, possessed great interest at court. Thus it is most probable that the same was suffered to remain vested in feoffees for the use of the parish, as it continues at the present day. The *Stone-field* is now let to Mr. Rhodes, at £.84 *per annum*, for the remainder of a lease, which will shortly expire, when it is expected the ground will be let on building leases, with considerable advantage to the parish.

The great increase in the value of land near the Metropolis since the reign of Henry VIII. is exemplified in the *Stone-field*. This plot of ground, then let at the annual rent of £.4, has lately been valued in the fee simple at the sum of £.22,800, on an application being made by the Corporation of London to purchase the same as an eligible spot for the removal of Smithfield Market.

unto Communion, printed by Robert Redman, beginning of the 16th century. *Ames's Typographical Antiquities*, by Herbert, vol. I. p. 400.
  [4] James Robinson, LL. B. vicar 1545. See List of Vicars, p. 281.

### THE NEW CHURCH.

The present church was built by the before-mentioned Mr. Steem-son, under the direction of Mr. Launcelot Dowbiggin [1], who furnished the design, and superintended the work till its completion. The contract entered into with the builder was as under :

                                                                      £.
For the Church and the Tower, the sum of........5622
The Spire, Vane, &c...............................................577
The Stone Ballustrades..............................................23
The Stone Portico in front..........................................97
                                        _____

                                              £.6319.
                                        _____

The foundation stone was laid on the 28th August, 1751, by James Colebrooke, Esq. (the largest landed proprietor in the parish), in which was placed a copper plate, engraved with the following inscription :

" This Church
" was built at the
" expence of the parish,
" and
" the first stone thereof
" was laid by
" JAMES COLEBROOKE, Esq.
" the 28th day of August,
" in the year of our Lord
1751."

[1] This architect made a design for the new bridge at Blackfryars, containing 11 arches, which he estimated would cost £.140,000. It was submitted to the City, but the plan was not accepted. See Lond. Mag. for April 1756, which contains an engraving of the design.

Islington Church.

Upper Street. Islington.

Pub.d May 1.1819. for the Proprietor by R. Ackermann, 101. Strand.

*Plate XXI.*

Drawn and Engraved by E.Rich, pupil to J.Hawksworth.

*ISLINGTON CHURCH.*

It was finished and opened for divine service on Sunday, the 26th of May, 1754, having been just two years and three quarters in building.

The church is situate on the East side of the Upper-street, and nearly in the centre of the village. Though perhaps not formed according to strict architectural rule, it is nevertheless allowed to be a light and handsome edifice. It is built with brick, strengthened and adorned with stone groins, cornices, &c. in plain Rustic. It contains a nave, chancel, and two ailes, and is adorned at the West end with an elegant spire of Portland stone (see Plate XII). The floor is vaulted considerably above the level of the church-yard. The door in front is ornamented with a portico of a semicircular form, consisting of a dome supported by four columns of the Tuscan order, to which there is an ascent by a flight of five steps, arranged also semicircularly. The two side doors are from a Vitruvian model, and have a very neat appearance. At the East end is a window after the Venetian taste, divided into three compartments by pillars of the Ionic order; but the intercolumns are filled up with stone, and covered on the inside with the painted decorations of the altar. The roof is spanned the whole width of the church, without the support of pillars, and is covered with Westmoreland slates.

The steeple consists of a tower, rising square to the height of 87 feet, terminated by a cornice supporting four vases at the corners. Upon this is placed an octagonal ballustrade, from within which rises the base of the dome in the same form, supporting eight Corinthian double columns, with their shafts wrought with Rustic. Upon these the dome rests, and from its crown rises the spire, which is terminated by a ball and vane. The ceiling of the church is vaulted and disposed in a circular form in the centre, around which it is divided into compartments enriched with wreathed mouldings of flowers, &c. in stucco. The galleries are supported by Tuscan pillars, and are painted on the front in imitation of oak wainscoat. They contain 62 pews, framed of fir, and at the West end is a very handsome and good-toned organ in a mahogany case, placed here by the direction of the trustees for the new church, at the request of the inhabitants, in 1772. It was opened by Dr. Worgan.

The pews in the area of the building, which are 91 in number, together with the screen which divides the church from the vestibule, are framed of right wainscoat; and in the christening-pew is a neat marble font. The pulpit, reading-desk, &c. are of mahogany, and the sounding-board is supported by two Corinthian columns. The altar-piece is composed also of the same wood, divided into compart-ments by pillars and their entablature of the Doric order. The Deca-logue, &c. is painted in golden letters on a black ground; and above the pediment, in the place of the window, is a chaste and appropriate painting, representing the annunciation, having on each side emblems of the Law and the Gospel in *chiaro-'scuro*. These were painted by Mr. Nathaniel Clarkson, an inhabitant of Islington [1]. The church throughout exhibits an elegant plainness; and though commodious for its size, and no doubt sufficiently large at the time of its erection, it has, from the great increase of population, been for some time past found too small for the accommodation of the parishioners [2].

> The altitude of the tower, from the ground to
>     the stone ballustrade, is............................ ......87 feet.
> To the top of the Vane....................................164 feet.
> Extreme length of the Church.........................108 feet.
> Width .....................................................................60 feet.

In the tower is an agreeable set of bells, eight in number; the six which were in the old tower being re-cast in 1774, and two smaller ones added by subscription, to complete the octave. The tenor weighs

---

[1] He resided at the house the North-west corner of Church-street, where some figures in *chiaro-'scuro* of his painting, representing *Design, Sculpture, Architecture* &c. yet remain on the wainscot.

[2] An Act has been lately brought into Parliament to supply this deficiency, by enabling the parishioners to erect a Chapel of Ease.

Plate 13

*Drawn & engraved by W. Ellis.*

## ISLINGTON.

Islington Church, Interior

# TABLET IN ISLINGTON CHURCH.

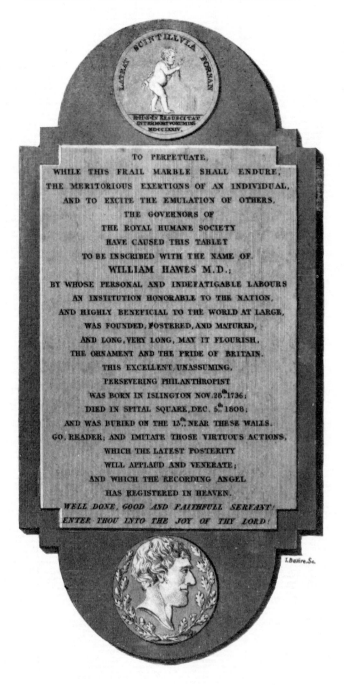

TO PERPETUATE,
WHILE THIS FRAIL MARBLE SHALL ENDURE,
THE MERITORIOUS EXERTIONS OF AN INDIVIDUAL,
AND TO EXCITE THE EMULATION OF OTHERS,
THE GOVERNORS OF
THE ROYAL HUMANE SOCIETY
HAVE CAUSED THIS TABLET
TO BE INSCRIBED WITH THE NAME OF.
WILLIAM HAWES M.D.;
BY WHOSE PERSONAL AND INDEFATIGABLE LABOURS
AN INSTITUTION HONORABLE TO THE NATION,
AND HIGHLY BENEFICIAL TO THE WORLD AT LARGE,
WAS FOUNDED, FOSTERED, AND MATURED,
AND LONG, VERY LONG, MAY IT FLOURISH,
THE ORNAMENT AND THE PRIDE OF BRITAIN.
THIS EXCELLENT, UNASSUMING,
PERSEVERING PHILANTHROPIST
WAS BORN IN ISLINGTON NOV.28.1736;
DIED IN SPITAL SQUARE, DEC. 5. 1808;
AND WAS BURIED ON THE 13. NEAR THESE WALLS.
GO, READER, AND IMITATE THOSE VIRTUOUS ACTIONS,
WHICH THE LATEST POSTERITY
WILL APPLAUD AND VENERATE;
AND WHICH THE RECORDING ANGEL
HAS REGISTERED IN HEAVEN.
*WELL DONE, GOOD AND FAITHFULL SERVANT*
*ENTER THOU INTO THE JOY OF THY LORD!*

16 cwt. and was re-cast in 1808, in order to improve the tone. Around each bell is an inscription, of which the following is a copy :

1st bell.   Although I am but light and small,
           I will be heard above you all.

2d.        At proper times our voices we will raise,
           In sounding to our benefactors' praise[1].

3d.        If you have a judicious ear,
           You'll own our voices sweet and clear.

4th.       To honour both our God and King,
           Our voices shall in concert ring.

5th.       Whilst thus we join in cheerful sound,
           May love and loyalty abound :

6th.       In wedlock's bands all ye who join,
             With hand your heart unite ;
         So shall our tuneful tongues combine,
             To laud the nuptial rite.

7th.       Ye ringers all, that prize your health and happiness,
           Be sober, merry, wise, and you'll the same possess.

8th.       Cast 1808. Present, Edward Flower, Churchwarden,
         Thomas Whittomore, John Blount, Edward Manton,
              Thomas Meares and Son, of London, fecit.

The total expence of building the Church, including the internal materials and fittings up, was as follows[2] :

|  | £. | s. | d. |
|---|---|---|---|
| The contract for the building, as before stated........6319 | 0 | 0 |  |
| A brass chandelier to hold 36 lights..............................50 | 0 | 0 |  |
| The clock...............................................................73 | 0 | 0 |  |
| Dials to ditto..........................................................13 | 14 | 11 |  |
| Mr. Dowbiggin, Surveyor..........................................105 | 0 | 0 |  |
| Ditto      for extra trouble...............................18 | 18 | 0 |  |

Carried forward £.6579 12 11

[1] Alluding to their having been placed here by subscription.

[2] Biggerstaff's MS

|                                          | £.   | s. | d. |
|------------------------------------------|------|----|----|
| Brought over                             | 6579 | 12 | 11 |
| Church-yard walls, &c.                   | 93   | 10 | 0  |
| Messrs. Byfield and Green, for organ     | 400  | 0  | 0  |
| Bells and Frames, about                  | 210  | 0  | 0  |
| Extra bills and charges                  | 56   | 17 | 1  |
|                                          | £ 7340 | 0 | 0 |

In 1787, the Church underwent a thorough repair, when the tower was strengthened by the insertion of three tiers of iron bars or ties placed across in different directions. A flag-staff, 42 feet in height, which had stood at the South-west corner from the year 1776, was removed, and an electrical rod or conductor was affixed from the top of the spire to the ground, to preserve the building from the effects of lightning. The means used to effect these alterations were at once novel and ingenious. Thomas Birch, a basket-maker, undertook, for the sum of £.20, to erect a scaffold of wicker-work round the spire, and which he formed entirely of willow, hazel, and other sticks; it had a flight of stairs reaching in a spiral line from the octagonal balustrade to the vane, by which the ascent was as easy and safe as the stairs of a dwelling-house. This ingenious contrivance entirely superseded the use of a scaffold, which would have been more expensive, and is frequently attended with danger in works of this kind. The spire on this occasion presented a very curious appearance (see Plate VI.) being entirely enveloped as it were in a huge basket, within which the workmen were performing the necessary repairs in perfect safety[1]. The emolument received by the basket

[1] The late Alderman Sir William Staines is said to have been the first person who contrived this kind of scaffolding in some repairs done to the spire of St. Bride's Church, London, which was damaged by lightning in the year 1764, after having his scaffold-poles, &c. which had been erected in the usual way, carried away by a violent storm. (*Europ. Mag.* vol. LII. p. 338.) It was afterwards improved upon

maker on this occasion was very considerable, from the donations, not only of the inhabitants, but of others whose curiosity daily led them from London and the adjacent villages to view this surprizing piece of workmanship. The exhibition was advertized in the newspapers, and the price of admission to the wicker staircase was 6*d.* each person [1]. The Church on this occasion, was shut up for five months; and the whole expence of the improvements and repairs amounted to near £.800. [2]

In the vestry-room is a large drawing of the Church over the fire-place, between the two views of the old structure. On the frame is the following inscription: " South-west view of the Parish Church of " St. Mary Islington, drawn from actual measurement, and respect-" fully presented to the vestry by William Wickings, Easter 1793 [3]." The vestry-room also contains a large plan or survey of the parish on vellum, with a copy on a reduced scale, both inclosed in mahogany cases. These were made by Richard Dent in the years 1805 and 1806; and contain an accurate delineation of the site of every house, garden, field, &c. throughout the parish, with figures of reference to a terrier containing the names of the respective proprietors. Here is also an old plan or survey of the roads, made in the year 1735 (see Plate I.); and the following table of Benefactions:

by Birch in repairing the steeple at St. Alban's, Herts, and brought to the greatest perfection by him at Islington on the above occasion. A print of the Church, with the spire inclosed in the wicker-work, about seven inches square, was engraved and published by Matthew Skinner, of Camden-street, Islington, in Feb. 1788.

[1] Mr. Biggerstaff's MS. says, Birch collected upwards of £.50. by this exhibition.

[2] Biggerstaff's MS.

[3] There is a copper-plate engraving published from this drawing by I. Roffe.

## A Table of Benefactions to yᵉ Poor of the Parish of St. Mary Islingdon, alias Islington [1].

| | £. | s. | d. |
|---|---|---|---|
| Mr. William Cloudsley, per annum..............................40 | 40 | 0 | 0 |
| Mrs. Alice Owen, per annum....2 | 2 | 12 | 0 |
| Mr. Thomas Hobson, per ann.....5 | 5 | 4 | 0 |
| Mr. Nathaniel Loane, per ann.....5 | 5 | 4 | 0 |
| *Mrs. Anne Hodeson, per ann. ....2 | 2 | 0 | 0 |
| *Mr. George Smith, per ann.....0 | 0 | 13 | 4 |
| Mr. Martin, per annum.............0 | 0 | 5 | 0 |
| Mrs. Swinerton, a silver plate....1 | 1 | 0 | 0 |

Thomas Lord Coventry, Baron of Ailsboroug, Lord Keeper of yᵉ Privy Seale of England, two silver bowls gilt to yᵉ Communion-table; besides a noble benefactor to the parish.

Sir Thomas Fisher, Kt. and Bart. a silver plate to yᵉ Communion-table, a pulpit-cloth and cushion, and beautifying the pulpit.

Sir Thomas Fowler, Knt. and Bart. yᵉ beautifying and adorning the Communion-

table and yᵉ rails about it.

Mr. John Pitts, a benefactor to the beadle's silver-headed staff.

Sir Richard Fisher, Bart. a pulpit cloth and cushion of silver velvet.

| | £. | s. | d. |
|---|---|---|---|
| *Dr. William Crowne, for bread for the poor for ever, at one shilling per week...................2 | 2 | 12 | 0 |
| Mr. John Haines, per annum, bread to the poor...................2 | 2 | 0 | 0 |
| Mr. Ephraim Skinner [2], per annum, for a Catechist lecture,18 | 18 | 0 | 0 |

apulpit cloth, with cushion and table cloth, two cushions, two large Common Prayer Books covered with velvet, and linen for the Communion-table.

Mrs. Christian Norman, a velvet pall for the use of the poor.

Dame Sarah Temple, to purchase a freehold estate, for the education and putting

[1] Those benefactions in the above table marked thus (*) have been long since lost.

[2] In the parish Church of St. Olave Jewry is a marble monument to the memory of the above gentleman, which bears the following inscription : " Near this place " lieth the body of *Ephraim Skinner*, merchant, sometime his Majesty's Consul at " *Livorne*, whose exemplary piety towards God, integrity towards men, charity to " the poor, and humility towards all, made him live desired, and die lamented by " all that knew him.  He was born in the town of *Barnstaple*, in *Devon*, on St. An- " drew's day, anno 1637, died at *Islington* May 6, 1678, in the 44th year of " his age."

|                                                                 | £. | s. | d. |
|-----------------------------------------------------------------|----|----|----|
| forth of poor children for ever [1] ...500                      | 500 | 0 | 0 |
| *Mr. John Patin, per annum, for a sermon and bread to the poor...1 | 1 | 10 | 0 |
| *Dame Mary Sadlier, for bread for yᵉ poor for ever: the said Dame Mary being late widow of Doctor William Crowne, at one shilling per week ...50 | 50 | 0 | 0 |
| Mr. Benja. Smith, per annum, weekly, to the poor for ever...2 | 2 | 12 | 0 |
| Everard Sayer, Esq...20 | 20 | 0 | 0 |
| Mrs. Hull, per annum...6 | 6 | 0 | 0 |
| Mrs. Amey Hill, per annum...2 | 2 | 0 | 0 |
| Mr. John Parsons, per annum...6 | 6 | 0 | 0 |

1783 Mrs. Rosamond Marshall gave two silver plates for receiving the offering at the Communion.

1785 Mr. Henry Wright, a large folio Bible for the desk.

Mr. Samuel Pullin, a crimson velvet cushion and covering, trimmed with gold fringe and lace for the pulpit.

Joseph Mainwaring, jun. Esq. a crimson velvet covering and cushions trimmed with gold lace for the Communion table.

Mr. Charles Brown, a damask table-cloth and two napkins for the use of the Communion table.

1786 Francis Marshall, Esq. and Mrs. Rosamond Marshall, each £.100. three per cent. Consols, the interest to be distributed to poor housekeepers annually 6 0 0

1787 Mr. Nathaniel Clarkson, the painting at the East window of this Church, designed and executed by himself.

Joseph Mainwaring, jun. Esq. a carpet at the Communion-table.

Mr. Charles Brown, a silk line and tassel for the cover of the font.

Mrs. Elizabeth Pickford, the curtain at the East window of the Church.

1800 Alexander Aubert, Esq. Lieutenant-Col.-Commandant of the Loyal

An estate at North Mims, in Herts, was purchased, pursuant to the will of this lady, the present rent of which is £.48. 5s. 9d. per annum. This is applied in the maintenance, clothing, and education, of three boys at a private academy on Hanwell-heath, kept by Mr. Compson.

| £. s. d. | | £. s. d. |
|---|---|---|
| Islington Volunteers. His Majesty's coat of arms in this Church, front of the organ. | | John Biggerstaff, jun. the clock in the front of the organ. |

The site of the church and church-yard occupies 1 acre and 20 perches. An inclosed cemetery or burying-ground, containing 3 roods and 2 perches, was annexed to the latter, by virtue of an Act passed for that purpose, (33 Geo. III.), intituled "An Act for enlarging the "church-yard or cemetery of the Parish-church of St. Mary Isling- "ton, in the County of Middlesex." The copyhold of this ground cost £.1200, and £.108 was paid for the enfranchisement. It was con- secrated by the Bishop of the Diocese, December 18, 1793. The iron rails were placed upon the dwarf wall in front of the church about the year 1802.

### MONUMENTAL INSCRIPTIONS IN THE CHURCH.

Those marked thus (*) were removed from the old Church.

On a mural monument on the North side of the altar near the gal- lery :

* " Juxta heic
Ad imum Pulpiti gradum
Conditur quod claudi potuit
GULIELMI CAVE, S. TH. PR.
Canonici Windesoriensis,
Carolo II. à sacris domesticis,
Hujus Ecclesiæ per XXVIII annos vicarii ;
Natus est Decemb. XXX, An. MDCXXXVII.
Obiit Aug. IV. Ann. MDCCXIII.

Quatuor filiis et filiabus eodem
circiter loco ex Australi
Latere conditis accessit tandem
Anna (Gualt. Stonehouse,
S. T. B. filia unica), mater
Pientissima, conjux charissima,
quæ quidem obiit Jan. x, MDCXCI.
Quisquis es, viator, homo cum sis,
Ossa nostra ne violes; depositi cineres
Quiescant in pace; abi mortalitatis memor,
nec te incautum rapiat suprema dies."

Arms : *Azure, fretty Argent*, Cave ; *impaling, Argent, on a fess between three hawks volant Sable, a leopard's face between two mullets Or.*

## On a black marble slab in the middle aile near the pulpit :

* " Here lyes the body of Mr. Robert Gery, late vicar of this parish, and rector of Allhallows the Great in London for seventeen years, prebendary of Lincoln, the son of William Gery, D. D. by Mary, daughter to Robert Sanderson, Bishop of Lincoln. He married Elizabeth, the daughter of Dr. William Cave, Canon of Windsor, and late vicar of this parish, by whom he left two children, Thomas and Anne. He died October 1, 1707, aged 55."

Arms : *Two bars, each charged with three muscles, a lion's face in dexter chief; impaling the arms of* Cave. *Crest, a goat's head erased.*

## On an oval marble tablet near the East end of the North aile :

* "To the memory of
Cornelius Yeate, M. A.
Archdeacon of Wilts,
and vicar of this parish.
He departed this life April 20th, 1720,
in the 60th year of his age,
and was buried in the Church-yard, near
the North-east corner of the Chancel.
" Who then is that faithful and wise Steward
" whom his Lord shall make ruler over
" his household, to give them their portion
" of meat in due season?
" Blessed is that servant whom his Lord
" when he cometh shall find so doing."

### At the East end of the church:

*" Here lyes the body of Mary Woodrofe, wife of David Woodrofe, of Staple-inn, in the county of Middlesex, gent. and sister to the Reverend Dr. Cave, who was minister of this parish thirty years.

She was both just, generous, and charitable. She lived a pious and a holy life, and died in the true Protestant faith of the Church of England, in the 70th year of her age, anno Domini 1705.

*Vivit post funera virtus.*"

Arms: *Gules, on a chevron Argent, three stags' heads erased Azure, a chief per fess nebulé Sable and Argent; impaling the arms of* Cave.

## On a white marble tablet against the wall on the South gallery stairs:

*" Sacred to the memory of Ann Harwood, wife of John Harwood, LL. D. F. R. S. who dyed September the 4th, 1729, aged 55. And of the said John Harwood, who dyed December the 30th, 1730, aged 72. As also of their youngest and eldest sons Thomas and John Harwood, who departed this life, Thomas, March the 24th, 1734, aged 19; John, February the 8th, 1736, aged 28. Likewise in the same vault is interred the body of Anne Jermy, only daughter of the abovementioned Dr. Harwood, LL. D. and relict of Seth Jermy, Esq. Vict'ling office. She departed this life, generally lamented, the 10th day of June, 1765, in the 59th year of her age. Who all lie interred in a vault at the East side of the church-yard, close to the wall."

Arms: *Argent, a chevron between three stags' heads caboshed Gules; impaling Azure, a chevron Or, between two swans proper, in chief, and a pair of shears in base.*

### An oval tablet in the North aile
*" To the memory
of William Danvers,
Gentleman, who died
the 13th July, 1740, aged
eighteen years, and was
buried in the Church-yard,
near the North-east corner
of the Chancel."

### Within the rails of the Communion-table:

" Here lyes interred the body of
Richard Meredith, of the
County of Gloucester, Gentleman,
Who by Margaret his wife now living, daughter of Edward Corbet, of Ponts-
bury, in the County of Salop, D. D. left issue one son, George, of Grays-inn,
Gent. also buried here 12th Sept. 1714, ætat. 29, and two daughters, viz. Ka-
therine and Mary, both ........................"

Arm *A Lion rampant, collared and chained ; impaling two birds. Crest, a demy
Lion rampant.*

### Within the rails of the Communion-table:

" Here lyeth the body of Vere Boothe,
only daughter of the Right Honourable George Lord Delamer,
by his first wife the Right Honourable Lady Catherine Clynton,
eldest daughter of the Right Honourable Theophilds, Earle of Lincolne,
who died the 14th of November, 1717,
in the 74th year of her age."

Arms : *Three boars heads erased, erected: quartering, six cross crosslets fitche ;
3. 2. 1. a chief charged with two mullets.*

### Within the rails of the Communion-table:

" Underneath this stone are interred the remains of Mrs. Elizabeth Smith, wife of
Richard Smith, Esq. of this parish, who died the 7th of July, 1766, aged 58
years.

Likewise, the remains of Richard-Turner Smith, grandson of the above Richard
Smith, and son of Benjamin Smith, Esq. who died the 6th of April, 1767,
aged 13 months and 18 days.

Likewise the remains of Samuel Smith, grandson of the said Richard Smith, and
son of the Rev. Mr. Richard Smith, who died the 9th of April 1771, aged
1 day.

Also the remains of the aforesaid Rev. Richard Smith, late vicar of this parish,
and son of the said Richard Smith, Esq. who died the 15th day of Feb. 1772,
aged 32 years."

### A black marble slab in the Chancel:

" In memory of Elizabeth Eddowes, of Wrexham, in Denbighshire, late of this parish, who died March 29th, 1760.

The most tender, affectionate, and best of sisters, best of friends! whose virtuous, pious, spotless life, rendering their *loss* her infinite *gain*, alone can console her surviving brothers and sisters, to whom her memory will be ever dear, from their grateful sense of her tender care and regard for them in early life."

Arms : *Ermine, a Lion rampant.*

## On a Portland slab adjoining the above :

"Beneath this stone are interred the remains of Mrs. Dorothy Aubert,
late of *Highbury House,*
who died Nov. 30th 1804, in the 80th year of her age.
Also the remains of
*Alexander Aubert,* Esq.
late of *Highbury House,* who departed this life
the 19th of October, 1805,
aged 75 years.
Also the remains of Mrs. Henrietta Aubert,
who departed this life the 27th of December, 1805,
aged 68 years."

## On a flat stone near the pulpit stairs :

" Mrs. Judith Gatehouse, died June the 25th, 1767, aged 60 years.
Also Mr. John Wills, late of this parish, who departed this life Jan. 15, 1771,
aged 80 years. Likewise Mrs. Sarah Wills, wife of the above Mr. John Wills,
who departed this life on the 21st day of April, 1778, aged 72 years."

## On a black marble slab in the chancel :

" To the memory of Mr. Henry Barne, late of this parish, Gent. formerly of London, merchant, who departed this life April 1st, 1757, aged 42 years."

Arms *Three lions' faces, a mullet in chief; quartering, a chevron between three birds.*

At the East end of the South aile is a neat marble monument, inclosed with iron rails, to perpetuate the memory of *Dame Alice Owen,* containing the inscription in gilt letters from her monument in the old Church, ending at the words " *Queen Elizabeth*," (see p. 292) to which is subjoined the following :

" In the year 1751 the old Church being taken down to be re-built occasioned a large monument to the memory of the Lady Owen to be taken down likewise, which, by length of time and removing, was so much decayed and impaired as rendered it unfit to be replaced ; in order therefore to preserve the memory of so good a Lady, the Worshipful Company of Brewers (Trustees to her Charities) caused this monument to be erected in the year 1754 [1]."

Arms : *Argent, a pomegranate tree proper, fruited Or, on a mount.* Wilkes, *her paternal coat.*

### On a marble table adjoining the altar on the right hand :

" Sacred to the memory of Philadelphia, late wife of
Thomas Cogan, Esq.
of this parish,
who died the 24th of April 1792, aged 59 years.
Also of the said Thomas Cogan, Esq.
who died the 18th of June, 1792,
aged 82 years.

Arms : *Gules, three aspen leaves Argent ; quartering, Paly of six Or and Azure. On a chief of the second a griffin passant of the first, and impaling Or, on a chevron Gules between three demi lions rampant issuant Azure, as many cross crosslets Or,* Stephens.

### A marble table at the end of the South aile :

" Sacred to the memory of
Margaret, the wife of Richard Singleton, Esq.
(of this parish,) who died the 1st of May 1793,
aged 34 years.
Also the said Richard Singleton, Esq.

---

[1] It may be proper to observe, that the benevolent person here commemorated is improperly styled " *Lady*," as neither of her husbands was a Knight. On pulling down the Church in 1751, the remains of this monument, consisting of the effigies of Mrs. Owen, with a ruff band about her neck, in the habit of her time, also several of her children, were removed to her free-school, where several mutilated figures still remain preserved over the door, with this inscription : " *Part of Lady* " *Owen's Monument,* 1753."

T T

who died the 5th of Feb. 1801,
aged 53 years.
Likewise Mary Singleton, daughter of the above,
who died in her infancy."

### A marble tablet adjoining the above:
" To the memory of
Mr. John Biggerstaff, sen.
late vestry-clerk of this parish,
who died the 29 of December, 1804,
in the 73d year of his age :
After serving his office with great integrity and ability
upwards of 37 years, so truly esteemed, and so sincerely
lamented by the *parishioners*, that they voted
unanimously, on Easter Tuesday 1805, for the erection
of this tablet."

### A marble tablet adjoining the altar on the left hand:
" Sacred to the memory of Richard Smith, Esq.
merchant of London, who died
on the 13th Oct. 1776, aged 69.
Also of Elizabeth his second wife,
and of his son the Rev. Richard Smith, rector [1] of this parish.
And also of Lucy his third wife, who died the 14th of April, 1795,
aged 77."

Arms : *Argent, on a bend Sable, between two unicorns heads erased Azure, horned and crined, three lozenges of the field. Impaling Sable, a castle Or.*

### On a small marble tablet, end of the North aile:
" In memory of
the Rev. John Ditton, B. A.
formerly of Pembroke Hall, Cambridge,
and afterwards, during a period of 35 years and upwards,
the much respected lecturer of this parish,
who died March 16th, 1776,
in the 61st year of his age,

-------------------------------------------------

[1] So by mistake on the tablet.

and was buried under the vestry-room,
at the North-west angle of the church.

*O ! thou great Arbiter of life and death,*
*Our gracious Saviour from eternal woe ;*
*Thy call I follow to the land unknown,*
*I trust in thee, and know in whom I trust.*"

**On a handsome tablet of white and variegated marble, near the above:**

" Near this tablet
are deposited the remains
of John Eddowes, Esq.
late of New Bridge-street, London,
who died Aug. the 30, 1802, in the 81st year of his age.
In the same grave are likewise the remains
of Elizabeth Eddowes, sister to the above ;
and of Mrs. Sarah Freeman, wife of John Freeman, Esq.
of Lamb's Conduit-street, London, likewise sister to
the above, who died Feb. 28, 1803,
aged 75 years."

Arms : *Quarterly,* 1. *Party per bend sinister Ermine and Ermines, a lion rampant langued Or ;* 2. *Gules, a chevron Argent, between three heads armed, in helmets, with beavers open proper ;* 3. *Gules, three chevronels Argent ;* 4. *Argent, a cross fleury engrailed between four blackbirds proper.* Crest, *a head armed, beaver open, proper, on a wreath Argent and Sable.* Motto, A . VIMVO . DVW . DERVID.

**In the North-east corner of the church is a handsome pyramidical monument of white and veined marble, representing Christ raising Jairus's daughter, sculptured in alto-relievo, and the motto, " Weep " not, she is not dead, but sleepeth. St. Luke, chap. viii. ver. 52." It bears the following inscription :**

" In the vault of this church
are deposited the mortal remains of
Miss Mary-Elizabeth Ward,
eldest daughter of George Ward, Esq. and Mary his wife,
who was born 11 Dec. 1790;
and, in humble hope of divine mercy,
departed this life 18th May, 1808.
Also of

John Ward, born 4 June, 1786, died 17 May, 1794 ;
Robert-Dawes Ward, born 31 March, 1789, died 3d March, 1790 ;
Julia-Christian Ward, born 25 July, 1807, died 24 Feb. 1808 ;
children of the same parents."

## A tablet in the South aile :

" In the vault beneath this church
lieth the body of
James Christian,  Esq.
late of this parish, who died the 18th Nov. 1808,
aged 76 years."

## On a tablet in the South aile :

" Near this place lieth the body of Mary, wife of
Thomas Rowe, of this parish, and daughter of
John and Sarah Mortimer, of Walthamstow, in the county of Essex,
who departed this life the 1st of August, 1777, aged 44 years.
Also,
the body of the abovesaid Thomas Rowe, a descendant
of the antient family of that name in the parish of
Walthamstow, in the county of Essex,
who departed this life the 3d of August, 1790,
aged 58 years."

Arms : *Quarterly, 1 and 4. Gules, a quatrefoil Or ; 2 and 3. Argent, a chevron Azure, charged with three bezants between as many quatrefoils slipped and divided palewise Gules and Vert.  Crest, a stag's head Gules, horned Or.*  Motto, TRAMITE RECTO.

## On a pyramidical monument in the South aile :

" In the vault beneath this church are deposited the remains of
Mrs. Elizabeth Simpson, late wife of Mr. Alexander Simpson,
merchant, of Gibraltar,
and daughter of Mr. Henry Cowper, of the same place,
who died the 5th day of November, 1786,
aged 19 years,
possessing many amiable virtues,
and much lamented by all that knew her."

## Within the rails of the communion-table:

" Here lies interred the body of Mr. Richard Tuckwell, late of Cow-lane, London, coachmaker, who departed this life on the 13th of December, 1747, aged 58 years.   He was an affectionate husband, a tender father, and a sincere friend.   Also the body of Mrs. Elizabeth Tuckwell, late wife of the abovesaid Mr. Richard Tuckwell, who departed this life the 11th of October 1758, aged 73 years."

## On a tablet at the East end of the South aile:

" To perpetuate,
while this frail marble shall endure,
the meritorious exertions of an individual,
and to excite the emulation of others ;
the Governors of the
ROYAL HUMANE SOCIETY
have caused this tablet to be inscribed,
with the name of
WILLIAM HAWES, M. D.
by whose personal and indefatigable labours,
an Institution, honourable to the Nation,
and highly beneficial to the World at large,
was founded, fostered, and matured.
And long, very long, may it flourish,
the Ornament and the Pride of Britain !

This excellent, unassuming,
persevering Philanthropist,
was born in Islington Nov. 28, 1736;
died in Spital-square Dec. 5, 1808,
and was buried on the 13th near these walls.
Go, Reader ! and imitate those virtuous actions,
which the latest posterity will applaud and venerate,
and which the Recording Angel
has registered in Heaven.
*Well done, good and faithful Servant !*
*Enter thou into thy joy of the Lord.*"

[At the bottom of the tablet is a medallion of the Doctor, within a wreath of oak leaves; and at the top, a copy of the Humane Society's medal, with the motto, " *Lateat scintillula forsan.*"]

A monument near the above :
" Sacred to the memory of William Parry,
Clk, D. D. ob. 4 May, 1810, æt. 72."

Arms : *Or, a bar between three lozenges Sable, a cross moline Gules in chief ; impaling, Gules, a saltire between four garbes Or.* Crest, *five battle-axes fretty, in a wreath proper.* Motto. *Cedant arma togæ.*

*At the Eastern extremity of the North aile is a black stone slab, bearing the effigies in brass of two figures, a male and a female, in praying attitudes : their lower half, and the inscription, are covered by the pews. They, without doubt, represent the figures of Henry Saville and his lady, daughter of Thomas Fowler, Esq. whose epitaph is given in p. 298. At the top of the stone are two escutcheons, also in brass ; one bears on a bend three owls with a mullet in chief, the arms of Saville, quartering those of Wyatt. The other is charged with the coat of Fowler, impaling the above. See Plate II. fig. 3.

*An adjoining slab, also half covered by the pews, bears a handsome brass canopy ; part of it has been stolen away by some sacrilegious hand, as also two escutcheons from the upper part of the stone. This, it is most likely, belonged also to the families of Fowler or Fisher.

At the East end of the Church are funeral hatchments, belonging to the families of *Pullin, Wilson, Moorhouse, Blackstone,* and *Burton.*

In the Church vault are two iron coffins, in which are deposited the bodies of —— Giles and his wife, formerly inhabitants of the City gardens : likewise one of cedar, with a cover similar to the gable roof of a house ; this contains the body of Justice Palmer, mentioned in p. 251, and was made according to his own directions, with a view of resisting the attacks of worms, and to prevent any other coffin being placed upon him.

William Baxter, an eminent Philologist and Antiquary, author of the " Glossarium Antiquitatum Romanarum, &c." is said to have been buried at Islington [1] in 1723; but his name does not appear in the Register.

Anthony Wood, in the first edition of his Athenæ Oxonienses, vol. I. says, that John Bell, Bishop of Worcester, who was employed by Henry the VIIIth in the business of his divorce, was buried in Islington Church; but he was, without doubt, interred in that of St. James Clerkenwell. A monumental brass, containing his effigies in his Bishop's robes, which was removed on the pulling down of that edifice, is engraved in Malcolm's " Londinium Redivivum," from the original, which is still carefully preserved.

### INSCRIPTIONS IN THE CHURCH-YARD.

On the North and South sides of the Church, near the walls, are six several slab stones, which appear to have been removed from the interior of the old structure, where they recorded the interment of persons of note, having been formerly charged with figures and escutcheons in brass of considerable size, of which they have been shamefully deprived.

Such was the rage for demolishing every relick of superstition after the Reformation, and during the Civil War between Charles I. and the Parliament, that even the hallowed sepulchres of the dead could not escape the sacrilegious hands of the enthusiasts. Weever tells us [2], that Dr. Hanmer (vicar of this parish in 1583) at the time he held the living of Shoreditch, " for covetousness of the brass which he con-" verted into coyned silver, he plucked up many (brass) plates fixed on the grave " stones, and left no memory of such as had been buried under them."

In the 2d year of Elizabeth a proclamation was issued against the breaking or defacing the monuments of the dead; this was followed by another, both of which, as we are informed by Weever, " tooke small effect."

Had the brasses remained on the stones above mentioned at the time the old Church was pulled down, they would doubtless have been reinstated in the new

---

[1] History and Antiquities of Tottenham, p. 89.
[2] Funeral Monuments, p. 427.

building, as was the stone and brass to the memory of Henry Saville and his wife (see p. 326) : we may therefore attribute to the enthusiastic zeal of the times, or to the more impure motives that actuated the Rev. Divine at Shoreditch, these depredations of a similar kind, committed at Islington, and which the lover of antiquity will always reflect upon with indignation.

Among the tomb-stones which are gone to decay, or have been removed from the Church-yard, are those containing the following inscriptions ; viz. Edward Sympson, son of Giles, 1665.—Thomas Satterthwaite, 1688.—John Patten, of the parish of St. Giles in the Fields, founder, 1696 ; Thomas, his son, 1693.—John Biddle, born, lived, and died, in the parish of St. Andrew Holborn.—William Taylor, 14 Oct. 1700, in 72d year.—Lewis Protheroe, Churchwarden of this parish, 28 Nov. 1733, in his 58th year.—Thomas Willis, Gent. of Buckby in Northamptonshire, 1620.—Christopher White, " Professor of Chemistry to both the Universities," and another bearing the name of Edgerley, with the following quaint inscription :

" As Death once travelling the Northern road
" Stopt in this town some short abode
" Enquiring where *true merit* lay,
" H' envy'd and snatch'd this youth away."

The following is an abbreviated alphabetical list of all the inscriptions in the Church-yard, the only omissions are those of children, which in some instances are also given. Those marked thus * are in the new cemetery, the letter h. denotes on head stones, s. slabs, a. altar tombs, and a. r. altar tombs railed.

## A.

h. *Abbet, Edward,* of St. James Clerkenwell, died Sept. 1, 1722, aged 69. Also his first wife.

h. *Abbot, John,* of St. Dunstan's East.

h. *Agar, Elizabeth,* of Canterbury, co. Kent, died Nov. 30, . . . . , aged 57.

h. *Akers, Elizabeth,* wife of William, of this parish, died 6 May, 1736, in 57th year.

h. *Albright, John,* citizen and goldsmith of London, 23 June, 1771, 78.

h. *Alcock, Mrs. Jane,* 20 April, 1768, in her 24th year. Mary Brice her mother, Nov. 13, 1777, 61. Margaret-Jane Brice, Mar. 5, 1590, 40. Robert Brice, Aug. 13, 1791, 43.

*Alcock.* See *Sebbon.*

h. *Alexander, Mary,* daughter of Jane Brown, of this parish, Sept. 24, 1790, 33 ; said Jane Brown, 25 April, 1781, 66. Han-

nah, wife of Thomas Duddy, of this parish, 24 June, 1805, 66.

*h *Allan, Donald,* 17 April, 1803, 39.

h. *Allen, Benjamin,* of St. Anne, Westminster, 1756, 52.

*Allen.* See *Porter.*

h. *Althroup, Jane,* of this parish, 5 Aug. 1761, 78.

h. *Anderson, Capt. Robert,* 6 July, 1789, 61, many years captain and commander in the Mediterranean trade.

h. *Armstrong, George,* of St. James, Clerkenwell, 13 May, 1808, 46. Anne his daughter, 16. Marian, daughter of William Armstrong, 17.

h. *Armstrong, Mary,* wife of William, of this parish, May 3, 1784, 55. Mary her daughter, wife of Thomas Wood, of this parish, 6 May, 1793, 33. William Sexton, of this parish, brother to said Mary Armstrong, 21 Nov. 1805, 81, many years brass-founder, in St. John-street, West Smithfield.

\*h. *Armstrong, John,* Nov. 29, 1798, 52.

h. *Arnold, Wm.* citizen and stationer of London, and this parish, Dec. 5, 1766, in his 53d year.

h. *Arnott, Wm.* 26 Aug. 1729, 27. John Arnott, citizen and currier of London, Mar. 30, 1750, 71. Mary his wife, Nov. 3, 1756, 78. John their son, Nov. 27, 1762, 47. Mary Haughter their daughter, 23 April, 1766, 55.

a. *Askew, Eliz.* daughter of Anthony, M. D. and Elizabeth his wife, May 24, 1764, in her 2d year.

\*h. *Atkins, John,* 10 Oct. 1803, 54.

\*h. *Atkins, Joseph,* of North Kilworth, Leicestershire, 20 Mar. 1798, 70. William his son, 13 Mar. 1803, 47.

s. *Atkinson, Susanna,* Feb. 1783, 67. Also *Ellen Soreton,* a friend of the above.

\*h. *Austin, John,* Dec. 2, 1810, 39.

## B.

\*h. *Bacon, Sarah,* 26 May, 1796, aged 25.

h. *Bailey, James,* citizen and stationer of London, Mar. 28, 1776, in 70th year. Sarah his wife, Jan. 14, 1784, in 72d year.

h. *Baker, Daniel,* many years a respectable inhabitant of this parish, June 6, 1781, in 51st year. Daniel his son, Feb. 12, 1808, aged 42.

h. *Baker, Joseph,* of London, merchant, 9 Sept. 1778, 87. Also his two wives, Frances, Jan. 1, 1739, 50; Mary, Jan. 29, 1764, 64. His only daughter Sarah, June 7, 1749, 31. Edward his brother, Jan. 21, 1779, 74. Martha, relict of Edward, Aug. 14, 1780, 80.

h. *Baker, Francis,* pearl-ash merchant, of London, son of John Baker, Litton, Derbyshire, 20 April, 1778, 40. Charlotte his widow, July 4, 1784, 39.

h. *Baldwin, Hannah,* wife of Richard, citizen and stationer of London, 3 July, 1758, 61. Said Richard, Jan. 5, 1777, in 85th year.

h. *Bantam, Eliz.* 11 Jan. 1753, in 59th year.

s. *Barber, Francis,* of this parish, 23 April, 1772, 38.

h. *Barfoot, Wm.* of Coleman-street, London, May 6, 1807, in 65th year. Catherine, wife of Thomas, of Pentonville, 19 Feb. 1808, in 35th year.

h. *Barnard, Wm.* 14 May, 1806, 57. Ann his

sister in law, 14 Sept. 1804, 52. Mary, 28 Oct. 1809, 32.

h. *Barnes, Wm.* of Orange-street, Bloomsbury, 18 July, 1793, 40.

\*h. *Barnes, George,* July 20, 1807, "upwards of 30 years the faithful foreman of Mr. Thomas Poynder, of Bishopsgate-street, London, and by his attention and integrity acquired and preserved the confidence of his employer, and the esteem of all who knew him."

h. *Barr, Eleanor,* wife of Henry, bricklayer, of Knightsbridge, 12 Oct. 1764, in 36th year.

h. *Bartholomew, Robert,* 6 Feb. 1766, 56. Elizabeth his wife, 20 July, 1784, 67. William Burdett, grandson, 19 Aug. 1788, 25.

\*h. *Bartley, Sophia,* youngest daughter of Nehemiah and Sarah, late of Bristol, 19 Feb. 1808, 17.

*Barwell.* See *Morris.*

h. *Barwick, John,* 6 April, 1755, 57.

h. *Bate, Thomas,* of this parish, 3 May, 1807, 52.

h. *Bateman, Edward,* "a just and faithful apprentice, and a true Christian," July 13, 1797, 19.

*Bateman.* See *Willet.*

h. *Bates, Deborah,* wife of Charles, of St. Botolph, Aldersgate, Dec. 21, 1775, 51. Said Charles, 8 April, 1785, 60.

*Batt.* See *Taylor.*

h. *Battin, Sarah,* wife of William, of this parish, March 27, 1785, 32. Frances Vincent her sister, April 17, 1785, 34.

\*a. *Beard, Thomas,* citizen and mason of London, 35 years an inhabitant of this parish, 12 May, 1803, 76.

\*h. *Becket, Mrs. Jane,* daughter of Rev. Timothy Perkins, M. A. rector of Haselingfield, Cambridgeshire, born 6 Nov. 1754, died 19 Oct. 1808.

h. *Beckman, Nicholas-Francis,* Jan. 4, 1792, 62.

h. *Beldon, James,* of St. Giles's in the Fields, Dec. 20, 1729, 44.

a. *Bell, Mary,* a lady eminent for the practice of every Christian virtue. Her days were marked with misfortune, and her sole comfort arose from the hopes of attaining a better life, and the dutiful affection of her children. She was born in his Majesty's colony of Rhode Island, in North America, and lived there honoured and beloved by all who knew her, till, in the year 1779, and in the 50th year of her age, she was obliged, though a widow with eight children, to quit it, and take refuge in *Great Britain*, from the vindictive spirit of a rebellion, whose object is the destruction of its empire, and the destruction of its glory. She died of the small-pox, on the 16th of Sept. anno Dom. 1781." Temperance Heatly, granddaughter of Mary Bell, 2 April, 1799. Eliz. wife of S. Middleton, esq. (daughter) 30 May, 1810, 38.

a. *Bellas, Richard,* citizen and vintner of London, 20 Oct. 1725, in 37th year. Mary his wife, late wife of Castle Thorpe, citizen and vintner, 13 Aug. 1731, 43.

h. *Bellman, Johans,* 23 Oct. 1768, 73. Grace his wife, 6 Jan. 1782, 86.

h. *Bennet, Wm.* 3 Feb. 1793, 75. Sarah his mother, 13 Oct. 1761, 78.
*Bennet.* See *Crane.*

h. *Bernonville, Thomas,* of Hatton-garden, gent. 21 Jan. 1777, in 69th year.

b. *Bewes, Daniel,* of Brianstone-street, Portman-square, born at Ruthwaite in Cumberland, died 17 Oct. 1792, 70. Mary Little, niece to Mr. Steel, of Cross-street, Islington, born at Seaton in Cumberland, died 27 Jan. 1806, 67.

h. *Bickerdike, Robert,* April 4, 1791, 48. Frances his wife, Sept. 28, 1784, 52.

h. *Biddle, Susanna,* wife of Edward, of this parish, Sept. 8, 1746, in 45th year. Edward, Oct. 3, 1747, 52.
*Bigelston.* See *Davenport* and *Johnson.*

*h. *Biggerstaff, John, sen.* vestry-clerk of this parish 37 years, died Dec. 29, 1804, in 73d year. John his son, 20 July, 1806, in 42d year.

*h. *Birch, Eliz.* wife of Richard, of this parish, citizen and wire-drawer of London, June 27, 1803, 61. Susanna his second wife, Feb. 15, 1807, 59.

h. *Birchinghough, Peter,* March 28, 1761, 43. Sarah his wife, July 13, 1760, 33.

s. *Birchmore, Edward,* of this parish, citizen and coachmaker, Aug. 1761.

h. *Bird, Mary,* of this parish, 13 Aug. 1786, 42.

Farewell, vain world, I've seen enough of thee
And now am careless what thou say'st of me ;
Thy smiles I court not, nor thy frowns I fear,
My soul's at rest, my head lies quiet here.
The faults you saw in me take care to shun,
Look you at home, there's enough to be done."

h. *Birkenhead, James,* of Gutter-lane, jeweller, Jan. 16, 1787, 66. Elizabeth his wife, 1 May, 1791, in 63d year.

h. *Black, Wm.* 15 May, 1777, 52. Elizabeth his wife, 13 May, 1798, 84.

h. *Blackbourne.* Hic situm est quod mortale fuit viri verè Reverendi Johannis Blackbourne, A. M. ecclesiæ Anglicanæ presbyteri, Pontificiorum æque ac Novatorum Mallei, docti, clari, strenui, prompti; qui (uti verbo dicam, cætera enim quis nescit ?) cum eo non dignus erat, usque adeo degener, mundus, ad beatorum sedes translatus est 17º die Novembris, A. D. MDCCXLI, ætatis suæ LVIII. Cui tandem hic restituta est Philadelphia, olim ejus relicta, postea vera conjux Ric. Heyborne, civis Londini, quæ obiit 10º die Januarii, A.D. MDCCL, ætat. suæ LXX.

*Blackwell.* See *Socket.*

h. *Bletsoe, Dorothy,* wife of William, of St. Sepulchre, Dec... 1693, in 46th year.
*Bleuler.* See *Shuttleworth.*
*Blott.* See *Cliften.*
*Boeden.* See *Davis.*
*Bolton.* See *Bond.*

a. *Bolton, Arabella,* wife of Samuel, of this parish, 1 Jan. 1781, 71. Said Samuel, Esq. 1 Jan. 1789, 78.

h. *Bond, Edward,* of Lombard-street, gunmaker, 27 May, 1790, 58. Mary Bolton, of the Minories, 18 Nov. 1797, 82.

*h. *Bond, Thomas,* 13 May, 1809, 55. Martha, 6 Dec. 1809, 60.

h. *Booth, John,* late of Barnard's-inn, London, attorney at law, and one of the Society of Antiquaries, 10 Jan. 1757, 63. Margaret his sister, 20 Jan. 1755, 40.

*h. *Bottrill, Thomas,* of this parish, 23 June, 1805, 36.

h. *Boughey, John,* of St. Helen's, Bishopsgate, tobacconist, 13 Dec. 1805, 55.

a. *Boustred, George,* of Crouch-end, 18 July, 1796, in 61st year.

h. *Boustred, John,* of this parish, 9 Nov. 1765, 75. John his son, 25 Nov. 1770, 43. Mary his wife, 19 Feb. 1771, 69. Charlotte, wife of George, of Hornsey, March 4, 1782, 51.

h. *Boyce, Ann,* wife of William.

*h. *Branburgh, Sarah,* 3 Aug. 1807, 38.
Death's fatal stroke dissolves our dearest ties,
Our fond embrace of all terrestrial joys;
O! may the resurrection sweetly prove,
Our endless union, in celestial love.

h. *Brandon, Mary,* 22 Sept. 1758, 47. Susanna, 25 Oct. 1760, 22. Thomas, Mar. 20, 1764, 39.

h. *Brathwaite, William,* of this parish, May 27,

1730, 53. Hannah his wife. Benjamin, of this parish, 3 July, 1756.

*h. *Brayne, Sarah,* widow of Joseph, of Clerkenwell, Feb. 21, 1807, 63.

h. *Brewster, John,* March 9, 1757, 22. Faith his mother, Sept. 28, 1767, 62. John her husband, Aug. 6, 1778, 72.

h. *Brice, Charles,* of this parish, Sept. 24, 1766, 78. Robert, 6 Dec. 1785, 70. Hannah Raynham, 21 May, 1789, 46.

h. *Brice, Susanna,* Jan. 1, 1771, 29. Thomas her son, who died at Cape Coast Castle, Africa, 19 Nov. 1792, 23. John his father, 28 Sept. 1795, 55.

*Brice.* See *Alcock.*

*h. *Bridel, Victoria-Louisa,* a child of remarkable strength and health, died 24 July, 1804, in the 14th year of her age, of a mortification of the bowels caused by a stoppage arising from swallowing cherry-stones.

*h. *Bridgens, Wm.* Aug. 3, 1807, 45. Hannah his wife, Dec. 2, 1807, 53.

h. *Bridges, Humphrey,* July 26, 1770, 42.

Reader, prepare to follow me,
For as I am so shall ye be ;
Thy body too must come to dust,
Therefore prepare, for die you must.
For life 's uncertain, death is sure :
Sin is the wound, and Christ the cure.
Repent in time, and sin no more.

*Brock.* See *Powell.*

a. *Brogden, James,* Aug. 19, 1799, 71. Mary his wife, Jan. 25, 1800, 74.

h. *Brooks, John,* of St. Giles, Cripplegate, 27 Nov. 1775, 37.

*h. *Brown, Sarah,* wife of William, of St. John-street, cheesemonger, Jan. 22, 1803, 26. And Thomas her infant son, March 13, 1803.

A much-lov'd wife, array'd in youthful bloom,
Snatch'd from my circling arms to grace the tomb,
Lies sleeping here : and with her, join'd in death,
A darling child, to whom she first gave breath,
A tender plant I fondly hop'd to raise,
To cheer the sorrows of my future days.
In vain to raise its drooping head I try'd,
It felt a mother's loss — languish'd and dy'd.
Sought, through Death's passage, for a mother gone,
And found, and join'd her near th' eternal throne.

*a. *Brown, John,* son of Thomas and Mary, of the parish of Allhallows, Honey-lane, 10 Oct. 1807, 22.

*Brown.* See *Alexander* and *Watkins.*

h. *Browne, Sarah,* wife of Andrew-William, of this parish, Aug. 9, 1758, 42.

Grace was in all her steps,
Heav'n in her eye,
In all her gestures dignity and love.

*Budgen.* See *Newman.*

h. *Bull, Margaret,* wife of William, 9 May, 1809, in 51st year.

h. *Bull, Henry,* Oct. XXIV, MDCCXXXIX. Mary his mother, Nov. 20, 1741, in 55th year.

*Burch.* See *Parsons.*

*Burdett.* See *Bartholomew.*

*h. *Burgie, James,* died in this parish 20 May, 1757, aged 30. John, of Mark-lane, London, merchant, 29 April, 1808, 34.

h. *Burgis, Mary,* wife of William, of St. Mary Axe, glazier, 29 April, 1750, in 36th year.

*Burr.* See *Chamberlayne.*

h. *Burrows, John,* of Newington Green, 5 Sept. 1790, 52. Ann his wife, 7 Dec. 1797, 52.

h. *Burton, Thomas,* Dec. 25, 1760, 50. Susanna his wife, May 25, 1766, 56. Richard their son, April 15, 1785, in 33d year.

h. *Burton, Mary,* wife of Francis, July 27, 1783, in 36th year. Also Francis, born June 11, 1747, died Jan. 23, 1802.

h. *Buswell, Charles,* of Arthingworth in Northamptonshire, Oct. 22, 1786, 49.

May Christ conduct my soul to bliss !
All else is naught, compar'd with this.
Give another wish, kind heaven,
To meet friends, wife, and children seven.

h. *Butler, Cornelia,* wife of John, of this parish, gent. Nov. 7, 1749, in 72d year. Said John, Aug. 21, 1750, in 68th year.

## C.

a tablet. *Cadman, Susannah,* wife of Charles, 9 Aug. 1793, in 30th year.

a. *Cafe, John,* of Blackford, co. Somerset, citizen and goldsmith of London, Aug. 7, 1757, 40.

*h. *Calcutt, Charles,* of this parish, Aug. 12, 1807, 29.

*h. *Caldwell, Sarah,* 9 Nov.

*h. *Campbell, Archibald,* late Capt. of an independant Company, 13 Oct. 1794, 25.

h. *Campion, Eliz.* Nov. 2, 1727, 52. Thomas, 20 Dec. 1731, 61. William Farr, jun. Oct. 7, 1764, 32.

h. *Capp, Alice,* of Highbury-place, 10 April, 1784, 73.

*a. *Careless, Eliz.* wife of Robert, of this parish, 16 Jan. 1799, in 63d year; said Robert, gent. 26 Aug. 1805, 67.

h. *Carleton, Lough,* esq. 12 April, 1792, 65. John, his son, 12 Feb. 1798, 43.

h. *Carr, Ann,* wife of James, of St. George, Bloomsbury, Feb. 3, 1770. in 67th year. Said James, April 12, 1773.

s. *Carr, Henry,* March 27, 1769, 36. "A faithful servant."

*h. *Cart, Jane,* wife of John, 14 Dec. 1763, 26. Elizabeth, his second wife, born in 1737, died 15 April, 1806. "John and Elizabeth Cart were married 39 years."

h. *Carter, Zacharias,* of Princes-street, Drury-lane, June 21, 1776, 58. Susannah, his wife, March 2, 1786, 69.

*h. *Cary, Col. James,* of South Carolina, 9 Dec. 1794, 62.

h. *Cater, Isabella,* wife of John, of Newington-green, in this parish, gent. 5 April, 1769, in 37th year.

h. *Catherall, Eliz.* wife of Robert, of this parish, Dec. 6, 1757, in 56th year. Robert, June 7, 175 . . aged 67.

*h. *Cave, Edward,* of this parish, 15 Feb. 1807, 50.

*h. *Cawthorn, John,* of this parish, 7 April, 1799, 48.

h. *Chadwick, Marmaduke,* citizen and glover of London, of St. Botolph, Aldersgate, 11 Dec. 1764, 39. Edmund Wrigley, citizen and innholder, 19 Aug. 1769, in 36th year.

h. *Chamberlayne, Mary,* 30 May, 1775, 84. Elizabeth Burr, Nov. 20, 1797, 71.

h. *Chandler, Thomas,* of St. James Clerkenwell, Sept. 26, 1780, 39.

h. *Chapman, Eliz.* wife of Richard, of this parish, builder, (interred in the Church-vault) Nov. 24, 1810, 39.

h. *Charron, Wm.* son of Andrew and Catharine, of this parish, Sept. 19, 1780, aged 6 years 1 month.

Happy the babe who is ordain'd by fate
To shorter labour and a lighter weight ;
Receiv'd but yesterday the gift of breath,
Ordered to-morrow to return to death.

Said Andrew, 7 Nov. 1793, in 63d year. Catharine, his widow, 12 Jan. 1807, 72.

*h. *Chatel, Mary-Jane,* daughter of Samuel and Mary, of this parish, 15 April 1797, 37.

*h. *Cheese, Ann,* 30 Sept. 1799, 66.

*h. *Child, Francis,* 23 Dec. 1810, 65.

h. *Chilton, Eleanor,* 30 Sept. 1799, 52. Thomas, her husband, 29 Jan. 1803, 55.
Death, like an overflowing stream,
Sweeps us away : our life's a dream,
An empty tale, a morning flow'r
Cut down and wither'd in an hour.
Our age to seventy years are set,
How short the time, how frail the state ;
And if to eighty we arrive
We rather sigh and groan than live.

*Chubb.* See *Haynes.*

h. *Chumley, Matthew,* of this parish, Oct. 1, 1765, in 57th year, Elizabeth, his daughter, 20 Jan. 1771, 20.

h. *Circuitt, Richard,* of Leadenhall market, butcher, 18 April, 1801, 52. And 2 children.

h. *Clare, Mary,* wife of John, of Lincoln's-inn, gent. May 17, 1772, 24.

*h. *Clark, Ann-Dorothy,* 28 March 1809, 32.

*h. *Clark, John,* of this parish, Sept. 21, 1801, 73. Guido, his son, of St. Andrew, Holborn, Feb. 18, 1802, 45.

*Clark.* See *Prince.*

h. *Clarke, Edmund,* Sept. 10, 1743, 72. Martha, his wife, Feb. 10, 1755, 84.

*Clarke.* See *Macdonald.*

h. *Claridge, Eliz.* June 9, 1787, 17.

h. *Clayton, Aaron,* esq. capt. of 69th reg. of foot, of this parish, Dec. 3, 1774, in 65th year.

h. *Cliften, Mary,* wife of Peter, of St. James, Clerkenwell, May 11, 1788, 27. William Blott, of St. Giles, Cripplegate, her father, April 16, 1793, 57. Lucy, his wife, 11 Sept. 1796, 49.

a. *Cloudesley.* "Here lyes the body of Richard Cloudesley, a good benefactor to this parish, who died 9 Hen. VIII. anno Domini 1517." Repaired and re-insculpt 1802[1].

h. *Clutterbuck, Susannah,* wife of Edmund, 6 July 1761, 40. Said Edmund, gent. 8 Dec. 1797, in 77th year.

h. *Colchin, William,* Feb. 15, 1788, in 50th year.

---

[1] This tomb is kept in repair by the parish. It was repaired, polished, and the letters restored, A. D. 1690, Nicholas Rufford, James Porter, Churchwardens; also in 1733, John Booth and Lewis Protheroe, Churchwardens.

h. *Cole, Elizabeth,* wife of Benjamin, of Fleet-street, July 31, 1763, 75. Said Benjamin, 23d June, 1766, in 72d year.

h. *Cole, Joseph,* citizen and skinner of London, 1st Feb. 1741, in 76th year. Elizabeth, his wife, 26 Jan. 1745, in 80th year. Richard, their son, 29 May, 1760.

*Cole.* See *Whittenbury.*

*Coleman.* See *Newton.*

h. *Collet, Eleanor,* wife of Joseph, of this parish, 10 May, 1805, 65. Said Joseph, 15 July, 1805, 55.

h *Collins, Mary,* wife of Joseph, citizen and cook of London, April 2, 1752, 53. Said Joseph, 14 April, 1766, 68.

h. *Collins, Rebecca,* wife of Wm. of St. Bride's, July 29, 1763, 55.

*h. *Collison, Stephen,* April 19, 1800, 41.

*Coney.* See *Taverner.*

h. *Cooper, Mary,* daughter of George, of Jewin-street, London, Aug. 11, 1740, in 25th year. Mary, his wife, 24 March 1741, in 48th year.

h. *Cooper, Edward,* of St. Sepulchre, Middlesex, March 7, 1790, 75. Charles Till, Feb. 12, 1807, 52.

*a. *Cooper, William,* nephew of John Scott, esq. of this parish, 21 Dec. 1803, 13.

h. *Corneg, Theophilus-John,* of this parish, printer, 12 Dec. 1777, 73.

h. *Corneck, John,* of this parish, bricklayer, Aug. 17, 1747, 41. Sarah, his wife, Oct. 6, 1762, 48.

h. *Cotton, Elizabeth,* Aug. 1, 1743, 66. And Paul, her son.

*h. *Coward, Susannah,* wife of John, of this parish, 26 Aug. 1809, 63.

Whatsoever thy hand findeth to do, do it with thy might, for there is no work nor device, nor knowledge, nor wisdom in the grave, whither thou goest. Eccles. chap. ix. v. 10.

h. *Courthorpe, William,* of Paternoster-row, senior warden of the Company of Upholders, 62.

h. *Cox, Thomas,* citizen and draper of London, Aug. 7, 1740, 56.

h. *Coxall, Eliz.* Feb. 2, 1771, 48. Edward, of this parish, gardener, 9 June, 1776, 55.

h. *Cradock, William,* and *Sarah* his wife, descended from a respectable family in Leicestershire. He was born at Uxbridge in May 1710, and died in Westminster, Dec. 22, 1779. She was born at Wellingborough April 26, 1712, and died at Islington, Aug. 3, 1795. They are deposited by their joint desire near the grave of a justly beloved daughter Mrs. Anne Nichols, who died Feb. 18, 1776.

a. *Crane, Edward,* of this parish, 3 May, 1746, 82. Mary, his wife, Nov. 12, 1755, 72. James, Oct. 12, 1785, 64. Also Jane Senior, May 9, 1770, 41. Also Mary Bennett, June 3, 1782, 61.

h. *Crane, Thomas,* citizen and turner of London, Feb. 18, 1763, 70. Mary, his wife, June 12, 1730, in 85th year.

h. *Cremer, Susannah,* wife of Peter, of St. James, Clerkenwell, Aug. 23, 1781, in 62d year. Mary, their daughter, May 27, 1797, 53. Peter, Sept. 1, 1803, 93. Joseph, son, 13 Nov. 1806, 49.

h. *Crick, Elizabeth,* of this parish, spinster, Jan. 15, 1773, 57.

Afflictions sore long time I bore,
Physicians were in vain,
Till death did seize, and God did please
To ease me of my pain.

h. *Crook, James,* of this parish, 22 Dec. 1797, 72. James, his son, 5 April, 1801, 42. Mary, 25 April, 1803. 75.

h. *Cropley, Thomas,* May 28, 1718, 26.

a. *Cross, William,* of London, merchant, 29 April, 1785, 60. Edward, of Fleet-street, seedsman, 13 July, 1793, 62.

h. *Crowder, William,* of St. Luke's, 6 Oct. 1805, 57.

*Cummins.* See *Ton.*

## D.

*a. *Damant, Annabella,* wife of William Castell, of Lammas, in Norfolk, gent. 26 June, 1809, 26.

*h. *Damont, John,* March 20, 180.. 31.

s. *Dannalld, John,* of Newington-green, a person of approved integrity and great usefulness. Frances, his wife, Feb 9, 1701. Nathaniel, their son, 1694.

h. *Davenport, William,* gent. July 19, 1781, in 29th year. Hannah Vernon, May 21, 1782, 23. Sarah Bigelston, May 3, 1809, 35.

*h. *Davies, Philip,* April 6, 1807, 65. Susannna, his wife, 11 April, 1801, 56.

a. r. *Davis, Eliz.* wife of John, of this parish, carpenter and citizen of London, 31 Jan. 1765, 68. Eliz. Boeden, his niece, 17 June, 1775, in 25th year. John Davis[1], 23 Aug. 1793, in 84th year. Jane, his 2d wife, 13 June, 1801, in 81st year.

[1] Founder of the eight almshouses on the South side of Queen's Head-lane.

s. r. *Davis, Ann,* 8 March, 1747, in 19th year. Samuel, her father, 9 Feb. 1748, in 56th year. John, his son, Jan. 19, 1775, 49. Elizabeth, daughter, Sept. 5, 1775, 44. Ann, wife of Samuel, 4 Nov. 1794, in 90th year. Samuel, son of the above Samuel and Ann, March 13, 1797, 59.

*h. *Davis, John,* gent. late of Carey-street, Lincoln's-inn, 22 April, 1797, 38.
*Davis.* See *Glover.*

h. *Dawson, Wm.* June 20, 1774, 36. Eliz. his wife, Jan. 15, 1800, 74.

h. *Day, Philip,* of the Poultry, London, Feb. 6, 1803, 72. Mary, his daughter, April 25, 1789, 17. George, his son, 4 Dec. 1804, 25.

h. *Deakin, Francis,* of this parish, 18 April, 1780, 51.
Beneath this stone doth honest Deakin lie.
The good, the great, the virtuous, all must die.
He acted well his part while here on earth,
To heav'n now call'd enjoys a better birth.
Friend to the poor, a friend to all he knew,
His virtues many, and his faults but few,
Those few, were only Nature's common lot,
Think of his goodness—faults may be forgot.

*h. *Deans, David,* 18 Jan. 1803, 54.

*h. *De Camp,* Mrs. of Green-man's-lane, Islington, 23d April 1808, 70.

h. *Dennis, Samuel,* of this parish, April 3, 1743, 67.

h. *Denton, Wm.* of this parish, victualler, 17 Sept. 1781, 41.

*h. *Denys, Elizabeth,* 27 Nov. 1802, 45.

h. *Dickinson, Mary,* of St. Martin's in the Fields, 5 Jan. 1786, in 69th year.

h. *Dobson, James,* citizen and innholder, of St. Michael, Bassishaw, London, 9 Jan. 1762, in 34th year

*a. *Donald, David,* esq. [1] formerly a planter in the parish of Hanover, in the island of Jamaica, and late of this parish, died Sept. 30, 1807, aged 63.

a tablet. *Donaldson, James,* late of the East India House, Feb. 6, 1787, 55.

h. *Dore, Moses,* 12 June, 1779, 69. Rebecca, his wife, 24 April, 1792, 90.

h. *Dorrington, Thomas,* of St. Andrew, Holborn, April 15, 1752.

h. *Dorrington, Matthew,* of St. Andrew, Holborn, bricklayer, Oct. 8, 1735, in 67th year.

*h. *Dorrington, James,* 30 Sept. 1806, 55.

h. and a. *Dowbiggen, Launcelot,* citizen and joyner, of London, July 24, 1759, aged 70. "Architect to this Church in the year 1754." Rebecca, wife to the son of the above, March 9, 1798, 72. Samuel, son of Launcelot, Nov. 19, 1809, 85.
*Dower.* See *Terrett.*

*h. *Drewitt, James,* Purser in the Royal Navy, died off Ushant of a fever, 12 March 1801, 45.

a. *Dring, Rebecca,* 1 June, 1782.

h. *Dring, Ann,* wife of John, of this parish, Nov. 16, 1767, in 37th year. John, of the Feathers tavern, Strand, June 15, 1783, 50. Frederick-John, his son, March 15, 1784, 20.
*Duddy.* See *Alexander.*

h. *Dungate, Mary,* daughter of Joseph and Rebecca, 2d May, 1766, 15. Joseph, gent. April 21, 1780, 54. Mary, wife of Joseph and grandmother to said Mary, Sept. 25, 1770, 75. Joseph, gent. April 21, 1780, 54.

h. *Dunsdon, Hannah,* daughter of John and Mary, maltster, of Tulbrock, near Burford, Oxfordshire, April 9, 1721, 23.

h. *Dupont, Sarah,* wife of Peter, of this parish, 3 Jan. 1751, in 65th year. Abraham, brother of Peter, Dec. 18, 1770, in 61st year.

**E.**

h. *Eaton,* 1754. John and Ann, son and daughter of Thomas and Elizabeth, of this parish. Said Elizabeth, 11 July, 1784, 67. Said Thomas, 16 Sept. 1794, 82.

h. *Eaton, Eliz.* wife of John, of this parish, Sept. 2, 1793, 29; and several children.

*a. r. *Eburne, Thomas,* esq. of this parish, 1 March, 1799, in 71st year, and in the third choir vault under the Church lies Susanna his daughter, 16 Dec. 1794, 19.

h. *Edwards, Rachael,* wife of William, of this

---

[1] This eccentric character, who lived in Cumberland-row, had his coffin made some time previous to his decease, and placed it in one of his rooms for a corner cupboard. He is said to have returned one upon the hands of the Undertaker, because it did not exactly please him with respect to size on his getting into it.

parish, 24 Oct. 1737, 59. Said William, 30 July, 1742, 65.

h. *Edwards, Maria,* wife of Francis, May 22, 1796, 55 ; and two children.

*h. *Eicke, Bonaventure,* May 15, 1799, 56.

h. *Elborough, Mary,* wife of Jacob, of this parish, 15 Jan. 1773, 29. Esther his wife, 16 May, 1793, 51. Said Jacob, 20 Aug. 1794, 52.

*h. *Elkin, John,* son of John and Barbara, of this parish, 17 Aug. 1805, 29. George-Elisha his brother, 8 Sept. 1806, 26. John their father, 15 Feb. 1807, 56.

*h. *Elkin, Charlotte,* daughter of John and Barbara, 21 Dec. 1807, 19.

h. *Ellis, Joseph,* 1 Aug. 1793, 58.

h. *Ellis, George,* of St. Clement Danes, pastry cook, Sept. 3, 1736, in 51st year.

*h. *Ellis, Catherine,* of this parish, daughter of Francis, late Deputy of Cornhill Ward, London, 11 Sept. 1807, 67.

*Ellis.* See *Weed.*

h. *Ellston, Mary,* 24 Feb. 1807, 92. John Ward 11 July, 1809, 54.

*h. *Engall, Mary,* 11 June 1804, 30.

*h. *Evans, Thomas,* son of Jeremiah, goldsmith, of Foster-lane, London, March 16, 1802, in 21st year.

h. *Evans, William,* of Bearbinder-lane, citizen, 4 July, 1805, 36.

## F.

*Farmer.* See *Jefferson.*
*Farr.* See *Campion.*
*Fawsett.* See *Lane.*

h. *Feary, Wm.* 16 April, 1779, 50.

a. *Fellowe, Thomas,* esq. 17 Feb. 1735, 53. Elizabeth his wife, 4 Oct. 1752, 52.

Arms: *A fesse crenelle between three lions heads crowned, erased. Impaling a chevron ingrailed Ermine, between six crosses paitee fitchy.*

h. *Fenning, Mary,* of this parish, widow, 25 April, 1780, 73.

h. *Ferrall, Russell,* of Watling-street, cork-cutter, 26 April, 1764, 52. Mary his wife, Nov. 14, 1767, 49.

s. r. *Field, Martha,* Feb. 17, 1806, 61.
*Field.* See *Spindle.*

*h. *Fifield, Robert,* of this parish, 24 Oct. 1794, 60. William his son, 13 March, 1799, in 28th year.

*h. *Finch, Priscilla-Ann,* wife of Thomas, of this parish, 31 March, 1802.

h. *Fisher, Elizabeth,* 26 May, 1776, 27.

h. *Fletcher, Ann,* wife of William, of Fleet-street, London, 28 May, 1749, 31.
*Fletcher.* See *Morris.*

s. *Floyd, John.*

h. *Fortescue, Francis,* Nov. 29, 1758, 58. Sarah, wife of John Vere, of Shoe-lane, Fleet-street, daughter of the aforesaid, Oct. 27, 1776, 30. Sarah, wife of said Francis, Jan. 15, 1780, 72.

*h. *Fossett,* three daughters of Joseph and Sarah, of this parish, died 20, 25, and 27 Nov. 1801; Eliz. aged 7 years 3 months; Louisa, 9 years 5 months; Maria, 3 years 9 months.

h. *Foster, John,* and two sons, died 1701. Elizabeth his wife, 1712. Deborah, wife of Thomas, son of the above, 1739. Said Thomas, Sept. 1763, in 68th year, and " clerk of this parish 28 years."

*h. *Francillon, Charlotte,* wife of ......, of this parish, 28 March, 1806, 36.

a. *Francis, Susanna,* Oct. 1, 1792, 52. Richard her husband, Aug. 19, 1808, 70.

h. *Freemantle, Jane,* 6 Dec. 1761, 39. Margaret, wife of Richard, citizen and goldsmith of London, 25 Oct. 1767, 40.

h. *Frost, Laurence,* citizen of London.

h. *Fryer, Anthony,* attorney at law, of the Middle Temple, June 16, 1784, in 79th year.
Who in his life-time he a pleasure took, Instructing youth from the most sacred book.

h. *Fullard, William,* 10 Nov. 1781, 42.

## G.

h. *Galloway, John,* of this parish, April 26, 1770, 48. Ann Swain his daughter, Nov. 6, 1779, 24. Mary his wife, April 20, 1783, 55. John his son, Jan. 31, 1787, 27. Jane, June 22, 1789, 27. Martha ..........

*h. *Gander, James,* of Hart-street, Bloomsbury, 21 June, 1809, 36.
*Gant.* See *Sterry.*
*Gardner.* See *Mucklow.*

*h. *Garnham, Robert,* of this parish, 2 Feb. 1799, 45.

s. *Gaskin, John,* citizen and leatherseller of London, 27 Oct. 1766, 56. Mabel Gaskin, 19 April, 1791, 84. The honoured parents of George Gaskin, D. D. lecturer of this parish.

h. *Gaskins, Wm.* Jan. 28, 1785, 69.

h. *Gawen, John,* late master of the workhouse

of this parish, which office he discharged
with credit to himself, tenderness to the
poor, and integrity to the parish, for the
space of 15 years; and, after a lingering
illness, departed this life Jan. 30, 1792,
58. Charlotte his widow, 28 July,
1794, 60.

*h. *Gee, Mary*, wife of Benjamin, of Kingsland Green, June 20, 1805, 75. Mary
their daughter, 10 March, 1806, 45.
Benjamin, 13 March, 1807, in 89th year.
Sarah, wife of William Taylor, of Ches-
hunt, Herts, daughter of said Benjamin
and Mary, 19 April, 1809, 45.

*George.* See *Hart.*

h. *Gibbons, Ann*, wife of Thomas, esq. of
Chad's row, Battle-bridge, July 13, 1772,
77. Said Thomas Gibbons, 20 Nov.
1779, 76.

    Livest thou, Thomas? Yes, with God
      on high.
Art thou not dead? Yes, and here I lye.
I that with man on earth did live to die,
Died for to live with Christ eternally.

    Also Mary, relict of Thomas Gibbons,
Esq. son of the above, Dec. 21, 1781, in
39th year.

h. *Gibson, William*, notary-public, of London,
Nov. 15, 1774, 62.

h. *Gibson, Sarah*, wife of William, of St. Andrew, Holborn, April 28, 1753, 28.

*Gibson.* See *Pickard.*

*h. *Giles, Ann*, wife of John, of this parish,
20 June, 1801, 64.

h. *Gill, Elizabeth*, of this parish, May 27,
1782, 73. Henry Harrup, Aug. 3, 1785,
35. Hester his wife, Aug. 12, 1788, 36.

h. *Gleeson, Thomas*, 20 March, 1809, 56.

h. *Glover, William*, July 15, 1758, 72. Elizabeth Davis his daughter, July 29, 1758,
40. Also Mary Martin his daughter, 44.
And Edward Martin, of this parish, victualler, Jan. 6, 1772, 66, and Elizabeth
his wife.

*h. *Goddard, Sarah*, wife of William, 27 Jan.
1801, 30.

*h. *Goddard, John*, of this parish, 23 Jan.
1795, 66.

*h. *Godfrey, Eliz.* wife of Rev. Richard, M. A.
formerly of Emmanuel College, Cambridge,
and vicar of Poslingford, Suffolk, born 16
Aug. 1730, died 13 Jan. 1805.

h. *Goff, Elias*, of St. Andrew, Holborn, Feb. 17,
1741, 56.

*h. *Goff, Thomas*, of this parish, citizen and
merchant taylor of London, 28 Nov.
1805, 67.

*h. *Golden, Robert*, architect, late of Red
Lion-street, Holborn, 28 Sept. 1809, 72.

*h. *Gallop, William-Nesbitt*, late of Exeter, 7
July, 1800, 34.

h. *Goodall, Daniel*, of this parish, June 25,
1777, 38. Ann his wife, 10 March, 1790,
44. Samuel his son, Nov. 4, 1777, aged
14 months 14 days.

    When the Archangel's trump shall blow
      And souls to bodies join,
    Thousands may wish their stay below
      Had been as short as mine.

h. *Goodall, Jane*, wife of William, late of
Fawey, in Cornwall, 15 Dec. 1781, 28.

s. r. *Gordon, John*, esq. lieut.-col. of his majesty's 50th reg. of foot, 10 June, 1782, 47.

*a. *Gordon, William*, of this parish, formerly
of Lad-lane, warehouseman, April 18,
1788, 70. John Gray, of this parish, 6
July, 1798, 40.

h. *Goslee, William*, 12 May, 1749, 63. Susanna his wife, 11 March, 1775, 86.
Thomas Parsons, son in law, 8 Feb.
1778, 60.

h. *Goslen, John*, of St. Martin, Ludgate, gent.
Jan. 2, 1784, 49.

*Gould.* See *Royds.*

h. *Grammar*, four children of Samuel and
Frances, of this parish. Said Frances,
23d April, 1801, 46. Joseph their son,
Feb. 9, 1802, 15. Said Samuel, 14 Mar.
1810, 60.

H. S. E.

a. *Grattan*,     *Johannes*,
           Hibernicus,
Et non ignotâ prosapiâ in comitatu Kidariensi
          Qui
  Ob egregiam indolis suavitatem
    mores mansuetissimos
        ac
  (quod jam nunc pluris est) ob
  integerrimam vitæ probitatem
    permultis adamatus,
      in hac regione,
    Fortunâ usque adversante,
annos plu-quam triginta commoratus est;
    atque ibidem denique,
      longè a suis,
  Filio unico in Indiâ Orientali militante,
    decessit XIV Septembris,
anno Salutis MDCCLXXXII, æt. suæ LX.
    Hæc pauca inscribens
Impar hocce amoris et reverentiæ testimonium
      rite posuit
      filius iste,
      eheu!
    mœstissimus.

Gray. See Gordon.

h. Green, Ann, wife of John, of this parish, July 30, 1785, 52. Said John, April 23, 1796, 67.

*a. Green, Joseph, of this parish, 18 Feb. 1802, in 60th year.

Green. See Nichols.

h. Greenhough, Mary, wife of Robert, of this parish, gent. Oct. 1761. Said Robert, 3 Oct. 1770, 48.

*h. Greenland, Mrs. Ann, 14 Aug. 1802, 70.

h. Greenop, Elizabeth, of this parish, Sept. 6, 1774, 40. Joseph her husband, of St. John's, Clerkenwell, Nov. 30, 1797, 63. Elizabeth-Amelia their daughter, June 12, 1798, 28.

*h. Greensill, Joseph, Esq. of this parish, 27 Aug. 1808, 67.

h. Griffes, Edward, of this parish, 7 May, 1777, 50. Mary his wife, 19 April, 1779, 54.

Arms : Sable, a chevron between three fleurs de lis Argent; impaling, Sable, a fess between six cross crosslets fitchy Argent.

h. Griegg, Mary, wife of Thomas, glass-engraver, 5 Nov. 1790, 36. J. Griegg, Apr. 20, 1796, 28.

h. Grimstead, Wm.-Hendrick, of this parish, Sept. 21, 1726.

h. Guest, James, 27 Oct. 1788, 45. Elizabeth his daughter, 25 Jan. 1809, 25.

# H.

*s. Haddock, Ann, late of Halifax, Yorkshire, 22 April, 1798, 33.

*a. r. Haist, Joseph, Esq. 28 July, 1807, in 64th year.

*h. Halfpenny, Anna-Catharina, formerly of Red Lion-street, Holborn, 22 Nov. 1798, in 45th year.

h. Hall, George, of Kingsland-green, 12 April, 1780, 53.

h. Ham, Ann, wife of James, bricklayer, of this parish, Nov. 18, 1793, 29.

*h. Hamley, Osbertus, of Clerkenwell, 21 July, 1795, 65. Susanna his wife, 28 Dec. 1796, 57.

h. Hance, Robert, of this parish, 11 July, 1807, 43. Ann his wife, 17 Sept. 1788, 40.

h. Handcock, Richard, of this parish, Oct. 4, 1791, 51.

h. Harding, John, of this parish, 27 Jan. 1802, 60.

*h. Hardwick, Temperance, 7 Oct. 1802, 78.

h. Harnett, Ann, 13 March, 1733, 45.
Behold the silent grave, it doth embrace
A virtuous wife, with Rachel's comely face;
Sarah's obedience, Lydia's open heart,
Martha's care, and Mary's better part.

h. Harris, Mrs. R.-E. of Pentonville, 10 Nov. 1809, 25.

h. Harrison, John, gent. of this parish, July 13, 1783, 62.

h. Harrison, Samuel, of St. Andrew, Holborn.

h. Harrison, John, 27 Nov. 1693, 54.

h. Harrison, Elizabeth, 9 Jan. 1771, 93. Also Mrs. Christian Walker, 2 Aug. 1776, 59.
We must, through much tribulation, enter into the kingdom of God.

Harrup. See Gill.

h. Hart, William, of St. James, Clerkenwell, tallow-chandler, citizen and bowyer of London, Dec. 16, 1737, in 45th year. Ann George his relict, 28 June, 1754, 56. William George, Nov. 12, 1758, 44.

*h. Hartop, Mary, wife of James, of this parish, June 22, 1798, in 39th year.

*h. Hartop, Samuel-Goodman, 18 June, 1807, in 49th year.

a. Hatley, Philip, of the parish of St. George the Martyr, March 25, 1744, in 60th year. Susanna, May 28, 1746, 25. Mary, wife of Philip, July 28, 1726, 45. Jane Pullen, of St. Andrew, Holborn, daughter of Philip and Mary Hatley, Dec. 2, 1742, 23. Philip, of the said parish, April 3, 1782, 62.

s. Hatton, Sarah, wife of Edward, of London, gent. Aug. 18, 1808, near 36.

*h. Harvey, Martha, of this parish, 24 Sept. 1751, in 56th year.

*h. Harvey, William, of Camden-street, in this parish, Feb. 25, 1803, 56.

Haughter. See Arnott.

h. Haughton, Jeffery, 19 May, 1785, in 75th year.

h. Hawes, Ann, wife of Edward, of this parish, daughter of Henry Laban, of Chatham, Kent, 10 Feb. 1689, 36.

*h. Hawes, William, M. D. 5 Dec. 1808, 72.

h. Hawes, Elizabeth, wife of Benjamin, of this parish, Aug. 9, 1783, 71. Said Benjamin, 4 July, 1789, in 80th year. James their nephew, 20 Jan. 1789, in 55th year. Mary his wife, 2 Feb. 1803, in 70th year.

*h. Hawkins, John, late of the Stock-exchange, 23 Sept. 1801, in 43d year.

s. Haygarth, James, of St. Pancras, 20 March, 1796, in 60th year. Jane his wife, 26 April, 1775, 29. Elizabeth Flude, mother to the above, 3 July, 1796, in 81st year. Sarah, second wife of said James, 7 Dec. 1800, 48.

*h. *Haylett, Alice,* wife of William, of Bouverie-street, Fleet-street, London, 29 March, 1806, 55. William, 26 Dec. 1807, 41.

*a. *Hayne, Susanna,* daughter of Lieut. Arthur Hayne, of His Majesty's Royal Navy, Dec. 26, 1798, 16. Jennett her sister, 6 April, 1801, 21.

h. *Haynes, John,* of this parish, collar-maker, and churchwarden in 1754, when this church was re-built, died May 30, 1756, 57. Elizabeth Chubb his daughter, Oct. 19, 1767, 24. Mary his wife, Jan. 20, 1787, 80.

h. *Healy, Michael,* May 1761, 37. Patrick, March 3, 1772, 52.

*h. *Henshall, Mary,* wife of William, 14 Aug. 1804, 34.

h. *Henwood, Daniel,* of this parish, 1 Dec. 1780, 67. Dorothy his wife, June 8, 1782, 61.

h. *Herd[1], John,* late of the Custom-house, gent. and many years an inhabitant of this parish, who was barbarously murdered by footpads, on Friday the 17th of May, 1782, aged 31.

*a. *Herrieres, Eliz.* wife of Isaac, of this parish, 27 March, 1773, 42.

*Hetherington, Helen,* daughter of John and Elizabeth, of Newington Green, 16 Feb. 1801, in her 19th year.

*h. *Hewitt, John,* 25 April, 1798, 28. Honnor his mother 27 May, 1799, 62.

a. *Hickman, Eliz.* wife of Edward, of this parish, 26 May, 1773, 51. Said Edward, 25

---

[1] This gentleman, who had lodgings at Canonbury-house, whither he generally repaired pretty early of an evening, had been detained in town on the above fatal day till about 11 o'clock, in settling some matters relative to the marriage of his niece, which was to have taken place the next day, with a Captain Best, of the 92d regiment, who, with two servants, was accompanying him to Islington. In the foot-path between the Shepherd and Shepherdess and the Prebend-field, not many yards from the porter's resting-block, they were attacked by four footpads. Mr. Herd, who was a very stout man, six feet high, and who had been often heard to declare that he would never submit to be robbed, offered some resistance; when one of the villains discharging a blunderbuss, blew off the fore part of his head; one of the servants, who was armed with a pistol, which he attempted to fire at the thieves, received a wound on the arm with a cutlass, Captain Best and the other escaped unhurt. Gray, a notorious ruffian, who perpetrated the above horrid murder, was not long after taken, and executed, as was also Stunell, and several others of this desperate gang. — The following tribute to the memory of Mr. Herd (intended to have been inscribed on his monument) was written by his friend Mr. William Woodfall, the celebrated Reporter of the Parliamentary Debates, who at that time also resided in Islington:

"Stop! youthful passenger!
and read, with steady attention, the following lines:
Here rests, from the cares, the toils, and follies of human nature,
the remains of
*John Herd.*
He once (perhaps like thee) was engaged in a multiplicity of pursuits
after fame, honours, wealth, and pleasures; but was suddenly
arrested in the midst of his career, in the bloom of life,
and plunged into eternity, by four villains, in the fields leading
from the Shepherd and Shepherdess to Islington, as he was endeavouring
to prevent being robbed, on Tuesday the 17th of May, 1782.
He was a cheerful companion, and a sincere friend;
His frailties (few) rest upon the bosom of his God.
His virtues make his memory revered amongst his numerous acquaintance.
His life was amiable, his death lamented.
This inscription was by a friend engraven upon his tomb, as a lasting testimony of friendship,
and for a memento to his youthful companions, and others whom chance may lead to visit
this shrine, not to go unprepared for their final dissolution, which may be as sudden and dreadful as his.

Drop, youthful passenger, the friendly tear
Of sympathy, of soft compassion here.
And since not youth, in all its blooming pride,
Death's fatal stroke can alter or avoid;
Learn so to spend thy short uncertain day,
That thou canst brave his pow'r, and take his sting away."

Dec. 1777, 77. George, grandson, 28 Dec. 1796, 22. George, son, 20 Nov. 1801, 48.

*h. *Hickman, Sarah*, late of St. Mary-le-bone, 21 Feb. 1809, 73.

*Higgs.* See *Tawlks*.

*Hill.* See *Prince.*

*h. *Hincheliff, Mary*, wife of James, of this parish, 15 June, 1807, 31.

*a. *Hoby, Lucy*, wife of James, of Colebrooke-row, July 8, 1806, 46.

h. *Hogarth, Frances*, wife of Andrew, March 4, 1775, 40.

*Holmes.* See *Whitworth* and *Meekes*.

h. *Hood, James*, 13 March, 1792, 44.

*h. *Hooper, William*, of Doctors Commons, London, 24 Feb. 1805, 55.

*h. *Horth, Fanny*, second daughter of John and Ann, late of Norwich, 26 July, 1808, 14.

a. *Hose, John*, 24 March, 1769, 70. Elizabeth his wife, 22 Nov. 1738, 36. Anthony Woolley, 5 Nov. 1773, 40. John-William his son, 15 Oct. 1786, 24. Thomas, son of John Hose, 29 Dec. 1787, 53.

h. *How, Alice*, wife of Benjamin, 26 Nov. 1778, 57. Ann Slade their daughter, 12 Jan. 1784, 32. Samuel their son, Oct. 26, 1788, 31.

*h. *How, Benjamin*, jun. of this parish, Jan. 10, 1795, 44. John, Nov. 16, 1796, 37. Benjamin their father, July 27, 1801, in 79th year. Hannah, wife of Jeremiah, Aug. 11, 1807, 50.

*h. *How, Margaret*, 22 April, 1798, 85.

*h. *Howard, Susannah*, 27 July, 1803, 77. Thomas, her husband, 23 April, 1808, 80.

h. *Howes, Samuel Barnardiston*, of Newington Butts, 6 June, 1806, in 45th year.

h. *Hughes, Robert*, June 5, 1774, 68.

h. *Humphreys, Sarah*, April 17, 1778, 33.

*h. *Humphreys, James D. G.* late of Powick, in Worcestershire, 31 Aug. 1800, 24.

*h. *Humphrey, Hester*, late of Tetbury, Gloucestershire, late of this parish, 28 Jan. 1802, 40.

*h. *Humphreys, Catharine*, wife of Thomas, of Princes-square, St. George's in the East, March 29, 1801, 25. Thomas, Sept. 1, 1804, 34.

a. r. *Humphries, Valentine*, of Smyrna, 23d April, 1786.

h. *Hunter, Elizabeth*, wife of Thomas, Sept. 22, 1808, 54. Lydia, of this parish, 12 Feb. 1762, 39. Robert, March 18, 1789, 67.

h. *Hurley, Mary*, wife of Henry, of this parish, 4 April, 1743, 74. Henry, 30 Oct. 1754, 77. Elizabeth Rogers, granddaughter, 4 May, 1809, 68.

h. *Husday, Isaac*, Dec. 25, 1728, 60.

*Hussey.* See *Nicholls.*

h. *Hutchason, Richard*, citizen and clockmaker, London, May 9, 1747.

s. *Hutchinson, Mary*, widow of John, esq. of Beckenham, Kent, 24 Sept. . . . . aged 67.

## I.

h. *Jarvis, Sarah*, wife of Edward, citizen and baker, of London, Feb. 9, 1749.

h. *Jarvis, James*, citizen and blacksmith, 18 May, 1763, 59. Susannah, his wife, Feb. 28, 1762, 50.

h. *Jarvis, Stephen*, citizen and blacksmith, of London, 9 Oct. 1742, 76. Elizabeth, his wife, Dec. 24, 1742, 72. Judith, wife of George Kier, of Bridge-street, Westminster, 5 March 1783, in 32d year.

h. *Jarvis, David*, citizen of London, May 26, 1777, 42.

h. *Jarvis, Ann*, relict of David, of Fetter-lane, London, 23 June, 1792, 49.

h. *Jeays, Jane*, wife of Thomas, Aug. 17, 1777, 31.

s. *Jefferson, James*, (of Witney, co. Oxon) clothier, 12 May, 1730, 33. Elizabeth-Farmer, his relict, 20 Jan. 1772, in 66th year. James Jefferson, late of Chancery-lane, London, attorney, and deputy clerk of the peace for Middlesex and Westminster, and Treasurer of the said county, son of the above, Dec. 28, 1772, 45. Ann his relict, 11 Feb. 1775, 39.

h. *Jennings, John*, gent. of the General Post Office, London, July 23, 1767, in 22d year. Ann, late of Budge-row, widow, Oct. 2, 1777, 58.

h. *Jennings, John*, citizen and broiderer of London, 10 March 1761, 68. Mary his widow, 12 June, 1774, in 79th year.

h. *Inglish, Jane*, wife of James, 30 Sept. 1774.

h. *Ingram, John*, of Saffron-hill, St. Andrew, Holborn, July 1735. Mary, wife of John, jun. Aug. 6, 1741, 26.

h. *Ingram, Hubert*, 2 Oct. 1737, 42. Ann his daughter, 22 July, 1765, 32.

s. *Johnson, Amy*, a good and virtuous woman, 28 Dec. 1764. Mary-Barber Bigelston, wife of William, of St. Ann, Westminster, 5 April, 1801, 28.

h. *Johnson, Eliz.* April 10, 1757, 84. Martha White, Sept. 20, 1761, 48. Katherine Johnson, June 21, 1763, 63. Elizabeth Thomas, Oct. 9, 1791, 46.

*h. *Johnson, Sarah,* formerly of Derby, 8 May, 1796, 53.

*h. *Johnson, Amy,* wife of John, of this parish, Nov. 9, 1798, 49.

*h. *Johnson, George,* Aug. 7, 1801, 60.

*a. *I'on, George,* esq. of this parish, March 31, 1795, 80. Frances his wife, Oct. 3, 1795, 81. Hannah Cummins, of this parish, 5 Nov. 1800, 52.

h. *Jones, Robert,* of St. Bride's parish, 14th March, 1775, 41. Hannah his wife, Dec. 1, 1787, 51.

h. *Jones, Samuel,* of the city of Hereford, late of Islington, traveller, born 12 Aug. 1727; died 27 Aug. 1795.

h. *Jones, Robert,* 11 June, 1772, 33. Thomas his brother, Oct. 18, 1777, 42. Jane, wife of Thomas, 3 Aug. 1795, 75.

h. *Jones, Samuel,* brother of Robert and Thomas, Sept. 14, 1779, 33. John, Aug. 31, 1780, 41. Thomas, Aug. 12, 1780, 39. Hugh, brother of the above.

*h. *Jones, Samuel,* 23 May, 1810, 28.

*h. *Jones, Richard,* of this parish, 13 Dec. 1810, 68.

*h. *Jones, Elizabeth,* wife of John, of Newcastle-court, Temple-bar, 1 Jan. 1802, in 33d year.

a. r. *Irish, Mary,* wife of John, of Kingsland, in this parish, 22 Oct. 1766, 49. Said John, late of Chipping Ongar, Essex, 9 Aug. 1776, in 83d year.

h. *Ives, Anna-Maria,* 8 Nov. 1795, 19.
> Who are thou art it matters not:
> One question to you as your stopp'd.
> Ask thyself,
> Is it thus, O my soul, and is it true
> That thou art mortal and immortal too?
> Must this proud flesh, to worms a banquet give,
> And must my soul, through endless ages live?

Also *John Ives,* 2 Jan. 1802, 67.

### K.

h. *Kay, John,* of Gray's-inn, gent. 18 Aug 1779, 60.
> If for the poor to take a friendly part,
> To guard th' oppressed from th' oppressors art,
> The laws to practise in a mode direct,
> To shew true justice, and ill acts detect,
> Can to the good, departed worth endear,
> Here drop the kindest tributary tear.

Also *Mary,* wife of Thomas Manley, of Wood-street, London, 27 Nov. 1782, 52.

s. *Keen, Stephen,* ob. 1712.

*h. *Keene, Margaret,* 9 April, 1809, 55.

*Kendal.* See *Watkinson.*

h. *Kershaw, Charles,* 2 Nov. 1786, in 67th year. Eliz. his wife, 21 April 1787, 71.

*h. *Kershaw, Edmund,* of Newington-green, 9 June, 1808, 67.

*h. *Kestin, Edward,* Oct. 15, 1803, 37. Also Betty, wife of Thomas Williams, and formerly wife of the above, 29 Sept. 1808, 26.

*Kier.* See *Jarvis.*

h. *Knight, Thomas,* victualler, Aug. 30, 1769, 62. John Rockett, victualler, Oct. 29, 1775, 45. Ann his wife, of St. James's, Westminster, formerly wife of said Thomas Knight, Jan. 22d, 1786, 70.

h. *Knowles, Ann,* of this parish, 4 Feb. 1789, 83. Sarah her sister, 17 Oct. 1802, 85.

### L.

*h. *Laing, Catharine,* 22 March, 1803, 70.

*Lammas.* See *Porter.*

h. *Lander, Hannah,* wife of Samuel of St. George, Hanover-square, April 26, 1746, 42. John Martin, May 27, 1762, 72. Also Jane Wilkin, a true believer of the third record, who knew that Christ is the eternal God, Dec. 13, 1792, 82, in full assurance of a joyful resurrection.

h. *Lane, Mary,* wife of James, of this parish, 17 Dec. 1759, in 28th year. Mary, wife of James Willes, their daughter, 4 July, 1776, in 20th year. Ann Scofield, mother of said Mary Lane, aged 97.

h. *Lane, James,* of Canonbury House, 17 Mar. 1783, 67. Sarah Schofield his sister, 17 Aug. 1800, 68.

h. *Lane, James,* sen. 7 Dec. 1722, 74. Jane Fawsett his daughter, 1 Feb. 1722-3, 38. John his son, 22 Feb. 1769, 77.

*Lanfear.* See *Stanfield.*

h. *Langhorn, Joseph,* clerk in the General Post Office, Dec. 25, 1768, 48.

*h. *Laroche, Eliz.* wife of Michael, 1 Nov. 1799, 37.

h. *Laycock, Charles,* Oct. 20, 1779, in 37th year. Charles his father, Oct. 29, 1779, 63. Mary his wife, March 21, 1790, 81.

a. r. *Laycock, Charles,* of Stratford, co. Essex, 10 March, 1807, 43. Mrs. Christian Mayor, 23 Sept. 1807, 46. Daniel Sebbon, 31 May, 1810, aged 83.

s. *Lea, Rebecca,* wife of William, esq. of this parish, 27 April 1777, in 55 year. Said William, 5 Jan. 1789, 70.
> Arms: *a chevron between three lions faces, impaling, Ermine, an eagle displayed.*

*h. *Leavey, Jane,* 17 Feb. 1800, 68.

h. *Lee, John,* late of Cross-street, in this parish, Sept. 13, 1783, in 37th year. Mrs. Mary Wheeler, June 27, 1795, 80.

h. *Lee, Leonard,* of St. Giles's in the Fields, salesman, April 7, 1762, 55.

*a. *Lee, Richard,* esq. of this parish, 3 Mar. 1799, 81.

h. *Leeo, Timothy,* Oct. 6, 1787, 42. Margaret, wife of John, June 1, 1792, 57. John, 28th March, 1801, 49.

h. *Leeson, Daniel,* esq. of Burton upon Trent, late of Gray's Inn, 7 Feb. 1808, 59. William, of Staples Inn, Esq. his brother, 26 Dec. 1809, 54.

*h. *Leicester,* Rev. *Francis,* 27 Nov. 1800, 66. Mary, (spinster) Feb. 9, 1805, 68. Jeremy Thomas Leicester, esq. March 25, 1809, 68.

*Lens.* See *Millington.*

*Lever.* See *Pankhurst.*

h. *Lewin, Thomas,* son of John and Ann, of St. Andrew, Holborn, May 11, 1688, aged 10 years and two months.

h. *Lewis, Samuel,* 5 Feb. 1787, 71. Samuel his son, 19 Jan. 1790, 19. Mary his wife, 10 Feb. 1803, 63.

*h. *Lewis, Edward,* 21 June, 1806, 34.

h. *Liford, John,* 22 April, 1755, 52.

*a. *Lightfoot, Samuel,* merchant, 8 April, 1798, 38.

s. *Lindsay, Eliz.* wife of Alexander, of St. Clement Danes, May 9, 1782, 42. Said Alexander, July 9, 1808, 71.

s. *Lindsay, Maria.* " Hic requiescit in Domino Maria uxor Johannis Lindsay, ecclesiæ Anglicanæ Presbyteri, de quâ nil dicere non fas est, satis non tutum. Vi'n' verbo dicam? In illa omnis enituit quæ fœminam optimam ornaret virtus, cujus ad exemplum si vixeris, Amice Lector, mori non est quod timeas. Vale. Obiit in festo Omnium Animarum, A. D. MDCCXXVII. ætat. suæ 43."

h. *Lindsay, John.* " Hic etiam restant exuviæ reverendi Johannis Lindsay, Aulæ Mariæ apud Oxonienses olim alumni; qui ecclesiæ Anglicanæ exinde minister (beneficiis ejus opulentis licet interiori stimulo recusatis) animo in adversis æquo magnoque, sincerâ fide, nudâque veritate, honos posteris effulsit. Eruditione insuper eximius, vitæ integer propositique tenax, spectatâ pietate insignis, moresque præcipuè ingenuus vixit. Cursu tandem benè peracto fortiter diuque pro fide certando emeritus, obdormientis more, benedicens, obiit Jun.

28. A. D. 1768, ætat. 82. *En virtus! en prisca fides!*"

h. *Lingart, Eliz.* daughter of David and Jane, April 18, 1723, 20.

*Little.* See *Bewes.*

h. *Lloyd, Joseph,* farrier, 2 July, 1796, 60.

h. *Lloyd,* Mrs. *Christian,* wife of Benjamin, of Chancery-lane, attorney, 6 Jan. 1783, 32.

*a. r. *Lloyd, Sarah,* daughter of Robert and Sarah, 30 April, 1799, in 27th year.

*a. *Lloyd, Sophia,* wife of John, of the East India House, 14 Jan. 1801, in 33d year.

*h. *Lloyd, Mary,* wife of Rev. John, rector of Tothill, Lincolnshire, 22 Sept. 1802, 64. Said Rev. John, 17th Feb. 1810, 74.

h. *Looker, Anna,* wife of Thomas, of St. Bride's, watchmaker, Sept. 18, 1737, 36.

*h. *Lovie, Wm.* jeweller, 3 Oct. 1808, 22.

h. *Ludgate, Susannah,* Nov. 11, 1785, 75. Thomas, of this parish, 29 June, 1791, 74.

h. *Lyndahl, Ann,* May 17, 1789, 75. Mary Rant, 8 July, 1790, 74.

Be ye also ready. Matt. xxiv. v. 44.

h. *Lyng, Benjamin,* 4 Nov. 1767, 54.

h. *Lyon, Sarah,* April 16, 1808, 72. Benjamin her husband, June 30, 1808, 75.

## M.

h. *Maccascree, Nathaniel,* of St. Botolph Aldersgate, distiller, 19 Aug. 1753, 44.

*a. r. *M'Call, John,* esq. late of Jamaica (and four sons of George M'Call, esq. of the City of Glasgow, North Britain) 18 May, 1808, 34.

h. *Macdonald, Ann,* of this parish, 20 Dec. 1765, 44. Catherine, July 31, 1776, 24. Lydia Clarke, 28 Feb. 1794, 31.

h. *Macdonald, Sarah,* of this parish, 19 July, 1783, 28. Thomas, 5 Dec. 1783, 23. Donald their father, 25 Sept. 1793, 73.

*h. *Mac Intosh, Wm.* of this parish, 16 Nov. 1795, 54.

*h. *Major, John,* 22 Aug. 1799, 41.

h. *Malkin, Thomas,* 24 March, 1803, 65.

*Manley.* See *Kay.*

h. *Mansel, Ann,* March 1, 1779, 30. Jane, wife of Richard South, of this parish, 9 Feb. 1795, in 33d year.

h. *Markland, George,* of St. George, Hanover-square, 18 Nov. 1747, in 89th year.

h. *Marshall, John,* of this parish, Nov. 19, 1787, 52.

a. *Martin, Mary,* 10 Sept. 1792, 64.

*Martin.* See *Glover* and *Lander.*

*h. *Matthews, Mary,* wife of William, of this parish, April 21, 1788, 50. Said William, July 18, 1808, 73. Mary, his second wife, Oct. 23, 1808, 57.

a. *Mauger, Peter,* of the island of Jersey, and since of Abchurch-lane, London, died at Islington, 14 June, 1764, in 49th year.

s. *Maxey, Martha,* wife of Joseph, of London, merchant, 11 Sept. 1732, 48.

"H. S. E.

" Josephus Maxey, ex honestâ familiâ in agro Nordovicensi ortus, ingenuisque artibus instructus, ad Hispaniensem Mercaturam se transtulit ; negotiator sine dolo probus ; filius parentum observantissimus ; maritus charissimæ conjugis amantissimus ; erga amicos suavitate, erga omnes benevolentiâ paucos invenies pares ; erga Deum verò tum piâ humilitate, tum purâ religione, vix ullum superiorem. Obiit 21 Dec$^{is}$ die, An° Sal. 1742, ætat. 80."

*h. *May, Hannah,* 28 Aug. 1801, 4 years 5 months.

*Mayor.* See *Laycock.*

h. *Meekes, Thomas,* of this parish, plaisterer and citizen of London, 21 Aug. 1759, 55. Eliz. wife of Robert Holmes, of this parish, March 5, 1776 ; and Ann their daughter ; also Robert Holmes, 18 July, 1793, 61. Ann his widow, 26 Nov. 1808, 62.

a. *Mellor, Wm.* 16 Dec. 1763, 53.

*h. *Mence, Wm.* of this parish, 16 March, 1809, 74.

*h. *Mendham, Eliz.* 8 May, 1810, 66.

Arms: *Argent on a canton Sable, a fleur de lis of the field, impaling, Sable, a lion rampant langued Argent.*

*h. *Metcalf, George,* 12 Oct. 1799, 50. Harrietta his daughter, 2 July, 1805, in 17th year.

h. *Middlebrook, John,* May 19th, 1786, 45. William, 8 April, 1793, 45.

h. *Middleton, Henry,* June 17, 1755, 38. Bridget his wife, June 19, 1762, 70.

h. *Millard, Ann,* wife of George, plumber, of Berwick-street, St. James's, 23 June, 1780, 35.

*h. *Miller, Ann,* Sept. 7, 1805, 33.

h. *Millington, Thomas,* of St. Luke's, jeweller, March 6, 1756, 58. William his son, Aug. 22, 1760, 36. Thomas his son, of Gutter-lane, jeweller, 14 Feb. 1772, 49. William Lens, 30 Nov. 1801, 44.

h. *Mills, Benjamin,* of St. Andrew, Holborn, 12 Jan. 1745, 70, and Jane his wife.

*Minton.* See *Palmer.*

h. *Mirfield, Joshua,* 21 June, 1760, 53. Mary, 30 Sept. 1762, 19 ; and Esther.

h. *Mizen, Mary,* wife of Robert, of this parish, 17 March 1800, in 34th year.

*h. *Moorhouse, Evan,* of this parish, 19 Oct. 1810, 30.

s. *Mordaunt, Sir John,* late of Tangier, Knt. Banneret, 12 Sept. 1723, 86.

h. *Morel, Lewis,* 31 Oct. 1761, 57. Dorothy his wife, 5 Dec. 1761, 58.

h. *Morgan, Thomas,* 16 Aug. 1793, 45.

*h. *Morgan, Wm.* late of this parish, chemist and druggist, 10 July, 1800, 47.

s. *Morris, Henry,* of St. Clement Danes, Sept. 17, 1724, 70. Ann his wife, Feb. 1714, 54. George Barwell, July 24, 1748, 59. John Summers, 25 June 1772, 45. Hannah Fletcher, 9 June, 1782, 53. Edmund her husband, 12 Oct. 1801, 75.

*h. *Morris, Edward,* gent. 20 Jan. 1807, in 59th year.

*h. *Morris, Charles,* of St. Martin's in the Fields, 23 Nov. 1808, 40.

*Morrison.* See *Munday.*

h. *Morton, Eliz.* of St. James, Westminster, 5 March 1757, 20. Sarah, of St. Martin's in the Fields, Feb. 28, 1760, 60.

*a. *Morton, Sarah,* relict of John Burridge, of Leadenhall-street, 14 May, 1795, 77.

h. *Mousley, John,* of St. James, Clerkenwell, 7 Dec. 1766, 68. Jane, 9 Jan. 1777, 42. John, jun. her husband, 28 Jan. 1777, 46. Elizabeth, Oct. 18, 1780, 81.

*h. *Moxon, Francis,* Oct. 25, 1801, in 75th year.

Be not slothful, but followers of those who through faith and patience inherit the promise.

a tablet. *Mucklow, William,* esq. March 25, 1788, 59. Mary his wife, 19 March 1806, 85. Henry-Lasher Gardner, esq. their son-in-law, 29 Feb. 1808, 64. Susannah Mucklow, sister of William, 19 Jan. 1809, 73.

+
I H S

h. *Mulvey, Hugh,* Oct. 24, 1797, 48.

Requiescat in pace.

Garrett his brother, 13 Feb. 1808, 54.

*h. *Munday, Thomas,* gent. Feb. 19, 1802, 87. Mary Morrison his niece, 17 Dec. 1807, 74.

a. *Munn, John,* Feb. 6, 1791, 71. Jane, May 26, 1793, 21. Elizabeth, wife of John, 23 Dec. 1799, 74. Mary, 28 Jan. 1802, 40.

h. *Musson, Francis,* of Grantham, Lincolnshire, 20 March 1748, 42.

## N.

h. *Nash, Winifred,* Jan. 9, 1751, 62. Winifred Yardley her daughter.

h. *Naylor, James,* citizen and plumber, of Shoe-lane, 18 March, 1786, in 37th year.

*a. *Neave, David,* 19 April 1807, 67.
"He was a good husband, an affectionate father, and a sincere Christian."

h. *Needham, George,* of Wood-street, London, 20 Oct. 1787, 63.

*a. *Needham, Isaac,* esq. receiver of fines and forfeitures of His Majesty's Customs, born April 10, 1733, died Sept. 16, 1808.

h. *Newbank, Thomas,* Oct. 24, 1787, 56. Edward, Sept. 2, 1788, 50. Elizabeth his wife, Oct. 24, 1795, in 55th year.

s. *Newby, Mary,* wife of Richard, of this parish, 13 Feb. 1763, in 34th year. Ann, 15 Feb. 1796, in 39th year. Richard her husband, 27 Feb. 1801, in 79th year.

a. *Newman, Wm.* Alderman of the City of London, 12 Dec. 1802, 77. Grace his wife, 11 May 1781, 54. Sarah, 27 Sept. 1769, 15. Mary Budgen, 2 April, 1774, 25; their daughters; and 4 grandchildren.
*Newman.* See *Porter.*

h. *Newton, Peter,* March 31, 1764, 40. Peter his father, Dec. 22, 1773, 72. Miss Coleman grand-daughter, Oct 1, 1782, 21.

h. *Nicholl, Ann,* wife of Thomas, of Knightrider-street, March 27, 1773, 49.

h. *Nicholls, Edward,* of this parish, 18 Dec. 1765, in 48th year. Ann Hussey his widow, 14 Feb. 1789, 63.

h. *Nichols, Isabella,* March 31, 1749, 66. Edward Nichols [her son,] of this parish, baker, Jan. 29, 1779, 60. Ann his relict, Dec. 27, 1783, 64. Nicholas-Read Nichols [their youngest son,] Sept. 23, 1778, 26. Ann, wife of John Nichols, esq. of St. Bride's, Feb. 18, 1776, 36. William Bowyer, her only son, April 6, 1776, 1 year and 5 days.

h. *Nichols, Martha,* second wife of John Nichols, 29 Feb. 1788, in 33d year. Thomas Cleiveland, her second son, April 2d, 1782, 10 months. Charles Howard, her third son, Nov. 13, 1786, 10 months. Charles Green, of Hinckley, brother to Martha Nichols, March 16, 1785, 27. See also *Cradock* and *Read.*

s. r. *Nockells, Wm.* citizen and bowyer of London, April 29, 1727, in 70th year. Elizabeth Plees, daughter, 6 Aug. 1728, 45.
*Norbury.* See *Phillips.*

s. *Norman, I.* born 1688, died July 10, 1739.
This modest stone, what few vain marbles can,
May truly say, here lies an honest man. A. Pope.

h. *Norman, Ann,* wife of Edward, of this parish, 14 Aug. 1790, 60. Said Edward, 22 Dec. 1802, 61.

s. *Norman, Wm.* of this parish, yeoman, and Christian his wife, and Christian, late wife of William Strode, of this parish, gent. their only daughter, 17 Nov. 1698.

## O.

a. *Oddy, Anne,* "Sub hoc marmore jacet quod mortale fuit Annæ Oddy (nuper uxoris Philippi Oddy hujus parochiæ generosi) quæ 30 Martij 1732, anno ætatis suæ 61, & connubij quadragesimo, spiritum Deo resignavit, corpus sepulchro reliquit, in Christo dormiens, cui fide, spe, et charitate constantissime vixit.
In memoriam virtutis et amoris ipsius charissimæ uxoris hoc monumentum posuit dolens maritus, P. O.
Ad te quacunque vocas, dulcissime Jesu."
O.
P. A.
Here also lies the last remains of Philip Oddy, Gent. died Jan. 14, 1738, in his 87th year.

*h. *Odell, Samuel,* of this parish, 17 Oct. 1808, 53.

h. *Oldershaw, Sarah,* daughter of Thomas and Sarah, April 1, 1780, 21. Sarah her mother, 9 April, 1781, 44.

*h. *Oliver, Mrs. B.* late of Derby, 9 Nov. 1799, 29. John her husband, 10 April, 1806, 38.

h. *Orange, Wm.* of this parish, victualler, 17 Oct. 1764, in 33d year.

h. *Ord, Thomas,* of Newington-green, gent. June 10, 1770, in 81st year.
*Orton.* See *Simpson.*

*h. *Oxley, Thomas,* of Hellingley, co. Suffolk, late gardener to Dr. Saunders of Highbury, 19 Oct. 1797, 29.

## P.

h. *Page, John,* of East Norton, co. Leicester, Nov. 9, 1758, 26. Thomas Rowe, of this parish, 14 Aug. 1763, 36.

*a. r. *Page, Elizabeth,* 28 Jan. 1808, 49.

h. *Paine, Mary,* 23 Jan. 1792, in 77th year. Elizabeth Page her daughter, 28 Jan. 1801, 58.

h. *Palmer, Benjamin,* 5 March, 1784, 19. Mary, wife of Arthur Minton, of St. George, Hanover-square, 21 Jan. 1794, 30.

*h. *Palmer, Martha,* of this parish, 10 Aug. 1800, 52.

*h. *Palmer, Hannah,* daughter of Thomas and Dorothy, of this parish, 21 July, 1797, 22. Thomas, 13 April, 1800, 70. Dorothy his wife, 22 Jan. 1804, 70.

h. *Pamplyn, Rebecca,* wife of Wm. of this parish, 11 June, 1763, 62. Said William, Nov. 20, 1764, 52.

h. *Pankhurst, Thomas,* Aug. 15, 1805, 40. Houghton Lever, July 14, 1808, 27.

h. *Park, Elizabeth,* Jan. 1754. William her husband, of this parish, 8 April, 1760, in 60th year.

h. *Parker, Rebecca,* wife of Francis, of this parish, 25 Nov. 1779, 41. Said Francis, Dec. 13, 1782, 48.

h. *Parker, Robert,* jun. 15 Dec. 1736, in 23d year.

Requiescat in pace. Amen.

h. *Parker, Ann,* wife of Robert, 10 April, 1738, in 46th year.

Requiescat in pace. Amen.

*a. r. *Parry, Eliz.* wife of Roger, of Colebrooke-row, 9 Feb. 1798, 46. Thomas, late of Dulass, Herefordshire, 1 July, 1800, 24. Martha, 27 Nov. 1802, 11.

h. *Parsons, Eleanor,* of St. Andrew, Holborn, 26 April, 1747, 52. Ann Payne, spinster, of same place, 14 Oct. 1749, 50. Mary Burch of same place, 28 Sept. 1757, 72. Thomas Burch, bachelor, her son, Aug. 30, 1779, in 54th year.

*Parsons.* See *Goslee.*

h. *Patterick, John,* of St. Giles in the Fields, 16 July, 1767, 57.

a. *Paty, John,* bricklayer, of St. Botolph, Bishopsgate, citizen of London, Dec. 3, 1789, in 51st year. Rosamond his widow, 8 June, 1808, 66.

*Payne.* See *Parsons.*

*h. *Pear,* John, of this parish, Aug. 21, 1808, 50.

h. *Pearson, Henry,* citizen and vintner of London, and of the parish of St. Sepulchre, 30 Sept. 1746, in 46th year.

*Peart.* See *Taylor.*

h. *Peill, Leonard,* 13 Nov. 1763, 33.

*h. *Pemberton, Thomas,* 30 Sept. 1794, 62.

*h. *Penn, Wm.* son of John and Elizabeth, April 11, 1800, in 24th year. Said John, 9 Oct. 1806, 71.

*h. *Penny, Theodosia,* wife of Thomas, 17 March, 1798, 78. Said Thomas, 29 Aug. 1805, 74.

*h. *Percival, William-James,* son of Richard and Margaret, of this parish, 16 July, 1809, 15.

h. *Perkins, Mary,* 2 Feb. 1809, 62.

*h. *Perry, Thomas,* 13 Feb. 1800, 33. John Reay, late of the parish of Hackney, Nov. 14, 1800, 34.

*Perry.* See *Stone.*

*h. *Phillips, Frances,* wife of Job, of the Inner Temple and Upper Holloway, esq. sister to Sir Edward Berry, of Catton, co. Norfolk, bart. 21 Dec. 1810, 37.

s. *Phillips, Catherine,* Dec. 11, 1770. Mary, Oct. 8, 1771. Coningsbury Norbury, esq. aged 72.

h. *Pickard, Joseph,* of St. Botolph, Aldgate, Nov. 16, 1785, 42. Sarah Gibson, formerly his wife, Feb. 19, 1790, 41.

h. *Pickersgill, Catherine,* 20 May, 1748, 73.

*a. *Pickford, Elizabeth,* 14 July, 1806, 88.— Catherine, her granddaughter, 7 March, 1808, 24.

*s. *Piercy, Capt. John Wintersgill,* late of the Hon. East India Company's service, 31 Jan. 1802, 39.

h. *Pigott, Christopher,* 14 May 1735, 62.

*h. *Playfair, Thomas,* 14 Feb. 1809, 67. George, 15 March, 1810, in 32d year.

*Plees.* See *Nockells.*

h. *Poe, Peter,* 8 March, 1793, 77. Rebecca, his wife, both of this parish, 18 Sept. 1805, in 86th year. Rebecca Watts, their daughter, 14 Feb. 1806, 62.

h. *Poole, William,* of St. Mary-le-bow, 2 Jan. 1795, 70. William, his son, 18 Feb. 1788, 31. Martha, Aug. 6, 1802, 35.

h. *Poole, Sarah,* of Islington, Dec. 5, 1741, in 80th year. Dr. Robert Poole, who, with indefatigable labour, instituted the Small Pox Hospital in the year 1746, 30 May 1752, 43.

*h. *Poole, Thomas,* esq. of Highgate, April 26, 1795, 60.

h. *Pooley, Mary,* of this parish, 20 Sept. 1794, 60.

h. *Porter, Ann,* wife of Richard, of this parish, 1 Oct. 1791, 37.

h. *Porter, Hannah,* daughter of Robert Newman, and wife of Wm. Porter, citizen and embroiderer of London, Sept. 8, 1732, 34. Robert Newman, citizen and merchant taylor of London, June 10, 1736, 76. Elizabeth, his daughter, wife of John Allen, citizen and founder of London, 27 Mar. 1743, 44. Martha Lammas, his daughter, Feb. 13, 1743, 51.

a. *Poulter, Ann,* wife of Edward, of St. Andrew, Holborn, gent. 26 March, 1718, 65. Mary, wife of Edward, jun. 11 Oct. 1714, 34. Elizabeth, wife of Thomas,

1735. Edward, sen. gent. May 11, 1727, 73. John, son of Thomas, also George, son of Thomas, Aug. 2, 1744, 29.

h. *Powell, Richard*, Feb. 6, 1773, 40. Elizabeth Brock, his relict, Nov. 4, 1799, 56.

a. *Powell.* " S. Æternæ memoriæ perpetuæque securitati Rebeccæ Powell, virginis honestissimæ, castissimæ, pientissimæ ; quæ ipso in flore ætatis annos xxiii circiter nata præmaturâ, proh dolor, proh pietas & prisca virtus ! multumque deflendâ morte obiit desideratissima, Maii 27, anno salutis nostræ 1759. Hoc monumentum, tam propter rarissimas animi dotes, quam incomparabilem corporis venustatem, meritò ponendum mœrens curavit avunculus charissimus Z. Brooke, S. T. P."

*h. *Powell, Mary*, wife of William, of St. Anne, Blackfryars, 2 Jan. 1798, 60.

*Powell.* See *Wilson.*

h. *Price, John*, of this parish, schoolmaster, 27 Sept. 1793, 49.

h. *Price, Sarah*, 1744.

h. *Price, Jane*, wife of John, of this parish, victualler, 29 Oct. 1730, in 56th year ; also John Price, shipwright.

*h. *Price, Henrietta*, 14 Sept. 1806, 22.

b. *Prince, John*, of this parish, Sept. 12, 1737, 63. Jonathan his son, April 16, 1737, 29. Thomas Hill, Aug. 19, 1743, 44. Martha Prince, Feb. 15, 1755, 82. Martha Clark, daughter of John and Martha Prince, March 14, 1760, 52. George Prince, May 16, 1774, 58. Joseph Clark, of St. John-street, husband of said Martha, 26 July, 1775, 58.

*h. *Pugh, Richard*, 21 Dec. 1806, 54.

a. *Pullin, John*, of St. James, Clerkenwell, Feb. 28, 1742, in 65th year. Samuel his brother, July 20, 1745, in 73d year. Thomas, son of said John, Nov. 28, 1746, in 33d year. Elizabeth, wife of said John, May 25, 1753, in 67th year. Mary, wife of said Samuel, Jan 25, 1767, in 84th year. Samuel, son of said John and Elizabeth, of this parish, 23 Jan. 1775, in 63d year. Henry their son, 10 Oct. 1775, 59. Elizabeth their daughter, 16 April, 1780, in 70th year. Mary their daughter, 21 May, 1793, in 75th year. John Pullin, of Enfield, July 17, 1793, 67.

## R.

*Rant.* See *Lyndahl.*

*h. *Rathbon, Eliz.* a woman of exemplary piety and extraordinary understanding, a true Christian, and a sincere friend, and one who experienced in an uncommon degree the vicissitudes of this transitory life, born at Liverpool, died at Islington, 18 Dec. 1808, in 68th year.

*Raven.* See *Wilmer* and *Thomas.*

h. *Rawlins, Mary-Ann*, 5 Jan. 1789, 17. . Jane Rebecca, 31 Jan. 1790, 16.

h. *Rayboll, Josiah*, of this parish, farmer, 18 Feb. 1753, 58. Elizabeth his daughter, 28 Aug. 1754, 26. Sarah his wife, July 11, 1776.

*Raynham.* See *Brice.*

h. *Read, Nicholas*, of this parish, baker, Feb. 22, 1745, 72. Catherine his widow, April 20, 1749, 76. Isabella Nichols their sister, March 31, 1749, 66. See *Nichols.*

h. *Read, Hannah*, of Worcestershire, late of St. Giles's in the Fields, 18 May, 1784, 59.

*Reay.* See *Perry.*

+
I. H. S.

h. *Reed, John*, April 9, 1798, 51.

Requiescat in pace.

*a. *Reeves, Hannah-Maria*, wife of William, of Colebrooke-row, 27 April, 1802, 45. Said William, 17 April, 1803, in 64th year.

*h. *Revell, Ann*, wife of Charles, of Canonbury-place, Feb. 28, 1798, 50.

*h. *Richardson, Eliz.* 24 Jan. 1801, 39.

h. *Ricket, Jeremiah*, of this parish, 21 January 1787, 64. Mary his wife, 28 Sept. 1794, 67.

h. *Roberts, Sarah*, Aug. 27, 1759, 50.

h. *Roberts, Thomas*, of St. James, Clerkenwell, 3 March, 1805, 58. Eliz. his wife, April 3, 1809, 43.

h. *Robinson, Catherine.*

*Rockett.* See *Knight.*

s. *Rogers, James-Terret*, grandson of James Terret, of this parish, 12 Aug. 1778, in 21st year. Lucy Rogers, Nov. 27, 1780, in 21st year. Mary, March 4, 1781, 18.

*Rogers.* See *Hurley.*

*Rowe.* See *Page.*

h. *Rowland, Susannah*, wife of Joseph, of this parish, 1764, 42.

*s. *Royds, Susannah*, daughter of James, esq. of Rochdale, in Lancashire, 22 Feb. 1801, 14. Mary Gould, 11 Feb. 1804, in 13th year.

h. *Rudyard, Richard*, gent. natus 14 Aug. 1659, denatus 23 Aug. 1727.

Requiescat in pace.

a. *Rufford*, Capt. *Nicholas*, of this parish, 20 Mar. 1711, in 72d year. Mary, daughter of Nicholas, 29 May, 1711, in 20th year. Judith, wife of Nicholas, 22 Sept. 1707, 40; by whom he had three sons and six daughters. Elizabeth, daughter of Nicholas and Judith, 14 June, 1712, 15. Elizabeth, wife of Nicholas, 18 Jan. 1685, 45. Also the mother of said Nicholas, Feb. 1674, 60; and three of his brothers, William, Andrew, and Comfort.

h. *Ryder, Charles*, of this parish, Nov. 2, 1808, 48, and seven children.

### S.

h. *Sale, William*, of this parish, calf salesman, 27 June, 1807, 54.

h. *Salter, John*, gent. of St. Chad's Wells, Battle Bridge, July 17, 1798, 72.

*h. *Sambrook, Thomas*, 31 July 1810, 27.

h. *Sanders, Mary*, " *a pious young woman*," born Feb. 18, 1759, died April 19, 1778.

h. *Sanders*, Capt. *Thomas*, 11 Aug. 1781, in 29th year.

*h. *Sanders, Martha*, June 16, 1800, 20.

*h. *Sanders, Sukey*, wife of Thomas, of this parish, butcher, 14 Feb. 1796, in 24th year.

> Naked as from the earth we came,
>   And crept to life at first,
> So to the earth we soon return,
>   And mingle with our dust.
> The dear delights we here enjoy,
>   And fondly call our own,
> Are but short favours borrowed now
>   To be repaid anon.

h. *Saunders, Wm.* 15 April 1777, 47.

*h. *Saxby, Susanna*, Sept. 26, 1795, 68. James, April 30, 1806, in 68th year.

h. *Schlomer, Nicholas*, 13 Aug. 1791, 89. Susanna, 22 July, 1799, in 95th year.

*Scofield*. See *Lane*.

h. *Scott, Judith*, 24 Jan. 1792, aged 102 years.

h. *Scott*. Rev. *Thomas*, M. A. Lecturer of this parish, July 18th 1740, in 51st year, much lamented. Also Isaac Scott, 19 April, 1749, aged 47, a tender husband and affectionate father.

s. *Sebbon, John*, 3 Oct. 1737, 33.

*Sebbon*. See *Laycock*.

s. *Sebbon, Walter*, of this parish, 16 May, 1786, in 93d year. Sarah, his daughter, wife of Thomas Skinner, of this parish, 20 Jan. 1803, in 77th year. Said Thomas Skinner, 1 June, 1803, in 79th year. Elizabeth Alcock, daughter of said Walter, 20 May, 1806, 84.

*h. *Seddon, Eliza-Marchant*, eldest daughter of Thomas and Eliza, of Pentonville, 6 Oct.

1807, 11. Said Thomas, late Treasurer to the Sons of Commerce, 2 June 1809, 36.

*Senior*. See *Crane*.

*Sexton*. See *Armstrong*.

h. *Seymour, Jane*, wife of Robert, of St. Leonard, Shoreditch, June 14, 1806, in 41st year.

> No trust on self, on firmer ground she
>   stood ;
> Her hope was founded in a Saviour's blood.
> A sinner sav'd, who in death's trying hour
> Did cast her soul, on Jesu's love and pow'r,
> And now with myriads of the ransom'd
>   race,
> Ascribes her bliss to free and sovereign
>   grace.
> As such her happy lot, then why complain,
> My loss though great, is her eternal gain.

h. *Sharp, Richard*, of St. Andrew, Holborn, Oct. 21, 1747, in 56th year. John, his son, April 24, 1745, in 29th year.

h. *Sharpe, Wm.* Jan. 28, 1716, 61. Elizabeth his wife, Dec. 6, 1746, 85.

h. *Sharpley, Eliz.* Oct. 12, 1774, 22. Edward her brother, Oct. 6, 1781, in 30th year.

h. *Shelswell, Daniel*, 6 June 1752, 30. John Shepard, brother-in-law, 4 Sept. 1768, 60.

*Shepard*. See *Shelswell*.

h. *Shepperson, Thomas*, 4 Feb. 1807, 57.

*Sherwood*. See *Taylor*.

h. *Shipston, John*, esq. June 11, 1766, 67.

h. *Shury, James*, 8 March, 1779, 56.

a. *Shuttleworth, Henry-Raynes*, optician, of Ludgate-street, London, June 19th, 1798, 66. Elizabeth, his wife, June 16, 1781, 46. Eliz. Bleuler, their daughter, Aug. 15, 1794, 31.

h. *Simmons, Eliz.* 15 Nov. 1810, 25.

*h. *Simmons, Mary*, 19 Sept. 1810, 46, and several children.

h. *Simpson, John*, May 27, 1764, 19. Ann Orton, his sister, March 11, 1767, 23. William Orton, Sept. 23, 1781, 46. Ann Simpson, mother of the above John and Ann, May 10, 1786, 77.

*h. *Singer, Luke*, of this parish, 4 June 1803, 43. Hannah his wife, 5 Jan. 1810, 52.

s. *Sirdefield, Mary*, daughter of Finney and Mary, of Newgate-street, London, July 14, 1795, 18.

> Mary possessed a well-disposed mind,
>   Religion dawn'd upon her early youth,
> Pure were her sentiments, by grace refin'd,
>   And stedfast virtue deck'd her lips with
>   truth.

Mary, mother of the above, June 14, 1798, 52 ; and Ann, her second daughter, late wife of M. Stockley, 9 Feb. 1806, in 24th year.

b. *Skay, Beale,* citizen and cooper of London, 31 March 1758, 46.

*h. *Skelton, George,* of this parish, 18 Feb. 1795, 37.

*Skelton.* See *Spencer.*

*Skinner.* See *Sebbon.*

h. *Skirrow, William,* late of Salter, Lancashire, 1 Feb. 1767, 31. John his brother, late of Queen-street, Cheapside, 9 May 1780, 46. Frances, widow of John, 12 Nov. 1800, 71.

*Slade.* See *How.*

*h. *Smart, Amelia,* 17 Aug. 1807, 59, wife of James, of this parish.

h. *Smith, Mary,* 21 Nov. 1786, 69.

h. *Smith, Mary,* 1 Feb. 1793, 28.

h. *Smith, Thomas-Jesup,* 24 July, 1802, 17.

h. *Smith, Rev. Thomas,* buried in the Church vault ; Sunday morning and Thursday afternoon Lecturer of St. Giles, Cripplegate, London, supported by the Worshipful Company of Haberdashers, and also author of the Treatise of Resignation to the Will of God, and the use and abuse of the Passions of the Soul, and of several other Treatises, died 12 April 1782, aged 76.

h. *Smith, James,* of this parish, farrier, Nov. 13, 1784, 41.

*h. *Smith, Maria-Hinckley,* daughter of George and Mary, of Finsbury-terrace, St. Luke's, 11 Sept. 1805, in 19th year.

*h. *Smith, Launcelot,* of Melmerby, Cumberland, and late of Kingston, Jamaica, merchant, Sept. 30, 1799, 48.

h. *Snape, Mary,* wife of John, of this parish, 28 Aug. 1758, in her 64th year.

*h. *Soames, Henry,* of this parish, Jan. 4, 1797, 73.

*h. *Sobey, Jane,* 13 May, 1807, 90.

*h, *Sockett, Thomas,* Oct. 28, 1802, 22. Ann Blackwell, Oct. 29, 1796, in 32d year.

*Soreton.* See *Atkinson.*

*South.* See *Mansel.*

*h. *Spence, Samuel,* 5 April, 1801, in 45th year.

*a. *Spencer, Eliz.* wife of William, esq. of this parish, 1 March, 1803, 83. Said William, 25 Dec. 1805, in 86th year. Mrs. Sarah Skelton his daughter, Aug. 12, 1807, 51.

a. *Spencley, Mary,* wife of Allen, of this parish, 15 March, 1772, 58. Thomas, 25 March, 1773, 26. Said Allen, 1 July, 1781, 66.

a. *Spiller, Wm.* of Mile End Old Town, parish of Stepney, March 7, 1748-9, 65.

Reader, behold this monument of death ;
Contains a Saint depriv'd of mortal breath,
How sweetly sleeps the soul that dies in peace,
Earnest of endless joys which ne'er can cease.
A true believer in the third record,
Which does declare Christ is the only Lord,
Here patient waits the last great trumpet's sound,
Whilst Nature shakes and trembles all around ;
The faithful seed shall then arise and shine,
In measure glorious, like their God divine.
With joyful acclamations they'll ascend, )
Surrounding their redeeming dying friend )
With Hallelujahs that will never end. )

h. *Spindle, Eliz.* 23 June, 1793, 73. William Field, 14 April, 1797, 37.

h. *Spragg, John,* of this parish, 29 Dec. 1784, in 62d year, Sarah, wife of Carlos Ceasar, of Holborn-bridge, citizen, daughter of said John, 31 Dec. 1784, in 21st year. George-John, son of James and Elizabeth Cross, and grandson of the above John Spragg, of this parish, May 20, 1781, 16 months. Also Sophia their daughter, July 6, 1784, aged 17 months. Also Elizabeth, wife of the above John Spragg.

*h. *Spratley, Thomas,* of St. Giles, Cripplegate, 2 Aug. 1794, in 49th year. Jane Purden his wife, June 10, 1804, in 63d year, late of St. Mary, Islington.

*h. *Stabb, Rebecca,* 27 Oct. 1804, 64, late of Tor, co. Devon.

s. *Stanfield, Sarah,* wife of Joseph, of this parish, gent. 30 Aug. 1789, 59. Sarah, their only child, wife of Ambrose Lanfear, of Cheapside, 3 April, 1802, 35. Elizabeth, second wife of said Joseph, 11 Sept. 1809, 64.

h. *Staniland, Susanna,* Feb. 20, 1768, 55.

h. *Staveley, Ann,* of Woodstock, Oxon, Feb. 8, 1776, 59.

*h. *Stanynought, Eliz.* 19 Nov. 1805, 68.

h. *Stedman, Christopher,* of Leadenhall-street, March 16, 1774, 54. Elizabeth his wife, June 4, 1798, 65.

h. *Steell, Mary,* wife of John, of this parish, May 30, 1782, 79. John, 3d April, 1799, 90. Jeremiah, esq. son of the above, 10 March, 1809, 64.

h. *Sterry, Patience,* wife of William, of this parish, Sept. 13, 1770, 69. William, 30th Jan. 1776, 76. Also Martha Gant, 29 April, 1795, 73.

h. *Stevens, Mary,* 10 Oct. 1783, 66.

*h. *Stevenson, Charlotte,* daughter of James and Jane, of this parish, Sept. 29, 1798, 9. Said Jane, 2 June, 1808, 61.

a. r. *Steyman, Mary,* wife of Johan Conrad, gent. of this parish, July 18, 1766, 67.

h. *Stirn, Michael,* of this parish, victualler, April 2, 1761, 46.

His life though short he laboured to improve,
In trade, in virtue, and in social love,
His heart was good, religiously inclin'd,
His temper sweet, benevolent, and kind,
His manner open, generous, and free,
He was a man, such as a man should be.

*Stockley.* See *Sirdefield.*

*h. *Stogdon, T.* 26 Jan. 1800, 74.

*h. *Stokes, Amy,* wife of Henry, of this parish, Feb. 8, 1807, 35.

h. *Stone, Anne,* July 26, 1719, 58. John Perry her son, March 5, 1743, 31. Margaret Stone, daughter in law, July, 1746, 20. Robert Stone, of Whitecross-street, St. Luke's, 1752, 56.

h. *Stonehouse, Wm.* of this parish, Nov. 30, 1776.

*h. *Storer, Eliz.* Sept. 9, 1805, in 31st year.

———— But that I am forbid
To tell the secrets of my prison house,
I could a tale unfold, whose lightest word
Would harrow up thy soul.————

*h. *Strank, Eleanor,* daughter of Eleanor, of this parish, 1 July, 1795, 16.

h. *Streetin, Mary,* wife of Richard, of this parish, 5 Feb. 1811, 53.

*Strode.* See *Norman.*

h. *Style, Nathaniel,* citizen and liveryman of the Company of Clockmakers, 30 Aug. 1781, 80. Richard his nephew, 22 May, 1796, in 69th year.

*Summers.* See *Morris.*

h. *Sutter, Mary,* Dec. 11, 1759, in 27th year.

When God ordains the fatal blow,
The heart may wish, the tear may flow,
But can't the dead restore.
Yet comfort dawns from realms divine,
There, souls their kindred souls shall join,
And meet to part no more.

h. *Sutton, Robert,* 9 May, 1789, 47.

*h. *Swift, Eliz.* wife of John, of Fenchurch-street, 19 Jan. 1797, 65, and two grand-daughters.

*Swain.* See *Galloway.*
*Sweet.* See *Wilby.*

## T.

*h. *Taitt, Mary,* eldest daughter of James, esq. and Mary his wife, 14 Sept. 1804, 83.

h. *Tapp, Mary,* wife of Charles, Nov. 1774, 88.

h. *Taverner, John,* Jan. 1, 1759, in 59th year. Mary his wife, Oct. 8, 1764, 58. Mary Coney, their daughter, Feb. 5, 1771, 36. Martha, wife of William, Dec. 14, 1778, in 25th year.

h. *Taverner, Margaret,* wife of Thomas.

h. *Tawlks, Ann,* 19 Jan. 1768, 66. Peter Higgs, 26 Dec. 1769, 35.

h. *Tayler, Margaret,* wife of John, of Hoxton, 21 Sept. 1808, 53.

h. *Taylor, Rebecca,* Oct. 15, 1792, 66.

a. *Taylor, Wm.* 14 Oct. 1700, in 72d year. Ann his relict, 15 Sept. 1719, in 76th year. Robert Whitehead, 19 May, 1771, 67. Elizabeth his daughter, wife of Benjamin Batt, 17 Jan. 1787, 50. Mary, wife of Wm. Sherwood, of this parish, Nov. 25, 1788, 74. Mary Sherwood, daughter of said William, Feb. 3, 1791, 52. Joseph Peart, esq. of West Butterwick, co. Lincoln, Nov. 23, 1798, 53.

*Taylor.* See *Gee.*

*a. *Temple, Anne,* wife of Paul, 2 March 1795, 60. Said Paul, 9th June, 1797, 69.

s. *Terrett,* Mrs. *Frances,* Nov. 23, 1753, in 59th year. James, Feb. 29, 1760, in 70th year. Esther their daughter, wife of Robert Dower, of this parish, Aug. 8, 1773, in 43d year. Said Robert, 1 July, 1793, 72.

s. *Terry, James,* of Aldersgate-street, tobacconist. Ann his wife and two daughters. Also James their only son, 177..

*Testar.* See *Whitby.*

h. *Thomas, Susannah,* of St. Bride's, London, Aug. 6, 1790, in 72d year.

h. *Thomas, Daniel,* of St. Bride's, April 29, 1763, in 40th year.

h. *Thomas, James,* of St. Magnus the Martyr, London Bridge, citizen and brush-maker, 27 Feb. 1756, in 32d year.

h. *Thomas, Susanna,* Mar. 14, 1750, 32. William, Feb. 24, 1765, 52. Also Sarah Raven, Oct. 19, 1779, 61. William, son of the above William and Susanna Thomas, 4 Dec. 1802, 58.

*Thomas.* See *Johnson.*

*Thompson, Elizabeth,* wife of Edward, of this parish, 22 April, 1789, 79. Edward, 6 Dec. 1792, in 82d year.

h. *Thompson, William,* of St. Faith, London, Dec. 2, 1741, in 49th year. Rebecca Walker, 2d Oct. 1805, 28.

*Thompson, John,* of this parish, innholder, Sept. 9, 1790, 52. Elizabeth Whittenbury, his mother, Oct. 9, 1791, 76. Elizabeth, his wife, April 9, 1793, 52. Sarah, their daughter, 11 Sept. 1793, 22. Mary Thompson, 5 May, 1798, 29. Elizabeth, 22 Dec. 1801, 33.

h. *Thompson, Andrew,* of this parish, 23d Jan. 1788, 49. Mary, his relict, late wife of John Ufford, esq.

*h. *Thompson, Elizabeth,* wife of James, 10 Sept. 1805, 47. John, brother of James, 2 Jan. 1809, 56.

*h. *Thorn, William,* 3 March, 1804, 47.

h. *Tibbs, Sarah,* March 7, 1764, 35.

*Till.* See *Cooper.*

h. *Treacy, Elizabeth,* wife of Thomas, of this parish, 26 Aug. 1806, 53. Said Thomas, 17 May, 1809, 60; and 7 children. Also Elizabeth White, their daughter, 13 Oct. 1803, 27.

h. *Truelove, Frances,* wife of John, of this parish, 12 April, 1743, 68. Said John, . . . .

h. *Turbet, Robert,* of Durham, 3 May, 1771, in 29th year.

## V.

*Vere.* See *Fortescue.*
*Vernon.* See *Davenport.*
*Ufford.* See *Thompson.*

h. *Vicaridge, Charles,* sen. of this parish, citizen and fishmonger of London, 22 Aug. 1732, in 72d year.

*Vincent.* See *Battin.*
*Underwood.* See *Weed.*

h. *Upton, Thomas,* wife of George, of this parish, May 3, 1741, in 66th year. George, Aug. 5, 1750, in 73d year.

## W.

h. *Walker, James,* of the parish of St. Bartholomew, Aug. 6, 1762, in 37th year.

*h. *Walker, George,* son of William and Elizabeth, of Hailybury House, Herts, 11 April, 1797, 12.

*Walker.* See *Thompson* and *Harrison.*

h. *Walker, Deborah-Sophia,* wife of Rev. Thomas, LL. B. formerly curate of this parish, 11 Feb. 1811, 62[1].

h. *Waller, Thomas Bates,* 16 Mar. 1775, 37.

+
### I. H. S.
* *Walsh, Patrick,* Oct. 25, 1802, 42.
Requiescat in pace. Amen.

h. *Walters, George,* of St. Andrew, Holborn, taylor.

*h. *Walton, Elizabeth,* daughter of William and Jane Ann, of this parish, 27 July 1801, 10 years; Frances her sister, 18 Feb. 1811, 21.

*h.*Walton, Frances,* of this parish, 9 Aug. 1797, 62. Joseph, her husband, 8 Dec. 1800, 70.

*h. *Ward, Francis,* 1 May, 1807, 46.

*h. *Ward, John,* 1 Dec. 1806, 33.
A loving husband, father dear,
A faithful friend, lies buried here;
Free from malice, void of pride,
So he liv'd, and so he died.
Mary, his wife, 2 Sept. 1808, 30.

*Ward.* See *Elston.*

*h. *Wardell, Margaret,* wife of John, late of Ship Yard, near Temple Bar, parish of St. Clement Danes, April 24, 1803, 54.

h. *Warner, Ann,* of St. Bride's, London, Sept. 21, 1757, 69. Edward, her husband, Feb. 10, 1763, in 75th year.

h. *Warner, Edward,* of St. Bride's, London, 3 March, 1778, 52.

h. *Warner, Samuel,* of St. Andrew, Holborn, Sept. 16, 1745, in 43d year. Ann, his wife, Dec. 13, 1778, in 71st year.

*a. *Warren, John,* son of John and Rebecca, 14 March, 1811, 26.

h. *Wartering, Thomas,* of this parish, Aug. 13, 1781, 60. Margaret, his wife, 12 Nov. 1793, 71.

h. *Watkins, Samuel,* of this parish, gardener, 19 June, 1707, 77. Esther, his daughter, wife of John Brown, of this parish, gardener, 26 April, 1743, 77. Said John, her husband.

h. *Watkinson, Ann,* widow of William, of Bradninch, Devon, Nov. 21, 1776, 66. Ann Kendall, her mother, June 1757, 75.

*h. *Watson, Margaret,* wife of James, biscuit baker, 16 Jan. 1794, 55.

*Watts.* See *Poe.*

a. *Wear,* Mr. and Mrs. of Johnson's Court, St. Dunstan's in the West; he died 27 Feb. 1753; she died 1 July . . . .

h. *Weed, Thomas,* of St. Giles's in the Fields, baker, Aug. 15, 1785, 74. John Underwood, of the same parish, baker, his nephew, Dec. 26, 1785, 44. Ann Underwood, his mother, July 30, 1785, 64. George Ellis, nephew to Thomas Weed, Aug. 2, 1786, 44.

---

[1] This inscription is on the head-stone of Elizabeth Harrison and Christian Walker.

*a. r. *Welby, Gulielmi,* hujusce parochiæ, arm. qui ex hâc vitâ decessit 18 Maij, A. D. 1809, ætatis suæ 85.

h. *Welchon, Elizabeth,* wife of Samuel, attorney at law, of this parish, 14 Dec. 1792, 33.

*h. *Welchon, Thomas,* 16 March, 1796, 63.

*h. *Wells, Harriet,* daughter of Richard and Bridget, of the island of Jamaica, 21 Mar. 1797, 24. Catherina, her sister, 28 Feb. 1803, 30.

h. *Wentworth, George,* of this parish, 23 Dec. 1784, 70.

An urn railed. *Werg, Charles,* May 31, 1780, 74.

*h. *Wheeler, John,* of Fleet Street, carpenter, 17 Oct. 1800, 65. William, his son, 30 Dec. 1803, 35.

*Wheeler.* See *Lee.*

h. *Whieldon, Joseph,* of Holloway, April 10, 1795, in 41st year. Thomas, his brother, Dec. 24, 1798, 48. Hannah, his sister, March 23, 1805, in 61st year.

h. *Whitamore, Anne,* wife of Nathaniel, of Holloway, Oct. 9, 1742, 58. Nathaniel, Jan. 26, 1760, in 76th year.

h. *Whitby, Elizabeth,* daughter of James and Hannah Testar, of Battle Bridge, 10th June, 1792, 19. Thomas Testar, 10 Dec. 1793, 17. Hannah Testar, their mother, 5 Dec. 1793, 41.

*h. *White, John,* son of Peter and Rebecca, 12 Sept. 1798, 28.

*h. *White, Thomas,* 29 June, 1800, 52.
The Lord to me short warning gave ;
I trust in him my soul to save :
In health and spirits in the morn I rose,
Death took me hence before the evening's close.

*h. *White, Thomas,* formerly of Coleman Street, late of this parish, 17 Sept. 1803, 67. Susanna his wife, 10 Sept. 1810, 68.
*White.* See *Treacy* and *Johnson.*

*h. *White, Mary,* 6 March, 1808, 45. Joseph, her husband, 1 June, 1810, 56, both of this parish.

h. *Whitehead, Elizabeth,* of this parish, 15 Jan. 1732, 74.

*h. *Whitehead, Elizabeth,* 21 Nov. 1798, 75. Ann, her daughter, 20 Feb. 1805, in 46th year.
*Whitehead.* See *Taylor.*

h. *Whittenbury, Joseph,* 27 April, 1783, 31. Martha Cole, 3d Sept. 1788, 42.
*Whittenbury.* See *Thompson.*

*h. *Whittingham, Ann,* 6 April, 1797, 21. Ann her mother, 18 Feb. 1803, 62. Eleanor, 21 June, 1803, 28.

h. *Whitworth, James,* June 21, 1780, 38.

Hannah Holmes, his wife, June 3, 1798, 61.

*h. *Whyte, Margaret,* 3 Sept. 1795, 25.

h. *Wickings, Ann,* wife of William, of this parish, daughter of Mr. St. John Jones, of Crooked-lane, London, 25 Feb. 1802, in 41st year, and four children.

h. *Wicksteed, Ann,* wife of Randle, April 23, 1750, 65.

h. *Widt, Alice,* of the Lower-street, April 9th, 1793, 63.

h. *Wiggen, Henry,* born at Whaley, Lancashire, 24 years wharfinger at Fresh wharf, near London Bridge, died in this parish, 28 July, 1784, 50.

h. *Wilby, Eliz.* Aug. 31, 1740. Also Eusebius Sweet, 24 Jan. 1746, 72. Mary Sweet, March 14, 1753, 74.

*h. *Wilcox, William,* citizen and draper, of this parish, 4 Feb. 1810, in 61st year.

h. *Wildman, William,* 4 March, 1772, 58. Francis his son 15 April, 1774, 20. Bridget his wife, 29 April, 1774, 48.
*Wilkin.* See *Lander.*

h. *Wilkinson, Edward,* of this parish, baker, 18 Oct. 1755, in 43d year, and 7 children. Ann, 12 Oct. 1756, 42.

*h. *Wilkinson, Esther,* wife of John Lightfoot, of Hornsey-lane, in this parish, 27 Oct. 1794, in 28th year.

h. *Willet, Hannah,* wife of Thomas, of St. James, Clerkenwell, March 10, 1768, in 28th year. Jane, wife of Thomas Bateman, of St. Sepulchre, mother of the above, March 1, 1772, 67.

h. *Williams, Eliz.* wife of Job, of this parish, 8 April, 1776, 41. Said Job, 24 March, 1807, in 72d year. Jane his wife, 3 Feb. 1810, 74.

h. *Williams, John,* oilman, of St. Sepulchre's, Jan 25, 1776, 64.

*h. *Williams, Sarah,* 22 Dec. 1800, 56. Benj. of this parish, 4 Nov. 1804, 64.
*Williams.* See *Kestin.*
*Willes.* See *Lane.*

a. *Willis, Charles,* 28 April 1807, 32.

*h. *Willison, Mary,* 12 Jan. 1797, 12.

h. *Willmer, Elizabeth,* of this parish, spinster, daughter of Abraham, of Great Ilford, co. Essex, 4 Oct. 1738, 54. Also, Walter George Raven, of this parish, upholder, April 13, 1768, 23. William Raven, citizen and stationer, Aug. 9, 1773, 53.

h. *Wilson, Thomas,* 3 April 1795, 34.

h. *Wilson, Richard,* of Gray's Inn, gent. 16 April 1728, 30. Elizabeth, Feb. 9, 1737. Sarah Powell, Oct. 3, 1786, 59.

\*h. *Wilson*, Rev. *James*, late chaplain to the 67th regiment of foot, 16 Aug. 1802, 69.

\*a. *Wilson, Anne*, wife of John, Esq. of Canonbury, 7 July 1801, 56. John, 13 Dec. 1801, 64.

\*h. *Wing, Samuel*, late of Aldermanbury, Dec. 15, 1808, 53.

h. *Wingate, John*, of this parish, 11 Oct. 1790, 54. William, his son, 8 Dec. 1804, 35.

An obelisk. *Witham, James*, citizen and brewer, of St. Giles, Cripplegate, son of Robert, of Worsthorn, Lancashire, Dec. 1, 1761, 64.

+

Catherine, wife of Benjamin, of Redcross-street, London, brewer, Jan. 18, 1765, 55.

+ *Requiescat in pace.*

Benjamin, brother and successor to the said James, 7 July 1767, 55.

*Requiescat in pace.*

h. *Wolfe, Samuel*, 3 Aug. 1776, 52.

*Wood. See Armstrong.*

\*h. *Woodhall, Sarah*, wife of John, of Upper Holloway, in this parish, formerly of Basinghall-street, London, smith, Dec. 6, 1796, in her 64th year. The said John, April 11, 1797, in his 67th year. Mary, wife of John, of Basinghall-street, son of the above, died suddenly Sept. 29, 1803, in her 47th year.

h. *Woodhouse, Richard*, gent. citizen of London, June 8, 1743, 48.

\*h. *Woodward, Elizabeth*, wife of William, 23 Dec. 1802, in her 31st year. And two daughters, Elizabeth and Mary-Anne.

h. *Woolley, Dorothy*, **wife of William**, citizen and victualler of London, June . . 1735, aged 34 ; and two sons.

*Woolley. See Hose.*

h. *Wootton, Ann*, wife of Joseph, 20 April 1733, in her 46th year. The said Joseph, Aug. 1735, 63.

\*h. *Worcester, John*, 28 Feb. 1807, 85. Mrs. Mary, 7 Feb. 1795, 78. William, their son, born 19 May 1751, died 10 May 1809.

h. *Worboys, Thomas*, April 7, 1785, 37.

h. *Worsley, John*, citizen and carpenter, of this parish, 4 March 1774, 46.

\*h. *Wright, Mary*, wife of Gabriel, of this parish, Dec. 23, 1795, in her 46th year. Mary, sister to Gabriel, 7 May 1802, 59. The said Gabriel, 29 Jan. 1804, in his 64th year.

*Wrigley. See Chadwick.*

h. *Wythes, Elizabeth*, wife of Thomas, of Duke-street, Lincoln's inn fields, in the parish of St. Giles, 25 Feb. 1777, in her 57th year.

## Y.

*Yardley. See Nash.*

h. *Yates, John*, of St. James's, Clerkenwell, carpenter, 25 Oct. 1797, 37.

h. *Yates, Ann*, wife of William, of this parish, Sept. 21, 1782, 42. Also, Mary his wife, 18 Dec. 1793, 34. The said William, 31 May 1795, 56.

s. *Yeate, Cornelius*, late vicar, April 12, 1720.

### THE PARISH REGISTER.

THE earliest date of the Register is 1557. It is, for the most part, very fairly written, and very accurately kept, except during the Civil War and Interregnum; at which period there is an *hiatus* of several years. The following is an average statement of Baptisms and Burials, as taken from the Register, by Mr. Lysons:

| | Average of Baptisms. | Average of Burials. |
|---|---|---|
| 1580—1589 | $38\frac{1}{5}$ | $47\frac{3}{10}$ |
| 1630—1639 | $58\frac{3}{5}$ | $73\frac{4}{5}$ |
| 1680—1689 | $67\frac{1}{2}$ | $127\frac{4}{5}$ |
| 1730—1739 | $88\frac{7}{10}$ | $231\frac{4}{5}$ |
| 1780—1784 | $155\frac{1}{5}$ | $228\frac{1}{5}$ |
| 1784—1789 | $160\frac{4}{5}$ | $219\frac{4}{5}$ |
| 1790—1793 | $174$ | $235\frac{1}{2}$ |
| 1793—1794 | $77$ | $74\frac{2}{3}$ |
| 1795—1799 | $95\frac{4}{5}$ | $67\frac{3}{5}$ |
| 1800—1804 | $112\frac{2}{5}$ | $78\frac{2}{5}$ |
| 1805—1809 | $119\frac{1}{5}$ | $73\frac{2}{5}$ |

The general disproportion of the burials has arisen principally from the circumstance mentioned in p. 43; to which may be added, that there are numbers of nursed children, who die, and are interred at Islington, and many funerals are brought from the Metropolis.

Several persons died of the plague at Islington in 1577, 1578, and 1592. In 1593, 106 persons fell victims to that distemper; the whole number of burials that year being 187. In 1603, there were 322 burials; in 1625, 213; in 1665, 696, of which 593 were persons who died of the plague. 94 died in one week, from Aug. 29 to Sept. 5 [1]. In the months of August and September, the number of burials was above 490 [2]. In the former part of this year, before the plague broke out, the average of burials did not exceed two or three in a week [3].

## EXTRACTS FROM THE REGISTER [4].

" William Perriam and Margery Huchyson, married April 6, " 1562."—Sir William Perriam, Lord Chief Baron of the Exchequer

[1] The following is an extract from the " *City Remembrancer* :" " A citizen broke " out of his house in Aldersgate-street, and attempted, but was refused going into " the *Angel*, or the *White Horse*, at ISLINGTON. At the *Pyed Horse* he pretended " going into Lincolnshire, that he was entirely free from infection, and required only " lodgings for one night. They had but a garret bed empty, and that but one " night, expecting drovers with cattle next day. A servant shewed him the room, " which he gladly accepted. He was well dressed; and, with a sigh, said, he had " seldom lain in such a lodging, but would make shift, as it was but for one " night, and in a dreadful time. He sat down on the bed, desiring a pint of warm " ale, which was forgot. Next morning one asked, what was become of the gen- " tleman? The maid, starting, said, she had never thought more of him; he " bespoke warm ale, but I forgot it.—A person going up, found him dead cross " the bed; his cloaths were pulled off, his jaw fallen, his eyes open, in a most " frightful posture, the rug of the bed clasped hard in one hand. The alarm was " great, having been free from the distemper, which spread immediately to the " houses round about. Fourteen died of the plague that week in Islington."

*Great Plague* 1665.

[2] Weekly Bills of Mortality. The Parish Register is defective in the latter part of this year.

[3] Ibid.

[4] The following interments are recorded before the commencement of the Register; viz. " In July 1556, the Lady Broke, wife to the Lord Broke, Chief Baron, " died of an infectious fever, and was brought from *Canbury* to Islington church

in the reign of Queen Elizabeth, had a considerable estate at Islington [1].

" Henry, the sonne of Mr. Henry Yelverton, was baptized July 7, " 1566."—This was, no doubt, the celebrated Sir Henry Yelverton, who is said to have been born at Easton Mauduit, in Northampton-shire, on the 29th of June. From the date of his baptism, how-ever, it seems much more likely that he was a native of Islington, where his father Sir Christopher (then Mr. Yelverton, and a student at Gray's-inn) had, it is probable, country lodgings. Sir Henry Yelverton was Attorney General to King James; but having given offence, as it is said, to the favourite Buckingham, he was accused in the Star-chamber of illegal proceedings in his office, and by a sen-tence of that court deprived of his place, imprisoned in the Tower, and heavily fined. Being afterwards brought before the Lords, he made a speech, which was so offensive to the King and his favourite, that he was fined 10,000 marks for the reflections which he had cast on his Majesty, and 5,000 for the insult offered to Buckingham. By one of those unaccountable changes which occur among politicians of all ages, he became soon afterwards in great favour with the very man whose enmity had cost him so dear, and was, through his in-terest, made a Judge of the Common Pleas, in which situation he continued till his death, anno 1630. Sir Henry Yelverton was esteemed one of the first lawyers of his time. His Reports were pub-lished several years after his death by Serjeant Wilde. Some of his Speeches in Parliament are also extant [2].

---

" to burial, with six long torches, and six tapers of three pounds apiece, for six " women, and other lights, and a herald, yeoman, and other solemnities."

*Strype's Memorials*, vol. III.

In December 1556, Sir Richard Bruton, sometime of the Privy Chamber to King Henry VIII. was buried at Islington. *Ibid.*

[1] Harl. MSS. No. 366. (See p. 49.)

[2] Lysons's Environs.

" Mr. Modye, my Lady of Worcester's priest, was buried the 26
" daie of August, 1569. — The Ladye of Worcester, late wife to the
" Earle of Worcester, was buried the 25th daie of Julye, between
" 11 and one of the clocke in the mornynge, being St. James's daye,
" in the South chappell, neare unto the towre, 1584."— Lady Worcester was daughter of Sir Anthony Browne, Standard-bearer to
Henry VII. and relict of Henry the second Earl of Worcester (of
the Somerset family), who died in 1549 [1].

" Thomas Fowler and Mary Mosse, married March 18, 1571.
" Mrs. Mary, wife of Thomas Fowler, Esq. buried April 25, 1586,"
first wife of Sir Thomas Fowler the elder, not mentioned in any of
the monumental inscriptions.

" Mrs. Jane, wife of Thomas Fowler, Esq. buried Oct. 14, 1601,"
second wife of Sir Thomas.   " Mary, the wife and lady of Sir
" Thomas Fowler the elder, buried Jan. 6, 1621, at night."

" Thomas, son of Thomas Fowler, Gent. baptized Jan. 2, 1602
" (buried Nov. 8, 1603); Samuel, son of Sir Thomas Fowler (ju-
" nior), baptized April 23, 1604; John, Sept. 2, 1605 (buried
" Sept. 3, 1638); Jane, baptized Nov. 12, 1606; William, baptized
" Nov. 29, 1607; Mary, Jan. 31, 1609; Elizabeth, April 9, 1610;
" Penelope, Nov. 12, 1611 (buried March 25, 1613); Theophilus,
" baptized June 30, 1613 (buried Oct. 20); Martha, baptized Mar.
" 28, 1615 (buried Jan. 14, 1634); Alice, baptized Oct. 15, 1617;
" Sarah, wife of Sr Thomas Fowler the younger, was buried Sept.
" 28, 1618."   This Sir Thomas Fowler was created a Baronet in
1628.

" Edmund Fowler and Anne Bowes, married Feb. 10, 1606;
" Ann, wife of Sr Edmund Fowler, buried March 8, 1638; Thomas,
" son of Sr Edmund, May 25, 1638."   Sir Edmund was a younger
brother of Sir Thomas Fowler, Bart. and on whose death the title
became extinct.

[1] Collins's Peerage.

" S<sup>r</sup> Thomas Fisher, Knt. and Mrs. Mary Fowler, married March
" 2, 1619." Sir Thomas Fisher, who was created a Baronet in 1627,
married the daughter of Sir Thomas Fowler, Bart. " Edmund, son
" of S<sup>r</sup> Thomas Fisher, baptized March 20, 1626 (buried March 21);
" Sarah, baptized Dec. 20, 1627," (married Sir Hugh Ducie, K. B.);
" Richard, baptized Jan. 22, 1629; Ursula, April 13, 1630," (married Sir Thomas Halton, Bart.); " S<sup>r</sup> Thomas Fisher, buried May
" 25, 1636."

" Anne, daughter of S<sup>r</sup> Thomas and Elizabeth Fisher, baptized
" Nov. 26, 1667; S<sup>r</sup> Thomas Fisher (the second Baronet), buried
" Sept. 9, 1670; S<sup>r</sup> Thomas Fisher, junior (the third Baronet),
" April 14, 1671; Dame Ann Fisher (probably wife of S<sup>r</sup> Richard)
" Sept. 29, 1693; S<sup>r</sup> Richard Fisher, Bart. (in whom it is supposed
" the title became extinct), Oct. 14, 1707; Lady Browne Fisher,
" March 24, 1740."

" Mr. Thomas Skinner, of Broad-street, and Mrs. Susan, daugh-
" ter of the Lady Fisher, married Sept. 7, 1647; Mr. Nathaniel
" Tench and Ann Fisher were married July 19, 1666." Fisher
Tench, of Low Layton, co. Essex, Esq. was created a Baronet in
1715.

" Thomas, son of S<sup>r</sup> Thomas Morgan, buried Dec. 29, 1590."

" Diana, daughter of S<sup>r</sup> William Wilde, Knt. buried Jan. 1,
" 1593."

" William, the son of Mr. . . . Dru, Esq. Recorder of the City of
" London, buried May 15, 1593."—Edward Drew Serjeant at Law,
was Recorder of London from 1592 to 1594. He succeeded Sir Edward Coke.

" William . . . . . . . servant to Sir Charles Pereseye, Knt. was
" slaine at Ring-Crosse May . . . and buried the same day, 1597."

" William Wynche, the first that was executed at Ring-Crosse,
" was buried at Islington the 9th of September, 1600."

" Edward, son of Sir Thomas Reeresby, Knt. baptized Sept. 28,
" 1598."

" Richard, son of Sir Thomas Holte, was baptized Oct. 2, 1604. " Katherine, his daughter, buried Aug. 3, 1605." Sir Thomas Holte was created a Baronet in 1612.

" John, son of Sir Edward Dimmock, baptized April 28, 1625."

" Ann, daughter of L^d William Compton, baptized the 6th day " of September, 1605." She married Ulick Burgh (son of the Earl of Clanrickard) who was created a Marquis by Charles the First.

" Edward Clark and Catherine Stonehouse, married Aug. 17, " 1608. Mary, daughter of S^r James Stonehouse, baptized March " 23d, 1623. W^m, son of S^r James Stonehouse by his wife " Ann, buried Jan. 16, 1622. Thomas, buried July 3, 1624." Sir James Stonehouse was created a Baronet in 1641, but having no male issue at his death, the title became extinct in that branch. The Stonehouse family were for many years impropriators of the Rectory.

" S^r Henry Ascough, Knt. and Mary Southwell, married Feb. 9, " 1608."

" S^r George Wharton, sonne of L^d Wharton, was buried the 10th " of November 1609. James Steward, Esq. godsonne to King " James, was buried the 10th of November 1609." These two persons (the latter of whom was eldest son of Walter, first Lord Blantyre, Lord Treasurer of Scotland) were both servants to King James the First. Some reproachful words having passed betwixt them, being inflamed with a desire of revenge, and having first searched each others breasts for secret armour, they fought a duel near Islington, wherein they killed each other.

> With ruthless spears and ruthless hate
> They rush'd; victorious both, both shar'd one common fate.

It is said that when the King heard of this sad accident he was very sorry, and ordered them both to be buried in one grave. There was published at the time " A lamentable Ballad of a Combate lately " fought near London between S^r James Steward and S^r George " Wharton, Knights, who were bothe slaine at that time." It is reprinted in the History of Canonbury.   The following are copies of the letters that passed between these desperadoes, and which led to the above fatal event[1].

" Mr. George Wharton's challenge to Sir James Stewart before
" they fought :

  " S^r,

  " Your misconstruing of my message gives me cause to thinke you
" extreme vaineglorious; a humour w^ch y^e valiant detests.   And
" whereas you unjustly said I durst not meet you in y^e field to fight
" w^th you, you shall finde y^t you are much mistaken.   For I will
" fight w^th you w^th what weapon you shall appoint,  and meet
" you where you will, being contented to give you this advantage,
" not valuing y^e worst you can doe.

                              " GEORGE WHARTON."


            " Sir James Stewart's Answere :

  " S^r,

  " Your message being eyther ill delyverd, or else not accepted,
" you have since, though ill advised, retracted and repented it; for
" your messenger willed me from you, that eyther of us should make
" choyce of a friend to debate y^e matter.   To which, I confesse, I
" did but lightly hearken, since I knew oddes which no breath could
" make even.   And now you have to acknowledge noe other speeches
" than you charged me with, which is, that I said you durst not
" meet me in the field to fight.   True it is, your barbarous and un-
" civil insolency in such a place, and before such a company (for
" whose respect I am only sorry for what I then did or said), made
" me doe and saye y^t w^ch I nowe will make good.   Wherein since
" you finde yourself behind, I am ready to doe you all the right you
" can expect; and to that end have I sent you the length of my

[1] From the Harl. MSS. 787. f. 596.

" rapyer w<sup>ch</sup> I will use, with a dagger, and soe meet you at y<sup>e</sup> farther
" end of *Islington* (as I understande nearer you than me) at three of
" the clock in y<sup>e</sup> afternoone ; w<sup>ch</sup> things I scorne to take as advan-
" tages, but as my due, and w<sup>ch</sup> I have made indifferent.   And in
" respect I cannot send any of my friendes w<sup>th</sup>out hazard of disco-
" very, I have sent my servant herewith, who is onely acquainted
" with this business.                           JAMES STUARTE."


" John Egerton, son of Sir John Egerton, Knt. was buried
" April 22, 1610."   Islington seems to have been remarkably fatal
to the duellists of that day.   Mr. Egerton was killed in a duel on the
20th of April.   He is said to have been put to death basely by his
antagonist, one Edward Morgan, who was himself " sorely hurt[1]."
Mr. Egerton was third son of Sir John Egerton, Knt. whose son
Rowland was created a Baronet by James the First, and was ancestor
of Lord Grey de Wilton.

" S<sup>r</sup> Valentine Browne, Knt. and Ann Foulston, married Feb. 19,
" 1610."

" Penélope, the daughter of S<sup>r</sup> Maximilian Dallison, baptized the
" 9th May, 1611."

" A servant of Sir Oliver Butler's, buried Sept. 1, 1612 ; Mrs.
" Mary Fitzwilliams, from S<sup>r</sup> Oliver Butler's, Nov. 20, 1617."

" Mrs. Sisely Kempe, the wife of Nicholas Kempe, esq. buried
" June 19, 1617.   Nicholas Kempe, Knight, Sept. 14, 1624." (See
p. 296.)   This gentleman, who was an inhabitant of Islington, bequeathed 2000 marks to the University of Oxford.   (Vide Gutch's
Annals, vol. II. p. 353.)

" John, son of S<sup>r</sup> John Miller, baptized April 22, 1619 ; Thomas
" Aug. 17, 1620 ; Mary Feb. 27, 1623 ; Henry April 27, 1625 ;
" Benjamin, son of S<sup>r</sup> John and Mary Miller, Jan. 7, 1631."

" William, son of S<sup>r</sup> Stephen Stonor, baptized Oct. 5, 1621."

[1] Winwood's Memorials, vol. III. p. 154.

" Sir William Foster and Ann Ley, widow, married April 29,
" 1623."

" Thomas, son of Sir Henry Fines, buried April 15, 1626."

" William, the son of Sir Thomas Coventrye, beinge at that time
" L$^d$ Keeper of the Greate Seale of England, was baptized the 4$^{th}$ of
" October, 1627." He was knighted by Charles II. and made a
Commissioner of the Treasury. Bishop Burnet calls him the best
speaker in the House of Commons. He died unmarried in 1686.

" Mr. Alexander Steward, brother to Sir James Steward, was bu-
" ried April 29, 1629."

" Ann, daughter of Sir Simon and Ann Dewes, baptized May 13,
" 1630." Sir Symonds Dewes was an eminent antiquary, and made
very large Historical and Topographical Collections, which are now
in the College of Arms and in the British Museum, where is a very
curious life of Sir Symonds, written by himself, of which some extracts have been published. According to his own account, he had
been enabled in his enquiries, to correct Camden's Britannia in almost
every page. He employed the latter part of his life in copying records
and other antient documents, and in collecting coins and manuscripts.
At the age of thirty he had completed his principal work, viz. The
Journals of the Parliaments in the reign of Elizabeth. This was revised and published by Paul Bowes, Esq. in 1682, and is still in print.

" Fostino Menandye, Gent. and servant to the Earl of Exeter, bu-
" ried Nov. 25, 1630."

" Philipp, the daughter of the Right Honourable Sir Humphrey
" and Judith May, baptized December 17, 1630." Sir Humphrey
May was Master of the Rolls.

" Robert, the son of the Honourable John and the R$^t$ Honourable
" the Lady Lucy Roberts, baptized the 7th day of Feb. 1633."

" Ann, the daughter of Edward and Ann Mountegue, the Right
" Honourable the L$^d$ Mandefield, was baptized the 17th day of Fe-
" bruary, 1635, (buried March 3d.") Lord Mandeville was afterwards Earl of Manchester.

" Sr Henrie Robinson, buried the 21 day of Dec. 1637, in the
" vault with his mother. Ann, daughter of Sir Henry, Sept. 15,
" 1638." He was son of Mrs. Alice Owen by her first husband.

" William, son of Benjamin Hewling, baptized Oct. 28, 1665."
The unfortunate William Hewling, who was executed at Lyme, Sept.
12, 1685, for being concerned in the Duke of Monmouth's rebellion.
His brother Benjamin was executed at Taunton a few days afterwards.
The youth, beauty, and amiable qualities of these misguided men, excited a more general commiseration of their fate, than that of others
who suffered, perhaps more unjustly, under the stern rigour of the
merciless Jefferies. William Hewling's corpse was interred in the
Church-yard at Lyme, whither it was attended by 200 persons, men
and women of the first rank in the town [1].

" John, son of John Playford, baptized Oct. 6, 1665." Playford,
the celebrated writer on musick, lived many years at Islington, where
his wife kept a boarding-school for young ladies, opposite the Church,
and which was advertised at the end of one of his publications in
1679. His son John was a printer of musick.

" Thomas Lee, Esq. and Dame Mary Shipman, married Feb. 18,
" 1667."

" Sr Nicholas Crispe and Judith Adrian, married April 30, 1674."

" John Shurley, buried Dec. 30, 1679." John Shirley, who died
at Islington on the 28th of December that year, and was buried in
the Church-yard, published the Life of Sir Walter Ralegh, and some
Chirurgical tracts [2].

" The Lady Partridge, buried Nov. 4, 1675."

" William Dusey, a Knight, from St. Bride's, buried Aug. 4,
" 1683."

" Sir Robert Ducy, Bart. May 30, 1703." Sir Robert Ducie
succeeded his brother William, Viscount Downe of the Kingdom

---

[1] Lysons's Environs.

[2] Ant. Wood's Athen. Oxon. vol. II.

of Ireland (who died in 1697), in the title of Baronet. His daughter Elizabeth married Edward Morton, Esq. ancestor of the present Lord Ducie.

"Susanna Creed and her daughter Hester, killed by a clap of "thunder in their beds, buried the 10th day of Aug. 1690."

"Fisher, son of Sir Thomas Halton and Elizabeth his wife, was "baptized Aug. 5, 1694 (buried Nov. 25); Mary, their daughter, "baptized Oct. 31, 1695." Sir Thomas was son of Sir William Halton, by Ursula, daughter of Sir Thomas Fisher, Bart. Sir Thomas Halton's Lady was Elizabeth, daughter of John Cressener, Esq. of Islington. Mary Halton married James Nicoll, Esq. of Munfield, in Sussex [1]. "Madam Ursula Halton was buried at Islington, Aug. "13, 1716. Dame Elizabeth Halton, Sept. 10, 1716. S$^r$ Thomas "Halton, Bart. Sept. 14, 1726. Fenwick, son of S$^r$ Thomas, Feb. "13, 1732. Dame Frances Halton, (wife of S$^r$ William and "daughter of Sir George Dalston) April 21, 1747. Sir William "Halton (by mistake *Haughton* in the Register) Feb. 18, 1754, "aged 74. Dame Margaret Dalston, mother of Lady Halton, was "buried at Islington, May 5, 1715."

"S$^r$ Charles Hobby, buried April 23, 1715."

"S$^r$ John Night, buried Feb. 8, 1718."

"Job, Joshua, and Robert, sons of Richard and Ann Sale, were "baptized Aug. 18, 1731." They were all buried the 24th.

"Samuel Humphrys, stranger, buried Jan. 15th, 1736-7." (See page 250.)

"William, son of Thomas and Catharine Hawes, baptized Nov. "17th, 1736." The amiable and benevolent founder of the Humane Society.

"John Blackbourn, buried Nov. 19, 1741." An eminent Divine, and a Bishop among the Nonjurors. He republished Bale's " Chro-"nycle concerning Syr Johan Oldecastell," with an Appendix, and

---

[1] Kimber's Baronetage.

an edition of Bacon's Works, in four volumes folio [1]; (see his epitaph, p. 330.)

" Dr. Robert Poole, buried June 3d, 1752." Dr. Poole published Travels to France, in two volumes octavo, and a book called the Physical *Vade Mecum*. To both these works his portrait is prefixed. It is said in his epitaph, that with indefatigable industry, in the year 1746, he instituted the Small Pox Hospital. (See p. 204.)

" The Rev. John Lindsay, buried July 2, 1768, aged 81." A learned Nonjuring Divine, and an intimate friend of Blackbourne. He was author of " A short History of the Regal Succession, with " Remarks on Whiston's Scripture Politics," and translated Mason's Vindication of the Church of England, with a large Preface, containing a Series of the English Bishops since the Reformation; this preface is dated, Islington, 1727. Mr. Lindsay was 50 years minister of a Chapel in Aldersgate-street. He was buried near the tomb of his friend in the Church-yard, at the East end of the Church. (See his epitaph, p. 341.)

" John Hyacynth de Magelhaens, buried Feb. 13, 1790, aged 67." This man was F. R. S. and Member of several foreign academies, and had been formerly an Augustine Monk at Lisbon. He was great grandson to the celebrated navigator Ferdinando Magelhaens, who gave name to the strait discovered by him in 1519. He was also related to the Jesuit Magelhaens, who travelled over China from 1640 to 1648, till he was carried to the Court of Pekin, where he resided 29 years and died in 1677. Having renounced the Roman Catholic religion, he came to reside in England about the year 1764. He was a studious, ingenious, and learned man, particularly distinguished among the literati in this and other enlightened Countries, for his intimate acquaintance with most branches of natural philosophy, and no less ingenious for his experiments therein, particularly in mechanics. He was author and translator of many noted and ingenious

[1] Nichols's Anecdotes of Bowyer.

works, particularly an edition of " Cronstedt's Essay towards a System
" of Mineralogy."   Among his smaller works, was much esteemed a
tract on impregnating common water with fixed air, and his celebrated
invention to imitate the qualities and effects of all medical waters,
Bath, Pyrmont, Spa, Tunbridge, &c.   He also published several
other Treatises in Chemistry, an Account of various Philosophical
Instruments, and a Narrative of the last days of Rousseau, to which his
name is not affixed.   His languages were Portuguese, Spanish, Italian,
English, French, a little Dutch, and good Latin ; and he was particularly known in the Low Countries, having travelled there with young
foreigners.   He possessed a Canonry in the Austrian Netherlands,
and bore the character of a mild, charitable, and humane Christian.
All the Literati in Europe knew something of his merit, and most of
them were desirous to know more.   He died in lodgings at Islington ; and having desired that where the tree fell, there it might lie,
and that no tomb-stone should mark the place of his interment, he
was accordingly buried privately, but genteelly, in the Church-yard,
about 15 yards parallel with the East end of the Church on the North
side.

" Capt. George Tufnell, aged 21, buried 11 Aug. 1797, from St.
" Peter the Great, Colchester."

" Elizabeth Emma Thomas, buried 29th October, 1808."

The following extraordinary circumstances took place on the interment of this person ; *viz.*

On Saturday the 29th of October, the corpse was brought from a
house in Charter-house-square, and buried in the Church-yard ; on
the following Monday a head stone was placed over her grave, with
the following inscription :

" In memory of
" Mrs. Elizabeth Emma Thomas,
" who died the 28th October, 1808,
" aged 27 years.
" She had no fault, save what travellers give the moon :
" The light was lovely, but she died too soon."

A letter was received by the Coroner, intimating a strong suspicion that there had been some foul play with regard to the deceased, grounded on the circumstances of her dying, being buried, and a stone erected to her memory, in the short space of three days. Whereupon application was made to the parish officers, to have the grave opened; which was done on the following Thursday morning, and the body removed into the Church for the inspection of the Coroner's jury. On examining the corpse, a large wire pin was found sticking in the heart of the deceased, having been thrust through the left side of the body, and which served to confirm the suspicion that had been previously entertained respecting the manner of her death.

It however appeared in evidence that the deceased, having been for some time previously indisposed, had received proper medical assistance, but fell a victim to the violence of her disorder on the day above mentioned. Further, that a gentleman with whom she lived, being under the necessity of embarking immediately for the Continent, was desirous of seeing her previously interred, and paying the last honours to her remains; and it was at her own request that the pin was inserted (after the body had been placed in the coffin) by the medical gentleman who attended the deceased; in order to prevent the possibility of her being buried alive. These circumstances being proved by corroborative testimony, and nothing whatever appearing to criminate any of the parties concerned, the Jury returned their verdict, " *Died by* " *the Visitation of God.*"

The relatives of the deceased immediately applied to Doctors Commons for a faculty to remove the body to another place for interment; which being granted, the corpse was taken in a new coffin on the 8th of the following November to the Tabernacle in Tottenham Court Road, and there buried a second time. The stone bearing the foregoing inscription yet remains in the new burying-ground.

" William Tufnell, esq. aged 40, May 6th, 1809."

" Sir John Burton, aged 65, Dec. 1, 1809."

## THE PREBEND MANOR.

THIS Manor is bounded by the upper and lower parts of the Manor of Highbury on the North and South, the parish boundary line on the East, and the Manor of Canonbury and public highway on the West. It is the corps of one of the Prebends of St. Paul's, and is called in old records Iseldon extra London. The prebendal stall in the cathedral is the eleventh on the North side of the choir, and has written over it, " ISLINGTON. *In Convertendo Dom. Capt.*" It is rated in the King's Books at £.11. 10s. 10d. and is taxed at eight marks.

King William the Conqueror in or about the year 1065 restored to the Canons of St. Paul's certain estates of which they had been unjustly deprived; among these were nine cassats of lands in Islington [1], probably the two estates mentioned in the Domesday Survey. The extent of this manor being scarcely one hide, and the Even or Iveney Grove-field (see p. 54) only 6 acres 31 perches, which comprizes the whole property in this parish now belonging to the Church, can therefore include but a small portion of the lands the clergy of St. Paul's originally possessed here, which in Domesday Book is stated at four hides; and this serves to confirm the opinion mentioned in p. 99, respecting their estates in this parish having passed into the family of Berners [2].

In the Ecclesiastical taxation of Pope Nicholas IV. A. D. 1290, (temp. Edward I.) when that Pontiff granted a tenth of all Ecclesias-

[1] Records of the Dean and Chapter of St. Paul's, Lib. L. f. 12. and MSS. Bib. Lansdowne, Brit. Mus. No. 372.

[2] The present occupier of the Even Grove-field is Mr. Ambler of Newgate-market, who pays a reserved rent of £1. 8s. 4d. to the Dean and Chapter of St. Paul's. This rent was formerly paid in half yearly sums of 11s. 4d. with two capons, or 5 shillings, at Christmas. MSS. Bib. Lansd. Brit. Mus. No. 372. The ground is situate within the boundary line of Highbury Manor, on the East side of the road leading to Ball's Pond. Several acres of ground near to this spot have been lately taken for the purpose of building, upon a part of which, facing the road, it is intended to erect a large and handsome edifice for a manufactory of floor cloths.

tical revenues to the King to defray the expences of the Holy War; the Prebend Manor is thus noticed :

" Bona Mag'ri Will'i de Monteforti in Iseldon, decani S'ci Pauli,
" £.3. 17s. 5d.
" Decima 7s. 3½d."

The Customs of the Manor, together with the number of copyholders and houses it contained in 1649, will be seen from the following extract of the Survey thereof, taken in that year by order of the Parliament.

|  | £. | s. | d. |
|---|---|---|---|
| " The rents of assize due to the Lord of the said " Manno' by the several tenants being copyholders " of inheritance at fines certaine, are *per annum* | iiij | xiiij | iiij |

" MEMORANDUM.   All the customary tenants hold
" together in the said Manno' as followeth ; viz.
" Messuages or tenements in all *fourty-sixe*, and
" ninety-eight acres of pasture or meadow ground,
" be it more or less.
" MEMORANDUM.  The aforesaid tenants pay to the
" Lord of the said Mano', a fine certaine upon
" every alienation or descent, viz. 6s. 8d. for every
" messuage or tenement, and 6s. 8d. for every
" acre of land.  Only the Company of Cloth-
" workers pay their fine once in every twenty
" years, being £.11. 1s. 8d.
" At the Court Leet the tenants of the Manor of
" Canbury doe service.
" Perquisites belonging to the said Manno' are
" waiftes, strayes, and felons goods.
" The Courts Baron and Courts Leet, fines and
" amerciaments of Courts, fines upon descent or

*£.   s.   d.*

" alienation, waiftes, strayes, and felons goods,
" and all other profits and perquisites within the
" said Manor to the Royaltie thereof belonging
" or appertaining, we estimate to be worth com-
" mu'ibus annis - - - - - - - - - - - - - -   xj

" MEMORANDUM. Y$^t$ the *£*.4. 14*s.* 4*d.* rents of
" assize before mentioned is included in the said
" sum of *£*.11. being intended by us for the whole
" yearly value of the said Manor.

" MEMORANDUM. The customary tenants of the said Manor are
" copyholders of inheritance, and theire rents of assize due to the
" Lord of the said Manno' payable once every yeare, viz. the five
" and twentieth of March, are as followeth :

| " Yearely Rents : | *£.* | *s.* | *d.* |
|---|---|---|---|
| " William Nicholls - - - - - - | — | iij | — |
| " Benjamin Pierson - - - - - - | — | i | iij |
| " The Widd' Pitts - - - - - - - | — | — | vj |
| " Robert Pierson - - - - - - - | — | j | iij |
| " John Harvey - - - - - - - - | — | j | iij |
| " John Smith - - - - - - - - - | — | ii | vj |
| " George Carleton - - - - - - | — | — | ix |
| " The Company of Clothworkers | i | xiij | ix |
| " Maurice Gething - - - - - - | — | ii | xi |
| " Sir John Miller - - - - - - - | — | xvij | vij |
| " Sir Edmond Fowler - - - - - | — | xi | vj |
| " Thomas Tomlinson - - - - - | — | xiij | — |
| " Henry Swinnerton - - - - - | — | v | — |

Total   iiij   xiiij   iiij

18 Dec. 1649.

" RICHARD ROCKE,
" JOSEPH HUTCHINSON, } Surveyors."
" BENJAMIN WARDEN,

The Manor was sold by the Parliament in the same year to the above-named Maurice Gething, Citizen of London, for £.275.[1] There are no demesnes belonging to it.

List of Prebendaries of ISELDON or ISLINGTON, in old records Isledon extra London. (Principally from Newcourt.)

1. ALGAR, the son of Derman.
2. ULFRAN, the Bishop's chaplain; he was a Canon here, and a priest in 1104 and 1114.
3. RICHARD, the son of the Chancellor.
4. HENRY, nephew to Gilbert.
5. JOCELIN, a native of Lombardy, Archdeacon of Westminster and Bishop of Sarum. He was suspended, with the Bishop of London and some other Bishops, in the cause of Becket 1170, and died in 1184, having first taken the habit of a Cisterian Monk.
6. ROBERT WARELWAST, Dean of Salisbury, Bishop of Exeter 1150 or 1155; he died in 1159, and was buried at Plympton.
7. JOHN DE GREENFORD, Dean of Chichester, elected Bishop of that See 1173, died in 1180.
8. RICHERUS or Richard, de Andele.
9. ROBERT BANASTER occurs, Archdeacon of Essex in 1168 and 1194. His obit was kept 13 kal. Junii.
10. ROBERT THE TREASURER.
11. PETER DE SANCTA MARIA. He was Rector of Fering, in Essex, Treasurer of St. Paul's, and had also the Prebends of Kentish Town and Mora.
12. RALPH FURNIS.
13. GALFRIDUS DE LUCY occurs Prebendary of Isledon, and perhaps of Totenhale, in which last, (if he be the same) he is named Galfridus filius Decani. He is said to be Canon of this Church about 1224; was Archdeacon of London in the time of Eustace

[1] Parliamentary Surveys, St. Pauls' Cathedral.

the Bishop, and Robert de Watford the Dean; and appears to
be Dean of St. Paul's in 1231, William de Fauconberg being
Treasurer the same year; which William was succeeded in that
office by Alexander de Swerford that very year; for it appears
that the said Alexander was Treasurer of St. Paul's Jan. 12;
and if so, then, if William de Fauconberg was Treasurer when
Galfry de Lucy was Dean, as is said above, the said Galfry must
be Dean in 1231. He likewise occurs Dean in 1234. On the
Feast of St. Peter ad Vincula, 1239, there was an agreement
made between him and the Chapter of St. Paul's on the one
part, and R. de Wendover on the other, about the manor of
Sandon. And about the middle of the same year, the Bishop
being absent, he accursed all those who had presumptuously
attempted to lay hands on Ranulph de Brito, a Canon of this
church, and put his own church under jurisdiction. According
to the Registry of Bermondsey, he died July 30, 1240; but,
according to the records of his own church, there was a controversy moved before him and his Chapter in the year 1241, about
some lands alledged by Roger de Horset to belong to his prebend
of Portpool. He died in September, the same year, according to
Matthew Paris, p. 576; which seems to be farther confirmed by
the patent 26 Hen. III. 1241, wherein John de Mansel was
presented to the prebend of Totehale, quæ fuit (as it is there
expressed) Magistri Galfridi de Lucy, quondam Decani S. Pauli,
London. He founded a chauntry in the church of St. Paul; to
which church he gave his manor, house, and lands at Acton, reserving one hundred shillings per annum to be paid to a priest
celebrating divine service there, for the health of his soul, and for
the souls of Eustace de Fauconberg Bishop of London, and
Philip de Fauconberg Archdeacon of Huntingdon; and paying
20 s. yearly on the day of the said Galfry's obit, which, according to an obituary of St. Paul's, was held 7 id. Septembris; and
a mark at the obit of the said Philip de Fauconberg.

14. WILLIAM DE HAVERSHULL, a great favourite with King Henry III. He had the King's letters of presentation to the church of Luffenham, directed to Hugh Bishop of Lincoln Nov. 6, and again Feb. 22 following, 1228; the like to the church of Wensington, by reason the see of Winton was void Nov. 9, 1241. The King made him his Treasurer the year before, viz. 1240, in the place of Hugh de Pateshull, elected Bishop of Coventry and Lichfield on the kalends of July that year. In the aforesaid year, 1241, he had the King's letters directed to the Dean and Chapter of Litchfield, for the prebend which was William de Radley's Bishop of Norwich, and which the King besides granted to William de Glocester, dated March 6. He had likewise that King's letter of presentation to the church of Preston in Amounderness, July 3, 1243, which church was valued at £.100 a year; and the King gave it to his brother Jeffery after the death of the said William de Havershull. He died on the vigil of St. Bartholomew, 10 kal. Sept. 1252, being at the time of his death a Canon of this Church and the King's Treasurer, in whose service he had with great diligence spent many years. His anniversary was kept on 10 kal. Sept. according to one obituary of this church, and according to another on the 9th, and a pittance of 14s. *per annum* allowed for it. His executors assigned lxiv s. *per annum* to find a chaplain to celebrate for his soul at the altar of St. Chad, where the body of Alexander de Swerfore is buried.

15. FULCO LOVELL, prebendary of Caddington Major and Isledon, was Archdeacon of Colchester July 1, 1267; also in 1268 or 1269; for then, with Godfrey de S. Dunstan, having the custody of the Bishopric of London (Henry de Sandwich the Bishop being under excommunication), he made an agreement with the King to pay him for the tenths of the benefices within the city and diocese of London, according to their true value, 3300 marks. In 1270, with John de Witham the King's chaplain,

he had the custody of the abbey of Bileig in Essex, by reason of a difference there between the abbot and convent. Feb. 6, 1280, he was assigned the sole coadjutor to John de Chishull Bishop of London, who died within three days after; of whose death Fulco Lovell and Godfry de Mortuo-Mari, Archdeacon of London, were sent to give notice to the King, who, on the 18th of that month, granted them licence to chuse another Bishop; upon which they elected this Fulco Lovell; but he, either because he reaped greater profit from his ecclesiastical benefices (which were more than twenty) than he could hope for from the Bishopric of London, or for fear the Archbishop should reject him, by reason of his pluralities, or rather (as he pretended) out of his infirmity of body, or other matters of conscience, refused it. He died, according to Murimoth and the Annals of London, Nov. 21, 1287, but more truly, according to the manuscript of Florilegus, Nov. 21, 1285; for, in six days after, one Hugo de Kendale had the King's letters of presentation to the church of Ledered, void by the death of Fulco Lovell, directed to the Bishop of Winton, dated Nov. 27, 1285. His anniversary was kept 11 kal. Dec. for which there was an allowance of 50 s. *per annum*. When he was dying, he founded a chauntry of two priests at the altar of St. John Baptist in the church of St. Paul, to celebrate for his soul.

16. PHILIP LOVELL, prebendary also of Caddington Major and of Wildland, from being steward to the Earl of Winchester, was called up to the King's service about the feast of St. Michael 1251; but was grievously accused by his enemies for taking very rich vessels from a wealthy Jew, privately, to ease him of the King's tax; and private gifts from others for the same cause: but at last, by the advice and means of John Mansell, a principal chancellor of the King's, he procured the royal favour, but not without the payment of 1000 marks; nevertheless he was removed from his office of treasurer; not without a great deal of shame. But the next year, by the intercession of Alexander

King of Scotland, who had newly married the King's daughter, and to whom the said Philip (when the Earl of Winchester's steward) had oftentimes been very kind and respectful, the King forgave the said Philip all his offences; but in 1258, the said Philip being then the King's Clerk, Special Counsellor, and Treasurer, upon an information given against him of the damages he had done the King's forest, the King was so incensed against him that he commanded him to be taken into custody; and, though he gave noble sureties until he should make his innocence appear, yet it stuck so by him that, on the festival of St. Thomas the Martyr, the next year, he died at his Church at Hamestable through grief, as it was said, because he was not reconciled to the King.

17. HUGH DE DODINGH.

18. PETER DE AURIVALL.

19. RALPH DUNGON, Dungeon, or Dunion, made his will, whereby it appears that he was at that time parson of Wygmerstock, Stotesdon, and Dugarvan, for to those his churches, and to the poor of these parishes, he gave legacies; he gave also 100 marks to purchase a yearly rent to sustain a priest daily celebrating in this church, for his and the souls of all his parents. His obit was kept Oct. 13, for which there was a pittance of 26s. 8d. per annum.

20. WILLIAM DE MONTFORD. He was elected Dean of St. Paul's 1285. In 1289 he attested a certain ordination of the Chancellor of London, dated 16 kal. Aug. He died suddenly towards the end of the year 1294 in the King's chamber, and at the time of his death, besides his Deanry, held the Archdeaconry of Salop and seven rectories with cure of souls.

21. JOHN DE LUCO, de Luc, or de Luca, was a prebendary of Wildland in 1281, and occurs in 1289.

22. WILLIAM DE SARDENE, prebendary also of Eald-street. He was Official of the Arches in 1297.

23. RALPH DE BALDOCK.  Educated at Merton College, Oxford. Prebendary also of Holborn and of Newington; Archdeacon of Middlesex 1274.  In 1290 he was at the Court of Rome; was elected Dean of St. Paul's Oct. 18, 1294, and with his Chapter, in 1298, made statutes concerning the habits of perpetual chaplains.  He was elected Bishop of London 1304; but the Archbishop of Canterbury having suspended three of the Canons of St. Paul in his visitation of that church, whilst the See was vacant, these Canons (whereof Peter de Dene was one) required their places (or votes) in the election, but were refused, upon which they appealed to the Pope, and afterwards from the confirmation also.  Upon the day appointed for the hearing at Rome, both the Bishop elect and the said Peter appeared personally; but Peter renouncing his appeal, the Pope ratified the confirmation of the Bishop elect, and commanded his consecration, which was accordingly performed at Lyons Jan. 30, 1306. He was for a short time Lord Chancellor of England, but resigned that office within a year.

24. RICHARD DE NEWPORT, Archdeacon of Middlesex 1304, Dean of St. Paul's 1314; Bishop of London 1317; died Aug. 24, 1318, at the vicar's (or parson's) house at Ilford; was forthwith carried thence in the night to Stepney, and buried on the 28th of the same month in the Cathedral Church of St. Paul.

25. GERARD de INGOLISME.

26. THOMAS DE CHARLTON.

27. THOMAS DE ASTLEY, Prebendary of Holywell, Archdeacon of Middlesex, and Treasurer of St. Paul's.  He was also a Prebendary in the Churches of Exeter, Litchfield, and Sarum; was ratified by King Edward the Third in the Prebends of Swytherton and in South Neweton, in the monastical church of Wilton, and in the church of Reculver, and in Canterbury, Jan. 21, 1345; and died in or before 1349.

28. ROBERT DE REDDESWELL, professor of the Civil Law, rector of

Kelvedon, Essex, 1321; Treasurer of St. Paul's 1329; Prebendary of Wildland 1330; Archdeacon of Middlesex 1333; died 1377.

29. HENRY DE IDESWORTH. He occurs Prebendary of Holborn by the name of Henry de Ides; and was parson of Stanwell, in Middlesex, Feb. 20, 1328. The King gave him the Prebend of Illeton, in the Church of Wells, Oct. 3 following. He was present Nov. 16, 1331, with the Dean and Chapter of St. Paul's, at the making of the Statute of not leasing out of their manors for term of life without the consent of the Chapter. He likewise occurs Prebendary of Kentish Town.

30. HUMPHRY DE HASTANG, Prebendary of Langebragg, in the free chapel of Penrith, 1338, Archdeacon of Coventry and Prebendary of Nassington 1340; Prebendary of Isledon 1343; after which he had the King's licence to give certain lands, &c for the maintainance of a chaplain to celebrate in the church of Bradelegh, for the souls of Ralph Baron of Stafford and Margaret his wife, Jan. 25, 1343; and on April 6, 1347, he again gave him the said Prebendary of Nassington. He died before July 26, 1349, for then the King disposed of his Prebend of Langebrug, as void by his death.

31. WILLIAM DE ROTHWELL, Rector of Eastwood, Essex, from 1327 to 1350; and Archdeacon of Essex 1351, on the presentation of Edward the Third, during the vacancy of the See of London. Newcourt (I. 72), says he was Chaplain to that Prince, who gave him the eighth Prebend in St. Stephen's collegiate church at Westminster 1351; and that of Croperdy, in the county of Oxford, in the church of Lincoln, the same year. Browne Willis confirms (Cath. II. 260, 262) Newcourt's account; and adds, that he died in the reign of Edward the Third, and was buried at Rothwell, in Northamptonshire, his native town. His epitaph, from a brass, (copied in Nichols's Hist. Canonbury, and Gough's Sepulchral Monuments,) records two

other places of preferment, *Ferrying* and *Yelmeton*, the one a Prebend in the Church of Chichester, in the gift of the Bishop of that Diocese, who at that time was Robert Stratford, Lord Chancellor, the other a vicarage in Devonshire, in the gift of the Prebendary of King's Leynton, in the church of Salisbury. Mr. Brydges, in his History of Northamptonshire, by a strange oversight, says William de Rothwell was chaplain and vicar of Rothwell when the vicarage was first ordained, 1220, and succeeded 1222 by another vicar (II. 62. Reg. Hug. Wells Ep. Linc.) But not to mention that this is too early a date for brass plates, the above extracts clearly show the person for whom the epitaph was intended lived above a century later.

32. WILLIAM DE LOTHBURY occurs Prebendary of Isledon March 6, 1357.

33. JOHN DE SUYNLO, or Sweinleigh, was the King's chaplain, who gave him the Prebend which William de Cusancia had in the collegiate church of St. Stephen, Westminster, Aug. 6, 1361, and the custody of the free chapel of St. Anne de Alvedelee in twelve days after. He had the King's letters of presentation to the church of Walpole, in the Diocese of Ely, Oct. 8, the same year, and on the 21st of that month the King gave him the Prebend of Isledon. On Feb. 20, 1366, he resigned his Prebend of St. Stephen, (which the King thereupon gave to Alexander South,) as he did this Prebend of Isledon in September before, as appears above, and was succeeded therein by

34. WILLIAM DE HYNDELEE, who was afterwards admitted rector of St. Alphage May 20, 1385, which he resigned June 5, 1386, and was admitted the same day rector of Bardfield Parva, by way of exchange with Adam Wylying, *alias* de Wynshynham. Bardfield he exchanged Dec. 4, 1397, for the church of Borley, both in Essex, with William Wigor, which he resigned 1399, but how or when he voided this Prebend appears not.

35. ADAM HOLME, who, with his brother Roger Holme, Chancellor of St. Paul's, and John Pirywell, were executors to Adam de Bury, Lord Mayor of London in 1364, and, according to the will of the said Adam de Bury, by which he ordained that out of his personal estate provision should be made to find three chaplains, perpetually to celebrate divine service in a certain chapel newly built in this Cathedral Church, near the North door, for the health of his soul and the souls of all the faithful deceased, did by their deed, dated April 30, 1367, assign to the Dean and Chapter of St. Paul's, divers lands and rents for the maintenance of the said Chaplains, which the said Roger, being Chancellor of London, as also a Canon resident and Prebendary of Kentish Town, before the death of the testator increased to the number of seven, to celebrate for ever, in the said chapel dedicated to the Holy Ghost, towards the building whereof he was at extraordinary costs. Hence it was called Holme's College, and their Common Hall in St. Paul's Church-yard on the South side, near to a carpenter's yard, which college was suppressed in the reign of King Edward VI. This Roger Holme did likewise restore and establish a certain chauntry of one priest, for the soul of John de Wengam, sometime chief chaunter in this Cathedral, which was then utterly come to nothing.

36. WILLIAM STORTFORD, Treasurer of St. Paul's 1387, Archdeacon of Middlesex 1393, Prebendary of Isledon 1399. His will was made in Aug. 1416, and proved Nov. 4.

37. RICHARD BRUTON succeeded Stortford both in his Archdeaconry of Middlesex and Prebend of Isledon, to which he was admitted Nov. 20, 1416, and died before March 17, 1417, (perhaps he was the same that was collated to the Prebend of Rugmore in 1409) for on that day he was succeeded by

38. RICHARD CLIFFORD, in his Prebend of Isledon, as void by the said Bruton's death, and on May 2, 1418, in the Archdeaconry of Middlesex. This was not that Richard Clifford who was Bishop of Lon-

3 c

don, but, perhaps, his nephew; and was collated to the Prebend of Chiswick Dec. 21, 1398, upon the resignation of the last named Richard, who, being made Bishop of Worcester in 1401, collated this our Richard Clifford to the church of Hampton upon Avon, in that diocese, in 1402, May 4, and being afterwards translated to London in 1407, conferred on this our Richard Clifford the Prebend of Twyford in 1408, and afterwards the Prebend of Pancras in 1417, as also that of Isledon and this Archdeaconry, as above, which last became void by his death before Sept. 6, 1422.

39. JOHN RYDER, June 21, 1419.

40. WILLIAM BRIGGEFORD, was vicar of Braughing: the time of his admission appears not, but he resigned it before Aug. 28, 1428. In 1438, Feb. 14, he was collated to the church of Hadham Magna; both in Herts; to this Prebend in 1442, March 8, which he resigned April 15, 1447, and was on the same day collated to that of Newington; but how long he held that and Hadham appears not.

41. WILLIAM SAY, B. D. collated to this Prebend April 15, 1447, elected Dean of St. Paul's, April 21, 1457. He was afterwards Prebendary of Newington, which he resigned in 1464, and by way of exchange had that of Wenlakesbarn conferred on him the same year, July 20, he being then Doctor of Divinity; and the same year was made one of the King's Privy Counsel. He was Prolocutor in a Synod held at London in 1463. He was made rector of the brotherhood of Jesus Chapel under the choir of St. Paul's Church, anno 1459, founded, or rather confirmed by King Henry VI. where, after the death of the said William, a chauntry was founded in 17 Henry VII. for one priest to perform divine service in a certain chapel there, where the body of the said William was interred, for his soul and the souls of several of his relations, and a yearly allowance of 40s. assigned for the keeping of his anniversary for ever. To which was afterwards added ano-

ther chauntry, founded in 18th Henry VIII. by William Vale, citizen and cutler of London, who by his testament gave several messuages for the maintenance of a priest to celebrate and pray for the soul of the said William Say in the forementioned chapel for ever. This our Dean died on the 23d Nov. 1468, whereby his Deanry and Prebend of Wenlakesbarn became void, and therefore could not be the same William Say who Stow saith was Master of the Hospital of St. Anthony in 1474.

42. HENRY EWEN, M. A. Nov. 6, 1451.

43. JAMES GOLDWELL, LL. D. occurs rector of Rivenhall, in Essex, and Prebendary of Wildland, to which he was collated Oct. 28, 1457, and resigned it in 1458; was collated to the Prebend of Sneating Oct. 16 the same year, and leaving that, was collated to the Prebend of Isledon May 16th, 1459. He was made Archdeacon of Essex Aug. 5, 1461, having about that time resigned Rivenhall, as he did Isledon and his Archdeaconry about 1472. He had been rector of St. John the Evangelist, London, to which he was admitted May 20th, 1455, but resigned it before Jan. 30, the same year. He was educated in All Souls College, Oxon, to which he was a benefactor. He was President of St. George's Hall there, and lastly, being Dean of Sarum and Secretary to King Edward IV. was promoted to the Bishoprick of Norwich, and had restitution of his temporalities Feb. 25, 1473. He repaired and for the most part rebuilt the church of Great Chart, in Kent, which seems to have been the place of his nativity, and died in 1499.

44. JOHN MORTON, LL. D. Oct. 26, 1472, Prebendary of Chiswick, 1478.

45. WILLIAM KEMPE (a kinsman doubtless of Thomas Kempe, at this time Bishop of London) was collated by him to this Prebend Oct. 27, 1473; to the rectory of Stepney, Feb. 26, 1476; to the Prebendary of Kentish Town, March 2, 1478, being then B. D.; to the rectory of Orsett, Essex, March 28, 1489. This

Prebend he left on or before March 31, 1487; Stepney and Orsett he resigned before December 23, 1522; and Kentish Town before May 9, 1523. William Kempe, clerk, was admitted to the church of Layer Bretton, in Essex, May 24, 1550, which became void by his death before Jan. 18, 1552, but it is doubtful whether he was the same with our Prebendary.

46. RALPH BYRD was admitted rector of Wideford, Herts, April 29, 1454. The time of his voiding it appears not, but probably when he was admitted to the sinecure rectory of Chigwell, in Essex, which was May 12, 1460. In 1470, Nov. 8, he was collated to the Prebend of St. Pancras, which being afterwards appropriated to the office of Penitentiary in the church of St. Paul, together with the advowson of the said church of Chigwell, he left about the beginning of 1486. Nov. 10 he was admitted rector of Wrabnes and vicar of Ramsey, both in Essex, by the name of *Bride*, July 2, 1512.

47. JOHN WANDYSFORD, B. D. Jan. 12, 1482.

48. WILLIAM HARYNDON or HARRINGTON, who was collated to this Prebend in 1497, was admitted rector of St. Anne, Aldersgate, London, 1505, which he resigned in 1510. He voided this Prebend by his death before Nov. 25, 1523.

49. GALFR. WHARTON was collated to the Prebend of Isledon Nov. 25, 1523; to the rectory of Fulham March 23 following; to the Archdeaconry of London March 29, 1526; and was admitted to the vicarage of Sawbridgeworth (Herts) April 17 following: all which preferments became void by his death, about Oct. 1529. He was admitted vicar of Totenham (Middlesex) May 21, 1525, and resigned it in 1526. He was Vicar-general to Cuthbert Tunstall, Bishop of London.

50. ROBERT RYDELEY was collated to the rectory of St. Botolph, Bishopsgate, July 3, 1523, which he resigned before March 21 that year, and on that day was collated to the prebend of Mora; and on Feb. 20, 1526, was admitted rector of

St. Edmund, Lombard-street; his **Prebend of Mora** he resigned April 3, 1527, and was on the same day collated to that of St. Andrew's, which he resigned about Oct. 30, 1529, and on that very day had this Prebend of Isledon, and the sinecure rectory of Fulham, conferred on him; both which, together with his said church of St. Edmund, became void by his death before June 12, 1536.

51. JOHN SPENDLOVE, or SPENDLOWE, was collated to the sinecure rectory of Little Badow in Essex, by the Bishop of London, to whom it devolved by lapse Dec. 4, 1535. He had several other preferments in this diocese. He was collated to this Prebend June 12, 1536, but resigned it in 1537, and was the same year collated to the Prebend of Holywell. In 1533, he was admitted to the church of Finchley in Middlesex; and in 1534, Sept. 29, to the Prebend of Mapesbury, which he resigned the next month. To the sinecure rectory of Hackney (Middlesex) in 1537, which he resigned in 1571, as he did that of Little Badow in 1575. Lastly, he was admitted to the church of St. Andrew Undershaft in 1555, which he resigned the year following. Of the churches of Finchley, Hackney, and the Prebend of Holywell, he was deprived soon after Queen Mary came to the Crown; but, upon Queen Elizabeth succeeding, he was restored to them all; two of which, viz. Finchley, and the Prebend of Holywell, he held to the time of his death, which happened before Sept. 14, 1581. But whether he was deprived of Badow, and restored to it again, doth not appear.

52. ELIZEUS AMBROSE, Nov. 16, 1537.

53. RICHARD FLETCHER, D. D. sometime fellow of Corpus Christi College, in Cambridge. He was admitted to the Prebend of Isledon Sept. 30, 1572, being then M A. which he resigned in 1589. In the mean time he was made Dean of Peterborough, in 1583, was present with Mary Queen of Scots when she suffered death at Fotheringhay in Northamptonshire, in Feb. 1586,

where he persuaded her to renounce her religion, to her great disturbance. In 1589, he was made Bishop of Bristol, Dec. 14, and about that time Bishop Almoner; thence he was translated to Worcester, in February 1593; and soon after to London, being elected thereto Dec. 30, 1594. He fell under the displeasure of Queen Elizabeth, by marrying a second wife, the handsome widow of Sir John Baker, of Sissinghurst, and was forbid the Court a year, and suspended from the exercise of his episcopal functions for six months. This disgrace is supposed to have shortened his life. He died while sitting in his chair, and smoking tobacco, June 15, 1596, and was buried in his own cathedral church. He left nine children, of whom the eldest was John Fletcher the Dramatic Poet.

54. THOMAS MARTEN, M. A. Oct. 24, 1589.

55. SIMON ROGERS, M. A. was collated to the Prebend of Totenhale Feb. 13, 1601, which he resigned before May 29, 1602; and afterwards was collated to this Prebend in 1603, which he resigned in 1604.

56. WILLIAM ROGERSON, B. D. June 25, 1604.

57. GRANADO CHESTER, of the family of Chester of Herts. He was M. A. of Cambridge, and incorporated in the same degree at Oxford July 13, 1619. He was afterwards B. and D. D. and dignified in this church as above.

58. WILLIAM HALL, M. A. Aug. 17, 1660. He was collated by the Dean and Chapter of this church to the rectory of St. Michael Bassishaw, London, Aug. 30, 1660, which, as also his Prebend, became void by his death before April 21, 1662.

59. MARK FRANK, D. D. was on one and the same day, viz. Dec. 19, 1660, collated to the Archdeaconry of St. Alban's, and to the Treasurership of St. Paul's, he being then B. D.; to the Prebend of Isledon April 21, 1662, he being then D. D.; and was admitted rector of Barley, Herts, Feb. 2 following; all which became void by his death before June 7, 1664.

60. JOHN HALL, M. A. July 11, 1664.

61. EDWARD STILLINGFLEET, D. D. of St. John's College, Cambridge, rector of Sutton, co. Bedford, 1657, which he resigned for the rectory of St. Andrew, Holborn, Jan. 1664-5; preacher at the Rolls chapel, Prebendary of Islington Feb. 9, 1666-7; Canon Residentiary of St. Paul's 1670; exchanged his Prebend for that of Newington, Oct. 11, 1672; Archdeacon of London 1676; Dean of St. Paul's 1677; consecrated Bishop of Worcester, Oct. 13, 1689; died March 27, 1699[1]. He was greatly distinguished for his numerous polemic writings, particularly " Origines Sacræ; " or, a Rational Account of the Grounds of Natural and Revealed " Religion ;" a work, which for extensive and profound learning, solidity of judgment, strength of argument, and perspicuity of expression, has been justly esteemed one of the best defences of revealed religion that ever was published in our own or any other language.

62. WILLIAM HOLDER, D. D. Nov. 16, 1672. He was Sub-dean of the King's chapel, rector of Therfield, in Herts, and one of the Canons Residentiary of St. Paul's Church.

63. EDMUND KIDBY, M. A. April 9, 1688, vicar of East and West Haningfield, Essex, died 1718.

64. PTOLOMEY JAMES, 1718. He was Minister of St. Helen's, in Bishopsgate-street, and died suddenly April 26, 1729. He left his estate to be divided between the Corporation of the Sons of the Clergy and the Hospital of Bethlem, for the incurables there.

65. MR. DREW, 1729—1745.

66. JOSEPH BUTLER, M. A. rector of Shadwell, 1741; installed Prebendary of Islington in 1745. This gentleman was nephew to Dr. Butler, Bishop of Durham, who died in 1752. He departed this life at his native town of Wantage, Berks, Aug. 1798, and was at the time of his decease, the oldest incumbent in London.

[1] See Bibl. Top. Brit. No. IX. p. 52.

67 ROBERT NARES, B. D. the present Prebendary, was installed
1798. This excellent Divine and very learned Critic (son of Dr.
Nares, the celebrated musical composer, and nephew of Mr. Justice Nares) was presented to the rectory of Sharnford in Leicestershire 1798, which he resigned in 1799 on being collated to
the archdeaconry of Stafford. He was also for some time preacher
at Lincoln's Inn, and one of the Assistant Librarians at the
British Museum ; but relinquished those situations in 1805, on
being presented to the vicarage of St. Mary at Reading, where
he regularly resides, highly respected as a worthy man and a con-
scientious parish priest. He has published a curious " Treatise
" on Orthoëpy," and several other valuable works ; particularly a
complete Course of Warburtonian Lectures.

On the site of Cumberland-row, before the present houses were built
(A. D. 1766,) there stood a row of almshouses; but to what Company
or individual they owed their foundation, or what objects the charity embraced, cannot at this time be discovered. About 30 years ago,
a house in this row was destroyed by fire, by which accident a poor woman was also burnt to death. A similar accident, but attended with
less dreadful consequences, happened on the 2d of Jan. 1799, at the
house of Mr. Ridley, an eminent copper-plate-engraver in Colebrooke
row, by which the upper part of the premises was destroyed, together with many valuable engravings.

At the back of Colebrooke-row is a nursery-ground, containing six
acres, in the occupation of Thomas Watson ; it was first converted to
this use, on Mr. W. Watson his brother and predecessor's ceasing to
occupy the ground in Church-street, mentioned in p. 273. The row
of houses last mentioned was built on land belonging to the family
whose name it bears in the year 1768. The house at the South end
was originally a public house, but has been for several years a
boarding school for young ladies. The white plaster tenement at the
back of this row, and abutting on the nursery ground, was for some

time the residence of the celebrated William Woodfall, Reporter of the Parliamentary Debates. The house at the other end of the row, facing the South, was about 40 years since an academy for young gentlemen, and kept by the Rev. John Rule, M. A. whose custom it was to have dramatic performances exhibited by his pupils at their breakings up. A piece performed on one of these occasions called " The Agreeable Surprize," translated from the French of De Marivaux, was published in a volume bearing the title of " Poetical Blos- " soms, or the Sports of Genius; being a Collection of Poems upon se- " veral Subjects, by the young Gentlemen of Mr. Rule's Academy at " Islington," printed for the authors, duodecimo, 1766, price 1s. 6d. The house and premises next to the one last mentioned was about the same period known as the Castle public house and tea gardens, of which mention is made in the 26th paper of the Connoisseur. Adjoining to this the celebrated Colley Cibber had lodgings, and here he died on the 12th Dec. 1757 [1]. His daughter Mrs. Clarke, than whom few women ever passed through a greater variety of adventures and occupations, kept a public house in Islington, where she died in great distress in 1760.

At the house No. 1 in Bird's-buildings, some years ago resided —— Penn, a very ingenious artizan, who there fabricated a convex burning glass of most extraordinary powers, for Mr. Parker, an eminent glass manufacturer in Fleet-street. He erected an out-building at the bottom of his garden (lately converted into a dwelling) for the purpose of carrying on his operations, and at length succeeded in producing the most powerful burning lens that had ever been constructed. Its diameter was three feet, and the completing the machine with its necessary apparatus is said to have cost his employer upwards of £.700. Its powers were astonishing : the most hard and solid substances of the mineral world, as platina, iron, steel, flint stone, &c. were melted in a few seconds on being exposed to its intense focus; and it is

---

[1] Communicated by Mr. Nichols.

3 D

stated that a diamond weighing 10 grains exposed to this lens for 30 minutes, was reduced to six grains, during which operation it opened and foliated like the leaves of a flower, and emitted whitish fumes, and when closed again it bore a polish and retained its form. A full description of this extraordinary machine, with a comparative statement of its effect upon a variety of substances, will be found in the new edition of the Cyclopædia by Dr. Rees, from which it appears that a subscription was proposed for raising the sum of 700 guineas, towards indemnifying the charges of Mr. Parker, and retaining this very curious and useful machine in our own country; but from the failure of the subscription, and some other concurring circumstances, that gentleman was induced to dispose of it to Capt. Macintosh, who accompanied Lord Macartney in the embassy to China, and it was left, much to the regret of philosophers in Europe, at Pekin; where it remains in the hands of persons who most probably know neither its value nor use.

Near to this spot, on the West bank of the New River, just at the place where it emerges from underneath the road, is a small yard and barn, about ten years since in the occupation of that singular character the Honourable Baron Ephraim Lopez Pereira D'Aguilar, who resided at No. 21 in Camden-street. This eccentric being was by birth a Jew, and was born at Vienna about the year 1740. He succeeded to the title and estate of his father Baron Diego D'Aguilar, a Portuguese, who died in England in 1759. In 1757 the subject of the present sketch was naturalized, and about the same time married the daughter of Moses Mendez Da Costa, Esq. a rich merchant of London. Miss Da Costa had an immense fortune, but which as it appears was all settled upon her previously to their marriage. By this lady the Baron had two daughters, who inherited their mother's property after her decease, which happened in the year 1763.

In 1767 the Baron took for his second wife the widow of Benjamin Da Costa, Esq. a respectable merchant. With this virtuous and

BARON  D'AGUILAR,

MERCHANT,

*Late of Broad Street Buildings,*

Bethnal Green, Iflington, Sydenham, Twickenham, &c.&c.

Exterior of Nelson's Lodgings in Camden Passage.
Watercolour by T. H. Shepherd, circa 1835.

accomplished female he also received a very considerable fortune, but which was also vested in her by their marriage settlement. During his first and the former part of his second marriage, the Baron lived in very great style in the house built by his father-in-law, Mendez Da Costa, Esq. in Broad Street-buildings. He kept an elegant equipage of carriages, horses, and (as he often boasted) between 20 and 30 servants of various descriptions. He however soon afterwards, having lost a considerable estate in America, by reason of the war with that country, and being not altogether satisfied with his matrimonial connexion, began to change his mode of living ; he removed from Broad-street, became rude, slovenly, and careless, both in his person and manners, affected the appearance of poverty, and totally withdrew himself from his family connexions and the gay world.

But of all the traits in his character, this, in comparison with many subsequent actions of his life, will be found liable to the least censure. The character of a gentleman became entirely lost in him ; although abounding in wealth, he contracted habits of the most mean and penurious kind, and acted with the greatest cruelty towards his wife, whom he locked up in a hay-loft, and otherwise treated with the utmost brutality. For this conduct however a prosecution was instituted against him with success in the Court of King's Bench, on which occasion he had the effrontery to appear in open court during the whole of the trial, and on a verdict being given against him, boldly petitioned the Bench to make his wife pay half the expences, on account of his *poverty*.

This unfortunate lady died six or seven years before the Baron. Previous to her death he took a house in Shaftesbury-place, Aldersgate-street, whither he usually retired at night to sleep, also the one in Camden-street, together with the premises before described, which he converted into a *sort* of farm, and where he spent a considerable portion of his time during the day. With the most consummate hypocrisy, and in spite of the avaricious disposition which he had acquired, he would affect to be extremely humane and charitable, to any **poor** starving ragged female whom chance might throw in his way; such he would take home to his dwelling, and provide with food and comfortable garments. He would also invite orphans and friend- less children to his houses, whom he occasionally made his servants, increasing their wages with their years, but intended ultimately, with the former, to be the victims of his lust, or the ministers of his de- baucheries. His house exhibited a scene of the most abandoned de- pravity, several females and their families all living together with him at the same time.

A numerous progeny of illegitimate issue was the result of this practice, and he was extremely regular in keeping the account of his outgoings on this head. When any parish officer made application to him for the usual indemnification, after being informed of the demand necessary to exonerate him entirely from the burthen, he would reach down his ledger, and with the greatest *sang froid* remark how much greater the sum charged was, than what he had been accustomed to pay on similar occasions!

Besides the premises before mentioned, the Baron had a piece of ground and two houses at Bethnal-green: these were shut up, and crammed with rich household furniture, &c. part of the establishment of his house in Broad Street-buildings, and which he never used after quitting that place. He had also a mansion at Twickenham, which he had formerly used as his country house; this was also shut up, and he allowed a man a small pittance monthly to keep an eye upon the premises. He likewise employed a poor shoemaker to take care of another shut-up house at Sydenham, together with a few cattle upon the premises; these, after the poor man had done every thing in his power to keep them alive, the whole of the provender being con- sumed, and not seeing or hearing from the Baron, were literally starved to death. With D'Aguilar this was indeed a common mode of treat- ing the brute creation; and when remonstrated with on the inhuma- nity of the practice, he would answer that he did it *in order that his cattle might know their master*.

He had a strange propensity to farming, and it was shocking and disgusting to witness the manner in which the affairs of his farm yard at this place were conducted. It was a perfect dunghill; and among the inhabitants of the village and others properly denominated, *The Starvation Farm*, from the wretched appearance exhibited by every living object upon it. The pittance of food allotted to his wretched cattle, was always apportioned, and frequently given by the Baron's own hand; and so strange and unaccountable was the character of the man in this respect, that he suffered nearly the whole of his stock to languish and die by inches for want of provender. In the heap of dung and filth that had accumulated on the premises from the time he commenced farming (for he never suffered the place to be cleansed) between 30 and 40 carcases of different animals were supposed to have been deposited, which had all in this manner been starved to death. A man whom he employed to look after his cattle, &c. on the farm, had orders, when any of the stock died, to bury them in the general heap. This man having upon one occasion sold the body of a starved calf to a vender of dog's meat, and the transaction coming to the ears of the Baron, he was instantly summoned before him, to answer the serious charge of embezzling his master's property: the affair however ended in the man being turned off the premises, after the deduction of 1s. 10d. out of his wages, being the sum he received for the dead carcase. His cows he would sometimes send from the *Starvation Farm* to his field at Bethnal Green to grass, and oblige his servant to go daily thither to fetch the milk they afforded for the use of his family at Islington.

Such was the state of famine to which the Baron's *live* stock at this place has been sometimes reduced, that they have been known literally to devour each other. His hogs have been often observed making a meal upon a starveling fowl that has been unable to escape from their famished jaws. The wretched situation of these poor animals would frequently rouse the indignation of the spectators, who assembled in crowds to hoot and pelt the Baron, for he was often to be seen about

the premises, in a very mean dress, besmeared with dung and filth [1].
On these occasions he would never take any notice of the justly incensed
mob, but seize the first opportunity of quietly making his escape.
The wretch was once threatened with a prosecution by the New River
Company, on the discovering a skeleton of one of his cattle which had
been thrown into the stream. At this place he also kept, safely locked
up, his old favourite coach; it was a cumbrous machine, and had been
formerly drawn by six horses, which now formed a part of the live
stock on his farm.

Having thus totally forsaken all genteel society, and given himself
up to the most wretched and abandoned pursuits, he never cared to
see any of his family, or his former respectable connexions. He
would, sarcastically, tell his sons-in-law that they were *gentlemen*,
and not fit associates for him; and his daughters, that they were too
*fine* to sit in his company. As the human character is oftentimes
found to exhibit strange and unaccountable contradictions, so it was
with the Baron. The large estate which he lost in America, he never attempted to recover; nor would he suffer any person to interfere
in the business, though with a probability of success. He is said to
have been an excellent scholar; to have written with great elegance
and facility; and he had some of his natural children educated under the first masters, and behaved towards them with the greatest
parental tenderness. His benevolence towards the poor, in some few
instances, redounded highly to his praise; but his bounty was chiefly
confined to the most wretched and unfortunate of the female sex, who
frequently found an asylum at his *sleeping-house* in Shaftesbury-
place. As his farm at Islington might be compared with the stable of
Augeas, so this nocturnal habitation was an absolute chaos of household goods, merchandize, filth, &c. forming altogether such a rude
and incongruous mass, that it was with the greatest difficulty that
any stranger could enter it.

[1] See Portraits of Baron D'Aguilar and a View of the "*Starvation Farm*," at Islington, in Granger's Wonderful Museum," 1802, 8vo.

In his last illness, which was occasioned by an inflammation in his bowels, notwithstanding the weather was very severe, and the dangerous nature of his complaint, he would not allow a fire in his house, nor admit a doctor into his presence. He, however, followed the prescriptions of a medical man, to whom he sent his water every day, with a fee of one guinea. His youngest daughter affectionately sent several times to him in his last moments, begging permission to see him; but with dreadful imprecations, to which he was much addicted, he declared she should never enter his presence. He died at his house in Shaftesbury-place, on the 16th of March, 1802, at the age of 62. His body was afterwards removed to Islington, and thence carried to the Jews' burying-ground at Mile-end, where it was interred.

Thus lived and died the Baron D'Aguilar, a most singular character, who possessed both the means and the ability for the exercise of virtuous and munificent actions; but whose life was, for the most part, absorbed in habits the most unnatural, inhuman, and degrading. He left two legitimate daughters, who, by his dying intestate, administered, and came into possession of all his property, while a number of poor objects, who had natural claims to his protection, and who had been supported by him in his life-time, were left altogether destitute.

The Baron's effects at Islington were sold by auction, which lasted two days; his stock of *lean* cattle sold for £.128, and his favourite coach, which was almost dropping to pieces, was bought for the sum of £.7, by a person in the village, for the sake of the springs. He had a valuable library at Shaftesbury-place, consisting of Hebrew, English, and foreign literature, which was also sold. His diamonds, jewels, &c. were reported to be worth £.30,000; and his plate consisted of seven hundred-weight, in articles of various descriptions. He had, moreover, a stock of about 40 bags of cochineal, and 12 bags of fine indigo, probably worth near £.10,000. These articles the Baron had purchased many years before his death at a high price, upon speculation, and hoarded them up in his house, resolving never to part with them till he had a desirable profit. The total bulk of his property is supposed to have been upwards of £.200,000.

A house in Camden-passage, near the West end of Camden-street, was for some time the residence of the amiable but eccentric Alexander Cruden, whose life and manners, though as much at variance with the common rules that actuate and govern mankind as the subject of the last memoir, affords, nevertheless, a pleasing transition from the contemplation of a course of base degeneracy and depravity in the one, to a life of virtue, integrity, and every quality that can tend to exalt the human character, in the other. The subject of the present sketch, whose literary labours will always entitle him to the veneration of every student of the Sacred Writings, was an occasional inhabitant of Islington for a number of years, having resided at intervals in the Upper-street, Old Paradise-row, and the place above-mentioned, where he drew his last breath. He was the second son of Mr. William Cruden, a merchant, and one of the chief magistrates of Aberdeen, at which place he was born, in the year 1701. After receiving a course of education at the grammar-school of that city, and taking the degree of M. A. at the Marischal College, with a view to the ministry, at the age of 18 he came to London, and engaged himself with several families in the capacity of a private tutor: thus his thoughts appear to have been diverted from the Church as a profession, though he retained through life the impression that he was intended for the exercise of the ministry, and all his labours and studies certainly took that direction.

Previously to his leaving Aberdeen, his eccentric disposition had begun to manifest itself, insomuch that some remarkable things in his words and actions were construed into insanity; and it appears that a disappointment in love which he had experienced was attended with such horrid circumstances [1], as were enough to have affected the reason of any man of tender affections. Under this impression he was kept in a place of confinement for some time previous to his departure from his native country.

After visiting the Isle of Man, in the capacity of private tutor, in 1732, we find him again in London, employed as corrector of the press, and bookseller, in which latter business he opened a shop under the Royal Exchange. The year after he began to complete the work which entitles him to be ranked among the friends of Sacred Literature. He had long meditated " A COMPLETE CON-" CORDANCE OF THE HOLY SCRIPTURES OF THE OLD AND NEW " TESTAMENT," designed (as he expresses himself) " to promote " the Study and Knowledge of the Scriptures." If the merit of labour only be given to this work, it is a labour which has been seldom equalled, and which cannot be exceeded : it seems, indeed, so vast a performance for one man, nay so much beyond human patience, that while the Divine and the private Christian are thankful for such assistance in their study of the sacred writings, as no other work affords, they cannot cease to wonder by what means it could have been procured. A bare inspection of the volume, in any of its copious articles, will afford a stupendous proof of patience and perseverance. In this work he surpassed all his predecessors, of whose labours he could avail himself but little; since, in order to make a correct Concordance, it was absolutely necessary for him to begin as if no such work had ever preceded ; and this he did with uncommon zeal and attachment to the plan he had laid down. Habits of industry were familiar to him ; and such was his affection for what he considered as eminently useful, that he executed the whole before he had

---

[1] See Mr. A. Chalmers's Life of Cruden, prefixed to the last Edition of his Concordance, in 1810, which also contains a good likeness of Mr. Cruden.—It may not be amiss here to mention, that every single extract in this last edition was accurately compared with the original by a man of equal industry with Mr. Cruden, whose name deserves to be recorded — Mr. Deodatus Bye, a worthy, unassuming Printer.

received any encouragement from the publick. The first edition of his Concordance was dedicated to Queen Caroline, who had given some reason to expect a gratuity on its presentation to her; but her death happening in the same month that the book was presented (November 1737), he was unfortunately deprived of his patroness.

This, together with other disappointments, occasioned some embarrassment in his affairs; and his work, however liked, did not produce him any immediate return of profit. These circumstances appear to have affected his mind very deeply; he disposed of his stock in trade, and shut up his shop. Being now without support, without friends, and without hope, he became a prey to his phrenetic disorder, which occasioned his being sent to a private mad-house at Bethnal-green. That his disorder was of the most harmless kind, appears from a pamphlet he published on his release, intituled, " The London " Citizen extremely injured; giving an Account of his Adventures " during the Time of his severe and long Campaign at Bethnal-green for " Nine Weeks and Six Days; the Citizen being sent there in March 1738 " by Robert Wightman, a notoriously conceited whimsical Man; where " he was chained, handcuffed, strait-waistcoated, and imprisoned, &c. " &c." In this pamphlet he gives a distinct account of facts, such as proves that he was neither deficient in memory nor judgment, but certainly in a style singularly whimsical. He also commenced an action against Dr. Munro, and other defendants, who obtained a verdict in their favour. This trial Mr. Cruden published, with remarks on the economy of private mad-houses, which he dedicated to the late King. Certain it is that the abuses of these receptacles soon became so notorious and shameful to the character of the nation, that they were at length subjected to a new law.

After this, Mr. Cruden, who never appeared to be a lunatic in the eyes of his employers, lived chiefly by correcting the press; and, under his inspection, several editions of the Greek and Roman classics were published with great accuracy. To booksellers he rendered himself useful in every employment where the talents of a scholar were requisite. His manners were extremely simple and inoffensive; he was always to be trusted, and performed his engagements with the strictest fidelity. In these occupations he employed several years, until we find him a third time under confinement. No information that can be obtained throws any light on the causes of this harsh treatment; no person can recollect a single act which seemed to require the rigours of lunatic discipline, or that he indicated any thing like a mischievous disposition. When released, he again published his case, under the whimsical title of " The Adventures of Alexander the Corrector;" in three parts. If this work be a faithful transcript of his mind, it is evident that he was at least harmless [1]. The only circumstances by which he was convicted of lunacy, in the general opinion, were those which might have in former ages convicted many persons of higher distinction. These were, an extraordinary zeal for doing good in ways not generally adopted by mankind. He seems to have considered himself as appointed to be a general reformer; and in his attempts to reform, he departed from accustomed rules, and was sometimes irregular in invading the province of the Divine and the Legislator. The following may be given as a curious instance of his whimsical turn of mind: in Sept. 1753, after his release, he wanted to persuade those who had been the means of his confinement to submit to be imprisoned in Newgate, in compensation for the injuries they had brought upon him. To his sister he proposed what he thought very mild terms, namely, the choice of four prisons, *viz.* Newgate, Reading, and Aylesbury jails, and the prison in Windsor Castle. On her refusal, he commenced actions against her and three

[1] Maitland relates (History of London, vol. I, p. 712) that " Alexander Cruden, citizen and stationer, much disordered in mind, and lately patient in a mad-house, insisted on being put in nomination at the election for city representatives in the year 1754;" but adds, in a note, " In order to efface any ill impressions which may " be made on the memory of this gentleman, it is an act of justice to acquaint the " reader that, upon the strictest enquiry, we find him to be a person of sound mo- " rals, unaffected piety, a sincere well-wisher to all good men, and the useful author " of the best Concordance (in any language) to the Bible."

others, which were tried in February 1754, when a verdict was given
for the defendants. He published this trial, which he also dedicated
to the King, but who refused the honour which he requested of presenting it to his Majesty in person.

As a Reformer he called himself "*Alexander the Corrector*," and
gave out that he was commissioned from Heaven to reform the manners of the age, and particularly to restore the due observance of the
Sabbath. If there was madness in this, it was in the hopes that an
unprotected individual might succeed where laws and societies,
strengthened by every possible authority, have failed. It was like the
hopeless plan of " raising one from the dead," to convince those who
had neglected " Moses and the Prophets." In such attempts, however, consisted the whole of Mr. Cruden's real or supposed lunacy. He
went to Oxford and Cambridge, and in person exhorted the young
ladies and gentlemen, whom he found in the public walks on the
Sabbath, to go home, and keep that day holy. Such advice from the
pulpit would have been only the performance of a solemn duty; in
Mr. C. it was deemed madness. This feature in his character brings
to mind an excellent remark made by Dr. Johnson on Smart the
poet: " Madness frequently discovers itself merely by unnecessary
" deviation from the usual modes of the world. My poor friend Smart
" shewed the disturbance of his mind by falling upon his knees, and
" saying his prayers, in the street, or in any other unusual place.
" Now although, rationally speaking, it is GREATER MADNESS NOT
" TO PRAY AT ALL than to pray as Smart did, I am afraid there are
" so many who do not pray, that their understanding is not called in
" question." Dr. Johnson said at another time of Mr. Smart, what is
far more applicable to our author, " I did not think he ought to be
" shut up; his infirmities were not noxious to society."

Among the other singularities of Mr. Cruden, may be reckoned his
application for the honour of knighthood, which was refused him.
He would traverse the streets, and with a piece of sponge which he
carried in his pocket for the purpose; obliterate from the walls, win-

dow shutters, &c. No. 45, wherever he found it chalked, from his aversion to the celebrated John Wilkes, against whom he wrote a pamphlet. All expressions contrary to good morals which he chanced to meet with in his peregrinations, were also effaced by him in the same manner; and he would enter any mob or tumultuous assembly with the authority of a magistrate, and strenuously exhort the contending parties to depart quietly to their homes, which advice, from his respectable appearance, and the gently reproving manner in which it was delivered, frequently produced the desired effect.

But these singularities occupied comparatively but little of Mr. Cruden's attention; his best hours were devoted to study, and the enlargement of his Concordance, the second edition of which was published in 1761, and dedicated to his present Majesty, to whom he had the honour of presenting it in person. At this time he was corrector of the press to the Public Advertizer, a paper once in high estimation, and then printed by Mr. Henry Woodfall. His opinion, however, seems to have been, that it was incumbent on him to go about doing good. And under the influence of that philanthropic spirit which gave life to all his actions, in the year 1762, by his fervent applications to the Earl of Halifax, then Secretary of State, he succeeded in rescuing from the gallows one *Potter*, a poor sailor, who had been capitally convicted at the Old Bailey for uttering a forged seaman's will. His benevolence did not stop here; he visited the man in prison, prayed with him, exhorted him, taught him the principles of religion, and in a word made a convert of the poor wretch, who had scarcely ever heard of a God, except when his name was taken in vain. The tenderness indeed with which Mr. C. visited, exhorted, fed, and clothed, this convert, the anxiety he felt, and the unceasing application he made, deserve to be remembered with approbation, and may be perused with much interest in a publication he issued the same year, intituled, " The History of Richard Potter, &c."

Mr. Cruden's success in reforming this poor criminal induced him to continue his labours among the other felons in Newgate; he visited them daily, gave them copies of the New Testament, Catechisms, &c. catechized them himself, and bestowed small pecuniary rewards on the most apt scholars. His want of success in this instance did not cause him to relax in the least in his meritorious efforts, and regard for the eternal welfare of his fellow creatures, which was ever a predominant trait in his character. Upon another occasion, the consolation and friendly relief which he administered to a man (a total stranger) who had left his home with the dreadful resolution of committing suicide, were the means of inducing him to forego his purpose, and return to the bosom of his family.

In 1769 Mr. Cruden visited the place of his nativity, and in a public hall gave a lecture on the cause of reformation, and exhorted all ranks to mend their ways. Among other endeavours to reform his townsmen he had the fourth commandment printed in the form of a hand-bill, and distributed them to all persons without distinction whom he met in the streets on Sunday. For young people he always had his pockets full of religious tracts, and some of considerable price, which he bestowed freely on such as promised to read them. It was highly pleasing to behold the tender regard, and winning manners by which he endeavoured to allure children to read their Bibles, Catechisms, &c. In the case of persons somewhat more advanced, he had a mode of treatment which almost approached to waggery. To a young clergyman, whom he thought too conceited and *modern*, he very gravely and formally presented a little Catechism used by children in Scotland, called " *The Mother's Catechism, dedicated to the young* " *and ignorant."*

After residing about a year at Aberdeen he returned to London, and resumed his lodgings at Islington, where he died on the morning of Nov. 1, 1770, in the 69th year of his age. When the person of the house went to inform him that breakfast was ready, he was found dead on his knees in the posture of prayer. He had complained for some days of an asthmatic affection ; one of the paroxysms of which probably terminated his life. His body was interred in the burial-ground of a Dissenting Meeting House in Deadman's-place, Southwark[1]. As he never married, he bequeathed his moderate savings to his relations, except a certain sum to the City of Aberdeen, to be employed in the purchase of religious books for the use of the poor, and he founded a bursary (or exhibition) of £.5. sterling *per annum*, to assist in educating a student at the Marischal College.

Mr. Cruden was much employed as an editor, and wrote many prefaces and recommendations to books, the titles of which cannot now be recollected. In 1749 he wrote "An Account of the History and " Excellency of the Scriptures," which was prefixed to " A Compen- " dium of the Holy Bible," 12mo. He compiled also, " A Scrip- " ture Dictionary, or Guide to the Holy Scriptures," 2 vols. 8vo. printed at Aberdeen a little after his death. He likewise formed that very elaborate verbal index which belongs to Bishop Newton's edition of Milton's Works, an undertaking inferior only to his Concordance.

In private life Mr. Cruden was courteous and affable; and so firm in his religious opinions (which were Calvinistic) that he would repel any one that attempted to attack them, with considerable warmth. He was never neglectful however of shewing his faith by his works. To the poor he was as liberal of his money as of his advice, and seldom indeed separated the one from the other. It is well known, that he often gave more than he retained for his own uses, and such liberality from one who was labouring for the wants of the passing day must have proceeded from motives the most honourable and exalted. To such young men, especially from Aberdeen, as were recommended to him, he acted like a father and affectionate friend, and was particularly careful to fortify their minds against the temptations of London by religious advice. He attended in London the places of worship belonging to the Ministers of the Calvinistic persuasion among the Dissenters. During the greatest part of his life he joined in Communion with Dr. Guise's Independant Meeting; but about the year

---

[1] From the information of Mr. Powell the undertaker.

1761-2, when age and infirmities obliged that gentleman to resign, and Dr. Stafford succeeded him, Mr. Cruden attended Dr. Conder, on the Pavement, Moorfields, and went to Dr. Guise's Meeting on the first Sunday in every month only, when the Sacrament was administered.

While we lament that so useful a life should have been sometimes clouded by mental infirmity, we cannot but venerate the character of a man whom neither infirmity nor neglect could debase, who sought consolation where only it can be found, whose sorrows always served to instruct him in the distresses of others, and who employed his prosperity to relieve those who in every sense were ready to perish.

Near to the *Carved Lion*, fronting Bird's-buildings, was formerly an ale-brewery belonging to a person named Emery, but which has been discontinued many years. An upright stone on the North side of Langley Church-yard, Bucks, contains an inscription to the memory of Mr. Thomas Emery, brewer [1], of Islington, who died Nov. 7, 1755, aged 30; Mary his wife, Aug. 6, 1778; and others of the family.

THE OLD QUEEN'S HEAD public house in the Lower-street, is one of the most perfect specimens of antient domestic architecture remaining in the neighbourhood of London, or perhaps in the whole kingdom (see Plate XIII.). It is a strong wood and plaster building [2], consisting of three lofty stories projecting over each other in

---

[1] The brewery was continued by the son, who afterwards settled in St. John's-street.

[2] The mode of erecting dwelling-houses for several centuries previous to the reign of Elizabeth, was more like the art of *ship-building*, than any thing to which it can be now compared. Immense beams of oak, or more frequently chesnut wood, placed in perpendicular, diagonal, and transverse directions, and strongly morticed or rivetted together, formed the shell or carcase of almost every domestic building. "The common run of houses," as Strutt observes, " (especially among the middling " sort of people) were built with wood. They generally made large porches before " their principal entrance, with great halls and large parlours; the frame work was

ALEXANDER CRUDEN.

*BIBLIA Anchora est mea: Et CHRISTUS est mihi Anchora et Omnia.*

Lower Street. Islington.

front, and forming bay windows, supported by brackets and carved figures. The centre projects several feet beyond the other part of the building, and forms a commodious porch, to which there is a descent of several steps. This is supported in front by carya-tides of carved oak, crowned with Ionic scrolls, standing on each side the entrance. The floor of the parlour in the front of the house is four feet below the surface of the highway, though a tradition prevails that the house originally was entered by an ascent of several steps. This indeed is not improbable, when the antiquity of the building is considered, and the vast accumulation of matter upon the road in the course of several centuries : add to this, that the New River, which passes under the highway directly in front of the house, has, in the formation of its banks, and the turning an arch over it, occasioned a considerable rise in this place.

The interior of this house is constructed in a similar manner to

" constructed with beams of timber of such enormous size, that the materials of " one house as they built antiently would make several of equal size according to " the present mode of building. The common method of making walls was to nail " laths to the timber frame, and strike them over with a rough plaster, which was " afterwards whitened and ornamented with fine mortar, and this last was often " beautified with figures and other curious devices. The houses in the cities and " towns, were built each story jetting forth over the former story, so that when the " streets were not very wide, the people at the top from opposite houses, might not " only talk and converse with each other, but even shake hands together. Their " houses were covered with tiles, shingles, slates, or lead, except in the City of " London, where shingles were forbid." *Manners and Customs of the People of England,* vol. II. p. 85. Houses built in the manner above described, though per-haps of too combustible a nature for populous neighbourhoods, were without doubt more calculated for strength and durability than the greater part of our modern erec-tions of brick. While we are almost daily witnesses to the fact of new houses *falling to the ground* before they are well out of the builder's hands, many of the wooden fabricks of our ancestors, which have stood the test of centuries, yet remain *standing* reproaches to either the want of skill or the want of honesty in our modern professors of the building art, calling themselves surveyors and *architects ! !*

that of most of the old buildings in this parish, having oak pannelled wainscots and stuccoed cielings: the latter in the parlour before-mentioned is ornamented with dolphins, cherubs, acorns, &c. surrounded by a wreathed border of fruit and foliage. Near the centre of the cieling is the medallion of a character, apparently Roman, crowned with bays; also a small shield, containing the initials " I. M." surrounded by cherubim and glory (Plate II. fig. 14). The chimney-piece is supported by two figures carved in stone, hung with festoons, &c. The stone slab immediately over the fire-place exhibits the story of Danaë and Actæon in relief, with mutilated figures of Venus, Bacchus, and Plenty (Plate II. fig. 13).

The origin and history of this house is involved in the greatest obscurity; neither the records of the prebend, nor any historical document, throws any light upon the subject; therefore all that can be said repecting it, being founded on traditionary report or probable conjecture, might very properly be summed up in the words of the poet:

> " Perhaps, for History is silent here,
> " And we may guess at will — perhaps some Cit,
> " Grown wealthy, here retir'd in peace to pass
> " His latter days. — Some courtier here, perchance,
> " Erst liv'd in pomp and feast and revelry.
> " How alter'd now the scene ! — how chang'd the fate !"
>
> Fox.

It however appears that the house was about the beginning of the last century possessed by a family named *Roome*, who were respectable citizens, and who had been proprietors of the premises for a considerable time. One of this family bequeathed the estate to Lady Edwards, and it is now the property of I. T. Hope, Esq. who married her daughter.

The Old Queen's Head has been coupled with the name of our gallant countryman Sir Walter Raleigh, who has been said, if not

Queen's Head Public House Islington.

Published May 1.1819. for the Proprietor, by R.Ackermann. 101. Strand.

Queen's Head Interior.

to have built, at least to have patronized this house, and to have made it one of his smoking taverns, where,

" At his hours of leisure,
" He'd puff his pipe, and take his pleasure."

A further conjecture has been founded on the circumstance of his having, in the 30th year of Elizabeth's reign, obtained a patent " to " make lycences for keeping of taverns, and retailing of wynes " throughout Englande;" namely, that this was one of the taverns so licensed by him, and that the Queen's Head was adopted as the sign of the house, in *compliment* to his royal mistress.

Mr. Ellis mentions a tradition (Campag. Lond. p. 96), that this house was at one time the residence of the Lord Treasurer Burleigh, and observes, that in the yard belonging to a neighbouring tenement were, some time previous, two lions carved in wood, the supporters of the *Cecil* arms, which appeared to have belonged to the Old Queen's Head. It has also been related by some aged persons in the parish as a tradition received from their forefathers, that Queen Elizabeth's sadler resided here [1]; whilst others assert that it was the summer residence of her great favourite the Earl of Essex, and the occasional resort of her Majesty [2].

Having mentioned these several circumstances merely as matters of tradition, and respecting which the reader may form his own opinion, it may be proper to remark that this building, as most of the antient edifices already described, was evidently erected about the time of Elizabeth. The heavy Gothic ornaments prevailing throughout the

[1] Thomas Cure, Esq. sadler to Edward VI. Mary, and Elizabeth, appears to have dwelt in Southwark. He died the 24 May, 1588, and lies buried in the Church of St. Mary Overy, to which parish he was a considerable benefactor.

[2] A curious inscription in verse, referring to this tradition, is inscribed on a large pewter tankard in the bar of the Old Queen's Head. It was written by the eccentric *John Cranch* in the year 1796, at which time the vessel was presented to the landlord by a convivial party which had dined at the house.

whole of these structures, intermingled with the volute, the astragal, and other detached portions after the Grecian taste, are alone sufficient to refer us back with certainty to the period above mentioned.

A print of the Old Queen's Head, and some of the decorations of the interior, may be seen in the Gentleman's Magazine for June 1794; and an engraving of the house, in Britton's "Architectural Antiquities." A more correct view than either is contained in the European Mag. for March 1808.

In Queen's Head-lane (formerly called Boon's-lane) is a row of alms-houses founded by John Heath, Esq. in 1640, for the reception of ten decayed members of the Company of Clothworkers, who receive annually, from the Trustees of that Corporation, a suit of clothes, a chaldron of coals, and £20. in money for their maintenance. The sum originally vested in the Company by Mr. Heath for the endowment of the above charity appears to have been £.1500.

On the opposite side of the lane is another row of very neat almshouses, respecting which the following particulars are recorded on a stone in front of the building:

In the year of our Lord
1794
these eight Alms-houses were erected and endowed
for the reception and maintenance
of aged and poor persons
by Mrs. JANE DAVIS,
in pursuance of the will of her deceased husband,
Mr. John Davis, late of this parish.
The Rev. George Strahan,
John Jackson, Esq.
Edmund Clutterbuck, Esq. }Trustees.
Mr. Edward Martin,
Mr. Thomas Craven,

This charity is open to both men and women, who are admitted by the Trustees on producing proper testimonials, and are allowed £.10. *per annum* each, towards their maintenance. Robert Careless, Esq.

who died 26th Aug. 1805, left £.100. to this charity; but his benefaction was rendered abortive by the insolvency of one of the Trustees
who had received the legacy. A portrait of Mrs. Davis the founder
is preserved in one of the alms-houses, to which it was presented by
Mr. Powell of Cross-street.

Near to the Old Queen's Head is a large handsome brick mansion,
frequently called *Sandys House*, from having been some years since
the residence of an eccentric character, bearing that name; it is
now in the occupation of Mrs. Hardcastle.

Further to the North, where the " City Farm House" now stands,
was formerly a very old public house called *The Crown* (see Plate
III.) It contained several fragments of antiquity, in carved work,
stained glass, &c. and had probably been once the residence of
some opulent merchant, or person of distinction. In the window of a
large room on the ground floor were the arms of England, the City
of London, the Mercers Company[1], and another coat[2]; also the
red and white roses united, with other ornaments that seemed to
refer to the reign of Henry VII. or Henry VIII. as the period of its
erection.

[1] Gules, a demy virgin couped below the shoulders, issuing from the clouds, all
proper, vested Or, crowned with an Eastern crown of the last, her hair dishevelled,
and wreathed round the temples with roses of the second, all within an orle of clouds,
proper. Mr. Ellis (Campag. Lond. p. 100.) is incorrect in affirming this " buxom
" well-looking damsel" (which has been always borne as the Mercers Arms) to be a
portrait of Elizabeth, the wife of Henry VII. The original in stained glass is yet
preserved in a window in the house of Mr. Clifton, apothecary, on the terrace, Lower-
street, and of which the engraving, Plate V. fig 6. is a reduced copy.

[2] Azure, three escutcheons Argent; impaling, Azure, a chevron between three
eagles' heads erased Or. There was also in the same window the representation of
a cross of Calvary, overspread with vines. These, together with the arms above
mentioned (except the Mercers), also the figures of St. Anthony and some other
Saints, are yet preserved in a window of an upper room at the City Farm House,
which room is used as a chapel for the poor maintained in that building.

Many years previous to the pulling down of this building it had been converted into a public house or inn, the common fate of most of the old respectable dwellings in this parish : it was latterly kept by a person named *Pressey*, and was much resorted to by strolling players, who often engaged a principal room in the house for the exhibition of dramatic pieces. The building which occupies its site, was erected about 15 years ago : it is an establishment belonging to an individual named *Sutton*, for the purpose of *farming* the poor belonging to parishes in the City, who are here kept and employed in the same manner as in a parish workhouse. The building at present contains about 200 paupers, and bears in front the following inscription : " City Farm House, pursuant to Act of Parliament of 22d Geo. III. [1]"

Nearly opposite the end of Cross-street, in the Lower-street, is a spacious and substantial brick building, called *Fisher House*, having been sometime the residence of the family bearing that name. It was probably built by Sir Thomas Fisher about the beginning of the 17th century. It bears in front the initials $_{WE}^{P}$ and in the inside of the building is the coat of Fowler, Bart. and that of Fisher [2]; impaling, Or, a lion rampant Gules : these are placed over opposite doors on the landing place of a large staircase. We are informed by Anthony Wood that Ezekiel Tongue, author of several Tracts against the Papists, and some Treatises in Natural History, about the year 1660 kept an academy

[1] It is to be hoped that those officers of parishes, who are induced to form *contracts* for the maintenance of the poor committed to their care, are possessed of sufficient philanthropy and liberality, not to consider merely the *cheapest* way of going to work, but to be certain that the money paid shall afford a sufficient provision for these unfortunate objects, with a reasonable profit to the *contractor;* and that such provision, both in regard to food, raiment, and other necessaries, is duly and impartially administered. It is to be feared that many abuses are practised in houses of the above description ; and those parish officers who do not, by frequent inspection and enquiry, ascertain that the comforts of the poor are properly attended to, are not only deficient in that which is a great public duty, but stand highly responsible in the eyes of God.

[2] Or, 3 demy lions rampant, and a chief indented Gules.

for teaching young ladies Latin and Greek in a large gallery of a house at Islington belonging to Sir Thomas Fisher [1]. It is very probable that this was the house referred to, and that *Tongue* was patronized by the worthy Baronet, who allotted him a gallery in his mansion for the purpose of following his academical pursuits.

Fisher House has been nearly 30 years appropriated to the reception of insane persons, and is now kept for that purpose by Dr. Sutherland, Physician to St. Luke's Hospital [2]. It had been previously occupied as a lodging-house.

In Britannia-row, is an extensive manufactory of cut glass chandeliers, lustres, &c. belonging to Messrs. Bull and Smith. In the same place is also a considerable manufactory of watch springs. At the South end of *Frog-lane*, nearly facing Britannia-row, was formerly a public house called FROG HALL, on the front of which was exhibited the ludicrous sign of a plough drawn by frogs.

Near to this spot are eight alms-houses for so many poor widows of Members of the Clothworkers Company, who have each an annual allowance of about £.20. a gown, and a chaldron of coals. This charity was originally endowed in 1538 by Margaret Countess of Kent, widow of Richard Earl of Kent, who caused alms-houses to be built at White Fryars, in the room whereof these were subsequently erected here, as is recorded on the Table of Benefactions in the Clothworkers Hall, Mincing-lane. From this table it also appears, that Lady Anne Packington gave to the Company houses and land at Islington in 1560.

[1] Athen. Oxon. vol. II.

[2] A pamphlet intituled, "The Discovery, or the Mysterious Separation of *Hugh Doherty* and his wife, 1807," duodecimo; contains some particulars respecting Fisher House.

Brothers, the pretended prophet, was confined here for some time, until he was liberated by the authority of the Lord Chancellor Erskine in 1806.

**THE END.**

## ADDITIONS AND CORRECTIONS.

P. 11. The following is the return of the Population, &c. of Islington (in May 1811) made by the Overseers of the Parish in pursuance of the Act 51st Geo. III.; viz. Total number of Houses (including 185 unfinished and 72 uninhabited) 2656. Males 6244. Females 8821. Total 15,065.

P. 62. Mrs. Snell died at Clapham Nov. 30, 1810. By the decease of this Lady a moiety of the Manor of St. John of Jerusalem descends to William Hood, Esq. of Bardon Park, co. Leicester, and a Bencher of the Inner Temple. See *Gent. Mag.* vol. LXXX. p. 660.

P. 74. Another tradition has been mentioned respecting the etymology of *Copenhagen House;* viz. that towards the beginning of the 17th century, upon some political occasion, great numbers of Danes were induced to leave that kingdom, and take up their abode in London; whereupon this house was opened under the above name by an emigrant from Copenhagen, and became a place of resort for his countrymen resident in the metropolis. This tradition probably refers to the reign of James I. who was visited in London by his brother-in-law the King of Denmark, at which time it is very probable that there was a considerable influx of persons from the Danish capital. " *Coopen-*" Hagen" is the name given to the place in the map accompanying Camden's Britannia, fol. 1695.

P. 77. last line but two, for *Ware* read *Wase.*

P. 171. The dividend of a share of the New River for the year 1809 was £.472. 5s. 8d. the property tax being deducted. A very erroneous opinion prevails in the public mind respecting the *original* value of a share in this concern, it being generally considered that they were first issued at a certain definite price, in the same way as our modern dock and canal shares. It has been already stated (p. 165) that the expence of the undertaking amounted to £.500,000, of which there can be little doubt, when we consider the immense quantity of land it was necessary to purchase for the channel of the stream, in its course of nearly 40 miles, besides the variety of inevitable and heavy expences attending the completion of the work : supposing, therefore, that this sum is correct, and that it was paid by the original shareholders, it may be properly divided by 72, the original and present number of the shares, and this will shew the sum of £.6944. and a fraction to have been the original cost of every share. It therefore appears, that the increase in the value of the New River shares, so far from being to the surprizing extent generally imagined, has by no means kept pace with that of the Liverpool, the Manchester and Salford Water-works, and many other concerns of a similar nature recently established.

P. 216. Before the City-road was made, the New River was in that place carried over "*the hollow*," (as it was locally denominated) in a wooden trough lined with lead, similar to the one at Highbury, described in p. 159, but considerably smaller, under which there was a way for cattle and foot passengers.

P. 225. line 22. *dele* " and Baronet."

P. 252. During the two last winters an Assembly termed the " Ca-" nonbury Assembly," has been established at Canonbury-tavern; and a book club bearing the name of the " Canonbury Book Society" has been formed. The number consists of twelve gentlemen, who meet to dine at each other's houses, in rotation, on the first Thursday in every month.

P. 264. bottom of page, insert " ment in Europe, America, or In-" dia, where."

P. 279. The Advowson or right of presentation to the vicarage of this parish has been lately purchased by William Wilson, Esq. of Nether Worton, Oxfordshire, a branch of the very respectable family of that name residing at Highbury.

P. 326. line 15. for " the coat of Fowler impaling the above," read " the above impaling the coat of Fowler ;" this requires a similar correction in the corresponding engraving, Plate II. fig. 3.

P. 336. second column, line 3. for " *Gallop*," read *Gollop*.

In 1665 there was collected in *Islington*, for the relief of the poor Protestants in Piedmont, £.15. 11s. 5d.

3 G

# INDEX

# APPENDIX

Some roads which have changed their name since 1811:

Back Road now Liverpool Road
Church Street now Gaskin Street
Frog Lane now Danbury Street
Hopping Lane now St. Paul's Road
Lower Street now Essex Road
Maiden Lane now York Road